Communications
in Computer and Information Science 1601

More information about this series at https://link.springer.com/bookseries/7899

Davide Ciucci · Inés Couso · Jesús Medina ·
Dominik Ślęzak · Davide Petturiti ·
Bernadette Bouchon-Meunier ·
Ronald R. Yager (Eds.)

Information Processing and Management of Uncertainty in Knowledge-Based Systems

19th International Conference, IPMU 2022
Milan, Italy, July 11–15, 2022
Proceedings, Part I

Springer

Editors
Davide Ciucci ⓘ
University of Milano-Bicocca
Milan, Italy

Jesús Medina ⓘ
University of Cádiz
Cádiz, Spain

Davide Petturiti ⓘ
University of Perugia
Perugia, Italy

Ronald R. Yager ⓘ
Iona College
New Rochelle, NY, USA

Inés Couso ⓘ
University of Oviedo
Oviedo, Spain

Dominik Ślęzak ⓘ
University of Warsaw
Warsaw, Poland

Bernadette Bouchon-Meunier ⓘ
Sorbonne Université
Paris, France

ISSN 1865-0929   ISSN 1865-0937 (electronic)
Communications in Computer and Information Science
ISBN 978-3-031-08970-1   ISBN 978-3-031-08971-8 (eBook)
https://doi.org/10.1007/978-3-031-08971-8

Preface

We are very pleased to present you with the proceedings of the 19th International Conference on Information Processing and Management of Uncertainty in Knowledge-Based Systems (IPMU 2022). The conference was held during July 11–15, 2022, in Milan, Italy. The IPMU conference is organized every two years with the aim of bringing together scientists working on methods for the management of uncertainty and aggregation of information in intelligent systems. Since 1986, the IPMU conference has been providing a forum for the exchange of ideas between theoreticians and practitioners working in these areas and related fields.

Following the IPMU tradition, the Kampé de Fériet Award for outstanding contributions to the field of uncertainty and management of uncertainty was presented. Past winners of this prestigious award are Lotfi A. Zadeh (1992), Ilya Prigogine (1994), Toshiro Terano (1996), Kenneth Arrow (1998), Richard Jeffrey (2000), Arthur Dempster (2002), Janos Aczel (2004), Daniel Kahneman (2006), Enric Trillas (2008), James Bezdek (2010), Michio Sugeno (2012), Vladimir N. Vapnik (2014), Joseph Y. Halpern (2016), Glenn Shafer (2018) and Barbara Tversky (2020). In this 2022 edition, the award was given to Tomaso Poggio for his interdiciplinary work on human and machine intelligence and his fundamental research in computational neuroscience, in particular concerning the computational analysis of vision and learning.

The program included the keynote talk of Tomaso Poggio, as recipient of the Kampé de Feriet Award, and keynote talks by Cesar Hidalgo (Artificial and Natural Intelligence Toulouse Institute, France), Marianne Huchard (Laboratory of Informatics, Robotics, and Microelectronics, France) and Andrzej Skowron (University of Warsaw, Poland).

To celebrate the 40th anniversary of the seminal paper "Rough Sets" by Z. Pawlak, a panel session on rough sets was organized. The panel session witnessed the participation and discussion of renowned researchers on rough sets, including Salvatore Greco, Ernestina Menasalvas, and Andrzej Skowron, to whom we are grateful for their contribution. The participants shared their memories and experiences related to rough set-based decision making, applications of rough set approximations, and rough set contributions to machine learning, emphasizing the strong points of rough sets and the ways of using them in hybrid solutions.

The IPMU 2022 program consisted of 14 special sessions and 124 papers authored by researchers from 38 different countries. The conference followed a single-blind review process, respecting the usual conflict-of-interest standards. All submitted papers were judged by at least two reviewers and in most cases by three or more – even up to five – referees. Furthermore, all the papers were examined by the program chairs. As a result of the reviewing process, 124 submissions were accepted as full papers, which are included in the two volumes of the proceedings.

The organization of the IPMU 2022 conference was possible with the assistance, dedication, and support of many people and institutions. We are particularly thankful to the organizers of special sessions. Such sessions, dedicated to a variety of topics and organized by experts, have always been a characteristic feature of IPMU conferences. We would like to pass on our special thanks to Célia Da Costa Pereira, who helped evaluate all special session proposals. We would like to acknowledge all members of the IPMU 2022 Program Committee, as well as the additional reviewers who played an essential role in the reviewing process, ensuring a high-quality conference. Thank you very much for all your work and efforts. We gratefully acknowledge the technical co-sponsorship of the IEEE Computational Intelligence Society and the European Society for Fuzzy Logic and Technology (EUSFLAT).

We also acknowledge the support received from the University of Milano-Bicocca, and in particular from the Department of Information, Systems and Communications; from the Springer team who managed the publication of these proceedings; and from the EasyChair platform used to handle submissions and the review process. Our very special and greatest gratitude goes to the authors who submitted the results of their work and presented them at the conference. Without you this conference would not take place. Thank you!

We hope that these proceedings provide the readers with multiple ideas leading to numerous research activities, significant publications, and intriguing presentations at future IPMU conferences.

July 2022

Davide Ciucci
Inés Couso
Jesús Medina
Dominik Ślęzak
Davide Petturiti
Bernadette Bouchon-Meunier
Ronald R. Yager

Organization

General Chair

Davide Ciucci — University of Milano-Bicocca, Italy

Program Chairs

Inés Couso — University of Oviedo, Spain
Jesús Medina — University of Cádiz, Spain
Dominik Ślęzak — University of Warsaw, Poland

Executive Directors

Bernadette Bouchon-Meunier — LIP6, CNRS, France
Ronald R. Yager — Iona College, USA

Special Session Chair

Célia da Costa Pereira — Université Côte d'Azur, France

Publication Chair

Davide Petturiti — University of Perugia, Italy

Virtual Conference Chair

Rafael Peñaloza — University of Milano-Bicocca, Italy

Web Chair

Marco Viviani — University of Milano-Bicocca, Italy

International Advisory Board

Joao Paulo Carvalho — Instituto Superior Tecnico/INESC-ID, Portugal
Giulianella Coletti — University of Perugia, Italy
Miguel Delgado — University of Granada, Spain
Mario Fedrizzi — University of Trento, Italy
Laurent Foulloy — Université de Savoie, France

Salvatore Greco	University of Catania, Italy
Julio Gutiérrez-Ríos	Universidad Politécnica de Madrid, Spain
Eyke Hüllermeier	Paderborn University, Germany
Uzay Kaymak	Eindhoven University of Technology, The Netherlands
Anne Laurent	University of Montpellier, France
Marie-Jeanne Lesot	Universite Pierre et Marie Curie - Paris 6, France
Luis Magdalena	Universidad Politécnica de Madrid, Spain
Christophe Marsala	Universite Pierre et Marie Curie - Paris 6, France
Benedetto Matarazzo	University of Catania, Italy
Jesús Medina	University of Cádiz, Spain
Manuel Ojeda-Aciego	University of Malaga, Spain
Maria Rifqi	LEMMA, Université Panthéon-Assas, France
Lorenzo Saitta	Università del Piemonte Orientale, Italy
Olivier Strauss	Université de Montpellier, France
Enric Trillas	Universidad Politécnica de Madrid, Spain
Llorenç Valverde	Universitat de les Illes Balears, Spain
José Luis Verdegay	University of Granada, Spain
María Amparo Vila	University of Granada, Spain

Program Committee

Michał Baczyński	University of Silesia in Katowice, Poland
Gleb Beliakov	Deakin University, Australia
Vaishak Belle	University of Edinburgh, UK
Rafael Bello	Universidad Central "Marta Abreu" de las Villas, Cuba
Radim Bělohlávek	Palacky University Olomouc, Czech Republic
Salem Benferhat	CNRS, Université d'Artois, France
Isabelle Bloch	LTCI, Télécom Paris, France
Ulrich Bodenhofer	University of Applied Sciences Upper Austria, Austria
Humberto Bustince	UPNA, Spain
Joao Paulo Carvalho	Instituto Superior Tecnico/INESC-ID, Portugal
Giulianella Coletti	University of Perugia, Italy
Ana Colubi	University of Oviedo, Spain
María Eugenia Cornejo Piñero	Universidad de Cádiz, Spain
Chris Cornelis	Ghent University, Belgium
Keeley Crockett	Manchester Metropolitan University, UK
Bernard De Baets	Ghent University, Belgium
Guy De Tre	Ghent University, Belgium
Sébastien Destercke	CNRS, Université de Technologie de Compiègne, France

Antonio Di Nola	University of Salerno, Italy
Didier Dubois	IRIT-CNRS, France
Sylvie Galichet	LISTIC, Université de Savoie, France
Lluis Godo	Artificial Intelligence Research Institute, IIIA-CSIC, Spain
Fernando Gomide	University of Campinas, Brazil
Gil González-Rodríguez	University of Oviedo, Spain
Przemysław Grzegorzewski	Polish Academy of Sciences, Poland
Janusz Kacprzyk	Systems Research Institute, Polish Academy of Sciences, Poland
Uzay Kaymak	Eindhoven University of Technology, The Netherlands
Jim Keller	University of Missouri, USA
Frank Klawonn	Ostfalia University of Applied Sciences, Germany
Erich Peter Klement	Johannes Kepler University Linz, Austria
Lászlo T. Kóczy	Budapest University of Technology and Economics, Hungary
Vladik Kreinovich	University of Texas at El Paso, USA
Tomas Kroupa	CTU in Prague, Czech Republic
Rudolf Kruse	OVGU Magdeburg, Germany
Christophe Labreuche	Thales R&T, France
Jérôme Lang	CNRS, Université Paris-Dauphine, France
Anne Laurent	University of Montpellier, France
Marie-Jeanne Lesot	Universite Pierre et Marie Curie - Paris 6, France
Weldon Lodwick	University of Colorado at Denver, USA
Luis Magdalena	Universidad Politécnica de Madrid, Spain
Christophe Marsala	Universite Pierre et Marie Curie - Paris 6, France
Trevor Martin	University of Bristol, UK
Sebastià Massanet	University of the Balearic Islands, Spain
Gilles Mauris	Université de Savoie, France
Jerry Mendel	University of Southern California, USA
Radko Mesiar	STU Bratislava, Slovakia
Enrique Miranda	University of Oviedo, Spain
Javier Montero	Universidad Complutense de Madrid, Spain
Susana Montes	University of Oviedo, Spain
Jacky Montmain	École des Mines d'Alès, France
Serafín Moral	University of Granada, Spain
Zbigniew Nahorski	Polish Academy of Sciences, Poland
Vilém Novák	University of Ostrava, Czech Republic
Manuel Ojeda-Aciego	University of Malaga, Spain
Endre Pap	Singidunum University, Serbia
Gabriella Pasi	Università degli Studi di Milano-Bicocca, Italy

Irina Perfilieva	University of Ostrava, Czech Republic
Fred Petry	Naval Research Lab, USA
Vincenzo Piuri	University of Milan, Italy
Olivier Pivert	IRISA-ENSSAT, France
Henri Prade	IRIT-CNRS, France
Anca Ralescu	University of Cincinnati, USA
Mohammed Ramdani	Hassan II University of Casablanca, Morocco
Eloísa Ramírez-Poussa	Universidad de Cádiz, Spain
Marek Reformat	University of Alberta, Canada
Adrien Revault d'Allonnes	LIASD, France
Maria Rifqi	LEMMA, Université Panthéon-Assas, France
Thomas A. Runkler	Siemens Corporate Technology, Germany
Daniel Sánchez	University of Granada, Spain
Mika Sato-Ilic	University of Tsukuba, Japan
Roman Słowiński	Poznań University of Technology, Poland
Grégory Smits	IRISA/University of Rennes 1, France
Joao Sousa	IST, University of Lisbon, Portugal
Martin Štěpnička	University of Ostrava, Czech Republic
Umberto Straccia	ISTI-CNR, Italy
Eulalia Szmidt	Systems Research Institute, Polish Academy of Sciences, Poland
Marco Elio Tabacchi	University of Palermo, Italy
Andreja Tepavčević	University of Novi Sad, Serbia
Settimo Termini	University of Palermo, Italy
Vicenç Torra	University of Skövde, Sweden
Barbara Vantaggi	Sapienza Università di Roma, Italy
Marley Vellasco	Pontifical Catholic University of Rio de Janeiro, Brazil
José Luis Verdegay	University of Granada, Spain
Thomas Vetterlein	Johannes Kepler University Linz, Austria
Susana Vieira	Universidade de Lisboa, Portugal
Qiang Wei	State Key Laboratory of Mathematical Engineering and Advanced Computing, China
Sławomir Zadrożny	Systems Research Institute, Polish Academy of Sciences, Poland

Special Session Organizers

Stefano Aguzzoli	University of Milan, Italy
Michał Baczyński	University of Silesia in Katowice, Poland
Valerio Basile	University of Turin, Italy
Salem Benferhat	CNRS, Université d'Artois, France
Matteo Bianchi	University of Milan, Italy

Stefania Boffa · University of Milano-Bicocca, Italy
Humberto Bustince · UPNA, Spain
Federico Cabitza · University of Milano-Bicocca, Italy
Andrea Campagner · University of Milano-Bicocca, Italy
Juan Luis Castro · University of Granada, Spain
Martine Ceberio · University of Texas at El Paso, USA
Yurilev Chalco-Cano · Universidad de Tarapacá, Chile
Pablo Cordero · University of Malaga, Spain
Nahuel Costa Cortez · University of Oviedo, Spain
Tiago da Cruz Asmus · Universidade Federal do Rio Grande, Brazil
Bernard De Baets · Ghent University, Belgium
Rocío De Andrés · University of Salamanca, Spain
José Ángel Diaz-García · University of Granada, Spain
Graçaliz P. Dimuro · Universidade Federal do Rio Grande, Brazil
Krzysztof Dyczkowski · Adam Mickiewicz University in Poznań, Poland
Javier Fernández · UPNA, Spain
Carlos Fernández Basso · University of Granada, Spain
Tommaso Flaminio · Artificial Intelligence Research Institute, IIIA-CSIC, Spain
Brunella Gerla · University of Insubria, Italy
Lluis Godo · Artificial Intelligence Research Institute, IIIA-CSIC, Spain
Przemysław Grzegorzewski · Polish Academy of Sciences, Poland
Karel Gutiérrez · University of Granada, Spain
Beatriz Hernández Jiménez · Universidad Pablo de Olavide, Spain
Jan Hula · University of Ostrava, Czech Republic
Balasubramaniam Jayaram · Indian Institute of Technology Hyderabad, India
Katarzyna Kaczmarek-Majer · Systems Research Institute, Polish Academy of Sciences, Poland
Vladik Kreinovich · University of Texas at El Paso, USA
Carlos López-Molina · Universidad Publica de Navarra, Spain
Domingo López-Rodríguez · University of Malaga, Spain
Dario Malchiodi · University of Milan, Italy
Nicolás Marín · Univesity of Granada, Spain
Sebastià Massanet · University of the Balearic Islands, Spain
Corrado Mencar · University of Bari Aldo Moro, Italy
Enrique Miranda · University of Oviedo, Spain
Javier Montero · Universidad Complutense de Madrid, Spain
Ignacio Montes · University of Oviedo, Spain
Ángel Mora · University of Malaga, Spain
Petra Murinová · University of Ostrava, Czech Republic
Vilém Novák · University of Ostrava, Czech Republic

Irina Perfilieva   University of Ostrava, Czech Republic
Silvia Prieto Herráez   Universidad de Salamanca, Spain
Raúl Pérez-Fernández   Universidad de Oviedo, Spain
Barbara Pekała   University of Rzeszów, Poland
Rosana Rodríguez-López   Universidad de Santiago de Compostela, Spain
Luciano Sánchez   Universidad de Oviedo, Spain
Teresa Scantamburlo   Ca' Foscari University of Venice, Italy
Olivier Strauss   Université de Montpellier, France
Karim Tabia   Artois University, France
Sara Ugolini   Artificial Intelligence Research Institute,
                                      IIIA-CSIC, Spain
Amanda Vidal   Artificial Intelligence Research Institute,
                                      IIIA-CSIC, Spain
Anna Wilbik   Maastricht University, The Netherlands

Additional Reviewers

Angulo Castillo, Vladimir   Hoffmann, Frank
Antonucci, Alessandro   Holcapek, Michal
Badia, Guillermo   Hryniewicz, Olgierd
Baldi, Paolo   Jabbour, Said
Behounek, Libor   Kmita, Kamil
Ben Amor, Nahla   Kreinovich, Vladik
Benavoli, Alessio   Król, Anna
Bianchi, Matteo   Lapenta, Serafina
Cabañas, Rafael   Leray, Philippe
Cao, Nhung   Llamazares, Bonifacio
Carvalho, Thiago   Mir, Arnau
Casalino, Gabriella   Miś, Katarzyna
Cornejo Piñero, Maria Eugenia   Murinová, Petra
Diaz-Garcia, J. Angel   Muñoz-Velasco, Emilio
Doria, Serena   Nanavati, Kavit
Elouedi, Zied   Ojeda-Aciego, Manuel
Erreygers, Alexander   Ojeda-Hernandez, Manuel
Fernandez-Peralta, Raquel   Peelman, Milan
Figueroa-García, Juan Carlos   Pelessoni, Renato
Flaminio, Tommaso   Petturiti, Davide
Garcia Calvés, Pere   Pekala, Barbara
Godo, Lluis   Quaeghebeur, Erik
González-Arteaga, Teresa   Riera, Juan Vicente
Gupta, Megha   Rodriguez, Ricardo Oscar
Gupta, Vikash Kumar   Rodríguez, Domingo
Guyot, Patrice   Romaniuk, Maciej
Helbin, Piotr   Ruiz, M. Dolores

Runkler, Thomas A.
Rutkowska, Aleksandra
Seliga, Adam
Stupnanova, Andrea
Toulemonde, Gwladys
Troffaes, Matthias
Truong, Phuong

Vannucci, Sara
Vemuri, Nageswara Rao
Vicig, Paolo
Yang, Xiang
Yepmo, Véronne
Yoon, Jin Hee

Contents – Part I

Aggregation Theory Beyond the Unit Interval

Aggregation on a Cartesian Product of Bounded Partially Ordered Sets   3
    Raúl Pérez-Fernández and Bernard De Baets

Flexible-Dimensional EVR-OWA as Mean Estimator for Symmetric
Distributions   11
    Juan Baz, Diego García-Zamora, Irene Díaz, Susana Montes,
    and Luis Martínez

Sugeno Integral Extended to Undefined Inputs   25
    Michal Burda, Martina Daňková, and Viktor Pavliska

Sugeno Integral Based Pandemic Risk Assessment   34
    Luca Anzilli and Marta Cardin

On the Aggregation of n-distances   47
    Tomasa Calvo Sánchez and Pilar Fuster-Parra

Formal Concept Analysis and Uncertainty

Fuzzy Rough Set Decision Algorithms   63
    Fernando Chacón-Gómez, Maria Eugenia Cornejo, Jesús Medina,
    and Eloísa Ramírez-Poussa

Relational Extension of Closure Structures   77
    Manuel Ojeda-Hernández, Inma P. Cabrera, Pablo Cordero,
    and Emilio Muñoz-Velasco

Computing the Mixed Concept Lattice   87
    Francisco Pérez-Gámez, Pablo Cordero, Manuel Enciso,
    Domingo López-Rodríguez, and Ángel Mora

On the Definition of Fuzzy Relational Galois Connections Between Fuzzy
Transitive Digraphs   100
    Inma P. Cabrera, Pablo Cordero, Emilio Muñoz-Velasco,
    Manuel Ojeda-Aciego, and Bernard De Baets

Study on the Necessity Operator to Factorize Formal Contexts
in a Multi-adjoint Framework   107
    Roberto G. Aragón, Jesús Medina, and Eloísa Ramírez-Poussa

Encoding Non-global Time Representations into the Lattice of Divisibility   118
  Francisco José Valverde-Albacete, Carmen Peláez-Moreno,
  Inma P. Cabrera, Pablo Cordero, and Manuel Ojeda-Aciego

On the Effects of Conjunctions in the Solution Set of Multi-adjoint Fuzzy
Relation Equations   130
  David Lobo, Víctor López-Marchante, and Jesús Medina

Comparing Attribute Reduction in Multi-adjoint Concept Lattices
and the CR-method   142
  María José Benítez-Caballero and Jesús Medina

Determining Cause-Effect Relations from Fuzzy Relation Equations   155
  Clemente Rubio-Manzano, Daniel Alfonso-Robaina,
  Juan Carlos Díaz-Moreno, Annette Malleuve-Martínez, and Jesús Medina

Fuzzy Implication Functions

Monodistances from Fuzzy Implications   169
  Kavit Nanavati, Megha Gupta, and Balasubramaniam Jayaram

On the Additional Properties of Fuzzy Polynomial Implications of Degree 4 . . .   182
  Michał Baczyński, Raquel Fernandez-Peralta, Sebastia Massanet,
  Arnau Mir, and Juan Vicente Riera

Preservation of the Ordering Property Under the Quadratic Polynomial
Construction of Fuzzy Implication Functions   194
  Mateusz Pieszczek and Michał Baczyński

On a New Contrapositivisation Technique for Fuzzy Implications
Constructed from Triangular Conorms   206
  Fernando Neres, Benjamín Bedregal, and Regivan Santiago

Construction of Fuzzy Implications from the Bandler-Kohout Subproduct   219
  Katarzyna Miś

Fuzzy Mathematical Analysis and its Applications

On Conflicts of Linguistic Fuzzy Rules   233
  Nhung Cao, Radek Valášek, and Martin Štěpnička

A Review on Differentiability and Optimality Conditions in Fuzzy
Environments   245
  Beatriz Hernández-Jiménez, Rafaela Osuna-Gómez,
  Yurilev Chalco-Cano, and Tiago Mendoça da Costa

Selected Dynamical Properties of Fuzzy Dynamical Systems 258
  Jiří Kupka

Parameterized Metrics and Their Applications in Word Combinatorics 270
  Raivis Bēts, Alexander Šostak, and Emīls Miķelis Miķelsons

CI Approach to Numerical Methods for Solving Fuzzy Integral Equations 282
  Irina Perfilieva and Tam Pham

A Characterization for Generalized Hukuhara Differentiable
Interval-Valued Functions and Some Rules of Calculus 294
  Juan Carlos Blanche-Alcócer and Yurilev Chalco-Cano

Generalized Sets and Operators

Selection of Relevant Features Based on Optimistic and Pessimistic
Similarities Measures of Interval-Valued Fuzzy Sets 307
  Barbara Pękala, Krzysztof Dyczkowski, Jarosław Szkoła,
  and Dawid Kosior

Applications of Monads in Semiring-Valued Fuzzy Sets 320
  Jiří Močkoř

Similarity for Multisets and Heterogeneous Sets 332
  Ryszard Janicki

Attribute Ranking with Bipolar Information 345
  Christophe Marsala

Information Fusion Techniques based on Aggregation Functions, Pre-aggregation Functions, and Their Generalizations

On Construction Methods of (Interval-Valued) General Grouping Functions ... 359
  Graçaliz P. Dimuro, Tiago Asmus, Jocivania Pinheiro, Helida Santos,
  Eduardo Borges, Giancarlo Lucca, Iosu Rodriguez-Martinez,
  Radko Mesiar, and Humberto Bustince

Aggregation Functions in Flexible Classification by Ordinal Sums 372
  Miroslav Hudec, Erika Mináriková, and Radko Mesiar

Honeycomb-Based Polygonal Chains Aggregation Functions 384
  Grzegorz Moś

Polarization Measures in Bi-partition Networks Based on Fuzzy Graphs   398
Clara Simón de Blas, Juan Antonio Guevara, Jaime Morillo,
and Daniel Gómez González

On Rational Bivariate Aggregation Funcions   410
Isabel Aguiló, Sebastia Massanet, and Juan Vicente Riera

Parameterized Pre-aggregation Function with Interval Values in Medical
Decisions Making   421
Krzysztof Balicki and Paweł Drygaś

Int-FLBCC: Exploring Fuzzy Consensus Measures via Penalty Functions   434
Guilherme Schneider, Bruno Moura, Eduardo Monks, Helida Santos,
Adenauer Yamin, and Renata Reiser

Aggregated Fuzzy Equivalence Relations in Clustering Process   448
Olga Grigorenko and Valerijs Mihailovs

Fuzzy-Valued Distance Between Fuzzy Numbers Based on a Generalized
Extension Principle   460
Juscelino Araújo, Benjamin Bedregal, and Regivan Santiago

On an Application of Integral Transforms for Lattice-Valued Functions
in Image Processing   471
Michal Holčapek and Viec Bui Quoc

Interval Uncertainty

Why People Tend to Overestimate Joint Probabilities   485
Olga Kosheleva and Vladik Kreinovich

Necessary and Possibly Optimal Items in Selecting Problems   494
Sébastien Destercke and Romain Guillaume

Anomaly Detection in Crowdsourced Work with Interval-Valued Labels   504
Makenzie Spurling, Chenyi Hu, Huixin Zhan, and Victor S. Sheng

Atanassov's Intuitionistic Fuzzy Sets Demystified   517
Eulalia Szmidt and Janusz Kacprzyk

Towards Explainable Summary of Crowdsourced Reviews Through Text
Mining   528
Aaron Moody, Chenyi Hu, Huixin Zhan, Makenzie Spurling,
and Victor S. Sheng

A New Similarity Measure for Real Intervals to Solve the Aliasing Problem ... 542
*Pedro Huidobro, Noelia Rico, Agustina Bouchet, Susana Montes,
and Irene Díaz*

Knowledge Acquisition, Representation and Reasoning

Similarity Fuzzy Semantic Network for Social Media Analysis 557
Juan Luis Castro and Manuel Francisco

Management of Uncertain Data in Event Graphs 568
Valerio Bellandi, Fulvio Frati, Stefano Siccardi, and Filippo Zuccotti

Possibilistic Preference Networks and Lexicographic Preference Trees –
A Comparison 581
Nahla Ben Amor, Didier Dubois, Henri Prade, and Syrine Saidi

Generating Contextual Weighted Commonsense Knowledge Graphs 593
Navid Rezaei, Marek Z. Reformat, and Ronald R. Yager

Logical Structures of Opposition and Logical Syllogisms

Modelling of Fuzzy Peterson's Syllogisms Related to Graded Peterson's
Cube of Opposition 609
Karel Fiala and Petra Murinová

Comparing Hexagons of Opposition in Probabilistic Rough Set Theory 622
Stefania Boffa, Davide Ciucci, and Petra Murinová

Analysis of Peterson's Rules for Syllogisms with Intermediate Quantifiers 634
Vilém Novák and Petra Murinová

On Modeling of Fuzzy Peterson's Syllogisms Using Peterson's Rules 647
Petra Murinová and Vilém Novák

Mathematical Fuzzy Logics

Cutting of Partial Fuzzy Relations and Their Compositions – The Case
of the Dragonfly Operations 663
Nhung Cao and Martin Štěpnička

Rotations of Gödel Algebras with Modal Operators 676
*Tommaso Flaminio, Lluis Godo, Paula Menchón,
and Ricardo O. Rodriguez*

On Operations of Restriction and Freezing on Monadic Fuzzy Quantifiers
Over Fuzzy Domains 689
    Antonín Dvořák and Michal Holčapek

Involutions on Different Goguen L-fuzzy Sets 703
    S. Cubillo, C. Torres-Blanc, L. Magdalena, and P. Hernández-Varela

On the Order-Compatibility of Fuzzy Logic Connectives on the Generated
Clifford Poset 714
    Kavit Nanavati and Balasubramaniam Jayaram

Theoretical and Applied Aspects of Imprecise Probabilities

Decision Making with State-Dependent Preference Systems 729
    Christoph Jansen and Thomas Augustin

Inner Approximations of Credal Sets by Non-additive Measures 743
    Enrique Miranda, Ignacio Montes, and Andrés Presa

A Robust Bayesian Estimation Approach for the Imprecise Plackett–Luce
Model 757
    Tathagata Basu, Sébastien Destercke, and Benjamin Quost

A Discussion About Independence and Correlation in the Framework
of Coherent Lower Conditional Probability 770
    Giulianella Coletti, Sara Latini, and Davide Petturiti

Markov and Time-Homogeneity Properties in Dempster-Shafer Random
Walks 784
    Andrea Cinfrignini, Davide Petturiti, and Barbara Vantaggi

Correlated Boolean Operators for Uncertainty Logic 798
    Enrique Miralles-Dolz, Ander Gray, Edoardo Patelli, and Scott Ferson

Author Index 813

Contents – Part II

Data Science and Machine Learning

Nonlinear Weighted Independent Component Analysis 3
Andrzej Bedychaj, Przemysław Spurek, Aleksandra Nowak, and Jacek Tabor

Statistical Models for Partial Orders Based on Data Depth and Formal
Concept Analysis 17
Hannah Blocher, Georg Schollmeyer, and Christoph Jansen

BEUD: Bifold-Encoder Uni-Decoder Based Network for Anomaly
Detection 31
Mohith Rajesh, Chinmay Kulkarni, and S. S. Shylaja

Prescriptive Analytics for Optimization of FMCG Delivery Plans 44
*Marek Grzegorowski, Andrzej Janusz, Stanisław Łażewski,
Maciej Świechowski, and Monika Jankowska*

A Multilevel Clustering Method for Risky Areas in the Context
of Avalanche Danger Management 54
*Fanny Pagnier, Frédéric Pourraz, Didier Coquin, Hervé Verjus,
and Gilles Mauris*

Fast Text Based Classification of News Snippets for Telecom Assurance 69
Artur Simões and Joao Paulo Carvalho

Decision Making Modeling and Applications

Reciprocal Preference-Aversion Structures 85
J. Tinguaro Rodríguez, Camilo Franco, and Javier Montero

Calibration of Radiation-Induced Cancer Risk Models According
to Random Data 99
Luis G. Crespo, Tony C. Slaba, Floriane A. Poignant, and Sean P. Kenny

A Novel Variable Selection Approach Based on Multi-criteria Decision
Analysis 115
Shengkun Xie and Jin Zhang

Fintech Lending Decisions: An Interpretable Knowledge-Base System
for Retail and Commercial Loans 128
    Swati Sachan

Intuitionistic Fuzzy Selected Element Reduction Approach (IF-SERA)
on Service Quality Evaluation of Digital Suppliers 141
    Esra Çakır, Mehmet Ali Taş, and Emre Demircioğlu

A New Approach to Polarization Modeling Using Markov Chains 151
    Juan Antonio Guevara, Daniel Gómez, Javier Castro,
    Inmaculada Gutiérrez, and José Manuel Robles

Intervals and Possibility Degree Formulae for Usage Prioritization
of Cartagena Coastal Military Batteries 163
    Juan Miguel Sánchez-Lozano, Manuel Fernández-Martínez,
    Marcelino Cabrera-Cuevas, and David A. Pelta

Stability of Preferences over Time: Preferences on COVID-19 Vaccine
from Spanish and French People 173
    Silvia Prieto-Herráez and Rocio de Andrés Calle

On the Notion of Influence in Sensory Analysis 185
    Jacky Montmain, Abdelhak Imoussaten, Sébastien Harispe,
    and Pierre-Antoine Jean

Study of the Instability of the Sign of the Nonadditivity Index in a Choquet
Integral Model 197
    Paul Alain Kaldjob Kaldjob, Brice Mayag, and Denis Bouyssou

The d-Interaction Index in MCDA 210
    Brice Mayag and Bertrand Tchantcho

E-Health

Analysis of Graphical Causal Models with Discretized Data 223
    Ofir Hanoch, Nalan Baştürk, Rui Jorge Almeida,
    and Tesfa Dejenie Habtewold

Population and Individual Level Meal Response Patterns in Continuous
Glucose Data 235
    Danilo Ferreira de Carvalho, Uzay Kaymak, Pieter Van Gorp,
    and Natal van Riel

Analyzing Patient Feedback Data with Topic Modeling 248
Jasper Arendsen, Emil Rijcken, Kalliopi Zervanou, Kim Rietjens,
Femke Vlems, and Uzay Kaymak

A Framework for Active Contour Initialization with Application to Liver
Segmentation in MRI 259
Arnau Mir-Fuentes, Arnau Mir, Felipe Antunes-Santos,
F. Javier Fernandez, and Carlos Lopez-Molina

Fuzzy Methods in Data Mining and Knowledge Discovery

Improving Text Clustering Using a New Technique for Selecting
Trustworthy Content in Social Networks 275
J. Angel Diaz-Garcia, Carlos Fernandez-Basso,
Karel Gutiérrez-Batista, M. Dolores Ruiz, and Maria J. Martin-Bautista

Fuzzy System-Based Solutions for Traffic Control in Freeway Networks
Toward Sustainable Improvement 288
Mehran Amini, Miklos F. Hatwagner, and Laszlo T. Koczy

Contextual Sentence Embeddings for Obtaining Food Recipe Versions 306
Andrea Morales-Garzón, Juan Gómez-Romero,
and Maria J. Martín-Bautista

A Fuzzy-Based Approach for Cyberbullying Analysis 317
J. Angel Diaz-Garcia, Carlos Fernandez-Basso, Jesica Gómez-Sánchez,
Karel Gutiérrez-Batista, M. Dolores Ruiz, and Maria J. Martin-Bautista

Flexible Division Queries Based on RL-Instances 329
Patricia Córdoba-Hidalgo, Nicolás Marín, and Daniel Sánchez

Soft Computing and Artificial Intelligence Techniques in Image Processing

Image Segmentation Losses with Modules Expressing a Relationship
Between Predictions 343
Petr Hurtik, Vojtech Molek, and Hana Zámečníková

Fuzzy Clustering to Encode Contextual Information in Artistic Image
Classification 355
Javier Fumanal-Idocin, Zdenko Takáč, Ľubomíra Horanská,
Humberto Bustince, and Oscar Cordon

New Aggregation Strategies in Color Edge Detection with HSV Images 367
Pablo A. Flores-Vidal, Daniel Gómez, Javier Castro, and Javier Montero

Representing Vietnamese Traditional Dances and Handling Inconsistent
Information 379
  Salem Benferhat, Zied Bouraoui, Truong-Thanh Ma, and Karim Tabia

Laplace Operator in Connection to Underlying Space Structure 394
  Hana Zámečníková and Irina Perfilieva

Noise Reduction as an Inverse Problem in F-Transform Modelling 405
  Jiří Janeček and Irina Perfilieva

Selection of Keypoints in 2D Images Using F-Transform 418
  Irina Perfilieva and David Adamczyk

3D Shapes Classification Using Intermediate Parts Representation 431
  Jan Hula, David Mojzisek, and David Adamczyk

Content-Aware Image Smoothing Based on Fuzzy Clustering 443
  Felipe Antunes-Santos, Carlos Lopez-Molina, Arnau Mir-Fuentes,
  Maite Mendioroz, and Bernard De Baets

Soft Methods in Statistics and Data Analysis

A Probabilistic Tree Model to Analyze Fuzzy Rating Data 457
  Antonio Calcagnì and Luigi Lombardi

Distance Metrics for Evaluating the Use of Exogenous Data in Load
Forecasting 469
  Ramón Christen, Luca Mazzola, Alexander Denzler, and Edy Portmann

On the Role of the Considered Measure in a Quantile-Based Graded
Version of Stochastic Dominance 483
  Raúl Pérez-Fernández and Juan Baz

Bootstrapped Kolmogorov-Smirnov Test for Epistemic Fuzzy Data 494
  Przemyslaw Grzegorzewski and Maciej Romaniuk

Connections Between Granular Counts and Twofold Fuzzy Sets 508
  Corrado Mencar and Didier Dubois

Testing Independence with Fuzzy Data 520
  Przemyslaw Grzegorzewski

Learning from Categorical Data Subject to Non-random Misclassification
and Non-response Under Prior Quasi-Near-Ignorance Using an Imprecise
Dirichlet Model 532
    Aziz Omar, Timo von Oertzen, and Thomas Augustin

Uncertainty, Heterogeneity, Reliability and Explainability in AI

Uncertainty in Predictive Process Monitoring 547
    Pietro Portolani, Alessandro Brusaferri, Andrea Ballarino,
    and Matteo Matteucci

Set-Based Counterfactuals in Partial Classification 560
    Gabriele Gianini, Jianyi Lin, Corrado Mio, and Ernesto Damiani

Logic Operators and Sibling Aggregators for Z-grades 572
    Guy De Tré, Milan Peelman, and Jozo Dujmović

Canonical Extensions of Conditional Probabilities and Compound
Conditionals 584
    Tommaso Flaminio, Angelo Gilio, Lluis Godo, and Giuseppe Sanfilippo

Classifier Probability Calibration Through Uncertain Information Revision 598
    Sara Kebir and Karim Tabia

Evidential Hybrid Re-sampling for Multi-class Imbalanced Data 612
    Fares Grina, Zied Elouedi, and Eric Lefevre

A Parallel Declarative Framework for Mining High Utility Itemsets 624
    Amel Hidouri, Said Jabbour, Badran Raddaoui, Mouna Chebbah,
    and Boutheina Ben Yaghlane

Towards an FCA-Based Approach for Explaining Multi-label Classification 638
    Hakim Radja, Yassine Djouadi, and Karim Tabia

Characterizing the Possibilistic Repair for Inconsistent Partially Ordered
Assertions 652
    Sihem Belabbes and Salem Benferhat

Coherent Upper Conditional Previsions with Respect to Outer Hausdorff
Measures and the Mathematical Representation of the Selective Attention 667
    Serena Doria

Handling Disagreement in Hate Speech Modelling 681
    Petra Kralj Novak, Teresa Scantamburlo, Andraž Pelicon,
    Matteo Cinelli, Igor Mozetič, and Fabiana Zollo

What Is the Cost of Privacy? 696
    Petr Dvořáček and Petr Hurtik

Integrating Prior Knowledge in Post-hoc Explanations 707
    Adulam Jeyasothy, Thibault Laugel, Marie-Jeanne Lesot,
    Christophe Marsala, and Marcin Detyniecki

PANDA: Human-in-the-Loop Anomaly Detection and Explanation 720
    Grégory Smits, Marie-Jeanne Lesot, Véronne Yepmo Tchaghe,
    and Olivier Pivert

Weak and Cautious Supervised Learning

SSFuzzyART: A Semi-Supervised Fuzzy ART Through Seeding
Initialization 735
    Siwar Jendoubi and Aurélien Baelde

Informed Weak Supervision for Battery Deterioration Level Labeling 748
    Luciano Sánchez, Nahuel Costa, David Anseán, and Inés Couso

Rough-set Based Genetic Algorithms for Weakly Supervised Feature
Selection 761
    Andrea Campagner and Davide Ciucci

Choosing the Decision Hyper-parameter for Some Cautious Classifiers 774
    Abdelhak Imoussaten

Author Index 789

Aggregation Theory Beyond the Unit Interval

Aggregation on a Cartesian Product of Bounded Partially Ordered Sets

Raúl Pérez-Fernández[1]([✉]) and Bernard De Baets[2]

[1] Department of Statistics and O.R. and Mathematics Didactics,
University of Oviedo, Oviedo, Spain
perezfernandez@uniovi.es
[2] KERMIT, Department of Data Analysis and Mathematical Modelling,
Ghent University, Coupure Links 653, 9000 Gent, Belgium
bernard.debaets@ugent.be

Abstract. Aggregation functions on bounded partially ordered sets have been extensively studied for more than thirty years. In this paper, we study aggregation functions on a specific type of bounded partially ordered set: a Cartesian product of several bounded partially ordered sets. In particular, we position this type of aggregation into the recently-introduced framework of aggregation on sets equipped with a betweenness relation (besets), which are a natural generalization of partially ordered sets. The main result is that, depending on the considered set of bounds for the beset associated with the Cartesian product of several bounded partially ordered sets, we obtain two alternative notions: classical aggregation functions w.r.t. the product order on the entire Cartesian product of the bounded partially ordered sets or componentwise aggregation functions acting separately on each of the bounded partially ordered sets.

Keywords: Aggregation · Cartesian product · Poset · Beset

1 Introduction

Aggregation functions formalize the process of combining several objects into a single one [2,7]. The objects to be aggregated typically are elements of a bounded partially ordered set [9] (bounded poset, for short). However, it is nowadays more and more common to study aggregation functions on structures that are not equipped with an order relation [5]. Prominent such examples are the aggregation of rankings [13] and the aggregation of elements of the unit simplex [15]. For this reason, the present authors recently revisited the definition of an aggregation function [12] by substituting the bounded poset by a more general structure, namely a set equipped with a betweenness relation [10] (beset, for short).

Here, we devote our attention to aggregation functions on a specific type of bounded poset: the Cartesian product of several bounded posets. This type

R. Pérez-Fernández—This research has been partially supported by the Spanish Ministry of Science and Technology (TIN-2017-87600-P).

of structure arises naturally in the context of multivariate data, where several attributes are considered at the same time, yet each of the attributes is modelled by a single bounded poset (e.g., when jointly studying the quality and price of a certain product). Typical examples of the Cartesian product of several bounded posets are real bounded hypercubes (the unit hypercube being the most prominent real bounded hypercube), for which there exists a large literature on aggregation functions in the field of multivariate statistics (see, e.g., [6]). In this work, we will position the aggregation on the Cartesian product of several bounded posets as an example of aggregation on a bounded beset. The most interesting discovery is the importance of the choice of the set of bounds for the beset, which will result in either classical aggregation functions w.r.t. the product order on the entire Cartesian product of the bounded posets or componentwise aggregation functions acting separately on each of the bounded posets. Interestingly, in the context of the aggregation of multivariate data, the former type of functions are related to the property of monotonicity w.r.t. the product order, whereas the latter type of functions are related to the property of componentwise monotonicity. For more details on these two types of monotonicity properties, we refer to [6], and for a more general taxonomy of monotonicity properties for the aggregation of multivariate data, we refer to [11].

The remainder of the paper is structured as follows. We first introduce the notion of an aggregation function on a bounded beset in Sect. 2. The particular case in which the considered bounded beset is a Cartesian product of bounded posets is studied in Sect. 3. We end with a short discussion in Sect. 4.

2   Aggregation on Besets

An order relation on X is a binary relation $\leq$ that is reflexive (i.e., $x \leq x$, for any $x \in X$), antisymmetric (i.e., $x \leq y$ and $y \leq x$ imply $x = y$, for any $x, y \in X$) and transitive (i.e., $x \leq y$ and $y \leq z$ imply $x \leq z$, for any $x, y, z \in X$). The pair $(X, \leq)$ is called a partially ordered set (poset, for short). A bounded poset is a poset $(X, \leq, 0, 1)$ for which the elements $0, 1 \in X$ respectively are a lower bound (i.e., $0 \leq x$, for any $x \in X$) and an upper bound (i.e., $x \leq 1$, for any $x \in X$).

Aggregation functions [2,7] are typically described as functions that combine several objects of a bounded poset into a single one, while satisfying some desirable properties, namely the boundary conditions and increasingness (in the present context, more appropriately called order preservation).

Definition 1. *Consider a bounded poset $(X, \leq, 0, 1)$ and $n \in \mathbb{N}$. A function $A : X^n \to X$ is called an (n-ary) aggregation function on $(X, \leq, 0, 1)$ if*

(i) it satisfies the boundary conditions, i.e., $A(0, \ldots, 0) = 0$ and $A(1, \ldots, 1) = 1$;
(ii) it is order-preserving, i.e., for any $(x_1, \ldots, x_n), (y_1, \ldots, y_n) \in X^n$ such that $x_i \leq y_i$ for any $i \in \{1, \ldots, n\}$, it holds that

$$A(x_1, \ldots, x_n) \leq A(y_1, \ldots, y_n).$$

Unfortunately, although this definition may seem very general at first sight, it is actually quite restrictive in terms of the objects that may be aggregated. For instance, as was already mentioned in the introduction, the aggregation of rankings [13] and the aggregation of elements of the unit simplex [15] are two largely studied examples of aggregation processes on structures that are not (bounded) posets. For this purpose, the present authors recently proposed to further generalize the definition of an aggregation function by substituting the structure of a poset with the more general structure of a beset [12]. A beset is simply a set equipped with a betweenness relation, which is a ternary relation representing whether an object is in between two other objects. The study of betweenness relations dates back several decades and several axiomatic definitions have been explored (see, e.g., [1,4,8,14]). For data aggregation, we restrict to the one in [10], which provides a set with natural and interesting semantics. In particular, it assures that the binary relation R_o defined from the betweenness relation B via $(x, y) \in R_o$ if $(o, x, y) \in B$, for any fixed $o \in X$, is assured to be an order relation [16], thus allowing to understand a beset as a family of posets.

Definition 2. *A ternary relation B on a non-empty set X is called a betweenness relation if it satisfies the following three properties:*

(i) Symmetry in the end points: for any $x, y, z \in X$, it holds that

$$(x, y, z) \in B \Leftrightarrow (z, y, x) \in B.$$

(ii) Closure: for any $x, y, z \in X$, it holds that

$$((x, y, z) \in B \wedge (x, z, y) \in B) \Leftrightarrow y = z.$$

(iii) End-point transitivity: for any $o, x, y, z \in X$, it holds that

$$((o, x, y) \in B \wedge (o, y, z) \in B) \Rightarrow (o, x, z) \in B.$$

A set X equipped with a betweenness relation B is called a beset and denoted by (X, B).

As for posets, we could define the notion of a set of bounds of a beset.

Definition 3. *Given a beset (X, B), a non-empty subset S of X is called a set of bounds of (X, B) if, for any $y \in S$ and any $x, z \in X \backslash S$, it holds that $(x, y, z) \notin B$. We thus refer to (X, B, S) as a bounded beset.*

The definition of an aggregation function on a poset could thus be naturally generalized in order to deal with besets.

Definition 4. *Consider a bounded beset (X, B, S) and $n \in \mathbb{N}$. A function $A : X^n \to X$ is called an (n-ary) aggregation function on (X, B, S) if*

(i) it satisfies the boundary conditions, i.e., $A(o, \ldots, o) = o$, for any $o \in S$;

(ii) it is betweenness-preserving, i.e., for any $o \in S$ and any $(x_1, \ldots, x_n)$, $(y_1, \ldots, y_n) \in X^n$ such that $(o, x_i, y_i) \in B$ for any $i \in \{1, \ldots, n\}$, it holds that

$$\big(A(o, \ldots, o), A(x_1, \ldots, x_n), A(y_1, \ldots, y_n)\big) \in B.$$

As proven in [12], Definition 1 for an aggregation function on a bounded poset $(X, \leq, 0, 1)$ and Definition 4 for an aggregation function on a bounded beset (X, B, S) are equivalent in case $S = \{0, 1\}$ and B is the betweenness relation $B_\leq$ induced by $\leq$, i.e.,

$$B_\leq = \big\{(x, y, z) \in X^3 \mid (x = y) \vee (y = z) \vee (x \leq y \leq z) \vee (z \leq y \leq x)\big\}. \tag{1}$$

Theorem 1. [12] *Consider a bounded poset $(X, \leq, 0, 1)$, the associated bounded beset $(X, B_\leq, \{0, 1\})$ and $n \in \mathbb{N}$. A function $A : X^n \to X$ is an aggregation function on $(X, B_\leq, \{0, 1\})$ (in the sense of Definition 4) if and only if it is an aggregation function on $(X, \leq, 0, 1)$ (in the sense of Definition 1).*

3   Aggregation on a Cartesian Product of Bounded Posets

3.1   The Beset Structure of a Cartesian Product of Bounded Posets

Consider m bounded posets $(X_j, \leq_j, 0_j, 1_j)$, $j \in \{1, \ldots, m\}$. Each order relation $\leq_j$ induces a betweenness relation B_j on X_j, as in Eq. (1). The ternary relation $\mathbf{B}$ on $\mathbf{X} = X_1 \times \ldots \times X_m$ defined by

$$\mathbf{B} = \{(\mathbf{x}, \mathbf{y}, \mathbf{z}) \in X_1 \times \ldots \times X_m \mid (\forall j \in \{1, \ldots, m\})((x_j, y_j, z_j) \in B_j)\},$$

is a betweenness relation, hereinafter called the product betweenness relation of $B_1, \ldots, B_m$. Therefore, the structure $(\mathbf{X}, \mathbf{B})$ is a beset.

Note that the betweenness relation $\mathbf{B}$ does not coincide with the betweenness relation $B_{\leq_\pi}$ induced by the product order relation $\leq_\pi := \leq_1 \times \ldots \times \leq_m$ on $\mathbf{X}$. For instance, consider $X_1 = X_2 = [0, 1]$ and $\leq_1 = \leq_2$ the usual order relation on $\mathbb{R}$. Given $\mathbf{x} = (0, 1)$, $\mathbf{y} = (0.5, 0.5)$ and $\mathbf{z} = (1, 0)$, it follows that $(\mathbf{x}, \mathbf{y}, \mathbf{z}) \in \mathbf{B}$, but $(\mathbf{x}, \mathbf{y}, \mathbf{z}) \notin B_{\leq_\pi}$. However, since it will be key in the upcoming subsection, it is important to remark that both betweenness relations share at least all triplets for which one of the end-points is either $\mathbf{0} := (0_1, \ldots, 0_m)$ or $\mathbf{1} := (1_1, \ldots, 1_m)$. More precisely, it holds that $(\mathbf{0}, \mathbf{x}, \mathbf{y}) \in \mathbf{B}$ is equivalent to $(\mathbf{0}, \mathbf{x}, \mathbf{y}) \in B_{\leq_\pi}$. Similarly, $(\mathbf{1}, \mathbf{x}, \mathbf{y}) \in \mathbf{B}$ is equivalent to $(\mathbf{1}, \mathbf{x}, \mathbf{y}) \in B_{\leq_\pi}$.

3.2   Classical Aggregation Functions on a Cartesian Product of Bounded Posets

It has been seen that $(\mathbf{X}, \mathbf{B})$ is a beset. It can easily be verified that $\mathbf{S}_0 = \{\mathbf{0}, \mathbf{1}\}$ is a set of bounds of $(\mathbf{X}, \mathbf{B})$. Similarly to Theorem 1, it turns out that aggregation functions on $(\mathbf{X}, \mathbf{B}, \mathbf{S}_0)$ are precisely classical aggregation functions on the Cartesian product of the bounded posets.

Proposition 1. *Consider m bounded posets $(X_j, \leq_j, 0_j, 1_j)$, $j \in \{1, \ldots, m\}$, and the associated bounded besets $(X_j, B_{\leq_j}, \{0_j, 1_j\})$, $j \in \{1, \ldots, m\}$, and $n \in \mathbb{N}$. A function $A : \mathbf{X}^n \to \mathbf{X}$ is an aggregation function on $(\mathbf{X}, \mathbf{B}, \mathbf{S}_0)$ if and only if it is an aggregation function on $(\mathbf{X}, \leq_\pi, \mathbf{0}, \mathbf{1})$.*

Proof. From Theorem 1, it follows that a function $A : \mathbf{X}^n \to \mathbf{X}$ is an aggregation function on $(\mathbf{X}, B_{\leq_\pi}, \mathbf{S}_0)$ if and only if it is an aggregation function on $(\mathbf{X}, \leq_\pi, \mathbf{0}, \mathbf{1})$. We simply need to prove that a function $A : \mathbf{X}^n \to \mathbf{X}$ is an aggregation function on $(\mathbf{X}, B_{\leq_\pi}, \mathbf{S}_0)$ if and only if it is an aggregation function on $(\mathbf{X}, \mathbf{B}, \mathbf{S}_0)$. Since the betweenness relation does not play a role in the boundary conditions, only the betweenness preservation needs to be verified. The result then follows from the fact that $(\mathbf{0}, \mathbf{x}, \mathbf{y}) \in \mathbf{B}$ is equivalent to $(\mathbf{0}, \mathbf{x}, \mathbf{y}) \in B_{\leq_\pi}$, and that $(\mathbf{1}, \mathbf{x}, \mathbf{y}) \in \mathbf{B}$ is equivalent to $(\mathbf{1}, \mathbf{x}, \mathbf{y}) \in B_{\leq_\pi}$. $\square$

3.3   Componentwise Aggregation Functions on a Cartesian Product of Bounded Posets

In this section, we consider a different set of bounds $\mathbf{S}_1 = \{0_1, 1_1\} \times \ldots \times \{0_m, 1_m\}$ of $(\mathbf{X}, \mathbf{B})$. Since $\mathbf{S}_0 \subseteq \mathbf{S}_1$, it follows from Proposition 1 that aggregation functions on $(\mathbf{X}, \mathbf{B}, \mathbf{S}_1)$ are aggregation functions on the Cartesian product of the bounded posets. In particular, this set of bounds characterizes all aggregation functions on the Cartesian product of the bounded posets that can be decomposed into m aggregation functions, one on each of the bounded posets. This type of aggregation function has been studied, for instance, in the context of triangular norms on product lattices [3].

Proposition 2. *Consider m bounded posets $(X_j, \leq_j, 0_j, 1_j)$, $j \in \{1, \ldots, m\}$, the associated bounded besets $(X_j, B_{\leq_j}, \{0_j, 1_j\})$, $j \in \{1 \ldots, m\}$, and $n \in \mathbb{N}$. A function $A : \mathbf{X}^n \to \mathbf{X}$ is an aggregation function on $(\mathbf{X}, \mathbf{B}, \mathbf{S}_1)$ if and only if there exist m aggregation functions $A'_j : X_j^n \to X_j$ on $(X_j, \leq_j, 0_j, 1_j)$, $j \in \{1, \ldots, m\}$, such that $A(\mathbf{x}^1, \ldots, \mathbf{x}^n) = (A'_1(\mathbf{x}_1^1, \ldots, \mathbf{x}_1^n), \ldots, A'_m(\mathbf{x}_m^1, \ldots, \mathbf{x}_m^n))$ for any $\mathbf{x}^1, \ldots, \mathbf{x}^n \in \mathbf{X}$.*

Proof. Left-to-right implication. Consider an aggregation function $A : \mathbf{X}^n \to \mathbf{X}$ on $(\mathbf{X}, \mathbf{B}, \mathbf{S}_1)$. We first prove that, for $j \in \{1, \ldots, m\}$, the function $A_j : \mathbf{X}^n \to \mathbf{X}$, representing the j-th projection after applying A, only depends on the values at the j-th components of the inputs. Consider $\mathbf{x}^1, \ldots, \mathbf{x}^n, \mathbf{y}^1, \ldots, \mathbf{y}^n \in \mathbf{X}$ such that $\mathbf{x}_j^i \leq \mathbf{y}_j^i$ and $\mathbf{y}_\ell^i = 0_\ell$ when $\ell \neq j$, for any $i \in \{1, \ldots, n\}$. For any $i \in \{1, \ldots, n\}$, it follows that $(\mathbf{x}_j^i, \mathbf{y}_j^i, 1_j) \in B_j$ and $(\mathbf{x}_\ell^i, \mathbf{y}_\ell^i, 0_\ell) \in B_\ell$ for any $\ell \neq j$, thus $(\mathbf{x}^i, \mathbf{y}^i, \mathbf{s}) \in \mathbf{B}$, where $\mathbf{s} \in \mathbf{S}_1$ is such that $\mathbf{s}_j = 1_j$ and $\mathbf{s}_\ell = 0_\ell$ for any $\ell \neq j$. It follows that

$$\left(A(\mathbf{x}^1, \ldots, \mathbf{x}^n), A(\mathbf{y}^1, \ldots, \mathbf{y}^n), A(\mathbf{s}, \ldots, \mathbf{s})\right) \in \mathbf{B}.$$

In particular, it holds that

$$\left(A_j(\mathbf{x}^1, \ldots, \mathbf{x}^n), A_j(\mathbf{y}^1, \ldots, \mathbf{y}^n), A_j(\mathbf{s}, \ldots, \mathbf{s})\right) \in B_j.$$

Since $A_j(\mathbf{s}, \ldots, \mathbf{s}) = 1_j$, the above implies that

$$A_j(\mathbf{x}^1, \ldots, \mathbf{x}^n) \leq A_j(\mathbf{y}^1, \ldots, \mathbf{y}^n).$$

Note that, for any $\mathbf{z}^1, \ldots, \mathbf{z}^n \in \mathbf{X}$ such that $\mathbf{z}_j^i = \mathbf{y}_j^i$ for any $i \in \{1, \ldots, n\}$, it holds that $\mathbf{y}^i \leq_\pi \mathbf{z}^i$ for any $i \in \{1, \ldots, n\}$. Therefore, since A is an aggregation function on $(\mathbf{X}, \leq_\pi, \mathbf{0}, \mathbf{1})$ (see Proposition 1 and note that $\mathbf{S}_0 \subset \mathbf{S}_1$), we conclude that for any $\mathbf{x}^1, \ldots, \mathbf{x}^n, \mathbf{z}^1, \ldots, \mathbf{z}^n \in \mathbf{X}$ such that $\mathbf{x}_j^i \leq \mathbf{z}_j^i$, it holds that

$$A_j(\mathbf{x}^1, \ldots, \mathbf{x}^n) \leq A_j(\mathbf{z}^1, \ldots, \mathbf{z}^n).$$

Therefore, we finally obtain that, for any $\mathbf{x}^1, \ldots, \mathbf{x}^n, \mathbf{z}^1, \ldots, \mathbf{z}^n \in \mathbf{X}$ such that $\mathbf{x}_j^i = \mathbf{z}_j^i$, it holds that

$$A_j(\mathbf{x}^1, \ldots, \mathbf{x}^n) = A_j(\mathbf{z}^1, \ldots, \mathbf{z}^n).$$

We conclude that we have m functions $A_j' : X_j^n \to \mathbf{X}$ satisfying $A_j'(\mathbf{x}_j^1, \ldots, \mathbf{x}_j^n) = A_j(\mathbf{x}^1, \ldots, \mathbf{x}^n)$, for any $\mathbf{x}^1, \ldots, \mathbf{x}^n \in \mathbf{X}$. Next, we prove that each A_j' is an aggregation function on $(X_j, \leq_j, 0_j, 1_j)$. Consider $j \in \{1, \ldots, m\}$. The boundary conditions are fulfilled since it holds that

$$A_j'(0_j, \ldots, 0_j) = A_j(\mathbf{0}, \ldots, \mathbf{0}) = 0_j,$$

and

$$A_j'(1_j, \ldots, 1_j) = A_j(\mathbf{1}, \ldots, \mathbf{1}) = 1_j.$$

Consider any $\mathbf{x}_j^1, \ldots, \mathbf{x}_j^n, \mathbf{y}_j^1, \ldots, \mathbf{y}_j^n \in X_j$ such that $\mathbf{x}_j^i \leq \mathbf{y}_j^i$ for any $i \in \{1, \ldots, n\}$. If we consider $\mathbf{x}_\ell^i = 0_\ell$ and $\mathbf{y}_\ell^i = 1_\ell$ for any $i \in \{1, \ldots, n\}$ and any $\ell \neq j$, then we have $\mathbf{x}^i \leq_\pi \mathbf{y}^i$ for any $i \in \{1, \ldots, n\}$. Order preservation is fulfilled since it holds that

$$A_j'(\mathbf{x}_j^1, \ldots, \mathbf{x}_j^n) = A_j(\mathbf{x}^1, \ldots, \mathbf{x}^n)$$
$$\leq A_j(\mathbf{y}^1, \ldots, \mathbf{y}^n)$$
$$= A_j'(\mathbf{x}_j^1, \ldots, \mathbf{x}_j^n),$$

where the inequality follows from A being an aggregation function on $(\mathbf{X}, \leq_\pi, \mathbf{0}, \mathbf{1})$ (see Proposition 1 and note that $\mathbf{S}_0 \subset \mathbf{S}_1$).

Right-to-left implication. Consider m aggregation functions $A_j' : X_j^n \to X_j$ on $(X_j, \leq_j, 0_j, 1_j)$, $j \in \{1, \ldots, m\}$, such that

$$A(\mathbf{x}^1, \ldots, \mathbf{x}^n) = (A_1'(\mathbf{x}_1^1, \ldots, \mathbf{x}_1^n), \ldots, A_m'(\mathbf{x}_m^1, \ldots, \mathbf{x}_m^n)),$$

for any $\mathbf{x}^1, \ldots, \mathbf{x}^n \in \mathbf{X}$. For any $\mathbf{o} \in \mathbf{S}_1$, it follows that

$$A(\mathbf{o}, \ldots, \mathbf{o}) = (A_1'(\mathbf{o}_1, \ldots, \mathbf{o}_1), \ldots, A_m'(\mathbf{o}_m, \ldots, \mathbf{o}_m))$$
$$= (\mathbf{o}_1, \ldots, \mathbf{o}_m) = \mathbf{o}.$$

Therefore, A satisfies the boundary conditions. Similarly, for any $\mathbf{o} \in \mathbf{S}_1$ and any $(\mathbf{x}^1, \ldots, \mathbf{x}^n), (\mathbf{y}^1, \ldots, \mathbf{y}^n) \in \mathbf{X}^n$ such that $(\mathbf{o}, \mathbf{x}^i, \mathbf{y}^i) \in \mathbf{B}$ for any $i \in \{1, \ldots, n\}$, it holds that

$$(\mathbf{o}_j, \mathbf{x}_j^i, \mathbf{y}_j^i) \in B_{\leq_j},$$

for any $j \in \{1, \ldots, m\}$. Since each A_j' is an aggregation function on $(X_j, \leq_j, 0_j, 1_j)$, it follows that

$$(A_j'(\mathbf{o}_j, \ldots, \mathbf{o}_j), A_j'(\mathbf{x}_j^1, \ldots, \mathbf{x}_j^n), A_j'(\mathbf{y}_j^1, \ldots, \mathbf{y}_j^n)) \in B_{\leq_j},$$

for any $j \in \{1, \ldots, m\}$. Therefore, by definition of A and $\mathbf{B}$, it follows that

$$(A(\mathbf{o}, \ldots, \mathbf{o}), A(\mathbf{x}^1, \ldots, \mathbf{x}^n), A(\mathbf{y}^1, \ldots, \mathbf{y}^n)) \in \mathbf{B}.$$

We conclude that A preserves the betweenness relation $\mathbf{B}$ and thus is an aggregation function on $(\mathbf{X}, \mathbf{B}, \mathbf{S}_1)$. □

4 Conclusion

In this paper, we have explored the aggregation of elements of a Cartesian product of bounded posets. This problem setting arises naturally in the context of multivariate data, where more than one attribute is studied at the same time but each attribute is linked to a single bounded poset. In particular, we have positioned the aggregation on a Cartesian product of bounded posets in the recently-introduced framework of aggregation on a bounded beset. Interestingly, depending on the choice of set of bounds of the beset, we obtain either classical aggregation functions w.r.t. the product order on the entire Cartesian product of the bounded posets or componentwise aggregation functions acting separately on each of the bounded posets.

References

1. Bankston, P.: Road systems and betweenness. Bull. Math. Sci. **3**(3), 389–408 (2013)
2. Beliakov, G., Pradera, A., Calvo, T.: Aggregation Functions: A Guide for Practitioners. Studies in Fuzziness and Soft Computing, vol. 221. Springer, Heidelberg (2007)
3. De Baets, B., Mesiar, R.: Triangular norms on product lattices. Fuzzy Sets Syst. **104**(1), 61–75 (1999)
4. Fishburn, P.C.: Betweenness, orders and interval graphs. J. Pure Appl. Algebra **1**(2), 159–178 (1971)
5. Gagolewski, M.: Data Fusion. Theory, Methods and Applications. Institute of Computer Science, Polish Academy of Sciences, Warsaw (2015)
6. Gagolewski, M.: Penalty-based aggregation of multidimensional data. Fuzzy Sets Syst. **325**, 4–20 (2017)
7. Grabisch, M., Marichal, J.L., Mesiar, R., Pap, E.: Aggregation Functions. Cambridge University Press, Cambridge (2009)
8. Huntington, E.V., Kline, J.R.: Sets of independent postulates for betweenness. Trans. Am. Math. Soc. **18**(3), 301–325 (1917)

9. Komornikova, M., Mesiar, R.: Aggregation functions on bounded partially ordered sets and their classification. Fuzzy Sets Syst. **175**(1), 48–56 (2011)
10. Pérez-Fernández, R., De Baets, B.: On the role of monometrics in penalty-based data aggregation. IEEE Trans. Fuzzy Syst. **27**(7), 1456–1468 (2019)
11. Pérez-Fernández, R., De Baets, B., Gagolewski, M.: A taxonomy of monotonicity properties for the aggregation of multidimensional data. Inf. Fusion **52**, 322–334 (2019)
12. Pérez-Fernández, R., De Baets, B.: Aggregation theory revisited. IEEE Trans. Fuzzy Syst. **29**(4), 797–804 (2020)
13. Pérez-Fernández, R., Rademaker, M., De Baets, B.: Monometrics and their role in the rationalisation of ranking rules. Inf. Fusion **34**, 16–27 (2017)
14. Pitcher, E., Smiley, M.F.: Transitivities of betweenness. Trans. Am. Math. Soc. **52**(1), 95–114 (1942)
15. Wilkin, T., Beliakov, G.: Robust aggregation of compositional and interval-valued data: the mode on the unit simplex. Fuzzy Sets Syst. (2021). https://doi.org/10.1016/j.fss.2021.01.007
16. Zhang, H.P., Pérez-Fernández, R., De Baets, B.: Topologies induced by the representation of a betweenness relation as a family of order relations. Topology Appl. **258**, 100–114 (2019)

Flexible-Dimensional EVR-OWA as Mean Estimator for Symmetric Distributions

Juan Baz[1]($\boxtimes$)(iD), Diego García-Zamora[2](iD), Irene Díaz[3](iD), Susana Montes[1](iD), and Luis Martínez[2](iD)

[1] Department of Statistics and O.R. and Mathematics Didactics,
University of Oviedo, Oviedo, Spain
{bazjuan,montes}@uniovi.es

[2] Department of Computer Science, University of Jaén, Jaén, Spain
{dgzamora,martin}@ujaen.es

[3] Department of Computer Science, University of Oviedo, Oviedo, Spain
sirene@uniovi.es

Abstract. In the field of statistics, linear combinations of order statistics, also known as L-statistics, have been widely used for the estimation of the mean of a population, which is equivalent to considering Ordered Weighted Averaging (OWA) operators over simple random samples. If previous data are available or the distribution of the deviation from the mean is known, it is possible to compute optimal OWA weights that minimize the Mean Squared Error of the estimation. However, the optimal weights can only be used for a specific sample size, while in real Statistics the number of values that must be aggregated may change. In order to overcome this limitation, this contribution proposes a method based on the use of the recently defined Extreme Value Reductions (EVRs) to fit the cumulative optimal OWA weights and then use these EVRs to compute new weights for a different sample size. In addition, theoretical and simulated results are provided to show that, if sample sizes that are similar to the original one are considered, the weights generated by using EVRs are also similar to the optimal ones.

Keywords: Mean Estimation · EVR-OWA operator · Extreme Values Reduction · Flexible Sample Size

1 Introduction

Estimating the mean of a population is a classical problem in statistics [21]. One of the approaches that has been considered in the literature consists of using linear combinations of order statistics, or L-statistics, in which the values of the

This research has been partially supported by the Spanish Ministry of Science and Technology (TIN-2017-87600-P and PGC2018-098623-B-I00), the Spanish Ministry of Economy and Competitiveness (PGC2018-099402-B-I00) and by the Spanish Ministry of Universities (FPU2019/01203).

© Springer Nature Switzerland AG 2022
D. Ciucci et al. (Eds.): IPMU 2022, CCIS 1601, pp. 11–24, 2022.
https://doi.org/10.1007/978-3-031-08971-8_2

random sample are multiplied by a weight depending on their position when sorted from the lower to the higher one, and then added. This topic of statistics has been developed from 1952 [17], to the most recent contributions [9,16]. From the aggregation theory point of view, this linear combination of order statistics is equivalent to applying an Ordered Weighted Averaging (OWA) operator, see [4], to the random sample.

In some cases, the distribution of the deviation from the mean is known, or there are real data available that can be used to compute the optimal weights to minimize the Mean Squared Error (MSE) when estimating the mean using order statistics. In these situations, this optimal weighting is expected to be combined with a new random sample to obtain the best possible estimation. However, in some cases, the size of the new random sample could be different from the size of the former sample. One of the most notable examples is the case of censored samples [2,3,18], which are commonly applied in survival analysis [15], where the sample size can be reduced due to external factors. However, it is also possible that the sample size grows because of an increase in, for example, the frequency of the measure or the number of experts. For all of these cases, it is no longer possible to use the optimal weights determined for a specific sample.

In order to overcome this drawback, this contribution proposes a method for estimating the mean of a population with symmetric distribution based on the EVR-OWA operator introduced by García-Zamora et al. [11] which allow generating OWA weights for different values of the sample size. In particular, starting with optimal weights for a sample size, the cumulative weights are fitted using a family of Extreme Values Reductions (EVR) [10,11]. Subsequently, the weights for other sample sizes are computed by using the fitted EVR. Theoretical results that endorse this procedure are provided and the behavior of the method is explored by using simulated data from logistic and hyperbolic secant distributions.

The remainder of the paper is structured as follows. In Sect. 2, the main concepts and basic results involving mean estimation and the EVR-OWA operator are introduced. The use of the OWA operator for mean estimation is discussed in Sect. 3. The theoretical aspects regarding the convergence of the cumulative weights are included in Sect. 4. Section 5 is devoted to the definition and study of the behavior of the proposed procedure. Finally, the conclusions and some comments about future work are discussed in Sect. 6.

2   Preliminaries

In this section, we introduce the general concepts needed for understanding the contribution. In particular, we will show some basic definitions and results concerning mean estimation and the EVR-OWA operator.

2.1   Mean Estimation

First, let us recall the basic concepts about mean estimation based on order statistics. Rohatgi et al. [21] has been used as the main reference.

Consider a random variable X. We denote its density and cumulative distribution functions as f and F, respectively. The support of the variable, that is, $\{x \in \mathbb{R} \mid f(x) > 0\}$, is denoted as S. Now, consider a random sample, that is, a (finite) sequence of random variables $X_1, \ldots, X_n$ such that they are all independent and have the same distribution as X.

Even though the expression for the density and cumulative distribution function of X are known, it depends on one or more unknown parameters. If Θ denotes the set of possible values for the unknown parameter θ, an estimator of θ is a function of the random sample whose image is Θ.

Definition 1. *Let $X_1, \ldots, X_n$ be a sequence of independent and identically distributed (iid for short) random variables with density function f_θ depending on some unknown parameters $\theta \in \Theta$. An estimator is a measurable function $f : \mathbb{R}^n \to \Theta$ that does not depend on the value of the unknown parameters.*

In classical statistics, scholars and researchers have defined and studied the desirable properties that an estimator for a certain parameter should satisfy. Here, we are going to focus on unbiasedness and efficiency.

Definition 2. *Let $X_1, \ldots, X_n$ be a sequence of random variables with the same density function f_θ depending on some unknown parameter $\theta \in \Theta$. An estimator T is called unbiased if $E[T] = \theta$ for any $\theta \in \Theta$.*

The efficiency regards on the Mean Squared Error (MSE) between two estimators for a parameter.

Definition 3. *Let $X_1, \ldots, X_n$ be a sequence of iid random variables with density function f_θ depending on the unknown parameter $\theta \in \Theta$ and T_1, T_2 two estimators of θ. It is said that T_1 is more efficient than T_2 if $MSE(T_1) \leq MSE(T_2)$ for any $\theta \in \Theta$ and exists $\theta_0 \in \Theta$ such that $MSE(T_1) < MSE(T_2)$.*

A relation between the bias and the efficiency of an estimator can be done by using the well-known Fréchet-Cramér-Rao inequality [6,8,20]. Since the EVR-OWA, and any other OWA operator, relies on the order of the aggregated values, when used over a random sample, we need to use the concept of order statistic.

Definition 4. *[21] Let $X_1, \ldots, X_n$ be a sequence of random variables. The function $X_{(k)}$ of $(X_1, \ldots, X_n)$ that takes the value k-th smaller value in each possible observation $(x_1, \ldots, x_n)$ of $(X_1, ..., X_n)$ is known as the k-th order statistic or the statistic of order k (of the sequence $X_1, \ldots, X_n$).*

The use of order statistics in estimation has been a classic research line in statistics [17,22–24] and continues to be an important topic today [1,7,9,13,16].

2.2   The EVR-OWA Operator

Here, there are provided some basics about OWA operators [27,28] and García-Zamora et al. method [11] to generate positive symmetric weights for OWA operators that give more importance to intermediate values.

Ordered Weighted Averaging Operators. OWA operators are a family of aggregation functions [4] which allow assigning importance to the aggregated values according to their position with respect to the median value. Formally:

Definition 5. *Let* $w \in [0,1]^n$ *be a weighting vector such that* $\sum_{i=1}^{m} w = 1$. *The OWA Operator* $\Psi_w : [0,1]^n \to [0,1]$ *associated to* w *is defined by:*

$$\Psi_w(\vec{x}) = \sum_{k=1}^{n} w_k x_{\sigma(k)} \ \forall \ \vec{x} \in [0,1]^n$$

where σ *is a permutation of the* n-*tuple* $(1,2,...,n)$ *such that* $x_{\sigma(1)} \geq x_{\sigma(2)} \geq ... \geq x_{\sigma(n)}$.

Note that OWA operators allow generalizing other classical aggregation functions. For example, if the weighting vector is chosen as $w = (\frac{1}{n}, \frac{1}{n}, ..., \frac{1}{n}) \in [0,1]^n$, the aggregation function obtained is the arithmetic mean, while from $w = (1,0,...,0) \in [0,1]^n$ or $w = (0,...,0,1) \in [0,1]^n$ the maximum operator and the minimum operator are obtained, respectively.

Also notice that the OWA operator orders the elements from the greatest to the smallest and the order statistics from the smallest to the greatest. Thus, when an OWA operator is applied to a random sample, the k-th weight is associated with the $(n+1-k)$-th order statistics. In the case of symmetric distributions, which will lead to symmetric weights, these two ordinations are, in fact, equivalent.

Linear RIM Quantifiers to Compute OWA Weights. In order to define weights for OWA operators Yager [28] proposed the use of Fuzzy Linguistic Quantifiers [29]. Specifically, given a Regular Increasing Monotonous (RIM) quantifier, namely an increasing function $Q : [0,1] \to [0,1]$ such that $Q(0) = 0$ and $Q(1) = 1$, the weights for an OWA operator to aggregate $n \in \mathbb{N}$ elements were computed as follows:

$$w_k = Q\left(\frac{k}{n}\right) - Q\left(\frac{k-1}{n}\right) \ \text{ for } k = 1,2,...,n.$$

Note that the final values of the weights strongly depend on the choice of a suitable linguistic quantifier. One of the most widely extended choices [14,19] is the linear RIM quantifier $Q_{\alpha,\beta} : [0,1] \to [0,1]$, $0 \leq \alpha < \beta \leq 1$ defined by:

$$Q_{\alpha,\beta}(x) = \begin{cases} 0 & 0 \leq x < \alpha \\ \frac{x-\alpha}{\beta-\alpha} & \alpha \leq x \leq \beta \\ 1 & x \geq \beta \end{cases},$$

which allow modifying the importance of the intermediate values by changing the values of α and β.

The EVR-OWA Operator. In order to overcome some limitations of the linear RIM quantifier, García-Zamora et al. proposed the use of Extreme Values Reductions (EVRs) [11] as RIM linguistic quantifiers:

Definition 6 *[10]. Let* $\hat{D} : [0,1] \to [0,1]$ *be a function satisfying:*

1. $\hat{D}$ *is an automorphism in the interval* $[0,1]$,
2. $\hat{D}$ *is a function of class* $\mathcal{C}^1$,
3. $\hat{D}$ *satisfies* $\hat{D}(x) = 1 - \hat{D}(1-x) \; \forall \; x \in [0,1]$,
4. $\hat{D}'(0) < 1$ *and* $\hat{D}'(1) < 1$,
5. $\hat{D}$ *is convex in a neighborhood of* 0 *and concave in a neighborhood of* 1,

then $\hat{D}$ *will be called Extreme Values Reduction (EVR) in the interval* $[0,1]$.

The main property of such functions is the fact that they reduce distances between the most extreme values of the interval $[0,1]$ whereas increase the distances between the intermediate values [10] (see Fig. 1).

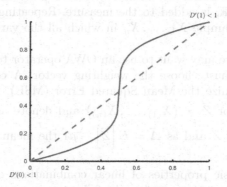

Fig. 1. Scheme of an EVR

For instance, some examples of EVRs are the functions $s_\alpha : [0,1] \to [0,1]$, $\alpha \in]0, \frac{1}{2\pi}]$ defined by

$$\hat{s}_\alpha(x) = x + \alpha \cdot \sin(2\pi x - \pi) \; \forall \; x \in [0,1]$$

and the polynomial functions $p_\alpha : [0,1] \to [0,1]$, $\alpha \in]0,1]$ defined as

$$p_\alpha(x) = (1 - \alpha)x + 3\alpha x^2 - 2\alpha x^3 \; \forall \; x \in [0,1].$$

Consequently, the EVR-OWA operator was defined as an OWA operator whose weights were computed by using an EVR [11]:

Definition 7. *Let* $\hat{D}$ *be an Extreme Values Reduction and consider* $n \in \mathbb{N}$. *Then, the family* $W = \{w_1, w_2, ..., w_n\}$, *where*

$$w_k = \hat{D}\left(\frac{k}{n}\right) - \hat{D}\left(\frac{k-1}{n}\right) \; \forall \; k \in \{1, 2, ..., n\},$$

receives the name of order n weights associated with the EVR $\hat{D}$, and the OWA operator $\Psi_{\hat{D}}$ defined with respect to these weights.

The latter procedure for computing the weights of the OWA operator can be seen as a particular example of an Extended Ordered Weighted Averaging (EOWA), we refer to [5], for which the weighting triangles are computed using an EVR.

3   OWA Operator for Mean Estimation

Regarding the concepts of the previous section, applying an OWA operator to a random sample is equivalent to making a weighted average of the order statistics, i.e. an L-statistic. In this section, we will explore the use of the OWA operator as an estimator when there is symmetric noise.

Suppose that a quantity of interest takes the value μ. When measuring this quantity, a symmetric noise, i.e., a random variable with mean 0 such as $f(x) = f(-x)$ for any $x \in \mathbb{R}$, is added to the measure. Repeating the same measure gives us a random sample $X_1, \ldots, X_n$ in which all the variables have mean μ and are symmetric.

In this context, we may want to use an OWA operator to estimate the value of μ. However, we must choose the weighting vector. A common criterion in statistics is to minimize the Mean Squared Error (MSE). Let us consider the order statistics vector $\vec{Z} = \left(X_{(1)}, \ldots, X_{(n)} \right)$ and denote as $\Sigma = \text{Var} \left[\vec{Z} \right]$ the covariance matrix of $\vec{Z}$ and as $\vec{\Delta} = E \left[\vec{Z} \right] - \mu \vec{1}$ the mean drift from μ of the components of $\vec{Z}$.

By using the basic properties of linear combinations of random variables (see [21]), the MSE to estimate μ has the following expression

$$E \left[\left(\mu - \Psi_w \left(\vec{X} \right) \right)^2 \right] = \vec{w}' \left(\Sigma + \vec{\Delta}\vec{\Delta}' \right) \vec{w}.$$

From this expression, computing the optimal weights is equivalent to solving an optimization problem, for instance using Lagrange's multipliers procedure.

Proposition 1. *Let $X_1, \ldots, X_n$ a random sample in which any variable has mean μ. Then, the weighting vector $\vec{w}$ (verifying that $\sum_{i=1}^{n} w_i = 1$, $w_i \geq 0, i = 1, 2, \ldots, n$) which minimize $E \left[(\mu - \Psi_w(\vec{x}))^2 \right]$ is*

$$\vec{w} = \frac{\left(\Sigma + \vec{\Delta}\vec{\Delta}' \right)^{-1} \vec{1}}{\vec{1}' \left(\Sigma + \vec{\Delta}\vec{\Delta}' \right)^{-1} \vec{1}}.$$

Notice that we allow the weights to have a negative value. Although this does not coincide with the classical definition of the OWA weights, for our approach, this is a desirable flexibilization in the definition of the operator. Firstly, we are making greater the feasible region, thus the result is at least as good as in the positive weights case. Secondly, the closed expression of Proposition 1, only achievable by allowing negative weights, eases the computations in the main result of the next section. We also remark here that, even though it is possible to construct examples where negative weights appear, in most cases, among which are the most widely used distributions, all the weights are positive.

Therefore, we have optimal weights that depend on the distribution of the noise and the size of the random sample considered. Notice that multiplying the noise by a factor α does not change the optimal weights, since the only change would be a factor α^2 multiplying $\Sigma + \vec{\Delta}\vec{\Delta}'$. In Fig. 2, the simulated optimal weights for the Logistic and Hyperbolic secant distributions, when $n = 20$, are presented. The density functions, respectively f_L and f_{Hs}, of these distributions are as follows:

$$f_L(x) = \frac{1}{4\sigma}\text{sech}^2\left(\frac{x - \mu}{2\sigma}\right) \; \left(\mu \in \mathbb{R}, \sigma \in \mathbb{R}^+\right), \qquad f_{Hs}(x) = \frac{1}{2}\text{sech}\left(\frac{\pi x}{2}\right),$$

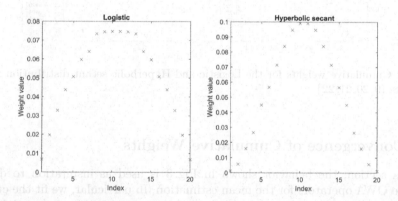

Fig. 2. Optimal weights for the Logistic and Hyperbolic secant distribution when $n = 20$.

As we indicated in the Introduction, many real-life problems require dealing with a non-fixed random sample size. In these cases, even we have an expression of our optimal weights, which could be computed from previous data, we cannot apply the OWA operator to our new data because the number of aggregated values changes. In this direction, one may wonder if there exists any relation between optimal weights when having the same distribution but different sample sizes. If we can find a connection, we can use the optimal weights initially calculated for a specific sample size to calculate a suitable weighting vector for a different value of n.

However, it is difficult to compare weighting vectors with different length. To fix that, we can follow the same idea that is used in the generation of weights presented in Subsect. 2.2, but in the other direction. Given a weighting vector

$\vec{w}$, let us define a cumulative weight function $W : \{0, \frac{1}{n}, \ldots, \frac{n-1}{n}, 1\} \to \mathbb{R}$ such that:

$$W\left(\frac{k}{n}\right) = \sum_{i=1}^{k} w_i$$

Surprisingly, when we represent the cumulative weight functions for different but close values of n, using the distributions considered in Fig. 2, we can see that the points seem to distribute in a common line (see Fig. 3).

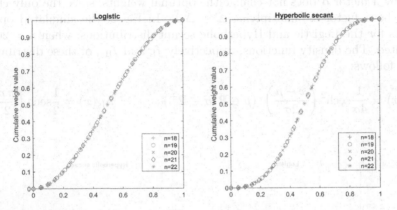

Fig. 3. Cumulative weights for the Logistic and Hyperbolic secant distribution when $n \in \{18, 19, 20, 21, 22\}$.

4   Convergence of Cumulative Weights

In this section, the behavior shown in Fig. 3 is used as inspiration to define flexible OWA operators for the mean estimation. In particular, we fit the cumulative weights with a function f and then, if necessary, generate new weights as $w_i = f\left(\frac{i}{n}\right) - f\left(\frac{i-1}{n}\right)$, $i \in \{1, \ldots, n\}$. However, it is necessary to state a theoretical result that sustain this procedure. In this section, we will give a result in this regard by proving that, if the distribution is sufficiently regular, then the cumulative weight points converge to a function on the unit interval. The most easy example is the Gaussian distribution. In this case, since the optimal weights are the balanced ones [17], then the cumulative weights are always over the graph of the identity function defined over the unit interval.

Before proving the main result, let us prove a useful lemma that allows to ease the computations when the distribution is symmetric.

Lemma 1. *Let $X_1, \ldots, X_n$ a sequence of idd random variables with symmetric distribution and mean μ. Then, the weighting vector $\vec{w}$ (verifying that $\sum_{i=1}^{n}$, $w_i = 1, w_i \geq 0$ $i = 1, 2, \ldots, n$) which minimizes $E\left[\left(\mu - \Psi_w(\vec{X})\right)^2\right]$ also minimizes $Var\left[\Psi_w(\vec{X})\right]$.*

Proof. Since the distribution is symmetric, we have that $Cov\left[X_{(i)}, X_{(j)}\right] = Cov\left[X_{(n-i+1)}, X_{(n-j+1)}\right]$, $E[X_{(i)}] - \mu = \mu - E[X_{(n-i+1)}]$ and $E\left[X_{\left(\frac{n}{2}\right)}\right] = \mu$ (if n is even) for any $i, j \in \{1, \ldots, n\}$. Thus, Σ is a persymmetric matrix (see [12]) and $\vec{\Delta}$ holds $\Delta_i = -\Delta_{n-i+1}$ and $\Delta_{\frac{n}{2}} = 0$ (if n is even).

By performing the same procedure as in Proposition 1, the weights that minimize the variance are

$$\vec{w} = \frac{\Sigma^{-1}\vec{1}}{\vec{1}'\Sigma^{-1}\vec{1}},$$

and since the inverse of a persymmetric matrix is persymmetric [12], the resultant weights hold $w_i = w_{n-i+1}$ for any $i \in \{1, \ldots, n\}$. The result follows by noticing that $\vec{w}'\vec{\Delta} = 0$ ∎

In conclusion, since we are considering symmetric distributions, the optimal weights depend only on Σ. Since we want to find an expression in the limit when $n \to \infty$, we should study the asymptotic behavior of Σ.

Lemma 2. *[25,26] Let $X_1, \ldots, X_n$ be a sequence of iid random variables with density function f and cumulative distribution F such that f is continuous and strictly positive in $F^{-1}((0,1))$ and there exists $\epsilon > 0$ such that*

$$\lim_{x \to \infty} |x|^\epsilon \left[1 - F(x) + F(-x)\right] = 0.$$

Then, for any $\delta > 0$ and $p, q \in [\delta, 1-\delta], p \leq q$:

$$\lim_{n \to \infty} (n+2)Cov\left(X_{(nq)}, X_{(np)}\right) = \frac{(1-p)q}{f\left(F^{-1}(p)\right) f\left(F^{-1}(q)\right)}$$

uniformly.

Remark 1. Note that Σ^{-1} may be heuristically approximated when n goes to infinity as $\Sigma^{-1} \sim (n+1)(n+2)DQD$ [25], where D is a diagonal matrix that satisfies $D_{i,i} = f\left(F^{-1}(\frac{i}{n+1})\right)$ for any $i \in \{1, \ldots, n\}$ and $Q = (q_{ij})$ is the matrix

$$Q = \begin{pmatrix} 2 & -1 & 0 & 0 & 0 & \cdots & 0 \\ -1 & 2 & -1 & 0 & 0 & \cdots & 0 \\ 0 & -1 & 2 & -1 & 0 & \cdots & 0 \\ \vdots & \ddots & \ddots & \ddots & \ddots & \cdots & \vdots \\ 0 & \cdots & 0 & -1 & 2 & -1 & 0 \\ 0 & 0 & \cdots & 0 & -1 & 2 & -1 \\ 0 & 0 & 0 & \cdots & 0 & -1 & 2 \end{pmatrix}$$

In the next result, we give sufficient conditions that ensure the convergence of the cumulative weights and also state the expression of the limit.

Theorem 1. *Let $X_1, \ldots, X_n$ be a sequence of iid random variables with support S and symmetric distribution whose density function and cumulative distribution are respectively denoted as f and F. Let us assume that f is bounded, continuous, twice differentiable, and strictly positive on $F^{-1}((0,1))$. Suppose that:*

– *There exists a sequence $k(n)$ such that $\frac{k(n)}{n^3} \to \infty$ satisfying that for any $\delta > 0$ and $p, q \in [\delta, 1 - \delta], p \leq q$*

$$\lim_{n \to \infty} k(n)(n+1)^2 \left((n+2) f \left(F^{-1}(p) \right) f \left(F^{-1}(q) \right) \Sigma_{np,nq} - p(1-q) \right) = 0$$

uniformly,

– $\int_0^1 f\left(F^{-1}(x)\right) \left(\frac{d^2}{dx^2} f\left(F^{-1}(x)\right) \right) dx < \infty.$

Then, for any $q \in [0,1] \cup \mathbb{Q}$ with irreducible fraction $\frac{a}{b}$:

$$\lim_{n \to \infty} W^{(nb)}(q) = \begin{cases} \dfrac{L + \int_0^q f(F^{-1}(x))\left(\frac{d^2}{dx^2} f(F^{-1}(x))\right) dx}{2L + \int_0^1 f(F^{-1}(x))\left(\frac{d^2}{dx^2} f(F^{-1}(x))\right) dx} & \text{if } \lim_{x \to \inf S} \dfrac{f(x)^2}{F(x)} = L < \infty \\ \dfrac{1}{2} & \text{otherwise} \end{cases}.$$

Proof. For the sake of simplicity, we provide here a sketch of the proof because developing the necessary computations would require several pages. Let us denote the inverse of the covariance matrix of the order statistics of dimension n as $\Sigma(n)^{-1}$. Consider the following sequence:

$$W^{(nb)}(q) = \frac{\sum_{i=1}^{na} \sum_{j=1}^{nb} \left(\Sigma(nb)^{-1} \right)_{i,j}}{\sum_{i=1}^{nb} \sum_{j=1}^{nb} \left(\Sigma(nb)^{-1} \right)_{i,j}}.$$

The imposed convergence conditions guarantee that the following equality holds:

$$\lim_{n \to \infty} \sum_{i=1}^{na} \sum_{j=1}^{nb} (DQD)_{i,j} = \lim_{n \to \infty} \sum_{i=1}^{na} \sum_{j=1}^{nb} \left(\Sigma(nb)^{-1} \right)_{i,j},$$

where D and Q are the matrices defined in Remark 1.

By substituting the expression of the elements of DQD and using the symmetry of the distribution, the following expression is obtained:

$$\lim_{n \to \infty} W^{(nb)}(q) = \lim_{n \to \infty} \frac{f\left(F^{-1}\left(\frac{1}{n}\right)\right)^2 + \frac{1}{n} \int_0^q f\left(F^{-1}(x)\right) \left(\frac{d^2}{dx^2} f\left(F^{-1}(x)\right) \right) dx}{2 f\left(F^{-1}\left(\frac{1}{n}\right)\right)^2 + \frac{1}{n} \int_0^1 f\left(F^{-1}(x)\right) \left(\frac{d^2}{dx^2} f\left(F^{-1}(x)\right) \right) dx}.$$

Note that the limit of the first term of the numerator multiplied by n is equivalent to $\lim_{x \to \inf S} \frac{f(x)^2}{F(x)} = L$. If this limit converges, we have the first case of the Theorem. If the limit diverges, the integral terms are negligible, and the limit is 0.5. Due to the continuity of f, the sequence must be convergent (it cannot be oscillatory). $\blacksquare$

Although these conditions may be too restrictive, and some of them, as the fast convergence of the moments of the ordered statistics, are hard to check, in our numerical experiments the convergence holds for all the considered distributions. Moreover, even if we simulate distributions that do not satisfy some condition (for instance, the density function of the Laplace distribution is not differentiable), the convergence still holds.

5   EVR-OWA Operator as Mean Estimator for Symmetric Distributions

In this section, we define a method to fit the cumulative weights associated with symmetric distributions based on EVRs. We also consider here the limit case $\hat{D}(x) = x \; \forall \; x \in [0,1]$, which corresponds to the balanced weights associated with Gaussian distribution. In this case, we consider a family of EVRs consisting of functions of the form:

$$\hat{D}_{\alpha,\beta,\lambda} = \lambda s_\alpha + (1-\lambda)p_\beta$$

where $\alpha \in \left[0, \frac{1}{2\pi}\right]$, $\beta, \lambda \in [0,1]$.

This family consists of convex combinations of EVRs of the families s_α and p_α, defined in Sect. 2.2, and the limit case corresponding to the identity function. This family has been considered because it has a good behavior regarding the logistic and hyperbolic secant distributions, but it can be extended to a more wide family if needed.

We have applied the latter family to fit the cumulative weights, when $n = 20$, for the logistic and hyperbolic secant distributions. The results are shown in Fig. 4, in addition to the cumulative weights for $n = 21$ and $n = 19$.

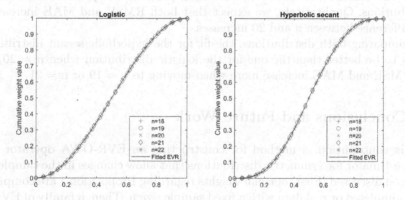

Fig. 4. EVRs fitted to the cumulative weights when $n = 20$ and cumulative weights for $n = \{18, 19, 20, 21, 22\}$ for the Logistic and Hyperbolic secant distributions.

In particular, the optimal parameters are, in the case of the logistic distribution, $\alpha = 0.1592, \beta = 1, \lambda = 0.0325$ and, in the case of the hyperbolic secant distribution, $\alpha = 0.1591, \beta = 0.7361, \lambda = 0.9730$. As it is shown in Fig. 4, the fit seems reasonable not only for $n = 20$ but also for $n = 19$ and $n = 21$. We have also computed the Root Mean Squared Error (RMSE) and the Mean Absolute Error (MAE) of the fit for the three values of n, which can be consulted in Table 1.

Table 1. Root Squared Mean and Mean Absolute Errors of the EVR fitted for the case $n = 20$ when $n \in \{19, 20, 21\}$ for the logistic and hyperbolic secant distributions.

Distribution	Sample size	RMSE ($\times 10^{-3}$)	MAE ($\times 10^{-3}$)
Logistic	18	0.94	0.72
	19	1.19	0.92
	20	0.80	0.62
	21	0.83	0.66
	22	0.94	0.73
Hyperbolic secant	18	1.59	1.19
	19	1.14	0.89
	20	0.60	0.37
	21	1.19	0.98
	22	0.98	0.66

As we can see, the RMSE and MAE are lower when $n = 20$, as expected because we have fitted the EVRs using these points. However, the increase when the value of n is changed is not too high, and it seems reasonable to approximate the constructed EVR-OWA for $n \in \{18, 19, 21, 22\}$, for the considered distributions. Qualitatively, we expect that both RMSE and MAE increase as the difference between n and 20 increases.

Comparing both distributions, the fit for the hyperbolic secant distribution seems to be better than the one for the logistic distribution when $n = 20$, but the RMSE and MAE increase more when moving to $n = 19$ or $n = 21$.

6   Conclusions and Future Work

In this contribution, a method for constructing an EVR-OWA operator as a mean estimator for symmetric distributions that allow changes in the sample size has been discussed. First, optimal weights regarding Proposition 1 are computed, using simulated or real data with a fixed sample size n. Then, a family of EVRs is used to fit the cumulative weights. Finally, we use the fitted function to generate weights associated to another sample sized different to n.

In order to justify the use of this method, we have presented Theorem 1, which states that when n goes to infinity, under some particular conditions, the cumulative weights converge.

The method have been illustrated using the Logistic and Hyperbolic secant distributions for $n = 20$, considering the convex linear combination of sinusoidal and polynomial EVRs, see Fig. 4. Keeping in mind the RMSE and the MAE of the fit (see Table 1), we conclude that we have to obtain reasonably adequate results when considering $n = 19$ or $n = 21$.

As future work, we want to extend the study to non-symmetric distributions and also to real data. In this regard, the EVR functions are too limited and we need a more general family of functions defined over the unit interval. From a theoretical point of view, we need to extend Theorem 1 for non-symmetric distributions, and we also wonder if some distribution requirements can be relaxed.

References

1. Ahsanullah, M., Alzaatreh, A.: Parameter estimation for the log-logistic distribution based on order statistics. REVSTAT **16**(4), 429–443 (2018)
2. Almongy, H.M., Almetwally, E.M., Alharbi, R., Alnagar, D., Hafez, E.H., Mohie El-Din, M.M.: The Weibull generalized exponential distribution with censored sample: estimation and application on real data. Complexity **2021** (2021). Article ID: 6653534
3. Alzeley, O., Almetwally, E.M., Gemeay, A.M., Alshanbari, H.M., Hafez, E., Abu-Moussa, M.: Statistical inference under censored data for the new exponential-x fréchet distribution: simulation and application to leukemia data. Comput. Intell. Neurosci. **2021** (2021). Article ID: 2167670
4. Beliakov, G., Bustince Sola, H., Calvo Sánchez, T.: A Practical Guide to Averaging Functions. SFSC, vol. 329. Springer, Cham (2016). https://doi.org/10.1007/978-3-319-24753-3
5. Calvo, T., Mayor, G., Torrens, J., Suñer, J., Mas, M., Carbonell, M.: Generation of weighting triangles associated with aggregation functions. Int. J. Uncertainty Fuzziness Knowl. Based Syst. **8**(04), 417–451 (2000)
6. Cramér, H.: A contribution to the theory of statistical estimation. Scand. Actuar. J. **1946**(1), 85–94 (1946)
7. Dytso, A., Cardone, M., Veedu, M.S., Poor, H.V.: On estimation under noisy order statistics. In: 2019 IEEE International Symposium on Information Theory (ISIT), pp. 36–40. IEEE (2019)
8. Fréchet, M.: Sur l'extension de certaines évaluations statistiques au cas de petits échantillons. Revue de l'Institut International de Statistique, pp. 182–205 (1943)
9. Gao, W., Zhang, T., Yang, B.B., Zhou, Z.H.: On the noise estimation statistics. Artif. Intell. **293**, 103451 (2021)
10. García-Zamora, D., Labella, Á., Rodríguez, R.M., Martínez, L.: Non linear preferences in group decision making. extreme values amplifications and extreme values reductions. Int. J. Intell. Syst. (2021). https://doi.org/10.1002/int.22561
11. García-Zamora, D., Labella, Á., Rodríguez, R.M., Martín, L.: Symmetric weights for OWA operators prioritizing intermediate values. the EVR-OWA operator. Inf. Sci. **584**, 583–602 (2022)
12. Golub, G.H., Van Loan, C.F.: Matrix Computations. Johns Hopkins Studies in the Mathematical Sciences, Johns Hopkins University Press, Baltimore (1996)
13. Hassan, A.S., Abd-Allah, M.: Exponentiated Weibull-Lomax distribution: properties and estimation. J. Data Sci. **16**(2), 277–298 (2018)
14. Herrera-Viedma, E., Herrera, F., Chiclana, F.: A consensus model for multiperson decision making with different preference structures. IEEE Trans. Syst. Man Cybern. A Syst. Hum. **32**, 394–402 (2002). https://doi.org/10.1109/TSMCA.2002. 802821
15. Klein, J.P., Moeschberger, M.L.: Survival Analysis. SBH, Springer, New York (2003). https://doi.org/10.1007/b97377
16. Kumar, D., Kumar, M., Joorel, J.S.: Estimation with modified power function distribution based on order statistics with application to evaporation data. Ann. Data Sci. 1–26 (2020). https://doi.org/10.1007/s40745-020-00244-6

17. Lloyd, E.: Least-squares estimation of location and scale parameters using order statistics. Biometrika **39**(1/2), 88–95 (1952)
18. Narisetty, N., Koenker, R.: Censored quantile regression survival models with a cure proportion. J. Econom. **226**(1), 192–203 (2022)
19. Palomares, I., Estrella, F.J., Martínez, L., Herrera, F.: Consensus under a fuzzy context: Taxonomy, analysis framework AFRYCA and experimental case of study. Inf. Fusion **20**, 252–271 (2014)
20. Radhakrishna Rao, C.: Information and accuracy attainable in the estimation of statistical parameters. Bull. Calcutta Math. Soc. **37**(3), 81–91 (1945)
21. Rohatgi, V.K., Saleh, A.M.E.: An Introduction to Probability and Statistics. Wiley, Hoboken (2015)
22. Sarhan, A.: Estimation of the mean and standard deviation by order statistics, Part II. Ann. Math. Stat. **26**(3), 505–511 (1955)
23. Sarhan, A.: Estimation of the mean and standard deviation by order statistics, Part III. Ann. Math. Stat. **26**(4), 576–592 (1955)
24. Sarhan, A.E.: Estimation of the mean and standard deviation by order statistics. Ann. Math. Stat. **25**(2), 317–328 (1954)
25. Stephens, M.: Asymptotic calculations of functions of expected values and covariances of order statistics. Can. J. Stat. **18**(3), 265–270 (1990)
26. Stigler, S.M.: Linear functions of order statistics. Ann. Math. Stat. **40**(3), 770–788 (1969)
27. Yager, R.: Families of OWA operators. Fuzzy Sets Syst. **59**(2), 125–148 (1993)
28. Yager, R.: Quantifier guided aggregation using OWA operators. Int. J. Intell. Syst. **11**(1), 49–73 (1996)
29. Zadeh, L.: A computational approach to fuzzy quantifiers in natural languages. Comput. Math. Appl. **9**, 149–184 (1983). https://doi.org/10.1016/0898-1221(83)90013-5

Sugeno Integral Extended to Undefined Inputs

Michal Burda[iD], Martina Daňková[(✉)][iD], and Viktor Pavliska[iD]

Institute for Research and Applications of Fuzzy Modeling, University of Ostrava,
CE IT4Innovations, 30. dubna 22, 701 03 Ostrava, Czech Republic
{Michal.Burda,Martina.Dankova,Viktor.Pavliska}@osu.cz

Abstract. In this contribution, we introduce an extension of the Sugeno integral to undefined inputs and outputs. Undefined inputs are encoded by a single dummy value out of the domain as well as the range of the Sugeno integral; moreover, all internal operations of the integral are extended to deal with this encoding.

Keywords: Generalized Integral · Sugeno Integral · Undefined Values · Partial Function · Partial Fuzzy Relation

1 Introduction

The Sugeno integral [1] as a special type of aggregation operators provides a salient basis for various application areas, e.g., decision making [2], fuzzy systems [3], generalized fuzzy quantifiers [4]. Accordingly, it is a central concept for modeling preferences acting on uncertain or vague states.

There are several generalizations of the Sugeno integral, e.g., handling attributes with distinct domains using qualitative utility functions [2], with different internal operation; for an overview, we refer to [5] or [6]. Computation of the Sugeno integral in case of undefined inputs can be processed as in [7], where four specific extensions to undefined inputs or outputs were introduced. Such generalization is important mainly due to the practical need to deal with missing data employing undefinedness, mainly from the area of database systems and data processing.

Here, we propose a generalization of the Sugeno integral to undefined values that differs from the one given in [7] (see Observation 4). We deal with extensions of particular internal operations as given in [8] (Sect. 3), and we combine them so that they fulfill specific algebraic properties (Definition 2). This speci fication restricts our combinations of extended operation in the definition of the generalized Sugeno integral (Definition 4) that allows us to prove the essential property (Theorem 1), i.t., the representation of the extended Sugeno integral using alpha-level sets, which is particularly useful in practical calculations. Based on that, we propose an algorithm of computation and discuss its time complexity in Sect. 4.2.

© Springer Nature Switzerland AG 2022
D. Ciucci et al. (Eds.): IPMU 2022, CCIS 1601, pp. 25–33, 2022.
https://doi.org/10.1007/978-3-031-08971-8_3

2   Classical Sugeno Integral

In the sequel, we use the unit interval $[0,1]$ with the standard ordering $\leq$ and the induced lattice operations $\wedge$ and $\vee$. Moreover, let us consider a measure space (U, μ), where U be the finite universe of discourse, and μ be a $[0,1]$-valued fuzzy measure on U (i.e., $\mu(\emptyset) = 0$ and for all $A, B \in \mathcal{P}(U) : A \subseteq B$ implies $\mu(A) \leq \mu(B)$) so that $\mu : \mathcal{P}(U) \rightarrow [0,1]$, where $\mathcal{P}(U)$ denotes the power set of U.

We denote by $\mathcal{F}$ the set of all total functions $U \rightarrow [0,1]$, that is, $\mathrm{Dom}(f) = U$ for all $f \in \mathcal{F}$.

Definition 1. (see [9]**).** *The Sugeno integral of the function $f \in \mathcal{F}$ is defined by:*

$$(S) \int_U f d\mu = \bigvee_{E \subseteq U} \left(\mu(E) \wedge \bigwedge_{x \in E} f(x) \right).$$

The above formula can be written in the following form:

$$(S) \int_U f d\mu = \bigvee_{\alpha \in [0,1]} (\alpha \wedge \mu(F_\alpha)),$$

where $F_\alpha = \{x \in U : f(x) \geq \alpha\}$.

Example 1. Consider $U = \{a, b, c, d, e\}$, and a fuzzy measure μ defined for each $X \subseteq U$ as follows:

$$\mu(X) = \frac{|X|}{|U|}.$$

Moreover, let a function $f : U \rightarrow [0,1]$ be so that $f(a) = 1$, $f(b) = 0.7$, $f(c) = 0.7$, $f(d) = 0.2$, $f(e) = 0$.

To compute the Sugeno integral $(S) \int_U f d\mu$, it suffices to consider the α-cuts. For $\alpha \in \{0, 0.2, 0.7, 1\}$, the corresponding F_α (see Definition 1) equals

$$F_1 = \{a\}, \ F_{0.7} = \{a, b, c\}, \ F_{0.2} = \{a, b, c, d\}, \ F_0 = \{a, b, c, d, e\},$$

and the measures are

$$\mu(F_1) = 0.2, \ \mu(F_{0.7}) = 0.6, \ \mu(F_{0.2}) = 0.8, \ \mu(F_0) = 1,$$

from which we obtain

$$(S) \int_U f d\mu = \bigvee_{\alpha \in \{0, 0.2, 0.7, 1\}} (\alpha \wedge \mu(F_\alpha))$$

$$= (0 \wedge 1) \vee (0.2 \wedge 0.8) \vee (0.7 \wedge 0.6) \vee (1 \wedge 0.2) = 0.6 \ .$$

3   Undefined Values as Inputs or Outputs

In the following, we extend a lattice structure with a dummy element $*$ interpreting undefinedness. Being undefined can be handled in various different ways (see [8]), e.g., ignorable nonsense, non-ignorable undefined value (sort of fatal error). This fact is reflected in our definition of an extended structure based on a lattice, where each operation can handle $*$ differently.

Definition 2. *Let $\mathcal{L} = \langle L, \wedge, \vee \rangle$ be a lattice with $L \neq \emptyset$. Then, we define*

$$\mathcal{L}_* = \langle L_*, \wedge_*, \vee_* \rangle,$$

where $L_* = L \cup \{*\}$, $* \notin L$, and operations $\wedge_*$ and $\vee_*$ extend $\wedge$ and $\vee$, respectively, to L_* so that they are commutative, associative, idempotent, and $\forall a, b \in L$:

$$a \leq b \;\Rightarrow\; (a \wedge_* *) \vee_* (b \wedge_* *) = (b \wedge_* *). \tag{1}$$

Notice that in [10,11], the authors also deal with extended structures by a value representing undefinedness. There, an underlying structure is a residuated lattice, and they approach tasks distinct from ours related to the field of fuzzy relational equations.

Example 2. Consider the following extensions of $\wedge$ and $\vee$:

– *Bochvar extensions:*

$$a \wedge_B b = \begin{cases} a \wedge b & \text{if } a, b \neq *; \\ * & \text{otherwise.} \end{cases} \qquad a \vee_B b = \begin{cases} a \vee b & \text{if } a, b \neq *; \\ * & \text{otherwise.} \end{cases}$$

– *Sobociński extensions:*

$$a \wedge_S b = \begin{cases} a \wedge b & \text{if } a, b \neq *; \\ a & \text{if } b = *; \\ b & \text{if } a = *; \\ * & \text{otherwise.} \end{cases} \qquad a \vee_S b = \begin{cases} a \vee b & \text{if } a, b \neq *; \\ a & \text{if } b = *; \\ b & \text{if } a = *; \\ * & \text{otherwise.} \end{cases}$$

– *Kleene extensions:*

$$a \wedge_K b = \begin{cases} a \wedge b & \text{if } a, b \neq *; \\ 0 & \text{if } a = 0 \text{ or } b = 0; \\ * & \text{otherwise.} \end{cases} \qquad a \vee_K b = \begin{cases} a \vee b & \text{if } a, b \neq *; \\ 1 & \text{if } a = 1 \text{ or } b = 1; \\ * & \text{otherwise.} \end{cases}$$

It is easy to verify that all variants $\langle L_*, \wedge_i, \vee_j \rangle$, for $i, j \in \{B, K, S\}$, except $\langle L_*, \wedge_K, \vee_S \rangle$, satisfy Definition 2.

Observation 1. *The unit interval $[0, 1]$ with the standard ordering is a complete distributive lattice. An extended structure in the sense of Definition 2 usually violates background lattice properties. E.g., for the Bochvar extension $\langle L_*, \wedge_B, \vee_B \rangle$, the absorption laws are violated for any $a \in [0, 1]$: $a \vee_B (a \wedge_B *) = * \neq a$.*

Observation 2. *In the case of* $\langle L_*, \wedge_{\mathrm{B}}, \vee_{\mathrm{S}} \rangle$, *i.e., the Bochvar extension of* $\wedge$ *and the Sociński extension of* $\vee$, $*$ *is the smallest element in the induced ordering* $\leq_*$. *The following is valid for all* $a, b \in L$: $a \leq_* b$ *iff* $a \wedge_* b = a$ *and* $a \vee_* b = b$. *Consequently,* $\mathcal{L}_*$ *is a lattice.*

Dually, $*$ *is the greatest element for* $\langle L_*, \wedge_{\mathrm{S}}, \vee_{\mathrm{B}} \rangle$, *i.e., the Bochvar extension of* $\vee$ *and Sociński extension of* $\wedge$. *Hence, the structure* $\langle L_*, \wedge_{\mathrm{S}}, \vee_{\mathrm{B}} \rangle$ *is a lattice too.*

Observation 3. *For* $\langle L_*, \wedge_{\mathrm{K}}, \vee_{\mathrm{K}} \rangle$, $x \wedge_{\mathrm{K}} * = *$ *for all* $x > 0$ *and* $0 \wedge_{\mathrm{K}} * = 0$. *Hence it suggests that* $*$ *is smaller than any* $x > 0$ *and greater than* 0. *On the other hand,* $x \vee_{\mathrm{K}} * = *$ *for all* $x < 1$ *and* $1 \vee_{\mathrm{K}} * = 1$, *which suggests that* $*$ *is greater than any* $x < 1$ *and smaller than* 1. *This is because* $\langle L_*, \wedge_{\mathrm{K}}, \vee_{\mathrm{K}} \rangle$ *is not a lattice – the absorption laws do not hold for any* $x \in (0, 1)$: $x \vee_{\mathrm{K}} (x \wedge_{\mathrm{K}} *) = * \neq x$.

4 Sugeno Integral for Undefined Inputs

From now on, we denote by $\mathcal{F}$ the set of all functions (including partial) $U \to [0, 1]$, that is, $\mathrm{Dom}(f) \subseteq U$, for all $f \in \mathcal{F}$.

Definition 3. *Let* $f \in \mathcal{F}$. *Then we define*

$$\tilde{f}(x) =_{df} \begin{cases} f(x) & , \textit{for } x \in \mathrm{Dom}(f); \\ * & , \textit{otherwise.} \end{cases}$$

We call $\tilde{f}$ *the* representation *of* f *on* $[0, 1]_*$.

In the sequel, let us consider a structure $\mathcal{L}_* = \langle [0, 1]_*, \wedge_*, \vee_* \rangle$ satisfying Definition 2.

Definition 4. *The* $*$-*extended Sugeno integral of the partial function* $f \in \mathcal{F}$ *represented by* $\tilde{f}$ *is defined by:*

$$(S)_* \int_U \tilde{f} d\mu = \bigvee_{E \subseteq U}^* \left(\mu(E) \wedge_* \bigwedge_{x \in E}^* \tilde{f}(x) \right).$$

Convention 1. *In the case of known extension classes, we will use the following abbreviations and the respective names of the extended integrals:*

$\mathcal{L}_*$	$(S)_* \int_U \tilde{f} d\mu$	Name of the Integral
$\langle [0,1]_*, \wedge_{\mathrm{B}}, \vee_{\mathrm{B}} \rangle$	$(S)_B \int_U \tilde{f} d\mu$	Bochvar-like Sugeno integral
$\langle [0,1]_*, \wedge_{\mathrm{S}}, \vee_{\mathrm{S}} \rangle$	$(S)_S \int_U \tilde{f} d\mu$	Sobo-like Sugeno integral
$\langle [0,1]_*, \wedge_{\mathrm{K}}, \vee_{\mathrm{K}} \rangle$	$(S)_K \int_U \tilde{f} d\mu$	Kleene-like Sugeno integral

Observation 4. *It is easy to see that:*

- *The Bochvar-like Sugeno integral evaluates to* ∗ *whenever* Dom(*f*) ≠ *U*.
- *The Sobociński extension of operations ensures that the Sobociński-like Sugeno integral is always given by a value from* [0, 1], *because μ takes values from* [0, 1], *and if* $\tilde{f} \equiv *$ *then* $(S)_* \int_U \tilde{f} d\mu = \mu(U)$. *Note that the Sobociński extension of the Sugeno integral given in [7, Definition 4] yields* ∗ *in the case of* $\tilde{f} \equiv *$.
- *The Kleene-like Sugeno integral for a strictly partial f (i.e.,* Dom(*f*) ⊂ *U) is not reduced to Bochvar-style Sugeno integral only if there exists E ⊆ U : x ∈ E : f(x) = 1 and μ(E) = 1.*

4.1 Representation Using Alpha-Level Sets

Definition 4 involves all subsets of the universe U, whose enumeration can be computationally extremely complex in case of higher cardinalities of U. Therefore, it is highly desirable to find a simplification of the computation. A standard approach is given by the alpha-level sets representation, i.e., the computation that uses a system of subsets based on the functional values of the input function.

The incorporation of ∗ as an additional functional value does not allow to prove directly the alpha-level sets representation for arbitrary extensions of operations. We need to put additional constraints on the choice of extensions as given in Definition 2. Only then, we can prove the required representation (Theorem 1).

Lemma 1. *Let* $E \subseteq U$, $e \in U$ *and* $E' = E \cup \{e\}$ *such that*

$$\bigwedge_{x \in E} {}_* \tilde{f}(x) = \bigwedge_{x \in E'} {}_* \tilde{f}(x). \tag{2}$$

Then

$$\left(\mu(E) \wedge_* \bigwedge_{x \in E} {}_* \tilde{f}(x) \right) \vee_* \left(\mu(E') \wedge_* \bigwedge_{x \in E'} {}_* \tilde{f}(x) \right) = \left(\mu(E') \wedge_* \bigwedge_{x \in E'} {}_* \tilde{f}(x) \right). \tag{3}$$

Proof. Since μ is a fuzzy measure, it is obvious that $\mu(E), \mu(E') \in [0, 1]$ and $\mu(E) \leq \mu(E')$. For simplicity, let

$$A = \bigwedge_{x \in E} {}_* \tilde{f}(x) = \bigwedge_{x \in E'} {}_* \tilde{f}(x).$$

Then the Eq. (3) may be simplified as follows:

$$(\mu(E) \wedge_* A) \vee_* (\mu(E') \wedge_* A) = (\mu(E') \wedge_* A). \tag{4}$$

The proof of this lemma will be divided into two cases.

1) If $A \in [0,1]$ then (4) is trivially valid.

2) For $A = *$, we can continue by perceiving that $\mu(E) \leq \mu(E')$ is equivalent to $\mu(E) \vee \mu(E') = \mu(E')$. By applying property (1), we can easily check the validity of (4).

Theorem 1. *The Sugeno integral*

$$(S)_* \int_U \tilde{f}d\mu = \bigvee_{E \subseteq U} \left(\mu(E) \wedge_* \bigwedge_{x \in E} \tilde{f}(x) \right) \tag{5}$$

may be computed from α-cuts as follows:

$$(S)_* \int_U \tilde{f}d\mu = \bigvee_{\alpha \in \mathcal{R}} (\alpha \wedge_* \mu(F_\alpha)), \tag{6}$$

where

$$\mathcal{R} = \{\tilde{f}(x) : x \in U\},$$
$$F_\alpha = \{x \in U : \alpha \wedge_* \tilde{f}(x) = \alpha\}.$$

Proof. Let $(S)_* \int_U \tilde{f}d\mu = r$ and let E denote such subset of U that

$$\mu(E) \wedge_* \bigwedge_{x \in E} \tilde{f}(x) = r.$$

Let

$$\alpha = \bigwedge_{x \in E} \tilde{f}(x).$$

Let us create a set E' by joining E with a set of all $x \in U$ such that $\alpha \wedge_* \tilde{f}(x) = \alpha$. Clearly

$$\bigwedge_{x \in E'} \tilde{f}(x) = \alpha = \bigwedge_{x \in E} \tilde{f}(x).$$

The application of Lemma 1 results in

$$r \vee_* \left(\mu(E') \wedge_* \bigwedge_{x \in E'} \tilde{f}(x) \right) = \left(\mu(E') \wedge_* \bigwedge_{x \in E'} \tilde{f}(x) \right).$$

However, $E \subseteq E' \subseteq U$ and r is the supremum among all subsets of U, hence

$$r = \mu(E') \wedge_* \bigwedge_{x \in E'} \tilde{f}(x).$$

Note also that $E' = F_\alpha$ and $\alpha \in \mathcal{R}$. Therefore, it is obvious that Eq. (6) surely finds r as the solution of the Sugeno integral (5).

Observation 5. *Let $f(x) \neq *$ for all $x \in U$. Then*

$$(S)_* \int_U f d\mu = (S) \int_U f d\mu.$$

Example 3. Consider a finite universe $U = \{a, b, c, d, e\}$. Let us define a fuzzy measure μ for each $X \subseteq U$ as follows:

$$\mu(X) = \frac{|X|}{|U|}.$$

Moreover, consider a function $\tilde{f}$ such that

$$\tilde{f}(a) = 1, \ \tilde{f}(b) = 0.7, \ \tilde{f}(c) = 0.7, \ \tilde{f}(d) = *, \ \tilde{f}(e) = 0.$$

In the case of the Sobociński-style Sugeno integral, we get

$$F_1 = \{a, d\}, \ F_{0.7} = \{a, b, c, d\}, \ F_0 = \{a, b, c, d, e\}, \ F_* = \{d\},$$

and the measures are $\mu(F_1) = 0.4$, $\mu(F_{0.7}) = 0.8$, $\mu(F_0) = 1$, $\mu(F_*) = 0.2$. Finally, we get

$$(S)_S \int_U \tilde{f} d\mu = \bigvee_{\alpha \in \{0, 0.2, 0.7, 1, *\}}^S (\alpha \wedge_S \mu(F_\alpha))$$

$$= (0 \wedge_S 1) \vee_S (0.7 \wedge_S 0.8) \vee_S (1 \wedge_S 0.4) \vee_S (* \wedge_S 0.2) = 0.7.$$

For Kleene-style Sugeno integral, we firstly get $F_1 = \{a\}$, $F_{0.7} = \{a, b, c\}$, $F_0 = \{a, b, c, d, e\}$, $F_* = \{a, b, c, d\}$ and therefore $\mu(F_1) = 0.2$, $\mu(F_{0.7}) = 0.6$, $\mu(F_0) = 1$, $\mu(F_*) = 0.8$. Then

$$(S)_K \int_U \tilde{f} d\mu = \bigvee_{\alpha \in \{0, 0.2, 0.7, 1, *\}}^K (\alpha \wedge_K \mu(F_\alpha))$$

$$= (0 \wedge_K 1) \vee_K (0.7 \wedge_K 0.6) \vee_K (1 \wedge_K 0.2) \vee_K (* \wedge_K 0.8) = *.$$

4.2 Algorithm of Computation

A basic description of the algorithm is given by Algorithm 1. The essential idea of the algorithm is to utilize the alpha-level representation of Sugeno integral as discussed in the previous section. We can show that the time complexity of the SUGENO algorithm is $O(nK(n) + n \log(n) + nL(n))$ if the time complexity of an evaluation of $\tilde{f}$ is $O(K(n))$ and of an evaluation of the measure μ is $O(L(n))$.

Algorithm 1. The algorithm for computation of the Sugeno integral of a function $\tilde{f}$ with the fuzzy measure μ.

---

function SUGENO($\tilde{f}, \mu, U$)
    $\mathcal{R} \leftarrow \{\tilde{f}(x) \colon x \in U\}$
    $r \leftarrow \{0, *\} \setminus \{0 \vee_* *\}$ (so that $r \vee_* a = a$ for all $a \in [0,1]^*$)
    while $\mathcal{R} \neq \emptyset$ **do**
        $\alpha \leftarrow$ such α that $(\forall b \in \mathcal{R})(b \wedge_* \alpha = b)$
        $\mathcal{R} \leftarrow \mathcal{R} \setminus \{\alpha\}$
        $F_\alpha \leftarrow \{x \in U \colon \alpha \wedge_* \tilde{f}(x) = \alpha\}$
        $r \leftarrow r \vee_* (\alpha \wedge_* \mu(F_\alpha))$
    end while
    return r
end function

---

5 Conclusion

In this contribution, we introduced a generalization of the Sugeno integral to input and out undefined values. This generalization deals with undefined values encoded by a dummy value $*$. Different nature of undefinedness is captured by specific extensions of operations that handle it. We allowed (by means of Definition 2) only those combinations of extended operations that allowed us to simplify the integral calculation using alpha-levels (see Theorem 1). We also gave a basic algorithm of computation of extended Sugeno integrals with undefined inputs and touched a problem of its complexity.

Acknowledgement. This research was partially supported by Czech Science Foundation through the grant 20-07851S.

References

1. Sugeno, M.: Theory of fuzzy integrals and its application, Tokyo Institute of Technology, Doctoral Thesis (1974)
2. Couceiro, M., Dubois, D., Prade, H., Waldhauser, T.: Decision-making with Sugeno integrals. Order **33**, 517–535 (2016). Sugeno Integral and Decision Modeling
3. Torra, V., Narukawa, Y.: The interpretation of fuzzy integrals and their application to fuzzy systems. Int. J. Approximate Reasoning **41**(1), 43–58 (2006). Aggregation Operators and Decision Modeling
4. Dvořák, A., Holčapek, M.: Type $\langle 1, 1 \rangle$ fuzzy quantifiers determined by fuzzy measures on residuated lattices. Part I. Basic definitions and examples. Fuzzy Sets Syst. **242**, 31–55 (2014)
5. Gagolewski, M.: Data Fusion. Institute of Computer Science, Polish Academy of Sciences (2015)
6. Grabisch, M., Marichal, J.-L., Mesiar, R., Pap, E.: Aggregation Functions. Encyclopedia of Mathematics and Its Applications, vol. 124. Cambridge University Press, New York (2009)

7. Běhounek, L., Daňková, M.: Aggregation operators with undefined inputs or outputs. Int. J. Uncertainty Fuzziness Knowl. Based Syst. **30**(1), 19–41 (2022). https://doi.org/10.1142/S0218488522500027

8. Běhounek, L., Novák, V.: Towards fuzzy partial logic. In: IEEE International Symposium on Multiple-Valued Logic (ISMVL), pp. 139–144. IEEE (2015)

9. Dubois, D., Prade, H., Rico, A., Teheux, B.: Generalized Sugeno integrals. In: 2016 16th International Conference on Information Processing and Management of Uncertainty in Knowledge-Based Systems (IPMU 2016), vol. II, Eindhoven, Netherlands, pp. 363–374. https://hal.archives-ouvertes.fr/hal-01445233

10. Štěpnička, M., Cao, N., Běhounek, L., Burda, M., Dolný, A.: Missing values and dragonfly operations in fuzzy relational compositions. Int. J. Approximate Reasoning **113**, 149–170 (2019). https://doi.org/10.1016/j.ijar.2019.07.004

11. Štěpnička, M., Cao, N.: On solvability of systems of partial fuzzy relational equations. Fuzzy Sets Syst. (submitted)

Sugeno Integral Based Pandemic Risk Assessment

Luca Anzilli[1]([⊠]) [iD] and Marta Cardin[2] [iD]

[1] Dipartimento di Scienze dell'Economia, Università del Salento, Lecce, Italy
luca.anzilli@unisalento.it
[2] Department of Economics, Ca' Foscari University of Venice, Venice, Italy
mcardin@unive.it

Abstract. Complex situations such as pandemics generally lead to consider different sources of information in the analysis. We propose a general framework for coronavirus risk assessment based on multi-criteria decision aiding (MCDA) where input variables are indicators expressed on the basis of qualitative-ordinal scales. The proposed approach, based on Sugeno Utility Functionals, makes the problem setting easy to interpret and allows us to reflect the policy-makers' opinions on the importance of each indicator or subset of indicators. Interestingly, our approach is related to if-then rule-based systems adopted by some Governments for pandemic risk assessment and restriction policy planning.

Keywords: Sugeno integral · Multiple criteria decision making · Local utility function · Coronavirus pandemic · Aggregation functions

1 Introduction

The coronavirus (COVID-19) pandemic crisis poses unprecedented challenges for governments and international organisations. To respond to the pandemic emergency, governments have had to face complex decision problems by implementing containment policies in a very short time. The need to classify parts of the country according to the severity of the pandemic has led to the adoption of a number of models for assigning each individual territorial unit to a specific risk class (e.g. the colour-coded maps).

During the early phases, the models helped establish the global risk scale and motivated actions. However, most of the models used are able to reap the benefits of specific interventions in terms of reduced transmission, without saying anything about the relative economic and social costs. The pandemic has devastated many aspects of daily life in which governments around the world have had to submit their citizens to long periods of lockdown. Many organizations have been forced to undergo a significant transformation, rethinking the key elements of their business processes and the use of technology to maintain operations, within an evolving landscape of guidelines and new procedures [7]. Measurement of these costs is important to identify which interventions work

© Springer Nature Switzerland AG 2022
D. Ciucci et al. (Eds.): IPMU 2022, CCIS 1601, pp. 34–46, 2022.
https://doi.org/10.1007/978-3-031-08971-8_4

best and which are most costly. The models initially adopted must therefore be progressively modified to include new information on the circulation of the virus and on the socio-economic difficulties that have arisen. So, models that encompass both epidemiological and socio-economic aspects are needed [9].

In this paper we propose a general framework for pandemic risk assessment and restriction policies planning based on multi-criteria decision analysis (MCDA). Decision theory constructs can offer helpful guidance for transparent policymaking that addresses severe uncertainty in sensible ways. The proposed approach acknowledges both the importance of rigorous risk evaluation against multiple factors and, at same time, the necessity of providing policy-makers with flexible tool for decision support. MCDA methods can also be usefully employed when scarce data are available and the most of information is based on experts' subjective judgments. In complex situations such as pandemics, i.e. when different sources of information have to be considered in the analysis, it may be useful to employ a qualitative approach for risk assessment. The rationale is to refrain from using numbers that seem arbitrary or hard to collect, namely address decision problems in the ordinal setting. There are two advantages to using a qualitative approach: (i) a gain in robustness and the need for less data; (ii) qualitative methods lend themselves to a logical representation (which makes proposed choices more easily explainable) [3].

The approach we propose is based on the Sugeno integral that is used in MCDA as a tool for guiding decision support. Sugeno integrals [3,8] are commonly used as qualitative aggregation functions using finite scales under the commensurability assumption between them. The definition of these integrals is based on a monotonic set-function, named capacity or fuzzy measure, that aims to qualitatively represent the likelihood of sets of possible states of nature, the importance of sets of criteria, etc. In pandemic scenarios, where more indicators are typically considered for risk assessment, the choice of the set-monotonic function in the Sugeno integral allows taking into account the subjective opinions of the policy-maker in the face of the importance weights assigned to groups of indicators, not necessarily singletons. Since indicators evaluations are usually expressed over different scales, we employ the Sugeno utility functionals as qualitative aggregation operators. The use of local utility functions increases the expressive power of the Sugeno integrals and, moreover, allows the individual evaluations of each indicator to be adapted to the subjective level of risk perception of the decision makers.

Section 2 introduces basic notions on Sugeno integrals and Sugeno Utility Functionals. In Sect. 3 we formalize our general risk assessment model. In Sects. 4 and 5 we discuss some relationships between Sugeno integrals and rule sets and, as an application, we deal with the Italian pandemic system.

2   Preliminaries

We introduce Sugeno integrals and Sugeno Utility functionals. The Sugeno integral is an aggregation function particularly suited for the aggregation of ordinal inputs and it is defined with respect to a fuzzy measure that reflects the user's perception of the importance of each criteria subset in the considered problem. We consider a finite set of inputs $N = \{1, 2, \ldots, n\}$, which can be either decision criteria, optimisation objectives or any other aggregation variables. Let $(E, \leq)$ be a finite totally ordered set with a least element 0 and a greatest element 1.

Definition 1. *A set function* $m : 2^N \rightarrow E$ *is a* capacity (fuzzy measure) *if* $\forall A, B \subseteq N$: $A \subseteq B \implies m(A) \leq m(B)$, *and* $m(\emptyset) = 0$, $m(N) = 1$.

Definition 2. *The Sugeno integral w.r.t.* m *is the function* $\mathcal{S}_m \colon E^n \rightarrow E$ *defined by*

$$\mathcal{S}_m(\boldsymbol{x}) = \bigvee_{A \subseteq N} \left(m(A) \wedge \bigwedge_{i \in A} x_i \right). \tag{1}$$

The following alternative expression holds

$$\mathcal{S}_m(\boldsymbol{x}) = \bigvee_{i=1}^{n} \left(x_{(i)} \wedge m(\{(i), \ldots, (n)\}) \right) \tag{2}$$

where $x_{(1)} \leq x_{(2)} \leq \cdots \leq x_{(n)}$.

Sugeno integrals allow aggregating values belonging to the same scale. The so-called Sugeno Utility Functionals (SUF) generalize Sugeno integrals and enable the fusion of values coming from different scales [1, 2, 4].

Let $X_1, \ldots, X_n$ be finite totally ordered sets called *attribute domains*, and $\boldsymbol{X} = X_1 \times \cdots \times X_n$. We denote the lower bounds of $X_1, \ldots, X_n$ by 0 and their upper bounds by 1. A function $\varphi_i \colon X_i \rightarrow E$ is called *local qualitative normalization* function if it is nondecreasing and if it satisfies $\varphi_i(0) = 0$ and $\varphi_i(1) = 1$. The *global qualitative normalization* function $\varphi \colon \boldsymbol{X} \rightarrow E^n$ is

$$\varphi(\boldsymbol{x}) = (\varphi_1(x_1), \varphi_2(x_2), \ldots, \varphi_n(x_n)), \qquad x \in \boldsymbol{X}. \tag{3}$$

Definition 3. *The Sugeno Utility Functional (SUF) w.r.t* m *and* φ *is the function* $\mathcal{S}_{m,\varphi} \colon \boldsymbol{X} \rightarrow E$ *defined by*

$$\mathcal{S}_{m,\varphi}(\boldsymbol{x}) = \mathcal{S}_m(\varphi(\boldsymbol{x})) = \mathcal{S}_m(\varphi_1(x_1), \varphi_2(x_2), \ldots, \varphi_n(x_n)). \tag{4}$$

3   Sugeno Integral Based Risk Assessment Model

We now propose the risk assessment model following a MCDA methodology based on Sugeno integrals. One of the benefits offered by the qualitative approach is that it allows us to handle with the ambiguity of setting thresholds between risk classes.

Let us consider a finite set of indicators $\mathcal{C} = \{C_1, C_2, \ldots, C_n\}$. As usually done, we will refer to set $\mathcal{C}$ as the set $N = \{1, 2, \ldots, n\}$. Then, a subset $A \subseteq N$

identifies a subset of indicators. In our modelization, a subset $A \subseteq N$ describes a scenario in which all indicators C_i, with $i \in A$, have extremely risky values and all others indicators C_i, with $i \in N \setminus A$, are inside the normal range. The risk associated with a scenario $A \subseteq N$ is expressed on the scale E, being E a finite totally ordered set. For example $E = \{VL, L, M, H, VH\}$, with $VL < L < M < H < VH$, where $VL = $ "Very Low", $L = $ "Low", $M = $ "Medium", $H = $ "High" and $VH = $ "Very High". We denote the lower bound of E by 0 and its upper bound by 1. We introduce a fuzzy measure $m : 2^N \to E$, that assigns to each scenario $A \subseteq N$ the corresponding risk degree $m(A)$. This fuzzy measure has to be elicited from experts' opinions (see, e.g., [11] for an interactive elicitation protocol for the Sugeno integral involving decision maker's opinions).

However, in a more general setting, each indicator C_i will not only be classified as "not risky" or "extremely risky", but intermediate evaluations between these two extreme values will also be considered. We denote by $x_i \in E$, with $i \in N$, the individual risk degree associated with indicator C_i expressed on the ordinal scale E. In order to infer the risk degree associated with a scenario represented by an input vector $\boldsymbol{x} = (x_1, x_2, \ldots, x_n) \in E^n$ we have to construct, using the information expressed by the fuzzy measure m, an overall evaluation function $F : E^n \to E$ that associates to each vector of (individual) risk evaluations $\boldsymbol{x} \in E^n$ an overall risk degree $F(\boldsymbol{x}) \in E$.

We observe that a subset $A \subseteq N$ refers to a scenario in which all indicators C_i, with $i \in A$, have extremely risky values, i.e. $x_i = 1$, for all $i \in S$, and all other indicators C_i, with $i \in N \setminus A$, are inside the normal range, i.e. $x_i = 0$. Then, the scenario described by a subset $A \subseteq N$ can be represented by the vector $\boldsymbol{\delta}^A \in \{0,1\}^n \subseteq E^n$ defined by $\delta_i^A = 1$ if $i \in A$ and 0 otherwise.

Since $m(A)$ is the risk degree associated with subset A, i.e. to scenario $\boldsymbol{\delta}^A$, we have to require that $F(\boldsymbol{\delta}^A) = m(A)$ for all $A \subseteq N$. Thus, F has to be equal to m on $\{0,1\}^n$. The goal is now to extend F over E^n. We propose to approach this interpolation-type problem by using as function F the Sugeno integral.

Then the risk level $\Phi(\boldsymbol{x})$ assigned to a scenario $\boldsymbol{x}$ is defined as (see Definition 2)

$$\Phi(\boldsymbol{x}) = S_m(\boldsymbol{x}) = \bigvee_{A \subseteq N} \left(m(A) \wedge \bigwedge_{i \in A} x_i \right). \tag{5}$$

Example 1. Let us suppose that risk assessment procedure outlined by a Government is based on three risk indicators $C = \{C_1, C_2, C_3\}$. The individual risk assigned to each indicator is expressed on the ordinal scale $E = \{VL, L, M, H, VH\}$. Let m the fuzzy measure on C defined according to Table 1. Each territorial unit (region) is assigned to different levels of risk, expressed on the ordinal scale E, based on the considered three indicators. Let T^1, T^2 and T^3 be three territorial units whose evaluations are described by the vectors $\boldsymbol{x}^1 = (L, M, VL)$, $\boldsymbol{x}^2 = (H, VL, VL)$ and $\boldsymbol{x}^3 = (VL, H, M)$, respectively. Then, from (5), the overall risk degrees assigned to T^1, T^2 and T^3 are given by, respectively,

$$\Phi(\boldsymbol{x}^1) = L, \qquad \Phi(\boldsymbol{x}^2) = VL, \qquad \Phi(\boldsymbol{x}^3) = M.$$

Remark 1. We observe that $\Phi(\delta^A) = \mathcal{S}_m(\delta^A) = m(A)$. For example, if $\boldsymbol{x} = (VH, VL, VH)$ that is $\boldsymbol{x} = (1,0,1) = \delta^A$, being $A = \{C_1, C_3\}$, from Table 1 we have $\Phi(\boldsymbol{x}) = M = m(\{C_1, C_3\})$.

Table 1. Fuzzy measure m

A	$m(A)$
$\emptyset$	VL
$\{C_1\}$	VL
$\{C_2\}$	L
$\{C_3\}$	VL
$\{C_1, C_2\}$	L
$\{C_1, C_3\}$	M
$\{C_2, C_3\}$	H
$\{C_1, C_2, C_3\}$	VH

Subsets of Indicators. In a more general setting, we may consider k subsets of indicators $\mathcal{C}^1, \mathcal{C}^2, \ldots, \mathcal{C}^k$ and, for $j = 1, \ldots, k$, let n_j be the number of indicators belonging to $\mathcal{C}^j$. For all $j = 1, \ldots, k$ and $i = 1, \ldots, n_j$, we denote by C_i^j the i-th indicator of subset $\mathcal{C}^j$. We denote by $x_i^j \in E$ the evaluation of indicator C_i^j. For each subset $\mathcal{C}^j$ we denote $\boldsymbol{x}^j = (x_1^j, \ldots, x_{n_j}^j)$. For each $j = 1, \ldots, k$ the risk degree assigned to $\mathcal{C}^j$ is defined by $\Phi(\boldsymbol{x}^j) = \mathcal{S}_{m^j}(\boldsymbol{x}^j)$ being m^j a fuzzy measure on $\mathcal{C}^j = \{C_1^j, \ldots, C_{n_j}^j\}$. The overall evaluation of $\boldsymbol{x} = (\boldsymbol{x}^1, \ldots, \boldsymbol{x}^k)$ can be expressed as

$$\Phi(\boldsymbol{x}) = \mathcal{S}_m \left(\mathcal{S}_{m^1}(\boldsymbol{x}^1), \ldots, \mathcal{S}_{m^k}(\boldsymbol{x}^k) \right)$$

where m is a fuzzy measure on $\{\mathcal{C}^1, \mathcal{C}^2, \ldots, \mathcal{C}^k\}$.

Different Scales. In practise, each considered indicator may have its own scale, which requires an extension of the above model. We assume that there are possibly distinct scales $X_1, X_2, \ldots, X_n$, one per indicator, that are finite totally ordered set, and, without danger of ambiguity, we denote the lower and upper bounds of X_i by 0 and 1, respectively, for all $i = 1, \ldots, n$. We denote by $x_i \in X_i$ the evaluation of indicator C_i expressed on the ordinal scale X_i. Thus each scenario can be represented by a vector $\boldsymbol{x} = (x_1, x_2, \ldots, x_n) \in \boldsymbol{X}$, where $\boldsymbol{X} = X_1 \times X_2 \cdots \times X_n$. For each indicator C_i we let $\varphi_i(x_i)$ be the evaluation x_i expressed on the scale E, where $\varphi_i \colon X_i \to E$ is a *local qualitative normalization* function. In this more general framework, the expression (5) can be generalised as SUF (see (4))

$$\Phi(\boldsymbol{x}) = \mathcal{S}_{m,\varphi}(\boldsymbol{x})$$

where φ is a *global qualitative normalization* function as defined in (3).

In the case when k subsets of indicators $\mathcal{C}^1, \mathcal{C}^2, \ldots, \mathcal{C}^k$ are considered, we first define the risk index of each $\mathcal{C}^j$ as

$$\Phi(\boldsymbol{x}^j) = \mathcal{S}_{m^j, \varphi^j}(\boldsymbol{x}^j)$$

where $x^j = (x_1^j, \ldots, x_{n_j}^j)$ is the evaluation vector related to subset of indicators $\mathcal{C}^j$, m^j a fuzzy measure on $\mathcal{C}^j = \{C_1^j, \ldots, C_{n_j}^j\}$ and φ^j is a global qualitative normalization function such that $\varphi^j(x^j) = (\varphi_1^j(x_1^j), \ldots, \varphi_{n_j}^j(x_{n_j}^j))$.

The overall risk degree $\Phi(x) \in E$ associate to a scenario $x \in X$ is defined as

$$\Phi(x) = \mathcal{S}_{m,\varphi}\left(\mathcal{S}_{m^1,\varphi^1}(x^1), \ldots, \mathcal{S}_{m^k,\varphi^k}(x^k)\right). \tag{6}$$

4 Decision Rules and Sugeno Integrals

In this section we study the representation of a set of if-then rules by Sugeno Utility Functionals. A decision rule r is an implication of the form:

$$\text{IF } (x_1 = a_1^r \text{ and } x_2 = a_2^r \text{ and } \ldots \text{ and } x_n = a_n^r) \quad \text{THEN } y = b^r \tag{7}$$

where $a_i^r \in X_i$ and $b^r \in E$. We also denote the rule r as $(a_1^r, a_2^r, \ldots, a_n^r) \to b^r$.

We will consider set of rules that are representable with generalized Sugeno integrals that are monotonic operators and so we consider only monotone rule sets.

Definition 4. *A set of rules R of the form (7) is said to be nondecreasing if for each pair of rules $(a_1^r, a_2^r, \ldots, a_n^r) \to b_1^r$ and $(c_1^r, c_2^r, \ldots, c_n^r) \to b_2^r$ such that $a_i^r \leq c_i^r$ for every $i, 1 \leq i \leq n$, it follows that $b_1^r \leq b_2^r$.*

Let R be a nondecreasing set of rules of the form (7). We denote by $f_R : X \to E$ the smallest nondecreasing function compatible with R that is defined by

$$f_R(x) = \bigvee_{r \in R} f_r(x), \quad x \in X$$

where, for each rule r, the function $f_r : X \to E$ is defined by

$$f_r(x_1, x_2, \ldots, x_n) = \begin{cases} b^r & \text{if } \forall i = 1, \ldots, n \quad x_i \geq a_i^r \\ 0 & \text{otherwise.} \end{cases}$$

Definition 5. *We say that a rule set R is SUF-representable if there exists a fuzzy measure $m : 2^N \to E$ and a global qualitative normalization function $\varphi : X \to E^n$ such that for all $x \in X$ we have $\mathcal{S}_{m,\varphi}(x) = f_R(x)$.*

Note that we consider a representation of rule sets by nondecreasing functions. For a nondecreasing function $f : X \to E$ the following result can be proved.

Proposition 1. *([2]) For any non decreasing function $f : X \to E$ such that $f(0, \ldots, 0) = 0$ and $f(1, \ldots, 1) = 1$ there exists a set of SUFs S such that*

$$f = \bigvee_{S \in \mathcal{S}} S$$

that is $f(x) = \bigvee_{S \in \mathcal{S}} S(x)$ for all $x \in X$.

Now we consider the representation of a decision rule r by a Sugeno Utility Functional.

Proposition 2. *A rule $r\colon (a_1^r, a_2^r, \ldots, a_n^r) \to b^r$ of the form (7) can be represented as a SUF, that is there exist a fuzzy measure $m_r : 2^N \to E$ and a global qualitative normalization function $\varphi_r\colon X \to E^n$ such that for all $x \in X$*

$$\mathcal{S}_{m_r, \varphi_r}(x) = f_r(x).$$

Proof. Let us denote

$$A^r = \{i \in N\colon a_i^r > 0\}$$

and let m_r be the fuzzy measure such that, for all $A \subseteq N$,

$$m_r(A) = \begin{cases} b^r & A \supseteq A^r, \ A \neq N \\ 1 & A = N \\ 0 & \text{otherwise.} \end{cases}$$

Moreover we define a function $\varphi_r(x) = (\varphi_1^r(x_1), \varphi_2^r(x_2), \ldots, \varphi_n^r(x_n))$ by

$$\varphi_i^r(x_i) = \begin{cases} b^r & \text{if } x_i \geq a_i^r, \ x_i \neq 1 \\ 1 & \text{if } x_i = 1 \\ 0 & \text{otherwise.} \end{cases}$$

Then we can easily prove that $\mathcal{S}_{m_r, \varphi_r}(x) = f_r(x)$. $\qquad\square$

Following the approach in [2], we give some conditions on the representation of a rule set R by Sugeno Utility Functionals.

Let us denote $A^r = \{i \in N\colon a_i^r > 0\}$. Let m be the capacity defined by

$$m(A) = \bigvee\{b^r\colon r \in R, \quad A^r \subseteq A\} \tag{8}$$

for $\emptyset \subsetneq A \subsetneq N$, and $m(\emptyset) = 0$, $m(N) = 1$. Let φ be the function defined by

$$\varphi_i(x_i) = \bigvee\{b^r\colon r \in R, \quad 0 < a_i^r \leq x_i\} \tag{9}$$

for all $i = 1, \ldots, n$ and $x_i \neq 0, 1$, and $\varphi_i(0) = 0$ and $\varphi_i(1) = 1$.

Note that the functions φ_i are local qualitative normalization functions.

The following result can be easily proved using the approach proposed Sect. 4.3 of [2]

Proposition 3. *A rule set R SUF-representable if and only if $\mathcal{S}_{m,\varphi}(x) = f_R(x)$ where m and φ are defined by (8) and (9), respectively.*

Now we study rule sets in which the antecedent part $(a_1^r, a_2^r, \ldots, a_n^r)$ of each rule r is a n-tuple of 0s and 1s. We will show that, if the monotonicity property is satisfied, these types of rule sets are SUF-representable.

Proposition 4. *Let R be a nondecreasing rule set such that $X_i = \{0, 1\}$ for all $i = 1, 2, \ldots, n$. Then R is SUF-representable, that is $\mathcal{S}_{m,\varphi}(\boldsymbol{x}) = f_R(\boldsymbol{x})$, where m and φ are defined by (8) and (9), respectively.*

Proof. Since $X_i = \{0, 1\}$ for $i = 1, \ldots, n$, from (9) the functions φ_i are defined by $\varphi_i(0) = 0$, $\varphi_i(1) = 1$. If $\boldsymbol{x} = (x_1, \ldots, x_n) \in \{0, 1\}^n$ and $A_{\boldsymbol{x}} = \{i \in N : x_i = 1\}$ we have $\mathcal{S}_{m,\varphi}(\boldsymbol{x}) = \mathcal{S}_m(\varphi(\boldsymbol{x})) = \mathcal{S}_m(\varphi_1(x_1), \varphi_2(x_2), \ldots, \varphi_n(x_n)) = m(A_{\boldsymbol{x}})$ and so, from (8),

$$\mathcal{S}_{m,\varphi}(\boldsymbol{x}) = m(A_{\boldsymbol{x}}) = \bigvee_{r \in R} \{b^r : A^r \subseteq A_{\boldsymbol{x}}\}. \tag{10}$$

Furthermore, recalling that

$$f_r(\boldsymbol{x}) = f_r(x_1, x_2, \ldots, x_n) = \begin{cases} b^r & \text{if} \quad \forall i = 1, \ldots, n \quad x_i \geq a_i^r \\ 0 & \text{otherwise} \end{cases}$$

we have

$$f_r(\boldsymbol{x}) = \begin{cases} b^r & \text{if} \quad A^r \subseteq A_{\boldsymbol{x}} \\ 0 & \text{otherwise} \end{cases}$$

Thus

$$f_R(\boldsymbol{x}) = \bigvee_{r \in R} f_r(\boldsymbol{x}) = \bigvee_{r \in R} \{b^r : A^r \subseteq A_{\boldsymbol{x}}\}. \tag{11}$$

From (10) and (11) it follows that $\mathcal{S}_{m,\varphi}(\boldsymbol{x}) = f_R(\boldsymbol{x})$. Thus, by Proposition 3, the rule set R is SUF-representable. □

The next proposition provides a characterization of rule sets that are SUF-representable. Firstly, we recall a definition and some notation that are useful in the proof of this result.

If $\boldsymbol{X}$ is a chain the *median* function is a function med $: \boldsymbol{X}^3 \to \boldsymbol{X}$ given by

$$\text{med}(x_1, x_2, x_3) = (x_1 \wedge x_2) \vee (x_1 \wedge x_3) \vee (x_2 \wedge x_3).$$

This definition is typically studied in the context of distributive lattices.

If $\boldsymbol{x}$ is an element of $\boldsymbol{X}$, $\boldsymbol{x}_i^a$ denotes the element of $\boldsymbol{X}$ whose k-th component is a if $k = i$ and x_k otherwise.

Proposition 5. *A rule set R SUF-representable if and only if for every element $\boldsymbol{x}$ of $\boldsymbol{X}$ and for every $i, 1 \leq i \leq n$*

$$\text{either } f_R(\boldsymbol{x}) = f_R(\boldsymbol{x}_i^0) \text{ or } f_R(\boldsymbol{x}) = f_R(\boldsymbol{x}_i^1) \text{ or } f_R(\boldsymbol{x}) = \varphi_i(x_i) \tag{12}$$

$$\text{and } f_R(\boldsymbol{x}) > f_R(\boldsymbol{x}_i^0) \Rightarrow \varphi_i(x_i) \geq f_R(\boldsymbol{x}), \tag{13}$$

$$f_R(\boldsymbol{x}) < f_R(\boldsymbol{x}_i^1) \Rightarrow \varphi_i(x_i) \leq f_R(\boldsymbol{x}) \tag{14}$$

where φ is defined by (9).

Proof. By Theorem 2.12 in [5] a nondecreasing function $f \colon X \to E$ is a Sugeno utility functional if and only if it satisfies the following property

$$f(x_i^0) < f(x_i^a) \quad \text{and} \quad f(y_i^a) < f(y_i^1) \Rightarrow f(x_i^a) \leq f(y_i^a) \tag{15}$$

for all $x, y \in X$ and for all $i = 1, \dots, n$ and $a \in X$.

Let f_R be a nondecreasing function $f_R \colon X \to E$ defined with respect to a nondecreasing set of rules R that satisfies conditions (12) and (13). Then if we consider $x, y \in X$, $1 \leq i \leq n$ and $a \in X$ such that $f_R(x_i^0) < f_R(x_i^a)$ and $f_R(y_i^a) < f_R(y_i^1)$ we see that $f_R(xi^a) \leq \varphi_i(a) \leq f_R(y_i^a)$ hence $f_R(x_i^a) \leq f_R(y_i^a)$.

Conversely if a rule set R is SUF-representable the function f_R is a Sugeno utility functional and then by Theorem 2 in [6] for every element x of X and for every $i, 1 \leq i \leq n$,

$$f_R(x) = \mathrm{med}(f_R(x_i^0), \varphi_i(x_i), f_R(x_i^1))$$

and this implies that condition (12) is satisfied. Moreover if $f_R(x) > f_R(x_i^0)$ therefore

$$f_R(x_i^0) < f(x) = \mathrm{med}(f_R(x_i^0), \varphi_i(x_i), f_R(x_i^1)) = \varphi_i(x_i) \wedge f_R(x_i^1) \leq \varphi_i(x_i)$$

and if $f_R(x) < f_R(x_i^1)$ hence

$$f_R(x_i^1) > f_R(x) = \mathrm{med}(f_R(x_i^0), \varphi_i(x_i), f_R(x_i^1)) = \varphi_i(x_i) \vee f_R(x_i^0) \geq \varphi_i(x_i).$$

then also conditions (13) and (14) are satisfied.   □

5   The Italian System

Following [10], the Italian system employs two algorithms for the evaluation of epidemic probability (P) risk and epidemic impact (I) risk. Probability (P) and Impact (I) risks are evaluated by using suitable indicators.

Probability indicators:

P_1: Evidence of new cases reported in the last 5 days in the Region;
P_2: Evidence of an increase in transmission;
P_3: Evidence of widespread transmission in the Region that can not be managed effectively with local measures.

Impact indicators:

I_1: Evidence of new ceses reported in the past 5 days in individuals aged > 50 in the Region;
I_2: Signs of health service overload;
I_3: Evidence of new outbreaks in the last 7 days in nursing homes/hospitals or other places hosting vulnerable populations.

We observe that the two algorithms used for the evaluation of epidemic probability (P) risk and epidemic impact (I) risk can be expressed by suitable Rule sets. First, we consider the epidemic probability (P) risk assessment. We let $X_1 = X_2 = X_3 = \{0, 1\}$ and denote by $x_i \in X_i$ the evaluation of indicator P_i. Let $\boldsymbol{X} = X_1 \times X_2 \times X_3 = \{0, 1\}^3$ and $\boldsymbol{x} = (x_1, x_2, x_3) \in \boldsymbol{X}$. A decision rule r is an implication of the form

Table 2. Rule set R_P for Probability (P)

	P_1	P_2	P_3	P
r_1:	0	0	0	VL
r_2:	0	0	1	VL
r_3:	0	1	0	VL
r_4:	0	1	1	VL
r_5:	1	0	0	L
r_6:	1	0	1	L
r_7:	1	1	0	M
r_8:	1	1	1	H

Table 3. Rule set R_I for Impact (I)

	I_1	I_2	I_3	I
r_1:	0	0	0	VL
r_2:	0	0	1	VL
r_3:	0	1	0	VL
r_4:	0	1	1	VL
r_5:	1	0	0	L
r_6:	1	0	1	L
r_7:	1	1	0	M
r_8:	1	1	1	H

$$\text{IF } (x_1 = A_1 \text{ and } x_2 = A_2 \text{ and } x_3 = A_3) \quad \text{THEN } P = B$$

where $A_i \in X_i = \{0, 1\}$ and $B \in E = \{VL, L, M, H\}$. In this way, the Probability evaluation algorithm (as described in [10]) can be formalised by the Rule set R_P shown in Table 2. Similarly, the Impact (I) can be obtained as the output of the Rule set R_I shown in Table 3. We now deal with the problem of translating the rule sets R_P and R_I into Sugeno Utility Functionals. Let $\{P_1, P_2, P_3\}$ the set of criteria and $E = \{VL, L, M, H\}$. We define the fuzzy measure $m_P : \mathcal{P}(\{P_1, P_2, P_3\}) \to E$ as shown in Table 4, being $\mathcal{P}(\{P_1, P_2, P_3\})$ the power set of $\{P_1, P_2, P_3\}$. Let $\varphi_P : \boldsymbol{X} \to E^3$ be the global qualitative utility function defined by

$$\varphi_P(\boldsymbol{x}) = (\varphi_1(x_1), \varphi_2(x_2), \varphi_3(x_3)) \tag{16}$$

where, for all $i = 1, 2, 3$, the functions $\varphi_i : X_i \to E$ are defined by

$$\varphi_i(0) = VL, \qquad \varphi_i(1) = H. \tag{17}$$

The next result follows from Proposition 4.

Table 4. Fuzzy measure m_P

A	$m_P(A)$
$\emptyset$	VL
$\{P_1\}$	L
$\{P_2\}$	VL
$\{P_3\}$	VL
$\{P_1, P_2\}$	M
$\{P_1, P_3\}$	L
$\{P_2, P_3\}$	VL
$\{P_1, P_2, P_3\}$	H

Table 5. Rule set for Risk matrix

	P	I	$Risk$
r_1:	VL	VL	VL
r_2:	VL	L	L
r_3:	VL	M	L
r_4:	VL	H	M
r_5:	L	VL	L
r_6:	L	L	L
r_7:	L	M	M
r_8:	L	H	M
r_9:	M	VL	L
r_{10}:	M	L	M
r_{11}:	M	M	M
r_{12}:	M	H	H
r_{13}:	H	VL	M
r_{14}:	H	L	M
r_{15}:	H	M	H
r_{16}:	H	H	VH

Table 6. Fuzzy measure m

A	$m(A)$
$\emptyset$	VL
$\{P\}$	M
$\{I\}$	M
$\{P, I\}$	VH

Proposition 6. *Let m_P be the fuzzy measure defined in Table 4 and φ_P as defined in (16) and (17). Then, the Sugeno Utility Functional (SUF) (see (4))*

$$\mathcal{S}_{m_P, \varphi_P}(\boldsymbol{x}) = \mathcal{S}_{m_P}(\varphi_P(\boldsymbol{x})) = \mathcal{S}_{m_P}(\varphi_1(x_1), \varphi_2(x_2), \varphi_3(x_3)) \qquad (18)$$

translates the Rule set R_P described in Table 2.

For example, in the rule r_3, we have $\boldsymbol{x} = (0, 1, 0)$ and so $\varphi_P(\boldsymbol{x}) = (VL, H, VL)$ and $\mathcal{S}_{m_P, \varphi_P}(\boldsymbol{x}) = \mathcal{S}_{m_P}(\varphi_P(\boldsymbol{x})) = (VL \wedge H) \vee (VL \wedge VL) \vee (H \wedge VL) = VL$. In the rule r_7, we have $\boldsymbol{x} = (1, 1, 0)$ and so $\varphi_P(\boldsymbol{x}) = (H, H, VL)$ and $\mathcal{S}_{m_P, \varphi_P}(\boldsymbol{x}) = \mathcal{S}_{m_P}(\varphi_P(\boldsymbol{x})) = (VL \wedge H) \vee (H \wedge M) \vee (H \wedge VL) = M$.

In a similar way, the Rule set R_I shown in Table 3 can be expressed by the SUF $\mathcal{S}_{m_I, \varphi_I}(\boldsymbol{x}) = \mathcal{S}_{m_I}(\varphi_I(\boldsymbol{x})) = \mathcal{S}_{m_I}(\varphi_1(x_1), \varphi_2(x_2), \varphi_3(x_3))$.

The variables P and I are then aggregated, using a risk matrix (see [10]), to obtain the final Risk value assigned to a region. This risk matrix can be expressed by the Rule set shown in Table 5. With respect to the Rule set shown in Table 5, we compute in Table 6 the fuzzy measure m defined in (8). The functions φ_i ($i = 1, 2$) defined in (9) are the functions $\varphi_i \colon E \to E'$, being $E' = \{VL, L, M, H, VH\}$, given by $\varphi_i(VL) = VL$, $\varphi_i(L) = M$, $\varphi_i(M) = H$ and $\varphi_i(H) = VH$.

However, the SUF $\mathcal{S}_{m,\varphi}(\boldsymbol{x})$ does not translate the rule set shown in Table 5. For example, if we consider the rule r_3, we have $\boldsymbol{x} = (VL, M)$ and so $\varphi(\boldsymbol{x}) = (VL, H)$ and $\mathcal{S}_{m,\varphi}(\boldsymbol{x}) = \mathcal{S}_m(\boldsymbol{v}) = (VL \wedge VH) \vee (H \wedge M) = M$. Then, from Proposition 3, the rule set shown in Table 5 is not SUF-representable.

Remark 2. We observe that the SUF $\mathcal{S}_{m,\varphi}(\boldsymbol{x})$ translates a rule subset $R' \subset R$, being R the rule set shown in Table 5. Moreover, from Proposition 1, the whole rule set can be expressed by a set of SUFs.

6   Conclusions

In this study, we formulated a general model, based on Sugeno integrals, for risk assessment and planning of restriction policies to address emergency situations such as pandemics. The proposed approach makes the problem setting easy to interpret and allows incorporating the subjective opinions of policy-makers. Furthermore, we have shown how Sugeno integrals are related, in the monotone case, with if-then rule sets and, as an application, we revisited the Italian pandemic risk model in terms of Sugeno utility functionals. In future work we will explore more properties and benefits of the proposed approach and also the relationships with the models adopted by the governments of other countries.

References

1. Brabant, Q., Couceiro, M., Dubois, D., Prade, H., Rico, A.: Extracting decision rules from qualitative data via Sugeno utility functionals. In: Medina, J., et al. (eds.) IPMU 2018. CCIS, vol. 853, pp. 253–265. Springer, Cham (2018). https://doi.org/10.1007/978-3-319-91473-2_22
2. Brabant, Q., Couceiro, M., Dubois, D., Prade, H., Rico, A.: Learning rule sets and Sugeno integrals for monotonic classification problems. Fuzzy Sets Syst. **401**, 4–37 (2020). https://doi.org/10.1016/j.fss.2020.01.006
3. Couceiro, M., Dubois, D., Fargier, H., Grabisch, M., Prade, H., Rico, A.: New directions in ordinal evaluation: Sugeno integrals and beyond. In: Doumpos, M., Figueira, J.R., Greco, S., Zopounidis, C. (eds.) New Perspectives in Multiple Criteria Decision Making. MCDM, pp. 177–228. Springer, Cham (2019). https://doi.org/10.1007/978-3-030-11482-4_7
4. Couceiro, M., Dubois, D., Prade, H., Rico, A.: Enhancing the expressive power of Sugeno integrals for qualitative data analysis. In: Kacprzyk, J., Szmidt, E., Zadrożny, S., Atanassov, K.T., Krawczak, M. (eds.) IWIFSGN/EUSFLAT -2017. AISC, vol. 641, pp. 534–547. Springer, Cham (2018). https://doi.org/10.1007/978-3-319-66830-7_48

5. Couceiro, M., Dubois, D., Prade, H., Waldhauser, T.: Decision-making with Sugeno integrals. Order **33**(3), 517–535 (2016)
6. Couceiro, M., Waldhauser, T.: Axiomatizations and factorizations of Sugeno utility functions. Int. J. Uncertain. Fuzziness Knowl. Based Syst. **19**(04), 635–658 (2011)
7. Dwivedi, Y.K., et al.: Impact of covid-19 pandemic on information management research and practice: transforming education, work and life. Int. J. Inf. Manage. **55**, 102211 (2020)
8. Grabisch, M., Marichal, J.L., Mesiar, R., Pap, E.: Aggregation Functions, Encyclopedia of Mathematics and Its Applications, vol. 127 (2009)
9. Metcalf, C.J.E., Morris, D.H., Park, S.W.: Mathematical models to guide pandemic response. Science **369**(6502), 368–369 (2020)
10. Paroni, L., et al.: The traffic light approach: indicators and algorithms to identify Covid-19 epidemic risk across Italian regions. Frontiers Public Health **9** (2021). https://doi.org/10.3389/fpubh.2021.650243
11. Rico, A., Viappiani, P.: Incremental elicitation of capacities for the Sugeno integral with a maximin approach. In: Davis, J., Tabia, K. (eds.) SUM 2020. LNCS (LNAI), vol. 12322, pp. 156–171. Springer, Cham (2020). https://doi.org/10.1007/978-3-030-58449-8_11

On the Aggregation of n-distances

Tomasa Calvo Sánchez[1] and Pilar Fuster-Parra[2,3]

[1] Department of Computer Science, Universidad de Alcalá, 28871 Alcalá de Henares, Madrid, Spain
tomasa.calvo@uah.es

[2] Departament de Ciències, Matemàtiques i Informàtica, Universitat de les Illes Balears, 07122 Palma, Illes Balears, Spain
pilar.fuster@uib.es

[3] Institut d' Investigació Sanitària Illes Balears (IdISBa), Hospital Universitari Son Espases, 07120 Palma, Illes Balears, Spain

Abstract. This work deals with the aggregation of n-distances and S-generalized n-distances. The necessary conditions that a function has to satisfy to aggregate a collection of n-distances (respectively, S-generalized n-distances) into a new n-distance (respectively, S-generalized n-distance) are given. The last distances are introduced and discussed, in this work, as a generalization of the first ones. We also provide some relationship between both classes of distances. Moreover, we present several equivalent relations between an S-generalized n-distance and a new type of n-T-indisguishability operator.

Keywords: Aggregation function · distance · metric space · n-distance · S-generalized n-distance · n-T-indistinguishability operator · t-norms

1 Introduction

Aggregation functions [1, 7] are defined to combine several numerical values into a single representative one, which are increasing functions with some boundary conditions. They have been successfully employed in a plethora of theoretical and applied fields.

The notion of metric space [9] is of key importance in many areas like analysis, topology, geometry, statistics, and data analysis.

Let us recall that a *metric space* is a pair (X, d), where X is a non-empty set and d is a distance on X, i.e., d is a function $d : X^2 \to \mathbb{R}_+$ (where $\mathbb{R}_+$ denotes $[0, +\infty)$) satisfying the following conditions:

(A1) $d(x_1, x_2) = 0$ if and only if $x_1 = x_2$ (identity),

This research was funded by FEDER/Ministerio de Ciencia, Innovación y Universidades-Agencia Estatal de Investigación/_Proyecto PGC2018-095709-B-C21, and by Spanish Ministry of Economy and Competitiveness under contract DPI2017-86372-C3-3-R (AEI, FEDER, UE).

(A2) $d(x_1, x_2) = d(x_2, x_1)$ (symmetry),
(A3) $d(x_1, x_2) \leq d(x_1, z) + d(z, x_2)$ for all $x_1, x_2, z \in X$ (triangle inequality).

Generalizations of the concept of distance with $n \geq 3$, n an integer, have been studied by several authors [5,12,13]. The three conditions above are generalized to a function $d : X^n \to \mathbb{R}_+$ and studied in [10], so that considering $n \geq 2$ an integer, and given a non-empty set X, (X, d^n) is an n-metric space if d^n is a function $d^n : X^n \to \mathbb{R}_+$ satisfying the following conditions:

(N1) $d^n(x_1, \ldots, x_n) = 0$ if and only if $x_1 = \ldots = x_n$,
(N2) $d^n(x_1, \ldots, x_n) = d^n(x_{\pi(1)}, \ldots, x_{\pi(n)})$ for any permutation π of $1, \ldots, n$,
(N3) $d^n(x_1, \ldots, x_n) \leq \sum_{i=1}^{n} d^n(x_1, \ldots, x_n)_{x_i = z}$ for all $x_1, \ldots, x_n, z \in X$.

Where condition (N3) is referred to as the simplex inequality [5] (triangle inequality if $n = 2$). When $n = 2$ the concept of 2-distance on a non empty set is the same that the concept of distance on a non-empty set.

The metric spaces are generalized in such a way that instead of pairwise comparing elements of a non-empty set X through a distance d, where $d(x_1, x_2)$ would measure how far is the element x_1 from the element x_2, the concept of n-distance acts globally on n-tuple of elements of X evaluating how different or separated are the elements of the n-tuple. This is very characteristic when working in data analysis, where we are dealing with data.

In this work, we pay special attention in the preservation of the properties of n-distances and S-generalized n-distances by means of aggregation functions. The former notions appear in Definitions 1 and 4.

The antecedents of partial T-indistinguishability operators were introduced by Trillas in [16], so that given a t-norm $T : [0,1] \to [0,1]$, a T-indistinguishability operator on a (non-empty) set X is a fuzzy relation $E : X \times X \to [0,1]$ verifying for all $x, y, z \in X$ the following properties: (i) $E(x, x) = 1$, (ii) $E(x, y) = E(y, x)$, (iii) $T(E(x, y), E(y, z)) \leq E(x, z)$. A T-indistinguishability operator is a mathematical tool for classifying objects when a measure presents some kind of uncertainty. They are also known as measures of similarity, in fact, the greater $E(x, y)$ the more similar are x and y. The relation between different classes of T-indistinguishability operators and different types of pseudo metrics has been studied by several authors, see for instance [2–4,6,8,14]. Here, we investigate this kind of relations between the class of n-distances and the new class of n-T-indistinguishability operators.

The paper is organized as follows. In Sect. 2 we provide the conditions that a function F has to hold to aggregate a collection of n-distances into a new one. The next Section is devoted to the study of the S-generalized n-distances, the relationship with the n-distances and the problem of the aggregation of these distances is also analyzed. In Sect. 4, the relations between an S-generalized n-distance and an n-T-indistinguishability operator are given. Finally, in Sect. 5 we conclude the paper by proposing topics for further research.

2   Aggregation of n-distances

In this section, we deal with the problem of combining by means of a function, a collection of n-distances into a single representative one. Let us introduce the notion of n-distance aggregation function.

Definition 1. *Let $n, m \in \mathbf{N}$, X a nonempty set. A function $F : \mathbb{R}_+^m \to \mathbb{R}_+$ will be called an n-distance aggregation function, if for each family of m n-distances on X, $d_1^n, d_2^n, \ldots, d_m^n$, the function F is an n-distance on X, where $F(d_1^n, d_2^n, \ldots, d_m^n)$ is given by*

$$F(d_1^n, d_2^n, \ldots, d_m^n)(x_1, \ldots, x_n) = F(d_1^n(x_1, \ldots, x_n), \ldots, d_m^n(x_1, \ldots, x_n)),$$

for each $x_1, \ldots, x_n \in X$.

For the shake of simplicity, the n-distance aggregation function F would also be denoted as:

$$d^F(x_1, \ldots, x_n) = F(d_1^n, d_2^n, \ldots, d_m^n)(x_1, \ldots, x_n).$$

Example 1. Let $n, m \in \mathbf{N}$, X a nonempty set. Consider $\{d_1^n, \ldots, d_m^n\}$ a collection of m n-distances on X, the function $F : \mathbb{R}_+^m \to \mathbb{R}_+$, given by

$$F(d_1^n, d_2^n, \ldots, d_m^n)(x_1, \ldots, x_n) = \left(\sum_{i=1}^m d_i^n(x_1, \ldots, x_n) \right)^{1/2}$$

provide us that $F(d_1^n, d_2^n, \ldots, d_m^n)$ is an n-distance on X.

In order to provide necessary conditions to characterize n-distance aggregation functions, let us remember the following definitions.

Definition 2. *A function $F : \mathbb{R}_+^m \to \mathbb{R}_+$ is a subadditive function whenever*

$$F\left(\sum_{i=1}^n z_1^i, \ldots, \sum_{i=1}^n z_m^i \right) \leq \sum_{i=1}^n F(z_1^i, \ldots, z_m^i).$$

Definition 3. *A function $F : \mathbb{R}_+^m \to \mathbb{R}_+$ is a non-decreasing function if for all $(a_1, \ldots, a_m), (b_1, \ldots, b_m) \in \mathbb{R}_+^m$ such that $(a_1, \ldots, a_m) \leq (b_1, \ldots, b_m)$ then*

$$F(a_1, \ldots, a_m) \leq F(b_1, \ldots, b_m).$$

The next result provides a sufficient condition to ensure that a function aggregates n-distances.

Proposition 1. *Let $d_1^n, d_2^n, \ldots, d_m^n$ a collection of n-distances defined on the same set X and $F : \mathbb{R}_+^m \to \mathbb{R}_+$. If F holds the following conditions:*

(i) $F(z_1, \ldots, z_m) = 0$ if and only if $z_k = 0$ for some $k \in \{1, \ldots, m\}$,
(ii) F is a non-decreasing function, and
(iii) F is subadditive function,

then $d^F(x_1, \ldots, x_n) = F(d_1^n, \ldots, d_m^n)(x_1, \ldots, x_n)$, *for all* $x_1, \ldots, x_n \in X$, *is also an n-distance.*

Proof. First we will prove the condition (N1), so that if $x_1 = \ldots = x_n$ then $d_i^n(x_1, \ldots, x_n) = 0$, $i = 1, \ldots, m$ therefore $d^F(x_1, \ldots, x_n) = 0$. Reciprocally, if $d^F(x_1, \ldots, x_n) = F(d_1^n(x_1, \ldots, x_n), \ldots, d_m^n(x_1, \ldots, x_n)) = 0$ then there is a $k \in \{1, \ldots, m\}$ such that $d_k^n(x_1, \ldots, x_n) = 0$ therefore $x_1 = \ldots = x_n$.

The symmetry of d^F (condition (N2)) follows directly from the symmetry of each n-distance d_i^n, $i = 1, \ldots, m$.

Now, we have to show the condition (N3), that is

$$d^F(x_1, \ldots, x_n) = F(d_1^n(x_1, \ldots, x_n), \ldots, d_m^n(x_1, \ldots, x_n)) \leq$$

$$F\left(\sum_{i=1}^n d_1^n(x_1, x_2, \ldots, x_n)_{x_i=z}, \ldots, \sum_{i=1}^n d_m^n(x_1, x_2, \ldots, x_n)_{x_i=z} \right) \leq$$

$$\sum_{i=1}^n F(d_1^n(x_1, x_2, \ldots, x_n)_{x_i=z}, \ldots, d_m^n(x_1, x_2, \ldots, x_n)_{x_i=z}) = \sum_{i=1}^n d^F(x_1, \ldots, x_n)_{x_i=z}$$

where the first inequality follows from the monotonicity of F and the second is due to its subadditive property. $\qquad\square$

In the following example the function F verifies conditions of Proposition 1.

Example 2. The homogeneous and linear function $F : \mathbb{R}_+^m \to \mathbb{R}_+$ defined by $F(z_1, \ldots, z_m) = \sum_{i=1}^m \lambda_i z_i$, with $\lambda_i \geq 0$ and $\lambda_k \neq 0$ for some $k \in \{1, \ldots, m\}$, is an example of n-distance aggregation function.

Remark 1. The Proposition 1 is also valid for only one n-distance. In this case we obtain sufficient conditions for any F function that transforms an n-distance d^n in another n-distance $F(d^n)$.

It can easily see that the functions

(i) $F_1(x) = \frac{x}{1-x}$,
(ii) $F_2(x) = \min\{1, x\}$

verify properties (i), (ii) and (iii) of Proposition 1, and therefore if d^n is an n-distance then $\frac{d^n}{1-d^n}$, $\min\{1, d^n\}$ are n-distances with range $[0, 1]$, and therefore these transformations give a way to normalize any n-distance.

The reciprocal of Proposition 1 is not necessarily true as the following example shows.

Example 3. Let $d_1^n, d_2^n, \ldots, d_m^n$ a collection of drastic n-distances defined on the same set X and $F : \mathbb{R}_+^3 \to \mathbb{R}_+$ defined as $F(x, y, z) = x \cdot y \cdot z$. The drastic n-distances $i = 1, \ldots, m$:

$$d_i^n(x_1, \ldots, x_n) = \begin{cases} 0 & \text{if } x_1 = \ldots = x_n \\ 1 & \text{otherwise.} \end{cases}$$

Then $F(d_i^n, d_j^n, d_k^n)$ is also a drastic n-distance. However, F is not a subadditive function:

$$F((d_1^n + (d_1^n)')(x_1, \ldots, x_n), (d_2^n + (d_2^n)')(x_1, \ldots, x_n), (d_3^n + (d_3^n)')(x_1, \ldots, x_n)) \not\leq$$

$$F(d_1^n, d_2^n, d_3^n)(x_1, \ldots, x_n) + F((d_1^n)', (d_2^n)', (d_3^n)')(x_1, \ldots, x_n)$$

Now, considering $x_1 \neq \ldots \neq x_n$ we have:

$$8 = 2 \cdot 2 \cdot 2 = F(2,2,2) \not\leq F(1,1,1) + F(1,1,1) = 1 + 1 = 2.$$

The following proposition gives a necessary condition to be d^F an n-distance.

Proposition 2. *Let $d_1^n, d_2^n, \ldots, d_m^n$ a collection of n-distances ($d_i^n \neq d_j^n$ for some $i, j \in \{1, \ldots, m\}$) defined on the same set X and if $F : \mathbb{R}_+^m \to \mathbb{R}_+$ aggregates n-distances then*

$$F(d_1^n, \ldots d_m^n)(x_1, \ldots, x_n) = 0$$

if and only if $d_i^n(x_1, \ldots, x_n) = 0$ for some $i \in \{1, \ldots, m\}$.

Proof. If there was a list $(z_1, \ldots, z_m)$ of non-constant elements (i.e., $\exists i, j \in \{1, \ldots, m\}$ such that $z_i \neq z_j$) and with $z_i \neq 0 \; \forall i \in \{1, \ldots, m\}$ such that $F(z_1, \ldots, z_m) = 0$, it would be possible to find a non-constant list $(x_1, \ldots, x_n)$ (i.e., $\exists i, j \in \{1, \ldots, m\}$ such that $x_i \neq x_j$) and $d_1^n, d_2^n, \ldots, d_m^n$ n-distances such that $d_i^n(x_1, \ldots, x_n) = z_i$ for all $i \in \{1, \ldots, m\}$.

Then as F is a n-distance if $F(d_1^n, \ldots d_m^n)(x_1, \ldots, x_n) = 0$ we have that $d_1^n(x_1, \ldots, x_n) = \ldots = d_m^n(x_1, \ldots, x_n)$ which is a contradiction because $(z_1, \ldots, z_m)$ is a non-constant list.

Reciprocally, let us suppose $\exists i \in \{1, \ldots, m\}$ such that $d_i^n(x_1, \ldots, x_n) = 0$ and $F(z_1, \ldots, z_m) \neq 0$ so, as F is an n-distance $\exists j \in \{1, \ldots, m\}, j \neq i$ such that $d_j^n(x_1, \ldots, x_n) \neq 0$, but as d_i^n is an n-distance and $d_i^n(x_1, \ldots, x_n) = 0$ then $x_1 = \ldots = x_n$, and therefore $d_j^n(x_1, \ldots, x_n)$ sould also be equal to 0, which is a contradiction and we can ensure that $F(z_1, \ldots, z_m) = 0$. $\square$

Throughout the following sections we will assume that the reader is familiar with the basics of triangular norms (see [11] for a deeper treatment of the topic).

3   On S-generalized n-distances

Inspired by the generalization of the concept of distance based on the simplex inequality [10] and the notion of S-generalized metrics defined on $([0,1], \leq, 0)$ (see [16,17]), the notion of S-generalized n-distance is introduced by replacing the sum of the simplex inequality of condition (N3) (triangle inequality in case $n = 2$) by a t-conorm, i.e., $d^n(x_1, \ldots, x_n)_{x_1=z} + \ldots + d^n(x_1, \ldots, x_n)_{x_n=z}$ is replaced by $S(d^n(x_1, \ldots, x_n)_{x_1=z}, \ldots, d^n(x_1, \ldots, x_n)_{x_n=z})$.

Definition 4. *Let $n \geq 2$ be an integer and S a t-conorm. Given a non-empty set X, (X, d^n) is an n-metric space with respect to the conorm S, if d^n is a function $d^n : X^n \to [0,1]$ satisfying the following conditions:*

(G1) $d^n(x_1,\ldots,x_n) = 0$ *if and only if* $x_1 = \ldots = x_n$,

(G2) $d^n(x_1,\ldots,x_n) = d^n(x_{\pi(1)},\ldots,x_{\pi(n)})$ *for any permutation* π *of* $1,\ldots,n$,

(G3) $d^n(x_1,\ldots,x_n) \leq S(d^n(x_1,\ldots,x_n)_{x_1=z},\ldots,d^n(x_1,\ldots,x_n)_{x_n=z})$,

    for all $x_1,\ldots,x_n,z \in X$,

then d^n *is called an* S-generalized n-distance.

Remark 2. (i) Let d_1^n, d_2^n be S-generalized n-distances with $S \leq S_L$ and S_L the Łukasiewicz t-conorm $(S_L(x,y) = \min\{x+y,1\})$, then the bounded sum $d_1^n \oplus d_2^n$ is a S_L-generalized n-distance. Observe that

$$d_i^n(x_1,\ldots,x_n) \leq S(d_i^n(x_1,\ldots,x_n)_{x_1}^z,\ldots,d_i^n(x_1,\ldots,x_n)_{x_n}^z)$$

for all $x_1,\ldots,x_n,z \in X$ and $i = 1,2$, and $d_i^n(x_1,\ldots,x_n)_{x_i}^z = d_i^n(x_1,\ldots,x_n)_{x_i=z}$. Now, for all $x_1,\ldots,x_n, z \in X$ and $i = 1,2$ we have,

$$d_1^n \oplus d_2^n(x_1,\ldots,x_n) = d_1^n(x_1,\ldots,x_n) \oplus d_2^n(x_1,\ldots,x_n)$$

$$= S_L(d_1^n(x_1,\ldots,x_n), d_2^n(x_1,\ldots,x_n)) \leq$$

$$S_L(S(d_1^n(x_1,\ldots,x_n)_{x_1}^z,\ldots,d_1^n(x_1,\ldots,x_n)_{x_n}^z), S(d_2^n(x_1,\ldots,x_n)_{x_1}^z,\ldots,d_2^n(x_1,\ldots,x_n)_{x_n}^z)) \leq$$

$$S_L(S_L(d_1^n(x_1,\ldots,x_n)_{x_1}^z,\ldots,d_1^n(x_1,\ldots,x_n)_{x_n}^z), S_L(d_2^n(x_1,\ldots,x_n)_{x_1}^z,\ldots,d_2^n(x_1,\ldots,x_n)_{x_n}^z)) =$$

by associativity of S_L

$$S_L(S_L((d_1^n, d_2^n)(x_1,\ldots,x_n)_{x_1}^z,\ldots,(d_1^n, d_2^n)(x_1,\ldots,x_n)_{x_n}^z))$$

$$= S_L((d_1^n \oplus d_2^n)(x_1,\ldots,x_n)_{x_1}^z,\ldots,(d_1^n \oplus d_2^n)(x_1,\ldots,x_n)_{x_n}^z)).$$

Observe that any S_L-generalized n-distance is also an S_D-generalized n-distance.

(ii) If d^n is an S_M-generalized n-distance, with S_M the maximum t-conorm $(S_M(x,y) = \max\{x,y\})$ then $\lambda \cdot d^n$ is an S_M-generalized n-distance, and therefore an S-generalized n-distance.

Proposition 3. *Let S be a continuous Archimedean t-conorm with normed additive generator $\hat{s}$. Then:*

(i) d^n *is an* S-generalized n-distance *if and only if* $\hat{s} \circ d^n$ *is an* n-distance.

(ii) d^n *is an* n-distance *if and only if* $\hat{s}^{-1} \circ d^n$ *is an* S-generalized n-distance.

Proof. In both cases we will only show the third condition, i.e., condition (N3) for n-distances and (G3) for S-generalized n-distances because conditions (N1), (N2), (G1) and (G2) follow directly.

(i) Taking into account the representation theorem of a continuous t-conorm, we see that for an S-generalized n-distance d^n verifies condition (G3)

$$d^n(x_1,\ldots,x_n) \leq S(d^n(z,x_2,\ldots,x_n),\ldots,d^n(x_1,\ldots,x_{n-1},z))$$

$$= \hat{s}^{-1}(\textstyle\sum_{i=1}^n (\hat{s} \circ d^n(x_1,\ldots,x_n))_{x_i=z}),$$

is equivalent to the next inequality as $\hat{s}$ is strictly increasing,

$$\hat{s} \circ d^n(x_1, \ldots, x_n) \leq \sum_{i=1}^{n}(\hat{s} \circ d^n(x_1, \ldots, x_n))_{x_i = z},$$

therefore $\hat{s} \circ d^n$ satisfies the third condition (N3) of an n-distance.

(ii) We proceed in a similar way of the previous case. The third condition of a n-distance d^n (N3) is

$$d^n(x_1, \ldots, x_n) \leq d^n(z, x_2, \ldots, x_n) + \ldots + d^n(x_1, \ldots, x_{n-1}, z)$$

or equivalently,

$$(\hat{s} \circ \hat{s}^{-1})d^n(x_1, \ldots, x_n) \leq$$

$$(\hat{s} \circ \hat{s}^{-1})(d^n(z, x_2, \ldots, x_n)) + \ldots + (\hat{s} \circ \hat{s}^{-1})(d^n(x_1, \ldots, x_{n-1}, z))$$

which is equivalent

$$(\hat{s}^{-1} \circ d^n)(x_1, \ldots, x_n) \leq$$

$$\hat{s}^{-1}(\hat{s}((\hat{s}^{-1} \circ d^n)(z, x_2, \ldots, x_n))) + \ldots + \hat{s}((\hat{s}^{-1} \circ d^n)(x_1, \ldots, x_{n-1}, z)))$$

and considering the representation theorem of t-conorm we have that

$$(\hat{s}^{-1} \circ d^n)(x_1, \ldots, x_n) \leq S((\hat{s}^{-1} \circ d^n)(z, x_2, \ldots, x_n), \ldots, (\hat{s}^{-1} \circ d^n)(x_1, \ldots, x_{n-1}, z))$$

therefore $\hat{s}^{-1} \circ d^n$ is an S-generalized n-distance.   □

The following Proposition shows that any S-norm aggregates S-generalized n-distances.

Proposition 4. *Let $d_j^n, j = 1, \ldots, m$ be a collection of S-generalized n-distances. Then $S(d_1^n, \ldots, d_m^n)$ is an S-generalized n-distance.*

Proof. The proof of conditions (G1) and (G2) of an S-generalized n-distance of $S(d_1^n, \ldots, d_m^n)$ follows directly. We show the condition (G3) of Definition 4. We know that each $d_j^n, j = 1, \ldots, m$ satisfies

$$d_j^n(x_1, \ldots, x_n) \leq S(d_j^n(z, \ldots, x_n), \ldots, d_j^n(x_1, \ldots, z)).$$

Applying S in the two sides of the above inequalities and due to its increasingness we have

$$S(d_1^n, \ldots, d_m^n)(x_1, \ldots, x_n) \leq$$

$$S(S(d_1^n(z, \ldots, x_n), \ldots, d_1^n(x_1, \ldots, z)), \ldots, S(d_m^n(z, \ldots, x_n), \ldots, d_m^n(x_1, \ldots, z))).$$

Considering the associativity of S we have

$$S(d_1^n, \ldots, d_m^n)(x_1, \ldots, x_n) \leq$$

$$S(S(d_1^n(z, \ldots, x_n), \ldots, d_m^n(z, \ldots, x_n)), \ldots, S(d_1^n(x_1, \ldots, z), \ldots, d_m^n(x_1, \ldots, z)))$$

$$= S(S(d_1^n \ldots, d_m^n)(z, \ldots, x_n), \ldots, S(d_1^n \ldots, d_m^n)(x_1, \ldots, z)).   □$$

The next result provides a sufficient condition to ensure that a function aggregates S-generalized n-distances.

Proposition 5. *Let* $d_1^n, d_2^n, \ldots, d_m^n$ *a collection of S-generalized n-distances defined on the same set X and $F : \mathbb{R}_+^m \to \mathbb{R}_+$. If F holds the following conditions:*

(i) $F(z_1, \ldots, z_m) = 0$ *if and only if $z_k = 0$ for some $k \in \{1, \ldots, m\}$,*
(ii) *F is a non-decreasing function, and*
(iii) *F holds the following inequality*

$$F\left(S(d_1^n(x_1, x_2, \ldots, x_n)_{x_i=z}), \ldots, S(d_m^n(x_1, x_2, \ldots, x_n)_{x_i=z})\right) \leq$$

$$S(F\left(d_1^n(x_1, x_2, \ldots, x_n)_{x_i=z}, \ldots, d_m^n(x_1, x_2, \ldots, x_n)_{x_i=z}\right)$$

then $d^F(x_1, \ldots, x_n) = F(d_1^n, \ldots, d_m^n)(x_1, \ldots, x_n)$, for all $x_1, \ldots, x_n \in X$, is also an S-generalized n-distance.

Proof. First we will prove the condition (G1), so that if $x_1 = \ldots = x_n$ then $d_i^n(x_1, \ldots, x_n) = 0$, $i = 1, \ldots, m$ therefore $d^F(x_1, \ldots, x_n) = 0$. Reciprocally, if $d^F(x_1, \ldots, x_n) = F(d_1^n(x_1, \ldots, x_n), \ldots, d_m^n(x_1, \ldots, x_n)) = 0$ then there exists a $k \in \{1, \ldots, m\}$ such that $d_k^n(x_1, \ldots, x_n) = 0$ therefore $x_1 = \ldots = x_n$.

The symmetry of d^F (condition (G2)) follows directly from the symmetry of each S-generalized n-distance. d_i^n, $i = 1, \ldots, m$.

Now, we have to show the condition (G3), for that we will use the two following notations

$$S(d_j^n(z, \ldots, x_n), \ldots, d_j^n(x_1, \ldots, z)) = S(d_j^n(x_1, x_2, \ldots, x_n)_{x_i=z}), j = 1, \ldots, m$$

and

$$S\left(F\left(d_1^n(x_1, x_2, \ldots, x_n)_{x_i=z}, \ldots, d_m^n(x_1, x_2, \ldots, x_n)_{x_i=z}\right)\right) =$$

$$S\left(F\left(d_1^n(z, x_2, \ldots, x_n), \ldots, d_m^n(z, x_2, \ldots, x_n)\right), \ldots, F\left(d_1^n(x_1, x_2, \ldots, z), \ldots, d_m^n(x_1, x_2, \ldots, z)\right)\right).$$

To show (G3)

$$d^F(x_1, \ldots, x_n) = F(d_1^n(x_1, \ldots, x_n), \ldots, d_m^n(x_1, \ldots, x_n)) \leq$$

$$F\left(S(d_1^n(x_1, x_2, \ldots, x_n)_{x_i=z}), \ldots, S(d_m^n(x_1, x_2, \ldots, x_n)_{x_i=z})\right) \leq$$

$$S(F\left(d_1^n(x_1, x_2, \ldots, x_n)_{x_i=z}, \ldots, d_m^n(x_1, x_2, \ldots, x_n)_{x_i=z}\right) =$$

$$S(F(d_1^n, \ldots, d_m^n)(z, \ldots, x_n), \ldots, F(d_1^n, \ldots, d_m^n)(x_1, \ldots, z)),$$

where the first inequality follows from the monotonicity of the function F and the second is due to the condition (G3).

4   On n-distances, S-generalized n-distances and n-T-indistinguishabilities

Pseudo-distances are related to T-indistinguishabilities [11]. In the following we will relate n-distances to a special type of T-indistinguishability called n-T-indistinguishability. Let us remember the notion of T-indistinguishability. According to [16] (see also [15]), a T-equivalence on a (nonempty) set X is a fuzzy relation $E : X \times X \to [0,1]$ satisfying for all $x, y, z \in X$ the following axioms:

(E1) $E(x,x) = 1$,
(E2) $E(x,y) = E(y,x)$,
(E3) $T(E(x,y), E(y,z)) \leq E(x,z)$.

Following [15], a T-equivalence E is said to be a T-equality when for all $x, y \in X$ the following condition is fulfilled:

(E1)' $E(x,y) = 1 \Leftrightarrow x = y$.

Definition 5. *Let $n \in \mathbb{N}$, T be a t-norm, and X a non empty set. A function $\mathcal{E}^n : X^n \to [0,1]$ is an n-T-indistinguishability in X if and only if satisfies for all $x_1, \ldots, x_n, z \in X$ the following axioms:*

(M1) $\mathcal{E}^n(x_1, \ldots, x_n) = 1$ if $x_1 = \cdots = x_n$,
(M2) $\mathcal{E}^n(x_1, \ldots, x_n) = \mathcal{E}^n(x_{\pi(1)}, \ldots, x_{\pi(n)})$,
(M3) $\mathcal{E}^n(x_1, \ldots, x_n) \geq T(\mathcal{E}^n(z, x_2, \ldots, x_n), \mathcal{E}^n(x_1, z, \ldots, x_n), \ldots, \mathcal{E}^n(x_1, \ldots, x_{n-1}, z))$.

An n-T-indistinguishability $\mathcal{E}^n$ is said that separates points (T-equality) if in addition verifies

(M4) $\mathcal{E}^n(x_1, \ldots, x_n) = 1 \to x_1 = \cdots = x_n$.

Example 4. Let $\mathcal{E}^n : X^n \to [0,1]$ defined by

$$\mathcal{E}^n(x_1, \ldots, x_n) = \begin{cases} 1 & \text{if } x_1 = \ldots = x_n, \\ 0 & \text{otherwise.} \end{cases}$$

$\mathcal{E}^n$ is an n-T_M-indistinguishability which separates points. Observe that any n-T_M-indistinguishability is an n-T-indistinguishability with any T.

Proposition 6. *Let T be a continuous and Archimedean t-norm, and t the additive generator of T, then*

(i) If $d^n : X^n \to \mathbb{R}_+^n$ is an n-distance on X, then $\mathcal{E}_d^n : X^n \to [0,1]$ defined by $\mathcal{E}_d^n = t^{(-1)} \circ d^n$ is an n-T-indistinguishability on X.
(ii) If $\mathcal{E}^n : X^n \to [0,1]$ is an n-T-indistinguishability in X, then $d_{\mathcal{E}}^n : X^n \to \mathbb{R}_+^n$ given by $d_{\mathcal{E}}^n = t \circ \mathcal{E}$ is an n-distance if and only if $\mathcal{E}$ separates points.

Proof. (i) Let us see that condition (M1) is verified,

$$\mathcal{E}_d^n(x,\ldots,x) = t^{(-1)}(d^n(x,\ldots,x))$$
$$= t^{(-1)}(0)$$
$$= 1.$$

Condition (M2) follows directly because the symmetry of d^n, and inequality (M3) is also verified:

$$\mathcal{E}_d^n(x_1,\ldots,x_n) = t^{(-1)}(d^n(x_1,\ldots,x_n))$$
$$\geq t^{(-1)}(\textstyle\sum_{i=1}^n d^n(x_1,\ldots,x_n)_{x_i=z})$$
$$= t^{(-1)}(\textstyle\sum_{i=1}^n t(\mathcal{E}_d^n(x_1,\ldots,x_n)_{x_i=z}))$$
$$= T(\mathcal{E}_d^n(x_1,\ldots,x_n)_{x_1=z},\ldots,\mathcal{E}_d^n(x_1,\ldots,x_n)_{x_n=z}).$$

(ii) Let us see that condition (M1) is verified,

$$d_{\mathcal{E}}^n(x,\ldots,x) = t(\mathcal{E}(x,\ldots,x))$$
$$= t(1)$$
$$= 0.$$

Condition (M2) follows directly because of symmetry of d^n, and inequality (M3) is also verified:

$$d_{\mathcal{E}}^n(x_1,\ldots,x_n) = t(\mathcal{E}(x_1,\ldots,x_n))$$
$$\leq t(T(\mathcal{E}(x_1,\ldots,x_n)_{x_1=z},\ldots,\mathcal{E}(x_1,\ldots,x_n)_{x_n=z}))$$
$$= \textstyle\sum_{i=1}^n t(\mathcal{E}(x_1,\ldots,x_n)_{x_i=z})$$
$$= \textstyle\sum_{i=1}^n d_{\mathcal{E}}^n(x_1,\ldots,x_n)_{x_i=z}.$$

With respect to condition (M4) note that,

$$d_{\mathcal{E}}^n(x_1,\ldots,x_n) = 0 \leftrightarrow t(\mathcal{E}(x_1,\ldots,x_n)) = 0$$
$$\leftrightarrow \mathcal{E}(x_1,\ldots,x_n) = 1. \qquad \square$$

Note that, if T is a non continuous t-norm Proposition 6 is not verified as the following example shows.

Example 5. For any $n \geq 3$, the map $d_S^n : (\mathbb{R}^2)^n \to \mathbb{R}_+$ which associates to any $(\mathbf{x_1},\ldots,\mathbf{x_n}) \in (\mathbb{R}^2)^n$ the surface area bounded by $S(\mathbf{x_1},\ldots,\mathbf{x_n})$ is an n-distance [10]. Let us consider the Archimedean non-continuous Drastic t-norm T_D defined by

$$T_D(x,y) = \begin{cases} 0 & \text{if } (x,y) \in [0,1[^2, \\ \min(x,y) & \text{otherwise,} \end{cases}$$

with additive generator:

$$t_D(x) = \begin{cases} 2 - x & \text{if } x \in [0,1), \\ 0 & \text{if } x = 1, \end{cases}$$

and

$$t_D^{(-1)}(x) = \begin{cases} 0 & \text{if } x \in (2,\infty], \\ 2 - x & \text{if } x \in (1,2], \\ 1 & \text{if } x \in [0,1]. \end{cases}$$

Considering $\mathbf{x_1} = (0,0), \mathbf{x_2} = (2,0), \mathbf{x_3} = (0,2)$ and $\mathbf{z} = (\frac{1}{2}, \frac{1}{2})$, we have,

$$d_S(\mathbf{x_1}, \mathbf{x_2}, \mathbf{x_3}) = S(\mathbf{x_1}, \mathbf{x_2}, \mathbf{x_3}) = \frac{2 \cdot 2}{2} = 2 \rightarrow t_D^{(-1)}(2) = 0,$$

$$d_S(\mathbf{z}, \mathbf{x_2}, \mathbf{x_3}) = S(\mathbf{z}, \mathbf{x_2}, \mathbf{x_3}) = \frac{(2\sqrt{2}) \cdot \frac{\sqrt{2}}{2}}{2} = 1 \rightarrow t_D^{(-1)}(1) = 1,$$

$$d_S(\mathbf{x_1}, \mathbf{z}, \mathbf{x_3}) = S(\mathbf{x_1}, \mathbf{z}, \mathbf{x_3}) = \frac{2 \cdot \frac{1}{2}}{2} = \frac{1}{2} \rightarrow t_D^{(-1)}(1) = 1,$$

$$d_S(\mathbf{x_1}, \mathbf{x_2}, \mathbf{z}) = S(\mathbf{x_1}, \mathbf{x_2}, \mathbf{z}) = \frac{2 \cdot \frac{1}{2}}{2} = \frac{1}{2} \rightarrow t_D^{(-1)}(1) = 1,$$

and therefore property (M3) of Definition 5 is not verified

$$t_D^{(-1)}(2) = 0 \not\geq T_D(t_D^{(-1)}(1), t_D^{(-1)}(1), t_D^{(-1)}(1)) = T_D(1,1,1) = 1.$$

The following Proposition 7 relates S-generalized n-distances to n-indistinguis-habilities through the concept of strong negation. Let us remember that a non-increasing function $N : [0,1] \rightarrow [0,1]$ is called a *negation* [11] if $N(0) = 1$ and $N(1) = 0$; a negation is called *strict negation* if, additionally, N is continuous and strictly decreasing; a negation is called *strong* negation if it is an involution, i.e., $N \circ N = id_{[0,1]}$. The most important negation is the standard negation $N(x) = 1 - x$. When the t-conorm S is the dual of the t-norm T with respect to a strong negation N we have,

$$S(x,y) = N(T(N(x), N(y))),$$

$$T(x,y) = N(S(N(x), N(y))).$$

Proposition 7. *Let T be a continuous t-norm and T^* its dual t-conorm w.r.t. a strong negation N.*

(i) *If d^n is an S-generalized n-distance then $\mathcal{E}_d^n = N \circ d^n$ is an n-T-indistinguishability operator on X, where T is the n-dual t-norm associated with S.*

(ii) *If $\mathcal{E}^n$ is an n-T-indistinguishability operator on X then $d_{\mathcal{E}}^n = N \circ \mathcal{E}^n$ is a T^*-generalized n-distance.*

Proof. To show (i) we start the property (M3) of the involved definitions, since the two other, (M1) and (M2), can be proven easily. If d^n is an S-generalized n-distance then satisfies the condition (G3) of Definition 4, i.e.,

$$d^n(x_1, \ldots, x_n) \leq S(d^n(z, x_2, \ldots, x_n), \ldots, d^n(x_1, x_2, \ldots, z))$$

equivalently,

$$d^n(x_1, \ldots, x_n) \leq N(T(N \circ d^n(z, x_2, \ldots, x_n), \ldots, N \circ d^n(x_1, x_2, \ldots, z)))$$

and composing with N we obtain

$$N \circ d^n(x_1, \ldots, x_n) \geq T(N \circ d^n(z, x_2, \ldots, x_n), \ldots, N \circ d^n(x_1, x_2, \ldots, z))$$

or equivalently,

$$\mathcal{E}_d^n(x_1, \ldots, x_n) \geq T(\mathcal{E}_d^n(z, x_2, \ldots, x_n), \ldots, \mathcal{E}_d^n(x_1, x_2, \ldots, z)).$$

Therefore $\mathcal{E}_d^n$ is an n-T-indistinguishability operator.

Similarly, we can prove the case (ii). If $\mathcal{E}^n$ is an n-T-indistinguishability operator w.r.t. T, from the condition (M3) of its definition we obtain that

$$\mathcal{E}^n(x_1, \ldots, x_n) \geq T(\mathcal{E}^n(z, x_2, \ldots, x_n), \ldots, \mathcal{E}^n(x_1, x_2, \ldots, z))$$

$$N \circ \mathcal{E}^n(x_1, \ldots, x_n) \leq N \circ T(\mathcal{E}^n(z, x_2, \ldots, x_n), \ldots, \mathcal{E}^n(x_1, x_2, \ldots, z))$$

T is replaced by the dual of S,

$$N \circ \mathcal{E}^n(x_1, \ldots, x_n) \leq N \circ N \circ S(N \circ \mathcal{E}^n(z, x_2, \ldots, x_n), \ldots, N \circ \mathcal{E}^n(x_1, x_2, \ldots, z))$$
$$\leq S(N \circ \mathcal{E}^n(z, x_2, \ldots, x_n), \ldots, N \circ \mathcal{E}^n(x_1, x_2, \ldots, z))$$

Simplifying,

$$d_{\mathcal{E}}^n(x_1, \ldots, x_n) \leq S(d_{\mathcal{E}}^n(z, x_2, \ldots, x_n), \ldots, d_{\mathcal{E}}^n(x_1, x_2, \ldots, z)),$$

where $d_{\mathcal{E}}^n = N \circ \mathcal{E}^n$, so that d is an S-generalized n-distance.

Moreover, if
$\mathcal{E}_d^n(x, \ldots, x) = 1 \leftrightarrow N \circ \mathcal{E}_d^n(x, \ldots, x) = N(1) = 0$ then $d_{\mathcal{E}}^n(x, \ldots, x) = 0$. So, that the first condition of an n-T-indistinguishability (M1) is equivalent to the first condition of a T^*-generalized n-distance (G1).

The symmetry condition in the two above concepts is also an equivalent property.   □

5   Conclusions

We have studied the problem of the aggregation of n-distances and of S-generalized n-distances. Namely, we present the necessary conditions of a function defined on $[0, 1]^m$ that aggregates a collection of n-distances or S-generalized n-distances into a new n-distance or S-generalized n-distance. We point out that the former distances are introduced and discussed, in this work, as a generalization of the first ones. Moreover, we also provide some relationship between both classes of distances. Finally, we present several equivalent relations between an S-generalized n-distance and a new type of n-T-indistinguishability operator.

Some possible applications are: (i) Networks: considering n villages $n \geq 3$ and an n-distance d^n measuring the distance among them may help to determine the best position to locate a transmitter; (ii) Systems of Communication: to minimize cost of transportation; (iii) Image Processing: when comparing pictures through an n-distance, etc.

After the considerations made in this work we will investigate the problem of the aggregation of other classes of generalized distances or multidistances.

References

1. Beliakov, G., Pradera, A., Calvo, T.: Aggregation Functions: A Guide for Practitioners. Springer, Heidelberg (2007). https://doi.org/10.1007/978-3-540-73721-6
2. De Baets, B., Mesiar, R.: Pseudo-metrics and T-equivalences. J. Fuzzy Math. **5**, 471–481 (1997)
3. De Baets, B., Mesiar, R.: Metrics and T-equalities. J. Math. Anal. Appl. **267**, 531–547 (2002)
4. Calvo, T., Fuster-Parra, P.: Aggregation of partial T-indistinguishability operators and partial pseudo-metrics. Fuzzy Sets Syst. **403**, 119–138 (2021)
5. Deza, M.M., Deza, E.: Other distances. In: Encyclopedia of Distances, pp. 683–722. Springer, Heidelberg (2016). https://doi.org/10.1007/978-3-662-52844-0_29
6. Gottwald, S.: On T-norms which are related to distances of fuzzy sets. BUSEFAL **50**, 25–30 (1992)
7. Grabisch, M., Marichal, J.L., Mesiar, R., Pap, E.: Aggregation Functions. Cambridge University Press, New York (2009)
8. Höhle, U.: Fuzzy equalities and indistinguishability. In: Proceedings of EUFIT 1993, vol. 1, Aachen, pp. 358–363 (1993)
9. Hausdorff, F.: Grundzüge der Mengenlehre. Veit and Company, Leipzig (1914)
10. Kiss, G., Marichal, J.-L., Teheux, B.: A generalization of the concept of distance based on the simplex inequality. Beiträge zur Algebra und Geometrie/Contrib. Algebra Geom. **59**(2), 247–266 (2018). https://doi.org/10.1007/s13366-018-0379-5
11. Klement, E.P., Mesiar, R., Pap, E.: Triangular Norms. Kluwer Academic Publishers, Alphen aan den Rijn (2000)
12. Martín, J., Mayor, G.: Multi-argument distances. Fuzzy Set Syst. **167**, 92–100 (2010). https://doi.org/10.1016/j.fss.2010.10.018
13. Molinari, F.: About a new family of multidistances. Fuzzy Set Syst. **195**, 118–122 (2012). https://doi.org/10.1016/j.fss.2011.10.014
14. Pradera, A., Trillas, E., Castiñeira, E.: On the aggregation of some classes of fuzzy relations. In: Bouchon-Meunier, B., Gutierrez, J., Mag-dalena, L., Yager, R. (eds.) Technologies for Constructing Intelligent Systems, pp. 125–147. Springer, Heidelberg (2002). https://doi.org/10.1007/978-3-7908-1796-6_10
15. Recasens, J.: Indistinguishability Operators: Modelling Fuzzy Equalities and Fuzzy Equivalence Relations. Springer, Heidelberg (2010). https://doi.org/10.1007/978-3-642-16222-0
16. Trillas, E.: Assaig sobre les relacions d'indistingibilitat. In: Proceedings Primer Congrés Català de Lògica Matemàtica, Barcelona, pp. 51–59 (1982)
17. Schweizer, B., Sklar, A.: Probabilistic Metris Spaces. North-Holland (1983)

Formal Concept Analysis
and Uncertainty

Fuzzy Rough Set Decision Algorithms

Fernando Chacón-Gómez[✉], Maria Eugenia Cornejo, Jesús Medina,
and Eloísa Ramírez-Poussa

Department of Mathematics, University of Cádiz, Cádiz, Spain
{fernando.chacon,mariaeugenia.cornejo,jesus.medina,eloisa.ramirez}@uca.es

Abstract. Decision rules are a powerful tool for the management of information from a relational database, allowing the extraction of conclusions. A decision algorithm collects a characteristic set of decision rules and its efficiency is one of its most interesting properties, since it allows us to know the usefulness of the decision algorithm and to compare it with other algorithms. This paper focuses on the generalization of the notions of decision algorithm and efficiency to the fuzzy case.

Keywords: Rough Set Theory · Fuzzy Rough Set Theory · Decision Rules · Decision Algorithm

1 Introduction

Rough set theory (RST) was introduced by Pawlak [17,18] in the 1980s as a formal tool to deal with imprecise or incomplete information contained in databases. In this theory, a relational dataset is interpreted as a decision table, that is, a set of objects, a set of attributes and a collection of mappings characterizing the objects by the attributes. RST studies the relationship among the objects by using the attributes in order to summarize and extract information from the considered dataset.

In RST, the characterization of decision tables by a set of decision rules [8,19–21,24] is a powerful tool for the management of information from relational databases since they allow the extraction of significant conclusions. In addition, decision rules are accompanied by some measurements which provide us with valuable information of them. A characterization of decision tables from a decision algorithm is given in [20], which shows the interest of this notion. Another fundamental notion is the efficiency of a decision algorithm because it allows to measure the usefulness of the decision algorithm and compare with other algorithms as well.

Partially supported by the 2014-2020 ERDF Operational Programme in collaboration with the State Research Agency (AEI) in project PID2019-108991GB-I00, and with the Department of Economy, Knowledge, Business and University of the Regional Government of Andalusia in project FEDER-UCA18-108612, and by the European Cooperation in Science & Technology (COST) Action CA17124.

© Springer Nature Switzerland AG 2022
D. Ciucci et al. (Eds.): IPMU 2022, CCIS 1601, pp. 63–76, 2022.
https://doi.org/10.1007/978-3-031-08971-8_6

The fuzzy paradigm has already been developed and applied to RST in different papers [3,4,6,7,10–15,22], due to its great flexibility to deal with databases containing uncertainty information. A complete overview about different recent fuzzy generalisations of RST can be seen in [9]. In order to increase the potential of Fuzzy Rough Set Theory (FRST), this paper focuses on generalizing the classical notions related to decision rules to the fuzzy framework, paying special attention to the notions of decision algorithm and efficiency. Furthermore, different examples have been introduced through the paper to illustrate all the new definitions.

2   Basic Notions in RST

This section includes some preliminary definitions of RST [19,20]. First of all, it is convenient to recall that databases are represented as decision tables in this framework.

Definition 1. *Let U and $\mathcal{A}$ be non-empty sets of objects and attributes, respectively. A decision table is a tuple $(U, \mathcal{A}_d, V_{\mathcal{A}_d}, \overline{\mathcal{A}_d})$ such that $\mathcal{A}_d = \mathcal{A} \cup \{d\}$ with $d \notin \mathcal{A}$, $V_{\mathcal{A}_d} = \{V_a \mid a \in \mathcal{A}_d\}$, where V_a is the set of values associated with attribute $a \in \mathcal{A}_d$ over U, and $\overline{\mathcal{A}_d} = \{\bar{a} \colon U \to V_a \mid a \in \mathcal{A}_d\}$. In this case, the attributes of $\mathcal{A}$ are called* condition attributes *and d is called* decision attribute.

Notice that only one decision attribute is being considered in this definition. However, a similar study could be carried out when more than one decision attribute is worked.

Next, an equivalence relation is defined on the set of objects of a decision table. This equivalence relation will be useful to compare objects according to a given subset of attributes.

Definition 2. *Let $(U, \mathcal{A}_d, V_{\mathcal{A}_d}, \overline{\mathcal{A}_d})$ be a decision table. The* indiscernibility *mapping $I \colon \mathcal{P}(\mathcal{A}_d) \to \mathcal{P}(U \times U)$ is defined, for each $B \subseteq \mathcal{A}_d$, as the equivalence relation*

$$I(B) = \{(x, y) \in U \times U \mid \bar{a}(x) = \bar{a}(y), \text{ for all } a \in B\}$$

which is called B-indiscernibility relation. Each class of $I(B)$ can be written as $[x]_{I(B)} = \{y \in U \mid (x, y) \in I(B)\}$. The partition determined by $I(B)$ on the set of objects U is denoted as $U/I(B) = \{[x]_{I(B)} \mid x \in U\}$.

The positive region is another interesting notion of RST which is introduced below.

Definition 3. *Let $(U, \mathcal{A}_d, V_{\mathcal{A}_d}, \overline{\mathcal{A}_d})$ be a decision table and $B \subseteq \mathcal{A}$. The* positive region *of the partition $U/I(\{d\})$ with respect to B is defined as*

$$POS_B(\{d\}) = \bigcup_{X \in U/I(\{d\})} B_*(X)$$

where $B_*(X) = \{x \in U \mid [x]_{I(B)} \subseteq X\}$.

In the following, we recall some basic definitions of FRST which are required to study decision rules in the fuzzy environment [4]. The first one is essential to compare a pair of objects of a decision table according to an attribute.

Definition 4. *Let $(U, \mathcal{A}_d, \mathcal{V}_{\mathcal{A}_d}, \overline{\mathcal{A}_d})$ be a decision table and $a \in \mathcal{A}_d$. An a-indiscernibility relation is a $[0,1]$-fuzzy tolerance relation $R_a : U \times U \to [0,1]$, that is, a reflexive and symmetrical fuzzy relation.*

Next notion is useful to compare pairs of objects by using the total set of attributes $\mathcal{A}$ instead of a singleton. Aggregation operators [4] play a key role in the following definition.

Definition 5. *Let $(U, \mathcal{A}_d, \mathcal{V}_{\mathcal{A}_d}, \overline{\mathcal{A}_d})$ be a decision table and $R_a : U \times U \to [0,1]$ be an a-indiscernibility relation, for all $a \in \mathcal{A}$. The $\mathcal{A}$-indiscernibility relation $R_{\mathcal{A}} : U \times U \to [0,1]$ is defined for each pair of objects $x, y \in X$ as*

$$R_{\mathcal{A}}(x,y) = @(R_{a_1}(x,y), \dots, R_{a_m}(x,y))$$

where $@ : [0,1]^m \to [0,1]$ is an aggregation operator, that is, an increasing operator on each argument satisfying that $@(1, \dots, 1) = 1$ and $@(0, \dots, 0) = 0$.

Finally, we recall the generalization of positive region (Definition 3) to the fuzzy setting, from the notion of fuzzy implication [2].

Definition 6. *Let $(U, \mathcal{A}_d, \mathcal{V}_{\mathcal{A}_d}, \overline{\mathcal{A}_d})$ be a decision table, $B \subseteq \mathcal{A}$ and $I : [0,1] \times [0,1] \to [0,1]$ be a fuzzy implication, that is, it is increasing in the left argument (consequent), decreasing in the right argument (antecedent) and it satisfies $I(0,0) = I(1,1) = 1$ and $I(0,1) = 0$. The fuzzy $\mathcal{A}$-positive region is defined, for each $y \in U$, as:*

$$POS_{\mathcal{A}}(y) = \inf\{I(R_d(y,x), R_{\mathcal{A}}(x,y)) \mid x \in U\}$$

2.1 Decision Rules

As it was commented in [20], decision tables describe decisions in terms of conditions that must be satisfied in order to carry out the decision specified in the decision table. In addition, a set of decision rules can be associated with every decision table, which can be also seen as a logical description of approximation of decisions. This fact facilitates the interpretation of decision tables, so that the study of decision rules is justified. Before presenting the notion of decision rule, we need to define a formal language to describe approximations in logical terms.

Definition 7. *Let $S = (U, \mathcal{A}_d, \mathcal{V}_{\mathcal{A}_d}, \overline{\mathcal{A}_d})$ be a decision table and $B \subseteq \mathcal{A}$. The set of formulas associated with B, denoted as $For(B)$, is built from attribute-value pairs (a, v), where $a \in B$ and $v \in V_a$, by means of the conjunction and disjunction logical connectives, $\wedge$ and $\vee$ respectively.*

For each $\Phi \in For(B)$, the set of objects $x \in U$ that satisfies Φ in S is defined, for all $a \in B$ and $v \in V_a$, as:

$$\|\Phi\|_S = \|(a,v)\|_S = \{x \in U \mid \bar{a}(x) = v\}$$

Given $\Phi, \Psi \in For(B)$, *the set of objects that satisfies* $\Phi \wedge \Psi$ *in* S *is defined as* $\|\Phi \wedge \Psi\|_S = \|\Phi\|_S \cap \|\Psi\|_S$ *and the set of objects that satisfies* $\Phi \vee \Psi$ *in* S *is defined as* $\|\Phi \vee \Psi\|_S = \|\Phi\|_S \cup \|\Psi\|_S$.

Once we have presented the formal language associated with a subset of attributes, we can introduce the notion of decision rule.

Definition 8. *Let* $S = (U, \mathcal{A}_d, \mathcal{V}_{\mathcal{A}_d}, \overline{\mathcal{A}_d})$ *be a decision table and* $B \subseteq A$. *A decision rule in* S *is an expression* $\Phi \to \Psi$ *where* $\Phi \in For(B), \Psi \in For(\{d\})$ *where* $B, \{d\}$ *are condition and decision attributes, respectively. In addition, we say that an object* $x \in U$ *satisfies a decision rule* $\Phi \to \Psi$ *if* $x \in \|\Phi \wedge \Psi\|_S$.

Next, we introduce the definitions of *support*, *strength* and *certainty* of a decision rule. Specifically, the *support* takes into account the number of objects satisfying the decision rule, the *strength* represents the proportion of objects satisfying the decision rule and the *certainty* provides us with the probability of the consequent be fulfilled the antecedent. Hence, these measures offer interesting information about decision rules and they have already been applied to mining patterns in [5,23].

Definition 9. *Let* $S = (U, \mathcal{A}_d, \mathcal{V}_{\mathcal{A}_d}, \overline{\mathcal{A}_d})$ *be a decision table and* $\Phi \to \Psi$ *be a decision rule in* S, *with* $\Phi \in For(B)$ *and* $\Psi \in For(\{d\})$. *We call*

- support *of the decision rule* $\Phi \to \Psi$ *to the number:*

$$supp_S(\Phi, \Psi) = |\|\Phi \wedge \Psi\|_S|$$

- strength *of the decision rule* $\Phi \to \Psi$ *to the number:*

$$\sigma_S(\Phi, \Psi) = \frac{supp_S(\Phi, \Psi)}{|U|}$$

- certainty *of the decision rule* $\Phi \to \Psi$ *to the number:*

$$cer_S(\Phi, \Psi) = \frac{|\|\Phi \wedge \Psi\|_S|}{|\|\Phi\|_S|}$$

From the notion of certainty, we will say that $\Phi \to \Psi$ is a *true decision rule* if $cer_S(\Phi, \Psi) = 1$. Otherwise, except if $cer_S(\Phi, \Psi) = 0$, it will be called a *not entirely true decision rule.*

Notice that, the strength of a decision rule is called support of an association rule in formal concept analysis [1,16]. In addition, the value of the certainty of a decision rule corresponds to the confidence factor of an association rule, although the meaning is slightly different.

These measures play a fundamental role in the study of decision algorithms and their efficiency, as it is shown in the next section.

2.2   Decision Algorithm

With every decision table, we can associate a decision algorithm which is a set of decision rules verifying certain conditions. Consequently, decision algorithms can be seen as a logical description of basic properties of the data, what favors the optimal treatment of information contained in decision tables. The formal definition of decision algorithm is given below [20].

Definition 10. *Let* $S = (U, \mathcal{A}_d, \mathcal{V}_{\mathcal{A}_d}, \overline{\mathcal{A}_d})$ *be a decision table and* $Dec(S) = \{\Phi_i \to \Psi_i\}_{i \in I}$ *be a set of decision rules of* S, *where the index set is* $I = \{1, \ldots, m\}$ *and* $m \geq 2$. *We say that:*

1. $Dec(S)$ *is a set of* pairwise mutually exclusive (independent) *decision rules, if each pair of decision rules* $\Phi \to \Psi, \Phi' \to \Psi' \in Dec(S)$ *satisfies that* $\Phi = \Phi'$ *or* $\|\Phi \wedge \Phi'\|_S = \varnothing$, *and* $\Psi = \Psi'$ *or* $\|\Psi \wedge \Psi'\|_S = \varnothing$.
2. $Dec(S)$ *covers* U, *if* $\| \bigvee_{i=1}^{m} \Phi_i \|_S = \| \bigvee_{i=1}^{m} \Psi_i \|_S = U$.
3. *The decision rule* $\Phi \to \Psi \in Dec(S)$ *is admissible in* S *if* $supp_S(\Phi, \Psi) \neq 0$.
4. $Dec(S)$ *preserves the consistency of* S *if*

$$POS_{\mathcal{A}}(\{d\}) = \bigvee_{\Phi \to \Psi \in Dec^+(S)} \|\Phi\|_S$$

where $Dec^+(S)$ *is the set of true decision rules of* $Dec(S)$.

The set of decision rules $Dec(S)$ *satisfying the previous properties is called* decision algorithm in S.

Notice that, from the first three items in Definition 10, we can deduce that the sum of the support of all decision rules is the cardinal of the set of objects, since each object is only represented in one decision rule. Consequently, the sum of the strength of all decision rules is 1.

Now, we present the notion of *efficiency* of a decision algorithm which is fundamental to compare decision algorithms and it will be one of the cornerstone of this paper.

Definition 11. *Let* $S = (U, \mathcal{A}_d, \mathcal{V}_{\mathcal{A}_d}, \overline{\mathcal{A}_d})$ *be a decision table,* $B \subseteq \mathcal{A}$ *and* $Dec(S)$ *a decision algorithm. We call* efficiency *of the decision algorithm* $Dec(S)$ *to the number*

$$\eta(Dec(S)) = \sum_{\Phi \in For(B)} \eta_\Phi(Dec(S))$$

where

$$\eta_\Phi(Dec(S)) = \max\{\sigma_S(\Phi, \Psi) \mid \Phi \to \Psi \in Dec(S)\}$$

According to Definition 11, we obtain that the efficiency of a decision algorithm only takes into account the decision rule with largest value of strength for each antecedent, this rule is called *representative decision rule of the antecedent*. Thus, the efficiency of a decision algorithm provides an accuracy degree of the classification of the objects of the maximal subsets of representative decision rules of the decision table.

Notice that, a similar definition could be done using the certainty. However, the obtained value will not be bounded by 1. Hence, since the strength and certainty are related, the efficiency considers in some way the certainty but with the goal of obtaining a value between 0 and 1.

3   Decision Rules in Fuzzy Rough Set Theory

This section is devoted to the study of decision tables in the fuzzy environment, by using decision rules. To do this, we need to extend the notions presented in Sect. 2.1 to the fuzzy framework.

First of all, it is important to mention that the notion of set of formulas in FRST is the same as in Definition 7, that is attribute-value pairs (a, v), due to the value v can be any element of an arbitrary set associated with the attribute a. This generalization provides enough flexibility to be considered in the fuzzy setting. However, the meaning of $\|\Phi\|_S$ is different.

Definition 12. *Let $S = (U, \mathcal{A}_d, \mathcal{V}_{\mathcal{A}_d}, \overline{\mathcal{A}_d})$ be a decision table and $B \subseteq \mathcal{A}$. Given $\Phi \in For(B)$, the mapping $\|\Phi\|_S \colon U \longrightarrow [0, 1]$ is defined, for each object of the universe, as:*

$$\|\Phi\|_S(x) = E_a(\bar{a}(x), v)$$

where $E_a \colon V_a \times V_a \to [0, 1]$ is a $[0, 1]$-fuzzy tolerance relation. Therefore, $\|\Phi\|_S(x)$ represents how much the object x satisfies the formula Φ, through the relationship between the value of the attribute a in the object x and the value of the attribute a in the formula Φ.

Given $\Phi, \Psi \in For(B)$, $\|\Phi \wedge \Psi\|_S(x)$ and $\|\Phi \vee \Psi\|_S(x)$ represent how much the object x satisfies the formula $\Phi \wedge \Psi$ and how much the object x satisfies the formula $\Phi \vee \Psi$, respectively, both are defined as follows:

$$\|\Phi \wedge \Psi\|_S(x) = \inf\{\|\Phi\|_S(x), \|\Psi\|_S(x)\}$$
$$\|\Phi \vee \Psi\|_S(x) = \sup\{\|\Phi\|_S(x), \|\Psi\|_S(x)\}$$

Notice that, the infimum and the supremum generalize the intersection and the union of sets, respectively, in the fuzzy environment, so that $\|\Phi \wedge \Psi\|_S(x)$ and $\|\Phi \vee \Psi\|_S(x)$ generalize the conjunction and disjunction of formulas in the classical environment given in Definition 7.

On the other hand, the definition of decision rule in FRST also coincides with the one given in Definition 8 the formulas are composed by conjunction or disjuncion of attribute-value pairs (a, v) in both frameworks.

In the following, we will include an example in order to illustrate the formal language and the notions related to decision rules in FRST.

Example 1. Consider the decision table $(U, \mathcal{A}_d, \mathcal{V}_{\mathcal{A}_d}, \overline{\mathcal{A}_d})$ where the set of objects is $U = \{x_1, x_2, x_3, x_4, x_5, x_6, x_7\}$ and the set of attributes is $\mathcal{A} = \{a_1, a_2, a_3\}$. This decision table is represented in Table 1. From these data, we will compute the decision rules obtained by using the conjunction and considering the whole set of attributes. After that, we will calculate how much each object $x_j \in U$, with $j \in \{1, 2 \ldots, 7\}$, satisfies each antecedent of the decision rules. We also make the corresponding computations in order to know the degree of satisfaction of each object $x_j \in U$ in all consequents of the decision rules.

Table 1. Decision table $(U, \mathcal{A}_d, \mathcal{V}_{\mathcal{A}_d}, \overline{\mathcal{A}_d})$ given in Example 1.

	a_1	a_2	a_3	d
x_1	0.34	0.31	0.75	0
x_2	0.21	0.71	0.5	1
x_3	0.52	0.92	1	0
x_4	0.85	0.65	1	1
x_5	0.43	0.89	0.5	0
x_6	0.21	0.47	0.25	1
x_7	0.09	0.93	0.25	0

First of all, we calculate decision rules considering the whole set of attributes by using the conjunction, and so we obtain one rule for each object.

$$r_1 : (a_1, 0.34) \wedge (a_2, 0.31) \wedge (a_3, 0.75) \rightarrow (d, 0)$$
$$r_2 : (a_1, 0.21) \wedge (a_2, 0.71) \wedge (a_3, 0.5) \rightarrow (d, 1)$$
$$r_3 : (a_1, 0.52) \wedge (a_2, 0.92) \wedge (a_3, 1) \rightarrow (d, 0)$$
$$r_4 : (a_1, 0.85) \wedge (a_2, 0.65) \wedge (a_3, 1) \rightarrow (d, 1)$$
$$r_5 : (a_1, 0.43) \wedge (a_2, 0.89) \wedge (a_3, 0.5) \rightarrow (d, 0)$$
$$r_6 : (a_1, 0.21) \wedge (a_2, 0.47) \wedge (a_3, 0.25) \rightarrow (d, 1)$$
$$r_7 : (a_1, 0.09) \wedge (a_2, 0.93) \wedge (a_3, 0.25) \rightarrow (d, 0)$$

On the one hand, to know the degree of satisfaction of each object in all antecedents of decision rules we compute $\|\Phi_i\|_S(x_j)$, where Φ_i is the antecedent of the decision rule r_i and $x_j \in U$, with $i, j \in \{1, 2 \ldots, 7\}$. With this purpose, we have considered the $[0, 1]$-fuzzy tolerance relation $E_a : V_a \times V_a \rightarrow [0, 1]$ defined as $E_a(\bar{a}(x), v) = 1 - |\bar{a}(x) - v|$, for all $a \in \mathcal{A}_d$, $x \in U$ and $v \in [0, 1]$. Since we have extracted the decision rules from each object, we obtain that $\|\Phi_i\|_S(x_j) = \|\Psi_i\|_S(x_j) = 1$, when $i = j$. Table 2 shows the rest of calculations.

On the other hand, we compute $\|\Psi_i\|_S(x_j)$ in order to know the degree of satisfaction of each object in all consequents of decision rules, where Ψ_i is the consequent of the decision rule r_i and $x_j \in U$, with $i, j \in \{1, 2 \ldots, 7\}$. In an easier way, we obtain that:

$$\|\Psi_i\|_S(x_j) = \begin{cases} 1 & \text{if } \bar{d}(x_j) = v \\ 0 & \text{otherwise} \end{cases} \tag{1}$$

$\square$

Table 2. Degree of satisfaction of each object in all antecedents of decision rules.

	$\|\Phi_1\|_S$	$\|\Phi_2\|_S$	$\|\Phi_3\|_S$	$\|\Phi_4\|_S$	$\|\Phi_5\|_S$	$\|\Phi_6\|_S$	$\|\Phi_7\|_S$
x_1	1	0.6	0.39	0.49	0.42	0.5	0.38
x_2	0.6	1	0.5	0.36	0.78	0.75	0.75
x_3	0.39	0.5	1	0.67	0.5	0.25	0.25
x_4	0.49	0.36	0.67	1	0.5	0.25	0.24
x_5	0.42	0.78	0.5	0.5	1	0.58	0.66
x_6	0.5	0.75	0.25	0.25	0.58	1	0.54
x_7	0.38	0.75	0.25	0.24	0.66	0.54	1

In the following, we need to consider a family of $[0,1]$-fuzzy tolerance relations known as *separable relations* [25] in order to introduce the notions of *support*, *strength* and *certainty* of a decision rule in the fuzzy framework. The interpretation of these notions is analogous to the one given in the classical case.

Definition 13. *Let $S = (U, \mathcal{A}_d, \mathcal{V}_{\mathcal{A}_d}, \overline{\mathcal{A}_d})$ be a decision table, $\Phi \to \Psi$ be a decision rule in S and $E = \{E_a : V_a \times V_a \to [0,1] \mid a \in \mathcal{A}_d\}$ be a family of $[0,1]$-fuzzy tolerance relations such that $E_a(\bar{a}(x), v) = 1$ if and only if $\bar{a}(x) = v$. We call:*

- *E-support of the decision rule $\Phi \to \Psi$ to the number:*

$$supp_S^E(\Phi, \Psi) = |\|\Phi \wedge \Psi\|_S| = \sum_{x \in U} \|\Phi \wedge \Psi\|_S(x) = \sum_{x \in U} \|\Phi\|_S(x) \wedge \|\Psi\|_S(x)$$

- *E-strength of the decision rule $\Phi \to \Psi$ to the number:*

$$\sigma_S^E(\Phi, \Psi) = \frac{supp_S^E(\Phi, \Psi)}{|U|}$$

- *E-certainty of the decision rule $\Phi \to \Psi$ to the number:*

$$cer_S^E(\Phi, \Psi) = \frac{|\|\Phi \wedge \Psi\|_S|}{|\|\Phi\|_S|}$$

Analogously to the classical environment, we say that $\Phi \to \Psi$ is a *true decision rule* if $cer_S^E(\Phi, \Psi) = 1$. Otherwise, except if $cer_S^E(\Phi, \Psi) = 0$, it is a *not entirely true decision rule*.

Next, Table 3 shows E-support, E-strength and E-certainty for each decision rule computed in Example 1. The results are obtained by using Table 2, Eq. (1) and Definition 13.

4   Decision Algorithms in Fuzzy Rough Set Theory

This section focuses on the generalization of the notion of decision algorithm to the fuzzy case. To reach this goal, we need firstly to define a fuzzy tolerance relation which allows us to compare formulas, as the mapping given below.

Table 3. E-Support, E-strength and E-certainty of decision rules of Example 1.

Rule	$supp_S^E$	σ_S^E	cer_S^E
r_1	2.19	0.31	0.58
r_2	2.11	0.3	0.45
r_3	2.14	0.31	0.6
r_4	1.61	0.23	0.58
r_5	2.58	0.37	0.58
r_6	2	0.29	0.52
r_7	2.29	0.33	0.6

Definition 14. *Given a decision table* $(U, \mathcal{A}_d, V_{\mathcal{A}_d}, \overline{\mathcal{A}_d})$, *we define the* $[0,1]$-*fuzzy tolerance relation* R_{Fd}: $For(\mathcal{A}_d) \times For(\mathcal{A}_d) \rightarrow [0,1]$, *for all* $\Phi, \Phi' \in For(\mathcal{A}_d)$, *as follows:*

$$R_{Fd}(\Phi, \Phi') = 1 - \max\{|\,\|\Phi\|_S(x) - \|\Phi'\|_S(x)|\ |\ x \in U\}$$

Given $\alpha \in [0,1]$, *the* R_{Fd}-α-*block is defined for each* $\Phi \in For(\mathcal{A}_d)$ *as:*

$$[\Phi]_\alpha = \{\Phi' \in For(\mathcal{A}_d) \mid \alpha \leq R_{Fd}(\Phi, \Phi')\}$$

Notice that, R_{Fd} is not a transitive fuzzy tolerance relation and therefore, we have defined tolerance blocks instead of equivalence classes. In addition, according to the previous definition, we can deduce that α determines if two elements are related enough to belong to the same block.

Now, we can introduce the notion of decision algorithm to the fuzzy case.

Definition 15. *Let* $S = (U, \mathcal{A}_d, V_{\mathcal{A}_d}, \overline{\mathcal{A}_d})$ *be a decision table,* $\alpha_1, \alpha_2, \alpha_4 \in [0,1]$, $\alpha_3 \geq 0$ *and* $Dec(S) = \{\Phi_i \rightarrow \Psi_i\}_{i \in I}$ *be a set of decision rules of* S, *where the index set is* $I = \{1, \ldots, m\}$ *and* $m \geq 2$. *We say that:*

1. *$Dec(S)$ is a set of $\alpha_1\alpha_2$-pairwise mutually exclusive (independent) decision rules, if each pair of decision rules $\Phi \rightarrow \Psi, \Phi' \rightarrow \Psi' \in Dec(S)$ satisfies that $\Phi = \Phi'$ or $\|\Phi \wedge \Phi'\|_S(x) \leq \alpha_1$ and $\Psi = \Psi'$ or $\|\Psi \wedge \Psi'\|_S(x) \leq \alpha_2$, for all $x \in U$.*
2. *$Dec(S)$ covers U, if $|\|\bigvee_{i=1}^{m} \Phi_i\|_S| = |\|\bigvee_{i=1}^{m} \Psi_i\|_S| = |U|$.*
3. *The decision rule $\Phi \rightarrow \Psi \in Dec(S)$ is α_3-admissible in S if $\alpha_3 < supp_S(\Phi, \Psi)$.*
4. *$Dec(S)$ preserves the α-consistency of S with a degree α_4 if the next inequality holds for all $x \in U$:*

$$\left| POS_{\mathcal{A}}(x) - \bigvee_{\Phi \rightarrow \Psi \in Dec_\alpha^+(S)} \|\Phi\|_S(x) \right| \leq \alpha_4$$

where $\alpha \in [0,1]$ *and*

$$Dec_\alpha^+(S) = \{\Phi \rightarrow \Psi \in Dec(S) \mid \text{ if there exists } \Phi' \rightarrow \Psi' \in Dec(S)$$
$$\text{ such that } \Phi' \in [\Phi]_\alpha \text{ then } \Psi' \in [\Psi]_\alpha\}$$

The set of decision rules $Dec(S)$ satisfying the previous properties for the values $\alpha_1, \alpha_2, \alpha_3, \alpha_4$ is called $(\alpha_1, \alpha_2, \alpha_3, \alpha_4)$-decision algorithm in S.

Observe that, none of the decision rules contained in the set $Dec_\alpha^+(S)$ lead to contradictions, that is, this set does not include decision rules for which there exists another decision rule whose antecedents are both included in the R_{Fd}-α-blocks of their antecedents but their consequents do not belong to both R_{Fd}-α-blocks of their consequents. Therefore, the set $Dec_\alpha^+(S)$ is generalizing to the set $Dec^+(S)$ included in Definition 10. As a consequence, when $\alpha_k = 0$, for each $k \in \{1, 2, 3, 4\}$, we obtain Definition 10 itself.

Finally, we introduce the generalization of the concept of efficiency.

Definition 16. *Let $S = (U, \mathcal{A}_d, V_{\mathcal{A}_d}, \overline{\mathcal{A}_d})$ be a decision table and $Dec(S)$ be an $(\alpha_1, \alpha_2, \alpha_3, \alpha_4)$-decision algorithm. Given $0 \le \alpha \le 1$, we call α-efficiency of the $(\alpha_1, \alpha_2, \alpha_3, \alpha_4)$-decision algorithm $Dec(S)$ to the number*

$$\eta^\alpha(Dec(S)) = \sum_{\Phi \in For(\mathcal{A})} \eta_\Phi^\alpha(Dec(S))$$

where

$$\eta_\Phi^\alpha(Dec(S)) = \max\{\sigma_S(\Phi', \Psi') \mid \Phi' \to \Psi' \in Dec(S), \Phi' \in [\Phi]_\alpha\}$$

being Φ, Φ' two antecedents and Ψ' a consequent of the decision rules of $Dec(S)$.

Notice that, although $0 \le R_{Fd}(\Phi, \Phi') \le 1$, for all Φ, Φ' antecedents of decision rules of $Dec(S)$, the α-efficiency is not bounded by 1. It can be checked taking into account that the sum of the E-strength of all decision rules of a decision algorithm is not bounded by 1, as we will show in the following example. Thence, it is difficult to extract conclusions due to the loss of its probabilistic character. Moreover, the α-efficiency is a decreasing map due to the value of α gives a degree of flexibility. Finally, it is convenient to emphasize that, when the relations E_a are booleans and $\alpha > 0$, the α-efficiency coincides with Definition 11, because in this case $R_{Fd}(\Phi, \Phi') = 1$ if $\Phi = \Phi'$ and $R_{Fd}(\Phi, \Phi') = 0$ otherwise.

Finally, these notions are illustrated in the following example.

Example 2. Coming back to the environment of Example 1, we will compute the minimum/maximum values of α_k with $k \in \{1, 2, 3, 4\}$ in order to ensure that $Dec(S) = \{r_1, r_2, r_3, r_4, r_5, r_6, r_7\}$ forms a $(\alpha_1, \alpha_2, \alpha_3, \alpha_4)$-decision algorithm. First of all, we calculate the value of α_1 by using Table 2 and Definition 15. Specifically, taking into account the first item of Definition 15, we compute the value

$$\max\{\|\Phi \wedge \Phi'\|_S(x) \mid \Phi, \Phi' \in For(\mathcal{A}), \Phi \ne \Phi', x \in U\} = 0.78$$

Therefore, any value $\alpha_1 \ge 0.78$ satisfies that $\|\Phi \wedge \Phi'\|_S(x) \le \alpha_1$ for all $\Phi, \Phi' \in For(\mathcal{A})$, with $\Phi \ne \Phi'$, and $x \in U$. Clearly, $\alpha_2 \ge 0$ and we do not have to consider more requirements because d is a boolean attribute. Now, for the computation of α_3, we consider the third item of Definition 15 obtaining:

$$\min\{supp_S^E(\Phi, \Psi) \mid \Phi \to \Psi \in Dec(S)\} = 1.61$$

Hence, for any value $\alpha_3 < 1.61$, the decision rules in $Dec(S)$ are α_3-*admissible in* S.

Finally, for the computation of α_4, we need to define the mappings involved in the fuzzy $\mathcal{A}$-positive region $POS_{\mathcal{A}}$, as well as the set $Dec_\alpha^+(S)$, given $\alpha \in [0, 1]$.

On the one hand, in order to determine the fuzzy $\mathcal{A}$-positive region $POS_{\mathcal{A}}$, we need to choose an a-indiscernibility relation, an $\mathcal{A}$-indiscernibility relation and a fuzzy implication. We will consider the a-indiscernibility relation $R_a \colon U \times U \to [0, 1]$ defined, for all $a \in \mathcal{A}_d$, as:

$$R_a(x, y) = 1 - |\bar{a}(x) - \bar{a}(y)|$$

It is easy to see that $R_a(x, y) = 1$ if and only if $\bar{a}(x) = \bar{a}(y)$. In addition, we will consider the $\mathcal{A}$-indiscernibility relation $R_{\mathcal{A}} \colon U \times U \to [0, 1]$ defined as:

$$
\begin{aligned}
R_{\mathcal{A}}(x, y) &= @(R_{a_1}(x, y), R_{a_2}(x, y), R_{a_3}(x, y)) \\
&= \frac{R_{a_1}(x, y) + 2(R_{a_2}(x, y) + R_{a_3}(x, y))}{5}
\end{aligned}
$$

for all $x, y \in [0, 1]$. In this case, $R_{\mathcal{A}}(x, y) = 1$ if and only if $x = y$. It is important to mention that $R_{\mathcal{A}}$ is an aggregation operator and the attribute a_1 is the least important in the decision table since it has the least weight according to the definition of $R_{\mathcal{A}}$.

To sum up, R_a, $R_{\mathcal{A}}$ and the Łukasiewicz implication, defined as $z \leftarrow_L y = \min\{1, 1 + z - y\}$ for all $y, z \in [0, 1]$, will be the mappings used for computing the fuzzy $\mathcal{A}$-positive region $POS_{\mathcal{A}}$.

On the other hand, we need to define the set $Dec_\alpha^+(S)$ to calculate α_4. To do this, we will fix $\alpha = 0.75$ and, applying Definition 14, we calculate the relation between each pair of antecedents of all rules in $Dec(S)$, see Table 4.

Table 4. Relation between each pair of antecedents of decision rules of Example 1.

R_{Fd}	Φ_1	Φ_2	Φ_3	Φ_4	Φ_5	Φ_6	Φ_7
Φ_1	1	0.6	0.39	0.49	0.42	0.5	0.38
Φ_2	0.6	1	0.5	0.36	0.78	0.75	0.75
Φ_3	0.39	0.5	1	0.07	0.5	0.25	0.25
Φ_4	0.49	0.36	0.67	1	0.5	0.25	0.24
Φ_5	0.42	0.78	0.5	0.5	1	0.58	0.66
Φ_6	0.5	0.75	0.25	0.25	0.58	1	0.54
Φ_7	0.38	0.75	0.25	0.24	0.66	0.54	1

The R_{Fd}-0.75-block of each antecedent is calculated by using Definition 14, obtaining $[\Phi_1]_{0.75} = \{\Phi_1\}$, $[\Phi_2]_{0.75} = \{\Phi_2, \Phi_5, \Phi_6, \Phi_7\}$, $[\Phi_3]_{0.75} = \{\Phi_3\}$, $[\Phi_4]_{0.75} = \{\Phi_4\}$, $[\Phi_5]_{0.75} = \{\Phi_2, \Phi_5\}$, $[\Phi_6]_{0.75} = \{\Phi_2, \Phi_6\}$ and $[\Phi_7]_{0.75} = \{\Phi_2, \Phi_7\}$. In a similar way, the R_{Fd}-0.75-block of each consequent is given as $[\Psi_i]_{0.75} = \{1, 3, 5, 7\}$ if i is odd and $[\Psi_j]_{0.75} = \{2, 4, 6\}$ if j is even. Therefore, $Dec^{+}_{0.75}(S) = \{r_1, r_3, r_4, r_6\}$. Consider the fourth item of Definition 15, we obtain that:

$$\max\{|POS_A(x) - \bigvee_{\Phi \to \Psi \in Dec^{+}_{0.75}(S)} \|\Phi\|_S(x)| \mid x \in U\}$$

$$= \max\{|0.29 - 1|, |0.12 - 0.75|, |0.17 - 1|, |0.17 - 1|, |0.12 - 0.58|, |0.21 - 1|,$$
$$|0.21 - -0.54|\}$$

$$= 0.83$$

As a consequence, for any value $\alpha_4 \geq 0.83$, we have that $Dec(S)$ preserves the 0.75-consistency of S with a degree α_4. In conclusion, $Dec(S)$ is a $(\alpha_1, \alpha_2, \alpha_3, \alpha_4)$-decision algorithm.

Now, we will compute some α-efficiencies corresponding to this decision algorithm, by using Definition 16.

– The 1-efficiency of the decision algorithm $Dec(S)$ is determined by the R_{Fd}-1-blocks. Since $\Phi \neq \Phi'$ for all $\Phi, \Phi' \in For(\mathcal{A})$ it is obtained that $[\Phi]_1 = \{\Phi\}$ for each $\Phi \in For(\mathcal{A})$. As a consequence,

$$\eta^1(Dec(S)) = \sum_{\Phi \to \Psi \in Dec(S)} \sigma^E_S(\Phi, \Psi) = 2.14$$

Notice that the efficiency is greater than 1 because the tolerance relations are not boolean, which leads us to conclude that the sum of the E-support of all decision rules of $Dec(S)$ is greater than $|U|$.

– The 0.75-efficiency of the decision algorithm $Dec(S)$ is determined by the R_{Fd}-0.75-blocks, which have been computed previously. From Table 3, it is easy to check that the decision rules with antecedents whose R_{Fd}-0.75-blocks are not singleton and can be ranked in order of E-strength, from the greatest to the lowest, are r_5, r_7, r_2 and r_6. As a consequence, the 0.75-efficiency of this decision algorithm $Dec(S)$ is:

$$\eta^{0.75}(Dec(S)) = \sigma^E_S(\Phi_1, \Psi_1) + \sigma^E_S(\Phi_5, \Psi_5) + \sigma^E_S(\Phi_3, \Psi_3) + \sigma^E_S(\Phi_4, \Psi_4)$$
$$+ \sigma^E_S(\Phi_5, \Psi_5) + \sigma^E_S(\Phi_2, \Psi_2) + \sigma^E_S(\Phi_7, \Psi_7)$$
$$= 2.22$$

– Finally, we will compute the 0-efficiency. Since $R_{Fd}(\Phi, \Phi') \geq 0$, for each pair Φ, Φ' of antecedents of the decision rules of $Dec(S)$, we obtain that $[\Phi_i]_0 = \{\Phi_1, \Phi_2, \Phi_3, \Phi_4, \Phi_5, \Phi_6, \Phi_7\}$ for each $i \in \{1, 2, \ldots, 7\}$. As a consequence,

$$\eta^0_\Phi(Dec(S)) = \max\{\sigma_S(\Phi', \Psi') \mid \Phi' \to \Psi' \in Dec(S)\}$$
$$= \sigma_S(\Phi_5, \Psi_5)$$
$$= 0.37$$

for all $\Phi \in For(\mathcal{A})$. Therefore, the 0-efficiency of the decision algorithm $Dec(S)$ is

$$\eta^0(Dec(S)) = \max\{\sigma_S^E(\Phi, \Psi) \mid \Phi \to \Psi \in Dec(S)\}|U|$$
$$= 0.37 \cdot 7$$
$$= 2.59$$

$\square$

From these computations, and taking into account that α-efficiency is a decreasing mapping in α, we can conclude that considering different levels of flexibility in the comparison of the antecedents of the decision rules of $Dec(S)$, given by the value of α, does not result in significant changes in the value of α-efficiency. The main reason is that the E-strength of all decision rules of $Dec(S)$ are similar, as it can be seen in Table 3. In addition, we have shown that the α-efficiency of a decision algorithm is not bounded by 1, as we remarked previously.

5   Conclusions and Further Work

In this paper, we have studied decision rules and decision algorithms in the fuzzy framework. For this purpose, we have introduced the generalization of classic notions of decision rule, support, strength and certainty. In addition, we have presented the fuzzy notions of decision algorithm and efficiency. Different examples have been worked in order to illustrate these new definitions.

As a future work, we will continue studying the relationships among these notions, both in the classical and fuzzy settings. Specifically, in the fuzzy case, we are interested in obtaining theoretical properties related to the given notions of support, strength, certainty and efficiency. For example, we will study new possible definitions of α-efficiency, in order to obtain as result a value in the unit interval. Furthermore, we will explore examples whose decision attribute is not boolean and real problems with many decision rules to check the usefulness of the introduced decision algorithms.

References

1. Agrawal, R., Imieliński, T., Swami, A.: Mining association rules between sets of items in large databases. SIGMOD Rec. **22**(2), 207–216 (1993)
2. Baczyński, M., Jayaram, B.: An Introduction to Fuzzy Implications, pp. 1–35. Springer, Berlin (2008). https://doi.org/10.1007/978-3-540-69082-5_1
3. Cock, M.D., Cornelis, C., Kerre, E.E.: Fuzzy rough sets: the forgotten step. IEEE Trans. Fuzzy Syst. **15**(1), 121–130 (2007)
4. Cornelis, C., Medina, J., Verbiest, N.: Multi-adjoint fuzzy rough sets: definition, properties and attribute selection. Int. J. Approximate Reasoning **55**, 412–426 (2014)

5. de Sá, C.R., Azevedo, P., Soares, C., Jorge, A.M., Knobbe, A.: Preference rules for label ranking: mining patterns in multi-target relations. Inf. Fusion **40**, 112–125 (2018)
6. Dubois, D., Prade, H.: Rough fuzzy sets and fuzzy rough sets. Int. J. Gen Syst **17**, 06 (1990)
7. Feng, T., Fan, H.-T., Mi, J.-S.: Uncertainty and reduction of variable precision multigranulation fuzzy rough sets based on three-way decisions. Int. J. Approximate Reasoning **85**, 36–58 (2017)
8. Li, J., Mei, C., Lv, Y.: Incomplete decision contexts: approximate concept construction, rule acquisition and knowledge reduction. Int. J. Approximate Reasoning **54**(1), 149–165 (2013)
9. Mardani, A., Nilashi, M., Antucheviciene, J., Tavana, M., Bausys, R., Ibrahim, O.: Recent fuzzy generalisations of rough sets theory: a systematic review and methodological critique of the literature. Complexity **2017**, 1–33 (2017)
10. Medina, J.: Towards multi-adjoint property-oriented concept lattices. In: Yu, J., Greco, S., Lingras, P., Wang, G., Skowron, A. (eds.) RSKT 2010. LNCS (LNAI), vol. 6401, pp. 159–166. Springer, Heidelberg (2010). https://doi.org/10.1007/978-3-642-16248-0_26
11. Medina, J.: Multi-adjoint property-oriented and object-oriented concept lattices. Inf. Sci. **190**, 95–106 (2012)
12. Medina, J.: Relating attribute reduction in formal, object-oriented and property-oriented concept lattices. Comput. Math/ Appli. **64**(6), 1992–2002 (2012)
13. Morsi, N.N., Yakout, M.M.: Axiomatics for fuzzy rough sets. Fuzzy Sets Syst. **100**, 327–342 (1998)
14. Nakamura, A.: Fuzzy rough sets. Note Multiple-Valued Logic Japan **9**, 1–8 (1988)
15. Nanda, S., Majumdar, S.: Fuzzy rough sets. Fuzzy Sets Syst. **45**, 157–160 (1992)
16. Pasquier, N., Bastide, Y., Taouil, R., Lakhal, L.: Efficient mining of association rules using closed itemset lattices. Inf. Syst. **24**(1), 25–46 (1999)
17. Pawlak, Z.: Information systems theoretical foundations. Inf. Syst. **6**(3), 205–218 (1981)
18. Pawlak, Z.: Rough sets. Int. J. Comput. Inf. Sci. **11**, 341–356 (1982)
19. Pawlak, Z.: Rough Sets: Theoretical Aspects of Reasoning About Data. Kluwer Academic Publishers, Norwell (1992)
20. Pawlak, Z.: Rough sets and decision algorithms. In: Ziarko, W., Yao, Y. (eds.) RSCTC 2000. LNCS (LNAI), vol. 2005, pp. 30–45. Springer, Heidelberg (2001). https://doi.org/10.1007/3-540-45554-X_3
21. Stawicki, S., Ślęzak, D., Janusz, A., Widz, S.: Decision bireducts and decision reducts - a comparison. Int. J. Approximate Reasoning **84**, 75–109 (2017)
22. Wang, C.Y.: Topological structures of l-fuzzy rough sets and similarity sets of l-fuzzy relations. Int. J. Approximate Reasoning **83**, 160–175 (2017)
23. Yadav, D., Chowdary, C.R.: Ooimasp: origin based association rule mining with order independent mostly associated sequential patterns. Expert Syst. Appl. **93**, 62–71 (2018)
24. Yao, Y.: Three-way decisions with probabilistic rough sets. Inf. Sci. **180**(3), 341–353 (2010)
25. Zedam, L., Bouremel, H., De Baets, B.: Left- and right-compatibility of order relations and fuzzy tolerance relations. Fuzzy Sets and Systems **360**, 65–81 (2019), Theme: Fuzzy Relations

Relational Extension of Closure Structures

Manuel Ojeda-Hernández[✉] [iD], Inma P. Cabrera[iD], Pablo Cordero[iD],
and Emilio Muñoz-Velasco[iD]

Universidad de Málaga, Andalucía Tech, Málaga, Spain
{manuojeda,ipcabrera,pcordero,ejmunoz}@uma.es

Abstract. Closure is a key concept in several branches of mathematics. This work presents a definition of fuzzy closure relation and relational closure system on fuzzy transitive digraphs. The core of the paper is the study of the properties of these structures. As expected, fuzzy closure relations and relational closure systems are related, but the relationship among them is not one-to-one. Last section of the paper shows the search for some characterizations for that one-to-one relation to hold.

Keywords: Fuzzy relation · Closure operator · Closure system · Transitive digraph

1 Introduction

The notion of closure operator, introduced by E.H. Moore in 1910 [17], plays a major role in computer science and both pure and applied mathematics [8]. The extension to the fuzzy framework, the so-called fuzzy closure operators [1,3], appear in several areas of fuzzy logic and its applications, next we list only a few of them: fuzzy mathematical morphology [11,16], fuzzy relational equations [10], approximate reasoning [4,9] and fuzzy logic in narrow sense [14], and its applications such as fuzzy logic programming [15] or formal concept analysis of data with fuzzy attributes [20].

In the classical case, there is a one-to-one correspondence relating the notions of closure operator and closure system. For each ordered structure there is a definition of closure system. Thus, the notion of fuzzy closure system has been defined on $\mathbb{L}$-ordered sets [13], on fuzzy preposets [5] and fuzzy preordered structures [6].

This paper is in line with the work done in [18,19], where the relationship between fuzzy closure operators and fuzzy closure systems is studied in the

Supported by the State Agency of Research (AEI), the Spanish Ministry of Science, Innovation, and Universities (MCIU), the European Social Fund (FEDER), the Junta de Andalucía (JA), and the Universidad de Málaga (UMA) through the FPU19/01467 (MCIU) internship and the research projects with reference PGC2018-095869-B-I00, TIN2017-89023-P (MCIU/AEI/FEDER, UE) and UMA2018-FEDERJA-001 (JA/UMA/FEDER, UE).

© Springer Nature Switzerland AG 2022
D. Ciucci et al. (Eds.): IPMU 2022, CCIS 1601, pp. 77–86, 2022.
https://doi.org/10.1007/978-3-031-08971-8_7

framework of complete fuzzy lattices. Our aim is to study the extension of closure operators to relational structures on fuzzy transitive digraphs, i.e., sets with a transitive binary relation.

The starting point of this paper is the definition of fuzzy closure relation, in the framework of fuzzy transitive digraphs, the background was given, though in a crisp setting in [7]. This extension is inspired by the notion of closure operator in the crisp case, where they are isotone, inflationary and idempotent. Then, a definition of relational closure system is given as the sets such that a certain family of fuzzy sets is normal. This idea extends the notion of closure system in [12] where the sets were crisp and non-emptyness was required.

Then, these two concepts are put together and, as awaited, there is a relationship between fuzzy closure relations and relational closure systems, that is, for each fuzzy closure relation κ we can induce a relational closure system C_κ and vice versa. Despite the relationship being one-to-one in the crisp case, this does not hold in our framework. Although, the results show that the iteration of relational closure systems and fuzzy closure relations is somewhat close to the original, i.e., for any fuzzy closure relation κ, the fuzzy closure relation κ_{C_κ} is similar to κ in some way or another. The same holds true for a relational closure system C and C_{κ_C}. In the last section, the conclusions of our research are shown and some hints of future work are presented.

2 Preliminary Notions

The framework considered in this work is that of $\mathbb{L}$-fuzzy set theory, where $\mathbb{L}$ is a complete residuated lattice. The reader is assumed to be familiar with the terminology of fuzzy sets, fuzzy relations and complete residuated lattices. However, some particular concepts and results are highlighted in this section in order to follow the arguments easily.

A complete residuated lattice is an algebra $\mathbb{L} = (L, \leq, 0, 1, \otimes, \rightarrow)$, where $(L, \leq)$ is a complete lattice, 0 is the bottom element, 1 is the top element, and the following adjointness property holds for all $p, q, r \in L$:

$$p \otimes q \leq r \qquad \text{if and only if} \qquad p \leq q \rightarrow r. \tag{1}$$

Basic consequences of this property, such as $q \rightarrow 1 = 1$ and ($p \leq q$ if and only if $p \rightarrow q = 1$), will be used throughout this paper without explicit mentioning.

The basic properties of residuated lattices can be found in [2, Chapter 2].

A fuzzy set X is said to be *normal* if $Core(X) := \{a \in A : X(a) = 1\} \neq \varnothing$, i.e., $X(a) = 1$ for some $a \in A$.

An $\mathbb{L}$-*fuzzy relation* between two universes A and B is a mapping $\mu \colon A \times B \rightarrow \mathbb{L}$, where $\mu(a, b)$ denotes the degree of relationship between the elements a and b. Given a fuzzy relation μ and an element $a \in A$, the *afterset* a^μ of a is the fuzzy set $a^\mu \colon B \rightarrow \mathbb{L}$ defined by $a^\mu(b) = \mu(a, b)$. A fuzzy relation μ is said to be *total* if the aftersets a^μ are normal, for all $a \in A$.

The composition of an $\mathbb{L}$-fuzzy relation μ between two universes A and B and an $\mathbb{L}$-fuzzy relation ν between B and a universe C is the $\mathbb{L}$-fuzzy relation $\mu \circ \nu$ between A and C defined by

$$\mu \circ \nu(a, c) = \bigvee_{b \in B} (\mu(a, b) \otimes \nu(b, c)).$$

A fuzzy relation $\rho \colon A \times A \to \mathbb{L}$ is said to be:

- *transitive* if $\rho(a, b) \otimes \rho(b, c) \le \rho(a, c)$, for all $a, b, c \in A$.

It is equivalent to either of the following two conditions:

$$\rho(a, c) \le \bigwedge_{b \in A} \rho(c, b) \to \rho(a, b) \quad \text{or} \quad \rho(a, c) \le \bigwedge_{b \in A} \rho(b, a) \to \rho(b, c)$$

for all $x, z \in A$.

Definition 1. $\mathbb{A} = \langle A, \rho \rangle$ *is said to be a* fuzzy T-digraph *if ρ is a transitive fuzzy relation on A.*

Given a relation R on a crisp set A, it is possible to lift R to the powerset 2^A by defining different *powerings* among which the so-called Plotkin powering is remarkable [7]. The adaptation of this powering to the present fuzzy framework is explained next.

Definition 2. *Consider a fuzzy T-digraph (A, ρ). We define the* full fuzzy powering *as follows, for any $X, Y \colon A \to \mathbb{L}$:*

$$\rho_\propto(X, Y) = \bigwedge_{x \in A} \bigwedge_{y \in A} (X(x) \otimes Y(y) \to \rho(x, y)) .$$

In the particular case of a *singleton* in the first argument of the fuzzy powering, the expressions in the above definition is greatly simplified. Indeed, for all $a \in A$, it holds:

$$\rho_\propto(a, Y) = \bigwedge_{y \in A} (Y(y) \to \rho(a, y)).$$

In [7], the concept of clique was fundamental for the characterisation of closure relations. It is expected that the fuzzy extension of this concept appears naturally in the study of fuzzy closure relations.

Definition 3. *Let A be a fuzzy T-digraph. A fuzzy set $X \colon A \to \mathbb{L}$ is called a* clique *if $\rho_\propto(X, X) = 1$.*

The following two lemmas are technical results that will be useful throughout the paper.

Lemma 1. *Consider a fuzzy T-digraph A and fuzzy sets $X, Y, Z \colon A \to \mathbb{L}$. If Y is normal, then $\rho_\propto(X, Y) \otimes \rho_\propto(Y, Z) \le \rho_\propto(X, Z)$.*

Lemma 2. *Consider a fuzzy T-digraph A and fuzzy sets $X, Y: A \to \mathbb{L}$. If X and Y are normal cliques, then for all $x_0 \in Core(X)$ and $y_0 \in Core(Y)$, it holds that*

$$\rho_\propto(X, Y) = \rho_\propto(x_0, Y) = \rho_\propto(X, y_0) = \rho(x_0, y_0).$$

In order to extend the definition of a closure relation to the fuzzy framework, we need the notions of isotone fuzzy relations between fuzzy T-digraphs (antitone fuzzy relations are introduced due to being analogous but will not be used).

Definition 4. *Consider two fuzzy T-digraphs $\langle A, \rho_A \rangle$ and $\langle B, \rho_B \rangle$. A fuzzy relation $\mu: A \times B \to \mathbb{L}$ is said to be:*

- *isotone if $\rho_A(a_1, a_2) \leq \rho_\propto(a_1^\mu, a_2^\mu)$, for all $a_1, a_2 \in A$.*
- *antitone if $\rho_A(a_1, a_2) \leq \rho_\propto(a_2^\mu, a_1^\mu)$, for all $a_1, a_2 \in A$.*

Definition 5. *Let A be a fuzzy T-digraph. A fuzzy relation $\mu: A \times A \to \mathbb{L}$ is said to be:*

- *inflationary if $\rho_\propto(a, a^\mu) = 1$.*
- *idempotent if $\rho_\propto(a^{\mu \circ \mu}, a^\mu) = 1$ and $\rho_\propto(a^\mu, a^{\mu \circ \mu}) = 1$, for all $a \in A$.*

3   On Closure Relations

In this section, we study the extension of closure operators to the fuzzy framework as relational structures, as well as the relationship with their counterpart, the so-called relational closure systems. This work walks the fine line between generality and the preservation of properties from the classical framework.

Definition 6. *Let (A, ρ) be a fuzzy T-digraph and $\kappa \in L^{A \times A}$ a total fuzzy relation. The fuzzy relation κ is said to be a fuzzy closure relation if the following properties hold:*

(i) *κ is inflationary.*
(ii) *κ is isotone.*
(iii) *$\rho_\propto(a^{\kappa \circ \kappa}, a^\kappa) = 1$, for all $a \in A$.*

Note that by isotonicity and inflationary we get that $\rho_\propto(a^\kappa, a^{\kappa \circ \kappa}) = 1$ for all $a \in A$. Thus, we get idempotency since $\rho_\propto(a^\kappa, a^{\kappa \circ \kappa}) = 1$ and $\rho_\propto(a^{\kappa \circ \kappa}, a^\kappa) = 1$. Therefore, condition (iii) in the definition above can be replaced by:

(iii') *κ is idempotent.*

Lemma 3. *Let A be a fuzzy T-digraph and $\kappa: A \times A \to \mathbb{L}$ a fuzzy closure relation, then a^κ and $a^{\kappa \circ \kappa}$ are cliques, for all $a \in A$.*

Proof. Since κ is total both a^κ and $a^{\kappa \circ \kappa}$ are normal fuzzy sets for all $a \in A$. Then, by inflationary and isotony of κ we have $\rho_\propto(a^\kappa, a^{\kappa \circ \kappa}) = 1$ and by idempotency, $\rho_\propto(a^{\kappa \circ \kappa}, a^\kappa) = 1$. Using Lemma 1 we get,

$$1 = \rho_\propto(a^\kappa, a^{\kappa \circ \kappa}) \otimes \rho_\propto(a^{\kappa \circ \kappa}, a^\kappa) \leq \rho_\propto(a^\kappa, a^\kappa)$$
$$1 = \rho_\propto(a^{\kappa \circ \kappa}, a^\kappa) \otimes \rho_\propto(a^\kappa, a^{\kappa \circ \kappa}) \leq \rho_\propto(a^{\kappa \circ \kappa}, a^{\kappa \circ \kappa})$$

Hence, both a^κ and $a^{\kappa \circ \kappa}$ are normal cliques.

Now we introduce the counterpart of fuzzy closure relations in our framework. This concept will play the role closure systems play in the classical case. First, given a fuzzy T-digraph (A, ρ) and $X \subseteq A$, we define the fuzzy set of minima as:

$$m(X)(a) = X(a) \otimes \rho_\propto(a, X)$$

It can be shown that the fuzzy set $m(X)$ is a clique for all $X \subseteq A$.

Definition 7. *Let (A, ρ) be a fuzzy T-digraph. A subset $C \subseteq A$ is said to be a relational closure system if for all $a \in A$, the fuzzy set $m(a^\rho \cap C)$ is normal.*

Remark 1. Observe that, since C is a crisp set, it is equivalent to use the intersection or the product. We will use the notation $(a^\rho \cap C)$ for sets but $\otimes$ in written out proofs. Also, since C is crisp, the definition of $m(a^\rho \cap C)$ can be simplified to 0 if $x \notin C$ and for $x \in C$ as follows:

$$m(a^\rho \cap C)(x) = a^\rho(x) \otimes \bigwedge_{y \in C} a^\rho(y) \to \rho(x, y)$$

In order to simplify the notation, we introduce the following auxiliary notions that appear naturally while working with fuzzy closure relations and relational closure systems in fuzzy T-digraphs.

Definition 8. *Let $\mathbb{A} = (A, \rho)$ be a fuzzy T-digraph*

- *Given $C \subseteq A$, the set $C^\circ = \{x \in C \mid \rho(x, x) = 1\}$ is said to be the* reflexive kernel *of C.*
- *The so-called* symmetric kernel relation *is the fuzzy relation $\approx$ on L^A defined as:*

$$X \approx Y = \rho_\propto(X, Y) \otimes \rho_\propto(Y, X), \quad \text{for } X, Y \in L^A.$$

The following result is the main theorem of this paper. It shows that the notions of relational closure system and fuzzy closure relation are very closely related in the framework of fuzzy T-digraphs.

Theorem 1. *Let (A, ρ) be a fuzzy T-digraph, $C \subseteq A$ a set and $\kappa \in L^{A \times A}$ a fuzzy relation.*

(i) *If C is a relational closure system, then $\kappa_C \in L^{A \times A}$ defined by $a^{\kappa_C} = m(a^\rho \cap C)$ is a fuzzy closure relation.*

(ii) *If κ is a fuzzy closure relation, then $C_\kappa = \{x \in A \mid (x^\kappa \approx \{x\}) = 1\}$ is a relational closure system. Moreover, it holds that $Core(\kappa) \subseteq Core(\kappa_{C_\kappa})$.*

(iii) *If C is a relational closure system, then*

$$C_{\kappa_C} = \bigcup_{z \in C} \{x \in A \mid (\{x\} \approx \{z\}) = 1\}.$$

Furthermore, it holds that $C^\circ \subseteq C_{\kappa_C} \subseteq A^\circ$.

(iv) If κ is a fuzzy closure relation, then $Core(a^{\kappa_{C_\kappa}}) = \{x \in A \mid (\{x\} \approx a^\kappa) = 1\}$. In particular, $(a^{\kappa_{C_\kappa}} \approx a^\kappa) = 1$, for all $a \in A$.

Proof.

(i) By $a^{\kappa_C} \leq a^\rho$, is is clear that κ_C is inflationary. Now, for isotonicity, by using the definition of m and transitivity, we get for all $x, y \in C$

$$\rho(a_1, a_2) \otimes a_1{}^{\kappa_C}(x) \otimes a_2^{\kappa_C}(y) = \rho(a_1, a_2) \otimes m(a_1^\rho \cap C)(x) \otimes m(a_2^\rho \cap C)(y)$$
$$\leq \rho(a_1, a_2) \otimes \rho(a_1, x) \otimes \bigwedge_{z \in C} (\rho(a_1, z) \to \rho(x, z)) \otimes \rho(a_2, y)$$
$$\leq \rho(a_1, y) \otimes (\rho(a_1, y) \to \rho(x, y)) \leq \rho(x, y)$$

The inequality holds trivially if $x \notin C$ or $y \notin C$. Hence, for all $a_1, a_2 \in A$:

$$\rho(a_1, a_2) \leq \rho_\propto(a_1^{\kappa_C}, a_2^{\kappa_C}).$$

Therefore, κ_C is isotone.
For κ_C idempotent we have to show that $\rho_\propto(a^{\kappa_C \circ \kappa_C}, a^{\kappa_C}) = 1$.
Consider $x, y, z \in C$, since a^{κ_C} is a clique we get

$$a^{\kappa_C}(x) \otimes x^{\kappa_C}(y) \otimes a^{\kappa_C}(z) \leq \rho(x, z) \otimes x^{\kappa_C}(y)$$
$$\leq \bigwedge_{w \in C} (\rho(x, w) \to \rho(y, w)) \otimes \rho(x, z)$$
$$\leq (\rho(x, z) \to \rho(y, z)) \otimes \rho(x, z)$$
$$\leq \rho(y, z).$$

If any of the elements x, y, z is not in C, the inequality holds trivially. Therefore,

$$a^{\kappa_C \circ \kappa_C}(y) \otimes a^{\kappa_C}(z) = \bigvee_{x \in A} (a^{\kappa_C}(x) \otimes x^{\kappa_C}(y)) \otimes a^{\kappa_C}(z) \leq \rho(y, z)$$

which is $\rho_\propto(a^{\kappa_C \circ \kappa_C}, a^{\kappa_C}) = 1$.

(ii) We will prove that $m(a^\rho \cap C_\kappa)$ is normal by showing that $Core(a^\kappa) \subseteq Core(m(a^\rho \cap C_\kappa))$.
Let $x_0 \in Core(a^\kappa)$. Notice that $\rho_\propto(a^\kappa, a^{\kappa \circ \kappa})$ and $\rho_\propto(a^{\kappa \circ \kappa}, a^\kappa)$ can be computed in terms of x_0.

$$\rho_\propto(a^{\kappa \circ \kappa}, a^\kappa) = \bigwedge_{x,y} a^{\kappa \circ \kappa}(x) \otimes a^\kappa(y) \to \rho(x, y)$$
$$= \bigwedge_{x,y,z} a^\kappa(z) \otimes z^\kappa(x) \otimes a^\kappa(y) \to \rho(x, y)$$
$$\leq \bigwedge_{x,y} a^\kappa(x_0) \otimes (x_0)^\kappa(x) \otimes a^\kappa(y) \to \rho(x, y)$$
$$= \bigwedge_{x,y} (x_0)^\kappa(x) \otimes a^\kappa(y) \to \rho(x, y) = \rho_\propto(x_0^\kappa, a^\kappa).$$

The argument for $\rho_\propto(a^\kappa, a^{\kappa \circ \kappa}) = \rho_\propto(a^\kappa, x_0^\kappa)$ is analogous, thus

$$(a^{\kappa \circ \kappa} \approx a^\kappa) = (x_0^\kappa \approx a^\kappa).$$

Besides, by inflationary of κ we have that $a^\kappa \leq a^\rho$ and $\rho(a, x_0) = 1$. Next, since κ is idempotent, using Lemma 2 we have,

$$(a^{\kappa \circ \kappa} \approx a^\kappa) = (x_0^\kappa \approx a^\kappa) = (x_0^\kappa \approx \{x_0\}) = 1.$$

Hence, $x_0 \in Core(a^\rho \cap C_\kappa)$.
Besides, we now prove $\rho_\propto(x_0, a^\rho \cap C_\kappa) = 1$.

$$\rho_\propto(x_0, a^\rho \cap C_\kappa) = \bigwedge_{y \in C_\kappa} \rho(a, y) \to \rho(x_0, y)$$

The last infimum is 1 because for all $y \in C_\kappa$ we have,

$$\rho(a, y) \leq \rho_\propto(a^\kappa, y^\kappa) = \rho_\propto(a^\kappa, y^\kappa) \otimes \rho_\propto(y^\kappa, y) \leq \rho_\propto(a^\kappa, y) = \rho(x_0, y)$$

Hence, $x_0 \in Core(m(a^\rho \cap C_\kappa))$ and $m(a^\rho \cap C_\kappa)$ is normal.

(iii) This item will be proved by showing the double inclusion.
Let $x \in C_{\kappa C}$. Since C is a relational closure system, there exists some $x_0 \in Core(m(x^\rho \cap C))$. By definition of $C_{\kappa C}$, $(\{x\} \approx m(x^\rho \cap C)) = 1$. Then, by Lemma 2, $(\{x\} \approx \{x_0\}) = 1$. Therefore,

$$C_{\kappa C} \subseteq \bigcup_{z \in C} \{x \in A \mid \{x\} \approx \{z\} = 1\}.$$

For the converse inclusion, let $x \in A$ be such that there is some $z \in C$ that satisfies $(\{x\} \approx \{z\}) = 1$. By $\rho(x, z) = 1$, it yields $z \in Core(x^\rho \cap C)$. Then, we check that $\rho_\propto(z, x^\rho \cap C) = 1$,

$$\rho_\propto(z, x^\rho \cap C) = \bigwedge_{y \in C} \rho(x, y) \to \rho(z, y) \geq \rho(z, x) = 1.$$

Therefore, $z \in Core(m(x^\rho \cap C))$. Then, by $m(x^\rho \cap C)$ being a clique, we get,

$$\rho_\propto(x, m(x^\rho \cap C)) = \bigwedge_{a \in A} m(x^\rho \cap C)(a) \to \rho(x, a)$$

$$= \bigwedge_{a \in A} (m(x^\rho \cap C)(z) \otimes m(x^\rho \cap C)(a)) \to \rho(x, a)$$

$$\geq \bigwedge_{a \in A} \rho(z, a) \to \rho(x, a) \geq \rho(x, z) = 1$$

The argument for $\rho_\propto(m(x^\rho \cap C), x) = 1$ is analogous.
Therefore, $(\{x\} \approx m(x^\rho \cap C)) = 1$ and $x \in C_{\kappa C}$.
Then, the chain of inclusions follows directly.

(iv) By items (i) and (ii) above, we have that κ_{C_κ} is a fuzzy closure relation and $Core(a^\kappa) \subseteq Core(a^{\kappa_{C_\kappa}})$. Let $x_0 \in Core(a^\kappa)$. Then, by Lemma 3, we have that $a^{\kappa_{C_\kappa}}$ is a clique and, therefore, for all $x \in Core(a^{\kappa_{C_\kappa}})$, using Lemma 2 we have that $(\{x\} \approx a^\kappa) = (a^{\kappa_{C_\kappa}} \approx a^\kappa) = (x_0 \approx x_0)$. Since a^κ is a clique we get $\rho(x_0, x_0) \geq \rho_\times(a^\kappa, a^\kappa) = 1$, thus $(\{x\} \approx a^\kappa) = 1$.

Conversely, assuming $(\{y\} \approx a^\kappa) = 1$, by the isotonicity of κ, we get that $(y^\kappa \approx a^{\kappa \circ \kappa}) = 1$. Now, as κ is idempotent, we have that $(a^{\kappa \circ \kappa} \approx a^\kappa) = 1$, hence

$$1 = (y^\kappa \approx a^{\kappa \circ \kappa}) \otimes (a^{\kappa \circ \kappa} \approx a^\kappa) \otimes (a^\kappa \approx \{y\}) \leq (y^\kappa \approx \{y\}),$$

which is equivalent to $y \in C_\kappa$. In addition, by the inflationary of κ we get $a^\kappa \leq a^\rho$, which, due to the the hypothesis, proves that $y \in Core(a^\rho)$. Last, we show $y \in Core(m(a^\rho \cap C_\kappa))$. The argument for $\rho_\times(y, a^\rho \cap C_\kappa) = 1$ is similar to the one in (ii) but the final string of inequalities differs in the last part, i.e., for any $x \in C_k$

$$\rho(a, x) \leq \rho_\times(a^\kappa, x) = \rho_\times(y, a^\kappa) \otimes \rho_\times(a^\kappa, x) \leq \rho(y, x)$$

Therefore, we have proved $Core(a^{\kappa_{C_\kappa}}) = \{x \in A \mid (\{x\} \approx a^\kappa) = 1\}$. In particular, $(Core(a^{\kappa_{C_\kappa}}) \approx Core(a^\kappa)) = (a^{\kappa_{C_\kappa}} \approx a^\kappa) = 1$, for all $a \in A$.

The following corollary shows some interesting properties concerning the conditions for relational closure systems and fuzzy closure relations to be fixed in some way by the iteration of the operations described in the theorem.

Corollary 1. *Let (A, ρ) be a fuzzy T-digraph, $C \subseteq A$ a relational closure system and $\kappa \in L^{A \times A}$ a fuzzy closure relation.*

(i) $Core(\kappa_{C_\kappa}) = Core(\kappa)$ *if and only if* $(\{x\} \approx a^\kappa) = 1$ *implies* $x \in Core(a^\kappa)$ *for all* $x, a \in A$.

(ii) $C_{\kappa_C} = C^\circ$ *if and only if for all* $x \in A$ *and* $z \in C$, $(\{x\} \approx \{z\}) = 1$ *implies* $x \in C$.

Proof. Straightforward.

The following example shows the results in Theorem 1. Moreover, it shows that in general $C_{\kappa_C} \subseteq C$ and $C \subseteq C_{\kappa_C}$ do not hold for a given relational closure system $C \subseteq A$.

Example 1. Let $A = \{1, 2, 3, 4\}$ with the Łukasiewicz logic and the fuzzy relation given by

ρ	a	b	c	d
a	0.1	1	1	1
b	0.1	1	1	1
c	0.1	1	1	1
d	0.1	0.1	0.1	1

The subset $C = \{a, c, d\}$ is a relational closure system, and it is a simple computation to prove that $C_{\kappa_C} = \{b, c, d\}$ and $C \nsubseteq C_{\kappa_C} \nsubseteq C$. Although, notice that the chain of inclusions in Theorem 1 holds since $C^\circ = \{c, d\} \subseteq \{b, c, d\} = C_{\kappa_C} = A^\circ$. However if we chose the set $D = \{d\}$, which is a relational closure system as well, $C = C^\circ = C_{\kappa_D} \subsetneq A^\circ$.

4 Conclusions and Further Work

In this paper, the definition of fuzzy closure relation has been introduced in the context of fuzzy T-digraphs. Following the spirit of [7], this definition extends inflationary, isotonicity and idempotency to the fuzzy framework, this definition is remarkably simplified by the use of Plotkin's full fuzzy powering. Next, we have introduced the counterpart of fuzzy closure relations. These structures are called relational closure systems and are crisp sets $C \subseteq A$ such that the fuzzy set $m(a^\rho \cap C)$ is normal for all $a \in A$. As expected, these structures are related, but the relationship is not one-to-one.

As prospect of future work, a study of the conditions that ensure the relationship to be one-to-one will be made. Also, the concept of relational closure system could be brought to the fuzzy framework by considering it as a fuzzy set instead of a crisp one.

References

1. Bělohlávek, R.: Fuzzy closure operators. J. Math. Anal. Appl. **262**, 473–489 (2001)
2. Bělohlávek, R.: Fuzzy Relational Systems. Springer, Cham (2002). https://doi.org/10.1007/978-1-4615-0633-1
3. Bělohlávek, R., De Baets, B., Outrata, J., Vychodil, V.: Computing the lattice of all fixpoints of a fuzzy closure operator. IEEE Trans. Fuzzy Syst. **18**(3), 546–557 (2010). https://doi.org/10.1109/TFUZZ.2010.2041006
4. Bělohlávek, R.: Pavelka-style fuzzy logic in retrospect and prospect. Fuzzy Sets Syst. **281**, 61–72 (2015). https://doi.org/10.1016/j.fss.2015.07.007
5. Cabrera, I.P., Cordero, P., García-Pardo, F., Ojeda-Aciego, M., De Baets, B.: On the construction of adjunctions between a fuzzy preposet and an unstructured set. Fuzzy Sets Syst. **320**, 81–92 (2017)
6. Cabrera, I.P., Cordero, P., García-Pardo, F., Ojeda-Aciego, M., De Baets, B.: Galois connections between a fuzzy preordered structure and a general fuzzy structure. IEEE Trans. Fuzzy Syst. **26**(3), 1274–1287 (2018)
7. Cabrera, I.P., Cordero, P., Muñoz-Velasco, E., Ojeda-Aciego, M., De Baets, B.: Relational Galois connections between transitive fuzzy digraphs. Math. Meth. Appl. Sci. **43**(9), 5673–5680 (2020). https://doi.org/10.1002/mma.6302
8. Caspard, N., Monjardet, B.: The lattices of closure systems, closure operators, and implicational systems on a finite set: a survey. Discret. Appl. Math. **127**(2), 241–269 (2003). https://doi.org/10.1016/S0166-218X(02)00209-3
9. Cordero, P., Enciso, M., Mora, A., Vychodil, V.: Parameterized simplification logic I: reasoning with implications and classes of closure operators. Int. J. Gen. Syst. **49**(7), 724–746 (2020). https://doi.org/10.1080/03081079.2020.1831484

10. De Baets, B.: Analytical solution methods for fuzzy relational equations. In: Dubois, D., Prade, H. (eds.) Fundamentals of Fuzzy Sets. The Handbooks of Fuzzy Sets Series, vol 7. Springer, Boston (2000). https://doi.org/10.1007/978-1-4615-4429-6_7

11. Elorza, J., Fuentes-González, R., Bragard, J., Burillo, P.: On the relation between fuzzy closing morphological operators, fuzzy consequence operators induced by fuzzy preorders and fuzzy closure and co-closure systems. Fuzzy Sets Syst. **218**, 73–89 (2013). https://doi.org/10.1016/j.fss.2012.08.010

12. García-Pardo, F., Cabrera, I.P., Cordero, P., Ojeda-Aciego, M.: On closure systems and adjunctions between fuzzy preordered sets. In: Baixeries, J., Sacarea, C., Ojeda-Aciego, M. (eds.) ICFCA 2015. LNCS (LNAI), vol. 9113, pp. 114–127. Springer, Cham (2015). https://doi.org/10.1007/978-3-319-19545-2_7

13. Guo, L., Zhang, Q., Li, Q.: Fuzzy closure systems on L-ordered sets. Math. Log. Q. **57**(3), 281–291 (2011)

14. Hájek, P.: Metamathematics of Fuzzy Logic. Trends in Logic. Springer, Netherlands (2013). https://doi.org/10.1007/978-94-011-5300-3

15. Kuhr, T., Vychodil, V.: Fuzzy logic programming reduced to reasoning with attribute implications. Fuzzy Sets Syst. **262**, 1–20 (2015). https://doi.org/10.1016/j.fss.2014.04.013

16. Madrid, N., Medina, J., Ojeda-Aciego, M., Perfilieva, I.: Toward the use of fuzzy relations in the definition of mathematical morphology operators. J. Fuzzy Set Valued Anal. **2016**(1), 87–98 (2016)

17. Moore, E.H.: Introduction to a Form of General Analysis, vol. 2. Yale University Press (1910)

18. Ojeda-Hernández, M., Cabrera, I.P., Cordero, P., Muñoz-Velasco, E.: On (fuzzy) closure systems in complete fuzzy lattices. In: 2021 IEEE International Conference on Fuzzy Systems (FUZZ-IEEE), pp. 1–6 (2021). https://doi.org/10.1109/FUZZ45933.2021.9494404

19. Ojeda-Hernández, M., Cabrera, I.P., Cordero, P., Muñoz-Velasco, E.: Closure systems as a fuzzy extension of meet-subsemilattices. In: Joint Proceedings of the 19th World Congress of the International Fuzzy Systems Association (IFSA), the 12th Conference of the European Society for Fuzzy Logic and Technology (EUSFLAT), and the 11th International Summer School on Aggregation Operators (AGOP), pp. 40–47. Atlantis Press (2021). https://doi.org/10.2991/asum.k.210827.006

20. Poelmans, J., Kuznetsov, S.O., Ignatov, D.I., Dedene, G.: Formal concept analysis in knowledge processing: a survey on models and techniques. Expert Syst. Appl. **40**(16), 6601–6623 (2013). https://doi.org/10.1016/j.eswa.2013.05.007

Computing the Mixed Concept Lattice

Francisco Pérez-Gámez[1]([✉])[ID], Pablo Cordero[1][ID], Manuel Enciso[2][ID],
Domingo López-Rodríguez[1][ID], and Ángel Mora[1][ID]

[1] Departamento de Matemática Aplicada, Universidad de Málaga, Málaga, Spain
{franciscoperezgamez,pcordero,dominlopez,amora}@uma.es
[2] Departamento de Lenguajes y Ciencias de la Computación, Universidad de Málaga,
Málaga, Spain
enciso@uma.es

Abstract. The classical approach on Formal Concept Analysis (FCA) extracts knowledge from a binary table $\mathbb{K} = (G, M, I)$ taking into account the existing relationships (given by the binary relation I) between objects G and attributes M. Thus, this classical setting accounts only for *positive information*. Particularly, FCA allows to define and compute the concept lattice $\mathbb{B}(\mathbb{K})$ from this positive information. As an extension of this framework, some works consider not only this positive information, but also the negative information that is explicit when objects have no relation to specific attributes (denoted by $\overline{\mathbb{K}}$). These works, therefore, use the apposition of *positive* and *negative* information to compute the *mixed* concept lattice $\mathbb{B}^{\#}(\mathbb{K})$. In this paper, we propose to establish the relationships between extents and intents of concepts in $\mathbb{B}(\mathbb{K})$, $\mathbb{B}(\overline{\mathbb{K}})$ and $\mathbb{B}^{\#}(\mathbb{K})$ and how to address an incremental algorithm to compute $\mathbb{B}^{\#}(\mathbb{K})$ merging the knowledge on $\mathbb{B}(\mathbb{K})$, $\mathbb{B}(\overline{\mathbb{K}})$ previously obtained with classical methods.

Keywords: Formal concept analysis · Mixed attributes · Concept lattice

1 Introduction

In the classical paradigm of formal concept analysis (FCA) [4,5], the fundamental data model is a structure (called formal context) that represents a binary relationship between a set of objects and their attributes. From this formal context, we can define formal concepts, which represent sets of objects that share common attributes. In addition, we can define an ordering relationship between concepts in the sense of *specialisation-generalisation*, which endows such a set of

Partially supported by the Spanish Ministry of Science, Innovation, and Universities (MCIU), State Agency of Research (AEI), Junta de Andalucía (JA), Universidad de Málaga (UMA) and European Regional Development Fund (FEDER) through the projects PGC2018-095869-B-I00 (MCIU/AEI/FEDER), TIN2017-89023-P (MCIU/AEI/FEDER), PRE2018-085199 and UMA2018-FEDERJA-001 (JA/UMA/FEDER).

© Springer Nature Switzerland AG 2022
D. Ciucci et al. (Eds.): IPMU 2022, CCIS 1601, pp. 87–99, 2022.
https://doi.org/10.1007/978-3-031-08971-8_8

concepts with the structure of a complete lattice. This paradigm has been used successfully in problems such as the construction of recommender systems [1,3] or in the analysis of data from social networks [2,7,9].

According to the classical scheme, FCA is not suitable for handling negative information (indicating the absence of some property in an object, in contrast to the presence which is assumed by default to be positive information). But some practical applications require such information to be explicitly contemplated, hence the need to study from a formal perspective the mixture of the two types of information.

Early attempts to handle mixed information in FCA tried to model the problem by apposing the *positive* context and its negation [6,10], so that the number of attributes is doubled and, therefore, the computational treatment of the problem has a higher complexity. Moreover, as mentioned in [11], real applications often have sparse data in the positive context and are very dense in the negative context, or vice versa, which generates a large amount of redundancy in the expression of information. Some works deal with positive and negative information [8,11,13,14] more efficiently, but they do not study the relationship between the different types of information at the concept lattice level.

In the present proposal, we build on the line of work of [13,14], in which, instead of relying on the apposition of positive and negative contexts, the concept formation operators, i.e. the Galois connection inducing a closure system, are redefined to allow for the mixing of information types without the need to duplicate the context. The treatment of mixed information under a unified framework improves the expressiveness of the model significantly.

The main aim of the paper is to relate the closed sets of the positive and negative contexts to those that can be obtained by means of the new derivation operators, which we denote by $\Uparrow$ and $\Downarrow$, instead of the traditional $\uparrow$ and $\downarrow$. To do so, we will define *embedding* and *projection* operators, which represent, in turn, a Galois connection between the individual lattices and the mixed lattice.

Thanks to these operators, we can demonstrate the isomorphism between the individual lattices and sub-semilattices of the mixed lattice, and the relationship between the extents and intents of the different lattice types. In addition, we will present results that establish the decomposition or representation of a mixed concept in terms of a pair of suitable positive and negative concepts. Thanks to these theoretical results, we will be able to propose an algorithm for the computation of the lattice of mixed concepts from the positive and negative lattices.

The rest of this work is structured as follows: in Sect. 2, we find the preliminary notions and definitions that will be used throughout this work. In Sect. 3, we present the main theoretical results that relate the individual concept lattices to the mixed lattice, and we provide an incremental algorithm able to compute this mixed lattice from the individual concept lattices. Finally, in Sect. 4, we present the conclusions and the proposal of future works in this line.

2   Preliminary Notions

Formal concept Analysis (FCA) is a useful tool to extract knowledge from a collection of data stored on a formal context $\mathbb{K} = (G, M, I)$, where G is a set of objects, M is a set of attributes and I represents the relation between them.

In a formal context $\mathbb{K} = (G, M, I)$, we can define a Galois connection used to extract the concepts behind the data. The Galois connection is formed by the mappings $\uparrow : 2^G \rightarrow 2^M$ and $\downarrow : 2^M \rightarrow 2^G$ defined in the following way. $A^\uparrow = \{m \in M \mid (g, m) \in I$ for all $g \in A\}$, that is, all the attributes shared by the objects in A and $B^\downarrow = \{g \in G \mid (g, m) \in I$ for all $m \in B\}$, i.e., all the objects that satisfy all the attributes in B. In [15] it is proved that these two maps form a Galois connection, therefore their compositions $\uparrow\downarrow$ and $\downarrow\uparrow$ are closure operators.

Using these notions we are able to extract knowledge: We say that a pair (A, B) with $A \subseteq G$ and $B \subseteq M$ is a formal concept if $A^\uparrow = B$ and $B^\downarrow = A$. So (A, B) is a formal context if all the objects in A share all the attributes in B and they do not share any other attributes. In addition, given two formal concepts (A, B) and (C, D) we can define a order relation between then with $(A, B) \leq (C, D)$ if and only if $A \subseteq C$ or, equivalently, if and only if $D \subseteq B$. It is well-known that the set with all formal concepts together with the order form a complete lattice that will be denoted by $\mathbb{B}(\mathbb{K})$.

The classical FCA paradigm only consider the information provided by the incidence relation I, and does not model the *negative* information contained therein, that is, the information provided by the pairs $(g, m) \notin I$. In this paper we want to extend to consider the positive and the negative information. Recently some authors work with this view like [8,11,13,14]. In [11] we find an approach that, given a formal context $\mathbb{K} = (G, M, I)$, they built a new one $(\mathbb{K} \mid \overline{\mathbb{K}}) = (G, M \cup \overline{M}, I^*)$ being $I^*(g, m) = I(g, m)$ for all $m \in M$ and $I^*(g, \overline{m}) = \min(1, 1 - I(g, m))$ otherwise. Here, the attributes in M are called positive attributes and the attributes in $\overline{M}$ are called negative attributes. This approach duplicates the number of attributes so the methods loses efficiency.

Here, we follow the working line of [14] which, instead of duplicating the number of attributes, define a new Galois connection over $\mathbb{K}$, i.e., the formal context does not change. The new connection is denoted by $\Uparrow$ and $\Downarrow$ to difference them from the Galois connection defined before. We define mixed context as any formal context $\mathbb{K}$ provided with the new Galois connection. We define the new operators $\Uparrow : 2^G \rightarrow 2^{M \cup \overline{M}}$ and $\Downarrow : 2^{M \cup \overline{M}} \rightarrow 2^G$ as follows:

$$X^\Uparrow = \{m \in M \mid (g, m) \in I \ \forall g \in X\} \cup \{\overline{m} \in \overline{M} \mid (g, m) \notin I \ \forall g \in X\}$$

$$Y^\Downarrow = \{g \in G \mid (g, m) \in I \ \forall m \in Y\} \cap \{g \in G \mid (g, m) \notin I \ \forall \overline{m} \in Y\}$$

These two operators form a Galois connection and, as consequence, both compositions are closure operators. Consequently, using the closure operators we can build a concept lattice over the mixed context of $\mathbb{K}$. We denote by $\mathbb{B}^\#(\mathbb{K})$ the lattice built by using the derivation operators $\Uparrow$ and $\Downarrow$, and we denote by $\mathbb{B}(\mathbb{K})$ the concept lattice formed by using the classic operators $\uparrow$ and $\downarrow$. Observe that with this new derivation operators we obtain the same concept lattice that the concept lattice build with the formal context with the double of attributes so we can process the same information without duplicating the number of columns and, as consequence, this view is more efficient.

Let A be a set of attributes, now we present some functions that allow us to capture the positive and negative information related to this set:

$$\text{Pos}(A) = A \cap M, \qquad \text{Neg}(A) = \overline{A} \cap M$$

where $\overline{A} = \{\overline{m} \in \overline{M} : m \in A\} \cup \{m \in M : \overline{m} \in A\}$.

Given a formal context $\mathbb{K}$ we define its complement as $\overline{\mathbb{K}} = (G, M, \overline{I})$ being $\overline{I}$ defined by $(g, m) \in \overline{I}$ if and only if $(g, m) \notin I$.

Lemma 1 ([12]). *Let $\mathbb{K}$ be a formal context. The following statements are fulfilled:*

1. *If $A \subseteq M$, then $A^{\Downarrow} = A^{\downarrow}$ (in $\mathbb{K}$).*
2. *If $A \subseteq \overline{M}$, then $A^{\Downarrow} = A^{\downarrow}$ (in $\overline{\mathbb{K}}$).*
3. *If $B \subseteq G$, then $\text{Pos}(B^{\Uparrow}) = B^{\uparrow}$ (in $\mathbb{K}$) and $\text{Neg}(B^{\Uparrow}) = B^{\uparrow}$ (in $\overline{\mathbb{K}}$).*

The following example will be used to show the main results in this work.

Example 1. Let $\mathbb{K}$ be a formal context given by Table 1(a). The apposition (concatenation by columns) of $\mathbb{K}$ and its complement $\overline{\mathbb{K}}$ is in Table 1(b). As usual, we follow the notation $\mathbb{K}|\overline{\mathbb{K}}$ for the concatenated formal context. In addition, we define $M = \{a, b, c, d\}$ and $\overline{M} = \{\overline{a}, \overline{b}, \overline{c}, \overline{d}\}$.

Table 1. Formal contexts for the example.

	a	b	c	d			a	b	c	d	$\overline{a}$	$\overline{b}$	$\overline{c}$	$\overline{d}$
o1		×	×			o1	×		×	×	×			
o2	×	×				o2	×	×				×		×
o3	×			×		o3	×		×		×		×	
o4		×				o4		×		×	×		×	×
o5		×	×	×		o5	×	×	×	×				
o6	×		×			o6	×		×		×			×
o7		×	×			o7		×	×		×			×
(a)						(b)								

The following example shows the difference between the two Galois connection defined over $\mathbb{K}$, that is, between $(^{\uparrow}, ^{\downarrow})$ and $(^{\Uparrow}, ^{\Downarrow})$.

$$\{c, d\}^{\downarrow\uparrow} = (\{c, d\}^{\downarrow})^{\uparrow} = \{o5\}^{\uparrow} = \{b, c, d\}$$

$$\{c, d\}^{\Downarrow\Uparrow} = (\{c, d\}^{\Downarrow})^{\Uparrow} = \{o5\}^{\Uparrow} = \{b, c, d, \overline{a}\}$$

Furthermore, we can check the results of Lemma 1, since $\{c, d\}^{\Downarrow} = \{c, d\}^{\downarrow} = \{o5\}$ and $\text{Pos}(\{o5\}^{\Uparrow}) = \text{Pos}(\{b, c, d, \overline{a}\}) = \{b, c, d\} = \{o5\}^{\uparrow}$.

Finally, we can see that $^{\downarrow}$ is defined on 2^{M} whereas $^{\Downarrow}$ is in $2^{M \cup \overline{M}}$ so it does not make sense to write $\{c, \overline{b}\}^{\downarrow}$. Instead, we have to rely on $^{\Downarrow}$ to compute the desired *extent* using mixed attributes: $\{c, \overline{b}\}^{\Downarrow} = \{o4, o6\}$.

3   Main Results

Hereinafter, we will consider a formal context $\mathbb{K} = (G, M, I)$ and its *negative* context $\overline{\mathbb{K}}$, both equipped with their corresponding concept-forming operators $(^{\downarrow}, ^{\uparrow})$, and the mixed context equipped with $(^{\Downarrow}, ^{\Uparrow})$. The main objective of this work is to characterise the elements of the mixed lattice $\underline{\mathbb{B}}^{\#}(\mathbb{K})$ in terms of those of the positive and negative lattices.

We divide this study into two strategies. The first part of this section will be devoted to studying how the individual positive and negative lattices can be mapped into the mixed lattice, analysing their inclusion and the isomorphism relationship between these lattices and sub-semilattices of the $\underline{\mathbb{B}}^{\#}(\mathbb{K})$. The second part will focus on analysing how to decompose the concepts of the mixed lattice in terms of concrete concepts of the individual lattices, allowing the definition of the algorithm for the computation of the mixed lattice from the latter.

3.1   Embedding of $\underline{\mathbb{B}}(\mathbb{K})$ and $\underline{\mathbb{B}}(\overline{\mathbb{K}})$ into $\underline{\mathbb{B}}^{\#}(\mathbb{K})$

Here, as mentioned above, we present theoretical results that allow us to study the inclusion relation of the positive and negative lattices within the $\underline{\mathbb{B}}^{\#}(\mathbb{K})$. We will start by studying how the extents of the mixed lattice have a higher level of granularity than the extents of the individual lattices. We will use the following notation in order to make the results of this work easier to read:

Notation 1. *Let us denote:*

$\text{Ext}(\mathbb{K}) := \{A \subseteq G : A \text{ is the extent of a concept in } \underline{\mathbb{B}}(\mathbb{K})\}$
$\text{Int}(\mathbb{K}) := \{B \subseteq M : B \text{ is the intent of a concept in } \underline{\mathbb{B}}(\mathbb{K})\}$
$\text{Ext}^{\#}(\mathbb{K}) := \{A \subseteq G : A \text{ is the extent of a concept in } \underline{\mathbb{B}}^{\#}(\mathbb{K})\}$
$\text{Int}^{\#}(\mathbb{K}) := \{B \subseteq M \cup \overline{M} : A \text{ is the intent of a concept in } \underline{\mathbb{B}}^{\#}(\mathbb{K})\}$

With this notation, we refer to the set of extents and intents of concepts in $\underline{\mathbb{B}}(\mathbb{K})$ and $\underline{\mathbb{B}}^{\#}(\mathbb{K})$, respectively. Analogously, we can denote the corresponding ones in the negative lattice $\overline{\mathbb{K}}$.

Lemma 2. *For a given formal context* $\mathbb{K} = (G, M, I)$, *we have* $\text{Ext}(\mathbb{K}) \subseteq \text{Ext}^{\#}(\mathbb{K})$ *and* $\text{Ext}(\overline{\mathbb{K}}) \subseteq \text{Ext}^{\#}(\mathbb{K})$.

We continue the example above to give a graphical representation of the situation stated in the previous theoretical result.

Example 2. We continue with the same contexts of Example 1. In Fig. 1, we show the concept lattices $\underline{\mathbb{B}}(\mathbb{K})$, $\mathbb{B}(\overline{\mathbb{K}})$ and $\underline{\mathbb{B}}^{\#}(\mathbb{K})$ of the *positive*, *negative* and *mixed* formal contexts. We have used a colour code to represent the relationships of $\text{Ext}(\mathbb{K})$ and $\text{Ext}(\overline{\mathbb{K}})$ with $\text{Ext}^{\#}(\mathbb{K})$. We have marked in blue the concepts whose extents are present in $\underline{\mathbb{B}}(\mathbb{K})$, and in orange those present in $\underline{\mathbb{B}}(\overline{\mathbb{K}})$. Note that some concepts are in grey since their extent appears in both $\underline{\mathbb{B}}(\mathbb{K})$ and $\underline{\mathbb{B}}(\overline{\mathbb{K}})$. We can observe that the concepts in the mixed context contain those of the other two contexts and provide additional information and granularity.

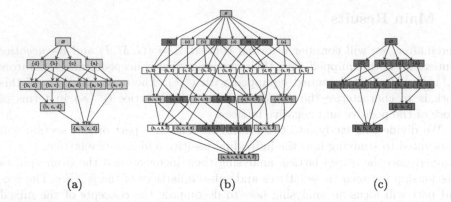

Fig. 1. Concept lattices associated with (a) the *positive* context $\mathbb{K}$ in Table 1(a); (b) the mixed context; (c) the *negative* formal context $\overline{\mathbb{K}}$.

The Lemma 2 allows us to define the following operators:

$$
\begin{array}{l|l}
e_+ : \mathbb{B}(\mathbb{K}) \to \mathbb{B}^{\#}(\mathbb{K}) & e_- : \mathbb{B}(\overline{\mathbb{K}}) \to \mathbb{B}^{\#}(\mathbb{K}) \\
(A, B) \mapsto e_+(A, B) := (A, A^{\Uparrow}) & (A, B) \mapsto e_-(A, B) := (A, A^{\Uparrow})
\end{array}
$$

Note that these mappings are well-defined since, by Lemma 2, every extent of $\mathbb{B}(\mathbb{K})$ and $\mathbb{B}(\overline{\mathbb{K}})$ is also an extent of $\mathbb{B}^{\#}(\mathbb{K})$. We can say that these operators define *embeddings* of $\mathbb{B}(\mathbb{K})$ and of $\mathbb{B}(\overline{\mathbb{K}})$ into $\mathbb{B}^{\#}(\mathbb{K})$. We shall now study their properties:

Theorem 1. *For a formal context* $\mathbb{K} = (G, M, I)$, *the embedding mappings* e_+ *and* e_- *are* $\wedge$-*preserving and injective.*

Let us now recall the projection operators $\pi_+ : \mathbb{B}^{\#}(\mathbb{K}) \to \mathbb{B}(\mathbb{K})$ and $\pi_- : \mathbb{B}^{\#}(\mathbb{K}) \to \mathbb{B}(\overline{\mathbb{K}})$ introduced in [12] and defined as

$$
\pi_+(A, B) := (\mathrm{Pos}(B)^{\downarrow}, \mathrm{Pos}(B)) \quad\Big|\quad \pi_-(A, B) := (\overline{\mathrm{Neg}(B)}^{\Downarrow}, \overline{\mathrm{Neg}(B)})
$$

For these mappings, we have the following result:

Theorem 2 ([12]). *The maps* $\pi_+ : \mathbb{B}^{\#}(\mathbb{K}) \to \mathbb{B}(\mathbb{K})$ *and* $\pi_- : \mathbb{B}^{\#}(\mathbb{K}) \to \mathbb{B}(\overline{\mathbb{K}})$ *are* $\vee$-*preserving and surjective.*

We can go even further in the study of their properties. According to the following theoretical result, these *embedding* and *projection* operators establish Galois connections between the individual lattices ($\mathbb{B}(\mathbb{K})$ and $\mathbb{B}(\overline{\mathbb{K}})$) and the mixed lattice.

Theorem 3. *For a formal context* $\mathbb{K} = (G, M, I)$, *we have:*

1. e_+, e_-, π_+ *and* π_- *are monotone.*
2. $\pi_+ \circ e_+ = \mathrm{id}_{\mathbb{B}(\mathbb{K})}$ *and* $\pi_- \circ e_- = \mathrm{id}_{\mathbb{B}(\overline{\mathbb{K}})}$.
3. (e_+, π_+) *and* (e_-, π_-) *are isotone Galois connections.*

In our case, (e_+, π_+) and (e_-, π_-) are not only Galois connections: by Theorem 3, $\pi_+ \circ e_+$ and $\pi_- \circ e_-$ are the identity mappings in $\mathbb{B}(\mathbb{K})$ and $\mathbb{B}(\overline{\mathbb{K}})$, respectively, and this condition allows us to say that they are **Galois injections** (also called Galois surjections). Let us introduce the following notation:

Notation 2. *Consider a formal context* $\mathbb{K} = (G, M, I)$ *and the operators* e_+, e_-, π_+ *and* π_- *defined as above. Then, we denote* $\sigma_+ := e_+ \circ \pi_+$ *and* $\sigma_- := e_- \circ \pi_-$, *where both maps are* $\underline{\mathbb{B}}^{\#}(\mathbb{K}) \to \underline{\mathbb{B}}^{\#}(\mathbb{K})$.

As a consequence of Theorem 3, we have:

Corollary 1. σ_+ *and* σ_- *are closure operators in* $\underline{\mathbb{B}}^{\#}(\mathbb{K})$.

We now finish the study of the embeddings of the individual lattices within the mixed lattice by showing that the system of closures induced by the above closure operators coincides with the embeddings of the individual lattices within $\mathbb{B}^{\#}(\mathbb{K})$. Let us denote $\mathcal{C}_+$ and $\mathcal{C}_-$ the set of closed sets according to operators σ_+ and σ_-, respectively. Then, we have:

Proposition 1. *The closed sets of* σ_+ *and* σ_- *are the embeddings of* $\mathbb{B}(\mathbb{K})$ *and* $\mathbb{B}(\overline{\mathbb{K}})$ *into* $\mathbb{B}^{\#}(\mathbb{K})$, *respectively. That is*

$$\mathcal{C}_+ = e_+(\mathbb{B}(\mathbb{K})) \quad \text{and} \quad \mathcal{C}_- = e_-(\mathbb{B}(\overline{\mathbb{K}}))$$

Example 3. We continue with the formal context presented in Example 1. Here, we present in Table 2 the embeddings of the lattices of $\mathbb{K}$ and $\overline{\mathbb{K}}$. In the table, we only list the intents of the corresponding concepts for the sake of clarity.

Table 2. Embedding of the individual concept lattices $\mathbb{B}(\mathbb{K})$ and $\mathbb{B}(\overline{\mathbb{K}})$ into $\mathbb{B}^{\#}(\mathbb{K})$. Only intents are shown in this table.

$(A, B) \in \underline{\mathbb{B}}(\mathbb{K})$	$e_+(A, B)$	$(A, B) \in \underline{\mathbb{B}}(\overline{\mathbb{K}})$	$e_-(A, B)$
$\varnothing$	$\varnothing$	$\varnothing$	$\varnothing$
$\{d\}$	$\{d\}$	$\{\overline{d}\}$	$\{\overline{d}\}$
$\{c\}$	$\{c\}$	$\{\overline{c}\}$	$\{\overline{c}\}$
$\{b\}$	$\{b\}$	$\{\overline{c}, \overline{d}\}$	$\{a, b, \overline{c}, \overline{d}\}$
$\{b, d\}$	$\{b, d, \overline{a}\}$	$\{\overline{b}\}$	$\{\overline{b}\}$
$\{b, c\}$	$\{b, c, \overline{a}\}$	$\{\overline{b}, \overline{d}\}$	$\{c, \overline{b}, \overline{d}\}$
$\{b, c, d\}$	$\{b, c, d, \overline{a}\}$	$\{\overline{b}, \overline{c}\}$	$\{a, d, \overline{b}, \overline{c}\}$
$\{a\}$	$\{a\}$	$\{\overline{a}\}$	$\{\overline{a}\}$
$\{a, d\}$	$\{a, d, \overline{b}, \overline{c}\}$	$\{\overline{a}, \overline{d}\}$	$\{c, \overline{a}, \overline{d}\}$
$\{a, c\}$	$\{a, c, \overline{b}, \overline{d}\}$	$\{\overline{a}, \overline{c}\}$	$\{b, d, \overline{a}, \overline{c}\}$
$\{a, b\}$	$\{a, b, \overline{c}, \overline{d}\}$	$\{\overline{a}, \overline{b}, \overline{d}\}$	$\{c, \overline{a}, \overline{b}, \overline{d}\}$
$\{a, b, c, d\}$	$\{a, b, c, d, \overline{a}, \overline{b}, \overline{c}, \overline{d}\}$	$\{\overline{a}, \overline{b}, \overline{c}, \overline{d}\}$	$\{a, b, c, d, \overline{a}, \overline{b}, \overline{c}, \overline{d}\}$

Finally, we state a result that is direct consequence of Corollary 1 and Proposition 1.

Corollary 2. $\mathbb{B}(\mathbb{K})$ *and* $\underline{\mathbb{B}}(\overline{\mathbb{K}})$ *are isomorphic to* $\wedge$*-subsemilattices of* $\underline{\mathbb{B}}^{\#}(\mathbb{K})$.

3.2   Decomposition of Concepts in $\underline{\mathbb{B}}^{\#}(\mathbb{K})$

In this part, we approach the problem of the decomposition or representation of mixed concepts in terms of concepts from the positive and negative lattices. The first result uses the closure operators σ_+ and σ_- to decompose mixed concepts.

Theorem 4. *Let* $\mathbb{K} = (G, M, I)$ *be a formal context and let* $(A, B) \in \underline{\mathbb{B}}^{\#}(\mathbb{K})$. *Then* $(A, B) = \sigma_+(A, B) \wedge \sigma_-(A, B)$.

Example 4. We continue with the formal context in Example 2. The mixed context presents an aggregate of 30 concepts. In Table 3, we show some of the concepts in $\underline{\mathbb{B}}^{\#}(\mathbb{K})$ together with their decomposition. To avoid massive listings, we have selected those concepts in which decomposition appear non-purely positive or negative sets $\sigma_+(A, B)$ and $\sigma_-(A, B)$, that is, such that $\mathrm{Neg}(\sigma_+(A, B)) \neq \varnothing$ or $\mathrm{Pos}(\sigma_-(A, B)) \neq \varnothing$.

Table 3. Decomposition of some of the concepts in $\underline{\mathbb{B}}^{\#}(\mathbb{K})$ of Example 1.

$(A, B) \in \underline{\mathbb{B}}^{\#}(\mathbb{K})$	$\sigma_+(A, B)$	$\sigma_-(A, B)$
$\{c, \overline{b}, \overline{d}\}$	$\{c\}$	$\{c, \overline{b}, \overline{d}\}$
$\{c, \overline{a}, \overline{d}\}$	$\{c\}$	$\{c, \overline{a}, \overline{d}\}$
$\{c, \overline{a}, \overline{b}, \overline{d}\}$	$\{c\}$	$\{c, \overline{a}, \overline{b}, \overline{d}\}$
$\{b, d, \overline{a}\}$	$\{b, d, \overline{a}\}$	$\{\overline{a}\}$
$\{b, d, \overline{a}, \overline{c}\}$	$\{b, d, \overline{a}\}$	$\{b, d, \overline{a}, \overline{c}\}$
$\{b, c, \overline{a}\}$	$\{b, c, \overline{a}\}$	$\{\overline{a}\}$
$\{b, c, \overline{a}, \overline{d}\}$	$\{b, c, \overline{a}\}$	$\{c, \overline{a}, \overline{d}\}$
$\{b, c, d, \overline{a}\}$	$\{b, c, d, \overline{a}\}$	$\{\overline{a}\}$
$\{a, d, \overline{b}, \overline{c}\}$	$\{a, d, \overline{b}, \overline{c}\}$	$\{a, d, \overline{b}, \overline{c}\}$
$\{a, c, \overline{b}, \overline{d}\}$	$\{a, c, \overline{b}, \overline{d}\}$	$\{c, \overline{b}, \overline{d}\}$
$\{a, b, \overline{c}, \overline{d}\}$	$\{a, b, \overline{c}, \overline{d}\}$	$\{a, b, \overline{c}, \overline{d}\}$
$\{a, b, c, d, \overline{a}, \overline{b}, \overline{c}, \overline{d}\}$	$\{a, b, c, d, \overline{a}, \overline{b}, \overline{c}, \overline{d}\}$	$\{a, b, c, d, \overline{a}, \overline{b}, \overline{c}, \overline{d}\}$

As a consequence of this theorem, and of the theoretical results of the previous section, we have the following decomposition result. This will help us provide an algorithm to compute $\underline{\mathbb{B}}^{\#}(\mathbb{K})$ from $\mathbb{B}(\mathbb{K})$ and $\underline{\mathbb{B}}(\overline{\mathbb{K}})$.

Theorem 5. *Let* $\mathbb{K} = (G, M, I)$ *be a formal context and let* $(A, B) \in \underline{\mathbb{B}}^{\#}(\mathbb{K})$. *Then* $(A_+, B_+) = \pi_+(A, B) \in \mathbb{B}(\mathbb{K})$ *and* $(A_-, B_-) = \pi_-(A, B) \in \underline{\mathbb{B}}(\overline{\mathbb{K}})$ *verify that* $(A, B) = (A_+ \cap A_-, B_+ \cup B_-)$.

Furthermore, we can say:

Theorem 6. *Let* $\mathbb{K} = (G, M, I)$ *be a formal context. The mappings:*

$$\phi : \text{Ext}(\mathbb{K}) \times \text{Ext}(\overline{\mathbb{K}}) \rightarrow \text{Ext}^{\#}(\mathbb{K}) \quad \bigg| \quad \psi : \text{Int}(\mathbb{K}) \times \text{Int}(\overline{\mathbb{K}}) \rightarrow \text{Int}^{\#}(\mathbb{K})$$
$$(A_1, A_2) \quad \mapsto \quad A_1 \cap A_2 \quad \bigg| \quad (B_1, B_2) \quad \mapsto (B_1 \cup B_2)^{\Downarrow\Uparrow}$$

are well defined and surjective.

The meaning of the last two theorems is that we can compute all intents of $\mathbb{B}^{\#}(\mathbb{K})$ by traversing the intents of $\mathbb{B}(\mathbb{K})$ and $\mathbb{B}(\overline{\mathbb{K}})$, taking their union, and computing the closure. In fact, we can say that:

Corollary 3. *Let* $\mathbb{K} = (G, M, I)$ *be a formal context. Then*

$$\text{Int}^{\#}(\mathbb{K}) = \{B = B_1 \cup B_2, B_1 \in \text{Int}(\mathbb{K}), B_2 \in \text{Int}(\overline{\mathbb{K}}), \text{ and } B = B^{\Downarrow\Uparrow}\}$$

Now, for the sake of readability, let us introduce the notation for the following mappings:

Notation 3. *Let* $\Delta_+^- := \pi_- \circ e_+ : \mathbb{B}(\mathbb{K}) \rightarrow \mathbb{B}(\overline{\mathbb{K}})$ *and* $\Delta_-^+ := \pi_+ \circ e_- : \mathbb{B}(\overline{\mathbb{K}}) \rightarrow \mathbb{B}(\mathbb{K})$.

Lemma 3. *Consider a formal context* $\mathbb{K} = (G, M, I)$:

1. *If* $(A, B) \in \mathbb{B}(\mathbb{K})$ *and we call* $(C, D) = \Delta_+^-(A, B) = \pi_-(A, A^{\Uparrow}) \in \mathbb{B}(\overline{\mathbb{K}})$, *then,*
   $(A, B \cup D) = e_+(A, B) \in \mathbb{B}^{\#}(\mathbb{K})$.
2. *If* $(A, B) \in \mathbb{B}(\overline{\mathbb{K}})$ *and we call* $(C, D) = \Delta_-^+(A, B) = \pi_+(A, A^{\Uparrow}) \in \mathbb{B}(\mathbb{K})$, *then,*
   $(A, B \cup D) = e_-(A, B) \in \mathbb{B}^{\#}(\mathbb{K})$.

Thus, Δ_+^- and Δ_-^+ can be used to find concepts in the other simple lattice that complete (by union) a concept in $\mathbb{B}^{\#}(\mathbb{K})$. In addition, $e_+(A, B) = (A, B \cup D)$ is the greatest concept (in the sense of the order $\leq$ in $\mathbb{B}^{\#}(\mathbb{K})$) such that its intent contains B: $e_+(A, B) = \sup\{(R, S) \in \mathbb{B}^{\#}(\mathbb{K}) : B \subseteq S\}$, and analogously in $\mathbb{B}(\overline{\mathbb{K}})$. This can be checked in Table 2, where we can see that the embeddings produce the intents in $\mathbb{B}^{\#}(\mathbb{K})$ with the minimum cardinality containing B.

3.3 An Algorithm for Computing the Mixed Lattice

In this, section, we present an algorithm to compute the mixed concept lattice $\mathbb{B}^{\#}(\mathbb{K})$ from the individual positive and negative lattices. It is based in the previous theoretical results about the decomposition of the intents of the mixed lattice. Furthermore, we will make use of other technical results to improve the performance of the algorithm:

Lemma 4 ([14]). *Let* $\mathbb{K} = (G, M, I)$ *be a formal context, and consider the associated mixed context. Then, the top concept of* $\mathbb{B}^{\#}(\mathbb{K})$ *is* $(G, G^{\Uparrow})$ *and its bottom concept is* $(\varnothing, M\overline{M})$.

For the second result, we need to define the notion of *consistent* set.

Definition 1. *A set A is said to be* consistent *if $A \cap \overline{A} = \varnothing$ or, equivalently, if* $\mathrm{Pos}(A) \cap \mathrm{Neg}(A) = \varnothing$, *that is, if it does not contain a given attribute and its negation.*

Lemma 5 ([13]). *Let $\mathbb{K} = (G, M, I)$ be a formal context, and consider the associated mixed lattice $\underline{\mathbb{B}}^{\#}(\mathbb{K})$. The intent of all the concepts but $(\varnothing, M\overline{M})$ are consistent sets.*

These results allow us to propose the Algorithm 1. This algorithm iterates through all the concepts in the positive lattice $\mathbb{B}(\mathbb{K})$, and for each concept (A, B) it computes the concept (C, D) given by Lemma 3, so that $(A, B \cup D)$ is indeed a mixed concept and is added to the result $\mathbb{L}$ (lines 3 – 4). Then, a queue Q is built consisting of all proper subconcepts of (C, D), excluding the bottom of $\mathbb{B}(\overline{\mathbb{K}})$ (line 5). This way, we avoid duplicating concepts in the enumeration. After this, the algorithm picks one element (C_1, D_1) of the queue in each iteration, builds the following candidate intent B_* and its corresponding intent $X = A \cap C_1$ (lines 7 – 8). If $X = \varnothing$, this means that B_* (and its closure $B_*^{\Downarrow\Uparrow} = X^{\Uparrow}$) is not *consistent*, therefore they cannot be the intents of any concept in the mixed lattice, according to Lemma 5. In this case, all the subconcepts of (C_1, D_1) will verify this same condition, hence they are removed from the queue Q (lines 9 – 11). The last comprobation (lines 12 – 13) adds (X, B_*) to $\mathbb{L}$ only if B_* is closed in the mixed context. Finally, the algorithm returns $\mathbb{L} \cup \{\varnothing, M\overline{M}\}$, since this latter is the only known (Lemma 4) concept not included in the previous steps (line 14).

Algorithm 1: Compute Mixed Concepts

Input: $\mathbb{B}(\mathbb{K})$: The lattice associated to $\mathbb{K}$. $\mathbb{B}(\overline{\mathbb{K}})$: The lattice associated to $\overline{\mathbb{K}}$.
Output: $\underline{\mathbb{B}}^{\#}(\mathbb{K})$

1 $\mathbb{L} := \varnothing$
2 **for** $(A, B) \in \mathbb{B}(\mathbb{K})$ **do**
3      $\quad (C, D) := \Delta_+^-(A, B) = \pi_-(A, A^{\Uparrow})$
4      $\quad \mathbb{L} \leftarrow \mathbb{L} \cup \{(A, B \cup D)\}$
5      $\quad Q := \{(C_1, D_1) \in \mathbb{B}(\overline{\mathbb{K}}) : \bot < (C_1, D_1) < (C, D)\}$
6      $\quad$ **for** $(C_1, D_1) \in Q$ **do**
7          $\quad\quad B_* := B \cup D_1$
8          $\quad\quad X := B_*^{\Downarrow} = A \cap C_1$
9          $\quad\quad$ **if** $|X| = 0$ **then**
10             $\quad\quad\quad$ Remove from Q all subconcepts of (C_1, D_1)
11             $\quad\quad\quad$ Go to line #6
12         $\quad\quad$ **if** $B_* = X^{\Uparrow}$ **then**
13             $\quad\quad\quad \mathbb{L} \leftarrow \mathbb{L} \cup \{(X, B_*)\}$

14 **return** $\underline{\mathbb{B}}^{\#}(\mathbb{K}) = \mathbb{L} \cup \{(\varnothing, M\overline{M})\}$

Next, we sketch a single step of Algorithm 1, starting in a specific concept $(A, B) \in \mathbb{B}_+(\mathbb{K})$, to show the procedure in more detail.

1. For $(A, B) = (\{o1, o2, o5, o7\}, \{b\})$, we compute $D = \varnothing$ using the operator Δ_+^-. Then $(A, B \cup D) = (A, B)$ is added to $\mathbb{L}$.
2. The queue is $Q = \{\{\overline{d}\}, \{\overline{c}\}, \{\overline{c}, \overline{d}\}, \{\overline{b}\}, \{\overline{b}, \overline{d}\}, \{\overline{b}, \overline{c}\}, \{\overline{a}\}, \{\overline{a}, \overline{d}\}, \{\overline{a}, \overline{c}\}, \{\overline{a}, \overline{b}, \overline{d}\}\}$.
3. We loop over the items in Q:
   (a) For $D_1 = \{\overline{d}\}$, we have $B_* = \{b, \overline{d}\}$ and $X = \{o2, o7\}$. Since $X^{\Uparrow} = B_*$, (X, B_*) is added to $\mathbb{L}$.
   (b) For $D_1 = \{\overline{c}\}$, it is $B_* = \{b, \overline{c}\}$ and $X = \{o1, o2\}$. As before, (X, B) is added to $\mathbb{L}$.
   (c) For $D_1 = \{\overline{c}, \overline{d}\}$, we have $B_* = \{b, \overline{c}, \overline{d}\}$ and $X = \{o2\}$. This pair is rejected since B_* is not closed: $X^{\Uparrow} = \{a, b, \overline{c}, \overline{d}\} \neq B_*$.
   (d) For $D_1 = \{\overline{b}\}$, we can compute $B_* = \{b, \overline{b}\}$ and then $X = \varnothing$. This means B_* is not consistent, so the algorithm removes $\{\{\overline{b}\}, \{\overline{b}, \overline{d}\}, \{\overline{b}, \overline{c}\}, \{\overline{a}, \overline{b}, \overline{d}\}\}$ from Q.
   (e) For $D_1 = \{\overline{a}\}$, we have $B_* = \{b, \overline{a}\}$ and $X = \{o1, o5, o7\}$. B_* is closed so we add (X, B_*) to $\mathbb{L}$.
   (f) For $D_1 = \{\overline{a}, \overline{d}\}$, it is $B_* = \{b, \overline{a}, \overline{d}\}$ and $X = \{o7\}$, but B_* is not closed: $X^{\Uparrow} = \{b, c, \overline{a}, \overline{d}\} \neq B_*$, so (X, B_*) is rejected.
   (g) For $D_1 = \{\overline{a}, \overline{c}\}$, we have $B_* = \{b, \overline{a}, \overline{c}\}$ and $X = \{o1\}$. As before, B_* is not closed so (X, B_*) is rejected.

Note that, if $\mathbb{B}(\mathbb{K})$ and Q are traversed in lectic order, then $\mathbb{B}^{\#}(\mathbb{K})$ is also built in lectic order.

4   Conclusions and Future Work

The classical FCA paradigm studies the presence of an attribute for an object and does not consider the absence of the attribute as information explicitly. In this paper, we adopt the line of modelling both positive and negative information, and present a line of work on the relationship between the concept lattices of formal contexts consisting of only positive or negative information, and the concept lattice when the mixture of both types of information is considered.

This line of work has as its starting point a series of theoretical results presented in this article. These results tell us how the individual lattices map onto the mixed lattice, thanks to some *embedding* and *projection* operators that, jointly, form Galois connections between the $\mathbb{B}(\mathbb{K})$ and $\mathbb{B}(\overline{\mathbb{K}})$ and the mixed lattice $\mathbb{B}^{\#}(\mathbb{K})$. Furthermore, we establish decomposition or representation results of the mixed concepts according to the closure operators induced by these Galois connections.

These decomposition results have allowed us to present a proposal of an algorithm for the computation of the concepts of the mixed lattice from the concepts of the individual lattices. Note that this algorithm requires to have precomputed $\mathbb{B}(\mathbb{K})$ and $\mathbb{B}(\overline{\mathbb{K}})$. But they can be computed in parallel.

As future work we aim to optimise this algorithm and exploit its *divide and conquer* strategy to build pyramid-like algorithms for the computation of massive concept lattices. Furthermore, the application of logic inference systems for mixed attributes may propose new strategies in this sense. In addition, we plan to apply all this results to the study of the minimal generators of the mixed lattice and of the implication bases of mixed contexts.

References

1. Cordero, P., Enciso, M., López, D., Mora, A.: A conversational recommender system for diagnosis using fuzzy rules. Expert Syst. Appl. **154**, 113449 (2020)
2. Cordero, P., Enciso, M., Mora, A., Ojeda-Aciego, M., Rossi, C.: Knowledge discovery in social networks by using a logic-based treatment of implications. Knowl. Based Syst. **87**, 16–25 (2015)
3. Cordero, P., Enciso, M., Mora, Á., Ojeda-Aciego, M., Rossi, C.: A formal concept analysis approach to cooperative conversational recommendation. Int. J. Comput. Intell. Syst. **13**, 1243–1252 (2020)
4. Ganter, B., Obiedkov, S.: More expressive variants of exploration. In: Conceptual Exploration, pp. 237–292. Springer, Heidelberg (2016). https://doi.org/10.1007/978-3-662-49291-8_6
5. Priss, U.: Diagrammatic representation of conceptual structures. In: Braud, A., Buzmakov, A., Hanika, T., Le Ber, F. (eds.) ICFCA 2021. LNCS (LNAI), vol. 12733, pp. 281–289. Springer, Cham (2021). https://doi.org/10.1007/978-3-030-77867-5_19
6. Gasmi, G., Yahia, S.B., Nguifo, E.M., Bouker, S.: Extraction of association rules based on literalsets. In: Song, I.Y., Eder, J., Nguyen, T.M. (eds.) DaWaK 2007. LNCS, vol. 4654, pp. 293–302. Springer, Heidelberg (2007). https://doi.org/10.1007/978-3-540-74553-2_27
7. Ibrahim, M.H., Missaoui, R., Vaillancourt, J.: Identifying influential nodes in two-mode data networks using formal concept analysis. IEEE Access **9**, 159549–159565 (2021)
8. Konecny, J.: Attribute implications in L-concept analysis with positive and negative attributes: validity and properties of models. Int. J. Approximate Reasoning **120**, 203–215 (2020)
9. Messaoudi, A., Missaoui, R., Ibrahim, M.-H.: Detecting overlapping communities in two-mode data networks using formal concept analysis. Revue des Nouvelles Technologies de l'Information, Extraction et Gestion des connaissances, RNTI-E-, **35** 189–200 2019
10. Missaoui, R., Nourine, L., Renaud, Y.: Generating positive and negative exact rules using formal concept analysis: problems and solutions. In: Medina, R., Obiedkov, S. (eds.) ICFCA 2008. LNCS (LNAI), vol. 4933, pp. 169–181. Springer, Heidelberg (2008). https://doi.org/10.1007/978-3-540-78137-0_13
11. Missaoui, R., Nourine, L., Renaud, Y.: Computing implications with negation from a formal context. Fund. Inform. **115**(4), 357–375 (2012)
12. Rodríguez-Jiménez, J.M., Cordero, P., Enciso, M., Mora, A.: Negative attributes and implications in formal concept analysis. Procedia Comput. Sci. **31**, 758–765 (2014)

13. Rodríguez-Jiménez, J., Cordero, P., Enciso, M., Rudolph, S.: Concept lattices with negative information: a characterization theorem. Inf. Sci. **369**, 51–62 (2016)
14. Rodríguez-Jiménez, J.M., Cordero, P., Enciso, M., Mora, A.: Data mining algorithms to compute mixed concepts with negative attributes: an application to breast cancer data analysis. Math. Methods Appli. Sci. **39**(16), 4829–4845 (2016)
15. Wille, R.: Restructuring lattice theory: an approach based on hierarchies of concepts. Ordered Sets **83**, 445–470 (1982)

On the Definition of Fuzzy Relational Galois Connections Between Fuzzy Transitive Digraphs

Inma P. Cabrera[1], Pablo Cordero[1], Emilio Muñoz-Velasco[1],
Manuel Ojeda-Aciego[1]([✉]), and Bernard De Baets[2]

[1] Departamento Matemática Aplicada, Universidad de Málaga, Málaga, Spain
{ipcabrera,pcordero,ejmunoz,aciego}@uma.es
[2] KERMIT, Department of Data Analysis and Mathematical Modelling,
Ghent University, Ghent, Belgium
Bernard.DeBaets@UGent.be

Abstract. We continue the study of different generalizations of the notion of Galois connection. Previously, we had focused on the cases in which both the domain and codomain had the structure of either a transitive digraph or a fuzzy transitive digraph. Here, we extend it to the fuzzy relational framework. Specifically, we present a suitable notion of fuzzy relational Galois connection between fuzzy transitive digraphs where both components are now fuzzy relations and the underlying truth value algebra is a complete Heyting algebra. The resulting notion of fuzzy relational Galois connection inherits interesting characterisations of the notion of (crisp) relational Galois connection.

Keywords: Galois connection · Transitive digraph · Fuzzy relation

1 Introduction

The notion of Galois connection [17] has been playing an important role in both mathematics and computer science [7] since it was introduced. One of our research lines is focused on the problem of constructing Galois connections: in a nutshell, given a mapping $f\colon A \to B$ between different structures (for instance, the domain A being a lattice and the codomain B a plain set), one wants to establish necessary and sufficient conditions under which it is possible to equip B with a desired structure and construct a mapping $g\colon B \to A$ such that the couple (f, g) is a Galois connection. It is important to note that the fact that A and B need not have the same structure rules out the application of Freyd's adjoint functor theorem.

There have been different efforts to extend the notion of Galois connection to the fuzzy setting, and the degrees of freedom that come along with such efforts usually result in different levels of generality, and this is no different for the notion of fuzzy Galois connection [1,2,8,9,11–16,18]. In previous works [3,4]

© Springer Nature Switzerland AG 2022
D. Ciucci et al. (Eds.): IPMU 2022, CCIS 1601, pp. 100–106, 2022.
https://doi.org/10.1007/978-3-031-08971-8_9

we explored the construction problem mentioned in the previous paragraph in various fuzzy settings, satisfactorily extending the problem to Galois connections between a fuzzy domain A and fuzzy range B. However, the proposed notion still has crisp functions as components, hence not obtaining a truly fuzzy notion of Galois connection.

Our approach to solve this situation is based on considering relations as components of the Galois connection. Recently, we focused on the cases of the domain A having the structure of a transitive digraph [5] or fuzzy transitive digraph [6], studying Galois connections whose left and right components are *crisp* relations satisfying certain reasonable properties expressed in terms of the so-called full powering. In this work, we expound for the first time an adequate notion of *fuzzy relational Galois connection* between fuzzy transitive digraphs, with both components now being *fuzzy* relations. The underlying algebraic setting for the truth values we are working with is that of a complete Heyting algebra. This notion of fuzzy relational Galois connection will be shown to inherit interesting equivalent characterizations of the notion of crisp Galois connection discussed in detail in [6].

2   Preliminary Notions

The framework considered in this work is that of $\mathbb{L}$-fuzzy set theory, where $\mathbb{L}$ is a complete Heyting algebra, which is an algebra $\mathbb{L} = (L, \leq, \perp, \top, \rightarrow)$, where $(L, \leq)$ is a complete lattice, $\perp$ is the bottom element, $\top$ is the top element, and the following adjointness property holds for all $p, q, r \in L$:

$$p \wedge q \leq r \qquad \text{if and only if} \qquad p \leq q \rightarrow r.$$

An $\mathbb{L}$-*fuzzy set* on a universe A (also called $\mathbb{L}$-*fuzzy subset* of A) is a mapping $X \colon A \rightarrow \mathbb{L}$ from A to the algebra $\mathbb{L}$ of membership degrees, where $X(a)$ denotes the degree to which element a belongs to X[1]. A fuzzy set X is said to be *normal* if $X(a) = \top$ for some $a \in A$. Any element $a \in A$ induces a *singleton*, i.e., a fuzzy set $a \colon A \rightarrow \mathbb{L}$ defined by $a(x) = \top$ if $x = a$ and $a(x) = \perp$ otherwise.

An $\mathbb{L}$-*fuzzy relation* between two universes A and B is a mapping $\mu \colon A \times B \rightarrow \mathbb{L}$, where $\mu(a, b)$ denotes the degree of relationship between the elements a and b. Given a fuzzy relation μ and an element $a \in A$, the *afterset* a^μ of a is the fuzzy set $a^\mu \colon B \rightarrow \mathbb{L}$ defined by $a^\mu(b) = \mu(a, b)$. A fuzzy relation μ is said to be *total* if the aftersets a^μ are normal, for all $a \in A$.

The composition of an $\mathbb{L}$-fuzzy relation μ between two universes A and B and an $\mathbb{L}$-fuzzy relation ν between B and a universe C is the $\mathbb{L}$-fuzzy relation $\mu \circ \nu$ between A and C defined by

$$\mu \circ \nu(a, c) = \bigvee_{b \in B} (\mu(a, b) \wedge \nu(b, c)).$$

An $\mathbb{L}$-fuzzy relation on a universe A is a mapping $\rho \colon A \times A \rightarrow \mathbb{L}$, and is said to be:

---

[1] For convenience, hereafter, we will always omit the prefix $\mathbb{L}$.

– *reflexive* if $\rho(a, a) = \top$, for all $a \in A$.
– *transitive* if $\rho(a, b) \wedge \rho(b, c) \leq \rho(a, c)$, for all $a, b, c \in A$; or, equivalently, $\rho \circ \rho(a, c) \leq \rho(a, c)$, for all $a, c \in A$.

Definition 1. $\mathbb{A} = \langle A, \rho \rangle$ *is said to be a* fuzzy T-digraph *if* ρ *is a transitive fuzzy relation on* A.

In order to extend the definition of a relational Galois connection to the fuzzy framework considered in this paper, we need the notions of antitone and inflationary fuzzy relations between fuzzy T-digraphs.

Definition 2. *Consider two fuzzy T-digraphs* $\langle A, \rho_A \rangle$ *and* $\langle B, \rho_B \rangle$. *A fuzzy relation* $\mu \colon A \times B \to \mathbb{L}$ *is said to be:*

– *antitone if* $\rho_A(a_1, a_2) \wedge \mu(a_1, b_1) \wedge \mu(a_2, b_2) \leq \rho_B(b_2, b_1)$, *for all* $a_1, a_2 \in A$ *and* $b_1, b_2 \in B$.
– *isotone if* $\rho_A(a_1, a_2) \wedge \mu(a_1, b_1) \wedge \mu(a_2, b_2) \leq \rho_B(b_1, b_2)$, *for all* $a_1, a_2 \in A$ *and* $b_1, b_2 \in B$.

Definition 3. *Let* $\langle A, \rho \rangle$ *be a fuzzy T-digraph. A fuzzy relation* $\mu \colon A \times A \to \mathbb{L}$ *is said to be:*

– *inflationary if* $\mu(a_1, a_2) \leq \rho(a_1, a_2)$, *for all* $a_1, a_2 \in A$.
– *idempotent if* $\rho(x, y) = \rho(y, x) = \top$, *for all* $a \in A$, $x \in a^{\mu}$ *and* $y \in a^{\mu \circ \mu}$.

We recall that in the characterisation of relational Galois connections in the crisp case, a key role was played by the notion of clique [5]. Not surprisingly, a fuzzy version of this notion will play a similar role here.

Definition 4. *Let* $\langle A, \rho \rangle$ *be a fuzzy T-digraph. A fuzzy set* $X \colon A \to \mathbb{L}$ *is called a* clique *if, for all* $x, y \in A$, *it holds that*

$$X(x) \wedge X(y) \leq \rho(x, y).$$

3 Fuzzy Powerings: Extending Relations to Fuzzy Powersets

Given a relation R on a set A, it is possible to lift R to the powerset 2^A by defining the following *powerings*, for all $X, Y \in 2^A$, which correspond to the construction of the Hoare, Smyth and full powersets, respectively:

$$X \, R_H \, Y \quad \Longleftrightarrow \quad (\forall x \in X)(\exists y \in Y)(xRy)$$
$$X \, R_S \, Y \quad \Longleftrightarrow \quad (\forall y \in Y)(\exists x \in X)(xRy)$$
$$X \, R_\propto \, Y \quad \Longleftrightarrow \quad (\forall x \in X)(\forall y \in Y)(xRy).$$

Note that if R is reflexive and transitive, then the two first relations defined above are actually preorder relations, specifically those used in the construction of the, respectively, Hoare and Smyth powerdomains; the third one need not be either reflexive nor transitive, and was introduced as a convenient tool to develop relational Galois connections. Nevertheless, it satisfies the following weakened version of transitivity:

$$\text{if } X R_\propto Y, \text{ and } Y R_\propto Z, \text{ where } Y \neq \varnothing, \text{ then } X R_\propto Z. \tag{1}$$

Furthermore, it is worth noting that the powerings can be defined for any relation not necessarily being a preorder.

The adaptation of these powerings to the present fuzzy framework is explained next [10].

Definition 5. *Consider a fuzzy T-digraph* $\langle A, \rho \rangle$. *We define the Hoare, Smyth and full fuzzy powerings as follows, for any* $X, Y \colon A \to \mathbb{L}$:

(i) $\rho_H(X, Y) = \bigwedge\limits_{x \in A} \left(X(x) \to \bigvee\limits_{y \in A} (Y(y) \wedge \rho(x, y)) \right)$;

(ii) $\rho_S(X, Y) = \bigwedge\limits_{y \in A} \left(Y(y) \to \bigvee\limits_{x \in A} (X(x) \wedge \rho(x, y)) \right)$;

(iii) $\rho_\propto(X, Y) = \bigwedge\limits_{x \in A} \bigwedge\limits_{y \in A} (X(x) \wedge Y(y) \to \rho(x, y))$.

As in the crisp case, both Hoare and Smyth powerings are reflexive and transitive fuzzy relations on L^A whenever ρ is. Once again, full fuzzy powering is somehow transitive in the same sense as in (1).

Lemma 1. *Consider a fuzzy T-digraph* $\langle A, \rho \rangle$ *and fuzzy sets* $X, Y, Z \colon A \to \mathbb{L}$. *If* Y *is normal, then* $\rho_\propto(X, Y) \wedge \rho_\propto(Y, Z) \leq \rho_\propto(X, Z)$.

In the particular case of *singletons* in the first argument of the fuzzy powerings, the expressions in the above definitions are greatly simplified. Indeed, for all $a \in A$, it holds:

(i) $\rho_H(a, Y) = \bigvee\limits_{y \in A} (Y(y) \wedge \rho(a, y))$;

(ii) $\rho_S(a, Y) = \rho_\propto(a, Y) = \bigwedge\limits_{y \in A} (Y(y) \to \rho(a, y))$.

Notice that cliques can be characterized in terms of this relations: a fuzzy set $X \colon A \to \mathbb{L}$ is called a clique if $\rho_\propto(X, X) = \top$.

The following lemma establishes the relationship between the fuzzy powerings defined above.

Lemma 2. *Consider a fuzzy T-digraph* $\langle A, \rho \rangle$, *a fuzzy set* $X \colon A \to \mathbb{L}$ *and* $a \in A$.

(i) *If* X *is a normal fuzzy set, then*

$$\rho_S(a, X) = \rho_\propto(a, X) \leq \rho_H(a, X).$$

(ii) If X is a clique, then

$$\rho_H(a, X) \le \rho_S(a, X) = \rho_\propto(a, X).$$

Finally, notions of antitone/isotone fuzzy relations, inflationarity and idempotency can be stated in terms of the full fuzzy powering $\propto$.

Consider two fuzzy T-digraphs $\langle A, \rho_A \rangle$ and $\langle B, \rho_B \rangle$. A fuzzy relation $\mu\colon A \times B \to \mathbb{L}$ is said to be:

- *antitone* if $\rho_A(a_1, a_2) \le \rho_{B\propto}(a_2^\mu, a_1^\mu)$, for all $a_1, a_2 \in A$ and $b_1, b_2 \in B$.
- *isotone* if $\rho_A(a_1, a_2) \le \rho_{B\propto}(a_1^\mu, a_2^\mu)$, for all $a_1, a_2 \in A$ and $b_1, b_2 \in B$.

Let $\langle A, \rho \rangle$ be a fuzzy T-digraph. A fuzzy relation $\mu\colon A \times A \to \mathbb{L}$ is said to be:

- *inflationary* if $\rho_\propto(a, a^\mu) = \top$, for all $a \in A$.
- *idempotent* if $\rho_\propto(a^{\mu \circ \mu}, a^\mu) = \top$ and $\rho_\propto(a^\mu, a^{\mu \circ \mu}) = \top$, for all $a \in A$.

4   Fuzzy Relational Galois Connections Between Fuzzy T-Digraphs

The next definition follows the classical approach of Galois connection instantiated on fuzzy transitive digraphs.

Definition 6. *Consider two fuzzy T-digraphs $\langle A, \rho_A \rangle$ and $\langle B, \rho_B \rangle$ and two total fuzzy relations $\mu\colon A \times B \to \mathbb{L}$ and $\nu\colon B \times A \to \mathbb{L}$. We say that the couple (μ, ν) is a fuzzy relational Galois connection if both μ and ν are antitone and both $\mu \circ \nu$ and $\nu \circ \mu$ are inflationary.*

This definition is usually followed by a characterization in terms of the so-called Galois condition. We explore if it remains valid on this framework.

Definition 7. *Consider two fuzzy T-digraphs $\langle A, \rho_A \rangle$ and $\langle B, \rho_B \rangle$ and two total fuzzy relations $\mu\colon A \times B \to \mathbb{L}$ and $\nu\colon B \times A \to \mathbb{L}$. We say that the couple (μ, ν) satisfies the fuzzy Galois condition if the following holds for all $a_1, a_2 \in A$ and $b_1, b_2 \in B$:*

(i) $\rho_A(a_1, a_2) \wedge \mu(a_1, b_1) \wedge \nu(b_2, a_2) \le \rho_B(b_2, b_1)$;
(ii) $\rho_B(b_2, b_1) \wedge \mu(a_1, b_1) \wedge \nu(b_2, a_2) \le \rho_A(a_1, a_2)$;

or, equivalently, for all $a \in A$ and $b \in B$:

(i) $\rho_{AH}(a, b^\nu) \le \rho_{BS}(b, a^\mu)$;
(ii) $\rho_{BH}(b, a^\mu) \le \rho_{AS}(a, b^\nu)$.

The following example shows that the fuzzy Galois condition is not sufficient to ensure that a couple of fuzzy relations is a fuzzy relational Galois connection.

Example 1. Consider the fuzzy T-digraphs $\mathbb{A} = \langle \{a_1, a_2, a_3, a_4\}, \rho_A \rangle$ and $\mathbb{B} = \langle \{b_1, b_2, b_3\}, \rho_B \rangle$, and the fuzzy relations $\mu : A \times B \to [0, 1]$ and $\nu : B \times A \to [0, 1]$ defined below:

ρ_A	a_1	a_2	a_3	a_4
a_1	0.5	1	1	0
a_2	0.5	1	1	0
a_3	0.5	0.5	1	0
a_4	0	0	0	1

ρ_B	b_1	b_2	b_3
b_1	1	0	0
b_2	0	1	1
b_3	0	1	1

μ	b_1	b_2	b_3
a_1	1	0.5	0
a_2	1	0.4	0
a_3	1	0.3	0
a_4	0	0	1

ν	a_1	a_2	a_3	a_4
b_1	0	0.5	1	0
b_2	0	0	0	1
b_3	0	0	0	1

It is routine to check that (μ, ν) satisfies the fuzzy Galois condition, although it is not a fuzzy relational Galois connection, since $\mu \circ \nu$ is not inflationary. Indeed, for instance, $(\mu \circ \nu)(a_1, a_4) = 0.5 \not\leq \rho_A(a_1, a_4) = 0$. □

As said above, we need to add the clique condition to the aftersets in order to get the desired characterization.

Theorem 1. *Consider two fuzzy T-digraphs $\langle A, \rho_A \rangle$ and $\langle B, \rho_B \rangle$ and two total fuzzy relations $\mu \colon A \times B \to \mathbb{L}$ and $\nu \colon B \times A \to \mathbb{L}$. The couple (μ, ν) is a fuzzy relational Galois connection between $\langle A, \rho_A \rangle$ and $\langle B, \rho_B \rangle$ if and only if the following conditions hold:*

(i) (μ, ν) satisfies the fuzzy Galois condition;
(ii) a^μ and b^ν are cliques, for all $a \in A$ and $b \in B$.

Now, by using Lemma 2, we can give the previous result in terms of the full powering where the fuzzy Galois condition can be expressed as an equality.

Corollary 1. *Consider two fuzzy T-digraphs $\langle A, \rho_A \rangle$ and $\langle B, \rho_B \rangle$ and two total fuzzy relations $\mu \colon A \times B \to \mathbb{L}$ and $\nu \colon B \times A \to \mathbb{L}$. The couple (μ, ν) is a fuzzy relational Galois connection between $\langle A, \rho_A \rangle$ and $\langle B, \rho_B \rangle$ if and only if the following conditions hold, for all $a \in A$ and $b \in B$:*

(i) $\rho_{A\alpha}(a, b^\nu) = \rho_{B\alpha}(b, a^\mu)$;
(ii) a^μ and b^ν are cliques.

5   Conclusions and Future Works

A new generalization of the notion of Galois connection has been introduced. Building upon previous approaches, we have given a suitable notion of *fuzzy relational Galois connection* between fuzzy transitive digraphs where both components are fuzzy relations and the underlying truth values belong to a complete Heyting algebra. The resulting notion inherits interesting properties of the notion of crisp relational Galois connection.

As immediate future work, working with this definition, we will focus on the characterisation of existence and the construction of the right adjoint to a mapping from a fuzzy T-digraph to an unstructured set.

Acknowledgements. Partially supported by the Spanish Ministry of Science, Innovation, and Universities (MCIU), State Agency of Research (AEI), Junta de Andalucía (JA), Universidad de Málaga (UMA) and European Regional Development Fund (FEDER) through the projects PGC2018-095869-B-I00 and TIN2017-89023-P (MCIU/AEI/FEDER), and UMA2018-FEDERJA-001 (JA/UMA/FEDER).

References

1. Bělohlávek, R.: Fuzzy Galois connections. Math. Log. Q. **45**(4), 497–504 (1999)
2. Bělohlávek, R., Osička, P.: Triadic fuzzy Galois connections as ordinary connections. Fuzzy Sets Syst. **249**, 83–99 (2014)
3. Cabrera, I., Cordero, P., Garcia-Pardo, F., Ojeda-Aciego, M., De Baets, B.: On the construction of adjunctions between a fuzzy preposet and an unstructured set. Fuzzy Sets Syst. **320**, 81–92 (2017)
4. Cabrera, I., Cordero, P., Garcia-Pardo, F., Ojeda-Aciego, M., De Baets, B.: Galois connections between a fuzzy preordered structure and a general fuzzy structure. IEEE Trans. Fuzzy Syst. **26**(3), 1274–1287 (2018)
5. Cabrera, I., Cordero, P., Muñoz-Velasco, E., Ojeda-Aciego, M., De Baets, B.: Relational Galois connections between transitive digraphs: characterization and construction. Inf. Sci. **519**, 439–450 (2020)
6. Cabrera, I., Cordero, P., Muñoz-Velasco, E., Ojeda-Aciego, M., De Baets, B.: Relational Galois connections between transitive fuzzy digraphs. Math. Methods Appl. Sci. **43**(9), 5673–5680 (2020)
7. Denecke, K., Erné, M., Wismath, S.L.: Galois Connections and Applications, vol. 565. Springer, Dordrecht (2004). https://doi.org/10.1007/978-1-4020-1898-5
8. Djouadi, Y., Prade, H.: Interval-valued fuzzy Galois connections: Aaebraic requirements and concept lattice construction. Fund. Inform. **99**(2), 169–186 (2010)
9. Frascella, A.: Fuzzy Galois connections under weak conditions. Fuzzy Sets Syst. **172**(1), 33–50 (2011)
10. Georgescu, G.: Fuzzy power structures. Arch. Math. Logic **47**(3), 233–261 (2008)
11. Georgescu, G., Popescu, A.: Non-commutative fuzzy Galois connections. Soft. Comput. **7**(7), 458–467 (2003)
12. Georgescu, G., Popescu, A.: Non-commutative fuzzy structures and pairs of weak negations. Fuzzy Sets Syst. **143**(1), 129–155 (2004)
13. Gutiérrez-García, J., Lai, H., Shen, L.: Fuzzy Galois connections on fuzzy sets. Fuzzy Sets Syst. **352**, 26–55 (2018)
14. Gutiérrez-García, J., Mardones-Pérez, I., de Prada-Vicente, M., Zhang, D.: Fuzzy Galois connections categorically. Math. Logic Q. **56**(2), 131–147 (2010)
15. Konecny, J.: Isotone fuzzy Galois connections with hedges. Inf. Sci. **181**, 1804–1817 (2011)
16. Oh, J.-M., Kim, Y.-C.: Fuzzy Galois connections on Alexandrov L-topologies. J. Intell. Fuzzy Syst. **40**(1), 251–270 (2021)
17. Ore, Ø.: Galois connexions. Trans. AMS **55**, 493–513 (1944)
18. Yao, W., Lu, L.-X.: Fuzzy Galois connections on fuzzy posets. Math. Log. Q. **55**(1), 105–112 (2009)

Study on the Necessity Operator
to Factorize Formal Contexts
in a Multi-adjoint Framework

Roberto G. Aragón$^{(\boxtimes)}$ ⓘ, Jesús Medina ⓘ, and Eloísa Ramírez-Poussa ⓘ

Department of Mathematics, University of Cádiz, Cádiz, Spain
{roberto.aragon,jesus.medina,eloisa.ramirez}@uca.es

Abstract. Dubois and Prade have already shown that the necessity operator is helpful in the decomposition of Boolean data tables into independent sub-tables. In this paper, we carry out a preliminary study on the properties satisfied by the necessity operator to factorize formal contexts. We will see what properties this operator satisfies in the classical framework and how these properties are translated into more general frameworks, such as the fuzzy framework provided by the multi-adjoint paradigm.

Keywords: formal concept analysis · factorization · multi-adjoint framework · modal operators

1 Introduction

Formal Concept Analysis (FCA for short) is a mathematical theory developed by Ganter and Wille [16] that allows to extract knowledge from relational databases. This formal theory is used to represent the information by means of the algebraic structure of a complete lattice and it also allows us to discover the existing dependencies among data. Specifically, FCA uses the duality between objects and attributes/properties in a Boolean data table, and different approaches have been analyzed in order to gather valuable information from both, the theoretical and applied perspectives.

Different fuzzy extensions of FCA have been already developed [2,9]. One of them is the fuzzy generalization provided by the multi-adjoint framework [21]. The latter was introduced as a generalization of different existing fuzzy approaches and the advantages of the use of this framework have been studied in some papers such as [1,12,13,19].

One of the strategies applied to FCA, in order to reduce the complexity of data processing, is the factorization of formal contexts by developing algorithms that allow obtaining factors (smaller tables) of Boolean tables [8,15]. In [15], the authors used the proper tools of possibility theory to obtain independent subcontexts from a formal context, by means of the modal operators that can be

© Springer Nature Switzerland AG 2022
D. Ciucci et al. (Eds.): IPMU 2022, CCIS 1601, pp. 107–117, 2022.
https://doi.org/10.1007/978-3-031-08971-8_10

defined on the context. Furthermore, we also can find different fuzzy extensions of factorization algorithms, as the ones presented in [3–7,18].

In this paper, we are interested in obtaining a factorization mechanism to simplify the analysis of multi-adjoint contexts, following the philosophy considered in [15]. With that goal, we present an initial study about the necessity operators applied to both, classical FCA and the generalized multi-adjoint framework. This study provides a first step to know different properties that allow us to better understand the behavior of the factorization procedure in the classical environment and how these properties are transferred to the considered fuzzy framework, with the goal of being able to determine subsequently independent subcontexts of a multi-adjoint context.

The paper is organized in the following way: the preliminary notions and results necessary to develop this work are recalled in Sect. 2. Afterwards, the contribution is presented in two parts: the study corresponding to the classical framework is presented in Sect. 3 and the generalization to the multi-adjoint framework is introduced in Sect. 4. Finally, conclusions and future works are presented in Sect. 5.

2   Preliminaries

In this section, we recall some notions related to FCA and its fuzzy generalization to the multi-adjoint framework, that have been considered to develop this work. In order to present the preliminary notions as clearly as possible, we will divide this section into two parts: the first one will be focused on basic notions of FCA and classical modal operators and the second one is focused on the generalizations of the same notions to the multi-adjoint framework.

2.1   Formal Concept Analysis

Firstly, a context in FCA is a triple (A, B, R) where A is a set of attributes, B is a set of objects and $R \subseteq A \times B$ is a relationship such that $(a, b) \in R$, if the object $b \in B$ possesses the attribute $a \in A$. Moreover, The mappings $\uparrow : 2^B \to 2^A$ and $\downarrow : 2^A \to 2^B$ defined as follow:

$$X^\uparrow = \{a \in A \mid (a, b) \in R \text{ for all } b \in X\}$$
$$Y^\downarrow = \{b \in B \mid (a, b) \in R \text{ for all } a \in Y\}$$

with $X \subseteq B$ and $Y \subseteq A$, are called *derivation operators*. The pair $(\uparrow, \downarrow)$ forms an antitone Galois connection. Furthermore, a pair (X, Y), with $X \subseteq B$ and $Y \subseteq A$, satisfying that $X^\uparrow = Y$ and $Y^\downarrow = X$, is called a *concept*. The subset X is called the *extent* of the concept and the subset Y is called the *intent*, and they are denoted by $\text{Ext}((X, Y))$ and $\text{Int}((X, Y))$, respectively. In addition, all the concepts together with the inclusion ordering on the left argument has the algebraic structure of a complete lattice, which is called *concept lattice* and it is denoted by $\mathcal{C}(A, B, R)$.

The derivation operators previously presented are not the only operators that can be defined on a formal context, there are other modal operators that can be defined for each subset of objects $X \subseteq B$ and $Y \subseteq A$ [14,17,22]. Consider the mappings $\uparrow_\pi : 2^B \to 2^A$, $\downarrow^N : 2^A \to 2^B$, defined as follow:

$$X^{\uparrow_\pi} = \{a \in A \mid \text{ there exists } b \in X, \text{ such that } (a,b) \in R\}$$
$$Y^{\downarrow^N} = \{b \in B \mid \text{ for all } a \in A, \text{ if } (a,b) \in R, \text{ then } a \in Y\},$$

are called *possibility and necessity operator*, respectively. Analogously, the mappings $\uparrow_N : 2^B \to 2^A$, $\downarrow^\pi : 2^A \to 2^B$ are defined as:

$$X^{\uparrow_N} = \{a \in A \mid \text{ for all } b \in B, \text{ if } (a,b) \in R, \text{ then } b \in X\}$$
$$Y^{\downarrow^\pi} = \{b \in B \mid \text{ there exists } a \in Y, \text{ such that } (a,b) \in R\}$$

The pairs $(\uparrow_\pi, \downarrow^N)$ and $(\uparrow_N, \downarrow^\pi)$ form isotone Galois connections and, as a consequence, they can be used to obtain concept lattices. The obtained concept lattices are called *property-oriented concept lattice* and *object-oriented concept lattice* [10,20].

2.2   Multi-adjoint Framework

As we previously commented, in this work we also consider the fuzzy generalization of FCA given by the multi-adjoint framework [21]. Then, we recall the fuzzy generalizations of the previous notions to the multi-adjoint frame.

First of all, the operators called adjoint triples [11] need to be recalled.

Definition 1. *Let* $(P_1, \leq_1)$, $(P_2, \leq_2)$, $(P_3, \leq_3)$ *be posets and* $\& : P_1 \times P_2 \to P_3$, $\swarrow : P_3 \times P_2 \to P_1$, $\nwarrow : P_3 \times P_1 \to P_2$ *be mappings, then* $(\&, \swarrow, \nwarrow)$ *is an* adjoint triple *with respect to* P_1, P_2, P_3 *if:*

$$x \leq_1 z \swarrow y \quad \text{iff} \quad x \& y \leq_3 z \quad \text{iff} \quad y \leq_2 z \nwarrow x \tag{1}$$

where $x \in P_1$, $y \in P_2$ *and* $z \in P_3$. *The condition* (1) *is called* adjoint property.

Furthermore, in order to define the notion of multi-adjoint context, we have to fix an algebraic structure called multi-adjoint frame.

Definition 2. *A* multi-adjoint frame *is a tuple* $(L_1, L_2, P, \&_1, \ldots, \&_n)$, *where* $(L_1, \preceq_1)$ *and* $(L_2, \preceq_2)$ *are complete lattices,* $(P, \leq)$ *is a poset and* $(\&_i, \swarrow^i, \nwarrow_i)$ *is an adjoint triple with respect to* L_1, L_2, P, *for all* $i \in \{1, \ldots, n\}$.

Once a multi-adjoint frame is fixed, the notion of multi-adjoint context is defined as follows.

Definition 3. *Let* $(L_1, L_2, P, \&_1, \ldots, \&_n)$ *be a multi-adjoint frame, a* multi-adjoint context *is a tuple* (A, B, R, σ) *such that* A *and* B *are non-empty sets (usually interpreted as attributes and objects, respectively),* R *is a* P-*fuzzy relation* $R : A \times B \to P$ *and* $\sigma : A \times B \to \{1, \ldots, n\}$ *is a mapping which associates any element in* $A \times B$ *to some particular adjoint triple of the frame.*

In addition, the generalization of derivation operators $\uparrow: L_2^B \to L_1^A$ and $\downarrow: L_1^A \to L_2^B$ are given as follows:

$$g^\uparrow(a) = \inf\{R(a,b) \swarrow^{\sigma(a,b)} g(b) \mid b \in B\}$$
$$f^\downarrow(b) = \inf\{R(a,b) \searrow_{\sigma(a,b)} f(a) \mid a \in A\}$$

for all $g \in L_2^B$, $f \in L_1^A$ and $a \in A$, $b \in B$, where L_2^B and L_1^A denote the set of mappings $g: B \to L_2$ and $f: A \to L_1$, respectively.

Equivalently, a *multi-adjoint concept* is a pair $\langle g, f \rangle$, where $g \in L_2^B$ is a fuzzy subset of objects and $f \in L_1^A$ is a fuzzy subset of attributes, satisfying that $g^\uparrow = f$ and $g^\downarrow = g$. Furthermore, the notion of multi-adjoint concept lattice is formalized in the following definition.

Definition 4. *The* multi-adjoint concept lattice *associated with a multi-adjoint frame* $(L_1, L_2, P, \&_1, \ldots, \&_n)$ *and a multi-adjoint context* (A, B, R, σ) *given, is the set*

$$\mathcal{M} = \{\langle g, f \rangle \mid g \in L_2^B, f \in L_1^A \text{ and } g^\uparrow = f, f^\downarrow = g\}$$

where the ordering is defined by $\langle g_1, f_1 \rangle \preceq \langle g_2, f_2 \rangle$ *if and only if* $g_1 \preceq_2 g_2$ *(equivalently* $f_2 \preceq_1 f_1$*), for all* $\langle g_1, f_1 \rangle, \langle g_2, f_2 \rangle \in \mathcal{M}$.

Similarly to what we have shown for the classical environment, the operators $\uparrow$ and $\downarrow$ are not the only operators that can be defined on a multi-adjoint context. The classical definitions of the necessity and possibility operators were also generalized in a fuzzy framework [19] where two complete lattices $(L_1, \preceq_1), (L_2, \preceq_2)$ and a poset $(P, \leq)$ are fixed. A multi-adjoint property-oriented frame is given by $(L_1, L_2, P, \&_1, \ldots, \&_n)$, where $(\&_i, \swarrow^i, \searrow_i)$ is an adjoint triple with respect to P, L_2, L_1 for all $i \in \{1, \ldots, n\}$. In this multi-adjoint algebra, the necessity and possibility operators are the mappings $\downarrow^N: L_1^A \to L_2^B$, $\uparrow^\pi: L_2^B \to L_1^A$, defined as:

$$g^{\uparrow^\pi}(a) = \sup\{R(a,b) \,\&_{\sigma(a,b)}\, g(b) \mid b \in B\}$$
$$f^{\downarrow^N}(b) = \inf\{f(a) \searrow_{\sigma(a,b)} R(a,b) \mid a \in A\}$$

for all $a \in A, b \in B, g \in L_2^B$ and $f \in L_1^A$. A multi-adjoint object-oriented frame is the tuple $(L_1, L_2, P, \&_1, \ldots, \&_n)$, where $(\&_i, \swarrow^i, \searrow_i)$ is an adjoint triple with respect to L_1, P, L_2 for all $i \in \{1, \ldots, n\}$. In this algebra these operators are given by the mappings $\uparrow^N: L_2^B \to L_1^A$, $\downarrow^\pi: L_1^A \to L_2^B$ defined as:

$$g^{\uparrow^N}(a) = \inf\{g(b) \swarrow^{\sigma(a,b)} R(a,b) \mid b \in B\}$$
$$f^{\downarrow^\pi}(b) = \sup\{f(a) \,\&_{\sigma(a,b)}\, R(a,b) \mid a \in A\}$$

for all $a \in A, b \in B, g \in L_2^B$ and $f \in L_1^A$. Notice that the pairs of operators $(\uparrow^\pi, \downarrow^N)$ and $(\uparrow^N, \downarrow^\pi)$ are isotone Galois connections.

Once a multi-adjoint frame has been fixed, we can obtain a multi-adjoint object-oriented frame and a multi-adjoint property-oriented frame by considering the dual orderings on the lattices and the poset of the multi-adjoint frame. For a more detailed information about the existing relationship among the multi-adjoint, the multi-adjoint objecto-riented and the multi-adjoint property-oriented frames, we refer the readers to [19]. Additionally, a multi-adjoint property-oriented concept lattice is denoted by $\mathcal{M}_{\pi N}$, and a multi-adjoint object-oriented concept lattice is denoted by $\mathcal{M}_{N\pi}$.

3   Properties of the Factorization in Classic FCA

In [15], one of the four set-functions of possibility theory is used to characterize independent subcontexts of a given context. In particular, the pair of operator of actual necessity, $(^{\uparrow N}, ^{\downarrow^N})$ is considered to decompose the relation R of a context (A, B, R), by computing the following intersection:

$$R^* = \bigcap \{ (X \times Y) \cup (X^c \times Y^c) \mid X \subseteq B, Y \subseteq A, X^{\uparrow N} = Y, Y^{\downarrow^N} = X \}$$

where X^c and Y^c are the complements of X and Y, respectively.

From the study presented in [15], we can bring to light some interesting properties from a pair of non-empty subsets $X \subseteq B$, $Y \subseteq A$, that satisfies the following equalities:

$$X^{\uparrow N} = Y \text{ and } Y^{\downarrow^N} = X, \tag{2}$$

The set of all pairs satisfying Expression (2) will be denoted by $\mathcal{C}_N$, that is,

$$\mathcal{C}_N = \{ (X, Y) \mid X \subseteq B, Y \subseteq A, X^{\uparrow N} = Y, Y^{\downarrow^N} = X \}$$

Therefore, in this section, we analyze these properties since it would allow us to know better how the decomposition of Boolean data tables into independent subcontexts works. This fact is essential to be able to extend this factorization procedure to more general environments, such as the fuzzy case provided by the multi-adjoint framework. In the following, we assume that the data table has neither empty rows nor attributes that are possessed by all objects in the context.

The first property relates the equalities given in Expression (2) to the formal concepts associated with the context.

Proposition 1. Let (A, B, R) be a formal context and $(X, Y) \in \mathcal{C}_N$. If $X^\uparrow \neq \varnothing$, then the pair $(X, X^\uparrow)$ is a concept, that is, $X^{\uparrow\downarrow} = X$.

Dually, we can obtain that the pair $(Y^\downarrow, Y)$ is a concept, when the condition $Y^\downarrow \neq \varnothing$ holds.

The following result shows when the top element of the independent subcontext differentiates from the top of the original concept lattice.

Proposition 2. Let (A, B, R) be a formal context and $(X, Y) \in \mathcal{C}_N$. If $X^\uparrow \neq \varnothing$, then there is no concept $(X_0, Y_0) \in \mathcal{C}(A, B, R)$ such that $(X, X^\uparrow) < (X_0, Y_0) < (B, \varnothing^{\downarrow\uparrow})$.

Consequently, in the previous result it is shown a comparison of the pair $(X, X^\uparrow)$ with the top element of the concept lattice associated with the original concept, and it has been proved that this top element is the concept directly greater than $(X, X^\uparrow)$. A similar result can be stated by duality for the pair $(Y^\downarrow, Y)$.

Now, the following result analyzes the relationship between $(X, X^\uparrow)$ and $(Y^\downarrow, Y)$, when they are concepts.

Proposition 3. *Given a formal context (A, B, R) and a pair $(X, Y) \in \mathcal{C}_N$ and the inequalities $X^\uparrow \neq \varnothing$ and $Y^\downarrow \neq \varnothing$, then we have that the concept generated by $(X, X^\uparrow)$ is greater than $(Y^\downarrow, Y)$, that is, $Y^\downarrow \subseteq X$.*

Observe that in all the previous results, we are requiring that there exists at least one attribute in the subcontext which is shared by all the objects of the considered subcontext, that is, if we consider the context $(X, Y, R_{X \times Y})$ where $R_{X \times Y}$ denotes the restriction of the relation R to the subsets X and Y, it is satisfied that $X^\uparrow \neq \varnothing$ (equivalently $Y^\downarrow \neq \varnothing$ indicates the existence of at least one object that possesses all the attributes of the subcontext). These requirements guarantee that the concept lattices associated with independent subcontexts do not have any concept in common, i.e., the factorization gives rise to a partition of the original concept lattice.

Notice that the pairs $(X, X^\uparrow)$ and $(Y^\downarrow, Y)$ do not necessarily have to be concepts from the original concept lattice. This occurs when the condition $X^\uparrow = \varnothing$ (or $Y^\downarrow = \varnothing$) is not taken into account. In this case, we can find more than one concept that satisfies Proposition 2 and 3, that is, there exist maximal elements satisfying these properties (equivalently with the minimal elements, when $Y^\downarrow = \varnothing$ holds). Therefore, when several independent subcontexts satisfy this condition, the top elements of the concept lattices associated with these independents subcontexts coincide, and it is the top element of the original context (similarly, when the condition $Y^\downarrow = \varnothing$ holds, the bottom elements of the concept lattices coincide).

4   Properties of the Factorization in the Multi-adjoint Framework

As we commented in the introduction, we are interested in generalizing the factorization of formal contexts into independent subcontexts in the fuzzy environment provided by the multi-adjoint framework. With that goal, in this section we study how the properties presented in the previous section are translated into the multi-adjoint framework.

Since we present an initial study, in order to simplify the results but without loss of generality, we will consider a multi-adjoint frame with only one adjoint triple. Therefore, we fix the multi-adjoint frame $(L_1, L_2, P, \&, \nearrow, \nwarrow)$ and the context (A, B, R), where the mapping σ does not appear since it is not necessary in this situation where we are considering a single adjoint triple.

In addition, we also consider the pair (g, f), with $g \in L_2^B$ and $f \in L_1^A$, satisfying the equalities given in Expression (2) but considering the generalized versions of the necessity operators, given in Sect. 2.2. Specifically, we will consider the set:

$$\mathcal{F}_N = \{(g, f) \mid g \in L_2^B, f \in L_1^A, f^{\downarrow^N} = g, g^{\uparrow_N} = f\}$$

Before generalizing Proposition 1, we need to present certain properties that are satisfied in a context given in a multi-adjoint framework. The next result shows the relation between the possibility and necessity operators applied to the same fuzzy set of objects g of the considered pair (g, f).

Proposition 4. *Given a pair of fuzzy sets $(g, f) \in \mathcal{F}_N$, we have that $g^{\uparrow_\pi} \preceq_1 g^{\uparrow_N}$.*

The following property relates the closure operator that arises from the composition of the mappings of the pair $(\uparrow_\pi, \downarrow^N)$ to the composition of the necessity operators $\uparrow_N$ and $\downarrow^N$.

Proposition 5. *Let (g, f) be a pair of fuzzy sets such that $(g, f) \in \mathcal{F}_N$. Then, $g^{\uparrow_\pi \downarrow^N} = g^{\uparrow_N \downarrow^N} = g$.*

Once the previous properties have been stated, we can introduce the generalized version of Proposition 1 in the multi-adjoint framework. Observe that, in this case the concept belongs to a multi-adjoint property-oriented concept lattice instead of a multi-adjoint concept lattice.

Proposition 6. *Given $(g, f) \in \mathcal{F}_N$, it is satisfied that $\langle g, g^{\uparrow_\pi} \rangle \in \mathcal{M}_{\pi N}$.*

Hence this result asserts that the pair $(g, g^{\uparrow_\pi})$ is always a concept, as long as the pair (g, f) is in $\mathcal{F}_N$.

On the other hand, if we look at Proposition 3, we can realize that the property $Y^\downarrow \subseteq X$ makes that the pair (X, Y) determines a block of concepts. However, within the multi-adjoint framework, assuming that $(g, f) \in \mathcal{F}_N$ does not imply the property $f^\downarrow \preceq_2 g$, in general, as we illustrate in the following example.

Example 1. We will consider the multi-adjoint frame

$$([0, 1]_4, [0, 1]_4, [0, 1]_4, \leq, \leq, \leq, \&_P^*)$$

where $[0, 1]_4$ denotes a regular partition of $[0, 1]$ into 4 pieces, and $\&^*_P$ is the discretization of the product conjunctor, defined for all $a, b \in [0, 1]_4$, as:

$$\&^*{}_P(a, b) = \frac{\lceil 4 \cdot a \cdot b \rceil}{4}$$

where $\lceil \_ \rceil$ is the ceiling function. The corresponding residuated implications $\nearrow^*_P, \nwarrow^*_P \colon [0, 1]_4 \times [0, 1]_4 \to [0, 1]_4$ are defined as:

$$c \nearrow^*_P b = \frac{\lfloor 4 \cdot (c \leftarrow b) \rfloor}{4}, \quad c \nwarrow^*_P a = \frac{\lfloor 4 \cdot (c \leftarrow a) \rfloor}{4}$$

where $\lfloor \_ \rfloor$ is the floor function and $\leftarrow : [0,1] \times [0,1] \rightarrow [0,1]$ is the residuated implication of the product t-norm, defined for all $b, c \in [0,1]$ as:

$$c \leftarrow b = \begin{cases} 1 & \text{if } b \leq c \\ \dfrac{c}{b} & \text{otherwise} \end{cases}$$

The multi-adjoint context is given by the set of attributes $A = \{a_1, a_2, a_3\}$, the set of objects $B = \{b_1, b_2, b_3\}$ and the relation $R : A \times B \rightarrow [0,1]_4$ defined in Table 1.

Table 1. Fuzzy relation of Example 1.

R	b_1	b_2	b_3
a_1	0.5	0.5	1
a_2	0.25	1	0
a_3	0	0.75	0.25

The list of concepts and the associated concept lattice are given in Fig. 1.

$C_0 = \langle \{b_2/0.5\}, \{a_1/1.0, a_2/1.0, a_3/1.0\} \rangle$

$C_1 = \langle \{b_1/0.25, b_2/0.5\}, \{a_1/1.0, a_2/1.0\} \rangle$

$C_2 = \langle \{b_2/0.75\}, \{a_1/0.5, a_2/1.0, a_3/1.0\} \rangle$

$C_3 = \langle \{b_2/0.5, b_3/0.25\}, \{a_1/1.0, a_3/1.0\} \rangle$

$C_4 = \langle \{b_1/0.5, b_2/0.5\}, \{a_1/1.0, a_2/0.5\} \rangle$

$C_5 = \langle \{b_1/0.25, b_2/1.0\}, \{a_1/0.5, a_2/1.0\} \rangle$

$C_6 = \langle \{b_1/0.5, b_2/1.0\}, \{a_1/0.5, a_2/0.5\} \rangle$

$C_7 = \langle \{b_1/0.5, b_2/0.5, b_3/1.0\}, \{a_1/1.0\} \rangle$

$C_8 = \langle \{b_1/1.0, b_2/1.0\}, \{a_1/0.5, a_2/0.25\} \rangle$

$C_9 = \langle \{b_1/1.0, b_2/1.0, b_3/1.0\}, \{a_1/0.5\} \rangle$

$C_{10} = \langle \{b_2/1.0\}, \{a_1/0.5, a_2/1.0, a_3/0.75\} \rangle$

$C_{11} = \langle \{b_2/0.75, b_3/0.25\}, \{a_1/0.5, a_3/1.0\} \rangle$

$C_{12} = \langle \{b_2/1.0, b_3/0.25\}, \{a_1/0.5, a_3/0.75\} \rangle$

$C_{13} = \langle \{b_2/1.0, b_3/0.5\}, \{a_1/0.5, a_3/0.5\} \rangle$

$C_{14} = \langle \{b_2/1.0, b_3/1.0\}, \{a_1/0.5, a_3/0.25\} \rangle$

$C_{15} = \langle \{b_2/0.5, b_3/0.5\}, \{a_1/1.0, a_3/0.5\} \rangle$

$C_{16} = \langle \{b_2/0.5, b_3/1.0\}, \{a_1/1.0, a_3/0.25\} \rangle$

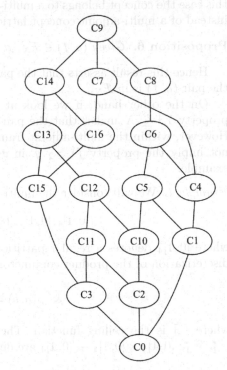

Fig. 1. List of concepts and multi-adjoint concept lattice of Example 1.

Note that, when $L_1 = L_2 = P$ the multi-adjoint, the multi-adjoint property-oriented and the multi-adjoint object-oriented frames coincide. Then, the same adjoint triples are considered in all these frameworks, for a more detailed information about this issue we refer the reader to [19].

Now, we consider the following fuzzy subsets of attributes and objects:

$$f(a_1) = 0.25 \qquad f(a_2) = 0.5 \qquad f(a_3) = 0.5$$
$$g(b_1) = 0.5 \qquad g(b_2) = 0.5 \qquad g(b_3) = 0.25$$

In order to prove that $g^{\downarrow} \leq f$ does not hold, we have to prove that the fuzzy sets g and f satisfy that $g^{\uparrow_N} = f$ and $f^{\downarrow^N} = g$. Thus, we compute $g^{\uparrow_N}$ and $f^{\downarrow^N}$:

$$g^{\uparrow_N}(a_1) = 0.25 \qquad g^{\uparrow_N}(a_2) = 0.5 \qquad g^{\uparrow_N}(a_3) = 0.5$$
$$f^{\downarrow^N}(b_1) = 0.5 \qquad f^{\downarrow^N}(b_2) = 0.5 \qquad f^{\downarrow^N}(b_3) = 0.25$$

We can easily check that (g, f) satisfies that $g^{\uparrow_N} = f$ and $f^{\downarrow^N} = g$, for all $\dot{a} \in A$ and $b \in B$. Now, we have to compute $f^{\downarrow}$:

$$f^{\downarrow}(b_1) = 0 \qquad f^{\downarrow}(b_2) = 1 \qquad f^{\downarrow}(b_3) = 0$$

We can verify that $f^{\downarrow}(b_1) = 0 \leq 0.5 = g(b_1)$ and $f^{\downarrow}(b_3) = 0 \leq 0.25 = g(b_3)$, but $f^{\downarrow}(b_2) = 1 \nleq 0.5 = g(b_2)$. In fact, if we compute all pairs (g_i, f_i) such that $g_i^{\uparrow_N} = f_i$ and $f_i^{\downarrow^N} = g_i$, with $g_i \in L_2^B$, $f_i \in L_1^A$, we obtain the following pairs excluding the trivial ones:

$$(g_1, f_1) = (\{b_1/0.5, b_2/0.25, b_3/0.25\}, \{a_1/0.25, a_2/0.25, a_3/0.25\})$$
$$(g_2, f_2) = (\{b_1/0.5, b_2/0.5, b_3/0.25\}, \{a_1/0.25, a_2/0.5, a_3/0.5\})$$
$$(g_3, f_3) = (\{b_1/1, b_2/0.25, b_3/0.5\}, \{a_1/0.5, a_2/0.25, a_3/0.25\})$$
$$(g_4, f_4) = (\{b_1/1, b_2/0.5, b_3/0.5\}, \{a_1/0.5, a_2/0.5, a_3/0.5\})$$
$$(g_5, f_5) = (\{b_1/1, b_2/0.5, b_3/0.75\}, \{a_1/0.75, a_2/0.5, a_3/0.5\})$$
$$(g_6, f_6) = (\{b_1/1, b_2/0.5, b_3/1\}, \{a_1/1, a_2/0.5, a_3/0.5\})$$
$$(g_7, f_7) = (\{b_1/1, b_2/0.75, b_3/0.5\}, \{a_1/0.5, a_2/0.75, a_3/1\})$$
$$(g_8, f_8) = (\{b_1/1, b_2/0.75, b_3/0.75\}, \{a_1/0.75, a_2/0.75, a_3/1\})$$
$$(g_9, f_9) = (\{b_1/1, b_2/0.75, b_3/1\}, \{a_1/1, a_2/0.75, a_3/1\})$$
$$(g_{10}, f_{10}) = (\{b_1/1, b_2/1, b_3/0.5\}, \{a_1/0.5, a_2/1, a_3/1\})$$
$$(g_{11}, f_{11}) = (\{b_1/1, b_2/1, b_3/0.75\}, \{a_1/0.75, a_2/1, a_3/1\})$$

Considering any pair (g_i, f_i) given in the previous list, we can look at the fuzzy subset g_i and look for the greatest extent of the concepts that is lesser than g_i. Analogously, we do the same for the fuzzy subset f_i looking for the smallest intent of the concepts that is greater than f_i. However, not always results in a block.

For instance, if we consider the pair (g_4, f_4) we obtain that:

$$\text{Ext}(C_{15}) = \{b_2/0.5, b_3/0.5\} \leq \{b_1/1, b_2/0.5, b_3/0.5\} = g_4,$$
$$\text{Ext}(C_4) = \{b_1/0.5, b_2/0.5\} \leq \{b_1/1, b_2/0.5, b_3/0.5\} = g_4,$$
$$f_4 = \{a_1/0.5, a_2/0.5, a_3/0.5\} \leq \{a_1/0.5, a_2/1.0, a_3/0.75\} = \text{Int}(C_{10}).$$

As we can observe, we do not obtain a block of concepts. In fact, the concepts C_4, C_{15} and C_{10} are incomparable elements of the concept lattice. □

Therefore, if we compute all pairs (g, f) in a given multi-adjoint context, we do not obtain independent blocks of the multi-adjoint concept lattice, that is, the existence of pairs (g, f) satisfying the equalities given in Expression (2) in the multi-adjoint framework, does not guarantee that there are independent subcontexts.

5   Conclusions and Future Work

In this paper, we have presented a preliminary study on the properties related to the necessity operator when a factorization of a formal context is carried out. We have proved several properties that the independent subcontexts, extracted by the necessity operator, satisfy in the classical framework. Furthermore, we have also analyzed how these properties are translated into the multi-adjoint framework.

In the near future, we will continue with the study of more properties related to independent subcontexts in both, the classical and the fuzzy framework provided by the multi-adjoint paradigm, in order to overcome the drawbacks found in this paper. We will also complement this work with some existing mechanisms in the references. In addition, we will consider alternative ways to address the decomposition of formal contexts into smaller subcontexts and we will explore different ways to aggregate the information provided by the independent subcontexts.

References

1. Antoni, L., Cornejo, M.E., Medina, J., Ramirez, E.: Attribute classification and reduct computation in multi-adjoint concept lattices. IEEE Trans. Fuzzy Syst. **29**, 1 (2020)
2. Bělohlávek, R.: Fuzzy concepts and conceptual structures: induced similarities. In: Joint Conference on Information Sciences, pp. 179–182 (1998)
3. Bělohlávek, R.: Optimal decompositions of matrices with entries from residuated lattices. J. Logic Comput. **22**, 1–21 (2011)
4. Belohlavek, R., Krmelova, M.: Beyond boolean matrix decompositions: toward factor analysis and dimensionality reduction of ordinal data. In: 2013 IEEE 13th International Conference on Data Mining, pp. 961–966 (2013)
5. Belohlavek, R., Outrata, J., Trnecka, M.: Factorizing boolean matrices using formal concepts and iterative usage of essential entries. Inf. Sci. **489**, 37–49 (2019)
6. Belohlavek, R., Trnecka, M.: A new algorithm for boolean matrix factorization which admits overcovering. Discrete Appli. Math. **249**, 6–52 (2018). Concept Lattices and Applications: Recent Advances and New Opportunities
7. Bělohlávek, R., Trneckova, M.: Factorization of matrices with grades via essential entries. Fuzzy Sets Syst. **360**, 97–116 (2019)
8. Belohlavek, R., Vychodil, V.: Discovery of optimal factors in binary data via a novel method of matrix decomposition. J. Comput. Syst. Sci. **76**(1), 3–20 (2010). Special Issue on Intelligent Data Analysis

9. Burusco, A., Fuentes-González, R.: The study of L-fuzzy concept lattice. Math. Soft Comput. **3**, 209–218 (1994)
10. Chen, Y., Yao, Y.: A multiview approach for intelligent data analysis based on data operators. Inf. Sci. **178**(1), 1–20 (2008)
11. Cornejo, M.E., Medina, J., Ramírez-Poussa, E.: A comparative study of adjoint triples. Fuzzy Sets Syst. **211**, 1–14 (2013)
12. Cornejo, M.E., Medina, J., Ramírez-Poussa, E.: Attribute reduction in multi-adjoint concept lattices. Inf. Sci. **294**, 41–56 (2015)
13. Cornejo, M.E., Medina, J., Ramírez-Poussa, E.: Characterizing reducts in multi-adjoint concept lattices. Inf. Sci. **422**, 364–376 (2018)
14. Dubois, D., de Saint-Cyr, F.D., Prade, H.: A possibility-theoretic view of formal concept analysis. Fund. Inform. **75**(1–4), 195–213 (2007)
15. Dubois, D., Prade, H.: Possibility theory and formal concept analysis: characterizing independent sub-contexts. Fuzzy Sets Syst. **196**, 4–16 (2012)
16. Ganter, B., Wille, R.: Formal Concept Analysis. Springer, Heidelberg (1999). https://doi.org/10.1007/978-3-642-59830-2
17. Gediga, G., Düntsch, I.: Modal-style operators in qualitative data analysis. In: Proceedings IEEE International Conference on Data Mining, pp. 155–162 (2002)
18. Georgescu, G., Popescu, A.: Non-dual fuzzy connections. Arch. Math. Log. **43**(8), 1009–1039 (2004)
19. Medina, J.: Multi-adjoint property-oriented and object-oriented concept lattices. Inf. Sci. **190**, 95–106 (2012)
20. Medina, J.: Relating attribute reduction in formal, object-oriented and property-oriented concept lattices. Comput. Math. Appli. **64**(6), 1992–2002 (2012)
21. Medina, J., Ojeda-Aciego, M., Ruiz-Calviño, J.: Formal concept analysis via multi-adjoint concept lattices. Fuzzy Sets Syst. **160**(2), 130–144 (2009)
22. Yao, Y., Chen, Y.: Rough set approximations in formal concept analysis. In: Peters, J.F., Skowron, A. (eds.) Transactions on Rough Sets V. LNCS, vol. 4100, pp. 285–305. Springer, Heidelberg (2006). https://doi.org/10.1007/11847465_14

Encoding Non-global Time Representations into the Lattice of Divisibility

Francisco José Valverde-Albacete[1]([⊠]) [ID], Carmen Peláez-Moreno[2] [ID],
Inma P. Cabrera[3] [ID], Pablo Cordero[3] [ID], and Manuel Ojeda-Aciego[3] [ID]

[1] Depto. Teoría de Señal y Comunicaciones, Sistemas Telemáticos y Computación,
Univ. Rey Juan Carlos, Madrid, Spain
francisco.valverde@urjc.es

[2] Depto. Teoría de Señal y Comunicaciones, Univ. Carlos III de Madrid,
Madrid, Spain
carmen@tsc.uc3m.es

[3] Dpt. Matemática Aplicada, Univ. de Málaga, Málaga, Spain
{ipcabrera,pcordero,aciego}@uma.es

Abstract. In this paper we provide an embedding of finite lattices into
$(\mathbb{N}, |)$, the lattice of divisibility of natural numbers. For that purpose,
we explore two representations: vector clocks, a device to provide a virtual time used in distributed systems that has gained traction as a finite
lattice representation, and the log-prime function that transforms natural numbers into sequences of prime exponents. Using a generalized
log-prime function and its inverse we describe how to embed any finite
(width, height) lattice into $(\mathbb{N}, |)$ and provide examples for such process,
prior to analysing the affordances of such encoding vis-a-vis the representation of non-global, distributed time. We also discuss how this representation may help improve the affordances of using complete lattices
in data analysis both for time- and non-time related data.

1 Motivation: Modelling Imprecise, Local Time

Distributed systems can be considered a set of concurrently executing processes
$\{P_i\}_{i=1}^n$ and the computations they execute. The finest-grained computation is
an *event* $e \in E$, atomic actions that occur in processes, and build up the trace

CPM and FJVA have been partially supported by the Department of Research and
Innovation of Madrid Regional Authority, in the EMPATIA-CM research project (reference Y2018/TCS-5046), and Grant PDC2021-121071-I00 funded by MCIN/AEI/
10.13039/501100011033 and by the European Union "NextGenerationEU/PRTR" for
this work. IPC, PC and MOA have been partially supported by the Spanish Ministry of
Science, Innovation, and Universities (MCIU), State Agency of Research (AEI), Junta
de Andalucía (JA), Universidad de Málaga (UMA) and European Regional Development Fund (FEDER) through the projects PGC2018-095869-B-I00 and TIN2017-
89023-P (MCIU/AEI/FEDER), and UMA2018-FEDERJA-001 (JA/UMA/FEDER).

© Springer Nature Switzerland AG 2022
D. Ciucci et al. (Eds.): IPMU 2022, CCIS 1601, pp. 118–129, 2022.
https://doi.org/10.1007/978-3-031-08971-8_11

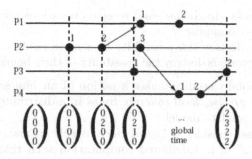

Fig. 1. *Happened before* relation of a distributed system execution as a time diagram (above) and clock vectors (below) of some of the events in it (from [10])

of each process $\{C_i\}_{i=1}^n$ as an arbitrary sequence of events $C_i \in E^\omega$. In fact, we may only consider the following types of events [4,10]:

1. An *internal event* causes a change of state.
2. A *send event* causes a message to be sent to a different process.
3. A *receive event* causes a message to be received and the local state update by the value of the message.

Some events can influence or *cause* later events. This notion of *internal causality* about what can be perceived within the distributed system is related to *external causality*—that is, in the "real world"—but distinct. As the relations of potential cause and effect between events are fundamental to the design of distributed algorithms [1], the *happened before* relation was proposed [9].

Definition 1. *In the context of distributed computation:*

- *an event c can be the cause of an event e, or c happened before e, $c \to e$ iff*
  1. *both occur in the same node and c was executed first, or,*
  2. *being at different nodes, if e could know about the occurrence of c thanks to some message received from some node that knows about c.*
- *They are said to be* concurrent *if neither event can know about the other, $c\|e \iff c \not\to e$ and $e \not\to c$.*

It is well-known that, given a set of events E in a distributed computation and the *happened before* relation $\to$, then $(E, \to)$ is a partial order [4,9,10]. Note that this is an implicit definition of the *flow of time as occurrence of events*.

An instance of such a *happened before* order for a particular distributed system is shown in Fig. 1 (see below for the vector clocks.) This is an expressive model, yet anchored in very basic properties:

1. Only atomic events—in chains—and send operations are adequate loci for join-irreducibles to appear[1].

---

[1] Recall that an element x of a finite lattice L is join-irreducible if $x = a \vee b$ implies $x = a$ or $x = b$. And lattice-dually for meet-irreducibles.

2. Only atomic events—in chains—and receive operations are adequate loci for meet-irreducibles to appear.
3. Send operations destroy the possibility of a node being a meet-irreducible, while receive operations destroy the possibility of their being join-irreducibles.

Note how this internal causality makes a notion of an *imprecise, global virtual time* emerge out of *precise, local concrete times* in a distributed system. This is the notion that we want to model.

For such purpose consider a *logical clock*, a rule to assign a number $C(e)$ to each event $e \in E$ of a distributed computation such that it preserves the causality relation [2],

$$c \to e \Rightarrow C(c) < C(e). \tag{1}$$

Several types of numbers may be used—either $\mathbb{N}$, $\mathbb{Z}$, $\mathbb{Q}$ or $\mathbb{R}$ [10]—to timestamp events [9]. In Fig. 1, natural numbers have been used above each of the events for a process P_i to signify clock events, and these are imposed by the index of the event in the sequence for its process C_i. In such virtual time, we may refer to $\downarrow e = \{c \in E \mid c \to e\}$ for each $e \in E$ as the *past of e*, and to $\uparrow e$ as its *future*.

However, for such *scalar* logical clocks the converse of (1) does not hold [2, §.3], therefore they cannot faithfully capture concurrency, that is, unrelatedness in this relation. Notice that the *causal history (past) of an event* [1] is simply the sequence of uniquely identified events in the past of such event. Such identifiers for past events have two components: an *identifier* for the process that generated it, and a *local time* e.g. a clock to distinguish the past event in the sequence of events generated by the process. Send, receive and atomic events just register themselves in such histories. *Vector clocks* [4,10] are an encoding of these histories that can be used to capture the *happened before* relation.

Definition 2 (Vector Clock of a Process). *Let $\{P_i\}_{i=1}^n$ be the processes in a distributed system. Let $v_i \in \mathbb{N}^n$ be a vector assigned to process P_i with initial values $v_i[j] = 0, 1 \leq j \leq n$. Then v_i is a vector clock for process P_i if:*

1. *For each event e internal to P_i, just before the event occurs we increment it $v_i[i] := v_i[i] + d$ (d may be any conventional but finite value, typically $d = 1$).*
2. *Every message sent from P_i has v_i piggybacked onto it, after incrementing.*
3. *Upon receiving a message from P_i timestamped as v_i, process P_j updates its own vector clock as $v_j = max(v_j, v_i)$.*

The relevance of vector clocks for our purposes stems from the fact that they are a very productive representation for orders [6]. Notice that the encoding above guarantees the following properties:

Proposition 1 ([2]). *For an event $e \in E$ in P_i tagged with clock $e.v_i$:*

1. *The component $e.v_i[j]$ equals the number of events of P_j in the past of e:*

$$e.v_i[j] = |\{e \in p_j\} \cap \downarrow e|$$

Furthermore, the component $e.v_i[j]$ also describes the time of the latest event in P_j that happened before e.

2. *For any pair of elements* $c, e \in E$, $c \to e \iff c.v_i \le e.v_j$ *even if* $i \ne j$.
3. *The size of the vector clocks is the dimension of the partial order* $(E, \to)$.

Figure 1 shows the vector clocks worked out for a number of events. The properties cited above are evident for the last of the clocks.

In a number of previous papers, we have been exploring different alternative representations for complete lattices in terms of lattices of antichains [15] and partitions [17] following Wille's injunction in [18] to look for a broader gamut of representations for lattices than the usual one in Formal Concept Analysis (FCA) [5].

In this paper we want to tackle this sense of a "local, imprecisely advancing time" with techniques related to FCA. Prior results—e.g. the Dedeking-McNeille completion—suggest that we discuss this issue in terms of the embeddings of the irreducibles of a (finite) lattice into the lattice of divisibility, since the latter has antichains and chains of arbitrary cardinality.

For that purpose we first recall in Sect. 2 basic facts about the lattice of divisibility and primes. We next present our results in Sect. 3 pivoting around a function that helps transform natural numbers into a representation close to that of vector clocks. We finally discuss these results in the wider setting of affordances for the practice of FCA.

2 Theory: The Lattice of Divisibility

In this section, we recall the basics of the divisibility relation in the set of natural numbers which are required for the rest of the paper.

Given $m, n \in \mathbb{N}$, we say that "m is a *factor or divisor* of n", denoted $m \mid n$, if and only if there exists $k \in \mathbb{N}$, such that $m \cdot k = n$. The *divisibility relation* is reflexive, antisymmetric and transitive, hence a partial order relation. We will also use the usual terms related to divisibility (i.e. factor, divisor, prime, coprime, composite, etc.) with their standard meaning.

The poset $\langle \mathbb{N}, \mid \rangle$ has rather strong properties, since it is a distributive lattice whose join and meet are, respectively, the least common multiple (lcm) and the greatest common divisor (gcd). Moreover, $\langle \mathbb{N}, \mid \rangle$ also satisfies the Descending Chain Condition (DCC), its bottom is 1 and the primes are its atoms.

It is worth noticing that the completion of the lattice seems to have different solutions. One is to consider 0 as the top, see [3], but for reasons to be explained later, we do not.

Because ideals in orders are important for representation issues, and primes have a special status in $\langle \mathbb{N}, \mid \rangle$ associated to the prime factorization property, we state the following:

Proposition 2. *Let* $\langle \mathbb{N}, \mathrm{lcm}, \mathrm{gcd} \rangle$ *be the lattice of divisibility. Then*

1. *The set of primes is a maximum antichain.*
2. $n \in \mathbb{N}$ *is join-irreducible iff* $n = p^r$ *where* p *is prime and* $r \in \mathbb{N}$.
3. *For* $n \in \mathbb{N}$, *the join-irreducibles of* $\downarrow n$, *denoted* $\mathcal{J}(\downarrow n)$, *are the elements of the form* p^r *such that* p *is prime and* $p^r \mid n$.

4. $\mathcal{J}(\downarrow p^r)$ *is a chain of height* r *and length* $r + 1$ *(1 is the bottom).*
5. *For* $n \in \mathbb{N}$, *there exists* $m_n \in \mathbb{N}$ *such that* $\downarrow m_n$ *is a Boolean lattice isomorphic to* 2^n.

Since there are chains of arbitrary length and antichains of arbitrary width in the lattice of primes, we want to introduce the question whether any finite (complete) lattice can be embedded within it. At the same time, there is a lot of structure already in it, so it may be the fact that not every complete lattice can be embedded within $\langle \mathbb{N}, | \rangle$.

There are two strong results about this:

Proposition 3 ([3] Ex. 5.5, p. 125).

1. *Every finite distributive lattice can be embedded into* $\langle \mathbb{N}, | \rangle$.
2. *There are countable distributive lattices which cannot be embedded in* $\langle \mathbb{N}, | \rangle$.

Therefore, it would seem we have to stick to finite lattices if we want to maintain full representational capabilities. Still, the lattices obtained from data are of this kind and this is a useful enterprise.

3   Results

3.1   The Log-Prime and Exponential-Prime Functions

An Abstract Algebra Look. Recall that a semiring $\langle S, \oplus, \otimes, \epsilon, e \rangle$ is an algebra whose additive law $\langle S, \oplus, \epsilon \rangle$ is a commutative monoid, its multiplicative law $\langle S, \otimes, e \rangle$ a monoid, $\oplus$ distributes left and right over $\otimes$, the neutral element for addition ϵ and that for multiplication e are distinct, and ϵ is absorptive for $\otimes$, that is, for all $a \in S, a \otimes \epsilon = \epsilon \otimes a = \epsilon$ [8, Ch.1, S.5]. A semiring is *commutative* if the multiplicative law is commutative, and *idempotent* if the additive law is idempotent $a \oplus a = a$.

Furthermore, a dioid $\langle D, \oplus, \otimes, \epsilon, e \rangle$ is a semiring with an underlying partial order $\langle D, \leq \rangle$, where $a \leq b \iff \exists c \in D, b = a \oplus c$, compatible both with addition and multiplication so that if $a \leq b$, then, for all $c \in D$ we have $c \oplus a \leq c \oplus b$ and $c \otimes a \leq c \otimes b$ and commutatively [8, Ch.1, S.6].

From the point of view of abstract algebra:

- If we complete $\mathbb{N}$ to $\overline{\mathbb{N}} = \mathbb{N} \cup \{\infty\}$ then $\langle \overline{\mathbb{N}}, \gcd, \times, \infty, 1 \rangle$ is a commutative idempotent semiring, and the divisibility relation is precisely the partial order that renders it a dioid. The infinite acts as the bottom of the operation in the sense that $\gcd(a, \infty) = a$ and $a \times \infty = \infty$. This ∞ therefore is to be understood as a number all of whose prime exponents are infinite (see below).
- On the other hand, $\langle \mathbb{N}, \mathrm{lcm}, \times, 1 \rangle$ is only an idempotent pre-semiring, lacking absorptive property even if we complete $\mathbb{N}_{\geq 0} = \mathbb{N} \cup \{0\}$, since $\mathrm{lcm}(0, a)$ is undefined. We will see below how the logprime function suggests a value for this other completion.

The Logprime Function and Its Inverse. Let ∞^ω and 0^ω represent countable sequences of ∞ and 0 respectively, and consider $\langle \mathbb{N}^\omega_{\geq 0} \cup \{\infty^\omega\}, \min, +, \infty^\omega, 0^\omega \rangle$ where $\mathbb{N}^\omega_{\geq 0}$ represents the set of eventually zero sequences of nonnegative natural numbers with component-wise minimum as additive law, and the component-wise sum as the multiplicative law. Then we have:

Proposition 4. *There exists an isomorphism of commutative idempotent dioids from* $\langle \overline{\mathbb{N}}, \gcd, \times, \infty, 1 \rangle$ *to* $\langle \mathbb{N}^\omega_{\geq 0} \cup \{\infty^\omega\}, \min, +, \infty^\omega, 0^\omega \rangle$.

Proof. Let $\mathbb{P} = \{p_1, p_2, \dots\}$ be the set of prime numbers in increasing order. The logprime function represents each number by the vector of its prime exponents:

$$\log_\mathbb{P} : \overline{\mathbb{N}} \to \mathbb{N}^\omega_{\geq 0} \qquad\qquad \exp_\mathbb{P} : \mathbb{N}^\omega_{\geq 0} \to \overline{\mathbb{N}} \qquad (2)$$

$$n = \prod_{i=1}^\infty p_i^{r_i} \mapsto [r_i]_{i=1}^\infty \qquad\qquad s = [s_i]_{i=1}^\infty \mapsto n = \prod_{i=1}^\infty p_i^{s_i}$$

The isomorphism is just the logprime function for natural numbers completed with $\log_\mathbb{P}(\infty) = \infty^\omega$, and its inverse, $\exp_\mathbb{P}(\infty^\omega) = \infty$.   □

If we adopt a notation reminiscent of the writing of numbers in base b, we write the sequence with the exponent for the highest prime with non-zero exponent at the leftmost position, e.g. $\log_\mathbb{P}(20) = \log_\mathbb{P}(5^1 \cdot 3^0 \cdot 2^2) = 1.0.2$.

3.2   Embedding Finite Lattices Within the Lattice of Divisibility

It is easy to see that the vector clock algorithms of [4, 10] do not cater to all possible lattices. In particular, they do not consider any element to be

1. the meet of multiple other elements, since they only admit *sending* to a single node.
2. the join of several other elements, since they only admit *receiving* from a single node.

This is important for the concept of *logical clock* but of course not for lattice representations. For that purpose, we will:

1. Consider also the analogue of *multicast events* where the same message gets simultaneously sent to a number of other processes. The appearance of multicast and the granularity of "local time" are accountable for the appearance of nodes with multiple lower or upper covers.
2. Furthermore, since sending and receiving operations destroy the qualities of join- and meet-irreducibility, we will not consider that they are *not* clock-advancing.

For these reasons our vectors cannot be considered clocks, despite resembling them.

Next we introduce a procedure for encoding the elements of a finite lattice in terms of vectors of counts:

Pseudocode. (Encoding a finite lattice $\mathcal{L}$ into $\langle \mathbb{N}, | \rangle$)

1. Find $\mathcal{J}(\mathcal{L})$ and use Dilworth's theorem on it to find a chain cover $\{C_i\}_{i=1}^k$ for it, where $\mathtt{width}(\mathcal{J}(\mathcal{L})) = k$.
2. Assign vector counters on the elements of $\mathcal{J}(\mathcal{L})$ using the modified vector clock rule with diagrams similar to that of Fig. 1:
   (a) Increase the counter for C_i on finding a $\vee$-irreducible for internal events.
   (b) Do not increase the counter on *send* or *receive*.
3. Assign vector counters to the rest of the elements of the lattice as a join of $\vee$-irreducibles.
4. Consider the vectors as the prime powers of the first k primes and use the $\exp_{\mathbb{P}}$ function of Sect. 3.1 to find a representation of each element of $\mathcal{L}$ into $\mathbb{N}$.

This pseudocode is used in the next example, but first, note that:

- The algorithm provides a representation in terms of $\vee$-irreducibles: the manipulation of representations is by joins in the lattice of primes, essentially the lcm. This representation is an upward count of $\vee$-irreducibles on each chain, and these map quite directly to chains of prime powers. The requirement of finite height, therefore is for the procedure to be able to finish going over each individual chain.
- In order to be able to encode the chains into the prime powers—the last step—we must have gone through them beforehand therefore a terminating algorithm implicitly demands that we use lattices of finite width for actual data processing. As a tool for theoretical encoding, though, we could dispense with this finite width requirement.
- In order to find an analogue procedure for the $\wedge$-irreducibles we just have to apply the procedure above to the dual of the set of $\wedge$-irreducibles $\mathcal{M}(\mathcal{L}) \cong \mathcal{J}(\mathcal{L}^\delta)$. Note that, in general, $\mathtt{width}(\mathcal{J}(\mathcal{L})) \neq \mathtt{width}(\mathcal{M}(\mathcal{L}))$ so one of the two representations may offer an advantage in succinctness over the other.

An Example. Adapted from [3, Fig. 2.10, p.45], is depicted in Fig. 2a with its main quantitative characteristics described in the table in Fig. 2b. The join irreducibles are labelled with a white numbered square below them, and the meet irreducibles with a grey numbered square above them.

First we cover $\mathcal{J}(\mathcal{L})$ with the chains $C_1 = \{2 < 5 < 10\}$, $C_2 = \{9\}$ and $C_3 = \{1 < 3 < 6\}$. So to create time vectors for the $\vee$-irreducibles we have to use $\mathtt{width}(\mathcal{J}(\mathcal{L})) = k = 3$ primes.

These vector clocks with three dependent timelines are represented in column 2 of Table 1. In column 3 the formula to work out the encoding is shown: whether it is the actual algorithm—marked as j—or the join of which nodes—as a formula. Note how the constants for $\mathcal{J}(L)$ in Table 2b appear in this encoding: its width is the length of the encoding $k = 3$, while its height is one less than the maximum coordinate of $\top$, $h(\mathcal{J}(L)) = 2$.

Following our principle of using the lattice of dual primes to represent the "intents", we use the $\vee$-irreducibles of $\mathcal{L}^\delta$ to represent the $\wedge$-irreducibles of $\mathcal{L}$. For this purpose we consider the singleton chains $C_1' = \{10\}, C_2' = \{9\}, C_3' =$

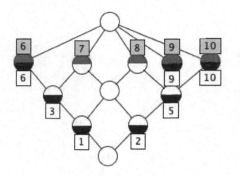

subset	size	height	width
$\mathcal{J}(\mathcal{L})$	7	2	3
$\mathcal{M}(\mathcal{L})$	5	0	5
$\mathcal{J}(\mathcal{L}) \cup \mathcal{M}(\mathcal{L})$	9	2	5

(a) Lattice diagram   (b) Lattice description

Fig. 2. Example lattice. a) Concept numbers shown in every join- or meet irreducible. The only numbers not shown are $\top$, $\bot$ and $4 = 1 \wedge 2$. b) Main characteristics of the lattice $\mathcal{L}$, including sets of join- $\mathcal{J}(\mathcal{L})$ and meet-irreducibles $\mathcal{M}(\mathcal{L})$, cardinalities, heights and widths.

$\{8\}, C_4' = \{7\}$ and $C_5' = \{6\}$ to find a chain-cover for $\mathcal{M}(\mathcal{L}) \cong \mathcal{J}(\mathcal{L}^\delta)$ with $k' = 5$. The results of the encoding are shown in column 4 of Table 1. In column 5 the formula to work out the encoding is shown: whether it is the actual algorithm— marked as m—or the join of the encoding of what nodes. Note also how the height of $\mathcal{M}(\mathcal{L})$ and the number of $\wedge$-irreducibles appear in the "intent" of $\bot$.

Figures 3a and 3b show the embedded copies of $\mathcal{L}$ into $\langle \mathbb{N}, | \rangle$ and $\langle \mathbb{N}, | \rangle^\delta$.

3.3   Affordances of the Embedding

In this section we briefly explore the *affordances* [7] of the representation above. In the context of *extended cognition* (Order) Mathematics can be understood as

Table 1. Two prime power encoding of the lattice in Fig. 2.

node	∨-irr. encoding	formula	∧-irr. encoding	formula
$\top$	3.1.3	$6 \vee 7 \vee 8 \vee 9 \vee 10$	0.0.0.0.0	$7 \wedge 8$
10	0.0.3	j	0.0.0.0.1	m
9	0.1.2	j	0.0.0.1.0	m
8	1.0.2	$4 \vee 5$	0.0.1.0.0	m
7	2.0.1	$3 \vee 4$	0.1.0.0.0	m
6	3.0.0	j	1.0.0.0.0	m
5	0.0.2	j	0.0.1.1.1	$8 \vee 9 \vee 10$
4	1.0.1	$1 \vee 2$	0.1.1.0.0	$7 \vee 8$
3	2.0.0	j	1.1.0.0.0	$6 \vee 7$
2	0.0.1	j	0.1.1.1.1	$4 \vee 5$
1	1.0.0	j	1.1.1.0.0	$3 \vee 4$
$\bot$	0.0.0	$1 \wedge 2$	1.1.1.1.1	$1 \vee 2$

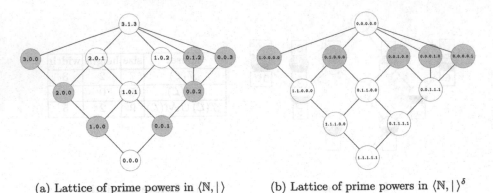

(a) Lattice of prime powers in $\langle \mathbb{N}, | \rangle$ (b) Lattice of prime powers in $\langle \mathbb{N}, | \rangle^\delta$

Fig. 3. A dually isomorphic pair of lattices of prime powers.

providing a "Landscape of Affordances" [11], an affordance being *a possibility for action provided by the "environment"*, in this case, the data[2].

Recall the last note below the pseudocode. Due to it we can actually conceive each element of the lattice $\mathcal{L}$ to be represented by a pair of vectors:

1. One of length $\mathtt{width}(\mathcal{J}(\mathcal{L})) = k$ describing the structure of the element in terms of its $\vee$-irreducibles, as encoded in prime powers of $\langle \mathbb{N}, | \rangle$
2. A second one, of length $\mathtt{width}(\mathcal{M}(\mathcal{L})) = l$ describing the structure of the elements in terms of its $\wedge$-irreducibles—represented as $\vee$-irreducibles in the dual $\langle \mathbb{N}, | \rangle^\delta$

We use this idea in an embedding similar to Dedekind and MacNeille's initial encoding of their eponymous completion—but based in a specific representation of the lower and upper bounds in the lattice of divisibility, which is the embedding we are looking for:

Proposition 5. *Any finite (height, width) lattice $\mathcal{L} = \langle L, \leq \rangle$ can be embedded (encoded) as a pair of sublattices of the lattice of divisibility.*

Proof. Let $\mathtt{width}(\mathcal{J}(\mathcal{L})) = k$ and $\mathtt{width}(\mathcal{M}(\mathcal{L})) = l$. Recall that $\mathfrak{B}(L, L, \leq) \cong \mathfrak{B}(\mathcal{J}(\mathcal{L}) \cup \mathcal{M}(\mathcal{L}), \mathcal{J}(\mathcal{L}) \cup \mathcal{M}(\mathcal{L}), \leq)$ since $\mathcal{J}(\mathcal{L}) \cup \mathcal{M}(\mathcal{L})$ is both join- and meet-dense. Consider rather the embedding $\iota(l) = (\downarrow l \cap \mathcal{J}(\mathcal{L}), \uparrow l \cap \mathcal{M}(\mathcal{L}))$ that proves the isomorphism $\mathcal{L} \cong \mathfrak{B}(\mathcal{J}(\mathcal{L}), \mathcal{M}(\mathcal{L}), \leq)$ with the inherited order [5], and call this pair $\iota(l) = (A, B)$.

Call the *(prime) past* π_p and *(prime) future* ϕ_p, of each element $l \in L$

$$\pi_{\mathbb{P}} : L \to \mathbb{N}^k \qquad\qquad \phi_{\mathbb{P}} : L \to \mathbb{N}^l \qquad\qquad (3)$$

the vectors obtained by applying the previous procedure to the lattice using the $\vee$-irreducibles and the $\wedge$-irreducibles, the latter encoded as the $\vee$-irreducibles

---

[2] In the words of Gibson, "The affordances of the environment are what it offers the animal, what it provides or furnishes [7]".

of $\mathcal{L}^\delta$. Use this to define $\lambda : 2^L \times 2^L \to \mathbb{N}^\omega \times \mathbb{N}^\omega, \lambda(A, B) = (v_\pi, v_\phi)$ with $v_\pi = \mathrm{lcm}_{l \in A} \pi_\mathbb{P}(l)$ for $A \subseteq \mathcal{J}(\mathcal{L})$ and $v_\phi = \mathrm{lcm}_{l \in B} \phi_\mathbb{P}(l)$ for $B \subseteq \mathcal{J}(\mathcal{L}^\delta)$. Then $\kappa = \lambda \circ \iota$ is the required embedding. $\qquad\square$

Note that:

1. This suggests a "conceptual" representation akin to that of FCA. In the same way that the Dedekind-MacNeille completion is the concept lattice of its doubling context $\mathfrak{B}(L, L, \leq)$ [5]. But note that the images $\Pi(L) = \{\pi_\mathbb{P}(l) \mid l \in L\}$ and $\Phi(L) = \{\pi_\mathbb{P}(l) \mid l \in L\}$ are not related by a context, and therefore there are no patent "polars", hence they are "ignorant" of one another.
2. Instead of using the product encoding [3, 7.38] suggest using, e.g. the projection on the first component for the representation. In our case the analogue would be selecting only either of the divisibility sublattices. Due to the reason argued before this cannot be the case for our encoding: *the past does not univocally determine the future, nor vice-versa*, any more than join-irreducibles determine meet-irreducibles or viceversa.

We suggest in this paper that this double structure is necessary to provide *an affordance for modelling diverging (through join-irreducibles) and converging (through meet-irreducibles) trajectories.* Furthermore, since trajectories in time and space can be mutually understood by analogy from each other, *this encoding can be used for conceptualizing and reasoning either non-synchronous, local time between processors or, alternatively, diverging and converging trajectories in directed graphs.*

4   Discussion and Conclusions

This paper is part of an ongoing project to develop new models and abstractions for lattice-oriented data processing. So far we have touched upon lattices of antichains [15]—to model independence between subcontexts—, lattices of partitions [17]—to deal with noise and indiscernibility between attributes or objects—and preliminary applications to showcase their use [14,16]. We have also explored the gamut of lattices associated to a single semifield-valued context [13] and its relationship to linear algebra in exotic semirings [12].

The original motivation of the exploration of the lattice of divisibility—prime sublattices—was for the purpose of encoding large lattices as sets of vectors with values in an idempotent semifields, using the log-prime and exp-prime functions, but this is now left for future work. Note also that these are lattices that obey the lcm of divisibility lattices—the join operation—therefore they are aligned with dualizations of the usual concept lattices, e.g. the lattices issuing from a co-Galois connection [13]. Each of these provide different *affordances* of FCA, in particular, and Lattice Theory, in general.

We were forced to discard basic vector clocks as a representation for lattices, since they do not allow us to model multiple upper or lower covers. Vector clocks are a formalism for describing non-global, logical clocks to model a *virtual time* for distributed computations [9,10]. Regardless, vector clocks have already proven effective and efficient in modelling a large class of lattices [6]. No results are known, to the best of our knowledge, whether *every lattice can be encoded as a vector clock diagram*, but our results clarify the basic idea proposed by [2] that they could be encoded using prime factorizations of numbers.

The interest of such "time vectors" for our purposes lies in that they provide a real-world application field—distributed computations—that is very different from the usual one ascribed to lattice, that of hierarchy. The affordances of this new model would be to offer a magnitude that evolves non-uniformly along a main axis, e.g. a "perceived time" or increasing scalar magnitude. However, by virtue of the analogy between space and time this could also help in conceptualizing converging and diverging trajectories, e.g. in artificial and natural networks, a different but related issue.

Dually, this brings into our standard perception of what a concept lattice stands for—the mutual determination of objects and attributes—this idea that the fully determined or undetermined objects and attributes exist only in the top and bottom of the lattices. All other concepts in between express a "degree of determinacy" in the relationship that emerges from the totality of the lattice to some extent, as if determination information percolated non-uniformly along the different chains embedded in the lattice. The discussion of these cognitively interesting affordances is also left for future work.

References

1. Baquero, C., Preguiça, N.M.: Why logical clocks are easy. ACM Commun. **59**, 43–47 (2016)
2. Charron-Bost, B.: Concerning the size of logical clocks in distributed systems. Inf. Process. Lett. **39**(1), 11–16 (1991)
3. Davey, B., Priestley, H.: Introduction to lattices and order, Cambridge, UK (2002)
4. Fidge, C.J.: Timestamps in message-passing systems that preserve the partial ordering. Austral. Comput. Sci. Comm. **10**(1), 56–65 (1988)
5. Ganter, B., Wille, R.: Formal Concept Analysis. Springer, Heidelberg (1999). https://doi.org/10.1007/978-3-642-59830-2
6. Garg, V.K.: Introduction to Lattice Theory with Computer Science Applications. f. John Wiley & Sons, Hoboken, March 2016
7. Gibson, J.J.: The Ecologial Approach to Visual Perception. Lawrence Erlbaum Associates (1979)
8. Gondran, M., Minoux, M.: Graphs, Dioids and Semirings. New Models and Algorithms. Operations Research Computer Science Interfaces series. Springer (2008). https://doi.org/10.1007/978-0-387-75450-5
9. Lamport, L.: Time, clocks, and the ordering of events in a distributed system. Commun. ACM **21**(7), 558–565 (1978)
10. Mattern, F.: Virtual time and global states of distributed systems. In: Corsnard, M., Quinton, P., (eds.) Parallel and Distributed Algorithms Proceeding of International Workshop on Parallel and Distributed Algorithm, October 1988

11. Rietveld, E., Denys, D., van Westen, M.: Ecological-enactive cognition as engaging with a field of relevant affordances: the skilled intentionality framework, SIF. In: The Oxford Handbook of {4E} Cognition, pp. 41–70. Oxford University Press (2018)
12. Valverde-Albacete, F.J., Peláez-Moreno, C.: K-formal concept analysis as linear algebra over idempotent semifields. Inf. Sci. **467**, 579–603 (2018)
13. Valverde-Albacete, F.J., Peláez-Moreno, C.: Four-fold formal concept analysis based on complete idempotent semifields. Math. MDPI **9**(2), 173 (2021)
14. Valverde-Albacete, F.J., Peláez-Moreno, C., Cabrera, I.P., Cordero, P., Ojeda-Aciego, M.: A data analysis application of formal independence analysis. In: Concept Lattices and their Applications, CLA 2018, pp. 1–12. Palacky University Olomouc (2018)
15. Valverde-Albacete, F.J., Peláez-Moreno, C., Cabrera, I.P., Cordero, P., Ojeda-Aciego, M.: Formal independence analysis. In: Medina, J., et al. (eds.) IPMU 2018. CCIS, vol. 853, pp. 596–608. Springer, Cham (2018). https://doi.org/10.1007/978-3-319-91473-2_51
16. Valverde Albacete, F.J., Pelaez-Moreno, C., Cabrera, I.P., Cordero, P., Ojeda-Aciego, M.: Exploratory data analysis of multi-label classification tasks with formal context analysis. In: Trnecka, M., Valverde Albacete, F.J. (eds.) Concept Lattices and their Applications CLA, pp. 171–183. Tallinn University of Technology (2020)
17. Valverde-Albacete, F.J., Peláez-Moreno, C., Cordero, P., Ojeda-Aciego, M.: Formal equivalence analysis. In: Proceedings of the 11th Conference of the European Society for Fuzzy Logic and Technology, EUSFLAT 2019 (2019)
18. Wille, R.: Restructuring lattice theory: an approach based on hierarchies of concepts. In: Ordered Sets, Banff, Alta., 1981, pp. 445–470. Reidel, Dordrecht-Boston (1982)

On the Effects of Conjunctions in the Solution Set of Multi-adjoint Fuzzy Relation Equations

David Lobo[✉][iD], Víctor López-Marchante[iD], and Jesús Medina[iD]

Department of Mathematics, University of Cádiz, Cádiz, Spain
{david.lobo,victor.lopez,jesus.medina}@uca.es

Abstract. A multi-adjoint fuzzy relation equation is defined from a sup-composition operator, which combines different conjunctions. The choice of such compositions has a direct impact on the resolution of the equation. This paper presents a first approach to the consequences of modifying the sup-composition associated with a multi-adjoint fuzzy relation equation in its solution set. Firstly, we show that greater conjunctions lead to lower greatest solutions. Then, two counterexamples are presented to highlight that, in general, an existing ordering in the conjunctions does not lead to comparable minimal solutions. Nevertheless, if the minimal solutions are comparable, we show that greater conjunctions lead to lower minimal solutions.

Keywords: Fuzzy Sets · Fuzzy Relation Equation · Property-oriented concept lattice · Adjoint triples

1 Introduction

Since their introduction in 1976 by Sanchez [16], fuzzy relation equations (FRE) have had a great impact in the literature [8,9,15,17], spreading to fields like decision making [3], bipolarity [4,5], optimization [2] and image processing [1]. In 2013, FRE were generalized to the multi-adjoint paradigm [10], enabling the coexistence of several conjunctions in a sup-composition of fuzzy relations, under the requirement of belonging to adjoint triples. A complete study on the resolution of multi-adjoint FRE was presented in [11], where the complete solution set is characterized in terms of an associated multi-adjoint property-oriented concept lattice [13].

The consideration of a problem in a multi-adjoint framework provides a user with a large flexibility, due to the generality of the underlying algebraic structure [12–14]. In particular, the user can consider different conjunctors associated

Supported by the 2014–2020 ERDF Operational Programme in collaboration with the State Research Agency (AEI) in project PID2019-108991GB-I00, and with the Department of Economy, Knowledge, Business and University of the Regional Government of Andalusia in project FEDER-UCA18-108612, and by the European Cooperation in Science & Technology (COST) Action CA17124.

© Springer Nature Switzerland AG 2022
D. Ciucci et al. (Eds.): IPMU 2022, CCIS 1601, pp. 130–141, 2022.
https://doi.org/10.1007/978-3-031-08971-8_12

with the variables [10]. Since the definition of the sup-composition operator is strongly related to the considered conjunctions, the resolution of FRE with this composition is markedly influenced by the underlying conjunctions.

For example, if & represents the usual product in the unit interval, then the expression

$$0.5 \, \& \, y = 0.25$$

holds for $y = 0.5$; but if $\& \colon [0,1] \times [0,1] \to [0,1]$ is defined as $x \, \& \, y = x^2 y$, then

$$0.5 \, \& \, y = 0.25$$

implies that $y = 1$. As a consequence, we can assert that, in general, a sup-composition that produces higher values does not lead to the same solution set than a sup-composition that produces lower values. Thus, it is very important analysing the relationships among the set of solutions of solvable multi-adjoint FRE changing the considered conjunctors.

The main goal of this paper is to introduce a preliminary study on how a change in the sup-composition associated with a multi-adjoint FRE affects to its solution set. In particular, we focus here on the impact of conjunctions on the greatest and minimal solutions of a multi-adjoint FRE.

We will show that greater conjunctions lead to lower greatest solutions. Concerning the minimal solutions, in general, an existing ordering in the conjunctions does not lead to comparable minimal solutions, although if we consider two comparable minimal solutions (associated with two multi-adjoint FRE with different compositions), then the minimal solution associated with the smaller conjunctor is greater than the minimal solution associated with the greater.

2   Multi-adjoint Fuzzy Relation Equations

In this section, we briefly recall some notions that are necessary for a correct understanding of this paper. The study presented is developed under the framework that was first presented in [10].

Adjoint triples generalize left-continuous t-norms and its residuated implications, under the consideration of possible non-commutative and non-associative conjunctions. Consequently, two different residuated implications can be defined associated with these conjunctions.

Definition 1 [6]. *Let $(P_1, \preceq_1)$, $(P_2, \preceq_2)$, $(P_3, \preceq_3)$ be posets and $\& \colon P_1 \times P_2 \to P_3$, $\swarrow \colon P_3 \times P_2 \to P_1$, $\nwarrow \colon P_3 \times P_1 \to P_2$ mappings, then $(\&, \swarrow, \nwarrow)$ is an adjoint triple with respect to P_1, P_2, P_3 if*

$$x \preceq_1 z \swarrow y \quad iff \quad x \& y \preceq_3 z \quad iff \quad y \preceq_2 z \nwarrow x$$

for each $x \in P_1$, $y \in P_2$, $z \in P_3$.

Given two conjunctions $\&_i, \&_j \colon P_1 \times P_2 \to P_3$, we will say that $\&_i \preceq \&_j$ if $x \&_i y \preceq_3 x \&_j y$ for all $x \in P_1, y \in P_2$. The following proposition states that this order is reversed for their residuated implications, if they exist.

Proposition 1. *Let* $(\&_i, \diagup^i, \diagdown_i)$, $(\&_j, \diagup^j, \diagdown_j)$ *be adjoint triples such that* $\&_i \preceq \&_j$. *Then,* $z \diagup^j y \preceq_1 z \diagup^i y$ *and* $z \diagdown_j x \preceq_2 z \diagdown_i x$, *for all* $x \in P_1$, $y \in P_2$ *and* $z \in P_3$.

In the examples, in order to simplify the computations, adjoint triples associated with the discretization of the Gödel, product and Łukasiewicz t-norms will be considered. Recall that the the Gödel t-norm $\&_G$ is defined as $x \&_G y = \min\{x, y\}$ for all $x, y \in [0,1]$; the product t-norm $\&_p$ is defined as $x \&_P y = xy$ for all $x, y \in [0,1]$ and the Łukasiewicz t-norm $\&_L$ is defined as $x \&_L y = \max\{0, x + y - 1\}$ for all $x, y \in [0,1]$. The three preceding t-norms are ordered as follows.

$$\&_L \preceq \&_P \preceq \&_G$$

A discretization of a t-norm $\&: [0,1] \times [0,1] \to [0,1]$ is the operator[1] $\&^*: [0,1]_m \times [0,1]_n \to [0,1]_k$, where $n, m, k \in \mathbb{N}$, defined as:

$$x \&^* y = \frac{\lceil k \cdot (x \& y) \rceil}{k}$$

for all $x \in [0,1]_m$ and $y \in [0,1]_n$, where $\lceil \_ \rceil$ is the ceiling function. The discretization of the corresponding residuated implications $\diagup^*: [0,1]_k \times [0,1]_n \to [0,1]_m$ and $\diagdown_*: [0,1]_k \times [0,1]_m \to [0,1]_n$ is defined as:

$$z \diagup^* y = \frac{\lfloor m \cdot (z \leftarrow y) \rfloor}{m} \qquad z \diagdown_* x = \frac{\lfloor n \cdot (z \leftarrow x) \rfloor}{n}$$

for all $z \in [0,1]_k$ and $y \in [0,1]_n$, where $\lfloor \_ \rfloor$ is the floor function and $\leftarrow$ is the residuated implication of the t-norm $\&$. We have that $(\&^*, \diagup^*, \diagdown_*)$ is an adjoint triple with respect to $[0,1]_n$, $[0,1]_m$ and $[0,1]_k$ [7,14].

Proposition 2. *Let* $[0,1]_n$ *be the regular partition of the unit interval in n pieces and* $\overline{\&}_G$, $\overline{\&}_P$ *and* $\overline{\&}_L$ *the discretization of the Gödel, product and Łukasiewicz t-norms, respectively. It holds that* $\overline{\&}_L \preceq \overline{\&}_P \preceq \overline{\&}_G$.

The concept of multi-adjoint property-oriented frame was introduced in [13] with the aim of allowing the use of several adjoint triples for the same triplet of posets. For computational reasons, we will assume that two of the posets are lattices.

Definition 2 [13]. *Let* $(L_1, \preceq_1)$, $(L_2, \preceq_2)$ *be two lattices,* $(P, \preceq_3)$ *a poset and* $\{(\&_i, \diagup^i, \diagdown_i) \mid i \in \{1, \ldots, n\}\}$ *a set of adjoint triples with respect to* P, L_2, L_1. *The tuple*

$$(L_1, L_2, P, \preceq_1, \preceq_2, \preceq_3, \&_1, \diagup^1, \diagdown_1, \ldots, \&_n, \diagup^n, \diagdown_n)$$

is called multi-adjoint property-oriented frame.

---

[1] $[0,1]_m$ denotes a regular partitions of $[0,1]$ into m pieces, for example, $[0,1]_4 = \{0, 0.25, 0.5, 0, 75, 1\}$ divides the unit interval into four pieces.

To improve readability, if $L_1 = L_2 = P$, the property-oriented multi-adjoint frame will be denoted as

$$(P, \preceq_3, \&_1, \nearrow^1, \nwarrow_1, \ldots, \&_n, \nearrow^n, \nwarrow_n)$$

The consideration of different adjoint triples in the frame allows a useful flexibility. For example, we can consider the following family of left-continuous t-norms of Yager [18]. For each $p > 0$, we define the t-norm $T_p \colon [0,1] \times [0,1] \to [0,1]$ as

$$T_p(x,y) = 1 - \min\{1, \sqrt[p]{(1-x)^p + (1-y)^p}\}$$

for all $x, y \in [0,1]$. This family verifies that, if $0 < p_1 \leq p_2$, then $T_{p_1}(x,y) \leq T_{p_2}(x,y)$, for all $x, y \in [0,1]$. This family enables to associate some variables with greater conjunctions and others with lower ones, depending on the preferences of the user.

In what follows, we recall some notions and results concerning multi-adjoint FRE. For more details, we refer the reader to [10].

A multi-adjoint FRE is an equality of the form $R \odot S = T$, where R, S and T are fuzzy relations, $\odot$ is a sup-composition operator and R or S is an unknown relation. Composition operators between fuzzy relations can be defined in several ways, but in this paper we will focus on the following.

Definition 3 [10]. *Let U, V, W be sets, $(P_1, \preceq_1), (P_2, \preceq_2), (P_3, \preceq_3)$ posets, being P_3 an upper-semilattice and $R \in P_1^{U \times V}$, $S \in P_2^{V \times W}$, $T \in P_3^{U \times W}$ three fuzzy relations. Given a set of adjoint triples $\{(\&_i, \nearrow^i, \nwarrow_i) \mid i \in \{1, \ldots, n\}\}$ with respect to P_1, P_2, P_3 and a mapping $\sigma \colon V \to \{1, \ldots, n\}$, the operator $\odot_\sigma \colon P_1^{U \times V} \times P_2^{V \times W} \to P_3^{U \times W}$ defined as*

$$R \odot_\sigma S(u,w) = \bigvee\nolimits_3 \{R(u,v) \&_{\sigma(v)} S(v,w) \mid v \in V\} \tag{1}$$

is called sup-$\&_\sigma$-composition.

The definition of multi-adjoint FRE follows from the sup-composition operator defined in Definition 3.

Definition 4 [10]. *A multi-adjoint FRE with sup-$\&_\sigma$-composition is an equality of the form*

$$R \odot_\sigma X = T \tag{2}$$

where X is an unknown fuzzy relation.

We say that a multi-adjoint FRE is *solvable* if there exists at least one solution, that is, a relation X satisfying (2). Otherwise, we say that the multi-adjoint FRE is *unsolvable*. A dual equation can be developed if given an equality $R \odot_\sigma S = T$, the unknown relation is R.

In case P_2 is a lower-semilattice and the multi-adjoint FRE (2) is solvable, its greatest solution exists and can be computed as a meet of implications.

Proposition 3 [10]. *Let $R \odot_\sigma X = T$ be a solvable equation and $(P_2, \preceq_2)$ a lower-semilattice. Its greatest solution $\overline{X}$ is given by*

$$\overline{X}(v, w) = \bigwedge\nolimits_2 \{T(u, w) \searrow_{\sigma(v)} R(u, v) \mid u \in U\}$$

for each $(v, w) \in V \times W$.

In [10, 11], some results concerning the solvability and the computation of the solution set of a multi-adjoint FRE are introduced based on FCA techniques. We will retrieve the most relevant ones in the scope of this paper. Firstly, the notion of context is recalled.

Definition 5 [13]. *Let $(L_1, L_2, P, \&_1, \ldots, \&_n)$ be a multi-adjoint property-oriented frame. A context is a tuple (A, B, R, σ) where A and B are non-empty sets, $R \colon A \times B \to P$ is a fuzzy relation and $\sigma \colon A \times B \to \{1, \ldots, n\}$ is a mapping.*

Given a multi-adjoint frame and a context, two mappings can be defined between the fuzzy subsets of *attributes* A, that is $L_1^A = \{f \mid f \colon A \to L_1\}$, and the fuzzy subsets of *objects* B, that is $L_2^B = \{g \mid g \colon B \to L_2\}$. Specifically, the mappings $\uparrow_\pi \colon L_2^B \to L_1^A$ and $\downarrow^N \colon L_1^A \to L_2^B$ are defined as

$$g^{\uparrow_\pi}(a) = \bigvee\nolimits_1 \{R(a, b) \&_{\sigma(a,b)} g(b) \mid b \in B\} \tag{3}$$

$$f^{\downarrow^N}(b) = \bigwedge\nolimits_2 \{f(a) \searrow_{\sigma(a,b)} R(a, b) \mid a \in A\} \tag{4}$$

for each $f \in L_1^A$ and $g \in L_2^B$, where $\bigvee_1$ and $\bigwedge_2$ represent the suprema and infima of $(L_1, \preceq_1)$ and $(L_2, \preceq_2)$, respectively. The pair of mappings $(\uparrow_\pi, \downarrow^N)$ forms an isotone Galois connection [13]. This leads to the definition of *multi-adjoint property-oriented concept lattice.*

Consider the order relation $\preceq_{\pi N}$ defined as $(g_1, f_1) \preceq_{\pi N} (g_2, f_2)$ if and only if $f_1 \preceq_1 f_2$, or equivalently, if and only if $g_1 \preceq_2 g_2$. The multi-adjoint property-oriented concept lattice associated with the multi-adjoint property-oriented frame is given by

$$\mathcal{M}_{\pi N}(A, B, R, \sigma) = \left\{(g, f) \in L_2^B \times L_1^A \mid g = f^{\downarrow^N}, f = g^{\uparrow_\pi}\right\} \tag{5}$$

The set $\mathcal{M}_{\pi N}$ endowed with the order $\preceq_{\pi N}$ is a complete lattice [13]. Given a concept (g, f), the mapping g is called *extent* of the concept and f is called the *intent* of the concept. The set of intents is denoted as $\mathcal{I}(\mathcal{M}_{\pi N})$ and the extents are denoted as $\mathcal{E}(\mathcal{M}_{\pi N})$.

The following definition assigns a context to a multi-adjoint FRE.

Definition 6 [10]. *The* multi-adjoint context associated with the multi-adjoint FRE $R \odot_\sigma X = T$ *is the property-oriented multi-adjoint context (U, V, R, σ).*

The following results are based on the notion of multi-adjoint concept lattice. The resolution procedure consists of associating a multi-adjoint FRE with a context and, consequently, a multi-adjoint property-oriented concept lattice is associated with it too.

The concept lattice $(\mathcal{M}_{\pi N}(U, V, R, \sigma), \preceq_{\pi N})$ of the context associated with a multi-adjoint FRE characterizes its solvability.

Proposition 4 [10]. *Let (U, V, R, σ) be the multi-adjoint context associated with a multi-adjoint FRE $R \odot_\sigma X = T$ and $(\mathcal{M}_{\pi N}, \preceq_{\pi N})$ the concept lattice associated with that context. Then $R \odot_\sigma X = T$ is solvable if and only if $T_w \in \mathcal{I}(\mathcal{M}_{\pi N})$ for all $w \in W$, where $T_w(u) = T(u, w)$, for all $u \in U$, $w \in W$.*

The solution set of a multi-adjoint FRE can be characterized in terms of its associated context. To recall such characterization, given a lattice $(L, \preceq)$ and $x \in L$, we will denote the lower bounds of x as $(x]$. Additionally, we define the set of predecessors of x as

$$\text{Pre}_L(x) = \{x' \in L \mid x' \prec x \text{ and there is no } x'' \in L \text{ such that } x' \prec x'' \prec x\}$$

Proposition 5 [11]. *Let (U, V, R, σ) be the multi-adjoint context associated with a solvable multi-adjoint FRE $R \odot_\sigma X = T$. If U, V are finite sets, the solution set of the multi-adjoint FRE is*

$$\left\{X \in L_2^{V \times W} \mid X_w \in \left(T_w^{\downarrow N}\right] \setminus \bigcup \left\{(g] \mid g \in Pre_{\mathcal{E}(\mathcal{M}_{\pi N})}\left(T_w^{\downarrow N}\right)\right\} \text{ for each } w \in W\right\}$$

Propositions 4 and 5 will be used together in the examples of Sect. 3, in order to determine the solution set of a particular multi-adjoint FRE.

3   Effects of Conjunctions in the Solution Set of a Multi-adjoint FRE

A question that naturally arises due to the flexibility of the multi-adjoint paradigm is whether the election of a sup-composition in the definition of a multi-adjoint FRE has direct consequences in its solution set. The solution set obtained from considering two different sup-compositions with the same coefficient matrix and independent term are expected to preserve some kind of ordering whenever the sup-compositions are comparable.

From now on, let

$$(L_1, L_2, P, \preceq_1, \preceq_2, \preceq_3, \&_1, \nearrow^1, \searrow_1, \ldots, \&_n, \nearrow^n, \searrow_n)$$

be a property-oriented multi-adjoint frame and U, V, W sets.

The partial order in the set of conjunctions induces a partial order in a set of sup-composition operators. Given two sup-composition operators $\odot_\sigma, \odot_{\sigma'} : P^U \times L_2^V \to L_1^W$, we say that $\odot_\sigma \preceq \odot_{\sigma'}$ if $\&_{\sigma(v)} \preceq \&_{\sigma'(v)}$ for all $v \in V$.

Notice that, the solution set of a multi-adjoint FRE has structure of upper-semilattice [10], as usual [9]. Consequently, any multi-adjoint FRE has a greatest solution and a (possibly empty) set of minimal solutions.

Proposition 3 characterizes the analytic expression of the greatest solution of a multi-adjoint FRE, which is given by a meet of values obtained from implications. Taking into account that greater conjunctions entail lower implications and the meet operator is an order-preserving mapping, the following proposition shows that greater conjunctions lead to lower greatest solutions.

Theorem 1. *Let $R \odot_\sigma X = T$ and $R \odot_{\sigma'} X = T$ be two solvable multi-adjoint FRE such that $\odot_\sigma \preceq \odot_{\sigma'}$ and $\overline{X}_\sigma, \overline{X}_{\sigma'}$ their greatest solutions respectively. Then, $\overline{X}_{\sigma'} \preceq_2 \overline{X}_\sigma$.*

Once it has been shown the relation between greatest solutions, it is natural wondering if it is possible obtaining a similar result with respect to minimal solutions. For example, it seems reasonable that, if $\odot_\sigma \preceq \odot'_\sigma$ and the multi-adjoint FRE $R \odot_\sigma X = T$ and $R \odot_{\sigma'} X = T$ are solvable, then at least one of the following statements holds:

a) For each minimal solution $X_{\sigma'}$ of $R \odot_{\sigma'} X = T$, there exists a minimal solution X_σ of $R \odot_\sigma X = T$ such that $X_{\sigma'} \preceq_2 X_\sigma$.
b) For each minimal solution X_σ of $R \odot_\sigma X = T$, there exists a minimal solution $X_{\sigma'}$ of $R \odot_{\sigma'} X = T$ such that $X_{\sigma'} \preceq_2 X_\sigma$.

Nevertheless, neither (a) nor (b) holds, in general. Moreover, as we show next in two counterexamples, they do not even hold for FRE with a non-multi-adjoint nature, that is, for FRE defined with a simple conjunction.

To improve readability, if $\sigma(v) = i$ for all $v \in V$, we will denote the sup-composition operator $\odot_\sigma$ as $\odot_i$. Furthermore, when working with the t-norms $\&_G, \&_p, \&_L$, we will abuse of notation by denoting sup-composition operators as $\odot_G, \odot_p$ and $\odot_L$, instead of using a number.

Example 1. Consider the sets $U = \{u_1, u_2\}$, $V = \{v_1, v_2\}$, $W = \{w\}$ and the multi-adjoint frame

$$([0,1]_8, \leq, \overline{\&}_p, \nearrow^p, \searrow_p, \overline{\&}_G, \nearrow^G, \searrow_G) \tag{6}$$

where $\overline{\&}_p$ is the discretization of the product t-norm and $\overline{\&}_G$ is the discretization of the Gödel t-norm, both discretized in $[0,1]_8$. By Corollary 2, it holds that $\overline{\&}_p \preceq \overline{\&}_G$.

Consider the FRE

$$R \odot_p X = T \tag{7}$$

and the FRE

$$R \odot_G X = T \tag{8}$$

where

$$R = \begin{pmatrix} 0.5 & 0.25 \\ 0.25 & 0.25 \end{pmatrix}, \qquad T = \begin{pmatrix} 0.25 \\ 0.25 \end{pmatrix}$$

The relevant part of their associated concept lattices is shown in Figs. 1 and 2, respectively. In both cases, there exists a concept whose intent is T. Therefore, applying Proposition 4, we conclude that FRE (7) and (8) are both solvable.

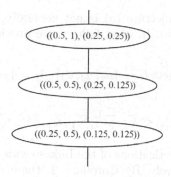

Fig. 1. Sublattice of the concept lattice associated with FRE (7)

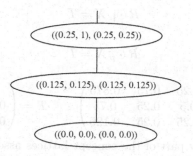

Fig. 2. Sublattice of the concept lattice associated with FRE (8)

On the one hand, by Proposition 3, the greatest solutions of FRE (7) and (8) are determined, in both cases, by the extent of the concept with intent T, which come out to be

$$\overline{X}_p = \begin{pmatrix} 0.5 \\ 1 \end{pmatrix} \quad \text{and} \quad \overline{X}_G = \begin{pmatrix} 0.25 \\ 1 \end{pmatrix}$$

On the other hand, by Proposition 5, predecessors of the concept whose intent is T determine the solution set of a FRE. Carrying out the corresponding computations, we obtain that, FRE (7) has a minimum solution,

$$X_{p,1} = \begin{pmatrix} 0 \\ 0.625 \end{pmatrix}$$

while FRE (8) has two minimal solutions

$$X_{G,1} = \begin{pmatrix} 0.25 \\ 0 \end{pmatrix} \quad X_{G,2} = \begin{pmatrix} 0 \\ 0.25 \end{pmatrix}$$

Clearly, $X_{1,1} \nparallel X_{2,1}$, what contradicts the conjecture (a).

□

Example 1 shows that conjecture (a) is not generally true. However, there is still place for conjecture (b). In what follows, we provide a counterexample to conjecture (b).

Example 2. Consider the sets $U = \{u_1, u_2, u_3\}$, $V = \{v_1, v_2, v_3\}$, $W = \{w\}$ and the multi-adjoint frame

$$([0,1]_8, \leq, \overline{\&}_L, \nearrow^L, \nwarrow_L, \overline{\&}_p, \nearrow^p, \nwarrow_p) \tag{9}$$

where $\overline{\&}_L, \overline{\&}_p$ are the discretizations of the Łukasiewicz t-norm and the product t-norm in $[0,1]_8$, respectively. By Corollary 2, these conjunctions verify that $\overline{\&}_L \preceq \overline{\&}_p$.

Consider the FRE

$$R \odot_L X = T \tag{10}$$

and the FRE

$$R \odot_p X = T \tag{11}$$

where

$$R = \begin{pmatrix} 0.25 & 0.75 & 0.875 \\ 0.5 & 0.25 & 0.75 \\ 0.25 & 0.25 & 0.125 \end{pmatrix} \qquad T = \begin{pmatrix} 0.5 \\ 0.375 \\ 0.125 \end{pmatrix}$$

Figures 3 and 4 show part of the concept lattices associated with FRE (10) and (11). In both cases, there exists a concept whose intent is T and hence, applying Proposition 4, we conclude that FRE (10) and (11) are solvable.

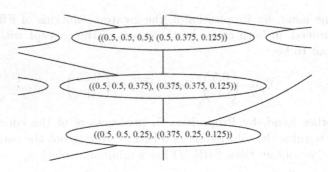

Fig. 3. Sublattice of the concept lattice associated with FRE (10)

Now, applying Proposition 5, we conclude that $R \odot_L X = T$ has a greatest solution

$$\overline{X}_L = \begin{pmatrix} 0.875 \\ 0.75 \\ 0.625 \end{pmatrix}$$

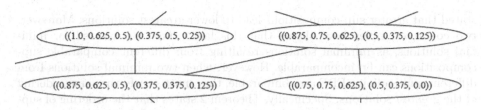

Fig. 4. Sublattice of the concept lattice associated with FRE (11)

and two minimal solutions

$$X_{L,1} = \begin{pmatrix} 0.875 \\ 0.75 \\ 0 \end{pmatrix} \qquad X_{L,2} = \begin{pmatrix} 0.875 \\ 0 \\ 0.625 \end{pmatrix}$$

Concerning $R \odot_p X = T$, there exists a greatest solution

$$\overline{X}_p = \begin{pmatrix} 0.5 \\ 0.5 \\ 0.5 \end{pmatrix}$$

and a minimum one

$$X_{p,1} = \begin{pmatrix} 0 \\ 0 \\ 0.5 \end{pmatrix}$$

Since $X_{p,1} \not\parallel X_{L,1}$, this contradicts the conjecture (b). $\square$

The counterexamples of conjectures (a) and (b) prove that there is not a natural way of establishing a biunivocal correspondence between the minimal solutions of $R \odot_\sigma X = T$ and the minimal solutions of $R \odot_{\sigma'} X = T$.

In addition, Examples 1 and 2 show that, in spite of the possible existing order between two sup-compositions $\odot_\sigma$ and $\odot_{\sigma'}$, a minimal solution of $R \odot_\sigma X = T$ might be incomparable with all minimal solutions of $R \odot_{\sigma'} X = T$, and vice versa. Nevertheless, the following result states that if two minimal solutions are comparable, then there is only one possible ordering. Specifically, greater sup-compositions give rise to lower minimal solutions.

Theorem 2. *Let $R \odot_\sigma X = T$ and $R \odot_{\sigma'} X = T$ be two solvable multi-adjoint FRE such that $\odot_\sigma \preceq \odot_{\sigma'}$. If X_σ is a minimal solution of $R \odot_\sigma X = T$ and $X_{\sigma'}$ is a minimal solution of $R \odot_{\sigma'} X = T$ such that X_σ and X'_σ are comparable, it holds that $X_{\sigma'} \preceq_2 X_\sigma$.*

4   Conclusions and Future Work

A first study on the consequences of changing the sup-composition associated with a multi-adjoint fuzzy relation equation has been presented. Theorem 1 has stated that greater sup-compositions lead to lower greatest solutions. Moreover, two counterexamples have shown that this fact cannot be assured for minimal solutions, as minimal solutions resulting from different comparable sup-compositions can be incomparable. However, when two minimal solutions from different multi-adjoint FRE are comparable, they must satisfy the same ordering of the greatest solutions. Specifically, Theorem 2 states that the ordering of sup-compositions reverses the ordering in minimal solutions whenever they are comparable. Future work will aim for conditions that assure comparability between minimal solutions of multi-adjoint FRE with comparable sup-compositions.

References

1. Alcalde, C., Burusco, A., Díaz-Moreno, J.C., Medina, J.: Fuzzy concept lattices and fuzzy relation equations in the retrieval processing of images and signals. Int. J. Uncertain. Fuzz. Knowl.-Based Syst. **25**(Supplement-1), 99–120 (2017). https://doi.org/10.1142/s0218488517400050
2. Aliannezhadi, S., Abbasi Molai, A.: A new algorithm for geometric optimization with a single-term exponent constrained by bipolar fuzzy relation equations. Iran. J. Fuzzy Syst. **18**(1), 137–150 (2021). https://doi.org/10.22111/ijfs.2021.5879
3. Cornejo, M.E., Díaz-Moreno, J.C., Medina, J.: Multi-adjoint relation equations: a decision support system for fuzzy logic. Int. J. Intell. Syst. **32**(8), 778–800 (2017). https://doi.org/10.1002/int.21889
4. Cornejo, M.E., Lobo, D., Medina, J.: On the solvability of bipolar max-product fuzzy relation equations with the standard negation. Fuzzy Sets Syst. **410**, 1–18 (2021). https://doi.org/10.1016/j.fss.2020.02.010
5. Cornejo, M.E., Lobo, D., Medina, J., De Baets, B.: Bipolar equations on complete distributive symmetric residuated lattices: the case of a join-irreducible right-hand side. Fuzzy Sets Syst. (2022). https://doi.org/10.1016/j.fss.2022.02.003
6. Cornejo, M.E., Medina, J., Ramírez-Poussa, E.: Algebraic structure and characterization of adjoint triples. Fuzzy Sets Syst. (2021). https://doi.org/10.1016/j.fss.2021.02.002
7. Cornejo, M.E., Medina, J., Ramírez-Poussa, E.: A comparative study of adjoint triples. Fuzzy Sets Syst. **211**, 1–14 (2013). https://doi.org/10.1016/j.fss.2012.05.004
8. De Baets, B.: Analytical solution methods for fuzzy relation equations. In: Dubois, D., Prade, H. (eds.) The Handbooks of Fuzzy Sets Series, vol. 1, pp. 291–340. Kluwer, Dordrecht (1999)
9. Di Nola, A., Sanchez, E., Pedrycz, W., Sessa, S.: Fuzzy Relation Equations and Their Applications to Knowledge Engineering. Kluwer Academic Publishers, Norwell (1989)
10. Díaz, J.C., Medina, J.: Multi-adjoint relation equations: definition, properties and solutions using concept lattices. Inf. Sci. **253**, 100–109 (2013). https://doi.org/10.1016/j.ins.2013.07.024
11. Díaz-Moreno, J.C., Medina, J.: Using concept lattice theory to obtain the set of solutions of multi-adjoint relation equations. Inf. Sci. **266**, 218–225 (2014). https://doi.org/10.1016/j.ins.2014.01.006
12. Medina, J., Ojeda-Aciego, M., Ruiz-Calviño, J.: Formal concept analysis via multi-adjoint concept lattices. Fuzzy Sets Syst. **160**(2), 130–144 (2009). https://doi.org/10.1016/j.fss.2008.05.004

13. Medina, J.: Multi-adjoint property-oriented and object-oriented concept lattices. Inf. Sci. **190**, 95–106 (2012). https://doi.org/10.1016/j.ins.2011.11.016
14. Medina, J., Ojeda-Aciego, M., Valverde, A., Vojtáš, P.: Towards biresiduated multi-adjoint logic programming. In: Conejo, R., Urretavizcaya, M., Pérez-de-la-Cruz, J.-L. (eds.) CAEPIA/TTIA -2003. LNCS (LNAI), vol. 3040, pp. 608–617. Springer, Heidelberg (2004). https://doi.org/10.1007/978-3-540-25945-9_60
15. Pedrycz, W.: Fuzzy relational equations with generalized connectives and their applications. Fuzzy Sets Syst. **10**(1–3), 185–201 (1983). https://doi.org/10.1016/S0165-0114(83)80114-6
16. Sanchez, E.: Resolution of composite fuzzy relation equations. Inf. Control **30**(1), 38–48 (1976). https://doi.org/10.1016/S0019-9958(76)90446-0
17. Turunen, E.: On generalized fuzzy relation equations: necessary and sufficient conditions for the existence of solutions. Acta Universitatis Carolinae. Mathematica et Physica **28**(1), 33–37 (1987). http://eudml.org/doc/246361
18. Yager, R.R.: An approach to inference in approximate reasoning. Int. J. Man Mach. Stud. **13**(3), 323–338 (1980). https://doi.org/10.1016/S0020-7373(80)80046-0

Comparing Attribute Reduction in Multi-adjoint Concept Lattices and the CR-method

María José Benítez-Caballero[✉][iD] and Jesús Medina[iD]

Department of Mathematics, Universidad de Cádiz (Puerto Real), Cádiz, Spain
{mariajose.benitez,jesus.medina}@uca.es

Abstract. One of the main goal in several fields is to describe a general method to reduce the size of any kind of database. One of these methods is the clarification and reduction method (CR-method). In this paper, the relationship between the CR-method and the reduction mechanism in multi-adjoint formal concept analysis is studied.

Keywords: multi-adjoint formal concept analysis · CR-method · attribute reduction

1 Introduction

Formal Concept Analysis (FCA), introduced by Wille in the eighties [26], is one of the most powerful mathematical tools in order to manage and obtain information collected in databases. Usually, the mathematical representation of these databases is called formal context and it is composed of a set of objects, a set of properties studied over the set of objects, usually called attributes, and the relation between them.

In this environment, the notion of concept is considered as a minimal unit of information. It is a pair composed of a subset of objects verifying a subset of attributes, and vice versa. Furthermore, an order can be considered providing a hierarchy among the concepts, giving the algebraic structure of complete lattice [12]. The way of building concepts changes depending on the nature of the data [2,6,23]. Specifically, if the databases is working in a fuzzy background, there are several approaches [3,5,15]. In this paper, we are focused on multi-adjoint formal concept analysis [20,21]. In this framework, adjoint triples [8] are considered in the definition of the concept-forming operators [20]. The use of a specific adjoint triple for each pair object-attribute allows us to describe different degrees of relevance over the sets of objects and attributes.

Partially supported by the 2014–2020 ERDF Operational Programme in collaboration with the State Research Agency (AEI) in project PID2019-108991GB-I00, and with the Department of Economy, Knowledge, Business and University of the Regional Government of Andalusia in project FEDER-UCA18-108612, and by the European Cooperation in Science & Technology (COST) Action CA17124.

D. Ciucci et al. (Eds.): IPMU 2022, CCIS 1601, pp. 142–154, 2022.
https://doi.org/10.1007/978-3-031-08971-8_13

One of the main goals in applications is to reduce the size of the given database. With this goal, the notion of reduct arose, as a minimal set of attributes keeping the original information. In FCA, this notion is deeply studied in several papers [7,13,18,19].

In this paper, we are going to study the reduction method presented in [17] and compare it with the one given in the multi-adjoint concept lattice framework [1,20]. For example, we will prove that an attribute belonging to a reduct obtained with the CR-method also belongs to a reduct given by the multi-adjoint reduction mechanism.

This paper is structured as follows: first of all, some preliminaries notions and results are recalled in Sect. 2. Then, we are able to study the connection between the two methods in Sect. 3. In Sect. 4, a specific example is detailed. Finally, some conclusions and future work is presented in Sect. 5.

2   Preliminaries

2.1   Multi-adjoint Formal Concept Analysis

The adjoint triples are a generalization of the triangular norm and its residuated implication [16]. In this paper, we consider adjoint triple in order to define concept-forming operators.

Definition 1. *Let* $(P_1, \leq_1)$, $(P_2, \leq_2)$, $(P_3, \leq_3)$ *be posets and* $\&\colon P_1 \times P_2 \to P_3$, $\swarrow\colon P_3 \times P_2 \to P_1$, $\nwarrow\colon P_3 \times P_1 \to P_2$ *be mappings, then* $(\&, \swarrow, \nwarrow)$ *is an adjoint triple with respect to* P_1, P_2, P_3 *if the following double equivalence holds:*

$$x \leq_1 z \swarrow y \quad \text{iff} \quad x \& y \leq_3 z \quad \text{iff} \quad y \leq_2 z \nwarrow x \tag{1}$$

for all $x \in P_1$, $y \in P_2$ *and* $z \in P_3$. *This double equivalence is called* adjoint property.

In a multi-adjoint concept lattice environment, the considered posets $(P_1, \leq_1)$ and $(P_2, \leq_2)$ must be complete lattices [20]. In the following, we are going to recall the notion of multi-adjoint frame.

Definition 2. *A* multi-adjoint frame $\mathcal{L}$ *is a tuple:*

$$(L_1, L_2, P, \preceq_1, \preceq_2, \leq, \&_1, \swarrow^1, \nwarrow_1, \ldots, \&_n, \swarrow^n, \nwarrow_n)$$

where $(L_1, \preceq_1)$ *and* $(L_2, \preceq_2)$ *are complete lattices,* $(P, \leq)$ *is a poset and, for all* $\{i = 1, \ldots, n\}$, $(\&_i, \swarrow^i, \nwarrow_i)$ *is an adjoint triple with respect to* L_1, L_2, P. *Multi-adjoint frames are denoted as* $(L_1, L_2, P, \&_1, \ldots, \&_n)$.

Given a frame, a *multi-adjoint context* is a tuple consisting of sets of objects, attributes and a fuzzy relation among them; in addition, the multi-adjoint approach also includes a function which assigns an adjoint triple to each pair of objects and attributes.

Definition 3. *Let us consider* $(L_1, L_2, P, \&_1, \ldots, \&_n)$ *a multi-adjoint frame, a context is a tuple* $(\mathcal{O}, \mathcal{P}, \mathcal{R}, \sigma)$ *where* $\mathcal{O}$ *is the set of objects and* $\mathcal{P}$ *is the set of attributes, both non-empty sets,* $\mathcal{R}$ *is a P-fuzzy relation* $\mathcal{R} \colon \mathcal{O} \times \mathcal{P} \to P$ *and* $\sigma \colon \mathcal{O} \times \mathcal{P} \to \{1, \ldots, n\}$ *is a mapping which associates an specific adjoint triple in the frame with any element in* $\mathcal{O} \times \mathcal{P}$.

Now, we will reformulate the concept-forming operators when a multi-adjoint frame and a context for that frame are considered. Let $L_1^{\mathcal{O}}$ and $L_2^{\mathcal{P}}$ be set of fuzzy subsets $g \colon \mathcal{O} \to L_1$ and $f \colon \mathcal{P} \to L_2$, respectively, the concept-forming operators, $\uparrow_\sigma \colon L_1^{\mathcal{O}} \longrightarrow L_2^{\mathcal{P}}$ and $\downarrow^\sigma \colon L_2^{\mathcal{P}} \longrightarrow L_1^{\mathcal{O}}$, are defined, for all $g \in L_1^{\mathcal{O}}$, $f \in L_2^{\mathcal{P}}$ and $a \in \mathcal{P}$, $x \in \mathcal{O}$, as:

$$g^{\uparrow_\sigma}(a) = \inf\{\mathcal{R}(x, a) \swarrow^{\sigma(x,a)} g(x) \mid x \in \mathcal{O}\} \tag{2}$$

$$f^{\downarrow^\sigma}(x) = \inf\{\mathcal{R}(x, a) \nwarrow_{\sigma(x,a)} f(a) \mid a \in \mathcal{P}\} \tag{3}$$

The defined operators form a Galois connection [20]. Hence, the definition of a concept is as usual: a pair $\langle g, f \rangle$ is called a *multi-adjoint concept* if $g \in L_1^{\mathcal{O}}$, $f \in L_2^{\mathcal{P}}$ and that equalities $g^{\uparrow_\sigma} = f$ and $f^{\downarrow^\sigma} = g$; with $(\uparrow_\sigma, \downarrow^\sigma)$, holds. The set g is the *extent* of the concept, meanwhile, the set f is the *intent*.

Definition 4. *The* multi-adjoint concept lattice *associated with a multi-adjoint frame* $(L_1, L_2, P, \&_1, \ldots, \&_n)$ *and a context* $(\mathcal{O}, \mathcal{P}, \mathcal{R}, \sigma)$ *is the set*

$$\mathcal{M}(\mathcal{O}, \mathcal{P}, \mathcal{R}, \sigma) = \{\langle g, f \rangle \mid g \in L_1^{\mathcal{O}}, f \in L_2^{\mathcal{P}} \text{ and } g^{\uparrow_\sigma} = f, f^{\downarrow^\sigma} = g\}$$

in which the ordering is defined by $\langle g_1, f_1 \rangle \preceq \langle g_2, f_2 \rangle$ *if and only if* $g_1 \preceq_2 g_2$ *(equivalently* $f_2 \preceq_1 f_1$*).*

The ordering just defined above provides $\mathcal{M}(\mathcal{O}, \mathcal{P}, \mathcal{R}, \sigma)$ with the structure of a complete lattice [20]. We will denote a multi-adjoint concept lattice as $(\mathcal{M}, \preceq)$, when no confusion with the context exists.

From now on, we are writing $\uparrow$ and $\downarrow$ as an alternative of $\uparrow_\sigma$ and $\downarrow^\sigma$, respectively, in order to simplify the notation.

2.2 Attribute Classification in Multi-adjoint Concept Lattices

In this section, the notions and results related to the attribute reduction mechanism in multi-adjoint concept lattices will be recalled [9,10]. Hereinafter, a multi-adjoint frame $(L_1, L_2, P, \&_1, \ldots, \&_n)$ and a context $(\mathcal{O}, \mathcal{P}, \mathcal{R}, \sigma)$ will be fixed.

The following definition presents the most natural extension of a consistent set in the multi-adjoint framework.

Definition 5. *A set of attributes* $Y \subseteq \mathcal{P}$ *is called a* consistent set *of* $(\mathcal{O}, \mathcal{P}, \mathcal{R}, \sigma)$ *if* $\mathcal{M}(\mathcal{O}, Y, \mathcal{R}_Y, \sigma_{Y \times \mathcal{O}}) \cong_E \mathcal{M}(\mathcal{O}, \mathcal{P}, \mathcal{R}, \sigma)$, *where* $\cong_E$ *denotes an isomorphism preserving extents. This is equivalent to say that, for all* $\langle g, f \rangle \in \mathcal{M}(\mathcal{O}, \mathcal{P}, \mathcal{R}, \sigma)$, *there exists a concept* $\langle g', f' \rangle \in \mathcal{M}(\mathcal{O}, Y, \mathcal{R}_Y, \sigma_{Y \times \mathcal{O}})$ *such that* $g = g'$.

Moreover, if $\mathcal{M}(\mathcal{O}, Y \setminus \{a\}, \mathcal{R}_{Y \setminus \{a\}}, \sigma_{Y \setminus \{a\} \times \mathcal{O}}) \not\cong_E \mathcal{M}(\mathcal{O}, \mathcal{P}, \mathcal{R}, \sigma)$, *for all* $a \in Y$, *then* Y *is called a* reduct *of* $(\mathcal{O}, \mathcal{P}, \mathcal{R}, \sigma)$.

The core *of* $(\mathcal{O}, \mathcal{P}, \mathcal{R}, \sigma)$ *is the intersection of all the reducts of* $(\mathcal{O}, \mathcal{P}, \mathcal{R}, \sigma)$.

A classification of the attributes can be described by means of the definition of reduct. Specifically, an attribute can be sorted into three groups.

Definition 6. *Given a multi-adjoint formal context $(\mathcal{O}, \mathcal{P}, \mathcal{R}, \sigma)$ and the set $\mathcal{Y} = \{Y \subseteq \mathcal{P} \mid Y \text{ is a reduct}\}$ of all the reducts of $(\mathcal{O}, \mathcal{P}, \mathcal{R}, \sigma)$, the set of attributes $\mathcal{P}$ can be split into the following three parts:*

1. *Absolutely necessary attributes (core attribute) $C_f = \bigcap_{Y \in \mathcal{Y}} Y$.*
2. *Relatively necessary attributes $K_f = (\bigcup_{Y \in \mathcal{Y}} Y) \smallsetminus (\bigcap_{Y \in \mathcal{Y}} Y)$.*
3. *Absolutely unnecessary attributes $I_f = \mathcal{P} \smallsetminus (\bigcup_{Y \in \mathcal{Y}} Y)$.*

One of the main goal in several fields is to reduce the set of attributes. In formal concept analysis, the reduction mechanism is based on the classification of the attributes from the irreducible elements in the concept lattice. Therefore, the definition of irreducible element of a lattice will be needed.

Definition 7. *Given a lattice $(L, \preceq)$, such that $\wedge, \vee$ are the meet and the join operators. An element $x \in L$ verifying that*

1. *If L has a top element $\top$, then $x \neq \top$.*
2. *If $x = y \wedge z$, then $x = y$ or $x = z$, for all $y, z \in L$.*

is called meet-irreducible *($\wedge$-irreducible) element of L. Condition (2) is equivalent to*

2'. *If $x < y$ and $x < z$, then $x < y \wedge z$, for all $y, z \in L$.*

Hence, if x is $\wedge$-irreducible, then it cannot be represented as the infimum of strictly greater elements.

A join-irreducible ($\vee$-irreducible) element of L is defined dually.

In order to recall a characterization of the meet-irreducible elements of a multi-adjoint concept lattice, we need to consider a multi-adjoint concept lattice $(\mathcal{M}, \preceq)$ associated with a multi-adjoint frame $(L_1, L_2, P, \&_1, \ldots, \&_n)$, a context $(\mathcal{O}, \mathcal{P}, \mathcal{R}, \sigma)$, where L_1, L_2, P, $\mathcal{P}$ and $\mathcal{O}$ are finite and the following specific family of fuzzy subsets of $L_2^{\mathcal{P}}$.

Definition 8. *For each $a \in \mathcal{P}$, the fuzzy subsets of attributes $\phi_{a,\beta} \in L_2^{\mathcal{P}}$ defined, for all $\beta \in L_2$, as*

$$\phi_{a,\beta}(a') = \begin{cases} \beta & \text{if } a' = a \\ 0 & \text{if } a' \neq a \end{cases}$$

will be called fuzzy-attributes. *The set of all fuzzy-attributes will be denoted as $\Phi = \{\phi_{a,\beta} \mid a \in \mathcal{P}, \beta \in L_2\}$.*

The following result presents a characterization of the meet-irreducible elements of a multi-adjoint concept lattice [10]. Also, the join-irreducible elements can be considered producing a similar result.

Theorem 1 [10]. *The set of $\wedge$-irreducible elements of $\mathcal{M}$, $M_F(\mathcal{O}, \mathcal{P}, \mathcal{R}, \sigma)$, is:*

$$\left\{ \langle \phi_{a,\beta}^{\downarrow}, \phi_{a,\beta}^{\downarrow\uparrow} \rangle \mid \phi_{a,\beta}^{\downarrow} \neq \bigwedge \{\phi_{a_i,\beta_i}^{\downarrow} \mid \phi_{a_i,\beta_i} \in \Phi, \phi_{a,\beta}^{\downarrow} \prec_2 \phi_{a_i,\beta_i}^{\downarrow} \} \text{ and } \phi_{a,\beta}^{\downarrow} \neq g_\top \right\}$$

where $\top$ is the maximum element in L_1 and $g_\top : \mathcal{O} \to L_1$ is the fuzzy subset defined as $g_\top(x) = \top$, for all $x \in \mathcal{O}$.

As a way to simplify notation, we will denote $M_F(\mathcal{P})$ instead of $M_F(\mathcal{O}, \mathcal{P}, \mathcal{R}, \sigma)$.

The following definition describes the set of all the attributes generating a given concept.

Definition 9. *Given a multi-adjoint frame $(L_1, L_2, P, \&_1, \ldots, \&_n)$, a context $(\mathcal{O}, \mathcal{P}, \mathcal{R}, \sigma)$ associated with the concept lattice $(\mathcal{M}, \preceq)$ and a concept C of $(\mathcal{M}, \preceq)$, the set of attributes generating C is the set:*

$$Atg(C) = \{a \in \mathcal{P} \mid \text{there exists} \quad \beta \in L_2 \quad \text{such that} \quad \langle \phi_{a,\beta}^{\downarrow}, \phi_{a,\beta}^{\downarrow\uparrow} \rangle = C\}$$

Now, we will list the three attribute classification theorems. The first one characterizes the absolutely necessary attributes.

Theorem 2 [9]. *Given an attribute $a \in \mathcal{P}$, then $a \in C_f$ if and only if there exists a meet-irreducible concept C of $(\mathcal{M}, \preceq)$ satisfying that $a \in Atg(C)$ and $card(Atg(C)) = 1$.*

The characterization of the relatively necessary attributes is given as follows:

Theorem 3 [9]. *Given an attribute $a \in \mathcal{P}$, then $a \in K_f$ if and only if $a \notin C_f$ and there exists $C \in M_F(\mathcal{P})$ with $a \in Atg(C)$ and $card(Atg(C)) > 1$, satisfying that $(\mathcal{P} \setminus Atg(C)) \cup \{a\}$ is a consistent set.*

Moreover, we will need a characterization over the set of absolutely unnecessary attributes when the attributes generating a concept are considered. This idea is recalled in the following proposition.

Theorem 4 [9]. *Given an attribute $a \in \mathcal{P}$, then $a \in I_f$ if and only if, for any $C \in M_F(\mathcal{P})$, $a \notin Atg(C)$, or if $a \in Atg(C)$ then $(\mathcal{P} \setminus Atg(C)) \cup \{a\}$ is not a consistent set.*

2.3   Clarification and Reduction Method

In this section, we are going to recall some notions of the clarification and reduction of a formal context presented in [14], in which only the attribute part is going to be considered. This method is applied in the aforementioned paper in the three-way concept lattices [22], the variable threshold concept lattices [25] and the generalized one-sided concept lattices [24]. Moreover, it can be adapted to be applied to the multi-adjoint framework [20]. Hence, we will recall this method from a context $(\mathcal{O}, \mathcal{P}, \mathcal{R})$, and the derivation operators $^{\downarrow}$, $^{\uparrow}$ in the classical case.

The main idea of clarification is to eliminate the duplicate columns by merging them. Therefore, a clarified formal context, denoted as $(\mathcal{O}, \mathcal{P}^\bullet, \mathcal{R}^\bullet)$, with

$\mathcal{P}^\bullet = \{[a] \mid a \in \mathcal{P}\}$, where the classes are defined as $[a] = \{a_i \in \mathcal{P} \mid a_i^\downarrow = a^\downarrow\}$. For any object $x \in \mathcal{O}$ and class attribute $[a] \in \mathcal{P}^\bullet$, the relation is defined as $\mathcal{R}^\bullet(x, [a]) = 1$ if and only if $\mathcal{R}(x, a_i) = 1$, with $a_i \in [a]$.

Then, the clarified formal context is reduced. In this paper, this clarified and reduced formal context will be denoted as CR-formal context. In order to do that, the reducible attributes are eliminated from the formal context. An attribute $[a] \in \mathcal{P}^\bullet$ is a *reducible attribute* if the concept $\langle [a]^\downarrow, [a]^{\downarrow\uparrow} \rangle$ is a meet-reducible concept in the clarified context $(\mathcal{O}, \mathcal{P}^\bullet, \mathcal{R}^\bullet)$.

In [17], this method is called *CR-method* and it was adapted to several extensions of FCA, with the following scheme:

Scaling. In the first step, the original attributes are split into several scale attributes. In some FCA frameworks, this step is trivial, as in three-way concept lattices or attribute-induced three-ways concept lattices. In the particular case of crisp-fuzzy variable threshold concept lattice, the original formal context is scaled into the formal context $\langle \mathcal{O}, \mathcal{P} \times L, \mathcal{R}^\times \rangle$, where the context lattice is isomorphic to the original one. In this case, the relation is defined as $\mathcal{R}^\times(x, a_\delta) = 1$ if and only if $\delta \leq \mathcal{R}(x, a)$, for all $x \in \mathcal{O}$, $a \in \mathcal{P}$ and $\delta \in L$. The value δ will be called as *scaled value*.

Clarification and Reduction. Now, the scaled formal context is clarified and reduced, using the ideas previously mentioned.

Discernibility Function. The following step is to create a conjunctive normal form (CNF) using the attributes of the last formal context:

$$\bigwedge_{[a] \in \mathcal{P}^\bullet} \left(\bigvee_{a_i \in [a]} a_i \right)$$

This CNF is called *discernibility function*.

Replacement. We replace the scaled attributes by the original ones, as final step. The disjunctive normal form (DNF) of the replaced discernibility function describes the reducts of the original formal context.

3   Comparison Between Both Methods

In this section, we will study the relationship between the reduction obtain with the CR-method and the general reduction mechanism given in the multi-adjoint formal context framework.

The first important requirement is that in a multi-adjoint frame it is needed, for example, that $P = L_1$, because we need to write the equality $\delta \leq \mathcal{R}(x, a)$ of the scaling step in the multi-adjoint frame. Hence, from now on, we will consider a context $(\mathcal{O}, \mathcal{P}, \mathcal{R}, \sigma)$ and a multi-adjoint frame $(L_1, L_2, L_1, \&_1, \ldots, \&_n)$, where the adjoint conjunctors satisfy the boundary condition with the top element on the second argument, that is, $x \&_i \top_2 = x$, for all $i \in \{1, \ldots, n\}$, $x \in L_1$ and the top element $\top_2$ of the complete lattice $(L_2, \preceq_2)$. The following results connects the scaled relationship and the value taken by the concept-forming operator.

Proposition 1. *Let $\mathcal{R}^\times$ be the scaled relation of the formal context $(\mathcal{O}, \mathcal{P}, \mathcal{R}, \sigma)$, an attribute $a \in \mathcal{P}$ and a truth value $\delta \in L$. If $\mathcal{R}^\times(x, a_\delta) = 1$ for an object $x \in \mathcal{O}$, then $\phi_{a,\delta}^{\downarrow}(x) = \top_2$.*

On the other hand, we cannot ensure what value is going to take $\phi_{a,\delta}^{\downarrow}(x)$ when $\delta \npreceq_1 \mathcal{R}(x, a)$, due to this value will depend on the considered adjoint triple and domain. For example, if we consider the Gödel adjoint triple, we obtain that $\phi_{a,\delta}^{\downarrow}(x) = \mathcal{R}(x, a)$.

Moreover, we can obtain a relation among the scaled values and the truth values used to build the fuzzy attributes.

Proposition 2. *Let $(\mathcal{O}, \mathcal{P}, \mathcal{R})$ be a formal context, $a \in \mathcal{P}$ an attribute, $\delta \in L_1$, and the set of truth values $\Psi_\delta = \{\beta \in L_1 \mid \phi_{a,\delta}^{\downarrow} = \phi_{a,\beta}^{\downarrow}\}$, we have that δ is a scaled value of the attribute a if and only if*

$$\delta = \max\{\beta \mid \beta \in \Psi_\delta\}$$

Both previous results, Proposition 2 and Proposition 1, are fundamental for proving the following theorem, which is the most interesting result and relates the irreducible elements between both approaches, when the lattice associated with the scaled values is linear.

Theorem 5. *Given an attribute $a \in \mathcal{P}$ and a truth value $\delta \in L_2$, we have that, if $(L_1, \preceq_1)$ is totally ordered and $a_{\geq \delta}$ is an irreducible attribute with the CR-method, then $\phi_{a,\delta}$ generates a join-irreducible concept in the multi-adjoint concept lattice framework.*

This result asserts that if an attribute is irreducible with the CR-method, then that attribute also belongs to a reduct obtained with the multi-adjoint reduction mechanism. However, if an attribute can be classified as an absolutely or relatively necessary attribute in a multi-adjoint framework, this attribute can be or not irreducible attribute in CR-method. Therefore, the reduction obtained using multi-adjoint philosophy is more accurate and preserves some information, which is missing with the CR-method. These comments are illustrated in the following example.

4   Worked Example

In this section, we will consider a modification of the variable threshold formal concept described in [17]. We have the formal context $(\mathcal{O}, \mathcal{P}, \mathcal{R})$, where we study four objects, $\mathcal{O} = \{x_1, x_2, x_3, x_4\}$, and the set of attributes is composed of six attributes $\mathcal{P} = \{a, b, c, d, e, f\}$. The relationship between them is shown in Table 1.

Table 1. Relation of the formal context

	a	b	c	d	e	f
x_1	0.5	0.7	0.7	0.5	0.7	0.7
x_2	0.6	0.7	1.0	0.5	1.0	0.7
x_3	1.0	0.9	1.0	0.1	1.0	1.0
x_4	1.0	0.9	0.9	0.1	0.9	0.7

The first step in the CR-method is to scale the formal context, obtaining the scaled formal context presented in Table 2.

Table 2. Scaled formal context

	$a_{\geq 0.6}$	$a_{\geq 1.0}$	$b_{\geq 0.9}$	$c_{\geq 0.9}$	$c_{\geq 1.0}$	$d_{\geq 0.5}$	$e_{\geq 0.9}$	$e_{\geq 1.0}$	$f_{\geq 1.0}$
x_1	0	0	0	0	0	1	0	0	0
x_2	1	0	0	1	1	1	1	1	0
x_3	1	1	1	1	1	0	1	1	1
x_4	1	1	1	1	0	0	1	0	0

As we can see in Table 2, some attributes produce the same column, as $a_{\geq 0.6}$, $c_{\geq 0.9}$ and $e_{\geq 0.9}$. Moreover, the attribute $f_{\geq 1.0}$ can be described as, for example, the infimum of columns $a_{\geq 1.0}$ and $c_{\geq 1.0}$. Therefore, the attribute $f_{\geq 1.0}$ can be eliminated. Consequently, the CR-formal context will be the one shown in Table 3.

Table 3. Clarified and reduced formal context

	$\{a_{\geq 0.6}, c_{\geq 0.9}, e_{\geq 0.9}\}$	$\{a_{\geq 1.0}, b_{\geq 0.9}\}$	$\{c_{\geq 1.0}, e_{\geq 1.0}\}$	$\{d_{\geq 0.5}\}$
x_1	0	0	0	1
x_2	1	0	1	1
x_3	1	1	1	0
x_4	1	1	0	0

The following step is to create the discernibility function using the attributes of the CR-formal context, which is equal to:

$$(a_{\geq 0.6} \vee c_{\geq 0.9} \vee e_{\geq 0.9}) \wedge (a_{\geq 1.0} \vee b_{\geq 0.9}) \wedge (c_{\geq 1.0} \vee e_{\geq 1.0}) \wedge d_{\geq 0.5}$$

In addition, we will replace the scaled attributes with the original ones, obtaining

$$(a \lor c \lor e) \land (a \lor b) \land (c \lor e) \land d = (a \lor b) \land (c \lor e) \land d$$
$$= (a \land c \land d) \lor (a \land d \land e) \lor (b \land c \land d) \lor (b \land d \land e)$$

Now, we are going to study the original formal context from the point of view of the multi-adjoint concept lattice framework. We consider the multi-adjoint formal context $(\mathcal{O}, \mathcal{P}, \mathcal{R}, \sigma)$, where σ assigns the discretized Gödel adjoint triple on the granular interval $[0,1]_{10}$ [11] to every attribute. The concept lattice associated with this context is shown in Fig. 1.

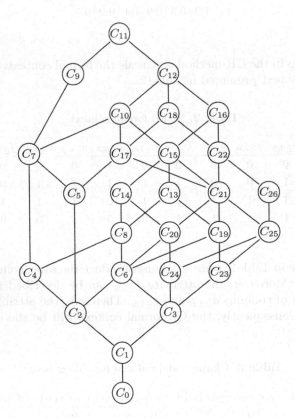

Fig. 1. Concept lattice of the context in example of Sect. 4.

Let us consider the attribute a with the truth value $\delta = 0.6$. By the definition of the concept-forming operator described in Expression (3), we have that

$$\phi^{\downarrow}_{a,0.6}(x_1) = \inf\{\mathcal{R}(x,a) \nwarrow \phi_{a,\delta}(a') \mid a' \in \mathcal{P}\}$$
$$= \inf\{0.5 \nwarrow 0.6, 0.7 \nwarrow 0, 0.7 \nwarrow 0, 0.5 \nwarrow 0, 0.7 \nwarrow 0, 0.7 \nwarrow 0\}$$
$$= 0.5$$

Making this computation over all the objects, we obtain that[1]

$$\phi_{a,0.6}^{\downarrow} = \{0.5/x_1, 1/x_2, 1/x_3, 1/x_4\} = \{0.5/x_1, x_2, x_3, x_4\}$$

As we can see, the objects x_2, x_3 and x_4 are taking the value 1, as well as in the scaled, clarified and reduce formal context, due to $0.6 \leq \mathcal{R}(x_i, a)$, for all $i \in \{2, 3, 4\}$.

Moreover, as we can see in Table 2, we have two scaled values for attribute a. The first one is $\delta = 0.6$ which is the only truth value considered to define the fuzzy attribute generating concept C_{18}. On the other hand, the concept C_{26} is generated by the fuzzy attributes $\phi_{a,\beta}$ with $\beta = \{0.7, 0.8, 0.9, 1.0\}$ and the other scaled value for attribute a is $\delta = 1.0$, the maximum truth value as Proposition 2 asserts.

Table 4. Fuzzy-attributes generating meet-irreducible concepts of the formal context of the example in Sect. 4.

C_i	Generated by
C_9	$\phi_{d,0.2}, \phi_{d,0.3}, \phi_{d,0.4}, \phi_{d,0.5}$
C_{10}	$\phi_{c,1.0}, \phi_{e,1.0}$
C_{12}	$\phi_{c,0.8}, \phi_{c,0.9}, \phi_{e,0.8}, \phi_{e,0.9}$
C_{13}	$\phi_{f,0.8}, \phi_{f,0.9}, \phi_{f,1.0}$
C_{14}	$\phi_{b,1}$
C_{16}	$\phi_{b,0.8}, \phi_{b,0.9}$
C_{18}	$\phi_{a,0.6}$
C_{26}	$\phi_{a,0.7}, \phi_{a,0.8}, \phi_{a,0.9}, \phi_{a,1.0}$

As we can see in Table 4, we have that all of the attributes used to built the reducts in the CR-method are also attributes generating meet-irreducible concepts. Moreover, attribute f could be eliminated when the CR-method is considered due to the column associated with the scaled attribute $f_{\geq 1.0}$ can be described as an infimum of others columns, which shows that f is a reducible attribute. However, when the multi-adjoint framework is considered, the attribute f is absolutely necessary, due to the fuzzy attributes $\phi_{f,\beta}$, for all $\beta = \{0.8, 0.9, 1.0\}$, is the only attribute generating the meet-irreducible concept C_{13} (Table 5).

---

[1] Note that, if the truth value is the top one, we can ignore it. On the other hand, we can remove the object with the bottom truth value.

Table 5. Meet-irreducible concepts of the formal context of example in Sect. 4.

C_i	$\text{Ext}(C_i)$	$\text{Int}(C_i)$
C_9	$\{x_1, x_2, 0.1/x_3, 0.1/x_4\}$	$\{0.5/a, 0.7/b, 0.7/c, 0.5/d, 0.7/e, 0.7/f\}$
C_{10}	$\{0.7/x_1, x_2, x_3, 0.9/x_4\}$	$\{0.5/a, 0.7/b, c, 0.1/d, e, 0.7/f\}$
C_{12}	$\{0.7/x_1, x_2, x_3, x_4\}$	$\{0.5/a, 0.7/b, 0.9/c, 0.1/d, 0.9/e, 0.7/f\}$
C_{13}	$\{0.7/x_1, 0.7/x_2, x_3, 0.7/x_4\}$	$\{0.5/a, 0.9/b, c, 0.1/d, e, f\}$
C_{14}	$\{0.7/x_1, 0.7/x_2, 0.9/x_3, 0.9/x_4\}$	$\{0.5/a, b, c, 0.1/d, e, 0.7/f\}$
C_{16}	$\{0.7/x_1, 0.7/x_2, x_3, x_4\}$	$\{0.5/a, 0.9/b, 0.9/c, 0.1/d, 0.9/e, 0.7/f\}$
C_{18}	$\{0.5/x_1, x_2, x_3, x_4\}$	$\{0.6/a, 0.7/b, 0.9/c, 0.1/d, 0.9/e, 0.7/f\}$
C_{26}	$\{0.7/x_1, 0.6/x_2, x_3, x_4\}$	$\{a, 0.9/b, 0.9/c, 0.1/d, 0.9/e, 0.7/f\}$

Moreover, using the classification Theorems 2, 3 and 4, we obtain two reducts: $Y_1 = \{a, b, c, d, f\}$ and $Y_2 = \{a, b, e, d, f\}$, which contain the attribute f. Therefore, the CR-method dismiss relevant data (in the fuzzy case), unlike the multi-adjoint attribute reduction procedure.

5   Conclusion and Future Work

As it have been shown through the paper, the multi-adjoint reduction mechanism and the CR-method can be related in interesting ways. One of the most relevant properties is that an irreducible attribute by the CR-method is also an absolutely or relatively necessary attribute with the attribute multi-adjoint classification.

In the future, we will perform a deeper study of the properties and possible relationships of the CR-method with multi-adjoint formal concept analysis considering different adjoint triples, as the left-sided adjoint triple [4]. Furthermore, we will study how the reduction and the relation between the mechanisms are affected when an attribute value reduction is also considered. That is, if we also take into consideration to erase a specific value, taken by an attribute, instead of eliminating or keeping the whole attribute.

References

1. Antoni, L., Cornejo, M.E., Medina, J., Ramírez-Poussa, E.: Attribute classification and reduct computation in multi-adjoint concept lattices. IEEE Trans. Fuzzy Syst. **29**(5), 1121–1132 (2021). https://doi.org/10.1109/TFUZZ.2020.2969114
2. Antoni, L., Krajči, S., Krídlo, O.: Constraint heterogeneous concept lattices and concept lattices with heterogeneous hedges. Fuzzy Sets Syst. **303**, 21–37 (2016). https://doi.org/10.1016/j.fss.2015.12.007, http://www.sciencedirect.com/science/article/pii/S0165011415005874
3. Bělohlávek, R.: Concept lattices and order in fuzzy logic. Ann. Pure Appl. Log. **128**, 277–298 (2004). https://doi.org/10.1016/j.apal.2003.01.001

4. Benítez-Caballero, M.J., Medina, J., Ramírez-Poussa, E.: Characterizing one-sided formal concept analysis by multi-adjoint concept lattices. Mathematics **10**(7) (2022). https://doi.org/10.3390/math10071020
5. Burusco, A., Fuentes-González, R.: Construction of the *L*-fuzzy concept lattice. Fuzzy Sets Syst. **97**(1), 109–114 (1998). https://doi.org/10.1016/S0165-0114(96)00318-1
6. Burusco, A., Fuentes-González, R.: Concept lattices defined from implication operators. Fuzzy Sets Syst. **114**, 431–436 (2000). https://doi.org/10.1016/S0165-0114(98)00182-1
7. Cornejo, M.E., Medina, J., Ramírez-Poussa, E.: Attribute and size reduction mechanisms in multi-adjoint concept lattices. J. Comput. Appl. Math. **318**, 388–402 (2017). https://doi.org/10.1016/j.cam.2016.07.012, http://www.sciencedirect.com/science/article/pii/S0377042716303314
8. Cornejo, M.E., Medina, J., Ramírez-Poussa, E.: Algebraic structure and characterization of adjoint triples. Fuzzy Sets Syst. (2021). https://doi.org/10.1016/j.fss.2021.02.002, https://www.sciencedirect.com/science/article/pii/S0165011421000348
9. Cornejo, M.E., Medina, J., Ramírez-Poussa, E.: Characterizing reducts in multi-adjoint concept lattices. Inf. Sci. **422**, 364–376 (2018). https://doi.org/10.1016/j.ins.2017.08.099, http://www.sciencedirect.com/science/article/pii/S0020025517302943
10. Cornejo, M.E., Medina, J., Ramírez-Poussa, E.: Attribute reduction in multi-adjoint concept lattices. Inf. Sci. **294**, 41–56 (2015). https://doi.org/10.1016/j.ins.2014.09.033, http://www.sciencedirect.com/science/article/pii/S0020025514009451
11. Cornejo, M.E., Medina, J., Ramírez-Poussa, E.: Multi-adjoint algebras versus non-commutative residuated structures. Int. J. Approx. Reason. **66**, 119–138 (2015)
12. Davey, B., Priestley, H.: Introduction to Lattices and Order, 2nd edn. Cambridge University Press, Cambridge (2002)
13. Dias, S.M., Vieira, N.J.: A methodology for analysis of concept lattice reduction. Inf. Sci. **396**, 202–217 (2017). https://doi.org/10.1016/j.ins.2017.02.037, http://www.sciencedirect.com/science/article/pii/S0020025517305388
14. Ganter, B., Wille, R.: Formal Concept Analysis: Mathematical Foundation. Springer, Heidelberg (1999). https://doi.org/10.1007/978-3-642-59830-2
15. Georgescu, G., Popescu, A.: Concept lattices and similarity in non-commutative fuzzy logic. Fund. Inform. **53**(1), 23–54 (2002)
16. Hájek, P.: Metamathematics of Fuzzy Logic. Trends in Logic. Kluwer Academic, Alphen aan den Rijn (1998)
17. Konecny, J.: On attribute reduction in concept lattices: methods based on discernibility matrix are outperformed by basic clarification and reduction. Inf. Sci. **415**, 199–212 (2017)
18. Kumar, C.A., Srinivas, S.: Concept lattice reduction using fuzzy k-means clustering. Expert Syst. Appl. **37**(3), 2696–2704 (2010). https://doi.org/10.1016/j.eswa.2009.09.026, http://www.sciencedirect.com/science/article/pii/S0957417409008070
19. Li, L., Zhang, J.: Attribute reduction in fuzzy concept lattices based on the T-implication. Knowl.-Based Syst. **23**(6), 497–503 (2010). https://doi.org/10.1016/j.knosys.2010.03.006, http://www.sciencedirect.com/science/article/pii/S0950705110000419
20. Medina, J., Ojeda-Aciego, M., Ruiz-Calviño, J.: Formal concept analysis via multi-adjoint concept lattices. Fuzzy Sets Syst. **160**(2), 130–144 (2009)

21. Medina, J.: Multi-adjoint property-oriented and object-oriented concept lattices. Inf. Sci. **190**, 95–106 (2012). https://doi.org/10.1016/j.ins.2011.11.016
22. Ren, R., Wei, L.: The attribute reductions of three-way concept lattices. Know.-Based Syst. **99**(C), 92–102 (2016). https://doi.org/10.1016/j.knosys.2016.01.045
23. Rodriguez-Jimenez, J., Cordero, P., Enciso, M., Rudolph, S.: Concept lattices with negative information: a characterization theorem. Inf. Sci. **369**, 51–62 (2016). https://doi.org/10.1016/j.ins.2016.06.015, http://www.sciencedirect.com/science/article/pii/S0020025516304364
24. Shao, M.W., Li, K.W.: Attribute reduction in generalized one-sided formal contexts. Inf. Sci. **378**, 317–327 (2017). https://doi.org/10.1016/j.ins.2016.03.018, http://www.sciencedirect.com/science/article/pii/S0020025516301657
25. Shao, M.W., Yang, H.Z., Wu, W.Z.: Knowledge reduction in formal fuzzy contexts. Knowl.-Based Syst. **73**, 265–275 (2015). https://doi.org/10.1016/j.knosys.2014.10.008, http://www.sciencedirect.com/science/article/pii/S095070511400375X
26. Wille, R.: Restructuring lattice theory: an approach based on hierarchies of concepts. In: Ferré, S., Rudolph, S. (eds.) ICFCA 2009. LNCS (LNAI), vol. 5548, pp. 314–339. Springer, Heidelberg (2009). https://doi.org/10.1007/978-3-642-01815-2_23

Determining Cause-Effect Relations from Fuzzy Relation Equations

Clemente Rubio-Manzano[1](✉), Daniel Alfonso-Robaina[2],
Juan Carlos Díaz-Moreno[3], Annette Malleuve-Martínez[2], and Jesús Medina[3]

[1] Universidad del Bío-Bío, Concepción, Chile
clrubio@ubiobio.cl
[2] Universidad Tecnológica de la Habana CUJAE, Havana, Cuba
{dalfonso,amalleuve}@ind.cujae.edu.cu
[3] Universidad de Cádiz, Cádiz, Spain
{juancarlos.diaz,jesus.medina}@uca.es

Abstract. This paper will study how fuzzy relation equations can be applied to determine a set of rules that simulate the interrelations among the determinant variables considered in the strategic management model focused on the enterprise architecture, to get a complete Integration Management System in the Enterprise (SMEA-IMSE). The proposed procedure will be applied to the first state of this model on real data.

Keywords: Fuzzy relation equations · fuzzy rules · cause-effect relationships · enterprise architecture

1 Introduction

Fuzzy relation equations (FRE) were introduced by E. Sanchez [14] as a mathematical tool based on the composition of fuzzy relations and focused on solving medical problems. From its introduction, FRE has been developed in theoretical and practical aspects. For instance, FRE has also been considered in approximate reasoning, automatic control or decision making.

This paper continues the study introduced in [1,13] on the strategic management model focused on the enterprise architecture (EA), which is an important research field in the business sector [3,9,15]. In [1,13], the relationship among the determinant variables considered in the model, which have been given by the study of the literature and the information offered by the experts, was studied through the use of FRE.

In this paper, taking in advantage of two theoretical results, we have introduced a mechanism based on FRE for computing the most representative cause-effect relationships from a whole dataset (observation of the variables). This

Partially supported by the 2014–2020 ERDF Operational Programme in collaboration with the State Research Agency (AEI) in project PID2019-108991GB-I00, and with the Department of Economy, Knowledge, Business and University of the Regional Government of Andalusia in project FEDER-UCA18-108612, and by the European Cooperation in Science & Technology (COST) Action CA17124.

ⓒ Springer Nature Switzerland AG 2022
D. Ciucci et al. (Eds.): IPMU 2022, CCIS 1601, pp. 155–166, 2022.
https://doi.org/10.1007/978-3-031-08971-8_14

procedure has been applied to the real case of the EA, in which the theoretical study of EA literature [10,11] fixed cause-effect relations. For the development of the EA, being able to identify the variable causes in each of the systems is of great importance in order to have a priority in the implementation of the improvement actions in business management. Carrying out this type of analysis with the use of FRE contributes to discovering new knowledge in business management that is not explicitly observed when it is carried out based on the perceptions of experts.

Hence, we have compared the cause-effect relations given by the theoretical study with the ones given by the mechanism introduced in this paper and, we have highlighted that the proposed mechanism has provided new remarkable relations, which have been well valued by the experts in the topic.

2 Preliminaries

2.1 Fuzzy Relation Equations

Different algebraic operators have been considered to define the composition of fuzzy relations. For example, the first composition considered the maximum and the minimum on the unit interval [14]. Recently, more flexible operators have been considered [7,8,12], which have a better adjustment to real cases. For example, the structure considered in [8] will be recalled in this section to be used later.

Given a complete lattice $(L, \preceq)$, an *adjoint pair* $(\odot, \leftarrow)$ is a pair of mappings $\odot: L \times L \longrightarrow L$ and $\leftarrow: L \times L \longrightarrow L$, such that satisfy the adjoint property, that is:

$$x \odot y \preceq z \quad \text{iff} \quad y \preceq z \leftarrow x$$

for all $x, y, z \in L$. Note that this property is equivalent to $\odot$ preserves the supreme in the second argument: $x \odot \bigvee \{y \mid y \in Y\} = \bigvee \{x \odot y \mid y \in Y\}$, for all $Y \subseteq L$.

Given an adjoint pair $(\odot, \leftarrow)$, a fuzzy relation equation is given by:

$$R \circ X = T \tag{1}$$

where $R: U \times V \longrightarrow L, T: U \times W \longrightarrow L$ are known fuzzy relations, $X: V \times W \longrightarrow L$ is unknown and $R \circ X$ is defined for each $u \in U, w \in W$, as

$$(R \circ X)(u, w) = \bigvee \{R(u, v) \odot X(v, u) \mid v \in V\}$$

The solvability of these equations was also studied in [8], obtaining that a fuzzy relation equation $R \circ X = T$ has a solution if and only if

$$(R \Rightarrow T)(v, w) = \bigwedge \{T(u, w) \leftarrow R(u, v) \mid u \in U\}$$

is a solution and, in that case, it is the maximum solution. When the equation is not solvable, an approximation can be computed [5]. In this last paper, two procedures for computing approximate solutions were introduced and justified, which were called conservative approximation and optimistic approximation. In this article we will consider the former one, which is the greatest solution of the next inequality:

$$R \circ X \leq T \tag{2}$$

In the study presented in this paper, for illustrating the given procedures, we will consider the linear lattice $L = [0, 1]$, the Łukasiewicz conjunction and its residuated implication, as adjoint pair: $x \odot y = \max\{0, x + y - 1\}$ and $z \leftarrow y = \min\{1, 1 - y + z\}$, for all $x, y, z \in [0, 1]$. Notice that other algebraic operator can be considered for the computations. In the future, the comparison among the use of different structures will be analyzed.

2.2 Enterprise Architecture to Strategic Management

This section recalls Stage 1 of the Strategic Management model focusing on the Enterprise Architecture presented in [1,13], which will be the basic model in which the study of the paper will be carried out.

The Strategic Management model focuses on Enterprise Architecture to achieve a level of Integration of the Enterprise Management System. The scope of this research is aimed at the first stage of the model analyzed in [1], where five variables of the basic strategic design are worked on. In this stage, the strategic direction of the organization is highlighted and the emphasis is placed on five variables:

- **Strategic Team (ST, a_1)** emphasizes the work of management using IT to implement the strategy.
- **Communication among Stakeholders (CS, a_2)** analyses the communication relationships between internal and external stakeholders to add value to key processes through IT or other channels.
- **Strategic Project (SP, a_3)** defines or redefines the strategic plan, taking into account the classic components of a strategic design, but emphasizing the use of IT.
- **Diagnosis, Design and Redesign of the Key Processes (DDRKP, a_4)** aims to diagnose, design and/or redesign key processes and relationships that increase the added value of products and services.
- **Diagnosis, Design and Redesign of the Functional Processes (DDRFP, a_5)** whose objective is to diagnose, design and/or redesign the functional processes and their relationships that ensure the operation of key processes.

These variables are of great importance in the development of the model, since it is the basic stage of any strategic project, so the bases for integration are guaranteed from analyzing the basic elements of a strategic exercise, which is why it is not enough for the development of the EA but if they are necessary to develop them in a strategic way as well as to prioritize the external and internal relations of the business system.

In this stage, teamwork begins to be seen from the corporate strategic think-ing of the company, thus involving the experts, leaders and manager of the company to conduct the strategic process together with the personnel involved in the different areas of work of the company.

One of the characteristics that differentiates the proposal from the EA model is achieved with greater emphasis at this stage than predictability, since it offers tools to carry out preventive and flexible actions within decision-making in the company's management system.

In the implementation of the proposed model, the need to define and identify the processes and information flows has been evidenced, as well as the commit-ment of the company's directors to manage the changes proposed in this stage. At the end of this stage, the companies must have defined the company strategy including IT.

In this stage as in the other two of the model proposed in [1,13], it is very important to improve the performance of each of these variables to know the influence of each of them on the rest of the system so that the company can increase its performance more optimally in the management of the EA approach with a strategic approach.

Hence, we will focus the attention on the cause-effect relations among the variables of the first stage studied in [1,13], in order to find out which variables are the most important for improving company performance of the considered companies. The proposed mechanism is exportable to the other two states and other studies in which the cause-effect relations among the variables is critical.

From variables involved at Stage 1 and detailed above, a theoretical study of EA literature [10,11] established cause-effect relations existing among the variables (see Fig. 1), whose dependencies are the following:

1. $a_2, a_3 \rightarrow a_1$
2. $a_3 \rightarrow a_2$
3. $a_1, a_2, a_3, a_5 \rightarrow a_4$
4. $a_1, a_2, a_3 \rightarrow a_5$

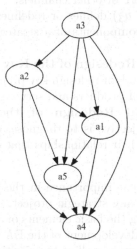

Fig. 1. Diagram established between the variables involved at Stage 1

For example, the first dependence means that CS and SP have a direct effect on ST, in this case, we would say that the Communication among the Stakeholders, and the Strategic Project affect to the Strategic Team.

3   Analysing Theoretical Cause-Effect Relationships

This section takes into consideration the established cause-effect relations existing among the variables, in each stage, obtained from a theoretical study of EA literature [10,11], as previously was commented.

In order to complement the theoretical study from the EA literature [10,11], another mechanism that assess the obtained set of cause-effect relations was introduced in [1] based on Fuzzy Relation Equations and their relationship with decision making and fuzzy dependence rules [5,6].

Specifically, the dataset introduced in [1], which was obtained from experts (managers and specialists) of several real companies, were considered (Table 1) in order to compute a truth value (weight) to each crisp cause-effect relation given by the theoretical study of the EA literature. We will recall here the procedure associated with Stage 1, the theoretical details can be seen in the paper [1].

Table 1 includes real data from six heterogeneous companies from different sectors, sizes and characteristics at Stage 1. These values can be considered as "observed" values for the variables for each company in the abduction reasoning framework.

Table 1. Input Matrix for Stage 1

Var.	E_1	E_2	E_3	E_4	E_5	E_6
a_1	7.56	6.26	2.25	3.17	7.81	6.22
a_2	6.44	6.26	3.91	4.80	15.64	7.60
a_3	8.78	7.19	4.20	5.23	7.59	7.82
a_4	9.00	6.32	3.10	5.30	7.66	8.02
a_5	8.78	6.16	3.83	3.88	7.70	7.63

Next, the procedure will be illustrated for the rules associated with a given variable. Considering effect a_1 of Stage 1, there exist two cause-effect relations with head a_1, $(a_2 \rightarrow a_1, a_3 \rightarrow a_1)$. Therefore, two weighted rules arise:

$$\langle a_2 \leftarrow a_1, \vartheta_1 \rangle \qquad \langle a_3 \leftarrow a_1, \vartheta_2 \rangle$$

where $\vartheta_1, \vartheta_2 \in [0,1]$ are the weights to each cause-effect relation. The procedure proposed in [1] takes advantage of the relationship of fuzzy dependence rules and FRE given in [5,6] to compute these weights. Specifically, the following fuzzy relation equation $R \circ X = T$ is considered

$$\begin{pmatrix} 0.644 & 0.878 \\ 0.626 & 0.719 \\ 0.391 & 0.42 \\ 0.481 & 0.523 \\ 0.564 & 0.759 \\ 0.76 & 0.782 \end{pmatrix} \circ \begin{pmatrix} \vartheta_1 \\ \vartheta_2 \end{pmatrix} = \begin{pmatrix} 0.756 \\ 0.626 \\ 0.225 \\ 0.317 \\ 0.781 \\ 0.622 \end{pmatrix}$$

where the matrix R (causes) includes the observed values for a_2, a_3 by columns, T (effect) the observed values of a_1, and X represents the weights of the fuzzy rules.

From the theory of fuzzy relation equations, $R \circ X = T$ is solvable if and only if $R \Rightarrow T$ is a solution, which it would be the greatest solution. However, $R \circ X = T$ is not solvable and it is necessary to consider an approximation [5].

$$R \circ (R \Rightarrow T) = \begin{pmatrix} 0.644 & 0.878 \\ 0.626 & 0.719 \\ 0.391 & 0.42 \\ 0.481 & 0.523 \\ 0.564 & 0.759 \\ 0.76 & 0.782 \end{pmatrix} \circ \begin{pmatrix} 0.834 \\ 0.794 \end{pmatrix} = \begin{pmatrix} 0.672 \\ 0.513 \\ 0.225 \\ 0.317 \\ 0.553 \\ 0.594 \end{pmatrix} = T^* < T$$

The non-solvability of the system arise for instance by the inherent uncertainty of the answers of the experts, the computation error, etc.

Hence, the *conservative approximation* presented in [5] is considered to obtain a lower approximation of the truth values of the rules. Therefore, the truth values of the rules will be $\vartheta_1 = 0.834$ and $\vartheta_2 = 0.794$:

$$\langle a_1 \leftarrow a_2, 0.834 \rangle \qquad \langle a_1 \leftarrow a_3, 0.794 \rangle$$

Table 2 displays the weights associated with the other cause-effect relationships.

Table 2. Fuzzy dependencies rules for Stage 1

$a_1 \leftarrow a_2, 0.834$	$a_4 \leftarrow a_3, 0.890$
$a_1 \leftarrow a_3, 0.794$	$a_4 \leftarrow a_5, 0.927$
$a_2 \leftarrow a_3, 0.766$	$a_5 \leftarrow a_1, 0.989$
$a_4 \leftarrow a_1, 0.985$	$a_5 \leftarrow a_2, 0.907$
$a_4 \leftarrow a_2, 0.919$	$a_5 \leftarrow a_3, 0.865$

From this procedure, only the cause-effect relationships given by the theoretical study of EA are considered. The following section studies the possibility of considering FRE for providing cause-effect relationships.

4 FRE to Detect Cause-Effect Relationships

This section will consider all of the variables as possible causes of the one selected variable (effect) and the observed values (Table 1) to determine the cause-effect relations via FRE. Hence, since in the resolution of equation $R \circ X = T$ we are considered now all of the observed values (for example, for a_1 as effect, we will consider all of the rest of variables instead of only a_2 and a_3), it is important to know how the solutions of equation $R \circ X = T$ change when the matrix R change. The first result shows that, if the equations are solvable, that is, we do not need to use the conservative approximation, the greatest solution "does not" change.

Proposition 1. *Given the fuzzy relations $R_1 \colon U \times V_1 \longrightarrow L$, $R_2 \colon U \times V_2 \longrightarrow L$, $T \colon U \times W \longrightarrow L$ and $X \colon V \times W \longrightarrow L$, where X is unknown, $V_1 \subseteq V_2$ and $R_{2|U \times V_1} = R_1$, that is, $R_1(u, v_1) = R_2(u, v_1)$, for all $u \in U$ and $v_1 \in V_1$. If $R_1 \circ X = T$ and $R_2 \circ X = T$ are solvable, then the greatest solution of the FRE $R_2 \circ X = T$ is equal to the greatest solution of the FRE $R_1 \circ X = T$ on the subset V_1.*

Proof. Given the greatest solution $\bar{X}_1$ of $R_1 \circ X = T$ and the greatest solution $\bar{X}_2$ of $R_2 \circ X = T$, we need to prove that $\overline{X_{2|V_1 \times W}} = \overline{X}_1$, which holds from the following chain of equalities.

$$\overline{X}_1(v_1, w) = (R_1 \Rightarrow T)(v_1, w)$$
$$= \bigwedge \{T(u, w) \leftarrow R_1(u, v_1) \mid u \in U\}$$
$$= \bigwedge \{T(u, w) \leftarrow R_2(u, v_1) \mid u \in U\}$$
$$= (R_2 \Rightarrow T)(v_1, w)$$
$$= \overline{X}_2(v_1, w)$$

for all $v_1 \in V_1$ and $w \in W$. □

The following proposition proves that, if the equation is not solvable, then a similar result arises for the conservative approximations and an interesting relationship among the new obtained independent terms T^*, as well.

Proposition 2. *Given the fuzzy relations $R_1 \colon U \times V_1 \longrightarrow L$, $R_2 \colon U \times V_2 \longrightarrow L$, $T \colon U \times W \longrightarrow L$ and $X \colon V \times W \longrightarrow L$, where X is unknown and $V_1 \subseteq V_2$ and $R_{2|U \times V_1} = R_1$. Then, the conservative approximation of the FRE $R_2 \circ X = T$ is equal to the conservative approximation of the FRE $R_1 \circ X = T$ on the subset V_1. Moreover, $T_1^* \leq T_2^*$.*

Proof. The proof of the first part follows similarly to the proof of Proposition 1 because the conservative approximations $R_1 \circ X = T$ and $R_2 \circ X = T$ are just $(R_1 \Rightarrow T)$ and $(R_2 \Rightarrow T)$, respectively. However, the independent term changes in both FRE. Specifically, the new independent terms are:

$$T_1^* = R_1 \circ (R_1 \Rightarrow T)$$
$$T_2^* = R_2 \circ (R_2 \Rightarrow T)$$

and we obtain the following chain of equalities.

$$R_1 \circ (R_1 \Rightarrow T)(u, w) = \bigvee\{R_1(u, v_1) \odot (R_1 \Rightarrow T)(v_1, w) \mid v_1 \in V_1\}$$
$$\overset{(1)}{=} \bigvee\{R_2(u, v_1) \odot (R_2 \Rightarrow T)(v_1, w) \mid v_1 \in V_1\}$$
$$\overset{(2)}{\leq} \bigvee\{R_2(u, v_2) \odot (R_2 \Rightarrow T)(v_2, w) \mid v_2 \in V_2\}$$
$$= R_2 \circ (R_2 \Rightarrow T)(u, w)$$

for all $u \in U$ and $w \in W$, where (1) holds by the hypothesis and the first part of the proof, and (2) by the supremum property because of $V_1 \subseteq V_2$.   □

As a consequence of the previous result, the more variables are considered the better independent matrix is obtained closer to the original observed values (matrix T). Therefore, it is interesting to take into account all variables in order to model the problem.

Moreover, from this result we also can give a procedure to determine the relationship among the variables, providing representative cause-effect relations. Specifically, given an effect variable v_{i_0}, if the matrix T^* obtained from all of the rest of variables does not change when we remove a variable v_{j_0}, then we can assert that v_{j_0} does not affect to the computation of v_{i_0} and the cause-effect relationship $v_{j_0} \rightarrow v_{i_0}$ does not need to be considered. The following example shows this procedure on Stage 1 of the Strategic Management model focusing on the Enterprise Architecture presented in [1,13].

Example 1. In this example, we will consider the dataset represented in Table 1 and we start from the FRE:

$$\begin{pmatrix} 0.644 & 0.878 & 0.9 & 0.878 \\ 0.626 & 0.719 & 0.632 & 0.616 \\ 0.391 & 0.42 & 0.31 & 0.383 \\ 0.481 & 0.523 & 0.53 & 0.388 \\ 0.564 & 0.759 & 0.766 & 0.77 \\ 0.76 & 0.78 & 0.802 & 0.763 \end{pmatrix} \circ \begin{pmatrix} \vartheta_1 \\ \vartheta_2 \\ \vartheta_3 \\ \vartheta_4 \end{pmatrix} = \begin{pmatrix} 0.756 \\ 0.626 \\ 0.225 \\ 0.317 \\ 0.781 \\ 0.622 \end{pmatrix}$$

and we reduce step by step the variables (columns) in the matrix R. From this equation we have

$$R \circ (R \Rightarrow T) = \begin{pmatrix} 0.644 & 0.878 & 0.9 & 0.878 \\ 0.626 & 0.719 & 0.632 & 0.616 \\ 0.391 & 0.42 & 0.31 & 0.383 \\ 0.481 & 0.523 & 0.53 & 0.388 \\ 0.564 & 0.759 & 0.766 & 0.77 \\ 0.76 & 0.78 & 0.802 & 0.763 \end{pmatrix} \circ \begin{pmatrix} 0.834 \\ 0.794 \\ 0.787 \\ 0.842 \end{pmatrix} = \begin{pmatrix} 0.72 \\ 0.513 \\ 0.225 \\ 0.317 \\ 0.612 \\ 0.605 \end{pmatrix} = T_{a_1}^* < T$$

Therefore, the approximate solution is $\vartheta_1 = 0.834$, $\vartheta_2 = 0.794$, $\vartheta_3 = 0.787$, and $\vartheta_4 = 0.842$, and it will not change if matrix R is reduced by columns, as Proposition 2 shown.

Now, we will apply the procedure given above to variable a_1 as cause and the rest of variables $A_{a_1} = \{a_2, a_3, a_4, a_5\}$ as effect. In Tables 3 and 4, every column is associated with a non-empty subset of A_{a_1} and shows the values obtained by the vector $T_{a_1}^*$ obtained from the corresponding equation. The last row includes the average of the differences between the vector T and the vectors $T_{a_1}^*$ obtained from each subset of variables in A_{a_1}.

Table 3. Matrices $T_{a_1}^*$ with four and three variables.

$T_{a_1}^*$	a_2, a_3, a_4, a_5	a_2, a_3, a_4	a_2, a_3, a_5	a_2, a_4, a_5	a_3, a_4, a_5
	0.72	0.687	0.72	0.72	0.72
	0.513	0.513	0.513	0.46	0.513
	0.225	0.225	0.225	0.225	0.225
	0.317	0.317	0.317	0.317	0.317
	0.612	0.553	0.612	0.612	0.612
	0.605	0.594	0.605	0.605	0.605
Difference with T	0.056	0.073	0.056	0.065	0.056

Table 4. Matrices $T_{a_1}^*$ with two and one variable.

$T_{a_1}^*$	a_2, a_3	a_2, a_4	a_2, a_5	a_3, a_4	a_3, a_5	a_4, a_5	a_2	a_3	a_4	a_5
	0.672	0.687	0.72	0.687	0.72	0.72	0.478	0.672	0.687	0.72
	0.513	0.46	0.46	0.513	0.513	0.458	0.46	0.513	0.419	0.458
	0.225	0.225	0.225	0.214	0.225	0.225	0.225	0.214	0.097	0.225
	0.317	0.317	0.317	0.317	0.317	0.317	0.315	0.317	0.317	0.23
	0.553	0.553	0.612	0.553	0.612	0.612	0.398	0.553	0.553	0.612
	0.594	0.594	0.605	0.589	0.605	0.605	0.594	0.576	0.589	0.605
Difference with T	0.075	0.082	0.065	0.076	0.056	0.065	0.143	0.08	0.111	0.079

Taking into account the smallest difference, which is given by the consideration of all of the variables in A_{a_1}, that is 0.056, only two subsets give this value: $\{a_2, a_3, a_5\}$ and $\{a_3, a_5\}$. Thus, we can assert that a_3 and a_5 are the variables that most influence variable a_1, and so the most representative cause-effect relations are:

$$\langle a_1 \leftarrow a_3, 0.794 \rangle, \qquad \langle a_1 \leftarrow a_5, 0.842 \rangle$$

Note that the weights are not determinant for choosing these relations. For instance, the weight 0.794 associated with a_3 is less than the weight 0.834 associated with a_2.

This procedure can be applied to the rest of variables. The most interesting subsets and differences are given in Table 5. Column entitles "Differences" shows the difference between T and $T_{a_i}^*$ for each considered subset, with $i \in \{2, 3, 4, 5\}$.

Therefore, the proposed methodology based on FRE shows a new cause-effect relations among the variables. Next, the new causes in the relations are given in blue and the variable not required are cross out in red.

1. $a_2, a_3, a_5 \rightarrow a_1$
2. $a_1, a_3 \rightarrow a_2$
3. $a_1, a_2, a_3, a_5 \rightarrow a_4$
4. $a_1, a_2, a_3, a_4 \rightarrow a_5$

Table 5. The most representative differences between T and $T_{a_i}^*$.

Subset of A_{a_2}	Differences
A_{a_2}	0.125
a_1, a_3, a_4	0.125
a_1, a_3, a_5	0.125
a_1, a_3	0.125
a_1	0.24
a_3	0.131

Subset of A_{a_3}	Differences
A_{a_3}	0.023
a_1, a_2, a_4	0.023
a_2, a_4, a_5	0.023
a_2, a_4	0.026
a_4, a_5	0.029
a_4	0.045

Subset of A_{a_4}	Differences
A_{a_4}	0.057
a_1, a_2, a_5	0.06
a_1, a_3, a_5	0.057
a_1, a_3	0.067
a_1, a_5	0.074
a_3, a_5	0.069

Subset of A_{a_5}	Differences
A_{a_5}	0.05
a_1, a_2, a_3	0.052
a_1, a_2, a_4	0.05
a_1, a_3, a_4	0.054
a_1, a_2	0.052
a_1, a_3	0.058

Moreover, new cause-effect relations arise with respect to variable (effect) a_3. We can consider $a_1, a_2, a_4 \rightarrow a_3$ or $a_2, a_4, a_5 \rightarrow a_3$. However, these relations are not considered as cause-effect rules, because a_3 is a cause in a natural way and it cannot be an effect.

Note that, the relationship associated with the effect a_2 includes the cause a_1, although the difference from considering only a_3 is very small and it could be given by some small errors (noise) taking the data (checklists) from the managers of the companies. Hence, we can assert that the relationship given by the theoretical study for this effect "coincides" with our proposal. The relation with a_3 as effect does not need all the rest of variables, and a_2 could not be considered. Hence, the theoretical study is improved in this case with the proposed methodology based on FRE.

Finally, the relation with a_5 as effect swaps cause a_3 by a_4. Anyway, the difference between the sets $\{a_1, a_2, a_4\}$ and $\{a_1, a_2, a_3\}$ is very small: 0.002. Moreover, from this last set, we also see that in this case a_3 is not needed because from the set $\{a_1, a_2\}$ the same difference arises.

The experts in EA have also analyzed the new proposal, besides the previous comment on a_3, they assert that it provides interesting information, refuting previous cause-effect rules, removing some of them, and offering new ones. They basically agree the changes except, for instance, the inclusion of the rule $a_5 \rightarrow a_1$, because it is not natural. If only variable a_3 is considered as cause of effect a_1, a small difference arises from the original one. In Table 4, we see that this difference is 0.08 instead of 0.056, which is the value considering all of the variables. Hence, the final set of cause-effect rules (model) can also be considered as consistent.

Consequently, from the comments above, we can assert that the procedure introduced in this paper based on FRE offers a mechanism for complementing the theoretical study of EA to help the decision making of the considered companies.

5   Conclusions and Further Work

We have proved two basic results in order to define a mechanism for determining cause-effect relationships among variables in a given problem. In this paper, we have applied this mechanism to a simple real case given by one of the three states theoretically studied in [10, 11] and analysed in [1]. Consequently, new interesting cause-effect relations have been obtained with interesting consequences in the specific domain of EA.

In the future, we will continue with this study. For example, we will analyze the relationship with concept lattices [2, 4] in order to study whether the determination of the variables more representative is related to the research fields of attribute reduction and attribute implications in concept lattices. Moreover, we will use the introduced methodology to real examples with many interacting variables.

References

1. Alfonso-Robaina, D., Díaz-Moreno, J.C., Malleuve-Martinez, A., Medina, J., Rubio-Manzano, C.: Modeling enterprise architecture and strategic management from fuzzy decision rules. Stud. Comput. Intell. **819**, 139–147 (2020)
2. Aragón, R.G., Medina, J., Ramírez-Poussa, E.: Reducing concept lattices by means of a weaker notion of congruence. Fuzzy Sets Syst. **418**, 153–169 (2021). Algebra

3. Braun, C., Winter, R.: Integration of it service management into enterprise architecture. In: Proceedings of the 2007 ACM Symposium on Applied Computing, pp. 1215–1219. ACM (2007)
4. Cornejo, M.E., Díaz-Moreno, J.C., Medina, J.: Generalized quantifiers in formal concept analysis. J. Comput. Appl. Math. **404**, 113772 (2022)
5. Cornejo, M.E., Díaz-Moreno, J.C., Medina, J.: Multi-adjoint relation equations: a decision support system for fuzzy logic. Int. J. Intell. Syst. **32**(8), 778–800 (2017)
6. Díaz-Moreno, J.C., Medina, J.: Multi-adjoint relation equations: definition, properties and solutions using concept lattices. Inf. Sci. **253**, 100–109 (2013)
7. Díaz-Moreno, J.C., Medina, J.: Using concept lattice theory to obtain the set of solutions of multi-adjoint relation equations. Inf. Sci. **266**, 218–225 (2014)
8. Díaz-Moreno, J.C., Medina, J., Turunen, E.: Minimal solutions of general fuzzy relation equations on linear carriers. An algebraic characterization. Fuzzy Sets Syst. **311**, 112–123 (2017)
9. Johnson, P., Ekstedt, M., Silva, E., Plazaola, L.: Using enterprise architecture for CIO decision-making: on the importance of theory. In: Second Annual Conference on Systems Engineering Research (2004)
10. Malleuve, A., Alfonso, D., Lavandero, J.: Study of elements behavior for integration management system with enterprise architecture approach. Dyna Colombia **84**(203), 349–355 (2017)
11. Malleuve-Martínez, A., Alfonso-Robaina, D., Lavandero-García, J., Ramos-Díaz, V.C.: Strategic management model with enterprise architecture approach for integration management system in enterprises. Dyna **85**(207), 297–305 (2018)
12. Medina, J.: Minimal solutions of generalized fuzzy relational equations: clarifications and corrections towards a more flexible setting. Int. J. Approx. Reason. **84**, 33–38 (2017)
13. Rubio-Manzano, C., Díaz-Moreno, J.C., Alfonso-Robaina, D., Malleuve, A., Medina, J.: A novel cause-effect variable analysis in enterprise architecture by fuzzy logic techniques. Int. J. Comput. Intell. Syst. **13**, 511–523 (2020)
14. Sanchez, E.: Resolution of composite fuzzy relation equations. Inf. Control **30**(1), 38–48 (1976)
15. Winter, R., Fischer, R.: Essential layers, artifacts, and dependencies of enterprise architecture. In: 10th IEEE International Enterprise Distributed Object Computing Conference Workshops, EDOCW 2006, pp. 30–30. IEEE (2006)

Fuzzy Implication Functions

Monodistances from Fuzzy Implications

Kavit Nanavati[ID], Megha Gupta[ID], and Balasubramaniam Jayaram[✉][ID]

Department of Mathematics, Indian Institute of Technology Hyderabad,
Hyderabad 502284, Telangana, India
{ma20resch01004,ma16m18p100001}@iith.ac.in, jbala@math.iith.ac.in

Abstract. In the literature there have been a few works [1–4] that have
dealt with obtaining metrics from associative, commutative, and monotonically increasing fuzzy logic connectives such as t-norms, t-conorms,
copulas, and quasi-copulas. Recently, it has been shown [9] that a distance function d_I can also be obtained from fuzzy implications which
do not satisfy any of the above properties. This work studies the above
distance along two aspects. Firstly, we investigate those implications I
that satisfy a particular form of transitivity, viz. the $S_{\mathbf{LK}}$ transitivity,
that is both necessary and sufficient for the proposed distance to be
a metric. In the recent past, monodistances w.r.t. a ternary relation,
called the betweenness relation, defined on a set, have garnered a lot of
attention for their important role in decision making and penalty-based
data aggregation. One of the major challenges herein is that of obtaining monodistances on a given betweenness set $(\mathcal{X}, \mathrm{B})$. By characterising
betweenness relations that can be obtained from a bounded below poset,
our second contribution in this work is in showing that a monodistance
on such betweenness sets $(\mathcal{X}, \mathrm{B})$ can be obtained through d_I. Our work
seems to suggest that fuzzy implications are rather a natural choice for
constructing monodistances.

Keywords: Fuzzy Implication · $S_{\mathbf{LK}}$-transitivity · Monodistance ·
Betweenness Relation

1 Introduction

The idea of constructing a distance function from fuzzy logic connectives such
as t-norms, and its dual t-conorms, was originally introduced by Alsina in [4],
where it was shown that this distance function turns out to be a metric if the
t-norm is a copula. Following this, there have been many works (see [1–4,10])
that have dealt with constructing distance functions from fuzzy logic connectives
such as t-norms and t-conorms, copulas, quasi-copulas, and symmetric difference
functions. Mostly all these works have considered only associative, monotonic,
or commutative fuzzy logic operations on $[0, 1]$ to define distance functions.

Supported by SERB under the project MTR/2020/000506.

© Springer Nature Switzerland AG 2022
D. Ciucci et al. (Eds.): IPMU 2022, CCIS 1601, pp. 169–181, 2022.
https://doi.org/10.1007/978-3-031-08971-8_15

1.1   Motivation for This Work

In [9], the construction of a distance function d_I from fuzzy implications I which are non-associative, mixed-monotonic, and non-commutative fuzzy logic connectives on $[0, 1]$, is given. However, these distance functions are not always metrics.

Viewing a fuzzy implication I as a binary relation on $[0, 1]$, a sufficient and necessary condition for d_I to be a metric was shown to be the satisfaction of a type of transitivity w.r.t. the Łukasiewicz t-conorm, see Definition 3. Our first motivation for this work is to explore the functional inequality deeper w.r.t. different families and transformations of fuzzy implications.

It was also shown that d_I is a monodistance w.r.t. the natural betweenness relation that can be obtained from a totally/linearly ordered set. However, one of the major challenges is to define a monodistance on any given betweenness set $(\mathcal{X}, B)$. Our second motivation is to investigate if d_I can be a source of such monodistances even when the betweenness relation is not obtained from a chain.

1.2   Contributions of This Work

The following are the main contributions of this work:

- Provide further characterizations of fuzzy implications that satisfy $S_{\mathbf{LK}}$-transitivity and the type of metrics obtainable from them.
- Characterize betweenness relations that can be induced from a bounded below poset.
- Using the above characterisation, present a way of obtaining monodistances from fuzzy implications on a betweenness set that has been induced by a partial order, that is not necessarily linear, thus providing a partial positive answer to the challenge mentioned above.

2   Distance Functions from Fuzzy Implications

In the literature there have been a few works [1–4] that have dealt with obtaining metrics from associative, commutative, and monotonically increasing fuzzy logic connectives such as t-norms, t-conorms, copulas, and quasi-copulas. Recently, it has been shown [9] that a distance function can also be obtained from fuzzy logic connectives such as fuzzy implications which do not satisfy any of the above properties.

In this section, we begin by recalling the related definitions and show the important role played by the S-transitivity in making it a metric. For the definitions employed in this work, we refer the readers to see [6–8]. We shall denote the set of all fuzzy implications by $\mathbb{FI}$.

Definition 1. *A symmetric function* $d : \mathcal{X} \times \mathcal{X} \to [0, \infty[$ *is called a **distance function** on* $\mathcal{X}$ *if it satisfies the following property for any* $x, y \in \mathcal{X}$:

$$x = y \implies d(x, y) = 0 . \tag{P1}$$

*Further, it is called a **metric** if the converse of* (P1) *holds, and it also satisfies the triangle inequality, i.e., for any* $x, y, z \in \mathcal{X}$,

$$d(x, z) \leq d(x, y) + d(y, z) . \tag{P2}$$

Definition 2 [9]. *Let* $I \in \mathbb{FI}$ *and define* $d_I : [0, 1] \times [0, 1] \to [0, 1]$ *as*

$$d_I(x, y) = \begin{cases} 0, & \text{if } x = y , \\ I(\min(x, y), \max(x, y)), & \text{otherwise} . \end{cases}$$

Clearly, d_I is a distance function on $[0, 1]$. Note that d_I satisfies the converse of (P1) if I satisfies the following condition:

$$I(x, y) > 0, \text{whenever } x \leq y, \quad x, y \in [0, 1]. \tag{1}$$

We would like to mention that throughout the paper, we will only consider fuzzy implications that satisfy (1).

Now, let us recall [9] the notion of S-transitive fuzzy relations, where S is a t-conorm.

Definition 3. *Given a t-conorm* S, *a fuzzy relation* $R : \mathcal{X} \times \mathcal{X} \to [0, 1]$ *is said to be an* S-**transitive relation** *if for all* $x, y, z \in \mathcal{X}$, *we have*

$$S(R(x, y), R(y, z)) \geq R(x, z) .$$

Note that S-transitivity has already been defined in a different context [5, 14], wherein the triangle inequality is generalised to S-transitivity and is termed as S-triangle inequality.

Since a fuzzy implication is also a mapping from the unit square to the unit interval, viewing it as a fuzzy relation on $[0, 1]$, in [9], it was shown that d_I can be made a metric provided I satisfies S-transitivity w.r.t. the Łukasiewicz t-conorm, $S_{\mathbf{LK}}(x, y) = \min(1, x + y)$.

Theorem 1 [9]. d_I *is a metric iff* I *is* $S_{\mathbf{LK}}$-*transitive.*

This clearly shows the usefulness of S-transitive fuzzy relations as much as their counterparts, T-transitive fuzzy relations. Hence, it leads to an interesting problem of investigating the fuzzy implications that are $S_{\mathbf{LK}}$-transitive.

3 $S_{\mathbf{LK}}$-Transitive Fuzzy Implications

In this section, we discuss the sufficient conditions under which some families and transformations of fuzzy implications satisfy $S_{\mathbf{LK}}$-transitivity.

3.1 S_{LK}-Transitivity of $I \in \mathbb{FI}$ Obtained from Other FLCs

Certain families of fuzzy implications are constructed by generalising classical tautologies. Typically these are obtained from other fuzzy logic connectives (FLCs). Below we study the satisfaction of S_{LK}-transitivity by some of the major families obtained through such constructions, viz. R-, (S, N)-, and QL-implications.

Lemma 1. An $I \in \mathbb{FI}$ satisfying the identity principle, i.e. $I(x, x) = 1$ for all $x \in [0, 1]$, generates a discrete metric, i.e.,

$$d_I(x, y) = \begin{cases} 0, & \text{if } x = y, \\ 1, & \text{otherwise}. \end{cases}$$

Definition 4. An $I \in \mathbb{FI}$ is called an R-**implication** if there exists a t-norm T such that for all $x, y \in [0, 1]$,

$$I(x, y) = \sup\{z \in [0, 1] \mid T(x, z) \le y\}.$$

We denote an R-**implication** by I_T.

From Lemma 1 the following result follows:

Corollary 1. An R implication I_T only generates a discrete metric.

Definition 5. An $I \in \mathbb{FI}$ is called an (S,N)-**implication**, denoted $I_{S,N}$, if there exists a t-conorm S, and a fuzzy negation N such that for all $x, y \in [0, 1]$,

$$I(x, y) = S(N(x), y).$$

Lemma 2 (cf. [9]). Every $I_{S,N}$ where either $S \le S_{LK}$ or $N \ge N_C$ satisfies S_{LK}-transitivity and hence generates a metric, where $N_C(x) = 1 - x$.

Not every (S, N)-implication satisfies S_{LK}-transitivity as shown below.

Example 1. Consider the $I_{S,N}$ obtained from

$$S(x, y) = \min(x + y + xy, 1), \qquad N(x) = \begin{cases} 1, & \text{if } x = 0, \\ \frac{1}{3}, & \text{if } x < 0.11, \\ 0, & \text{otherwise}. \end{cases}$$

Then $I_{S,N}(0.1, 0.11) + I_{S,N}(0.11, 0.45) = \dfrac{0.279}{3} \not\ge \dfrac{0.280}{3} = I_{S,N}(0.1, 0.45)$.

Definition 6. An $I \in \mathbb{FI}$ is called a QL-**implication**, denoted $I_{T,S,N}$, if there exists a t-norm T, a t-conorm S, and a fuzzy negation N such that

$$I_{T,S,N}(x, y) = S(N(x), T(x, y)), \qquad x, y \in [0, 1].$$

Table 1. Some examples of fuzzy implications satisfying S_{LK}-transitivity

Name	Family	Formula
Kleene-Dienes	(S,N)-	$I_{KD}(x,y) = \max(1-x,y)$
Weber	(S,N)-	$I_{WB}(x,y) = \begin{cases} 1, & \text{if } x < 1, \\ y, & \text{otherwise}. \end{cases}$
I_{PR}	QL-	$I_{PR}(x,y) = 1 - (\max(x(1+xy^2 - 2y),0))^{\frac{1}{2}}$
I_{PC}	QL-	$I_{PC}(x,y) = 1 - (\max(x(x+xy^2 - 2y),0))^{\frac{1}{2}}$

Lemma 3 [9]. *Let S be a t-conorm such that $S \leq S_{LK}$, then $d_{I_{T,S,N}}$ obtained from the QL-implication $I_{T,S,N}$ is a metric.*

Lemma 4. *$d_{I_{T,S,N}}$ generated from the QL-implication $I_{T,S,N}$, is a discrete metric when one of the following is true:*

(i) $T = T_M(x,y) = \min(x,y)$,

(ii) $T = T_D(x,y) = \begin{cases} \min(x,y), & \text{if } \max(x,y) = 1, \\ 0, & \text{otherwise}. \end{cases}$,

(iii) S is a positive t-conorm.

3.2 S_{LK}-Transitivity of Transformations of Fuzzy Implications

In this section, we show that one can construct metrics using different transformations of fuzzy implications.

Let Φ denote the family of all increasing bijections $\phi : [0,1] \to [0,1]$ such that $\phi(0) = 0$ and $\phi(1) = 1$.

Define the family of bijections that are super-additive and sub-additive on admissible arguments $x,y \in [0,1]$, denoted by Φ^+ and Φ_+ respectively, as follows:

$$\Phi^+ := \{\phi \in \Phi \mid \phi(x+y) \geq \phi(x) + \phi(y)\},$$
$$\Phi_+ := \{\phi \in \Phi \mid \phi(x+y) \leq \phi(x) + \phi(y)\}.$$

Definition 7 (cf. [15]). *Given $\phi \in \Phi$, and an $I \in \mathbb{FI}$, the following transformations of I always yield an implication:*

(i) $I_\phi^{[1]}(x,y) = \phi^{-1}(I(\phi(x),\phi(y)))$,

(ii) $I_\phi^{[2]}(x,y) = \phi(I(x,\phi^{-1}(y)))$,

(iii) $I_\phi^{[3]}(x,y) = \phi(I(\phi^{-1}(x),y))$,

(iv) $I_\phi^{[4]}(x,y) = \phi(I(x,y))$.

Lemma 5. *Let I be S_{LK}-transitive.*

(i) If $\phi \in \Phi^+$ then $I_\phi^{[1]}$ is S_{LK}-transitive.

(ii) If $\phi \in \Phi_+$ then $I_\phi^{[4]}$ is S_{LK}-transitive.

While similar sufficient conditions are hard to obtain for $I_\phi^{[2]}$ and $I_\phi^{[3]}$, Example 3 below presents some transformations under which $S_{\mathbf{LK}}$-transitivity is preserved.

Example 2. Let $\phi(x) = x^2$. Thus, $\phi^{-1}(x) = \sqrt{x}$. Clearly, $\phi \in \Phi^+$ since

$$\phi(x+y) = (x+y)^2 \geq x^2 + y^2 \geq \phi(x) + \phi(y).$$

Let $I = I_{\mathbf{RC}}$. Then,

$$I_\phi^{[1]}(x,y) = \sqrt{I_{\mathbf{RC}}(x^2, y^2)} = \sqrt{1 - x^2 + x^2 y^2} \ ,$$

$$d_{I_\phi^{[1]}}(x,y) = \begin{cases} 0, & \text{if } x = y \ , \\ \sqrt{1 - x^2 + x^2 y^2}, & \text{if } x < y \ , \\ \sqrt{1 - x^2 + x^2 y^2}, & \text{if } y < x \ . \end{cases}$$

Example 3. Let $\phi(x) = \sin\left(\frac{\pi}{2}x\right)$. Thus, $\phi^{-1}(x) = \frac{2}{\pi}\sin^{-1}(x)$. Since

$$\phi(x+y) = \sin\left(\frac{\pi}{2}(x+y)\right) = \sin\left(\frac{\pi}{2}x\right)\cos\left(\frac{\pi}{2}y\right) + \sin\left(\frac{\pi}{2}y\right)\cos\left(\frac{\pi}{2}x\right)$$

$$\leq \sin\left(\frac{\pi}{2}x\right) + \sin\left(\frac{\pi}{2}y\right) = \phi(x) + \phi(y) \ ,$$

we see that $\phi \in \Phi_+$. Once again letting $I = I_{\mathbf{RC}}$, we obtain

$$I_\phi^{[2]}(x,y) = \sin\left(\frac{\pi}{2}I_{\mathbf{RC}}\left(x, \frac{2}{\pi}\sin^{-1}(y)\right)\right) = \sin\left(\frac{\pi}{2}\left[1 - x + \frac{2}{\pi}x\sin^{-1}(y)\right]\right)$$

$$d_{I_\phi^{[2]}}(x,y) = \begin{cases} 0, & \text{if } x = y \ , \\ \sin\left(\frac{\pi}{2}[1 - x + \frac{2}{\pi}x\sin^{-1}(y)]\right), & \text{if } x < y \ , \\ \sin\left(\frac{\pi}{2}[1 - y + \frac{2}{\pi}y\sin^{-1}(x)]\right), & \text{if } y < x \ . \end{cases}$$

$$I_\phi^{[3]}(x,y) = \sin\left(\frac{\pi}{2}I_{\mathbf{RC}}\left(\frac{2}{\pi}\sin^{-1}(x), y\right)\right) = \sin\left(\frac{\pi}{2} - \sin^{-1}(x) + y\sin^{-1}(x)\right) \ .$$

$$d_{I_\phi^{[3]}}(x,y) = \begin{cases} 0, & \text{if } x = y \ , \\ \sin\left(\frac{\pi}{2} - \sin^{-1}(x) + y\sin^{-1}(x)\right), & \text{if } x < y \ , \\ \sin\left(\frac{\pi}{2} - \sin^{-1}(y) + x\sin^{-1}(y)\right), & \text{if } y < x \ . \end{cases}$$

$$I_\phi^{[4]}(x,y) = \sin\left(\frac{\pi}{2}I_{\mathbf{RC}}(x,y)\right) = \sin\left(\frac{\pi}{2}[1 - x + xy]\right) \ .$$

$$d_{I_\phi^{[4]}}(x,y) = \begin{cases} 0, & \text{if } x = y \ , \\ \sin\left(\frac{\pi}{2}[1 - x + xy]\right), & \text{if } x < y \ , \\ \sin\left(\frac{\pi}{2}[1 - x + xy]\right), & \text{if } y < x \ . \end{cases}$$

3.3 $S_{\mathbf{LK}}$-Transitivity of $I \in \mathbb{FI}$ Obtained from Unary Generators

Yet another way to obtain fuzzy implications are through unary operations on $[0, 1]$. Yager proposed this approach formally in [16] using the additive generators of Archimedean t-norms. Since then there have been many such proposals.

In this section, we discuss the $S_{\mathbf{LK}}$-transitivity of f-implications using the representation theorem for the family of f-implications given in [15].

Definition 8 ([6], **Definition 3.1.1**). *Let $f : [0,1] \to [0,\infty]$ be a strictly decreasing and continuous function with $f(1) = 0$. With the understanding $0 \cdot \infty = 0$, $I_f \in \mathbb{FI}$ and is called an f-implication, when defined as follows:*

$$I_f(x,y) = f^{-1}(x \cdot f(y)), \text{ for all } x,y \in [0,1] \ .$$

Example 4. Following are prototypical examples of f-implications and they satisfy $S_{\mathbf{LK}}$-transitivity:

(i) Yager: $I_{\mathbf{YG}}(x,y) = \begin{cases} 1, & \text{if } x = y = 0 \ , \\ y^x, & \text{otherwise} \ . \end{cases}$

(ii) Reichenbach: $I_{\mathbf{RC}}(x,y) = 1 - x + xy \ .$

Remark 1. Let us denote the family of all f-implications whose generators f satisfy $f(0) = 1$ by $I_{\mathbb{F},1}$ and those with $f(0) = \infty$ by $I_{\mathbb{F},\infty}$. Clearly, the family of all f-implications $I_{\mathbb{F}} = I_{\mathbb{F},\infty} \cup I_{\mathbb{F},1}$.

Theorem 2 ([15], **Corollary 5.9**).

(i) $I_f \in I_{\mathbb{F},1}$ *iff* $I_f(x,y) = I_{\mathbf{RC}_\phi}^{[2]}(x,y) = \phi(I_{\mathbf{RC}}(x,\phi^{-1}(y))) = 1 - x + x\phi^{-1}(y).$

(ii) $I_f \in I_{\mathbb{F},\infty}$ *iff* $I_f(x,y) = I_{\mathbf{YG}_\phi}^{[2]}(x,y) = \begin{cases} 1, & \text{if } x = y = 0 \ , \\ \phi\left([\phi^{-1}(y)]^x\right), & \text{otherwise} \ . \end{cases}$

$I_\phi^{[2]}$ defined in Example 3 is an $S_{\mathbf{LK}}$-transitive f-implication. Table 2 lists examples of metrics obtained from $I_{\mathbf{YG}}$, $I_{\mathbf{RC}}$ and the fuzzy implications given in Table 1.

Remark 2. Note that the metrics d_I are obtained on $[0,1]$, but as given in [9], one can easily lift them to any $\mathcal{X} \neq \emptyset$. Let $f : \mathcal{X} \to [0,1]$. Define $d_I^* : \mathcal{X} \times \mathcal{X} \to [0,1]$ as follows: for any $x,y \in \mathcal{X}$,

$$d_I^*(x,y) = d_I(f(x),f(y)) = \begin{cases} 0, & \text{if } x = y \ , \\ I(\min(f(x),f(y)), \max(f(x),f(y))), & \text{otherwise} \ . \end{cases}$$
(2)

Clearly, d_I^* is a distance function on $\mathcal{X}$ and it is a metric if d_I is a metric.

4   Monodistances from Fuzzy Implications

Recently, monodistances w.r.t betweenness relations have garnered a lot of attention, mainly due to their application in decision making and penalty based data aggregation (see [11–13]). We recall the definitions of these notions and show that d_I is essentially a monodistance on the $([0,1], B_\leq)$-set.

In this section, we generalize the above result and show that one can easily obtain a monodistance on a betweenness set induced from a partially ordered set(poset). Our quest also leads us to characterize the betweenness sets obtained from bounded below posets.

Table 2. Some examples of metrics obtained from implications

Implication	Type	Metric
$I_{\mathbf{KD}}$	(S,N)-	$d_{I_{\mathbf{KD}}}(x,y) = \begin{cases} 0, & \text{if } x=y, \\ \max(1-x,y), & \text{if } x<y, \\ \max(1-y,x), & \text{if } x>y. \end{cases}$
$I_{\mathbf{WB}}$	(S,N)-	$d_{I_{\mathbf{WB}}}(x,y) = \begin{cases} 1, & \text{if } x \neq y, \\ 0, & \text{otherwise}. \end{cases}$
$I_{\mathbf{PR}}$	QL-	$d_{I_{\mathbf{PR}}}(x,y) = \begin{cases} 0, & \text{if } x=y, \\ 1-\max(x(1+xy^2-2y),0)^{\frac{1}{2}}, & \text{if } x<y, \\ 1-\max(y(1+yx^2-2x),0)^{\frac{1}{2}}, & \text{if } x>y. \end{cases}$
$I_{\mathbf{PC}}$	QL-	$d_{I_{\mathbf{PC}}}(x,y) = \begin{cases} 0, & \text{if } x=y, \\ 1-\max(x(x+xy^2-2y),0)^{\frac{1}{2}}, & \text{if } x<y, \\ 1-\max(y(y+yx^2-2x),0)^{\frac{1}{2}}, & \text{if } x>y. \end{cases}$
$I_{\mathbf{YG}}$	Yager-	$d_{I_{\mathbf{YG}}}(x,y) = \begin{cases} 0, & \text{if } x=y, \\ y^x, & \text{if } x<y, \\ x^y, & \text{if } x>y. \end{cases}$
$I_{\mathbf{RC}}$	Yager-	$d_{I_{\mathbf{RC}}}(x,y) = \begin{cases} 0, & \text{if } x=y, \\ 1-\min(x,y)+xy, & \text{otherwise}. \end{cases}$

Definition 9. *Let* B *be a ternary relation on an* $\mathcal{X} \neq \emptyset$. *Then* B *is said to be a* **betweenness** *relation if* B *satisfies the following for any* $o,x,y,z \in \mathcal{X}$:

$$(x,y,z) \in B \iff (z,y,x) \in B, \tag{BS}$$
$$(x,y,z) \in B \wedge (x,z,y) \in B \iff y=z, \tag{BU}$$
$$(o,x,y) \in B \wedge (o,y,z) \in B \implies (o,x,z) \in B. \tag{BT}$$

Remark 3. (i) $(\mathcal{X}, B)$ is known as a Betweenness set or a B-set. Also, $(x,y,z) \in$ B is read as 'y is in between x and z'.

(ii) The minimal betweenneess relation B_0 on $\mathcal{X}$ is defined as follows:

$$B_0 = \{(x,y,z) \in \mathcal{X}^3 \mid x=y \vee y=z\}.$$

(iii) For an arbitrary but fixed $o \in \mathcal{X}$, the following is a partial order on $\mathcal{X}$:

$$x \preceq y \text{ iff } (o,x,y) \in B. \tag{3}$$

(iv) Conversely, a betweenness relation B can be defined from a partial order $\preceq$ on $\mathcal{X}$ as follows:

$$B_{\preceq} = B_0 \cup \{(x,y,z) \in \mathcal{X}^3 \mid x \preceq y \preceq z \vee z \preceq y \preceq x\}. \tag{4}$$

We present a more generalised definition of monodistance than what is presented in [11].

Definition 10 (cf. [11], Definition 6). *Consider a betweenness set* $(\mathcal{X}, \mathrm{B})$. *A distance function* $d : \mathcal{X} \times \mathcal{X} \rightarrow [0, \infty)$ *is called a monodistance (w.r.t.* B) *if for every* $(x, y, z) \in \mathrm{B}$, *it holds that:*

$$\max(d(x, y), d(y, z)) \leq d(x, z) . \tag{MC}$$

Note that if a monodistance d satisfies the converse of (P1), and (P2), then we will refer to it as a monometric.

Let us define a betweenness relation $\mathrm{B}_{\leq}$ on $[0, 1]$, as given in (4), where $\leq$ denotes the usual total order on it.

From (MC), it can be easily seen that d satisfies mixed monotonicity w.r.t. $\mathrm{B}_{\leq}$, i.e., it is decreasing in the first variable and increasing in the second variable. In fact, in [9], it was shown that d_I is a monodistance on $([0, 1], \mathrm{B}_{\leq})$. Clearly, fuzzy implications are both a natural choice and rich source for construction of monodistances.

Further, if we are given a totally ordered set $(\mathcal{X}, \leq)$, and let $(\mathcal{X}, \mathrm{B}_{\leq})$ be the corresponding B-set, then one can easily show that d_I^* defined on $\mathcal{X}$ is a monodistance on $(\mathcal{X}, \mathrm{B}_{\leq})$. For more details, see [9].

Thus the natural question to ask is if the above results hold on a poset, which is not a chain. In the rest of the section, we present a positive answer to this poser.

4.1   Monodistances on the B-Sets Obtained from a Poset

We begin by discussing the case where the betweenness set is obtained from a partially ordered set as in (4).

Theorem 3. *Let* $(\mathcal{X}, \preceq)$ *be a poset, and* $(\mathcal{X}, \mathrm{B}_{\preceq})$ *the B-set obtained as given in* (4). *Then there exists a non-trivial, i.e., a non-discrete, monodistance on* $(\mathcal{X}, \mathrm{B}_{\preceq})$.

Sketch of the Proof: Given $(\mathcal{X}, \preceq)$, using an order-preserving map $f : \mathcal{X} \rightarrow [0, 1]$, i.e., $x \preceq y$ implies $f(x) \leq f(y)$, it can be shown that the distance function d_I^* defined as in (2), is indeed a monodistance on $(\mathcal{X}, \mathrm{B}_{\preceq})$.

Remark 4. (i) Note that f in Theorem 3 can also be a constant function, in which case, we will get the discrete metric d_I^*, which is always a trivial monometric on $(\mathcal{X}, \mathrm{B}_{\preceq})$.
(ii) Further, the existence of non-constant f is not difficult to illustrate. For instance, if the cardinality of $\mathcal{X}$ is either finite or countable then the following f is one such order preserving map:

$$f(x) = 1 - \frac{1}{h(x) + 1} ,$$

where $h(x)$ gives the maximum of the heights of x from the minimal element of each of its chains. Example 5 provides yet another mapping with a clear visualisation of this projection in Fig. 1 (a). In fact, one can define a suitable f even in the case when $\mathcal{X}$ is of infinite cardinality, but where every chain of the poset $(\mathcal{X}, \preceq)$ is finite, as shown in Example 6. In the case when $\mathcal{X}$ is of infinite cardinality, but where at least one chain of the poset $(\mathcal{X}, \preceq)$ is infinite, one can define a suitable f by making use of any of the injections that are available between $\mathbb{R}$ and $[0, 1]$.

The following is an example of a monodistance on a $(\mathcal{X}, B_{\preceq})$-set where the cardinality of $\mathcal{X}$ is finite.

Example 5. Consider $\mathcal{X} = \{o, x, y, z\}$. Let $(\mathcal{X}, \preceq)$ be a partially ordered set as given in Fig. 1 (a). Then

$$B_{\preceq} = B_0 \cup \{(o, x, z), (z, x, o), (o, y, z), (z, y, o)\}.$$

Now, define a mapping $f : \mathcal{X} \to [0, 1]$ as in Table 3 (a):

Table 3. (a) The mapping f (b) The pairwise distance matrix on $\mathcal{X}$ under d_I^*

$\mathcal{X}$	o	x	y	z
f	0.25	0.5	0.5	0.75

d_I^*	o	x	y	z
o	0	0.875	0.875	0.9375
x	0.875	0	0.75	0.875
y	0.875	0.75	0	0.875
z	0.9375	0.875	0.875	0

A geometric visualisation of the mapping f is given in Fig. 1 (a).

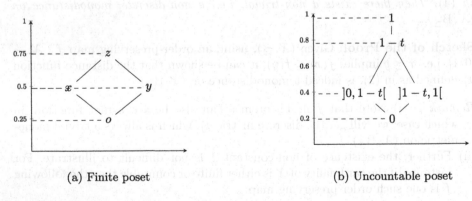

(a) Finite poset   (b) Uncountable poset

Fig. 1. Hasse Diagrams of the posets in Examples 5 and 6.

Consider $I = I_{\mathbf{RC}}$. We obtain the distance function d_I^* on $\mathcal{X}$ as given in Table 3 (b). Clearly, d_I^* is a monodistance w.r.t. $B_{\preceq}$. In fact, it is a monometric on $B_{\preceq}$ as $I_{\mathbf{RC}}$ satisfies $S_{\mathbf{LK}}$-transitivity.

The following is an example of a monodistance on $(\mathcal{X}, B_{\preceq})$, where $\mathcal{X}$ is an uncountable set.

Example 6. Let $\mathcal{X} = [0,1]$ and let $t_0 \in {]0,1[}$ be arbitrary but fixed. Consider the poset $(\mathcal{X}, \preceq)$ whose hasse diagram is given in Fig. 1 (b). Let $(\mathcal{X}, B_{\preceq})$ be the B-set obtained from $\preceq$ through (4).

Now, define a mapping $f : \mathcal{X} \to {]0,1[}$ as in Table 4 (a). Note that the second column should be read as f mapping the entire open interval $]0, 1 - t_0[$ to 0.4 and similarly $f(]1 - t_0, 1[) = 0.4$.

Table 4. (a) The mapping f (b) The pairwise distance matrix on $\mathcal{X}$ under d_I^*

(a)

$\mathcal{X}$	0	$]0, 1-t_0[$	$]1-t_0, 1[$	$1-t_0$	1
f	0.2	0.4	0.4	0.8	1

(b)

d_I^*	0	$y \in]0, 1-t_0[$	$y \in]1-t_0, 1[$	$1-t_0$	1
0	0	0.88	0.88	0.96	1
$x \in]0, 1-t_0[$	0.88	0	0.76	0.92	1
$x \in]1-t_0, 1[$	0.88	0.76	0	0.92	1
$1-t_0$	0.96	0.92	0.92	0	1
1	1	1	1	1	0

Consider $I = I_{\mathrm{RC}}$. We obtain the distance function d_I^* on $\mathcal{X}$ as given in Table 4 (b). Clearly, d_I^* is a monodistance w.r.t. $B_{\preceq}$. In fact, it is a monometric on $B_{\preceq}$ as I_{RC} satisfies S_{LK}-transitivity.

4.2   B-Sets Obtainable from a Poset: A Characaterisation

While Theorem 3 extends the result from [9] to the setting of posets, the existence of a monodistance on an arbitrary B-set is not clear.

In the following result, by providing a characterisation of betweenness sets obtained from a bounded below poset, we illustrate the scope and applicability of Theorem 3.

Theorem 4. *Let $(\mathcal{X}, B)$ be a betweenness set. Then B is induced from a bounded below poset iff there exists an $e \in \mathcal{X}$ such that the following property is true:*

$$
x \neq y \neq z \in \mathcal{X} \text{ and } (x, y, z) \in B \iff \begin{cases} \{(e, x, y), (e, y, z)\} \subset B \\ \text{or} \quad \{(e, y, x), (e, z, y)\} \subset B \, . \end{cases} \tag{5}
$$

Theorem 5. *Let $(\mathcal{X}, B)$ be a betweenness set s.t. B satisfies (5) with a special element $e \in \mathcal{X}$. Let us define the relation $x \preceq_e y \iff (e, x, y) \in B$. Then the following are true.*

(i) $(\mathcal{X}, \preceq_e)$ is a poset bounded below by e.
(ii) The natural betweenness obtained from $\preceq_e$ coincides with B, i.e., $B = B_{\preceq_e}$.

Corollary 2. *Let $(\mathcal{X}, B)$ be a betweenness set s.t. B satisfies (5) with a special element $e \in \mathcal{X}$. Then there exists a monodistance m on $(\mathcal{X}, B)$.*

5   Concluding Remarks

In this submission, we have studied distance functions that can be obtained from fuzzy implications. Firstly, we have investigated those families of fuzzy implications that satisfy $S_{\mathbf{LK}}$-transitivity, which is both necessary and sufficient for the proposed distance to be a metric. This also highlights the usefulness of S-transitivity as much as T-transitive fuzzy relations.

Secondly, we have demonstrated that implications are a natural choice for the construction of monodistances. In fact, by characterising the betweenness relations obtained from a given partial order, we have shown the existence of monodistances on them, built using these distance functions.

References

1. Aguiló, I., Calvo, T., Martín, J., Mayor, G., Suñer, J.: On distances derived from symmetric difference functions. In: 2015 Conference of the International Fuzzy Systems Association and the European Society for Fuzzy Logic and Technology (IFSA-EUSFLAT-15). Atlantis Press (2015)
2. Aguiló, I., Martín, J., Mayor, G., Suñer, J.: On distances derived from t-norms. Fuzzy Sets Syst. **278**, 40–47 (2015)
3. Alsina, C.: On quasi-copulas and metrics. In: Cuadras, C.M., Fortiana, J., Rodriguez-Lallena, J.A. (eds.) Distributions With Given Marginals and Statistical Modelling. Springer, Dordrecht (2002). https://doi.org/10.1007/978-94-017-0061-0_1
4. Alsina, C.: On some metrics induced by copulas. In: General Inequalities 4, pp. 397–397. Springer, Cham (1984). https://doi.org/10.1007/978-3-0348-6259-2_38
5. Ashraf, S.: Fuzzy dissimilarity and generalization of Valverde's theorem on t-indistinguishability relations. Fuzzy Sets Syst. **275**, 144–154 (2015)
6. Baczyński, M., Jayaram, B.: Fuzzy Implications, Studies in Fuzziness and Soft Computing, vol. 231. Springer, Heidelberg (2008). https://doi.org/10.1007/978-3-540-69082-5
7. Klement, E.P., Mesiar, R., Pap, E.: Triangular Norms, Trends in Logic, vol. 8. Kluwer Academic Publishers, Dordrecht (2000)
8. Klir, G.J., Yuan, B.: Fuzzy Sets and Fuzzy Logic: Theory and Applications. Prentice-Hall Inc., Hoboken (1995)
9. Nanavati, K., Gupta, M., Jayaram, B.: Metrics from fuzzy implications and their application. In: 9th International Conference on Pattern Recognition and Machine Intelligence (PREMI) (2021)
10. Ouyang, Y.: A note on metrics induced by copulas. Fuzzy Sets Syst. **191**, 122–125 (2012)
11. Pérez-Fernández, R., Baets, B.D.: The role of betweenness relations, monometrics and penalty functions in data aggregation. In: Proceedings of IFSA-SCIS 2017, pp. 1–6. IEEE (2017)
12. Pérez-Fernández, R., De Baets, B.: On the role of monometrics in penalty-based data aggregation. IEEE Trans. Fuzzy Syst. **27**(7), 1456–1468 (2019)
13. Pérez-Fernández, R., Rademaker, M., De Baets, B.: Monometrics and their role in the rationalisation of ranking rules. Inf. Fusion **34**, 16–27 (2017)
14. Valverde, L.: On the structure of F-indistinguishability operators. Fuzzy Sets Syst. **17**(3), 313–328 (1985)

15. Vemuri, N.R., Jayaram, B.: Representations through a monoid on the set of fuzzy implications. Fuzzy Sets Syst. **247**, 51–67 (2014)
16. Yager, R.R.: On some new classes of implication operators and their role in approximate reasoning. Inf. Sci. **167**(1–4), 193–216 (2004)

On the Additional Properties of Fuzzy Polynomial Implications of Degree 4

Michał Baczyński[1], Raquel Fernandez-Peralta[2,3],
Sebastia Massanet[2,3]([⊠]), Arnau Mir[2,3], and Juan Vicente Riera[2,3]

[1] Faculty of Science and Technology, University of Silesia in Katowice, Bankowa 14, 40-007 Katowice, Poland
michal.baczynski@us.edu.pl
[2] Soft Computing, Image Processing and Aggregation (SCOPIA) Research Group, Department of Mathematics and Computer Science, University of the Balearic Islands, 07122 Palma, Balearic Islands, Spain
{r.fernandez,s.massanet,arnau.mir,jvicente.riera}@uib.es
[3] Health Research Institute of the Balearic Islands (IdISBa), 07010 Palma, Spain

Abstract. It is well known that fuzzy implication functions have a very flexible definition that encompasses lots of different potential families. Therefore, the additional properties that the family members fulfill define the behavior these operators will have when modeling fuzzy conditionals or applied to any other application. In this way, in this paper, we study the additional properties of fuzzy polynomial implications of degree 4, a recent family of fuzzy implications which has been recently introduced as a family whose members have a simple expression, appealing for applied researchers. It is proved that members of this family fulfill some of the additional essential properties of fuzzy implication functions.

Keywords: Fuzzy implication function · Fuzzy polynomial implication · Exchange principle · Fuzzy connectives

1 Introduction

In the scientific literature of fuzzy implication functions (see [2,3,6] and references therein), almost 150 families of fuzzy implication functions have been introduced. These families have different construction methods, have very different final expressions, fulfill different additional properties, and therefore, some families are more adequate than others for a specific application.

In the last decade, a new line of research has emerged in which the goal is to propose the construction of new families of fuzzy implication functions focusing not on the proper construction method itself (from other logical connectives or univariate functions) but on the shared final expression that these implications have [7,8,11,12]. Within these studies, fuzzy polynomial implications (see [7]), those fuzzy implication functions whose expression is given by a bivariate polynomial, must be highlighted. Polynomials present relatively simple expressions, easily to be implemented on a computer, which is a crucial characteristic

© Springer Nature Switzerland AG 2022
D. Ciucci et al. (Eds.): IPMU 2022, CCIS 1601, pp. 182–193, 2022.
https://doi.org/10.1007/978-3-031-08971-8_16

when choosing a type of function to model an operator in a specific application. Moreover, they are always continuous, and, in comparison with other families of functions such as exponential or rational functions, they do not propagate as many errors from inputs to outputs. In [7], all fuzzy polynomial implications of degree less or equal to 4 were fully characterized in terms of conditions on the coefficients of the bivariate polynomial. However, while the most well-known additional properties for these operators were analyzed for fuzzy polynomial implications of degree less or equal to 3, no additional property was studied for those operators of degree 4. Consequently, this paper aims to fill this gap and to study the additional properties of this family of fuzzy implication functions, providing characterizations for the subfamilies that fulfill a concrete additional property.

The paper is structured as follows. First, in Sect. 2, those results and concepts needed to understand this paper are recalled. Then, in Sect. 3, we include the definition of fuzzy polynomial implications and the characterization theorem for the subfamily of degree 4, which will be crucial for the results presented in the next section. Specifically, we study the most well-known additional properties of fuzzy implication functions, always providing a characterization result for those properties which are satisfied by a subset of the family. The paper ends with some conclusions and future work.

2   Preliminaries

In this section, we list those concepts and the results needed to follow this work. First, we give the definition of a fuzzy negation.

Definition 2.1 ([4, **Definition 1.1**]). *A decreasing function* $N: [0,1] \to [0,1]$ *is a* fuzzy negation *if* $N(0) = 1$ *and* $N(1) = 0$. *A fuzzy negation* N *is*

(i) strict, *if it is continuous and strictly decreasing.*
(ii) strong, *if it is an involution, i.e.,* $N(N(x)) = x$ *for all* $x \in [0,1]$.

Next, we recall the definition of fuzzy implication functions.

Definition 2.2 ([4, **Definition 1.15**]). *A binary operator* $I: [0,1]^2 \to [0,1]$ *is called a* fuzzy implication function, *if it satisfies:*

(I1) $I(x,z) \geq I(y,z)$ *when* $x \leq y$, *for all* $z \in [0,1]$.
(I2) $I(x,y) \leq I(x,z)$ *when* $y \leq z$, *for all* $x \in [0,1]$.
(I3) $I(0,0) = I(1,1) = 1$ *and* $I(1,0) = 0$.

From the definition, we can deduce that $I(0,x) = 1$ and $I(x,1) = 1$ for all $x \in [0,1]$ while the symmetrical values $I(x,0)$ and $I(1,x)$ are not determined. In fact, $I(x,0)$ is always a fuzzy negation and denoted by N_I, the natural negation of I.

Some additional properties (see [2,4]) of fuzzy implication functions which will be used in this work are:

– The *left neutrality principle*,

$$I(1, y) = y, \quad y \in [0, 1]. \tag{NP}$$

– The *exchange principle*,

$$I(x, I(y, z)) = I(y, I(x, z)), \quad x, y, z \in [0, 1]. \tag{EP}$$

– The *law of importation* with respect to a t-norm T,

$$I(T(x, y), z) = I(x, I(y, z)), \quad x, y, z \in [0, 1]. \tag{LI}$$

– The *ordering property*,

$$x \le y \iff I(x, y) = 1, \quad x, y \in [0, 1]. \tag{OP}$$

– The *identity principle*,

$$I(x, x) = 1, \quad x \in [0, 1]. \tag{IP}$$

– The *iterative boolean law*,

$$I(x, I(x, y)) = I(x, y), \quad x, y \in [0, 1]. \tag{IB}$$

Additionally to these additional properties, we will also consider the invariance with respect to powers of a continuous t-norm[1], a property which was introduced in [9].

Definition 2.3 ([9]). *Let I be a fuzzy implication function and T be a continuous t-norm. It is said that I is invariant with respect to T-powers, or simply that it is T-power invariant when*

$$I(x, y) = I\left(x_T^{(r)}, y_T^{(r)}\right) \tag{PI$_T$}$$

holds for all real number $r > 0$ and for all $x, y \in [0, 1]$ such that $x_T^{(r)}, y_T^{(r)} \neq 0, 1$.

Finally, we recall the definitions of two important families of these operators, namely, (S, N)-implications and Yager's f-generated implications.

Definition 2.4 ([2, **Definition 2.4.1**]). *A function $I: [0, 1]^2 \to [0, 1]$ is called an (S, N)-implication if there exist a t-conorm S and a fuzzy negation N such that I is given by*

$$I_{S,N}(x, y) = S(N(x), y), \quad x, y \in [0, 1].$$

Definition 2.5 ([2, **Definition 3.1.1**]). *Let $f: [0, 1] \to [0, \infty]$ be a continuous and strictly decreasing function with $f(1) = 0$. The function $I_f: [0, 1]^2 \to [0, 1]$ defined by*

$$I_f(x, y) = f^{-1}(x \cdot f(y)), \quad x, y \in [0, 1],$$

understanding $0 \cdot \infty = 0$, is called an f-generated implication.

---

[1] We refer the reader to [9] for more details on powers of continuous t-norms.

3   Fuzzy Polynomial Implications

In [7], the authors introduced the family of fuzzy polynomial implications as those fuzzy implication functions whose expression is a polynomial of two variables. Formally, their definition is as follows.

Definition 3.1. *Let* $n \in \mathbb{N}$. *A binary operator* $I \colon [0,1]^2 \to [0,1]$ *is called a* fuzzy polynomial implication of degree n *if it is a fuzzy implication function and its expression is given by*

$$I(x,y) = \sum_{\substack{0 \leq i,j \leq n \\ i+j \leq n}} a_{ij} x^i y^j,$$

for all $x, y \in [0,1]$, $a_{ij} \in \mathbb{R}$ *and there exist some* $0 \leq i, j \leq n$ *with* $i + j = n$ *such that* $a_{ij} \neq 0$.

While a characterization of all fuzzy polynomial implications (of any degree) remains an open problem, in [7] characterizations for degrees $n \leq 4$ were presented. Let us recall the characterization for degree 4 which involves 19 conditions on the coefficients of the polynomial.

Theorem 3.2 ([7]). *Let* $I \colon [0,1]^2 \to [0,1]$ *be a binary operator. Then* I *is a fuzzy polynomial implication of degree* 4 *if, and only if,* I *is given by*

$$I(x,y) = x(1-y)(\alpha(x-1)^2 + \beta(x-1) + \gamma y^2 + \delta xy + \epsilon y - 1) + 1 \quad (1)$$

with $\alpha, \beta, \gamma, \delta, \epsilon \in \mathbb{R}$ *such that* $(\alpha, \gamma, \delta) \neq (0,0,0)$ *and the following conditions are satisfied:*

(1). $\alpha - \beta - \epsilon \leq 1$,
(2). $\delta + \epsilon + 1 \geq 0$,
(3). $\alpha - \beta + \gamma + \epsilon \leq 1$,
(4). $\gamma + \delta + \epsilon \leq 1$,
(5). *If* $\alpha < 0$ *and* $-2\alpha \leq \beta - \delta \leq -4\alpha$, *then* $(\beta - \delta)^2 + 4\alpha(\delta + \epsilon + 1) \leq 0$,
(6). *If* $\alpha < 0$ *and* $2\alpha \leq \beta + \delta \leq 0$, *then* $(\beta + \delta)^2 - 4\alpha(\gamma + \delta + \epsilon - 1) \leq 0$,
(7). *If* $\gamma < 0$ *and* $\gamma \leq \epsilon \leq -2\gamma$, *then* $\gamma^2 + \epsilon^2 + \gamma(-3\alpha + 3\beta + \epsilon + 3) \leq 0$,
(8). *If* $\gamma < 0$ *and* $\gamma \leq \delta + \epsilon \leq -2\gamma$, *then* $\gamma^2 + (\delta + \epsilon)^2 + \gamma(\delta + \epsilon + 3) \leq 0$.
(9). *If* $\alpha < 0$, $\gamma < 0$, $3\alpha\gamma - \delta^2 > 0$, $2\delta^2 \leq 3\beta\gamma - \delta(\gamma + 2\epsilon) \leq 6\alpha\gamma$ *and* $\delta^2 - 4\alpha\gamma \leq -\beta\delta + 2\alpha(\delta + \epsilon) \leq 2\alpha\gamma - \delta^2$ *then* $-4\alpha\left(\gamma^2 + \gamma(\delta + \epsilon + 3) + (\delta + \epsilon)^2\right) - 3\beta^2\gamma + 2\beta\delta(\gamma + 2(\delta + \epsilon)) + (\gamma + 4)\delta^2 \leq 0$.
(10). *If* $\alpha < 0$, $\gamma < 0$, $\delta^2 = 3\alpha\gamma$, $6\alpha(\delta + \epsilon) + \delta(\delta - 3\beta) = 0$, *and one or more of the following conditions hold:*
   (a) $-1 \leq \frac{\beta - 2\alpha}{\delta} < 1$,
   (b) $2\alpha \leq \beta - \delta \leq 0$,
   (c) $-1 \leq \frac{\beta}{\delta} \leq 1$,
   (d) $2\alpha \leq \beta + \delta \leq 0$,
   then $4\alpha(\delta + \epsilon + 1) + (\beta - \delta)^2 \leq 0$.
(11). $\alpha - \beta \leq 1$,
(12). $\beta \leq 1$,

(13). $\beta + \gamma + 2\delta + \epsilon \leq 1$,

(14). If $\alpha < 0$ and $2\alpha \leq \beta \leq -\alpha$, then $\alpha^2 + \beta^2 - \alpha\beta + 3\alpha \leq 0$,

(15). If $\alpha < 0$ and $2\alpha \leq \beta+\delta \leq -\alpha$, then $\alpha^2-\alpha(\beta+3\gamma+4\delta+3\epsilon-3)+(\beta+\delta)^2 \leq 0$,

(16). If $\gamma < 0$ and $0 \leq \epsilon \leq -2\gamma$, then $\epsilon^2 + 4\gamma(-\alpha + \beta + 1) \leq 0$,

(17). If $\gamma < 0$ and $0 \leq 2\delta + \epsilon \leq -2\gamma$, then $(2\delta + \epsilon)^2 - 4(\beta - 1)\gamma \leq 0$.

(18). If $\alpha < 0$, $\gamma < 0$, $3\alpha\gamma - \delta^2 > 0$, $-4\alpha\gamma \leq -2\beta\gamma + \delta\epsilon \leq 2\alpha\gamma - 2\delta^2$ and
$0 \leq -4\alpha\delta + 2\beta\delta - 3\alpha\epsilon \leq 6\alpha\gamma - 2\delta^2$ then $-4\alpha^2\gamma + 4\alpha(\beta - 3)\gamma - \alpha(2\delta + \epsilon)(2\delta + 3\epsilon) - 4\beta^2\gamma + 4\beta\delta(\delta + \epsilon) + 4\delta^2 \leq 0$.

(19). If $\alpha < 0$, $\gamma < 0$, $\delta^2 = 3\alpha\gamma$, $4\alpha\delta + 3\alpha\epsilon - 2\beta\delta = 0$, and one or more of the following conditions hold:
  (a) $-1 \leq \frac{\beta-2\alpha}{\delta} \leq 0$,
  (b) $2\alpha \leq \beta \leq -\alpha$,
  (c) $-1 \leq \frac{\alpha+\beta}{\delta} \leq 0$,
  (d) $2\alpha \leq \beta + \delta \leq -\alpha$,
  then $\alpha^2 + \beta^2 - \alpha\beta + 3\alpha \leq 0$.

As it can be seen, the expression of these fuzzy polynomial implications depends on five constants. In the next section, we will study the most important additional properties on fuzzy implication functions for this family.

4   Study of Additional Properties

First of all, we recall some additional properties which are fulfilled for fuzzy polynomial implications of any degree (and consequently, for degree 4).

Proposition 4.1 ([7]). *Let I be a fuzzy polynomial implication. Then the following statements hold:*

(i) I *is continuous.*

(ii) $I(x,y) = 1$ *if, and only if, $x = 0$ or $y = 1$.*

(iii) I *does not satisfy either* **(IP)** *or* **(OP)**.

(iv) N_I *is a strict negation.*

From the previous result, we can conclude the following fact.

Corollary 4.2. *The family of fuzzy polynomial implications do not intersect the family of R-implications.*

Proof. All R-implications fulfill **(IP)** (see Theorem 2.5.4 in [2]), a property which is never satisfied by fuzzy polynomial implications. □

From this point, the results are only valid for fuzzy polynomial implications of degree 4. The first result deals with the left neutrality principle.

Theorem 4.3. *Let $I: [0,1]^2 \rightarrow [0,1]$ be a binary operator. Then I is a fuzzy polynomial implication of degree 4 satisfying* **(NP)** *if, and only if, I is given by*

$$I(x,y) = x(1-y)(\alpha(x-1)^2 + \beta(x-1) + \delta y(x-1) - 1) + 1, \qquad (2)$$

for all $x, y \in [0,1]$, with $\alpha, \beta, \delta \in \mathbb{R}$ such that $(\alpha, \delta) \neq (0,0)$ and the Conditions (1), (3), (5), (6), (11)–(15) hold when $\gamma = 0$ and $\epsilon = -\delta$.

Proof. From Theorem 3.2 we know that I is a fuzzy polynomial implication of degree 4 if, and only if, I is given by Expression (1) with the coefficients satisfying Conditions (1)–(19). Now, considering Expression (1), it holds that I satisfies **(NP)** if, and only if, $I(1,y) = y$ for all $y \in [0,1]$ and consequently,

$$y = I(1,y) = (1-y) \cdot (\gamma y^2 + \delta y + \epsilon y - 1) + 1 \Leftrightarrow \begin{cases} \gamma = 0, \\ \epsilon = -\delta. \end{cases}$$

The result follows setting $\gamma = 0$ and $\epsilon = -\delta$ in Expression (1) and taking into account that with these parameter values Conditions (2), (4), (7)–(10) and (16)–(19) are trivially fulfilled. $\square$

Although this result fully characterizes the members of this family fulfilling the left neutrality principle, the large number of conditions makes difficult to find parameter values of (α, β, γ) satisfying all the conditions and consequently, providing examples of fuzzy polynomial implications of degree 4 that satisfy **(NP)** is not an easy task. To overcome this problem, next result defines a convex polyhedron in $\mathbb{R}^3$ which defines a whole family of fuzzy polynomial implications of degree 4 satisfying such property.

Proposition 4.4. *Let $I \colon [0,1]^2 \to [0,1]$ be a binary operator given by*

$$I(x,y) = x(1-y)(\alpha(x-1)^2 + \beta(x-1) + \delta y(x-1) - 1) + 1$$

with $(\alpha, \beta, \delta) \subset \mathbb{R}^3$ such that

$$(\alpha, \beta, \delta) = \sum_{i=1}^{5} \lambda_i V_i, \quad \lambda_i \in [0,1], \quad \sum_{i=1}^{5} \lambda_i = 1,$$

$(\alpha, \delta) \neq (0,0)$ *and*

$$V_i \in \{(0,0,1), (0,-1,0), (0,1,0), (0,1,-2), (2,1,0)\}.$$

Then I is a fuzzy polynomial implication of degree 4 satisfying **(NP)**.

Proof. Consider $\alpha \geq 0$. Applying Theorem 4.3, I given by

$$I(x,y) = x(1-y)(\alpha(x-1)^2 + \beta(x-1) + \delta y(x-1) - 1) + 1$$

is a fuzzy polynomial implication of degree 4 if, and only if, $(\alpha, \delta) \neq (0,0)$ and α, β, δ satisfy Conditions (1), (3), (11), (12) and (13) since the other ones are trivially satisfied. These conditions, jointly with $\alpha \geq 0$, constitute a system of linear inequalities whose set of solution defines a convex polyhedron. Applying a vertex enumeration algorithm to this system, the vertices of the convex polyhedron are given by:

$$V_i \in \{(0,0,1), (0,-1,0), (0,1,0), (0,1,-2), (2,1,0)\}.$$

     $\square$

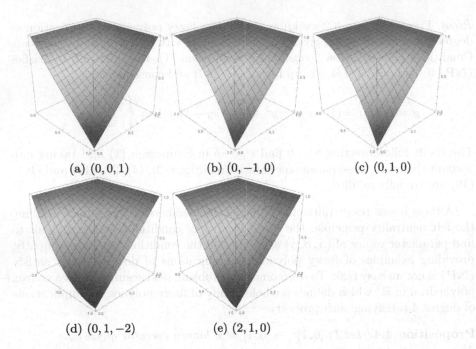

(a) $(0,0,1)$ (b) $(0,-1,0)$ (c) $(0,1,0)$

(d) $(0,1,-2)$ (e) $(2,1,0)$

Fig. 1. Fuzzy polynomial implications that satisfy **(NP)** obtained through the vertices of the convex polyhedron given in Proposition 4.3. Note that the second and third implications have a smaller degree than 4 since $(\alpha, \delta) = (0, 0)$.

In Fig. 1, the fuzzy polynomial implications obtained through the vertices of the convex polyhedron are depicted.

The following result proves that some family members satisfy the exchange principle.

Theorem 4.5. *Let* $I \colon [0,1]^2 \to [0,1]$ *be a binary operator. Then* I *is a fuzzy polynomial implication of degree 4 satisfying* **(EP)** *if, and only if,* I *is given by*

$$I(x,y) = x(1-y)(\alpha(x-1)^2 + \beta(x-1) - 1) + 1, \qquad (3)$$

with $\alpha, \beta \in \mathbb{R}$ *such that* $\alpha \neq 0$ *and the Conditions* (5), (6), (11), (12), (14) *hold when* $\gamma = \delta = \epsilon = 0$.

Proof. Again by Theorem 3.2 we know that I is a fuzzy polynomial implication of degree 4 if, and only if, I is given by Expression (1) with the coefficients satisfying Conditions (1)-(19).

At this point, if I satisfies **(EP)**, since N_I is continuous, according to Corollary 1.5.18 from [2], I satisfies **(NP)** and consequently, I is given by Expression (2). Now, it can be computed that the coefficient of $x^2 y^4 z^4$ in $I(x, I(y,z)) - I(y, I(x,z))$ (which must be 0 due to **(EP)**) is $-\delta^3$ and therefore, $\delta = 0$, obtaining already Expression (3). Note that being $\delta = \epsilon = 0$, Conditions

(1) and (3) are equal to Condition (11); Condition (13) is equal to Condition (12); Condition (15) is equal to Condition (14) and Conditions (2), (4), (7)–(10) and (16)–(19) are trivially satisfied. Therefore, only Conditions (5), (6), (11), (12) and (14) have to be fulfilled.

On the other hand, it is a tedious but straightforward computation to check that fuzzy implication functions given by Expression (3) satisfy **(EP)**.   □

Similarly to what we have done for the left neutrality principle, next result provides some insights on some values (α, β) satisfying all the conditions leading to examples of fuzzy polynomial implications of degree 4 that satisfy **(EP)**.

Proposition 4.6. *Let $I: [0,1]^2 \to [0,1]$ be a binary operator given by*

$$I(x,y) = x(1-y)(\alpha(x-1)^2 + \beta(x-1) - 1) + 1$$

with $(\alpha, \beta) \subset \mathbb{R}^2$ such that

$$(\alpha, \beta) = \lambda_1 \cdot (2,1) + \lambda_2 \cdot (0,1) + (1 - \lambda_1 - \lambda_2) \cdot (0,-1),$$

*with $0 \leq \lambda_1, \lambda_2 \leq 1$ and $\alpha > 0$. Then I is a fuzzy polynomial implication of degree 4 satisfying **(EP)**.*

Proof. Consider $\alpha \geq 0$. Applying Theorem 4.5, I given by

$$I(x,y) = x(1-y)(\alpha(x-1)^2 + \beta(x-1) - 1) + 1$$

is a fuzzy polynomial implication of degree 4 if, and only if, $\alpha \neq 0$ and α, β satisfy Conditions (1) and (12), namely $\alpha - \beta \leq 1$ and $\beta \leq 1$, since the other ones are trivially satisfied. These two last conditions delimit the triangle with vertices $(2,1)$, $(0,1)$ and $(0,-1)$ and the result follows.   □

In Fig. 2, the fuzzy polynomial implications obtained through the vertices of the aforementioned triangle are depicted.

The analysis of the exchange principle is crucial to determine the intersection of the family of fuzzy polynomial implications of degree 4 with the family of (S,N)-implications.

Theorem 4.7. *Let $I: [0,1]^2 \to [0,1]$ be a binary operator, S a t-conorm and N a fuzzy negation. Then the following statements are equivalent:*

(i) I is a fuzzy polynomial implication of degree 4 and an (S,N)-implication obtained from S and N.
(ii) I is given by

$$I(x,y) = x(1-y)(\alpha(x-1)^2 + \beta(x-1) - 1) + 1,$$

with $\alpha, \beta \in \mathbb{R}$ such that $\alpha \neq 0$ and the Conditions (5), (6), (11), (12), (14) hold when $\gamma = \delta = \epsilon = 0$.

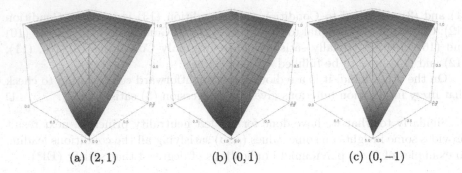

(a) $(2,1)$ (b) $(0,1)$ (c) $(0,-1)$

Fig. 2. Fuzzy polynomial implications satisfying **(EP)** obtained through the vertices of the triangle given in Proposition 4.5. Note that while the first one is of degree 4, the other ones have a smaller degree since $\alpha = 0$.

Moreover, in this case, $S(x,y) = S_P(x,y) = x + y - xy$ for all $x,y \in [0,1]$ and $N(x) = x(\alpha(x-1)^2 + \beta(x-1) - 1) + 1$ with $\alpha, \beta \in \mathbb{R}$ satisfying the conditions specified in (ii).

Proof. First, we will prove (i)$\Rightarrow$(ii). Since I is an (S,N)-implication, it satisfies **(EP)**. Consequently, being a fuzzy polynomial implication of degree 4 satisfying **(EP)**, by Theorem 4.5, I is given by

$$I(x,y) = x(1-y)(\alpha(x-1)^2 + \beta(x-1) - 1) + 1,$$

with $\alpha, \beta \in \mathbb{R}$ fulfilling the aforementioned conditions.

Reciprocally, by Theorem 4.5, I is a fuzzy polynomial implication of degree 4 that satisfies **(EP)**. Moreover, its natural negation given by

$$N_I(x) = I(x,0) = x(\alpha(x-1)^2 + \beta(x-1) - 1) + 1,$$

for all $x \in [0,1]$, is strict. Thus, by using Theorem 5.2 in [1], I is an (S,N)-implication generated from the fuzzy negation N_I and a t-conorm S. It can be checked that $S_P(N_I(x), y) = I(x,y)$ finishing the proof.   □

Next example provides some fuzzy implication functions satisfying the additional properties studied so far.

Example 4.8. (i) The fuzzy polynomial implication of degree 4 given by

$$I(x,y) = 1 - 2x + 2x^2 - x^3 + xy - x^2y + x^3y + xy^2 - x^2y^2$$

for all $x,y \in [0,1]$ which corresponds to Expression (2) with $\alpha = -1$, $\beta = 0$ and $\delta = 1$ satisfies **(NP)**. This operator does not belong to the subfamily introduced in Proposition 4.4.

(ii) The fuzzy polynomial implication of degree 4 given by

$$I(x,y) = 1 - 2x + 2x^2 - x^3 + 2xy - 2x^2y + x^3y$$

for all $x, y \in [0, 1]$ which corresponds to Expression (3) with $\alpha = -1$ and $\beta = 0$ satisfies **(EP)**. This implication cannot be retrieved from Proposition 4.6 and by Theorem 4.7, it is a (S, N)-implication generated from $S_\mathbf{P}$ and $N(x) = 1 - 2x + 2x^2 - x^3$ for all $x \in [0, 1]$.

Closely related to the exchange principle, the law of importation has gained importance in the last decades due to its applications [5]. Next result shows that there is only one fuzzy polynomial implication of degree 4 satisfying this property.

Theorem 4.9. *Let* $I \colon [0, 1]^2 \to [0, 1]$ *be a binary operator. Then* I *is a fuzzy polynomial implication of degree 4 satisfying* **(LI)** *with a t-norm* T *if, and only if,* $T(x, y) = T_\mathbf{P}(x, y) = xy$ *and* I *is given by* $I(x, y) = 1 - x^3 + x^3 y$ *for all* $x, y \in [0, 1]$.

Proof. Suppose first that I is a fuzzy polynomial implication of degree 4 satisfying **(LI)** with a t-norm T. Since it satisfies **(LI)**, it is well known that it satisfies **(EP)** and therefore, by Theorem 4.7 it is an (S, N)-implication generated by $S_\mathbf{P}$. Now, by Theorem 7.3.2 in [2], T must be the dual t-norm of $S_\mathbf{P}$ that is $T = T_\mathbf{P}$. Let us consider $I(T_\mathbf{P}(x, y), z) - I(x, I(y, z))$ for all $x, y, z \in [0, 1]$. Since I satisfies **(LI)** with $T = T_\mathbf{P}$, this must be 0. However, taking in this formula the family given by Expression (3) (those that satisfy **(EP)** and therefore, candidates to satisfy **(LI)**), we get that the coefficient of $x^3 y^3 z$ is $-\alpha^2 - \alpha$. Since $\alpha \neq 0$, the only possible value is $\alpha = -1$. Taking this and computing the coefficient of $x^3 y^2 z$, we get $2 + \beta$ and therefore, $\beta = -2$. This implies that $I(x, y) = 1 - x^3 + x^3 y$, for all $x, y \in [0, 1]$.

Reciprocally, the result is immediate taking into account that $I(x, y) = 1 - x^3 + x^3 y$ is Yager's f-generated implication with $f(x) = \sqrt[3]{1 - x}$. $\quad\square$

This result allows us to fully determine the intersection of fuzzy polynomial implications of degree 4 with the family of Yager's f-generated implications.

Theorem 4.10. *Let* $I \colon [0, 1]^2 \to [0, 1]$ *be a binary operator and* $f \colon [0, 1] \to [0, +\infty]$ *be a continuous and strictly decreasing function. Then the following statements are equivalent:*

(i) I is a fuzzy polynomial implication of degree 4 and a Yager's f-generated implication.

(ii) I is given by
$$I(x, y) = 1 - x^3 + x^3 y, \quad x, y \in [0, 1].$$

Moreover, in this case $f(x) = \sqrt[3]{1 - x}$.

Proof. The result is immediate by Theorem 4.9 since all Yager's f-generated implications satisfy **(LI)** with $T_\mathbf{P}$ (see Theorem 7.3.10 in [2]). $\quad\square$

To end this section, we will prove that no fuzzy polynomial implication of degree 4 (in fact, of any degree) satisfies either **(IB)** or **(PI$_T$)**.

Proposition 4.11. *Let I be a fuzzy polynomial implication. Then I does not satisfy* **(IB)**.

Proof. First, by Proposition 6 in [7], there are no fuzzy polynomial implications of degree less or equal to one. Therefore, I has degree n with $n \in \mathbb{N}$ and $n \geq 2$. By Proposition 5 in [7], there exists a polynomial $q(x, y)$ of degree $n - 2$ such that $I(x, y) = x(1 - y)q(x, y) + 1$ for all $x, y \in [0, 1]$. Now, on the one hand, we obtain that

$$I(x, I(x,y)) = x(1 - I(x,y))q(x, I(x,y)) + 1 = -x^2(1-y)q(x,y)q(x, I(x,y)) + 1$$

which is a polynomial of degree at least $3 + 2(n - 2) = 2n - 1$. On the other hand, the right hand side of **(IB)** stands for $I(x,y)$ which has degree n. Since $2n - 1 > n$ when $n \geq 2$, I does not satisfy **(IB)**.   □

Proposition 4.12. *Let I be a fuzzy polynomial implication and T a continuous Archimedean t-norm. Then I does not satisfy* **(PI$_T$)**.

Proof. By Lemma 6 in [10], if I satisfies **(PI$_T$)**, then $I(x,x)$ is constant for all $x \in (0, 1)$. In this case, since $I(0, 0) = I(1, 1) = 1$, by the continuity of I, $I(x,x) = 1$ for all $x \in [0, 1]$. A contradiction arises with Proposition 4.1-(ii). Consequently, I does not satisfy **(PI$_T$)**.   □

5   Conclusions and Future Work

In this paper, fuzzy polynomial implications of degree 4 have been deeply investigated from the point of view of their additional properties. Indeed, the most important additional properties on fuzzy implication functions have been analyzed, leading to complete characterization results whenever some members of the family fulfill a concrete additional property. In this way, we have proved that while an infinite number of fuzzy polynomial implications of degree 4 satisfy the exchange principle and the left neutrality principle, only one of these fuzzy implication functions satisfy the law of importation. From these results, the intersections of fuzzy polynomial implications of degree 4 with the well-known families of (S, N), R and Yager's f-generated implications have been presented.

As future work, we want to study the fulfillment of the law of importation and the exchange principle for fuzzy polynomial implications of any degree n.

Acknowledgements. This paper is part of the R+D+i Project PID2020-113870GB-I00- "Desarrollo de herramientas de Soft Computing para la Ayuda al Diagnóstico Clínico y a la Gestión de Emergencias (HESOCODICE)", funded by MCIN/AEI/10.13039/501100011033/. Raquel Fernandez-Peralta benefits from the fellowship FPU18/05664 granted by the Spanish Ministry of Science, Innovation and Universities within the Training University Lecturers (FPU) program. The research activities co-financed by the funds granted under the Research Excellence Initiative of the University of Silesia in Katowice.

References

1. Baczyński, M., Jayaram, B.: On the characterization of (S, N)-implications. Fuzzy Sets Syst. **158**, 1713–1727 (2007)
2. Baczyński, M., Jayaram, B.: Fuzzy Implications, Studies in Fuzziness and Soft Computing, vol. 231. Springer, Berlin Heidelberg (2008). https://doi.org/10.1007/978-3-540-69082-5
3. Baczynski, M., Jayaram, B., Massanet, S., Torrens, J.: Fuzzy implications: past, present, and future. In: Kacprzyk, J., Pedrycz, W. (eds.) Springer Handbook of Computational Intelligence, pp. 183–202. Springer, Heidelberg (2015). https://doi.org/10.1007/978-3-662-43505-2_12
4. Fodor, J., Roubens, M.: Fuzzy Preference Modelling and Multicriteria Decision Support. Kluwer Academic Publishers, Dordrecht (1994)
5. Jayaram, B.: On the law of importation $(x \wedge y) \longrightarrow z \equiv (x \longrightarrow (y \longrightarrow z))$ in fuzzy logic. IEEE Trans. Fuzzy Syst. **16**(1), 130–144 (2008)
6. Mas, M., Monserrat, M., Torrens, J., Trillas, E.: A survey on fuzzy implication functions. IEEE Trans. Fuzzy Syst. **15**(6), 1107–1121 (2007)
7. Massanet, S., Mir, A., Riera, J.V., Ruiz-Aguilera, D.: Fuzzy implication functions with a specific expression: the polynomial case (2022). Submitted to Fuzzy Sets and Systems
8. Massanet, S., Riera, J.V., Ruiz-Aguilera, D.: On fuzzy polynomial implications. In: Laurent, A., Strauss, O., Bouchon-Meunier, B., Yager, R.R. (eds.) IPMU 2014. CCIS, vol. 442, pp. 138–147. Springer, Cham (2014). https://doi.org/10.1007/978-3-319-08795-5_15
9. Massanet, S., Recasens, J., Torrens, J.: Fuzzy implication functions based on powers of continuous t-norms. Int. J. Approx. Reason. **83**, 265–279 (2017)
10. Massanet, S., Recasens, J., Torrens, J.: Some characterizations of T-power based implications. Fuzzy Sets Syst. **359**, 42–62 (2019)
11. Massanet, S., Riera, J.V., Ruiz-Aguilera, D.: On (op)-polynomial implications. In: Alonso, J.M., Bustince, H., Reformat, M. (eds.) 2015 Conference of the International Fuzzy Systems Association and the European Society for Fuzzy Logic and Technology (IFSA-EUSFLAT-15), Gijón, Spain, 30 June 2015. Atlantis Press (2015)
12. Massanet, S., Riera, J.V., Ruiz-Aguilera, D.: On rational fuzzy implication functions. In: 2016 IEEE International Conference on Fuzzy Systems (FUZZ-IEEE), pp. 272–279 (2016)

Preservation of the Ordering Property Under the Quadratic Polynomial Construction of Fuzzy Implication Functions

Mateusz Pieszczek[ID] and Michał Baczyński[✉][ID]

Faculty of Science and Technology, University of Silesia in Katowice,
Bankowa 14, 40-007 Katowice, Poland
{mpieszczek,michal.baczynski}@us.edu.pl

Abstract. In recent academic studies, new ways of constructing fuzzy implication functions have been developed. One of the proposed constructions is a ternary polynomial one of the form $I_F(x, y) := F(x, y, I(x, y))$, where F is a polynomial, and I is a fuzzy implication. In the particular case of quadratic polynomials, under additional conditions, construction preserves properties like the left neutrality principle, the law of contraposition, or the identity principle of the initial fuzzy implication I. In this paper, we looked at the preservation of the ordering property under such quadratic polynomial construction. Additionally, we took a look at the case of arbitrary degree polynomials and their preservation of boundary conditions of a fuzzy implication.

Keywords: Fuzzy implication function · Quadratic construction · Ordering property · Polynomial construction · Fuzzy connectives

1 Introduction

There exist a vast number of developing branches in fuzzy logic. One of the most prominent is the topic of fuzzy conditionals and inferences. Usually, they are implemented using some kind of fuzzy implications. Because of that, fuzzy implication functions received a lot of attention and literature dedicated to their theoretical aspects and applications (for instance, see [4,5]).

Our article is concerned with the problem of construction methods of fuzzy implication functions. Those construction methods can use other fuzzy connectives, like conjunction or disjunction. Still, in particular, we can use some given fuzzy implication functions to construct new ones. Examples like upper, lower, and medium contrapositivisations, convex combinations, reciprocal implications, residual implications can be seen in [5]. We also have more recent studies, e.g. other types of contrapositivisations [2], several threshold generation methods [7–9], ⊛-composition methods [11,12] and FNI-method [3,10].

© Springer Nature Switzerland AG 2022
D. Ciucci et al. (Eds.): IPMU 2022, CCIS 1601, pp. 194–205, 2022.
https://doi.org/10.1007/978-3-031-08971-8_17

In the article [6], the authors proposed construction based on three-dimensional polynomials. Given a polynomial $F\colon [0,1]^3 \to \mathbb{R}$ and some fuzzy implication function they were interested in functions of the form $I_F(x,y) = F(x,y,I(x,y))$. In the case of quadratic polynomials, they showed in the article the necessary conditions for the function I_F to be fuzzy implication and conditions for it to satisfy properties like identity principle, left neutrality property, etc. The problem of the preservation of the ordering property was left open. Later in the article [1] the ordering property was considered but with additional assumptions of satisfying extra properties like the left neutrality property or the law of contraposition for the classical negation.

In this paper, we will provide and prove the necessary conditions for function I_F to be fuzzy implication satisfying the ordering property. In the proof, we do not consider any other property, so our result is more general than shown in [1].

2   Preliminaries

First, let us bring notions that we will use throughout this article. We recall the definition of a fuzzy negation.

Definition 2.1 (see [5, Definition 1.4.1]). *We call a decreasing function $N\colon [0,1] \to [0,1]$ a **fuzzy negation** if $N(0) = 1$ and $N(1) = 0$. Additionally we say that N is*

1. ***strict**, if it is continuous and strictly decreasing.*
2. ***strong**, if it is an involution.*

We will denote the classical negation as N_C, where $N_C(x) = 1 - x$, for $x \in [0,1]$. Next, we will define a fuzzy implication function.

Definition 2.2 (see [5, Definition 1.1.1]). *We call a function $I\colon [0,1]^2 \to [0,1]$ a **fuzzy implication**, if it satisfies the following boundary and the monotonicity conditions*

1. *$I(x,z) \geq I(y,z) \iff x \leq y$, for all $z \in [0,1]$,*
2. *$I(x,y) \leq I(x,z) \iff y \leq z$, for all $x \in [0,1]$,*
3. *$I(0,0) = I(1,1) = 1$ and $I(1,0) = 0$.*

By $\mathcal{FI}$, we will denote the class of all fuzzy implication functions.

Remark 2.3. If I is a fuzzy implication function, then for any $x \in [0,1]$, it is true that $I(0,x) = I(x,1) = 1$.

We are usually interested in implications that satisfy some additional properties, which are commonly derived from classical logic tautologies. We will remind the reader of some properties, which will be used in later parts.

Definition 2.4 ([5, Definition 1.3.1]). *Let I be a fuzzy implication. Then we say that I satisfies*

– the **left neutrality property**, if

$$I(1, y) = y, \quad y \in [0, 1]. \tag{NP}$$

– the **identity principle**, if

$$I(x, x) = 1, \quad x \in [0, 1]. \tag{IP}$$

– the **ordering property**, if

$$x \leq y \iff I(x, y) = 1, \quad x, y \in [0, 1]. \tag{OP}$$

– the **law of contraposition** with respect to fuzzy negation N, if

$$I(N(y), N(x)) = I(x, y), \quad x, y \in [0, 1]. \tag{CP(N)}$$

– the **exchange principle**, if

$$I(x, I(y, z)) = I(y, I(x, z)), \quad x, y, z \in [0, 1]. \tag{EP}$$

By $\mathcal{FI}_{\mathbf{NP}}$ we will denote class of all fuzzy implication functions satisfying (**NP**). Likewise for other properties mentioned above.

3   Construction of Fuzzy Implication from Other Implications

In the scientific literature, there are many methods for constructing fuzzy implications. For other examples, one can look into, e.g., [4] or other articles mentioned in the introduction. We will only remind the construction based on the convex linear combination because it is a base for other construction methods. In particular, it is used in polynomial construction.

Proposition 3.1 ([5, **Lemma 6.2.1**]). *Let I_1 and I_2 be fuzzy implication functions and $\lambda \in [0, 1]$. The binary function $I : [0, 1]^2 \to [0, 1]$ given by*

$$I(x, y) = (1 - \lambda)I_1(x, y) + \lambda I_2(x, y), \quad \text{for all } x, y \in [0, 1], \tag{1}$$

is a fuzzy implication function.

It is easy to check that under this construction if implications I_1 and I_2 satisfy any of properties (**NP**), (**IP**), (**OP**), **CP(N)** then I_F will also satisfy that property. In general it is not true for (**EP**).

3.1 Construction of Fuzzy Implications Using Quadratic Polynomials

In the article [6] the authors considered some construction of fuzzy implications using polynomial transformations and in particular quadratic polynomials. Let us assume that I is a fuzzy implication, and $F\colon [0,1]^3 \to \mathbb{R}$ is a ternary polynomial of the form

$$F(x,y,z) = ax^2 + by^2 + cz^2 + dxy + exz + fyz + gx + hy + iz + j. \quad (2)$$

The authors of [6] were looking for prerequisites on F such that function I_F given by

$$I_F(x,y) := F(x,y,I(x,y)), \quad x,y \in [0,1], \quad (3)$$

is a fuzzy implication function. We can see that for linear case problem trivialise.

Proposition 3.2 ([6, Proposition 3.1]). *Let I be fuzzy implication and $F\colon [0,1]^3 \to \mathbb{R}$ be a linear function, i.e.,*

$$F(x,y,z) = ax + by + cz + d, \quad x,y \in [0,1]. \quad (4)$$

Then the following statements are equivalent:

1. *For each fuzzy implication I, I_F given by (3)is also fuzzy implication.*
2. *The function F is given by the projection $F(x,y,z) = z$, that is, $a = b = d = 0$ and $c = 1$, and therefore $I_F \equiv I$.*

Proper quadratic functions will give us more interesting results. With the assumption that F is a quadratic polynomial, results presented in [6] give us necessary and sufficient conditions for I_F to be a fuzzy implication function. We will now state those results. From boundary conditions of fuzzy implication function, we can reduce the number of coefficients of the function F to necessary ones.

Proposition 3.3 ([6, Proposition 3.2]). *Let F be a quadratic function of the form (2) and I a fuzzy implication function. Then the following statements are equivalent:*

1. *I_F fulfils the boundary conditions $I_F(1,0) = 0$ and $I_f(0,x) = I_F(x,1) = 1$ for all $x \in [0,1]$.*
2. *$a = b = 0$, $e = -(d+g)$, $h = -f$, $j = -g$, and $i = 1 - c + g$.*

Next, for I_F to be a fuzzy implication, it is enough for coefficients to lay in a convex hull of five specific points. During proof we mainly use Proposition 3.1 which allows us to only check boundary cases.

Theorem 3.4 ([6, Theorem 3.1]). *Let I be a fuzzy implication function and let F be a quadratic polynomial of the form (2). Then for a function $I_F\colon [0,1]^2 \to [0,1]$ such that $I_F(x,y) = F(x,y,I(x,y))$ following statements are equivalent:*

1. I_F is a fuzzy implication function for each fuzzy implication function I.
2. I_F is of the form

$$I_F(x,y) = cI^2(x,y) + dxy - (d+g)xI(x,y) \tag{5}$$
$$+fyI(x,y) + gx - fy + (1-c+g)I(x,y) - g,$$

where

$$(c,d,f,g) = \sum_{i=1}^{5} \lambda_i V_i, \quad \lambda_i \in [0,1], \quad \sum_{i=1}^{5} \lambda_i = 1,$$

and

$$V_1 = (1,0,0,0), V_2 = (-1,0,0,0), V_3 = (0,0,-1,0),$$
$$V_4 = (0,0,0,-1), V_5 = (0,1,0,-1).$$

Example 3.5. We can look at boundary cases of Theorem 3.4, which are functions F_i corresponding to vertices V_i for $i \in \{1,2,3,4,5\}$. It means that for polynomial F_i coefficients are of the form $(c,d,f,g) = V_i$.

$$I_{F_1}(x,y) = I^2(x,y), \qquad\qquad I_{F_2}(x,y) = 2I(x,y) - I^2(x,y),$$
$$I_{F_3}(x,y) = I(x,y) + y - yI(x,y), \qquad I_{F_4}(x,y) = xI(x,y) - x + 1.$$
$$I_{F_5}(x,y) = 1 - x + xy.$$

From them, F_1, F_2 and F_5 are constructions which could already be found in the literature. In fact I_{F_5} is just the Reichenbach implication. On the other hand F_3 and F_4 are actually original constructions originally proposed in [6]. If for example we take some well known implications

$$I_{RC}(x,y) = 1 - x + xy,$$
$$I_{LK}(x,y) = \min(1, 1 - x + y),$$
$$I_{KD}(x,y) = \max(1 - x, y),$$

then we can construct following implications

$$(I_{RC})_{F_3}(x,y) = 1 - x + 2xy - xy^2,$$
$$(I_{RC})_{F_4}(x,y) = 1 - x^2 + x^2y,$$
$$(I_{LK})_{F_3}(x,y) = \min(1, 1 - (x-y)(1-y)),$$
$$(I_{LK})_{F_4}(x,y) = \min(1, 1 - x^2 + xy),$$
$$(I_{KD})_{F_3}(x,y) = \max(1 - x + xy, 2y - y^2),$$
$$(I_{KD})_{F_4}(x,y) = \max(1 - x^2, 1 - x + xy).$$

4   Preserving Properties Under Quadratic Construction

In certain applications, we might be interested in preserving some additional properties of initial implication I. Authors of [6] proved preservation of some properties, under the transformation of the form (5). They made exhaustive characterisation for I_F, to satisfy **(NP)**, **(IP)** and **(CP(N_C))**. Now we will state their results.

Proposition 4.1 ([6, **Proposition 4.1**]). *Let I be a fuzzy implication function and function I_F be of the form (5). Then the next items hold:*

1. *If I satisfies **(NP)**, then I_F fulfils **(NP)** if and only if $f + c = 0$.*
2. *If I satisfies **(IP)**, then I_F fulfils **(IP)** if and only if $d = 0$.*
3. *If I satisfies **(CP(N_C))**, then I_F fulfils **(CP(N_C))** if and only if $d + g - f = 0$.*

Proposition 4.2 ([6, **Theorem 4.1**]). *Let $F: [0,1]^3 \to \mathbb{R}$ be a quadratic function of the form (2) and I_F the binary function given by (3). Then the following statements are equivalent:*

1. *For each I in $\mathcal{FI}_{IP,NP}$, the function I_F is also in $\mathcal{FI}_{IP,NP}$, that is I_F is a fuzzy implication function that satisfy **(IP)** and **(NP)**.*
2. *$I_F = I_{\alpha,\beta}$, where $I_{\alpha,\beta}$ is given by*

$$I_{\alpha,\beta}(x,y) = \alpha I(x,y)^2 + \beta x I(x,y) - \alpha y I(x,y) - \beta x$$
$$+ \alpha y + (1 - \alpha - \beta) I(x,y) + \beta,$$

with α, β fulfilling the conditions $0 \le \beta \le 1$, $0 \le \alpha \le 1 - \beta$, and $I \in \mathcal{FI}$.

Proposition 4.3 ([6, **Theorem 4.2**]). *Let $F: [0,1]^3 \to \mathbb{R}$ be a quadratic function of the form (2) and I_F the binary function given by (3). Then the following statements are equivalent:*

1. *For each I in $\mathcal{FI}_{IP,CP(N_C)}$, the function I_F is also in $\mathcal{FI}_{IP,CP(N_C)}$, that is I_F is a fuzzy implication function that satisfies **(IP)** and **(CP(N_C))**.*
2. *$I_F = I_{\alpha,\beta}$, where $I_{\alpha,\beta}$ is given by*

$$I_{\alpha,\beta}(x,y) = \alpha I(x,y)^2 + \beta x I(x,y) - \beta y I(x,y) - \beta x$$
$$+ \beta y + (1 - \alpha - \beta) I(x,y) + \beta,$$

with α, β fulfilling the conditions $0 \le \beta \le 1$, $\beta - 1 \le \alpha \le 1 - \beta$, and $I \in \mathcal{FI}$.

Proposition 4.4 ([6, **Theorem 4.3**]). *Let $F: [0,1]^3 \to \mathbb{R}$ be a quadratic function of the form (2) and I_F the binary function given by (3). Suppose that $I_F = I_{\alpha,\beta}$, where*

$$I_{\alpha,\beta}(x,y) = \alpha I(x,y)^2 + \beta xy + \alpha x I(x,y) - \alpha y I(x,y) - (\alpha + \beta)x \qquad (6)$$
$$+ \alpha y + (1 - 2\alpha - \beta) I(x,y) + \alpha + \beta,$$

*with α, β such that $0 \le \beta \le 1$ and $0 \le \alpha \le 1 - \beta$. Then for each I in $\mathcal{FI}_{NP,CP(N_C)}$, the function $I_{\alpha,\beta}$ is also in $\mathcal{FI}_{NP,CP(N_C)}$, that is $I_{\alpha,\beta}$ is a fuzzy implication function that satisfies **(NP)** and **(CP(N_C))**.*

Proposition 4.5 ([6, **Theorem 4.4**]). *Let* $F \colon [0,1]^3 \to \mathbb{R}$ *be a quadratic function of the form* (2) *and* I_F *the binary function given by* (3). *Suppose that for each* I *in* $\mathcal{FI}_{NP,CP(N_C)}$, *the function* I_F *is also in* $\mathcal{FI}_{NP,CP(N_C)}$. *Then* $I_F = I_{\alpha,\beta}$ *given by* (6) *with* α, β *such that* $0 \leq \beta \leq 1$ *and* $-\beta \leq \alpha \leq 1 - \beta$.

Remark 4.6. We can observe that regions of pairs (α, β) in Propositions 4.4 and 4.5 are not the same. In fact it is an open problem whether $I_{-1,1}$ is a fuzzy implication. If it would be, we would have a characterisation of functions preserving **(NP)** and **(CP(N_C))**. If its not we would have to put additional restrictions.

Additionally, we have a result considering all three properties.

Proposition 4.7 ([6, **Theorem 4.5**]). *Let* I *be a fuzzy implication function that satisfies* **(IP),(NP)** *and* **(CP(N_C))** *and function* I_F *be of the form* (5). *Then the following statements are equivalent:*

1. I_F *is a fuzzy implication function that satisfies* **(IP)**, **(CP(N_C))** *and* **(NP)**.
2. I_F *is given by*

$$I_F(x,y) = \alpha I(x,y)^2 + \alpha x I(x,y) - \alpha y I(x,y) - \alpha x + \alpha y + (1-2\alpha)I(x,y) + \alpha, \quad (7)$$

where $0 \leq \alpha \leq 1$.

4.1   Preservation of Ordering Property Under Quadratic Construction

Later the authors of [1] extended the results presented in [6], with consideration of **(OP)**. What they showed is conditional preservation of **(OP)** assuming other properties are also preserved.

Proposition 4.8 ([1, **Theorem 4.1**]). *Let* F *be a quadratic function of the form* (2) *and* I_F *be the binary function given by* (3). *Suppose that* $I_F = I_{\alpha,\beta}$, *where*

$$I_{\alpha,\beta}(x,y) = \alpha I(x,y)^2 - \beta x I(x,y) - \alpha y I(x,y) + \beta x + \alpha y + (1-\alpha+\beta)I(x,y) - \beta, \quad (8)$$

with α, β *such that* $-1 \leq \beta \leq 0$ *and* $0 \leq \alpha \leq 1+\beta$. *Then for each* I *in* $\mathcal{FI}_{NP,OP}$, *the function* $I_{\alpha,\beta}$ *is also in* $\mathcal{FI}_{NP}, OP$, *that is* $I_{\alpha,\beta}$ *is a fuzzy implication function that fulfils* **(NP)** *and* **(OP)**.

Proposition 4.9 ([1, **Theorem 4.2**]). *Let* F *be a quadratic function of the form* (2) *and* I_F *the binary function given by* (5). *Suppose that for each* I *in* $\mathcal{FI}_{NP}, OP$, *the function* I_F *is also in* $\mathcal{FI}_{NP}, OP$ $I_F = I_{\alpha,\beta}$. *Then* $I_F = I_{\alpha,\beta}$ *given by* (8) *with* α, β *such that* $-1 \leq \beta \leq 0, -1 \leq \alpha + \beta \leq 1$ *and* $\alpha \geq 0$.

Remark 4.10. Similarly as for **(NP)** and **(CP(N_C))** the regions for parameters in Propositions 4.8 and 4.9 are not equal. We do not know weather function $I_{2,-1}$ is a fuzzy implication. Therefore we do not have full characterisation. There might exist function $I_{\alpha,\beta}$ that satisfies the **(NP)** and **(CP(N_C))**, but is not a fuzzy implication function.

Proposition 4.11 ([1, **Theorem 4.3**]). *Let F be a quadratic function of the form (2) and I_F be a binary function given by (5). Suppose that $I_F = I_{\alpha,\beta}$, where*

$$I_{\alpha,\beta}(x,y) = \alpha I(x,y)^2 - \beta x I(x,y) + \beta y I(x,y) + \beta x + \alpha y + (1 - \alpha + \beta)I(x,y) - \beta, \quad (9)$$

with α, β such that $-1 \leq \beta \leq 0$ and $1 + \beta \leq \alpha \leq -1 - \beta$. Then for each I in $\mathcal{FI}_{\mathbf{CP(N_C)}}, \mathbf{OP}$, the function $I_{\alpha,\beta}$ is also in $\mathcal{FI}_{\mathbf{CP(N_C)}}, \mathbf{OP}$, that is $I_{\alpha,\beta}$ is a fuzzy implication function that fulfils (CP(N_C)) and (OP).

Proposition 4.12 ([1, **Theorem 4.4**]). *Let F be a quadratic function of the form (2) and I_F the binary function given by (5). Suppose that for each I in $\mathcal{FI}_{\mathbf{CP(N_C)}}, \mathbf{OP}$, the function I_F is also in $\mathcal{FI}_{\mathbf{CP(N_C)}}, \mathbf{OP}$ $I_F = I_{\alpha,\beta}$. Then $I_F = I_{\alpha,\beta}$ given by (9) with α, β such that $-1 \leq \beta \leq 0, -1 \leq \alpha + \beta \leq 1$.*

Remark 4.13. Again joining Propositions 4.11 and 4.12 regions do not match so without prove of $I_{2,-1}$ being fuzzy implication, we do not get a characterisation.

Building on top of results from [6] and [1] what we managed to prove are conditions for I_F to satisfy (**OP**) without any additional assumptions.

Theorem 4.14. *Let F be a quadratic function of the form (2) and I be a fuzzy implication such that it satisfies (OP), i.e.,*

$$x \leq y \iff I(x,y) = 1, \quad x,y \in [0,1], \quad (10)$$

Let I_F be a binary function given by (5). Then I_F is a fuzzy implication that satisfies (OP) if and only if $d = 0$.

Proof. Let $I : [0,1]^2 \to [0,1]$ be a fuzzy implication, which satisfies (**OP**) and the function I_F be of the form (5).

1. Assume I_F satisfies (**OP**). Also, let $x,y \in [0,1]$, such that $x \leq y$. Then $I_F(x,y) = 1$. Thus

$$cI^2(x,y) + dxy - (d+g)xI(x,y) + fyI(x,y) \quad (11)$$
$$+ gx - fy + (1 - c + g)I(x,y) - g = 1.$$

Because I satisfies (**OP**), then $I(x,y) = 1$, which reduces (11) to

$$dx(y - 1) = 0.$$

It holds for any $x,y \in [0,1]$, such that $x \leq y$. Therefore we conclude that $d = 0$.

2. Now lets assume that $d = 0$. Then I_F is of the form (5) is reduced to

$$I_F(x,y) = cI^2(x,y) - gxI(x,y) + fyI(x,y) \quad (12)$$
$$+ gx - fy + (1 - c + g)I(x,y) - g.$$

Now we will prove that I_F satisfies **(OP)**.

($\Longrightarrow$)

Lets assume that $x \leq y$. Because I satisfies **(OP)**, then $I(x,y) = 1$. Thus (12) reduces to

$$I_F(x,y) = c - gx + fy + gx - fy + 1 - c + g - g,$$

which after further reduction gives that $I_F(x,y) = 1$. Therefore,

$$x \leq y \Longrightarrow I_F(x,y) = 1. \tag{13}$$

($\Longleftarrow$)

Now let us assume that $I_F(x,y) = 1$. Then from (12) we get the series of equivalent transformations

$$1 = cI^2(x,y) - gxI(x,y) + fyI(x,y) + gx - fy + (1 - c + g)I(x,y) - g,$$

$$0 = [I(x,y) - 1] \cdot [cI(x,y) - gx + fy + 1 + g]. \tag{14}$$

If $I(x,y) = 1$, then because I satisfies **(OP)**, we get that $x \leq y$. Therefore, let us check the other case and assume that $I(x,y) \in [0,1)$. As I satisfies **(OP)**, it implies that $x > y$. Then from (14) we get that

$$cI(x,y) - gx + fy + 1 + g = 0. \tag{15}$$

We recall, that from Theorem 3.4 we know that

$$c = \lambda_1 - \lambda_2, \quad d = \lambda_5, \tag{16}$$

$$f = -\lambda_3, \quad g = -\lambda_4 - \lambda_5, \tag{17}$$

$$\sum_{i=1}^{5} \lambda_i = 1, \quad \text{where } \lambda_i \in [0,1], \quad \text{for } i \in \{1,2,3,4,5\}. \tag{18}$$

Because $d = 0$, then $\lambda_5 = 0$. Using substitution (16) and (17), we can write (15) as

$$(\lambda_1 - \lambda_2)I(x,y) + \lambda_4 x - \lambda_3 y + \lambda_1 + \lambda_2 + \lambda_3 + \lambda_4 - \lambda_4 = 0,$$

thus

$$\lambda_1[I(x,y) + 1] + \lambda_2[1 - I(x,y)] + \lambda_3[1 - y] + \lambda_4 x = 0. \tag{19}$$

We know that because $I(x,y) \in [0,1)$ thus

$$I(x,y) + 1 > 0 \quad \text{and} \quad 1 - I(x,y) > 0.$$

Additionally, because $x, y \in [0,1]$ and $x > y$ we can conclude that

$$1 - y > 0 \quad \text{and} \quad x > 0.$$

Also we recall that $\lambda_1, \lambda_2, \lambda_3, \lambda_4$ are non-negative. All elements of (19) are non-negative thus

$$\lambda_1 = \lambda_2 = \lambda_3 = \lambda_4 = 0,$$

which contradicts (18). Therefore

$$I_F(x, y) = 1 \quad \Longrightarrow \quad x \leq y. \tag{20}$$

From both (13) and (20) we receive that I_F satisfies **(OP)**, i.e.,

$$I_F(x, y) = 1 \quad \Longleftrightarrow \quad x \leq y,$$

which ends our proof.

□

Example 4.15. If we look at notation from Theorem 3.4, then condition $d = 0$ translates to $\lambda_5 = 0$. Which means that construction based on, e.g. F_3 will preserve **(OP)**. Well known examples of implications satisfying **(OP)** are the Goguen I_{GG}, the Gödel I_{GD}, the Rescher I_{RS}, and the Fodor I_{FD} implications:

$$I_{GG}(x, y) = \begin{cases} 1, & \text{if } x \leq y, \\ \frac{y}{x}, & \text{if } x > y, \end{cases} \qquad I_{RS}(x, y) = \begin{cases} 1, & \text{if } x \leq y, \\ 0, & \text{if } x > y, \end{cases}$$

$$I_{GD}(x, y) = \begin{cases} 1, & \text{if } x \leq y, \\ y, & \text{if } x > y, \end{cases} \qquad I_{FD}(x, y) = \begin{cases} 1, & \text{if } x \leq y, \\ \max(1 - x, y), & \text{if } x > y. \end{cases}$$

For those polynomial F_3 gives us the following functions:

$$(I_{GG})_{F_3}(x, y) = \begin{cases} 1, & \text{if } x \leq y, \\ \frac{y}{x} + y - \frac{y^2}{x}, & \text{if } x > y, \end{cases}$$

$$(I_{RS})_{F_3}(x, y) = I_{GD}(x, y),$$

$$(I_{GD})_{F_3}(x, y) = \begin{cases} 1, & \text{if } x \leq y, \\ 2y - y^2, & \text{if } x > y, \end{cases}$$

$$(I_{FD})_{F_3}(x, y) = \begin{cases} 1, & \text{if } x \leq y, \\ \max(1 - x + xy, 2y - y^2), & \text{if } x > y. \end{cases}$$

All of those functions are fuzzy implications satisfying **(OP)**.

5   Polynomial Construction of Arbitrary Degree

Articles [6] and [1] only considered quadratic polynomials. We shortly looked at polynomials of arbitrary degrees. What we have, is a characterization of F such that I_F satisfies boundary conditions of fuzzy implication.

Theorem 5.1. *Let I be a fuzzy implication function, $n \in \mathbb{N}$ and $F \colon \mathbb{R}^3 \to \mathbb{R}$ be a polynomial function of the form*

$$F(x, y, z) = \sum_{i,j,k=0}^{n} a_{(i,j,k)} x^i y^j z^k. \tag{21}$$

Then the function of the form $I_F(x,y) = F(x,y,I(x,y))$ satisfies five boundary conditions of a fuzzy implication function

$$I_F(0,0) = I_F(1,1) = 1, \quad I_F(1,0) = 0,$$
$$I_F(0,y) = 1, \quad y \in [0,1],$$
$$I_F(x,1) = 1, \quad x \in [0,1],$$

if and only if the following five equations hold

$$\sum_{k=0}^{n} a_{(0,0,k)} = 1, \quad \sum_{i,j,k=0}^{n} a_{(i,j,k)} = 1, \quad \sum_{i=0}^{n} a_{(i,0,0)} = 0,$$

$$\bigwedge_{1 \le j \le n} \sum_{k=0}^{n} a_{(0,j,k)} = 0, \quad \bigwedge_{1 \le i \le n} \sum_{j,k=0}^{n} a_{(i,j,k)} = 0.$$

The proof quickly follows from putting equations or boundary conditions into (21). The more critical problem that remains open is the monotonicity of function I_F for F of the form (21). We would need to find roots of partial derivatives of F, which is manageable in the quadratic case but would need more explanation in the general case.

6   Conclusions

In this paper, we managed to provide necessary and sufficient conditions for fuzzy implications constructed with quadratic polynomials to satisfy **(OP)** without any additional conditions. Additionally, we presented conditions for a polynomial of the arbitrary degree to satisfy boundary conditions of fuzzy implication function.

Problems shown in Remarks 4.6, 4.10 and 4.13 are still open. Moreover, the problem of polynomials of higher dimensions is only barely touched in Theorem 5.1. The question of whether we can give some reasonable conditions on polynomials of the form (21), such that the resulting function will satisfy the monotonicity of fuzzy implication, remains unanswered.

Acknowledgements. The research activities co-financed by the funds granted under the Research Excellence Initiative of the University of Silesia in Katowice.

References

1. Aguiló, I., Massanet, S., Riera, J.-V.: On the preservation of some additional properties via the quadratic polynomial construction method of fuzzy implication functions. In: Joint Proceedings of the 19th World Congress of the International Fuzzy Systems Association (IFSA), The 12th Conference of the European Society for Fuzzy Logic and Technology (EUSFLAT), and The 11th International Summer School on Aggregation Operators (AGOP). Atlantis Studies in Uncertainty Modelling, vol. 3, pp. 687–694. Atlantis Press (2021)

2. Aguiló, I., Suñer, J., Torrens, J.: New types of contrapositivisation of fuzzy implications with respect to fuzzy negations. Inf. Sci. **322**, 223–236 (2015)
3. Aguiló, I., Suñer, J., Torrens, J.: A new look on fuzzy implication functions: *FNI*-implications. In: Carvalho, J.P., Lesot, M.-J., Kaymak, U., Vieira, S., Bouchon-Meunier, B., Yager, R.R. (eds.) IPMU 2016. CCIS, vol. 610, pp. 375–386. Springer, Cham (2016). https://doi.org/10.1007/978-3-319-40596-4_32
4. Baczyński, M., Beliakov, G., Bustince, H., Pradera, A.: Advances in Fuzzy Implication Functions. Studies in Fuzziness and Soft Computing, vol. 300. Springer, Heidelberg (2013). https://doi.org/10.1007/978-3-642-35677-3
5. Baczyński, M., Jayaram, B.: Fuzzy Implications. Studies in Fuzziness and Soft Computing, vol. 231. Springer, Heidelberg (2008). https://doi.org/10.1007/978-3-540-69082-5
6. Kolesárová, A., Massanet, S., Mesiar, R., Riera, J.-V., Torrens, J.: Polynomial constructions of fuzzy implication functions: the quadratic case. Inf. Sci. **494**, 60–79 (2019)
7. Massanet, S., Torrens, J.: On some properties of threshold generated implications. Fuzzy Sets Syst. **205**, 30–49 (2012)
8. Massanet, S., Torrens, J.: Threshold generation method of construction of a new implication from two given ones. Fuzzy Sets Syst. **205**, 50–75 (2012)
9. Massanet, S., Torrens, J.: On the vertical threshold generation method of fuzzy implication and its properties. Fuzzy Sets Syst. **226**, 32–52 (2013)
10. Shi, Y., Van Gasse, B., Ruan, D., Kerre, E.E.: On dependencies and independencies of fuzzy implication axioms. Fuzzy Sets Syst. **161**(10), 1388–1405 (2010)
11. Vemuri, N.-R., Jayaram, B.: Representations through a monoid on the set of fuzzy implications. Fuzzy Sets Syst. **247**, 51–67 (2014)
12. Vemuri, N.-R., Jayaram, B.: The ⊛-composition of fuzzy implications: closures with respect to properties, powers and families. Fuzzy Sets Syst. **275**, 58–87 (2015)

On a New Contrapositivisation Technique for Fuzzy Implications Constructed from Triangular Conorms

Fernando Neres[1]([envelope]), Benjamín Bedregal[2], and Regivan Santiago[2]

[1] Departamento de Ciência e Tecnologia - DCT, Universidade Federal Rural do Semi-Árido - UFERSA, Caraúbas, Rio Grande do Norte, Brazil
fernandoneres@ufersa.edu.br
[2] Departamento de Informática e Matemática Aplicada - DIMAp, Universidade Federal do Rio Grande do Norte - UFRN, Natal, Rio Grande do Norte, Brazil
{bedregal,regivan}@dimap.ufrn.br

Abstract. We introduce a new contrapositivisation technique for fuzzy implications constructed from triangular conorms, which generalizes the medium contrapositivisation, and we study some of its properties; we present some characterizations of the operator that defines this new contrapositivisation technique concerning N-compatibility and the action of an automorphism. Finally, we present one method of how to obtain triangular conorms from the contrapositivisators operators of (S,N)-implications.

Keywords: contrapositivisation $\cdot$ $(S \cdot N)$-contrapositivisation $\cdot$ fuzzy implication $\cdot$ fuzzy logic $\cdot$ N-compatibility $\cdot$ aggregation function

1 Introduction

The contrapositive symmetry of a fuzzy implication I with respect to a fuzzy negation N, denoted by $(\mathbf{CP})(N)$, is important in many applications of fuzzy implications [4]. Usually, this property is studied with respect to their natural negation N_I. Nevertheless, some fuzzy implications do not satisfy $(\mathbf{CP})(N_I)$, even if N_I is strong [4].

The idea of contrapositivisation for fuzzy implications consists in transform any fuzzy implication I into a contrapositive fuzzy implication I', even if I is not contrapositive [13]. In the literature there are few works on this topic.

In [4], Baczyński and Jayaram, proposed three contrapositivisation techniques called *upper*, *lower* and *medium* built from the t-norm minimum and/or t-conorm maximum and a fuzzy negation, and studied their respective properties. In [1], Aguiló et al. proposed two new contrapositivisation techniques built from a fuzzy negation N called N-lower and N-upper, and studied their respective properties. In [13], Neres et al. introduced a new contrapositivisation technique constructed from bivariate aggregation functions and fuzzy negations, which generalizes the upper and lower contrapositivisations.

D. Ciucci et al. (Eds.): IPMU 2022, CCIS 1601, pp. 206–218, 2022.
https://doi.org/10.1007/978-3-031-08971-8_18

In this paper, we introduce a new contrapositivisation technique for a fuzzy implication I constructed from a triangular conorm S and a fuzzy negation N, which we denote by I_N^S and call (S,N)-*contrapositivisation*; we characterize the operator I_N^S through some of the main properties commonly associated with fuzzy implications; we show that I_N^S generalizes the medium contrapositivisation; we present conditions for the N-compatibility of I_N^S; we study the action of an automorphism under the operator I_N^S, and finally, we present one method of how to obtain triangular conorms from the operator I_N^S and a fuzzy negation N'.

This paper is organized as follows. Section 2 contains some basic definitions and results required in this paper. Section 3 contains some of the main contrapositivisation techniques already proposed in the literature. Section 4 contains the main contributions of this work, that is, the (S,N)-contrapositivisations and some of their characterizations. And, in Sect. 5, are presented the conclusions and some proposals for future investigations.

2   Preliminaries

In this section we will present some definitions and results already known in the literature, which will be useful for the development of this paper.

Definition 2.1 ([4]). *A function $N : [0,1] \to [0,1]$ is a* fuzzy negation *if:*

(N1) N *satisfies the boundary conditions:* $N(0) = 1$ *and* $N(1) = 0$.
(N2) N *is non-increasing: if* $x \leq y$, *then* $N(y) \leq N(x)$.

A fuzzy negation N is called **strong** *if it is an involution, i.e.,*

(N3) $N(N(x)) = x$, *for all* $x \in [0,1]$.

Example 2.1. $N_\perp(x) = \begin{cases} 1, & \text{if } x = 0 \\ 0, & \text{if } x \in]0,1] \end{cases}$ (least negation), $N_\top(x) = \begin{cases} 0, & \text{if } x = 1 \\ 1, & \text{if } x \in [0,1[\end{cases}$ (greatest negation), $N_Z(x) = 1 - x$ (Zadeh negation) and $N_K(x) = 1 - x^2$.

Definition 2.2 ([4,11]). *A function $S : [0,1]^2 \to [0,1]$ is a* triangular conorm *(t-conorm for short) if for all $x, y, z, w \in [0,1]$, the following conditions holds:*

(S1) *Commutativity:* $S(x,y) = S(y,x)$.
(S2) *Associativity:* $S(x, S(y,z)) = S(S(x,y), z)$.
(S3) *Monotonicity: If $x \leq z$ and $y \leq w$, then* $S(x,y) \leq S(z,w)$.
(S4) *Boundary condition:* $S(x,0) = x$.

Remark 2.1 ([6,11]). Every t-conorm S satisfies the following conditions:

(S5) $S(1,x) = S(x,1) = 1, \forall x \in [0,1]$.
(S6) $S(0,x) = x, \forall x \in [0,1]$.

(S7) $S(x,y) \geq x, \ \forall x,y \in [0,1]$.
(S8) $S(x,y) \geq y, \ \forall x,y \in [0,1]$.

Example 2.2. $S_{max}(x,y) = \max\{x,y\}$ (*maximum t-conorm*) and $S_{LK}(x,y) = \min\{x+y,1\}$ (*Łukasiewicz t-conorm*).

Definition 2.3 ([4,6]). *A t-conorm S is called*

i continuous, *if it is continuous in both the arguments.*
ii idempotent, *if* $S(x,x) = x$, *for all* $x \in [0,1]$.
iii positive, *if* $S(x,y) = 1$ *implies* $x = 1$ *or* $y = 1$.

Definition 2.4 ([6]). *Let* $n > 1$ *be an integer number. A function* $\mathcal{A} : [0,1]^n \rightarrow [0,1]$ *is an* n-ary aggregation function *if the following conditions hold:*

($\mathcal{A}$1) $\mathcal{A}(0,\ldots,0) = 0$.
($\mathcal{A}$2) $\mathcal{A}(1,\ldots,1) = 1$.
($\mathcal{A}$3) $\mathcal{A}$ *is non-decreasing.*

The set of all *bivariate aggregation functions* will be denoted by $\mathcal{BAF}$.

Example 2.3. $T_{min}(x,y) = \min\{x,y\}$, $T_P(x,y) = xy$ and any t-conorm are particular types of bivariate aggregation functions.

Definition 2.5 ([6]). *A bivariate aggregation function* $\mathcal{A}$ *is called*

(i) symmetric, *if* $\mathcal{A}(x,y) = \mathcal{A}(y,x)$, *for all* $x,y \in [0,1]$.
(ii) idempotent, *if* $\mathcal{A}(x,x) = x$, *for all* $x \in [0,1]$.

Example 2.4. T_{min} and S_{max} are symmetric and idempotent aggregations.

Definition 2.6 ([2,4]). *A function* $I : [0,1]^2 \rightarrow [0,1]$ *is said to be a* fuzzy implication *if it satisfies the following conditions:*

(I1) $I(x,z) \geq I(y,z)$, *whenever* $x \leq y$ *and* $z \in [0,1]$.
(I2) $I(x,y) \leq I(x,z)$, *whenever* $y \leq z$ *and* $x \in [0,1]$.
(I3) $I(0,0) = 1$.
(I4) $I(1,1) = 1$.
(I5) $I(1,0) = 0$.

Remark 2.2. Every fuzzy implication I satisfies the following conditions:

(I6) $I(0,y) = 1, \ \forall y \in [0,1]$. (left boundary condition).
(I7) $I(x,1) = 1, \ \forall x \in [0,1]$. (right boundary condition).

The set of all fuzzy implications will be denoted by $\mathcal{FI}$.

Example 2.5. $I_{LK}(x,y) = \min\{1, 1-x+y\}$ (Łukasiewicz implication), $I_{KD}(x,y) = \max\{1-x,y\}$ (Kleene-Dienes implication) and $I_{GD}(x,y) = \begin{cases} 1, & \text{if } x \leq y, \\ y, & \text{if } x > y. \end{cases}$ (Gödel implication).

Definition 2.7 ([4]). *A function* $I : [0,1]^2 \rightarrow [0,1]$ *is called an* (S,N)-*implication if there exist a t-conorm* S *and a fuzzy negation* N *such that, for all* $x,y \in [0,1]$,

$$I(x,y) = S(N(x),y). \qquad (1)$$

Among the various properties associated with fuzzy implications, we will consider the following:

Definition 2.8 ([4,7–9]). *A fuzzy implication* $I : [0,1]^2 \rightarrow [0,1]$ *satisfies:*

(NP) *if* $I(1,y) = y$, *for all* $y \in [0,1]$. (*left neutrality property*)
(IP) *if* $I(x,x) = 1$, *for all* $x \in [0,1]$. (*identity principle*)
(EP) *if* $I(x,I(y,z)) = I(y,I(x,z))$, *for all* $x,y,z \in [0,1]$. (*exchange principle*)
(OP) *if* $I(x,y) = 1 \iff x \le y$, *for all* $x,y \in [0,1]$. (*ordering property*)
(LOP) *if* $x \le y \implies I(x,y) = 1$, *for all* $x,y \in [0,1]$. (*left ordering property*)
(ROP) *if* $I(x,y) = 1 \implies x \le y$, *for all* $x,y \in [0,1]$. (*right ordering property*)

Definition 2.9 ([4]). *Let* $I \in \mathcal{FI}$ *and* N *be a fuzzy negation.* I *satisfies*

(CP) *if* $I(x,y) = I(N(y),N(x))$, *for all* $x,y \in [0,1]$. (*contrapositivity*)
(L-CP) *if* $I(N(x),y) = I(N(y),x)$, *for all* $x,y \in [0,1]$. (*left contrapositivity*)
(R-CP) *if* $I(x,N(y)) = I(y,N(x))$, *for all* $x,y \in [0,1]$. (*right contrapositivity*)

If I satisfies **(CP)** (resp. **(L-CP)**, **(R-CP)**) with respect to a fuzzy negation N, then we will denote this by **(CP)**(N) (resp. **(L-CP)**(N), **(R-CP)**(N)).

Proposition 2.1 ([4]). *If* $I : [0,1]^2 \rightarrow [0,1]$ *is any function and* N *is a strong fuzzy negation, then the following statements are equivalent:*

(i) I *satisfies* **(CP)***(N)*.
(ii) I *satisfies* **(L-CP)***(N)*.
(iii) I *satisfies* **(R-CP)***(N)*.

Definition 2.10 ([4]). *Let* $I \in \mathcal{FI}$. *The function* $N_I : [0,1] \rightarrow [0,1]$ *defined by*

$$N_I(x) = I(x,0), \qquad (2)$$

is called the natural negation *of* I *or the* negation induced by I.

Proposition 2.2 ([3,4]). *Let* I *be an* (S,N)-*implication. Then, it holds that:*

(i) $I \in \mathcal{FI}$ *and* $N_I = N$.
(ii) I *satisfies* **(NP)** *and* **(EP)**.
(iii) *If* N *is strong, then* I *satisfies* **(CP)***(N)*.

Definition 2.11 ([13]). *Let* $I \in \mathcal{FI}$ *and* N *be a fuzzy negation. We say that* N *is* N_I-*strong if and only if* $N_I(N(x)) = x$, *for all* $x \in [0,1]$.

Definition 2.12 ([2]). *A function* $\varphi : [0,1] \rightarrow [0,1]$ *is an* automorphism *if it is continuous, strictly increasing and satisfies the boundary conditions* $\varphi(0) = 0$ *and* $\varphi(1) = 1$, *i.e., if it is a non-decreasing bijection in* $[0,1]$.

Definition 2.13 ([2]). *Let $\varphi : [0,1] \to [0,1]$ be an automorphism. We say that two functions $f, g : [0,1]^n \to [0,1]$ are φ-conjugate if $g = f_\varphi$, where*

$$f_\varphi(x_1, \ldots, x_n) = \varphi^{-1}(f(\varphi(x_1), \ldots, \varphi(x_n))),$$

for all $x_1, \ldots, x_n \in [0,1]$.

Proposition 2.3 ([4]). *Let $I \in \mathcal{FI}$, φ be an automorphism, N be a fuzzy negation, S be a t-conorm and $\mathcal{A}$ be an n-ary aggregation function. Then, the following statements hold:*

(i) N_φ *is a fuzzy negation (in particular, if N is strong, then N_φ is a strong fuzzy negation).*
(ii) S_φ *is a t-conorm.*
(iii) I_φ *is a fuzzy implication.*
(iv) $\mathcal{A}_\varphi$ *is an n-ary aggregation function (in particular, if $\mathcal{A} \in \mathcal{BAF}$ is symmetric (resp. idempotent), then $\mathcal{A}_\varphi$ is a symmetric (resp. idempotent) bivariate aggregation function.)*

3   Contrapositivisation Techniques

Definition 3.1 ([4]). *Let $I \in \mathcal{FI}$ and N be a fuzzy negation. The functions $I_N^u, I_N^l, I_N^m : [0,1]^2 \to [0,1]$ defined by*

$$I_N^u(x,y) = S_{max}(I(x,y), I(N(y), N(x))), \tag{3}$$
$$I_N^l(x,y) = T_{min}(I(x,y), I(N(y), N(x))), \tag{4}$$
$$I_N^m(x,y) = T_{min}(S_{max}(I(x,y), N(x)), S_{max}(I(N(y), N(x)), y)), \tag{5}$$

for all $x, y \in [0,1]$, are called, respectively, the upper, lower *and* medium *contrapositivisations of I with respect to N.*

Proposition 3.1 ([4]). *Let $I \in \mathcal{FI}$ and N be a fuzzy negation. Then:*

(i) $I_N^u, I_N^l, I_N^m \in \mathcal{FI}$.
(ii) *If N is strong, then I_N^u, I_N^l and I_N^m satisfy* **(CP)***(N).*
(iii) *If N is strong and I satisfies* **(CP)***(N), then $I_N^u = I_N^l = I$.*
(iv) *If I satisfies* **(OP)***, then I_N^u and I_N^l satisfy* **(OP)***.*
(v) *If I satisfies* **(NP)***, then $N_{I_N^m} = N$ and I_N^m satisfies* **(NP)***.*

For more results on the upper, lower and medium contrapositivisations, see Subchapter 7.1 of Baczyński and Jayaram [4].

Definition 3.2 ([13]). *Let $I \in \mathcal{FI}$, $\mathcal{A} \in \mathcal{BAF}$ and N be a fuzzy negation. The function $I_N^{\mathcal{A}} : [0,1]^2 \to [0,1]$ defined by*

$$I_N^{\mathcal{A}}(x,y) = \mathcal{A}(I(x,y), I(N(y), N(x))) \tag{6}$$

is called the aggregated contrapositivisator *of I with respect to $\mathcal{A}$ and N. Moreover, when $\mathcal{A}$ is symmetric and N is strong, we will say that $I_N^{\mathcal{A}}$ is the* aggregated contrapositivisation *of I with respect to $\mathcal{A}$ and N.*

Proposition 3.2 ([13]). *Let $I \in \mathcal{FI}$, $A \in \mathcal{BAF}$ and N be a fuzzy negation. Then, it holds that:*

(i) $I_N^A \in \mathcal{FI}$.
(ii) *If A is symmetric and N is strong, then I_N^A satisfies* **(CP)** *(N)*.
(iii) *If $A = T_{min}$, then $I_N^A = I_N^l$.*
(iv) *If $A = S_{max}$, then $I_N^A = I_N^u$.*
(v) *If I satisfies* **(IP)**, *then I_N^A satisfies* **(IP)**.

For more results on the aggregated contrapositivisation, see Neres et al. [13].

4 (S,N)-Contrapositivisation

In this section we will introduce a new contrapositivisation technique for fuzzy implications constructed from triangular conorms and fuzzy negations, which generalizes the medium contrapositivisation.

Definition 4.1. *Let $I \in \mathcal{FI}$, S be a t-conorm and N be a fuzzy negation. The function $I_N^S : [0,1]^2 \to [0,1]$ defined by*

$$I_N^S(x,y) = T_{min}(S(I(x,y), N(x)), S(I(N(y), N(x)), y)) \tag{7}$$

is called the (S,N)-contrapositivisator of I with respect to S and N.

Proposition 4.1. *Let $I \in \mathcal{FI}$. Then, $I_N^S \in \mathcal{FI}$.*

Proof. (i) I_N^S satisfies **(I3)**, **(I4)** and **(I5)**. In fact,

$$I_N^S(0,0) \stackrel{\textbf{(I3),(I4)}}{=} T_{min}(S(1,1), S(1,0)) \stackrel{(S4),(S5)}{=} T_{min}(1,1) \stackrel{(A2)}{=} 1$$

$$I_N^S(1,1) \stackrel{\textbf{(I3),(I4)}}{=} T_{min}(S(1,0), S(1,1)) \stackrel{(S4),(S5)}{=} T_{min}(1,1) \stackrel{(A2)}{=} 1$$

$$I_N^S(1,0) \stackrel{\textbf{(I5)}}{=} T_{min}(S(0,0), S(0,0)) \stackrel{(S4)}{=} T_{min}(0,0) \stackrel{(A1)}{=} 0.$$

(ii) I_N^S satisfies **(I1)**. In fact, let $x, y, z \in [0,1]$ such that $x \leq y$. Hence,

$$x \leq y \underset{(N2),(I2)}{\stackrel{\textbf{(I1)}}{\Longrightarrow}} I(y,z) \leq I(x,z) \quad \text{and} \quad I(N(z), N(y)) \leq I(N(z), N(x))$$

$$\stackrel{(A3)}{\Longrightarrow} \quad S(I(y,z), N(y)) \leq S(I(x,z), N(x)) \qquad \text{and}$$
$$S(I(N(z), N(y)), z) \leq S(I(N(z), N(x)), z)$$

$$\stackrel{(A3)}{\Longrightarrow} \quad \min(S(I(y,z), N(y)), S(I(N(z), N(y)), z)) \leq$$
$$\leq \min(S(I(x,z), N(x)), S(I(N(z), N(x)), z))$$

$$\stackrel{(7)}{\Longrightarrow} \quad I_N^S(y,z) \leq I_N^S(x,z).$$

(iii) I_N^S satisfies (I2). The proof is analogous to that of item **(ii)**.   □

Proposition 4.1 tells us that a (S,N)-contrapositivisator is always a fuzzy implication, however, this implication is not always contrapositive for N.

Example 4.1. $(I_{LK})_{N_T}^{S_{max}}$ does not satisfy **(CP)**(N_T). In fact, let $y \in]0,1[$, then $(I_{LK})_{N_T}^{S_{max}}(1,y) = y$ and $(I_{LK})_{N_T}^{S_{max}}(N_T(y), N_T(1)) = (I_{LK})_{N_T}^{S_{max}}(1,0) = 0$.

Example 4.2. $(I_{GD})_{N_K}^{S_{LK}}$ does not satisfy **(CP)**(N_K). In fact, $(I_{GD})_{N_K}^{S_{LK}}(1,0.5) = 0.5$ and $(I_{GD})_{N_K}^{S_{LK}}(N_K(0.5), N_K(1)) = 0.4375$.

The next result provides conditions for I_N^S to be contrapositive for N.

Proposition 4.2. *Let $I \in \mathcal{FI}$, S be a t-conorm and N be a fuzzy negation. If N is strong, then I_N^S is a ·fuzzy implication which satisfies* **(CP)**(N).

Proof. By Proposition 4.1, one has that I_N^S is a fuzzy implication. In addition,

$$I_N^S(N(y), N(x)) \overset{(7),(N3)}{=} T_{min}(S(I(N(y), N(x)), y), S(I(x,y), N(x)))$$

$$= T_{min}(S(I(x,y), N(x)), S(I(N(y), N(x)), y)) \overset{(7)}{=} I_N^S(x,y).$$

Example 4.3. $(I_{LK})_{N_Z}^{S_{max}}$ satisfies **(CP)**(N_Z). In fact, since N_Z is strong, then $S_{max}(I_{LK}(N_Z(y), N_Z(x)), N_Z(N_Z(y))) = S_{max}(I_{LK}(N_Z(y), N_Z(x)), y)$ and, in addition, $S_{max}(I_{LK}(N_Z(N_Z(x)), N_Z(N_Z(y))), N_Z(x)) = S_{max}(I_{LK}(x,y), N_Z(x))$. But, T_{min} is commutative, hence, one obtains that $(I_{LK})_{N_Z}^{S_{max}}(N_Z(y), N_Z(x)) = (I_{LK})_{N_Z}^{S_{max}}(x,y)$. Similarly, one can prove that $(I_{LK})_{N_Z}^S$ satisfies **(CP)**(N_Z) for any t-conorm S.

Example 4.4. Analogously to Example 4.3, one concludes that $(I_{GD})_{N_Z}^S$ satisfies **(CP)**(N_Z) for any t-conorm S.

Corollary 4.1. *Let $I \in \mathcal{FI}$, S be a t-conorm and N be a fuzzy negation. If N is strong, then $I_N^S \in \mathcal{FI}$ and satisfies* **(L-CP)**(N) *and* **(R-CP)**(N).

Proof. It follows immediately from Propositions 2.1 and 4.2. □

Corollary 4.2. *Let $I \in \mathcal{FI}$, S be a t-conorm and N be a fuzzy negation. If N is strong, then $(I_N^S)_N^S$ is a fuzzy implication which satisfies* **(CP)**(N), **(L-CP)**(N) *and* **(R-CP)**(N). *In addition,*

$$(I_N^S)_N^S(x,y) = \begin{cases} S(I_N^S(x,y), N(x)), & \text{if } N(x) \le y, \\ S(I_N^S(x,y), y), & \text{if } N(x) > y. \end{cases}$$

Proof. It follows directly from Proposition 4.2, Corollary 4.1 and (S3). □

Definition 4.2. *Let $I \in \mathcal{FI}$, S be a t-conorm and N be a fuzzy negation. The (S,N)-contrapositivisator I_N^S is said be the (S,N)-contrapositivisation of I with respect to S and N, when N is strong.*

It follows from Proposition 4.2 that each (S,N)-contrapositivisation satisfies **(CP)**(N). The following proposition shows that the (S,N)-contrapositivisation generalizes the medium contrapositivisation.

Proposition 4.3. *Let $I \in \mathcal{FI}$, S be a t-conorm and N be a fuzzy negation. If $S = S_{max}$, then $I_N^S = I_N^m$.*

Proof. Straightforward.   □

The next result shows some of the main properties commonly associated with fuzzy implications, which are satisfied by a (S,N)-contrapositivisator.

Proposition 4.4. *Let $I \in \mathcal{FI}$, S, S' be two t-conorms and N be a fuzzy negation. Then, it holds that:*

(i) *If I satisfies **(NP)** and $N_I = N$, then $N_{I_N^S} = N$.*
(ii) *If I satisfies **(IP)**, then I_N^S satisfies **(IP)**.*
(iii) *If I satisfies **(OP)**, S is positive and N is strong, then I_N^S satisfies **(OP)**.*
(iv) *If I satisfies **(LOP)**, then I_N^S satisfies **(LOP)**.*
(v) *If I satisfies **(NP)** and N is N_I-strong, then I_N^S satisfies **(NP)**.*
(vi) *If N is strong and I is an (S',N)-implication, then $I_N^{S_{max}}$ satisfies **(EP)**.*

Proof. **(i)** For all $x \in [0,1]$, one has that

$$N_{I_N^S}(x) \overset{(2)}{=} I_N^S(x,0) \overset{(7)}{=} T_{min}(S(I(x,0),N(x)),S(I(1,N(x)),0)) =$$
$$\overset{\textbf{(NP)}}{\underset{N_I=N}{=}} T_{min}(S(N(x),N(x)),S(N(x),0)) \overset{(S3)}{=} S(N(x),0) \overset{(S4)}{=} N(x).$$

(ii) For all $x \in [0,1]$, one has that

$$I_N^S(x,x) \overset{(7)}{=} T_{min}(S(I(x,x),N(x)),S(I(N(x),N(x)),x))$$
$$\overset{\textbf{(IP)}}{=} T_{min}(S(1,N(x)),S(1,x)) \overset{(S5)}{=} T_{min}(1,1) = 1.$$

(iii) Let $x, y \in [0,1]$ such that $x \leq y$. So, $N(y) \leq N(x)$. Hence, it follows that

$$I_N^S(x,y) = T_{min}(S(I(x,y),N(x)),S(I(N(y),N(x)),y)) =$$
$$\overset{\textbf{(OP)}}{=} T_{min}(S(1,N(x)),S(1,y)) \overset{(S5)}{=} T_{min}(1,1) = 1.$$

Conversely, if $I_N^S(x,y) = 1$, then $S(I(x,y),N(x)) = 1$ and $S(I(N(y),N(x)),y) = 1$. As S is positive, so $(I(x,y) = 1$ or $N(x) = 1)$ and $(I(N(y),N(x)) = 1$ or $y = 1)$. But, I satisfies **(OP)** and N is strong, then follows immediately from both cases that $x \leq y$.

(iv) It follows directly from **(LOP)** and (S5).

(v) For all $y \in [0,1]$, one has that

$$I_N^S(1,y) \quad = \quad T_{min}(S(I(1,y),0), S(I(N(y),0),y)) =$$

$$\underset{\substack{(NP)\\N_I\text{-strong}}}{=} T_{min}(S(y,0), S(y,y)) \overset{(S3)}{=} S(y,0) \overset{(S4)}{=} y.$$

(vi) Since I is an (S',N)-implication and N is strong, then, by Proposition 2.2(iii), we conclude that I satisfies **(CP)**(N). Moreover, as $I(x,y) = S'(N(x),y)$, then $I(x,y) \geq N(x)$ (by (S7)) and $I(x,y) \geq y$ (by (S8)). Thereby,

$$I_N^{S_{max}}(x,y) \overset{(7)}{=} T_{min}(S_{max}(I(x,y),N(x)), S_{max}(I(N(y),N(x)),y)) =$$

$$\overset{(CP)}{=} T_{min}(S_{max}(I(x,y),N(x)), S_{max}(I(x,y),y)) = T_{min}(I(x,y),I(x,y)) = I(x,y).$$

Hence, as I satisfies **(EP)** (Proposition 2.2(ii)), so $I_N^{S_{max}}$ also satisfies **(EP)**. □

Now let's define the concept of N-compatibility for the contrapositivisation technique proposed in this paper.

Definition 4.3. *Let $I \in \mathcal{FI}$, S be a t-conorm and N be a strong fuzzy negation. Then, I_N^S is said to be N-compatible, if $N_{I_N^S} = N$.*

The next result establishes conditions for a (S,N)-contrapositivisation I_N^S to be N-compatible.

Proposition 4.5. *Let $I \in \mathcal{FI}$, S be a t-conorm and N be a fuzzy negation. If I satisfies (NP) and $N_I = N$, then I_N^S is N-compatible.*

Proof. Follows directly from Proposition 4.4(i).   □

Corollary 4.3. *Let $I \in \mathcal{FI}$, S, S' be two t-conorms and N be a fuzzy negation. If I is an (S',N)-implication, then I_N^S is N-compatible.*

Proof. The proof follows immediately from Propositions 2.2 and 4.5.   □

Proposition 4.6. *Let $I \in \mathcal{FI}$ satisfying (NP), S be a t-conorm and N be a fuzzy negation. If N_I is crisp, then I_N^S is N-compatible.*

Proof. For all $x \in [0,1]$, one has that

$$N_{I_N^S}(x) \overset{(2)}{=} I_N^S(x,0) \overset{(7)}{=} T_{min}(S(I(x,0),N(x)), S(I(1,N(x)),0)) =$$

$$\overset{(NP)}{=} T_{min}(S(N_I(x),N(x)), S(N(x),0)). \tag{8}$$

Suppose $N_I(x) = 0$. Then, by (S4), (S6) and (8), we get that $N_{I_N^S}(x) = T_{min}(N(x),N(x)) = N(x)$. Now, suppose $N_I(x) = 1$. So, by (S4), (S5) and (8), it follows that $N_{I_N^S}(x) = T_{min}(1,N(x)) = N(x)$.   □

Example 4.5. Since I_{LK} satisfies **(NP)** and $N_{I_{LK}} = N_Z$, then it follows from Proposition 4.5 that $(I_{LK})_{N_Z}^S$ is N_Z-compatible for any t-conorm S.

Example 4.6. Since I_{GD} satisfies **(NP)** and $N_{I_{GD}}$ is crisp, then by Proposition 4.6, one concludes that $(I_{GD})_N^S$ is N-compatible for any t-conorm S and fuzzy negation N.

Next, we show how an automorphism acts on a (S,N)-contrapositivisator.

Theorem 4.1. *Let $I \in \mathcal{FI}$, S be a t-conorm, N be a fuzzy negation and φ be an automorphism. Then, $(I_N^S)_\varphi = (I_\varphi)_{N_\varphi}^{S_\varphi}$.*

Proof. From Proposition 2.3, one has that I_φ, S_φ and N_φ are, respectively, a fuzzy implication, a t-conorm and a fuzzy negation. In addition, the fuzzy implication $(I_N^S)_\varphi$ coincides with the (S_φ, N_φ)-contrapositivisator $(I_\varphi)_{N_\varphi}^{S_\varphi}$. In fact,

$$
\begin{aligned}
(I_N^S)_\varphi(x,y) &= \varphi^{-1}(I_N^S(\varphi(x), \varphi(y))) \\
&= \varphi^{-1}(T_{min}(S(I(\varphi(x), \varphi(y)), N(\varphi(x))), S(I(N(\varphi(y)), N(\varphi(x))), \varphi(y)))) \\
&= \varphi^{-1}(T_{min}(S(I(\varphi(x), \varphi(y)), N(\varphi(x))), S(I(\varphi(N_\varphi(y)), \varphi(N_\varphi(x))), \varphi(y)))) \\
&= \varphi^{-1}(T_{min}(S(\varphi(I_\varphi(x,y)), \varphi(N_\varphi(x))), S(I(\varphi(N_\varphi(y)), \varphi(N_\varphi(x))), \varphi(y)))) \\
&= \varphi^{-1}(T_{min}(\varphi(S_\varphi(I_\varphi(x,y), N_\varphi(x))), S(\varphi(I_\varphi(N_\varphi(y), N_\varphi(x))), \varphi(y)))) \\
&= \varphi^{-1}(T_{min}(\varphi(S_\varphi(I_\varphi(x,y), N_\varphi(x))), \varphi(S_\varphi(I_\varphi(N_\varphi(y), N_\varphi(x)), y)))) \\
&= T_{min}(S_\varphi(I_\varphi(x,y), N_\varphi(x)), S_\varphi(I_\varphi(N_\varphi(y), N_\varphi(x)), y)) \\
&= (I_\varphi)_{N_\varphi}^{S_\varphi}(x,y).
\end{aligned}
$$

Corollary 4.4. *Let $I \in \mathcal{FI}$, S be a t-conorm, φ be an automorphism and N be a strong fuzzy negation. Then, $(I_N^S)_\varphi \in \mathcal{FI}$ and satisfies **(CP)**(N).*

Proof. Follows directly from Theorem 4.1 and Propositions 2.3 and 4.2. □

Proposition 4.7. *Let $I \in \mathcal{FI}$, S be a t-conorm, φ be an automorphism and N be a fuzzy negation. If N is strong, then $((I_\varphi)_{N_\varphi}^{S_\varphi})_{N_\varphi}^{S_\varphi}$ is a fuzzy implication which satisfies **(CP)**(N_φ), **(L-CP)**(N_φ) and **(R-CP)**(N_φ). In addition,*

$$
((I_\varphi)_{N_\varphi}^{S_\varphi})_{N_\varphi}^{S_\varphi}(x,y) = \begin{cases} S_\varphi((I_\varphi)_{N_\varphi}^{S_\varphi}(x,y), N_\varphi(x)), & \text{if } N_\varphi(x) \leq y, \\ S_\varphi((I_\varphi)_{N_\varphi}^{S_\varphi}(x,y), y), & \text{if } N_\varphi(x) > y. \end{cases}
$$

Proof. It follows directly from Proposition 2.3 and Corollary 4.2. □

The following result presents a method of how to obtain t-conorms from the (S,N)-contrapositivisators of (S',N)-implications.

Theorem 4.2. *Let $I \in \mathcal{FI}$, S, S' be two t-conorms, N, N' be two fuzzy negations and I_N^S be the (S,N)-contrapositivisator of I with respect to S and N. Define the function $\mathcal{J}_{I_N^S}^{N'} : [0,1]^2 \to [0,1]$ by*

$$
\mathcal{J}_{I_N^S}^{N'}(x,y) = I_N^S(N'(x), y). \tag{9}
$$

Then, it holds that:

(i) $\mathcal{J}_{I_N^S}^{N'}(x,1) = \mathcal{J}_{I_N^S}^{N'}(1,x) = 1$, *for all* $x \in [0,1]$.

(ii) *If* $N = N'$ *is strong, then* $\mathcal{J}_{I_N^S}^{N'}$ *satisfies (S1).*

(iii) *If* $S = S_{max}$, $N = N'$ *is strong and* I *is an* (S',N)*-implication, then* $\mathcal{J}_{I_N^S}^{N'}$ *satisfies (S2).*

(iv) $\mathcal{J}_{I_N^S}^{N'}$ *is non-decreasing in both variables, i.e.,* $\mathcal{J}_{I_N^S}^{N'}$ *satisfies (S3).*

(v) *If* $N = N'$ *is strong and* I *is an* (S',N)*-implication, then* $\mathcal{J}_{I_N^S}^{N'}$ *satisfies (S4).*

Proof. **(i)** It follows immediately from **(I6)** and **(I7)**. **(ii)** By Corollary 4.1, I_N^S satisfies **(L-CP)**(N'). Then, $\mathcal{J}_{I_N^S}^{N'}(x,y) = I_N^S(N'(x),y) = I_N^S(N'(y),x) = \mathcal{J}_{I_N^S}^{N'}(y,x)$, for all $x,y \in [0,1]$. **(iii)** By Proposition 4.4(vi), I_N^S satisfies **(EP)**, and by Corollary 4.1, I_N^S satisfies **(L-CP)**(N'). Hence, we get that

$$\mathcal{J}_{I_N^S}^{N'}(x, \mathcal{J}_{I_N^S}^{N'}(y,z)) \overset{(9)}{=} I_N^S(N'(x), I_N^S(N'(y),z)) \overset{\textbf{(L-CP)}(N')}{=} I_N^S(N'(x), I_N^S(N'(z),y))$$

$$\overset{\textbf{(EP)}}{=} I_N^S(N'(z), I_N^S(N'(x),y)) = \mathcal{J}_{I_N^S}^{N'}(z, \mathcal{J}_{I_N^S}^{N'}(x,y)) \overset{(ii)}{=} \mathcal{J}_{I_N^S}^{N'}(\mathcal{J}_{I_N^S}^{N'}(x,y),z).$$

(iv) Straightforward. **(v)** N is N_I-strong, since $N_I = N$ (Proposition 2.2) and N is strong; moreover, I satisfies **(NP)** (Proposition 2.2). Thereby, it follows from Proposition 4.4(v) that I_N^S satisfies **(NP)**. On the other hand, as $N = N'$ is strong, so I_N^S satisfies **(L-CP)**(N') (Corollary 4.1). Hence, for all $x \in [0,1]$,

$$\mathcal{J}_{I_N^S}^{N'}(x,0) \overset{(9)}{=} I_N^S(N'(x),0) \overset{\textbf{(L-CP)}(N')}{=} I_N^S(N'(0),x) = I_N^S(1,x) \overset{\textbf{(NP)}}{=} x,$$

for all $x \in [0,1]$. Therefore, $\mathcal{J}_{I_N^S}^{N'}$ satisfies (S4). $\qquad\square$

Corollary 4.5. *Let* $\mathcal{J}_{I_N^S}^{N'}$ *be the function defined by* Eq. (9). *If* $S = S_{max}$, $N = N'$ *is strong and* I *is an* (S',N)*-implication, then* $\mathcal{J}_{I_N^S}^{N'}$ *is a t-conorm.*

Proposition 4.8. *Let* $\mathcal{J}_{I_N^S}^{N'}$ *be the function defined by* Eq. (9) *and* φ *be an automorphism. If* $S = S_{max}$, $N = N'$ *is strong and* I *is an* (S',N)*-implication, then*
$$\left(\mathcal{J}_{I_N^S}^{N'}\right)_\varphi = \mathcal{J}_{(I_N^S)_\varphi}^{(N')_\varphi} = \mathcal{J}_{(I_\varphi)_{N_\varphi}^{S_\varphi}}^{(N')_\varphi}.$$

Proof. It follows from Corollary 4.5, Proposition 2.3 and Theorem 4.1. $\qquad\square$

5   Final Remarks

In this paper, we introduce a new contrapositivisation technique for fuzzy implications constructed from triangular conorms and fuzzy negations, which we call (S,N)-contrapositivisation; we investigate some of the properties that are satisfied by the (S,N)-contrapositivisators; we show that this new technique generalizes the medium contrapositivisation; we study briefly the N-compatibility of the (S,N)-contrapositivisators and investigate how an automorphism acts under such operators; in addition, we present one method of how to obtain triangular conorms from the (S,N)-contrapositivisators of (S',N)-implications.

As future research, we intend to introduce new methods of contrapositivisation for fuzzy implications and study their respective characterizations; develop a method of contrapositivisation that generalizes the (S,N)-contrapositivisation and investigate the contrapositivisation of the main classes of implications (see [4]) as well as of some new classes such as those proposed in [10,14,16]. In addition, we intend to investigate the notion of contrapositivisation for the main extensions of fuzzy logics [5,12,15,17].

Acknowledgments. This work is partially supported by the Brazilian National Council for Scientific and Technological Development CNPq under the Processes 312899/2021-1, 311429/2020-3 and 312053/2018-5.

References

1. Aguiló, I., Suñer, J., Torrens, J.: New types of contrapositivisation of fuzzy implications with respect to fuzzy negations. Inf. Sci. **322**, 223–236 (2015)
2. Baczyński, M., Beliakov, G., Bustince, H., Pradera, A. (eds.): Advances in Fuzzy Implication Functions. Studies in Fuzziness and Soft Computing, vol. 300. Springer, Heidelberg (2013). https://doi.org/10.1007/978-3-642-35677-3
3. Baczyński, M., Jayaram, B.: On the characterizations of (S, N)-implications. Fuzzy Sets Syst. **158**(15), 1713–1727 (2007)
4. Baczyński, M., Jayaram, B.: Fuzzy Implications. Studies in Fuzziness and Soft Computing, vol. 231. Springer, Heidelberg (2008). https://doi.org/10.1007/978-3-540-69082-5
5. Bedregal, B., Dimuro, G.P., Reiser, R.H.S.: An approach to interval-valued R-implications and automorphisms. In: Carvalho, J.P., Dubois, D., Kaymak, U., da Costa Sousa, J.M. (eds.) Proceedings of the Joint 2009 IFSA World Congress and 2009 EUSFLAT Conference, Lisbon, Portugal, 20–24 July 2009, pp. 1–6 (2009)
6. Beliakov, G., Pradera, A., Calvo, T.: Aggregation Functions: A Guide for Practitioners. Studies in Fuzziness and Soft Computing, vol. 221. Springer, Heidelberg (2007). https://doi.org/10.1007/978-3-540-73721-6
7. Dimuro, G.P., Bedregal, B.: On residual implications derived from overlap functions. Inf. Sci. **312**, 78–88 (2015)
8. Dimuro, G.P., Bedregal, B., Fernandez, J., Sesma-Sara, M., Pintor, J.M., Bustince, H.: The law of O-conditionality for fuzzy implications constructed from overlap and grouping functions. Int. J. Approx. Reason. **105**, 27–48 (2019)
9. Dimuro, G.P., Bedregal, B., Santiago, R.H.N.: On (G, N)-implications derived from grouping functions. Inf. Sci. **279**, 1–17 (2014)
10. Dimuro, G.P., et al.: On D-implications derived by grouping functions. In: 2019 IEEE International Conference on Fuzzy Systems, FUZZ-IEEE, New Orleans, LA, USA, 23–26 June 2019, pp. 1–6. IEEE (2019)
11. Klement, E.P., Mesiar, R., Pap, E.: Triangular Norms. Springer, Netherlands (2000). https://doi.org/10.1007/978-94-015-9540-7
12. Matzenauer, M., Reiser, R., Santos, H.S., Bedregal, B., Bustince, H.: Strategies on admissible total orders over typical hesitant fuzzy implications applied to decision making problems. Int. J. Intell. Syst. **36**(5), 2144–2182 (2021)

13. Neres, F., Bedregal, B., Santiago, R.: On a new contrapositivisation technique for fuzzy implications. In: VI Congresso Brasileiro de Sistemas Fuzzy (VI CBSF). Universidade Estadual Paulista (Unesp), São José do Rio Preto, São Paulo, Brasil, November 2021
14. Neres, F., Bedregal, B., Santiago, R.H.N.: (S, N, T)-Implications (2021). Preprint at https://arxiv.org/abs/2106.15746
15. Paiva, R., Bedregal, B., Santiago, R., Vieira, T.: Residuated implications derived from quasi-overlap functions on lattices. Int. J. Approx. Reason. **134**, 95–110 (2021)
16. Pinheiro, J., Bedregal, B., Santiago, R.H.N., Santos, H.: A study of (T, N)-implications and its use to construct a new class of fuzzy subsethood measure. Int. J. Approx. Reason. **97**, 1–16 (2018)
17. Zanotelli, R.M., Reiser, R., Bedregal, B.R.C.: n-dimensional (S, N)-implications. Int. J. Approx. Reason. **126**, 1–26 (2020)

Construction of Fuzzy Implications from the Bandler-Kohout Subproduct

Katarzyna Miś[✉][ID]

University of Silesia in Katowice, Bankowa 14, 40-007 Katowice, Poland
katarzyna.mis@us.edu.pl

Abstract. A sup $-T$ composition (where T is a triangular norm) of two fuzzy implications can be again a fuzzy implication. Motivated by this fact, in this contribution, we consider the Bandler-Kohout subproduct (BKS), which is a composition of fuzzy relations based on the infimum. We verify when such a composition of fuzzy connectives can provide a fuzzy implication and we investigate its properties. Further, we consider BKS as a method of constructing a new fuzzy implication from given t-norms or t-conorms. Moreover, we study essential properties of possibly built implications.

Keywords: fuzzy implication · t-norm · t-conorm · Bandler-Kohout subproduct · composition of fuzzy relations

1 Introduction

There are several possible compositions of fuzzy relations, however, one of them has large attention of researchers. This is sup $-T$ composition which was introduced in [14] for minimum t-norm and in general is understood as

$$(R \overset{T}{\circ} S)(x,y) = \sup_{z \in Z} T(R(x,z), S(z,y)), \quad (x,y) \in X \times Y,$$

for $R \in \mathcal{F}(X \times Z), S \in \mathcal{F}(Z \times Y)$ and a t-norm T [5]. Let us here recall that a notation $R \in \mathcal{F}(X \times Z)$ means R is a fuzzy binary relation (FBR), i.e., $R \colon X \times Z \to [0,1]$ for some nonempty sets X, Z. Hence, fuzzy implications $I, J \colon [0,1]^2 \to [0,1]$ are the particular cases of FBRs on $[0,1]$. Thus we may compose them and get a FBR in the following way:

$$(I \overset{T}{\circ} J)(x,y) = \sup_{z \in [0,1]} T(I(x,z), J(z,y)), \quad x,y \in [0,1]. \tag{1}$$

This FBR is not always a fuzzy implication. We know that $I \overset{T}{\circ} J$ is again a fuzzy implication if and only if $(I \overset{T}{\circ} J)(1,0) = 0$ (see [2, Theorem 6.4.4]). Moreover, for T which is left-continuous we can obtain an algebraic structure (a semigroup) with the operation $\overset{T}{\circ}$ (see [2, Chapter 6.4] for more details). Therefore, we see

© Springer Nature Switzerland AG 2022
D. Ciucci et al. (Eds.): IPMU 2022, CCIS 1601, pp. 219–229, 2022.
https://doi.org/10.1007/978-3-031-08971-8_19

that $I \overset{T}{\circ} J$ can give another fuzzy implication. Hence, $\sup -T$ composition is one of the constructing methods of fuzzy implications from old ones. There are several such methods like a convex combination or a min and a max operations of two fuzzy implications (see [11]). Moreover, a different composition of fuzzy implications I, J was considered in the following way [13]:

$$(I \circledast J)(x, y) = I(x, J(x, y)), \quad x, y \in [0, 1].$$

For this reason, one may ask what other methods of constructing fuzzy implications from two given ones are. Also, is it possible to use another known composition to build fuzzy implications?

The composition we examine in this paper is the Bandler-Kohout subproduct (BKS) (see e.g. [4]) which is defined as follows

$$(R \overset{I}{\vartriangleleft} S)(x, y) = \inf_{z \in Z} I(R(x, z), S(z, y)), \quad (x, y) \in X \times Y,$$

for $R \in \mathcal{F}(X \times Z), S \in \mathcal{F}(Z \times Y)$ and a fuzzy implication I.

In this contribution, we consider $\overset{I}{\vartriangleleft}$ as a possible direction for constructing fuzzy implications.

The paper is organised as follows. In Sect. 2 we provide some definitions and properties of fuzzy connectives used in the sequel. In Sect. 3 we present properties of the $\overset{I}{\vartriangleleft}$ composition and examples which justify some of the next results. They are given when I is an R-implication. We finish with plans for the future work and some conclusions.

2   Preliminaries

To make this work more self-contained, we placed some important definitions and facts here.

Definition 1 ([8]). *Let $n \in \mathbb{N}$. An aggregation function in $[0, 1]^n$ is a function $A^{(n)} \colon [0, 1]^n \to [0, 1]$ which satisfies the following conditions:*

(i) it is nondecreasing (in each variable),
(ii) $A^{(n)}(0, \ldots, 0) = 0$ and $A^{(n)}(1, \ldots, 1) = 1$.

Definition 2 ([6]). *A semicopula is a function $C \colon [0, 1]^2 \to [0, 1]$ if it satisfies the following conditions:*

(i) $C(x, 1) = C(1, x) = x, \quad x \in [0, 1]$,
(ii) C is non-decreasing with respect to each variable.

Definition 3 ([7,9]). *A function $T \colon [0, 1]^2 \to [0, 1]$ is called a **triangular norm** (**t-norm** in short) if it satisfies the following conditions for all $x, y, z \in [0, 1]$:*

(T1) $T(x, y) = T(y, x)$,
(T2) $T(x, T(y, z)) = T(T(x, y), z)$,
(T3) $T(x, y) \leq T(x, z)$ for $y \leq z$, i.e., $T(x, \cdot)$ is non-decreasing,
(T4) $T(x, 1) = x$.

Examples of t-norms are presented in Table 1, note that according to notations used there we have

$$T_{\mathbf{LK}} \leq T_{\mathbf{P}} \leq T_{\mathbf{M}}.$$

Definition 4 (see [9]). *A function* $S: [0, 1]^2 \to [0, 1]$ *is called a **triangular conorm (t-conorm** in short) if it satisfies the following conditions for all* $x, y, z \in [0, 1]$:

(S1) $S(x, y) = S(y, x)$,
(S2) $S(x, S(y, z)) = S(S(x, y), z)$,
(S3) $S(x, y) \leq S(x, z)$ for $y \leq z$, i.e., $S(x, \cdot)$ is non-decreasing,
(S4) $S(x, 0) = x$.

Examples of t-conorms are given in Table 2.

Table 1. Examples of t-norms

Name	Formula
minimum t-norm	$T_{\mathbf{M}}(x, y) = \min\{x, y\}$
product t-norm	$T_{\mathbf{P}}(x, y) = x \cdot y$
Łukasiewicz t-norm	$T_{\mathbf{LK}}(x, y) = \max\{0, x + y - 1\}$

Table 2. Examples of t-conorms

Name	Formula
maximum t-conorm	$S_{\mathbf{M}}(x, y) = \max\{x, y\}$
probabilistic t-conorm	$S_{\mathbf{P}}(x, y) = x + y - x \cdot y$
Łukasiewicz t-conorm	$S_{\mathbf{LK}}(x, y) = \min\{1, x + y\}$

Definition 5 ([2,7]). *A function* $I: [0, 1]^2 \to [0, 1]$ *is called a **fuzzy implication** if it satisfies the following conditions:*

(I1) *I is non-increasing with respect to the first variable,*
(I2) *I is non-decreasing with respect to the second variable,*
(I3) $I(0, 0) = I(1, 1) = 1$ *and* $I(1, 0) = 0$.

The family of fuzzy implication will be denoted by $\mathcal{FI}$.

Remark 1. Let us note that for $I \in \mathcal{FI}$ we immediately have $I(0, x) = 1$ and $I(x, 1) = 1$, $x \in [0, 1]$.

Table 3. Examples of fuzzy implications

Name	Formula
Gödel implication	$I_{\mathbf{GD}}(x,y) = \begin{cases} 1, & x \leq y, \\ y, & x > y. \end{cases}$
Łukasiewicz implication	$I_{\mathbf{LK}}(x,y) = \min\{1, 1 - x + y\}$
Goguen implication	$I_{\mathbf{GG}}(x,y) = \begin{cases} 1, & x \leq y, \\ \frac{y}{x}, & x > y. \end{cases}$

Basic examples of fuzzy implications are presented in Table 3.

Definition 6 (see [2]). *We say that a fuzzy implication I satisfies*

*(i) the **identity principle**, if*

$$I(x,x) = 1, \qquad x \in [0,1], \tag{IP}$$

*(ii) the **left neutrality property**, if*

$$I(1,y) = y, \qquad y \in [0,1], \tag{NP}$$

Definition 7 ([2, Definition 2.5.1]). *A function $I \colon [0,1]^2 \to [0,1]$ is called an R-implication if there exists a t-norm T such that*

$$I(x,y) = \sup\{t \in [0,1] : T(x,t) \leq y\}, \qquad x,y \in [0,1]. \tag{2}$$

If I is generated from a t-norm T, then it will be denoted by I_T.

Note that it is possible to generate an R-implication from just a fuzzy conjunction with specific properties (see [10]). Moreover, we will use the following useful characterization of some subclass of R-implications.

Theorem 1 ([2, Proposition 2.5.2]). *Let T be a t-norm. Then the following statements are equivalent:*

(i) T is left-continuous.

(ii) A pair (T, I_T) satisfies a residual principle

$$T(x,z) \leq y \iff I_T(x,y) \geq z, \qquad x,y,z \in [0,1]. \tag{RP}$$

(iii) The supremum in (2) is the maximum, i.e.,

$$I_T(x,y) = \max\{t \in [0,1] \mid T(x,t) \leq y\}, \qquad x,y \in [0,1].$$

3   BKS Composition

Firstly, let us recall basic property of monotonicity for BKS.

Remark 2 ([3, Properties 5.3]). Let $I \in \mathcal{FI}$ and let $R, R_1, R_2 \in \mathcal{F}(X \times Z)$, $S_1, S_2 \in \mathcal{F}(Z \times Y)$. Then

(i) $R_1 \subseteq R_2 \ \& \ dom(R_1) = dom(R_2) \ \Rightarrow \ R_2 \stackrel{I}{\triangleleft} S \subseteq R_1 \stackrel{I}{\triangleleft} S$,

(ii) $S_1 \leq S_2 \ \Rightarrow \ R \stackrel{I}{\triangleleft} S_1 \leq R \stackrel{I}{\triangleleft} S_2$.

Now, let us consider the following formula

$$(F_1 \stackrel{I}{\triangleleft} F_2)(x, y) = \inf_{z \in [0,1]} I(F_1(x, z), F_2(z, y)), \quad x, y \in [0, 1], \qquad (3)$$

where $I \in \mathcal{FI}, F_1, F_2 \in \mathcal{FC}$ and $\mathcal{FC}$ is a class of one of the following fuzzy connectives: t-norms, t-conorms or fuzzy implications. Can $\stackrel{I}{\triangleleft}$ be an operation in this class? After simple verifying border conditions for these chosen connectives, we see it is not possible.

Remark 3. Let $I \in \mathcal{FI}$ and let $\mathcal{FC}$ be defined as above. If $F_1, F_2 \in \mathcal{FC}$, then $F_1 \stackrel{I}{\triangleleft} F_2 \notin \mathcal{FC}$.

Proof. We will check one of the cases - when F_1, F_2 are t-conorms. $F_1 \stackrel{I}{\triangleleft} F_2(1, 0) = \inf_{z \in [0,1]} I(F_1(1, z), F_2(z, 0)) = \inf_{z \in [0,1]} I(1, z) = 0 \neq 1$ and $F_1 \stackrel{I}{\triangleleft} F_2$ is not a t-conorm since 0 can't be the neutral element of it.

Therefore, unfortunately, it is not possible to build any algebraic structure following the case of (1). Despite this fact we can use BKS composition to build a fuzzy implication. If F_1, F_2 are semicopulas or t-conorms (or in general aggregation functions with a neutral element 0), then $F_1 \stackrel{I}{\triangleleft} F_2 \in \mathcal{FI}$.

Proposition 1 (cf. [12, Remark 3.3, Proposition 3.4]). *Let C_1, C_2 be semicopulas (or aggregation functions with neutral element 0) and $I \in \mathcal{FI}$, then the following statements are equivalent:*

(i) I satisfies (IP).

(ii) $C_1 \stackrel{I}{\triangleleft} C_2 \in \mathcal{FI}$.

Further, we can define a finite sequence of the $\stackrel{I}{\triangleleft}$ composition.

Proposition 2. *Let $n \in \mathbb{N}$, $n > 2$, $C_1, \ldots, C_n$ be semicopulas and let $I_1, \ldots I_{n-1} \in \mathcal{FI}$. If I_{n-1} satisfies (IP), then*

$$C_1 \stackrel{I_1}{\triangleleft} (C_2 \stackrel{I_2}{\triangleleft} (\ldots (C_{n-1} \stackrel{I_{n-1}}{\triangleleft} C_n))) \in \mathcal{FI}. \qquad (4)$$

Proof. We know that $(C_{n-1} \overset{I_{n-1}}{\lhd} C_n) \in \mathcal{FI}$. Therefore, let $J = (C_{n-1} \overset{I_{n-1}}{\lhd} C_n)$ and let us show $C_{n-2} \overset{I_{n-2}}{\lhd} J \in \mathcal{FI}$.

$$(C_{n-2} \overset{I_{n-2}}{\lhd} J)(0,0) = \inf_{z \in [0,1]} I_{n-2}(0, J(z,0)) = 1,$$

$$(C_{n-2} \overset{I_{n-2}}{\lhd} J)(1,1) = \inf_{z \in [0,1]} I_{n-2}(z, 1) = 1,$$

$$(C_{n-2} \overset{I_{n-2}}{\lhd} J)(1,0) = \inf_{z \in [0,1]} I_{n-2}(z, J(z,0)) = I_{n-2}(1,0) = 0.$$

Also, it is obvious $C_{n-2} \overset{I_{n-2}}{\lhd} J$ satisfies (I1), (I2). Therefore, (4) is true by the iteration.

Among well-known families of fuzzy implications ((S, N)-implications, Yager's implications, R-implications) only all of the R-implications satisfy (IP). Therefore, in the sequel, we will focus on a case of $\overset{I}{\lhd}$ composition, when I is an R-implication.

Now, let us consider some examples which will be the reason for some other considerations.

Example 1. Let us consider the following t-norms - $T_{\mathbf{LK}}$ and $T_{\mathbf{P}}$ and let us check how $T_{\mathbf{LK}} \overset{I_{\mathbf{GD}}}{\lhd} T_{\mathbf{P}}$ looks like.

Let us take $x, y \in [0,1]$, for $x \leq y$ we have $T_{\mathbf{LK}}(x,z) \leq T_{\mathbf{P}}(x,z) \leq T_{\mathbf{P}}(y,z)$ for any $z \in [0,1]$, hence $(T_{\mathbf{LK}} \overset{I_{\mathbf{GD}}}{\lhd} I_{\mathbf{P}})(x,y) = 1$. For $x > y$ we have

$$(T_{\mathbf{LK}} \overset{I_{\mathbf{GD}}}{\lhd} T_{\mathbf{P}})(x,y) = \inf_{z \in [0,1]} I_{\mathbf{GD}}(T_{\mathbf{LK}}(x,z), T_{\mathbf{P}}(z,y))$$

$$= \inf_{z \leq 1-x} I_{\mathbf{GD}}(T_{\mathbf{LK}}(x,z), T_{\mathbf{P}}(z,y))$$

$$\wedge \inf_{z > 1-x \ \& \ z \leq \frac{1-x}{1-y}} I_{\mathbf{GD}}(T_{\mathbf{LK}}(x,z), T_{\mathbf{P}}(z,y))$$

$$\wedge \inf_{z > 1-x \ \& \ z > \frac{1-x}{1-y}} I_{\mathbf{GD}}(T_{\mathbf{LK}}(x,z), T_{\mathbf{P}}(z,y))$$

$$= \inf_{z \leq 1-x} I_{\mathbf{GD}}(0, zy) \wedge \inf_{z > 1-x \ \& \ z \leq \frac{1-x}{1-y}} I_{\mathbf{GD}}(x + z - 1, zy)$$

$$\wedge \inf_{z > 1-x \ \& \ z > \frac{1-x}{1-y}} zy$$

$$= 1 \wedge 1 \wedge \inf_{z > 1-x \ \& \ z > \frac{1-x}{1-y}} zy$$

$$= \frac{(1-x)y}{1-y},$$

therefore

$$(T_{\mathbf{LK}} \overset{I_{\mathbf{GD}}}{\lhd} I_{\mathbf{P}})(x,y) = \begin{cases} 1, & x \leq y, \\ \frac{y - xy}{1-y}, & x > y. \end{cases}$$

Example 2. Now, let us consider the same t-norms but another fuzzy implication - $I_{\mathbf{GG}}$. Then for $x, y \in [0,1]$, $(T_{\mathbf{LK}} \overset{I_{\mathbf{GG}}}{\triangleleft} T_{\mathbf{P}})(x,y) = 1$ if $x \leq y$ and for $1 > x > y$ we have

$$
\begin{aligned}
(T_{\mathbf{LK}} \overset{I_{\mathbf{GG}}}{\triangleleft} T_{\mathbf{P}})(x,y) &= \inf_{z \in [0,1]} I_{\mathbf{GG}}(T_{\mathbf{LK}}(x,z), T_{\mathbf{P}}(z,y)) \\
&= \inf_{z \leq 1-x} I_{\mathbf{GG}}(T_{\mathbf{LK}}(x,z), T_{\mathbf{P}}(z,y)) \\
&\wedge \inf_{z > 1-x \,\&\, z \leq \frac{1-x}{1-y}} I_{\mathbf{GG}}(T_{\mathbf{LK}}(x,z), T_{\mathbf{P}}(z,y)) \\
&\wedge \inf_{z > \frac{1-x}{1-y}} I_{\mathbf{GG}}(T_{\mathbf{LK}}(x,z), T_{\mathbf{P}}(z,y)) \\
&= \inf_{z \leq 1-x} I_{\mathbf{GG}}(0, zy) \wedge \inf_{z > 1-x \,\&\, z \leq \frac{1-x}{1-y}} I_{\mathbf{GG}}(x+z-1, zy) \\
&\wedge \inf_{z > \frac{1-x}{1-y}} I_{\mathbf{GG}}(x+z-1, zy) \\
&= 1 \wedge 1 \wedge \inf_{z > \frac{1-x}{1-y}} \frac{zy}{x+z-1} \\
&= \inf_{z > \frac{1-x}{1-y}} \frac{y}{1 + \frac{x-1}{z}} = \frac{y}{1 + x - 1} \\
&= \frac{y}{x},
\end{aligned}
$$

and if $x = 1$ we simply obtain $(T_{\mathbf{LK}} \overset{I_{\mathbf{GG}}}{\triangleleft} I_{\mathbf{P}})(1,y) = I_{\mathbf{GG}}(z, zy) = y$. Therefore

$$
(T_{\mathbf{LK}} \overset{I_{\mathbf{GG}}}{\triangleleft} I_{\mathbf{P}}) = I_{T_{\mathbf{P}}} = I_{\mathbf{GG}}.
$$

Example 3. Taking the t-norms from Example 2 with a different fuzzy implication $I_{\mathbf{LK}} = I_{T_{\mathbf{LK}}}$ we have $(T_{\mathbf{LK}} \overset{I_{\mathbf{LK}}}{\triangleleft} I_{\mathbf{P}})(x,y) = 1$, for $x, y \in [0,1]$ such that $x \leq y$ and for $x > y$ we have

$$
\begin{aligned}
(T_{\mathbf{LK}} \overset{I_{\mathbf{LK}}}{\triangleleft} T_{\mathbf{P}})(x,y) &= \inf_{z \in [0,1]} I_{\mathbf{LK}}(T_{\mathbf{LK}}(x,z), T_{\mathbf{P}}(z,y)) \\
&= \inf_{z \leq 1-x} I_{\mathbf{LK}}(T_{\mathbf{LK}}(x,z), T_{\mathbf{P}}(z,y)) \\
&\wedge \inf_{z > 1-x \,\&\, z \leq \frac{1-x}{1-y}} I_{\mathbf{LK}}(T_{\mathbf{LK}}(x,z), T_{\mathbf{P}}(z,y)) \\
&\wedge \inf_{z > 1-x \,\&\, z > \frac{1-x}{1-y}} I_{\mathbf{LK}}(T_{\mathbf{LK}}(x,z), T_{\mathbf{P}}(z,y)) \\
&= 1 \wedge 1 \wedge \inf_{z > 1-x \,\&\, z > \frac{1-x}{1-y}} 1 - (x+z-1) + zy \\
&= \inf_{z > 1-x \,\&\, z > \frac{1-x}{1-y}} 2 + z(y-1) - x \\
&= 2 + 1(y-1) - x = 1 - x + y,
\end{aligned}
$$

hence we have $T_{\mathbf{LK}} \overset{I_{\mathbf{LK}}}{\triangleleft} T_{\mathbf{P}} = I_{\mathbf{LK}}$.

After Example 3 we may ask when, for R-implications, $T_1 \overset{I_{T_1}}{\vartriangleleft} T_2$ is again the I_{T_1}? Let us recall here the following result used in the sequel.

Theorem 2 *[12, Corollary 3.8].* *If T is a t-norm, then*

$$T \overset{I_T}{\vartriangleleft} T = I_T. \tag{5}$$

Proposition 3. *Let T_1, T_2 be t-norms. If $T_1 \le T_2$, then*

$$T_1 \overset{I_{T_1}}{\vartriangleleft} T_2 = I_{T_1}$$

and

$$T_2 \overset{I_{T_1}}{\vartriangleleft} T_1 = I_{T_1}.$$

Proof. Note that in virtue of Theorem 2 it is enough to use the monotonicity (Remark 2). Therefore, for the first equality, we have

$$
\begin{aligned}
I_{T_1}(x,y) &= \inf_{z \in [0,1]} I_{T_1}(T_1(x,z), T_1(z,y)) \\
&\le \inf_{z \in [0,1]} I_{T_1}(T_1(x,z), T_2(z,y)) \le I_{T_1}(T_1(x,1), T_2(1,y)) \\
&= I_{T_1}(x,y),
\end{aligned}
$$

for $x, y \in [0,1]$. The second one is similar.

Now, we will show the reverse result (the case of Example 2) may hold as well.

Proposition 4. *Let T_1, T_2 be t-norms such that $T_1 \le T_2$ and T_2 is left-continuous. Then*

$$T_1 \overset{I_{T_2}}{\vartriangleleft} T_2 = I_{T_2}.$$

Proof. Let us take $x, y, z \in [0,1]$. If T_2 is left-continuous, then by (RP) we may write

$$I_{T_2}(x,y) \ge I_{T_2}(x,y) \Leftrightarrow T_2(x, I_{T_2}(x,y)) \le y.$$

Now we have

$$T_2(T_1(x,z), I_{T_2}(x,y)) \le T_2(T_2(x,z), I_{T_2}(x,y)) = T_2(z, T_2(x, I_{T_2}(x,y))) \le T_2(z,y),$$

so

$$T_2(T_1(x,z), I_{T_2}(x,y)) \le T_2(z,y) \Leftrightarrow I_{T_2}(T_1(x,z), T_2(z,y)) \ge I_{T_2}(x,y),$$

(again from (RP)) and for $z = 1$ we have $I_{T_2}(T_1(x,1), T_2(1,y)) = I_{T_2}(x,y)$. Therefore

$$\inf_{z \in [0,1]} I_{T_2}(T_1(x,z), T_2(z,y)) = I_{T_2}(x,y).$$

Now, let us consider two well-known properties of fuzzy implications - the left neutrality property and the identity principle. According to Example 1 BKS composition $\overset{I}{\lhd}$ of two t-norms doesn't always satisfy the left neutrality property even if I does.

Corollary 1. *Let T_1, T_2 be t-norms such that $T_1 \leq T_2$. Then*

(i) $T_1 \overset{I_{T_1}}{\lhd} T_2$ satisfies (NP).

(ii) $T_2 \overset{I_{T_1}}{\lhd} T_1$ satisfies (NP).

If, in addition, T_2 is left-continuous, then $T_1 \overset{I_{T_2}}{\lhd} T_2$ satisfies (NP).

Proof. In virtue of Propositions 3 and 4 in all of above three cases compositions $T_1 \overset{I_{T_1}}{\lhd} T_2, T_2 \overset{I_{T_1}}{\lhd} T_1, T_1 \overset{I_{T_2}}{\lhd} T_2$ are R-implications, which satisfy (NP) (see [2, Theorem 2.5.4]).

Let us take a look on the identity principle. Again, it depends on the relations between t-norms.

Proposition 5. *Let T_1, T_2 be t-norms and $I \in \mathcal{FI}$. If $T_1 \overset{I}{\lhd} T_2 \in \mathcal{FI}$ and $T_1 \leq T_2$, then $T_1 \overset{I}{\lhd} T_2$ satisfies (IP).*

Proof. If $T_1 \overset{I}{\lhd} T_2 \in \mathcal{FI}$, then I has to satisfy (IP) (see Proposition 1). Therefore, $I(T_1(x, z), T_2(z, x)) \geq I(T_2(x, z), T_2(z, x)) = 1$, $z \in [0, 1]$. Hence,

$$\inf_{z \in [0,1]} I(T_1(x, z), T_2(z, x)) = 1.$$

If (according to the above notation) $T_1 > T_2$ the situation can be completely different as the following example shows.

Example 4. Let us take $T_{\mathbf{P}} \overset{I_{\mathbf{GG}}}{\lhd} T_{\mathbf{LK}}$. Let us take $x, y \in [0, 1]$. If $x = 0$ or $y = 1$, then $(T_{\mathbf{P}} \overset{I_{\mathbf{GG}}}{\lhd} T_{\mathbf{LK}})(x, y) = 1$. However, if $x > 0$ and $y < 1$ we have

$$
\begin{aligned}
(T_{\mathbf{P}} \overset{I_{\mathbf{GG}}}{\lhd} T_{\mathbf{LK}})(x, y) &= \inf_{z \in [0,1]} I_{\mathbf{GG}}(xz, \max\{0, z + y - 1\}) \\
&= \inf_{z > 1-y} I_{\mathbf{GG}}(xz, \max\{0, z + y - 1\}) \\
&\quad \wedge \inf_{0 < z \leq 1-y} I_{\mathbf{GG}}(xz, \max\{0, z + y - 1\}) \\
&\quad \wedge I_{\mathbf{GG}}(0, \max\{0, y - 1\}) \\
&= \inf_{z > 1-y} I_{\mathbf{GG}}(xz, \max\{0, z + y - 1\}) \\
&\quad \wedge \inf_{0 < z \leq 1-y} I_{\mathbf{GG}}(xz, 0) \wedge I_{\mathbf{GG}}(0, 0) \\
&= \inf_{z > 1-y} I_{\mathbf{GG}}(xz, \max\{0, z + y - 1\}) \wedge I_{\mathbf{GG}}(x(1 - y), 0) \wedge 1 \\
&= \inf_{z > 1-y} I_{\mathbf{GG}}(xz, \max\{0, z + y - 1\}) \wedge 0 \wedge 1
\end{aligned}
$$

$$= 0.$$

Hence,

$$(T_{\mathbf{P}} \overset{I_{\mathbf{GG}}}{\lhd} T_{\mathbf{LK}})(x,y) = \begin{cases} 0, & y < 1 \text{ and } x > 0, \\ 1, & y = 1 \text{ or } x = 0, \end{cases}$$

which is the smallest fuzzy implication.

Finally, let us finish with the example that motivates us to further investigations and shows that BKS composition of t-conorms can give an interesting fuzzy implication.

Example 5. Let us consider $S_{\mathbf{P}} \overset{I_{\mathbf{GG}}}{\lhd} S_{\mathbf{M}}$. For $x \in (0,1]$, $y \in [0,1]$ we have

$$\inf_{z \in [0,1]} I_{\mathbf{GG}}(S_{\mathbf{P}}(x,z), S_{\mathbf{M}}(z,y)) = \inf_{z < y} I_{\mathbf{GG}}(x+z-xz, y) \wedge \inf_{z > y} I_{\mathbf{GG}}(x+z-xz, z)$$

$$= \frac{y}{x+y-xy} \wedge \inf_{z > y} \frac{z}{x+z-xz}$$

$$= \frac{y}{x+y-xy} \wedge \inf_{z > y} \frac{1}{\frac{x}{z} + 1 - x}$$

$$= \frac{y}{x+y-xy},$$

and for $x = 0$ $(S_{\mathbf{P}} \overset{I_{\mathbf{GG}}}{\lhd} S_{\mathbf{M}})(0,y) = 1$. Hence,

$$(S_{\mathbf{P}} \overset{I_{\mathbf{GG}}}{\lhd} S_{\mathbf{M}})(x,y) = \begin{cases} 1, & x = 0, \\ \frac{y}{x+y-xy}, & x > 0. \end{cases}$$

Thus we can see that for these particular t-conorms, we have obtained a new fuzzy implication. Therefore our future work will focus on considering this case deeper. Moreover, we can pose here some questions: What kind of fuzzy implications can we get? What are their properties and are they dependent on the properties of t-conorms?

Also, we will examine more of the principal properties of fuzzy implications built from $\overset{I}{\lhd}$ composition.

4   Conclusions

In this paper, we have considered the Bandler-Kohout subproduct. We have applied it as a constructing method of fuzzy implications. We have focused on a family of R-implications. We have shown throughout examples and results when $T_1 \overset{I_T}{\lhd} T_2$ $(T \in \{T_1, T_2\})$ can give new fuzzy implications and when (for some cases) we obtain again the same I_T implication.

Acknowledgment. The author would like to thank anonymous reviewers for their valuable comments and remarks.

References

1. Alsina, C., Frank, M., Schweizer, B.: Associative Functions: Triangular Norms and Copulas. World Scientific Publishing, Hackensack (2006)
2. Baczyński, M., Jayaram, B.: Fuzzy Implications. Studies in Fuzziness and Soft Computing, vol. 231. Springer, Heidelberg (2008). https://doi.org/10.1007/978-3-540-69082-5
3. De Baets, B., Kerre, E.: Fuzzy relational compositions. Fuzzy Sets Syst. **60**, 109–120 (1993)
4. Bandler, W., Kohout, L.J.: Fuzzy relational products as a tool for analysis and synthesis of the behaviour of complex natural and artificial systems. In: Wang, P.P., Chang, S.K. (eds.) Fuzzy Sets: Theory and Applications to Policy Analysis and Information Systems, pp. 341–367. Springer, Cham (1980)
5. De Baets, B.: Analytical solution methods for fuzzy relational equations. In: Dubois, D., Prade, H. (eds.) Fundamentals of Fuzzy Sets. The Handbooks of Fuzzy Sets Series, vol. 7, pp. 291–340. Springer, Cham (2000). https://doi.org/10.1007/978-1-4615-4429-6_7
6. Durante, F., Sempi, C.: Semicopulae. Kybernetika **41**(3), 315–328 (2005)
7. Fodor, J., Roubens, M.: Fuzzy Preference Modelling and Multicriteria Decision Support. Kluwer Academic Publishers, Dordrecht (1994)
8. Grabisch, M., Marichal, J., Mesiar, R., Pap, E.: Aggregation Functions (Encyclopedia of Mathematics and its Applications). Cambridge University Press, Cambridge (2009)
9. Klement, E.P., Mesiar, R., Pap, E.: Triangular Norms. Kluwer Academic Publishers, Dordrecht (2000)
10. Król, A.: Dependencies between fuzzy conjunctions and implications. In: Galichet, S., Montero, J., Mauris, G. (eds.) Proceedings of the 7th Conference of the European Society for Fuzzy Logic and Technology (EUSFLAT-2011) and LFA-2011. Advances in Intelligent Systems Research, vol. 1, pp. 230–237. Atlantis Press (2011)
11. Massanet, S., Torrens, J.: An overview of construction methods of fuzzy implications. In: Baczyński, M., Beliakov, G., Bustince Sola, H., Pradera, A. (eds.) Advances in Fuzzy Implication Functions. Studies in Fuzziness and Soft Computing, vol. 300. Springer, Cham (2013). https://doi.org/10.1007/978-3-642-35677-3_1
12. Miś, K., Baczyński, M.: Different forms of generalized hypothetical syllogism with regard to R-implications. In: Rutkowski, L., Scherer, R., Korytkowski, M., Pedrycz, W., Tadeusiewicz, R., Zurada, J.M. (eds.) ICAISC 2019. LNCS (LNAI), vol. 11508, pp. 304–313. Springer, Cham (2019). https://doi.org/10.1007/978-3-030-20912-4_29
13. Vemuri, N.R., Jayaram, B.: The ⊛-composition of fuzzy implications: closures with respect to properties, powers and families. Fuzzy Sets Syst. **275**, 58–87 (2015)
14. Zadeh, L.A.: Outline of a new approach to the analysis of complex systems and decision processes. IEEE Trans. Syst. Man Cyber. **3**, 28–44 (1973)

Fuzzy Mathematical Analysis and its Applications

On Conflicts of Linguistic Fuzzy Rules

Nhung Cao[ID], Radek Valášek, and Martin Štěpnička[✉][ID]

CE IT4Innovations – Institute for Research and Applications of Fuzzy Modeling,
University of Ostrava, 30. Dubna 22, 701 03 Ostrava, Czech Republic
{nhung.cao,radek.valasek,martin.stepnicka}@osu.cz

Abstract. In this paper, we study the conflict (or inconsistency) of linguistic fuzzy IF-THEN rules that use evaluative linguistic expressions. Firstly, we approach the so-called 1-coherence of the interpretation of perception-based logical deduction inference method, which is the method tailored to the linguistic fuzzy rules. This restrictive coherence of the used model enables the definition of conflicting rules, and consequently, it can be determined directly based on the existence of conflicting rules. Secondly, we focus on investigating the criteria to detect the conflicting rules in a given linguistic description. Based on the criteria, an algorithm for the automatic deduction of the pairs of rules which are in conflict is established. Finally, the paper demonstrates the efficient use of the proposed algorithm on an illustrative example.

Keywords: Linguistic fuzzy rules · Linguistic description ·
Perception-based logical deduction · Conflicting/Inconsistent rules ·
Coherence

1 Introduction and Motivation

Checking the consistency of fuzzy rules is particular important in fuzzy inference systems. It reveals the given system of fuzzy rules is well-formed, or shows the correlation between the rules which allows the analysis to get the comprehensibility of the rules or the search of some conditions (or hypothesis) to cancel the conflict/inconsistency of the rules if it exists.

Inconsistent (also conflicting) fuzzy rules are usually considered as rules having the same (or similar) antecedents and significantly different consequents [9,12,13,15]. The appearance of these rules usually leads to incorrect results derived from the inference process (cf. [18]). Therefore, the problem of finding conditions to ensure that a given system of fuzzy rules does not contain any conflict is of interest of many authors [6,8,9,15]. In [9], the concept of the *coherence* of the implicative model of fuzzy rules was proposed to check the consistency.

This paper addresses the first step of detecting conflicting *linguistic fuzzy rules*, i.e. rules, connected to the *Perception-based Logical Deduction* (abbr.

The authors announce the support of Czech Science Foundation through the grant 20-07851S.

PbLD) inference method [10, 16, 20]. They have a form similar to the implicative rules with the Łukasiewicz algebra of operations. However, unlike the relational model, PbLD does not aggregate conjunctively all rules when inferring any input, it uses a specific pre-selection procedure called *perception* to fire only some of them. Thus, there might be seemingly conflicting rules that are actually not conflicting at all as they never fire jointly. Because of this, the analysis of conflicting rules requires a specific approach.

2   Preliminaries

Let us recall some fundamental definitions relevant to the provided analysis. We consider fuzzy rules in the form:

$$\mathcal{R}_i := \text{IF } x \text{ is } A_i \text{ THEN } y \text{ is } B_i, \quad i = 1, \dots, m \tag{1}$$

in which, x and y are linguistic variables, and A_i and B_i are linguistic expressions. For the sake of simplicity, we will not distinguish between symbols for the linguistic variables and for the numerical values x, y from the input output universes X and Y, respectively, and analogously, between the linguistic expressions and the fuzzy sets $A_i \in \mathcal{F}(X)$, $B_i \in \mathcal{F}(Y)$ modeling their semantics.

The favourite Mamdani-Assilian interpretation, that does not have a sort of "built-in consistency checking mechanism" [1] and although some sort of consistency index has been proposed [5], according to some studies [11], there is no need to focus on consistency of rules that are disjunctively aggregated as semantically, there is not inconsistency at all.

So, we stem from the implicative rules that are very closely related to the studied linguistic fuzzy rules. Its model is a fuzzy relation $\hat{R} \in \mathcal{F}(X \times Y)$ given by

$$\hat{R}(x, y) = \bigwedge_{i=1}^{m} (A_i(x) \rightarrow B_i(y))$$

where $\rightarrow$ is a chosen fuzzy implication. The consistency is checked by the concept of *coherence* [9], i.e., by the fact that for any $x \in X$ there exists $y \in Y$ s.t. $\hat{R}(x, y) = 1$.

2.1   Linguistic Fuzzy IF-THEN Rules

If fuzzy rule base (1) is formed by *linguistic fuzzy rules*, i.e., rules with the linguistic expressions constructed using the theory o trichotomous *evaluative expressions* [17], the rule based is called *linguistic description* (abbr. *LD*) and have to be connected to the PbLD inference. An evaluative linguistic expression is structured as

⟨linguistic hedge⟩⟨atomic evaluative expression⟩ .

An atomic evaluative expression is one of the often used adjectives "small", "medium", and "big", which together form a basic trichotomy [18]. We may write in short this trichotomy as (Sm, Me, Bi). A linguistic hedge works as an adverb used for adjusting the semantics of atomic evaluative expressions. The hedges are distinguished to the *widening effect* and *narrowing effect*. Notice that ⟨linguistic hedge⟩ can be *empty* when it is necessary to use a pure atomic expression. In general, there can be an arbitrary finite number of hedges, however, it is usually limited to a small number that is sufficient for real applications [19,20]. Let us follow the previous works and restrict the number of hedges as mentioned in Table 1.

Table 1. Linguistic hedges and their denotations.

Narrowing effect		Widening effect	
Extremely	(Ex)	More or Less	(ML)
Significantly	(Si)	Roughly	(Ro)
Very	(Ve)	Quite Roughly	(QR)

Following [20], we define a linguistic expression Any whose fuzzy set model Any $\in \mathcal{F}(X)$ attains the normality at any point of the given universe, i.e., $\text{Any}(x) = 1$ for any $x \in X$.

We now recall the orderings of hedges and their respective evaluative expressions.

Definition 1 [10]. Given the set of linguistic hedges H = {Ex, Si, Ve, ML, Ro, QR}, the ordering $\leq_H$ is defined as follows:

$$\text{Ex} \leq_H \text{Si} \leq_H \text{Ve} \leq_H \langle\text{empty}\rangle \leq_H \text{ML} \leq_H \text{Ro} \leq_H \text{QR} .$$

Definition 2 [10,20]. Let A_i, A_j be evaluative expressions. Then we write $A_i \leq_{LE} A_j$ if

$$A_i := \langle\text{hedge}\rangle_i A \text{ and } A_j := \langle\text{hedge}\rangle_j A, \quad \text{and}$$
$$\langle\text{hedge}\rangle_i \leq_H \langle\text{hedge}\rangle_j ,$$

i.e., both expressions are constructed on the same atomic expression and the ordering $\leq_{LE}$ is then based on the ordering of hedges $\leq_H$. Furthermore, we define $A_i \leq_{LE} A_j$ whenever $A_j := \text{Any}$.

Notice that fuzzy sets interpreting evaluative expressions of the same atomic expression keep the inclusion ordering in a sense that if $A_1 \leq_{LE} A_2$ then $A_1 \subseteq A_2$, see Fig. 1.

If antecedents A_i, A_j are compound of several evaluative expressions connected by ∧ND, e.g.,

$$x \text{ is } A_i := (x_1 \text{ is } A_{i_1}) \text{ AND } \dots \text{ AND } (x_\ell \text{ is } A_{i_\ell}) \tag{2}$$
$$x \text{ is } A_j := (x_1 \text{ is } A_{j_1}) \text{ AND } \dots \text{ AND } (x_\ell \text{ is } A_{j_\ell}) \tag{3}$$

then $\leq_{LE}$ is defined per components, i.e., $A_i \leq_{LE} A_j$ iff $A_{i_k} \leq_{LE} A_{j_k}$ for all $k = 1, \dots, \ell$.

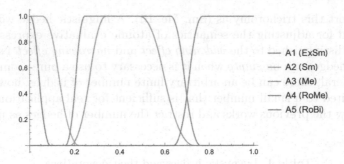

Fig. 1. Illustration of inclusive fuzzy sets modeling expressions of the same atomic expression. For instance, fuzzy set A_1 modeling the expression "Extremely Small" is narrower/more specific than A_2, which interprets the expression "Small".

Remark 1. *We denote $A_i \parallel_{\mathrm{LE}} A_j$ if neither $A_i \leq_{\mathrm{LE}} A_j$ nor $A_j \leq_{\mathrm{LE}} A_i$ holds.*

It is important mentioning that we adopt in this work a rather non-restrictive assumption, that a fuzzy rule base is comprised of fuzzy rules with ℓ antecedent variables ($\ell \geq 1$) and one consequent variable. Considering only one consequent is understandable, since, if a rule base consists of rules with s consequent variables then, in principle, such a rule base can be split into s separate rule bases in which each fuzzy rule has only one consequent variable.

Finally, we recall an important *partition axiom* introduced in [10].

Axiom 1. *Let A_1, A_2 be evaluative linguistic expressions with different atomic expressions modelled by $A_1, A_2 \in \mathcal{F}(X)$ for some X. Then there exists no $x_0 \in X$ s.t. $A_1(x_0) = A_2(x_0) = 1$.*

2.2 Perception-Based Logical Deduction Inference Method

The set $\mathbf{T}^{LD}$ containing all antecedent fuzzy sets of the rules from a given LD will be called *topic* of LD. Analogously, we may define $\mathbf{T}^K$ for any non-empty $K \subseteq LD$. Now, we may define the last ordering of evaluative expressions that is based on an observation (input) $x_0 \in X$.

Definition 3. *[10]. Let $A_i, A_j \in \mathbf{T}^{LD}$ and $x_0 \in X$. Then $A_i \leq_{x_0} A_j$ if either $A_i(x_0) > A_j(x_0)$; or $A_i(x_0) = A_j(x_0)$ and $A_i \leq_{\mathrm{LE}} A_j$.*

Note that if A_i is a compound expression given by (2) and $x_0 = (x_{0_1}, \dots, x_{0_\ell})$ then $A_i(x_0) = \bigwedge_{k=1,\dots,\ell} A_{i_k}(x_{0_k})$.

Definition 3 plays an essential role in the construction of the *local perception* function that determines the fuzzy rules to be fired.

Definition 4. [10]. Let LD be given. The *local perception* $P : X \to \mathcal{P}(\mathrm{T}^{LD})$ is defined by:

$$P(x_0) = \{A_i \mid A_i(x_0) > 0 \,\&\, \forall A_j : A_j \leq_{x_0} A_i \Rightarrow A_j = A_i\} \,.$$

For a given observation $x_0 \in X$, the perception returns a set of antecedent fuzzy sets that are minimal according to ordering $\leq_{x_0}$. These fuzzy sets identify the rules fired rules in the PbLD inference.

Lemma 1 states that at least for a single point, each given rule fires.

Lemma 1 [10]. *Let $A_i \in \mathrm{T}^{LD}$ for a given LD. Then there exists $x_0 \in X$ such that $P(x_0) = \{A_i\}$.*

Definition 5 [2,20]. For a given $x_0 \in X$, the *deduction rule* of PbLD is given by:

$$r_P(P(x_0)) = \bigcap \{C_i \mid C_i(y) = A_i(x_0) \to B_i(y) \,\&\, A_i \in P(x_0)\}, \ y \in Y \qquad (4)$$

where $\bigcap$ and $\to$ are respectively the Gödel intersection and Łukasiewicz implication.

Formula (4) can be replaced by a more comprehensible form. Indeed, for a given $x_0 \in X$, and for all $y \in Y$ the deduction rule of PbLD can be defined by:

$$R_P(x_0, y) = \bigwedge_{\substack{i \\ A_i \in P(x_0)}} (A_i(x_0) \to B_i(y)) \qquad (5)$$

resembling the relational implicative model [4,7,14] as R_P is a fuzzy relation on $X \times Y$ that differs from the implication model only by the restricted number of rules that are fired due to the local perception function.

3 Conflicting Linguistic Fuzzy Rules

3.1 1-Coherence of PbLD Interpretation and Conflicting Rules

The most natural approach to the conflicting rules and consistency of a linguistic description is to use the concept of coherence. However, we cannot take into account all rules like in the case of $\hat{R}$. Observing the local perception function, more rules fire if they are fired in the same degree lower than one (e.g. in the point when antecedents Small and Medium intersect) or in the case of more input variables within the intersection of kernels ($\mathrm{Ker}(A_i) = \{x \mid A_i(x) = 1\}$) of antecedents of several rules. As the first case can be actually tricky avoided by a well-chosen discretization of X in a computer, that will eliminate the existence of such intersecting points, the latter one seems crucial. Therefore, we will focus only on it and proceed with the definition of the 1-coherence of an LD.

Definition 6. A given LD is called *1-coherent* if for each $x_0 \in X$ such that $\exists \mathcal{R}_i \in LD : A_i(x_0) = 1$, there exists $y \in Y$ such that $R_P(x_0, y) = 1$.

The tiny formal difference compared to the original coherence of $\hat{R}$ defined in [7] has a strong impact on the fact that seemingly conflicting rules are not causing any inconsistency as they never fire at the same time.

Note that, due to the property $1 \to b = b$, we know that if $A_i(x_0) = 1$ for all $A_i \in P(x_0)$ then it holds that $r_P(P(x_0)) = \bigcap\{B_i \mid A_i \in P(x_0)\}$. Consequently, the condition $R_P(x_0, y) = 1$ for at least an output element y requires all the consequents of the fired rules to be built on the same atomic expression, see Axiom 1. In other words, PbLD interpretation is 1-coherent if there does not exist any two rules that can be jointly fired by the local perception at the maximal truth degree and that have consequents which are constructed on distinct atomic expressions. Therefore, such two rules are denoted as *conflicting rules*.

Definition 7. Let LD be a given linguistic description and let $\mathcal{R}_i, \mathcal{R}_j \in LD$. We say that $\mathcal{R}_i$ and $\mathcal{R}_j$ are *conflicting rules*, denoted by $\mathcal{R}_i \sim \mathcal{R}_j$, if $B_i \parallel_{LE} B_j$ and there exists an $x_0 \in X$ such that $A_i(x_0) = A_j(x_0) = 1$ and $A_i, A_j \in P(x_0)$.

It is clear that the LD is not 1-coherent if there exists a pair $(\mathcal{R}_i, \mathcal{R}_j)$ in LD such that $\mathcal{R}_i \sim \mathcal{R}_j$.

Remark 2. *From Definition 7, condition "an $x_0 \in X$ exists such that $A_i(x_0) = A_j(x_0) = 1$" is equivalent to that an $x_0 \in X$ exists such that $x_0 \in \mathrm{Ker}(A_i) \cap \mathrm{Ker}(A_j)$. Based on the properties of linguistic expressions [10, 16], it occurs if and only if the respective components of antecedents A_i and A_j (i.e., A_{i_k} and A_{j_k} for any k) are built on identical atomic expressions with help of the expression* Any.

3.2   How to Determine Conflicting Rules

Let us introduce the concept of compatible expressions that will be helpful in the clarity of the further analysis.

Definition 8. Consider two evaluative linguistic expressions C, D and their models $C, D \in \mathcal{F}(X)$ on a given universe X. We say that C, D are *compatible* expressions if $\mathrm{Ker}(C) \cap \mathrm{Ker}(D) \neq \emptyset$. If the condition is not met, i.e., if $\mathrm{Ker}(C) \cap \mathrm{Ker}(D) = \emptyset$, we say that C, D are *incompatible* expressions (fuzzy sets).

Note that incompatible expressions are built w.r.t. different atomic expressions, i.e. $C \parallel_{LE} D$. Note also that the notion of the compatibility of a pair of expressions can be extended to an arbitrary set of expressions.

Definition 7 on one hand clearly defines the conflicting rules, however, on the other hand, it cannot be directly used for the analysis of the consistency of an LD as we do not see immediately which rules can be jointly chosen by the perception to fire. Nevertheless, it helps us to determine at least the rules *suspicious from the conflict.*

Definition 9. Let LD be a given linguistic description and let $\mathcal{R}_i, \mathcal{R}_j \in LD$. We say that $\mathcal{R}_i$ and $\mathcal{R}_j$ are *suspicious from the conflict* if B_i, B_j are incompatible, and $\mathrm{Ker}(A_i) \cap \mathrm{Ker}(A_j) \neq \emptyset$, and either $A_i = A_j$ or $A_i \parallel_{LE} A_j$.

Clearly, all rules that are conflicting have to be firstly suspicious from the conflict but there might be suspicious rules that turn not to be conflicting. For the analysis of which of the suspicious rules are also conflicting, it will be helpful to split the given LD to a union of subsets of rules.

Convention 1. *In the sequel, let us consider a given LD in the form of union of γ distinct sets*

$$LD = G_1 \cup \cdots \cup G_\gamma, \tag{6}$$

*in which each set $G_r, r = 1, \ldots, \gamma$ contains all rules whose antecedents form the set of compatible expressions. Let us note that, due to the potential presence of the expression **Any**, the sets $G_1, \ldots, G_\gamma$ need not to be disjoint. However, even in such case, it is important to emphasize that, for each G_r and for any $\mathcal{R}^\star \in LD \setminus G_r$, the following holds:* $\mathrm{Ker}(A^\star) \cap \bigcap_{A \in \mathbf{T}^{G_r}} \mathrm{Ker}(A) = \emptyset$.

Example 1. *Consider $LD = \{\mathcal{R}_1, \ldots, \mathcal{R}_4\}$ where*

$$\mathcal{R}_1 := \textit{IF } x_1 \textit{ is Sm AND } x_2 \textit{ is \textbf{Any} THEN } y \textit{ is Bi}$$
$$\mathcal{R}_2 := \textit{IF } x_1 \textit{ is ML Sm AND } x_2 \textit{ is Sm THEN } y \textit{ is Ve Bi}$$
$$\mathcal{R}_3 := \textit{IF } x_1 \textit{ is Ex Sm AND } x_2 \textit{ is Ro Sm THEN } y \textit{ is Me}$$
$$\mathcal{R}_4 := \textit{IF } x_1 \textit{ is Sm AND } x_2 \textit{ is Bi THEN } y \textit{ is Bi }.$$

Then, $LD = G_1 \cup G_2$ where $G_1 = \{\mathcal{R}_1, \mathcal{R}_2, \mathcal{R}_3\}$ and $G_2 = \{\mathcal{R}_1, \mathcal{R}_4\}$.

Lemma 2. *Let $LD = G_1 \cup \cdots \cup G_\gamma$ as formulated in Convention 1. Then, for any $\mathcal{R}_i, \mathcal{R}_j \in LD$ which are suspicious from the conflict, there exists a set $G_r \in \{G_1, \ldots, G_\gamma\}$ such that $\{\mathcal{R}_i, \mathcal{R}_j\} \subseteq G_r$.*

Proof-sketch: By Definition 9, $\mathcal{R}_i, \mathcal{R}_j$ are rules with compatible antecedents. So, it is trivial that both rules belong to at least a single G_r.   □

Let us introduce one more denotation. For an LD and $K \subseteq LD$, by

$$K_{\min} = \{\mathcal{R}_k \in K \mid \forall A \in \mathbf{T}^K : A \leq_{\mathrm{LE}} A_k \Rightarrow A = A_k\}$$

we denote the set of the rules from K whose antecedents are minimal with respect to ordering $\leq_{\mathrm{LE}}$. The following Theorem provides a criterion for detecting the pairs of rules which are in conflict in a given linguistic description.

Theorem 1. *Let $\mathcal{R}_i, \mathcal{R}_j$ be rules in a given LD such that they are suspicious from the conflict. Then, $\mathcal{R}_i \sim \mathcal{R}_j$ in LD if and only if there exists no $\mathcal{R}_k \in LD$ such that*

$$\mathrm{Ker}(A_i) \cap \mathrm{Ker}(A_j) \subseteq \mathrm{Ker}(A_k) \quad \& \quad A_k <_{\mathrm{LE}} A_i \textit{ or } A_k <_{\mathrm{LE}} A_j . \tag{7}$$

Proof-sketch: Assume that $\mathcal{R}_i, \mathcal{R}_j$ are suspicious from the conflict and there is no $\mathcal{R}_k \in LD$ meeting condition (7). Then there is an $x_0 \in X$ such that $x_0 \in \mathrm{Ker}(A_i) \cap \mathrm{Ker}(A_j)$ and $x_0 \notin \mathrm{Ker}(A)$ for any $A \in \mathrm{T}^{LD \smallsetminus \{\mathcal{R}_i, \mathcal{R}_j\}}$ satisfying that $\mathrm{Ker}(A_i) \cap \mathrm{Ker}(A_j) \nsubseteq \mathrm{Ker}(A)$. On the other hand, $x_0 \in \mathrm{Ker}(A')$ for $A' \in \mathrm{T}^{LD \smallsetminus \{\mathcal{R}_i, \mathcal{R}_j\}}$ satisfying $\mathrm{Ker}(A_i) \cap \mathrm{Ker}(A_j) \subseteq \mathrm{Ker}(A')$. Let K be the set of $\mathcal{R}' \in LD$ with such antecedents A'. By assumption (7), there is no rule $\mathcal{R}_k$ in LD such that its antecedent A_k is strictly smaller than A_i or A_j, and $\mathrm{Ker}(A_k)$ includes the intersection of $\mathrm{Ker}(A_i)$ and $\mathrm{Ker}(A_j)$. Thus, based on the definition of perception function, we imply $A_i, A_j \in P(x_0)$. In particular, $P(x_0) = \{A_i, A_j\} \cup \mathrm{T}^{K_{\min}}$. Thus, $\mathcal{R}_i \nsim \mathcal{R}_j$.

Let there exists an $\mathcal{R}_k \in LD$ meeting condition (7), e.g., such that $A_k <_{\mathrm{LE}} A_i$ and $\mathrm{Ker}(A_i) \cap \mathrm{Ker}(A_j) \subseteq \mathrm{Ker}(A_k)$. Then, for any $x_0 \in X$ such that $A_i(x_0) = A_j(x_0) = 1$, it holds that $A_k(x_0) = 1$. The fact that $A_k <_{\mathrm{LE}} A_i$ directly implies $A_i \notin P(x_0)$ which means that $\mathcal{R}_i$ and $\mathcal{R}_j$ are not in conflict. $\square$

Below, we introduce Corollary 1 and Corollary 2 that allow to detect a pair of conflicting rules in LD by investigating only the involved sets G_r.

Corollary 1. *Let $LD = G_1 \cup \cdots \cup G_\gamma$ as expressed in Convention 1 and consider $G^\star \in \{G_1, \ldots, G_\gamma\}$. Let $\mathcal{R}_i, \mathcal{R}_j$ be rules in $G^\star$ that are suspicious from the conflict. Assume that $\{\mathcal{R}_i, \mathcal{R}_j\} \nsubseteq G_r$ for any $G_r \neq G^\star$. Then, $\mathcal{R}_i \nsim \mathcal{R}_j$ in LD if and only if no $\mathcal{R}_k$ exists in $G^\star$ meeting condition (7).*

Proof-sketch: By Convention 1, for any two rules $\mathcal{R} \in LD \smallsetminus G^\star$, $\mathcal{R}' \in G^\star$ the intersection of $\mathrm{Ker}(A)$ and $\mathrm{Ker}(A')$ is empty. Therefore, no rule from $LD \smallsetminus G^\star$ can satisfy (7). Combining this fact and the assumption that no $\mathcal{R}_k$ meeting condition (7) exists in $G^\star$, we get that there is no rule in LD satisfying condition (7). The conclusion is then derived by Theorem 1. $\square$

Corollary 2. *Let $LD = G_1 \cup \cdots \cup G_\gamma$ as expressed by Convention 1 and let $M \subseteq \{G_1, \ldots, G_\gamma\}$. Let $\{\mathcal{R}_i, \mathcal{R}_j\} \subseteq \bigcap_{G \in M} G$ be suspicious from the conflict. Assume that $\{\mathcal{R}_i, \mathcal{R}_j\} \nsubseteq G_r$ for any $G_r \notin M$. Then, $\mathcal{R}_i \nsim \mathcal{R}_j$ in LD if and only if no $\mathcal{R}_k$ satisfying condition (7) exists in $\bigcup_{G \in M} G$.*

Proof-sketch: We may proceed the proofsketch similarly to that of Corollary 1, noting that for any two rules $\mathcal{R}, \mathcal{R}' \in LD$ s.t. $\mathcal{R} \in LD \smallsetminus \bigcup_{G \in M} G$, and $\mathcal{R}' \in \bigcup_{G \in M} G$, we get $\mathrm{Ker}(A) \cap \mathrm{Ker}(A') = \emptyset$. $\square$

3.3   Algorithmic Implementation

The theoretical results introduced above result in the following algorithm for an automatic detection of conflicting rules in a given linguistic description.

Algorithm 1. *Input LD.*

(*I*) *Based on Convention 1, form subsets $G_r, r = 1, \ldots, \gamma$ of LD. For each G_r, proceed steps (1)-(4):*

(1) *Find all pairs of rules in G_r that are suspicious from the conflict. Denote the set of all such pairs by P_{G_r}.*

(2) Take pair $(\mathcal{R}_i, \mathcal{R}_j)$ in P_{G_r} and determine

$$K = \{\mathcal{R}_i, \mathcal{R}_j\} \cup \{\mathcal{R} \in G_r \mid \mathcal{R} \text{ satisfies } (7)\} \ .$$

Determine $K_{\min}$. Then,
- if $K_{\min} = \{\mathcal{R}_i, \mathcal{R}_j\}$, pair $(\mathcal{R}_i, \mathcal{R}_j)$ is marked to remain in P_{G_r}.
- if $K_{\min} \neq \{\mathcal{R}_i, \mathcal{R}_j\}$, find the pairs in $K_{\min}$ whose consequents are incompatible and mark them to be kept in P_{G_r}. Delete $(\mathcal{R}_i, \mathcal{R}_j)$ from P_{G_r}.
(3) Repeat step (2) for the other pairs in P_{G_r} that are different from the ones marked to remain in P_{G_r}.
(4) Denote the resulting set containing only the remaining pairs of rules $SP_{G_r} \subseteq P_{G_r}$.

(II) Take a pair $(\mathcal{R}_i, \mathcal{R}_j) \in SP_{G_r}$ for an $r = 1, \ldots, \gamma$. If there exists at least a single index $p \neq r$ such that $(\mathcal{R}_i, \mathcal{R}_j) \in P_{G_p}$ and $(\mathcal{R}_i, \mathcal{R}_j) \notin SP_{G_p}$, then by Corollaries 1-2 $(\mathcal{R}_i, \mathcal{R}_j)$ are not conflicting. Otherwise $\mathcal{R}_i \approx \mathcal{R}_j$.

Example 2. Let us consider the LD consisting of 11 rules provided in Table 2.

Table 2. Example of an LD for the demonstration of the proposed algorithm.

Rules	Antecedents		Consequents
	A_{i1}	A_{i2}	B_i
$\mathcal{R}_1$	Ve Sm	Ex Bi	Bi
$\mathcal{R}_2$	ML Sm	Bi	Bi
$\mathcal{R}_3$	Si Sm	Bi	Ve Sm
$\mathcal{R}_4$	Sm	Si Bi	Bi
$\mathcal{R}_5$	Si Sm	ML Bi	Me
$\mathcal{R}_6$	ML Sm	Ro Bi	ML Bi
$\mathcal{R}_7$	Me	Si Sm	Sm
$\mathcal{R}_8$	Ro Me	QR Sm	Sm
$\mathcal{R}_9$	ML Sm	Bi	ML Me
$\mathcal{R}_{10}$	QR Me	Sm	Bi
$\mathcal{R}_{11}$	QR Sm	QR Bi	Ro Bi

(I) $LD = G_1 \cup G_2$ s.t. $G_1 = \{\mathcal{R}_1, \mathcal{R}_2, \mathcal{R}_3, \mathcal{R}_4, \mathcal{R}_5, \mathcal{R}_6, \mathcal{R}_9, \mathcal{R}_{11}\}$, and $G_2 = \{\mathcal{R}_7, \mathcal{R}_8, \mathcal{R}_{10}\}$. We proceed with the steps (1)-(4) for G_1.

(1) $P_{G_1} = \{(\mathcal{R}_1, \mathcal{R}_5), (\mathcal{R}_1, \mathcal{R}_3), (\mathcal{R}_2, \mathcal{R}_9), (\mathcal{R}_2, \mathcal{R}_5), (\mathcal{R}_4, \mathcal{R}_5), (\mathcal{R}_4, \mathcal{R}_3)\}$.
(2) Take the first pair $(\mathcal{R}_1, \mathcal{R}_5)$. Then, $K = \{\mathcal{R}_1, \mathcal{R}_5, \mathcal{R}_3\}$ and $K_{\min} = \{\mathcal{R}_1, \mathcal{R}_3\}$. Consequents of $\mathcal{R}_1$ and $\mathcal{R}_3$ are incompatible so, pair $(\mathcal{R}_1, \mathcal{R}_3)$ is marked to remain in P_{G_1}. We delete pair $(\mathcal{R}_1, \mathcal{R}_5)$ from P_{G_1}.

(3) Step (2) is repeated for other pairs.
   Take $(\mathcal{R}_2, \mathcal{R}_9)$. We get $K = K_{min} = \{\mathcal{R}_2, \mathcal{R}_9\}$. Thus, $(\mathcal{R}_2, \mathcal{R}_9) \in SP_{G_1}$.
   Take $(\mathcal{R}_2, \mathcal{R}_5)$. Then, $K = \{\mathcal{R}_2, \mathcal{R}_5, \mathcal{R}_3\}$ and $K_{min} = \{\mathcal{R}_3\}$. There is no pair with incompatible consequents in K_{min} so, $(\mathcal{R}_2, \mathcal{R}_5)$ is deleted.
   Take $(\mathcal{R}_4, \mathcal{R}_5)$. Then, $K = \{\mathcal{R}_4, \mathcal{R}_5, \mathcal{R}_3\}$ and $K_{min} = \{\mathcal{R}_4, \mathcal{R}_3\}$. As consequents of $\mathcal{R}_4$ and $\mathcal{R}_3$ are incompatible, $(\mathcal{R}_4, \mathcal{R}_3) \in SP_{G_1}$. Pair $(\mathcal{R}_4, \mathcal{R}_5)$ is deleted.
(4) We get $SP_{G_1} = \{(\mathcal{R}_1, \mathcal{R}_3), (\mathcal{R}_2, \mathcal{R}_9), (\mathcal{R}_4, \mathcal{R}_3)\}$.
   Using analogous steps (1)-(4), we get $P_{G_2} = SP_{G_2} = \{(\mathcal{R}_8, \mathcal{R}_{10})\}$.

(II) No pair from SP_{G_1} belongs to SP_{G_2}. As $P_{G_2} = SP_{G_2}$, no pair from SP_{G_1} belongs to P_{G_2}. Similarly, the only pair from SP_{G_2} does neither belong to SP_{G_1} nor to P_{G_1}. Consequently, $\mathcal{R}_1 \sim \mathcal{R}_3, \mathcal{R}_4 \sim \mathcal{R}_3, \mathcal{R}_2 \sim \mathcal{R}_9, \mathcal{R}_8 \sim \mathcal{R}_{10}$.

Remark 3. *It is worth mentioning that the proposed algorithm can be applied after the simplification of a given linguistic description by eliminating the redundant rules. The algorithm for the automatic detection and deletion the redundant rules in a given system of fuzzy rules has been recently generalized [2,3] can be applied for such a purpose of the simplification. The size of the simplified system can be then significantly reduced and this may help to decrease the complexity in running the algorithm for detecting the conflicting rules.*

For instance, in Example 2, the application of the redundancy algorithm described in [3] finds rule $\mathcal{R}_1$ redundant and deletes it from the given LD. Based on $LD \setminus \{\mathcal{R}_1\}$, investigated pairs $(\mathcal{R}_1, \mathcal{R}_5)$ and $(\mathcal{R}_1, \mathcal{R}_3)$ do not appear in P_{G_1} when applying the proposed algorithm for detecting conflicting rules. The amount of investigated pairs is slightly reduced and we obtain only three pairs of conflicting rules: $\mathcal{R}_4 \sim \mathcal{R}_3, \mathcal{R}_2 \sim \mathcal{R}_9, \mathcal{R}_8 \sim \mathcal{R}_{10}$.

4   Conclusions and Remark

We have approached the consistency of linguistic descriptions via the concept of 1-coherence that is directly motivated by the coherence of implicative rules [7] however, it reflects the different shape of fuzzy sets modeling evaluative linguistic expressions and the necessarily tailored PbLD inference with the perception mechanism pre-selecting the rules to be fired. The 1-coherence of a given linguistic description is ensured whenever the LD contains no conflicting rules. Analogously to the analysis of redundancy in linguistic descriptions [2,10], also here there might be rules that are only seemingly conflicting. Therefore, we first have to define rules suspicious from the conflict and we investigate them further in the context of the other rules present in the linguistic description.

An algorithm for the automatic detection of the conflicting rules was designed based on the theoretical results provided in the paper and its functionality demonstrated on an illustrative example.

Let us emphasize that the algorithm results into a set of particular pairs of conflicting rules. The ambition of this research was not to "solve" the inconsistency, e.g., by removal of one of the conflicting rules for each pair. Such a step requires a further analysis often focusing on the previous generation of the rules – from which data samples or based on which expert opinions the incriminated rules got into the linguistic description. However, the algorithm provides an essential basis for such an analysis and potentially, for further development. One of such potential directions can stem from a sort of automatically computed inconsistency index. This can be feasible, e.g., by computing the similarity between fuzzy rules. Then the further analysis may, e.g., motivated by [13], establish a formula to calculate the conflicting indexes of considered pairs.

References

1. Bodenhofer, U., Daňková, M., Štěpnička, M., Novák, V.: A plea for the usefulness of the deductive interpretation of fuzzy rules in engineering applications. In: Proceedings of the 16th IEEE International Conference on Fuzzy Systems, London, pp. 1567–1572(2007)
2. Cao, N., Štěpnička, M., Dvořák, A., Valášek, R.: Redundancy criteria for linguistic fuzzy rules. unpublished, submitted to Expert Systems with Applications (2021)
3. Cao, N., Valášek, R.: On consistency of redundancy deduction of linguistic fuzzy rules. In: 2021 13th International Conference on Knowledge and Systems Engineering (KSE), pp. 1–6. IEEE (2021)
4. Coufal, D.: Coherence of radial implicative fuzzy systems. In: Proceedings of the 15th IEEE International Conference on Fuzzy Systems, Vancouver, BC, pp. 307–314 (2006)
5. Coufal, D.: Coherence Index of Radial Conjunctive Fuzzy Systems. In: Melin, P., Castillo, O., Aguilar, L.T., Kacprzyk, J., Pedrycz, W. (eds.) IFSA 2007. LNCS (LNAI), vol. 4529, pp. 502–512. Springer, Heidelberg (2007). https://doi.org/10.1007/978-3-540-72950-1_50
6. Coufal, D.: Coherence of radial implicative fuzzy systems. In: 2006 IEEE International Conference on Fuzzy Systems, pp. 307–314. IEEE (2006)
7. Dubois, D., Prade, H., Ughetto, L.: Checking the coherence and redundancy of fuzzy knowledge bases. IEEE Trans. Fuzzy Syst. **5**(6), 398–417 (1997)
8. Dubois, D., Prade, H.: What are fuzzy rules and how to use them. Fuzzy Sets Syst. **84**(2), 169–185 (1996)
9. Dubois, D., Prade, H., Ughetto, L.: Checking the coherence and redundancy of fuzzy knowledge bases. IEEE Trans. Fuzzy Syst. **5**(3), 398–417 (1997)
10. Dvořák, A., Štěpnička, M., Štěpničková, L.: On redundancies in systems of fuzzy/linguistic IF-THEN rules under perception-based logical deduction inference. Fuzzy Sets Syst. **277**, 22–43 (2015)
11. Dvořák, A., Štěpnička, M.: Mamdani-Assilian rules: with or without continuity? In: Proceedings of the 13th International Workshop on Fuzzy Logic and Applications (WILF 2021), vol. 3074. CEUR (2021)
12. Gacto, M.J., Alcalá, R., Herrera, F.: Interpretability of linguistic fuzzy rule-based systems: an overview of interpretability measures. Inf. Sci. **181**(20), 4340–4360 (2011)
13. Gutiérrez-Estrada, J.C., Pulido-Calvo, I., Bilton, D.T.: Consistency of fuzzy rules in an ecological context. Ecol. Model. **251**, 187–198 (2013)
14. Jones, H., Charnomordic, B., Dubois, D., Guillaume, S.: Practical inference with systems of gradual implicative rules. IEEE Trans. Fuzzy Syst. **17**(1), 61–78 (2008)

15. Klawonn, F., Novák, V.: The relation between inference and interpolation in the framework of fuzzy systems. Fuzzy Sets Syst. **81**(3), 331–354 (1996)
16. Novák, V.: Perception-based logical deduction. In: Computational Intelligence, Theory and Applications, pp. 237–250. Springer, Cham (2005). https://doi.org/10.1007/3-540-31182-3_21
17. Novák, V.: A comprehensive theory of trichotomous evaluative linguistic expressions. Fuzzy Sets Syst. **159**(22), 2939–2969 (2008)
18. Novák, V., Perfilieva, I., Dvořák, A.: Insight into Fuzzy Modeling. Wiley, New York (2016)
19. Štěpnička, M., Dvořák, A., Pavliska, V., Vavříčková, L.: A linguistic approach to time series modeling with the help of f-transform. Fuzzy Sets Syst. **180**(1), 164–184 (2011)
20. Štěpnička, M., Burda, M., Štěpničková, L.: Fuzzy rule base ensemble generated from data by linguistic associations mining. Fuzzy Sets Syst. **285**, 140–161 (2016)

A Review on Differentiability and Optimality Conditions in Fuzzy Environments

Beatriz Hernández-Jiménez[1](✉) , Rafaela Osuna-Gómez[2] ,
Yurilev Chalco-Cano[3] , and Tiago Mendoça da Costa[3]

[1] Universidad Pablo de Olavide, Sevilla, Spain
mbherjim@upo.es
[2] Universidad de Sevilla, Sevilla, Spain
rafaela@us.es
[3] Universidad de Tarapacá, Arica, Chile
ychalco@academicos.uta.cl, grafunjo@yahoo.com.br

Abstract. In this paper we present a review of the most important notions and characterizations of differentiability and necessary optimality conditions for a fuzzy multiobjective problem. As basis of this review, we first study the fundamental aspects of the notions of differentiability for interval valued functions, since the fuzzy environment and the interval environment are closely related. Those aspects are related to the different definitions of difference for intervals and their drawbacks, the different definitions and characterizations of the differentiability for interval-valued functions and their drawbacks and how they have been solved in the literature. Based on the most important and meaning results on interval valued functions you can find in the literature, a review on notions of differentiability in fuzzy context is given, both in the case of functions of one variable, and several variables. And finally we present the review results of the necessary optimality conditions for fuzzy multiobjective problems and the main conclusions.

Keywords: Fuzzy functions · Differentiability · Optimality conditions

1 Introduction

Throughout history it has been shown that the notion of differentiability for real functions has had a crucial importance for solving problems and its application to different fields such as physics, engineering, medicine, economics, among others.

Supported by the European Regional Development Fund (ERDF) and by the Ministry of Economy, Knowledge, Business and University, of the Junta de Andalucía, within the framework of the FEDER Andalucía 2014–2020 operational program. Specific objective 1.2.3. ("Promotion and generation of frontier knowledge and knowledge oriented to the challenges of society, development of emerging technologies") within the framework of the reference research project (UPO-1381297). ERDF co-financing percentage 80%.

D. Ciucci et al. (Eds.): IPMU 2022, CCIS 1601, pp. 245–257, 2022.
https://doi.org/10.1007/978-3-031-08971-8_21

Mathematical programming has developed all the tools for solving optimization problems in this case. In particular, multiobjective mathematical programming is really useful in order to model real situations where more than one objective exists. In order to solve problems closer to human reality, it is quite common to find a certain degree of incomplete, subjective, vague or inaccurate information in the situations to be modeled. So the need to use other tools that allow modelling that situations, giving rise to Interval Analysis, introduced in the works of Moore (1959) [15]. However, there exist some shortcomings in the algebraic operation "difference" given in these works, which do not allow developing a consistent differential theory in interval spaces and it has motivated the introduction of some different kinds of algebraic arithmetic in interval spaces (Lodwick 2015; Markov 1979; Plotnikova 2005 and its references). As the notion of differentiability is based on a difference, there exist some shortcomings in the different notions of differentiability given for an interval-valued function and its properties and/or characterizations along the literature. Let us show them and how they have been solved.

As the classical mathematical programming tools do not adequately reflect this lack of precision in the data, the Fuzzy Set Theory was introduced to manage the incomplete, vague, subjective or lack of accurate information that appears in many mathematical models or computations of some real-world phenomena. A significant and growing field is the Fuzzy Optimization that deals with the resolution of optimization problems with incomplete or vague data. In particular, Fuzzy Multiobjective Optimization is really useful in order to model situations where more than one objective exists.

This review is motivated by the importance of the notion of differentiability and its characterizations as basis to obtain optimality conditions, convexity notions and algorithms to find the solutions of an optimization problem. In the case of interval-valued functions there are some drawbacks due to the nature of the intervals space: the notion of difference used and the algebraic structure of this space, that it is not a linear one, among others. These drawbacks have leaded to notions of differentiability that can be improved, uncorrected characterizations of differentiability, on which convexity notions, optimality conditions, and even algorithms have been based for problems with interval-valued functions. So how them have been solved is essential, since they will be the basis also for the problems with fuzzy functions.

2   Preliminaries

Let us consider $I(\mathbb{R})$ the space of all closed and bounded intervals on $\mathbb{R}$, $I(\mathbb{R}) = \{[\underline{a}, \overline{a}] \, / \, \underline{a}, \overline{a} \in \mathbb{R} \text{ and } \underline{a} \leq \overline{a}\}$, equipped with standard addition and scalar multiplication operations. Let us consider $A, B \in I(\mathbb{R})$ and $\lambda \in \mathbb{R}$, Minkowski addition and scalar multiplication are defined by

$$A + B = [\underline{a}, \overline{a}] + [\underline{b}, \overline{b}] = [\underline{a} + \underline{b}, \overline{a} + \overline{b}], \qquad \lambda A = \begin{cases} [\lambda\underline{a}, \lambda\overline{a}] & \text{if } \lambda \geq 0 \\ [\lambda\overline{a}, \lambda\underline{a}] & \text{if } \lambda < 0. \end{cases} \tag{1}$$

If $\lambda = -1$, scalar multiplication gives the opposite of A but, in general, $A + (-A) \neq 0$ i.e. the opposite of A is not the inverse of A in Minkowski addition (unless $A = \{a\}$ is a singleton). In order to overcome this situation, Hukuhara [10] defined the H-difference: $A \ominus B = C \Longleftrightarrow A = B + C$. It has the property that $A \ominus A = \{0\}$, but the inconvenient that it does not always exist, a necessary condition for $A \ominus B$ to exist is that A contains a translation $\{c\} + B$ of B. So the generalization of Hukuhara difference (gH-difference) [21] was given to solve that inconvenience:

$$A \ominus_{gH} B = C \Leftrightarrow \begin{cases} (a) \ A = B + C & \text{if } \mu(B) \leq \mu(A) \\ (b) \ B = A + (-1)C & \text{if } \mu(B) > \mu(A), \end{cases} \qquad (2)$$

where $\mu(A)$ denotes the length of an interval A, i.e., $\mu(A) = \overline{a} - \underline{a}$. The gH-difference for two intervals always exists, and it can be calculated (Stefanini et al. 2009) [22]: $A \ominus_{gH} B = [\min\{\underline{a} - \underline{b}, \overline{a} - \overline{b}\}, \max\{\underline{a} - \underline{b}, \overline{a} - \overline{b}\}] = [\underline{a} - \underline{b} \vee \overline{a} - \overline{b}]$. So we use the Standard Interval Arithmetic (SIA) with the gH-difference (SIA generalized arithmetic).

We write $A = [\alpha \vee \beta]$ if α and β are the end-points of the interval $A \in I(\mathbb{R})$, but $\alpha \leq \beta$ is not necessarily satisfied.

Let us consider the order relation in $I(\mathbb{R})$ given by Ishibuchi et al. (1990) [11]. Given $A = [\underline{a}, \overline{a}]$ and $B = [\underline{b}, \overline{b}]$ two closed intervals in $\mathbb{R}$, we write,

i) $A \preceq B \Leftrightarrow \underline{a} \leq \underline{b}$ and $\overline{a} \leq \overline{b}$,
ii) $A \prec B \Leftrightarrow A \preceq B$ and $A \neq B$, i.e. $\underline{a} \leq \underline{b}$ and $\overline{a} \leq \overline{b}$, with a strict inequality,
iii) $A \prec B \Leftrightarrow \underline{a} < \underline{b}$ and $\overline{a} < \overline{b}$.

It is clear that $A \prec B \Rightarrow A \preceq B \Rightarrow A \preceq B$.

Given $n \in \mathbb{N}$, an application $F : S \subseteq \mathbb{R}^n \to I(\mathbb{R})$ such that $F(x) = [\underline{f}(x), \overline{f}(x)]$ is called an interval-valued function of several variables, where $\underline{f}, \overline{f} : S \to \mathbb{R}$ are real-valued functions, such that $\underline{f}(x) \leq \overline{f}(x)$, for all $x \in S$, and $\underline{f}$ and $\overline{f}$ are its endpoints functions. If $n = 1$, then F is called an interval-valued function of a real variable.

Based on the limit concept of set-valued function (Aubin et al. (1984)) [3], and on the gH-difference given by Stefanini (2008) [21], the following differentiability concept for interval-valued functions was introduced.

Definition 1. *(Stefanini et al. 2009) [22] Let $S \subseteq \mathbb{R}$ be an open and nonempty set and let $F : S \to I(\mathbb{R})$ be an interval-valued function, then the generalized Hukuhara derivative (gH-derivative, for short) of F at $x^* \in S$ is defined by*

$$F'_{gH}(x^*) = \lim_{h \to 0} \frac{F(x^* + h) \ominus_{gH} F(x^*)}{h}. \qquad (3)$$

If $F'_{gH}(x^*) \in I(\mathbb{R})$ satisfying (3) exists, we say that F is generalized Hukuhara differentiable (gH-differentiable, for short) at x^*.

The relationships between the $gH-$differentiability of an interval-valued function $F(x) = [\underline{f}(x), \overline{f}(x)]$ and the differentiability of its endpoint functions, $\underline{f}(x)$ and $\overline{f}(x)$, have been completely studied by Qiu(2021) [19].

Theorem 1. *[5, 19] Let S be an open and nonempty set $\mathbb{R}, x^* \in S$ and $F : S \to I(\mathbb{R})$ be an interval-valued function $(F(x) = [\underline{f}(x), \overline{f}(x)])$ continuous in $(x^* - \delta, x^* + \delta)$ for some $\delta > 0$. Then F is gH-differentiable at x^* if and only if one of the following cases holds:*

a) $\underline{f}$ *y* $\overline{f}$ *are differentiable at x^* and*

$$F'_{gH}(x^*) = [min\{(\underline{f})'(x^*), (\overline{f})'(x^*)\}, max\{(\underline{f})'(x^*), (\overline{f})'(x^*)\}]$$

b) *The lateral derivatives $(\underline{f})'_-(x^*), (\underline{f})'_+(x^*), (\overline{f})'_-(x^*)$ and $(\overline{f})'_+(x^*)$ exist and verify that $(\underline{f})'_-(x^*) = (\overline{f})'_+(x^*)$ y $(\underline{f})'_+(x^*) = (\overline{f})'_-(x^*)$. Moreover,*

$$F'_{gH}(x^*) = [min\{(\underline{f})'_-(x^*), (\overline{f})'_-(x^*)\}, max\{(\underline{f})'_-(x^*), (\overline{f})'_-(x^*)\}]$$

$$= [min\{(\underline{f})'_+(x^*), (\overline{f})'_+(x^*)\}, max\{(\underline{f})'_+(x^*), (\overline{f})'_+(x^*)\}]$$

The gH-difference coincides to other ones defined by Markov (1977) [13] and Chalco-Cano et al. (2011) [5]. Associated to before mentioned differences other notions of differentiability have been defined by Markov (1979) [14] and Chalco-Cano et al. (2011) [5], among others, but it has been demonstrated that they are equivalent to the gH-differentiability or more restrictive than it. So it can be considered that the gH-differentiability is the most general notion of differentiability for interval-valued functions as it has been shown in the literature [5–7,22].

3   Differentiability for Interval-Valued and Fuzzy Functions: New Necessary and Sufficient Conditions

Let us begin studying the notion of differentiability and its characterization for an interval-valued function $F : S \subseteq \mathbb{R} \to I(\mathbb{R})$ with S and open and nonempty set.

Markov (1979) [14] establishes a "difference" on interval spaces and based on it, introduces an interval version of the Gâteaux differentiability and demonstrates that calculus for interval-valued functions of a real variable can be developed. Specifically, Markov states that a necessary and sufficient conditions for the gH-differentiability of F at x^* is the existence of an interval $A \in I(\mathbb{R})$ and an interval-valued function $P : (-\epsilon, \epsilon) \to I(\mathbb{R})$ with $\lim_{h \to 0} P(h) = [0, 0]$, such that

$$F(x^* + h) \ominus_{gH} F(x^*) = hA + hP(h). \tag{4}$$

However, this condition, in general, is not necessary as it is shown in the following example, since the intervals space does not have a vector structure:

Example 1. [18] Let $F : (-1, 1) \to I(\mathbb{R})$ be the interval-valued function given by $F(x) = (1 - x^2)[1, 2]$. Using Theorem 1 a), F is gH–differentiable with $F'_{gH}(x) = -2x[1, 2]$. Since

$$F(x + h) \ominus_{gH} F(x) = [min\{-h^2 - 2xh, 2(-h^2 - 2xh)\}, max\{-h^2 - 2xh, 2(-h^2 - 2xh)\}]$$

for all $x \in (-1, 1)$ and $h \in \mathbb{R}$ such that $x + h \in (-1, 1)$, then given $x < 0$, there exists $\epsilon_1 > 0$ such that $h + 2x < 0$ for all $h \in (0, \epsilon_1)$, and consequently,

$$F(x + h) \ominus_{gH} F(x) = [-h^2 - 2xh, 2(-h^2 - 2xh)].$$

However, it does not exist any interval-valued function $P : B(-\epsilon, \epsilon) \to I(\mathbb{R})$, $P(h) = [\underline{p}(h), \overline{p}(h)]$ for all $h \in (-\epsilon, \epsilon)$, such that

$$[-h^2 - 2xh, -2(-h^2 - 2xh)] = h(-2x)[1, 2] + h[\underline{p}(h), \overline{p}(h)]. \tag{5}$$

Using a reasoning by contradiction, and setting $\tilde{\epsilon} = \min\{\epsilon, \epsilon_1\}$ and given $h \in (0, \tilde{\epsilon})$, it follows that $\underline{p}(h) = -h$ and $\overline{p}(h) = -2h$, that is, $\overline{p}(h) < \underline{p}(h)$, which contradicts the fact that P is an interval-valued function. Therefore, F is gH-differentiable but it does not exist an interval $A \in I(\mathbb{R})$ and an interval-valued function $P : (-\epsilon, \epsilon) \to I(\mathbb{R})$ such that (4) holds.

The right necessary and sufficient condition for gH-differentiability is given by Osuna-Gómez et al. (2022) in the following result:

Theorem 2. *[18] Let $S \subseteq \mathbb{R}$ be an open and nonempty set. An interval-valued function $F : S \to I(\mathbb{R})$ is gH-differentiable at $x^* \in S$ if and only if there exist an interval $A \in I(\mathbb{R})$ and an interval-valued function $P : (-\epsilon, \epsilon) \to I(\mathbb{R})$ with $\lim_{h \to 0} P(h) = [0, 0]$, such that*

$$(F(x^* + h) \ominus_{gH} F(x^*)) \ominus_{gH} hA = hP(h). \tag{6}$$

Remark 1. The gH-differentiability condition given in Theorem 2 is an interval version of the Fréchet differentiability. Moreover, Theorem 2 shows that the gH-differentiability concept given in Markov (1979) and Stefanini et al. (2009), which is an interval version of Gatêax differentiability, are equivalent to an interval version of the Fréchet differentiability for interval-valued functions of a real variable.

Remark 2. Let us remember that is classical differential calculus theory, where S is an open set and V is a normed vector space, a function $f : S \subseteq \mathbb{R} \to V$ is differentiable at $x^* \in S$ if and only if there exist a linear function $L_{x^*} : \mathbb{R} \to V$ given by $L_{x^*}(h) = f'(x^*)h$ and a function $p : (-\epsilon, \epsilon) \to V$ with $\lim_{h \to 0} p(h) = 0$, such that $f(x^* + h) - f(x^*) = L_{x^*}(h) + hp(h)$ for all $h \in \mathbb{R}$ with $x^* + h \in S$.

So making a comparison with the gH-differentiability for intervals space, and from the necessary and sufficient condition for gH-differentiability (Theorem 2), a similar result can be got.

Theorem 3. *[18] Given $F : S \to I(\mathbb{R})$, F is gH-differentiable at $x^* \in S$ if there exist the interval valued function $T_{x^*} : \mathbb{R} \to I(\mathbb{R})$ given by $T_{x^*}(h) = hF'_{gH}(x^*)$ and an interval valued function $P : (-\epsilon, \epsilon) \to I(\mathbb{R})$ with $\lim_{h \to 0} P(h) = [0, 0]$ such that $(F(x_0 + h) \ominus_{gH} F(x_0)) \ominus_{gH} T_{x^*}(h) = hP(h)$.*

However, the interval-valued function $T_{x^*}(h)$, satisfying Theorem 3, may not be linear since $I(\mathbb{R})$ it is not a vector space. It is easy to prove that $T_{x^*}(h) = hF'_{gH}(x^*)$ is a quasilinear interval-valued function in the sense pointed out by Assev (1986) [2] and Rojas-Medar et al. (2005) [20] (see [18] for more details).

Now we recall the $gH-$ differentiability concepts for interval-valued functions of several variables that were introduced in the literature, and present a short discussion about the shortcomings generated by such concepts. Moreover, we recall the new $gH-$differentiability concept which overcomes the shortcomings above mentioned [18] and that is equivalent to the $gH-$differentiability one for interval-valued functions of several variables given by Stefanini et al. (2019) [24].

In Ahmad et al. (2016) [1], Chalco-Cano et al. (2013) [7] and Luhandjula et al. (2014) [12], the following interval-valued $gH-$differentiability definitions for interval-valued-functions of several variables are considered.

Definition 2. *Let F be an interval-valued function defined on an open and non-empty set $S \subseteq \mathbb{R}^n$ and let $x^* = (x_1^*, \ldots, x_n^*) \in S$ be fixed. Given the interval-valued function $H_i : \mathbb{R} \to I(\mathbb{R})$ defined by $H_i(x_i) = F(x_1^*, \ldots, x_{i-1}^*, x_i, x_{i+1}^*, \ldots, x_n^*)$, if H_i is gH-differentiable at x_i^*, then we say that F has the ith partial gH-derivative at x^* that is defined and denoted by*

$$\frac{\partial F}{\partial x_i}(x^*) = H_i'(x_i^*) \in I(\mathbb{R}).$$

If there exists $\frac{\partial F}{\partial x_i}(x^*)$ for all $i \in \{1, \ldots, n\}$, then the $n-$tuple $\left(\frac{\partial F}{\partial x_1}(x^*), \ldots \frac{\partial F}{\partial x_n}(x^*) \right)$ of intervals is called the gradient of F and it is denoted by $\nabla_{gH} F(x^*)$.

Definition 3. *Given $S \subseteq \mathbb{R}^n$ an open and nonempty set, let $F : S \to I(\mathbb{R})$ be an interval-valued function and let $x^* \in S$ be fixed. F is said to be gH-differentiable at x^* if there exist all the partial gH-derivatives $\frac{\partial F}{\partial x_1}(x), \ldots, \frac{\partial F}{\partial x_n}(x)$ on some neighborhood of x^* and are continuous at x^*.*

Remark 3. Definition 3 says that, for n $= 1$, an interval valued-function $F : S \subseteq \mathbb{R} \to I(\mathbb{R})$ is $gH-$differentiable at $x_0 \in S$ if and only if there exist $F'_{gH}(x)$ in a neighborhood of x_0 and F'_{gH} is continuous at x_0. Therefore, Definition 3 does not coincide with Definition 1. Moreover, if F is a real-valued function, then Definition 3 is more restrictive than the classical real-valued differentiability concept.

Based on Theorem 2, Remark 2, and on the fact that a real-valued function $f : S \to \mathbb{R}$, defined on an open set $S \subseteq \mathbb{R}^n$, is differentiable at $x^* \in S$ if there exists a continuous and linear real-valued function $L_{x^*} : \mathbb{R}^n \to \mathbb{R}$ and a function $p : B(\mathbf{0}, \epsilon) \to \mathbb{R}$, where $\mathbf{0} = (0, \ldots, 0) \in \mathbb{R}^n$ and $B(\mathbf{0}, \epsilon) := \{x \in \mathbb{R}^n : \|x\| < \epsilon\}$, with $\lim_{v \to \mathbf{0}} p(v) = 0$ such that $f(x^* + v) - f(x^*) = L_{x^*}(v) + \|v\|p(v)$, the $gH-$differentiability definition for interval-valued functions of several real variables presented by Osuna-Gómez et al. (2022) that improves the previous ones is:

Definition 4. *[18] Given $\boldsymbol{0} = (0,\ldots,0) \in \mathbb{R}^n$ and $S \subseteq \mathbb{R}^n$ an open and nonempty set, let $F : S \to I(\mathbb{R})$ be an interval-valued function. We say that F is gH-differentiable at $x^* \in S$ if there exist a continuous and quasilinear interval-valued function $T_{x^*} : \mathbb{R}^n \to I(\mathbb{R})$ and an interval-valued function $P : B(\boldsymbol{0}, \epsilon) \subseteq \mathbb{R}^n \to I(\mathbb{R})$ with $\lim\limits_{v \to \boldsymbol{0}} P(v) = [0,0]$ such that*

$$(F(x^* + v) \ominus_{gH} F(x^*)) \ominus_{gH} T_{x^*}(v) = \|v\| P(v), \tag{7}$$

for all $v \in B(\boldsymbol{0}, \epsilon) := \{x \in \mathbb{R}^n : \|x\| < \epsilon\}$ with $(x^* + v) \in S$, and in this case, $T_{x^*}(v)$ is called the $gH-$derivative of F at x^*. If F is $gH-$differentiable at all $x \in S$, then F is said to be $gH-$differentiable.

The necessary and sufficient condition for gH-differentiability for an interval-valued function with several variables is given too:

Theorem 4. *[18] Given $\boldsymbol{0} = (0,\ldots,0) \in \mathbb{R}^n$ and $S \subseteq \mathbb{R}^n$ an open and nonempty set, let $F : S \to I(\mathbb{R})$ be an interval-valued function. Then F is gH-differentiable at $x^* \in S$ if and only if*

$$\lim_{v \to \boldsymbol{0}} \frac{(F(x^* + v) \ominus_{gH} F(x^*)) \ominus_{gH} T_{x^*}(v)}{\|v\|} = [0,0], \tag{8}$$

where $T_{x^*} : \mathbb{R}^n \to I(\mathbb{R})$ is a continuous and quasilinear interval-valued function that satisfies (7).

When $n = 1$, Definition 4 coincides with Definition 1 (see Stefanini et al. 2009).

On the other hand, based on the representation of an interval using its midpoint and its (semi)width, Stefanini et al. (2019) [24] presented a definition for gH-differentiability and a necessary and sufficient condition for it, respectively. But in Osuna-Gómez et al. (2022) it has been demonstrated that Definition 6 in [24] and Definition 4 are the same. Moreover to know exactly the continuous and quasilinear interval-valued function T_{x^*} given in Definition 4 we can use the formula given in Definition 6 in [24], that is consistent with the necessary and sufficient conditions for gH-differentiability (Theorem 4) even if $n = 1$ (Theorem 2).

4   Notion of gH-Differentiability for Fuzzy Functions with Several Real Variables

As an application of the study presented on gH-differentiability for interval-valued functions and based on the relation between interval and fuzzy environments, we recall now the notion of gH-differentiability for fuzzy functions with several real variables. Let us recall some basic notions about the fuzzy environment in order to understand the extension to fuzzy context.

A fuzzy set on $\mathbb{R}^n$ is a mapping defined as $u : \mathbb{R}^n \to [0,1]$. The α-level set of a fuzzy set, $0 \le \alpha \le 1$, is defined as

$$[u]^\alpha = \begin{cases} \{x \in \mathbb{R}^n | u(x) \ge \alpha\} & \text{if } \alpha \in (0,1], \\ cl(supp\ u) & \text{if } \alpha = 0, \end{cases}$$

where $cl(supp\ u)$ denotes the closure of the support of u, $supp(u) = \{x \in \mathbb{R}^n | u(x) > 0\}$.

Definition 5. *A fuzzy interval is a fuzzy set u on $\mathbb{R}$ with the following properties:*

1. u is normal, that is, there exists $x_0 \in \mathbb{R}$ such that $u(x_0) = 1$;
2. u is an upper semi-continuous function;
3. $u(\lambda x + (1 - \lambda)y) \ge min\{u(x), u(y)\}$, $x, y \in \mathbb{R}$, $\lambda \in [0,1]$;
4. $[u]^0$ is compact.

If there exist an unique $x_0 \in \mathbb{R}$ such that $u(x_0) = 1$, u is called a fuzzy number. Let $\mathcal{F}_C$ be the set of all fuzzy intervals on $\mathbb{R}$.

Obviously, if $u \in \mathcal{F}_C$, then $[u]^\alpha \in \mathbb{I}(\mathbb{R})$ for all $\alpha \in [0,1]$ and thus the α-level sets of a fuzzy interval are given by $[u]^\alpha = [\underline{u}_\alpha, \overline{u}_\alpha]$, $\underline{u}_\alpha, \overline{u}_\alpha \in \mathbb{R}$ for all $\alpha \in [0,1]$.

Let us consider $u, v \in \mathcal{F}_C$, represented by $[\underline{u}_\alpha, \overline{u}_\alpha]$ and $[\underline{v}_\alpha, \overline{v}_\alpha]$ respectively, and for any real number λ, we define the following operations:

$$(u + v)(x) = \sup_{y+z=x} min\{u(y), v(z)\}, \ (\lambda u)(x) = \begin{cases} u\left(\frac{x}{\lambda}\right), \text{ if } \lambda \ne 0, \\ 0, \quad\quad \text{ if } \lambda = 0, \end{cases}$$

$$u \ominus_{gH} v = w \Leftrightarrow \begin{cases} (i) \ u = v + w, \\ \text{or } (ii) \ v = u + (-1)w. \end{cases}$$

It is known that, for every $\alpha \in [0,1]$,

$$[u + v]^\alpha = [(\underline{u + v})_\alpha, (\overline{u + v})_\alpha] = [\underline{u}_\alpha + \underline{v}_\alpha, \ \overline{u}_\alpha + \overline{v}_\alpha], \tag{9}$$

$$[\lambda u]^\alpha = [(\underline{\lambda u})_\alpha, (\overline{\lambda u})_\alpha] = \lambda[u]^\alpha = \lambda[\underline{u}_\alpha, \overline{u}_\alpha] = [min\{\lambda\underline{u}_\alpha, \lambda\overline{u}_\alpha\}, max\{\lambda\underline{u}_\alpha, \lambda\overline{u}_\alpha\}], \tag{10}$$

and if $u \ominus_{gH} v$ exists then, in terms of α-level sets, we can deduce that (see [22, 23]):

$$[u \ominus_{gH} v]^\alpha = [u]^\alpha \ominus_{gH} [v]^\alpha = [min\{\underline{u}_\alpha - \underline{v}_\alpha, \overline{u}_\alpha - \overline{v}_\alpha\}, max\{\underline{u}_\alpha - \underline{v}_\alpha, \overline{u}_\alpha - \overline{v}_\alpha\}]. \tag{11}$$

We recall the usual order relations between fuzzy intervals [16]:

Definition 6. *For $u, v \in \mathcal{F}_C$, it is said that*

(1) $u \preceq v$ if $[u]^\alpha \preceq [v]^\alpha$ for every $\alpha \in [0,1]$.
(2) $u \preceq v$ if $u \preceq v$ and $u \ne v$, i. e. $[u]^\alpha \preceq [v]^\alpha$ for every $\alpha \in [0,1]$, and $\exists \alpha_0 \in [0,1]$, such that $[u]^{\alpha_0} \prec [v]^{\alpha_0}$.
(3) $u \prec v$ if $u \preceq v$ and $\exists \alpha_0 \in [0,1]$, such that $[u]^{\alpha_0} \prec [v]^{\alpha_0}$.

Note that $\preceq$ is a partial order relation on $\mathcal{F}_C$. Hence, $v \succeq u$ can be written instead of $u \preceq v$. We observe that if $u \prec v$ then $u \preceq v$ and therefore $u \preceq v$.

Let us consider $\tilde{f} : S \subseteq \mathbb{R}^n \to \mathcal{F}_C$ a fuzzy function or fuzzy mapping where S is an open and nonempty subset of $\mathbb{R}^n$. We associate with $\tilde{f}$ the family of interval-valued functions $f_\alpha : S \to I(\mathbb{R})$ where, for each $\alpha \in [0,1]$, $f_\alpha(x) = [\tilde{f}(x)]^\alpha = \left[\underline{f}_\alpha(x), \overline{f}_\alpha(x)\right] = [\underline{f}(x; \alpha), \overline{f}(x; \alpha,)]$, are the α-level sets of $\tilde{f}$.

As a particular case of fuzzy quasilinear operators [20], a fuzzy function is quasilinear if $\forall \lambda \in \mathbb{R}, x, y \in \mathbb{R}^n$

1. $\tilde{f}(\lambda x) = \lambda \tilde{f}(x)$.
2. $\tilde{f}(x + y) \preceq \tilde{f}(x) + \tilde{f}(y)$.

In Bede et al. (2013) [4] we find the notions of gH-differentiability and level-wise gH-differentiability for fuzzy functions of a single variable. The gH-differentiability for fuzzy functions on $\mathbb{R}$ is a more general concept than the H-differentiability and G-differentiability, but less general than level-wise gH-differentiability, that is based on the gH-differentiability of every interval-valued function f_α.

Osuna-Gómez et al. (2022) defined a level-wise gH-differentiable fuzzy function when $n \geq 1$, using the results obtained for interval-valued functions.

Definition 7. *[18] Let us consider $\tilde{f} : S \subseteq \mathbb{R}^n \to \mathcal{F}_C$, $f_\alpha(x) = \left[\underline{f}_\alpha(x), \overline{f}_\alpha(x)\right]$ for each $\alpha \in [0,1]$ and let $x^* \in S$ such that $x^* + v \in S$ for all $v \in \mathbb{R}^n$ with $||v|| < \epsilon$ ($\epsilon > 0$). We say that $\tilde{f}$ is level-wise gH-differentiable at $x^* \in S$ if and only if for each $\alpha \in [0,1]$, there exist two interval-valued functions, $T_{x^*}^\alpha$ continuous and quasilinear and P^α with $\lim_{v \to 0} P^\alpha(v) = [0,0]$ such that*

$$\left(f_\alpha(x^* + v) \ominus_{gH} f_\alpha(x^*)\right) \ominus_{gH} T_{x^*}^\alpha(v) = ||v|| P^\alpha(v)$$

The family of interval-valued functions $\{T_{x^*}^\alpha\}_{\alpha \in [0,1]}$ is called the level-wise gH-derivative of $\tilde{f}$ at x^*.

When $S \subseteq \mathbb{R}$ ($n = 1$), from Theorem 2, this definition coincides with Definition 23 in Bede et al. (2013) [4]. In the general case, $S \subseteq \mathbb{R}^n$ with $n > 1$ from the equivalence between definitions of gH-differentiability given in [18], it coincides with Definition 9-A in Stefanini et al. (2019) [24].

Example 2. [18] Let us consider the fuzzy fynction $\tilde{f} : S \subseteq \mathbb{R}^2 \to \mathcal{F}_C$, defined by

$$\tilde{f}(x_1, x_2) = (1, 1, 1) \cdot x_1^2 + (0, 0, 1) \cdot x_2^2$$

whose α-level sets for all $\alpha \in [0,1]$ are $\left[\tilde{f}(x_1, x_2)\right]^\alpha = [\underline{f}(x; \alpha), \overline{f}(x; \alpha)] = [x_1^2, x_1^2 + (1 - \alpha)x_2^2]$.

The gH-derivatives for the α-level sets interval-valued functions are:

$$[T_{x^*}(v)]^\alpha = [2x_1^* v_1 \vee 2x_1^* v_1 + 2(1 - \alpha)x_2^* v_2]$$

For each $\alpha \in [0,1]$, fixed x^* and $v \in \mathbb{R}^n$ the family of interval-valued functions given by $\{[T_x^*(v)]^\alpha\}_{\alpha \in [0,1]}$ define a fuzzy number.

So the fuzzy function $\tilde{f}$ is gH-differentiable in $\mathbb{R}^2$ according to Definition 9-B in Stefanini et al. (2019).

Let us notice that the family of level-wise gH-derivatives $\{T_{x^*}^\alpha\}_{\alpha \in [0,1]}$ does not have to determine a fuzzy number. Therefore although it is a more restrictive notion it makes sense to define the fuzzy gH-differentiability directly, without the use of the interval-valued functions associated. So Osuna-Gómez et al. (2022) defined them firstly for the case $n = 1$ and then $n > 1$, directly, as Bede et al. (2013) did in [4].

Theorem 5. *[18] Let $\tilde{f} : S \subseteq \mathbb{R} \to \mathcal{F}_C$ be a fuzzy function and $v \in S$ such that $x^* + v \in S$. Then there exists $\tilde{f}'(x^*) \in \mathcal{F}_C$ with*

$$\tilde{f}'(x^*) = \lim_{v \to 0} \frac{\tilde{f}(x^* + v) \ominus_{gH} \tilde{f}(x^*)}{v} \tag{12}$$

if and only if there exists $\tilde{u} \in \mathcal{F}_C$ and $\tilde{P} : (-\epsilon, \epsilon) \to \mathcal{F}_C$ with $\lim_{v \to 0} \tilde{P}(v) = \tilde{0}$ such that

$$(\tilde{f}(x^* + v) \ominus_{gH} \tilde{f}(x^*)) \ominus_{gH} v\tilde{u}(x^*) = v\tilde{P}(v). \tag{13}$$

Definition 8. *[18] Given $\mathbf{0} = (0, \ldots, 0) \in \mathbb{R}^n$ and $S \subseteq \mathbb{R}^n$ an open and nonempty set, let $\tilde{f} : S \to \mathcal{F}_C$ be a fuzzy function. We say that $\tilde{f}$ is gH-differentiable at $x^* \in S$ if there exist a continuous and quasilinear fuzzy function $\tilde{T}_{x^*} : S \subseteq \mathbb{R}^n \to \mathcal{F}_C$ and a fuzzy function $\tilde{P} : B(\mathbf{0}, \epsilon) \subseteq \mathbb{R}^n \to \mathcal{F}_C$ with $\lim_{v \to \mathbf{0}} \tilde{P}(v) = \tilde{0}$ such that*

$$(\tilde{f}(x^* + v) \ominus_{gH} \tilde{f}(x^*)) \ominus_{gH} \tilde{T}_{x^*}(v) = ||v||\tilde{P}(v), \tag{14}$$

for all $v \in B(\mathbf{0}, \epsilon) := \{x \in \mathbb{R}^n : ||x|| < \epsilon\}$, $\epsilon > 0$ with $(x^* + v) \in S$, and in this case, $\tilde{T}_{x^*}(v)$ is called the gH-derivative of $\tilde{f}$ at $x^* \in S$. If $\tilde{f}$ is gH-differentiable at all $x \in S$, then $\tilde{f}$ is said to be gH-differentiable.

This necessary and sufficient condition for fuzzy gH- differentiability coincides to Definition 20 given in [4] with $n = 1$ and Definition 8 can serve as the basis for further developments of fuzzy differentiability.

5   Optimality Conditions in Fuzzy Multiobjective Optimization

In order to define the optimum notion, some different techniques can be found in the literature, among them, defuzzification techniques, interval-optima and optimality notions by levels. Defuzzification techniques are used by Wu (2008) in [25, 26] and generally with the consequent loss of important information when substituting a fuzzy set for a crisp number. An approximation of a fuzzy set by a crisp interval, that is in certain sense, close to the former one is used by

Grzegorzewski 2002 in [8], and Luhandjula 2014 [12]. In particular, the Nearest Interval Approximation Operator (NIA), is among interval approximation operators, the one that minimizes a certain measure of the distance to the fuzzy number. But in 2021, Hernández-Jiménez et al. in [9] propose to use an optimality concept by levels, which means we will use the level sets that characterize the fuzzy set entirely to define the optimum. It has been demonstrated that this concept is more general than the aforementioned. Undoubtedly, the optimum notion should be determined by the decider's interest, so, in some cases, the crisp optima or interval-optima can be considered more satisfactory than the optimality notions by levels. However, by including the latter in the previous, the search mechanisms proposed in [9] are valid whatever the concept used.

Let us consider the following multiobjective fuzzy mathematical programming problem:

$$(P) \quad \text{Min} \ \left(\tilde{f}_1(x), ..., \tilde{f}_p(x) \right)$$

where $\tilde{f}_j : S \to \mathcal{F}_C$, $j = 1, ..., p$ are fuzzy functions defined on S, an open non-empty subset in $\mathbb{R}^n$, $n \geq 1$.

Definition 9. *[9] Let $\tilde{f} : S \to \mathcal{F}_C^p$ be a vector fuzzy function defined on $S \subseteq \mathbb{R}$. It is said that $x^* \in S$ is an efficient solution or Pareto solution if there exists no $x \in S$ such that $\tilde{f}_j(x) \preceq \tilde{f}_j(x^*)$, $\forall j = 1, ..., p$ and $\exists k$ such that $\tilde{f}_k(x) \prec \tilde{f}_k(x^*)$.*

The optimality notions by levels is a similar solution concept to the non-dominated solution than the one introduced by Pareto, and usually considered in real-valued multiobjective optimization. Really it coincides with the classic one when the functions are real-valued.

In order to search for the solutions of (P), with the necessary optimality conditions, we can exclude feasible solutions that are not optimums. Let us begin recalling the definition of a gH- differentiable fuzzy vector function given by Hernández-Jiménez et al. (2021) and the necessary optimality condition:

Definition 10. *[9] Given a fuzzy vector function $\tilde{f} = (\tilde{f}_1, ..., \tilde{f}_p) \in \mathcal{F}_C^p$, we say that $\tilde{f}$ is a vector gH-differentiable fuzzy function at $t_0 \in S$ if and only if $\tilde{f}_j$ is gH-differentiable at t_0, for all $j = 1, ..., p$.*

Theorem 6. *Let $\tilde{f} : S \to \mathcal{F}_C^p$ be a vector gH-differentiable fuzzy function at $x^* \in S$. If x^* is an efficient or Pareto solution for (P), then there exists a non-negative matrix $\Lambda \in \mathcal{M}^{p \times 2}$ such that $\Lambda \times \left[\tilde{f}'(x^*) \right]^0 = 0$.*

Remark 4. Identify possible candidates for Pareto solutions, is reduced to identify those feasible solutions whose 0 level set of the derivative contains the zero element. This coincides with the result for a unique objective function given by Osuna-Gómez et al. [17].

In the case $n > 1$ no necessary optimality conditions can be found in the literature for (P) with the most general notion of differentiability, so it is a future line of research.

6 Conclusions

In this paper a review on notions of differentiability in interval and fuzzy environment is presented and based on it the necessary optimality conditions that can be find in the literature are given. A future line of research is presented too in order to complete the study.

References

1. Ahmad, I., Singh, D., Dar Bilal, A.: Optimality conditions for invex interval valued nonlinear programming problems involving generalized H-derivative. Filomat **30**(8), 2121–2138 (2016). https://doi.org/10.2298/FIL1608121A
2. Assev, S.M.: Quasilinear operators and their application in the theory of multivalued mappings. Proc. Steklov Inst. Math. **167**, 23–52 (1986)
3. Aubin, J.-P., Cellina, A.: Differential Inclusions. Springer, Heidelberg (1984). https://doi.org/10.1007/978-3-642-69512-4
4. Bede, B., Stefanini, L.: Generalized differentiability of fuzzy-valued functions. Fuzzy Sets Syst. **230**, 119–141 (2013). https://doi.org/10.1016/j.fss.2012.10.003
5. Chalco-Cano, Y., Román-Flores, H., Jiménez-Gamero, M.D.: Generalized derivative and π−derivative for set-valued functions. Inf. Sci. **181**, 2177–2188 (2011)
6. Chalco-Cano, Y., Lodwick, W.A., Rufián-Lizana, A.: Optimality conditions of type KKT for optimization problems with interval-valued objective function via generalized derivative. Fuzzy Optim. Decis. Making **196**(1), 305–322 (2013)
7. Chalco-Cano, Y., Rufián-Lizana, A., Román-Flores, H., Jiménez-Gamero, M.D.: Calculus for interval-valued functions using generalized Hukuhara derivative and applications. Fuzzy Sets Syst. **219**, 49–67 (2013)
8. Grzegorzewski, P.: Nearest interval approximation of a fuzzy number. Fuzzy Sets Syst. **130**, 321–330 (2002)
9. Hernández-Jiménez, B., Ruiz-Garzón, G., Beato-Moreno, A., Osuna-Gómez, R.: A better aproach for solving a fuzzy multiobjective programming problem by level sets. Mathematics **9**, 992 (2021). https://doi.org/10.3390/math9090992
10. Hukuhara, M.: Integration des applications mesurables dont la valeur est un compact convexe. Funkcialaj Ekvacioj **10**, 205–223 (1967)
11. Ishibuchi, H., Tanaka, H.: Multiobjective programming in optimization of the interval objective function. Eur. J. Oper. Res. **48**, 219–225 (1990)
12. Luhandjula, M.K., Rangoaga, M.J.: An approach for solving a fuzzy multiobjetive programming problem. Eur. J. Oper. Res. **232**, 249–255 (2014)
13. Markov, S.: A non-standard subtraction of intervals. Serdica **3**, 359–370 (1977)
14. Markov, S.: Calculus for interval functions of a real variable. Computing **22**, 325–337 (1979)
15. Moore, R.E., Yang, C.T.: Interval Analysis I, Technical Report LMSD-285. Lockheed Aircraft Corporation, Missiles and Space Division, Sunnyvale (1959)
16. Osuna-Gómez, R., Chalco-Cano, Y., Rufián-Lizana, A., Hernández-Jiménez, B.: Necessary and sufficient conditions for fuzzy optimality problems. Fuzzy Sets Syst. **296**, 112–123 (2016). https://doi.org/10.1016/j.fss.2015.05.013
17. Osuna-Gómez, R., Hernández-Jiménez, B., Chalco-Cano, Y., Ruiz-Garzón, G.: Different optimum notions for fuzzy functions and optimality conditions associated. Fuzzy Optim. Decis. Making **17**(2), 177–193 (2017). https://doi.org/10.1007/s10700-017-9269-9

18. Osuna-Gómez, R., Costa, T.M., Chalco-Cano, Y., Hernández-Jiménez, B.: Quasi-linear approximation for interval-valued functions via generalized Hukuhara differentiability. Comp. Appl. Math. **41**, 149 (2022). https://doi.org/10.1007/s40314-021-01746-6

19. Qiu, D.: The generalized Hukuhara differentiability of interval-valued function is not fully equivalent to the one-sided differentiability of its endpoint functions. Fuzzy Sets Syst. **149**, 158–168 (2021)

20. Rojas-Medar, M.A., Jiménez-Gamero, M.D., Chalco-Cano, Y., Viera-Brandao, A.J.: Fuzzy quasilinear spaces and applications. Fuzzy Sets Syst. **152**(2), 173–190 (2005). https://doi.org/10.1016/j.fss.2004.09.011

21. Stefanini, L.: A generalization of Hukuhara difference for interval and fuzzy arithmetic. In: Dubois, D., Lubiano, M.A., Prade, H., Gil, M.A., Grzegorzewski, P., Hryniewicz, O. (Eds.), Soft Methods for Handling Variability and Imprecision. Advances in Soft Computing, vol. 48, Springer, Heidelberg (2008). https://doi.org/10.1007/978-3-540-85027-4_25

22. Stefanini, L., Bede, B.: Generalized Hukuhara differentiability of interval-valued functions and interval differential equations. Nonlin. Anal. **71**(34), 1311–1328 (2009). https://doi.org/10.1016/j.na.2008.12.005

23. Stefanini, L.: A generalization of Hukuhara difference and division for interval and fuzzy arithmetic. Fuzzy Sets Syst. **161**(11), 1564–1584 (2010). https://doi.org/10.1016/j.fss.2009.06.009

24. Stefanini, L., Arana-Jiménez, M.: Karush-Kuhn-Tucker conditions for interval and fuzzy optimization in several variables under total and directional generalized differentiability. Fuzzy Sets Syst. **362**, 1–34 (2019)

25. Wu, H.C.: Solutions of fuzzy multiobjective programming problems based on the concept of scalarization. J. Optim. Theory Appl. **139**, 361–378 (2008)

26. Wu, H.C.: Using the technique of scalarization to solve the multiobjective programming problems with fuzzy coefficients. Math. Comput. Model. **48**, 232–248 (2008)

Selected Dynamical Properties of Fuzzy Dynamical Systems

Jiří Kupka(✉)

Institute for Research and Applications of Fuzzy Modeling,
University of Ostrava, 30. Dubna 22, 701 03 Ostrava, Czechia
Jiri.Kupka@osu.cz
https://ifm.osu.cz/

Abstract. This paper summarizes knowledge on selected properties describing relations between various discrete dynamical systems. Mainly, those between the original (crisp) discrete dynamical system (X, φ) and its natural extensions provided by (either the standard or a more general form of) Zadeh's extension $(\mathcal{F}(X), z_{\varphi,g})$. Among discussed dynamical properties are the topological entropy and various properties related to famous Devaney chaos.

Keywords: Discrete dynamical system · Zadeh's extension ·
Dynamical properties · Devaney chaos · Topological entropy

1 Introduction

A discrete dynamical system is usually considered as a pair (X, φ), where X is a (usually compact) metric space and $\varphi : X \to X$ is continuous. The theory of such systems is very rich and among the most common open problems the question of dynamical complexity of the dynamical system (X, φ) belongs.

Since the seventies, a very natural question leading to a very complex (and likely never-ending) problem was raised by Bauer and Sigmund in [4] and then studied by many mathematicians. This problem led to investigating mutual properties between a given dynamical system (X, φ) and some natural extensions of (X, φ). Bauer and Sigmund considered the extension to the space $\mathcal{K}(X)$ of nonempty compact subsets of X, and to the space $\mathcal{M}(X)$ of invariant probabilistic measures on X, but the question can be considered in a bit wider setting – for instance for fuzzy dynamical systems.

Fuzzy dynamical systems were elaborated in a nice pioneering paper by P. Kloeden [14], in which such systems were systematically defined with the help of the standard Zadeh's extension. Fuzzy dynamical systems are not an unnatural concept as they naturally allow to study time evolution of an input value represented as a fuzzy set. A bit later it turned out that the standard Zadeh's extension is not always the best from the applied point of view and some generalizations (like the notion of interactivity [12] or the notion of Γ-fuzzification

© Springer Nature Switzerland AG 2022
D. Ciucci et al. (Eds.): IPMU 2022, CCIS 1601, pp. 258–269, 2022.
https://doi.org/10.1007/978-3-031-08971-8_22

[11] appeared) were developed. The latter notion was then transformed into the notion of a g-fuzzification in [16] with an appropriate mathematical structure. With the help of g-fuzzifications one can consider a fuzzy dynamical system $(\mathcal{F}(X), z_{\varphi,g})$ defined on the space $\mathcal{F}(X)$ of nonempty upper-semicontinuous fuzzy sets with compact support.

It is now natural to ask the following problem:

Question 1. What are the relations between a given discrete dynamical system (X, φ) and its generalized fuzzy extension $(\mathcal{F}(X), z_{\varphi,g})$?

In this paper we would like to provide some partial answers to that problem. Due to the page limit, we cannot fully explain the importance and motivation for various dynamical properties. While the question above was addressed in many papers primarily for the common Zadeh's extension (i.e. for g being equal to the identity map $id_{[0,1]}$ on [0,1]) – and dynamical properties like the topological entropy [7,8], several versions of Devaney chaos [17], some transitive and mixing properties [18], Martelli chaos [20], sensitivity [23], chain properties and Li-Yorke sensitivity [24], many standard dynamical properties including equicontinuity, rigidity and proximality [24] were studied among others – the notion of g-fuzzification was mentioned only occasionally (e.g. [20] or [25]). The purpose of this paper is to provide a short survey of results obtained for Zadeh's extension, with some additional remarks commenting the generalized version of Zadeh's extension.

The structure of this manuscript is very natural. In the next section we introduce the notions, definitions and facts used later. Then in Sect. 3 we start commenting results on the size of the topological entropy, and the properties related to famous Devaney definition of chaos such as density of periodic points or various transitivity notions are discussed in Sect. 4.

2 Definitions and Notation

Within this paper we assume that X denotes a (locally compact or compact) metric space (X, d_X) equipped with the metric d_X, $\mathbf{R}$ denotes the family of real numbers, and $I = [0, 1] \subseteq \mathbf{R}$. The family of continuous maps $\varphi : X \to X$ is denoted by $C(X)$. Below, $\mathbf{N}$ and $\mathbf{Z}$ denote the family of natural numbers and integers, respectively.

For a fuzzy set $A : X \to I$ and $\alpha \in I$ we consider its α-cut $[A]_\alpha = \{x \in X \mid A(x) \geq \alpha\}$, its support $supp(A) = \overline{\{x \in X \mid A(x) > 0\}}$, where $\overline{A}$ stands for the topological closure of $A \subseteq X$.

2.1 Spaces of Fuzzy Sets

Below we consider several metric spaces of objects induced from a (compact) metric space (X, d_X). A space $\mathcal{K}(X)$ denotes a family of all nonempty compact subsets of the space X. The space $\mathcal{K}(X)$ is equipped with the Hausdorff metric d_H, defined as, for $A, B \in \mathcal{K}(X)$,

$$d_H(A, B) = \inf\{\varepsilon > 0 \mid A \in U_\varepsilon(B) \text{ and } B \in U_\varepsilon(A)\},$$

where

$$U_\varepsilon(A) = \{x \in X \mid D(x, A) < \varepsilon\} \text{ for } D(x, A) = \inf_{y \in A} d_X(x, y).$$

Sometimes, by using $d_{H(X \times I)}$, we emphasize the space (i.e. $X \times I$) on which the Hausdorff metric is considered. In the case of $X \times I$, the Hausdorff metric $d_{H(X \times I)}$ is induced from the product metric of d_X and d_I. It is well-known that $(\mathcal{K}(X), d_H)$ is a metric space, which is compact, complete and separable provided X does have the same properties.

We are ready to define several spaces of fuzzy sets. By $\mathcal{F}(X)$ we consider a family of upper semicontinuous fuzzy sets $A : X \to I$ with compact supports. By $\mathcal{F}^1(X) \subseteq \mathcal{F}(X)$ we denote the family of *normal* fuzzy sets (i.e. $A(x) = 1$ for some $x \in X$), by $\mathcal{F}_0(X) \subseteq \mathcal{F}(X)$ we consider the family of nonempty fuzzy sets (i.e. $\mathcal{F}_0(X) = \mathcal{F}(X) \backslash \{\emptyset_X\}$, $\emptyset_X$ denoting a function (i.e. an *empty fuzzy set*) equal to 0 everywhere in X), and by $\mathcal{F}_1^1(X) \subseteq \mathcal{F}(X)$ we consider a family of *fuzzy numbers*, i.e. normal fuzzy sets for which every α-cut is nonempty and (topologically) connected.

In order to obtain some topological structures on $\mathcal{F}(X)$, $\mathcal{F}^1(X)$, $\mathcal{F}_0(X)$ and $\mathcal{F}_1^1(X)$ respectively, we need to introduce the most used metrics. For $A \in \mathcal{F}_0(X)$, we define two closed subsets defined by the undergraph of A, namely

$$end(A) = \{(x, y) \in X \times I \mid y \leq A(x)\} \text{ and } send(A) = end(A) \cap (supp(A) \times I).$$

Now we are ready to define metrics on spaces of fuzzy sets. Namely, for $A, B \in \mathcal{F}_0(X)$, we consider

$$d_E(A, B) = d_{H(X \times I)}(end(A), end(B)),$$

and

$$d_S(A, B) = d_{H(X \times I)}(send(A), send(B)).$$

Additionally, one can consider

$$d_\infty(A, B) = \sup_{\alpha \in (0, 1]} d_{H(X)}([A]_\alpha, [B]_\alpha).$$

For the metrics d_E, d_S and d_∞, one can consider metric topologies induced from them. A brief survey of those elementary notions as well as topological properties of these spaces can be found in [16] and references therein.

2.2   Induced Discrete Dynamical Systems

A pair (X, φ) denotes a *discrete dynamical system* if X is a (compact) metric space and $\varphi \in C(X)$ is continuous. For every discrete dynamical system

(X, φ) there are several natural extensions of this discrete dynamical system. The dynamical system (X, φ) is then called *crisp* or *non-fuzzy* (resp. *original*) discrete dynamical system.

Now, a *set-valued* (or *induced*) discrete dynamical system $(\mathcal{K}(X), s_\varphi)$ is naturally defined by $s_\varphi(L) = \varphi(L)$ for any $L \in \mathcal{K}(X)$. For a fuzzy set $A \in \mathcal{F}_0(X)$ and $g \in C(I)$, we can define its *g-fuzzification* (or *generalized fuzzification*) $z_{\varphi,g} : \mathcal{F}_0(X) \to \mathcal{F}_0(X)$ by

$$z_{\varphi,g}(A)(x) = \sup_{y \in \varphi^{-1}(x)} \{g(A(y))\}.$$

Clearly, $g = id_{[0,1]}$ gives the standard definition of Zadeh's extension. This expression naturally defines a *fuzzy (discrete) dynamical system* $(\mathcal{F}_0(X), z_{\varphi,g})$.

Naturally you will see that dynamical properties of g-fuzzifications depend on the properties of the map $g \in C(I)$. Therefore, we define the following classes of maps:

$D_m(I) := \{g : I \to I \,|\,$ the map g is a non-decreasing right-continuous map such that $g(0) = 0$, $g(1) = 1\}$.

Clearly, for every $g \in D_m(I)$, $z_{\varphi,g}$ *preserves the normality* of a fuzzy set $A \in \mathcal{F}^1(X)$. Also the following classes can be considered:

$C_m(I) = \{g \in D_m(I) \,|\, g$ is continuous$\}$, and

$C'_m(I) = \{g \in C_m(I) \,|\, g$ is strictly increasing at $0\}$.

Using of these classes depends on which metric (d_E, d_S or d_∞) is considered [16].

2.3 Elementary Notions from Topological Dynamics

In this subsection we want to introduce notions from topological dynamics used below. Thus, let (X, φ) denote a discrete dynamical system.

At the elementary level, dynamics in this dynamical system is given by so-called trajectories. For a given $x \in X$, a sequence $\{\varphi^n(x)\}_{n \in \mathbf{N}}$, defined inductively by $\varphi^1(x) = \varphi(x)$ and $\varphi^{n+1}(x) = \varphi(\varphi^n(x))$, for every $n \in \mathbf{N}$, is called a *trajectory* of the point x. An accumulation point $y \in X$ of the trajectory $\{\varphi^n(x)\}_{n \in \mathbf{N}}$ is called an *ω-limit point* of x (with respect to the map φ) – notation $y \in \omega_\varphi(x)$. A point x is called *periodic* if $\varphi^p(x) = x$ for some $p \in \mathbf{N}$. The number p is called a *period* of x and if $p = 1$ then x is called a *fixed* point. Naturally, all the notions above could be extended to trajectories of sets, fuzzy sets, etc.

A set $A \subseteq X$ is called *invariant* (more precisely φ-*invariant*) if $\varphi(A) \subseteq A$. The notion of invariance is needed for the definition of the topological entropy on spaces that are not compact.

We will also use some facts from symbolic dynamics. Namely, for $n \in \mathbf{N}$, $\Sigma_n = \{0, 1, 2, 3, \dots, n-1\}^{\mathbf{Z}}$, the symbol x_j denotes the j-th coordinate of $x \in \Sigma_n$. This means that every $x \in \Sigma_n$ can be written as $x = \dots x_{-2}x_{-1}x_0x_1x_2x_3 \dots$.

The metric δ_n on Σ_n is defined in the following way, for any two infinite sequences of symbols $x, y \in \Sigma_n$,

$$\delta_n(x, y) = \sum_{m \in \mathbf{Z}} \frac{|x_m - y_m|}{n^{|m|}}.$$

It is well known that the metric space (Σ_n, δ_n) is compact and separable. Among the mappings on Σ_n, so-called *shift* map σ_n is one of the best known. The map σ_n sends each coordinate x_i to x_{i-1}, i.e.

$$\sigma_n(\ldots x_{-1} x_0 x_1 x_2 x_3 \ldots) = \ldots x_0 x_1 x_2 x_3 x_4 \ldots.$$

2.4   Transitivity-Like Properties

For a given discrete dynamical system (X, φ), a map φ is called *transitive* if for every pair of nonempty open subsets $U, V \subseteq X$ there exists $n \in \mathbf{N}$ such that $\varphi^n(U) \cap V \neq \emptyset$. In this case we say that the space X *admits* a transitive map. It is well known (for a brief survey we refer to [15]) that there is a dichotomy for transitive maps. This means that they are either very regular (simple) or very non-regular (complex). It is also known that not all compact metric spaces (e.g. some infinite spaces with finitely many isolated points) admit a transitive map.

Further, the map φ is *totally transitive* if and only if φ^n is transitive for every $n \in \mathbf{N}$. The map φ is called *weakly mixing* if the product map $\varphi \times \varphi$ is transitive. The map φ is called *strongly mixing* (or shortly *mixing*) if, for every pair of nonempty open subsets $U, V \subseteq X$, there exists an $n \in \mathbf{N}$ such that $\varphi^k(U) \cap V \neq \emptyset$ for every $k \geq n$. Finally, the map φ is *topologically exact* (or simply *exact*) if for every nonempty subset $U \subseteq X$ there exists $n \in \mathbf{N}$ such that $\varphi^k(U) = X$ for every $k \geq n$.

Although the definitions above look simple, they usually lead to quite complicated behavior. On compact metric spaces, the relations among the properties above are the following:

exactness $\Rightarrow$ strong mixing $\Rightarrow$ weak mixing $\Rightarrow$ total transitivity $\Rightarrow$ transitivity.

2.5   Chaotic Properties

There are many chaotic properties which can be defined for discrete dynamical systems, and which differ from each other even for the simplest case of 1-dimensional (interval) maps ($\varphi \in C(I)$). Among the best known chaotic notions belong topological chaos (i.e. positive topological entropy (cf. the next subsection)), Li-Yorke chaos [21] and Devaney chaos [10]. For a brief survey of chaotic properties in one-dimensional dynamical systems we refer to [5].

Again, let a discrete dynamical system (X, φ) be given. A pair $x, y \in X$ is a *Li-Yorke pair* if

$$\limsup_{n \in \mathbf{N}} \{d_X(\varphi^n(x), \varphi^n(y))\} > 0$$

and

$$\liminf_{n \in \mathbf{N}} \{d_X(\varphi^n(x), \varphi^n(y))\} = 0.$$

We say that $S \subseteq X$ is *scrambled* if every pair of distinct points from S forms a Li-Yorke pair. Finally, we say that a given discrete dynamical system (X, φ) is *Li-Yorke chaotic* if there exists an uncountable *scrambled* set $S \subseteq X$.

The map φ *sensitively depends on initial conditions* if there exists a $\delta > 0$ such that for every $x \in X$ and every open neighborhood U of x there exists $y \in U$ such that $d_X(\varphi^k(x), \varphi^k(y)) > \delta$ for some $k \in \mathbf{N}$.

A map $\varphi \in \mathcal{C}(X)$ is *Devaney chaotic* [10] if the following conditions are satisfied:

(i) φ is transitive,
(ii) the set $P(\varphi)$ of periodic points of the map φ is (topologically) dense in X,
(iii) φ is sensitively dependent on initial conditions.

However, it was proved that the third condition is implied by the transitivity and the density of periodic points [3].

As we mentioned above, the transitivity is the weakest of several properties. And this fact led to several versions of Devaney chaos. Namely, the map φ is called *totally Devaney chaotic* if the transitivity (in the definition of Devaney chaos) is replaced by the total transitivity. Analogously, if the transitivity is replaced by the exactness, then φ is called *exactly Devaney chaotic*.

2.6 Topological Entropy

In this subsection we want to introduce an instrument commonly used in topological dynamics for measuring and evaluating the complexity of a discrete dynamical system under consideration.

Assume now that (X, d_X) is a metric space. We introduce the notion of topological entropy introduced in [6]. For $L \subset X$, $\varepsilon > 0$ and fixed $n \in \mathbb{N}$, one say that a set $E \subset L$ is $(n, \varepsilon, L, \varphi)$–*separated* (by the map φ) if for any $x, y \in E$, $x \neq y$, there is $k \in \{0, 1, ..., n - 1\}$ such that $d_X(\varphi^k(x), \varphi^k(y)) > \varepsilon$. Denote by $s_n(\varepsilon, L, \varphi)$ the cardinality of any maximal $(n, \varepsilon, L, \varphi)$–separated set in L and define

$$s(\varepsilon, L, \varphi) = \limsup_{n \to \infty} \frac{1}{n} \log s_n(\varepsilon, L, \varphi).$$

The construction continues as follows - it is known that $s(\varepsilon, L, \varphi)$ increases when ε decreases. Finally, the *topological entropy* of f is

$$h_{d_X}(\varphi) = \lim_{\varepsilon \to 0} s(\varepsilon, X, \varphi).$$

It is well known that there are some equivalent definitions, for instance the one in which the metric d_X is used to define so-called (n, ε)-*spanning sets*. As the index d_X in $h_{d_X}(f)$ indicates, the value of $h_{d_X}(f)$ depends on the metric d_X under consideration.

However, if the space (X, d_X) is both metric and compact, then different approaches (e.g. Bowen's and Adler's, Konheim and McAndrew's) coincide. If the space (X, d_X) is not compact, then we consider the following extension [9] of the entropy notion to non-compact spaces:

$$ent_{d_X}(\varphi) = \sup\left\{h_{d_X}(\varphi|_K) \mid K \in \mathcal{K}(X) \text{ satisfies } \varphi(K) \subseteq K\right\}.$$

Properties of the topological entropy have been deeply studied in many papers and monographs, among the most common properties belong the following two facts: the first one showing that the topological entropy increases with the increasing number of iterations, i.e. for every $n \in \mathbf{N}$

$$h(\varphi^n) = n \cdot h(\varphi) \quad (\text{resp. } ent(\varphi^n) = n \cdot ent(\varphi)),$$

and the second one showing that for $K \subseteq L \subseteq X$ one gets the monotonicity

$$h(\varphi_K) \leq h(\varphi_L) \quad (\text{resp. } ent(\varphi_K) = ent(\varphi_L)). \tag{1}$$

As an outcome of the calculation above we obtain a value in the interval $[0, \infty]$, where $h(\varphi) = 0$ means that (X, φ) possesses a simple behavior, while $h(\varphi) > 0$ indicates a *topological chaos*, Naturally, the higher the topological entropy of φ is, the more complex behavior of the dynamical system (X, φ) is observed. In a series of papers (see the next subsection) we studied how are topological entropies of the original system (X, φ) and its fuzzification $(\mathcal{F}(X), \varphi)$ related.

3   Topological Entropy of g-fuzzifications

The following facts on mutual relations between entropies of dynamical systems (X, φ), $(\mathcal{K}(X), s_\varphi)$ and $(\mathcal{F}(X), z_\varphi)$ have been observed in a series of papers (e.g. [7,8] and references therein). Due to the monotonicity condition (1) and the existence of natural isometries i_1, i_2, for $x \in X$ and $L \in \mathcal{K}(X)$,

$$i_1 : X \to \mathcal{K}(X) \ (i_1(x) = \{x\}), \ i_2 : \mathcal{K}(X) \to \mathcal{F}(X) \ (i_2(L) = \chi_L),$$

χ_L denoting the characteristic function of L, one can expect that

$$h(\varphi) \leq h(s_\varphi) \leq ent(z_\varphi).$$

However, it has been surprising that the assumptions for strict inequalities in the last expression can be so simple. Namely in [8], the following result, showing how fast the topological entropy can increase (regardless of which of metrics d_E, d_S, d_∞ is considered), was proved.

Theorem 1. *Let (X, φ) be a discrete dynamical system such that there exists a point $z_0 \in X$ such that $\{\varphi^n(z_0)\}_{n \in \mathbf{N}}$ converges to $o \in X$ and $\{\varphi^{-n}(z_0)\}_{n \in \mathbf{N}}$ converges to $a \in X$, $a \neq o$. Then,*

$$h(\varphi|_{\overline{\mathcal{O}(z_0)}}) = 0 < h(s_\varphi|_{\overline{\mathcal{O}(z_0)}}) < \infty = ent(z_\varphi|_{\overline{\mathcal{O}(z_0)}}),$$

where $\mathcal{O}(z_0) = \{z_i \in X \mid \varphi(z_i) = z_{i+1} \text{ for every } i \in \mathbf{Z}\}$ denotes the full orbit of z_0.

The careful reader could expect such a property due to the monotonicity of the topological entropy (1) however the fast growth present for the fuzzy extension was surprising. Namely, the assumptions of Theorem 1 are quite weak. For instance, a homeomorphism $h : I \to I$, $h(x) = x^2$, having zero topological entropy satisfies the assumptions of Theorem 1 (i.e. $ent(z_h) = \infty$). Thus, fuzzy dynamical systems shall be considered as really complex in general.

However, elements of $\mathcal{F}(X)$ (even of $\mathcal{F}(I)$) are usually very complex, for instance, they can be represented as the union of finitely many characteristic functions of Cantor sets. However, such fuzzy sets are not typically used as inputs in particular applications. The following result shows what can be expected when we restrict our attention to simpler spaces and fuzzy numbers only (regardless of which metric $d = \{d_E, d_S, d_\infty\}$ is considered).

Theorem 2. *[7] Let (I, φ) be a discrete dynamical system. Then*

$$h(\varphi) = ent(z_\varphi|_{\mathcal{F}_1^1(I)}). \tag{2}$$

Thus the topological entropies of the crisp map and its Zadeh's extension coincide on the space of fuzzy numbers. The above result was recently extended to various classes of maps. For example in [13], it was proved that, provided the crisp dynamical system does have a mixing regular periodic decomposition, then the topological entropies of the crisp dynamical system and its fuzzy extension also coincide.

However, Theorem 2 cannot be generalized in the sense that the equality (2) holds for every compact metric space X. For example, for some dendrites (i.e. locally connected compact connected spaces that contain no simple closed curve), the equality is broken by using the result of [1] even for set-valued extensions.

The results above clarified the situation with fuzzy dynamical systems defined with the help of Zadeh's extension. However, there are no published results on the size of the topological entropy of g-fuzzifications yet. (Although there are results describing an influence of the topological entropy in fuzzy dynamical systems [11].) The first result for g-fuzzifications is an analogy of Theorem 1. The following discrete dynamical system will be considered below.

Example 1. Let us consider a subsystem (S, σ_S) of the symbolic space (Σ_2, σ_2), where S is the family of sequences of two symbols (0 and 1), for which the symbol 1 appears at most once. Then denote $\sigma_S = \sigma_2|_S$. It is known [19] that

$$h(\sigma_S) = 0 < \log 2 = h(s_{\sigma_S}) = h(\sigma_2).$$

Theorem 3. *There exists a discrete dynamical system (S, σ) and $g \in \mathcal{D}_m(I)$ such that*

$$h(\sigma) = 0 < h(s_\sigma) < \infty = ent(z_{\sigma,g}).$$

Proof. Due to space reasons we present a short sketch of the proof only. Let us consider the discrete dynamical system (S, σ_S) from Example 1. This symbolic dynamical system (S, σ_S) was considered in a very technical proof of the result analogous to Theorem 1 ([8, Theorem 1]), which is valid for the standard Zadeh's extension only. While the idea of the proof can be used for our case, the proof itself is not working for g-fuzzifications for $g \in D_m(I)$ distinct from $id_{[0,1]}$. It is necessary to redefine the sets K_m in the proof of Theorem 1 in [8] in such a way that values of characteristic functions in K_m's are not dense in $[0,1]$ and adapt the rest of the proof accordingly.

We conclude this section by a remark that it is still unknown for what classes of interval maps g the following equality is valid

$$ent(z_\varphi) = ent(z_{\varphi,g}).$$

4   Transitivity

Let us discuss the notion of transitivity in this subsection. As it is mentioned in the introduction, the transitivity is a famous property, indicating either very regular (e.g. equicontinuous) behavior, or very non-regular (such as chaotic) behavior. For example, transitive interval maps ($\varphi \in C(I)$) are considered as chaotic, while transitive rational rotation on the unit circle provides an uninteresting (simple) behavior. It is also worth mentioning that not all spaces admit a transitive map. To be more precise - a space X admits a transitive map if there exists a map $\varphi \in C(X)$ for which φ is transitive.

It was shown in [18] that in general, the space $\mathcal{F}(X)$ does not admit a transitive fuzzification (for $g \neq id_{[0,1]}$). However, it was proved in another paper [17] that the space of **normal** fuzzy sets $\mathcal{F}^1(X)$ admits a transitive fuzzification (and the metric d_∞). This is the reason why only the space $\mathcal{F}^1(X)$ is considered below.

Under the assumption that $\mathcal{F}^1(X)$ admits a transitive g-fuzzification, one can define an operator between open subsets of X and $\mathcal{F}^1(X)$, which allows to prove the following statement (among other results). The following statements were proved for the levelwise metric d_∞.

Theorem 4. [17] Let (X, φ) be a discrete dynamical system. Then

$$(\mathcal{F}^1(X), z_\varphi) \text{ transitive} \Rightarrow (X, \varphi) \text{ transitive}. \tag{3}$$

It is very easy to find a counterexample showing that the implication converse to (3) is not valid in general. As it is mentioned above, the transitivity could imply a very regular behavior. In this case, e.g. for the rational rotation on the unit circle $\mathcal{S}^1$ (which is, to be precise, an isometry), the fuzzification on $\mathcal{F}^1(\mathcal{S}^1)$ is not complex. However, provided the transitivity indicating complex behavior (i.e. when the map is strongly mixing) is present, then the situation is different.

Theorem 5. [17] Let (X, φ) be a discrete dynamical system. Then

$$(X, \varphi) \text{ strongly mixing} \Rightarrow (\mathcal{F}^1(X), z_\varphi) \text{ transitive}. \tag{4}$$

For further related properties we refer to [17,23] and references therein.

As for g-fuzzifications, it can be easily shown [23] that in full generality, $(\mathcal{F}^1(X), z_{\varphi,g})$ does not admit a transitive fuzzification provided $g \in D_m(I)$ is such that $g \neq id_{[0,1]}$. This indicates that the transitivity need not be the best notion for studying complex behavior of fuzzy dynamical systems, and that stronger properties (like the exactness) should be considered instead.

Another direction could be considering some specific metric spaces X, for instance *almost meshed continua* (a class of continua containing topological graphs and dendrites with closed or countable set of endpoints) or spaces with so-called free arc [22].

5   Density of Periodic Points

Let us summarize results on the property "$P(\varphi)$ is dense in the respective space". Let (X, φ) be a discrete dynamical systems. Considering its extensions, the situation is quite nice between the set-valued and fuzzy extension. Namely (see [17]),

$$P(s_\varphi) \text{ is dense in } \mathcal{K}(X) \Leftrightarrow P(z_\varphi) \text{ is dense in } \mathcal{F}(X).$$

But the relations are more complicated when the system (X, φ) is considered. The results below were proved for the levelwise metric d_∞.

Theorem 6. *[17] Let (X, φ) be a discrete dynamical system. Then*

$$P(\varphi) \text{ is dense in } X \Rightarrow P(z_\varphi) \text{ is dense in } \mathcal{F}(X).$$

While the theorem above shows the positive relation, the converse relation is not valid in general as shown in [17]. As a counterexample it was enough to consider an adding machine map on Σ_2, which is an uncountable minimal system (i.e. the smallest nonempty, closed and invariant subsystem), and which forms many periodic clopen (i.e. closed and open) portions for the set-valued extension. Recently it was shown that the property

$$P(\varphi) \text{ is dense in } X(X) \Leftrightarrow P(s_\varphi) \text{ is dense in } \mathcal{K}(X).$$

depends on the space X under consideration. Namely in [2], the authors showed that it holds for so-called almost meshed continua.

As for g-fuzzifications, the situation is quite easy explainable. Namely, for every $g \in D_m(I)$, it is known (e.g. see [5]) that for every interval $J \subseteq I$ contiguous to fixed points v_0, v_1 and no other fixed point in the interior of J, we have $J \cap P(g) = \emptyset$ and all trajectories in the interior of J are monotone. This simple observation provides the following statement.

Theorem 7. *Let (X, φ) be a discrete dynamical system and $g \in D_m(I)$ be such that $I \setminus P(g) \neq \emptyset$. Then $P(z_{\varphi,g})$ is not dense in $\mathcal{F}(X)$.*

Note that every $g \in D_m(I)$ distinct from the identity map $id_{[0,1]}$ satisfies the assumptions of Theorem 7.

6   Devaney-Like Chaos

As simple consequences of results mentioned in Sects. 4 and 5 we have the following statement claiming that there is no relation between the original dynamical system (X, φ) and its g-fuzzification $(\mathcal{F}^1(X), z_{\varphi,g})$, if fully general situation is considered. Again, note that the metric d_∞ is considered.

Theorem 8. *Let (X, φ) be a given discrete dynamical system and $(\mathcal{F}^1(X), z_{\varphi,g})$, $g \neq id_{[0,1]}$, be its g-fuzzification. Then, for some $g \in D_m(I)$:*

1. (X, φ) Devaney chaotic $\not\Rightarrow$ $(\mathcal{F}^1(X), z_{\varphi,g})$ Devaney chaotic.
2. $(\mathcal{F}^1(X), z_{\varphi,g})$ Devaney chaotic $\not\Rightarrow$ (X, φ) Devaney chaotic.

While the situation is unpleasant for g-fuzzifications in general, because the density of periodic points is broken for $g \neq id_{[0,1]}$, one can find some positive results for stronger versions of Devaney chaos.

Theorem 9. *[17] Let (X, φ) be a given discrete dynamical system and $(\mathcal{F}^1(X), z_\varphi)$ be its fuzzification. Then,*

1. (X, φ) totally Devaney chaotic $\Rightarrow$ $(\mathcal{F}^1(X), z_\varphi)$ totally Devaney chaotic.
2. (X, φ) exactly Devaney chaotic $\Rightarrow$ $(\mathcal{F}^1(X), z_\varphi)$ exactly Devaney chaotic.

References

1. Acosta, G., Illanes, A., Mendez-Lango, H.: The transitivity of induced maps. Topol. Appl. **156**(5), 1013–1033 (2009)
2. Acosta, G., Hernandez-Gutierrez, R., Naghmouchi, I., Oprocha, P.: Periodic points and transitivity on dendrites. Ergod. Theory Dynamic. Syst. **37**(7), 2017–2033 (2017)
3. Banks, J., Brooks, J., Cairns, G., Davis, G., Stacey, P.: On Devaney's definition of Chaos. Am. Math. Month. **99**(4), 332–334 (1992)
4. Bauer, W., Sigmund, K.: Topological dynamics of transformations induced on the space of probability measures. Monatsheft. Math. **79**, 81–92 (1975)
5. Block, L., Coppel, W.: Dynamics in One-Dimension, Lecture Notes in Mathematics. Springer, Heidelberg (1992)
6. Bowen, R.: Entropy for group endomorphisms and homogeneous spaces. Trans. Am. Math. Soc. **153**, 401–414 (1971)
7. Cánovas, J.S., Kupka, J.: On the topological entropy on the space of fuzzy numbers. Fuzzy Sets Syst. **257**, 132–145 (2014)
8. Cánovas, J.S., Kupka, J.: Topological entropy of fuzzified dynamical systems. Fuzzy Sets Syst. **165**, 67–79 (2011)
9. Cánovas, J.S., Rodríguez, J.M.: Topological entropy of maps on the real line. Topol. Appl. **153**, 735–746 (2005)
10. Devaney, R.: An Introduction to Chaotic Dynamical Systems. Addison-Wesley (1989)
11. Diamond, P., Pokrovskii, A.: Chaos, entropy and a generalized extension principle. Fuzzy Sets Syst. **61**, 277–283 (1994)

12. Fuller, R., Keresztfalvi, T.: On generalization of Nguyen's theorem. Fuzzy Sets Syst. **41**, 371–374 (1991)
13. Kim, Ch., Chen, M., Ju, H.: Dynamics and topological entropy for Zadeh's extension of a compact system. Fuzzy Sets Syst. **319**, 93–100 (2017)
14. Kloeden, P.E.: Fuzzy dynamical systems. Fuzzy Sets Syst. **7**(3), 275–296 (1982)
15. Kolyada, S., Snoha, Ł: Topological transitivity. Scholarpedia **4**(2), 5802 (2009)
16. Kupka, J.: On fuzzifications of discrete dynamical systems. Inf. Sci. **181**(13), 2858–2872 (2011)
17. Kupka, J.: On Devaney chaotic induced fuzzy and set-valued dynamical systems. Fuzzy Sets Syst. **177**(1), 34–44 (2011)
18. Kupka, J.: Some chaotic and mixing properties of fuzzified dynamical systems. Inf. Sci. **279**, 642–653 (2014)
19. Kwietniak, D., Oprocha, P.: Topological entropy and chaos for maps induced on hyperspaces. Chaos Solitons Fract. **33**, 76–86 (2007)
20. Lan, Y., Mu, Ch.: Martelli chaotic properties of a generalized Form of Zadeh's extension principle. J. Appl. Math. **2014**, 956467 (2014)
21. Li, T., Yorke, J.: Period three implies Chaos. Am. Math. Month. **82**(10), 985–992 (1975)
22. Dirbák, M., Snoha Ł, Š.V.: Minimality, transitivity, mixing and topological entropy on spaces with a free interval. Ergod. Theory Dynamic. Syst. **33**(6), 1786–1812 (2013)
23. Wu, X., Chen, G.: Sensitivity and transitivity of fuzzified dynamical systems. Inf. Sci. **396**, 14–23 (2017)
24. Wu, X., Ding, X., Lu, T., Wang, J.: Topological dynamics of Zadeh's extension on upper semi-continuous fuzzy sets. Int. J. Bifurcat. Chaos **27**(10), 1750165 (2017)
25. Wu, X., Wang, L., Liang, J.: The chain properties and Li-Yorke sensitivity of Zadeh's extension on the space of upper semi-continuous fuzzy sets. Iranian J. Fuzzy Syst. **15**, 83–95 (2018)

Parameterized Metrics and Their Applications in Word Combinatorics

Raivis Bēts[1](✉) , Alexander Šostak[1,2] , and Emīls Miķelis Miķelsons[1,2]

[1] Institute of Mathematics and CS, University of Latvia, Riga 1459, Latvia
raivis.bets@lu.lv, aleksandrs.sostaks@lumii.lv, mm15121@edu.lu.lv
[2] Department of Mathematics, University of Latvia, Riga 1004, Latvia

Abstract. We develop a scheme for constructing a parameterized metric on the universe of infinite words. By illustrating the behavior of this parameterized metric with specific examples within the framework of combinatorics of words, we analyze the impact of a parameter-defining function and the impact of a t-conorm $\oplus$ involved in the construction on the outcome of metrics.

Keywords: Parameterized metric · Combinatorics on words · T-conorm

1 Introduction and Preliminaries

Recently some researchers, specifically people working in the field of automatic sequences, in stringology, in word cominatorics and other related areas of mathematics and theoretical computer science, became interested in the use of different analytical methods for the study of the structure of the sets of infinite words and languages. In particular, different metrics describing distance between infinite words, limits of sequences of words and topologies on the set of infinite words were studied in [1,3,5]. However, in our opinion ordinary metrics cannot be an appropriate tool for the study of problems of combinatorics on words, see comments in the introduction of Sect. 3. In our papers [2,14] we applied fuzzy metric with this aim. Although fuzzy metrics are much more suited than the ordinary ones, the scope of their applications is still quite restricted. Proceeding with the study of this problem we came to the idea that the best tool for research could be metrics parameterized by means of specially chosen t-conorms. Realizing our idea in this paper, we develop a scheme for constructing parameterized metrics on the universe of infinite words and study the properties of the obtained parameterized metric (Subsect. 2.2), analyze the scope of admissible t-conorms for such a parameterization (Subsect. 2.3), illustrate the results obtained by such parameterization (Sect. 3) and analyze the impact of the choice a parameter used for the parameterization (Subsect. 3.1) and the impact of the chosen t-conorm (Subsect. 3.2).

The work has been supported by ERDF within the project No. 1.1.1.2/16/I/001, application No. 1.1.1.2/VIAA/4/20/706 "Applications of Fuzzy Pseudometrics in Combinatorics on Words".

© Springer Nature Switzerland AG 2022
D. Ciucci et al. (Eds.): IPMU 2022, CCIS 1601, pp. 270–281, 2022.
https://doi.org/10.1007/978-3-031-08971-8_23

1.1   t-conorms

The notion of a t-norm was introduced in [9] and further studied and applied by many authors, see e.g., [7,12]. However we do not base our work on t-norms, but on its duals, namely on t-conorms.

Definition 1. *A binary operation* $\oplus : [0,1] \times [0,1] \rightarrow [0,1]$ *is called a t-conorm if for all* $\alpha, \beta, \gamma \in [0,1]$ *the following properties hold:*
$(\oplus_1)$ $\oplus$ *is commutative, that is* $\alpha \oplus \beta = \beta \oplus \alpha$;
$(\oplus_2)$ $\oplus$ *is associative, that is* $\alpha \oplus (\beta \oplus \gamma) = (\alpha \oplus \beta) \oplus \gamma$;
$(\oplus_3)$ $\oplus$ *is monotone, that is* $\alpha \leq \beta \Longrightarrow \alpha \oplus \gamma \leq \beta \oplus \gamma$;
$(\oplus_4)$ 0 *is the neutral element for* $\oplus$, *that is* $\alpha \oplus 0 = \alpha$.

It is easy to see that a t-conorm satisfies also the following condition:
$(\oplus_5)$ $\alpha \oplus 1 = 1$.
In our paper we interchangeably use a t-conorm both as a binary operation $\oplus : [0,1] \times [0,1] \rightarrow [0,1]$ and as a two variable function defined by $S : [0,1] \times [0,1] \rightarrow [0,1]$.

Example 1. Among the most important examples of t-conorms are:

- The Maximum t-conorm $\alpha \oplus^M \beta := \alpha \vee \beta$, where $\alpha \vee \beta = \max\{\alpha, \beta\}$. It is known and easy to check that $\oplus^M$ is the smallest t-conorm.
- The Probabilistic sum t-conorm $\alpha \oplus^P \beta := \alpha + \beta - \alpha \cdot \beta$.
- The Łukasiewicz t-conorm $\alpha \oplus^L \beta := \min\{\alpha + \beta, 1\}$.
- The so called Drastic t-conorm is defined by $\alpha \oplus^D \beta = \begin{cases} \alpha \vee \beta, & \text{if } \alpha \wedge \beta = 0, \\ 1, & \text{otherwise.} \end{cases}$

It is known and easy to check that $\oplus^D$ is the largest t-conorm.

1.2   Parameterized Pseudometrics

Many researchers used families of (pseudo)metrics, often endowed with a parameter, in order to characterize properties of the object of their study. For example, J.F. McClendon [8] considers a disjoint collection of metric spaces whose metrics are compatible with a given topology on the disjoint union of sets, V. Radu [10] applies families of metrics in his research on distribution functions, D. Schueth [11] in her research uses families of Riemannian metrics on simply connected manifolds, etc. On the other hand, we know few papers that have studied parameterized metrics as objects. Actually, the first work known to us, in which parameterized metrics appear in this role (under a grammatically confusing name of a parametric metric) is a recent work by N. Husseln et al. [6]. Revising the definition from [6] we introduce the following

Definition 2. *A parameterized pseudometric on a set X is a mapping $P :$ $X \times X \times T \rightarrow [0, \infty)$, where T is a set of parameters, satisfying the following conditions:*
(PPM1) $P(x, x, t) = 0$ *for any $x \in X$, and for any $t \in T$;*

(PPM2) $P(x, y, t) = P(y, x, t)$ for all $x, y \in X$ and for all $t \in T$;
(PPM3) $P(x, z, t) \leq P(x, y, t) + P(y, z, t)$ for all $x, y, z \in X$ and for all $t \in T$.
A parameterized pseudometric $P : X \times X \times T \to [0, \infty)$ is called a parameterized metric if it satisfies a stronger version of the 1st axiom
(PPM1') $P(x, y, t) = 0$ for any $t \in T$ if and only if $x = y$.

In our work the set of parameters is restricted to cases $T = (0, \infty)$ or $T = [0, \infty)$.

Definition 3. A parameterized pseudometric $P : X \times X \times T \to [0, \infty)$ is called increasing, if $t < t' \implies P(x, y, t) \leq P(x, y, t')$ $\forall x, y \in X$.
An increasing parameterized pseudometric $P : X \times X \times T \to [0, \infty)$ is called lower semicontinuous if $\lim_{t \to t_0, t < t_0} P(x, y, t) = P(x, y, t_0)$ $\forall x, y \in X, \forall t_0 \in T$.

2   Parameterized Metric on the Universe of Infinite Words

In this section we develop a scheme for the construction of parameterized metrics based on a pre-chosen suitable decreasing function φ and a continuous t-conorm satisfying certain properties. We recall that the usage of a t-conorm has been already studied for fuzzy metrics, see e.g., [4,13].

2.1   Parameter Regulating Function

In the construction of a parameterized metric we use a function $\varphi : (0, \infty) \to (0, 1)$ satisfying the following properties:

(1) φ is upper semicontinuous, particularly continuous;
(2) φ is decreasing, that is $t \leq s$, $t, s \in (0, \infty) \implies \varphi(t) \geq \varphi(s)$;
(3) $\lim_{t \to \infty} \varphi(t) = 0$;
(4) $\int_0^\infty \varphi(t) dt = 1$.

Although any function φ satisfying the above conditions can be taken, in the following we shall rely on the function $\varphi(t) = \frac{2k}{\pi} \cdot \frac{1}{t^2 + k^2}$ where $0 < k < \infty$ is a fixed number.

Based on the function φ we define the step function $\bar{\varphi} : (0, \infty) \to (0, 1)$ by setting:

$$\bar{\varphi}(t) = \varphi(1) \quad \text{if} \quad 0 < t \leq 1;$$
$$\bar{\varphi}(t) = \varphi(2) \quad \text{if} \quad 1 < t \leq 2;$$
$$\cdots\cdots\cdots \quad \cdots \quad \cdots\cdots\cdots$$
$$\bar{\varphi}(t) = \varphi(n) \quad \text{if} \quad n - 1 < t \leq n;$$
$$\cdots\cdots\cdots \quad \cdots \quad \cdots\cdots\cdots,$$

that is, $\bar{\varphi}(t) = \varphi(\lceil t \rceil)$, where $\lceil \cdot \rceil$ is the ceiling function. Obviously $\int_0^\infty \bar{\varphi}(t) = \sum_1^\infty \varphi(i) < 1$. In turn this means that the addition operation "+" in our case is just the Łukasiewicz t-conorm, that is, $\sum_{i=1}^n \varphi(i) = \bigoplus_{i=1,\dots,n}^L \varphi(i)$, and therefore $\int_0^\infty \bar{\varphi}(t) dt = \sum_{n=1}^\infty \varphi(n) = \lim_{n \to \infty} \bigoplus_{i=1,\dots,n}^L \varphi(i) \leq 1$. Further, let $\oplus$ be a t-conorm such that $\oplus \leq \oplus^L$. Then $\lim_{n \to \infty} \bigoplus_{i=1,\dots,n} \varphi(i) :=_{def} A \leq \lim_{n \to \infty} \bigoplus_{i=1,\dots,n}^L \varphi(i) < 1$.

2.2 Construction of a Parameterized Metric on the Set of All Infinite Words Based on a t-conorm $\oplus$

Let X be the universe of all infinite words. That is elements of X are sequences $x = (x_0, x_1, \ldots, x_n, \ldots)$, where $x_i \in \{0, 1\}$ for each $i = 0, 1, \ldots, n, \ldots$. For every i we define a function $\chi_i : X \times X \to \{0, 1\}$ by setting for $x = (x_0, x_1, \ldots, x_n, \ldots)$ and $y = (y_0, y_1, \ldots, y_n, \ldots)$ $\chi_i(x, y) = \begin{cases} 0, & \text{if } x_i = y_i, \\ 1, & \text{if } x_i \neq y_i \end{cases}$. One can easily prove the following.

Lemma 1. *Let* $\oplus : [0, 1] \times [0, 1] \to [0, 1]$ *be any t-conorm and* $\alpha \in [0, 1]$. *Then* $\alpha \cdot \chi_i(x, z) \leq \alpha \cdot \chi_i(x, y) \oplus \alpha \cdot \chi_i(y, z)$ *for any* $x, y, z \in X$ *and any* $i \in \mathbb{N} \cup \{0\}$.

Let $\oplus : [0, 1] \times [0, 1] \to [0, 1]$ be a t-conorm such that $\oplus \leq \oplus_{\mathrm{L}}$. Based on this t-conorm, we construct a step function $\bar{D} : X \times X \times (0, \infty) \to [0, 1]$ by induction on half open intervals $(n - 1, n]$ for all $n \in \mathbb{N}$:

$$
\begin{array}{lll}
i = 1 & \bar{D}(x, y, t) = \bar{\varphi}(t) \cdot \chi_0(x, y) & \text{for } t \in (0, 1]; \\
i = 2 & \bar{D}(x, y, t) = \bar{D}(x, y, 1) \oplus (\bar{\varphi}(t) \cdot \chi_1(x, y)) & \text{for } t \in (1, 2]; \\
i = 3 & \bar{D}(x, y, t) = \bar{D}(x, y, 2) \oplus (\bar{\varphi}(t) \cdot \chi_2(x, y)) & \text{for } t \in (2, 3]; \\
\cdots\cdots & \cdots\cdots\cdots\cdots\cdots & \cdots\cdots\cdots; \\
i = n & \bar{D}(x, y, t) = \bar{D}(x, y, n - 1) \oplus (\bar{\varphi}(t) \cdot \chi_{n-1}(x, y)) & \text{for } t \in (n - 1, n]; \\
\cdots\cdots & \cdots\cdots\cdots\cdots\cdots & \cdots\cdots\cdots
\end{array}
$$

Since $\oplus \leq \oplus_{\mathrm{L}}$, it is easy to notice that if $t \in (n - 1, n]$ then $\bar{D}(x, y, t) \leq \sum_{i=1}^{n} \varphi(i) \leq 1$. Therefore, the definition of the function $\bar{D}(x, y, t)$ for all (x, y) is correct and $\bar{D} : X \times Y \times (0, \infty) \to [0, A]$ where $\sum_{i=1}^{\infty} \varphi(i) = A$. Finally, we define a function $D : X \times Y \times (0, \infty) \to [0, 1]$ by normalizing the function $\bar{D} : X \times Y \times (0, \infty) \to [0, A]$:

$$
D(x, y, t) = \frac{\bar{D}(x, y, t)}{A}.
$$

Below we note basic properties of the function $D : X \times Y \times (0, \infty) \to [0, 1]$. The proof of the first three propositions is clear from the construction of the function $D : X \times Y \times (0, \infty) \to [0, 1]$.

Proposition 1. *For every* $x, y \in X$ *the function* $D(x, y, -) : (0, \infty) \to [0, 1]$ *is increasing:* $t < t' \implies D(x, y, t) \leq D(x, y, t')$.

Proposition 2. *For every* $t \in (0, \infty)$ *the function* $D(-, -, t) : (0, \infty) \to [0, 1]$ *is symmetric:* $D(x, y, t) = D(y, x, t)$.

Proposition 3. *Given* $x, y \in X$ *it holds* $D(x, y, t) = 0$ *for all* $t \in (0, 1)$ *if and only if* $x = y$.

Proposition 4. *Function* $D(x, y, -) : (0, \infty) \to [0, 1]$ *is lower semicontinuous for every* $x, y \in X$.

Proof. It is sufficient to prove lower semicontinuity for the function $\bar{D}(x, y, -)$: $(0, \infty) \to [0, 1]$. Obviously, this function is a constant and hence continuous on each open interval $(n - 1, n) \subset (0, \infty)$. Besides,

$$\lim_{t \to n^-} \bar{D}(x, y, -) = \bar{D}(x, y, n) < \lim_{t \to n^+} \bar{D}(x, y, -) = \bar{D}(x, y, n + 1)$$

in the case $x_n \neq y_n$ and

$$\bar{D}(x, y, n) = \lim_{t \to n^-} \bar{D}(x, y, -) = \lim_{t \to n^+} \bar{D}(x, y, -) = \bar{D}(x, y, n + 1)$$

in the case $x_n = y_n$. We complete the proof by taking into account that $\bar{D}(x, y, -) : (0, \infty) \to [0, 1]$ is increasing. □

Proposition 5. $\lim_{t \to \infty} D(x, y, t) = 1$ if and only if $x_i \neq y_i$ for all $i \in \mathbb{N} \cup \{0\}$.

Proof. If $x_i \neq y_i$ for every $i \in \mathbb{N} \cup \{0\}$, then $D(x, y, t) = \frac{1}{A} \bigoplus_{i=0}^{n} \varphi(i)$ for $t \in (n - 1, n]$ and hence, $\lim_{n \to \infty} D(x, y, t) = \frac{\lim_{n \to \infty} \bar{D}(x, y, t)}{A} = 1$. Otherwise, if, say, $x_j = y_j$, then $\chi_j(x, y) = 0$ and hence $\lim_{t \to \infty} D(x, y, t) \leq 1 - \frac{\varphi(j)}{A}$.

Remark 1. Proposition 3 and Proposition 5 may be viewed as a justification for the informal interpretation of the equality $\lim_{t \to \infty} D(x, y, t) = \alpha$ as *the degree of distinction between infinite words x and y.*

In order to formulate the next important property of the function $D(x, y, -)$: $(0, \infty) \to [0, 1]$ we need to define the dominance relation between two t-conorms. This is done patterned after the known relation of dominance between two t-norms, see e.g. [7].

Definition 4. *Given two t-conorms $S_1 : [0, 1] \times [0, 1] \to [0, 1]$ and $S_2 : [0, 1] \times [0, 1] \to [0, 1]$ we say that the t-conorm S_1 dominates the t-conorm S_2 if*

$$S_2((S_1(a, b), S_1(c, d)) \leq S_1(S_2(a, c), S_2(b, d)) \text{ for all } a, b, c, d \in [0, 1].$$

Proposition 6. *If the Łukasiewicz t-conorm $\oplus^L$ dominates the t-conorm $\oplus$ used in the construction of the function $D(x, y, -) : (0, \infty) \to [0, 1]$ then*

$$D(x, z, t) \leq D(x, y, t) + D(y, z, t) \text{ for all } x, y, z \in X, \text{ for all } t \in (0, \infty).$$

Proof. It is sufficient to prove this inequality for the function $\bar{D}(x, y, -)$: $(0, \infty) \to [0, 1]$, that is to show that $\bar{D}(x, z, t) \leq \bar{D}(x, y, t) + \bar{D}(y, z, t)$. We prove this by induction on the parameter n determining the restriction of this function to the interval $(0, n] \subset (0, \infty)$, $n \in \mathbb{N}$.

Let $n = 1$. Then $0 < t \leq 1$ and applying Lemma 1 for $\oplus = \oplus^L$ we have

$$\bar{D}(x, z, t) = \bar{\varphi}(1)\chi_1(x, z) \leq \bar{\varphi}(1)\chi_1(x, y) + \bar{\varphi}(1)\chi_1(y, z) = \bar{D}(x, y, t) + \bar{D}(y, z, t).$$

Assume that the inequality holds on the interval $(0, n - 1]$ that is

$$\bar{D}(x, z, t) \leq \bar{D}(x, y, t) + \bar{D}(y, z, t) \ \forall x, y, z \in X, \forall t \in (0, n - 1],$$

and let $t \in (n-1, n]$ Then by construction and taking into account the inductive assumption, Lemma 1 and the dominance of the Łukasiewicz t-conorm over $\oplus$ we have

$$D(x, z, t) = D(x, z, n-1) \oplus \bar{\varphi}(n) \cdot \chi_n(x, z) \le (\bar{D}(x, y, n-1) + D(y, z, n-1)) \oplus$$
$$(\bar{\varphi}(n) \cdot \chi_n(x, y) + \bar{\varphi}(n) \cdot \chi_n(y, z)) \le (\bar{D}(x, y, n-1) \oplus \bar{\varphi}(n) \cdot \chi_n(x, y)) + (\bar{D}(y, z, n-1) \oplus \bar{\varphi}(n) \cdot \chi_n(y, z)) = \bar{D}(x, y, t) + \bar{D}(y, z, t).$$ □

From Propositions 6, 4 and 3 and taking into account Lemma 2 proved in the next subsection, we get the main result of this section:

Theorem 1. *Let the t-conorm $\oplus$ used in the construction of D be dominated by the Łukasiewicz t-conorm $\oplus^{\text{L}}$. Then function $D(x, y, -) : (0, \infty) \to [0, 1]$ is a parameterized metric on the set of infinite words.*

From the construction of the parameterized metric D it is easy to get also the following

Theorem 2. *For every $t = t_0$ the function $D(-, -t_0) : X \times X \to [0, 1]$ is a pseudometric on the set X of infinite words. Specifically, $D(x, y, t_0) = 0$ if and only if $x_i = y_i$ for all $i \le \lfloor t_0 \rfloor$, where $\lfloor - \rfloor : \mathbb{R} \to \mathbb{Z}$ is the floor function.*

2.3   Analysis of Acceptable t-conorms

The construction of the parameterized metric $D(x, y, -) : (0, \infty) \to [0, 1]$ was based on a t-conorm $\oplus$. In the proof we needed two properties of this t-conorm. It must be less or equal than the Łukasiewicz t-conorm $\oplus^{\text{L}}$ (this was important in order that the resulting construction converge) and that it is dominated by the Łukasiewicz t-conorm (this was important to prove the triangle inequality for the resulting parameterized metric). In this section we are concerned about the scope of t-conorms satisfying these properties. One can easily prove the following Lemma:

Lemma 2. *If the t-conorm S_1 dominates the t-conorm S_2, then $S_1 \ge S_2$.*

A broad scope of t-conorms that can be used in our construction is presented by the family of Weber t-conorms, first defined in [15]. Recall that Weber t-conorms S_W^λ are defined for a parameter $\lambda \in [-1; +\infty]$ by

$$S_W^\lambda(x, y) = \min\{x + y - \frac{\lambda xy}{1 + \lambda}, 1\}.$$

For specific λ we get $S_W^0 = S_L$, i.e., Łukasiewicz t-conorm, $S_W^{-1} = S_D$, i.e., Drastic t-conorm and $S_W^\infty = S_P$, i.e., the probabilistic sum.

Theorem 3. *A Weber t-conorm S_W^λ is dominated by Łukasiewicz t-conorm S_L if and only if $\lambda \in [0, \infty]$.*

Proof. We have to prove that

$$(a \oplus^{\text{L}} b) \oplus^\lambda (c \oplus^{\text{L}} d) \le (a \oplus^\lambda c) \oplus^{\text{L}} (b \oplus^\lambda d) \ \forall a, b, c, d \in [0, 1].$$

Since in the case $a \oplus^{\text{L}} b = 1$ or $c \oplus^{\text{L}} d = 1$ the inequality is obvious, we can replace the Łukasiewicz t-conorm sign $\oplus_{\text{L}}$ by the ordinary sum and rewrite the provable inequality as $S_W^\lambda(a+b, c+d) \leq S_W^\lambda(a,c) + S_W^\lambda(b,d)$, which we have to justify for arbitrary $a, b, c, d \in [0,1]$. We have

$$S_W^\lambda(a+b, c+d) = \min\{\tfrac{a+b+c+d+\lambda(a+b+c+d)-\lambda(a+b)(c+d)}{1+\lambda}, 1\};$$

$$S_W^\lambda(a,c) = \min\{\tfrac{a+c+\lambda(a+c)-\lambda ac}{1+\lambda}, 1\}; \quad S_W^\lambda(b,d) = \min\{\tfrac{b+d+\lambda(b+d)-\lambda bd}{1+\lambda}, 1\}.$$

It is easy to notice that if $S_W^\lambda(a+b, c+d) = 1$, then $S_W^\lambda(a,c) + S_W^\lambda(b,d) \geq 1$, and hence the inequality can be simplified as

$$\tfrac{a+b+c+d+\lambda(a+b+c+d)-\lambda(a+b)(c+d)}{1+\lambda} \leq \tfrac{a+c+\lambda(a+c)-\lambda ac}{1+\lambda} + \tfrac{b+d+\lambda(b+d)-\lambda bd}{1+\lambda}.$$

In turn, this inequality under simple algebraic conversions reduces to the following inequality $\lambda(a+b)(c+d) \geq \lambda(ac+bd)$ that holds if and only if $\lambda \geq 0$.

Thus we have proved the theorem for all Weber t-conorms $\oplus^\lambda$ where $0 \leq \lambda < \infty$. To complete the proof, we separately consider the case $\lambda = \infty$, that is when the Weber t-conorm S_W^∞ reduces to the probabilistic sum t-conorm S_P. In this case $S_W^\infty(a+b, c+d) = a+b+c+d-(ac+bd+ad+bc)$; $S_W^\infty(a,c) = a+c-ac$, $S^\infty(b,d) = b+d-bd$, and again we have the obvious inequality $S_W^\infty(a+b, c+d) \leq S_W^\infty(a,c) + S_W^\infty(b,d)$. □

3 Examples of Application of the Constructed Parameterized Metrics in Word Combinatorics

Different metrics describing distance between infinite words have been an aim for some researchers working in the field of automatic sequences, combinatorics on words and other related areas of mathematics. One of the classical approaches is introduced in [5]. Let $x = (x_0, x_1, x_2, \ldots x_n, \ldots)$ and $y = (y_0, y_1, y_2, \ldots y_n, \ldots)$ be infinite words and let $\sigma(x,y) = \sum_{i=0}^\infty \tfrac{1}{2^i} \chi_i(x,y)$. Then $\sigma : X \times X \to [0,1]$ is a metric on the set of all infinite words. However, we consider the following three infinite words $x = (1, 0, 0, 0, 0, \ldots)$, $y = (0, 1, 1, 1, 1, \ldots)$ and $z = (0, 0, 0, 0, 0, \ldots)$, which contradict our intuition. Indeed, $\sigma(y,z) = 1$, and $\sigma(x,z) = 1$ also we expect x to be estimated "closer" to z than y to z. In the next subsection we show that our construction attempts to correct this shortcoming.

3.1 Analysis of the Impact of the Choice of a Parameter

In this subsection we will deal with two t-conorms – $\oplus^L$ and $\oplus^P$, which were used in the construction of a parameterized metric D. Let define $\lim_{t \to \infty} D(x,y,t) = \Delta(x,y)$ and recall that we shall rely on the function $\varphi(t) = \tfrac{2k}{\pi} \cdot \tfrac{1}{t^2+k^2}$, where $0 < k < \infty$ is a fixed number. This parameter k has a huge impact on the resulting distance between two infinite words. The larger a parameter k is, the smaller is the effect of the prefix on the final distance. To demonstrate this, we look at the example mentioned above.

Suppose we compare three infinite words mentioned above $x = (1, 0, 0, 0, ...)$, $y = (0, 1, 1, 1, ..)$ and $z = (0, 0, 0, 0, ...)$. In the case of $\oplus^L$ and $k = 1$ we get

$$\Delta(x, z) \approx 0.464393 \text{ and } \Delta(y, z) \approx 0.534679,$$

but in the case of $\oplus^P$ and $k = 1$ we get

$$\Delta(x, z) \approx 0.596872 \text{ and } \Delta(y, z) \approx 0.591365.$$

As we can see the values for both t-conorms are almost the same and this is due to the big impact of the first symbols in words. If we take, for example, $k = 100$, we already get

$$\Delta(x, z) \approx 0.006386 \text{ and } \Delta(y, z) \approx 0.929992$$

in the case of $\oplus^L$ and

$$\Delta(x, z) \approx 0.01048 \text{ and } \Delta(y, z) \approx 0.995859$$

in the case of $\oplus^P$, i.e., we get the expected inequality $\Delta(x, z) < \Delta(y, z)$. For a broader view, see Tables 1, 2, 3, and 4 and Figs. 1, 2, and 3. We can generalize this example and suppose that we have $x = (1^m 000\ldots)$, $y = (0^m 111\ldots)$ and $z = (0000\ldots)$, where $m \in \mathbb{N}$ and the symbol 0^m defines a string of the length m, which consists of zeroes (similarly 1^m – consists of ones). It seems natural that for bigger m the distance between words x and z become larger, but distance between y and z would be smaller. If we fix $k = 1$, in Table 1 we can see that starting from $m = 2$ in the case of $\oplus^L$ we already have the result that contradicts our intuition, that is $\Delta(x, z) > \Delta(y, z)$.

Table 1. The values of parameterized metric for $k = 1$ and various m

m	1	2	10	50
$\Delta(x, z)$	0.4646	0.6502	0.9119	0.9816
$\Delta(y, z)$	0.5347	0.3489	0.0872	0.0175

(a) Usage of $\oplus^L$

m	1	10	50
$\Delta(x, z)$	0.596872	0.946048	0.9895
$\Delta(y, z)$	0.591365	0.022309	0.0223

(b) Usage of $\oplus^P$

Table 2. The values of parameterized metric for $k = 10$ and various m

m	1	9	10	50
$\Delta(x, z)$	0.0651	0.4668	0.4997	0.8715
$\Delta(y, z)$	0.9283	0.5266	0.4937	0.1219

(a) Usage of $\oplus^L$

m	1	9	10	50
$\Delta(x, z)$	0.1011	0.5954	0.6275	0.9243
$\Delta(y, z)$	0.9594	0.6435	0.6110	0.1787

(b) Usage of $\oplus^P$

Increasing the parameter k allows us to improve the results of our construction and obtain values of distances more appropriate. As can be seen in Table 2 (Fig. 1 illustrates the general relation), if we fix $k = 10$, then for all $m \leq 9$ we get the expected inequality $\Delta(x, z) < \Delta(y, z)$.

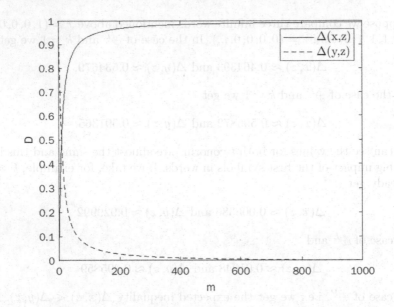

Fig. 1. The values of parameterized metric for $k = 10$ and various m using $\oplus_L$

Tables 3 and 4 illustrate that increasing the parameter k allows us to maintain the inequality $\Delta(x, z) < \Delta(y, z)$ for greater matching prefixes of y and z and unmatching prefixes of x and z. For $k = 100$ (Fig. 2 illustrates the general relation) the inequality stands for all $n \leq 90$, but for $k = 500$ this requirement can be achieved for all $m \leq 308$.

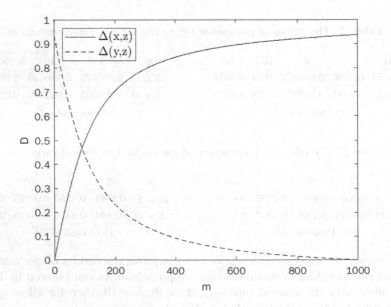

Fig. 2. The values of parameterized metric for $k = 100$ and various m using $\oplus_L$

Table 3. The values of parameterized metric for $k = 100$ and various m

m	1	90	91	200
$\Delta(x, z)$	0.0064	0.4666	0.4701	0.7045
$\Delta(y, z)$	0.9299	0.4698	0.4663	0.2318

(a) Usage of $\oplus^L$

m	1	90	91	200
$\Delta(x, z)$	0.0101	0.5902	0.5936	0.8001
$\Delta(y, z)$	0.9587	0.5924	0.5890	0.3268

(b) Usage of $\oplus^P$

Table 4. The values of parameterized metric for $k = 500$ and various m

m	1	308	309	500
$\Delta(x, z)$	0.0013	0.3515	0.3524	0.5000
$\Delta(y, z)$	0.7035	0.3532	0.3523	0.2048

(a) Usage of $\oplus^L$

m	1	308	309	500
$\Delta(x, z)$	0.0020	0.4689	0.4700	0.6225
$\Delta(y, z)$	0.7992	0.4707	0.4697	0.2929

(b) Usage of $\oplus^P$

An important result can be seen in Table 4 and Fig. 3. They both show that although the change of the sign of the inequality appears for the same length of prefix $m = 309$, the outcome values of both parameterized metrics differ a lot depending on the used t-conorm in the construction (see comment on Subsect. 3.2).

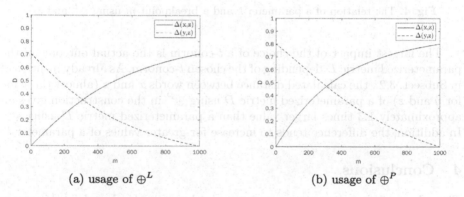

(a) usage of $\oplus^L$ (b) usage of $\oplus^P$

Fig. 3. The values of parameterized metric for $k = 500$ and various m using $\oplus^L$ and $\oplus^P$

3.2 Analysis of the Impact of a t-conorm $\oplus$

As it can be seen in Tables 3, 4 and in the Fig. 3, the choice of a t-conorm (in our approach the choice between $\oplus^L$ and $\oplus^P$) has almost no impact to the breakpoint (the length m of prefixes), where the inequality $\Delta(x, z) < \Delta(y, z)$ changes the sign. Actually, as we can see in Fig. 4, the relation between parameter k and the breakpoint m is independent on the choice of a t-conorm. The Probabilistic Sum t-conorm works a little better than the Łukasiewicz t-conorm, that is, for a fixed length of prefixes (coincide for y and z and differ for x and z), the t-conorm $\oplus^P$ used in the construction of a parameterized metric D gives us the expected inequality $\Delta(x, z) < \Delta(y, z)$ for smaller parameter k than the t-conorm $\oplus^L$, see Fig. 4.

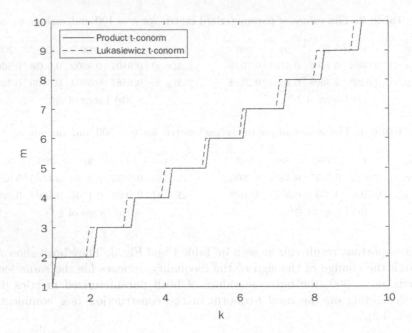

Fig. 4. The relation of a parameter k and a breakpoint m using $\oplus^L$ and $\oplus^P$

The largest impact of the choice of a t-conorm is the actual outcome of the parameterized metric D depending of the chosen t-conorm. As already mentioned in Subsect. 3.2., the calculated distance between words x and z (almost the same for y and z) of a parameterized metric D using $\oplus^P$ in the construction gives an approximately 1.3 times larger value than a parameterized metric D using $\oplus^L$. In addition, the difference tends to increase for greater values of a parameter k.

4   Conclusions

The scheme for constructing a parameterized metric developed in this paper can essentially be interpreted as a parameterization of a sequence of very special pseudometrics χ_i defined on the universe X of infinite words. As the next natural step in what follows, we see the extension of this special scheme for parameterization to a general parameterization scheme for sequences of arbitrary (probably, satisfying some assumptions) pseudometrics on some set X. Following the general construction scheme, an important and promising line of research, in our opinion, is the study of properties, especially topological and uniform ones, of the structures induced on the set X by such parameterized metrics. Of course, in this general scheme, too, it is necessary to study the impact of the parameter-defining function φ and the influence of the t-conorm $\oplus$ involved in the construction. At present we are working on these problems. We see another possible direction for expanding the research started in this article in proposing more general schemes for parameterizing a sequence or, possibly, families of metrics, in which, instead of the t-conorms used in this article, one could use arbitrary aggregation operators.

As for the possible applications of our construction, we have illustrated its display with some particular examples. These examples help to see the influence of the parameter-defining function as well as the impact of the t-conorm used in the construction. As the next practical goal, we see the use of this scheme to study some real-life problems in the field of combinatorics of words. Further, we guess that the scheme of parameterization, when extended to families of more general type of metrics mentioned in the previous paragraph, could get application in the analysis of other real-world problems, in particular related to theoretical computer science.

References

1. Afrouzi, G.A., Shakeri, S., Rasouli, S.H.: On the fuzzy metric spaces. J. Math. Comput. Sci. **2**(3), 475–482 (2011)
2. Bēts, R., Šostak, A.: Fragmentary fuzzy pseudometrics: basics of the theory and applications in combinatorics on words. Baltic J. Mod. Comput. 826–845 (2016)
3. Calude, C.S., Jürgensen, H., Staiger, L.: Topology on words (2009)
4. Grigorenko, O., Miñana, J.J., Šostak, A., Valero, O.: On t-Conorm based fuzzy (pseudo)metrics. Axioms **9**, 78 (2020)
5. Holmgren, R.A.: A First Course in Discrete Dynamical Systems, 2nd edn. Springer, New York(2000). https://doi.org/10.1007/978-1-4419-8732-7
6. Hussain, N., Khaleghizadeh, S., Salimi, P., Abdou, A.: A new approach to fixed point results in triangular intuitionistic fuzzy metric spaces. Abstr. Appl. Anal. **2014**, 690139 (2014)
7. Klement, E.P., Mesiar, R., Pap, E.: Triangular Norms. Kluwer Academy (2000)
8. McClendon, J.F.: Metric families. Pacific J. Math. **57**(2), 491–509 (1975)
9. Menger, K.: Probabilistic geometry. Proc. Natl. Acad. Sci. **27**, 226–229 (1951)
10. Radu, V.: Families of metrics for distribution functions. In: Proceedings 7th Conference on Probablity Theory Brasov, Romania, pp. 487–492 (1982)
11. Schueth, D.: Continuous families of isospherical metrics on simply connected manifolds. Annal. Math. Second Ser. **149**, 287–308 (1999)
12. Schweizer, B., Sklar, A.: Statisitcal metric spaces. Pacific J. Math. **10**, 215–229 (1960)
13. Šostak, A.: George-Veeramani fuzzy metrics revised. Axioms **7**, 60 (2018)
14. Šostak, A., Bets, R.: Fuzzy φ-pseudometrics and fuzzy φ-pseudometric spaces. Adv. Intell. Syst. Comput. **643**, 328–341 (2017)
15. Weber, S.: A general concept of fuzzy connectives, negation and implication based on t-norms and t-conorms. Fuzzy Sets Syst. **11**, 115–134 (1983)

CI Approach to Numerical Methods for Solving Fuzzy Integral Equations

Irina Perfilieva[1](✉)(iD) and Tam Pham[2]

[1] Institute for Research and Applications of Fuzzy Modelling, University of Ostrava,
30. dubna 22, 701 03 Ostrava, Czech Republic
irina.perfilieva@osu.cz
[2] Department of Mathematics, Faculty of Science, University of Ostrava,
30. dubna 22, 701 03 Ostrava, Czech Republic
p19171@student.osu.cz
https://ifm.osu.cz/, https://prf.osu.cz/

Abstract. The contribution is focused on what can be called a computational intelligence approach to numerical methods in fuzzy integral equations. We consider a fuzzy Fredholm integral equation of the second kind and propose a new numerical method for finding its approximate solution. The method is based on the technique called fuzzy (F-) transform, which refers to numerical methods that build a solution on a finite number of subdomains and then combine them into a final one. This approach allows us to transform the original Fredholm fuzzy integral equation into a system of algebraic equations. The solution of this algebraic system gives the corresponding parameters of the inverse F^1-transform. Therefore, we can estimate the approximate solution of the original problem. We discuss two types of numerical methods based on the F^0 and F^1-transforms and give numerical examples of both approaches. We study the convergence and approximation quality of a sequence of approximate solutions in terms of the number of subdomains. We compare numerical approaches based on F^0 and F^1 transforms with similar methods of numerical analysis.

Keywords: Fredholm integral equation · F^1-transform · fuzzy partition

1 Introduction

Integral equations are a very useful mathematics tool in many fields. Therefore, solving integral equations plays an important role in mathematical theory and there are many studies of this field such as the existence of solutions, approximation solutions, well-posed or ill-posed, regularization solutions, etc.

This work was supported by the ERDF/ESF project "Centre for the development of Artificial Intelligence Methods for the Automotive Industry of the region" No. $CZ.02.1.01/0.0/0.0/17 - 049/0008414$ and by SGS20/PrF-MF/2022 of the University of Ostrava.

D. Ciucci et al. (Eds.): IPMU 2022, CCIS 1601, pp. 282–293, 2022.
https://doi.org/10.1007/978-3-031-08971-8_24

In 1965, L.A. Zadeh suggested the fuzzy set theory. Since then, there are many fields where this theory has applications: statistics, numerical analysis, control engineering, decision making, image processing, etc.

From the very beginning, research on fuzzy integral equations has been greatly expanded thanks to the numerous efforts of many scientists around the world. This is due to the applicability of these equations to real dynamic processes that are associated with uncertainty. As a result, the theory of fuzzy integral equations is constantly enriched with new methods and theoretical studies substantiating them.

In our research, we consider the second kind of fuzzy Fredholm integral equation, which is given by

$$y(t) = f(t) + \int_0^T k(t,s)y(s)ds, \tag{1}$$

where $k : [0,T] \times [0,T] \longrightarrow \mathbb{R}$ is a function of two variables, $T \in \mathbb{R}$, and f is a given fuzzy-valued (source) function, and y is an unknown fuzzy-valued function, both are defined on $[0,T]$. We observe that, when f is an ordinary function, then Eq. (1) possesses a crisp solution. However, it is not always possible to find its explicit form. Therefore, research is focused on numerical methods, which differ in their solution requirements.

In [10], an operational method based on approximation by Chebyshev polynomials was proposed. The efficiency of this method depends on the chosen degree of polynomials. Hence, the numerical cost of this method is quite high. In [1], we suggested using the theory of fuzzy (F-)transforms to solve (1). The efficiency of this method depends on two factors: the number of partition elements and the degree of the approximating polynomial. This makes it possible to achieve high quality using low-degree polynomials that do not require large computational costs. In this article, we use the F^1-transform method based on first-degree polynomials that approximate functions on fuzzy partition elements that are smaller than the solution area. It is shown that the accuracy of the numerical method based on the F^1-transform is better than on the pure F^0-transform, and, with a reasonable partition, is comparable to the approximation using Chebyshev polynomials of much higher degree (and higher complexity).

1.1 The Fuzzy Fredholm Integral Equations

The general form of the fuzzy Fredholm integral equation (FFIE) of the second kind

$$y(t,r) - f(t,r) + \lambda \int_a^b k(t,s)y(s,r)ds. \tag{2}$$

is specified as follows: $\lambda = 1$, $a = 0$, and $b = T > 0$. The kernel $k(t,s)$ is defined on $D = [0,T] \times [0,T]$, and the fuzzy function $f : [0,T] \times [0,1] \longrightarrow \mathbb{R}$, where r is the level cut, is given.

Based on [10], the fuzzy Fredholm equation (2) can be rewritten as follows:

$$\underline{y}(t,r) = \underline{f}(t,r) + \int_0^T \Big(k_+(t,s)\underline{y}(s,r) - k_-(t,s)\overline{y}(s,r) \Big) ds$$

$$\overline{y}(t,r) = \overline{f}(t,r) + \int_0^T \Big(k_+(t,s)\overline{y}(s,r) - k_-(t,s)\underline{y}(s,r) \Big) ds \qquad (3)$$

where

$$k_+(t,s) = \begin{cases} k(t,s) & \text{if } k(t,s) \geq 0 \\ 0 & \text{otherwise,} \end{cases}$$

and

$$k_-(t,s) = \begin{cases} -k(t,s) & \text{if } k(t,s) \leq 0 \\ 0 & \text{otherwise.} \end{cases}$$

The system (3) can be now represented in terms of real-valued functions and written as

$$y(t,r) = f(t,r) + \int_0^T \mathbf{k}(t,s)y(s,r)ds, \qquad (4)$$

where $y(t,r) = [\underline{y}(t,r), \overline{y}(t,r)]^T$ and $f(t,r) = [\underline{f}(t,r), \overline{f}(t,r)]^T$

$$\mathbf{k}(t,s) = \begin{pmatrix} k_+(t,s) & -k_-(t,s) \\ -k_-(t,s) & k_+(t,s) \end{pmatrix}.$$

1.2 F^1-transform of Functions of Two Variables

In this section, we use the notion of the direct and the inverse F^1-transforms introduced in [7], for two-variable functions.

Below we repeat [7] to get the extension of the F^1-transform to functions with two variables. Let $f(x,y) \in C([a,b] \times [c,d])$, $n \geq 2$, and the rectangle $[a,b] \times [c,d] \subset \mathbb{R}^2$, has h_1-equidistant nodes $x_0, x_1, ..., x_n$, and h_2-equidistant nodes $y_0, y_1, ..., y_m$, where $a = x_0, x_n = b$ and $c = y_0, y_m = d$.

Let us denote the fuzzy partition $A_0(x), A_1(x), A_2(x), ..., A_n(x)$ which is h_1-uniform, and $B_0(y), B_1(y), B_2(y), ..., B_m(y)$ be h_2-uniform fuzzy partition. Then the inverse F^1-transform $\hat{f}_{n,m}(x,y)$ of $f(x,y)$ approximates $f(x,y)$, and is expressed by

$$\hat{f}_{n,m}(x,y) = \sum_{k=1}^{n-1} \sum_{l=1}^{m-1} F_k^l A_k(x) B_l(y), \qquad (5)$$

where for all $k = 1, ..., n - 1$ and $l = 1, ..., m - 1$,

$$F_k^l = c_{k,0}^{l,0} + c_{k,1}^{l,0}(x - x_k) + c_{k,0}^{l,1}(y - y_l)$$

where

$$c_{k,0}^{l,0} = \frac{\int_{x_{k-1}}^{x_{k+1}} \int_{y_{l-1}}^{y_{l+1}} f(x,y) A_k(x) B_l(y) dy dx}{h_1 h_2} \quad \text{for all } 1 \le k \le n-1,\ 1 \le l \le m-1,$$

$$c_{k,1}^{l,0} = \frac{\int_{x_{k-1}}^{x_{k+1}} \int_{y_{l-1}}^{y_{l+1}} f(x,y)(x - x_k) A_k(x) B_l(y) dy dx}{h_1 h_2} \quad \text{for all } 1 \le k \le n-1,\ 1 \le l \le m-1,$$

$$c_{k,0}^{l,1} = \frac{\int_{x_{k-1}}^{x_{k+1}} \int_{y_{l-1}}^{y_{l+1}} f(x,y)(y - y_l) A_k(x) B_l(y) dy dx}{h_1 h_2} \quad \text{for all } 1 \le k \le n-1,\ 1 \le l \le m-1,$$

Let $\varphi(x) = [A_1(x), A_1(x)(x - x_1), A_2(x), A_2(x)(x - x_2), ..., A_{n-1}(x), A_{n-1}(x)$ $(x - x_{n-1})]^T$, $\psi(y) = [B_1(y), B_1(y)(y - y_1), B_2(y), B_2(y)(y - y_2), ..., B_{m-1}(y), B_{m-1}(y)(y - y_{m-1})]^T$ and

$$F = \begin{pmatrix} c_{1,0}^{1,0} & c_{1,0}^{1,1} & \cdots & c_{1,0}^{m-1,0} & c_{1,0}^{m-1,1} \\ c_{1,1}^{1,0} & 0 & \cdots & c_{1,1}^{m-1,0} & 0 \\ & & \cdots & & \\ c_{n-1,0}^{1,0} & c_{n-1,0}^{1,1} & \cdots & c_{n-1,0}^{m-1,0} & c_{n-1,0}^{m-1,1} \\ c_{n-1,1}^{1,0} & 0 & \cdots & c_{n-1,1}^{m-1,0} & 0 \end{pmatrix}$$

be a real matrix of size $(2n - 2) \times (2m - 2)$. Then the approximation of f by the inverse F^1-transform given in (5) is written is the vector form as

$$f(x,y) \approx \hat{f}_{n,m}(x,y) = \varphi^T(x) F \psi(y). \tag{6}$$

2   Function Approximation

In system (3), we replace all vector-functions $y(t,r) = [\underline{y}(t,r), \overline{y}(t,r)]$, $f[t,r] = [\underline{f}(t,r), \overline{f}(t,r)]$ and $k_+(t,s), k_-(t,s)$ by their F^1-transform approximations.

Let $t_0, t_1, ..., t_n$ be h_1-equidistant nodes in $[0, T]$ where $0 = t_0, t_n = T$. Let $A_0(t), A_1(t), ..., A_n(t)$ be h_1-uniform fuzzy partition of $[0, T]$ with $A : [-1, 1] \to [0, 1]$ as a generating function. We denote $\varphi(t) = [A_1(t), A_1(t)(t - t_1), A_2(t), A_2(t)(t - t_2), ..., A_{n-1}(t), A_{n-1}(t)(t - t_{n-1})]^T$.

Similarly, $r_0, r_1, ..., r_m$ are the h_2-equidistant nodes in $[0, 1]$ where $0 = r_0, r_m = 1$. Let fuzzy partition $B_0(r), B_1(r), ..., B_m(r)$ of $[0, 1]$ be h_2-uniform with the generating function $B : [-1, 1] \to [0, 1]$. We denote $\psi(r) = [B_1(r), B_1(r)(r - r_1), B_2(r), B_2(r)(r - r_2), ..., B_{m-1}(r), B_{m-1}(r)(r - r_{m-1})]^T$.

Using (6), we obtain the following approximations for y, f, k_+, k_-

$$y(t,r) \approx [\varphi^T(t)\underline{Y}\psi(r), \varphi^T(t)\overline{Y}\psi(r)] \quad \text{on} \quad [0,T] \times [0,1],$$

$$f(t,r) \approx [\varphi^T(t)\underline{F}\psi(r), \varphi^T(t)\overline{F}\psi(r)] \quad \text{on} \quad [0,T] \times [0,1],$$

$$k_+(t,s) \approx \varphi^T(t)K_1\varphi(s) \quad \text{and} \quad k_-(t,s) \approx \varphi^T(t)K_2\varphi(s) \quad \text{on} \quad [0,T] \times [0,T], \quad (7)$$

where $\underline{Y}, \overline{Y}, \underline{F}, \overline{F}$ are $(2n-2) \times (2m-2)$ real matrices and K_1, K_2 are $(2n-2) \times (2n-2)$ real matrices.

2.1 Properties of φ and ψ

Theorem 1. *Let φ be defined as above. Let the $(2n-2) \times (2n-2)$ matrix P be defined by*

$$P := \int_0^T \varphi(t)\varphi^T(t)dt. \tag{8}$$

Let us denote

$$\alpha_1 = \int_{-1}^1 A^2(t)dt, \quad \alpha_2 = \int_{-1}^1 t^2 A^2(t)dt, \quad \alpha_3 = \int_0^1 tA^2(t)dt$$

$$\beta_1 = \int_0^1 A(t)A(1-t)dt, \quad \beta_2 = \int_0^1 tA(t)A(1-t)dt,$$

$$\beta_3 = \int_{-1}^0 tA(t)A(1+t)dt, \quad \beta_4 = \int_0^1 t(t-1)A(t)A(1-t)dt$$

Therefore, we have

$$P = \begin{pmatrix} h_1\alpha_1 & 0 & h_1\beta_1 & h_1^2\beta_3 & \dots & 0 & 0 \\ 0 & h_1^3\alpha_2 & h_1^2\beta_2 & h_1^3\beta_4 & \dots & 0 & 0 \\ h_1\beta_1 & h_1^2\beta_2 & h_1\alpha_1 & 0 & \dots & 0 & 0 \\ h_1^2\beta_3 & h_1^3\beta_4 & 0 & h_1^3\alpha_2 & \dots & 0 & 0 \\ \vdots & \vdots & \vdots & \vdots & \vdots & \vdots & \vdots \\ 0 & 0 & 0 & 0 & \dots & h_1\alpha_1 & 0 \\ 0 & 0 & 0 & 0 & \dots & 0 & h_1^3\alpha_2 \end{pmatrix}.$$

Proof. Based on the definition in [8], we have $A_i(t) = 0$ for all $t \in [0, t_{i-1}] \cup [t_{i+1}, T]$ and $A_i(t) = A(\frac{t-t_i}{h_1})$. Then the assertion follows from the direct calculation of the components of the matrix P.

For $k = 1, ..., n - 1$ and $l = 1, ..., m - 1$, let us denote

$$\omega_k : \mathbb{R} \to \mathbb{R}$$

$$t \mapsto \omega_k(t) = \begin{cases} e^{-\frac{1}{t_k - t}} & t_{k-1} + \frac{h_1}{2} < t < t_k \\ -e^{-\frac{1}{t - t_{k-1}}} & t_{k-1} < t < t_{k-1} + \frac{h_1}{2} \\ 0 & \text{otherwise} \end{cases}$$

$$\zeta_l : \mathbb{R} \to \mathbb{R}$$

$$r \mapsto \zeta_l(r) = \begin{cases} e^{-\frac{1}{r_l - r}} & r_{l-1} + \frac{h_2}{2} < r < r_l \\ -e^{-\frac{1}{r - r_{l-1}}} & r_{l-1} < r < r_{l-1} + \frac{h_2}{2} \\ 0 & \text{otherwise.} \end{cases} \qquad (9)$$

Theorem 2. *Assume that $A_0, \ldots, A_n$ is a fuzzy partition of $[0, T]$ and ω_k is as in (9). Let*

$$\omega(t) = \left[\frac{\omega_1(t)}{t - t_1} A_0(t), \ \omega_1(t) A_0(t), \ ..., \ \frac{\omega_{n-1}(t)}{t - t_{n-1}} A_{n-2}(t), \ \omega_{n-1}(t) A_{n-2}(t) \right]^T,$$

where ω_k is taken from (9). Then $Q = \int_{\mathbb{R}} \omega(t) \varphi^T(t) dt$ is a lower triangular matrix with non-zero diagonal.

Theorem 3. *Assume that $B_0, \ldots, B_m$ is a fuzzy partition of $[0, 1]$ and ζ_l is as in (9). Let*

$$\zeta(r) = \left[\frac{\zeta_1(r)}{r - r_1} B_0(r), \ \zeta_1(r) B_0(r), \ ..., \ \frac{\zeta_{m-1}(r)}{r - r_{m-1}} B_{m-2}(r), \ \zeta_{m-1}(r) B_{m-2}(r) \right]^T,$$

where ζ_l is taken from (9). Then $\hat{Q} = \int_{\mathbb{R}} \psi(r) \zeta^T(r) dr$ is a lower triangular matrix with non-zero diagonal.

3   General Scheme of the Proposed Method

By (7), we have

$$\begin{pmatrix} \varphi^T(t) \underline{Y} \psi(r) \\ \varphi^T(t) \overline{Y} \psi(r) \end{pmatrix} = \begin{pmatrix} \varphi^T(t) \underline{F} \psi(r) \\ \varphi^T(t) \overline{F} \psi(r) \end{pmatrix} + \int_0^T \begin{pmatrix} \varphi^T(t) K_1 \varphi(s) & -\varphi^T(t) K_2 \varphi(s) \\ -\varphi^T(t) K_2 \varphi(s) & \varphi^T(t) K_1 \varphi(s) \end{pmatrix} \begin{pmatrix} \varphi^T(s) \underline{Y} \psi(r) \\ \varphi^T(s) \overline{Y} \psi(r) \end{pmatrix} ds.$$
$$(10)$$

For the first row of (10), we have

$$\varphi^T(t) \underline{Y} \psi(r) = \varphi^T(t) \underline{F} \psi(r) + \int_0^T \left[\varphi^T(t) K_1 \varphi(s) \varphi^T(s) \underline{Y} \psi(r) - \varphi^T(t) K_2 \varphi(s) \varphi^T(s) \overline{Y} \psi(r) \right] ds$$

$$= \varphi^T(t) \left(\underline{F} + K_1 \left(\int_0^T \varphi(s) \varphi^T(s) ds \right) \underline{Y} - K_2 \left(\int_0^T \varphi(s) \varphi^T(s) ds \right) \overline{Y} \right) \psi(r).$$

Then we have

$$\varphi^T(t)\underline{Y}\psi(r) = \varphi^T(t)\left(\underline{F} + (K_1 P\underline{Y} - K_2 P\overline{Y})\right)\psi(r). \tag{11}$$

Multiplying (11) by $\omega(t)$ from the left and $\zeta^T(r)$ from the right and we have

$$\left(\omega(t)\varphi^T(t)\right)\underline{Y}\left(\psi(r)\zeta^T(r)\right) = \left(\omega(t)\varphi^T(t)\right)\left(\underline{F} + (K_1 P\underline{Y} - K_2 P\overline{Y})\right)\left(\psi(r)\zeta^T(r)\right).$$

Then integrating with respect to t and r, we have

$$Q\underline{Y}\hat{Q} = Q\left(\underline{F} + (K_1 P\underline{Y} - K_2 P\overline{Y})\right)\hat{Q} \tag{12}$$

By Theorems 2 and 3, Q^{-1} and $\hat{Q}^{-1}$ exist. Multiplying (12) by Q^{-1} from the left and $\hat{Q}^{-1}$ from the right, we obtain

$$\underline{Y} = \underline{F} + (K_1 P\underline{Y} - K_2 P\overline{Y}).$$

Repeating the same procedure with the second row of (10), we obtain

$$\begin{pmatrix} \underline{Y} \\ \overline{Y} \end{pmatrix} = \begin{pmatrix} \underline{F} \\ \overline{F} \end{pmatrix} + \begin{pmatrix} K_1 P\underline{Y} - K_2 P\overline{Y} \\ -K_2 P\underline{Y} + K_1 P\overline{Y} \end{pmatrix} = \begin{pmatrix} \underline{F} \\ \overline{F} \end{pmatrix} + \begin{pmatrix} K_1 P & -K_2 P \\ -K_2 P & K_1 P \end{pmatrix}\begin{pmatrix} \underline{Y} \\ \overline{Y} \end{pmatrix}.$$

Finally, we come to the linear system of equations

$$\begin{pmatrix} I - K_1 P & K_2 P \\ K_2 P & I - K_1 P \end{pmatrix}\begin{pmatrix} \underline{Y} \\ \overline{Y} \end{pmatrix} = \begin{pmatrix} \underline{F} \\ \overline{F} \end{pmatrix}. \tag{13}$$

4   Examples

In this section, we consider a number of examples with various kernels, source functions and lengths of the time intervals. In all these examples, we compute the error estimations, using absolute differences between exact and approximate solutions. The latter are considered at particular points as well as on the whole domains. In all examples, the domains have square shapes and by this, we use the same number n of fuzzy partition units. The value of n is a parameter of error functions. They are denoted by $\underline{E}_n(t,r) = |\underline{y}_n(t,r) - y(t,r)|$ and $\overline{E}_n(t,r) = |\overline{y}_n(t,r) - \overline{y}(t,r)|$.

In the selected examples, the kernels vary from smooth to sharp monotone or oscillating. We see that the proposed approximation has satisfactory quality for all considered cases. Moreover this quality is one order better than the one obtained using approximation by Chebyshev polynomial with high degrees [10].

Example 1. We use our method to solve the FFIE with the *smooth and non-monotone* kernel

$$k(t, s) = \sin s \sin t,$$

where $0 \leq s, t \leq \pi$, and fuzzy function $f = (\underline{f}, \overline{f})$, such that

$$\underline{f}(t, r) = \left(1 - \frac{\pi}{2}\right) \sin t(r^2 + r),$$
$$\overline{f}(t, r) = \left(1 - \frac{\pi}{2}\right) \sin t(4 - r^3 - r).$$

The exact solution has the parametric form $y = (\underline{y}, \overline{y})$

$$\underline{y}(t, r) = \sin t(r^2 + r),$$
$$\overline{y}(t, r) = \sin t(4 - r^3 - r).$$

Figure 1 shows graphs of exact $\underline{y}$ and approximate (based on F^1-transform) solution $\underline{y}_n$ of the equation from exercise 1. Obviously, the graphs of $\underline{y}_n$ and $\underline{y}$ almost coincide.

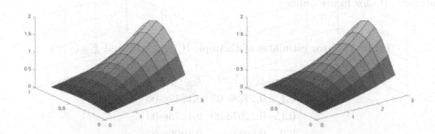

Fig. 1. Exact solution (left) and approximated solution (right) of Example 1.

Figure 2 shows the superiority of the F^1- transform approximate solution over the F^0-transform approximate solution of Example 1 at $t = \frac{1}{3}$.

Let us denote the absolute error estimate $\underline{E}_n(t, r) = |\underline{y}_n(t, r) - \underline{y}(t, r)|$. Table 1 shows values of $\underline{E}_n(t, r)$ computed at $t = 1/3$ using $n = 10$ and $n = 20$ fuzzy partition units. These estimates correspond to the estimates obtained in [10] using the Chebyshev polynomials of the 6th and 8th degrees. Recall that the proposed method is based on F-transform polynomials of the 1st degree, so we have clearly gained in complexity.

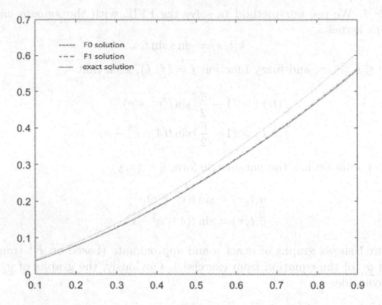

Fig. 2. The exact solution (blue), F^0 (green) and F^1 (red) transform solutions of Example 1. (Color figure online)

Table 1. Error estimates of Example 1: $\underline{E}_{10}(\frac{1}{3}, r)$ and $\underline{E}_{20}(\frac{1}{3}, r)$.

r	$\underline{E}_{10}(\frac{1}{3}, r)$	$\underline{E}_{20}(\frac{1}{3}, r)$
0.1	0.7828e-03	0.1242e-03
0.15	0.1267e-03	0.1173e-03
0.2	0.0011	0.1099e-03
0.25	0.4245e-03	0.1020e-03
0.3	0.0014	0.0935e-03
0.35	0.7647e-03	0.0844e-03
0.4	0.0017	0.0748e-03
0.45	0.0011	0.0646e-03
0.5	0.0021	0.0539e-03
0.55	0.0016	0.0427e-03
0.6	0.0026	0.0309e-03
0.65	0.002	0.0185e-03
0.7	0.0031	0.0056e-03
0.75	0.0026	0.0078e-03
0.8	0.0036	0.0218e-03
0.85	0.0031	0.0364e-03
0.9	0.0042	0.0515e-03

Example 2. We consider FFIE with the low-amplitude oscillating kernel $k(t, s) = 0.1\sin(\frac{t}{2})\sin s$, $0 \leq s, t \leq 2\pi$, and fuzzy function $f = (\underline{f}, \overline{f})$, where

$$\underline{f}(t, r) = \frac{1}{15}(13(r^2 + r) - 2(4 - r^3 - r))\sin(\frac{t}{2})$$

$$\overline{f}(t, r) = \frac{1}{15}(-2(r^2 + r) + 13(4 - r^3 - r))\sin(\frac{t}{2})$$

The exact solution has the form

$$\underline{y}(t, r) = \sin(\frac{t}{2})(r^2 + r), \quad \overline{y}(t, r) = \sin(\frac{t}{2})(4 - r^3 - r).$$

Figure 3 shows the exact solutions $\underline{y}$ and $\overline{y}$ and F^1-transform approximate solutions $\underline{y}_n$, $\overline{y}_n$ of Example 2 at $t = \frac{20\pi}{11}$, and with $n = 11$.

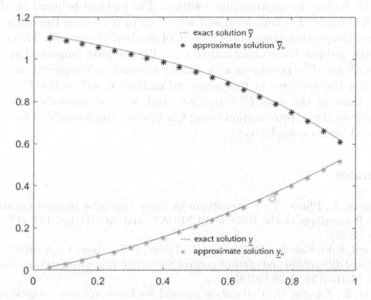

Fig. 3. Solutions of equations in Example 2: exact $\underline{y}$ (blue) and $\overline{y}$ (orange), and F^1-approximate solutions $\underline{y}_n$ and $\overline{y}_n$ by dotted lines. (Color figure online)

Let us denote

$$\underline{E}_n = \max_{t \in [0, 2\pi], r \in [0,1]} |\underline{y}_n(t, r) - \underline{y}(t, r)|; \quad \overline{E}_n = \max_{t \in [0, 2\pi], r \in [0,1]} |\overline{y}_n(t, r) - \overline{y}(t, r)|.$$

Table 2 shows the maximal error estimates of the approximate solutions in Example 2 for various numbers n of fuzzy partition units. We consider $n = 4$, $n = 12$, $n = 22$, $n = 22$, $n = 52$ and compare with the estimates obtained in [10] using Chebyshev polynomials of the same degree n as above. We see that for all considered values of n our estimates are one power order better. However, we emphasize once again that the meaning of n in our case is different, and the F-transform polynomials used have only the 1st degree.

Table 2. The maximal error estimate in Example 2 for various numbers n of fuzzy partition units.

n	4	12	22	32	52
$\underline{E}_n$	$9.3300e-02$	$3.3000e-03$	$4.1574e-04$	$1.1880e-04$	$2.4436e-05$
$\overline{E}_n$	$2.5180e-01$	$8.4000e-03$	$1.1000e-03$	$3.0589e-04$	$6.2944e-05$

5   Conclusion

In this contribution, we were focused on algorithmic aspects of solving the fuzzy Fredholm integral equation of the second kind. We used the theoretical background developed in our previous paper [1] and proposed a new numerical method for finding its approximate solution. The method is based on the technique called fuzzy (F-) transform and allows us to transform the original Fredholm fuzzy integral equation into a system of algebraic equations. This approach significantly reduces the computational cost. We compare numerical approaches based on F^0 and F^1-transforms with similar methods of numerical analysis. We showed that the accuracy of the numerical method based on the F^1-transform is better than on the pure F^0-transform, and, with a reasonable partition, is comparable to the approximation using Chebyshev polynomials of much higher degree (and higher complexity).

References

1. Perfilieva, I., Pham, T.: F^1-transform in fuzzy Fredholm integral equations. In: Joint Proceedings of the IFSA & EUSFLAT, and AGOP, pp. 158–163. Atlantis Press (2021)
2. Agarwal, R.P., Baleanu, D., Nieto, J.J., Torres, D.F., Zhou, Y.: A survey on fuzzy fractional differential and optimal control nonlocal evolution equations. J. Comput. Appl. Math. **339**, 3–29 (2018)
3. Alijani, Z., Kangro, U.: Collocation method for fuzzy Volterra integral equations of the second kind. Math. Model. Anal. **25**, 146–166 (2020)
4. Bica, A.M., Ziari, S.: Iterative numerical method for solving fuzzy Volterra linear integral equations in two dimensions. Soft. Comput. **21**(5), 1097–1108 (2017)
5. Dubois, D., Prade, H.: Operations on fuzzy numbers. Int. J. Syst. Sci. **9**, 613–626 (1978)
6. Khastan, A., Alijani, Z., Perfilieva, I.: Fuzzy transform to approximate solution of two-point boundary value problems. Math. Meth. Appl. Sci. **40**, 6147–6154 (2017)
7. Perfilieva, I.: Fuzzy transforms, fuzzy sets and systems: theory and applications. Fuzzy Sets Syst. **157**, 993–1023 (2006)
8. Perfilieva, I., Dankova, M., Bede, B.: Towards a higher degree F-transform. Fuzzy Sets Syst. **180**, 3–19 (2011)
9. Novak, V., Perfilieva, I., Dvorak, A.: Insight into Fuzzy Modeling. Wiley (2016)
10. Shiri, B., Perfilieva, I., Alijani, Z.: Classical approximation for fuzzy Fredholm integral equation. Fuzzy Sets Syst. **404**, 159–177 (2020)

11. Tomasiello, S., Macías-Díaz, J.E., Khastan, A., Alijani, Z.: New sinusoidal basis functions and a neural network approach to solve nonlinear Volterra–Fredholm integral equations. Neural Comput. Appl. **31**(9), 4865–4878 (2019)
12. Zadeh, L.A.: The concept of a linguistic variable and its application to approximate reasoning, Information. Science **8**, 199–249 (1975)
13. Zakeri, K.A., Ziari, S., Araghi, M.A.F., Perfilieva, I.: Efficient numerical solution to a bivariate nonlinear fuzzy Fredholm integral equation. IEEE Trans. Fuzzy Syst. **29**(2), 442–454 (2021)
14. Perfiljeva, I., Kreinovich, V.: Fuzzy transforms of higher order approximate derivatives: a theorem. Fuzzy Sets Syst. **180**, 55–68 (2011)
15. Kolmogorov, A.N., Fomin, S.V.: Elements of the Theory of Functions and Functional Analysis. Moskva, Nauka (1963). Russian translation

A Characterization for Generalized Hukuhara Differentiable Interval-Valued Functions and Some Rules of Calculus

Juan Carlos Blanche-Alcócer[1] and Yurilev Chalco-Cano[2(✉)] ⓘ

[1] Magíster en Ciencias con Mención en Matemática, Departamento de Matemática, Universidad de Tarapacá, Casilla 7D, Arica, Chile
jblanchea@academicos.uta.cl
[2] Departamento de Matemática, Universidad de Tarapacá, Casilla 7D, Arica, Chile
ychalco@academicos.uta.cl

Abstract. In this article we show a characterization for a gH-differentiable interval-valued function through of properties of the (lateral) differentiability of its length function. Then, we give a procedure to classify a gH-differentiable interval-valued function according to their four types of gH-differentiability. Furthermore, using this classification, we propose a procedure to determine the points at which the sum of two gH-differentiable functions is gH-differentiable as well as to determine their type of gH-differentiability.

Keywords: Interval-valued functions · generalized Hukuhara derivative · algebra of interval-valued functions

1 Introduction

The generalized Hukuhara differentiability (gH-differentiability, for short) for interval-valued functions is a very useful concept in the area of interval mathematical analysis. This concept has been very important in the development of various topics into interval analysis, for instance, interval differential equations [9,11,12] and set optimization problems [4,7]. Furthermore, this has been the initial step to later define the concept of gH-differentiability for fuzzy functions [2].

Obtaining the gH-derivative of an interval-valued function directly from the definition is a rather complex task. In contrast, the use of the (lateral) differentiability of its endpoint functions considerably simplifies the problem. In this

This article was partially supported by the project UTA-Mayor Number 4745-19 and by the European Regional Development Fund (ERDF) and by the Ministry of Economy, Knowledge, Business and University, of the Junta de Andalucía, within the framework of the FEDER Andalucía 2014–2020 operational program. Specific objective 1.2.3. "Promotion and generation of frontier knowledge and knowledge oriented to the challenges of society, development of emerging technologies" within the framework of the reference research project (UPO-1381297). ERDF co-financing percentage 80%.

© Springer Nature Switzerland AG 2022
D. Ciucci et al. (Eds.): IPMU 2022, CCIS 1601, pp. 294–303, 2022.
https://doi.org/10.1007/978-3-031-08971-8_25

direction, a characterization of the gH-differentiable interval-valued functions through of the (lateral) differentiability of its endpoint functions was obtained in [3,10]. From such characterization we can distinguish four types of gH-derivatives, usually called $(k)gH$-differentiability, with $k \in \{i, ii, iii, iv\}$ [5]. Also, the connection of the gH-derivative with the behavior of its length function has been shown [6,8]. In particular, if the length function is increasing (decreasing) then the function is $(i)gH$-differentiable ($(ii)gH$-differentiable, respectively) [8]. The switching points for gH-differentiability are points at which the monotonicity of the length function changes [3,6].

Several properties of the gH-differentiable interval-valued functions have been also obtained in [1,3,6,8,11,12]. In particular, some results on the algebra of gH-differentiable fuzzy functions have been presented in [1,5,8,12]. We note that the sum of two gH-differentiable interval-valued function is not always gH-differentiable [5]. Also, the calculation rules for the sum of two gH-differentiable interval-valued functions change according to the type of gH-differentiability of the interval-valued functions [5].

The main objective of this article is to present a new characterization for gH-differentiable interval-valued functions. In particular, we show a characterization for the $(k)gH$-derivatives through of properties of the (lateral) derivatives of its length function. From this result, we give a procedure for classify a gH-differentiable interval-valued function according to their four types of $(k)gH$-differentiability. Finally, we use this classification for propose a procedure (step to step) for determine the gH-differentiability of the sum of two gH-differentiable interval-valued functions.

2 Preliminaries

Let $\mathbb{I}$ denote the family of all bounded closed intervals in $\mathbb{R}$, i.e.,

$$\mathbb{I} = \{A = [\underline{a}, \overline{a}] \ / \ \underline{a}, \overline{a} \in \mathbb{R} \text{ and } \underline{a} \leq \overline{a}\}.$$

For A, B, $C \in \mathbb{I}$ and $\lambda \in \mathbb{R}$ we consider the following operations

$$A + B = [\underline{a}, \overline{a}] + [\underline{b}, \overline{b}] = [\underline{a} + \underline{b}, \overline{a} + \overline{b}], \tag{1}$$

$$\lambda \cdot A = \lambda [\underline{a}, \overline{a}] = \begin{cases} [\lambda \underline{a}, \lambda \overline{a}] \text{ if } \lambda \geq 0, \\ [\lambda \overline{a}, \lambda \underline{a}] \text{ if } \lambda < 0. \end{cases} \tag{2}$$

$$A -_H B = C \Leftrightarrow A = B + C \tag{3}$$

$$A \ominus_{gH} B = C \Leftrightarrow \begin{cases} (a) \ A = B + C, & \text{or} \\ (b) \ B = A + (-1)C. \end{cases} \tag{4}$$

From (1) and (2) we have that $-A = [-\overline{a}, -\underline{a}]$ and $B - A = B + (-A) = [\underline{b} - \overline{a}, \overline{b} - \underline{a}]$. The space $\mathbb{I}$ with operations (1) and (2) is not a linear space. In (3), $A -_H B$ denotes the Hukuhara difference (H-difference) while, in (4), $A \ominus_{gH} B$ denotes the generalized Hukuhara difference (gH-difference).

We note that the H-difference of two intervals does not always exist while the gH-difference always exists [11] and

$$A \ominus_{gH} B = \left[\min \left\{ \underline{a} - \underline{b}, \overline{a} - \overline{b} \right\}, \max \left\{ \underline{a} - \underline{b}, \overline{a} - \overline{b} \right\} \right].$$

We denote by $len(A)$ the width of the interval A, i.e., $len(A) = len\left([\underline{a}, \overline{a}] \right) = \overline{a} - \underline{a}$.

Lemma 1. *Given two intervals $A, B \in \mathbb{I}$, we have*

(a) *If $len(A) > len(B)$, then $A \ominus_{gH} B = A -_H B$;*
(b) *If $len(A) < len(B)$, then $A \ominus_{gH} B = (-B) -_H (-A)$;*
(c) *If $len(A) = len(B)$, then $A \ominus_{gH} B = \{\underline{a} - \underline{b}\} = \{\overline{a} - \overline{b}\}$;*

Henceforth $T = (a, b)$ will denote an open interval of $\mathbb{R}$. Let $F : T \to \mathbb{I}$ be an interval-valued function with $F(x) = [\underline{f}(x), \overline{f}(x)]$, where $\underline{f}(x) \le \overline{f}(x)$, $\forall x \in T$. The functions $\underline{f}$ and $\overline{f}$ are called the lower and the upper endpoint functions of F, respectively.

Based on the gH-difference, the following definition of differentiability for interval-valued functions was introduced in [11].

Definition 1. *Let $x_0 \in T$ and let $F : T \to \mathbb{I}$ be an interval-valued function, then the generalized Hukuhara derivative (gH-derivative, for short) of F at x_0 is defined as*

$$F'(x_0) = \lim_{h \to 0} \frac{F(x_0 + h) \ominus_{gH} F(x_0)}{h}. \tag{5}$$

If $F'(x_0) \in \mathbb{I}$ satisfying (5) exists, we say that F is generalized Hukuhara differentiable (gH-differentiable, for short) at x_0.

We say that F is gH-differentiable if it is gH-differentiable at x, for all $x \in T$.

Example 1. Let $F : T \to \mathbb{I}$ be defined by $F(x) = A \cdot g(x) = [\underline{a}, \overline{a}] \cdot g(x)$, where $g : T \to \mathbb{R}$ is a function. In this case, the endpoint functions are given by

$$\underline{f}(x) = \begin{cases} \underline{a}g(x) \text{ if } g(x) \ge 0, \\ \overline{a}g(x) \text{ if } g(x) < 0. \end{cases} \qquad \overline{f}(x) = \begin{cases} \overline{a}g(x) \text{ if } g(x) \ge 0, \\ \underline{a}g(x) \text{ if } g(x) < 0. \end{cases}$$

If g is differentiable, then F is gH-differentiable [3,11]. Also, in general, if g is differentiable it does not imply that $\underline{f}$ and $\overline{f}$ are differentiable.

Since the gH-difference and the difference introduced by Markov in [8] are equivalent concepts, the concepts of derivative are coincident.

Theorem 1 *[1]. Let $F : T \to \mathbb{I}$ be gH-differentiable at $x_0 \in T$. Then F is continuous at x_0.*

Obtaining the gH-derivative of an interval-valued function via (5) is a rather complex problem. However, the next result characterizes the gH-differentiability of F in terms of the differentiability of its endpoint functions $\underline{f}$ and $\overline{f}$.

Theorem 2. *Let $F : T \to \mathbb{I}$ be an interval-valued function which is continuous in $(x_0 - \delta, x_0 + \delta) \subset T$ for some $\delta > 0$. Then F is gH-differentiable at x_0 if and only if one of following cases hold:*

(i) $\underline{f}$ *and* $\overline{f}$ *are differentiable at x_0 and* $F'(x_0) = \left[\underline{f}'(x_0), \overline{f}'(x_0) \right]$.

(ii) $\underline{f}$ *and* $\overline{f}$ *are differentiable at x_0 and* $F'(x_0) = \left[\overline{f}'(x_0), \underline{f}'(x_0) \right]$.

(iii) $\underline{f}'_-(x_0), \underline{f}'_+(x_0), \overline{f}'_-(x_0), \overline{f}'_+(x_0)$ *exist and satisfy* $\underline{f}'_-(x_0) = \overline{f}'_+(x_0)$, $\underline{f}'_+(x_0) = \overline{f}'_-(x_0)$, *and* $F'(x_0) = \left[\underline{f}'_-(x_0), \underline{f}'_+(x_0) \right]$.

(iv) $\underline{f}'_-(x_0), \underline{f}'_+(x_0), \overline{f}'_-(x_0), \overline{f}'_+(x_0)$ *exist and satisfy* $\underline{f}'_-(x_0) = \overline{f}'_+(x_0)$, $\underline{f}'_+(x_0) = \overline{f}'_-(x_0)$, *and* $F'(x_0) = \left[\underline{f}'_+(x_0), \underline{f}'_-(x_0) \right]$.

Proof. It is an immediate consequence of Theorem 5 in [10].

Now, from Theorem 2 we can distinguish four cases of gH-differentiability. We say that an interval-valued function $F : T \to \mathbb{I}$ is $(k)gH$-differentiable if case k in Theorem 2 holds, for $k \in \{i, ii, iii, iv\}$.

Remark 1. Note that if $F : T \to \mathbb{I}$ is gH-differentiable at x_0 in more than one case, then F is gH-differentiable at x_0 in all four cases and $F'(x_0)$ is a trivial interval or singleton, i.e. $F'(x_0) = \{a\} = [a, a]$, for some $a \in \mathbb{R}$.

3   Characterization of gH-differentiable Interval-Valued Functions via Its Length Function

Given an interval-valued function $F : T \to \mathbb{I}$, we define its **length function** as the real function $L_F : T \to \mathbb{R}_0^+$ by

$$L_F(x) = len\left([\underline{f}(x), \overline{f}(x)] \right) = \overline{f}(x) - \underline{f}(x),$$

for all $x \in T$.

Lemma 2. *If $F : T \to \mathbb{I}$ is continuous, then L_F is continuous.*

The gH-differentiability of an interval-valued function is linked with the behavior of its length function. The first result on this connection was proved by Markov in [8].

Example 2. We consider the interval-valued function $F : \mathbb{R} \to \mathbb{I}$ defined by $F(x) = [-1, 1] \cdot x$. Then F is gH-differentiable and $F'(x) = [-1, 1]$. Now, $L_F(x) = 2|x|$, for all $x \in \mathbb{R}$, and so L_F is decreasing in $(-\infty, 0)$ and increasing in $(0, +\infty)$. Then, from Theorem 4 in [8], F is (i) gH-differentiable in $(-\infty, 0)$ and is (ii) gH-differentiable in $(0, +\infty)$. At point $x = 0$, L_F has lateral derivatives, with $(L_F)'_-(0) = -2$, $(L_F)'_-(0) = 2$, and L_F has a strict minimum at $x = 0$. We can see that F is (iv) $- gH$-differentiable.

Next we give a characterization of the $(k)\,gH$-differentiability through the properties of the length function which generalizes the result given in [8].

Theorem 3. *Let* $F : T \to \mathbb{I}$ *be* gH-*differentiable and* $x_0 \in T$, *with* $F'(x_0)$ *nontrivial. Then,*

(a) *F is $(i)\,gH$-differentiable at x_0 iff L_F is differentiable at x_0 and $L'_F(x_0) > 0$,*

(b) *F is $(ii)\,gH$-differentiable at x_0 iff L_F is differentiable at x_0 and $L'_F(x_0) < 0$,*

(c) *F is $(iii)\,gH$-differentiable at x_0 iff there are $(L_F)'_-(x_0)$ and $(L_F)'_+(x_0)$, with $(L_F)'_-(x_0) \neq (L_F)'_+(x_0)$, and L_F has a local strict maximum at x_0.*

(d) *F is $(iv)\,gH$-differentiable at x_0 iff there are $(L_F)'_-(x_0)$ and $(L_F)'_+(x_0)$, with $(L_F)'_-(x_0) \neq (L_F)'_+(x_0)$, and L_F has a local strict minimum at x_0.*

Proof. (a) ($\Longrightarrow$) We suppose that F is $(i)\,gH$-differentiable at x_0, then $\underline{f}$ and $\overline{f}$ are differentiable at x_0 and

$$F'(x_0) = \left[\underline{f}'(x_0), \overline{f}'(x_0) \right].$$

Then, L_F is differentiable at x_0. Moreover, since $F'(x_0)$ is nontrivial, $\underline{f}'(x_0) < \overline{f}'(x_0)$ and thus $L'_F(x_0) > 0$.

($\Longleftarrow$) Since F is gH-differentiable and $F'(x_0)$ is nontrivial, from Theorem 2, F is $(k)\,gH$-differentiable at x_0, for a unique $k \in \{i, ii, ii, iv\}$. If F is $(ii)\,gH$-differentiable at x_0, then L_F is differentiable at x_0 and $L'_F(x_0) < 0$ which is a contradiction. Also, if F is $(iii)\,gH$-differentiable (or $(iv)\,gH$-differentiable) at x_0, then L_F is not differentiable at x_0 which is a contradiction. Therefore, F is $(i)\,gH$-differentiable at x_0.

(b) It is proved in a similar way to the item (a).

(c) ($\Longrightarrow$) We suppose that F is $(iii)\,gH$-differentiable at x_0, then there exist $\left(\underline{f}\right)'_{-/+}(x_0)$ and $\left(\overline{f}\right)'_{-/+}(x_0)$ such that $\left(\underline{f}\right)'_-(x_0) = \left(\overline{f}\right)'_+(x_0)$ and $\left(\underline{f}\right)'_+(x_0) = \left(\overline{f}\right)'_-(x_0)$ hold. Moreover,

$$F'(x_0) = \left[\left(\underline{f}\right)'_-(x_0), \left(\underline{f}\right)'_+(x_0) \right].$$

Hence, there exist $(L_F)'_-(x_0)$ and $(L_F)'_+(x_0)$, and since $F'(x_0)$ is nontrivial, we have

$$\left(\underline{f}\right)'_-(x_0) < \left(\underline{f}\right)'_+(x_0) \implies \left(\underline{f}\right)'_+(x_0) - \left(\underline{f}\right)'_-(x_0) > 0$$

$$\implies \left(\overline{f}\right)'_-(x_0) - \left(\underline{f}\right)'_-(x_0) > 0$$

$$\implies (L_F)'_-(x_0) > 0.$$

In the same way, we have also that $(L_F)'_+(x_0) < 0$. Then, for some $\delta > 0$, $L_F(x_0) > L_F(x)$, for all $x \in (x_0 - \delta, x_0)$, and $L_F(x_0) > L_F(x)$, for all $x \in (x_0, x_0 + \delta)$. Therefore, L_F has a local strict maximum at x_0.

($\Longleftarrow$) Since F is gH-differentiable and $F'(x_0)$ is nontrivial, from Theorem 2, F is $(k)\,gH$-differentiable at x_0, for a unique $k \in \{i, ii, ii, iv\}$. From item (a) and (b), F is neither $(i)gH$-differentiable nor $(ii)gH$-differentiable at x_0. If F is $(iv)gH$-differentiable, then $(L_F)'_+ (x_0) > 0$ and so $L_F(x_0) < L_F(x)$, for all $x \in (x_0, x_0 + \delta)$, for some $\delta > 0$. This contradicts the fact that x_0 is a local strict maximum for L_F. Therefore, F is $(iii)gH$-differentiable at x_0.

(d) It is proved in a similar way to the item (c). $\qquad\qquad\square$

Theorem 3 allows us to classify a gH-differentiable interval-valued function by its four types of $(k)gH$-differentiability. In the following example we show this fact and give a procedure (step to step) for this classification.

Example 3. We consider the interval-valued function $F : (-2, 4) \to \mathbb{I}$ defined by $F(x) = [1, 2] \cdot g(x)$, with $g(x) = x^2 - 2x$. Since g is differentiable in $(-2, 4)$, F is gH-differentiable. Now, the function length $L_F : (-2, 4) \to \mathbb{I}$ is given by

$$L_F(x) = len\left([1, 2] \cdot (x^2 - 2x)\right) = \left|x^2 - 2x\right|.$$

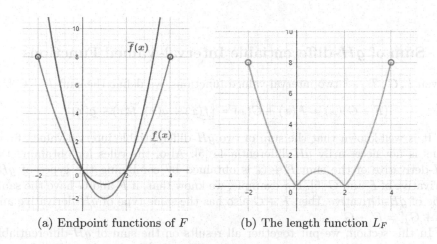

(a) Endpoint functions of F $\qquad$ (b) The length function L_F

Fig. 1. Graphics associate to F

Figure 1(a) shows the graphic of F and its endpoint functions $\underline{f}$ and $\overline{f}$ while Fig. 1(b) shows the graphic of the length function L_F.

Taking into account Remark 1 and Theorem 3, we classify F by its type of gH-differentiability on its domain:

(1) L_F is strict decreasing in $(-2, 0)$, then F is $(ii)gH$-differentiable in $(-2, 0)$.
(2) L_F has a local strict minimum at $x = 0$ and it is not differentiable at $x = 0$, then F is $(iv)gH$-differentiable at $x = 0$.
(3) L_F is strict increasing in $(0, 1)$, then F is $(i)gH$-differentiable in $(0, 1)$.
(4) L_F has a local strict maximum at $x = 1$ and it is differentiable at $x = 1$, then F is $(k)gH$-differentiable at $x = 1$, for all $k \in \{i, ii, iii, iv\}$.
(5) L_F is strict decreasing in $(1, 2)$, then F is $(ii)gH$-differentiable in $(1, 2)$.

(6) L_F has a local strict minimum at $x = 2$ and it is not differentiable at $x = 2$, then F is (iv) gH-differentiable at $x = 2$.

(7) L_F is strict increasing in $(2, 4)$, then F is (i) gH-differentiable in $(2, 4)$.

We can summarize the classification in a table, which will be more useful.

Interval or Point	Behavior of L_F	Type of gH-diff
$(-2, 0)$	strict decreasing	(ii) gH-differentiable
0	has minimum - is not differentiable	(iv) gH-differentiable
$(0, 1)$	strict increasing	(i) gH-differentiable
1	has maximum - is differentiable	(k) gH-differentiable
$(1, 2)$	strict decreasing	(ii) gH-differentiable
2	has minimum - is not differentiable	(iv) gH-differentiable
$(2, 3)$	strict increasing	(i) gH-differentiable

4   Sum of gH-differentiable Interval-Valued Functions

Given $F, G : T \to \mathbb{I}$ two interval-valued functions, we define the sum $F + G$ by

$$(F + G)(x) = F(x) + G(x) = \left[\underline{f}(x) + \underline{g}(x), \overline{f}(x) + \overline{g}(x) \right].$$

It is well-known that the sum of two gH-differentiable interval-valued functions is not necessarily gH-differentiable [5]. Also, the rules for obtaining the gH-derivative of the sum $F + G$ is obtained by combining the types of gH-derivative of F and G [5]. For example, we know that, if F and G have the same type of gH-derivative, then $F + G$ also has the same type of gH-derivative and $(F + G)' = F' + G'$.

In this section, we put together all results on the sum of gH-differentiable functions and fill in some missing rules. Then, with the results of the previous Section, we propose a procedure (step to step) to determine the gH-differentiability of the sum.

Theorem 4. *Let $F, G : T \to \mathbb{I}$ be two gH-differentiable interval-valued functions and $x_0 \in T$, with $F'(x_0)$ and $G'(x_0)$ nontrivial.*

1. *If F and G are (k) gH-differentiable for the same $k \in \{i, ii, iii, iv\}$ at x_0, then $F + G$ is (k) gH-differentiable at x_0 for the same k. Moreover,*

$$(F + G)'(x_0) = F'(x_0) + G'(x_0).$$

2. *If F is (i) gH-differentiable at x_0, G is (ii) gH-differentiable at x_0 and $len\,(F'(x_0)) > len\,(G'(x_0))$, then $F + G$ is (i) gH-differentiable at x_0. Moreover,*

$$(F + G)'(x_0) = F'(x_0) -_H (-1)G'(x_0).$$

3. If F is $(i)\,gH$-differentiable at x_0, G is $(ii)\,gH$-differentiable at x_0 and $len\,(F'(x_0)) < len\,(G'(x_0))$, then $F + G$ is $(ii)\,gH$-differentiable at x_0. Moreover,

$$(F + G)'(x_0) = G'(x_0) -_H (-1)F'(x_0).$$

4. If F is $(i)\,gH$-differentiable at x_0, G is $(ii)\,gH$-differentiable at x_0 and $len\,(F'(x_0)) = len\,(G'(x_0))$, then $F + G$ is $(k)\,gH$-differentiable at x_0, for all $k \in \{i, ii, iii, iv\}$. Moreover, $(F + G)'(x_0)$ is a trivial interval and

$$(F + G)'(x_0) = G'(x_0) -_H (-1)F'(x_0) = F'(x_0) -_H (-1)G'(x_0).$$

5. If F is $(iii)\,gH$-differentiable at x_0, G is $(iv)\,gH$-differentiable at x_0 and $len\,(F'(x_0)) > len\,(G'(x_0))$, then $F + G$ is $(iii)\,gH$-differentiable at x_0. Moreover,

$$(F + G)'(x_0) = F'(x_0) -_H (-1)G'(x_0)$$

6. If F is $(iii)\,gH$-differentiable at x_0, G is $(iv)\,gH$-differentiable at x_0 and $len\,(F'(x_0)) < len\,(G'(x_0))$, then $F + G$ is $(iv)\,gH$-differentiable at x_0. Moreover,

$$(F + G)'(x_0) = G'(x_0) -_H (-1)F'(x_0).$$

7. If F is $(iii)\,gH$-differentiable at x_0, G is $(iv)\,gH$-differentiable at x_0 and $len\,(F'(x_0)) = len\,(G'(x_0))$, then $F + G$ is $(k)\,gH$-differentiable at x_0, for all $k \in \{i, ii, iii, iv\}$. Moreover, $(F + G)'(x_0)$ is a trivial interval and

$$(F + G)'(x_0) = G'(x_0) -_H (-1)F'(x_0) = F'(x_0) -_H (-1)G'(x_0).$$

8. If F is $(i)\,gH$-differentiable at x_0 and G is $(iii)\,gH$-differentiable at x_0 (or $(iv)\,gH$-differentiable at x_0), then $F + G$ is not gH-differentiable at x_0.

9. If F is $(ii)\,gH$-differentiable at x_0 and G is $(iii)\,gH$-differentiable at x_0 (or $(iv)\,gH$-differentiable at x_0), then $F + G$ is not gH-differentiable at x_0.

Proof. 1. This is Theorem 3.1 in [5].

2. From Theorem 3.2 in [5], $F + G$ is either $(i)gH$-differentiable or $(ii)gH$-differentiable at x_0. Now, since $len\,(F'(x_0)) > len\,(G'(x_0))$, then $\overline{f}'(x_0) - \underline{f}'(x_0) > \overline{g}'(x_0) - \underline{g}'(x_0)$ and thus $\underline{f}'(x_0) + \underline{g}'(x_0) < \overline{f}'(x_0) + \overline{g}'(x_0)$. Therefore, $(F + G)'(x_0) = \left[\underline{f}'(x_0) + \underline{g}'(x_0), \overline{f}'(x_0) + \overline{g}'(x_0)\right]$ and so $F + G$ is $(i)\,gH$-differentiable at x_0.

3., 4., 5., 6. and 7. are proved from Theorem 3.2 in [5] and with similar arguments to 2.. Finally, 8. and 9. are showed in Theorem 3.3 in [5]. $\square$

Example 4. Let $F, G : \mathbb{R} \to \mathbb{I}$ be two interval valued functions defined by $F(x) = [1, 2] \cdot (x - 1)$ and $G(x) = [1, 2] \cdot (x^2 - 2x)$. Clearly, both F and G are gH-differentiable and

$$L_F(x) = |x - 1| \qquad \text{and} \qquad L_G(x) = |x^2 - 2x|.$$

We classify F and G by its types of gH-differentiability:

Interval or Point	Behavior of L_F	Type of gH-diff.
$(-\infty, 1)$	strict decreasing	(ii) gH-differentiable
$x = 1$	has minimum - is not differentiable	(iv) gH-differentiable
$(1, +\infty)$	strict increasing	(i) gH-differentiable

and

Interval or Point	Behavior of L_G	Type of gH-diff.
$(-\infty, 0)$	strict decreasing	(ii) gH-differentiable
$x = 0$	has minimum - is not differentiable	(iv) gH-differentiable
$(0, 1)$	strict increasing	(i) gH-differentiable
$x = 1$	has maximum - is differentiable	(k) gH-differentiable
$(1, 2)$	strict decreasing	(ii) gH-differentiable
$x = 2$	has minimum - is not differentiable	(iv) gH-differentiable
$(2, +\infty)$	strict increasing	(i) gH-differentiable

where (k) gH-differentiable in the table means that F is (k) gH-differentiable, for all $k \in \{i, ii, iii, iv\}$, equivalently, $F'(x_0)$ is a trivial interval.

Now, taking into account Theorem 4 and the classification of F and G, we can summarize the behavior of the gH-derivative of $F + G$ in the following table:

Interval or Point	Type of gH-diff. F	Type of gH-diff. G	Type of gH-diff. $F + G$
$(-\infty, 0)$	(ii) gH-differentiable	(ii) gH-differentiable	(ii) gH-differentiable
$x = 0$	(ii) gH-differentiable	(iv) gH-differentiable	Not gH-differentiable
$(0, \frac{1}{2})$	(ii) gH-differentiable	(i) gH-differentiable	(i) gH-differentiable
$x = \frac{1}{2}$	(ii) gH-differentiable	(i) gH-differentiable	(k) gH-differentiable
$(\frac{1}{2}, 1)$	(ii) gH-differentiable	(i) gH-differentiable	(ii) gH-differentiable
$x = 1$	(iv) gH-differentiable	(k) gH-differentiable	(iv) gH-differentiable
$(1, \frac{3}{2})$	(i) gH-differentiable	(ii) gH-differentiable	(ii) gH-differentiable
$x = \frac{3}{2}$	(i) gH-differentiable	(ii) gH-differentiable	(k) gH-differentiable
$(\frac{3}{2}, 2)$	(i) gH-differentiable	(ii) gH-differentiable	(i) gH-differentiable
$x = 2$	(i) gH-differentiable	(iv) gH-differentiable	Not gH-differentiable
$(2, +\infty)$	(i) gH-differentiable	(i) gH-differentiable	(i) gH-differentiable

5   Conclusion

In this paper we have given a characterization of a gH-differentiable interval-valued function via properties of the (lateral) derivative of its length function. We have used this result to introduce a useful procedure for classifying gH-differentiable functions according to their four types of gH-differentiability. In last Section, we have presented rules and a procedure for obtaining the gH-derivative of the sum of two gH-differentiable interval-valued functions.

The results and procedures will be a useful tool for calculating the gH-derivative of interval-valued functions.

For future work, extend the results and procedures to the entire algebra of gH-differentiable functions is desirable. Extend the results and procedures obtained in this article for gH-differentiable fuzzy functions is also desirable.

References

1. Armand, A., Allahviranloo, T., Gouyandeh, Z.: Some fundamental results on fuzzy calculus. Iran. J. Fuzzy Syst. **15**, 27–46 (2018)
2. Bede, B., Stefanini, L.: Generalized differentiability of fuzzy-valued functions. Fuzzy Sets Syst. **230**, 119–141 (2013)
3. Chalco-Cano, Y., Rufián-Lizana, A., Román-Flores, H., Jiménez-Gamero, M.D.: Calculus for interval-valued functions using generalized Hukuhara derivative and applications. Fuzzy Sets Syst. **219**, 49–67 (2013)
4. Chalco-Cano, Y., Lodwick, W.A., Rufián-Lizana, A.: Optimality conditions of type KKT for optimization problem with interval-valued objective function via generalized derivative. Fuzzy Optim. Decis. Making **12**, 305–322 (2013)
5. Chalco-Cano, Y., Maqui-Huamán, G.G., Silva, G.N., Jiménez-Gamero, M.D.: Algebra of generalized Hukuhara differentiable interval-valued functions: review and new properties. Fuzzy Sets Syst. **375**, 53–69 (2019)
6. Chalco-Cano, Y., Costa, T.M., Román-Flores, H., Rufián-Lizana, A.: New properties of the switching points for the generalized Hukuhara differentiability and some results on calculus. Fuzzy Sets Syst. **404**, 62–74 (2021)
7. Ghosh, D., Singh, A., Shukla, K.K., Manchanda, K.: Extended Karush-Kuhn-Tucker condition for constrained interval optimization problems and its application in support vector machines. Inf. Sci. **504**, 276–292 (2019)
8. Markov, S.: Calculus for interval functions of a real variable. Computing **22**, 325–337 (1979)
9. Malinowski, M.T.: Interval Cauchy problem with a second type Hukuhara derivative. Inf. Sci. **213**, 94–105 (2012)
10. Qiu, D.: The generalized Hukuhara differentiability of interval-valued function is not fully equivalent to the one-sided differentiability of its endpoint functions. Fuzzy Sets Syst. **419**, 158–168 (2021)
11. Stefanini, L., Bede, B.: Generalized Hukuhara differentiability of interval-valued functions and interval differential equations. Nonlinear Anal. **71**, 1311–1328 (2009)
12. Tao, J., Zhang, Z.: Properties of interval-valued function space under the gH-difference and their application to semi-linear interval differential equations. Adv. Difference Equ. **2016**(1), 1–28 (2016). https://doi.org/10.1186/s13662-016-0759-9

Generalized Sets and Operators

Selection of Relevant Features Based on Optimistic and Pessimistic Similarities Measures of Interval-Valued Fuzzy Sets

Barbara Pękala[1,2(✉)], Krzysztof Dyczkowski[3], Jarosław Szkoła[1], and Dawid Kosior[1]

[1] University of Rzeszów, Rzeszów, Poland
bpekala@ur.edu.pl
[2] University of Information Technology and Management, Rzeszów, Poland
[3] Adam Mickiewicz University, Poznań, Poland
chris@amu.edu.pl

Abstract. This paper presents the application of optimistic and pessimistic similarity measures of interval-valued fuzzy sets (IVFS) to the problem of selecting relevant attributes as input to classification algorithms. The paper presents a modified IV-Relief algorithm using the aforementioned measures. The theoretical considerations are supported by the analysis of the effectiveness of the proposed algorithm on a well-known breast cancer diagnostic data-set. The proposed methods extend existing classification methods so that they work on uncertain data.

Keywords: Similarity measure · Interval-valued fuzzy set · Future selection · Classification

1 Introduction

A very important practical issue in classification problems is the selection of appropriate attributes based on which the algorithms will be learned. Additionally, in many applications the algorithms must be able to operate on uncertain data. In this paper, we focus on the use of optimistic and pessimistic similarity measures that allow the selection of attributes whose values are represented using IVFS's. For this purpose, we apply the Relief algorithm adapted to interval data based on the degree of inclusion and similarity of fuzzy sets with IVFSs (see [22]). The effectiveness of attributes selection was made using k-nearest neighbors classification algorithm (k-NN). The fundamental novelty of the proposed approach is the use of a measure that takes into account similarity between intervals or IVFSs, representing the uncertainty of information and imprecision of the membership function in epistemic aspect.

Many researchers have proposed various operators and measures for IVFSs, and investigated different kinds of relationships between them and used them practical applications in solving real problems, including in medical diagnostics or decision making, e.g. [2,9–18].

© Springer Nature Switzerland AG 2022
D. Ciucci et al. (Eds.): IPMU 2022, CCIS 1601, pp. 307–319, 2022.
https://doi.org/10.1007/978-3-031-08971-8_26

The main goal is to find the minimum-sized subset of features that is necessary and sufficient to represent the objective concept and at the same time select the subset of features that maximizes the prediction accuracy or reduces the complexity of the model without significantly reducing the prediction accuracy. This article focuses on a Relief-based algorithm, a unique filter-style future selection algorithm that flexibly adapts to various data characteristics, for example, classification versus regression with modification by use of new optimistic and pessimistic similarity measures in the interval-valued fuzzy issue. The use of ranges to represent the uncertainty of data and the comparability measures related to the interval calculus take into account different epistemic, more or less restrictive (optimistic or pessimistic) approaches.

Therefore, the main goal concentrate on the new idea of similarity used in the selection of relevant features needed in diagnostic breast cancer, in particular:

1. To introduce similarity in the optimistic and pessimistic issues of interval-valued fuzzy relations and introduce precedence indicators in the optimistic and pessimistic issues.
2. To use new similarities in the optimistic and pessimistic and standard aspects in modifying the diagnostic model based on the generalized Relief algorithm by verifying using the kNN algorithm.

2   Interval-Valued Fuzzy Setting

For $X \neq \emptyset$ and $cardX = n$. By $L^I = \{[\underline{a}, \overline{a}] : \underline{a}, \overline{a} \in [0,1], \underline{a} \leqslant \overline{a}\}$ we denote the family of all compact sub-intervals of the unit interval we recall the notion of an **interval-valued fuzzy set (IVFS)** [6,7] A in X as a mapping $A : X \to L^I$ such that for each $x \in X$ $A(x) = [\underline{A}(x), \overline{A}(x)]$ attributes the degree of membership of an element x into A. The family of all IVFSs in X will be denoted by $IVFS(X)$. In the case of the IVFS the value membership function is not precisely defined (epistemic interpretation). It is only possible to indicate an upper and lower bound of its membership value. Therefore, IVFSs seem so useful in approximate reasoning with uncertain data.

2.1   Orders in the Interval Setting

Considering two IVFSs A and B in the same universe X we use simplified notation $A(x) = [\underline{A}(x), \overline{A}(x)] = [\underline{a}, \overline{a}]$ and $B(x) = [\underline{B}(x), \overline{B}(x)] = [\underline{b}, \overline{b}]$.

The best known partial order in L^I is designated as follows
$[\underline{a}, \overline{a}] \leqslant_2 [\underline{b}, \overline{b}] \Leftrightarrow \underline{a} \leqslant \underline{b}$ and $\overline{a} \leqslant \overline{b}$,
where $[\underline{a}, \overline{a}] <_2 [\underline{b}, \overline{b}]$ if and only if $[\underline{a}, \overline{a}] \leqslant_2 [\underline{b}, \overline{b}]$ and $(\underline{a} < \underline{b}$ or $\overline{a} < \overline{b})$.

The operations meet and join are defined in L^I in the following way
$[\underline{a}, \overline{a}] \vee [\underline{b}, \overline{b}] = [\max(\underline{a}, \underline{b}), \max(\overline{a}, \overline{b})], [\underline{a}, \overline{a}] \wedge [\underline{b}, \overline{b}] = [\min(\underline{a}, \underline{b}), \min(\overline{a}, \overline{b})].$

For a practical aspect, we need a linear order to be able to compare any two intervals, where we are focused on expanding the partial order $\leqslant_2$ to a linear one. Thus we recall the notion of so-called admissible order.

Definition 1 ([8], **Def. 3.1**). *An order $\leq_{Adm}$ in L^I is coined **admissible** if $\leq_{Adm}$ is linear in L^I and for all $a, b \in L^I$ $a \leq_{Adm} b$ whenever $a \leqslant_2 b$.*

Admissible orders were considered, e.g., in [9]. Below are some examples of admissible orders in L^I (see, e.g., [8]):

- the Xu-Yager order

$$[\underline{a}, \overline{a}] \leqslant_{XY} [\underline{b}, \overline{b}] \Leftrightarrow \underline{a} + \overline{a} < \underline{b} + \overline{b} \text{ or } (\overline{a} + \underline{a} = \overline{b} + \underline{b}, \quad \overline{a} - \underline{a} \leqslant \overline{b} - \underline{b})$$

- lexicographical orders

$$[\underline{a}, \overline{a}] \leqslant_{Lex1} [\underline{b}, \overline{b}] \Leftrightarrow \underline{a} < \underline{b} \text{ or } (\underline{a} = \underline{b}, \quad \overline{a} \leqslant \overline{b})$$
$$[\underline{a}, \overline{a}] \leqslant_{Lex2} [\underline{b}, \overline{b}] \Leftrightarrow \overline{a} < \overline{b} \text{ or } (\overline{a} = \overline{b}, \quad \underline{a} \leqslant \underline{b}).$$

2.2 Interval-Valued (I-V) Aggregation Functions

Now we review the notion of an aggregation function on L^I being a significant concept in numerous applications. What follows is the description of aggregation functions connected with $\leqslant_2$ and $\leqslant_{Adm}$. In the present section is the use of the concept $\leq$ for the either partial or admissible linear order, were $0_{L^I} = [0,0]$ and $1_{L^I} = [1,1]$ are as limit elements of L^I.

Definition 2 ([9,10]). *Let $n \in \mathbf{N}$, $n \geqslant 2$. An operation $\mathcal{A} : (L^I)^n \to L^I$ is called an interval-valued (I-V) aggregation function if it is increasing in connection to the order $\leq$ (partial or linear), i.e.*

$$\forall x_i, y_i \in L^I \quad x_i \leq y_i \Rightarrow \mathcal{A}(x_1, ..., x_n) \leq \mathcal{A}(y_1, ..., y_n) \tag{1}$$

and $\mathcal{A}(0_{L^I}, ..., 0_{L^I}) = 0_{L^I}$, $\mathcal{A}(1_{L^I}, ..., 1_{L^I}) = 1_{L^I}$.

Example 1. Presented earlier lattice operations $\wedge$ and $\vee$ are aggregation functions on L^I, where $A_1 = A_2 = \min$ and $A_1 = A_2 = \max$, respectively (as for the order $\leq_2$, however not $\leq_{Lex1}$, $\leq_{Lex2}$ or $\leq_{XY}$). List of other aggregate functions that can be applied on $\leq_2$:

- the arithmetic mean $\mathcal{A}_{mean}([\underline{x}, \overline{x}], [\underline{y}, \overline{y}]) = [\frac{\underline{x}+\underline{y}}{2}, \frac{\overline{x}+\overline{y}}{2}]$,
- the geometric mean $\mathcal{A}_{gmean}([\underline{x}, \overline{x}], [\underline{y}, \overline{y}]) = [\sqrt{\underline{x}\underline{y}}, \sqrt{\overline{x}\overline{y}}]$,
- the mean-power mean $\mathcal{A}_{meanpow}([\underline{x}, \overline{x}], [\underline{y}, \overline{y}]) = [\frac{\underline{x}+\underline{y}}{2}, \sqrt{\frac{\overline{x}^2+\overline{y}^2}{2}}]$,
- the mean-max $\mathcal{A}_{meanmax}([\underline{x}, \overline{x}], [\underline{y}, \overline{y}]) = [\frac{\underline{x}+\underline{y}}{2}, \max(\overline{x}, \overline{y})]$, $[\underline{x}, \overline{x}], [\underline{y}, \overline{y}] \in L^I$.

Moreover, an operation $\mathcal{A}_\alpha(x, y) = [\alpha \underline{x} + (1 - \alpha)\underline{y}, \alpha \overline{x} + (1 - \alpha)\overline{y}]$ is an I-V aggregation function on L^I in connection to $\leq_{Lex1}$, $\leq_{Lex2}$ and $\leq_{XY}$ (see [9]) for $x, y \in L^I$. Moreover, $\mathcal{A}_{mean}$ is the aggregation in connection to $\leqslant_{Lex1}$, $\leqslant_{Lex2}$ and $\leqslant_{XY}$, not only to $\leqslant_2$. Aggregate functions for interval values may also be built in other ways in connection to $\leq_2$ or $\leq_{Adm}$.

2.3 Inclusion and Similarity Degree Measures for IVFSs

Assessing the degree of inclusion or similarity is one of the more difficult issues in data analysis based on IVFSs representing uncertainty. We often have a situation where we have missing values in the input data this problem is one of the potential sources of uncertainty in the data, and then using a range/interval containing the missing value is an effective tool for predicting it. Therefore, in the case of the measure of similarity, the extensions of the set theory are used, i.e., IVFS Theory. Therefore, researchers are trying to soften the comparability relationship from the form defined by Zadeh, to a more consistent with fuzzy logic. Current approaches tend to move from binary discrimination to fuzzy interval values [9,12,13]. The general definition of inclusion specifies the *including degree*, which determines the level of uncertainty of the information. The following study proposes a measure that determines the degree to which one fuzzy set is contained in another fuzzy subset in different aspects.

2.3.1 Precedence Indicator

To begin with, we will introduce the precedence measure using the linear and partial order, and the method of measuring the uncertainty width, i.e. $w(a) = \overline{a} - \underline{a}$ of $a \in L^I$. Thus, we study a precedence indicator concept in which a strong inequality between inputs leads to the same value (the biggest) of the inclusion measure for these inputs. Moreover, a width of the interval is used in the reflexivity property.

Definition 3 ([15]).   *The function* Prec $: (L^I)^2 \to L^I$ *is perceived to be a* **precedence indicator** *if it fulfills the following conditions for any* $a, b, c \in L^I$:

P1 *if* $a = 1_{L^I}$ *and* $b = 0_{L^I}$ *then* $\mathrm{Prec}(a, b) = 0_{L^I}$;
P2 *if* $a < b$, *then* $\mathrm{Prec}(a, b) = 1_{L^I}$ *for any* $a, b \in L^I$;
P3 $\mathrm{Prec}(a, a) = [1 - w(a), 1]$ *for any* $a \in L^I$;
P4 *if* $a \leq b \leq c$, *then* $\mathrm{Prec}(c, a) \leq \mathrm{Prec}(b, a)$ *and* $\mathrm{Prec}(c, a) \leq \mathrm{Prec}(c, b)$.

Examples of the construction of precedence indicators satisfying Definition 3 are presented below.

Proposition 1 ([14]).   *For* $a, b \in L^I$ *the operation* $\mathrm{Prec}_{\mathcal{A}} : (L^I)^2 \to L^I$ *is the* **precedence indicator**

$$\mathrm{Prec}_{\mathcal{A}}(a, b) = \begin{cases} [1 - w(a), 1], & a = b, \\ 1_{L^I}, & a < b, \\ \mathcal{A}(N_{IV}(a), b), & otherwise \end{cases}$$

for interval-valued (I-V) fuzzy negation N_{IV} *(cf. [16]), as follows* $N_{IV}(a) = [n(\overline{a}), n(\underline{a})] \leq [1 - \overline{a}, 1 - \underline{a}]$, *where* n *is a fuzzy negation and* $\mathcal{A}$ *is a representable I-V aggregation such that* $\mathcal{A} \leq \vee$.

2.3.2 Similarity Measure

In this section, we recall and study the similarity measures between IVFSs.

This approach is inspired firstly by the fact that we reflect the total order of the intervals, and secondly, we determine the output value in such a way that the level of uncertainty of the results is strongly related to the uncertainty of the input, depending on the width of the intervals. In the construction method of this interval-valued (I-V) similarity, I-V aggregation functions, and I-V subsethood measures that take into account the width of the intervals are needed.

For $A, B \in IVFS(X)$ and $card(X) = n, n \in N, X \neq \emptyset$ we will use the following notion of partial order $A \preceq B \Leftrightarrow a_i \leq b_i$ for $i = 1, ..., n$, where $\leq$ is the same kind of orders (partial or linear) for each i and $a_i = A(x_i)$, $b_i = B(x_i)$. Let us note that if for $i = 1, ..., n$ we consider the same linear order $a_i \leq b_i$, then the order $A \preceq B$ between IVFSs A, B is a partial one.

Definition 4 ([15], cf. [18]). *Let $A_1 : [0, 1]^n \to [0, 1]$ be an aggregation function. Then operation $S : IVFS(X) \times IVFS(X) \to L^I$ is called a similarity measure, which satisfies the following items for $i = 1, ..., n$:*

(S_{V1}) $S(A, B) = S(B, A)$ for $A, B \in IVFS(X)$;
(S_{V2}) $S(A, A) = [1 - A_1(w_A(x_1), ..., w_A(x_n)), 1]$;
(S_{V3}) $S(A, B) = 0_{L^I}$, if $\{A(x_i), B(x_i)\} = \{0_{L^I}, 1_{L^I}\}$;
(S_{V4}) if $A \preceq B \preceq C$, then $S(A, C) \leq S(A, B)$ and $S(A, C) \leq S(B, C)$.

Proposition 2 ([15]). *Let Prec be an inclusion measure. If $\mathcal{A} = [A_1, A_2]$, $\mathcal{B} = [B_1, B_2]$ are representable I-V aggregation functions for which A_1 is as in Definition 4 and self-dual, $\mathcal{B}$ is symmetric with the neutral element 1_{L^I} and B_1 is idempotent aggregation function, then the operation $S : IVFS(X) \times IVFS(X) \to L^I$: $S(A, B) = \mathcal{A}_{i=1}^n(\mathcal{B}(\mathrm{Prec}(A(x_i), B(x_i)), \mathrm{Prec}(B(x_i), A(x_i))))$ is a similarity measure.*

Example 2. The operation $S : IVFS(X) \times IVFS(X) \to L^I$:
$S(A, B) = \mathcal{A}_{i=1}^n(\mathrm{Prec}_{\mathcal{A}}(A(x_i), B(x_i)) \wedge \mathrm{Prec}_{\mathcal{A}}(B(x_i), A(x_i)))$ is a similarity measure, where $\mathcal{A} \in \{\mathcal{A}_{mean}, \mathcal{A}_{meanpow}, \mathcal{A}_{meanmax}\}$ by adequate precedence indicators: $\mathrm{Prec}_{\mathcal{A}_{mean}}, \mathrm{Prec}_{\mathcal{A}_{meanpow}}$ and $\mathrm{Prec}_{\mathcal{A}_{meanmax}}$.

3 Possibility and Necessity Issue

Now we are going to discuss some alternative definitions connected with the epistemic issue. We observe a structure with a possible and necessary comparability relation (called "interval order" in the sense as Fishburn or Fodor, 1970–1994.

Necessary Relation

We define the following restricted case of comparability intervals, i.e., the necessary relation, which we may interpret as a conjunctive (ontic) relation and present that one interval contains collection of true values of each variable smaller than or equal to all true values from the second interval:

$\forall_{x^*} \forall_{y^*} x \preceq_\nu y \Leftrightarrow \overline{x} \leq \underline{y}$,

where $x, y \in L^I$, $x^*, y^* \in [0,1]$ and $\underline{x} \leq x^* \leq \overline{x}$ and $\underline{y} \leq y^* \leq \overline{y}$.

In L^I the relation $\preceq_\nu$ is anti-symmetric, transitive and has Ferrers property.

Possible Relation

Possibility relation describes more general situation, which we may write:

$\exists_{x^*} \exists_{y^*} x \preceq_\pi y \Leftrightarrow \underline{x} \leq \overline{y}$,

where $x, y \in L^I$, $x^*, y^* \in [0,1]$ and $\underline{x} \leq x^* \leq \overline{x}$ and $\underline{y} \leq y^* \leq \overline{y}$.

In the structure $(L^I, \preceq_\pi)$ the relation $\preceq_\pi$ is complete and has the Ferrers property (interval order). Relation $\preceq_\pi$ is more suitable for the epistemic (disjunctive) setting of the intervals. The relation $\preceq_\pi$ thus has a possibility interpretation (Dubois, 1988).

Moreover, we observe the following connections between the mentioned comparability relations: $x \preceq_\nu y \Rightarrow x \leq_2 y \Rightarrow x \preceq_\pi y$.

3.1 Aggregation Functions. Possible and Necessary

By replacing in the monotonicity condition the natural order $\preceq$ with the admissible linear orders or relations $\preceq_\pi$ and $\preceq_\nu$, new types of aggregation functions are obtained [17].

Definition 5. *An operation $\mathcal{A} : (L^I)^n \to L^I$ is called a possible aggregation (pos-aggregation) function (necessary aggregation (nec-aggregation) function) if $\mathcal{A}(0_{L^I}, ..., 0_{L^I}) = 0_{L^I}$, $\mathcal{A}(1_{L^I}, ..., 1_{L^I}) = 1_{L^I}$ and*

$$\underset{x_i, y_i \in L^I}{\forall} x_i \preceq_\pi y_i \Rightarrow \mathcal{A}(x_1, \ldots, x_n) \preceq_\pi \mathcal{A}(y_1, \ldots, y_n). \tag{2}$$

$$\left(\underset{x_i, y_i \in L^I}{\forall} x_i \preceq_\nu y_i \Rightarrow \mathcal{A}(x_1, \ldots, x_n) \preceq_\nu \mathcal{A}(y_1, \ldots, y_n). \right) \tag{3}$$

Example 3. The following operations are the possible $\mathcal{A}_\pi$ or necessary $\mathcal{A}_\nu$ aggregation functions:

$$\mathcal{A}_\pi([\underline{x}, \overline{x}], [\underline{y}, \overline{y}]) = \begin{cases} [1,1], & x = y = [1,1], \\ [\frac{y+\overline{x}}{2}, \frac{\overline{x}+\overline{y}}{2}], & \text{otherwise} \end{cases}$$

$$\mathcal{A}_\nu([\underline{x}, \overline{x}], [\underline{y}, \overline{y}]) = [\frac{\underline{x}+\underline{y}}{2}, \max(\frac{\underline{x}+\overline{y}}{2}, \frac{\overline{x}+\underline{y}}{2})].$$

3.2 Negation Functions. Possible and Necessary

By analogy with building aggregation possible and necessary if we use order to antytonicity in IV negation, then we obtained N_π and N_ν:

$N_1(x) = [1 - \overline{x}, 1 - \underline{x}]$, $(N_{IV}, N_\pi$ and $N_\nu)$,

$$N_2(x) = \begin{cases} [1,1], & x = [0,0], \\ [0,0], & x = [1,1], \quad (N_{IV} \text{ and } N_\pi). \\ [\frac{1-\underline{x}}{2}, 1 - \frac{\overline{x}}{2}], & \text{otherwise} \end{cases}$$

3.3 Precedence Indicator. Possible and Necessary

Now we consider two new classes of precedence indicators, i.e., in the sense of possible and necessary (optimistic and pessimistic).

3.3.1 Possible Precedence Indicator

Definition 6. *A function* $\mathrm{Prec}_\pi : (L^I)^2 \to L^I$ *is said to be a **possible precedence indicator** if it satisfies the following conditions for any* $a, b, c \in L^I$:

P1 *If* $a = 1_{L^I}$ *and* $b = 0_{L^I}$ *then* $\mathrm{Prec}_\pi(a, b) = 0_{L^I}$;
P2 *If* $a <_\pi b$ *and* $a \neq b$, *then* $\mathrm{Prec}_\pi(a, b) = 1_{L^I}$ *for any* $a, b \in L^I$;
P3 $\mathrm{Prec}_\pi(a, a) = [1 - w(a), 1]$ *for any* $a \in L^I$, *where* $w(a) = \overline{a} - \underline{a}$ *denotes the width of* $a \in L^I$;
P4 *If* $a \leq_\pi b \leq_\pi c$ *and* $a \subseteq b \subseteq c$, *then* $\mathrm{Prec}_\pi(c, a) \leq_\pi \mathrm{Prec}_\pi(b, a)$ *and* $\mathrm{Prec}_\pi(c, a) \leq_\pi \mathrm{Prec}_\pi(c, b)$, *where* $a \subseteq b$ *iff* $\underline{a} \geq \underline{b}$ *and* $\overline{a} \leq \overline{b}$.

Proposition 3. *Let* N_π *denote a possible interval-valued fuzzy negation (i.e. an antytonic operation that satisfies* $N_\pi(0_{L^I}) = 1_{L^I}$ *and* $N_\pi(1_{L^I}) = 0_{L^I}$, *such that* $N_\pi(a) \leq_\pi [1 - \overline{a}, 1 - \underline{a}]$, *where* n *is a fuzzy negation and* $\mathcal{A}$ *is a possible representable interval-valued aggregation such that* $\mathcal{A} \leq_\pi \vee$. *Then*

$$
\mathrm{Prec}_{\pi\mathcal{A}}(a, b) = \begin{cases} [1 - w(a), 1], & \text{if } a = b, \\ 1_{L^I}, & \text{if } a <_\pi b, \\ \mathcal{A}_\pi(N_\pi(a), b), & \text{otherwise} \end{cases}
$$

is the possible precedence indicator.

3.3.2 Necessary Precedence Indicator

Definition 7. *A function* $\mathrm{Prec}_\nu : (L^I)^2 \to L^I$ *is said to be a **necessary precedence indicator** if it satisfies the following conditions for any* $a, b, c \in L^I$:

P1 *If* $a = 1_{L^I}$ *and* $b = 0_{L^I}$ *then* $\mathrm{Prec}_\nu(a, b) = 0_{L^I}$;
P2 *If* $a <_\nu b$, *then* $\mathrm{Prec}_\nu(a, b) = 1_{L^I}$ *for any* $a, b \in L^I$;
P3 $\mathrm{Prec}_\nu(a, a) = [1 - w(a), 1]$ *for any* $a \in L^I$, *where* $w(a) = \overline{a} - \underline{a}$ *denotes the width of* $a \in L^I$;
P4 *If* $a \leq_\nu b \leq_\nu c$, *then* $\mathrm{Prec}_\nu(c, a) \leq_\nu \mathrm{Prec}_\nu(b, a)$ *and* $\mathrm{Prec}_\nu(c, a) \leq_\nu \mathrm{Prec}_\nu(c, b)$.

Proposition 4. *The operation*

$$
\mathrm{Prec}_\nu(a, b) = \begin{cases} [1 - w(a), 1], & \text{if } u - b, \\ 1_{L^I}, & \text{if } a <_\nu b, \quad \text{is the necessary} \\ [1 - \max(w(a), r(a, b)), 1 - r(a, b)], & \text{otherwise} \end{cases}
$$

precedence indicator, where $r(a, b) = \max(|\underline{a} - \underline{b}|, |\overline{a} - \overline{b}|)$.

3.4   Similarity Measure. Possible and Necessary

As a consequence of the use of precedence indicators, i.e., in the sense of possible and necessary (optimistic and pessimistic), we may obtain also similarities in the adequate, possible and necessary cases.

3.4.1   Possible Similarity Measure

Definition 8. *Let $\Psi : [0,1]^n \rightarrow [0,1]$ be an aggregation function. A function $S_\pi : (IVFS(X))^2 \rightarrow L^I$ which satisfies the following properties*

SP1 $S_\pi(A,B) = S_\pi(B,A)$ *for* $A, B \in IVFS(X)$;
SP2 $S_\pi(A,A) = [1 - \Psi(w(A(x_1)), ..., w(A(x_n))), 1]$;
SP3 $S_\pi(A,B) = 0_{L^I}$ *if* $\{A(x_i), B(x_i)\} = \{0_{L^I}, 1_{L^I}\}$, *for* $i = 1, ..., n$;
SP4 *if* $A \preceq_\pi B \preceq_\pi C$ *and* $A \subseteq B \subseteq C$, *then* $S_\pi(A,C) \leq_\pi S_\pi(A,B)$ *and* $S_\pi(A,C) \leq_\pi S_\pi(B,C)$,

*is called the **possible aggregation-based similarity measure** between interval-valued fuzzy sets, where* $A \preceq_\pi B \Leftrightarrow a_i \leq_\pi b_i$ *and* $A \subseteq B \Leftrightarrow a_i \subseteq b_i \Leftrightarrow \underline{a}_i \geq \underline{b}_i$ *and* $\overline{a}_i \leq \overline{b}_i$ *for* $i = 1, ..., n$.

Proposition 5. *Let* Prec_π *be a possible precedence indicator. If* $\mathcal{A}_\pi = [A_1, A_2]$, $\mathcal{B}_\pi = [B_1, B_2]$ *are possible representable I-V aggregation functions for which A_1 self-dual, $\mathcal{B}_\pi$ is symmetric with the neutral element 1_{L^I} and B_1 is idempotent aggregation function, then the action* $S_\pi : IVFS(X) \times IVFS(X) \rightarrow L^I$: $S_\pi(S,T) = \mathcal{A}_{\pi_{i=1}}^n (\mathcal{B}_\pi(\mathrm{Prec}_\pi(S(x_i), T(x_i)), \mathrm{Prec}_\pi(T(x_i), S(x_i))))$ *is a possible similarity measure.*

Example 4. The operation $S : IVFS(X) \times IVFS(X) \rightarrow L^I$: $S_\pi(A,B) = \mathcal{A}_{i=1}^n (\mathcal{B}(\mathrm{Prec}_\pi(A(x_i), B(x_i)), \mathrm{Prec}_\pi(B(x_i), A(x_i))))$ *is a similarity possible measure, where* $\mathcal{A} = \mathcal{A}_{mean}, \mathcal{B} = \wedge$

3.4.2   Necessary Similarity Measure

Definition 9. *Let $\Psi : [0,1]^n \rightarrow [0,1]$ be an aggregation function. A function $S_\nu : (IVFS(X))^2 \rightarrow L^I$ which satisfies the following properties*

SN1 $S_\nu(A,B) = S_\nu(B,A)$ *for* $A, B \in IVFS(X)$;
SN2 $S_\nu(A,A) = [1 - \Psi(w(A(x_1)), ..., w(A(x_n))), 1]$;
SN3 $S_\nu(A,B) = 0_{L^I}$ *if* $\{A(x_i), B(x_i)\} = \{0_{L^I}, 1_{L^I}\}$, *for* $i = 1, ..., n$;
SN4 *if* $A \preceq_\nu B \preceq_\nu C$, *then* $S(A,C) \leq_\nu S(A,B)$ *and* $S(A,C) \leq_\nu S(B,C)$,

*is called the **necessary similarity measure** between interval-valued fuzzy sets, where* $A \preceq_\nu B \Leftrightarrow a_i \leq_\nu b_i$ *for* $i = 1, ..., n$.

Example 5. The operation $S : IVFS(X) \times IVFS(X) \rightarrow L^I$: $S_\nu(A,B) = \mathcal{A}_{i=1}^n (\mathcal{B}(\mathrm{Prec}_\nu(A(x_i), B(x_i)), \mathrm{Prec}_\nu(B(x_i), A(x_i))))$ *is a similarity necessary measure, where* $\mathcal{A} = \mathcal{A}_{mean}, \mathcal{B} = \wedge$

4   Application. Attribute Selection Algorithm

In the literature, one can find various criteria for the division of the methods of selecting features, but most commonly the following division can be found [3,5,19–21]: ranking method (also called filter or filtration method), wrapped method, and embedded methods.

We introduce a new aspect/new similarity in interval-valued algorithm based on Relief algorithm (filtration method) (see e.g. [5] or [22]) in associated concepts of uncertainty in interval-valued settings, emphasizing the intuition behind how it works, how the feature weights generated by the algorithm can be interpreted, and why it is sensitive to feature interactions. As an individual evaluation filtering feature selection method, Relief calculates a proxy statistic for each feature that can be used to estimate feature 'quality' or 'relevance' to the target concept (i.e. predicting decision). These feature statistics are referred to as feature weights (W_i = weight of feature 'A_i'), or more casually as feature 'scores' that can range from -1 (worst) to $+1$ (best). We proposed the modification of the Relief algorithm, i.e., IVRelief, which operates on IVFSs, with respect to uncertainty in the data in epistemic issues.

4.1   Algorithm IVRelief - Interval-Valued Fuzzy Relief

A pseudo-code of IVRelief algorithm is presented in Algorithm 1. As an input to the algorithm, we have an n-element data set P, each vector of data has a features (attributes) with values from L^I and has assigned a positive or negative decision. Firstly, the set P is divided into two disjoint sets: P^+ of vectors with positive decision and P^- of vectors with negative decisions.

The algorithm starts with a vector W in weight of length a filled with zeros. For each record form, P is search for most similar vector from P^+ (using given similarity measure) - which is denoted as "nearHit" and most similar vector from P^- which is denoted as "nearMiss". For large data-sets, instead of using all records from P it is possible to randomly choose m vectors.

Algorithm 1: IVRelief Algorithm

---

input : a n element data set P composed of vectors of size a
output: a vector W of size a

$W \longleftarrow (0, 0, \ldots, 0)$;
for all $x \in P$ **do**
  find closest vector "nearHit" from P^+ using D;
  find closest vector "nearMiss" from P^- using D;
  for $j \leftarrow 1$ **to** a **do**
    $W_j \leftarrow W_j - \text{diff}(x_j, nearHit_j)/n + \text{diff}(x_j, nearMiss_j)/n$

Then the weight vector is updated using the function diff:

$$\text{diff}(a, b) = \begin{cases} 0, & D(a, b) \leq \gamma, \\ 1, & \text{otherwise}, \end{cases}$$

where $a, b \in L^I$ and γ is a fixed small parameter that determines the margin over which the intervals are indistinguishable. Moreover, D is distance measure based on similarity measure S, as $D = N_{IV}S$. As result of the algorithm, we obtain a vector W of scores that estimate the significance of features. We choose the attributes for future classification if their value of relevance is greater than the relevance threshold θ where $0 \leq \theta \leq 1$.

4.2   Application of K-NN Classifiers

The classification problem which we use is applied to assess the effectiveness of the method of selection of features. Here we consider uncertainty in an epistemic sense, i.e., the data are represented by interval values. In particular, we used techniques for the classification k-Nearest Neighbor classifier (k-NN). In this approach, the object subjected to the classification process belongs to the class to which most of its k-nearest neighbors belong. In this article, we introduce the modified algorithm presented in [22] of an interval-valued fuzzy classifier for helping decision-making processes based on imprecise (uncertain) data. Unlike the IV-kNN [22], the classification concept proposed here is based on the definition of precedence and similarity measures, related to the width of the compartments and in new aspects optimistic and pessimistic, it is the innovation of our approach.

4.2.1   Classification Method

Scheme IV-kNN (Algorithm IV-kNN) shows the basic steps of the proposed classification method, the modified method introduced in [22]. We recall some points and which we also change and we add the issue of selection of attributes:

I. IVFS is constructed for each instance/object.
II. In this part of the algorithm, we use one of the similarity measures from Example 2 to measure the similarity of the tested object to every other object.
III. Selection is made using one of the orders: $\{\leqslant_2, \leqslant_{Adm}, \leqslant_\pi, \leqslant_\nu\}$.
IV. Choosing the most similar objects for $k \in \{1, ..., n\}, n \in N$.
V. Aggregation of similarity measure values of the elements from each class individually. We use aggregations from Example 1 or 3.
VI. For the two obtained intervals matching each class, we use the following method leading to the decision. The interval classes "0" and "1", in addition, we may refrain from making decisions ("No Decision"). The method of searching for decisions consists in comparing the width of the intervals (the smaller width, the better) and the location of the intervals against the value 0.5 [22].

4.2.2   Data Set Description

The data-set is a Wisconsin (diagnostic) breast cancer data-set. This is one of the popular data-sets from UCI Machine Learning Repository (https://archive. ics.uci.edu/ml/index.php). Data contains information on 569 medical cases. Features are calculated from a digitized image of a fine needle aspirate (FNA) of a breast mass. They describe the characteristics of the cell nuclei present in the image.

Ten real-valued features are computed for each cell nucleus: *radius (mean of distances from center to points on the perimeter), texture (standard deviation of gray-scale values), perimeter, area, smoothness (local variation in radius lengths), compactness, concavity (severity of concave portions of the contour), concave points (number of concave portions of the contour), symmetry, fractal dimension.*

For each value, the standard deviation and the mean value of the trait measurements for the patient are given. On the basis of both of these values, the value of the interval is constructed (Step I of the algorithm IV-kNN):

[**mean − standard deviation, mean + standard deviation**]

after earlier fuzzified both values by normalization [22].

The decision attribute stores information about the diagnosis: malignant (0) or benign (1). The data-set consists of 212 malignant objects and 357 benign objects.

4.2.3   Results and Discussion

We will focus on reporting the conclusions of the algorithm evaluation in the following aspects:

1. Selection of aggregation construction with a similarity measure (including precedence measure) (Step II of IV-kNN algorithm using examples of ($\mathcal{A}_{IV}$, $\mathcal{A}_{\pi}$, $\mathcal{A}_{\mu}$)); 2. choosing ordering relations (Step III and one of the cases in Step VI of IV-kNN algorithm); 3. the selection of parameter γ and θ; 4. The selection IV negations (N_{IV}, N_{π}, N_{μ}) and IV similarity measures used in the IVRelief algorithm (examples 2, 4 and 5: S, S_{π} or S_{ν}). During the tests, it was assumed: The data was divided into a training part and a test part. The training part has 90% of all and the testing part has 10% from all objects. We test the algorithm using 10 times cross-validation. From the ten values obtained in this way for accuracy (ACC), sensitivity (SENS), specificity (SPEC), and precision (PREC) their arithmetic mean was calculated and presented as the value obtained by the algorithm with particular parameters. Modification of the value of k.

In studying the IVRelief algorithm we choose the distance (dual to the adequate similarity) in operation diff and for the parameter γ we check the different values and we present the optimal results for 0.01, similar for $0 \leq \theta \leq 0.01$. The presented results refer to the algorithm working for the best in dependencies from k (we tested $k \in \{1, 3, 5, ...\}$). Results of IVRelief - the vector weight: $W_1 = 0.012$, $W_2 = 0.042$, $W_3 = 0.007$, $W_4 = 0.075$, $W_5 = -0.05$, $W_6 = 0.04$, $W_7 = 0.054$, $W_8 = 0.117$, $W_9 = 0.128$, $W_{10} = -0.035$.

We consider three analysis cases concerns removing the attribute with the lowest weight among those indicated by the θ parameter, based on three kinds

Table 1. Compare algorithms and methods

Similarity	Case of test	ACC	SENS	SPEC	PREC
S	No feature removal	0.961	0.927	**0.993**	0.992
	With feature removal (IVRelief)	0.964	0.934	**0.993**	0.993
S_π	With feature removal (IVRelief)	0.928	0.967	0.750	0.937
S_ν	With feature removal (IVRelief)	**0.982**	**0.968**	0.972	**0.994**

of similarities: classic, possible and necessary (S, S_π and S_ν). We observe the results where we use different aggregation functions and different orders, especially for the classic similarity S we present aggregation functions created the best results, i.e. based on example 2 we use $\mathcal{A}_{mean}$ aggregation instead of $\mathcal{A}$ and $\mathcal{B} = \wedge$ and precedence measures built by $\mathcal{A}_{0.4}$, and by using, Xu-Yager order for comparability of intervals in steps III and VI of the IV-kNN algorithm (Table 1).

In the case of S_ν for $\mathcal{A}_{mean}$ and $Prec_\nu$ from Example 5, we observe the progress effectiveness of the presented method in comparing method with classic and possible similarity. Besides, we observe the best level of decision making 98,2% with the selection algorithm IVRelief by canceled attribute with negative values of weight. Moreover, what is important, we obtain a similar efficiency by using the presented algorithm for real data, which indicates a positive aspect of using interval fuzzy values, i.e. data uncertainty.

Conclusions and Future Plans The presented article was aimed at solving the problem of selecting appropriate features based on the Relief algorithm adapted to interval data using the degree of inclusion and similarity between IVFSs. The effectiveness of the selection of relevant attributes has been checked in the classification of uncertain data with the use of the modified k-nearest neighbors (k-NN) algorithm. The proposed approach includes the measure between intervals or IVFSs, i.e., the width of those intervals represents the imprecision of the membership functions and the uncertainty of information. In the future, we have to plan and study the presented algorithm for other data sets and other classification methods.

References

1. Zadeh, L.A.: Fuzzy sets. Inf. Contr. **8**, 338–353 (1965)
2. Dyczkowski, K.: Intelligent Medical Decision Support System Based on Imperfect Information. SCI, vol. 735. Springer, Cham (2018). https://doi.org/10.1007/978-3-319-67005-8
3. Kira, K., Rendell, L.A.: A practical approach to feature selection. In: Proceedings of the 9th International Workshop on Machine Learning, pp. 249–256 (1992)
4. Chapelle, O., Keerthi, S., Chapelle, O., Keerthi, S.: Multi-class feature selection with support vector machines. In: Proceedings of the American Statistical Association, ASA, Denver, CO, USA, 3–7 August (on CD-ROM) (2008)

5. Urbanowicz, R.J., Meekerb, M., La Cavaa, W., Olsona, R.S., Moore, J.H.: Relief-based feature selection: introduction and review. J. Biomed. Inform. **85**, 189–203 (2018)
6. Zadeh, L.A.: The concept of a linguistic variable and its application to approximate reasoning. Inf. Sci. **8**, 199–251, 301–357 (1975). Inf. Sci. **9**, pp. 43–80, 1975
7. Sambuc, R.: Fonctions ϕ-floues: application á l'aide au diagnostic en pathologie thyroidienne. Ph.D. Thesis, Université de Marseille, France (in French) (1975)
8. Bustince, H., Fernandez, J., et al.: Generation of linear orders for intervals by means of aggregation functions. Fuzzy Sets Syst. **220**, 69–77 (2013)
9. Zapata, H., Bustince, H., Montes, S., Bedregal, B., et al.: Interval-valued implications and interval-valued strong equality index with admissible orders. Int. J. Appr. Reas. **88**, 91–109 (2017)
10. Komorníková, M., Mesiar, R.: Aggregation functions on bounded partially ordered sets and their classification. Fuzzy Sets Syst. **175**, 48–56 (2011)
11. Pękala, B.: Uncertainty Data in Interval-Valued Fuzzy Set Theory. SFSC, vol. 367. Springer, Cham (2019). https://doi.org/10.1007/978-3-319-93910-0
12. Bustince, H.: Indicator of inclusion grade for interval-valued fuzzy sets. Application to approximate reasoning based on interval-valued fuzzy sets. Int. J. Appr. Reas. **23**(3), 137–209 (2000)
13. Takáč, Z., Minárová, M., Montero, J., Barrenechea, E., Fernandez, J., Bustince, H.: Interval-valued fuzzy strong S-subsethood measures, interval-entropy and P-interval-entropy. Inf. Sci. **432**, 97–115 (2018)
14. Pękala, B., et al.: Interval subsethood measures with respect to uncertainty for interval-valued fuzzy setting. Int. J. Comp. Int. Syst. **3**, 167–177 (2020)
15. Pękala, B., Dyczkowski, K., Grzegorzewski, P., Bentkowska, U.: Inclusion and similarity measures for interval-valued fuzzy sets based on aggregation and uncertainty assessment. Inf. Sci. **547**, 1182–1200 (2021)
16. Asiain, M.J., Bustince, H., Mesiar, R., Kolesarova, A., Takac, Z.: Negations with respect to admissible orders in the interval-valued fuzzy set theory. IEEE Trans. Fuzzy Syst. https://doi.org/10.1109/TFUZZ.2017.2686372
17. Bentkowska, U.: New types of aggregation functions for interval-valued fuzzy setting and preservation of pos-B and nec-B-transitivity in decision making problems. Inf. Sci. **424**, 385–399 (2018)
18. Bustince, H., Marco-Detchart, C., Fernandez, J., Wagner, C., Garibaldi, J.M., Takáč, Z.: Similarity between interval-valued fuzzy sets taking into account the width of the intervals and admissible orders. Fuzzy Sets Syst. **390**, 23–47 (2020)
19. Jović, A., Brkić, K., Bogunović, N.: A review of feature selection methods with applications. In: 38th International Convention on Information and Communication Technology, Electronics and Microelectronics, pp. 1200–1205. IEEE (2015)
20. Tang, J., Alelyani, S., Liu, H.: Feature selection for classification: a review. In: Data Classification: Algorithms and Applications, pp. 37–64 (2014)
21. Srivastava, M.S., Joshi, M.N., Gaur, M.M.: A review paper on feature selection methodologies and their applications. Int. J. Eng. Res. Dev. **7**(6), 57–61 (2013)
22. Pękala, B., Dyczkowski, K., Szkoła, J., Kosior, D.: Classification of uncertain data with a selection of relevant features based on similarities measures of Interval-Valued Fuzzy Sets. In: IEEE International Conference on Fuzzy System, pp. 1–8 (2021)

Applications of Monads in Semiring-Valued Fuzzy Sets

Jiří Močkoř[✉]

Centre of Excellence IT4Innovations, Institute for Research and Applications of Fuzzy Modeling, University of Ostrava, 30. Dubna 22, 701 03 Ostrava 1, Czech Republic
Jiri.Mockor@osu.cz
http://irafm.osu.cz/

Abstract. Many of the new fuzzy structures with value sets in complete MV-algebras, such as hesitant, intuitionistic, neutrosophic or fuzzy soft sets, can be transformed into one common type of fuzzy sets with values in special semirings. This transformation of fuzzy structures is then used to unify the various specific methods used in these new fuzzy structures, such as special fuzzy relations, fuzzy approximation, or fuzzy rough sets. The unification of these methods uses the existence of monads defined by special semirings.

1 Introduction

The current development of fuzzy mathematics and its applications leads to a significant expansion of fuzzy mathematical structures with values in various partially ordered structures. Examples of these new fuzzy structures are intuitionistic fuzzy sets [2,4,5,21,37,39], hesitant fuzzy sets [31,34,35,38], fuzzy soft sets [3,11,22–25,27,29], or neutrosophic fuzzy sets [18–20] and their mutual combinations, such as intuitionistic fuzzy soft sets [1,13], hesitant fuzzy soft sets [6,8,33,36], and many others. Although all of these fuzzy structures are different from each other, they still use a number of type-analog methods and tools that are commonly used in classical fuzzy sets. These tools in general include various specific modifications of fuzzy relations, variants of Zadeh's extension principle, analogies of upper and lower approximations of fuzzy structures, or generalizations of rough fuzzy structures. In most of these fuzzy structures, these methods are developed independently, including proofs of their theoretical properties.

It is therefore natural that, in addition to the efforts to create new fuzzy structures, there are also efforts to unify these structures and their methods or to create new fuzzy structures, which would comprise a wide range of existing fuzzy structures. One possible approach to this unification was published in [28], where we proved that most of these fuzzy structures with values in the

This work was partly supported from ERDF/ESF project CZ.02.1.01/0.0/0.0/17-049/0008414.

complete MV-algebra can be represented by the so-called $(\mathcal{R}, \mathcal{R}^*)$-fuzzy sets, i.e., mappings $X \to R$, where R is the (common) underlying set of special partially ordered semirings $\mathcal{R}$ and $\mathcal{R}^*$. This unification of fuzzy structures thus creates a precondition for the unification of methods used in these fuzzy structures, i.e., power set objects of fuzzy structures, and methods based on fuzzy relations such as rough fuzzy structures or various approximations of fuzzy structures.

Our goal in this paper is to focus on the second task, that is, the unification of the methods mentioned above in various fuzzy structures with values in the complete MV-algebra. Because many of the fuzzy structures can be commonly represented as $(\mathcal{R}, \mathcal{R}^*)$-fuzzy sets, to unify the methods used in these fuzzy structures, it is sufficient to create a generic variant of these methods for $(\mathcal{R}, \mathcal{R}^*)$-fuzzy sets. The basic tool we will use for this unification is the theory of monads of categories, as introduced in [26]. This theory allows us to use a monad to define the concept of a monadic relation, which can be used to construct the theoretical tools mentioned for $(\mathcal{R}, \mathcal{R}^*)$-fuzzy sets. This procedure can be briefly described by the following steps:

1. We choose the pair $(\mathcal{R}, \mathcal{R}^*)$ of adjoint semirings corresponding to the concrete $\mathcal{L}$-fuzzy structure.
2. Using $(\mathcal{R}, \mathcal{R}^*)$ we define the pair of monads $\mathbf{T}_{\mathcal{R}}, \mathbf{T}_{\mathcal{R}^*}^*$ in the category **Set** of sets.
3. For this pair of monads we can define the notion of a monadic relation.
4. Using the pair of monads and monadic relation, we can construct a monadic variant of Zadeh's extension principle, a monadic rough structure, or a monadic approximation of $(\mathcal{R}, \mathcal{R}^*)$-fuzzy sets.
5. The created concepts can be transformed back into the original fuzzy structures.

The details of the proofs and other concepts will be published elsewhere.

2   Semiring-Valued Fuzzy Sets

The notion of a semiring appears for the first time in [7] and was elaborated in [16]. We need to use semirings in which a partially ordered or preorder relation is defined, and this notion of a partially ordered semiring was first introduced in the [12].

Definition 1. *[7, 12] A partially preordered (or ordered) idempotent commutative semiring $\mathcal{R} = (R, \leq_R, +, \times, 0_R, 1_R)$ (or, shortly, po-semiring) is an algebraic structure with the following properties:*

(i) $(R, +, 0_R)$ is an idempotent commutative monoid,

(ii) $(R, \times, 1_R)$ is a commutative monoid,

(iii) $x \times (y + z) = x \times y + x \times z$ holds for all $x, y, z \in R$,

(iv) $0_R \times x = 0_R$ holds for all $x \in R$.

(v) $(R, \leq_R)$ is a partially preordered (or ordered) set such that for all $a, b, c \in R$ the following hold.

$$a \leq_R b \Rightarrow a +_R c \leq_R b +_R c, \quad a \times_R c \leq_R b \times_R c,$$
$$a \geq_R 0_R,$$

If a semiring $\mathcal{R}$ is such that for any subset $S \subseteq R$ there exists the sum of elements $r \in S$, then $\mathcal{R}$ is called a *complete* semiring. The sum of elements $x \in S$ is denoted by $\sum_{r \in S}^{\mathcal{R}} r$. The notion of a po-semiring homomorphism is defined as a standard homomorphism between algebraic structures.

Definition 2. *Let $\mathcal{R}$ and $\mathcal{S}$ be po-semirings. A po-semiring homomorphism Φ: $\mathcal{R} \to \mathcal{S}$ is a mapping $\Phi : R \to S$ between the underlying sets of these semirings such that*

1. *Φ is a homomorphism of semirings,*
2. *Φ is order-preserving.*

The basic value set structure we use is the so-called adjoint pair of complete po-semirings $(\mathcal{R}, \mathcal{R}^*)$ which was introduced in [28].

Definition 3 ([28]). *Let $\mathcal{R} = (R, \leq, +, \times, 0, 1)$ and $\mathcal{R}^* = (R, \leq^*, +^*, \times^*, 0^*, 1^*)$ be complete po-semirings with the same underlying set R. The pair $(\mathcal{R}, \mathcal{R}^*)$ is called the adjoint pair of po-semirings if there exists a po-semiring isomorphism $\Phi : R \to R^*$ and the following statements hold:*

1. *Φ is self-inverse, that is, $\Phi.\Phi = id_R$,*
2. *$\forall a, b \in R, \ a \leq b \Leftrightarrow a \geq^* b$,*
3. *$\forall a, b, c \in R, \quad a \times^* (b + c) = (a \times^* b) + (a \times^* c)$,*
4. *$\forall a, b, c \in R, \quad a + (b +^* c) = (a + b) +^* (a + c)$,*
5. *$\forall a, b \in R, \quad a +^* b \leq a + b$,*

The basic structure with which we will work is the fuzzy set with semi-ring values $((\mathcal{R}, \mathcal{R}^*)$-fuzzy sets, for short). As we showed in our previous paper [28], although this notion has not yet been used and this structure has not been studied, it represents many of the new fuzzy structures, such as intuitionistic, hesitant, neutrosophis, or fuzzy soft sets with values in complete MV-algebras. In the next part of this section, we repeat some basic definitions and properties of $(\mathcal{R}, \mathcal{R}^*)$-fuzzy sets which we use in the next part of the paper.

Definition 4 ([28]). *Let $(\mathcal{R}, \mathcal{R}^*)$ be the adjoint pair of po-semirings with the common underlying set R and isomorphism Φ. Let X be a set.*

1. *A mapping $s : X \to R$ is called the $(\mathcal{R}, \mathcal{R}^*)$-fuzzy set in X. The set of all $(\mathcal{R}, \mathcal{R}^*)$-fuzzy sets in X is denoted by $(\mathcal{R}, \mathcal{R}^*)^X$.*
2. *The operations on $(\mathcal{R}, \mathcal{R}^*)$-fuzzy sets and the external operation with elements of R are defined for arbitrary $s, t \in (\mathcal{R}, \mathcal{R}^*)^X$ and $a \in R$ by*
   (a) The intersection $s \sqcap t$ is defined by $(s \sqcap t)(x) = s(x) +^* t(x)$, $x \in X$,
   (b) The union $s \sqcup t$ is defined by $(s \sqcup t)(x) = s(x) + t(x)$, $x \in X$,

(c) The complement ¬s is defined by $(\neg s)(x) = \Phi(s(x))$,

(d) The external multiplication $\star$ by elements from R is defined by $(a \star s)(x) = a \times s(x)$,

(e) The preorder relation $\subseteq$ between $(\mathcal{R}, \mathcal{R}^*)$-fuzzy sets is defined by

$$s \subseteq t \Leftrightarrow (\forall x \in X) s(x) \leq t(x).$$

For illustration, we present two examples of adjoint *po*-semirings. In these examples, $\mathcal{L} = (L, \oplus, \otimes, \neg, 0_L, 1_L)$ is a complete MV-algebra, where we standardly set

$$x \vee y = (x \oplus \neg y) \otimes y, \quad x \wedge y = (x \otimes \neg y) \oplus y, \quad x \leq y \Leftrightarrow x \vee y = y.$$

Example 1 ([9]).

1. The reduct $\mathcal{L}^\vee = (L, \leq, \vee, \otimes, 0_L, 1_L)$ is the *po*-semiring.
2. The reduct $\mathcal{L}^\wedge = (L, \geq, \wedge, \oplus, 1_L, 0_L)$ is the *po*-semiring.
3. $(\mathcal{L}^\vee, \mathcal{L}^\wedge)$ is the adjoint pair of *po*-semirings, where the *po*-semiring isomorphism $\Phi : \mathcal{L}^\vee \to \mathcal{L}^\wedge$ is defined by $\Phi(\alpha) = \neg \alpha$.

Example 2 ([28]).

1. The *po*-semiring $\mathcal{R} = (R, \leq, +, \times, \mathbf{0}, \mathbf{1})$ is defined by
   (a) $R = L^3$,
   (b) $(\alpha, \beta, \gamma) + (\alpha_1, \beta_1, \gamma_1) := (\alpha \vee \alpha_1, \beta \wedge \beta_1, \gamma \wedge \gamma_1)$,
   (c) $(\alpha, \beta, \gamma) \times (\alpha_1, \beta_1, \gamma_1) := (\alpha \otimes \alpha_1, \beta \wedge \beta_1, \gamma \oplus \gamma_1)$,
   (d) $\mathbf{0} = (0_L, 1_L, 1_L)$, $\quad \mathbf{1} = (1_L, 1_L, 0_L)$,
   (e) $(\alpha, \beta, \gamma) \leq (\alpha', \beta', \gamma') \Leftrightarrow \alpha \leq \alpha', \beta \geq \beta', \gamma \geq \gamma'$.
2. The *po*-semiring $\mathcal{R}^* = (R, \leq^*, +^*, \times^*, \mathbf{0}^*, \mathbf{1}^*)$ is defined by
   (a) $(\alpha, \beta, \gamma) +^* (\alpha_1, \beta_1, \gamma_1) := (\alpha \wedge \alpha_1, \beta \vee \beta_1, \gamma \vee \gamma_1)$,
   (b) $(\alpha, \beta, \gamma) \times^* (\alpha_1, \beta_1, \gamma_1) := (\alpha \oplus \alpha_1, \beta \vee \beta_1, \gamma \otimes \gamma_1)$,
   (c) $\mathbf{0}^* = (1_L, 0_L, 0_L)$, $\quad \mathbf{1}^* = (0_L, 0_L, 1_L)$,
   (d) $(\alpha, \beta, \gamma) \leq^* (\alpha', \beta', \gamma') \Leftrightarrow (\alpha, \beta, \gamma) \geq_4 (\alpha', \beta', \gamma')$.

Let $\Phi : \mathcal{R} \to \mathcal{R}^*$ be defined by

$$(\alpha, \beta, \gamma) \in R, \quad \Phi(\alpha, \beta, \gamma) = (\gamma, \neg \beta, \alpha).$$

Then $(\mathcal{R}, \mathcal{R}^*)$ is the adjoint pair of *po*-semirings and Φ is the *po*-semiring isomorphism.

As we mentioned in Introduction, many of the new $\mathcal{L}$-valued fuzzy structures can be represented as $(\mathcal{R}, \mathcal{R}^*)$-fuzzy sets for appropriate semirings. Let us consider the following examples that were introduced in [28].

Example 3. [28] Let $\mathcal{L}$ be the complete MV-algebra. The following structures are isomorphic to the structure $((\mathcal{R}, \mathcal{R}^*)^X, \sqcup, \sqcap, \neg, \star)$ for some adjoint pair of semirings:

1. The algebraic structure $H(X)$ of all hesitant $\mathcal{L}$-fuzzy sets in X.
2. The algebraic structure $J(X)$ of all intuitionistic $\mathcal{L}$-fuzzy sets.

3. The algebraic structure $S(X)$ of all $\mathcal{L}$-fuzzy soft sets in X.
4. The algebraic structure $N(X)$ of all neutrosophic $\mathcal{L}$-fuzzy sets in X.

It should be noted that the adjoint pair of *po*-semirings corresponding to the algebraic structure of classical $\mathcal{L}$-fuzzy sets is the adjoint pair from Example 1 and the adjoint pair from Example 2 corresponds to the structure $N(X)$ of neutrosophic fuzzy sets.

3   Monads in $(\mathcal{R}, \mathcal{R}^*)$-Fuzzy Set Theory

Although the monad can be defined in an arbitrary category, for simplicity, we use only the monad in the category **Set** of sets as objects and mappings as morphisms and with "." as the composition of morphisms. For our purposes, we need the monads to have some other properties that more reflect properties of structures we know from the theory of fuzzy sets. One of these typical properties is that there is a point-wise ordered relation on the set of L-valued fuzzy sets. This property is then represented by the so-called partially ordered monads, which were introduced and elaborated in [10,14,15,17,30]. The following definition is modified from the definitions in [17] and [32].

Definition 5. $\mathbf{T} = (T, \Diamond, \eta, \ll)$ *is a* **partially preordered monad** *in the category* **Set***, where*

1. $T: \mathbf{Set} \to \mathbf{Set}$ *is the object function,*
2. $\ll = \{\leq_X : X \in \mathbf{Set}\}$*, where $\leq_X$ is a partially preordered relation on the set $T(X)$,*
3. *For arbitrary objects $X, Y \in \mathbf{Set}$, on the set $Hom(X, T(Y))$ the partially pre-order relation $\leq_{X,Y}$ is defined such that for arbitrary mappings $h, k: X \to T(Y)$,*

$$h \leq_{X,Y} k \Leftrightarrow \forall x \in X, \quad h(x) \leq_Y k(x),$$

4. η *is a system of mappings $\{\eta_X : X \to T(X) | X \in \mathbf{Set}\}$,*
5. *For each pair of mappings $f: X \to T(Y)$, $g: Y \to T(Z)$, there exists a composition (called a Kleisli composition) $g \Diamond f : X \to T(Z)$, which is associative,*
6. *For every mapping $f : X \to T(Y)$, $\eta_Y \Diamond f = f$ and $f \Diamond \eta_X = f$ hold,*
7. $\Diamond$ *is compatible with composition of mappings, i.e., for mappings $f : X \to Y$, $g : Y \to T(Z)$, we have $g \Diamond (\eta_Y . f) = g.f$,*
8. *For arbitrary mappings $f, f' : X \to T(Y), g, g' : Y \to T(Z)$, the following implications hold*

$$g \leq g' \Rightarrow g \Diamond f \leq_{X,Z} g' \Diamond f,$$
$$f \leq f' \Rightarrow g \Diamond f \leq_{X,Z} g \Diamond f'.$$

For two partially preordered monads in the category **Set** we can define the morphism between these monads.

Definition 6. *Let* $\mathbf{T} = (T, \Diamond, \eta, \ll_T)$ *and* $\mathbf{S} = (S, \Box, \tau, \ll_S)$ *be partially preordered monads in the category* **Set**. *We say that* $\Psi = \{\Psi_X : X \in \mathbf{Set}\} : \mathbf{T} \to \mathbf{S}$ *is a morphism from* $\mathbf{T}$ *to* $\mathbf{S}$, *if for arbitrary set* X, $\Psi_X : T(X) \to S(X)$ *is a preorder-preserving mapping and for arbitrary mappings* $f : A \to T(B)$ *and* $g : B \to T(C)$, *the following hold:*

$$\Psi_C.(g \Diamond f) = (\Psi_C.g) \Box (\Psi_B.f),$$
$$\Psi_A.\eta_A = \tau_A.$$

Using the monad in category **Set**, the notion of a monadic relation in **Set** can be defined according to [26].

Definition 7. *[26] Let* $\mathbf{T} = (T, \Diamond, \eta, \ll)$ *be a partially preordered monad in the category* **Set**. *A* $\mathbf{T}$*-relation* R *from a set* X *to a set* Y *is a mapping* $R : X \to T(Y)$, *denoted by* $R : X \rightsquigarrow Y$. *If* $S : Y \rightsquigarrow Z$ *is another* $\mathbf{T}$*-relation, its composition is a* $\mathbf{T}$*-relation* $S \Diamond R : X \rightsquigarrow Z$.

Analogously, as in the case of classical relations or fuzzy relations, we can define some special $\mathbf{T}$-relations.

Definition 8. *Let* $\mathbf{T} = (T, \Diamond, \eta, \ll)$ *be a partially preordered monad in the category* **Set** *and let* $R : X \rightsquigarrow X$ *be a* $\mathbf{T}$*-relation.*

1. $\mathbf{T}$ *is called a reflexive* $\mathbf{T}$*-relation, if* $\eta_X \leq_{X,X} R$.
2. $\mathbf{T}$ *is called a transitive* $\mathbf{T}$*-relation, if* $R \Diamond R \leq_{X,X} R$.

The basic step in our process of unifying methods in fuzzy structures is the construction of two partially preordered monads defined by an adjoint pair of *po*-semirings. These constructions we present in the following theorem.

Theorem 1. *Let* $(\mathcal{R}, \mathcal{R}^*)$ *be the adjoint pair of po-semirings with the adjoint semiring isomorphism* Φ, *where* $\mathcal{R} = (R, \leq, +, \times, 0_R, 1_R)$ *and* $\mathcal{R}^* = (R, \leq^*, +^*, \times^*, 0_R^*, 1_R^*)$. *Let the structures* $\mathbf{T}_{\mathcal{R}} = (T, \Diamond, \eta, \ll_T)$ *and* $\mathbf{T}_{\mathcal{R}^*}^* = (T^*, \Diamond^*, \eta^*, \ll_T^*)$ *be defined by*

1. $\ll_T = \{\leq_X : X \in \mathbf{Set}\}$, *where for* $f, g \in T(X)$, $f \leq_X g \Leftrightarrow f(x) \leq g(x)$ *for each* $x \in X$,
2. $\ll_T^* = \{\leq_X^* : X \in \mathbf{Set}\}$, *where for* $f, g \in T^*(X)$, $f \leq_X^* g \Leftrightarrow f(x) \leq^* g(x)$ *for each* $x \in X$,
3. $T : \mathbf{Set} \to \mathbf{Set}$ *is such that* $T(X) = R^X$,
4. $T^* : \mathbf{Set} \to \mathbf{Set}$ *is such that* $T^*(X) = R^X$,
5. *For mappings* $f : X \to T(Y)$ *and* $g : Y \to T(Z)$ *we set*

$$g \Diamond f : X \to T(Z), \quad (g \Diamond f)(x)(z) = \sum_{y \in Y}^{\mathcal{R}} f(x)(y) \times g(y)(z), \qquad (1)$$

$$g \Diamond^* f : X \to T(Z), \quad (g \Diamond^* f)(x)(z) = \sum_{y \in Y}^{\mathcal{R}^*} f(x)(y) \times^* g(y)(z). \qquad (2)$$

6. η_X and η_X^* are mappings $X \to T(X)$ defined by

$$\eta_X(x)(y) = \begin{cases} 1_R, & x = y, \\ 0_R, & x \neq y, \end{cases}, \quad \eta_X^*(x)(y) = \Phi(\eta_X(x)(y)).$$

Then $\mathbf{T}_\mathcal{R}$ and $\mathbf{T}^*{}_{\mathcal{R}^*}$ are partially preordered monads in category **Set** and $\Psi = \{\Psi_X : X \in \mathbf{Set}\} : \mathbf{T}_\mathcal{R} \to \mathbf{T}^*_{\mathcal{R}^*}$ is the morphisms of monads, where $\Psi_X : T(X) \to T^*(X)$ is defined by $\Psi_X(f)(x) = \Phi(f(x))$ for $f \in T(X)$ and $x \in X$.

Proof. Instead of proof, we only show that $\Psi : \mathbf{T}_\mathcal{R} \to \mathbf{T}^*_{\mathcal{R}^*}$ is a monad morphism. Let $f : A \to T(B)$ and $g : B \to T(C)$ be mappings. For $a \in A, c \in C$ we have

$$(\Psi_C.(g \lozenge f))(a)(c) = \Psi_C((g \lozenge f)(a))(c) = \Phi((g \lozenge f)(a)(c)) =$$

$$\Phi(\sum_{y \in B}^{\mathcal{R}} f(a)(y) \times g(y)(c)) = \sum_{y \in B}^{\mathcal{R}^*} \Phi(f(a)(y)) \times^* \Phi(g(y)(c)) =$$

$$\sum_{y \in B}^{\mathcal{R}^*} (\Psi_B.f)(a)(y) \times^* (\Psi_C.g)(y)(c) = ((\Psi_C.g) \lozenge^* (\Psi_B.f))(a)(c).$$

□

As we mentioned in the Introduction, using the notion of monads defined by the pair of adjoint *po*-semrings, some methods and procedures known from the theory of classical $\mathcal{L}$-fuzzy sets can be introduced for $(\mathcal{R}, \mathcal{R}^*)$-fuzzy sets. These methods mainly concern variants of Zadeh's extension principle, lower and upper approximations of $(\mathcal{R}, \mathcal{R}^*)$-fuzzy sets, or other types of approximation, such as rough fuzzy structures. In the next part, we present the details of these general methods for $(\mathcal{R}, \mathcal{R}^*)$-fuzzy sets. In all these examples, we suppose that $(\mathcal{R}, \mathcal{R}^*)$ is a pair of adjoint *po*-semirings with a *po*-semiring homomorphism Φ and with monads $\mathbf{T}_\mathcal{R}$ and $\mathbf{T}^*_{\mathcal{R}^*}$ defined by this adjoint pair.

3.1   Zadeh's Extension Principle for $(\mathcal{R}, \mathcal{R}^*)$-Fuzzy Sets

Zadeh's extension principle for $(\mathcal{R}, \mathcal{R}^*)$-fuzzy sets relates, in general, to the possibility of extending a mapping $f : X \to Y$ between two sets onto the direct mapping $f^\to : T(X) = R^X \to R^Y = T(Y)$ or the inverse mapping $f^\leftarrow : T(Y) \to T(X)$.

We introduce the definitions of the lower and upper variants of Zadeh's extension for $(\mathcal{R}, \mathcal{R}^*)$-fuzzy sets, which are based on the application of monads $\mathbf{T}_\mathcal{R}$ and $\mathbf{T}^*_{\mathcal{R}^*}$. This approach enables us to apply these Zadeh's extensions to any fuzzy structure which can be expressed as $(\mathcal{R}, \mathcal{R}^*)$-fuzzy sets.

Definition 9. Let $f : X \to Y$ be a mapping. Then the upper and lower direct Zadeh's extensions $f^\to$ and $f^\Rightarrow$, respectively, of the $(\mathcal{R}, \mathcal{R}^*)$-fuzzy sets are defined by

$$f^\to = (\eta_Y.f) \lozenge 1_{T(X)} : R^X \to R^Y, \tag{3}$$

$$f^\Rightarrow = (\eta_Y^*.f) \lozenge^* 1_{T(X)} : R^X \to R^Y, \tag{4}$$

By Theorem 1, these formulas can be transformed for arbitrary $s \in T(X)$ and $y \in Y$ into the following formulas:

$$f^{\rightarrow}(s)(y) = \sum_{z \in X}^{\mathcal{R}} 1_{T(X)}(s)(z) \times (\eta_Y . f)(z)(y) = \sum_{z \in X, f(z)=y}^{\mathcal{R}} s(z), \qquad (5)$$

$$f^{\Rightarrow}(s)(y) = \sum_{z \in X}^{\mathcal{R}^*} 1_{T(X)}(s)(z) \times^* (\eta_Y^* . f)(z)(y) = \sum_{z \in X, f(z)=y}^{\mathcal{R}^*} s(z). \qquad (6)$$

It is easy to prove that the following relationships hold between $f^{\rightarrow}$ and $f^{\Rightarrow}$:

$$f^{\Rightarrow}(s)(y) = \Phi(f^{\rightarrow}(\neg s)(y)), \quad f^{\rightarrow}(s)(y) = \Phi(f^{\Rightarrow}(\neg s)(y)),$$
$$f^{\Rightarrow}(s)(y) \le f^{\rightarrow}(s)(y).$$

Moreover, the following properties of the upper and lower Zadeh's extensions hold for $(\mathcal{R}, \mathcal{R}^*)$-fuzzy sets.

Lemma 1. *Let* $s, t \in (\mathcal{R}, \mathcal{R}^*)^X$ *and* $a \in R$ *and let* $f : X \to Y$ *be a mapping. Then the following statements are valid.*

1. $f^{\rightarrow}(a \star s) = a \star f^{\rightarrow}(s), \quad f^{\Rightarrow}(a \star s) = a \star^* f^{\Rightarrow}(s),$
2. $f^{\rightarrow}(s + t) = f^{\rightarrow}(s) + f^{\rightarrow}(t), \quad f^{\Rightarrow}(s +^* t) = f^{\Rightarrow}(s) +^* f^{\Rightarrow}(t),$ *where the additions of* s *and* t *are defined pointwise from the additions in* $\mathcal{R}$ *and* $\mathcal{R}^*$, *respectively.*
3. $s \le_X t \Rightarrow f^{\rightarrow}(s) \le_X f^{\rightarrow}(t), f^{\Rightarrow}(s) \ge_X^* f^{\Rightarrow}(t),$
4. $f^{\rightarrow}(\underline{a}) = f^{\Rightarrow}(\underline{a}) = \underline{a}$, *where* $\underline{a}$ *is the constant fuzzy set with the value* $a \in R$.

Analogously to classical $\mathcal{L}$-fuzzy sets, we can also define the inverse upper and lower Zadeh's extensions. Let $f : X \to Y$ be a mapping; then we can set

$$t \in T(Y), x \in X, \quad f^{\leftarrow}(t)(x) = f^{\Leftarrow}(t)(x) = t(f(x)).$$

In that case, the following statements hold for arbitrary $s \in T(X), t \in T(Y)$.

$$f^{\leftarrow} f^{\rightarrow}(s) \ge_X s, \quad f^{\Leftarrow} f^{\Rightarrow}(s) \ge_X^* s,$$
$$f^{\rightarrow} f^{\leftarrow}(t) = t = f^{\Rightarrow} f^{\Leftarrow}(t).$$

The lower and upper variants of the Zadeh's extension principle for $(\mathcal{R}, \mathcal{R}^*)$-fuzzy sets can be used to define the Zadeh's extension for arbitrary fuzzy structure, which can be expressed as the $(\mathcal{R}, \mathcal{R}^*)$-fuzzy set, e.g., $\mathcal{L}$-valued hesitant, intuitionistic, neutrosophic, or fuzzy soft sets. For illustration, we show how the Zadeh's extension looks for neutrosophic fuzzy sets.

Example 4. For this purpose, we use Example 2 to transform $\mathcal{L}$-neutrosophic fuzzy sets to $(\mathcal{R}, \mathcal{R}^*)$-fuzzy sets. Let $f : X \to Y$ is a mapping. Let $s : X \to R$ be the $(\mathcal{R}, \mathcal{R}^*)$-fuzzy set. For $x \in X$ we set $s(x) = (\alpha_x, \beta_x, \gamma_x) \in R$. According to (5)(6), and Example 2, for $y \in Y$ we obtain

$$f^{\rightarrow}(s)(y) = \sum_{z \in X, f(z)=y}^{\mathcal{R}} (\alpha_z, \beta_z, \gamma_z) = \left(\bigvee_{z,f(z)=y} \alpha_z, \bigwedge_{z,f(z)=y} \beta_z, \bigwedge_{z,f(z)=y} \gamma_z \right),$$

$$f^{\Rightarrow}(s)(y) = \sum_{z \in X, f(z)=y}^{\mathcal{R}^*} (\alpha_z, \beta_z, \gamma_z) = \left(\bigwedge_{z,f(z)=y} \alpha_z, \bigvee_{z,f(z)=y} \beta_z, \bigvee_{z,f(z)=y} \gamma_z \right),$$

$\square$

3.2   Approximations of $(\mathcal{R}, \mathcal{R}^*)$-Fuzzy Sets

The approximation of $\mathcal{L}$-fuzzy sets by $\mathcal{L}$-fuzzy relations is a method that is very often used in both the theory and applications of classical $\mathcal{L}$-fuzzy sets. Well-known methods, such as, e.g., fuzzy rough set theory, F-transform theory, or various special types of $\mathcal{L}$-fuzzy set approximations using various types of fuzzy relations depending on particular applications, are based on this method. It is therefore natural that most of these methods are equally interesting for all types of new fuzzy structures, which we mentioned in the Introduction.

Just as we have unified a large part of the new $\mathcal{L}$-fuzzy structures using the adjoint pair of semirings, we can also unify the approximations of these new fuzzy sets. As in the case of Zadeh's extension principle, we will again use the monads $\mathbf{T}_{\mathcal{R}}$ and $\mathbf{T}_{\mathcal{R}^*}^*$.

For a general monad $\mathbf{T}$ in the category $\mathbf{Set}$ and a $\mathbf{T}$-relation $S : X \rightsquigarrow Y$, the approximation of elements from $T(X)$ defined by S is a mapping $S^{\uparrow} : T(X) \rightarrow T(Y)$ introduced in the following definition.

Definition 10. *Let* $\mathbf{T} = (T, \Diamond, \eta, \ll)$ *be a partially preordered monad in* $\mathbf{Set}$ *and let* $S : X \rightsquigarrow Y$ *be a* $\mathbf{T}$-*relation. The approximation* $S^{\uparrow} : T(X) \rightarrow T(Y)$ *is defined by*

$$S^{\uparrow} = S \Diamond 1_{T(X)}.$$

In this part, we focus on the monads $\mathbf{T}_{\mathcal{R}}$ and $\mathbf{T}_{\mathcal{R}^*}^*$, respectively, and the corresponding relations. Because the object functions of these monads are equal T and are identical, any $\mathbf{T}_{\mathcal{R}}$-relation is also $\mathbf{T}_{\mathcal{R}^*}^*$-relation, and conversely. It follows that for arbitrary monadic relation $S : X \rightsquigarrow Y$ there are two possibilities for extending S to mappings $T(X) \rightarrow T(Y)$, i.e.,

$$S^{\uparrow} = S \Diamond 1_{T(X)}, \quad S^{\downarrow} = S \Diamond^* 1_{T(X)},$$

or, in explicit expressions for $s \in T(X), y \in Y$,

$$S^{\uparrow}(s)(y) = \sum_{z \in X}^{\mathcal{R}} 1_{T(X)}(s)(z) \times S(z)(y) = \sum_{z \in X}^{\mathcal{R}} s(z) \times S(z)(y), \qquad (7)$$

$$S^{\downarrow}(s)(y) = \Phi((\neg S)^{\rightarrow}(\neg s))(y) = \sum_{z \in X}^{\mathcal{R}^*} s(z) \times^* S(z, y). \qquad (8)$$

$S^{\downarrow}(f)$ and $S^{\uparrow}(f)$ are called the *lower and upper* **T**-*approximations* of f defined by S, respectively.

Using these approximations, we can define the notion of the *rough* $(\mathcal{R}, \mathcal{R}^*)$-*fuzzy sets*:

Definition 11. *Let* $(\mathcal{R}, \mathcal{R}^*)$ *be the adjoint pair of po-semirings, and let* $S:X \rightsquigarrow X$ *be a* $\mathbf{T}_{\mathcal{R}}$-*relation (or* $\mathcal{T}_{\mathcal{R}^*}^*$-*relation, equivalently). Then the rough* $(\mathcal{R}, \mathcal{R}^*)$-*fuzzy set of* $f \in (\mathcal{R}, \mathcal{R}^*)^X$ *defined by* S *is the pair*

$$(S^{\downarrow}(f), S^{\uparrow}(f)).$$

We present some basic properties of the lower and upper approximations of $(\mathcal{R}, \mathcal{R}^*)$-fuzzy sets.

Lemma 2. *Let* $(\mathcal{R}, \mathcal{R}^*)$ *be the adjoint pair of po-semirigs with the adjoint isomorphism* Φ *and let* $S : X \rightsquigarrow Y$ *be a* $\mathbf{T}_{\mathcal{R}}$-*relation. Let* $a \in \mathcal{R}$ *and* $s, t, s_i \in \mathcal{R}^X$, $i \in I$.

1. $S^{\uparrow}(\bigsqcup_{i \in I} s_i) = \bigsqcup_{i \in I} S^{\uparrow}(s_i)$, $S^{\downarrow}(\bigsqcap_{i \in I} s_i) = \bigsqcap_{i \in I} S^{\downarrow}(s_i)$,
2. $S^{\uparrow}(a \star s) = a \star S^{\uparrow}(s)$, $S^{\downarrow}(a \star^* s) = a \star^* S^{\downarrow}(s)$,
3. $s \leq t \Rightarrow S^{\downarrow}(s) \leq S^{\downarrow}(t)$, $S^{\uparrow}(s) \leq S^{\uparrow}(t)$,
4. $S^{\downarrow}(s) = \neg(S^{\uparrow}(\neg(s)))$, $S^{\uparrow}(s) = \neg(S^{\downarrow}(\neg(s)))$.
5. *If* S *is reflexive,* $S^{\downarrow}(s) \leq s \leq S^{\uparrow}(s)$ *is valid for all* $s \in \mathcal{R}$.
6. *Let* $R:X \rightsquigarrow Y$ *and* $S:Y \rightsquigarrow Z$ *be* $\mathbf{T}_{\mathcal{R}}$-*relations. We have*

$$S^{\uparrow}.R^{\uparrow} = (S \lozenge R)^{\uparrow}, \quad S^{\downarrow}.R^{\downarrow} = (S \lozenge^* R)^{\downarrow}.$$

Example 5. For illustration, we show how the rough $(\mathcal{R}, \mathcal{R}^*)$-fuzzy sets look for neutrosophic fuzzy sets, where $(\mathcal{R}, \mathcal{R}^*)$ is the adjoint pair of *po*-semirings from Example 2, corresponding to neutrosophis $\mathcal{L}$-fuzzy sets. Let $f : X \to R$ be the $(\mathcal{R}, \mathcal{R}^*)$-fuzzy set (i.e., the neutrospohic $\mathcal{L}$-fuzzy set) and $S:X \rightsquigarrow Y$ be a reflexive $\mathbf{T}_{\mathcal{R}}$-relation. For $x, y \in X$ we set $f(x) = (\alpha_x, \beta_x, \gamma_x) \in R$, $S(x)(y) = (\alpha_{xy}, \beta_{xy}, \gamma_{xy})$. According to (7),(8), and Example 2, for $y \in Y$ we obtain

$$S^{\uparrow}(f)(y) = \sum_{z \in X}^{\mathcal{R}} s(z) \times S(z)(y) = \left(\bigvee_{z \in X} \alpha_z \otimes \alpha_{zy}, \bigwedge_{z \in X} \beta_z \wedge \beta_{zy}, \bigwedge_{z \in X} \gamma_z \oplus \gamma_{zy}\right),$$

$$S^{\downarrow}(f)(y) = \sum_{z \in X}^{\mathcal{R}^*} s(z) \times^* S(z)(y) = \left(\bigwedge_{z \in X} \alpha_z \oplus \alpha_{zy}, \bigvee_{z \in X} \beta_z \vee \beta_{zy}, \bigvee_{z \in X} \gamma_z \otimes \gamma_{zy}\right).$$

□

4   Conclusions

The article follows our previous work [28], in which we proved that many of the new fuzzy structures can be represented as the so-called $(\mathcal{R}, \mathcal{R}^*)$-fuzzy sets, where $(\mathcal{R}, \mathcal{R}^*)$ is the appropriate adjoint pair of semirings. Therefore, a natural continuation of this unification is the unification of methods which could be used by these new structures. These potential methods naturally include methods based on the application of fuzzy relations in these structures, such as different types of transformations and approximations of fuzzy structures using fuzzy relations. We have shown that in the structure of $(\mathcal{R}, \mathcal{R}^*)$-fuzzy sets, it is possible to create a pair of monads that allow one to define relations and their compositions for $(\mathcal{R}, \mathcal{R}^*)$-fuzzy sets and use these for definitions of transformations and approximations. The methods defined in this way can then be applied retroactively to any new fuzzy structure, the elements of which can be transformed into $(\mathcal{R}, \mathcal{R}^*)$-fuzzy sets. This gives us a new tool for developing new fuzzy structures and their methods.

References

1. Agarwal, M., Biswas, K.K., Hanmandlu, M.: Generalized intuitionistic fuzzy soft sets with applications in decision-making. Appl. Soft Comput. **13**(8), 3552–3566 (2013)
2. Aggarwal, H., Arora, H.D., Kumar, V.: A decision-making problem as an applications of intuitionistic fuzzy set. Int. J. Eng. Adv. Technol. **9**(2), 5259–5261 (2019)
3. Aktas, H., Cagman, N.: Soft sets and soft groups. Inf. Sci. **177**, 2726–2735 (2007)
4. Atanassov, K.T.: Intuitionistic fuzzy sets. Fuzzy Sets Syst. **20**(1), 87–96 (1986)
5. Atanassov, K.T.: Intuitionistic fuzzy relations. In: Antonov, L. (ed.) III International School "Automation and Scientific Instrumentation", Varna, pp. 56–57 (1984)
6. Babitha, K., John, S.: Hesitant fuzzy soft sets. J. New Results Sci. **2**(3), 98–107 (2013)
7. Berstel, J., Perrin, D.: Theory of Codes. Academic Press (1985)
8. Das, S., Malakar, D., Kar, S., Pal, T.: Correlation measure of hesitant fuzzy soft sets and their application in decision making. Neural Comput. Appl. **31**(4), 1023–1039 (2017). https://doi.org/10.1007/s00521-017-3135-0
9. Di Nola, A., Gerla, B.: Algebras of Lukasiewicz logic and their semiring reducts. Contemp. Math. **377**, 131–144 (2005)
10. Eklund, P., Galán, M.Á.: Partially ordered monads and rough sets. In: Peters, J.F., Skowron, A. (eds.) Transactions on Rough Sets VIII. LNCS, vol. 5084, pp. 53–74. Springer, Heidelberg (2008). https://doi.org/10.1007/978-3-540-85064-9_4
11. Feng, F., Jun, Y.B., Zhao, X.Z.: Soft semirings. Comput. Math. Appli. **56**, 2621–2628 (2008)
12. Gan, A.P., Jiang, Y.L.: On ordered ideals in ordered semirings. J. Math. Res. Exposition **31**(6), 989–996 (2011)
13. Garg, H., Arora, R.: Generalized and group-based generalized intuitionistic fuzzy soft sets with applications in decision-making. Appl. Intell. **48**(2), 343–356 (2017). https://doi.org/10.1007/s10489-017-0981-5
14. Gähler, W.: General Topology - the monadic case, examples, applications. Acta Math. Hungar. **88**, 279–290 (2000)
15. Gähler, W.: Extension structures and completions in topology and algebra, Seminarberichte aus dem Fachbereich Mathematik, Band 70, FernUniversität in Hagen (2001)
16. Golan, J.S.: Semirings and Their Applications. Kluwer Academic Publishers, Dordrecht (1999)

17. Höhle, U.: Partially Ordered Monads. In: Many Valued Topology and its Applications. Kluwer Academic Publishers, Boston (2001)
18. Hu, Q., Zhang, X.: Neutrosophic triangular norms and their derived residuated lattices. Symmetry **11**, 817 (2019)
19. James, J., Mathew, S.C.: Lattice valued neutrosophis sets. J. Math. Comput. Sci. **11**, 4695–4710 (2021)
20. Zhang, X., Bo, C., Smarandache, F., Dai, J.: New inclusion relation of neutrosophic sets with applications and related lattice structure. Int. J. Mach. Learn. Cybern. **9**(10), 1753–1763 (2018). https://doi.org/10.1007/s13042-018-0817-6
21. Kozae, A.M., et al.: Intuitionistic fuzzy set and its application in Corona Covid-19. Appli. Comput. Math. **9**(5), 146–154 (2020)
22. Maji, P.K., et al.: Fuzzy soft-sets. J. Fuzzy Math. **9**(3), 589–602 (2001)
23. Maji, P.K., Biswas, R., Roy, A.R.: Soft set theory. Comput. Math. Appl. **45**, 555–562 (2003)
24. Maji, P.K., et al.: An application of soft sets in a decision making problem. Comput. Math. Appl. **44**, 1077–083 (2002)
25. Majumdar, P., Samanta, S.K.: Similarity measure of soft sets. New Math. Nat. Comput. **4**(1), 1–12 (2008)
26. Manes, E.G.: Algebraic Theories. Springer Verlag, Berlin (1976)
27. Molodtsov, D.: Soft set theory-First results. Comput. Math. Appl. **37**, 19–31 (1999)
28. Močkoř, J.: Semiring-valued fuzzy sets and F-transform. Mathematics **9**(23), 3107 (2021)
29. Mushrif, M.M., Sengupta, S., Ray, A.K.: Texture classification using a novel, soft-set theory based classification algorithm. In: Narayanan, P.J., Nayar, S.K., Shum, H.-Y. (eds.) ACCV 2006. LNCS, vol. 3851, pp. 246–254. Springer, Heidelberg (2006). https://doi.org/10.1007/11612032_26
30. Rodabaugh, S.E.: Relationship of algebraic theories to power set theories and fuzzy topological theories for lattice-valued mathematics. Int. J. Math. Math. Sci. **2007**, 1–71 (2007)
31. Rodríguez, R.M., et al.: Hesitant fuzzy sets: state of the art and future directions. Int. J. Intell. Syst. **29**(6), 495–524 (2014)
32. Gavin, S.: On the monadic nature of categories of ordered sets, Cahiers de Topologie et Géométrie Différentielle Catégoriques 52 (2011)
33. Suo, C., Li, Y., Li, Z.: A series of information measures of hesitant fuzzy soft sets and their application in decision making. Soft. Comput. **25**(6), 4771–4784 (2021). https://doi.org/10.1007/s00500-020-05485-4
34. Torra, V., Narukawa, Y.: On hesitant fuzzy sets and decision. In: Proceedings of the 2009 IEEE International Conference on Fuzzy Systems, FUZZ-IEEE, Jeju Island, Korea, pp. 1378–1382 (2009)
35. Torra, V.: Vincenc, Hesitant fuzzy sets. Int. J. Intell. Syst. **25**(6), 529–539 (2010)
36. Wang, J., Li, X.-E., Chen, X.: Hesitant fuzzy soft sets with application in multi-criteria group decision making problems. Sci. World J. **2015**, 806983 (2015)
37. Yahya, M., Begum, E.N.: A Study on Intuitionistic L-Fuzzy Metric Spaces. Annal. Pure Appli. Math. **15**(1), 67–75 (2017)
38. Xu, Z.: Hesitant Fuzzy Sets Theory. SFSC, vol. 314. Springer, Cham (2014). https://doi.org/10.1007/978-3-319-04711-9
39. Zhang, H.: Linguistic intuitionistic fuzzy sets and application in MAGDM. J. Appli. Math. **2014**, 432092 (2014)

Similarity for Multisets and Heterogeneous Sets

Ryszard Janicki[✉]

Department of Computing and Software, McMaster University, Hamilton,
ON L8S 4K1, Canada
janicki@mcmaster.ca

Abstract. Marczewski-Steinhaus similarity measure is extended to multisets and, newly introduced, heterogeneous sets. Various properties of these extensions are discussed, including axioms and consistent similarities. The results obtained for Marczewski-Steinhaus measure are applied to other popular similarity indexes.

Keywords: Similarity · Multisets · Types · Measure space · Consistent similarities

1 Introduction

While multisets [1,12,23] have in general a well developed theory and plenty of applications in various areas of science and technology [1,6,12,20], the part of them that deals with issues of similarity measure is rather sketchy and ad hoc. Particular definitions depend heavily on concrete applications. There is no part devoted to multisets in the popular *Encyclopedia of Distances* [3]. While the concept of *distance* has a well-established formal definition and has one universally accepted set of axioms [3,7,16], its counterpart, *similarity*, does not. The fact is that very often similarity *is not* just an inverse of some distance. There are many application oriented definitions of similarity and many of them cannot be expressed in terms of distances. There are also several different set of axioms for the concept of similarity (cf. [9,11,19,22]).

Many conceptually different similarities, while providing different numerical values, preserve the order they generate, i.e. if A is closer to B than to C with respect to one similarity, it does it also with respect to the other, and vice verse. To deal with this phenomenon the concept of *consistent* similarity measures has been introduced and discussed in [11].

In this paper we first extend the well known Marczewski-Steinhaus [3,14] similarity index to multisets, introduce the concept of *heterogeneous sets* (i.e. sets of elements of different types), and then extend this index to the heterogeneous sets. Next we discuss some similarity axioms to multisets and the use of these axioms for heterogeneous sets. At the end we extend the concept of consistent similarities to multisets and heterogeneous sets, and discuss other well known similarity indexes as: *Dice-Sørensen index* [4,21], *Braun-Blanquet index* [2,19] and *symmetric Tversky index* [11,22].

© Springer Nature Switzerland AG 2022
D. Ciucci et al. (Eds.): IPMU 2022, CCIS 1601, pp. 332–344, 2022.
https://doi.org/10.1007/978-3-031-08971-8_28

2   Similarity over Measure Space

Let U be a finite set and let $\mu : U \to \mathbb{R}$, where $\mathbb{R}$ is a set of real numbers and for each $x \in U$, $\mu(x) \geq 0$. The value $\mu(x)$ is called an *individual measure* of x. We extend μ element-wise to 2^U in the following way: for each $X \subseteq U$,

$$\mu(X) = \sum_{x \in X} \mu(x).$$

It can easily be shown that μ is a *finite measure* [7,16] and $(U, \mathbb{R}, \mu)$ is a *measure space* [7,16]. Note that *cardinality*, i.e. $\mu(x) = 1$ and $\mu(X) = |X|$, is a natural finite measure that is used quite often.

For every measure space we can define *Marczewski-Steinhaus similarity* index [14]: $\text{sim}_{MS} : 2^U \times 2^U \to \langle 0, 1 \rangle$ as

$$\text{sim}_{MS}(X, Y) = \frac{\mu(X \cap Y)}{\mu(X \cup Y)},$$

where $X, Y \subseteq U$. Marczewski-Steinhaus similarity is a generalization of older Jaccard similarity [8] which is given by $\text{sim}_J(X, Y) = \frac{|X \cap Y|}{|X \cup Y|}$, i.e. μ is just the cardinality. It is also *metrical*, since $1 - \text{sim}_{MS}(X, Y)$ is a proper metrics [3,14]. Moreover, it can also be considered as an adequate representation of other (not necessarily metrical) similarity indexes [11].

Consider the following example. Let E_1 and E_2 be elephants and $c_1, \ldots, c_6$ be chickens, $U = \{E_1, E_2, c_1, \ldots, c_6\}$, and let μ be the following measure (say 'of distinguishability of individual animals'): $\mu(E_1) = \mu(E_2) = 10$ and $\mu(c_i) = 1$ for $i = 1, \ldots, 6$. Consider now the sets $A = \{E_1, E_2, c_1, c_2, c_3, c_5\}$, $B = \{E_1, c_1, c_2, c_4\}$ and $C = \{c_1, c_2, c_3, c_4, c_5\}$. When we use Marczewski-Steinhaus similarity index, we have $\text{sim}_{MS}(A, B) = \frac{10+2}{10+10+5} = \frac{12}{25} = 0.48$, while $\text{sim}_{MS}(A, C) = \frac{4}{10+10+5} = \frac{4}{25} = 0.16$, which is consistent with common intuition.

However consider the set $D = \{E_2, c_1, c_2, c_4\}$. From some distance the set D looks almost as B, only elephants are different, B contains E_1 while D contains E_2. When applying the Marczewski-Steinhaus similarity index, we have: $\text{sim}_{MS}(D, B) = \frac{3}{10+10+3} = \frac{3}{23} = 0.13$, while $\text{sim}_{MS}(D, C) = \frac{3}{10+5} = \frac{1}{5} = 0.2$, so D is more similar to C than to B, despite the fact that there is no elephant in C at all, and this seems to be against common intuition! To solve this problem in full we need multisets [1,12] and heterogeneous sets.

3   Multisets

Let U be a finite set. A *function* $\text{m} : U \to \mathbb{N}$, where $\mathbb{N}$ is the set of all natural numbers (including zero) is called a *multiset* [1,12,23] over U. Let $[U \to \mathbb{N}] = \{\text{m} \mid \text{m} : U \to \mathbb{N}\} \subseteq U \times \mathbb{N}$ denote the set of all multisets over U. When dealing with multisets, usually the following notation is used. For each $x \in U$, $\text{m}(x)$

denotes the numbers of appearances of x in m, and is called the *coefficient* of x in m. The multiset m will then be represented by an abstract sum:

$$m = \sum_{x \in U} m(x)x.$$

For example if $U = \{a, b, c, d, e\}$, then the multiset defined by the equalities $m(a) = 3$, $m(b) = 1$, $m(c) = 0$, $m(d) = 183$, and $m(e) = 0$, is represented by the abstract sum $m = 3a + b + 183d$. Formally, directly from the fact that $m : U \to \mathbb{N}$, we also have $m = \{(a, 3), (b, 1), (c, 0), (d, 183), (e, 0)\} \subseteq U \times \mathbb{N}$.

For each multiset m, we define its cardinality as $|m| = \sum_{x \in U} m(x)$. We say that a multiset m is empty when $|m| = 0$, and that $x \in m$ if $m(x) > 0$. For $m = 3a + b + 183d$, $|m| = 187$, $a, b, d \in m$ and $c, e \notin m$. Interpretation $m(x) = 0$ as $x \neq m$ allows us to represent a multiset m as a set of pairs $\{(x, m(x) \mid m(x) > 0\} \subseteq U \times (\mathbb{N} \setminus \{0\})$. For example $m = 3a + b + 183d$ corresponds also to $m = \{(a, 3), (b, 1), (d, 183)\}$.

Moreover, for each two multisets m_1 and m_2, we define [1,12] intersection, $m_1 \cap m_2$, union, $m_1 \cup m_2$, and subtraction $m_1 \setminus m_2$ as follows: $m_1 \cap m_2 = \sum_{x \in U} \min(m_1(x), m_2(x)) \cdot x$, $m_1 \cup m_2 = \sum_{x \in U} \max(m_1(x), m_2(x)) \cdot x$, and, if $m_1(x) \geq m_2(x)$ for all $x \in U$, $m_1 \setminus m_2 = \sum_{x \in U} (m_1(x) - m_2(x)) \cdot x$.

Both measure space and Marczewski-Steinhaus similarity can be extended to multisets in a rather natural manner. Let U be a finite set, m be a multiset over U and let $(U, \mathbb{R}, \mu)$ be a *measure space*. We can now define a *measure of the multiset* m *induced by* μ simply as

$$\widehat{\mu}(m) = \sum_{x \in U} m(x) \cdot \mu(x).$$

The quadruple $(U, \mathbb{R}, m, \widehat{\mu})$ will be called *multiset measure space* over U.

For example if $U = \{a, b, c, d, e\}$, $m = 3a + b + 183d$, $\mu(a) = 3$, $\mu(b) = 2$, $\mu(c) = 1$, $\mu(d) = 3$, $\mu(e) = 5$, then $\widehat{\mu}(m) = 3 \cdot 3 + 1 \cdot 2 + 0 \cdot 1 + 183 \cdot 3 + 0 \cdot 5 = 560$.

Let m be a multiset over U. Define $\widehat{U} = U \times \{1, 2, 3, \ldots\}$ and we will write $a^{(i)}$ rather than (a, i). Let $\mathcal{S}_m : U \to 2^{\widehat{U}}$ be a mapping such that, for each $x \in U$, if $m(x) \neq 0$, $\mathcal{S}_m(x) = \{x^{(1)}, x^{(2)}, \ldots, x^{m(x)}\}$. We extend $\mathcal{S}_m$ to multisets in a standard component-wise manner, namely, $\mathcal{S} : [U \to \mathbb{N}] \to 2^{\widehat{U}}$, and for a multiset m,

$$\mathcal{S}(m) = \bigcup_{m(x) \neq 0} \mathcal{S}_m(x).$$

For each multiset m, the set $\mathcal{S}(m)$ can be considered as an adequate set representation of m. For example if $m = 3a + b + 2c$ then $\mathcal{S}(m) = \{a^{(1)}, a^{(2)}, a^{(3)}, b^{(1)}, c^{(1)}, c^{(2)}\}$.

We extend the measure μ to $\widehat{U}$ by $\mu(a^{(i)}) = \mu(a)$ for all $a \in U$.

Not every subset of $\widehat{U}$ is an image of some m via $\mathcal{S}$. For example consider the set $A = \{a^{(3)}, a^{(5)}, a^{(8)}, b^{(1)}, b^{(4)}\} \subseteq \widehat{U}$. There is no multiset m such that $\mathcal{S}(m) = A$. To make A an image of some multiset m, we need to change appropriately indexes in $a^{(i)}$ and $b^{(i)}$. Let $\mathcal{R} : 2^{\widehat{U}} \to 2^{\widehat{U}}$ be a mapping defined as follows. For each $A \subseteq U$, $\mathcal{R}(A)$ is the smallest set that satisfies the following: for each $x \in U$, if $|\{x^{(i)} \mid x^{(i)} \in A\}| = k_x > 0$ then $\{x^{(1)}, \ldots, x^{(k_x)}\} \subseteq \mathcal{R}(A)$. Note that $\mathcal{R}(A) = \{a^{(1)}, a^{(2)}, a^{(3)}, b^{(1)}, b^{(2)}\} = B$, and of course $B = \mathcal{S}(3a + 2b)$. Clearly for each $A \subseteq \widehat{U}$, there is a multiset m_A such that $\mathcal{R}(A) = \mathcal{S}(m_A)$, we will skip a simple algorithm for finding such m_A.

The mapping $\mathcal{S}$ provides a convenient bridge between multisets and sets, and often allows us to prove properties of multisets with techniques designed for standard sets. The properties described below are very useful in a variety of both proofs and applications.

Proposition 1. *Let* m, m_1, m_2 *be multisets over* U, *and* $A \subseteq \widehat{U}$.

1. $\mathcal{S}(m_1 \cup m_2) = \mathcal{S}(m_1) \cup \mathcal{S}(m_2)$,
2. $\mathcal{S}(m_1 \cap m_2) = \mathcal{S}(m_1) \cap \mathcal{S}(m_2)$,
3. $\widehat{\mu}(m) = \mu(\mathcal{S}(m))$,
4. *if* $m_1(x) \geq m_2(x)$ *for all* $x \in U$, *then* $\mathcal{S}(m_1 \backslash m_2) = \mathcal{R}(\mathcal{S}(m_1) \backslash \mathcal{S}(m_2))$,
5. $\mu(A) = \mu(\mathcal{R}(A))$,
6. *if* $m_1(x) \geq m_2(x)$ *for all* $x \in U$, *then* $\mu(\mathcal{S}(m_1 \backslash m_2)) = \mu(\mathcal{S}(m_1) \backslash \mathcal{S}(m_2))$.

Proof.(1) $x^{(i)} \in \mathcal{S}(m_1 \cup m_2) \iff \max(m_1(x), m_2(x)) \geq i \iff m_1(x) \geq i \vee m_1(x) \geq i \iff x^{(i)} \in \mathcal{S}(m_1)) \vee x^{(i)} \subset \mathcal{S}(m_1)) \iff x^{(i)} \in \mathcal{S}(m_1) \cup \mathcal{S}(m_2)$.

(2) $x^{(i)} \in \mathcal{S}(m_1 \cap m_2) \iff \min(m_1(x), m_2(x)) \geq i \iff m_1(x) \geq i \wedge m_1(x) \geq i \iff x^{(i)} \in \mathcal{S}(m_1)) \wedge x^{(i)} \in \mathcal{S}(m_1)) \iff x^{(i)} \in \mathcal{S}(m_1) \cap \mathcal{S}(m_2)$.

(3) $\mu(\mathcal{S}(m)) = \sum_{x^{(i)} \in \mathcal{S}(m)} \mu(x^{(i)})$. Since $\mu(x^{(i)}) = \mu(x)$, then we have $\sum_{x^{(i)} \in \mathcal{S}(m)} \mu(x^{(i)}) = \sum_{x \in U} m(x) \cdot x = \widehat{\mu}(m)$.

(4)   Suppose $m_1(x) \geq m_2(x)$ for all $x \in U$. We have $x^{(i)} \in \mathcal{S}(m_1 \backslash m_2) \iff 0 < i \leq m_1(x) - m_2(x)$. On the other hand, $x^{(i)} \in \mathcal{S}(m_1) \backslash \mathcal{S}(m_2) \iff m_2(x) < x \leq m_1(x)$. Hence $x^{(i)} \in \mathcal{R}(\mathcal{S}(m_1) \backslash \mathcal{S}(m_2)) \iff 0 < i \leq m_1(x) - m_2(x)$.

(5)   Since for all $a^{(i)}, a^{(j)} \in \widehat{U}$, $\mu(a^{(i)}) = \mu(a^{(j)}) = \mu(a)$.

(6)   A simple consequence of (4) and (5).   □

We can now define the Marczewski-Steinhaus similarity index for multisets as follows, for all multisets m_1, m_2 over U;

$$\text{sim}_{MS}^{(m)}(m_1, m_2) = \frac{\widehat{\mu}(m_1 \cap m_2)}{\widehat{\mu}(m_1 \cup m_2)}.$$

The mapping $\mathcal{S}$ provides a natural link between $\text{sim}_{MS}^{(m)}$ and sim_{MS}.

Proposition 2. *Let* m_1, m_2 *be multisets over* U. *Then we have:*

$$\text{sim}_{MS}^{(m)}(m_1, m_2) = \text{sim}_{MS}(\mathcal{S}(m_1), \mathcal{S}(m_2)).$$

Proof. By Proposition 1 we have $\widehat{\mu}(m_1 \cap m_2) = \mu(\mathcal{S}(m_1 \cap m_2)) = \mu(\mathcal{S}(m_1) \cap \mathcal{S}(m_2))$, and, $\widehat{\mu}(m_1 \cup m_2) = \mu(\mathcal{S}(m_1 \cup m_2)) = \mu(\mathcal{S}(m_1) \cup \mathcal{S}(m_2))$. □

We may now redefine our elephants and chickens example as follows: Let $U = \{elephant, chicken\}$, $m_A = 2 \cdot elephant + 4 \cdot chicken$, $m_B = elephant + 3 \cdot chicken$, $m_C = 5 \cdot chicken$, $m_D = elephant + 3 \cdot chicken$. In this case we have: $m_B = m_D$, $m_A \cup m_B = m_A$, $m_A \cap m_B = m_B$, $m_B \cup m_C = elephant + 5 \cdot chicken$ and $m_B \cap m_C = 3 \cdot chicken$. Hence $\text{sim}_{MS}^{(m)}(m_A, m_B) = \frac{10+3}{2 \cdot 10+4} = 0.54$, $\text{sim}_{MS}^{(m)}(m_B, m_C) = \frac{3}{10+5} = 0.2$ and $\text{sim}_{MS}^{(m)}(m_B, m_D) = 1.0$. We have now agreement with common intuition and this model works very well if we do not want to make any distinction between individual elephants and any distinction between individual chickens.

However this approach might be considered as some oversimplification if a distinction between individual elements is important, or at least should not be neglected. In this case we have $m_B = m_D$, while $B \neq D$ and in many cases we may not want to identify distinct, although intuitively similar sets.

4   Types, Heterogeneous Sets, Typed and Mixed Similarities

Heterogeneous sets, i.e. sets with elements of various types, can be interpreted as both standard sets and multisets.

Let U be a finite set (of *objects*) and T be a finite set (of *types*). We additionally assume $|T| \leq |U|$. Let $\tau : U \to T$ be a total mapping called *type* function. For every $x \in U$, $\tau(x)$ is a *type* of x. A triple (U, T, τ) is called a *heterogeneous set*[1].

Standardly a mapping f on a set X is extended to 2^X component-wise, i.e. $f(Y) = \{f(a) \mid a \in Y\}$, if $f(a)$'s are not sets, or $f(Y) = \bigcup_{a \in Y} f(a)$, if $f(a)$'s are sets, for all $Y \subseteq X$. The extension of τ to sets must be a little bit more sophisticated, it requires an extension of range as well.

Consider our example with $U = \{E_1, E_2, c_1, \ldots, c_6\}$. We might assume the types $T = \{elephant, chicken\}$, and $\tau(E_1) = \tau(E_2) = elephant$ and $\tau(c_i) = chicken$ for $i = 1, \ldots, 6$. However the types of sets are usually multisets. Consider our sets A, B, C and D. Intuitively we have $\tau(A) = 2 \cdot elephant + 4 \cdot chicken = m_A$, $\tau(B) = elephant + 3 \cdot chicken = m_B$, $\tau(C) = 5 \cdot chicken = m_C$, and $\tau(D) = elephant + 3 \cdot chicken = m_D$. All $\tau(A), \tau(B), \tau(C)$ and $\tau(D)$ are *multisets of types*. Note that with such interpretation of types of sets, we have $\tau(B) = \tau(D)$,

---

[1] Technically every multiset is a heterogeneous set with $T = \{1, \ldots, k_{max}\}$, where $k_{max} = \max\{m(a) \mid a \in m\}$. However, the interpretation and intuition are different in each case. Also hybrid sets of [13] and (real) multisets of [15] can be interpreted as special cases of heterogeneous sets.

which is intuitively expected. Hence an extension of the domain of τ to sets, i.e. 2^U, requires an extension of the range to mulitsets of types, i.e. $[T \to \mathbb{N}]$.

Formally we extend the domain of τ to sets and range to multisets of types as follows:

$$\tau : 2^U \to [T \to \mathbb{N}],$$

and, for every $X \subseteq U$:

$$\tau(X) = \sum_{t \in T} |\{x \in X \mid \tau(x) = t\}| \cdot t.$$

In other words, for every $X \subseteq U$, $\tau(X) : T \to \mathbb{N}$ is a *multiset* such that for each $t \in T$, the coefficient $\tau(X)(t)$ is given by:

$$\tau(X)(t) = |\{x \in X \mid \tau(x) = t\}|.$$

Summing up, $\tau : U \to T$, while extended τ, $\tau : 2^U \to [T \to \mathbb{N}]$. The extension is sound as for each $x \in U$, $\tau(\{x\}) = 1 \cdot \tau(x)$.

We will call a *multiset* $\tau(X)$: 'the *type* of a set X'.

Suppose that $(T, \mathbb{R}, \mu_T)$ is a *finite measure space* also over T, and $\widehat{\mu}_T$ is the multiset measure induces by μ_T. Hence for every $X \subseteq U$, $(T, \mathbb{R}, \tau(X), \widehat{\mu})$ is a multiset measure space over T.

We define *typed Marczewski-Steinhaus similarity index* as follows, for all $X, Y \subseteq U$:

$$\mathsf{sim}_{MS}^{(\tau)}(X, Y) = \frac{\widehat{\mu}_T(\tau(X) \cap \tau(Y))}{\widehat{\mu}_T(\tau(X) \cup \tau(Y))}.$$

The mappings τ and $\mathcal{S}$ make it possible to link together $\mathsf{sim}_{MS}^{(\tau)}$, $\mathsf{sim}_{MS}^{(m)}$ and sim_S.

Proposition 3. *For all $X, Y \subseteq U$, we have:*

$$\mathsf{sim}_{MS}^{(\tau)}(X, Y) = \mathsf{sim}_{MS}^{(m)}(\tau(X), \tau(Y)) = \mathsf{sim}_{MS}(\mathcal{S}(\tau(X)), \mathcal{S}(\tau(Y))).$$

Proof. Just from the definitions we have: $\mathsf{sim}_{MS}^{(\tau)}(X, Y) = \mathsf{sim}_{MS}^{(m)}(\tau(X), \tau(Y))$, and from Proposition 2 we have $\mathsf{sim}_{MS}^{(m)}(\tau(X), \tau(Y)) = \mathsf{sim}_{MS}(\mathcal{S}(\tau(X)), \mathcal{S}(\tau(Y)))$. $\square$

For our example if $\mu_T(elephant) = 10$ and $\mu_T(chicken) = 1$, we have $\mathsf{sim}_{MS}^{(\tau)}(A, B) = \mathsf{sim}_{MS}^{(\tau)}(A, D) = \frac{10+3}{20+4} = \frac{13}{24} = 0.54$, $\mathsf{sim}_{MS}^{(\tau)}(A, C) = \frac{4}{20+5} = \frac{4}{25} = 0.16$, $\mathsf{sim}_{MS}^{(\tau)}(C, D) = \frac{3}{10+5} = \frac{3}{15} = 0.2$ and $\mathsf{sim}_{MS}^{(\tau)}(B, D) = 1$. We may now say that the sets $B = \{E_1, c_1, c_2, c_4\}$ and $D = \{E_2, c_1, c_2, c_3\}$ are different, but indistinguishable with respect to measure μ_T, which does not distinguish between different elephants and between different chickens; and this was partially our goal.

Since $B \neq D$, the similarity $\mathsf{sim}_{MS}^{(\tau)}(B, D) = \mathsf{sim}_{MS}^{(\tau)}(B, B) = \mathsf{sim}_{MS}^{(\tau)}(D, D) = 1$ may not be entirely satisfactory. In some cases it may want to have fact that $B \neq D$ included in a given similarity measure.

Let U be a finite set (of *objects* and T be a finite set (of *types*), $(U, \mathbb{R}, \mu)$ be a *measure space* over U (with $\mu : U \to \mathbb{R}$), $(T, \mathbb{R}, \mu_T)$ be a *measure space* over T (with $\mu_T : T \to \mathbb{R}$), and $\widehat{\mu}_T$ be the multiset measure induces by μ_T. Additionally, let α and β be two positive numbers greater than zero and with $\alpha + \beta = 1$.

We may now define for example *mixed Marczewski-Steinhaus similarity index* as follows, for all $X, Y \subseteq U$:

$$\mathrm{sim}_{MS}^{(\alpha\beta)}(X, Y) = \alpha \cdot \mathrm{sim}_{MS}(X, Y) + \beta \cdot \mathrm{sim}_{MS}^{(\tau)}(X, Y).$$

For our example with $\alpha = 0.2$ and $\beta = 0.8$, we have $\mathrm{sim}_{MS}^{(\alpha\beta)}(A, B) = 0.2\frac{12}{25} + 0.8\frac{13}{24} = 0.53$, $\mathrm{sim}_{MS}^{(\alpha\beta)}(A, C) = 0.2\frac{4}{25} + 0.8\frac{4}{25} = 0.16$, $\mathrm{sim}_{MS}^{(\alpha\beta)}(B, D) = 0.2\frac{3}{23} + 0.8\frac{13}{13} = 0.83$ and $\mathrm{sim}_{MS}^{(\alpha\beta)}(C, D) = 0.2\frac{3}{15} + 0.8\frac{3}{15} = 0.2$. In this case $\mathrm{sim}_{MS}^{(\alpha\beta)}(B, D) = 0.83$ while $\mathrm{sim}_{MS}^{(\tau)}(B, B) = \mathrm{sim}_{MS}^{(\tau)}(D, D) = 1$, which is exactly what we might want.

The coefficient α defines the importance of individuals, while the coefficient β the importance of types.

5   Similarity Axioms

Similarity is usually defined as a (total) function $sim : 2^U \times 2^U \to \langle 0, 1 \rangle$. While such functions have been known since the beginning of the twentieth century [8], they do not have standard indisputable axiomatization [3]. Depending on the area of application, some desirable properties may vary [3,9,11,19,22], sometimes substantially [9,19]. The following axioms, proposed by Janicki and Lenarčič [10, 11], seem to be well motivated and are satisfied by most known indexes (however there are cases when they have to be weakened [9]). For all sets $A, B \subseteq U$:

$S1$ (Maximum) : $sim(A, B) = 1 \iff A = B$,
$S2$ (Symmetry) : $sim(A, B) = sim(B, A)$,
$S3$ (Minimum) : $sim(A, B) = 0 \iff A \cap B = \emptyset$,
$S4$ (Inclusion) :   if $a \in B \backslash A$ then $sim(A, B) < sim(A \cup \{a\}, B)$,
$S5$ (Exclusion) :   if $a \notin A \cup B$ and $A \cap B \neq \emptyset$ then $sim(A, B) > sim(A \cup \{a\}, B)$,
$S5'$ (Weak Excl.) : if $a \notin A \cup B$ then $sim(A, B) \geq sim(A \cup \{a\}, B)$

The only similarity measure we have discussed so far was Marczewski-Steinhaus [14] (and implicitly Jaccard [8] as a special case) index. The other popular and widely used indexes are: *Dice-Sørensen index* [4,21], *Braun-Blanquet index* [2,19], *Tversky index* [22][2], and *symmetric Tversky index* [11,22]. They were all originally defined with cardinality as a measure of sets, but they can all

---

[2]   Tversky index is asymmetric by design. When we consider X to be the prototype and Y to be the variant, then λ_1 corresponds to the weight of the prototype and λ_2 corresponds to the weight of the variant [22]. For other interpretations we assume $\lambda_1 = \lambda_2$. In this paper we deal with symmetric cases only.

be extended to an arbitrary finite measure μ[11], in the following natural way.

$Dice\text{-}S\text{ø}rensen\ \mu\text{-}index:$ $\mathrm{sim}_{\mu DS}(X,Y) = \dfrac{2\mu(X \cap Y)}{\mu(X) + \mu(Y)},$

$Tversky\ \mu\text{-}index:$ $\mathrm{sim}_{\mu T}(X,Y) = \dfrac{\mu(X \cap Y)}{\mu(X \cap Y) + \lambda_1 \mu(X \backslash Y) + \lambda_2 \mu(Y \backslash X)},$

$Symmetric\ Tversky\ \mu\text{-}index:$ $\mathrm{sim}_{\mu sT}(X,Y) = \dfrac{\mu(X \cap Y)}{\mu(X \cap Y) + \lambda \mu((X \cup Y) \backslash (X \cap Y))},$

$Braun\text{-}Blanquet\ \mu\text{-}index:$ $\mathrm{sim}_{\mu BB}(X,Y) = \dfrac{\mu(X \cap Y)}{\max(\mu(X), \mu(Y))}.$

As opposed to Marczewski-Steinhaus index, none of the above indexes is metrical. They all, with an exception of (asymmetric) Tversky μ-index satisfy the axioms presented above.

Proposition 4 [11]. *The indexes* $\mathrm{sim}_{MS}, \mathrm{sim}_{\mu DS}$ *and* $\mathrm{sim}_{\mu sT}$ *satisfy the axioms S1–S5 and the index* $\mathrm{sim}_{\mu BB}$ *satisfies S1–S4 and S5'.*   ◇

For multisets, the equivalent axioms look as follows:

$S1\mathrm{m}$ (Maximum) : $sim(\mathsf{m}_1, \mathsf{m}_2) = 1 \iff \mathsf{m}_1 = \mathsf{m}_2,$

$S2\mathrm{m}$ (Symmetry) : $sim(\mathsf{m}_1, \mathsf{m}_2) = sim(\mathsf{m}_2, \mathsf{m}_1),$

$S3\mathrm{m}$ (Minimum) : $sim(\mathsf{m}_1, \mathsf{m}_2) = 0 \iff \mathsf{m}_1 \cap \mathsf{m}_2 = \emptyset,$

$S4\mathrm{m}$ (Inclusion) : if $\mathsf{m}_2(a) > \mathsf{m}_1(a)$ then $sim(\mathsf{m}_1, \mathsf{m}_2) < sim(\mathsf{m}_1 + a, \mathsf{m}_2),$

$S5\mathrm{m}$ (Exclusion) : if $a \notin \mathsf{m}_1 \cup \mathsf{m}_1$ and $\mathsf{m}_1 \cap \mathsf{m}_2 \neq \emptyset$ then

$$sim(\mathsf{m}_1, \mathsf{m}_2) > sim(\mathsf{m}_1 + a, \mathsf{m}_2),$$

$S5'\mathrm{m}$ (Weak Excl.) : if $a \notin \mathsf{m}_1 \cup \mathsf{m}_2$ then $sim(\mathsf{m}_1, \mathsf{m}_2) \geq sim(\mathsf{m}_1 + a, \mathsf{m}_2).$

By mimicking the definitions of $\mathrm{sim}_{MS}^{(m)}(\mathsf{m}_1, \mathsf{m}_2)$ and $\mathrm{sim}_{MS}^{(\tau)}(X,Y)$ for both multisets and typed similarities, we can provide extensions to all the indexes above:

$Dice\text{-}S\text{ø}rensen:$ $\mathrm{sim}_{\mu DS}^{(m)}(\mathsf{m}_1, \mathsf{m}_2) = \dfrac{2\widehat{\mu}(\mathsf{m}_1 \cap \mathsf{m}_2)}{\widehat{\mu}(\mathsf{m}_1) + \widehat{\mu}(\mathsf{m}_2)},$

$\mathrm{sim}_{\mu DS}^{(\tau)}(X,Y) = \dfrac{2\widehat{\mu}_T(\tau(X) \cap \tau(Y))}{\widehat{\mu}_T(\tau(X)) + \widehat{\mu}_T(\tau(Y))},$

$Symm.\ Tversky:$ $\mathrm{sim}_{\mu sT}^{(m)}(\mathsf{m}_1, \mathsf{m}_2) = \dfrac{\widehat{\mu}(\mathsf{m}_1 \cap \mathsf{m}_2)}{\widehat{\mu}(\mathsf{m}_1 \cap \mathsf{m}_2) + \lambda \widehat{\mu}((\mathsf{m}_1 \cup \mathsf{m}_2) \backslash (\mathsf{m}_1 \cap \mathsf{m}_2))},$

$\mathrm{sim}_{\mu sT}^{(\tau)}(X,Y) = \dfrac{\widehat{\mu}_T(\tau(X) \cap \tau(Y))}{\widehat{\mu}_T(\tau(X) \cap \tau(Y)) + \lambda \widehat{\mu}_T((\tau(X) \cup \tau(Y)) \backslash (\tau(X) \cap \tau(Y)))},$

$Braun\text{-}Blanquet:$ $\mathrm{sim}_{\mu BB}^{(m)}(\mathsf{m}_1, \mathsf{m}_2) = \dfrac{\widehat{\mu}(\mathsf{m}_1 \cap \widehat{\mu}(\mathsf{m}_2)}{\max(\widehat{\mu}(\mathsf{m}_1), \widehat{\mu}(\mathsf{m}_1))},$

$\mathrm{sim}_{\mu BB}^{(\tau)}(X,Y) = \dfrac{\widehat{\mu}_T(\tau(X) \cap \tau(Y))}{\max(\widehat{\mu}_T(\tau(X)), \widehat{\mu}_T(\tau(Y)))},$

$All\ indexes:$ $\mathrm{sim}^{(\alpha\beta)}(X,Y) = \alpha \cdot \mathrm{sim}_{...}(X,Y) + \beta \cdot \mathrm{sim}^{(\tau)}(X,Y).$

The two useful results, that allow reducing Marczewski-Steinhaus similarity for multisets and heterogeneous (typed) sets to appropriate standard sets by using the mapping $\mathcal{S}$, i.e. Propositions 2 and 3, also hold for all indexes defined above.

Proposition 5. *Let* m_1, m_2 *be multisets over* U. *Then we have:*

1. $\mathrm{sim}_{\mu sT}^{(m)}(m_1, m_2) = \mathrm{sim}_{\mu DS}(\mathcal{S}(m_1), \mathcal{S}(m_2))$,
2. $\mathrm{sim}_{\mu sT}^{(m)}(m_1, m_2) = \mathrm{sim}_{\mu sT}(\mathcal{S}(m_1), \mathcal{S}(m_2))$,
3. $\mathrm{sim}_{\mu BB}^{(m)}(m_1, m_2) = \mathrm{sim}_{\mu BB}(\mathcal{S}(m_1), \mathcal{S}(m_2))$.

Proof. (1) and (3)   By Proposition 1(2,3) we have $\widehat{\mu}(m_1 \cap m_2) = \mu(\mathcal{S}(m_1 \cap m_2)) = \mu(\mathcal{S}(m_1) \cap \mathcal{S}(m_2))$, $\widehat{\mu}(m_1) + \widehat{\mu}(m_2) = \mu(\mathcal{S}(m_1)) + \mu(\mathcal{S}(m_2))$, and $\max(\widehat{\mu}(m_1), \widehat{\mu}(m_1)) = \max(\mu(\mathcal{S}(m_1)), \mathcal{S}(m_2))$, which clearly imply (1) and (3).
(2)   Proposition 1(1) gives us $\widehat{\mu}(m_1 \cup m_2) = \mu(\mathcal{S}(m_1 \cup m_2)) = \mu(\mathcal{S}(m_1) \cup \mathcal{S}(m_2))$, and from Proposition 1(1,2,4) we have $\widehat{\mu}((m_1 \cup m_2) \backslash (m_1 \cap m_2)) = \mu(\mathcal{R}(\mathcal{S}(m_1) \cup \mathcal{S}(m_2)) \backslash (\mathcal{S}(m_1) \cap \mathcal{S}(m_2)))$, which gives as the equation $\mathrm{sim}_{\mu sT}^{(m)}(m_1, m_2) = \frac{\mu(\mathcal{S}(m_1) \cap \mathcal{S}(m_2))}{\mu(\mathcal{S}(m_1) \cap \mathcal{S}(m_2)) + \lambda \mu(\mathcal{R}(\mathcal{S}(m_1) \cup \mathcal{S}(m_2)) \backslash (\mathcal{S}(m_1) \cap \mathcal{S}(m_2)))}$. By Proposition 1(6) we have $\mu(\mathcal{R}(\mathcal{S}(m_1) \cup \mathcal{S}(m_2)) \backslash (\mathcal{S}(m_1) \cap \mathcal{S}(m_2))) = \mu(\mathcal{S}(m_1) \cup \mathcal{S}(m_2)) \backslash (\mathcal{S}(m_1) \cap \mathcal{S}(m_2)))$, so $\mathrm{sim}_{\mu sT}^{(m)}(m_1, m_2) = \mathrm{sim}_{\mu sT}(\mathcal{S}(m_1), \mathcal{S}(m_2))$.   □

Proposition 6. *For all* $X, Y \subseteq U$, *we have:*

1. $\mathrm{sim}_{\mu DS}^{(\tau)}(X, Y) = \mathrm{sim}_{\mu DS}^{(m)}(\tau(X), \tau(Y)) = \mathrm{sim}_{\mu DS}(\mathcal{S}(\tau(X)), \mathcal{S}(\tau(Y)))$,
2. $\mathrm{sim}_{\mu sT}^{(\tau)}(X, Y) = \mathrm{sim}_{\mu sT}^{(m)}(\tau(X), \tau(Y)) = \mathrm{sim}_{\mu sT}(\mathcal{S}(\tau(X)), \mathcal{S}(\tau(Y)))$,
3. $\mathrm{sim}_{\mu BB}^{(\tau)}(X, Y) = \mathrm{sim}_{\mu BB}^{(m)}(\tau(X), \tau(Y)) = \mathrm{sim}_{\mu BB}(\mathcal{S}(\tau(X)), \mathcal{S}(\tau(Y)))$,

Proof. (1)   Just from the definitions we have: $\mathrm{sim}_{\mu DS}^{(\tau)}(X, Y) = \mathrm{sim}_{\mu DS}^{(m)}(\tau(X), \tau(Y))$, and from Proposition 5(1) we have $\mathrm{sim}_{\mu DS}^{(m)}(\tau(X), \tau(Y)) = \mathrm{sim}_{\mu DS}(\mathcal{S}(\tau(X)), \mathcal{S}(\tau(Y)))$.
(2) and (3)   Similarly as (1), using Proposition 5(2,3).   □

It appears that the axiom $S1$ is often too strong [9] so we add its weaker but indisputable version:

$$S1' \ (\text{Weak Maximum}): \quad A = B \implies sim(A, B) = 1.$$

The results corresponding to Proposition 4 also hold for others types of similarities measures.

Proposition 7

1. The indexes $\mathrm{sim}_{MS}^{(m)}, \mathrm{sim}_{\mu DS}^{(m)}$ and $\mathrm{sim}_{\mu sT}^{(m)}$ satisfy the axioms $S1m$–$S5m$.
2. If $\alpha > 0$ then the indexes $\mathrm{sim}_{SM}^{(\alpha\beta)}, \mathrm{sim}_{\mu DS}^{(\alpha\beta)}$ and $\mathrm{sim}_{\mu sT}^{(\alpha\beta)}$ satisfy the axioms $S1$–$S5$.
3. The index $\mathrm{sim}_{\mu BB}^{(m)}$ satisfies $S1m$–$S4m$ and $S5'm$,
4. If $\alpha > 0$ then the index $\mathrm{sim}_{\mu BB}^{(\alpha\beta)}$ satisfy the axioms $S1$–$S4$ and $S5'$.
5. The indexes $\mathrm{sim}_{MS}^{(\tau)}, \mathrm{sim}_{\mu DS}^{(\tau)}$ and $\mathrm{sim}_{\mu sT}^{(\tau)}$ satisfy the axioms $S1'$ and $S2$–$S5$.

6. *The index* $\text{sim}^{(\tau)}_{\mu BB}$ *and satisfies the axioms S1', S2–S4 and S5'.*

Proof. Sketch. The detailed proof is very straightforward, more or less like the similar proof in [11] for sets (Proposition 4 above), but rather lengthy due to the number of cases needed to consider.

(1) and (3)   From Proposition 4, Proposition 2 and Proposition 5.

(5) and (6)   The axioms $S2$–$S5$ follow from Proposition 4, Proposition 3 and Proposition 6. The axiom $S1m$ is obvious, the axiom $S1$ does not hold as the operator τ intentionally forgets about individual objects of the same type.

(2) and (4)   From (1), (3), (5) and (6). The condition $\alpha > 0$ guarantees the axiom $S1$. For $\alpha = 0$, (2) and (4) are reduced to (5) and (6).   □

The indexes $\text{sim}^{(\tau)}$ do not satisfy the axiom $S1$ since it may happen that $X \neq Y$ but $\tau(X) = \tau(Y)$. In the example at the end of Sect. 2, we have $B = \{E_1, c_1, c_2, c_4\}$ and $D = \{E_2, c_1, c_2, c_4\}$, clearly $B \neq D$, but $\tau(B) = \tau(D) = elephant + 3 \cdot chicken$, so $\text{sim}^{(\tau)}_{MS}(B, D) = 1$.

If we are only interested in qualitative similarity and not much in quantitative, many indexes may be considered as equivalent. Formally this can be expressed using the concept of *consistency* [11].

6   Consistency of Similarity Indexes

In some applications the fact that A is closer to B than C is more important than the exact numerical value of appropriate similarity indexes (as these values not always have straight interpretation). To deal with this problem the concept of *consistent similarities* has been proposed in [11].

We say that two similarity indexes sim_1 and sim_2 are *consistent* [11] if for all sets $A, B, C \subseteq U$,

$$sim_1(A, B) < sim_1(A, C) \iff sim_2(A, B) < sim_2(A, C).$$

In many applications consistent similarity indexes may be considered as exchangeable [11]. For example, optimal rough sets approximations are identical for consistent similarities [11], the same algorithm can be used.

Proposition 8 [11]. *The similarity indexes* $\text{sim}_{MS}, \text{sim}_{\mu DS}$ *and* $\text{sim}_{\mu sT}$ *are mutually consistent, while* $\text{sim}_{\mu BB}$ *is not consistent with any of* $\text{sim}_{MS}, \text{sim}_{\mu DS}$ *and* $\text{sim}_{\mu sT}$.   ◇

The concept of consistency can easily be extended to multisets.

We say that two similarity indexes sim_1 and sim_2 for multisets are *consistent* if for all multisets m_1, m_2, m_3 over U,

$$sim_1(m_1, m_2) < sim_1(m_1, m_3) \iff sim_2(m_1, m_2) < sim_2(m_1, m_3).$$

The results corresponding to Proposition 8 can also be formulated and proved for other types of similarities discussed in this paper.

Proposition 9

1. *The similarity indexes* $\text{sim}_{MS}^{(m)}, \text{sim}_{\mu DS}^{(m)}$ *and* $\text{sim}_{\mu sT}^{(m)}$ *are mutually consistent, while* $\text{sim}_{\mu BB}^{(m)}$ *is not consistent with any of* $\text{sim}_{MS}^{(m)}, \text{sim}_{\mu DS}^{(m)}$ *and* $\text{sim}_{\mu sT}^{(m)}$.

2. *The similarity indexes* $\text{sim}_{MS}^{(\tau)}, \text{sim}_{\mu DS}^{(\tau)}$ *and* $\text{sim}_{\mu sT}^{(\tau)}$ *are mutually consistent, while* $\text{sim}_{\mu BB}^{(\tau)}$ *is not consistent with any of* $\text{sim}_{MS}^{(\tau)}, \text{sim}_{\mu DS}^{(\tau)}$ *and* $\text{sim}_{\mu sT}^{(\tau)}$.

3. *The similarity indexes* $\text{sim}_{MS}^{(\alpha\beta)}, \text{sim}_{\mu DS}^{(\alpha\beta)}$ *and* $\text{sim}_{\mu sT}^{(\alpha\beta)}$ *are mutually consistent, while* $\text{sim}_{\mu BB}^{(\alpha\beta)}$ *is not consistent with any of* $\text{sim}_{MS}^{(\alpha\beta)}, \text{sim}_{\mu DS}^{(\alpha\beta)}$ *and* $\text{sim}_{\mu sT}^{(\alpha\beta)}$.

Proof. Sketch. The detailed proof is very straightforward, more or less like the similar proof in [11] for sets (Proposition 8 above), but rather lengthy due to the number of cases needed to consider.

(1)   From Proposition 8, Proposition 2 and Proposition 5.

(2)   From Proposition 8, Proposition 3 and Proposition 6.

(3)   From (1), (2) and the definition of $\text{sim}^{(\alpha\beta)}$.   □

It appears that extending the concepts of similarity indexes $\text{sim}_{MS}, \text{sim}_{\mu DS}$, $\text{sim}_{\mu sT}$ and $\text{sim}_{\mu DD}$ to multisets and typed sets is a rather smooth process, as all (or at least most of) main properties are preserved. This means that in many cases we might expect the results for multisets and heterogeneous sets very close to these for standard sets.

7   Final Comment

In many applications the data are obtained in an empirical manner, so, for example due to some errors, they may not have a desired structure. From the nature of the problem we know exactly what structure the data should have, but because the data are empirical, they do not. What is the 'best/optimal' approximation and how this approximation can be computed? Solution to this problem could be NP-hard even for simple structures as partial orders [9], and use of appropriate similarity measure is crucial. For many applications the multisets or, especially, *heterogeneous sets* - introduced in this paper, seem to be a better modelling tool than standard sets, so we need well defined concepts of similarity for multisets, which is the main motivation of this paper.

The similarity measures consistent with Marczewski-Steinhaus index sim_{MS} have been successfully used to define and analyze the concept of *optimal approximation* [10,11] for Pawlak's rough sets [17].

In this paper we have extended the Marczewski-Steinhaus similarity index to both multisets and heterogeneous sets. We have also proposed some axioms for multisets and discussed the use of these axioms for heterogeneous sets. We consider the concept of consistency for similarity measures as very important as it allows a greater choice of similarities for practical applications. In most cases it is not obvious which similarity index is the most appropriate, the concept of consistency makes this choice a little bit less important. In this paper we have shown that the concept of consistency can be extended to multisets and heterogeneous sets. Moreover we extend to multisets and heterogeneous sets, and discuss the properties of some other well known similarity indexes as: *Dice-Sørensen index* [4,21], *Braun-Blanquet index* [2,19] and *symmetric Tversky index* [11,22].

The mapping $\mathcal{S}$, introduced and discussed in Sect. 2, provides a convenient bridge between multisets and sets, and often allows us to prove properties of multisets with techniques designed for standard sets.

The results of this paper should make it possible to extend the idea of *optimal approximation* of [10,11] to rough multisets [5,6].

We also believe that the extension of rough multisets [5,6] to rough heterogeneous sets is feasible.

Acknowledgment. This research has been partially supported by a Discovery NSERC grant of Canada. The author gratefully acknowledges three anonymous referees for their helpful comments.

References

1. Blizard, W.D.: Multiset theory. Notre Dame J. Formal Logic **30**(1), 36–66 (1989)
2. Braun-Blanquet, J.: Pflanzensoziologie. Springer, Berlin (1928). https://doi.org/10.1007/978-3-662-02056-2
3. Deza, M.M., Deza, E.: Encyclopedia of Distances. Springer, Berlin (2012). https://doi.org/10.1007/978-3-642-30958-8
4. Dice, L.R.: Measures of the amount of ecologic association between species. Ecology **26**(3), 297–302 (1945)
5. Girish, K.P., John, S.J.: Rough multisets and information multisystems. Adv. Decis. Sci. **2011**, 1–18 (2011). https://doi.org/10.1155/2011/495392
6. Grzymała-Buse, J.W.: Learning from examples based on rough multisets. In: Raś, Z., Zemankova, M. (eds.) Methodologies for Intelligent Systems, pp. 325–332. Elsevier (1987)
7. Halmos, P.: Measure Theory. Van Nostrand, New York (1950)
8. Jaccard, P.: Étude comparative de la distribution florale dans une portion des Alpes et des Jura. Bull. de la Soc. Vaudoise des Sci. Nat. **37**, 547–549 (1901)
9. Janicki, R.: Approximations of arbitrary relations by partial orders. Int. J. Approx. Reason. **98**, 177–195 (2018)
10. Janicki, R., Lenarčič, A.: Optimal approximations with rough sets. In: Lingras, P., Wolski, M., Cornelis, C., Mitra, S., Wasilewski, P. (eds.) RSKT 2013. LNCS (LNAI), vol. 8171, pp. 87–98. Springer, Heidelberg (2013). https://doi.org/10.1007/978-3-642-41299-8_9
11. Janicki, R., Lenarčič, A.: Optimal approximations with rough sets and similarities in measure spaces. Int. J. Approx. Reason. **71**, 1–14 (2016)
12. Knuth, D.E.: The Art of Computer Programming, Volume 2: Seminumerical Algorithms. Addison-Wesley, Reading (1969)
13. Loeb, D.: Sets with a negative number of elements. Adv. Math. **91**, 64–74 (1992)
14. Marczewski, E., Steinhaus, H.: On a certain distance of sets and corresponding distance of functions. Colloq. Math. **4**, 319–327 (1958)

15. Monro, G.P.: The concept of multiset. Zeitschrift für Mathematische Logik und Grundlagen der Mathematik **33**(2), 171–178 (1987)
16. Munroe, M.E.: Introduction to Measure and Integration. Addison Wesley (1953)
17. Pawlak, Z.: Rough Sets. Kluwer, Dordrecht (1991)
18. Petrovsky, A.B.: Structuring techniques in multiset spaces. In: Fandel, G., Gal, T. (eds.) Multiple Criteria Decision Making. Lecture Notes in Economics and Mathematical Systems, vol. 448, pp. 174–184. Springer, Heidelberg (1997). https://doi.org/10.1007/978-3-642-59132-7_20
19. Rezai, H., Emoto, M., Mukaidono, M.: New similarity measure between two fuzzy sets. J. Adv. Comput. Intell. Intell. Inf. **10**(6), 946–953 (2006)
20. Samanthula, B.K., Jiang, W.: Secure multiset intersection cardinality and its application to Jaccard coefficient. IEEE Tran. Dependable Secure Comput. **13**, 591–604 (2016)
21. Sørensen, T.: A method of establishing groups of equal amplitude in plant sociology based on similarity of species and its application ro analysis of the vegetation on Danish commons. Biologishe Skrifter **5**(4), 1–34 (1957)
22. Tversky, A.: Features of similarity. Psych. Rev. **84**(4), 327–352 (1977)
23. Yager, R.R.: On the theory of bags. Int. J. Gen Syst **13**, 23–37 (1986)

Attribute Ranking with Bipolar Information

Christophe Marsala(✉)

Sorbonne Université, CNRS, LIP6, 75005 Paris, France
Christophe.Marsala@lip6.fr

Abstract. In this paper, we place ourselves in a machine learning context and we tackle the problem of the ranking of attributes through bipolar information. From a classical training set, bipolar sets (Atanassov intuitionistic fuzzy sets or interval-valued fuzzy sets) are constructed and could thus be used with bipolar information measures, such as entropies, in order to produce a novel approach to rank attributes. With such an approach, new means to highlight the lack of knowledge associated with the distribution of attribute values are offered.

Keywords: Bipolar information · Entropy · Interval-valued fuzzy sets · Intuitionistic fuzzy sets · Machine learning

1 Introduction

Interval-valued fuzzy sets (IVFS) [21], as (Atanassov) Intuitionistic Fuzzy Sets (IFS) [1] are representations of the imprecision that pointed out the knowledge about the membership of an element to a set. As it has already been shown in the literature, these two models of representation are very close [8].

These two models of representation are efficient to represent a lack of knowledge with regard to the membership of elements to a set. This lack of knowledge could be valued through the margin of hesitancy in the case of the IFS and through the gap between the membership functions in the case of the IVFS.

Such a capacity to offer a bipolar information that brings out also an information related to the lack of knowledge about data is a powerful property that could be used in machine learning. In this domain, one aims at building a model, in an inductive way, from a given training set and it relies on the underlying (and fundamental) hypothesis that this training set is representative of the whole universe of data. However, such an induction process encounters difficulties to be applied successfully in real-world problems. This has been recently underlined by leading machine learning researchers: *"From the early days, theoreticians of machine learning have focused on the* iid *assumption[1], which states that the test cases are expected to come from the same distribution as the training examples. Unfortunately, this is not a realistic assumption in the real world. [...] As a*

---

[1] iid *stands for* independent and identically distributed.

© Springer Nature Switzerland AG 2022
D. Ciucci et al. (Eds.): IPMU 2022, CCIS 1601, pp. 345–356, 2022.
https://doi.org/10.1007/978-3-031-08971-8_29

practical consequence, the performance of today's best AI systems tends to take a hit when they go from the lab to the field." [3].

Using IVFS or IFS in Machine learning is a very promising approach to introduce means to tackle a lack of representativeness of a training set. Some works have been done with IVFS or IFS in machine learning [4,18], but the construction of the IVFS/IFS in this context is still a challenge.

In this paper, three approaches to construct IVFS/IFS are presented and compared. In Sect. 2 a recall of approaches is done, then, in Sect. 3, ranking with entropies for such a representation is detailed. In Sect. 4, an experimental study is presented to bring out some main properties of the approaches. Finally, a conclusion and some future work are presented.

2 Background

2.1 Models for Bipolar Information

Interval-valued fuzzy sets have been introduced by L. A. Zadeh in 1975 [21]. In the following, the notations are those classically used in the literature [8,9].

Let $U = \{u_1, \ldots, u_n\}$ be a discrete universe and let A be a subset of U. An IVFS A of U is defined by a function F_A from U to $\mathbb{I}([0,1])$, the set of all closed intervals of $[0,1]$, such that for every $u \in U$,

$$F_A(u) = [\underline{f}_A(u), \overline{f}_A(u)] \text{ with } \underline{f}_A(u) \leq \overline{f}_A(u).$$

The IVFS A is then denoted $A = \{(u, [\underline{f}_A(u), \overline{f}_A(u)]) \mid u \in U\}$.

The interval between $\underline{f}_A(u)$ and $\overline{f}_A(u)$ represents the framing of the degree of membership of u to A. $\underline{f}_A(u)$ represents the minimum value that can be given to the degree of membership of u to A and $\overline{f}_A(u)$ the maximum value that can be given to this degree. Indeed, the bigger this interval, the less knowledge or reliable information about the membership of u to A.

Intuitionistic fuzzy sets have been introduced by Atanassov [1]. An IFS A of U is defined as:
$$A = \{(u, \mu_A(u), \nu_A(u)) \mid u \in U\}$$

with $\mu_A : U \to [0,1]$ and $\nu_A : U \to [0,1]$ such that $0 \leq \mu_A(u) + \nu_A(u) \leq 1$, $\forall u \in U$. The values $\mu_A(u)$ and $\nu_A(u)$ are respectively the membership degree and the non-membership degree of u to A.

The *margin of hesitancy* of the membership of u to A is defined as $\pi_A(u) = 1 - (\mu_A(u) + \nu_A(u))$, it is also called *intuitionistic index* of u to A. This index provides information about the lack of knowledge concerning A if any. When the margin of hesitancy according to A is equal to zero for all u, that is to say when $\mu_A(u) + \nu_A(u) = 1$, $\forall u \in U$, then A is a Zadeh's fuzzy set.

When the IFS A is such that $\mu_A(u) = \nu_A(u) = 0$, $\forall u \in U$, then it is called *completely intuitionistic* [5]. It corresponds to an IFS with a maximal margin of hesitancy, that states that there is no information concerning the membership or the non-membership to A for any element from U.

These two models of representation are very close, and particularly on a discrete universe of values as U. Indeed, it is possible to construct an IFS from an IVFS and, reciprocally, an IVFS from an IFS [8]. Let $A \subseteq U$, on the one hand, if A is the IFS $\{(u, \mu_A(u), \nu_A(u)) \mid u \in U\}$, its corresponding representation as an IVFS is $\{(u, [\underline{f}_A(u), \overline{f}_A(u)]) \mid u \in U\}$ with $\underline{f}_A(u) = \mu_A(u)$ and $\overline{f}_A(u) = 1 - \nu_A(u)$. On the other hand, if A is an IVFS $\{(u, [\underline{f}_A(u), \overline{f}_A(u)]) \mid u \in U\}$, its corresponding representation as an IFS is $\{(u, \mu_A(u), \nu_A(u)) \mid u \in U\}$ with $\mu_A(u) = \underline{f}_A(u)$ and $\nu_A(u) = 1 - \overline{f}_A(u)$.

Both representations, IFS and IVFS, can thus be viewed as two ways to highlight a lack of knowledge on the membership of an element to a set.

2.2   Training Set in Machine Learning

Let $\mathcal{X}$ be a universe of values, $\mathcal{U} = \{u_1, \ldots, u_n\} \subseteq \mathcal{X}$ be a discrete subset of $\mathcal{X}$, and $\mathcal{C} = \{+, -\}$ be a set of classes (we place ourselves in a binary class context[2]). Each element of $\mathcal{X}$ is considered to be associated with a class. The aim of supervised machine learning is to find relations between the elements of $\mathcal{U}$ and the classes in order to build a model $m : \mathcal{X} \to \mathcal{C}$ that can accurately associate the class for any element of $\mathcal{X}$.

A *training set* TS is a tuple $\langle \mathcal{U}, \mathcal{C}, (n_1^+, \ldots, n_n^+), (n_1^-, \ldots, n_n^-) \rangle$. The value n_i^+ ($i = 1, \ldots, n$) is the number of instances of u_i associated with class $+$, and n_i^- is the number of instances of u_i associated with class $-$. In the following, we denote $n^+ = \sum_{i=1}^{n} n_i^+$, $n^- = \sum_{i=1}^{n} n_i^-$, and $n_i = n_i^+ + n_i^-$, $\forall i = 1, \ldots, n$. It is assumed that $n^+ \neq 0$ and $n^- \neq 0$. From the set of values $n_1^+, \ldots, n_n^+$ (resp. $n_1^-, \ldots, n_n^-$) a probability distribution P^+ (resp. P^-) over $\mathcal{U}$ can be defined such that $P^+(u_i) = \frac{n_i^+}{n^+}$ (resp. $P^-(u_i) = \frac{n_i^-}{n^-}$). Thus, P^+ (resp. P^-) is the probability distribution over $\mathcal{U}$ restricted to elements associated with class $+$ (resp. $-$).

2.3   Approaches to Construct Ant IFS from a Probability Distribution

In this section, existing approaches to construct IFS are presented, they can be easily adapted to construct IVFS as explained in Sect. 2.1. We place ourselves in a machine learning context, as a consequence, we have decided to present all the approaches to build an IFS (or IVFS) according to this context.

The Fuzzy Generator Approach. In [6], the fuzzy generator approach has been introduced to build an IFS. This approach has shown a great efficiency in image segmentation [4,7], or in clustering problems [20] to cite a few. It is based

---

[2] In a multi-class context, the classical Machine learning "one-versus-all" approach can be used.

on the use of an intuitionistic fuzzy generator (IFG) whose definition has been proposed in [6]: a function $\Phi : [0,1] \rightarrow [0,1]$ is an intuitionistic fuzzy generator if $\Phi(x) \leq 1 - x$ for all $x \in [0,1]$. An instance of such a generator is:

$$N(x) = \frac{1-x}{1+\lambda x}, \text{ with } \lambda > 0, \ N(0) = 1 \text{ and } N(1) = 0. \tag{1}$$

From the definition of a fuzzy set, an IFS can be built with the use of an IFG [6]: let $A = \{(u, \mu_A(u)) \mid u \in \mathcal{U}\}$ be a fuzzy set on $\mathcal{U}$, and let Φ be an intuitionistic fuzzy generator, then $\tilde{A} = \{(u, \mu_A(u), \Phi(\mu_A(u))) \mid u \in \mathcal{U}\}$ is an intuitionistic fuzzy set on $\mathcal{U}$. In [4] and in [20], the IFG defined in Eq. (1) is used but other IFG can be used [7].

The Mass Assignment Approach. This approach enables to build an IFS [15,19] and it has been used recently in machine learning applications to select attributes [17,18]. It is based on the construction of a mass assignment m_A of a fuzzy set A of $\mathcal{U}$ from a probability distribution P by means of the mass assignment theorem [2]. Let p be a probability distribution over a set $\mathcal{U}$, a mass assignment m_A can be constructed as follows: $m_A(F_i) = \mu_i - \mu_{i+1}$ for $i = 1, \ldots, n-1$, and $m_A(F_n) = \mu_n$ where $F_i = \{u \in \mathcal{U} \mid p(u) \geq p_i\}$ and

$$\mu_i = |F_i|p_i + \sum_{j=i+1}^{n} (|F_j| - |F_{j-1}|)p_j.$$

According to [15], an IFS $A = \{(u, \mu_A(u), \nu_A(u)) \mid u \in \mathcal{U}\}$ could be deduced from two independent probability distributions on $\mathcal{U}$. Let p^+ be the probability distribution connected to the membership of the elements of $\mathcal{U}$ to the IFS A, and p^- be the probability distribution connected to their non-membership to the IFS A. The construction of an IFS from p^+ and p^- is based on the relation between $\mu_A(u)$, $\nu_A(u)$ and $\pi_A(u)$ (see Sect. 2) [15]:

1. the mass assignment m_A^+ is build from p^+ according to the mass assignment theorem. As stated in [15]: $m_A^+(u) = \mu_A(u) + \pi_A(u)$.
2. the mass assignment m_A^- is build from p^- with the mass assignment theorem. It is considered that $m_A^-(u) = \nu_A(u) + \pi_A(u)$.
3. the aggregation of m_A^+ and m_A^- is used to value μ_A and ν_A. For all $u \in \mathcal{U}$, $\mu_A(u) + \nu_A(u) + \pi_A(u) = 1$, it leads to $m_A^+(u) + m_A^-(u) = 1 + \pi_A(u)$ and thus for all $u \in \mathcal{U}$, $\pi_A(u) = m_A^+(u) + m_A^-(u) - 1$. Thus, values $\mu_A(u)$ and $\nu_A(u)$ are determined for any $u \in \mathcal{U}$.

As a consequence, from the two probability distributions P^+ and P^- defined from the training set TS, and following the mass assignment approach, an IFS $A \subseteq \mathcal{U}$ can be completely defined.

Discussion. In an unsupervised machine learning context, the IFG approach to construct an IFS is very efficient but its drawback lies in the choice of its hyper-parameter: the IFG. Moreover, according to the chosen IFG, other hyper-parameters may need to be set. For instance, in the case of the IFG defined in Eq. (1), it is also mandatory to choose a good value for λ.

Concerning the mass assignment approach to define an IFS, it has the drawback to produce a negative value for $\pi_A(u)$. Indeed, in this approach, a problem could appear as there is no guarantee that $m_A^+(u) + m_A^-(u) \geq 1$ for all $u \in \mathcal{U}$ thus $m_A^+(u) + m_A^-(u) - 1$ could be negative. In this case, $\pi_A(u)$ is set to 0 (this solution has been used below, in the experimental part). However, in machine learning, it offers the interesting property to have no hyper-parameter to set.

Both approaches enable the building an IFS from probability distributions. As a consequence, from a training set TS as defined above, a first set is to value the probability distributions P^+ and P^- before applying them. However, these probability distributions "hide" the real numbers of occurrences of each element for each class. It could be an inconvenience in machine learning.

2.4   Construction of an IFS/IVFS from a Training Set

In [12], an approach has been introduced to construct an IFS A of $\mathcal{U}$ from a set of values and is particularly adapted to machine learning. This method considers a supervised machine learning task, the IFS is built from a training set that provides a set of instances separated into classes. In [12], training sets associated with only 2 classes are considered but the approach could be generalised in multi-class problems with usual machine learning techniques.

There are 2 steps in this approach: 1) from the training set two weighted distributions are built taking into account the representativeness of the training set; 2) the IFS A is built by means of the two weighted distributions.

The main particularity of this approach lies in the fact that it considers a complete training set with the number of instances for each attribute value and each class. This approach differs from previously defined approaches that only consider a probability distribution over the class.

Representativeness and Weighted Distributions. In machine learning, the TS is used to highlight the relation between descriptive variables and the class (the induction process): the best model $m : \mathcal{X} \to \mathcal{C}$ that can give the correct class for any element of $\mathcal{X}$ is built. However, TS offers only a limited view concerning the whole $\mathcal{X}$, this brings out a question related to its representativeness and the lack of information that could be missing to have a precise and fully informed view on the whole $\mathcal{X}$. Indeed, the only way to train a model that perfectly fits any element of $\mathcal{X}$ is from a training set that is $\mathcal{X}$ itself. In other words, the more representative TS, the more accurate the induced m.

Representativeness Degree. As a consequence, a training set could be evaluated with regard to its representativeness. The representativeness degree gives information about how the training set is adequately representative of the whole description space in which the elements are defined. Ideally, the training set should provide enough knowledge to make a good generalisation of the relations to the classes it enables to observe. Thus, its representativeness should ensure that all its properties are also accurate for any element of $\mathcal{X}$.

A degree is proposed to value this representativeness. This degree could be set either by the user that appreciates the training set and considers its generality, or by means of an approximation deduced from the cardinality of the training set (in number of examples) and the dimensions of the whole description space defined by $\mathcal{X}$.

Let TS be the training set $\langle \mathcal{U}, \mathcal{C}, (n_1^+, \ldots, n_n^+), (n_1^-, \ldots, n_n^-) \rangle$, the *representativeness degree* $\rho \in [0,1]$ of TS is defined as:

- $\rho = 0$ when TS is not representative of $\mathcal{X}$. In this case, the knowledge it provides can not be generalised to elements of $\mathcal{X}$ not in $\mathcal{U}$.
- $\rho = 1$ when TS is completely representative of $\mathcal{X}$. In this case, the knowledge it provides can be fully generalised to any element of $\mathcal{X}$.
- when $0 < \rho < 1$, the greater ρ, the more representative TS.

In terms of probability distribution over the classes, the representativeness degree evaluates to which extent one could be confident in the fact that the probability distributions induced by $(n_i^+)_{i=1,..,n}$ and $(n_i^-)_{i=1,..,n}$ reflect the corresponding probability distributions on $\mathcal{X}$.

Lack-of-Knowledge Degree. The representativeness degree provides an information related to the TS. In order to take it into account at an example level, this degree is used to weight the information associated with any example $u \in \mathcal{U}$.

Definition 1. *Let* $TS = \langle \mathcal{U}, \mathcal{C}, (n_1^+, \ldots, n_n^+), (n_1^-, \ldots, n_n^-) \rangle$ *be a training set of* $\mathcal{X}$, *and* $\rho \in [0,1]$ *be the representativeness degree of* TS. *The* lack-of-knowledge degree *of* $u_i \in \mathcal{U}$ *is defined as* $l(u_i) = \rho * \frac{n_i}{n_{max}}$ *with* $n_{max} = \sup_{\{i=1,\ldots,n\}} n_i$.

It is easy to see that, for all $i = 1, \ldots, n$, $l(u_i) \in [0,1]$ as $\rho \in [0,1]$ and $0 \leq \frac{n_i}{n_{max}} \leq 1$.

The lack-of-knowledge degree is a way to take into account the representativeness of $\mathcal{U}$ to reduce the influence of an example of TS during the construction of A from P^+ and P^-.

Weighted Probability Distributions. By means of the lack-of-knowledge degree, it is possible to weight the influence of the information related to u with regard to the global information given by the training set.

Definition 2. *Let* $TS = \langle \mathcal{U}, \mathcal{C}, (n_1^+, \ldots, n_n^+), (n_1^-, \ldots, n_n^-) \rangle$ *be a training set of* $\mathcal{X}$, *and* $\rho \in [0,1]$ *be the representativeness degree of* TS. *The* weighted probability distributions *over* $\mathcal{U}$ *related to* $\mathcal{C}$ *are defined* $\forall i = 1, \ldots, n$ *as:*

$$P_w^+(u_i) = l(u_i) \frac{n_i^+}{n_i} \text{ and } P_w^-(u_i) = l(u_i) \frac{n_i^-}{n_i}.$$

It is easy to see that, for all $i = 1, \ldots, n$, as $l(u_i) \in [0,1]$ and $\frac{n_i^+}{n_i} \in [0,1]$ (resp. $\frac{n_i^-}{n_i} \in [0,1]$), we have $P_w^+(u_i) \in [0,1]$ (resp. $P_w^-(u_i) \in [0,1]$). Moreover, it is also easy to see that for all $u_i \in \mathcal{U}$:

$$P_w^+(u_i) + P_w^-(u_i) = l(u_i)\frac{n_i^+}{n_i} + l(u_i)\frac{n_i^-}{n_i} = l(u_i) \text{ and } 0 \leq l(u_i) \leq 1.$$

Construction of IVFS or IFS. A training set associated with its representativeness degree enables us to define either an IFVS or an IFS that keeps track of the information of the class: the class $+$ is associated with the information related to the membership of elements to A, and the class $-$ is associated with the information related to their non-membership to A.

Definition 3 (Construction of an IVFS). *Let* $TS = \langle \mathcal{U}, \mathcal{C}, (n_1^+, \dots, n_n^+), (n_1^-, \dots, n_n^-) \rangle$ *be a training set of* $\mathcal{X}$, *and* $\rho \in [0,1]$ *be its representativeness degree. The* interval-valued fuzzy set A *is defined as*

$$A = \{(u, [P_w^+(u), 1 - P_w^-(u)]) \mid u \in U\}.$$

Definition 4 (Construction of an IFS). *Let* $TS = \langle \mathcal{U}, \mathcal{C}, (n_1^+, \dots, n_n^+), (n_1^-, \dots, n_n^-) \rangle$ *be a training set of* $\mathcal{X}$, *and* $\rho \in [0,1]$ *be its representativeness degree. The* intuitionistic fuzzy set A *is defined as*

$$A = \{(u, P_w^+(u), P_w^-(u)) \mid u \in \mathcal{U}\}.$$

Discussion. The approach presented in this section enables the construction of an IVFS or an IFS from a given training set and its representativeness degree. Its main advantage is to consider the number of occurrences for each element and their association to the class. As a consequence, it could differentiate machine learning situations more deeply than approaches only based on probability distributions to build such a set.

3   Attributes Ranking with Bipolar Information

In many machine learning algorithms that train a model m from a training set TS, attributes need to be ranked according to their discriminative power with regard to the class [11]. This ranking is often constructed by means of an entropy, a measure that fulfils all the properties needed to highlight such a discriminative power. In our study, the entropies that could be used are measures suitable to handle IFS or IVFS (that are often similar). We focus here on entropies for IFS but the work is easily compatible with entropies of IVFS.

3.1   Entropies of IFS

An IFS $A = \{(u, \mu_A(u), \nu_A(u)) \mid u \in U\}$ is classically represented in a Cartesian space by the set of points $(\mu_A(u), \nu_A(u))$ defined in $[0,1] \times [0,1]$, for every element $u \in U$. In [13], a polar representation has been introduced to study the properties of the entropies of IFS, this representation makes easier the understanding of the behaviour of such measures. In this section, this polar representation is used to present the entropies.

For each $u \in U$ the polar coordinates: $(r_A(u), \theta_A(u))$, where $r_A(u)$ is its radius (*i.e.* the distance to $(0,0)$) and $\theta_A(u)$ is the polar angle (*i.e.* the angle between the abscissa axis and the vector from $(0,0)$ to $(\mu_A(u), \nu_A(u))$. Let A be an IFS, its polar representation is defined from its Cartesian representation as: $r_A(u) = \sqrt{\mu_A(u)^2 + \nu_A(u)^2}$ and $\theta_A(u)$ is such that $\tan\theta_A(u) = \frac{\nu_A(u)}{\mu_A(u)}$ if $\mu_A(u) \neq 0$ and $\theta_A(u) = \frac{\pi}{2}$ otherwise.

An entropy of IFS is a measure E, from 2^U to $[0,1]$. The three main entropies of an IFS A of U are [14]:

– the entropy introduced by Szmidt and Kacprzyk [16]:

$$E_1(A) = 1 - \frac{\sqrt{2}}{2n} \sum_{i=1}^{n} r_i \left| sin(\frac{\pi}{4} - \theta_i) \right|.$$

– the entropy introduced by Burillo and Bustince [5]:

$$E_2(A) = n - \sqrt{2} \sum_{i=1}^{n} r_i \sin(\theta_i + \frac{\pi}{4}).$$

– and the entropy proposed by Guo and Song [10]:

$$E_3(A) = \frac{1}{2n} \sum_{i=1}^{n} \left(1 - r_i\sqrt{2} \left| sin(\frac{\pi}{4} - \theta_i) \right| \right) \cdot \left(2 - r_i\sqrt{2} \sin(\frac{\pi}{4} + \theta_i) \right).$$

3.2   Ranking with Entropies

Under the polar representation, two monotonicity properties have been introduced [14]. Let A and B be two IFS of U.

Definition 5 (Radius monotonicity [14]). $E(A) \leq E(B)$ *if A is* better known than B. That is to say: $E(A) \leq E(B)$ if $r_A(u) \geq r_B(u)$ for all $u \in \mathcal{X}$.

Definition 6 (Polar angle monotonicity [14]). $E(A) \leq E(B)$ *when A is* more informative about the decision *than B. That is to say: $E(A) \leq E(B)$ when* $\left|\theta_A(u) - \frac{\pi}{4}\right| \geq \left|\theta_B(u) - \frac{\pi}{4}\right|$ for all $u \in \mathcal{X}$.

With a *radius monotonous* entropy, a better knowledge of the studied phenomenon entails a smaller value of such an entropy. A *polar-angle monotonous* entropy is useful to evaluate the easiness to make a decision.

It can be shown that E_1, E_2 and E_3 are radius monotonous, E_1 and E_3 are polar-angle monotonous, whereas E_2 is not polar-angle monotonous [14].

In machine learning, to rank attributes according to their discriminating power with regard to the class, the polar-angle monotonicity is essential. Thus, the use of entropies E_1 and E_3 should be favoured. This point is studied in the experimental part of this paper, in Sect. 4.

4   Experimental Study

4.1   Comparing the Approaches to Build IFS/IVFS

In order to compare the approaches to build the IFS/IVFS, we compare them on a toy dataset. This set is composed of 10 examples associated with classes, the number of occurrences for each instance of each class is given in Table 1 and Table 2. Both datasets have the same probability distribution over the class. They only differ by the number of occurrences of the instances.

Table 1. Case 1: more data for the class −

	u01	u02	u03	u04	u05	u06	u07	u08	u09	u10
Class +	0	0	34	165	301	301	165	34	0	0
Class −	250	256	234	160	100	100	160	234	256	250

Table 2. Case 2: more data for the class +

	u01	u02	u03	u04	u05	u06	u07	u08	u09	u10
Class +	0	0	68	330	602	602	330	68	0	0
Class −	125	128	117	80	50	50	80	117	128	125

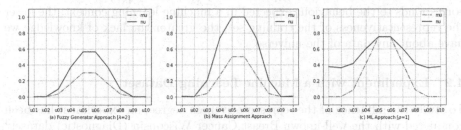

Fig. 1. IVFS constructed (case 1)

The IFVS constructed by means of the three approaches described in Sect. 2 are presented for the 2 datasets in Fig. 1 and Fig. 2. It is not surprising to see that the Fuzzy Generator approach and the Mass Assignment approach produce the same IVFS for both case 1 and case 2 because these two approaches only proceed from the probability distribution over the class. On the other hand, the Machine learning approach is sensitive to the number of occurrences and produces two different IVFS for both cases.

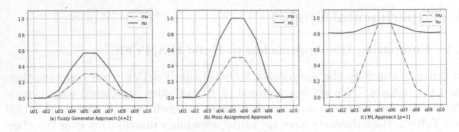

Fig. 2. IVFS constructed (case 2)

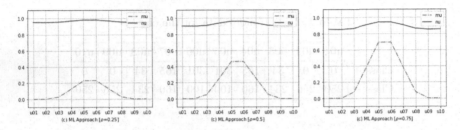

Fig. 3. IVFS constructed (case 2) when ρ varies

To study the influence of the representativeness degree ρ for this approach, various values for ρ have been used with case 2. The results are shown in Fig. 3. It can be seen that when ρ increases, the lack of knowledge about the IFS that is built is reduced (the gap between $\underline{f}_A(u)$ and $\overline{f}_A(u)$ is decreasing). It corresponds to the behaviour expected in a machine learning context: the lower the representativeness of the training set, the greater the lack of knowledge we have about any data of the universe.

4.2   Experiment with a Machine Learning Dataset

To study the influence of the representativeness degree, an experiment has been conducted with the well-known Breast Cancer Wisconsin (Diagnostic) dataset[3] from the Scikit-learn library. This dataset is composed of 569 examples, described by means of 30 variables and associated with 2 classes.

In order to construct IVFS, each numerical attribute is split into 7 numerical categories of equal size (quantiles). After the construction of the IVFS, its entropy of attributes related to the class is valued by means of the 3 entropies E_1, E_2 and E_3 presented in Sect. 3.1. Results with 4 different values for ρ ranging from 0.25 to 1 are given in Fig. 4. In this figure, it can be seen that the lower the representativeness degree ρ, the greater the entropy. Indeed, as shown previously, the representativeness degree aims at taking account a lack of information about the data (the lower the degree, the more important the lack of information), thus this can be directly valued by means of an entropy.

---

[3] https://archive.ics.uci.edu/ml/datasets.php.

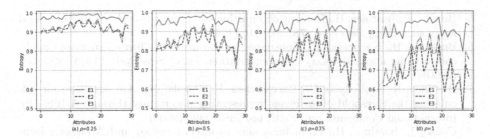

Fig. 4. Influence of the representativeness degree ρ (569 training instances)

As a consequence, it appears that the role of such a degree to build the IVFS is encouraging to rank the attributes in the case of a lack of knowledge regarding a dataset: a lack of knowledge increases the value of the entropy of an attribute and thus, it penalises it.

5 Conclusion

In this paper, three approaches are presented to build IVFS or IFS from a dataset. Two of them are based on the use of a probability distribution and the third one is particularly dedicated to the construction of such a set in machine learning. This last approach shows experimentally an interesting behaviour as it enables the construction of a different IVFS set when the number of occurrences varies. Moreover, this last approach is based on a representativeness degree that enables to take into account a lack of knowledge on the training set. This can be drawn from a comparison of the IVFS built from the same training set with different values for the representativeness degree. This comparison is done by means of 3 well-known entropies that highlight the relation between lack of knowledge and high value of entropy.

In future work, the introduction of this approach in a machine learning algorithm to build a rule set will be conducted, for instance with a dedicated algorithm to build decision trees.

References

1. Atanassov, K.T.: Intuitionistic fuzzy sets. Fuzzy Sets Syst. **20**, 87–96 (1986)
2. Baldwin, J.F., Lawry, J., Martin, T.P.: The application of generalised fuzzy rules to machine learning and automated knowledge discovery. Int. J. Uncertain. Fuzz. Knowl.-Based Syst. **6**(05), 459–487 (1998)
3. Bengio, Y., Lecun, Y., Hinton, G.: Deep learning for AI. Commun. ACM **64**(7), 58–65 (2021)
4. Bouchet, A., Montes, S., Ballarin, V., Díaz, I.: Intuitionistic fuzzy set and fuzzy mathematical morphology applied to color leukocytes segmentation. SIViP **14**(3), 557–564 (2019). https://doi.org/10.1007/s11760-019-01586-2

5. Burillo, P., Bustince, H.: Entropy on intuitionistic fuzzy sets and on interval-valued fuzzy sets. Fuzzy Sets Syst. **78**, 305–316 (1996)
6. Bustince, H., Kacprzyk, J., Mohedano, V.: Intuitionistic fuzzy generators application to intuitionistic fuzzy complementation. Fuzzy Sets Syst. **114**(3), 485–504 (2000)
7. Bustince, H., Mohedano, V., Barrenechea, E., Pagola, M.: An algorithm for calculating the threshold of an image representing uncertainty through A-IFSs. In: International Conference on IPMU, pp. 2383–2390 (2006)
8. Couso, I., Bustince, H.: From fuzzy sets to interval-valued and Atanassov intuitionistic fuzzy sets: a unified view of different axiomatic measures. IEEE Trans. Fuzzy Syst. **27**(2), 362–371 (2019)
9. Dubois, D., Prade, H.: Interval-valued fuzzy sets, possibility theory and imprecise probability. In: EUSFLAT-LFA'05, Barcelona, Spain, pp. 314–319, September 2005
10. Guo, K., Song, Q.: On the entropy for Atanassov's intuitionistic fuzzy sets: an interpretation from the perspective of amount of knowledge. Appl. Soft Comput. **24**, 328–340 (2014)
11. Marsala, C., Bouchon-Meunier, B.: Ranking attributes to build fuzzy decision trees: a comparative study of measures. In: IEEE International Conference on Fuzzy Systems (Fuzz-IEEE 2006), pp. 1777–1783 (2006)
12. Marsala, C.: Building intuitionistic fuzzy sets in machine learning. In: Proceedings of the 13th International Workshop on Fuzzy Logic and Applications (WILF 2021) (2021)
13. Marsala, C., Bouchon-Meunier, B.: Polar representation of bipolar information: a case study to compare intuitionistic entropies. In: Lesot, M.J., et al. (eds.) IPMU 2020. CCIS, vol. 1237, pp. 107–116. Springer, Cham (2020). https://doi.org/10.1007/978-3-030-50146-4_9
14. Marsala, C., Bouchon-Meunier, B.: Interpretable monotonicities for entropies of intuitionistic fuzzy sets or interval-valued fuzzy sets. In: Joint Proceedings of the 19th World Congress of the IFSA, the 12th Conference of the EUSFLAT, and the 11th International Summer School on AGOP, pp. 48–54. Atlantis Press (2021)
15. Szmidt, E., Baldwin, J.F.: Intuitionistic fuzzy set functions, mass assignment theory, possibility theory and histograms. In: Fuzz-IEEE 2006, pp. 35–41 (2006)
16. Szmidt, E., Kacprzyk, J.: New measures of entropy for intuitionistic fuzzy sets. In: Proceedings of the Ninth International Conference on Intuitionistic Fuzzy Sets (NIFS), Sofia, Bulgaria, vol. 11, pp. 12–20, May 2005
17. Szmidt, E., Kacprzyk, J., Bujnowski, P.: Attribute selection for sets of data expressed by intuitionistic fuzzy sets. In: Fuzz-IEEE 2020, pp. 1–7 (2020)
18. Szmidt, E., Kacprzyk, J., Bujnowski, P.: Three term attribute description of Atanassov's intuitionistic fuzzy sets as a basis of attribute selection. In: Fuzz-IEEE 2021, July 2021
19. Szmidt, E., Kukier, M.: A new approach to classification of imbalanced classes via Atanassov's intuitionistic fuzzy sets. In: Intelligent Data Analysis: Developing New Methodologies Through Pattern Discovery and Recovery, pp. 85–101. IGI Global (2009)
20. Yang, F., Liu, Z., Bai, X., Zhang, Y.: An improved intuitionistic fuzzy c-means for ship segmentation in infrared images. IEEE Trans. Fuzzy Syst. **30**(2), 332–344 (2020). https://doi.org/10.1109/TFUZZ.2020.3037972
21. Zadeh, L.: The concept of a linguistic variable and its application to approximate reasoning, part 1. Inf. Sci. **8**, 199–249 (1975). Reprinted in "Fuzzy Sets and Applications: selected papers by Zadeh, L.A.", Yager, R.R., Ovchinnikov, S., Tong, R.M., Nguyen, H.T. (eds.), pp. 219–269

Information Fusion Techniques based on Aggregation Functions, Pre-aggregation Functions, and Their Generalizations

On Construction Methods of (Interval-Valued) General Grouping Functions

Graçaliz P. Dimuro[1,2]([X]) [iD], Tiago Asmus[1,2] [iD], Jocivania Pinheiro[3] [iD],
Helida Santos[1,2] [iD], Eduardo Borges[1] [iD], Giancarlo Lucca[1] [iD],
Iosu Rodriguez-Martinez[2] [iD], Radko Mesiar[4] [iD], and Humberto Bustince[2] [iD]

[1] Universidade Federal do Rio Grande, Rio Grande, Brazil
{gracalizdimuro,tiagoasmus,helida,eduardoborges}@furg.br
[2] Universidad Publica de Navarra, Pamplona, Spain
{iosu.rodriguez,bustince}@unavarra.es
[3] Universidade Federal Rural do Semi-Árido, Mossoró, Brazil
vaniamat@ufersa.edu.br
[4] Slovak University of Technology, Bratislava, Slovakia
mesiar@math.sk

Abstract. Recently, several theoretical and applied studies on grouping functions and overlap functions appeared in the literature, mainly because of their flexibility when comparing them with the popular aggregation operators t-conorms and t-norms, respectively. Additionally, they constitute richer classes of disjunction/conjunction operations than t-norms and t-conorms. In particular, grouping functions have been applied as the disjunction operator in several problems, like decision making based on fuzzy preference relations. In this case, when performing pairwise comparisons, grouping functions allow one to evaluate the measure of the amount of evidence in favor of either of two given alternatives. However, grouping functions are not associative. Then, in order to allow them to be applied in n-dimensional problems, such as the pooling layer of neural networks, some generalizations were introduced, namely, n-dimensional grouping functions and the more flexible general grouping functions, the latter for enlarging the scope of applications. Then, in order to h andle uncertainty on the definition of the membership functions in real-life problems, n-dimensional and general interval-valued grouping functions were proposed. This paper aims at providing new constructions methods of general (interval-valued) grouping functions, also providing some examples.

Keywords: Grouping functions · general grouping functions · interval-valued general grouping functions

Supported by CNPq (301618/2019-4, 305805/2021-5), FAPERGS (19/2551-0001660-3), Spanish Ministry Science and Tech. (TIN2016-77356-P, PID2019-108392GB I00 (MCIN/AEI/10.13039/501100011033)), Navarra Servicios y Tecnologías, S.A. (NASERTIC).

1 Introduction

The concept of overlap functions was proposed by Bustince et al. [10], as aggregation functions [8] that may be non associate. They were originally developed for applications in image processing, in order to measure the degree of overlapping between two classes or objects. Its dual concept, namely, grouping functions, was also introduced by Bustince et al. [11]. Grouping functions have the original role of providing the measure of the amount of evidence in favor of either of two alternatives when one performs pairwise comparisons [5] in decision making problems based on fuzzy preference relations [12]. Grouping functions have been also used as the disjunction operator in several problems, e.g., in image thresholding technique [21] and for the development of a class of implication functions to construct fuzzy subsethood measures and entropy [16]. More recently, they have been used in the pooling layer of neural networks [27].

Overlap and grouping functions are richer classes when comparing with the well-known aggregation functions t-norms and t-conorms [22], respectively, since they are self-closed with respect to the convex sum and the aggregation by generalized composition of overlap and/or grouping functions [6,17], whereas t-norms and t-conorms are not. Additionally, the maximum t-conorm is the only idempotent t-conorm and the unique homogeneous t-conorm. Nevertheless, there exist an infinite number of idempotent, as well as, homogeneous grouping functions [6,17].

However, since overlap and grouping functions may be non associative, their extension to n-ary functions is not so immediate, which is a drawback whenever one has an n-dimensional problem to solve, as classification problems. Then, Gómez et al. [19] introduced the concept of n-dimensional overlap functions, with applications to fuzzy rule-based classification systems (FRBCSs). Those functions were also applied in decomposition strategies [18]. Gómez et al. [20] also introduced the concept of n-dimensional grouping functions, with an application to quantify the quality of a fuzzy community detection output based on n-dimensional operators.

After that, De Miguel et al. [14] proposed general overlap functions, a more flexible concept consisting of n-ary functions with less restrictive boundary conditions, applied to identify the matching degree in the fuzzy reasoning method of FRBCSs. Following analogous idea, Santos et al. [29] introduced the theoretical basis of general grouping functions, which is a resource that allows more flexibility to n-dimensional grouping functions and can be interpreted, e.g., as the quantity of evidence in favor of one alternative among multiple ones when performing n-ary comparisons in multi-criteria decision making based on n-ary fuzzy heterogeneous, incomplete preference relations [30].

Now observe that modeling fuzzy systems involves challenging tasks, such as the definition of adequate membership functions, mainly in the case of considering several experts. In the literature, the underlying uncertainty in this process is usually associated with the linguistic terms [24], by applying interval-valued (iv) fuzzy sets (IVFSs) [9]. As discussed by several authors [1,4,7], IVFSs can model not only uncertainty (regarding the membership function) but also vagueness (soft class boundaries). Then, IVFSs have provided good and interesting results in various applications, such as game theory [3], pest control [28] and classification problems [2].

Bedregal et al. [7] and Qiao and Hu [26] presented the notion of iv-overlap functions, and, more recently, general iv-overlap functions were proposed by Asmus et al. [4], with applications to interval-valued FRBCSs. Moreover, Asmus et al. [2] presented the concept of n-dimensional admissibly ordered iv-overlap functions, which are increasing functions concerning a total order, addressing their relevance in iv-FRBCSs.

Interval-valued grouping functions were introduced by Qiao and Hu [26] in 2017. Nevertheless, their proposal is limited to problems of two classes, which is an obstacle to be overcome in problems with n classes, as previously discussed. More recently, in 2020, Asmus et al. [13] introduced the concepts of n-dimensional and general iv-grouping functions, in such a way that the latter offers more flexibility than the former.

We point out that, although the works on general (interval-valued) grouping functions provided a simple construction method, we notice that they may be not suitable for some applications. In this direction, this paper aims at providing new constructions methods of general (interval-valued) grouping functions, also providing some examples. The paper is organized as follows. Section 2 presents preliminary concepts. In Sect. 3 we introduce new constructions methods of general grouping functions and, in Sect. 4, the ones for general iv-grouping functions. Section 5 is the Conclusion.

2 Preliminaries

In this section, we highlight some relevant concepts used in this work.

2.1 Aggregation Functions and Related Concepts

Definition 1 [8]. *A mapping $A: [0, 1]^n \rightarrow [0, 1]$ is said to be an aggregation function, if, for all $x_1, \ldots, x_n \in [0, 1]$: (A1)]A satisfies the boundary conditions: $A(0, \ldots, 0) = 0$ and $A(1, \ldots, 1) = 1$; (A2) A is increasing, i.e., for each $i \in \{1, \ldots, n\}$, if $x_i \leq y$ then $A(x_1, \ldots, x_n) \leq A(x_1, \ldots, x_{i-1}, y, x_{i+1}, \ldots, x_n)$.*

Definition 2 [8]. *An aggregation function $A: [0, 1]^n \rightarrow [0, 1]$ is said to be disjunctive if $A(\vec{x}) \geq \max(\vec{x}) = \max\{x_1, \ldots, x_n\}$ holds, for any $\vec{x} = (x_1, \ldots, x_n) \in [0, 1]^n$.*

Definition 3 [19]. *A mapping $Gn: [0, 1]^n \rightarrow [0, 1]$ is an n-dimensional grouping function if, for all $\vec{x} = (x_1, \ldots, x_n) \in [0, 1]^n$: (Gn1) Gn is commutative; (Gn2) $Gn(\vec{x}) = 0$ if and only if $x_i = 0$, for all $i = 1, \ldots, n$; (Gn3) $Gn(\vec{x}) = 1$ if and only if there exists $i \in \{1, \ldots, n\}$ with $x_i = 1$; (Gn4) Gn is increasing; (Gn5) Gn is continuous.*

Henceforth, we will refer to 2-dimensional grouping functions directly as grouping functions, originally defined by Bustince et al. [11].

Definition 4 [29]. *A mapping $GG: [0, 1]^n \rightarrow [0, 1]$ is said to be a general grouping function (GGF, for short) if, for all $\vec{x} = (x_1, \ldots, x_n) \in [0, 1]^n$: (GG1) GG is commutative; (GG2) If $\sum_{i=1}^n x_i = 0$, then $GG(\vec{x}) = 0$; (GG3) If there exists $i \in \{1, \ldots, n\}$ such that $x_i = 1$, then $GG(\vec{x}) = 1$; (GG4) GG is increasing; (GG5) GG is continuous.*

Example 1. Here, we discuss some examples of general grouping functions:

1. All grouping functions $G: [0, 1]^2 \rightarrow [0, 1]$ are GGF, but the opposite obviously is not true.

2. Take the bivariate general grouping function $GG_M \colon [0,1]^2 \to [0,1]$, defined by:

$$GG_M(x,y) = \min\{1, 2 - (1-x)^2 - (1-y)^2\}$$

for all $x, y \in [0,1]$. GG_M is not a grouping function, as $GG(0.5, 0.5) = 1$.

3. Take the grouping function $G_{Mp} \colon [0,1]^2 \to [0,1]$ (given in [15–17]) and the Łukasiewicz t-conorm $S_Ł \colon [0,1]^2 \to [0,1]$, defined, respectively, for all $x, y \in [0,1]$, by: $G_{Mp}(x,y) = \max\{1 - (1-x)^p, 1 - (1-y)^p\}$, $p > 0$ and $S_Ł(x,y) = \min\{1, x + y\}$. Then, the function $GG_{G_{Mp}}^{S_Ł} \colon [0,1]^2 \to [0,1]$, given, for all $x, y \in [0,1]$, by $GG_{G_{Mp}}^{S_Ł}(x,y) = G_{Mp}(x,y) \cdot S_Ł(x,y)$, is a GGF.

Definition 5 [4]. *A mapping $Gn \colon [0,1]^n \to [0,1]$ is said to be n-dimensional 0-grouping function if the condition (Gn2) in Definition 3 is replaced by: (Gn2') If $x_i = 0$, for all $i = 1, \ldots, n$, then $Gn(\vec{x}) = 0$. Similarly, a mapping $Gn \colon [0,1]^n \to [0,1]$ is said to be an n-dimensional 1-grouping function if the condition (Gn3) is replaced by: (Gn3') If there exists $i \in \{1, \ldots, n\}$ with $x_i = 1$, then $Gn(\vec{x}) = 1$.*

Remark 1. Observe that non-0-positive bivariate grouping and non-1-positive bivariate grouping functions were originally called as 0-grouping and 1-grouping functions [26], respectively. Also, if $Gn \colon [0,1]^n \to [0,1]$ is an n-dimensional grouping function, 0-grouping or 1-grouping function, then Gn is also a general grouping function.

2.2 Interval Mathematics and Interval-Valued Functions

Let $L([0,1])$ be the set of all closed subintervals of the unit interval $[0,1]$, $L([0,1]) = \{[x_1, x_2] | 0 \le x_1 \le x_2 \le 1\}$. Denote $\vec{x} = (x_1, \ldots, x_n) \in [0,1]^n$ and $\vec{X} = (X_1, \ldots, X_n) \in L([0,1])^n$. For any $X = [x_1, x_2]$, the left and right endpoints of X are represented, respectively, by $\underline{X}$ and $\overline{X}$, and therefore $\underline{X} = x_1$ and $\overline{X} = x_2$. Besides, for any $\vec{X} \in L([0,1])^n$, we have that $\underline{\vec{X}} = (\underline{X_1}, \ldots, \underline{X_n})$ and $\overline{\vec{X}} = (\overline{X_1}, \ldots, \overline{X_n})$.

The product order, given by $X \le_{Pr} Y \Leftrightarrow \underline{X} \le \underline{Y} \wedge \overline{X} \le \overline{Y}$, is a partial order defined for all $X, Y \in L([0,1])$. A mapping $F \colon L([0,1])^n \to L([0,1])$ is said to be $\le_{Pr}$-increasing if it is increasing with respect to the product order $\le_{Pr}$, i.e., $X_1 \le_{Pr} Y_1, \ldots, X_n \le_{Pr} Y_n \Rightarrow F(\vec{X}) \le_{Pr} F(\vec{Y})$ is satisfied, for all $\vec{X}, \vec{Y} \in L([0,1])^n$.

Let F be an interval-valued mapping. F is Moore-continuous if it is continuous with respect to the Moore metric [25] $d_M \colon L([0,1])^2 \to \mathbb{R}$, given, for all $X, Y \in L([0,1])$, by $d_M(X,Y) = \max(|\underline{X} - \underline{Y}|, |\overline{X} - \overline{Y}|)$. It is possible to generalize the Moore-metric to $L([0,1])^n$, as $d_M^n(\vec{X}, \vec{Y}) = \sqrt{d_M(X_1, Y_1)^2 + \ldots + d_M(X_n, Y_n)^2}$.

We recall some interval operations [25], given, for all $X, Y \in L([0,1])$, by:

Supremum: $\sup(X, Y) = [\max(\underline{X}, \underline{Y}), \max(\overline{X}, \overline{Y})]$;

Sum: $X + Y = [\underline{X} + \underline{Y}, \overline{X} + \overline{Y}]$;

Limited Sum: $X \dotplus Y = [\min(1, \underline{X} + \underline{Y}), \min(1, \overline{X} + \overline{Y})]$;

Subtraction: $X - Y = [\underline{X} - \overline{Y}, \overline{X} - \underline{Y}]$;

Definition 6 [23].   *An interval-valued mapping $\mathcal{A}\colon L([0,1])^n \to L([0,1])$ is called an n-dimensional interval-valued (iv-)aggregation function if: ($\mathcal{A}1$) $\mathcal{A}([0,0]\ldots,[0,0]) = [0,0]$ and $\mathcal{A}([1,1]\ldots,[1,1]) = [1,1]$; ($\mathcal{A}2$) $\mathcal{A}$ is $\leq_{Pr}$-increasing: for each $i \in \{1,\ldots,n\}$, if $X_i \leq_{Pr} Y$ then $\mathcal{A}(X_1,\ldots,X_n) \leq_{Pr} \mathcal{A}(X_1,\ldots,X_{i-1},Y,X_{i+1},\ldots,X_n)$.*

Definition 7 [26].   *An iv-function $\mathcal{G}\colon L([0,1])^2 \to L([0,1])$ is said to be an interval-valued (iv) grouping function if, for all $X,Y \in L([0,1])$: ($\mathcal{G}1$) $\mathcal{G}$ is commutative; ($\mathcal{G}2$) $\mathcal{G}(X,Y) = [0,0]$ if and only if $X = Y = [0,0]$; ($\mathcal{G}3$) $\mathcal{G}(X,Y) = [1,1]$ if and only if $X = [1,1]$ or $Y = [1,1]$; ($\mathcal{G}4$) $\mathcal{G}$ is $\leq_{Pr}$-increasing in the first component: $\mathcal{G}(Y,X) \leq_{Pr} \mathcal{G}(Z,X)$ when $Y \leq_{Pr} Z$; ($\mathcal{G}5$) $\mathcal{G}$ is Moore continuous.*

Definition 8 [13].   *A $\mathcal{G}n\colon L([0,1])^n \to L([0,1])$ is an n-dimensional interval-valued grouping function if it satisfies the following properties, for all $\vec{X} \in L([0,1])^n$: ($\mathcal{G}n1$) $\mathcal{G}n$ is commutative; ($\mathcal{G}n2$) $\mathcal{G}n(\vec{X}) = [0,0]$ if and only if $X_1 = \ldots = X_n = [0,0]$; ($\mathcal{G}n3$) $\mathcal{G}n(\vec{X}) = [1,1]$ if and only if there exists $i \in \{1,\ldots,n\}$ with $X_i = [1,1]$; ($\mathcal{G}n4$) $\mathcal{G}n$ is $\leq_{Pr}$-increasing in the first component: $\mathcal{G}n(X_1,\ldots,X_n) \leq_{Pr} \mathcal{G}n(Y,X_2,\ldots,X_n)$ when $X_1 \leq_{Pr} Y$; ($\mathcal{G}n5$) $\mathcal{G}n$ is Moore continuous.*

Observe that $\sup(\vec{X}) = [0,0]$ if and only if $X_1 = \ldots = X_n = [0,0]$. Besides, $\sup(\vec{X}) = [1,1]$ if and only if there exists $i \in \{1,\ldots,n\}$ with $X_i = [1,1]$.

Example 2. Examples of n-dimensional iv-grouping functions are, for all $\vec{X} \in L([0,1])$: (i) $\mathcal{G}n_S(\vec{X}) = \sup(\vec{X})$; (ii) $\mathcal{G}n_p(\vec{X}) = [1,1] - \prod_{i=1}^{n}([1,1] - X_i^p)$, for $p > 0$.

Definition 9 [13].   *A mapping $\mathcal{G}n\colon L([0,1])^n \to L([0,1])$ be an n-dimensional iv-0-grouping function if and only if the property ($\mathcal{G}n2$) from Definition 8 is replaced by: ($\mathcal{G}n2'$) If $X_1 = \ldots = X_n = [0,0]$. So, it follows that $\mathcal{G}n(\vec{X}) = [0,0]$, for all $\vec{X} \in L([0,1])^n$. Similarly, let a mapping $\mathcal{G}n\colon L([0,1])^n \to L([0,1])$ be an n-dimensional iv-1-grouping function if and only if ($\mathcal{G}n3$) is replaced by: ($\mathcal{G}n3'$) If there exists $i \in \{1,\ldots,n\}$ with $X_i = [1,1]$. So, it follows that $\mathcal{G}n(\vec{X}) = [1,1]$, for all $\vec{X} \in L([0,1])^n$.*

Example 3. Consider $\mathcal{G}n_S$ as being the n-dimensional interval-valued limited sum, defined by $\mathcal{G}n_S(\vec{X}) = X_1 \dot{+} \ldots \dot{+} X_n$. One may say that $\mathcal{G}n_S$ is an n-dimensional iv-1-grouping function. However, $\mathcal{G}n_S$ is not an n-dimensional iv-grouping function.

Definition 10 [13].   *Any function $\mathcal{G}\mathcal{G}\colon L([0,1])^n \to L([0,1])$ verifying the five properties given as follows is said to be a general interval-valued (iv) grouping function, for all $\vec{X} \in L([0,1])^n$: ($\mathcal{G}\mathcal{G}1$) $\mathcal{G}\mathcal{G}$ is commutative; ($\mathcal{G}\mathcal{G}2$) If $X_1 = \ldots = X_n = [0,0]$, then $\mathcal{G}\mathcal{G}(\vec{X}) = [0,0]$; ($\mathcal{G}\mathcal{G}3$) If there exists $i \in \{1,\ldots,n\}$ with $X_i = [1,1]$, then $\mathcal{G}\mathcal{G}(\vec{X}) = [1,1]$; ($\mathcal{G}\mathcal{G}4$) $\mathcal{G}\mathcal{G}$ is $\leq_{Pr}$-increasing in the first component: $\mathcal{G}\mathcal{G}(X_1,\ldots,X_n) \leq_{Pr} \mathcal{G}\mathcal{G}(Y,X_2,\ldots,X_n)$, when $X_1 \leq_{Pr} Y$; ($\mathcal{G}\mathcal{G}5$) $\mathcal{G}\mathcal{G}$ is Moore continuous.*

Example 4. The mapping given, for all $\vec{X} \in L([0,1])^n$, by

$$\mathcal{GG}_L(\vec{X}) = \begin{cases} [0,0] & \text{if } \overline{m} \leq \frac{1}{n}, \\ [0, \min(1, n \cdot \overline{m})] & \text{if } \min(1, \underline{m}) \leq \frac{1}{n} \text{ and } \min(1, \overline{m}) > \frac{1}{n}, \\ n \cdot (X_1 \dotplus \ldots \dotplus X_n) & \text{otherwise,} \end{cases}$$

with $\underline{m} = \min\left(1, \sum\limits_{i=1}^{n} \underline{X_i}\right)$ and $\overline{m} = \min\left(1, \sum\limits_{i=1}^{n} \overline{X_i}\right)$, is a general iv-grouping function, which is neither an n-dimensional iv-0-grouping function, nor an n-dimensional iv-1-grouping function. Thus, it is neither an n-dimensional iv-grouping function.

Proposition 1 [13]. *If $F \colon L([0,1])^n \to L([0,1])$ is a mapping that is either an n-dimensional iv-grouping, or an n-dimensional iv-0-grouping and an n-dimensional iv-1-grouping function, then F is also said to be a general iv-grouping function.*

3   About Construction Methods of General Grouping Functions

Santos et al. [29] presented some constructions methods of GGF. Here, we generalize such construction methods by using less restrictive constitutive base functions.

Theorem 1. *Take a continuous and disjunctive aggregation function $M \colon [0,1]^2 \to [0,1]$. Let $GG_A \colon [0,1]^n \to [0,1]$ be a GGF and let $F \colon [0,1]^n \to [0,1]$ be a commutative and continuous n-dimensional aggregation function. So, the mapping $M_{GG_A}^F \colon [0,1]^n \to [0,1]$ defined, for all $\vec{x} \in [0,1]^n$, by $M_{GG_A}^F(\vec{x}) = M(GG_A(\vec{x}), F(\vec{x}))$ is a GGF.*

Proof. Taking into account that GG_A and F are commutative, then **(GG1)** is satisfied by $M_{GG_A}^F$. Knowing that M, GG_A and F are increasing and continuous, conditions **(GG4)** and **(GG5)** are held by $M_{GG_A}^F$. Therefore, it remains to prove:

(GG2) Take $\vec{x} \in [0,1]^n$, such that $\sum\limits_{i=1}^{n} x_i = 0$. Therefore, $GG_A(\vec{x}) = F(\vec{x}) = 0$, and then $M_{GG_A}^F(\vec{x}) = M(0,0) = 0$.

(GG3) For some $\vec{x} \in [0,1]^n$, imagine there exists $i \in \{1, \ldots, n\}$ such that $x_i = 1$. Hence, $GG_A(\vec{x}) = 1$ and, since M is disjunctive, it follows that $M(1, F(\vec{x})) \geq \max(1, F(\vec{x})) = 1$. Thus, $M_{GG_A}^F(\vec{x}) = M(1, F(\vec{x})) = 1$.

Corollary 1. *Take a continuous and disjunctive aggregation function $M \colon [0,1]^2 \to [0,1]$. Let $Gn_A \colon [0,1]^n \to [0,1]$ be an n-dimensional grouping function and let $F \colon [0,1]^n \to [0,1]$ be a commutative and continuous n-dimensional aggregation function. So, the mapping $M_{Gn_A}^F \colon [0,1]^n \to [0,1]$ defined, for all $\vec{x} \in [0,1]^n$, by $M_{Gn_A}^F(\vec{x}) = M(Gn_A(\vec{x}), F(\vec{x}))$ is a general grouping function.*

Proof. Bearing in mind that all n-dimensional grouping functions are GGF, the proof follows straightforward from Theorem 1.

Example 5. Consider $M\colon [0,1]^2 \to [0,1]$ and $GG_A, F\colon [0,1]^n \to [0,1]$ given as $M(x,y) = \max(x,y)$, $GG_A(\vec{x}) = \min\left(1, n - \sum_{i=1}^n (1-x_i)^2\right)$ and $F(\vec{x}) = \min\{x_1^2, \ldots, x_n^2\}$, respectively. The GGF $M_{GG_A}^F$ is given as follows:

$$M_{GG_A}^F(\vec{x}) = \max\left(\min\left(1, n - \sum_{i=1}^n (1-x_i)^2\right), \min\{x_1^2, \ldots, x_n^2\}\right)$$

$$= \begin{cases} 1 & \text{if } n - \sum_{i=1}^n (1-x_i)^2 \geq 1, \\ n - \sum_{i=1}^n (1-x_i)^2 & \text{if } n - \sum_{i=1}^n (1-x_i)^2 < 1. \end{cases}$$

Example 6. Consider $M\colon [0,1]^2 \to [0,1]$ and $GG_A, F\colon [0,1]^n \to [0,1]$ given as $M(x,y) = \max(x,y)$, $GG_A(\vec{x}) = \min\left(1, n - \sum_{i=1}^n (1-x_i)^2\right)$ and $F(\vec{x}) = \min\left(1, \sum_{i=1}^n x_i\right)$, respectively. The GGF $M_{GG_A}^F$ is given as follows:

$$M_{GG_A}^F(\vec{x}) = \max\left(\min\left(1, n - \sum_{i=1}^n (1-x_i)^2\right), \min\left(1, \sum_{i=1}^n x_i\right)\right)$$

$$= \begin{cases} 1 & \text{if } \sum_{i=1}^n x_i \geq 1, \\ n - \sum_{i=1}^n (1-x_i)^2 & \text{if } \sum_{i=1}^n x_i < 1. \end{cases}$$

Example 7. Consider $M\colon [0,1]^2 \to [0,1]$ and $GG_A, F\colon [0,1]^n \to [0,1]$ given as $M(x,y) = \max(x,y)$, $GG_A(\vec{x}) = \min\left(1, n - \sum_{i=1}^n (1-x_i)^2\right)$ and $F(\vec{x}) = \max\left(0, \sum_{i=1}^n x_i - (n-1)\right)$, respectively. The GGF $M_{GG_A}^F$ is given by:

$$M_{GG_A}^F(\vec{x}) = \max\left(\min\left(1, n - \sum_{i=1}^n (1-x_i)^2\right), \max\left(0, \sum_{i=1}^n x_i - (n-1)\right)\right)$$

$$= \min\left(1, n - \sum_{i=1}^n (1-x_i)^2\right) = GG_A(\vec{x}).$$

One can have the extension of Theorem 1, to provide a method to construct a GGF through an aggregation of m functions:

Theorem 2. *Take $Mm\colon [0,1]^m \to [0,1]$ as a continuous and disjunctive aggregation function. Let $GG_A\colon [0,1]^n \to [0,1]$ be a GGF and consider commutative and continuous n-dimensional aggregation functions $F_2, \ldots, F_m\colon [0,1]^n \to [0,1]$. So, the mapping $Mm_{GG_A}^{F_2,\ldots,F_m}\colon [0,1]^n \to [0,1]$ defined, for all $\vec{x} \in [0,1]^n$, by $Mm_{GG_A}^{F_2,\ldots,F_m}(\vec{x}) = Mm(GG_A(\vec{x}), F_2(\vec{x}), \ldots, F_m(\vec{x}))$ is a GGF.*

The next corollary is also immediately obtained.

Corollary 2. *Take $Mm\colon [0,1]^m \to [0,1]$ as a continuous and disjunctive aggregation function. Let the mapping $Gn_A\colon [0,1]^n \to [0,1]$ be an n-dimensional grouping function and let $F_2, \ldots, F_m\colon [0,1]^n \to [0,1]$ be commutative and continuous n-dimensional aggregation functions. Therefore, the mapping $Mm_{Gn_A}^{F_2,\ldots,F_m}\colon [0,1]^n \to [0,1]$ given, for all $\vec{x} \in [0,1]^n$, by $Mn_{Gn_A}^{F_2,\ldots,F_m}(\vec{x}) = Mm(Gn_A(\vec{x}), F_2(\vec{x}), \ldots, F_m(\vec{x}))$ is a general grouping function.*

Example 8. Take $M_3\colon [0,1]^3 \to [0,1]$ and $GG_A, F_2, F_3\colon [0,1]^n \to [0,1]$ given as $M_3(\vec{x}) = \min(1, \sum_{i=1}^3 x_i)$, $GG_A(\vec{x}) = \min(1, \sum_{i=1}^n x_i)$, $F_2(\vec{x}) = \max(0, \sum_{i=1}^n x_i - (n-1))$ and $F_3(\vec{x}) = \prod_{i=1}^n x_i$, respectively. The GGF $M_{3GG_A}^{F_2,F_3} = \mathcal{M}_3$ is given by:

$$\mathcal{M}_3(\vec{x}) = \min\left(1, \min\left(1, \sum_{i=1}^n x_i\right) + \max\left(0, \sum_{i=1}^n x_i - (n-1)\right) + \prod_{i=1}^n x_i\right)$$

$$= \begin{cases} \sum_{i=1}^n x_i + \prod_{i=1}^n x_i & \text{if } \sum_{i=1}^n x_i + \prod_{i=1}^n x_i < 1, \\ 1 & \text{if } \sum_{i=1}^n x_i + \prod_{i=1}^n x_i \geq 1. \end{cases}$$

Example 9. Consider $M_4\colon [0,1]^4 \to [0,1]$ and $GG_A, F_2, F_3, F_4\colon [0,1]^n \to [0,1]$ given as $M_4(\vec{x}) = \max\{x_1, x_2, x_3, x_4\}$, $GG_A(\vec{x}) = \min(1, \sum_{i=1}^n x_i)$, $F_2(\vec{x}) = \min\{x_1^2, \cdots, x_n^2\}$, $F_3(\vec{x}) = \max\left(0, \sum_{i=1}^n x_i - (n-1)\right)$ and $F_4(\vec{x}) = \prod_{i=1}^n x_i$, respectively. The GGF $M_{4GG_A}^{F_2,F_3,F_4} = \mathcal{M}_4$ is given as follows:

$$\mathcal{M}_4(\vec{x}) = \max\{\min\left(1, \sum_{i=1}^n x_i\right), \min\{x_1^2, \ldots, x_n^2\}, \max\left(0, \sum_{i=1}^n x_i - (n-1)\right), \prod_{i=1}^n x_i\}$$

$$= \min\left(1, \sum_{i=1}^n x_i\right) = GG_A(\vec{x})$$

Remark 2. In the results about the construction methods of GGF presented by Santos et al. [29, Theorems 3.3, 3.4] and also Theorems 1 and 2 introduced here, one can notice that the construction methods performed by combining some aggregation functions allow one to obtain different GGF by either the composition of GGF (which are disjunctive) through a continuous (but not necessarily commutative or disjunctive) aggregation function [29, Theorems 3.3, 3.4] or the composition of one GGF with other(s) continuous and commutative (but not necessarily disjunctive) aggregation function(s) through a disjunctive and continuous (but not necessarily commutative) aggregation function.

4 On Construction Methods of iv-General Grouping Functions

Asmus et al. [13] presented constructions methods of iv-general grouping functions. Next, we provide some construction methods that are defined as interval extensions of the results in [13, Theorems 3.3, 3.4] and Theorems 1 and 2 introduced in Sect. 3 above. They enable one to construct general iv-grouping functions by two different ways: (i) aggregating general iv-grouping functions through a Moore continuous iv-aggregation function, or (ii) having the composition, through a Moore continuous and disjunctive iv-aggregation function, of at least one general iv-aggregation function and other commutative and Moore continuous iv-aggregation function.

Theorem 3. *Take the mapping* $\mathcal{M}\colon L([0,1])^2 \to L([0,1])$. *For any general iv-grouping functions* $GG_1, GG_2\colon L([0,1])^n \to L([0,1])$, *define the function* $\mathcal{M}_{GG_1}^{GG_2}\colon L([0,1])^n \to L([0,1])$, *for all* $\vec{X} \in L([0,1])^n$, *by* $\mathcal{M}_{GG_1}^{GG_2}(\vec{X}) = \mathcal{M}(GG_1(\vec{X}), GG_2(\vec{X}))$. *So,* $\mathcal{M}_{GG_1}^{GG_2}$ *is a general iv-grouping function iff* $\mathcal{M}$ *is a Moore continuous iv-aggregation function.*

Proof. ($\Rightarrow$) Consider that $\mathcal{M}_{\mathcal{GG}_1}^{\mathcal{GG}_2}$ is a general iv-grouping function. So, it is straightforward that $\mathcal{M}$ is Moore continuous and $\leq_{Pr}$-increasing ($\mathbf{A2}$). Next, take $\vec{X} \in L([0,1])^n$ and consider that $\sum\limits_{i=1}^{n} X_i = [0,0]$. So, by ($\mathcal{GG}2$), it follows that:

$$\mathcal{M}_{\mathcal{GG}_1}^{\mathcal{GG}_2}(\vec{X}) = \mathcal{M}(\mathcal{GG}_1(\vec{X}), \mathcal{GG}_2(\vec{X})) = [0,0]$$

and $\mathcal{GG}_1(\vec{X}) = \mathcal{GG}_2(\vec{X}) = [0,0]$. Hence, $\mathcal{M}([0,0],[0,0]) = [0,0]$ is verified. Now, take $\vec{X} \in L([0,1])^n$, such that there exists $i \in \{1,\ldots,n\}$ such that $X_i = [1,1]$. So, by ($\mathcal{GG}3$), it follows that: $\mathcal{M}_{\mathcal{GG}_1}^{\mathcal{GG}_2}(\vec{X}) = \mathcal{M}(\mathcal{GG}_1(\vec{X}), \mathcal{GG}_2(\vec{X})) = [1,1]$ and $\mathcal{GG}_1(\vec{X}) = \mathcal{GG}_2(\vec{X}) = [1,1]$. Thus, $\mathcal{M}([1,1],[1,1]) = [1,1]$ holds. This proves that $\mathcal{M}$ verifies property ($\mathbf{A1}$), and, hence, $\mathcal{M}$ is a Moore continuous iv-aggregation function.

($\Leftarrow$) Consider that $\mathcal{M}$ is a Moore continuous iv-aggregation function. It is straightforward that $\mathcal{M}_{\mathcal{GG}_1}^{\mathcal{GG}_2}$ is commutative by ($\mathcal{GG}1$), $\leq_{Pr}$-increasing by ($\mathcal{GG}4$) and Moore continuous by ($\mathcal{GG}5$). So, it remains to verify: ($\mathcal{GG}2$) Take $\vec{X} \in L([0,1])^n$ such that $\sum\limits_{i=1}^{n} X_i = [0,0]$. So, by ($\mathcal{GG}2$), it follows that $\mathcal{GG}_1(\vec{X}) = \mathcal{GG}_2(\vec{X}) = [0,0]$. Hence,

$$\mathcal{M}_{\mathcal{GG}_1}^{\mathcal{GG}_2}(\vec{X}) = \mathcal{M}(\mathcal{GG}_1(\vec{X}), \mathcal{GG}_2(\vec{X})) = \mathcal{M}([0,0],[0,0]) = [0,0],$$

by ($\mathbf{A1}$), as $\mathcal{M}$ is an iv-aggregation function.

($\mathcal{GG}3$) Imagine that there exists $i \in \{1,\ldots,n\}$ such that $X_i = [1,1]$, for some $\vec{X} = (X_1,\ldots,X_n) \in L([0,1])^n$. So, $\mathcal{GG}_1(\vec{X}) = \mathcal{GG}_2(\vec{X}) = [1,1]$ holds. Hence, $\mathcal{M}_{\mathcal{GG}_1}^{\mathcal{GG}_2}(\vec{X}) = \mathcal{M}(\mathcal{GG}_1(\vec{X}), \mathcal{GG}_2(\vec{X})) = \mathcal{M}([1,1],[1,1]) = [1,1]$, by ($\mathbf{A1}$), as $\mathcal{M}$ is an iv-aggregation function. Thus, $\mathcal{M}_{\mathcal{GG}_1}^{\mathcal{GG}_2}$ is a general iv-grouping function.

The following result is immediate.

Corollary 3. *Consider* $\mathcal{M}: L([0,1])^2 \to L([0,1])$. *For any* n-*dimensional iv-grouping functions* $\mathcal{G}n_1, \mathcal{G}n_2: L([0,1])^n \to L([0,1])$, *let* $\mathcal{M}_{\mathcal{G}n_1}^{\mathcal{G}n_2}: L([0,1])^n \to L([0,1])$ *be given, for all* $\vec{X} \in L([0,1])^n$, *by* $\mathcal{M}_{\mathcal{G}n_1}^{\mathcal{G}n_2}(\vec{X}) = \mathcal{M}(\mathcal{G}n_1(\vec{X}), \mathcal{G}n_2(\vec{X}))$. $\mathcal{M}_{\mathcal{G}n_1}^{\mathcal{G}n_2}$ *is a general iv-grouping function iff* $\mathcal{M}$ *is a Moore continuous iv-aggregation function.*

Proof. It is obtained straightforward from Theorem 3, considering that any n-dimensional iv-grouping function is also a general iv-grouping function.

Theorem 4. *Consider* $\mathcal{M}m: L([0,1])^m \to L([0,1])$. *For a tuple* $\overrightarrow{\mathcal{GG}} = (\mathcal{GG}_1,\ldots,\mathcal{GG}_m)$ *of general iv-grouping functions, let* $\mathcal{M}m_{\overrightarrow{\mathcal{GG}}}: L([0,1])^n \to L([0,1])$ *be given, for all* $\vec{X} \in L([0,1])^n$, *by:* $\mathcal{M}m_{\overrightarrow{\mathcal{GG}}}(\vec{X}) = \mathcal{M}m(\mathcal{GG}_1(\vec{X}),\ldots,\mathcal{GG}_m(\vec{X}))$. *So,* $\mathcal{M}m_{\overrightarrow{\mathcal{GG}}}$ *is a general iv-grouping function iff* $\mathcal{M}m$ *is a Moore continuous iv-aggregation function.*

Proof. The proof is similar to the one given in Theorem 3.

Other result, immediately obtained from the previous theorem, is:

Corollary 4. *Take* $\mathcal{M}m$: $L([0,1])^m \rightarrow L([0,1])$. *For a tuple* $\overrightarrow{\mathcal{G}n} = (\mathcal{G}n_1, \ldots, \mathcal{G}n_m)$ *of n-dimensional iv-grouping functions, let* $\mathcal{M}m_{\overrightarrow{\mathcal{G}n}}$: $L([0,1])^n \rightarrow L([0,1])$ *be defined, for all* $\vec{X} \in L([0,1])^n$, *by* $\mathcal{M}m_{\overrightarrow{\mathcal{G}n}}(\vec{X}) = \mathcal{M}m(\mathcal{G}n_1(\vec{X}), \ldots, \mathcal{G}n_m(\vec{X}))$. $\mathcal{M}m_{\overrightarrow{\mathcal{G}n}}$ *is a general iv-grouping function iff* $\mathcal{M}m$ *is a Moore continuous iv-aggregation function.*

Remark 3. Observe that Corollaries 3 and 4 could also be given by exchanging the tuple of n-dimensional iv-grouping functions by either a tuple of n-dimensional iv-0-grouping functions or a tuple of n-dimensional iv-1-grouping functions.

Theorem 5. *Take a Moore continuous and disjunctive iv-aggregation function* $\mathcal{M}$: $L([0,1])^2 \rightarrow L([0,1])$. *Let* $\mathcal{GG}_A, \mathcal{F}$: $L([0,1])^n \rightarrow L([0,1])$ *be a general iv-grouping function, and a commutative Moore continuous n-dimensional aggregation function, respectively. So,* $\mathcal{M}^{\mathcal{F}}_{\mathcal{GG}_A}$: $L([0,1])^n \rightarrow L([0,1])$ *given, for all* $\vec{X} \in L([0,1])^n$, *by* $\mathcal{M}^{\mathcal{F}}_{\mathcal{GG}_A}(\vec{X}) = \mathcal{M}(\mathcal{GG}_A(\vec{X}), \mathcal{F}(\vec{X}))$, *is a general iv-grouping function.*

Proof. Taking into account that $\mathcal{GG}_A$ and $\mathcal{F}$ are commutative, so the property ($\mathcal{GG}1$) is verified by $\mathcal{M}^{\mathcal{F}}_{\mathcal{GG}_A}$. Since $\mathcal{M}, \mathcal{GG}_A$ and $\mathcal{F}$ are $\leq_{Pr}$-increasing and Moore continuous, it follows that $\mathcal{M}^{\mathcal{F}}_{\mathcal{GG}_A}$ verifies properties ($\mathcal{GG}4$) and ($\mathcal{GG}5$). We still must verify:

($\mathcal{GG}2$) Take $\vec{X} = (X_1, \ldots, X_n) \in [0,1]^n$ such that $\sum_{i=1}^{n} X_i = 0$. Hence, $\mathcal{GG}_A(\vec{X}) = \mathcal{F}(\vec{X}) = [0,0]$. Therefore, $\mathcal{M}^{\mathcal{F}}_{\mathcal{GG}_A}(\vec{X}) = \mathcal{M}([0,0],[0,0]) = [0,0]$.

($\mathcal{GG}3$) Consider that, for some $\vec{X} = (X_1, \ldots, X_n) \in L([0,1])^n$, there exists $i \in \{1, \ldots, n\}$ such that $X_i = [1,1]$. Hence, $\mathcal{GG}_A(\vec{X}) = [1,1]$ and, considering that $\mathcal{M}$ is disjunctive, it follows that $\mathcal{M}([1,1], \mathcal{F}(\vec{X})) \geq_{Pr} \sup([1,1], \mathcal{F}(\vec{X})) = [1,1]$. Therefore, $\mathcal{M}^{\mathcal{F}}_{\mathcal{GG}_A}(\vec{X}) = \mathcal{M}([1,1], \mathcal{F}(\vec{X})) = [1,1]$.

Corollary 5. *Take a Moore continuous and disjunctive iv-aggregation function* $\mathcal{M}$: $L([0,1])^2 \rightarrow L([0,1])$, *and let the mappings* $\mathcal{G}n_A, \mathcal{F}$: $L([0,1])^n \rightarrow L([0,1])$ *be an n-dimensional iv-grouping function, and a commutative Moore continuous n-dimensional aggregation function, respectively.* $\mathcal{M}^{\mathcal{F}}_{\mathcal{G}n_A}$: $L([0,1])^n \rightarrow L([0,1])$ *given, for all* $\vec{X} \in L([0,1])^n$, *by* $\mathcal{M}^{\mathcal{F}}_{\mathcal{G}n_A}(\vec{X}) = \mathcal{M}(\mathcal{G}n_A(\vec{X}), \mathcal{F}(\vec{X}))$ *is a general iv-grouping function.*

Proof. Straightforward from Theorem 5 and Proposition 1.

Theorem 5 can be extended resulting in a construction method for a general iv-grouping function by aggregating m interval-valued functions.

Theorem 6. *Take a Moore continuous and disjunctive iv-aggregation function* $\mathcal{M}m$: $L([0,1])^m \rightarrow L([0,1])$. *Let* $\mathcal{GG}_A$: $L([0,1])^n \rightarrow L([0,1])$ *be a general iv-grouping function and let* $\mathcal{F}_2, \ldots, \mathcal{F}_m$: $L([0,1])^n \rightarrow L([0,1])$ *be commutative and continuous iv-aggregation functions. The mapping* $\mathcal{M}m^{\mathcal{F}_2, \ldots, \mathcal{F}_m}_{\mathcal{GG}_A}$: $L([0,1])^n \rightarrow L([0,1])$ *given, for all* $\vec{X} \in [0,1]^n$, *by* $\mathcal{M}m^{\mathcal{F}_2, \ldots, \mathcal{F}_m}_{\mathcal{GG}_A}(\vec{X}) = \mathcal{M}m(\mathcal{GG}_A(\vec{X}), \mathcal{F}_2(\vec{X}), \ldots, \mathcal{F}_m(\vec{X}))$ *is a general iv-grouping function.*

Proof. Similar to the proof given in Theorem 5.

At last, we have the following immediate result.

Corollary 6. *Take a Moore continuous and disjunctive iv-aggregation function* $\mathcal{Mm}$: $L([0,1])^m \rightarrow L([0,1])$, *and consider* $\mathcal{G}n_A$: $L([0,1])^n \rightarrow L([0,1])$ *is an n-dimensional iv-grouping function and let* $\mathcal{F}_2, \ldots, \mathcal{F}_m$: $L([0,1])^n \rightarrow L([0,1])$ *be commutative and continuous iv-aggregation functions. The mapping* $\mathcal{Mm}_{\mathcal{G}n_A}^{\mathcal{F}_2,\ldots,\mathcal{F}_n}$: $L([0,1])^n \rightarrow L([0,1])$ *given, for all* $\vec{X} \in [0,1]^n$, *by:* $\mathcal{Mm}_{\mathcal{G}n_A}^{\mathcal{F}_2,\ldots,\mathcal{F}_m}(\vec{X}) = \mathcal{Mm}(\mathcal{G}n_A(\vec{X}), \mathcal{F}_2(\vec{X}), \ldots, \mathcal{F}_m(\vec{X}))$ *is a general iv-grouping function.*

5 Conclusions

In this work, considering the contributions of grouping functions to several application areas, we focused on developments concerning new construction methods of general (also interval-valued) grouping functions. Also, we presented some examples to illustrate the construction methods. Future works is concerning in application of the provided methods in the pooling layer of neural networks, as initially proposed in [27].

References

1. Asmus, T.C., Dimuro, G.P., Bedregal, B., Sanz, J.A., Mesiar, R., Bustince, H.: Towards interval uncertainty propagation control in bivariate aggregation processes and the introduction of width-limited interval-valued overlap functions. Fuzzy Sets Syst. (2021). https://doi.org/10.1016/j.fss.2021.09.005. (In Press, Corrected Proof)
2. Asmus, T.C., Sanz, J.A.A., Pereira Dimuro, G., Bedregal, B., Fernandez, J., Bustince, H.: N-dimensional admissibly ordered interval-valued overlap functions and its influence in interval-valued fuzzy rule-based classification systems. IEEE Trans. Fuzzy Syst. 30(4), 1060–1072 (2022). https://doi.org/10.1109/TFUZZ.2021.3052342
3. Asmus, T.C., Dimuro, G.P., Bedregal, B.: On two-player interval-valued fuzzy Bayesian games. Int. J. Intell. Syst. 32(6), 557–596 (2017)
4. da Cruz Asmus, T., Dimuro, G.P., Bedregal, B., Sanz, J.A., Pereira, S., Jr., Bustince, H.: General interval-valued overlap functions and interval-valued overlap indices. Inf. Sci. 527, 27–50 (2020). https://doi.org/10.1016/j.ins.2020.03.091
5. Barzilai, J.: Consistency measures for pairwise comparison matrices. J. Multi-Criteria Decis. Anal. 7(3), 123–132 (1998)
6. Bedregal, B.C., Dimuro, G.P., Bustince, H., Barrenechea, E.: New results on overlap and grouping functions. Inf. Sci. 249, 148–170 (2013)
7. Bedregal, B., Bustince, H., Palmeira, E., Dimuro, G., Fernandez, J.: Generalized interval-valued OWA operators with interval weights derived from interval-valued overlap functions. Int. J. Approx. Reason. 90, 1–16 (2017)
8. Beliakov, G., Bustince Sola, H., Calvo Sánchez, T.: Averages on lattices, In: A Practical Guide to Averaging Functions. SFSC, vol. 329, pp. 305–345. Springer, Cham (2016). https://doi.org/10.1007/978-3-319-24753-3_8
9. Bustince, H., et al.: A historical account of types of fuzzy sets and their relationships. IEEE Trans. Fuzzy Syst. 24(1), 179–194 (2016)

10. Bustince, H., Fernandez, J., Mesiar, R., Montero, J., Orduna, R.: Overlap functions. Nonlinear Anal. Theory Methods Appl. **72**(3–4), 1488–1499 (2010)
11. Bustince, H., Pagola, M., Mesiar, R., Hüllermeier, E., Herrera, F.: Grouping, overlaps, and generalized bientropic functions for fuzzy modeling of pairwise comparisons. IEEE Trans. Fuzzy Syst. **20**(3), 405–415 (2012)
12. Chiclana, F., Herrera, F., Herrera-Viedma, E.: Integrating multiplicative preference relations in a multipurpose decision-making model based on fuzzy preference relations. Fuzzy Sets Syst. **122**(2), 277–291 (2001). https://doi.org/10.1016/S0165-0114(00)00004-X
13. da Cruz Asmus, T., Pereira Dimuro, G., Bustince, H., Bedregal, B., Santos, H., Sanz, J.A.: General interval-valued grouping functions. In: 2020 IEEE International Conference on Fuzzy Systems (FUZZ-IEEE), pp. 1–8 (2020)
14. De Miguel, L., et al.: General overlap functions. Fuzzy Sets Syst. **372**, 81–96 (2019)
15. Dimuro, G.P., et al.: On D-implications derived by grouping functions. In: FUZZ-IEEE 2019. IEEE International Conference on Fuzzy Systems, Proceedings, Los Alamitos, pp. 61–66. IEEE (2019)
16. Dimuro, G.P., Bedregal, B., Bustince, H., Jurio, A., Baczyński, M., Miś, K.: QL-operations and QL-implication functions constructed from tuples (O, G, N) and the generation of fuzzy subsethood and entropy measures. Int. J. Approx. Reason. **82**, 170–192 (2017)
17. Dimuro, G.P., Bedregal, B., Santiago, R.H.N.: On (G, N)-implications derived from grouping functions. Inf. Sci. **279**, 1–17 (2014)
18. Elkano, M., et al.: Enhancing multi-class classification in FARC-HD fuzzy classifier: on the synergy between n-dimensional overlap functions and decomposition strategies. IEEE Trans. Fuzzy Syst. **23**(5), 1562–1580 (2015)
19. Gómez, D., Rodríguez, J.T., Montero, J., Bustince, H., Barrenechea, E.: n-dimensional overlap functions. Fuzzy Sets Syst. **287**, 57–75 (2016)
20. Gómez, D., Rodríguez, J.T., Montero, J., Yáñez, J.: Fuzzy community detection based on grouping and overlapping functions. In: 2015 Conference of the International Fuzzy Systems Association and the European Society for Fuzzy Logic and Technology (IFSA-EUSFLAT-15), pp. 1514–1519. Atlantis Press, Paris (2015)
21. Jurio, A., Bustince, H., Pagola, M., Pradera, A., Yager, R.: Some properties of overlap and grouping functions and their application to image thresholding. Fuzzy Sets Syst. **229**, 69–90 (2013). https://doi.org/10.1016/j.fss.2012.12.009
22. Klement, E.P., Mesiar, R., Pap, E.: Triangular Norms. Kluwer, Dordrecht (2000)
23. Komorníková, M., Mesiar, R.: Aggregation functions on bounded partially ordered sets and their classification. Fuzzy Sets Syst. **175**(1), 48–56 (2011)
24. Mendel, J.M.: Computing with words and its relationships with fuzzistics. Inf. Sci. **177**(4), 988–1006 (2007). https://doi.org/10.1016/j.ins.2006.06.008
25. Moore, R.E., Kearfott, R.B., Cloud, M.J.: Introduction to Interval Analysis. SIAM, Philadelphia (2009)
26. Qiao, J., Hu, B.Q.: On interval additive generators of interval overlap functions and interval grouping functions. Fuzzy Sets Syst. **323**, 19–55 (2017)
27. Rodríguez-Martínez, I., Da Cruz Aamus, T., Pereira Dimuro, G., Ursúa-Medrano, P., Herrera, F., Bustince, H.: Feature downsampling on convolutional neural networks via grouping functions. In: Stupňanová, A., et al. (eds.) Book of Abstracts of the XVI International Conference on Fuzzy Set Theory and Applications, pp. 173–182. University of Ostrawa (2022)
28. Rodrigues, L.M., Dimuro, G.P., Franco, D.T., Fachinello, J.C.: A system based on interval fuzzy approach to predict the appearance of pests in agriculture. In: Proceedings of the 2013 Joint IFSA World Congress and NAFIPS Annual Meeting (IFSA/NAFIPS), Los Alamitos, pp. 1262–1267. IEEE (2003). https://doi.org/10.1109/IFSA-NAFIPS.2013.6608583

29. Santos, H., et al.: General grouping functions. In: Lesot, M.J., et al. (eds.) IPMU 2020. CCIS, vol. 1238, pp. 481–495. Springer, Cham (2020). https://doi.org/10.1007/978-3-030-50143-3_38

30. Ureña, R., Chiclana, F., Morente-Molinera, J., Herrera-Viedma, E.: Managing incomplete preference relations in decision making: a review and future trends. Inf. Sci. **302**, 14–32 (2015). https://doi.org/10.1016/j.ins.2014.12.061

Aggregation Functions in Flexible Classification by Ordinal Sums

Miroslav Hudec[1,2]($\boxtimes$) , Erika Mináriková[1] , and Radko Mesiar[3]

[1] Faculty of Economic Informatics, University of Economics in Bratislava,
Bratislava, Slovakia
{miroslav.hudec,erika.minarikova}@euba.sk

[2] Faculty of Economics, VSB - Technical University of Ostrava,
Ostrava, Czech Republic
miroslav.hudec@vsb.cz

[3] Faculty of Civil Engineering, Slovak University of Technology, Bratislava, Slovakia
radko.mesiar@stuba.sk

Abstract. The structure of ordinal sums of conjunctive and disjunctive functions is convenient for classification into the classes *Yes*, *No* and *Maybe* containing a tendency to the classes *Yes* and *No*. It especially holds when task is expressed by short vague requirements. The averaging part is covered by any averaging function. Concerning this part (class *Maybe*), functions having annihilator 0 usually are not suitable due to $A(1,0) = A(0,1) = 0$. The dual observation holds for functions having annihilator equal to 1. The classification by uninorms has reached to the same conclusion. This work proposes a parametric class of quasi-arithmetic means with the convex combination of the geometric mean and its dual geometric mean. Regarding classification into classes *Yes* and *No*, the parametrized family of nilpotent t–norms and t–conorms is proposed. This consideration creates the frame for learning function's parameter from the user inputs and labelled data. This research activity also contributes to the field of explainable computational intelligence. The results are supported by illustrative example. Finally, the discussion and the future research activities conclude the paper.

Keywords: Ordinal sums · Geometric mean and dual geometric mean · Łukasiewicz t-norm and t-conorm · Schweizer-Sklar family of t–norms and t–conorms · Classification

1 Introduction

In the process of recognition and differentiation of objects, entities cannot be always straightforwardly classified into classes *Yes* and *No* (e.g., healthy–sick). We need another class that can be labeled as *Maybe* and contains a corresponding tendency towards one of these two extreme poles [2,12,16].

In various tasks, domain experts have problems with the inclusion of black–box methods due to non–explainable solutions. In classification by the rule-based systems, domain experts should explicitly explain classification task by

© Springer Nature Switzerland AG 2022
D. Ciucci et al. (Eds.): IPMU 2022, CCIS 1601, pp. 372–383, 2022.
https://doi.org/10.1007/978-3-031-08971-8_31

the consistent set of IF–THEN rules, which is not always an easy task [1]. Next, well–designed (and of sufficient size) sets of labelled data are not always available for learning and validating.

In some tasks, experts are able to express vague, but relevant explanation, like: low values of considered attributes mean no interest at all (resp. reduced interest but not rejection), high values mean full acceptance (resp. increased interest), whereas a mix of high and low values indicates medium interest, which can be neutral, pessimistic (inclination to *No*), or optimistic (inclination to *Yes*).

For this class of classification problems, aggregation functions of mixed behaviour (ordinal sums of conjunctive and disjunctive functions) have been proposed [12]. Next, uni–norms, have been purposed for image edge detection and classification [11]. A problematic is classification for the borderline cases $A(0,1)$, $A(1,0) \in \{0,1\}$, i.e., the annihilator in averaging functions. This work is devoted to the further theoretical evaluations and extensions regarding the suitable subsets of averaging, conjunctive and disjunctive functions.

The remainder of paper is organized as follows. Section 2 briefly elaborates classification into three classes and introduces ordinal sums of conjunctive and disjunctive functions. Section 3 is devoted to averaging functions in classification, whereas Sect. 4 is dedicated to conjunctive and disjunctive functions. Section 5 provides experiments, discusses the obtained results and the implication for the future research. Finally, Sect. 6 concludes the paper.

2   Classification into Three Classes by Ordinal Sums of Conjunctive and Disjunctive Functions

This section studies classification aspects and ordinal sums, which are used throughout the paper.

2.1   Classification into Three Classes

When task deals with the uncertainty, classes should have flexible borders [15]. In Fig. 1, low values of two attributes indicate belonging to the class *No* (managed by conjunctive functions), high values to the class *Yes* (disjunctive functions), and the mix of low and high values to the class *Maybe* (averaging function) [12].

This approach handles classification when domain experts express requirements linguistically.

2.2   Preliminaries of Ordinal Sums

The main classification of aggregation functions is as follows [7]: conjunctive, averaging, disjunctive and mixed ones. More precisely, we can express conjunctive functions as $0 \leq A(\mathbf{x}) \leq x_i$ for each $i \in \{1, ..., n\}$, averaging functions as $x_i \leq A(\mathbf{x}) \leq x_j$ for some $i, j \in \{1, ..., n\}$, disjunctive functions as $x_i \leq A(\mathbf{x}) \leq 1$ for each $i \in \{1, ..., n\}$ and mixed as remaining aggregation functions.

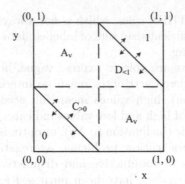

Fig. 1. An illustration of classification into three classes.

Ordinal sums in their origin were considered as extension methods for semi-groups [5], or for posets [3] as follows

$$x *_l y = \begin{cases} x *_l y & \text{for } (x,y) \in X_l \times X_l \\ x & \text{for } (x,y) \in X_l \times X_m, l \prec m \\ y & \text{for } (x,y) \in X_l \times X_m, l \succ m \end{cases} \quad (1)$$

where $(I, \prec), I \neq \emptyset$ is a totally ordered index set, $(X_l)_{l \in I}$ is a family of pairwise disjoint sets and $(G_l)_{l \in I} = (X_l, *_l)_{l \in I}$ is a family of semigroups.

In the framework of fuzzy sets theory, they were considered to build new t–norms/t–conorms from the scaled versions of existing ones [14].

The ordinal sum of conjunctive and disjunctive functions (belong to the class of mixed aggregation functions) has been proposed by De Baets and Mesiar [6].

Let us recall the main results of ordinal sums of conjunctive and disjunctive functions. For an n-ary aggregation function $B : [0,1]^n \to [0,1]$ and $[a,b] \subset \mathbf{R}$, denote $B_{[a,b]}(\mathbf{x}) = a + (b-a) \cdot B(\frac{x-a}{b-a})$ Note that then $B_{[a,b]}$ is an n-ary aggregation function on $[a,b]$. For $B_1, ..., B_k : [0,1]^n \to [0,1], k \geq 2$, and $0 \leq a_0 < a_1 < ... < a_k = 1$. Let $A_i : [a_{i-1}, a_i]^n \to [a_{i-1}, a_i]$ be given by $A_i = (B_i)_{[a_{i-1}, a_i]}$. Then the ordinal sum $A : [0,1]^n \to [0,1], A = (< a_{i-1}, a_i, A_i >)|i = 1, ..., k$ is given by

$$A(\mathbf{x}) = \sum_{i=1}^{k} (A_i(a_i \wedge (a_{i-1} \vee \mathbf{x})) - a_{i-1}) \quad (2)$$

is an aggregation function on $[0,1]$. If all $B_1, ..., B_k$ are t–norms (t–conorms, copulas, means) then also A is a t–norm (t–conorm, copula, mean).

Equivalently, $A(\mathbf{x}) = \sum_{i=1}^{k} (a_i - a_{i-1}) \cdot B_i(1 \wedge (0 \vee \frac{x - a_{i-1}}{a_i - a_{i-1}}))$. For our purposes, $n = k = 2$ is considered. Denoting $a_1 = a(a_0 = 0, a_2 = 1)$, we have two next forms of ordinal sums [12]

(i) $B_1, B_2 : [0,1]^2 \to [0,1]$,

$$A(x,y) = a \cdot B_1(1 \wedge \frac{x}{a}, 1 \wedge \frac{y}{a}) + (1-a) \cdot B_2(0 \vee \frac{x-a}{1-a}, 0 \vee \frac{y-a}{1-a}) \quad (3)$$

(ii) $A_1 : [0, a]^2 \to [0, a], A_2 : [a, 1]^2 \to [a, 1]$,

$$A(x, y) = A_1(a \wedge x, a \wedge y) + A_2(a \vee x, a \vee y) - a \qquad (4)$$

Then:

- if $(x, y) \in [0, a]^2$, $A(x, y) = a \cdot B_1(\frac{x}{a}, \frac{y}{a}) = A_1(x, y)$,
- if $(x, y) \in [a, 1]^2$, $A(x, y) = a + (1 - a) \cdot B_2(\frac{x-a}{1-a}, \frac{y-a}{1-a}) = A_2(x, y)$,
- if $(x, y) \in [0, a] \times [a, 1]$, $A(x, y) = a \cdot B_1(\frac{x}{a}, 1) + (1-a) \cdot B_2(0, \frac{y-a}{1-a}) = A_1(x, a) + A_2(a, y) - a$,
- if $(x, y) \in [a, 1] \times [0, a]$, $A(x, y) = a \cdot B_1(1, \frac{y}{a}) + (1-a) \cdot B_2(\frac{x-a}{1-a}, 0) = A_1(a, y) + A_2(x, a) - a$.

If B_1 is a conjunctive and B_2 is a disjunctive aggregation function, then A is conjunctive on $[0, a]^2$ and disjunctive on $[a, 1]^2$. Moreover, if B_1 has a neutral element $e = 1$, i.e., B_1 is a semicopula, and B_2 has a neutral element $e = 0$, i.e., B_2 is a dual semicopula [9], then, for $(x, y) \in [0, 1]^2 \setminus ([0, a]^2 \cup [a, 1]^2)$ it holds

$$A(x, y) = x + y - a \in [\min(x, y), \max(x, y)], \qquad (5)$$

i.e., A is averaging on this domain. It reflects the main requirement for classifying into the class *Maybe* [13]. The next section is devoted to the suitability of averaging functions for classification tasks.

3 Averaging Functions in Ordinal Sums for Classification

The result in (5) covers the whole range of averaging functions. Observe that averaging functions can be divided into the following categories

$$\mathcal{A}_v = \mathcal{A}_v^c \cup \mathcal{W} \cup \mathcal{A}_v^d$$

where $\mathcal{A}_v^c$ is a class of all averaging functions having the *ORNESS* measure lower than 0.5, $\mathcal{W}$ is a class of all means having *ORNESS* equal to 0.5 and $\mathcal{A}_v^d$ is a class of all averaging functions having the *ORNESS* measure greater than 0.5. Next, averaging functions are divided into functions having annihilator 0 (i.e., ORNESS measure lower than 0.25, which holds for two attributes) or having annihilator 1, and functions without annihilator [8].

In the classification square (see Fig. 1, two borderline cases: $A(0, 0) = 0$, $A(1, 1) = 1$ corresponds with the key property of aggregation functions (boundary condition), see e.g., [10]. Another two borderline cases $A(1, 0)$ and $A(0, 1)$ should be further examined. In the extreme case of a classification requirement: *IF x is low and y is high then Maybe*, i.e., $x = 0$, or $y = 1$, we might expect clear *No*, resp. clear *Yes*. It depends on the relevance of the clear satisfaction or rejection of the considered requirements. However, in the other cases, it is expected that $A(1, 0) = m$ and $A(0, 1) = m$ (symmetric case), where $m \in]0, 1[$. In this context, also holds: $A(0, m) = A(m, 0) \neq 0$ for $m > 0.5$, and $A(1, m) = A(m, 1) \neq 1$ for $m < 0.5$.

In the early expert systems MYCIN and PROSPECTOR [4] high values were considered as positive and low as negative on the scale $[-1, 1]$. However, the opposite evaluation also holds, when low values means *no alarm* or *significantly decreased alarm*. Cases $A(-1, 1)$ and $A(1, -1)$ were not defined, because two contradictory information should not be considered. When transforming the initial scale into $[0, 1]$, the neutral element becomes $1/2$. In this scaling, PROSPECTOR is $3 - \Pi$ function (see e.g., [18]), which is not defined on $A(0, 1)$ and $A(1, 0)$. In the other tasks, two extreme values (the highest one of one attribute and the lowest one of another attribute) indicate belonging to the class *Maybe* [13, 15].

This work proposes adopting averaging functions without annihilator 0 and 1, which also solves cases when $A(0, m) = A(m, 0) \neq 0$ for $m > 0.5$, and $A(1, m) = A(m, 1) \neq 1$ for $m < 0.5$. The first option is directly choosing averaging function like: arithmetic mean when neutral behaviour is required, quadratic mean when optimistic behaviour is required and the like [13]. But for the fine tuning classification results (to user's expectations or to labelled data), we need a general solution.

The parametric class of quasi–arithmetic means with the range between the geometric mean and its dual geometric mean as is shown in Fig. 2 can solve this problem. Generally, quasi–arithmetic means generalize averaging functions on the whole interval between $\min(x, y)$ and $\max(x, y)$. Each quasi–arithmetic mean on $[0, 1]$ is generated by an additive generator $g : [0, 1] \rightarrow [-\infty, \infty]$ (g is continuous and strictly monotone), as $QAM_g(x) = g^{-1}(\frac{g(x) + g(y)}{2})$. Considering the averaging part (5) we get

$$Avg_P(x, y) = g^{-1}(g(A_1(x, a))) + g(A_2(a, y)) - g(a)) \tag{6}$$

Next, the power–mean is a subclass when

$$g(t) = \begin{cases} t^r & \text{for } r \neq 0 \\ log(t) & \text{for } r = 0 \end{cases}$$

where for $r = -\infty$ we get *min*, whereas $r = \infty$ we get *max*. For $0 < r < \infty$ we get averaging functions without annihilator. Note that for $r = 0$ we get geometric mean. However, this is not the ideal solution when we should assign value of r to express inclination towards classes *Yes* and *No*. For the computational and users perspective, we should limit this interval and make it symmetric.

The immediate solution appears to be the convex (or multiplicative) combination of geometric mean and dual geometric mean

$$A(x, y) = \lambda G(x, y) + (1 - \lambda)G_d(x, y) \tag{7}$$

for $\lambda \in]0, 1[$. For $\lambda = 0.5$ we get neutral behaviour, for $0 < \lambda < 0.5$ we manage strict or pessimistic view, and for $0.5 < \lambda < 1$ we handle relaxed or optimistic view. Thus, adjusting λ is a more natural option than r in (6). When $\lambda = 0.5$ we get $\frac{\sqrt{xy}}{2} + \frac{1 - \sqrt{(1-x)(1-y)}}{2}$.

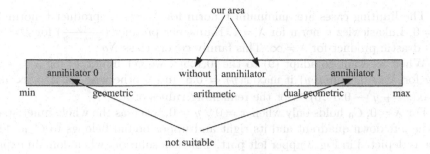

Fig. 2. A suitable subcategory of averaging functions.

Applying generator $g = log(t)$ for (6) and for $a = 0.5$ we get

$$A(x,y) = \lambda 2xy + (1 - \lambda)(1 - 2(1 - x)(1 - y)) \tag{8}$$

The next section focuses on conjunctive and disjunctive functions.

4   Conjunctive and Disjunctive Functions in Ordinal Sums for Classification

Conjunctive and disjunctive areas, $[0, 0.5]^2$ and $[0.5, 1]^2$, respectively, are dual and therefore an observation in one area holds for another. The conjunctive part consists of two areas $C_0 = 0$ (clear belonging to the class *No*, or 0) and $C_{>0} > 0$, where holds $C_{>0}(x, y) \leq \min(x, y)$ (equality holds for the idempotent conjunction, whereas inequality for Archimedean t–norms).

In the case of already mentioned MYCIN, the conjunctive part is equivalent with the product t–norm (i.e., $C(x, y) = 2xy$) which also holds for ordinal sums of conjunctive and disjunctive functions when product t–norm is adopted [12]. In these cases, result 0 is only on the dotted–dashed line in Fig. 3 on the upper left diagram. The dual observation holds for disjunctive part, where due to keeping disjunctive solution in $[0.5, 1]^2$, we get $D(x, y) = -1 + 2x + 2y - 2xy$.

Moving back to Fig. 1, we observe that the adjustable separation (diagonal line) in $[x, y]^2 \in [0, 0.5]^2$ is a valuable property for classification tasks.

The theory offers several parametrized families of t–norms and t–conorms. More about these families is in e.g., [10,14]. These families usually cover basic t–norms as limiting cases. Several families do not cover both strict and nilpotent behaviour, or one of these behaviours is only for a particular value of parameter. A suitable family for our purpose is the Schweizer–Sklar family [17] The family of t–norms is given as

$$T_\lambda^S(x,y) = \begin{cases} \min(x,y) & \text{for } \lambda = -\infty \\ T_P(x,y) & \text{for } \lambda = 0 \\ T_D(x,y) & \text{for } \lambda = \infty \\ (\max(x^\lambda + y^\lambda - 1, 0))^{\frac{1}{\lambda}} & \text{otherwise} \end{cases} \tag{9}$$

The limiting cases are: minimum t–norm for $\lambda = -\infty$, product t–norm for $\lambda = 0$, Łukasiewicz t–norm for $\lambda = 1$, Hamacher product $(\frac{xy}{x+y-xy})$ for $\lambda = -1$ and drastic product for $\lambda = \infty$. This family covers class No

When we want to adapt (9) to the $[0, 0.5]^2$, we get $\min(x, y)$ for $\lambda = -\infty$, $2xy$ for $\lambda = 0$, $\min(x, y)$ if $\max(x, y) = 0.5$ and 0 otherwise for $\lambda = \infty$ and $(\max(x^\lambda + y^\lambda - 0.5^\lambda, 0))^{\frac{1}{\lambda}}$ for the remaining values of λ.

For $\lambda = 0$, C_0 holds only when $x = 0 \vee y = 0$, whereas the whole inner space of the left down quadrant and its right and upper bound belongs to $C_{>0}$. This case is depicted in Fig. 3 upper left part. This is a solution, when domain expert wants clear 0 only in the case, when one attribute is clearly rejected and another has a low satisfaction value. This observation corresponds with the MYCIN.

In the opposite case, when the whole conjunctive quadrant should provide clear No, drastic product ($\lambda = \infty$), i.e., C_0 is everywhere except on the dotted– dashed lines of $[0, 0.5]^2$ depicted in Fig. 3 in the upper right diagram. Drastic product has mainly a theoretical meaning as a limiting and noncontinuous conjunctive function. However, it might be applicable in classification.

When the classification tasks requites clear 0 when both attributes have very low values (to express no alarm, for instance) and downward reinforcement for the other values, the simplest solution is for $\lambda = 1$ (Łukasiewicz t-norm). This case is in Fig. 3 second row left diagram. Next, by varying λ, the separation curve between C_0 and $C_{>0}$ can be set (Fig. 3, fourth and fifth diagram).

The Schweizer–Sklar family of t–conorms is given as [17]

$$S_\lambda^S(x, y) = \begin{cases} \max(x, y) & \text{for } \lambda = -\infty \\ S_P(x, y) & \text{for } \lambda = 0 \\ S_D(x, y) & \text{for } \lambda = \infty \\ 1 - (\max((1 - x)^\lambda + (1 - y)^\lambda - 1, 0))^{\frac{1}{\lambda}} & \text{otherwise} \end{cases} \quad (10)$$

Analogously, we can adapt this family to the $[0.5, 1]^2$ interval.

5   Illustrative Example and Discussion

This section provides example demonstrating the proposed approach followed by discussion.

5.1   Illustrative Examples

Let entities, e.g., flats are classified according to two compound attributes: distance and comfort. The former is a straightforward aggregation of atomic distances (e.g., *most of distances to the points of interest are short*). The latter is a result of aggregating atomic attributes like: *size approx.* 200 m^2 *and strong preference of balcony and spacious basement*, where the first compound attribute is marked as x, and the second compound attribute is marked as y.

The classification requirement is as follows: very high values of both attributes means full acceptance. When both values are very low, the flat should

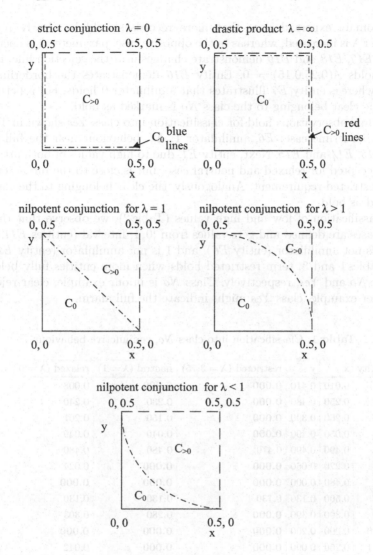

Fig. 3. Learning of the conjunctive part of classification by ordinal sums for class *No*.

be rejected. When one attribute is low and another one is high, the inclination is not provided. A set of labelled–data is not available. From the initial solution, domain expert decides, whether the classification result is acceptable, or parameters should be modified and in which direction.

For a better legibility, the whole set of entities is divided equally into three subsets: classified into class *No* (Table 1), classified into class Maybe (Table 2), and classified into class *Yes* (Table 3).

Let domain expert has not provided any further information for the class *No*. The classification is realized for $\lambda = 1$ (middle column of results in Table 1).

When domain expert declare that more records should be clearly rejected, parameter λ is increased, whereas in the opposite case, parameter λ is decreased. Entities *E17*, *E18* and *E19* demonstrate changes near the rejection line, i.e., for $\lambda = 1$ holds $A(0.25.0.15) = 0$. Entity *E16* demonstrates the borderline case $A(0, 0)$, whereas entity *E7* illustrates that annihilator 0 holds. For a better legibility, the clear belonging to the class *No* is marked as bold.

The dual observations hold for classification into class *Yes* shown in Table 3. Namely, borderline case: *E6*, annihilator 1: *E4*, behaviour near the full acceptance: *E13*, *E14* and *E15*. Next, entity *E1*, due to high values of both attributes is fully accepted for relaxed and neutral case, but is close to the full acceptance for the restricted requirement. Analogously, the clear belonging to the class *Yes* is marked as bold.

In classification of low and high values (Table 2), we observe that the borderline cases are defined and gets values from $]0, 1[$ interval (entities *E11*, *E12*). Next, 0 is not annihilator (entity *E6*), and 1 is not annihilator (entity *E13*).

In Tables 1 and 3, term restricted holds when more entities fully belong to the clear *No* and *Yes*, respectively. Class *No* is in our example, clear rejection. In another example, class *Yes* might indicate the full alarm.

Table 1. Classification into class *No*, conjunctive behaviour.

entity	x	y	restricted ($\lambda = 3.75$)	neutral ($\lambda = 1$)	relaxed ($\lambda = 0.05$)
E1	0.010	0.410	**0.000**	**0.000**	0.008
E2	0.250	0.480	**0.000**	0.230	0.240
E3	0.260	0.390	**0.000**	0.150	0.201
E4	0.050	0.490	**0.000**	0.040	0.049
E5	0.490	0.490	0.479	0.480	0.480
E6	0.220	0.060	**0.000**	**0.000**	0.024
E7	0.480	0.000	**0.000**	**0.000**	**0.000**
E8	0.500	0.130	0.130	0.130	0.130
E9	0.390	0.390	**0.000**	0.280	0.303
E10	0.000	0.200	**0.000**	**0.000**	**0.000**
E11	0.250	0.090	**0.000**	**0.000**	0.042
E12	0.400	0.000	**0.000**	**0.000**	**0.000**
E13	0.110	0.500	0.110	0.110	0.110
E14	0.100	0.100	**0.000**	**0.000**	0.017
E15	0.350	0.070	**0.000**	**0.000**	0.047
E16	0.000	0.000	**0.000**	**0.000**	**0.000**
E17	0.250	0.270	**0.000**	0.020	0.132
E18	0.250	0.230	**0.000**	**0.000**	0.112
E19	0.250	0.250	**0.000**	**0.000**	0.122
E20	0.110	0.320	**0.000**	**0.000**	0.068

Table 2. Classification into class *Maybe*, averaging behaviour.

entity	x	y	restricted ($\lambda = 0.85$)	neutral ($\lambda = 0.5$)	relaxed ($\lambda = 0.15$)
E1	0.420	0.960	0.828	0.880	0.932
E2	0.370	0.690	0.525	0.560	0.595
E3	0.260	0.960	0.565	0.720	0.875
E4	0.100	0.550	0.122	0.150	0.178
E5	0.500	0.500	0.500	0.500	0.500
E6	0.000	0.800	0.090	0.300	0.510
E7	0.000	0.500	0.000	0.000	0.000
E8	0.140	0.800	0.289	0.440	0.591
E9	0.310	0.570	0.361	0.380	0.399
E10	0.360	0.600	0.440	0.460	0.480
E11	1.000	0.000	0.150	0.500	0.850
E12	0.000	1.000	0.150	0.500	0.850
E13	1.000	0.200	0.490	0.700	0.910
E14	0.200	1.000	0.490	0.700	0.910
E15	0.430	0.730	0.637	0.660	0.683
E16	0.730	0.440	0.651	0.670	0.689
E17	0.010	0.630	0.051	0.140	0.229
E18	0.170	0.560	0.202	0.230	0.258
E19	0.450	0.710	0.645	0.660	0.675
E20	0.020	0.980	0.177	0.500	0.823

Table 3. Classification into class *Yes*, disjunctive behaviour.

entity	x	y	restricted ($\lambda = 3.75$)	neutral ($\lambda = 1$)	relaxed ($\lambda = 0.05$)
E1	0.690	0.960	**1.000**	**1.000**	0.977
E2	0.800	0.550	**1.000**	0.850	0.821
E3	0.960	0.690	**1.000**	**1.000**	0.977
E4	1.000	0.500	**1.000**	**1.000**	**1.000**
E5	0.880	1.000	**1.000**	**1.000**	**1.000**
E6	1.000	1.000	**1.000**	**1.000**	**1.000**
E7	0.500	0.500	0.500	0.500	0.500
E8	0.900	0.500	0.900	0.900	0.900
E9	1.000	0.770	**1.000**	**1.000**	**1.000**
E10	0.660	0.770	**1.000**	0.930	0.846
E11	0.880	0.610	**1.000**	0.990	0.908
E12	0.600	0.600	**1.000**	0.700	0.681
E13	0.750	0.730	**1.000**	0.980	0.868
E14	0.750	0.780	**1.000**	**1.000**	0.893
E15	0.750	0.750	**1.000**	**1.000**	0.878
E16	0.510	1.000	**1.000**	**1.000**	**1.000**
E17	0.510	0.660	0.692	0.670	0.667
E18	0.550	0.690	**1.000**	0.740	0.722
E19	0.600	0.900	**1.000**	**1.000**	0.921
E20	0.870	0.880	**1.000**	**1.000**	0.972

5.2   Discussion and Future Work

The theoretical work and the illustrative example have demonstrated the applicability and flexibility of ordinal sums of conjunctive and disjunctive functions by various functions. Also, all borderline cases behave as is expected. The overlap function is another option to cope with this task. Involving these new types of aggregation functions is a topic for the future work.

Classification into more classes is also a promising task. Dividing the class *Maybe* into several ones like slight or significant inclination to one of the opposites might cause problems with the continuity. On the other hand, a proper distinction between such classes emphasizes particular areas of inclinations.

The direction for future works should evolve around the convex combinations of other aggregation functions and any value from the open unit interval (not only 0.5) for dividing classification space into conjunctive, averaging, and disjunctive sub spaces to offer more flexibility. Finally, our future work will focus on the real-word classification problems in the medical domain.

This work can be considered as a contribution to the explainable computational intelligence field, where domain experts explain requirements by a short story. Consequently, the suitable functions and parameters are recognized. Next, when the overall result of classification is explained by e.g., linguistic summaries, domain expert is able to explain how the classification space should be modified. Also, when a set of labelled data is at disposal, the re–learning can be realized.

6   Conclusion

It is a challenging task to cover the diverse needs for classification by functions of mixed behaviour. Practice searches for the robust and explainable solutions to cover the whole range of classification, also when the requirements are explained by short story and labeled data might not be at disposal, or are available in an insufficient amount.

This work has proven that averaging functions without an annihilator are suitable for classification into the class *Maybe*. The flexibility is realized by the convex combination of geometric and dual geometric mean, without considering these two extreme cases. Concerning classification into classes *Yes* and *No*, the Schweizer–Sklar families of t–norms and t–conorms are the solutions for the considered requirements.

The topics for the future work should focus on the convex combinations of the other aggregation functions, evaluating any value from the open unit interval for dividing classification space, considering overlap functions, adopting more classes, and applying on real–world problems and data sets.

Acknowledgments. This paper was partially supported by SGS project No. SP2022/113 of the Ministry of Education, Youth and Sports of the Czech Republic. Also the supports of the projects APVV-18-0052, KEGA No. 025EU-4/2021 and VEGA No. 1/0466/19 of the Ministry of Education, Science, Research and Sport of the Slovak Republic are kindly announced.

References

1. Alonso, J.M., Castiello, C., Magdalena, L., Mencar, C.: Explainable Fuzzy Systems: Paving the way from Interpretable Fuzzy Systems to Explainable AI Systems. Springer, Cham (2021). https://doi.org/10.1007/978-3-030-71098-9
2. Bartoszuk, M., Gagolewski, M.: T-norms or t-conorms? How to aggregate similarity degrees for plagiarism detection. Knowl.-Based Syst. **231**, 107427 (2021)
3. Birkhoff, G.: Lattice Theory, 3rd edn, vol. XXV. AMS Colloqium Publications, American Mathematical Society, Providence (1967)
4. Buchanan, B., Shortliffe, E.: Rule-Based Expert Systems. The MYCIN Experiments of the Stanford Heuristic Programming Project. Addison-Wesley, Reading (1984)
5. Clifford, A.: Naturally totally ordered commutative semigroups. Am. J. Math. **76**, 631–646 (1954)
6. De Baets, B., Mesiar, R.: Ordinal sums of aggregation operators. In: Bouchon-Meunier, B., Gutiérrez-Rios, J., Magdalena, L., Yager, R. (eds.) Technologies for Constructing Intelligent Systems: Tasks, pp. 137–147. Springer, Heidelberg (2002). https://doi.org/10.1007/978-3-7908-1796-6_11
7. Dubois, D., Prade, H.: On the use of aggregation operations in information fusion processes. Fuzzy Sets Syst. **142**(1), 143–161 (2004)
8. Dujmović, J.: Soft Computing Evaluation Logic: The LSP Decision Method and Its Applications. Wiley, Hoboken (2018)
9. Durante, F., Sempi, C.: Semicopulae. Kybernetika **41**(3), 311–328 (2005)
10. Grabisch, M., Marichal, J.-L., Mesiar, R., Pap, E.: Aggregation Functions. Encyclopedia of Mathematics and its Applications, no. 127. Cambridge University Press, Cambridge (2009)
11. González-Hidalgo, M., Massanet, S., Mir, A., Ruiz-Aguilera, D.: A new edge detector based on uninorms. In: Laurent, A., Strauss, O., Bouchon-Meunier, B., Yager, R.R. (eds.) IPMU 2014. CCIS, vol. 443, pp. 184–193. Springer, Cham (2014). https://doi.org/10.1007/978-3-319-08855-6_19
12. Hudec, M., Mináriková, E., Mesiar, R., Saranti, A., Holzinger, A.: Classification by ordinal sums of conjunctive and disjunctive functions for explainable AI and interpretable machine learning solutions. Knowl.-Based Syst. **220**, 106916 (2021)
13. Hudec, M., Mesiar, R., Mináriková, E.: Applicability of ordinal sums of conjunctive and disjunctive functions in classification. In: the 19th World Congress of the International Fuzzy Systems Association (IFSA) and the 12th Conference of the European Society for Fuzzy Logic and Technology (EUSFLAT), 19–24 September, pp. 602–607. Atlantis Press, Bratislava (2021)
14. Klement, E., Mesiar, R., Pap, E.: Triangular Norms. Kluwer, Dordrecht (2000)
15. Meier, A., Werro, N.: A fuzzy classification model for online customers. Informatica **31**, 175–182 (2007)
16. Melin, P., Sánchez, D.: Optimal design of type-2 fuzzy systems for diabetes classification based on genetic algorithms. Int. J. Hybrid Intell. Syst. **17**(1–2), 15–32 (2021)
17. Schweizer, B., Sklar, A.: Associative functions and triangle inequalities. Publicationes Mathematicae Debrecen **8**, 169–186 (1961)
18. Yager, R., Rybalov, A.: Uninorm aggregation operators. Fuzzy Sets Syst. **80**, 111–120 (1996)

Honeycomb-Based Polygonal Chains Aggregation Functions

Grzegorz Moś[✉][iD]

Faculty of Science and Technology, University of Silesia in Katowice,
Katowice, Poland
`grzegorz.mos@us.edu.pl`

Abstract. Honeycomb-based structures appear in many scientific fields. Moreover, the number of such structures increases every day. Thus, new methods of analysis are needed. The aggregation functions are one of such methods. They are widely examined for numbers and considered for other objects, e.g., strings and graphs. This paper introduces a new way of representing the simplest structures based on a honeycomb grid with binary sequences. The invariance with respect to rotation and reflection is examined.

Keywords: Honeycomb · Polygonal chain · Aggregation function · Invariantness

1 Introduction

Honeycomb-based structures appear as chemical molecules in chemistry, polymers and materials in physics, graphs and lattices in mathematics (see [1,9,10], and [6]). Hence we need new methods of processing them. The aggregation functions are widely examined for various objects (cf. [5] and [3]). We represent the simplest honeycomb-based structures with binary sequences. The idea is to take a set of the coordinates of each vertice, a set of edges that connect the vertices, and labeling, which represent every case of the edge orientation. Our solution brings a more straightforward form of data to handle. Moreover, it allows using the methods used for strings. Then, we consider the structure's rotations and reflections concerning any line. These properties will be used as aggregation functions invariant properties. We show an example of the longest common subsequence alongside the invariant property with respect to structure rotations and invariant with respect to structure reflections. That shows that considered theses are essential in the theory of aggregation functions.

We will call the simplest structures based on a honeycomb grid the honeycomb-based polygonal chains because of their visual appearance.

2 Preliminary

The structures we are investigating are connected and open. We consider the disconnected case as a separated structures. Moreover, we will consider the non-open case in the next publications (Fig. 1).

© Springer Nature Switzerland AG 2022
D. Ciucci et al. (Eds.): IPMU 2022, CCIS 1601, pp. 384–397, 2022.
https://doi.org/10.1007/978-3-031-08971-8_32

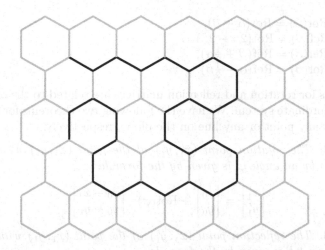

Fig. 1. Example of the honeycomb-based polygonal chain based on 29 vertices which contains 28 edges.

Firstly, we put together the fundamental theorems and principles of Euclidean geometry and binary sequences.

2.1 Geometry

The geometry foundations are necessary for representing the honeycomb-based structures with a binary sequence. The definitions and theorems can be found in many publications (cf. [2] and [8]). The rotation and reflection matrix notation makes the calculations and formulas clear and transparent.

Definition 1. *The rotation matrix* $\mathrm{Rot}(\varphi)$ *about the point* $(0,0)$ *by an angle* φ *is given by the formula*

$$\mathrm{Rot}(\varphi) = \begin{bmatrix} \cos(\varphi) & -\sin(\varphi) \\ \sin(\varphi) & \cos(\varphi) \end{bmatrix}. \tag{1}$$

Definition 2. *The reflection matrix* $\mathrm{Ref}(\varphi)$ *about a line* l *through the point* $(0,0)$ *which makes an angle* φ *with the x-axis is given by the formula*

$$\mathrm{Ref}(\varphi) = \begin{bmatrix} \cos(2\varphi) & \sin(2\varphi) \\ \sin(2\varphi) & -\cos(2\varphi) \end{bmatrix}. \tag{2}$$

These two mappings satisfy the following six identities. It is easy to prove them by applying the matrices product formula and the basics trigonometric identities.

Theorem 1. *Suppose* $\alpha, \beta \in \mathbb{R}$. *Then:*

1. $\mathrm{Rot}^{-1}(\alpha) = \mathrm{Rot}(-\alpha)$,
2. $\mathrm{Ref}^{-1}(\alpha) = \mathrm{Ref}(\alpha)$,

3. $\text{Rot}(\alpha) \cdot \text{Rot}(\beta) = \text{Rot}(\alpha + \beta)$,
4. $\text{Ref}(\alpha) \cdot \text{Ref}(\beta) = \text{Rot}(2\alpha - 2\beta)$,
5. $\text{Rot}(\alpha) \cdot \text{Ref}(\beta) = \text{Ref}(\beta + \frac{1}{2}\alpha)$,
6. $\text{Ref}(\alpha) \cdot \text{Rot}(\beta) = \text{Ref}(\alpha - \frac{1}{2}\beta)$.

The formulas for rotation and reflection matrices are related to the origin of the Cartesian coordinate system. We have the following two theorems for the general case, i.e., for any point or any line on the plane, respectively.

Theorem 2. *The rotation point (x_1', y_1') of the point (x_1, y_1) with respect to point (x_0, y_0) by an angle φ is given by the formula*

$$\begin{bmatrix} x_1' \\ y_1' \end{bmatrix} = \begin{bmatrix} x_0 \\ y_0 \end{bmatrix} + \text{Rot}(\varphi) \cdot \begin{bmatrix} x_0 - x_1 \\ y_0 - y_1 \end{bmatrix}. \tag{3}$$

Theorem 3. *The reflection point (x_1', y_1') of the point (x_1, y_1) with respect to the line $y = ax + b$ is given by the formula*

$$\begin{bmatrix} x_1' \\ y_1' \end{bmatrix} = \begin{bmatrix} 0 \\ b \end{bmatrix} + \text{Ref}(\varphi) \cdot \begin{bmatrix} x_1 \\ y_1 - b \end{bmatrix}, \tag{4}$$

where $\varphi = \tan^{-1}(a)$.

We omits proofs because of the simplicity of it.

2.2   Binary Sequence

A binary number is a number that is expressed in the base-2 numeral system (see [4]). It is widely used in logic gates in digital electronic circuits because of the simplicity of the language (cf. [7]). We will use it as a representation of a honeycomb-based polygonal chain. Thus, we will call such a representation a binary sequence instead of a binary number to distinguish the numerical approach.

Definition 3. *We will call the sequence*

$$B = (b_0, b_1, \ldots, b_{n-1}) \tag{5}$$

a binary sequence of length n, where $b_0, b_1, \ldots, b_{n-1} \in \{0, 1\}$. We will write down such a sequence for simplicity as

$$B = b_0 b_1 \ldots b_{n-1}. \tag{6}$$

There are two essential operations on binary sequences we will use later.

Definition 4. *We will call the replacement of a digit b_k, for $k \in \{0, 1, \ldots, n-1\}$, in a binary sequence B of the form (5) with a digit $b_k' = 1 - b_k$ as a bit reverse.*

Definition 5. *We will call the reverse of a binary sequence B of the form (5), i.e., the binary sequence*

$$B' = b_{n-1} b_{n-2} \ldots b_0, \tag{7}$$

as a binary sequence reverse.

We introduce the following comparison operators.

Definition 6. *Let $n \in \mathbb{N}$. We will say that the binary sequences $A = (a_0, a_1, \ldots, a_{n-1})$ and $B = (b_0, b_1, \ldots, b_{n-1})$ are equal whenever $a_k = b_k$ for $k \in \{0, 1, \ldots, n-1\}$. We will denote it as $A = B$.*

Definition 7. *Let $n_A, n_B \in \mathbb{N}$ such that $n_A \leq n_B$. We will say that the binary sequence $A = (a_0, a_1, \ldots, a_{n_A-1})$ precedes the binary sequence $B = (b_0, b_1, \ldots, b_{n_B-1})$ (which we denote as $A \leq B$) whenever either:*

(i) $A = B$,
(ii) $(\exists \, k \in \mathbb{N})(\forall \, m \in \{0, 1 \ldots, n_A - 1\}) \, a_m = b_{k+m}.$

3 Honeycomb-Based Polygonal Chains Foundations

3.1 Representation of a Structure with a Binary Sequence

We begin with an introduction to a new method of representing the structures with honeycomb-based shapes. Consider the shortest possible case with pointed out vertices $v_0 = (x_0, y_0)$ and $v_1 = (x_1, y_1)$:

Then, we can construct a structure of length 2, adding a vertice and connecting it to the vertice v_1. It can be done in two ways. We can append the vertice $v_2 = (x_2, y_2)$ above the vertice v_1. On the other hand, we can append the vertice $v_3 = (x_3, y_3)$ on the bottom right from the vertice v_1.

Notice that the angle between the vertices v_2, v_1, and v_3 is equal to $120°$. Thus, we are constructing either the point v_2 or v_3 taking the reflection of the v_0 with respect to v_1 and then, rotating it by $60°$ or $-60°$. Suppose v_0' is such a reflection with coordinates (x_0', y_0'):

where

$$\begin{cases} x_0' = x_1 + (x_1 - x_0) \\ y_0' = y_1 + (y_1 - y_0) \end{cases}. \tag{8}$$

Thus, we obtain the coordinates of the vertice v_2 rotating the vertice v_0' by the angle $60°$ with respect to the vertice v_1 from the Theorem 2 given by the formula

$$\begin{bmatrix} x_2 \\ y_2 \end{bmatrix} = \begin{bmatrix} x_1 \\ y_1 \end{bmatrix} + \text{Rot}(60°) \cdot \begin{bmatrix} x_1 - x_0 \\ y_1 - y_0 \end{bmatrix}. \tag{9}$$

Similarly, we obtain the vertice v_3 rotating the vertice v_0' by the angle $-60°$ with respect to the vertice v_1 given by the formula

$$\begin{bmatrix} x_3 \\ y_3 \end{bmatrix} = \begin{bmatrix} x_1 \\ y_1 \end{bmatrix} + \text{Rot}(-60°) \cdot \begin{bmatrix} x_1 - x_0 \\ y_1 - y_0 \end{bmatrix}. \tag{10}$$

Hence, we get the sequence of $\pm 60°$ angle rotations while constructing a honeycomb-based polygonal chain by adding up successive vertices in this manner. We will mark the $60°$ angle with 0 and the $-60°$ angle with 1. Thus, we can represent such a structure with a binary sequence.

Definition 8. *We will say that a tuple of vertices*

$$S = (v_0, v_1, \ldots, v_{n-1}, v_n),$$

where $v_k = (x_k, y_k)$, for $k \in \{0, 1, \ldots, n\}$, such that

$$\begin{bmatrix} x_k \\ y_k \end{bmatrix} = \begin{bmatrix} x_{k-1} \\ y_{k-1} \end{bmatrix} + \text{Rot}(\pm 60°) \cdot \begin{bmatrix} x_{k-1} - x_{k-2} \\ y_{k-1} - y_{k-2} \end{bmatrix}, \tag{11}$$

where $k \in \{2, 3, \ldots, n\}$, connected with the edges $e_k = (v_k, v_{k+1})$, for $k \in \{0, 1, \ldots, n-2, n-1\}$, is a honeycomb-based polygonal chain.

Definition 9. *We will say that a honeycomb-based polygonal chain*

$$S = (v_0, v_1, \ldots, v_{n-1}, v_n)$$

is represented by a binary sequence B of length $n-1$, i.e., by the sequence

$$B = b_0 b_1 \ldots b_{n-2},$$

whenever every $(x_k, y_k) = v_k \in S$ is of the form

$$\begin{bmatrix} x_k \\ y_k \end{bmatrix} = \begin{bmatrix} x_{k-1} \\ y_{k-1} \end{bmatrix} + \text{Rot}(\varphi_{k-2}) \cdot \begin{bmatrix} x_{k-1} - x_{k-2} \\ y_{k-1} - y_{k-2} \end{bmatrix}, \tag{12}$$

where $\varphi_{k-2} = (-1)^{b_{k-2}} \cdot 60°$ for $k \in \{2, 3, \ldots, n\}$.

Since a honeycomb-based polygonal chain has exactly two endpoints, we can represent such a structure with precisely two binary sequences. Moreover, a binary sequence represents exactly one honeycomb-based polygonal chain which is uniquely determined up to the positions of the first two vertices.

Remark 1. Two binary sequences represent a honeycomb-based polygonal chain (Fig. 2).

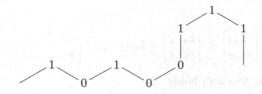

Fig. 2. Graph represented by the sequence 10100111.

Remark 2. A binary sequence represents exactly one honeycomb-based polygonal chain.

Example 1. The graph in the previous example is also represented by the sequence 00011010.

Thus, we will mark the beginning of such a sequence with an asterisks on the first vertice on the graph (Fig. 3).

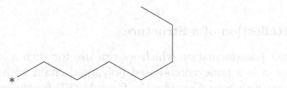

Fig. 3. Graph represented by the sequence 101000 with the asterisks at the beginning.

3.2 Rotation of a Structure

We noted before that the simplest honeycomb-based structures have two representations in the form of a binary sequence. Hence, we will call any alternative form a rotation of such a structure. We have the following formula for the next three consecutive points in such a graph from the Eq. (12).

$$\begin{bmatrix} x_k \\ y_k \end{bmatrix} = \begin{bmatrix} x_{k-1} \\ y_{k-1} \end{bmatrix} + \text{Rot}(\varphi) \cdot \begin{bmatrix} x_{k-1} - x_{k-2} \\ y_{k-1} - y_{k-2} \end{bmatrix}, \tag{13}$$

where $\varphi \in \{60°, -60°\}$ and k is restricted by the length of the structure. We have, from the Theorem 2 and applying the identities from Theorem 1, the following equality

$$\text{Rot}(-\varphi) \cdot \begin{bmatrix} x_k - x_{k-1} \\ y_k - y_{k-1} \end{bmatrix} = \begin{bmatrix} x_{k-1} \\ y_{k-1} \end{bmatrix} - \begin{bmatrix} x_{k-2} \\ y_{k-2} \end{bmatrix}. \tag{14}$$

Hence

$$\begin{bmatrix} x_{k-2} \\ y_{k-2} \end{bmatrix} = \begin{bmatrix} x_{k-1} \\ y_{k-1} \end{bmatrix} - \text{Rot}(-\varphi) \cdot \begin{bmatrix} x_k - x_{k-1} \\ y_k - y_{k-1} \end{bmatrix}. \tag{15}$$

Finally, we have

$$\begin{bmatrix} x_{k-2} \\ y_{k-2} \end{bmatrix} = \begin{bmatrix} x_{k-1} \\ y_{k-1} \end{bmatrix} + \mathrm{Rot}(-\varphi) \cdot \begin{bmatrix} x_{k-1} - x_k \\ y_{k-1} - y_k \end{bmatrix}. \tag{16}$$

Thus, the following theorem holds.

Theorem 4. *Suppose S is the honeycomb-based polygonal chain represented by a binary sequence B. Thus, the binary sequence obtained by reversing the whole sequence and reversing each bit is a rotation of the structure S.*

Definition 10. *We will say that the honeycomb-based polygonal chain S^{Rot} represented by a binary sequence B^{Rot} is a rotation of a honeycomb-based polygonal chain S represented by a binary sequence B whenever the sequence B^{Rot} is an inversion of the sequence B where every bit is inverted.*

Example 2. Consider the structure from the first example. It is represented by the binary sequence 10100111. The reversion of this sequence is of the form 11100101. We obtain the following sequence by reversion of the bits 00011010. This sequence appeared in the second example.

3.3   Reflection of a Structure

The next transformation which we can use for such a structures is a reflection. Suppose S is a honeycomb-based polygonal chain with $n + 1$ vertices and B is it's binary sequence. Consider the formula (12) for the next 3 consecutive points. Then, we take a reflection $v'_k = (x'_k, y'_k)$ of each vertice $v_k = (x_k, y_k)$ with respect to the line $y = ax + b$ for $k \in \{0, 1, \ldots, n\}$. Thus, from the Theorem 3, we have

$$\begin{bmatrix} x'_k \\ y'_k \end{bmatrix} = \begin{bmatrix} 0 \\ b \end{bmatrix} + \mathrm{Ref}(\theta) \cdot \begin{bmatrix} x_k \\ y_k - b \end{bmatrix}.$$

From the Theorem 1 we have

$$\begin{bmatrix} x_k \\ y_k \end{bmatrix} = \begin{bmatrix} 0 \\ b \end{bmatrix} + \mathrm{Ref}(\theta) \cdot \begin{bmatrix} x'_k \\ y'_k - b \end{bmatrix}.$$

Notice that

$$\begin{bmatrix} x_{k-1} - x_{k-2} \\ y_{k-1} - y_{k-2} \end{bmatrix} = \mathrm{Ref}(\theta) \cdot \begin{bmatrix} x'_{k-1} - x'_{k-2} \\ y'_{k-1} - y'_{k-2} \end{bmatrix},$$

for $\theta = \tan^{-1}(a)$. We have the following equation from (12) by applying the above formulas

$$\mathrm{Ref}(\theta) \cdot \begin{bmatrix} x'_k \\ y'_k \end{bmatrix} = \mathrm{Ref}(\theta) \cdot \begin{bmatrix} x'_{k-1} \\ y'_{k-1} \end{bmatrix} + \mathrm{Rot}(\varphi) \cdot \mathrm{Ref}(\theta) \cdot \begin{bmatrix} x'_{k-1} - x'_{k-2} \\ y'_{k-1} - y'_{k-2} \end{bmatrix}.$$

Hence, taking again the identities from Theorem 1, we have

$$\begin{bmatrix} x'_k \\ y'_k \end{bmatrix} = \begin{bmatrix} x'_{k-1} \\ y'_{k-1} \end{bmatrix} + \mathrm{Ref}^{-1}(\theta) \cdot \mathrm{Rot}(\varphi) \cdot \mathrm{Ref}(\theta) \cdot \begin{bmatrix} x'_{k-1} - x'_{k-2} \\ y'_{k-1} - y'_{k-2} \end{bmatrix}.$$

Consequently, we have

$$\begin{bmatrix} x'_k \\ y'_k \end{bmatrix} = \begin{bmatrix} x'_{k-1} \\ y'_{k-1} \end{bmatrix} + \mathrm{Rot}(-\varphi) \cdot \begin{bmatrix} x'_{k-1} - x'_{k-2} \\ y'_{k-1} - y'_{k-2} \end{bmatrix}. \tag{17}$$

The above reflection of each point of the structure S gives us a binary sequence derived from the binary sequence B in which every element is inverted. Thus, the following theorem holds.

Theorem 5. *Suppose S is the honeycomb-based polygonal chain represented by a binary sequence B. Thus, the structure represented by a binary sequence obtained by reversing each bit is a reflection of the structure S (Fig. 4).*

Definition 11. *We will say that the honeycomb-based polygonal chain S^{Ref_1} represented by a binary sequence B^{Ref_1} is a 1-type reflection of a honeycomb-based polygonal chain S represented by a binary sequence B whenever every bit of B^{Ref_1} is an inversion of every bit of B respectively.*

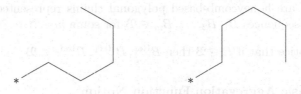

Fig. 4. Graphical representations of the structure 1000 (on the left) and the 1-type reflection 0111 (on the right).

We obtain the following type of reflection derived by a rotation of a 1-type reflection of S.

Theorem 6. *Suppose S is the honeycomb-based polygonal chain represented by a binary sequence B. Thus, the structure represented by a binary sequence obtained by reversing the whole sequence is a reflection of the structure S.*

Definition 12. *We will say that the honeycomb-based polygonal chain S^{Ref_2} represented by a binary sequence B^{Ref_2} is a 2-type reflection of a honeycomb-based polygonal chain S represented by a binary sequence B whenever the sequence B^{Ref_2} is a reverse of the sequence B.*

Remark 3. Notice that for a honeycomb-based polygonal chain S the following identities are satisfied (Fig. 5):

1. $(S^{\mathrm{Ref}_1})^{\mathrm{Ref}_1} = S = (S^{\mathrm{Ref}_2})^{\mathrm{Ref}_2}$,
2. $(S^{\mathrm{Ref}_1})^{\mathrm{Ref}_2} = S^{\mathrm{Rot}} = (S^{\mathrm{Ref}_2})^{\mathrm{Ref}_1}$,
3. $(S^{\mathrm{Ref}_2})^{\mathrm{Rot}} = S^{\mathrm{Ref}_1} = (S^{\mathrm{Rot}})^{\mathrm{Ref}_2}$,
4. $(S^{\mathrm{Ref}_1})^{\mathrm{Rot}} = S^{\mathrm{Ref}_2} = (S^{\mathrm{Rot}})^{\mathrm{Ref}_1}$.

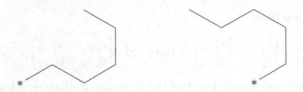

Fig. 5. Graphical representations of the structure 1000 (on the left) and the 2-type reflection 0001 (on the right).

4   Aggregation Functions

This section will introduce the concept of aggregation functions for a honeycomb-based polygonal chain. Then, we will introduce the property of invariants with respect to the rotations and reflections of such structures.

Suppose that $\mathfrak{B}$ is a set of all binary sequences which represent some honeycomb-based polygonal chains and suppose that the structures $S_1, S_2, \ldots, S_m$ are honeycomb-based polygonal chains represented respectively by the binary sequences $B_1, B_2, \ldots, B_m \in \mathfrak{B}$ for some $m \in \mathbb{N}$.

Remark 4. Notice that if $B \in \mathfrak{B}$ then $B^{\mathrm{Rot}}, B^{\mathrm{Ref}_1}, B^{\mathrm{Ref}_2} \in \mathfrak{B}$.

4.1   The Basic Aggregation Function Notion

We remind the basic definition of an aggregation function for numbers from [5].

Definition 13. *Suppose that $\mathbb{I}$ is nonempty real interval. An aggregation function in $\mathbb{I}^n$ is a function $A^{(n)} \colon \mathbb{I}^n \to \mathbb{I}$ that*

- *is nondecreasing (in each variable)*
- *fulfills the boundary conditions*

$$\inf_{x \in \mathbb{I}^n} A^{(n)}(x) = \inf \mathbb{I}$$

and

$$\sup_{x \in \mathbb{I}^n} A^{(n)}(x) = \sup \mathbb{I}$$

for $n \in \mathbb{N}$.

There are used two conditions in the above definition, i.e., the monotonicity and the boundary conditions. In order to introduce an aggregation function definition it is sufficient to state the comparison operator. We will consider two cases.

4.2   Rotations Invariantness Case

We assume that the honeycomb-based polygonal chain and its rotation are the same structure. Thus, we introduce the comparing operators which will handle this invariantness.

Definition 14. *Suppose that S_1 and S_2 are honeycomb-based polygonal chains represented by the binary sequences B_1 and B_2 respectively. We will say that S_1 and S_2 are equal (and denote it as $S_1 = S_2$) whenever $B_1 = B_2$ or $B_1^{Rot} = B_2$.*

Definition 15. *Suppose that S_1 and S_2 are honeycomb-based polygonal chains represented by the binary sequences B_1 and B_2 respectively. We will say that S_1 precedes S_2 (and denote it as $S_1 \leq S_2$) whenever either $B_1 \leq B_2$ or $B_1^{Rot} \leq B_2$.*

Remark 5. Note that the relation $\leq$ is a weak partial order on a set of all honeycomb-based polygonal chains.

Example 3. Let consider the structures S_1 and S_2 represented by $B_1 = 100$ and $B_2 = 1110$ respectively. Then $B_1^{Rot} = 110$. Hence $B_1^{Rot} \leq B_2$ and $S_1 \leq S_2$ (Fig. 6).

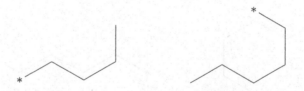

Fig. 6. Graphical representations of the structures 100 (on the left) and 1110 (on the right).

We state the monotonicity and the lower bound concepts which we will in the aggregation function definition.

Definition 16. *We will say that $A: \mathfrak{B}^m \to \mathfrak{B}$ is nondecreasing (in each variable) whenever, for every $(B_1, B_2. \ldots, B_m), (B_1', B_2', \ldots, B_m') \in \mathfrak{B}^m$,*

$$(\forall\, k \in \{1, 2, \ldots, m\})\ B_k \leq B_k' \implies A(B_1, B_2, \ldots, B_m) \leq A(B_1', B_2', \ldots, B_m').$$

Definition 17. *Let $B_1, B_2, \ldots, B_m, B \in \mathfrak{B}$. We will say that the function $\inf: \mathfrak{B}^m \to \mathfrak{B}$ is a infimum whenever*

$$\inf(B_1, B_2, \ldots, B_m) = B \iff (\forall\, k \in \{1, 2, \ldots, m\})\ B \leq B_k.$$

Remark 6. The above function is defined properly since $0 \leq B$ for every $B \in \mathfrak{B}$.

Definition 18. *The mapping $A\colon \mathfrak{B}^m \to \mathfrak{B}$ is an aggregation function whenever it is nondecreasing and*

$$\inf(B_1, B_2, \dots, B_m) \leq A(B_1, B_2, \dots, B_m)$$

for all $B_1, B_2, \dots, B_m \in \mathfrak{B}$.

The invariantness is a very important property in many aggregation functions (see [5]). Thus, the formal definition is expected.

Definition 19. *We will say that an aggregation function $A\colon \mathfrak{B}^m \to \mathfrak{B}$ is invariant with respect to rotations whenever*

$$A(B_1^{\mathrm{Rot}}, B_2^{\mathrm{Rot}}, \dots, B_m^{\mathrm{Rot}}) = A(B_1, B_2, \dots, B_m), \tag{18}$$

for $B_1, B_2, \dots, B_m \in \mathfrak{B}$.

Remark 7. Every aggregation function defined in the above way is invariant with respect to rotations since the comparison operators preserves this property.

Example 4. Consider the structures represented by the binary sequences 0001 and 1010. The longest common subsequence A_{LCS} for the above two structures is represented by a binary sequence 01, i.e., (Fig. 8)

$$A_{\mathrm{LCS}}(0001, 1010) = 01. \tag{19}$$

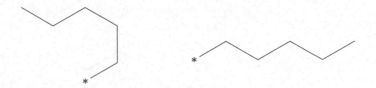

Fig. 7. Graphical representations of the structures 0001 (on the left) and 1010 (on the right).

Fig. 8. Graphical representation of the structure 01 (on the left) and 101 (on the right).

The binary sequence representing the rotation of the structure on the left-hand-side on the Fig. 7 is equal to 0111. Then we obtain again the longest common subsequence with respect to rotations given by the binary sequence 01. Thus

$$A_{\mathrm{LCS}}(0111, 1010) = 01.$$

Now, let consider the structure 10111. It is easy to notice that $0001 \leq 10111$ since $(0001)^{\mathrm{Rot}} = 0111$. Then we have (Fig. 9)

$$A_{\mathrm{LCS}}(0001, 1010) = 01 \leq 101 = A_{\mathrm{LCS}}(10111, 1010)$$

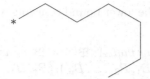

Fig. 9. Graphical representation of the structure 10111.

There are several properties which are expected to be satisfied by an aggregation function. The following definitions show two of them.

Definition 20. *We will say that an aggregation function* $A\colon \mathfrak{B}^m \to \mathfrak{B}$ *is idempotent whenever, for all* $B \in \mathfrak{B}$, *we have*

$$A(\underbrace{B, B, \ldots, B}_{m-\text{times}}) = B. \tag{20}$$

Remark 8. The function A_{LCS} is idempotent.

Definition 21. *We will say that an aggregation function* $A\colon \mathfrak{B}^m \to \mathfrak{B}$ *is symmetric whenever*

$$A(B_1, B_2, \ldots, B_m) = A(B_{\sigma(1)}, B_{\sigma(2)}, \ldots, B_{\sigma(m)}), \tag{21}$$

for all permutations σ, *i.e., for all bijections* $\sigma\colon \{1, 2, \ldots, m\} \to \{1, 2, \ldots, m\}$ *where* $B_1, B_2, \ldots, B_m \in \mathfrak{B}$.

Remark 9. The function A_{LCS} is symmetric.

4.3 Rotations and Reflections Invariantness Case

In this case, we assume that the honeycomb-based polygonal chain, its rotation and both reflections are the same structure. Thus, we introduce the comparing operators which will handle this extended invariantness.

Definition 22. *Suppose that* S_1 *and* S_2 *are honeycomb-based polygonal chains represented by the binary sequences* B_1 *and* B_2 *respectively. We will say that* S_1 *and* S_2 *are equal (and denote it as* $S_1 = S_2$) *whenever* $B_1 = B_2$ *or* $B_1^{\text{Rot}} = B_2$ *or* $B_1^{\text{Ref}_1} = B_2$ *or* $B_1^{\text{Ref}_2} = B_2$.

Definition 23. *Suppose that* S_1 *and* S_2 *are honeycomb-based polygonal chains represented by the binary sequences* B_1 *and* B_2 *respectively. We will say that* S_1 *precedes* S_2 *(and denote it as* $S_1 \leq S_2$) *whenever either* $B_1 \leq B_2$ *or* $B_1^{\text{Rot}} \leq B_2$ *or* $B_1^{\text{Ref}_1} \leq B_2$ *or* $B_1^{\text{Ref}_2} \leq B_2$.

Remark 10. Note that the relation $\leq$ is a weak partial order on a set of all honeycomb-based polygonal chains.

The monotonicity and the lower bound concepts will be similar as in the case of rotations invariantness.

Definition 24. *We will say that* $A\colon \mathfrak{B}^m \to \mathfrak{B}$ *is nondecreasing (in each variable) whenever, for every* $(B_1, B_2 \ldots, B_m), (B'_1, B'_2, \ldots, B'_m) \in \mathfrak{B}^m$,

$$(\forall\, k \in \{1, 2, \ldots, m\})\ B_k \le B'_k \implies A(B_1, B_2, \ldots, B_m) \le A(B'_1, B'_2, \ldots, B'_m).$$

Definition 25. *Let* $B_1, B_2, \ldots, B_m, B \in \mathfrak{B}$. *We will say that the function* $\inf\colon \mathfrak{B}^m \to \mathfrak{B}$ *is a infimum whenever*

$$\inf(B_1, B_2, \ldots, B_m) = B \iff (\forall\, k \in \{1, 2, \ldots, m\})\ B \le B_k.$$

Definition 26. *The mapping* $A\colon \mathfrak{B}^m \to \mathfrak{B}$ *is an aggregation function whenever it is nondecreasing and*

$$\inf(B_1, B_2, \ldots, B_m) \le A(B_1, B_2, \ldots, B_m)$$

for all $B_1, B_2, \ldots, B_m \in \mathfrak{B}$.

We state the extended definition of invariantness for this case.

Definition 27. *We will say that an aggregation function* $A\colon \mathfrak{B}^m \to \mathfrak{B}$ *is invariant with respect to reflections whenever it is invariant with respect to rotations and*

$$A(B_1^{\mathrm{Ref}_{i_1}}, B_2^{\mathrm{Ref}_{i_2}}, \ldots, B_m^{\mathrm{Ref}_{i_m}}) = A(B_1, B_2, \ldots, B_m), \tag{22}$$

for $B_k \in \mathfrak{B}$ *and* $\mathrm{Ref}_{i_k}, \in \{\mathrm{Ref}_1, \mathrm{Ref}_2\}$, *where* $k \in \{1, 2, \ldots, m\}$.

Remark 11. Every aggregation function defined in the above way is invariant with respect to rotations and reflections since the comparison operators preserve this property.

5 Summary and Future Work

The characterization with a binary sequence of a honeycomb-based polygonal chain was introduced in this paper. This form allows us to use many string aggregation function concepts. Then, the rotation and reflection properties were presented in the aggregation function. They are very intuitive and convenient to use.

The proposed concepts can be used, for example, by considering the chemical and physical properties of the molecules and materials. We want to use them to find the optimal paths increasing the chance of winning in the board game The Settlers of Catan.

Moreover, we want to extend these definitions and theory for more complex structures, i.e., for honeycomb-based structures containing a vertice of degree 3:

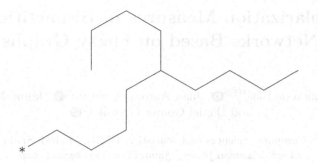

References

1. Coleman, M.M.: Fundamentals of Polymer Science: an Introductory Text, 2nd edn. (2019)
2. Gaulter, B., Gaulter, M.: Further Pure Mathematics. Oxford University Press, Oxford (2001)
3. Gagolewski, M.: Data Fusion: Theory, Methods, and Applications. No. 7 in Monograph Series: Information Technologies: Research and their Interdisciplinary Applications. Institute of Computer Science, Polish Academy of Sciences, Warsaw (2015)
4. Gillie, A.C.: Binary Arithmetic and Boolean Algebra. McGraw-Hill, New York (1965)
5. Grabisch, M. (ed.): Aggregation Functions. No. 127 in Encyclopedia of Mathematics and its Applications, Cambridge University Press, Cambridge (2009)
6. McCrum, N.G., Buckley, C.P., Bucknall, C.B.: Principles of Polymer Engineering, 2nd edn. Oxford University Press, Oxford, New York (1997)
7. Ndjountche, T.: Digital Electronics 2: Sequential and Arithmetic Logic Circuits. ISTE Ltd/Wiley, Hoboken (2016)
8. Pettofrezzo, A.J.: Matrices and Transformations. Dover Books on Advanced Mathematics, Dover Publ, New York (1978). Republ. of the 1966 edn
9. Wang, Z.: Recent advances in novel metallic honeycomb structure. Compos. B Eng. **166**, 731–741 (2019). https://doi.org/10.1016/j.compositesb.2019.02.011
10. Witek, H.A., Moś, G., Chou, C.P.: Zhang-Zhang polynomials of regular 3-and 4-tier benzenoid strips. MATCH Commun. Math. Comput. Chem. **73**(2), 427–442 (2015)

Polarization Measures in Bi-partition Networks Based on Fuzzy Graphs

Clara Simón de Blas[1]([✉])(iD), Juan Antonio Guevara[2](iD), Jaime Morillo[1], and Daniel Gómez González[2](iD)

[1] Computer Sciences and Statistics, URJC, Madrid, Spain
clara.simon@urjc.es, jamorillo.leal@gmail.com
[2] Facultad de Estudios Estadísticos, Universidad Complutense de Madrid, Madrid, Spain
juanguev@ucm.es, dagomez@estad.ucm.es

Abstract. In this paper we extend the definition of polarization in a network, by defining a new measure in fuzzy graphs. We will focus on the case of two communities in a fuzzy context. We present a well known problem in real life social networks to compare our results with the crisp case. Results shows improvements in detecting polarization masked in a crisp context.

Keywords: Polarization · Fuzzy set · Network Analysis · Aggregation Operators

1 Introduction

The analysis of social networks has become one of the hottest disciplines of data analysis due to its natural application in areas as diverse as: biology, medicine, transportation, communication, sociology, marketing, mathematics or computer science (see for example [3,6,8,14] among many others). The well-known term of social network analysis refers to the study of graphs. A graph is usually modeled as a set of nodes with relationships between its members. Most of the theoretical works of the SNA, as well as its applications, model the graph clearly without the existence of any type of uncertainty regarding the relationships that are generated [14]. In the same way, they suppose the knowledge of all the relations for all the nodes of a given graph.

Nevertheless, uncertainty related with the values or existence of the relation between nodes appears in a natural way when modeling real problems. Uncertainty modelling is one of the major issues deal by scientists in a wide range disciplinary areas. Depending on the source of the lack of knowledge that generates the uncertainty in the area in study, different techniques have been developed to complete the absence of information. Since the first human language was developed, based on a small set of phonemes, vagueness begin to emerge in

Supported by PGC2018-096509-B-I00 and PID2019-106254RB-I00 national projects.

© Springer Nature Switzerland AG 2022
D. Ciucci et al. (Eds.): IPMU 2022, CCIS 1601, pp. 398–409, 2022.
https://doi.org/10.1007/978-3-031-08971-8_33

language development, making difficulties to deduce the complete intention and interpret correctly a given message. Inspired in the imprecise aspects of human knowledge, Zadeh [22] introduce fuzzy sets as a method to deal with problems when the source of imprecision is the absence of sharply defined criteria of class membership.

The inclusion of soft computing in social network problems is clearly a significant improvement to deal with real problems since relationships is more natural to consider soft than something crisp. A clear example of this fact would be the problem of detecting communities in networks. Since clustering was one of the main problems in which the fuzzy approach seems more natural, the community detection solutions (clustering nodes in a network) are more realistic when are presented in a fuzzy way, where nodes are not always identified with a group or community and it is much more realistic to assume the existence of different degrees of memberships ([2,10,11]). In this paper, we are interested in a very important and structural property of complex network: the capability to measure the degree of polarization of the network. This structural property has been studied recently from different perspectives [1,5,12,15,17,19,21] with special relevance in social science. The polarization phenomenon refers to the existence of two highly cohesive groups with few or high interactions among the members of each vertex set, reflecting, possibly conflicting views.

The main contribution of this paper is the extension of the polarization measure proposed in [13] to the case of graphs, where relations between nodes may be crisp or soft, and nodes who belongs to several communities cannot be fully involved with all of them, as a result of limited time and resources. To this aim, we will consider the case where each vertex belongs to each group in a different extent. The polarization measure that we introduce here for networks, is based on aggregation operators and fuzzy sets.

This paper is organized as follow: in Sect. 2 we present some necessary definitions to understand the contribution of this paper. In Sect. 3, we present a novel and natural extension of the concept of polarization of [13] to the case of networks. In Sect. 4, we provide an example of the performance of this new measure to the Zachary karate Club case comparing with other polarization measures defined in literature, some conclusions and final remarks.

2 Preliminaries

2.1 Aggregation Operators: Overlapping and Grouping Functions

Since the beginning of fuzzy sets introduced by Zadeh [22], Aggregation Operators (AO) became a necessary discipline to deal with sets and membership functions. AO appears in a natural way when the soft information has to be aggregated. Although AO were originally defined to aggregate values from membership functions associated to fuzzy set, previous definition can be extended into a more general framework allowing to deal with more general objects than values into $[0, 1]$. Given two degrees of membership $x = \mu_A(c)$ and $y = \mu_B(c)$ of an object c into classes A and B, an overlap function is supposed to yield the degree z up to which the object c belongs to the intersection of both classes. Particularly, an overlap function was defined in [9] as a particular type of bivariate aggregation function characterized by a set of commutative, natural boundary and monotonicity properties. These authors extended the bivariate aggregation function to a n-dimensional case.

Definition 1. *[9] An n-dimensional aggregation function $G_O : [0,1]^n \longrightarrow [0,1]$ is a n-dimensional overlap function if and only if:*

1. *G_O is symmetric.*
2. *$G_O(x_1, \ldots, x_n) = 0$ if and only if $\prod_{i=1}^{n} x_i = 0$.*
3. *$G_O(x_1, \ldots, x_n) = 1$ if and only if $x_i = 1$ for all $i \in \{1, \ldots, n\}$.*
4. *G_O is increasing and continuous.*

In a similar way, the grouping concept can be also extended into a more general framework, Given n degrees of membership $x_i = \mu_{C_i}(c)$ for $i = 1, \ldots, n$ of an object c into classes $C_1, \ldots, C_n$, a grouping function is supposed to yield the degree z up to which the combination (grouping) of the n classes $C_1, \ldots, C_n$ is supported.

Definition 2. *[9] An n-dimensional function $G_G : [0,1]^n \longrightarrow [0,1]$ is a n-dimensional grouping function if and only if it satisfies the following conditions:*

1. *G_G is symmetric.*
2. *$G_G(x) = 0$ if and only if $x_i = 0$, for all $i = 1, \ldots, n$.*
3. *$G_G(x) = 1$ if and only if there exist $i \in \{1, \ldots, n\}$ with $x_i = 1$.*
4. *G_G is increasing and continuous.*

2.2 Polarization Measures

The measurement of polarization have been tackle from many perspectives having its origins on the field of economics as a natural evolution of the Gini index [5,7] at the end of the last century. Nonetheless, despite the fact that many measures have been proposed in the literature from different approaches [1,16,19], all of them have one aspect in common: they use crispy values to measure constructs that are fuzzy by nature. In [13], it is proposed a new Polarization measure based on the fuzzy sets which they call JDJ. These authors start from the premise that reality is not black or white but there are many nuances in the attitudes of people. In this sense, a crispy value that holds a specific position in the attitudinal axis by which the attitudes are being measured is missing all the nuances that this attitudes might hold. In this sense, it is common that an individual might be a supporter of a political party A but also agree with some statements proposed by another political party B. Thus, crispy values might not be sufficient to measure complex concepts such as Polarization in which attitudes are involve.

The polarization measure JDJ [13] is based on the one proposed by [5]. This measure is particularly interesting on the grounds of the fact that it includes not only metric aspects but theoretical aspects as well. To compute polarization, authors in [5] take into account three main aspects:

- High homophily within groups.
- High heterogeneity between groups.
- Few number of groups with significant size.

According to this, they proposed what they call the IA approach, where I is the identification of a given individual towards the group that he/she belong to and A is the alienation between individuals.

Then, Guevara et al. apply this idea to the fuzzy sets where a polarization measure is proposed according to the next. Let X be a one-dimensional variable by which the attitudes, positions or affectivity are being measured. Let assume that X has two extreme values or poles, being X_A and X_B. Also, let V be a finite set of individuals or nodes and let i be an individual that holds a value in X where $i \in V$. To take the idea of [5] into this field, authors add the membership degree of a given individual i to both extreme poles of the variable by which their attitude is being measured. So that, we have that μ_{X_A} and μ_{X_B} are functions for each $i \in V$. Thus, $\mu_A(i)$ is the membership degree of i towards the pole X_A whereas $\mu_{X_B}(i)$ is the membership degree of i towards the pole X_{X_B}, representing the closeness that an individual holds towards an extreme position. Then, polarization between two individuals is computed as the possibility of the next two situations:

- How individual i is close to the pole X_A and individual j is close to the pole X_B.
- How individual i is close to the pole X_B and individual j is close to the pole X_A.

In this vein, in [13] they are not only taking into account the approach proposed in [5] but adding a key aspect being the radicalization of the population. Finally, the polarization measure is the next:

$$JDJ_{pol}(V, \eta_{X_A}, \eta_{X_B}, \varphi, \phi) = \sum_{i,j \in V i \leq j} \varphi\left(\phi(\eta_{X_A}(i), \eta_{X_B}(j)), \phi(\eta_{X_B}(i), \eta_{X_A}(j))\right)$$

(1)

where $\phi : [0,1]^2 \longrightarrow [0,1]$ is an overlapping aggregation operator and $\varphi : [0,1]^2 \longrightarrow [0,1]$ is a grouping function.

This measure shows its highest value of polarization when 50% of the population hold the maximum value for μ_{X_A} and the minimum value for μ_{X_B}, while the other 50% holds the opposite, having the minimum value for μ_{X_A} and the maximum for μ_{X_B}. This scenario represents two main groups with same and maximum size in which all their members are radicalized towards extreme and opposite positions. Otherwise, the lowest values of JDJ are not only derived from the situation in which all the population represent the same values in μ_{X_A} and μ_{X_B} but this specific value must be an extreme one, holding the maximum value for μ_{X_A} and minimum for μ_{X_B} or vice versa. In this sense, in terms of probability there is a higher risk for polarization in those scenarios in which all the population hold the same attitude, being this attitude an extreme one rather than moderate one. According to this, authors state that the minimum value of polarization is the one in which not only there is not fragmentation or segregation but when there is an extended radicalization in the population.

2.3   Graphs, Community Detection. Crisp and Fuzzy Cases

Let $V = \{1, \ldots, n\}$ be a finite set of elements called nodes, and let $E = \{\{i, j\} \mid i, j \in V\}$ be a set of links or edges, it is, the set of neighboring or related elements of V. It is assumed that if the elements i, j are related, then $\exists \, e = \{i, j\} \in E$; otherwise, $\nexists \, e = \{i, j\} \in E$. Hence, the pair $G = (V, E)$ is a graph or network. A network can also be represented by means of its adjacency matrix, denoted A. It shows the direct connections between the elements of V in that sense: if $A_{ij} \neq 0$, then $\exists \, e = \{i, j\} \in E$; else, if $A_{ij} = 0$, then $\nexists \, e = \{i, j\} \in E$.

How to explain the community structure in a network is one of the most important problems in social network analysis (see [6,10,11]). Roughly speaking, a community in a network is a connected subgraph whose nodes are densely connected within itself but sparsely connected with the rest of the network. Most of the approaches assume that communities form a partition of the set of nodes. In this sense, given a graph $G = (V, E)$, we will say that $P = \{C_1, \ldots, C_k\}$ is a solution of the classical community detection problem if P is a partition of the set of V and the elements of P are connected in the graph. Nevertheless, real communities in complex network, often present overlap, such that each vertex may occur in more than one community.

As it is pointed in [20], two different types of overlapping could be possible in a given graph: the crisp case (where each node belongs fully to each community of which it is a member) and the fuzzy case (where each node belongs to each community to a different extent). Within the case of fuzzy community detection [10], there are two main challenges: the development of algorithms that produce a fuzzy clustering of the nodes in the network and the quantification of the quality of the algorithms performance. To conclude this section, let us refer to the approach developed in [20], in which a fuzzy partition is obtained from a crisp community detection solutions by the *Make Fuzzy* algorithm. Formally, given a graph $G = (V, E)$ with a crisp partition $P = \{C_1, \ldots, C_k\}$, they build the following fuzzy partition $\widetilde{P_{Gre}} = \{\mu_1, \ldots, \mu_k\}$, where $\mu_i : V \longrightarrow [0, 1]$ is defined as:

$$\mu_{C_i}(v) = \frac{|N(v) \cap C_i|}{|N(v)|}$$

where $N(v) = \{u \in V \; with \; (u, v) \in E\}$.

Example 1. Let $G = (V, E)$ be a network with 8 nodes $V = \{1, 2, 3, 4, 5, 6, 7, 8\}$ and ten edges $E = \{(1, 2), (1, 3), (2, 4), (3, 4), (4, 5), (4, 6), (5, 6)(5, 7), (6, 8), (7, 8)\}$, and let $P = \{C_1 = \{1, 2, 3, 4\}, C_2 = \{5, 6, 7, 8\}\}$ be a partition of the network in two communities. Then, the fuzzy partition $\widetilde{P_{gre}} = \{\mu_{C_1}, \mu_{C_2}\}$ is given by:

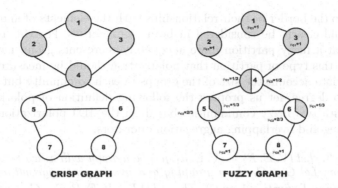

Fig. 1. Example 1. In grey nodes in C_1, in white nodes in C_2

3   Polarization Indices in Networks

One of the most common affections of the term polarization is associated when there are two opposite groups that break dialogue and communication. In terms of networks, we could think in the fact that there are few relations between them. In a network with two communities, the nodes of one community that link to a node of the other community make up what is called a boundary. Between two highly polarized communities the size of the border is very small or even null [12]. But also, it is important to note that the size of the two communities should be also affected the term polarization [5], since the highest polarization is reached when there exist two groups without relations (since they break their relations) and the size of the groups are similar. Is not the same polarization case if there are two groups of sizes $100k$ and $105k$ that is the size is $195k$ and $10k$.

Following other approaches developed in literature that deal with polarization in networks [12], our measure of polarization will be focus on the case in which we have a network with two communities (crisp or fuzzy). So our measure deals with the problem of measuring the polarization from a fuzzy networks $(V, E, \widetilde{P}) = (V, E, \mu_1, \mu_2)$ or a crisp one $(V, E, P) = (V, E, \{C_1, C_2\})$. How to extend the concept of polarization to a more general case, is a question that (we think) merits to be explore in a future.

In order to measure the polarization of a two community network $(V, E, P) = (V, E, \{C_1, C_2\})$, the most common approaches (see [18,21] for example), is to associate the concept of polarization with the case in which there exist two communities with similar size. In this sense, polarization can be seen as a measure of dispersion [5] over nominal variables, that for the case of two groups this measure is equivalent to the variance of a Bernoulli random variable. This fact, reflect the situation in which the network is partitioned into two groups with similar size that is one of the important factors in polarization. Nevertheless, the problems of this approach is to consider that the nodes of a community clearly belong to said community without differentiating that there are nodes that, due to their proximity to the border or their relationships with the elements of another community, could clearly be considered in both communities. For this reason, we consider that a fuzzy partition more adequately represents group membership and it is on this type of partition that polarization should be measured.

To take into account the size of the groups in each community but also their membership degree, let us propose the following definition of polarization for networks with two fuzzy communities based on the JDJ polarization measure with grouping and overlapping aggregation operators.

Definition 3. *Let* $(V, E, \widetilde{P}) = (V, E, \mu_1, \mu_2)$ *be a graph with a two fuzzy community partition. Let* G_G, G_O *be a grouping and overlapping aggregation operator as are defined in Definition 1 and 2. Then,* $JDJ_{pol}(V, E, \widetilde{P}, G_O, G_G)$ *polarization measure is defined as*

$$JDJ_{pol}(V, E, \widetilde{P}, G_O, G_G) = \frac{1}{(|N|/2)^2} \sum_{u,v \in V u \neq v} G_G \left(G_O(\mu_1(u), \mu_2(v)), G_O(\mu_2(u), \mu_1(v)) \right) \qquad (2)$$

Remark 1. Let us observed that the coefficient $\frac{1}{(|N|/2)^2}$ is just to guarantee that previous measure is in fact an index that belong to the unit interval and is equal to 1 if and only $N = C_1 \cup C_2$, $|C_1| = |C_2| =$, and $\mu_i(u) = 1$ if $u \in C_1$ and 0 otherwise. This measure can be viewed as the polarization average among each pair of elements in V. In order to make more interpretable this measure (loosing the boundary conditions) we could obtain the average of this sum changing the coefficient $\frac{1}{(|N|/2)^2}$ by $\frac{2}{(|N|(|N|-1))}$. The average represents the average polarization between each pair of nodes in the network. We can see this difference in the following example.

Example 2. Let us recall again in the Example 1 in which a fuzzy partition is given. Let $G_O(x, y) = xy$ and let $G_G(x, y) = Max(x, y)$ be two aggregation operators. If we want to obtain how the nodes 1 and 4 are polarizated in the fuzzy partition, we have to computed $Pol(1, 4) = Max\{\mu_1(1)\mu_2(4), \mu_2(1)\mu_1(4)\} = Max\{0.5, 0\} = 0.5$. In the following table we see some of the 28 pairwise comparison that has to be aggregate with the sum to obtain the polarization measure.

Table 1. Some pairwise polarization from the fuzzy clustering network of Table 1 $(V, E, \widetilde{P_{gre}})$

																	Average	JDJ
Node x	1	1	1	1	2	2	3	3	4	4	4	4	6	6	...		
Node y	2	4	5	7	4	5	7	8	5	6	7	8	7	8	...		
Pol.	0	0.5	0.66	1	0.5	0.66	1	1	0.5	0.5	0.5	0.5	0.33	0.33	...	0.541	0.94

From this results we can see that polarization is maximum between the internal nodes of different communities C_1 and C_2 $\{(1, 7), (1, 8), (2, 7), (2, 8), (3, 7), (3, 8)\}$ and minimum among internal nodes of the same community $\{(1, 2), (1, 3), (2, 3), (7, 8)\}$. Let us observed that our polarization measure could be applied to crisp partitions also. For example, if we consider the crisp partition $P = \{\{1,2,3,4\},\{5,6,7,8\}\}$, $JDJ_{pol}(V,E,P,Prod,Max)$ we can see that only when it is measure the polarization between two elements from different communities we are going to have a value different from 0 (1, in fact), so it is easy to check that

$$JDJ_{pol}(V,E,P,Prod,Max) = \tfrac{1}{(16)} \sum_{u,v \in V u \in C_1, v \in C_2} 1 = 16/16 = 1$$

Proposition 1. *Let $G = (V,E)$ be a graph with two communities $P = \{C_1, C_2\}$, then the following holds:*

$$JDJ_{pol}(V,E,P,G_O,G_G) = 4\frac{|C_1|}{|V|}\frac{|C_2|}{|V|} = 4Var(Ber(p)),$$

where p is the proportion of elements in the community C_1.

Proof. *Trivial from the fact that $G_G\left(G_O(\mu_1(u),\mu_2(v)), G_O(\mu_2(u),\mu_1(v))\right) = 1$, if and only if nodes u,v belong to different communities and 0 otherwise for any grouping G_G or overlapping G_O aggregation operators.*

From this proposition we can see that JDJ applied to crisp partitions in networks can be viewed as the classical way to measure polarizarion for two groups. Also we can see that maximum polarization is reached when we have two communities with the same size. Nevertheless, let us take into account that given the partition P, the JDJ measure is independent (as happen with the classical polarization measure) of the structure of the network. So polarization is the same if we eliminate the relations between communities C_1 and C_2:
$JDJ_{pol}(V,E,P,Prod,Max) =$
$= JDJ_{pol}(V,E \setminus \{(4.5)\},P,Prod,Max) =$
$= JDJ_{pol}(V,E \setminus \{(4.5),(4.6)\},P,Prod,Max)$. It is important to note that polarization from a theoretical point of view always focus on the fact that polarization is maximum when the groups breaks their relations, so we think that this performance of the classical (and our measure applied to crisp partition) should be improved.

In order to provide an alternative way to measure polarization in crisp networks (V,E,P) using the JDJ measure, we propose fuzzificate the crisp partition into a fuzzy one, to then obtain the JDJ value for the fuzzy partition. Formally, we propose the following definition.

Definition 4. *Let $(V,E,P) = (V,E,P = \{C_1,C_2\})$ be a graph with a two community partition, and let G_G, G_O be a grouping and overlapping aggregation operator. Then, the $JDJ_{pol,gre}(V,E,P,G_O,G_G)$ polarization fuzzy measure is defined as*

$$JDJ_{pol,gre,k}(V,E,P,G_O,G_G) = JDJ_{pol}(V,E,\widetilde{P_{gre}},G_O,G_G) \qquad (3)$$

where $\widetilde{P_{gre}} = (\mu_1,\mu_2)$ is obtained with the makefuzzy function, $\mu_{C_i}(v) = \frac{|N_k(v) \cap C_i|}{|N_k(v)|}$, where $N_k(v) = \{u \in V \text{ with } distance(u,v) \leq k\}$.

4   Some Computational Results and Conclusions

In this section we are going to compute our polarization measure in the well-known *karate club network*. To show how this measure is affected by small modifications of the network, we will add and remove edges by comparing the result obtained with the polarization measures based on the group sizes [4] and the *Frontier polarization measure* defined in [12] that is presented below.

Definition 5. *[12] Let $G = (V, E, P)$ be a network with a crisp partition $P = \{C_1, C_2\}$. Then*

$$Pol_{boundary}(V, E, P) = \sum_{v \in B} \frac{1}{|B|} 2 \left(\frac{|N(v) \cap C_{\delta(v)}|}{|N(v) \cap C_{\delta(v)}| + |N(v) \cap V \setminus \{C_{\delta(v)}\}|} - 0.5 \right),$$

where $B = \{u, v \in V \text{ with } (u, v) \in E \text{ and } u \in C_i, v \in C_j \ i \neq j\}$ is the nodes that have relations with member of the other group, $N(v) = N_{k=1}(v)$, and $C_{\delta(v)}$ is the community to which node v belong.

Let us consider the friendship network of Zachary karate Club shown in Fig. 2 without considering the edges weights. This network present the relations between 34 members of a US karate club in 1970s and let us consider the case in which the number of communities is two, computed with the edge and betweenness algorithm proposed by Girman and Newman.

In order to compare the performance of the measures $Pol_{boundary}$, Pol_{crisp}, the classical modularity $Mod(Q)$ function, and our proposal $JDJ_{pol,gre,k}$, we take the case of crisp partition of network $P = \{C_1, C_2\}$ in two groups obtained using the Girvan and Newman algorithm and stopping at the first partition of the graph. In Fig. 2 we can see this crisp partition. Obviously, the measures $Pol_{boundary}$, Pol_{crisp}, $Mod(Q)$ can not deal with fuzzy community detection solutions $(V, E, \widetilde{P})$ so here we only made the comparison for the crisp case.

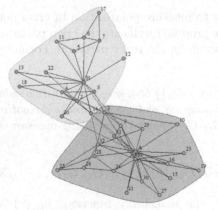

Nodes	$(\mu_{C_1}(v), \mu_{C_2}(v))$	Nodes	$(\mu_{C_1}(v), \mu_{C_2}(v))$
1	(0.1875,0,8125)	18	(0,1)
2	(0.22,0.77)	19	(1,0)
3	(0.5,0.5)	20	(0.33,0.66)
4	(0.16,0.83)	21	(1,0)
5	(0,1)	22	(0,1)
6	(0,1)	23	(1,0)
7	(0,1)	24	(1,0)
8	(0.25,0.75)	25	(1,0)
9	(0.8,0.2)	26	(1,0)
10	(1,0)	27	(1,0)
11	(0,1)	28	(1,0)
12	(0,1)	29	(1,0)
13	(0,1)	30	(1,0)
14	(0.4,0.6)	31	(0.75,0.25)
15	(1,0)	32	(0.83,0.16)
16	(1,0)	33	(1,0)
17	(0,1)	34	(0.88,0.12)

Fig. 2. The karate club network with two communities and modularity = 0.3599 and the fuzzy partition obtained from the makefuzzy function defined in [20].

To analyze the robustness of the different measures that we want to compare, in the following table we present the four measures previously mentioned obtained for the same partition (see Fig. 2) $P = \{C_1, C_2\}$ with

- $C_1 = \{H, 2, 4, 5, 6, 7, 8, 11, 12, 13, 14, 17, 18, 20, 22\}$
- $C_2 = \{A, 3, 9, 10, 15, 16, 19, 21, 23, 24, 25, 26, 27, 28, 29, 30, 31, 32\}$

in which the network has been modified by removing and adding edges.

Let us observed that since $|C_1| = 16$ and $|C_2| = 18$, the $Pol_{crisp}(V, E_k, P)$ will be the same for any graph E_k and as we have said previously in Proposition 1 will be

$$Pol_{crisp}(V, E_k, P) = \frac{|C_1|}{|V|}\frac{|C_2|}{|V|} = \frac{16}{34}\frac{18}{34}.$$

	Between Communities						Internal Edges				
Measure	Modularity	Pol_boundary	Crisp	JDJ	Edges Added/Erased	Measure	Modularity	Pol_boundary	Crisp	JDJ	Edges Added/Erased
Karate Original	0,4012	0,1265	0,9861	0,9569		Karate Original	0,4012	0,1265	0,9861	0,9569	
Added	0,391	0,1302	0,9861	0,9542	[15,20]	Added	0,3927	0,1311	0,9861	0,9563	[19,3]
Added	0,3967	0,1401	0,9861	0,9381	[15,20],[25,12]	Added	0,3974	0,1265	0,9861	0,9569	[18,6],[24,29]
Added	0,351	0,1414	0,9861	0,9206	[27,8],[33,11],[25,20]	Added	0,4023	0,1299	0,9861	0,9602	[14,8],[5,14],[10,9]
Added	0,3759	0,1019	0,9861	0,859	[19,13],[29,12],[3,17],[31,4]	Added	0,4104	0,1265	0,9861	0,9589	[17,6],[12,7],[30,23],[30,24]
Added	0,3574	0,14	0,9861	0,9245	[28,13],[25,14],[23,6],[10,14],[34,4]	Added	0,3904	0,1289	0,9861	0,9587	[23,16],[30,32],[12,6],[13,2],[11,5]
Added	0,3277	0,1039	0,9861	0,8704	],[24,11],[15,14],[28,12],[23,4],[23,13]	Added	0,3925	0,1349	0,9861	0,9606	1],[17,7],[20,17],[14,18],[17,14],[14,6]
Added	0,3204	0,1166	0,9861	0,8427	[33,20],[19,22],[28,14],[28,1],[15,22],[34,2],[30,20],[31,22],[33,7],[24,2],[10,2],[30,7],[16,5],[33,13],[29,18]	Added	0,3854	0,1368	0,9861	0,9623	[29,33],[9,28],[10,29],[10,9],[26,3],[33,24],[23,16],[4,5],[5,6],[8,34],[12,4],[18,8],[12,7],[4,11],[8,6],[15,16],[16,24],[19,24],[26,9],[23,30]
Added	0,26	0,1032	0,9861	0,741	[34,17],[30,12],[10,6],[27,6],[28,18],[32,13],[10,17],[29,5],[23,17],[19,20],[33,13],[31,],[26,12],[21,7],[19,2],[25,5],[32,14],[33,13],[30,4],[15,18],[2,3]	Added	0,3974	0,1367	0,9861	0,9615	[30,16],[23,24],[27,21],[21,31],[27,3],[13,12],[8,20],[5,18],[12,5],[12,6],[17,22],[13,6],[12,29],[2,22],[26,10],[24,30]
Deleted	0,4092	0,1468	0,9861	0,9593	[2,3]	Deleted	0,4075	0,1265	0,9861	0,9569	[24,30]
Deleted	0,4173	0,1234	0,9861	0,9662	[3,8],[1,32]	Deleted	0,382	0,1258	0,9861	0,9559	[16,34],[5,7]
Deleted	0,4089	0,2114	0,9861	0,9702	[2,3],[3,4],[3,8]	Deleted	0,4036	0,1265	0,9861	0,953	[1,20],[21,33],[1,18]
Deleted	0,4368	0,1854	0,9861	0,9701	[3,8],[1,3],[1,32],[14,34]	Deleted	0,4022	0,124	0,9861	0,9569	[1,10],[1,15],[1,32],[6,17]
Deleted	0,4285	0,2698	0,9861	0,9697	[3,14],[1,3],[3,4],[2,3],[2,31]	Deleted	0,4167	0,1083	0,9861	0,9569	[24,28],[3,10],[1,15],[3,9],[1,8]
Deleted	0,4844	NaN	0,9861	0,9861	[1,3],[1,9],[1,32],[2,3],[2,31],[3,4],[3,8],[3,14],[14,34],[20,34]	Deleted	0,395	0,1027	0,9861	0,9467	[1,15],[26,32],[1,32],[4,14],[23,31],[1,14],[2,4],[1,6],[24,26],[2,14]

Fig. 3. Different Polarization Measures for the Karate Club network adding and deleting edges.

As can be see from the Fig. 3, the JDJ polarization measure takes into consideration two important aspects in polarization: the size of the formed groups, which is also taken into consideration by traditional polarization measures (see Crisp polarization measure), and the frontier and relations that exist between groups, which is considered by $Pol_{Boundary}$. From the previous figure we can see that since the size of the groups are similar (18 and 16) the crisp polarization is high and obviously is the same for all modification of the network (highest value is reached in the case of two groups of 17 members). Let us observe the following some good performance of our measure:

- When a link between internal nodes (nodes that not belong to the frontier and are in the same community as for example $(6, 18)$) is added in the network, the JDJ polarization does not change (since the membership function of all members in the network does not change). With coincide with the idea of that in term of polarization nothing has changed.

- When a link between two nodes of the same community are added, but one of them are in the frontier and the other not. The polarization increase, since the frontier nodes be identify more with its community and then their antagonism with the other group.
- When a link between two communities are added, then the polarization is decreased since there exist more communication between communities.

Also it is important to see the main drawback of the measure proposed by [12] since it does not take into account the size of the groups as well as the nodes that are located far from the boundary. We can argue that only considering the boundary seems not sufficient to measure the polarization since having a high polarization score is invariant to the size of the groups that we are analyzing.

Let us observed also that since the polarization JDJ measure is the result of a composition of overlapping and grouping functions, it could be interesting to study in a future how the used of different functions G_G, G_O could affect to final results as well as some theoretical and desirable properties that could be imposed to these functions.

Finally, we can see also the relation with the modularity measure and the important differences between both concepts. Despite the fact that there is a correlation between modularity and polarization and high levels of modularity usually imply high levels of polarization these concepts are different. Modularity capture the internal density of the communities, so we can see how modularity increase when we delete links between communities from the original network. On the other hand, modularity usually increases when links inside communities are added but polarization could increase or not, depending on the types of nodes that we are connecting.

Acknowledgment. This research has been partially supported by the Government of Spain (grant PGC2018-096509-B-I00, PID2019-106254RB-I00).

References

1. Apouey, B.: Measuring health polarization with self-assessed health data. Health Econ. **16**(9), 875–894 (2007)
2. Biswas, A., Biswas, B.: FuzAg: fuzzy agglomerative community detection by exploring the notion of self-membership. IEEE Trans. Fuzzy Syst. **26**(5), 2568–2577 (2018)
3. de Blas, C.S., Martin, J.S., Gonzalez, D.G.: Combined social networks and data envelopment analysis for ranking. Eur. J. Oper. Res. **266**(3), 990–999 (2018)
4. Duclos, J.Y., Esteban, J., Ray, D.: Polarization: concepts, measurement, estimation. Econometrica **72**(6), 1737–1772 (2004). https://doi.org/10.1111/j.1468-0262.2004.00552.x
5. Esteban, J.M., Ray, D.: On the measurement of polarization. Econometrica J. Econ. Soc. **62**, 819–851 (1994)
6. Fortunato, S.: Community detection in graphs. Phys. Rep. **486**(3–5), 75–174 (2010)
7. Foster, J.E., Wolfson, M.C.: Polarization and the decline of the middle class: Canada and the us mimeo. Vanderbilt University (1992)

8. Gomez, D., González-Arangüena, E., Manuel, C., Owen, G., del Pozo, M., Tejada, J.: Centrality and power in social networks: a game theoretic approach. Math. Soc. Sci. **46**(1), 27–54 (2003)

9. Gómez, D., Rodriguez, J.T., Montero, J., Bustince, H., Barrenechea, E.: n-dimensional overlap functions. Fuzzy Sets Syst. **287**, 57–75 (2016)

10. Gomez, D., Rodríguez, J.T., Yanez, J., Montero, J.: A new modularity measure for fuzzy community detection problems based on overlap and grouping functions. Int. J. Approx. Reasoning **74**, 88–107 (2016)

11. Gómez, D., Zarrazola, E., Yáñez, J., Montero, J.: A divide-and-link algorithm for hierarchical clustering in networks. Inf. Sci. **316**, 308–328 (2015)

12. Guerra, P., Meira Jr, W., Cardie, C., Kleinberg, R.: A measure of polarization on social media networks based on community boundaries. In: Proceedings of the International AAAI Conference on Web and Social Media, vol. 7, pp. 215–224 (2013)

13. Guevara, J.A., Gómez, D., Robles, J.M., Montero, J.: Measuring polarization: a fuzzy set theoretical approach. In: Lesot, M.-J., et al. (eds.) IPMU 2020. CCIS, vol. 1238, pp. 510–522. Springer, Cham (2020). https://doi.org/10.1007/978-3-030-50143-3_40

14. Jackson, M.O.: Social and Economic Networks. Princeton University Press, Princeton (2010)

15. Morales, A.J., Borondo, J., Losada, J.C., Benito, R.M.: Measuring political polarization: Twitter shows the two sides of Venezuela. Chaos Interdisc. J. Nonlinear Sci. **25**(3), 033114 (2015). https://doi.org/10.1063/1.4913758

16. Permanyer, I., D'Ambrosio, C.: Measuring social polarization with ordinal and categorical data. J. Public Econ. Theory **17**(3), 311–327 (2015)

17. Permanyer, I.: The conceptualization and measurement of social polarization. J. Econ. Inequality **10**(1), 45–74 (2012). https://doi.org/10.1007/s10888-010-9143-2

18. Reynal-Querol, M.: Ethnic and religious conflicts, political systems and growth. Ph.D. thesis, London School of Economics and Political Science. University of London (2001)

19. Reynal-Querol, M.: Ethnic and religious conflicts, political systems and growth. Ph.D. thesis, London School of Economics and Political Science (University of London) (2001)

20. Gregory, S.: Fuzzy overlapping communities in networks. J. Stat. Mech. Theory Exp. **2**, PO2017 (2011)

21. Wang, Y.Q., Tsui, K.Y.: Polarization orderings and new classes of polarization indices. J. Public Econ. Theory **2**(3), 349–363 (2000)

22. Zadeh, L.A.: Fuzzy sets. Inf. Control **8**(3), 338–353 (1965)

On Rational Bivariate Aggregation Funcions

Isabel Aguiló[1,2], Sebastia Massanet[1,2(✉)], and Juan Vicente Riera[1,2]

[1] Department of Mathematics and Computer Science,
University of the Balearic Islands, 07122 Palma, Spain
{isabel.aguilo,s.massanet,jvicente.riera}@uib.es
[2] Health Research Institute of the Balearic Islands (IdISBa), 07010 Palma, Spain

Abstract. Aggregation functions play an essential role in many fields where it is necessary at some point to aggregate several input data into a representative output value. Due to this great number of applications, it is also necessary to investigate this type of functions from a theoretical point of view, with the intention of finding out which different families exist and which properties they satisfy. In this sense, aggregation functions that have simple expressions can be interesting for computational purposes. For this reason, in this work we study rational aggregation functions, that is, those whose expression is given by the quotient of two bivariate polynomial functions. A characterization of the binary rational aggregation functions of degree one (in both numerator and denominator) is presented. Moreover, specific characterizations of those that are symmetric and idempotent are also investigated.

Keywords: Aggregation functions · Rational Functions · Idempotence · Symmetry

1 Introduction

Aggregation functions play an essential role in many fields of sciences where it is essential at some point to merge several input data into a representative output value. For this reason, a large amount of literature can be found that develops both theoretical and practical aspects of this topic [2–4,6,8,17]. Depending on the context in which they are applied, it is important to know the type of aggregation function to be used and its properties. In this sense, four main families of aggregation functions are commonly accepted in the literature: the class of conjunctive aggregation functions (such as t-norms [9] or copulas [16]), the family of disjunctive aggregation functions (such as t-conorms or co-copulas [9]), the class of averaging aggregation functions (such as weighted means or Choquet integral [2]) and the family of mixed aggregation functions (such as uninorms [11] or null-norms [10]). On the other hand, the study of aggregation functions according to their expression is interesting not only from a practical point of view, since it can reduce the computational cost, but also from a theoretical point of view. In

© Springer Nature Switzerland AG 2022
D. Ciucci et al. (Eds.): IPMU 2022, CCIS 1601, pp. 410–420, 2022.
https://doi.org/10.1007/978-3-031-08971-8_34

this direction, we would like to point out that all rational Archimedean continuous t-norms were characterized in [7] (see also [1]) leading to the well-known Hamacher class (a clear example of rational binary aggregation function) which contains the t-norms given by the following expression

$$T_\alpha(x,y) = \frac{xy}{\alpha + (1-\alpha)(x+y-xy)}, \quad x,y \in [0,1]$$

with $\alpha \geq 0$ with the convention that $\frac{0}{0} = 0$ when $\alpha = x = y = 0$ or all the rational uninorms with neutral element $e \in (0,1)$ were characterized in [5], as those whose expression is given by

$$U_e(x,y) = \frac{(1-e)xy}{(1-e)xy + e(1-x)(1-y)}$$

if $(x,y) \in [0,1]^2 \setminus \{(0,1),(1,0)\}$ and either $U(1,0) = U(0,1) = 0$ or $U(0,1) = U(1,0) = 1$. Recently, some similar investigations for polynomial aggregation functions and polynomial or rational fuzzy implication functions have been made in the following papers [12–15].

Following this investigation line, in this work we want to investigate rational binary aggregation functions, that is, those whose expression is given by the quotient of two bivariate polynomial functions. In particular, rational binary aggregation functions of degree $(1,1)$ (both bivariate polynomials have degree 1) will be characterized. Also, concrete characterizations of those that are symmetric and idempotent are also studied.

The paper is structured as follows. After recalling the basic definitions and results which will be used throughout the paper, in Sect. 3 the definition of rational binary aggregation function of any degree is presented and some additional properties are studied. Then, rational binary aggregation functions of degree $(1,1)$ and those that are symmetric and idempotent will be characterized in Sect. 4. The paper ends with some conclusions and future work we want to investigate.

2   Preliminaries

Let us recall some concepts and results that will be used throughout this paper. First, we give the definition of a binary aggregation function.

Definition 1 ([3,4]). *A binary aggregation function $f : [0,1]^2 \to [0,1]$ is a binary mapping that satisfies the following properties:*

i) $f(0,0) = 0$ and $f(1,1) = 1$.
ii) f is increasing in each variable.

A binary aggregation function f is a conjunction when $f(1,0) = f(0,1) = 0$ and a disjunction when $f(1,0) = f(0,1) = 1$.

As we have already mentioned in the introduction, many families of aggregation functions have been introduced in the literature. One of such families which will play an important role in this paper is the family of weighted arithmetic means.

Definition 2 ([3,4]). *The* binary weighted arithmetic mean *is the binary function given by*

$$M_w(x_1, x_2) = w_1 x_1 + w_2 x_2$$

where $x_1, x_2 \in [0, 1]$ *and* $w = (w_1, w_2)$ *is the so-called weighting vector satisfying* $w_1, w_2 \in [0, 1]$ *and* $w_1 + w_2 = 1$.

Some additional properties of binary aggregation functions which will be used in this work are:

– The *idempotency*,

$$f(x, x) = x, \quad \text{for all } x \in [0, 1]. \tag{ID}$$

– The *symmetry*,

$$f(x_1, x_2) = f(x_2, x_1), \tag{SYM}$$

3 Rational Binary Aggregation Functions: Definition and Basic Properties

In this section we will introduce the notion of binary rational aggregation function and we will determine some conditions on the coefficients of a rational function in order to obtain a rational binary aggregation function.

Definition 3. *Consider* $n, m \in \mathbb{N}$. *A binary operator* $R : [0, 1]^2 \to [0, 1]$ *is called a* rational aggregation function of degree (n, m) *if it is an aggregation function and its expression is given by*

$$R(x, y) = \frac{p(x, y)}{q(x, y)} = \frac{\displaystyle\sum_{\substack{0 \le i, j \le n \\ i+j \le n}} a_{ij} x^i y^j}{\displaystyle\sum_{\substack{0 \le s, t \le m \\ s+t \le m}} b_{st} x^s y^t} \tag{1}$$

for all $x, y \in [0, 1]$ *where*

(i) $a_{ij} \in \mathbb{R}$ *for all* $0 \le i, j \le n$ *and* $i + j \le n$ *and there exists at least one* a_{ij} *with* $0 \le i, j \le n$ *and* $i + j = n$ *such that* $a_{ij} = 1$,

(ii) $b_{st} \in \mathbb{R}$ *for all* $0 \le s, t \le m$ *and* $s+t \le m$ *and there exist some* $0 \le s, t \le m$ *with* $s + t = m$ *such that* $b_{st} \ne 0$,

(iii) *the polynomials* $p(x, y)$ *and* $q(x, y)$ *have no factors in common*,

(iv) $q(x, y) \ne 0$ *for all* $x, y \in [0, 1]$.

Remark 1. Note that this definition encompasses all possible rational binary aggregation functions. First, any binary rational binary aggregation function whose numerator has degree n satisfies that there exists at least one a_{ij} with $0 \le i, j \le n$ and $i + j = n$ such that $a_{ij} \ne 0$. Therefore, dividing numerator and denominator by this a_{ij}, we obtain that there exists at least one a_{ij} with $0 \le i, j \le n$ and $i+j = n$ such that $a_{ij} = 1$. This condition ensures that the set of coefficients that define a concrete rational binary aggregation function according to Definition 3 is unique. Moreover, Condition (iv) ensures that the quotient is irreducible and therefore, the degree of the rational aggregation function is (n, m).

Remark 2. It is clear that when $b_{st} = 0$ for all $(s, t) \neq (0, 0)$, we obtain a polynomial aggregation function (for more details see [15]).

Next example shows the existence of infinite rational binary aggregation functions.

Example 1. The following expression provides a family of rational binary aggregation functions

$$R_{n,\lambda}(x, y) = \frac{1 - (1 - x)^{n-1}(1 - y) - (1 - \lambda)(1 - (1 - x)^{n-1})y}{1 - (1 - \lambda)(1 - (1 - x)^{n-1})y}$$

for all $x, y \in [0, 1]$ and $n \geq 2$. These rational binary aggregation functions have degree (n, n) if $\lambda \notin \{1, 2\}$, degree $(n, 0)$ if $\lambda = 1$ and degree $(n - 1, n)$ if $\lambda = 2$. Note that they satisfy $R_{n,\lambda}(0, 1) = R_{n,\lambda}(1, 0) = 1$ and therefore, it is a family of disjunctions. In particular, taking $\lambda = 2$ and $n = 2$, we obtain the rational binary aggregation function of degree $(1, 2)$ given by

$$R_{2,2}(x, y) = \frac{x + y}{1 + xy}$$

for all $x, y \in [0, 1]$. From this family, we can generate the following family of conjunctions given by

$$1 - R_{n,\lambda}(1 - x, 1 - y) = \frac{x^{n-1}y}{1 - (1 - \lambda)(1 - x^{n-1})(1 - y)}.$$

It is clear from this example that the standard duality between conjunctions and disjunctions given by $1 - F(1 - x, 1 - y)$ transforms rational binary aggregation functions in other rational binary aggregation functions.

A first result from the definition is the continuity of the rational binary aggregation functions.

Proposition 1. *All rational binary aggregation functions are continuous.*

However, it is clear that not every rational function is an aggregation function. Next result determines the necessary and sufficient conditions that a rational function must satisfy in order to be a rational binary aggregation function.

Theorem 1. *A rational binary function $R : [0, 1]^2 \rightarrow [0, 1]$ of degree (n, m) given by the irreducible quotient*

$$R(x, y) = \frac{p(x, y)}{q(x, y)} = \frac{\displaystyle\sum_{\substack{0 \leq i,j \leq n \\ i+j \leq n}} a_{ij} x^i y^j}{\displaystyle\sum_{\substack{0 \leq s,t \leq m \\ s+t \leq m}} b_{st} x^s y^t} \tag{2}$$

is a binary rational aggregation function if, and only if, the next properties hold:

(i) $R(0,0) = 0$ and $R(1,1) = 1$.

(ii) $\displaystyle\sum_{\substack{0 \le s,t \le m \\ s+t \le m}} b_{st} x^s y^t \ne 0$ for all $x, y \in [0,1]$.

(iii) $\frac{\partial R(x,y)}{\partial x} \ge 0$ for all $x, y \in [0,1]$.

(iv) $\frac{\partial R(x,y)}{\partial y} \ge 0$ for all $x, y \in [0,1]$.

The first property of the previous theorem provides some conditions on the coefficients a_{ij} and b_{st} of the rational function R in a direct way.

Proposition 2. *Let* $R : [0,1]^2 \to [0,1]$ *be a rational function of degree* (n,m) *given by the irreducible quotient*

$$R(x,y) = \frac{\displaystyle\sum_{\substack{0 \le i,j \le n \\ i+j \le n}} a_{ij} x^i y^j}{\displaystyle\sum_{\substack{0 \le s,t \le m \\ s+t \le m}} b_{st} x^s y^t}. \tag{3}$$

Then the following statements hold:

(i) $R(0,0) = 0$ *if, and only if,* $a_{00} = 0$.

(ii) $R(1,1) = 1$ *if, and only if,* $\displaystyle\sum_{\substack{0 \le i,j \le n \\ i+j \le n}} a_{ij} = \sum_{\substack{0 \le s,t \le m \\ s+t \le m}} b_{st}$.

However, the transfer of the properties (ii), (iii) and (iv) of Theorem 1 to properties on the coefficients of the polynomials is harder in general for rational aggregation functions of any degree. Consequently, and with the aim of characterizing some rational binary aggregation functions, from now on we will restrict the study to rational binary aggregation functions of degree $(1,1)$ since it is straightforward to show that there is no rational binary aggregation function of degree $(0,n)$. We point out that the case of rational binary aggregation functions of degree $(n,0)$ (those that are polynomial) was studied in [12].

4   Rational Binary Aggregation Functions of Degree (1,1)

In this section we will characterize the binary rational aggregation functions of degree $(1,1)$. The problem relies on choosing the coefficients of the polynomials $p(x,y)$ and $q(x,y)$ in order to generate a rational function satisfying all the conditions given in Definition 3. First of all from Proposition 2 it follows that $a_{00} = 0$. Thus, the expression of the rational function $R(x,y)$ can be written as

$$R(x,y) = \frac{a_{10}x + a_{01}y}{b_{00} + b_{10}x + b_{01}y}$$

for all $x, y \in [0,1]$. Based on this expression, next result provides a characterization of rational aggregation functions of degree $(1,1)$, obtaining two subfamilies depending on whether a_{10} or a_{01} are equal to 1.

Theorem 2. *A binary operator* $R : [0,1]^2 \to [0,1]$ *is a rational binary aggregation function of degree* $(1,1)$ *if, and only if,* R *is given by either*

$$R(x,y) = \frac{x + (b_{00} + b_{10} + b_{01} - 1)y}{b_{00} + b_{10}x + b_{01}y} \tag{4}$$

for all $x,y \in [0,1]$ *where the coefficients satisfy the following conditions:*

1. $b_{00} > 0$
2. $b_{00} + b_{01} \geq 0$,
3. $b_{00} + b_{10} \geq 1$,
4. $b_{00} + b_{10} + b_{01} \geq 1$,
5. $b_{10} < 1$.

or

$$R(x,y) = \frac{(b_{00} + b_{10} + b_{01} - 1)x + y}{b_{00} + b_{10}x + b_{01}y} \tag{5}$$

for all $x,y \in [0,1]$ *where the coefficients satisfy the following conditions:*

1. $b_{00} > 0$
2. $b_{00} + b_{01} \geq 1$,
3. $b_{00} + b_{10} \geq 0$,
4. $b_{00} + b_{10} + b_{01} \geq 1$,
5. $b_{01} < 1$.

We would like to highlight that these families of rational aggregation functions only depend on three parameters that must fulfill certain restrictions.

Remark 3. Note that characterizing this family of aggregation functions in terms of conditions on the parameters allows us to check in a simple way whether a rational function of degree $(1,1)$ is an aggregation function. For example, consider the rational function of degree $(1,1)$ given by $R(x,y) = \frac{x+6y}{2+3x+3y}$. It is easy to see that we have considered the parameters $b_{00} = 2$, $b_{10} = 3$ and $b_{01} = 2$ in Expression (5) and that the chosen parameter value $b_{10} = 3$ does not satisfy Condition 5 of the previous theorem. Indeed, it is immediate to check that $R(1,0) = \frac{7}{5} > 1$ and therefore it does not satisfy the boundary conditions.

The following examples show some aggregation functions constructed according to the conditions stated in Theorem 2.

Example 2. Let us suppose that $b_{00} = 2$, $b_{10} = \frac{1}{3}$ and $b_{01} = \frac{2}{3}$. It is immediate to check Conditions 1–5 for Expression (4) and then the rational binary aggregation function is given by

$$R(x,y) = \frac{x + 2y}{2 + \frac{1}{3}x + \frac{2}{3}y}$$

for all $x,y \in [0,1]$.

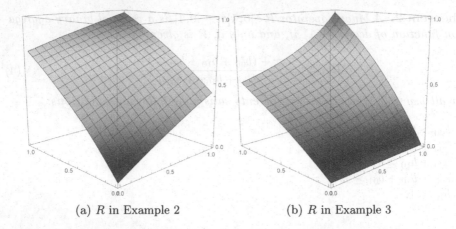

(a) R in Example 2   (b) R in Example 3

Fig. 1. Rational binary aggregation functions of degree $(1,1)$ obtained in Examples 2 and 3.

Example 3. Let us consider now $b_{00} = \frac{5}{3}$, $b_{10} = -1$ and $b_{01} = \frac{1}{3}$. It is easy to verify Conditions 1–5 for Expression (5) and then the rational binary aggregation function is given by

$$R(x,y) = \frac{y}{\frac{5}{3} - x + \frac{1}{3}y}$$

In Fig. 1, the rational binary aggregation functions obtained in Examples 2 and 3 are depicted.

Depending on the fields in which aggregation functions are going to be applied, it is crucial to know which additional properties they satisfy. Therefore, in the following results we will study the symmetry and idempotency properties for the family of binary rational aggregation functions of degree $(1,1)$.

Firstly, we will characterize the idempotent rational binary aggregation functions of degree $(1,1)$.

Proposition 3. *A binary operator $R : [0,1]^2 \to [0,1]$ is an idempotent rational binary aggregation function of degree $(1,1)$ if, and only if, R is given by either*

$$R(x,y) = \frac{x + (b_{00} - 1)y}{b_{00} + b_{10}(x - y)}$$

for all $x, y \in [0,1]$ where the coefficients satisfy the following conditions:

1. $b_{00} \geq 1$,
2. $0 < b_{10} \leq 1$,

or

$$R(x,y) = \frac{(b_{00} - 1)x + y}{b_{00} + b_{01}(y - x)}$$

for all $x, y \in [0,1]$ where the coefficients satisfy the following conditions:

1. $b_{00} \geq 1$,
2. $0 < b_{01} \leq 1$,

Next, we will provide some examples of idempotent rational binary aggregation functions constructed according to previous proposition.

Example 4. Some examples rational binary aggregation functions which are idempotent are the following ones:

i) $R(x,y) = \frac{x}{1+\frac{1}{2}(x-y)}$.

ii) $R(x,y) = \frac{x+y}{2+\frac{1}{2}(x-y)}$.

iii) Let us consider $c \in (0,1]$. Then,

$$R_c(x,y) = \frac{y}{1+c(y-x)}$$

is a family of idempotent binary rational aggregation function of degree (1,1).

These aggregation functions are shown in Fig. 2.

In the following result we will characterize the symmetric rational binary aggregation functions of degree $(1,1)$.

Proposition 4. *A binary operator $R : [0,1]^2 \to [0,1]$ is a symmetric rational binary aggregation function of degree $(1,1)$ if, and only if, R is given by*

$$R(x,y) = \frac{x+y}{2(1-b_{10}) + b_{10}(x+y)}$$

for all $x,y \in [0,1]$ where $b_{10} < 1$ with $b_{10} \neq 0$.

We can illustrate the previous result through the following example.

Example 5. Some examples rational binary aggregation functions of degree $(1,1)$ which are symmetric are the following ones:

i) $R(x,y) = \frac{x+y}{1+\frac{1}{2}(x+y)}$.

ii) $R(x,y) = \frac{x+y}{4-(x+y)}$.

These aggregation functions are shown in Fig. 3.

An immediate corollary which can be deduced from the study of the idempotence and the symmetry of these operators is the following one.

Corollary 1. *There are no rational binary aggregation functions of degree $(1,1)$ that are idempotent and symmetric.*

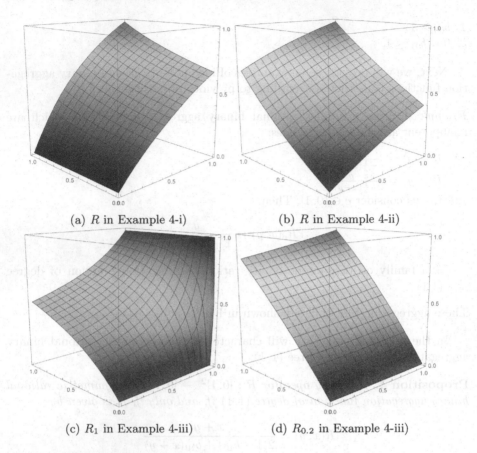

(a) R in Example 4-i)   (b) R in Example 4-ii)

(c) R_1 in Example 4-iii)   (d) $R_{0.2}$ in Example 4-iii)

Fig. 2. Idempotent rational binary aggregation functions of degree $(1, 1)$ obtained in Example 4.

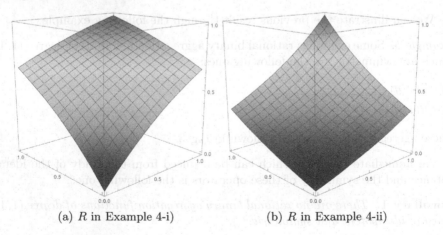

(a) R in Example 4-i)   (b) R in Example 4-ii)

Fig. 3. Symmetric rational binary aggregation functions of degree $(1, 1)$ obtained in Example 5.

5   Conclusions and Future Work

In this paper we have investigated rational binary aggregation functions. In particular, we have characterized all rational binary aggregation functions of degree $(1, 1)$ and we have also characterized those that are symmetric and idempotent.

As future work, first we want to analyze the performance and behavior of this family of aggregation functions in several applications where aggregation functions have proved to be useful. Then, we want to further investigate from the theoretical point of view this family. Namely, different properties such as associativity, the existence of left (right) neutral element or the existence of left (right) absorbing element have not been analyzed yet. The study of piece-wise binary aggregation functions in which each piece is given by a rational function is also worthy to study.

Acknowledgments. This paper is part of the R&D&I project PID2020-113870GB-I00- "Desarrollo de herramientas de Soft Computing para la Ayuda al Diagnóstico Clínico y a la Gestión de Emergencias (HESOCODICE)" funded by MCIN/AEI/10.13039/501100011033/.

References

1. Alsina, C., Frank, M.J., Schweizer, B.: Associative Functions: Triangular Norms and Copulas. Kluwer Academic Publishers, Dordrecht (2000)
2. Beliakov, G., Bustince Sola, H., Calvo Sánchez, T.: A Practical Guide to Averaging Functions. SFSC, vol. 329. Springer, Cham (2016). https://doi.org/10.1007/978-3-319-24753-3
3. Beliakov, G., Pradera, A., Calvo, T.: Aggregation Functions: A Guide for Practitioners. Studies in Fuzziness and Soft Computing. Springer, Cham (2007). https://doi.org/10.1007/978-3-540-73721-6
4. Calvo, T., Mayor, G., Mesiar, R.: Aggregation Operators: New Trends and Applications. Studies in Fuzziness and Soft Computing. Physica-Verlag HD (2002)
5. Fodor, J.C.: On rational uninorms. In: Proceedings of the First Slovakian-Hungarian Joint Symposium on Applied Machine Intelligence, Herlany, Slovakia, pp. 139–147 (2003)
6. Grabisch, M., Marichal, J.-L., Mesiar, R., Pap, E.: Aggregation Functions (Encyclopedia of Mathematics and Its Applications), 1st edn. Cambridge University Press, New York (2009)
7. Hamacher, H.: Über logische Aggregationen nicht binär explizierter Entscheidungskriterien - Ein axiomatischer Beiitrag zur normativen Entscheidungstheorie. In: Fischer, R.G. (ed.) Verlag, Frankfurt (1978)
8. Kerre, E.E., Nachtegael, M.: Fuzzy Techniques in Image Processing. Studies in Fuzziness and Soft Computing, vol. 52. Springer, New York (2000). https://doi.org/10.1007/978-3-7908-1847-5
9. Klement, E.P., Mesiar, R., Pap, E.: Triangular Norms. Kluwer Academic Publishers, Dordrecht (2000)
10. Mas, M., Mayor, G., Torrens, J.: t-Operators. Int. J. Uncertain. Fuzziness Knowl. Based Syst. **7**(1), 31–50 (1999)

11. Mas, M., Massanet, S., Ruiz-Aguilera, D., Torrens, J.: A survey on the existing classes of uninorms. J. Intell. Fuzzy Syst. **29**, 1021–1037 (2015)
12. Massanet, S., Riera, J.V., Ruiz-Aguilera, D.: On fuzzy polynomial implications. In: Laurent, A., Strauss, O., Bouchon-Meunier, B., Yager, R.R. (eds.) IPMU 2014. CCIS, vol. 442, pp. 138–147. Springer, Cham (2014). https://doi.org/10.1007/978-3-319-08795-5_15
13. Massanet, S., Riera, J.V., Ruiz-Aguilera, D.: On (OP)-polynomial implications. In: Alonso, J.M., Bustince, H., Reformat, M. (eds.) Proceedings of the 2015 Conference of the International Fuzzy Systems Association and the European Society for Fuzzy Logic and Technology (IFSA-EUSFLAT-2015), pp. 1208–1215. Atlantis Press (2015)
14. Massanet, S., Riera, J.V., Ruiz-Aguilera, D.: On rational fuzzy implication functions. In: Proceedings of IEEE World Congress on Computational Intelligence (IEEE WCCI), pp. 272–279 (2016)
15. Massanet, S., Torrens, J., Riera, J.V.: Aggregation functions given by polynomial functions. In: Proceedings of International Conference on Fuzzy Systems (FUZZ-IEEE), pp. 1–6 (2017)
16. Nelsen, R.B.: An Introduction to Copulas. Springer, New York (2006). https://doi.org/10.1007/0-387-28678-0
17. Torra, V., Narukawa, Y.: Modeling Decisions: Information Fusion and Aggregation Operators. Cognitive Technologies, Springer, Cham (2007). https://doi.org/10.1007/978-3-540-68791-7

Parameterized Pre-aggregation Function with Interval Values in Medical Decisions Making

Krzysztof Balicki[ID] and Paweł Drygaś[(⊠)][ID]

Institute of Computer Science, College of Natural Sciences,
University of Rzeszów, ul. Rejtana 16c, 35-959 Rzeszów, Poland
kbalicki@ur.edu.pl, paweldrs@gmail.com

Abstract. In this contribution the concept of parameterized operator in the interval-valued fuzzy sets, which is a pre-aggregation function, and their application in medical diagnosis is presented. Taking into account the widths of the intervals the type of interval operator measures are proposed in decision making problem. As it turns out, appropriate selection of the weight in the operator reduces the error in relation to one of the classes of decision.

Keywords: interval value aggregation function · interval value pre-aggregation function · interval order · general approximate reasoning

1 Introduction

Since the introduction of fuzzy sets by Zadeh [35], many new methods and theories behaving imprecision and uncertainty have been proposed. Interval-valued fuzzy sets ([27,36]) appeared very useful because of their flexibility in determining the grade of membership of elements into the concept under study (see [7]). Moreover, various applications of interval-valued fuzzy sets for solving real-life problems involving medical diagnosis, decision-making, pattern recognition or image thresholding were successfully proposed. Especially, many authors can be found in the literature who propose ([2,3,8,14–16,19,21,22,32,33,37,38]) different types of operators (interval-valued operators) study and used for the decision making problem. Also in classification the use of interval-valued fuzzy sets (IVFS) has led to improvements of the performance of some of the state-of-the-art algorithms for fuzzy rule-based classification systems ([28,29]). Moreover, the use of IVFS together with pre-aggregation functions provide better results than their fuzzy counterparts (see [5,30]).

The motivation to write this paper was to examine the effect on approximate inference has a parameter introduced in interval operator, i.e. an interval-valued pre-aggregation function. It was used in the generalized composition used in the inference algorithm. Interesting properties, in particular narrowing the range

© Springer Nature Switzerland AG 2022
D. Ciucci et al. (Eds.): IPMU 2022, CCIS 1601, pp. 421–433, 2022.
https://doi.org/10.1007/978-3-031-08971-8_35

values, of the introduced operator was the main motive for its use. Since the introduced operator is not monotonic due to none of the orders considered in [23], so the directional monotonicity is considered, that leads to the concept of pre-aggregation functions.

This work is composed of the following parts. Firstly, some notions and results useful in further considerations are recalled (Sect. 2). Next, we examine the parameterized operator in interval-valued fuzzy setting. E.g., the composition built with the new operator is examined (Sects. 3). Next, in Sect. 4 we propose an interval-valued multi conditional approximate reasoning algorithm based on the one presented in [12]. Finally, Sect. 5 provides an application of our definition of composition to a medical risk prediction problem.

2   Preliminaries

2.1   Interval-Valued Fuzzy Set Theory. Orders in the Interval-Valued Fuzzy Sets

Let $L^I = \{[\underline{a}, \overline{a}] : \underline{a}, \overline{a} \in [0,1], \underline{a} \leq \overline{a}\}$ denote a family of all subintervals of the unit interval. Let $X \neq \emptyset$.

Definition 1 (cf. [27,36]). *An interval-valued fuzzy set F in X is a mapping $F : X \to L^I$ such that $F(x) = [\underline{F}(x), \overline{F}(x)] \in L^I$ for $x \in X$. The classical monotonicity (partial order) for intervals is of the form*

$$[\underline{x}, \overline{x}] \leq_{L^I} [\underline{y}, \overline{y}] \Leftrightarrow \underline{x} \leq \underline{y} \ and \ \overline{x} \leq \overline{y}).$$

The family of all interval-valued fuzzy sets (relations) on the universe X ($X \times Y$) is denoted by $IVFS(X)$ ($IVFR(X \times Y)$).

The family of all interval-valued fuzzy sets on a given universe X with $\leq_{L^I}$ is partially ordered and moreover it is a complete lattice, with the operations joint and meet defined by

$$[\underline{x}, \overline{x}] \vee [\underline{y}, \overline{y}] = [\max(\underline{x}, \underline{y}), \max(\overline{x}, \overline{y})],$$

$$[\underline{x}, \overline{x}] \wedge [\underline{y}, \overline{y}] = [\min(\underline{x}, \underline{y}), \min(\overline{x}, \overline{y})].$$

Note that

$$\mathbf{1} = [1,1] \ and \ \mathbf{0} = [0,0]$$

are the greatest and the smallest element of $(L^I, \leq_{L^I})$, respectively.

Since in many real-life problems we need a linear order to be able to compare any two intervals, we are interested in extending the partial order $\leq_{L^I}$ to a linear one. The concept of, so called, admissible order would be useful there. We recall the notion of an admissible order, which was introduced in [4] and studied, for example, in [1] and [34]. The linearity of the order is needed in many applications of real problems, in order to be able to compare any two interval data [5].

Definition 2 ([4]). *An order $\leq_{Adm}$ in L^I is called admissible if it is linear and satisfies that for all $x, y \in L^I$, such that $x \leq_{L^I} y$, then $x \leq_{Adm} y$.*

Example 1 ([4]). The following are special cases of admissible linear orders on L^I:

- The Xu and Yager order:

$$[\underline{x}, \overline{x}] \leq_{XY} [\underline{y}, \overline{y}] \Leftrightarrow \underline{x} + \overline{x} < \underline{y} + \overline{y} \text{ or}$$

$$(\overline{x} + \underline{x} = \overline{y} + \underline{y} \text{ and } \overline{x} - \underline{x} \leq \overline{y} - \underline{y}).$$

- The first lexicographical order (with respect to the first variable), $\leq_{Lex1}$ defined as:

$$[\underline{x}, \overline{x}] \leq_{Lex1} [\underline{y}, \overline{y}] \Leftrightarrow \underline{x} < \underline{y} \text{ or } (\underline{x} = \underline{y} \text{ and } \overline{x} \leq \overline{y}).$$

2.2 Interval-Valued Aggregation Functions

Now we recall the concept of an aggregation function in L^I. Lets note, that we can consider aggregation with respect both to $\leq_{L^I}$ and $\leq_{Adm}$. Farther we will use the notation $\leq$ for both partial and admissible linear order.

Definition 3 ([20,34]). *An operation $\mathcal{A} : (L^I)^n \rightarrow L^I$ is called an interval-valued aggregation function if it is increasing with respect to the order $\leq$ (partial or total) and*

$$\mathcal{A}(\underbrace{0, ..., 0}_{n\times}) = 0, \quad \mathcal{A}(\underbrace{1, ..., 1}_{n\times}) = 1.$$

A special class of interval-valued aggregation functions is the one formed by the so called representable or decomposable interval-valued aggregation functions.

Definition 4 ([8,9]). *An interval-valued aggregation function $\mathcal{A} : (L^I)^n \rightarrow L^I$ is said to be representable if there exist aggregation functions $A_1, A_2 : [0,1]^n \rightarrow [0,1]$ such that*

$$\mathcal{A}(x_1, ..., x_n) = [A_1(\underline{x}_1, ... \underline{x}_n), A_2(\overline{x}_1, ..., \overline{x}_n)]$$

for all $x_1, ..., x_n \in L^I$, provided that $A_1 \leq A_2$.

Example 2. Lattice operations $\wedge$ and $\vee$ on L^I are examples of representable aggregation functions on L^I with respect to the partial order $\leq_{L^I}$, with $A_1 = A_2 = \min$ in the first case and $A_1 = A_2 = \max$ in the second one. However, $\wedge$ and $\vee$ are not interval-valued aggregation functions with respect to $\leq_{Lex1}$, $\leq_{Lex2}$ or $\leq_{XY}$. The following are other examples of representable interval-valued aggregation functions with respect to $\leq_{L^I}$.

- The projections:

$$\mathcal{A}_{P_1}([\underline{x}, \overline{x}], [\underline{y}, \overline{y}]) = [\underline{x}, \overline{x}], \quad \mathcal{A}_{P_2}([\underline{x}, \overline{x}], [\underline{y}, \overline{y}]) = [\underline{y}, \overline{y}].$$

– The representable product:

$$\mathcal{A}_{product}([\underline{x}, \overline{x}], [\underline{y}, \overline{y}]) = [\underline{xy}, \overline{xy}].$$

– The representable arithmetic mean:

$$\mathcal{A}_{mean}([\underline{x}, \overline{x}], [\underline{y}, \overline{y}]) = [\frac{\underline{x} + \underline{y}}{2}, \frac{\overline{x} + \overline{y}}{2}].$$

There are also other ways to build interval-valued aggregation functions with respect to $\leq_{L^I}$ or $\leq_{Adm}$.

Example 3. Let $A : [0, 1]^2 \to [0, 1]$ be an aggregation function. The function $\mathcal{A}_1 : (L^I)^2 \to L^I$, where

$$\mathcal{A}_1(x, y) = \begin{cases} [1, 1], & if \ (x, y) = ([1, 1], [1, 1]), \\ [0, A(\underline{x}, \overline{y})], & otherwise, \end{cases}$$

is a non-representable interval-valued aggregation function with respect to $\leq_{L^I}$.

2.3   Directional Monotonicity of IV Functions

In this part we recall the concept of the directional monotonicity of interval-valued fuzzy functions.

Definition 5 ([31])**.** *Let $v = (a_1, b_1, ..., a_n, b_n) \in (R^2)^n$ such that $(a_i, b_i) \neq \overrightarrow{0}$ for some $i \in \{1, ..., n\}$. A function $F : (L^I)^n \to L^I$ is said to be v-increasing if for all $x \in (L^I)^n$ and $c > 0$ such that $x + cv \in (L^I)^n$, it holds that*

$$F(x) \leq_{L^I} F(x + cv).$$

Theorem 1 ([31])**.** *Let $a, b > 0$ and $u, v \in (R^2)^n \setminus \{0\}$ such that for all $x \in (L^I)^n$ and $c > 0$ that satisfy $x + c(au + bv) \in (L^I)^n$, it holds that either $x + cau \in (L^I)^n$ or $x + cbv \in (L^I)^n$. Then, if a function $F : (L^I)^n \to L^I$ is both u-increasing and v-increasing, then F is $(au + bv)$-increasing.*

Definition 6 ([31])**.** *A function $F : (L^I)^n \to L^I$ is said to be an IV pre-aggregation function if it satisfies the following conditions:*

1) $F([0, 0], ..., [0, 0]) = [0, 0]$;
2) $F([1, 1], ..., [1, 1]) = [1, 1]$;
3) There exists a vector

$$v = ((a_1, b_1), ..., (a_n, b_n)) \in ((R^+)^2)^n,$$

such that F is v-increasing.

3   Parameterized Operators in Interval-Valued Fuzzy Setting

Now we will focus on an important element of this paper, i.e. a parameterized interval-valued operator.

Definition 7 (c.f. [13]). *Let* $n \in \mathbb{N}$, $i \in \{1, \ldots, n\}$ *and* $[\underline{x_i}, \overline{x_i}] \subset [0,1]$ *be intervals,* $t \in [0,1]$. *An operation* $W_t : (L^I)^n \to L^I$ *is given by*

$$W_t([\underline{x_1}, \overline{x_1}], \ldots, [\underline{x_n}, \overline{x_n}]) =$$

$$\left[\frac{\sum_{i=1}^n \underline{x_i} + t \sum_{i=1}^n \overline{x_i}(\overline{x_i} - \underline{x_i})}{n + t \sum_{i=1}^n (\overline{x_i} - \underline{x_i})}, \frac{\sum_{i=1}^n \overline{x_i} + t \sum_{i=1}^n \underline{x_i}(\overline{x_i} - \underline{x_i})}{n + t \sum_{i=1}^n (\overline{x_i} - \underline{x_i})} \right]. \tag{1}$$

Remark 1. If $t = 0$ then we obtain arithmetic mean.
If $t = 1$ then we obtain weak operator considered in [12, 26].

First, we consider the boundary conditions.

Theorem 2. *Let* $W_t : L^2 \to L$ *be the operator given by* (1). W_t *satisfy the boundary conditions, i.e.*

$$W_t(\mathbf{0}, \mathbf{0}) = \mathbf{0} \text{ and } W_t(\mathbf{1}, \mathbf{1}) = \mathbf{1};$$

Theorem 3. *Let* $W_t : L^2 \to L$ *be the operator given by* (1). W_t *is representable if and only if* $t = 0$.

Theorem 4. *Let* $W_t : L^2 \to L$ *be the operator given by* (1).

$$\underline{\min(x, y)} \leq \underline{W_t(x, y)};$$

$$\overline{W_t(x, y)} \leq \overline{\max(x, y)}.$$

Example 4. Let $t \in (0, 1]$, $x = [0, 1/4]$, $y = [0, 1/4]$, $u = [0, 0.5]$, $v = [0.5, 0.5]$. Then $\min(x, y) = [0, 1/4]$, $W_t(x, y) = [\frac{t}{4(t+4)}, \frac{1}{t+4}]$. This mean that operator W_t and min are not comparable.

Theorem 5. *Let* $W_t : L^2 \to L$ *be the operator given by* (1). *Then* W_t *is commutative, but it has no neutral element.*

Example 5. Let $t \in [0, 1]$ and $W_t : L^2 \to L$ be the operator given by (1). For $x = [0, 1]$ we have $W_t(x, x) = [t/(1+t), 1/(1+t)]$. In particular $W_0(x, x) = [0, 1]$, $W_1(x, x) = [1/2, 1/2]$.

Theorem 6. *Let* $t \in [0, 1]$ *and* $W : L^2 \to L$ *be the operator given by* (1). W_t *is idempotent if and only if* $t = 0$.

Theorem 7. *Let* $t \in [0, 1]$ *and* $W_t : L^2 \to L$ *be the operator given by* (1). W_t *is bisymmetric if and only if* $t = 0$.

Example 6. Let $x = [0, 0.5]$, $y = [0.1, 0.5]$, $z = [0.6, 1]$. Then we have $W_1(W_1(x, y), z) = [0.486674, 0.634756]$, $W_1(x, W_1(y, z)) = [0.308174, 0.454927]$.

Theorem 8. *Let $t \in [0, 1]$ and $W_t : L^2 \to L$ be the operator given by (1). Then W_t is not associative.*

Theorem 9. *Let $t \in [0, 1]$, $W_t : L^2 \to L$ be the operator given by (1). Then W_t is not transitive.*

Example 7. Let $t \in (0, 1]$, $x = [0.25, 0.375]$, $y = [0, 0]$ and $c = 0.08$. Then $W_1(x, y) = [0.139706, 0.191176]$;
$W_1(x + c[1, 0], y + c[0, 0]) = [0.169621, 0.190636]$,
i.e. weak operator W_1 is not $((1, 0), (0, 0))$ increasing.

Theorem 10. *Let $t \in (0, 1]$ $W_t : L^2 \to L$ be the operator given by (1).*

- W_t *is not* $((1, 0), (0, 0))$ *increasing;*
- W_t *is not* $((0, 1), (0, 0))$ *increasing;*
- W_t *is not* $((0, 0), (1, 0))$ *increasing;*
- W_t *is not* $((0, 0), (0, 1))$ *increasing.*

Corollary 1. *Let $t \in (0, 1]$. Operator W_t given by (1) is not increasing.*

Remark 2. If $t = 0$ then W_t is increasing.

Theorem 11. *Let $t \in (0, 1]$, $W_t : L^2 \to L$ be the operator given by (1). W_t is (a, b, a, b)- increasing for all $a \geq 0$, $b \geq 0$, $a + b > 0$.*

Theorem 12. *Let $t \in (0, 1]$, $W_t : L^2 \to L$ be operator given by (1). W_t is $(a, b, 0, 0)$- increasing for all $a \geq 0$, $b \geq 0$ such that $\frac{1}{3}a \leq b \leq 3a$.*

Proof. Let $t \in (0, 1]$. At the beginning we will show that W_t is $(3, 1, 0, 0)$-increasing. First observe, that $0 < c \leq \frac{1}{3}$. Using this inequality we get

$$c(3 - t(2c + \underline{x} + \overline{x})) > 0$$

and next

$$\underline{x} + 3c + \underline{y} + t(\overline{x} + c)(\overline{x} - \underline{x} - 2c) + t\overline{y}(\overline{y} - \underline{y}) \geq \underline{x} + \underline{y} + t\overline{x}(\overline{x} - \underline{x}) - t\overline{y}(\overline{y} - \underline{y})$$

and

$$2 + t(\overline{x} - \underline{x} + \overline{y} - \underline{y}) \geq 2 + t(\overline{x} - \underline{x} + \overline{y} - \underline{y} - 2c)$$

This implies

$$\frac{\underline{x} + 3c + \underline{y} + t(\overline{x} + c)(\overline{x} - \underline{x} - 2c) + t\overline{y}(\overline{y} - \underline{y})}{2 + t(\overline{x} - \underline{x} + \overline{y} - \underline{y} - 2c)} \geq \frac{\underline{x} + \underline{y} + t\overline{x}(\overline{x} - \underline{x}) - t\overline{y}(\overline{y} - \underline{y})}{2 + t(\overline{x} - \underline{x} + \overline{y} - \underline{y})}$$

and similarly

$$\frac{\overline{x} + c + \overline{y} + t(\underline{x} + 3c)(\overline{x} - \underline{x} - 2c) + t\underline{y}(\overline{y} - \underline{y})}{2 + t(\overline{x} - \underline{x} + \overline{y} - \underline{y} - 2c)} \geq \frac{\overline{x} + \overline{y} + t\underline{x}(\overline{x} - \underline{x}) - t\underline{y}(\overline{y} - \underline{y})}{2 + t(\overline{x} - \underline{x} + \overline{y} - \underline{y})}.$$

This means that W_t is $(3, 1, 0, 0)$- increasing. In a similar way, we can show that W_t is $(1, 3, 0, 0)$-increasing.

Using Theorem 1 we get that W is $(a, b, 0, 0)$-increasing for all a, b such that $\frac{1}{3}a \leq b \leq 3a$.

Example 8. Let $t = 1$, $v = (4, 1, 0, 0)$. Then W_t is not v-increasing, e.g. $x = [0, 0.15]$, $y = [0.85, 0.85]$, $c = 0.05$, and $W_t(x, y) = [0.405814, 0.465116]$, $W_t(x_{move}, y_{move}) = [0.405456, 0.506327]$

Theorem 13. *Let $t \in [0, 1]$. Operator $W_t : L^2 \to L$ given by (1) is IV pre-aggregation function.*

3.1 Preservation of Basic Properties by Operator W_t

In this article, we will only present some of the properties of the interval fuzzy relations that are listed below.

Definition 8. *A relation $R \in IVFR(X)$ is called*

(i) reflexive if $R(x, x) = \mathbf{1}$,
(ii) irreflexive if $R(x, x) = \mathbf{0}$,
(iii) W_t-transitive if $W_t(R(x, z), R(z, y)) \leq R(x, y)$.

We can observe that the examined operator preserves all of the listed properties.

Proposition 1 (cf. [12,23]). *Let $R_1, ..., R_n \in IVFR(X)$, $t \in [0, 1]$ and $W_t : (L^I)^n \to L^I$ be weak operator for $n \in N$.*

- *If there all $R_1, ..., R_n$ are reflexive/irreflexive, then $W_t(R_1, ..., R_n)$ is also reflexive/irreflexive,*
- *If the relations $R_1, ..., R_n \in IVFR(X)$ are symmetric, then $W_t(R_1, ..., R_n)$ is also symmetric,*
- *$R \in IVFR(X)$ is W_t-transitive if and only if R^{-1} is W_t-transitive and $R^{-1}(x, y) = R(y, x)$.*

3.2 Composition of Interval-Valued Fuzzy Relations

Based on the paper of Goguen [18] many authors study composition of fuzzy relations ([10,11]) or interval-valued fuzzy relations ([6,17,24,25]).

For arbitrary, non-empty sets X, Y, Z we define for relations $P \in IVFR(X \times Y)$, $R \in IVFR(Y \times Z)$ and for an interval-valued operation $\mathcal{B}$ the following:

- sup $-\mathcal{B}$ composition of relations P and R, denoted by $P \circ_{\vee_\mathcal{B}} R \in IVFR(X \times Z)$, where

$$(P \circ_{\vee_\mathcal{B}} R)(x, z) = \sup_{y \in Y} \mathcal{B}(P(x, y), R(y, z)).$$

- inf $-\mathcal{B}$ composition of relations P and R, denoted by $P \circ_{\wedge \mathcal{B}} R \in IVFR(X \times Z)$, where

$$(P \circ_{\wedge \mathcal{B}} R)(x, z) = \inf_{y \in Y} \mathcal{B}(P(x, y), R(y, z)).$$

Moreover, more general in respect to operations, but for finite sets $X, Y, Z \neq \emptyset$, interval-valued aggregation $\mathcal{A} : (L^I)^n \to L^I$ and the operation $\mathcal{B} : (L^I)^2 \to L^I$ with respect to the same order $\leq$ we have $\mathcal{A} - \mathcal{B}$ composition of relations P and R, denoted by $P \circ_{\mathcal{A}\mathcal{B}} R \in IVFR(X \times Z)$, where

$$(P \circ_{\mathcal{A}\mathcal{B}} R)_{ik} = \mathcal{A}_{j=1}^n (\mathcal{B}(P_{ij}, R_{jk})).$$

3.3   Basic Properties of $\mathcal{A} - W_t$ Composition

Now we consider some basic properties of composition built by studied operator W_t, interesting us with respect to the potential influence them to the application, i.e. monotonicity, symmetry or transititvity.

Proposition 2 (cf. [12,23]). *Let $\mathcal{A} : (L^I)^n \to L^I$ be an interval-valued aggregation function and $W_t : (L^I)^2 \to L^I$ be the operator with respect to the same order. Then the operation $\circ_{\mathcal{A}W_t}$ is monotonic with respect to the same order.*

Proposition 3 (cf. [12,23]). *Let $\mathcal{A} : (L^I)^n \to L^I$, be an interval-valued aggregation function and $W_t : (L^I)^2 \to L^I$ be the operator with respect to the same order.*

- *If $R, P \in IVFR(X)$ be symmetric relations, then*

$$R \circ_{\mathcal{A}W_t} P = (P \circ_{\mathcal{A}W} R)^{-1}.$$

- *If $R \in IVFR(X)$ is W_t-transitive, then $R \circ_{\mathcal{A}W_t} R \leq R$.*

4   Algorithm of General Approximate Reasoning

Based on [23] and [12], we will consider the following modification of the generalized approximate reasoning algorithm for interval-valued fuzzy set theory, where we propose use the parameterized operator.

5   Application

In this section, we apply the theoretical developments in a real-world problem, which consists in predicting the risk of suffering from a Cardio-Vascular Disease in ten years. CVDs are generally caused by some problem that hinders the blood flow, which could provoke affections in the heart. These class of diseases are associated with a high risk of suffering from severe illnesses such as thrombosis or heart attacks, which leads to a high death rate in many countries. So, it is important to predict the risk of suffering from CVDs so that doctors can appropriately treat their patients. In order to estimate such a risk, Spanish

---

Algorithm 1: General Approximate Reasoning

Input:
- Premises $\mathcal{D}_1, ..., \mathcal{D}_n, \mathcal{D}' \in IVFS(X)$;
- Conclusions $\mathcal{E}_1, ..., \mathcal{E}_n \in IVFS(Y)$;
- The interval-valued aggregation functions $\mathcal{A}, \mathcal{A}_k, \ k \in \{2, 3\}$;
- W_t operator given by (1);

Output: $\mathcal{E}'$

1 For each rule, the associated interval-valued fuzzy relation R_i is built, where $R_i \in IVFR(X \times Y)$ and

$$R_i(x, y) = \mathcal{A}_2(N_{IV}(\mathcal{D}_i(x)), \mathcal{E}_i(y))$$

for $i = 1, ..., n$ and $\mathcal{A}_2$ is an interval-valued aggregation function and N_{IV} is an interval-valued fuzzy negation;

2 The interval-valued aggregation functions $\mathcal{A}, \mathcal{A}_3$ and W_t are taken;

3 For each rule, it is calculated:

$$\mathcal{E}'_i(y) = \mathcal{A}_{x \in X}(W_t(\mathcal{D}'(x), R_i(x, y))), \text{ with } i = 1, ..., n;$$

4 It is computed: $\mathcal{E}' = \mathcal{A}_{3i=1,...,n}(\mathcal{E}'_i)$.

---

doctors use REGICOR tables that are composed of numbers representing the degree of suffering from a CVD based on some input variables like age, systolic and diastolic blood pressure, gender, presence or absence of diabetes and total or HDL cholesterol, among others. Later, the risk of suffering from a CVD can be categorized (low, medium or high) depending on the magnitude of these numbers. Consequently, this problem can be seen as a classification or a regression problem. In this paper, we tackle this problem as a regression one and, to face it, we propose to use an interval-valued fuzzy rule- based system to automatically predict the value of the risk. Specifically, for the sake of showing the behaviour of the theoretical developments, we only consider two input variables, which are the age and the systolic blood pressure of the patient, which are normalized in the range [0, 1]. The output variable is the risk of suffering from a CVD in the following ten years, which is ranged in [1, 19]. Dataset consists of 898 clinical cases obtained from the records of seven primary care health centers of Pamplona (Navarra, Spain) during 2008. Many of the values/data provided by the doctors have imperfect information associated with them, which has led us to use interval-valued fuzzy sets, as it was done in [12, 17, 23], where were considered this problem by different interval-valued aggregation functions in algorithm of approximate reasoning. Especially, in [12, 17, 23] there are present and applied the composition of interval-valued fuzzy relations using interval- valued aggregation functions. Now we present influence presented earlier IV operator on decision making problem in predicting the risk of suffering from a CVD in ten years.

5.1   Analyzing the Behaviour of the Different Aggregation Functions and Weak Operator when Accomplishing the Inference Process

We have tested the operator W_t and compare results with the results presented in [17], where authors received optimal results for the composition $\sup -T_L$, and with the results presented in [12], where the results for one of the classes were improved (operator W was used when accomplishing the inference process).

In [17] (Table 2) are presented the results obtained with the seven aggregation functions, when predicting the risk of the 898 patients composing our dataset, and in paper [12] the weak operator W was used for the same patients. Similarly, to mentioned papers we show the error obtained when predicting the risk of patients having low, moderate and high risk, respectively, whereas in the last one we present the error for all the patients. There we can observe that the results obtained with the Łukasiewicz t-norm are the best ones for patients having low and medium risks, moreover, regarding the total error, the fact that there is a larger number of patients having low (615 patients) or medium (252 patients) risk than patients having a high (31 patients) risk implies that the lowest total error of the system is provided when also using Łukasiewicz t-norm. Moreover, for the weak operator W we have $W = W_1$. This is the reason why we compare the W_t only with operator Łukasiewicz t-norm and weak operator W.

The results obtained are presented in the table below (Table 1).

Table 1. Results obtained when using the Łukasiewicz t-norm, the weak operator W and the parameterized operator W_t to perform the composition operation.

Composition	Low	Medium	High	Total
$\sup -T_L$ [17]	13.20	1.33	22.55	10.19
$\sup -W$	13.28	1.31	23.13	10.89
$\sup -W_t$	13.21	1.32	23.04	10.37

As we can see, we have received comparable results, comparably low error, so using the operator W_t for approximate reasoning seems to be a good solution. And this suggests the validity of examining the impact of the W_t operator examined in this paper on approximate reasoning for other types of data and/or on other methods of making decisions. Moreover, for this data set, the optimal parameter $t = 0$. was selected, which prompted the question of the existence of an optimal t parameter for data sets of different types. Such considerations are planned for future work.

6   Conclusions

In this paper some interval-valued operations with respect to the partial, linear or directional isotonicity were presented. But mainly concentrated on study basic properties of parameterized operator (IV pre-aggregation function). Moreover, application with new operator was proposed, especially in decision model of medical diagnosis support.

In the future, in addition to examining the effect of the W_t operator on approximate reasoning for other data types and other decision-making methods, we would like to consider other generalizations of operations. After introducing weak operation and the parametric family that generalized it, we observed that it is a generalization of the arithmetic mean. In the future, we would like to consider similar generalizations of other means or aggregations.

Acknowledgements. The authors would like to thank to the Editors and the anonymous reviewers for their most valuable comments and suggestions for a significant improvement of this article, and for indicating further generalizations of the operations under consideration.

References

1. Asiain, M.J., et al.: About the use of admissible order for defining implication operators. In: Carvalho, J.P., Lesot, M.-J., Kaymak, U., Vieira, S., Bouchon-Meunier, B., Yager, R.R. (eds.) IPMU 2016. CCIS, vol. 610, pp. 353–362. Springer, Cham (2016). https://doi.org/10.1007/978-3-319-40596-4_30
2. Barrenechea, E., Fernandez, J., Pagola, M., Chiclana, F., Bustince, H.: Construction of interval-valued fuzzy preference relations from ignorance functions and fuzzy preference relations: application to decision making. Knowl. Based Syst. **58**, 33–44 (2014)
3. Bentkowska, U., Pękala, B., Bustince, H., Fernandez, J., Jurio, A., Balicki, K.: N-reciprocity property for interval-valued fuzzy relations with an application to group decision making problems in social networks. Int. J. Uncertain. Fuzziness Knowl. Based Syst. **25**(Suppl. 1), 43–72 (2017)
4. Bustince, H., Fernandez, J., Kolesárová, A., Mesiar, R.: Generation of linear orders for intervals by means of aggregation functions. Fuzzy Sets Syst. **220**, 69–77 (2013)
5. Bustince, H., Galar, M., Bedregal, B., Kolesárová, A., Mesiar, R.: A new approach to interval-valued Choquet integrals and the problem of ordering in interval-valued fuzzy set applications. IEEE Trans. Fuzzy Syst. **21**(6), 1150–1162 (2013)
6. Bustince, H., Burillo, P.: Mathematical analysis of interval-valued fuzzy relations: application to approximate reasoning. Fuzzy Sets Syst. **113**, 205–219 (2000)
7. Bustince, H., et al.: A historical account of types of fuzzy sets and their relationships. IEEE Trans. Fuzzy Syst. **24**(1), 174–194 (2016)
8. Deschrijver, G., Kerre, E.E.: Implicators based on binary aggregation operators in interval-valued fuzzy set theory. Fuzzy Sets Syst. **153**(2), 229–248 (2005)
9. Deschrijver, G.: Quasi-arithmetic means and OWA functions in interval-valued and Atanassov's intuitionistic fuzzy set theory. In: EUSFLAT-LFA 2011, Aix les Bains, France, pp. 506–513 (2011)
10. Drewniak, J., Kula, K.: Generalized compositions of fuzzy relations. Int. J. Uncertain. Fuzziness Knowl.-Based Syst. **10**, 149–163 (2002)
11. Drewniak, J., Pękala, B.: Properties of fuzzy relations powers. Kybernetika **43**, 133–142 (2007)

12. Drygaś, P., Pękala, B., Balicki, K., Kosior, D.: Influence of new interval-valued pre-aggregation function on medical decision making. In: 2020 IEEE International Conference on Fuzzy Systems (FUZZ-IEEE) (2020). https://doi.org/10.1109/FUZZ48607.2020.9177801

13. Drygaś, P.: On a special class of interval-valued fuzzy operators. In: The 11th International Summer School on Aggregation Operators (AGOP) (2021)

14. Dyczkowski, K.: Intelligent Medical Decision Support System Based on Imperfect Information. The Case of Ovarian Tumor Diagnosis. Studies in Computational Intelligence. Springer, Cham (2018). https://doi.org/10.1007/978-3-319-67005-8

15. Dyczkowski, K., Wygralak, M.: On triangular norm-based generalized cardinals and singular fuzzy sets. Fuzzy Sets Syst. **133**(2), 211–226 (2003)

16. Dyczkowski, K., Wójtowicz, A., Żywica, P., Stachowiak, A., Moszyński, R., Szubert, S.: An intelligent system for computer-aided ovarian tumor diagnosis. In: Filev, D., et al. (eds.) Intelligent Systems'2014. AISC, vol. 323, pp. 335–343. Springer, Cham (2015). https://doi.org/10.1007/978-3-319-11310-4_29

17. Elkano, M., Sanz, J.A., Galar, M., Pękala, B., Bentkowska, U., Bustince, H.: Composition of interval-valued fuzzy relations using aggregation functions. Inf. Sci. **369**, 690–703 (2016)

18. Goguen, A.: L-fuzzy sets. J. Math. Anal. Appl. **18**, 145–174 (1967)

19. Jasiulewicz-Kaczmarek, M., Żywica, P.: The concept of maintenance sustainability performance assessment by integrating balanced scorecard with non-additive fuzzy integral. Eksploatacja i Niezawodnosc - Maintenance Reliab. **20**(4), 650–661 (2018)

20. Komorníková, M., Mesiar, R.: Aggregation functions on bounded partially ordered sets and their classification. Fuzzy Sets Syst. **175**, 48–56 (2011)

21. Paternain, D., Jurio, A., Barrenechea, E., Bustince, H., Bedregal, B., Szmidt, E.: An alternative to fuzzy methods in decision-making problems. Expert Syst. Appl. **39**(9), 7729–7735 (2012)

22. Pękala, B., Bentkowska, U., Bustince, H., Fernandez, J., Galar, M.: Operators on intuitionistic fuzzy relations. In: Proceedings of FUZZ IEEE 2015 (2015)

23. Pękala, B.: Uncertainty Data in Interval-Valued Fuzzy Set Theory. SFSC, vol. 367. Springer, Cham (2019). https://doi.org/10.1007/978-3-319-93910-0

24. Pękala, B., et al.: Operations on interval matrices. In: Kryszkiewicz, M., Peters, J.F., Rybinski, H., Skowron, A. (eds.) RSEISP 2007. LNCS (LNAI), vol. 4585, pp. 613–621. Springer, Heidelberg (2007). https://doi.org/10.1007/978-3-540-73451-2_64

25. Pękala, B., et al.: Properties of interval-valued fuzzy relations, Atanassov's operators and decomposable operations. In: Hüllermeier, E., Kruse, R., Hoffmann, F. (eds.) IPMU 2010. CCIS, vol. 80, pp. 647–655. Springer, Heidelberg (2010). https://doi.org/10.1007/978-3-642-14055-6_68

26. Pękala, B., Drygaś, P., Knap, M., Gil, D., Kwitkowski, B.: Preference and weak interval-valued operator in decision making problem. In: IEEE CIS International Conference on Fuzzy Systems 2021 - FUZZ-IEEE 2021, Luxembourg, July 2021

27. Sambuc, R.: Fonctions ϕ-floues: application á l'aide au diagnostic en pathologie thyroidienne. Ph.D. thesis, Université de Marseille, France (in French) (1975)

28. Sanz, J., Fernandez, A., Bustince, H., Herrera, F.: Improving the performance of fuzzy rule-based classification systems with interval-valued fuzzy sets and genetic amplitude tuning. Inf. Sci. **180**(19), 3674–3685 (2010)

29. Sanz, J., Fernández, A., Bustince, H., Herrera, F.: A genetic tuning to improve the performance of fuzzy rule-based classification systems with interval-valued fuzzy sets: degree of ignorance and lateral position. Int. J. Approximate Reasoning **52**(6), 751–766 (2011)

30. Sesma-Sara, M., Mesiar, R., Bustince, H.: Weak and directional monotonicity of functions on Riesz spaces to fuse uncertain data. Fuzzy Sets Syst. **386**, 145–160 (2020)
31. Sesma-Sara, M., De Miguel, L., Mesiar, R., Fernandez, J., Bustince, H.: Interval-valued pre-aggregation functions: a study of directional monotonicity of interval-valued functions. In: FUZZIEEE 2019 (2019)
32. Stachowiak, A., Dyczkowski, K., Wójtowicz, A., Żywica, P., Wygralak, M.: A bipolar view on medical diagnosis in OvaExpert system. In: Flexible Query Answering Systems 2015. AISC, vol. 400, pp. 483–492. Springer, Cham (2016). https://doi.org/10.1007/978-3-319-26154-6_37
33. Yager, R.R., Xu, Z.: Intuitionistic and interval-valued intuitionistic fuzzy preference relations and their measures of similarity for the evaluation of agreement within a group. Fuzzy Optim. Decis. Mak. **8**, 123–139 (2009)
34. Zapata, H., et al.: Interval-valued implications and interval-valued strong equality index with admissible orders. Int. J. Approximate Reasoning **88**, 91–109 (2017)
35. Zadeh, L.A.: Fuzzy sets. Inf. Control **8**, 338–353 (1965)
36. Zadeh, L.A.: The concept of a linguistic variable and its application to approximate reasoning. Inf. Sci. **8**, Part I, 199–251, Part II, 301–357, Inf. Sci. **9**, Part III, 43–80 (1975)
37. Żywica, P., Dyczkowski, K., Wójtowicz, A., Stachowiak, A., Szubert, S., Moszyński, R.: Development of a fuzzy-driven system for ovarian tumor diagnosis. Biocybern. Biomed. Eng. **36**(4), 632–643 (2016)
38. Żywica, P.: Modelling medical uncertainties with use of fuzzy sets and their extensions. In: Medina, J., Ojeda-Aciego, M., Verdegay, J.L., Perfilieva, I., Bouchon-Meunier, B., Yager, R.R. (eds.) IPMU 2018. CCIS, vol. 855, pp. 369–380. Springer, Cham (2018). https://doi.org/10.1007/978-3-319-91479-4_31

Int-FLBCC: Exploring Fuzzy Consensus Measures via Penalty Functions

Guilherme Schneider[1], Bruno Moura[1], Eduardo Monks[1],
Helida Santos[2,3](✉), Adenauer Yamin[1], and Renata Reiser[1]

[1] Universidade Federal de Pelotas, Pelotas, Brazil
{gbschneider,bmpdmoura,emmonks,adenauer,reiser}@inf.ufpel.edu.br
[2] Universidade Federal do Rio Grande, Rio Grande, Brazil
[3] Universidad Publica de Navarra - ISC, Pamplona, Spain
helida@furg.br

Abstract. The dynamic consolidation of resources in the infrastructures of services, programs, and information provided by cloud environments is a widely used strategy, modeling uncertainties to improve energy consumption in cloud computing. Determining the best configuration to reallocate overloaded hosts, underutilized or/and shallow load nodes may directly influence the resource utilization and the quality of service offered by the cloud-computing infrastructure. In this scenario, this work aims to address the uncertainty information related to computational power, communication cost, and RAM consumption in cloud environments based on the Int-FLBCC model. An interval-valued fuzzy logic approach is used, assuring reliability in the evaluation data through fuzzy consensus measures. The consensual analysis considers fusion data based on penalty functions. The evaluations considered two approaches: (i) consensus measures and penalty functions in fuzzy values related to membership functions; and (ii) consensus measures performed on fuzzy sets defining the input and output variables, building a new consensual analysis modeling the cohesion of several terms related to the same linguistic variables, and the coherence between fuzzy sets referring to the lowest and highest projections. Simulations pointed to promising results in the treatment of imprecision in Int-FLBCC.

Keywords: Consensus analysis · Penalty functions · Cloud computing · Interval-valued fuzzy logic

1 Introduction

The computing infrastructures generally used to run applications in Cloud Computing (CC) use resources like data centers known to demand large amounts of electrical energy, increasing providers' operating costs and harming the

This study was partially supported by CAPES, CNPq (309160/2019-7; 311429/2020-3), PqG/FAPERGS (21/2551-0002057-1) and FAPERGS/CNPq PRONEX (16/2551-0000488-9).

D. Ciucci et al. (Eds.): IPMU 2022, CCIS 1601, pp. 434–447, 2022.
https://doi.org/10.1007/978-3-031-08971-8_36

environment [12]. There have been estimated around 8.6 million data centers worldwide, including 3 million in the United States (US) [24] alone. Each data center typically hosts from 50,000 to 80,000 servers, demanding 25–30 MW of power consumption [27]. According to the Natural Resources Defense Council[1] report, in 2014, the USA data centers consumed 70 billion kilowatts/hour (kWh) corresponding to 1.8% of total US electricity consumption [26]. And, in 2020, US data centers used around 73 billion kWh.

The search for energy efficiency without losing performance led to the proposal of several concepts, with emphasis on CC, which consists of a distribution of computing services (allocation of servers, storage, database) with no need for the user to have large investments in equipment, and also with cost/payment associated with using time [23].

Within this context and related works [22], this study contemplates the migration and consolidation of Virtual Machines (VM) with an approach for efficient use of physical servers in CC environments. And, simultaneously, we seek to maintain a satisfactory standard via Quality of Service (QoS) and Service Level Agreements (SLA) [2]. The energy consumption minimization problem under QoS constraints is analytically complex and dependent on dynamic VM consolidation, which is an NP-Hard problem [13].

The main objective of this work is the conception of an approach that explores the premises and extensions of Fuzzy Logic (FL), dealing with the uncertainties of experts in specifying their preferences regarding the definition of membership functions, focusing on the consensus measures of fuzzy sets defined through penalty functions and thus, contributing to support decision making for the evaluation of loads on servers, and the resulting allocation of VM, considering the component *Int-FLBCC* (*Interval Fuzzy Load Balancing* for *Cloud Computing*) [22].

The paper is organized as follows. Sections 2 and 3 presents, respectively, Fuzzy Logic and Cloud Computing basic concepts. Section 4, provides the modeling of the *Int-FLBCC* component, including database detailing, fuzzification, rule base, inference and defuzzification. Section 4.3 describes the method for measuring consensus between fuzzy sets designed to evaluate *Int-FLBCC* modeling. Finally, in Sect. 5, the conclusions and future work are reported.

2 Preliminary Concepts on Fuzzy Logic

Zadeh proposed Type-2 Fuzzy Logic (T2FL) in 1975 as an extension of FL [20]. Its use is related to the insufficiency of the traditional Fuzzy Set Theory (FS) in modeling the uncertainties inherent to the definition of the membership functions of antecedents and consequences in a Fuzzy Inference System (FIS) [18]. These sets can be used when there is uncertainty on the degree, shapes, and/or parameters of the membership functions [15], providing a potential strategy for dealing with uncertainties in models based on multiple criteria obtained from different experts, or extracted from simulators.

---

[1] https://www.nrdc.org/.

T2FL is based on the theory of Type-2 Fuzzy Sets (T2FS), modeling the handling of uncertainties and allowing to specify an interval $\mu_{\tilde{A}} = [\underline{\mu_{\tilde{A}}}, \overline{\mu_{\tilde{A}}}]$ as the membership degree of such element x in a Fuzzy Set (FS) A [19]. Hence, T2FS extends the concepts of FL, modeling imprecision as an additional skill considering non-specificity as another important aspect of uncertainty. And in this context, reflecting this lack of specification throughout the extent of the membership degree, which is determined by an FS, in this case, a subinterval of the unit interval $[0, 1]$.

This work considers Interval-valued Fuzzy Sets, a class of Type-2 Fuzzy Logic (IT2FL) interpreting the membership degree of the element x of the universe χ in a fuzzy set A, as a numerical value in the membership interval $\mu_A(x)$. So it is not possible to specify exactly what this value is and, therefore, only provide limits (upper and lower) corresponding to the extremes of its range of relevance. The interval approach related to membership degree makes it possible to model the opinions of multiple experts when assigning membership degrees, aiding in decision making based on multiple criteria. One of the metrics that evaluates the imprecision in the different attributions of specialists is identified as the diameter of the interval membership degree.

Definition 1. *[15] Let $\chi \neq 0$ be a universe. A T2FS A is characterized by a type-2 membership function (T2MF) where $0 \leq \mu_{\tilde{A}}(x, u) \leq 1$, $x \in \chi$ and $u \in J_x \subseteq [0, 1]$. For each T2FS $\tilde{A}$ we have $\tilde{A} = \{((x, u), \mu_{\tilde{A}}(x, u)) \mid \forall x \in \chi, \forall u \in J_x \subseteq [0, 1]\}$.*

A T2FS assigns each element on χ to a function $A(x): [0, 1] \rightarrow [0, 1]$, which is defined as $\{(x, A(x, t)) : x \in \chi, t \in [0, 1]\}$, when $A(x, .): [0, 1] \rightarrow [0, 1]$ is given by $A(x, t) = A(x)(t)$, for each $x \in \chi$, $t \in [0, 1]$. And, an FS $A(x)$ is a real number in $[0, 1]$, for all $x \in \chi$.

The set of all closed intervals in $[0, 1]$ is $L([0, 1]) = \{[\underline{X}, \overline{X}]: \underline{X}, \overline{X} \in [0, 1]^2, \underline{X} \leq \overline{X}\}$.

Definition 2. *[28] An interval-valued fuzzy set A on the universe $\chi \neq \emptyset$ is a mapping $A: \chi \rightarrow L([0, 1])$, such that the membership degree of $x \in \chi$ is given by $A(x) = [\underline{A}(x), \overline{A}(x)]$, where $\underline{A}(x), \overline{A}(x) : \chi \rightarrow [0, 1]$ are mappings defining the lower and the upper bound of the membership interval $A(x)$.*

It is observed that the interval-valued fuzzy sets [11] are a particular case of T2FS. Let A be a T2FS $A(x) = [\underline{A}(x), \overline{A}(x)]$, $\forall x \in \chi$. Moreover, let $A, B \in T2FS$. For every $x \in \chi$, we have the operators:
(i) Complement: $A_C(x) = [1 - \overline{A}(x), 1 - \underline{A}(x)]$;
(ii) Union: $A(x) \cup B(x) = [\max(\underline{A}(x), \underline{B}(x)), \max(\overline{A}(x), \overline{B}(x))]$;
(iii) Intersection: $\mu_{A \cap B}(x) = [\min(\underline{A}(x), \underline{B}(x)), \min(\overline{A}(x), \overline{B}(x))]$.

We denote $A(x) = X$, $B(x) = Y$, $\forall x \in \chi$, U as the set of all real subintervals in the unit interval $[0, 1]$ and let $\mathbb{U}$ be the interval-valued fuzzy set values, the partial order $(\leq)$ on $\mathbb{U}$ is the Product Order [16] defined by: $X \leq Y \Leftrightarrow \underline{X} \leq \underline{Y} \wedge \overline{X} \leq \overline{Y}$.

The functions that qualify the intersections and unions in the fuzzy context are modeled by triangular norms and conorms, respectively. According to [19] and considering the intervals in $\mathbb{U}$, one has that an interval-valued triangular norm $\mathbb{T}\colon \mathbb{U}^2 \to \mathbb{U}$ is a mapping satisfying the commutativity, associativity, and monotonicity properties, and having $\mathbb{1} \in U$ as the neutral element. Some examples of frequently used t-norms are: Standard Intersection, Algebraic Product, Drastic Intersection, Łukasiewicz Product and Nilpotent Minimum. Similarly, an interval-valued triangular conorm $\mathbb{S}\colon \mathbb{U}^2 \to \mathbb{U}$ is a mapping satisfying the commutativity, associativity, and monotonicity properties, and having $\mathbb{0} \in U$ as the neutral element. The corresponding t-conorms are: Standard Union, Probabilistic Sum, Drastic Union, Łukasiewicz Sum and Nilpotent Maximum.

A system based on T2FL can estimate input and output functions, through the use of heuristics and interval-valued techniques. Figure 1 shows the architecture of an inference system based on T2FL. The main parts of a Type-2 Fuzzy Inference System (T2FIS) are briefly described as follows:

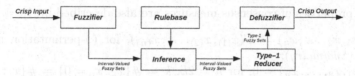

Fig. 1. Interval-Valued Fuzzy Inference System Architecture

(1) Fuzzifier: associating an input value with an interval-valued function and not simply with a single value in U. In other words, uncertainty related to input membership functions is inserted into the inference mechanism. Thus, for each input $A(x)$ an input vector $\mathbf{x} = (x_1, x_2, \ldots, x_n) \in \chi^n$ when $n \in \mathbb{N}^*$ is related to the vectors in $\mathbb{U}^n$: $(\overline{A}(x_1), \overline{A}(x_2), \ldots, \overline{A}(x_n))$ and $(\underline{A}(x_1), \underline{A}(x_2), \ldots, \underline{A}(x_n))$.

(2) Rulebase (RB): constituted by rules that classify the Linguistic Variables (LV) according to the interval-valued T2FS.

(3) Inference: performs the inference operations between input data and the RB demanded conditions, generating the action to be done in the T2FIS.

(4) Defuzzification: two main steps are considered in this part:

  (*i*) **Type-1 Reducer**: transforms the T2FS into an FS, when searching the best FS that represents the T2FS, necessarily satisfying the following premise: when all uncertainty disappears, the result of the T2FIS ends up being an FIS [31].

  (*ii*) **Defuzzlfler**: T2FIS uses the average of the lower and upper limits $\underline{y}$ and $\overline{y}$ from the output $B(x)$, $y = (\underline{Y} + \overline{Y})/2 = (\underline{B}(x) + \overline{B}(x))/2$, $\forall x \in \chi$, where $\underline{y}$ and $\overline{y}$ values are calculated by Karnik and Mendel iterative method (KM algorithm), obtained by a traditional method like the centroid, in the inference system.

2.1 Fuzzy Consensus Measures

Fuzzy consensus measures (FCM) are functions promoting a formal model to achieve a concordance analysis among fuzzy system inputs, often employed in decision-making contexts. According to [1], fuzzy consensus measures are functions defined on the unit interval $[0, 1]$ modeling the accordance related to values provided by a group of experts in modeling of a fuzzy system. Such consensus analysis is mainly concerned with two properties, namely: (i) the unanimity, interpreting the complete consensus when all inputs are the same; and (ii) the minimal consensus, resulting in a null-consensus whenever the inputs lie on the unit interval extremes (0 and 1).

Definition 3. *[1, Def 7]. A function $C \colon [0, 1]^n \to [0, 1]$ is called a FCM if it hols:*

(C1) $C(a, \dots, a) = 1$, $\forall a \in [0, 1]$ *(Unanimity)*;
(C2) $C(0, 1) = C(1, 0) = 0$ *(Minimum consensus for $n = 2$)*.

Other properties of consensus measures are also described in [1]:

(C3) $C(x_1, x_2, \dots, x_n) = C(x_{(1)}, x_{(2)}, \dots, x_{(n)})$, for ( )-permutation and $x \in [0, 1]^n$ *(Symmetry)*;
(C4) $C(x_1, x_2, \dots, x_n) = 0$, for $n = 2k$, $k = \#\{x_i \colon x_i = 0\} = \#\{x_i \colon x_i = 1\}$ *(Maximum Dissension)*;
(C5) $C(x_1, x_2, \dots, x_n) = C(N(x_1), N(x_2), \dots, N(x_n))$, when N is a strong fuzzy negation *(Reciprocity)*;
(C6) $C(x) = C(x, x) = C(x, \dots, x)$, $\forall x \in [0, 1]$ *(Replication Invariance)*;
(C7) For $n = 2k$, let half of the evaluations be equal, $\mathbf{a} = (a, \dots, a)$ where $\mathbf{a} \in [0, 1]^k$. If $|a - x_j| \leq |a - y_j|$ for $j = 1, \dots, k$, then $C(a, x_1, x_2, \dots, x_k) \geq C(a, y_1, y_2, \dots, y_k)$. *(Monotonicity w.r.t. the Majority)*.

2.2 Fuzzy Penalty Functions

A penalty function (PF) consists in a powerful tool to determine up to what extent a given output is similar (dissimilar) to a set of inputs. They have been widely studied in the context of consensus analysis in fuzzy systems based on decision making [1,6]. Penalty functions can dissuade decision makers from making extreme judgments that make consensual results unfeasible [32]. Aggregation methods based on penalty functions are also capable of proposing different weights, adapting the consensus analysis from the problem modeling to a specific situation [4,7].

The application and use of penalty functions is not restricted to the aggregation of expert opinions, but can be applied to distance measurements aiming at a consensus in benchmarking [14] experiments in current applications via simulations [9,17]. The diversity of definitions of fuzzy penalty functions has been formalized via preference relations [3], fuzzy subsethood measures [25], pre-aggregations [8] and many others fuzzy aggregators [5]. We will use the following definition:

Definition 4. *[30, Def. 10] A function $P : [0,1]^{n+1} \to \mathbb{R}$ is a PF if holds:*

P1: *$P(x_1, \ldots, x_n,, y) \geq c$, $\forall x_i \in [0,1]^n, i \in \mathbb{N}_n, y \in [0,1]$, and $c \in \mathbb{R}$;*
P2: *$P(x_1, \ldots, x_n, y) = c$ if and only if $x_i = y$, $\forall i \in \mathbb{N}_n$, and*
P3: *$P(\lambda(x_1, \ldots, x_n, y) + (1 - \lambda)(x'_1, \ldots x'_n, y')) \leq \max(P(x_1, \ldots, x_n, y), P(x'_1, \ldots, x'_n, y'))$, i.e. P is quasi-convex in y, for $x_1, \ldots, x_n, y, x'_1, \ldots, x'_n, y' \in [0,1]$.*

Example 1. Consider the quasi-convex function $f_{\|}(x,y) = |x - y|$ and a permutation $() : \{1, \ldots, n\} \to \{1, \ldots, n\}$. The function $P_{\|} : [0,1]^{n+1} \to \mathbb{R}$, given as

$$P_{\|}(x_1, \ldots, x_n, y) = \sum_{i=1}^{n} f_{\|}(x_{(i)} - y) = \sum_{i=1}^{n} |x_{(i)} - y|, \tag{1}$$

is a penalty function w.r.t. $N_S(x) = 1 - x$ and, in this case, the median average is the fusion value, see Sect. 4 [32].

3   Cloud Computing

CC models allow convenient, ubiquitous and on-demand access to a cluster of computing resources, such as network, servers, storage, applications and services, which can be quickly allocated and released with minimal management effort or interaction with the service provider [12]. CC models have five essential characteristics:

- **On-Demand Self-Service:** a consumer can unilaterally provision computing resources, such as server time and network storage, as needed, without requiring interaction with each service provider;
- **Broad Network Access:** the resources are available on the Internet and are accessed through standard mechanisms that allow the use on heterogeneous platforms, integrating mobile phones, tablets, notebooks and workstations;
- **Resource Pooling:** the provider's computing resources are pooled to serve multiple consumers using a multi-tenancy model, with different physical and virtual resources dynamically assigned according to consumer demand;
- **Fast Elasticity:** resources can be provisioned and released elastically, in some cases automatically by demand. To the consumer, the resources available for provisioning often appear limitless and can be consumed in any amount at any time;
- **Measured Services:** allowing resources to be monitored, controlled, and reported on. Providing transparency for both the provider and the service consumer.

Despite CC being widely present in industry and technological development, several challenger research proposals have been considered in the literature [33].

- **Automated Service Provisioning:** allocating and reallocating VMs according to the client's needs. The reallocations must respect the Service Level Objective (SLO) of the environment and seek to minimize the operational cost. However, it is not easy to determine how to map SLO to meet QoS requirements, such as defining CPU and memory utilization, as they sway every second. So, justifying the need for updates and optimizations in the online system to deal with these provisions.
- **Virtual Machine Migration:** virtualization has brought several advantages to Cloud Computing, such as the possibility of creating VMs in order to balance the load throughout the data center, and also, enabling robustness and fast provisioning response. The main benefits of VM migration are to optimize resource usage despite not being a simple task. Currently, detecting workload spikes and initiating a migration lacks the agility to respond to sudden, dynamic workload changes.
- **Server consolidation:** is an effective way to maximize resource utilization while minimizing the energy consumption of the CC environment. The technique of migrating VMs in real time is constantly used to consolidate VMs that are allocated on multiple, often underutilized, servers. However, the server consolidation problem in a data center is evaluated as a variant of the Packaging Problem (Bin-Packing), considered an NP-Hard computational problem [10].
- **Energy Management:** improving energy efficiency is also relevant and IT companies are constantly evolving, aiming at new technologies not only for financial reasons, but to comply with government regulations and environmental standards.

4   Int-FLBCC: Type-2 Fuzzy System Modelling

Int-FLBCC is responsible for checking the Usage Level (U) of the physical machine related to load balancing. It considers a rule base acting in three stages: Fuzzification, Inference and Defuzzification, returning as an output the utilization level of each physical machine in CC environments.

4.1   Modelling the Membership Functions in the Fuzzyfication Step

Through the study of the variables with a specialist, the LVs related to each of the uncertainty variables were transformed into FST2, using a trapezoidal function to represent their membership functions. The reading of the settings applied in the simulated CC environment is performed to measure three attributes: computational power (COP), communication cost (COC) and RAM consumption (RAM). These values are applied to a standard scale considering the interval

$[0; 10]$, and in order to obtain the membership degrees for COP, COC and RAM take Eqs. (2), (3) and (4), respectively.

$$COP = (h_i(MM)/\max COP \cdot 10) \tag{2}$$
$$COC = ((10 \cdot h_i(UtoB))/\min COC) \tag{3}$$
$$RAM = (h_i(UtoR)/\max Ram) \cdot 10 \tag{4}$$

where h_i represents the ith host of the cloud environment, MM is the Maximum MIPS (Millions of Instructions Per Second) available in host i considering all Processing Elements (PE), $UtoB$ represents the bandwidth usage on host i, $UtoR$ is the RAM use on host i, $\max PC$ is the total MIPS value of the best host in the CC environment, $\min COC$ is the lowest communication cost in the CC environment, and $\max RAM$ is the RAM consumption of the best host. And, Eqs. (2) (3) and (4) are associated to the T2FS of Figs. 2(a), 2(b), 2(c) and 2(d) modelling COP, COC, RAM and U variables, respectively. Next, see the description of the related Linguistic Terms (LT).

(i) COP: "Limited" (CPL), "Reasonable" (CPR) and "High" (PCH - best case), where $COP = a$ and $a \in [0; 10]$, as seen in Fig. 2(a).
(ii) COC: "Small" (CCS - best case), "Average" (CCA) and "Big" (CCB), where $COC = b$ and $b \in [0; 10]$, as seen in Fig. 2(b).
(ii) RAM: "Small" (RAMS - best case), "Average" (RAMA) and "High" (RAMH), where $RAM = c$ and $c \in [0; 10]$, as seen in Fig. 2(c).
(iii) U (output): "Low" (UL), "Average" (UA) and "High" (UH), where $U = d$ and $d \in [0; 10]$. The host usage (utilization) level U is also adapted for the standard scale as seen in Fig. 2(d).

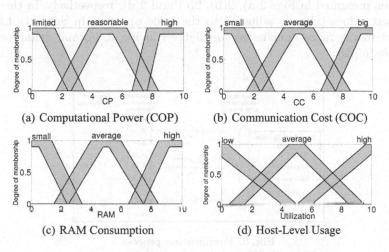

(a) Computational Power (COP)   (b) Communication Cost (COC)

(c) RAM Consumption   (d) Host-Level Usage

Fig. 2. Variables of the *Int-FLBCC* model.

Table 1. COP membership functions

COP	$\mu_A(x)$	$\mu_A(x)$
CPL	$\begin{cases} 1, & \text{if } 0 \le x < 1.5 \\ \frac{-x+3.5}{2}, & \text{if } 1.5 \le x < 3.5 \\ 0, & \text{otherwise.} \end{cases}$	$\begin{cases} 0.9, & \text{if } 0 \le x < 0.45 \\ -0.46x + 1.1, & \text{if } 0.45 \le x < 2.4 \\ 0, & \text{otherwise.} \end{cases}$
CPR	$\begin{cases} \frac{x-1.6}{2.2}, & \text{if } 1.6 \le x < 3.8 \\ 1, & \text{if } 3.8 \le x < 6.3 \\ \frac{-x+8.4}{2.1}, & \text{if } 6.3 \le x < 8.4 \\ 0, & \text{otherwise.} \end{cases}$	$\begin{cases} 0.45x - 1,17, & \text{if } 2.6 \le x < 4.6 \\ 0.9, & \text{if } 4.6 \le x < 5.4 \\ -0.45x + 3.33, & \text{if } 5.4 \le x < 7.4 \\ 0, & \text{otherwise.} \end{cases}$
CPH	$\begin{cases} x - 6.65, & \text{se } 6.65 \le x < 7.65 \\ 1, & \text{if } 7.65 \le x < 10 \\ 0, & \text{otherwise.} \end{cases}$	$\begin{cases} \frac{18x}{17} - 8.1, & \text{if } 7.65 \le x < 8.5 \\ 0.9, & \text{if } 8.5 \le x < 10 \\ 0, & \text{otherwise.} \end{cases}$

Table 2. COC membership functions

COC	μ_{B_x}	μ_{B_x}
CCS	$\begin{cases} 1, & \text{if } 0 \le x < 1.35 \\ \frac{-x+3.4}{2.05}, & \text{if } 1.35 \le x < 3.4 \\ 0, & \text{otherwise.} \end{cases}$	$\begin{cases} 0.9, & \text{if } 0 \le x < 0.5 \\ \frac{-0.9x+2.16}{1.9}, & \text{if } 0.5 \le x < 2.4 \\ 0, & \text{otherwise.} \end{cases}$
CCA	$\begin{cases} \frac{x-1.5}{2.5}, & \text{if } 1.5 \le x < 4 \\ 1, & \text{if } 4 \le x < 6 \\ \frac{-x+8.5}{2.5}, & \text{if } 6 \le x < 8.5 \\ 0, & \text{otherwise.} \end{cases}$	$\begin{cases} \frac{0.9x-2.25}{2.3}, & \text{if } 2.5 \le x < 4.8 \\ 0.9, & \text{if } 4.8 \le x < 5.2 \\ \frac{-0.9x+6.75}{2.3}, & \text{if } 5.2 \le x < 7.5 \\ 0, & \text{otherwise.} \end{cases}$
CCB	$\begin{cases} \frac{x-6.5}{2}, & \text{if } 6.5 \le x < 8.5 \\ 1, & \text{if } 8.5 \le x < 10 \\ 0, & \text{otherwise.} \end{cases}$	$\begin{cases} \frac{18x-13.5}{3.4}, & \text{if } 7.5 \le x < 9.2 \\ 0.9, & \text{if } 9.2 \le x < 10 \\ 0, & \text{otherwise.} \end{cases}$

Table 3. RAM membership functions

RAM	$\mu_A(x)$	$\mu_A(x)$
RAMS	$\begin{cases} 1, & \text{if } 0 \le x < 1.5 \\ \frac{-x+3.5}{2}, & \text{if } 1.5 \le x < 3.5 \\ 0, & \text{otherwise.} \end{cases}$	$\begin{cases} 0.9, & \text{if } 0 \le x < 0.45 \\ -0.4615x + 1.1076, & \text{if } 0.45 \le x < 2.4 \\ 0, & \text{otherwise.} \end{cases}$
RAMA	$\begin{cases} \frac{x-1.6}{2.2}, & \text{if } 1.6 \le x < 3.8 \\ 1, & \text{if } 3.8 \le x < 6.3 \\ \frac{-x+8.4}{2.1}, & \text{if } 6.3 \le x < 8.4 \\ 0, & \text{otherwise.} \end{cases}$	$\begin{cases} 0.45x - 1,17, & \text{if } 2.6 \le x < 4.6 \\ 0.9, & \text{if } 4.6 \le x < 5.4 \\ -0.45x + 3.33, & \text{if } 5.4 \le x < 7.4 \\ 0, & \text{otherwise.} \end{cases}$
RAMH	$\begin{cases} x - 6.65, & \text{if } 6.65 \le x < 7.65 \\ 1, & \text{if } 7.65 \le x < 10 \\ 0, & \text{otherwise.} \end{cases}$	$\begin{cases} \frac{18x}{17} - 8.1, & \text{if } 7.65 \le x < 8.5 \\ 0.9, & \text{if } 8.5 \le x < 10 \\ 0, & \text{otherwise.} \end{cases}$

Table 4. U membership functions

U	μ_{C_x}	μ_{C_x}
UL	$\begin{cases} 1, & \text{if } 0 \le x < 0.4 \\ -0.2178x + 1.089, & \text{if } 0.4 \le x < 5 \\ 0, & \text{otherwise.} \end{cases}$	$\begin{cases} -0.225x+0.9, & \text{if } 0 \le x < 4 \\ 0, & \text{otherwise.} \end{cases}$
UA	$\begin{cases} 0.25x-0.125, & \text{if } 0.5 \le x < 4.5 \\ 1, & \text{if } 4.5 \le x < 5.5 \\ -0.25x+2.375, & \text{if } 5.5 \le x < 9.5 \\ 0, & \text{otherwise.} \end{cases}$	$\begin{cases} 0.257x-0.3855, & \text{if } 1.5 \le x < 5 \\ -0.257x+2.185, & \text{if } 5 \le x < 8.5 \\ 0, & \text{otherwise.} \end{cases}$
UH	$\begin{cases} 0.222x-1.11, & mboxif\ 5 \le x < 9.5 \\ 1, & \text{if } 9.5 \le x, \\ 0, & \text{otherwise.} \end{cases}$	$\begin{cases} 0.225x-1.35, & \text{if } 6 \le x < 10 \\ 0, & \text{otherwise.} \end{cases}$

In CC environments, the host usage level is uncertain and imprecise due to several factors, such as sway in computing power, bandwidth and memory available at the time of execution of applications required by users. It is considered an online algorithm applying the T2FS approach that goes across the available hosts in the CC architecture, obtaining the usage level at each iteration.

In Tables 1, 2, 3 and 4 one finds the algebraic expressions of the membership functions presented in Figs. 2(a), 2(b), 2(c) and 2(d), respectively. In this step, the input values (already adjusted to the scale observed in Subsect. 4.1) are mapped to the fuzzy domain, as highlighted in Fig. 3. Formal definitions are available in [22].

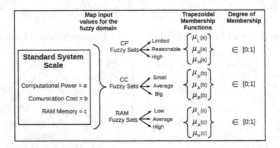

Fig. 3. Fuzzification process

4.2 Rule Base Acting on Inference System and the Defuzzification Step

The Rule Base of *Int-FLBCC* considers three factors: (i) the LVs name the FS, making the system modelling closer to the real world; (ii) "AND" logical connectives are used to create the relationship between the input variables; (iii) the implication functions follows the rule: If "x_1 is A_1" AND "x_2 is A_2" AND "x_3 is A_3" then "y is B", i.e. the *modus ponens* type (affirmative mode).

In the Inference process, operations occur between the FS, combining rule antecedents and implication functions via the *generalized modus ponens* operator. This phase occurs in three steps detailed below.

(i) Application of Fuzzy Operation: since the rules are formed by the "AND" fuzzy operator, the application uses the MIN (minimum) method on the values returned from the fuzzification;
(ii) Application of the Fuzzy Implication Method: combines the value obtained from the fuzzy operator and the output FS values of each rule, using the MIN (minimum) method on these combinations;
(iii) Application of the Fuzzy Aggregation Method: considers the composition of the fuzzy results of the output of each rule, using the MAX (maximum) method, thus creating a single fuzzy region to be analyzed on the next phase.

Defuzzification is the transformation of the region resulting from the inference, and the technique used was the Center of the Area. This method calculates the area centroid composed by the T2FIS output (union of all rule contributions demonstrated in Subsect. 4.2, defined as $u = \left(\sum_{i=1}^{N} u_i \cdot \mu_{OUT}(u_i) \right) / \sum_{i=1}^{N} \mu_{OUT}(u_i)$.

4.3 Consensus Measures Applied on the Int-FLBCC Approach

Let $\chi = \{u_1, \ldots, u_{100}\}$ and $x_i = \mu_X(u_i) \in [0, 1]$ be a fuzzy value in a fuzzy set X. The consensual analysis in [29] considers extended aggregation functions AM and exp_α, applied over $X \in \{H_{In}, M_{In}, L_{In}, H_{out}, M_{Out}, L_{Out}\}$ and defined by:

$$C_{AM}(X) = \frac{1}{n} \sum_{i=1}^{n} 1 - |x_{(i)} - x_{(n-i+1)}| \quad \text{and} \quad C_{\exp_\alpha}(X) = \frac{1}{\alpha} \ln \sum_{i=1}^{n} \frac{e^{1-|x_{(i)}-x_{(n-i+1)}|}}{n}.$$

Each consensus method is performed over the input of the linguistic variables related to the fuzzy sets of COP, COC and RAM, also including U, the output variable. We use $\alpha = 1$ and $n = 100$ to analyze the fuzzy consensus.

The final results for the crisp analysis of C_{AM} and $C_{\exp_\alpha}$ are described in Table 5, 2nd and 3rd columns, respectively. Closed values are observed in the consensus analysis for both aggregation operators. The highest consensus values are associated with "Low" linguistic term, as it has greater symmetry. The lowest consensus is associated with "Average" linguistic term. As for the upper/lower functions on the interval-valued case, the analysis helps to determine the size of the Footprint of Uncertainty (FOU). Knowing that the increase in the FOU will imply more uncertainty, by reducing the FOU it is expected to improve the precision in the detection of host loads, and in the recommendation for the migration of VMs.

The $C1$ and $C2$ properties are generalized from $\mathcal{L}_{[0,1]}$ to $\mathcal{L}_{\mathcal{F}_\chi}$.

Definition 5. *[21] For* $\chi = \{x_1, \ldots, x_m\} \in \mathcal{F}_\chi$, *a function* $C \colon \bigcup_{n=1}^{\infty} (\mathcal{F}_\chi)^n \to [0,1]$ *is a fuzzy consensus measure of fuzzy sets ($\mathcal{L}_{\mathcal{F}_\chi}$-FSCM) in $\mathcal{F}_\chi$ if the following holds:*

$C1 \colon C(X, \ldots, X) = 1, \forall X \in \mathcal{F}_\chi;$

$C2 \colon C(X_\chi, X_\emptyset) = C(X_\emptyset, X_\chi) = 0, \forall u \in \chi.$

Proposition 1. *The function* $\mathcal{C}_C \colon \bigcup_{n=1}^{\infty} (\mathcal{F}_{\chi_m})^n \to [0,1]$ *in Eq.(5) is an $\mathcal{L}_{\mathcal{F}_\chi}$-FSCM:*

$$\mathcal{C}_C(X_1, \ldots, X_n) = \frac{1}{m} \sum_{i=1}^{m} C(\mu_{X_1}(u_i), \ldots, \mu_{X_n}(u_i)). \tag{5}$$

In Table 5, columns 7 and 8, the final results are presented. The consensus based on $\mathcal{C}_{C_{AM}}$ and $\mathcal{C}_{C_{\exp}}$ functions are obtained by the average mean of the lower and upper analysis. The results indicated a high level of consensus between the functions developed. For $\mathcal{C}_{C_{AM}}$ the lowest consensus value was 0.7529 and the highest was 0.9101. And, for $\mathcal{C}_{C_{\exp}}$ the lowest and highest values were 0.7774 and 0.9148, respectively.

In Table 6, there is a summary of the results obtained with (weighted) penalty function in the Int-FLBCC consensual analysis. For AM, the highest consensus value is the U_A and the lowest value is in the linguist variable COP_H, with values 0.8598 and 0.4725, respectively. See, e.g., the highest values occurred in the medium linguist term of each variable. And, the lowest values were in the related low linguist terms. In the use of penalty functions via weighted arithmetic mean as presented in Tables 6 and 7, increments occur in the consensus analysis, since the highest value (0.9072) refers to U_A and the lowest value (0.8892) is related to COP_R.

Table 5. Int-FLBCC - Consensual Analysis

X	C_{AM}	C_{exp}	$[\underline{X},\overline{X}]$	C_{AM}	C_{exp}	C_{AM}	C_{exp}
COP_L	0.6600	0.7245	$\underline{L}_{In}$	0.7546	0.8028	0.8776	0.8962
			$\overline{L}_{In}$	0.5100	0.5989		
COP_R	0.9800	0.9803	$\underline{M}_{In}$	0.9640	0.9649	0.7780	0.7984
			$\overline{M}_{In}$	0.9900	0.9901		
COP_H	0.4900	0.5956	$\underline{H}_{In}$	0.9142	0.9339	0.7529	0.8257
			$\overline{H}_{In}$	0.4200	0.5267		
RAM_S	0.6351	0.7070	$\underline{L}_{In}$	0.7526	0.8013	0.8787	0.8970
			$\overline{L}_{In}$	0.5100	0.5989		
RAM_A	0.9938	0.9938	$\underline{M}_{In}$	0.9880	0.9882	0.7650	0.7774
			$\overline{M}_{In}$	0.9700	0.9803		
RAM_H	0.5900	0.6717	$\underline{H}_{In}$	0.6442	0.7229	0.8879	0.9114
			$\overline{H}_{In}$	0.4200	0.5267		
COC_S	0.6351	0.7070	$\underline{L}_{In}$	0.7480	0.7981	0.8936	0.9081
			$\overline{L}_{In}$	0.5351	0.6215		
COC_A	0.9938	0.9938	$\underline{M}_{In}$	0.9820	0.9822	0.7930	0.8078
			$\overline{M}_{In}$	0.9800	0.9802		
COC_B	0.5900	0.6717	$\underline{H}_{In}$	0.6921	0.7542	0.8989	0.9130
			$\overline{H}_{In}$	0.4900	0.5798		
U_L	0.5200	0.5755	$\underline{L}_{In}$	0.6490	0.6900	0.9101	0.9148
			$\overline{L}_{In}$	0.4692	0.5169		
U_A	0.9800	0.9801	$\underline{M}_{In}$	0.9824	0.9824	0.8150	0.8187
			$\overline{M}_{In}$	0.9800	0.9801		
U_H	0.5000	0.5560	$\underline{H}_{In}$	0.6940	0.7209	0.8732	0.8867
			$\overline{H}_{In}$	0.4405	0.4886		

Table 6. Penalty Consensual analysis

X	C_{AM}	$C_{penalty}$	$C_{Weighted-Penalty}$
COP_L	0.7432	0.7273	0.9007
COP_R	0.9990	0.7492	0.8892
COP_H	0.5230	0.4725	0.9050
RAM_S	0.7101	0.6888	0.8942
RAM_A	0.9999	0.7699	0.8925
RAM_H	0.6565	0.6201	0.8900
COC_S	0.7101	0.6888	0.8942
COC_A	0.9999	0.7699	0.8925
COC_B	0.6565	0.6415	0.8900
U_L	0.6566	0.7926	0.9072
U_A	0.9994	0.8598	0.9050
U_H	0.6366	0.7874	0.9048

Table 7. Weights in the Penalty Function

Y	$Weight$
$y < 0.2$	1
$0.2 < y \leq 0.6$	2
$0.6 < y \leq 1$	3

5   Conclusions

Int-FLBCC was developed in order to determine the usage level of physical machines in a CC environments, dynamically consolidating VM. The consensual analysis was performed on data referring to Computational Power, Communication Cost, RAM Consumption (as input data), and Usage Level (as output data). The problem of measuring the consensus degree was investigated, not only comparing fuzzy values, but in a more comprehensive way reporting to the fuzzy sets when modeling membership functions, associated with attributes in the fuzzy inference system. Such strategy contributes to better specify the FOU, by defining the region between upper and lower bound of each interval-valued membership functions. The preserved consensus measure degrees are obtained by average functions (AM, exp). We have a more realistic approach by taking an extended method based on weighted penalty functions. The confidence degree models the uncertainty, preserving the best selection option in CC environments. Future works intend to apply penalty methods [9] based on weighted averages, seeking to increase the evaluation of the accuracy of the uncertainty present in the CC environment.

References

1. Beliakov, G., Calvo, T., James, S.: Consensus measures constructed from aggregation functions and fuzzy implications. Knowl.-Based Syst. **55**, 1–8 (2014)
2. Beloglazov, A.: Energy-efficient management of virtual machines in data centers for cloud computing. Ph.D. thesis, University of Melbourne (2013)

3. Bustince, H., Barrenechea, E., Calvo, T., James, S., Beliakov, G.: Consensus in multi-expert decision making problems using penalty functions defined over a cartesian product of lattices. Inf. Fusion **17**, 56–64 (2014)
4. Bustince, H., Pagola, M., Barrenechea, E.: Construction of fuzzy indices from fuzzy DI-subsethood measures: application to the global comparison of images. Inf. Sci. **177**(3), 906–929 (2007)
5. Bustince, H., Fernandez, J., Burillo, P.: Penalty function in optimization problems: a review of recent developments. In: Pelta, D.A., Cruz Corona, C. (eds.) Soft Computing Based Optimization and Decision Models. SFSC, vol. 360, pp. 275–287. Springer, Cham (2018). https://doi.org/10.1007/978-3-319-64286-4_17
6. Calvo, T., Beliakov, G.: Aggregation functions based on penalties. Fuzzy Sets Syst. **161**(10), 1420–1436 (2010)
7. Calvo, T., Mesiar, R., Yager, R.R.: Quantitative weights and aggregation. IEEE Trans. Fuzzy Syst. **12**(1), 62–69 (2004)
8. Dimuro, G.P., Mesiar, R., Bustince, H., Bedregal, B., Sanz, J.A., Lucca, G.: Penalty-based functions defined by pre-aggregation functions. In: Medina, J., et al. (eds.) IPMU 2018. CCIS, vol. 854, pp. 403–415. Springer, Cham (2018). https://doi.org/10.1007/978-3-319-91476-3_34
9. Elkano, M., et al.: Consensus via penalty functions for decision making in ensembles in fuzzy rule-based classification systems. Appli. Soft Comput. **67**, 728–740 (2018)
10. Ferdaus, M.H., Murshed, M., Calheiros, R.N., Buyya, R.: Virtual machine consolidation in cloud data centers using ACO Metaheuristic. In: Silva, F., Dutra, I., Santos Costa, V. (eds.) Euro-Par 2014. LNCS, vol. 8632, pp. 306–317. Springer, Cham (2014). https://doi.org/10.1007/978-3-319-09873-9_26
11. Gehrke, M., Walker, C., Walker, E.: Some comments on interval valued fuzzy sets. Intl. J. Intell. Syst. **11**(10), 751–759 (1996)
12. Gourisaria, M.K., Samanta, A., Saha, A., Patra, S.S., Khilar, P.M.: An extensive review on cloud computing. In: Raju, K.S., Senkerik, R., Lanka, S.P., Rajagopal, V. (eds.) Data Engineering and Communication Technology. AISC, vol. 1079, pp. 53–78. Springer, Singapore (2020). https://doi.org/10.1007/978-981-15-1097-7_6
13. Hiltunen, M.A., Schlichting, R.D., Jung, G., Pu, C., Joshi, K.R.: Mistral: dynamically managing power, performance, and adaptation cost in cloud infrastructures. In: 2010 IEEE 30th Intefnational Conference on Distributed Computing System, ICDCS, pp. 62–73 (2010)
14. Hornik, K., Meyer, D.: Deriving consensus rankings from benchmarking experiments. In: Decker, R., Lenz, H.-J. (eds.) Advances in Data Analysis. SCDAKO, pp. 163–170. Springer, Heidelberg (2007). https://doi.org/10.1007/978-3-540-70981-7_19
15. Karnik, N.N., Mendel, J.M.: Introduction to type-2 fuzzy logic systems. In: 1998 IEEE International Conference on Fuzzy Systems Proceedings, vol. 2, pp. 915–920 (1998)
16. Klement, E., Mesiar, R., Pap, E.: Triangular norms. position paper I: basic analytical and algebraic properties. Fuzzy Sets Syst. **143**(1), 5–26 (2004)
17. Martínez-Panero, M.: Consensus perspectives: glimpses into theoretical advances and applications. In: Herrera-Viedma, E., García-Lapresta, J.L., Kacprzyk, J., Fedrizzi, M., Nurmi, H., Zadrozny, S. (eds.) Consensual Processes. Studies in Fuzziness and Soft Computing, vol. 267, pp. 179–193. Springer (2011). https://doi.org/10.1007/978-3-642-20533-0_11
18. Mendel, J.M.: Fuzzy sets for words: a new beginning. In: Fuzzy Systems, FUZZ 2003. The 12th IEEE International Conference on, vol. 1, pp. 37–42 (2003)

19. Mendel, J.M., John, R.I., Liu, F.: Interval type-2 fuzzy logic systems made simple. IEEE Trans. Fuzzy Syst. **14**(6), 808–821 (2006). https://doi.org/10.1109/TFUZZ. 2006.879986

20. Mendel, J., Hagras, H., Tan, W.W., Melek, W.W., Ying, H.: Introduction to type-2 fuzzy logic control: theory and applications. John Wiley & Sons (2014)

21. Moura, B.M.P., Schneider, G.B., Yamin, A.C., Pilla, M.L., Reiser, R.H.S.: IntfGrid: BoT tasks scheduling exploring fuzzy type-2 in computational grids. In: 2018 IEEE International Conference on Fuzzy Systems, FUZZ-IEEE, pp. 1–8, July 2018

22. Moura, B.M., Schneider, G.B., Yamin, A.C., Santos, H., Reiser, R.H., Bedregal, B.: Interval-valued fuzzy logic approach for overloaded hosts in consolidation of virtual machines in cloud computing. Fuzzy Sets Syst. (2021). https://doi.org/10. 1016/j.fss.2021.03.001

23. Nathani, A., Chaudhary, S., Somani, G.: Policy based resource allocation in IAAS cloud. Futur. Gener. Comput. Syst. **28**(1), 94–103 (2012)

24. Nayak, S.K., Panda, S.K., Das, S.: Renewable energy-based resource management in cloud computing: a review. In: Tripathy, A.K., Sarkar, M., Sahoo, J.P., Li, K.-C., Chinara, S. (eds.) Advances in Distributed Computing and Machine Learning. LNNS, vol. 127, pp. 45–56. Springer, Singapore (2021). https://doi.org/10.1007/978-981-15-4218-3_5

25. Santos, H.S., Couso, I., Bedregal, B.R.C., Takác, Z., Minárová, M., Asiain, A., Barrenechea, E., Bustince, H.: Similarity measures, penalty functions, and fuzzy entropy from new fuzzy subsethood measures. Int. J. Intell. Syst. **34**(6), 1281–1302 (2019)

26. Shehabi, A., et al.: United states data center energy usage report (2016)

27. Simmon, E.: Evaluation of cloud computing services based on nist sp 800–145 (2018). https://doi.org/10.6028/NIST.SP.500-322

28. Sola, H.B., Fernandez, J., Hagras, H., Herrera, F., Pagola, M., Barrenechea, E.: Interval type-2 fuzzy sets are generalization of interval-valued fuzzy sets: toward a wider view on their relationship. IEEE Trans. Fuzzy Syst. **23**(5), 1876–1882 (2015)

29. de Souza Oliveira, L., Argou, A., Dilli, R., Yamin, A., Reiser, R., Bedregal, B.: Exploring fuzzy set consensus analysis in IoT resource ranking. Eng. Appl. Artif. Intell. **109**, 104617 (2022)

30. Wilkin, T., Beliakov, G.: Weakly monotonic averaging functions. Int. J. Intell. Syst. **30**(2), 144–169 (2015)

31. Wu, D., Nie, M.: Comparison and practical implementation of type-reduction algorithms for type-2 fuzzy sets and systems. In: FUZZ-IEEE, pp. 2131–2138. IEEE (2011)

32. Yager, R.R., Rybalov, A.: Understanding the median as a fusion operator. Int. J. General Syst. **26**(3), 239–263 (1997)

33. Zhang, Q., Cheng, L., Boutaba, R.: Cloud computing: state-of-the-art and research challenges. J. Internet Serv. Appli. **1**(1), 7–18 (2010). https://doi.org/10.1007/s13174-010-0007-6

Aggregated Fuzzy Equivalence Relations in Clustering Process

Olga Grigorenko[(✉)][iD] and Valerijs Mihailovs[iD]

Institute of Mathematics and Computer Science, University of Latvia,
Raina bulv. 29, Riga 1459, Latvia
ol.grigorenko@gmail.com, tykon@inbox.lv
https://www.lumii.lv/

Abstract. The aim of the work is to involve fuzzy equivalence relations and aggregation of corresponding equivalence relations in a clustering process. Namely, we introduce fuzzy equivalence relations for different attributes of objects and then we aggregate these fuzzy equivalence relations to determine the similarities of objects. It is possible to involve different weights for attributes, thus defining the importance attributes in decision making process. In the work we also present illustrative examples.

Keywords: Fuzzy cluster analysis · Fuzzy equivalence relations · Aggregation of fuzzy relations

1 Introduction

Cluster analysis is a modelling and methodological tool for dealing with complex risk-evaluation, image processing, speech recognition, decision making and many others problems, when we need to place object into specific groups. We work in the field of fuzzy clustering which is a part of soft clustering, where objects or elements of an observing set could belong to two or more clusters. Specifically, the degree of belongingness of an object to a specific group is calculated.

The cluster analysis aim is often described as the placement of similar objects in a single cluster and distinguished objects in different clusters. In our approach we propose to introduce degrees of similarities by fuzzy equivalence relations and thus affect the placement of objects in clusters.

2 Preliminaries

2.1 Fuzzy Clustering Approach

If we are given a set of objects, also called a dataset,

$$\mathcal{D} = \{x_1, x_2, ..., x_n\},$$

The work has been supported by European Regional Development Fund within the project Nr.1.1.1.2/16/I/001, application Nr.1.1.1.2/VIAA/4/20/707 "Fuzzy relations and fuzzy metrics for customer behavior modeling and analyis".

containing n objects and each object is determined by m features (or attributes): $x_i = (x_i^1, x_i^2, ..., x_i^m)$, then the task of clustering is to group the objects of the set $\mathcal{D}$ into k subsets, denoted by $C_1, C_2, ..., C_k$. Thus k is the number of clusters. In fuzzy clustering the degree $u_{ij} \in [0, 1]$ is denoted, which indicates an object x_i degree of belongness to the cluster C_j. In other words, u_j is a membership function or a fuzzy set which takes values in unit interval and which arguments are objects. Thus $u_j(x_i)$ reveals the degree to which the element x_j belongs to the cluster C_j; this degree is denoted by u_{ij} for simplicity.

Further, if we defined some distance-like function $d : \mathbb{R}^m \times \mathbb{R}^m \to \mathbb{R}^+$, we could measure the degree of good separation of a dataset $\mathcal{D}$ in clusters $C_1, C_2, ..., C_k$, as follows:

$$F = \sum_{i=1}^{n} \sum_{j=1}^{k} u_{ij}^q d(x_i, c_j),$$

where c_j are the cluster centers and q is a fuzzifier. Formally speaking, the clustering problem is reduced to the problem of minimizing the function F.

2.2 T-norm as a Generalized Conjuction

We start with the definition of a t-norm which represents a generalized conjunction in fuzzy logic:

Definition 1 [6]. *A triangular norm (t-norm for short) is a binary operation $*$ on the unit interval $[0, 1]$, i.e. a function $* : [0, 1]^2 \to [0, 1]$ such that for all $a, b, c \in [0, 1]$ the following four axioms are satisfied:*

- $a * b = b * a$ *(commutativity);*
- $a * (b * c) = (a * b) * c$ *(associativity);*
- $a * b \leq a * c$ *whenever $b \leq c$ (monotonicity);*
- $a * 1 = a$ *(a boundary condition).*

Some of often used t-norms are mentioned below:

- $a *_M b = \min(a, b)$ minimum t-norm;
- $a *_P b = a \cdot b$ product t-norm;
- $a *_L b = \max(a + b - 1, 0)$ Łukasiewicz t-norm.

A t-norm $*$ is called Archimedean if and only if, for all pairs $(a, b) \in (0, 1)^2$, there is $n \in \mathbb{N}$ such that $a * a * ... * a$ (n times) $< b$. Product and Łukasiewicz t-norms are Archimedean while minimum t-norm is not.

We proceed recalling an important tool for the construction and study of t-norms involving single argument real function (additive generator) and addition. Later we use the same tool for constructing fuzzy equivalence relations.

Definition 2 [7]. *Let* $f : [a, b] \rightarrow [c, d]$ *be a monotone function, where* $[a, b]$ *and* $[c, d]$ *are closed subintervals of the extended real line* $[-\infty, \infty]$. *The pseudo-inverse*
$f^{(-1)} : [c, d] \rightarrow [a, b]$ *of* f *is defined by*

$$f^{(-1)}(y) = \begin{cases} \sup\{x \in [a, b] \mid f(x) < y\} & \text{if } f(a) < f(b), \\ \sup\{x \in [a, b] \mid f(x) > y\} & \text{if } f(a) > f(b), \\ a & \text{if } f(a) = f(b). \end{cases}$$

Definition 3 [7]. *An additive generator* $g : [0, 1] \rightarrow [0, \infty]$ *of a t-norm* $*$ *is a strictly decreasing function which is also right-continuous in* 0 *and satisfies* $g(1) = 0$, *such that for all* $(a, b) \in [0, 1]^2$ *we have*

$$g(a) + g(b) \in Ran(g) \cup [g(0), \infty],$$

$$a * b = g^{(-1)}(g(a) + g(b)).$$

where $Ran(g)$ *is the range of* g, $g^{(-1)}$ *- pseudo-inverse.*

2.3   Fuzzy Equivalence Relation

We continue with an overview of basic definitions and results on fuzzy equivalence relations.

Definition 4. *(see e.g. [9, 13]) A fuzzy binary relation* R *on a set* S *is a mapping* $R : S \times S \rightarrow [0, 1]$.

Definition 5. *(see e.g. [4]) A fuzzy binary relation* E *on a set* S *is called a fuzzy equivalence relation with respect to a t-norm* $*$ *(or* $*$-equivalence), *if and only if the following three axioms are fulfilled for all* $a, b, c \in S$:

1. $E(a, a) = 1$ *reflexivity;*
2. $E(a, b) = E(b, a)$ *symmetry;*
3. $E(a, b) * E(b, c) \leq E(a, c)$ $*$-transitivity.

The following result establishes principles of construction of fuzzy equivalence relations using pseudo-metrics.

Theorem 1 ([1]). *Let* $*$ *be a continuous Archimedean t-norm with an additive generator* g. *For any pseudo-metric* d, *the mapping*

$$E_d(a, b) = g^{(-1)}(\min(d(a, b), g(0)))$$

is a $*$-equivalence.

Let us consider two examples of fuzzy equivalences which will be used further in the algorithm:

Example 1. [Product t-norm]

Let $*_p$ be the product t-norm, that is $a *_p b = a \cdot b$. Then its additive generator $g_p : [0,1] \to [0,\infty]$ is

$$g_p(x) = \begin{cases} -ln(x) & x \neq 0 \\ \infty & x = 0. \end{cases}$$

Its pseudo-inverse is $g_p^{(-1)} : [0,\infty] \to [0,1]$ defined by

$$g_p^{(-1)}(y) = \begin{cases} e^{-y} & y \neq \infty \\ 0 & y = \infty. \end{cases}$$

Thus we obtain the corresponding fuzzy equivalence relations E_P for a metric d:

$$E_P(a,b) = e^{-d(a,b)}.$$

Example 2. [Łukasiewicz t-norm]

Let $*_L$ be the Łukasiewicz t-norm, that is

$$a *_L b = \begin{cases} a+b-1 & \text{if } a+b \leq 1 \\ 1 & \text{otherwise .} \end{cases}$$

Its additive generator is $g_L(x) = 1 - x$ with pseudo-inverse $g_L^{(-1)} : [0,\infty] \to [0,1]$ given by

$$g_L^{(-1)}(y) = \begin{cases} 1-y & y \in [0,1] \\ 0 & \text{otherwise .} \end{cases}$$

Thus we obtain the corresponding fuzzy equivalence relations E_L for a metric d:

$$E_L(a,b) = \max(1 - d(a,b), 0).$$

3   Fuzzy Clustering Approach

The most popular soft clustering algorithm implemented to search for an optimal partition is the well known fuzzy c-means algorithm ([2,3]), where the distance-like function d is $d(c,x) = ||c - x||^2$. We follow the fuzzy c-means algorithm and implement the degrees of belongingness as aggregated fuzzy equivalence relations. Namely we introduce a pointwise aggregation of m fuzzy equivalence relations defined for each feature separately. It is possible to involve weights $p_i, i = 1, ..., m$ to reveal the importance of features. Thus the algorithm is as follows for previously chosen number of clusters k and randomly assigned coefficients to each data point for being in the clusters (thus getting the membership matrix $U \subset [0,1]^{n \times k}$):

1. For a given dataset $\mathcal{D}$ and the membership matrix $U \in [0,1]^{n \times k}$ we calculate the best representatives or cluster centers (or centroids) using the following theorem:

Theorem 2. *Let $\mathcal{D}$ be a set of n objects or data points $(x_i \in \mathbb{R}^m)$ with weights $w_1, w_2, ..., w_n > 0$. The best representative c^* of the set $\mathcal{D}$ with weight $w_1, w_2, ..., w_n > 0$ denoted by $c^* = \arg\min\limits_{c \in \mathbb{R}^m} \sum\limits_{i=1}^{n} w_i \|c - x_i\|^2$ is its weighted centroid or barycenter:*

$$c^* = \left(\frac{1}{W} \sum_{i=1}^{n} w_i x_i^1, \frac{1}{W} \sum_{i=1}^{n} w_i x_i^2, ..., \frac{1}{W} \sum_{i=1}^{n} w_i x_i^m \right),$$

where $W = \sum\limits_{i=1}^{n} w_i$.

The theorem for $w_i = u_{ij}^q$ is used; thus cluster centers are:

$$c_j = \left(\frac{1}{U_j} \sum_{i=1}^{n} u_{ij}^q x_i^1, \frac{1}{U_j} \sum_{i=1}^{n} u_{ij}^q x_i^2, ..., \frac{1}{U_j} \sum_{i=1}^{n} u_{ij}^q x_i^m \right),$$

where $U_j = \sum\limits_{i=1}^{n} u_{ij}^q$.

2. Further we recalculate the membership matrix $U \in [0,1]^{n \times k}$ as follows:
   (a) Let $x_i = (x_i^1, x_i^2, x_i^3, ..., x_i^m)$ be an object and $c_j = (c_j^1, c_j^2, c_j^3, ..., c_j^m)$ be a cluster center, then let us build a fuzzy equivalence relation for each feature $l = 1, .., n$ $E^l(x_i^l, c_k^l)$ taking into account metric $d^l(x_i, c_j) = |x_i^l - c_j^l|$. For the different t-norms we obtain corresponding equivalence relations or similarities:
   $E_L^l(x_i^l, c_j^l) = \max(1 - |x_i^l - c_j^l|, 0);$
   $E_P^l(x_i, c_j) = e^{-|x_i^l - c_j^l|}.$
   Here we use the same metric d^l for each attribute l but they could differ. Using the fuzzy equivalence relation E_L the dataset should be standardized.
   (b) Further the idea is to fuse the information about all fuzzy equivalence relations E^l and get a global fuzzy equivalence relation E which includes the information about all fuzzy equivalence relations E^l and thereby the information about all similarities in the sets $\{x_1^l, x_2^l, ..., x_n^l\}$. Let us introduce the following mapping $A : [0,1]^k \rightarrow [0,1]$ which aggregates fuzzy equivalence relations:

$$E(x, y) = A(E^1(x, y), ..., E^m(x, y)).$$

It is natural to require from A at least the following properties:

(i) If $E^l(x^l, y^l) = 1$ for all l (that is x^l is similar to y^l for all l) the global degree should be also 1, that means that x should be similar to y. In other words: $A(1, ..., 1) = 1$.
(ii) If "x^l is similar to y^l" does not entirely fulfilled for every l, then the global degree of fulfillment should be 0 too: $A(0, ..., 0) = 0$.

(iii) If one degree $E^l(x, y)$ increases while the others are kept constant, the overall degree must not decrease, i.e. A should be non-increasing in each component.

That is exactly the definition of aggregation function:

Definition 6. *[10] An aggregation function is a mapping $A : [0,1]^m \to [0,1]$ which fulfills the following properties:*

- *$A(x^1, ..., x^m) \le A(y^1, ..., y^m)$ whenever $x^i \le y^i$ for all $i \in \{1, ..., m\}$ (monotonicity);*
- *$A(0, ..., 0) = 0$ and $A(1, ..., 1) = 1$ (boundary conditions).*

For more information about aggregation functions or aggregation operators see [10] and [11].

It is also natural to require that the global fuzzy relation should fulfill the same properties as the individual fuzzy relations.

The preservation of reflexivity is rather clear because of the boundary conditions of aggregation function. Preservation of symmetry is also obvious. The more interesting and complex question is about preservation of transitivity. Here we use the results about the preservation of transitivity studied in [12], where it is shown that preservation of transitivity is equivalent to the dominance of the t-norm $*$ by the aggregation operator A.

Definition 7 [12]. *Consider an m-argument aggregation function $A : [0,1]^m \to [0,1]$ and a t-norm $*$. We say that A dominates $*$ if for all $x^i \in [0,1]$ with $i \in \{1, ..., m\}$ and $y^i \in [0,1]$ with $i \in \{1, ..., m\}$ the following property holds:*

$$A(x^1, ..., x^m) * A(y^1, ..., y^m) \le A(x^1 * y^1, ..., x^m * y^m).$$

Theorem 3 [12]. *Let $*$ be a t-norm. An aggregation function A preserves transitivity of fuzzy relations if and only if A belongs to the class of aggregation functions which dominate $*$.*

Example 3 [12]. For any $m \ge 2$ and any $p = (p_1, ..., p_m)$ with $\sum_{i=1}^{m} p_i \ge 1$ and $p_i \in [0, \infty]$ m-ary aggregation function

$$A_p(x^1, ..., x^m) = \max(\sum_{i=1}^{m} x^i \cdot p_i + 1 - \sum_{i=1}^{m} p_i, 0)$$

dominates Łukasiewicz t-norm $*_L$.

Example 4 [12]. For any $m \ge 2$ and any $p = (p_1, ..., p_m)$ with $\sum_{i=1}^{m} p_i \ge 1$ and $p_i \in [0, \infty]$ m-ary aggregation function

$$A_p(x^1, ..., x^m) = \prod_{i=1}^{m} x^{i p_i}$$

dominates product t-norm $*_P$.

Theorem 4. *Let $*$ be a t-norm. If E_i for all $i \in \{1, ..., m\}$ are fuzzy equivalence relations (with respect to the t-norm $*$) then*

$$E(x, y) = A(E^1(x, y), ..., E^n(x, y))$$

is also a $*$-equivalence relation if A belongs to the class of aggregation functions which dominate $*$.

Therefore we built a new fuzzy equivalence relation by aggregating fuzzy equivalence relations E^l :

$$\mathbf{E}(x_i, c_k) = A(E^1(x_i^1, c_k^1), E^2(x_i^2, c_k^2), E^3(x_i^3, c_k^3), ..., E^n(x_i^n, c_k^n))$$

where we use aggregation operator A which preserve fuzzy equivalence relations.

Thus for different t-norms we obtain corresponding global equivalence relations or similarities:

$$\mathbf{E_L}(x_i, c_k) = \max(\sum_{l=1}^{m} E^l(x_i^l, c_k^l) \cdot p_l + 1 - \sum_{l=1}^{m} p_l, 0)$$

$$= \max(\sum_{l=1}^{m} (1 - |x_i^l - c_k^l|) \cdot p_l + 1 - \sum_{l=1}^{m} p_l, 0).$$

If $p_l = 1/m$ then (in this case we do not add additionally priorities for attributes since all weight are equal):

$$\mathbf{E_L}(x_i, c_k) = 1/m \sum_{l=1}^{m} (1 - |x_i^l - c_k^l|).$$

If p_l are not equal but $\sum_{l=1}^{m} p_l = 1$ then (in this case we add additionally priorities for attributes):

$$\mathbf{E_L}(x_i, c_k) = \sum_{l=1}^{m} p_l(1 - |x_i^l - c_k^l|).$$

For product t-norm we obtain the following equivalence relation:

$$\mathbf{E_P}(x_i, c_k) = \prod_{l=1}^{m} e^{-p_l|x_i^l - c_k^l|}.$$

If $p_l = 1/m$ then (in this case we do not add additionally priorities for attributes since all weight are equal):

$$\mathbf{E_P}(x_i, c_k) = \prod_{l=1}^{m} e^{-\frac{1}{m}|x_i^l - c_k^l|}.$$

Therefore we set $u_{ij} = \mathbf{E}(x_i, c_k)$, calculate F and come to the step 1.

Similarly as with the standard k-means algorithm or with the fuzzy c-means algorithm, this algorithm also produces monotonically decreasing sequence of objective function values F. Therefore the process stops when

$$\frac{F_{j-1} - F_j}{F_j} < \epsilon$$

for $\epsilon > 0$ and where F_j is a value of objective function obtained in j iteration.

4   Numerical Example

Let us look at well known dataset *MallCustomers* from Kaggle. Dataset contains information about customers, such as *Customer ID*, *age*, *genders*, *annual income* and *spending score*. We will segment this data by 2 features: *annual income* and *spending score* on 5 clusters. Thus the dataset's objects are in the square $[0, 150] \times [0, 100]$.

Implementation is done in Python. Here we illustrate the algorithm when similarities are defined by fuzzy equivalence relations with respect to the product t-norm:

$$\mathbf{E_P}(x_i, c_k) = \prod_{l=1}^{m} e^{-p_l |x_i^l - c_k^l|}.$$

```python
def fuzzy_distance(c, x, m=2, p=[p1, p2]):
    agg_dist = 1
    for i in range(m):
        agg_dist *= np.exp(-abs(c[i] - x[i]) * p[i])
    return agg_dist
```

The algorithm is following:

1. create (randomly) the membership matrix $U \in [0, 1]^{n \times k}$;
2. compute centroids based on the membership matrix;
3. update the membership matrix $U \in [0, 1]^{n \times k}$;
4. repeat steps 2–3.

```python
for it in range(n_iter):
    """ STEP 2: centroid computation """
    for j in range(k):
        weightSum = sum(np.power(weight[:, j], q))
        sumMM = 0
        for i in range(n):
            sumMM += np.multiply(np.power(weight[i, j], q), X[i, 0:m])
        C[j] = np.reshape(sumMM / weightSum, m)
```

```
""" STEP 3: weights update """
for i in range(n):
    distSum = 0
    for j in range(k):
        distSum += fuzzy_distance(C[j, 0:m], X[i, 0:m])
    for j in range(k):
        weight[i, j] = fuzzy_distance(C[j, 0:m], X[i, 0:m]) / distSum
```

The next figures demonstrate the process of clustering when $q = 2$ and weights for attributes are $p_1 = 0.1$, $p_2 = 0.9$ and $p_1 = p_2 = 0.5$.

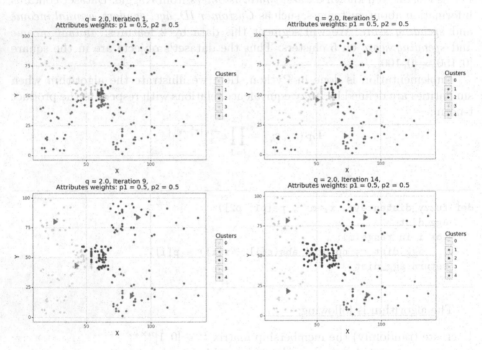

Fig. 1. A figure demonstrates the process of clustering when weights are 0.5 and 0.5. By the red triangles the placement of centroids is denoted. (Color figure online)

With a Fig. 1 we would like to demonstrate the example when we do not put the priorities for features. The results are similar to the results for fuzzy c-means algorithm, but condition $\frac{F_{j-1} - F_j}{F_j} < \epsilon$ is faster fulfilled.

With a Fig. 2 we would like to demonstrate the influence of weights involved for features. We can see that the influence of the feature (or coordinate for this example) with weight 0.1 is much lower than the influence of the feature with the weight of 0.9. The position of cluster centers along a line demonstrates the idea (Fig. 3).

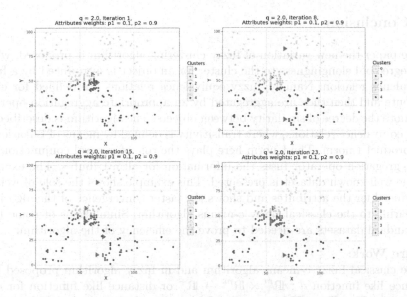

Fig. 2. A figure demonstrates the process of clustering when weights are 0.1 and 0.9 By the red triangles the placement of centroids is denoted. (Color figure online)

	Fuzzy Eq. based	Fuzzy C-Means
iteration	p1=p2=0.5, q=2	q=2
1	12.04%	2.17%
2	7.06%	2.55%
3	5.47%	1.36%
4	0.55%	1.65%
5	0.04%	2.11%
6	0.02%	2.04%
7	0.01%	1.62%
8	0.01%	1.62%
9	0.00%	2.15%
10	0.00%	1.97%
11	0.00%	1.35%
12	0.00%	0.63%
13	0.00%	0.58%
14	0.00%	0.45%
15	0.00%	0.26%
16	0.00%	0.14%
17	0.00%	0.07%
18	0.00%	0.03%
19	0.00%	0.02%
20	0.00%	0.01%
21	0.00%	0.01%
22	0.00%	0.00%

Fig. 3. A table demonstrates how fast the algorithm converges comparing to the fuzzy c-means algorithm.

5   Conclusion

In the paper the new variation of fuzzy clustering algorithm is proposed, where the degree of belongingness to the cluster for an object is introduced by a fuzzy equivalence relation. Namely, fuzzy equivalence relations are defined for every attribute and then they are aggregated by an appropriate aggregation operator to denote the degree of similarity between objects. The algorithm is described for fuzzy equivalence relations, where transitivity is defined by means of Łukasiewicz and product t-norm. The t-norm here plays the role of general conjunction but the aggregation operator fuses the information for all attributes. The example for one well known dataset is presented. This example shows the role of weights introduced for the attributes and shows the faster convergence of the algorithm comparing to the classical fuzzy c-means algorithm. Simulations or some tests on standard datasets are needed to prove the efficiency of the algorithm.

Future Work:
In the classical fuzzy c-means algorithm and in fuzzy algorithm proposed here distance like function $d : \mathbb{R}^m \times \mathbb{R}^m \to \mathbb{R}^+$ or distance like function for each feature $d^l : \mathbb{R} \times \mathbb{R} \to \mathbb{R}^+$ are utilized both directly in calculating function d and calculating membership degrees u_{ij}. Thus calculating cluster centers $c^* = arg \min\limits_{c \in \mathbb{R}^m} \sum\limits_{i=1}^{n} w_i \|c - x_i\|^2$ and cost function

$$F = \sum_{i=1}^{n} \sum_{j=1}^{k} u_{ij}^q d(x_i, c_j)$$

we double calculation of d^l. Therefore we propose to investigate how to find a cluster center, when the problem is to find $c^* = arg \min\limits_{c \in \mathbb{R}^m} \sum\limits_{i=1}^{n} w_i$, where w_i are introduced by means of fuzzy equivalence relations. In this situation the objective function will be $F = \sum_{i=1}^{n} \sum_{j=1}^{k} u_{ij}^q$.

References

1. De Baets, B., Mesiar, R.: Pseudo-metrics and T-equivalences. J. Fuzzy Math. **5**, 471–481 (1997)
2. Bezdek, J.C., Ehrlich, R., Full, W.: FCM: the fuzzy C-means clustering algorithm. Comput. Geosci. **10**, 191–203 (1984)
3. Bezdek, J.C., Keller, J., Krisnapuram, R., Pal, N.R.: Fuzzy Models and Algorithms for Pattern Recognition and Image Processing. Springer, Cham (2005). https://doi.org/10.1007/b106267
4. Bodenhofer, U.: A similarity-based generalization of fuzzy orderings preserving the classical axioms. Int. J. Uncertain. Fuzziness Knowl. Based Syst. **8**(5), 593–610 (2000)
5. Klement, E.P., Mesiar, R., Pap, E.: Generated triangular norms. Kibernetika **36**, 363–377 (2000)

6. Klement, E.P., Mesiar, R., Pap, E.: Triangular Norms. Kluwer Academic Publishing, Dodrecht (2000)
7. Klement, E.P., Mesiar, R., Pap, E.: Triangular norms. Position paper II. General constructions and parametrized families. Fuzzy Sets Syst. **145**, 411–438 (2004)
8. Klement, E.P., Mesiar, R., Pap, E.: Triangular norms: basic notions and properties. In: Klement, E.P., Mesiar, R. (eds.) Logical, Algebraic, Analytic and Probabilistic Aspects of Triangular Norms, pp. 17–60. Elsevier, Amsterdam (2005)
9. Fodor, J., Roubens, M.: Fuzzy Preference Modelling and Multicriteria Decision Support. Kluwer Academic Publishers, Dordrecht (1994)
10. Grabisch, M., Marichal, J.-L., Mesiar, R., Pap, E.: Aggregation Functions (Encyclopedia of Mathematics and its Applications). Cambridge University Press, Cambridge (2009)
11. Mesiar, R., Calvo, T., Mayor, G.: Aggregation Operators: New Trends and Applications (Studies in Fuzziness and Soft Computing). Physica-Verlag, Heidelberg (2002)
12. Saminger, S., Mesiar, R., Bodenhofer, U.: Domination of aggregation operators and preservation of transitivity. Int. J. Uncertain. Fuzziness Knowl. Based Syst. **10**(Suppl.), 11–35 (2002)
13. Zadeh, L.A.: Similarity relations and fuzzy orderings. Inf. Sci. **3**, 177–200 (1971)

Fuzzy-Valued Distance Between Fuzzy Numbers Based on a Generalized Extension Principle

Juscelino Araújo[1]([✉]) [iD], Benjamin Bedregal[2] [iD], and Regivan Santiago[2] [iD]

[1] Postgraduate Program in Systems and Computation, Federal University
of Rio Grande do Norte, Natal 59072-970, Brazil
`juscelino.araujo@ufrn.br`
[2] Department of Informatics and Applied Mathematics, Federal University
of Rio Grande do Norte, Natal 59072-970, Brazil

Abstract. This paper presents a generalization of the extension principle for fuzzy numbers. The minimum is substituted by a general binary aggregation function. It is used to extend the usual metric for real numbers to fuzzy numbers, generating a new family of fuzzy-valued distances between fuzzy numbers. Then, some conditions on these aggregation functions are studied to hold the fuzzy number properties of the generated distances.

Keywords: Fuzzy number · Binary aggregation function · Generalized extension principle

1 Introduction

In many situations, the uncertainties of measurements and systems are well modeled by fuzzy sets (Costa et al. [4], Asmus et al. [1], Souza et al. [14]). Moreover, many times it is necessary to compare such fuzzy sets. For example, using an appropriate distance between them. The use of classical metrics can hide the uncertainty in the system analyzed since real numbers will not bring any information about the fuzziness of the measurements. Therefore, other techniques should be employed.

Several ways of measuring distances between fuzzy sets were already studied. Kramosil and Michalek [11] extended to fuzzy sets the probabilistic metric spaces presented by Schweiser and Sklar [13]. George and Veeramani [7] adapted the approach of Kramosil and Michalék in order to gain new properties. Kaleva and Seikkala [8] introduced a concept of fuzzy metric space for measuring distances using fuzzy numbers.

The aim of this paper is to provide a new family of fuzzy-valued distances for fuzzy numbers based on a generalization of the extension principle (Zadeh [17], Yager [15]). Properties of binary aggregation functions are also studied in order to generalize the extension principle and keep the properties of fuzzy numbers.

© Springer Nature Switzerland AG 2022
D. Ciucci et al. (Eds.): IPMU 2022, CCIS 1601, pp. 460–470, 2022.
https://doi.org/10.1007/978-3-031-08971-8_38

One of the advantages of this approach is that two fuzzy numbers could compared using different distances just by changing the binary aggregation function used.

In Sect. 2 some results regarding fuzzy numbers and aggregation functions are presented. In Sect. 3 is proposed the new way to generalize the extension principle. Some examples are given, showing how the generalization proposed affects the resulting fuzzy sets. The conditions on the aggregation functions are studied in order to preserve the properties of fuzzy numbers of the resulting fuzzy set. Finally, in Sect. 4 the whole work is summarized and are presented some lines of research following the results found.

2   Preliminaries

In this paper, $\mathbb{R}$ is the set of real numbers.

Definition 1 (Fuzzy set [16]). *Let X be a non-empty set. A fuzzy set on X is a function $A : X \to [0,1]$ that assigns, to each element of X its degree of membership to A. The set of all fuzzy sets on X is denoted by $\mathcal{F}(X)$.*

Definition 2 (α-cut and support [10]). *Let A be a fuzzy set on a set X. Then $\forall \alpha \in (0,1]$, $A_\alpha := \{x \in X : A(x) \geq \alpha\}$ is the α-cut of A. And*

$$A_{0+} := \bigcup_{\alpha \in (0,1]} A_\alpha = \{x \in X : A(x) > 0\}$$

is the support of A.

Definition 3 (Fuzzy number [10]). *Let $A \in \mathcal{F}(\mathbb{R})$. A is called a fuzzy number if*

(i) $A_1 \neq \varnothing$ *(in this case, A is said to be normal);*
(ii) $\forall \alpha \in (0,1]$, A_α *is a compact interval;*
(iii) A_{0+} *is a bounded interval.*

Example 1. Consider the fuzzy set $A : \mathbb{R} \to [0,1]$ with $A_\alpha = [\alpha, 5 - 2\alpha]$ for each $\alpha \in (0,1]$, shown in Fig. 1. Note that A_α is compact for all $\alpha \in (0,1]$, $A_1 = [1,3] \neq \varnothing$ and $A_{0+} = (0,5)$ is bounded. Therefore, A is a fuzzy number.

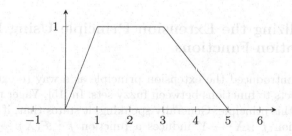

Fig. 1. The fuzzy number A with $A_\alpha = [\alpha, 5 - 2\alpha]$, $0 < \alpha \leq 1$.

Definition 4 (Non-negative fuzzy number [10]). *Let A be a fuzzy number. A is said to be non-negative if $A(t) = 0$ for all $t < 0$.*

Example 2. The fuzzy number A from Example 1 is non-negative.

We will denote by $\mathcal{E}$ the set of fuzzy number and by $\mathcal{E}_+$ the set of non-negative fuzzy numbers.

Definition 5 (Convex fuzzy number [16]). *A fuzzy number A is convex if, $\forall x, y, z \in \mathbb{R}$,*

$$x < y < z \Rightarrow A(y) \geq \min(A(x), A(z)).$$

Example 3. The fuzzy number from Example 1 is convex.

Definition 6 (Upper semi-continuous function) *Let $X \subseteq \mathbb{R}^n$. A function $f : X \to \mathbb{R}$ is upper semi-continuous (USC) if $\forall x \in X$, $\forall \varepsilon > 0$, $\exists \delta > 0$ such that for each $y \in X$,*

$$\|x - y\| < \delta \Rightarrow f(y) < f(x) + \varepsilon.$$

According to Dubois and Prade [6], the α-cuts of a fuzzy set are closed intervals if and only if it is convex and upper semi-continuous. If the support of a fuzzy set is bounded, then each α-cut will be bounded too. Thus, we may say that a fuzzy set is a fuzzy number if it is normal, convex, upper semi-continuous and has bounded support.

Definition 7 (n-ary aggregation function [3]). *An n-ary aggregation function is a function $\varphi : [0,1]^n \to [0,1]$ satisfying the following conditions:*

(i) $\varphi(0, \ldots, 0) = 0$ and $\varphi(1, \ldots, 1) = 1$ (boundary conditions);
(ii) If $x_i \leq y_i$ for all $i = 1, \ldots, n$, then $A(x_1, \ldots, x_n) \leq A(y_1, \ldots, y_n)$ (monotonicity).

Proposition 1 (USC aggregation function [9]). *An n-ary aggregation function φ is USC if $\forall (x_1, \ldots, x_n) \in [0,1]^n$, $\forall \varepsilon > 0$, $\exists \delta > 0$ such that for each $(y_1, \ldots, y_n) \in [0,1]^n$, if $y_i - x_i < \delta$ for all $i = 1, \ldots, n$, then $\varphi(y_1, \ldots, y_n) - \varphi(x_1, \ldots, x_n) < \varepsilon$.*

Example 4. The minimum, the arithmetic mean and the maximum are examples of USC aggregation functions.

3   Generalizing the Extension Principle Using Binary Aggregation Functions

In [17], Zadeh introduced the extension principle as a way to extend functions between crisp sets to functions between fuzzy sets. In [15], Yager made a further elaboration of this principle. Generally speaking, it states that, if X, Y are crisp sets, the function $f : X \to Y$ induces a function $f : \mathcal{F}(X) \to \mathcal{F}(Y)$, where $f(A)(y) = \sup_{x \in f^{-1}(\{y\})} A(x)$, for all fuzzy set A.

Operations between real numbers may also be extended to operations between fuzzy numbers. As seen in Klir and Yuan [10], if $*$ is one of the four arithmetic operations $(+, -, \times, /)$ and A and B are fuzzy numbers, then $A * B : \mathbb{R} \to [0, 1]$ is the fuzzy number defined by

$$(A * B)(z) = \sup_{x*y=z} \min(A(x), B(y)).$$

However, in order to the extended division be well defined is necessary that $0 \notin B_{0+}$. In Dubois and Prade [6] and Bednár [2], the extension principle is used to define distances between fuzzy sets. We want to generalize this approach using a binary aggregation function instead of the minimum. Dubois and Prade [5] present generalizations of the extension principle using triangular norms. Otto et al. [12], on the other hand, use idempotent monotonic combinations.

Restricting this analysis to the context of fuzzy numbers, given a binary aggregation function $\varphi : [0, 1]^2 \to [0, 1]$, let $\rho_\varphi : \mathcal{E} \times \mathcal{E} \to \mathcal{F}(\mathbb{R}_+)$ be the function defined in the following way: for each fuzzy numbers A and B,

$$\rho_\varphi(A, B)(x) = \sup_{|s-t|=x} \varphi(A(s), B(t)). \tag{1}$$

Example 5. Let B and C the fuzzy numbers whose α-cuts are $B_\alpha = [\alpha - 2, 1 - 2\alpha]$ and $C_\alpha = [0, 2 - \alpha]$, $\alpha \in (0, 1]$. They are shown in Fig. 2. Initially we may apply the classical extension principle to find the distance between B and C as seen in Dubois and Prade [6]. This is made using $\varphi = \min$ in (1). For $x \in [0, 1]$, the supremum of $\min(A(s), B(t))$, $|s - t| = x$, is attained when $t = 0$ (because $B(0) = 1$) and $s = -x$. Thus, for $x \in [0, 1]$,

$$\rho_{\min}(B, C)(x) = \min(A(-x), B(0)) = A(-x) = -\frac{(-x)}{2} + \frac{1}{2} = \frac{x}{2} + \frac{1}{2}.$$

For $x \in [1, 2]$, the supremum is attained when $s = -1$ and $t = x - 1$, because $A(-1) = 1$ and $x \in [1, 2] \Leftrightarrow x - 1 \in [0, 1] \Rightarrow B(x - 1) = 1$. Hence,

$$\rho_{\min}(B, C)(x) = \min(A(-1), B(x - 1)) = \min(1, 1) = 1.$$

And for $x \in [2, 4]$, the supremum is attained when $s \in [-2, -1]$, $t \in [1, 2]$ and $A(s) = B(t)$, since we don't want reduce $A(s)$ or $B(t)$ too much. Therefore,

$$A(s) = s + 2 = -t + 2 = B(t) \Rightarrow s = t.$$

Thus, $x = |s - t| = |-2t| = 2t \Rightarrow t = x/2$.

$$\rho_{\min}(B, C)(x) = B(x/2) = \frac{x}{2} + 2.$$

For $x > 4$, either $s = 0$ or $t = 0$, with the minimum resulting in zero. The fuzzy set $\rho_{\min}(B, C)(x)$ is shown in Fig. 3.

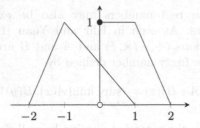

Fig. 2. The fuzzy numbers B and C with $B_\alpha = [\alpha - 2, 1 - 2\alpha]$ and $C_\alpha = [0, 2 - \alpha]$, $\alpha \in (0, 1]$.

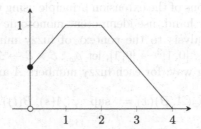

Fig. 3. The fuzzy set $\rho_{\min}(A, B)(x) = \sup\limits_{|s-t|=x} \varphi(A(s), B(t))$.

Example 6. Consider now the case $\varphi = f_\perp$, where $f_\perp$ is the binary aggregation function such that $f_\perp(a, b) = 1$ if $a = b = 1$ and $f_\perp(a, b) = 0$ otherwise. If B and C are the fuzzy number from Example 5, note that $\rho_{f_\perp}(B, C) = 1$ only when $A(s) = 1$ and $B(t) = 1$. Thus, $s = -1$ and $t \in [0, 2]$. Therefore, since $x = |s - t|$, we have $\rho_{f_\perp}(B, C) = 1$ if $x \in [1, 2]$ and $\rho_{f_\perp}(B, C) = 0$ otherwise. The fuzzy set $\rho_{f_\perp}(B, C)$ is shown in Fig. 4.

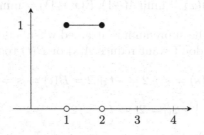

Fig. 4. The fuzzy set $\rho_{f_\perp}(A, B)(x) = \sup\limits_{|s-t|=x} f_\perp(A(s), B(t))$.

Example 7. Let $\varphi = T_L$, where T_L is the Łukaciewicz t-norm, i. e., $T_L(a,b) = \max(0, a + b - 1)$. If B and C are the fuzzy numbers from Example 5, let us analyze the behavior of $\rho_{T_L}(B,C)$.

If $x \in [0,1]$, the supremum of $\rho_{T_L}(B,C)(x)$ is attained when $s \in [-x]$ and $t = 0$, because $B(t) = 0$ for $t < 0$ and $A(s)$ is decreasing for $s > -1$. Then

$$\rho_{T_L}(B,C)(x) = A(-x) + B(0) - 1 = -\frac{(-x)}{2} + \frac{1}{2} + 1 - 1 = \frac{x}{2} + \frac{1}{2}.$$

For $x \in [1,2]$, the supremum is attained when $s = -1$ and $t = x - 1$, for the same reasons of Example 5. Thus,

$$\rho_{\min}(B,C)(x) = A(-1) + B(x-1) - 1 = 1 + 1 - 1 = 1.$$

And for $x \in [2,3]$, the supremum is attained by many ways. For example, if $s = -1$ and $t = x - 1$. Another way is $s = 1 - x$ and $t = 1$. Using this last case,

$$\rho_{T_L}(B,C)(x) = A(1-x) + B(1) - 1 = A(1-x) = -\frac{(1-x)}{2} + \frac{1}{2} = \frac{x-1}{2} + \frac{1}{2} = \frac{x}{2}.$$

For $x > 3$, if $|s - t| = x$ then $A(s) + B(t) < 1$. Thus, $T_L(A(s), B(t)) = \max(0, A(s) + B(t) - 1) = 0$ and $\rho_{T_L}(B,C)(x) = 0$. The fuzzy set $\rho_{T_L}(B,C)(x)$ is shown in Fig. 5.

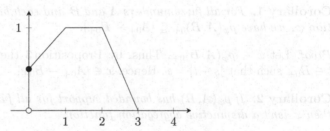

Fig. 5. The fuzzy set $\rho_{T_L}(A,B)(x) = \sup_{|s-t|=x} T_L(A(s), B(t))$.

We then investigate the conditions that φ must satisfy in order to make from $\rho_\varphi(A,B)$ a fuzzy non-negative number for all fuzzy numbers A and B. We use the following notation: if X and Y are two compact intervals, then $|X - Y| = \{|x - y| : x \in X, y \in Y\}$. For all compact intervals X and Y, the set $|X - Y|$ is a compact interval too.

Proposition 2. *For all fuzzy numbers A and B and each binary aggregation function φ, the fuzzy set $\rho_\varphi(A,B)$ is normal. Also, $|A_1 - B_1| \subseteq \rho_\varphi(A,B)_1$.*

Proof. Since A and B are fuzzy numbers, there exist $s_0, t_0 \in \mathbb{R}$ such that $A(s_0) = B(t_0) = 1$. And by the boundary conditions of φ we have $\varphi(A(s_0), B(t_0)) = 1$. Hence, $\rho_\varphi(A, B)(|s_0 - t_0|) = 1$. Also, if $x \in |A_1 - B_1|$ then there exist $s \in A_1$ and $t \in B_1$ such that $|s - t| = x$ and $\rho_\varphi(A, B)(x) \geq \varphi(A(s), B(t)) = \varphi(1, 1) = 1$. Hence, $x \in \rho_\varphi(A, B)_1$.

The Proposition 2 affirms an important fact: independently of the choice of the binary aggregation function, the resulting fuzzy set will always be normal. Some of the other conditions of a fuzzy number are not so easy to satisfy, as we will see ahead.

Proposition 3. *If $\rho_\varphi(A, B)$ has bounded support for all fuzzy numbers A and B, then φ has 0 as an absorbing element, i.e.,*

$$\forall x, y \in (0, 1], \ \varphi(x, 0) = \varphi(0, y) = 0.$$

Proof. Suppose that $\varphi(x, 0) > 0$ for some $x \in (0, 1]$. Then, let $s_0 \in A_x$. Thus, $\forall t \in \mathbb{R}, \varphi(A(s_0), B(t+s_0)) \geq \varphi(A(s_0), 0) > 0$. Therefore, the support of $\rho_\varphi(A, B)$ is the whole real line, which is a contradiction. The other case is analogous.

Example 8. Take the geometric mean m_G and the average mean m_A as binary aggregation functions. Note that m_G has 0 as an absorbing element and m_A has not. Therefore, if B and C are two fuzzy numbers, then $\rho_{m_G}(B, C)$ has bounded support, but $\rho_{m_A}(B, C)$ has not.

Corollary 1. *For all fuzzy numbers A and B and each binary aggregation function φ, we have $\rho_\varphi(A, B)_{0+} \subseteq |A_{0+} - B_{0+}|$.*

Proof. Let $x \in \rho_\varphi(A, B)_{0+}$. Thus, by Proposition 3 there exist $s \in A_{0+}$ and $t \in B_{0+}$ such that $|s - t| = x$. Hence, $x \in |A_{0+} - B_{0+}|$.

Corollary 2. *If $\rho_\varphi(A, B)$ has bounded support for all fuzzy numbers A and B, then φ isn't a disjunctive aggregation function.*

Proof. Every disjunctive aggregation function has 1 as an absorbing element and the absorbing element must be unique (see Beliakov et al. [3])

The remaining of this section deals with the question of how to prove that the α-cuts of $\rho_\varphi(A, B)$ are closed intervals. Firstly the convexity of $\rho_\varphi(A, B)$ in the sense of Zadeh [16] will be proved. Thereafter the conditions for upper semi-continuity are studied.

Lemma 1. *For all $\alpha_1, \alpha_2, \beta_1, \beta_2 \in (0, 1]$, if $\alpha_1 < \beta_1$ and $\alpha_2 < \beta_2$ then*

$$\min |A_{\alpha_1} - B_{\alpha_2}| \leq \min |A_{\beta_1} - B_{\beta_2}| \quad and \quad \max |A_{\alpha_1} - B_{\alpha_2}| \geq \max |A_{\beta_1} - B_{\beta_2}|.$$

Proof. See that if $\alpha_1 < \beta_1$ and $\alpha_2 < \beta_2$ then $A_{\alpha_1} \times B_{\alpha_2} \supseteq A_{\beta_1} \times B_{\beta_2}$. Hence, for each pair $(s, t) \in A_{\beta_1} \times B_{\beta_2}$, we have $|s - t| \in A_{\beta_1} \times B_{\beta_2} \subseteq A_{\alpha_1} \times B_{\alpha_2}$.

Lemma 2. *Let A and B be fuzzy numbers and φ a binary aggregation function. If $0 \leq x < y < \min|A_1 - B_1|$ then $\forall s, t \in \mathbb{R}$, $|s - t| = x$, $\exists u, v \in \mathbb{R}$, $|u - v| = y$, such that $\varphi(A(s), B(t)) \leq \varphi(A(u), B(v))$.*

Proof. Given $\alpha_1, \alpha_2 \in (0, 1]$, if $x \in |A_{\alpha_1} - B_{\alpha_2}|$ then $y > x \geq \min|A_{\alpha_1} - B_{\alpha_2}|$. Also, $y < \min|A_1 - B_1| \leq \max|A_1 - B_1| \leq \max|A_{\alpha_1} - B_{\alpha_2}|$ by Lemma 1. Hence, $y \in |A_{\alpha_1} - B_{\alpha_2}|$. Therefore, since $s \in A_{A(s)}$ and $t \in B_{B(t)}$, then $x \in |A_{A(s)} - B_{B(t)}|$. Thus, $y \in |A_{A(s)} - B_{B(t)}|$. Consequently, there exist $u \in A_{A(s)}$ and $v \in B_{B(t)}$ such that $|u - v| = y$. And since $A(u) \geq A(s)$ and $B(v) \geq B(t)$, we have $\varphi(A(s), B(t)) \leq \varphi(A(u), B(v))$.

Lemma 3. *Let A and B be fuzzy numbers and φ a binary aggregation function. If $z > y > \max|A_1 - B_1|$ then $\forall s, t \in \mathbb{R}$, $|s - t| = z$, $\exists u, v \in \mathbb{R}$, $|u - v| = y$, such that $\varphi(A(s), B(t)) \leq \varphi(A(u), B(v))$.*

Proof. Given $\alpha_1, \alpha_2 \in (0, 1]$, if $z \in |A_{\alpha_1} - B_{\alpha_2}|$ then $y < z \leq \max|A_{\alpha_1} - B_{\alpha_2}|$. Also, $y > \max|A_1 - B_1| \geq \min|A_1 - B_1| \geq \min|A_{\alpha_1} - B_{\alpha_2}|$ by Lemma 1. Hence, $y \in |A_{\alpha_1} - B_{\alpha_2}|$. Therefore, since $s \in A_{A(s)}$ and $t \in B_{B(t)}$, then $z \in |A_{A(s)} - B_{B(t)}|$. Thus, $y \in |A_{A(s)} - B_{B(t)}|$. The rest is identical to the proof of Lemma 2.

The following theorem states another strong fact: independently of the choice of the binary aggregation function, the resulting fuzzy set will be convex. On the other side, Lemmas 2 and 3 are related with the monotone increasing and monotone decreasing functions, respectively, that constitute another characterization of the fuzzy numbers, as in Klir and Yuan [10].

Theorem 1. *For all fuzzy numbers A and B and each binary aggregation function φ, the fuzzy set $\rho_\varphi(A, B)$ is convex, i.e., $\forall x, y, z \in \mathbb{R}$,*

$$x < y < z \Rightarrow \rho_\varphi(A, B)(y) \geq \min\left(\rho_\varphi(A, B)(x), \rho_\varphi(A, B)(z)\right).$$

Proof. If $y \in |A_1 - B_1|$ then by Proposition 2 we have $y \in \rho_\varphi(A, B)_1$. This case is trivial. If $y < \min|A_1 - B_1|$, by Lemma 2 we have that $\forall s, t \in \mathbb{R}$, $|s - t| = x$, $\exists u, v \in \mathbb{R}$, $|u - v| = y$, such that $\varphi(A(s), B(t)) \leq \varphi(A(u), B(v))$. Hence,

$$\rho_\varphi(A, B)(x) = \sup_{|s-t|=x} \varphi(A(s), B(t)) \leq \sup_{|u-v|=y} \varphi(A(u), B(v)) = \rho_\varphi(A, B)(y).$$

Analogously, if $y > \max|A_1 - B_1|$ then by Lemma 3 we have $\rho_\varphi(A, B)(z) \leq \rho_\varphi(A, B)(y)$. This completes the proof.

The upper semi-continuity is the last condition analyzed with the aim of obtaining a fuzzy number. This is intrinsically related to the upper semi-continuity of the binary aggregation function itself.

Lemma 4. *Let A and B be fuzzy numbers and φ be an USC binary aggregation function. Consider the function $\varphi \circ (A \times B) : \mathbb{R}^2 \to [0, 1]$ such that $(s, t) \mapsto \varphi(A(s), B(t))$. This function is USC.*

Proof. Fix $s_0, t_0 \in \mathbb{R}$. Since A and B are USC, then $\forall \gamma > 0$, $\exists \delta(\gamma) > 0$ such that $|s - s_0| < \delta(\gamma) \Rightarrow A(s) - A(s_0) < \gamma$ and $|t - t_0| < \delta(\gamma) \Rightarrow B(t) - B(t_0) < \gamma$. And since φ is USC, then $\forall \varepsilon > 0$, $\exists \gamma(\varepsilon) > 0$ such that

$$A(s) - A(s_0) < \gamma(\varepsilon), \ B(t) - B(t_0) < \gamma(\varepsilon) \Rightarrow \varphi(A(s), B(t)) - \varphi(A(s_0), B(t_0)) < \varepsilon.$$

Thus, for $\gamma(\varepsilon)$ there exists $\delta(\gamma(\varepsilon)) > 0$ such that

$$|s - s_0| < \delta(\gamma(\varepsilon)), \ |t - t_0| < \delta(\gamma(\varepsilon)) \Rightarrow A(s) - A(s_0) < \gamma(\varepsilon), \ B(t) - B(t_0) < \gamma(\varepsilon)$$
$$\Rightarrow \varphi(A(s), B(t)) - \varphi(A(s_0), B(t_0)) < \varepsilon.$$

Theorem 2. *If φ is an USC binary aggregation function then $\rho_\varphi(A, B)$ is USC for all fuzzy numbers A and B.*

Proof. Fix $x_0 \geq 0$. For all $\delta > 0$, if $|x - x_0| < \delta$ then for each pair $u, v \in \mathbb{R}$ with $|u - v| = x$, there exist $s, t \in \mathbb{R}$ with $|s - t| = x_0$ such that $|u - s| < \delta$ and $|v - t| < \delta$. On the other hand, by Lemma 4, $\varphi \circ (A \times B)$ is USC. Then $\forall \varepsilon > 0$, $\exists \delta(\varepsilon/2) > 0$ such that

$$|u - s| < \delta(\varepsilon/2), \ |v - t| < \delta(\varepsilon/2) \Rightarrow \varphi(A(u), B(v)) - \varphi(A(s), B(t)) < \varepsilon/2.$$

Therefore, if $|x - x_0| < \delta(\varepsilon/2)$ then for each pair $u, v \in \mathbb{R}$ with $|u - v| = x$ there exist $s, t \in \mathbb{R}$ with $|s - t| = x_0$ such that $\varphi(A(u), B(v)) - \varphi(A(s), B(t)) < \varepsilon/2$. Thus,

$$\begin{aligned}
\rho_\varphi(A, B)(x) &= \sup_{|u-v|=x} \varphi(A(u), B(v)) \\
&\leq \sup_{|s-t|=x_0} \varphi(A(s), B(t)) + \varepsilon/2 \\
&< \sup_{|s-t|=x_0} \varphi(A(s), B(t)) + \varepsilon \\
&= \rho_\varphi(A, B)(x_0) + \varepsilon.
\end{aligned}$$

This means $\rho_\varphi(A, B)$ is USC.

Example 9. The Łukasiewicz t-norm (see Example 7) is USC. Then $\rho_{T_L}(A, B)$ is a fuzzy number for all fuzzy numbers A and B.

The Theorems 1 and 2 allow us to conclude that the α-cuts of $\rho_\varphi(A, B)$ are closed intervals for all fuzzy numbers A and B when φ is an USC binary aggregation function. This leads to the following corollary:

Corollary 3. *If φ is a binary aggregation function which has 0 as an absorbing element and is upper semi-continuous on both arguments, then $\rho_\varphi(A, B)$ is a non-negative fuzzy number for all fuzzy numbers A and B.*

Proof. If φ has 0 as an absorbing element then by Proposition 3 we have that $\rho_\varphi(A, B)_{0+}$ is bounded. Hence, all α-cuts of $\rho_\varphi(A, B)$ are bounded. And they are also closed intervals by Theorems 1 and 2. Therefore, they are compact. And by Proposition 2 $\rho_\varphi(A, B)$ is normal. Hence, $\rho_\varphi(A, B) \in \mathcal{E}_+$.

4   Concluding Remarks

In this work we have generalized the extension principle changing the minimum for other binary aggregation functions and defined a new fuzzy-valued distance between fuzzy numbers. Some examples were given, showing the differences of the resulting fuzzy sets according to the binary aggregation function used in each case. Then we proceeded to analyze the conditions that had to be satisfied by the aggregation functions to generate fuzzy numbers from the new extension principle. And we found a sufficient condition to obtain such kind of aggregations.

Future lines of research include to find the methods and algorithms to compute the fuzzy numbers generated as distances. Moreover, such distances may belong to some kind of fuzzy-valued functions like the many definitions of fuzzy metrics (Kaleva and Seikkala [8], Bednár [2]). In each case, all properties must be verified. Another relevant point is that the complete characterization of this specific subset of binary aggregation functions which generalizes the extension principle requires more conditions. Regarding admissible orders on fuzzy numbers (Zumelzu et al. [18]), it is possible to wonder what aggregation functions that generalize the extension principle produce such kind of orders. And the possibility to extend the presented results to another kinds of fuzzy sets is also an interesting line of research.

Acknowledgements. The authors are also grateful to the reviewers for their valuable comments. This work was supported by the Brazilian Coordination for the Improvement of Higher Education Personnel (CAPES).

References

1. Asmus, T., Dimuro, G., Bedregal, B.: On two-player interval-valued fuzzy bayesian games: interval-valued fuzzy bayesian games. Int. J. Intell. Syst. **32**, 557–596 (2016)
2. Bednar, J.: Fuzzy distances. Kybernetika **41**, 375–388 (2005)
3. Beliakov, G., Pradera, A., Calvo, T.: Aggregation Functions: A Guide for Practitioners, 1st edn. Springer, Heidelberg (2007). https://doi.org/10.1007/978-3-540-73721-6
4. Costa, C., Bedregal, B., Neto, A.D.: Atanassov's intuitionistic probability and Markov chains. Knowl. Based Syst. **43**, 52–62 (2013)
5. Dubois, D., Prade, H.: Additions of interactive fuzzy numbers. IEEE Trans. Autom. Control **26**(4), 926–936 (1981)
6. Dubois, D., Prade, H.: Fuzzy Sets and Systems: Theory and Applications, 1st edn. Academic Press (1980)
7. George, A., Veeramani, P.: On some results in fuzzy metric spaces. Fuzzy Sets Syst. **64**, 395–399 (1994)
8. Kaleva, O., Seikkala, S.: On fuzzy metric spaces. Fuzzy Sets Syst. **12**, 215–229 (1984)
9. Klement, E.P., Mesiar, R., Pap, E.: Triangular Norms, 1st edn. Springer, Dordrecht (2000). https://doi.org/10.1007/978-94-015-9540-7
10. Klir, G.J., Yuan, B.: Fuzzy Sets and Fuzzy Logic: Theory and Applications, 1st edn. Prentice-Hall, Upper Sadle River (1995)

11. Kramosil, I., Michálek, J.: Fuzzy metrics and statistical metric spaces. Kybernetica **11**, 326–334 (1975)
12. Otto, K.N., Lewis, A.D., Antonsson, E.K.: Approximating α-cuts with the vertex method. Fuzzy Sets Syst. **55**(1), 43–50 (1993)
13. Schweizer, B., Sklar, A.: Statistical metric spaces. Pac. J. Math. **10**(1), 22 (1960)
14. Souza, E.L., Santiago, R.H.N., Canuto, A.M.P., Nunes, R.O.: Gradual complex numbers and their application for performance evaluation classifiers. IEEE Trans. Fuzzy Syst. **26**(2), 1058–1065 (2018)
15. Yager, R.R.: A characterization of the extension principle. Fuzzy Sets Syst. **18**(3), 205–217 (1986)
16. Zadeh, L.A.: Fuzzy sets. Inf. Control **8**, 338–353 (1965)
17. Zadeh, L.: The concept of a linguistic variable and its application to approximate reasoning-i. Inf. Sci. **8**(3), 199–249 (1975)
18. Zumelzu, N., Bedregal, B., Mansilla, E., Bustince, H., Diaz, R.: Admissible orders on fuzzy numbers. IEEE Trans. Fuzzy Syst. (2022). https://doi.org/10.1109/TFUZZ.2022.3160326

On an Application of Integral Transforms for Lattice-Valued Functions in Image Processing

Michal Holčapek[(✉)] and Viec Bui Quoc

CE IT4I - IRAFM, University of Ostrava,
30.dubna 22, 701 03 Ostrava 1, Czech Republic
michal.holcapek@osu.cz
http://irafm.osu.cz

Abstract. The integral transforms for lattice-valued functions have been introduced to generalize lower and upper fuzzy lattice-valued transforms that provide a lower and upper approximation of original functions. The paper aims to demonstrate the use of integral transforms in image processing, particularly, to filter a salt-and-pepper noise and compression and decompression of image. We consider the integral transforms defined with the help of the multiplication based Sugeno-like fuzzy integral and a fuzzy relation that serves as an integral kernel.

Keywords: Integral transform · Lattice-valued fuzzy transform ·
Residuated lattice · Integral kernel · Sugeno-like fuzzy integral

1 Introduction

In [7], integral transforms for lattice-valued functions have been introduced to build a general theoretical framework for transformations of functions whose function values belong to a weaker structure than real or complex numbers provide. The scheme of integral transforms for lattice-valued functions is in complete analogy with the standard integral transforms (e.g., Fourier or Laplace transforms), namely, by integrating the product of a function $f(x)$ and an integral kernel function $K(x, y)$ with respect to suitable limits, a new function $g(y)$ is created. For the considered theoretical framework, the complete residuated lattice was chosen as the basic algebraic structure for the functional values, because it is general enough to study the common properties of integral transforms for particular algebras as the BL-algebra, MV-algebra, or IMTL-algebra, which are popular in fuzzy set theory, fuzzy logic, and their applications.

The motivation for the integral transforms came from lattice-valued fuzzy transforms proposed by Perfilieva in [16] to approximate a function from below

This research was partially supported by the ERDF/ESF project AI-Met4AI No. CZ.02.1.01/0.0/0.0/17_049/0008414.

D. Ciucci et al. (Eds.): IPMU 2022, CCIS 1601, pp. 471–482, 2022.
https://doi.org/10.1007/978-3-031-08971-8_39

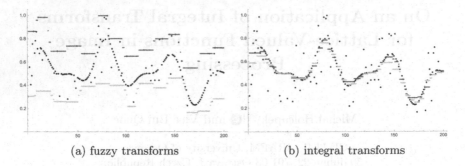

(a) fuzzy transforms   (b) integral transforms

Fig. 1. A comparison of noisy signal reconstructions based on lower and upper fuzzy transforms and integral transforms with multiplication based Sugeno-like fuzzy integral.

or above using an appropriate composition of the upper fuzzy transform $F^\uparrow$ and lower fuzzy transform $F^\downarrow$. The key element for fuzzy transforms is the concept of a fuzzy partition of the domain X of functions that are approximated, which is a system of fuzzy subsets of X whose cores[1] are non-empty and form a partition of X. For details, we refer to [11–15,18].

The proposed integral transforms generalize the lattice-valued fuzzy transforms in two directions, namely, the concept of fuzzy partition is replaced by a more general integral kernel, and the aggregation operators supremum and infimum that are used in the calculation of fuzzy transforms are replaced by Sugeno-like fuzzy integrals. More specifically, two types of integral transforms from $\mathcal{F}(X)$ to $\mathcal{F}(Y)$, i.e., from a set of all fuzzy sets on X to a set of all fuzzy sets on Y, were introduced by the following formulas:

$$F^{\otimes}_{(K,\mu)}(f)(y) = \int_X K(x,y) \otimes f(x)\,d\mu \text{ and } F^{\rightarrow}_{(K,\mu)}(f)(y) = \int_X K(x,y) \rightarrow f(x)\,d\mu,$$

where $K : X \times Y \to L$ is a fuzzy relation called the integral kernel and $\int_X$ is either a multiplication or residuum based Sugeno-like fuzzy integral on a fuzzy measure space $(X, \mathcal{F}, \mu)$. For details to various types of Sugeno-like fuzzy integrals, we refer to [3,4,7–9] and references therein.

Similarly to the lattice-valued fuzzy transform, in a current paper [6], we showed that the composition of integral transforms[2]

$$F^{\otimes}_{(K,\mu)} : \mathcal{F}(X) \to \mathcal{F}(Y) \text{ and } F^{\rightarrow}_{(K^{-1},\nu)} : \mathcal{F}(Y) \to \mathcal{F}(X),$$

where $K^{-1} : Y \times X \to L$ is given by $K^{-1}(y,x) = K(x,y)$ and ν is an appropriate fuzzy measure on a fuzzy measurable space $(Y, \mathcal{G})$, approximates original functions and can also remove the present random noise, in contrast to the fuzzy transform, as it is demonstrated in Fig. 1.

---

[1] The core of a fuzzy set A on X is the set of all elements of X for which the membership function of A gives 1 (see, Preliminary).

[2] The order of integral transforms in their composition provides a type of approximation of original functions.

This paper aims to present integral transforms for 2D lattice-valued functions and use the experience with the approximation of 1D functions in image processing, specifically filtering and compression/decompression of images. We show that filters based on integral transforms can be seen as a generalization of the known (weighted) median filter as well as minimum and maximum filters. Note that the median filter is a popular filter for removing salt-and-pepper noise. The minimum (also known as erosion) and maximum (dilation) filters are the most common morphological operations. The minimum filter erodes shapes on the image, whereas the maximum filter extends object boundaries [17].

The paper is structured as follows. The next section recalls the basic concepts used to construct the integral transform. The third section is devoted to integral transforms. The fourth section describes the method that is illustrated for salt-and-pepper filtering and compression/decompression of Lena image. The last section is a conclusion.

2 Preliminary

2.1 Algebra of Truth Values

For the purpose of the paper, we assume that the algebra of truth values is a *complete residuated lattice* on $[0, 1]$, i.e., an algebra $L = \langle [0, 1], \wedge, \vee, \otimes, \rightarrow, 0, 1 \rangle$ with four binary operations and two constants such that $\langle [0, 1], \wedge, \vee \rangle$ is a complete lattice, $\langle [0, 1], \otimes, 1 \rangle$ is a commutative monoid (i.e., $\otimes$ is associative, commutative and the identity $a \otimes 1 = a$ holds for any $a \in L$) and the adjointness property is satisfied, i.e.,

$$a \leq b \rightarrow c \quad \text{iff} \quad a \otimes b \leq c \tag{1}$$

holds for each $a, b, c \in [0, 1]$, where $\leq$ denotes the corresponding lattice ordering, i.e., $a \leq b$ if $a \wedge b = a$ for $a, b \in [0, 1]$. The operations $\otimes$ and $\rightarrow$ are called the *multiplication* and *residuum*, respectively. For details, we refer to [2].

Example 1. It is easy to prove that the algebra

$$L_T = \langle [0, 1], \min, \max, T, \rightarrow_T, 0, 1 \rangle,$$

where T is a left continuous t-norm (see, e.g., [10]) and $a \rightarrow_T b = \bigvee \{c \in [0, 1] \mid T(a, c) \leq b\}$, defines the residuum, is a complete residuated lattice. In this article, we consider complete residuated lattices determined by the Łukasiewicz, product, and minimum t-norms. Below we recall their definitions together with the corresponding residuum:

$$T_L(a, b) = \max(a + b - 1, 0), \qquad a \rightarrow_L b = \min(1, 1 - a + b),$$

$$T_P(a, b) = a \cdot b, \qquad a \rightarrow_P b = \begin{cases} 1, & \text{if } a \leq b, \\ \frac{b}{a}, & \text{otherwise}, \end{cases}$$

$$T_M(a, b) = \min(a, b), \qquad a \rightarrow_M b = \begin{cases} 1, & \text{if } a \leq b, \\ b, & \text{otherwise}. \end{cases}$$

2.2 Fuzzy Sets

Let L be a complete residuated lattice, and let X be a non-empty set. A function $A : X \to [0,1]$ is called a *fuzzy subset in* X. The set of all fuzzy sets on X is denoted by $\mathcal{F}(X)$. A fuzzy set A on X is called *crisp* if $A(x) \in \{0,1\}$ for any $x \in X$. The symbol $\emptyset$ denotes the empty fuzzy set on X, i.e., $\emptyset(x) = 0$ for any $x \in X$. The set of all crisp fuzzy sets on X (i.e., the power set of X) is denoted by $\mathcal{P}(X)$. A constant fuzzy set A on X (denoted as a_X) satisfies $A(x) = a$ for any $x \in X$, where $a \in L$. The set $\mathrm{Core}(A) = \{x \mid x \in X \,\&\, A(x) = 1\}$ is called the *core* of a fuzzy set A. A fuzzy set A is called *normal* if $\mathrm{Core}(A) \neq \emptyset$.

2.3 Fuzzy Measure Spaces

Definition 1. *Let X be a non-empty set. A subset $\mathcal{F}$ of $\mathcal{P}(X)$ is an* algebra of sets on X *provided that*

(M1) $X \in \mathcal{F}$,
(M2) if $A \in \mathcal{F}$, then $X \backslash A \in \mathcal{F}$,
(M3) if $A, B \in \mathcal{F}$, then $A \cup B \in \mathcal{F}$.

It is easy to see that if $\mathcal{F}$ is an algebra of sets, then the intersection of a finite number of sets belongs to $\mathcal{F}$. A pair $(X, \mathcal{F})$ is called a *measurable space* (on X) if $\mathcal{F}$ is an algebra of sets on X. Let $(X, \mathcal{F})$ be a measurable space and $A \in \mathcal{F}(X)$. We say that A is $\mathcal{F}$-*measurable* if $A \in \mathcal{F}$. Obviously, the sets $\{\emptyset, X\}$ and $\mathcal{P}(X)$ are algebras of sets on X.

Definition 2. *A map $\mu : \mathcal{F} \to [0,1]$ is called a* fuzzy measure *on a measurable space $(X, \mathcal{F})$ if*

(i) $\mu(\emptyset) = 0$ *and* $\mu(X) = 1$,
(ii) if $A, B \in \mathcal{F}$ such that $A \subseteq B$, then $\mu(A) \leq \mu(B)$.

A triplet $(X, \mathcal{F}, \mu)$ is called a *fuzzy measure space* whenever $(X, \mathcal{F})$ is a measurable space and μ is a fuzzy measure on $(X, \mathcal{F})$.

A negation on $[0,1]$ is a unary operation $\eta : [0,1] \to [0,1]$ such that η is a non-increasing map, $\eta(0) = 1$ and $\eta(1) = 0$ (see, e.g., [1]). A canonical example is a negation defined by the residuum on L, particularly, $\eta(a) = a \to 0$ for any $a \in [0,1]$. For a fuzzy measure μ on $(X, \mathcal{F})$, the map $\mu_\eta^c : \mathcal{F} \to [0,1]$ given by $\mu_\eta^c(A) = \eta(\mu(A^c))$ for any $A \in \mathcal{F}$, where A^c is the complement of A in X and η a negation, is a fuzzy measure called the η-*conjugate fuzzy measure to* μ (cf., [3]). In what follows, we use μ^c to denote the η-conjugate (conjugate, for short) fuzzy measure to μ with respect to $\eta(a) = 1 - a$ for $a \in [0,1]$.

Example 2. Let L be a complete residuated lattice, $X = \{x_1, \ldots, x_n\}$ be a finite non-empty set, and let $\mathcal{F}$ be an arbitrary algebra of sets. A *relative* fuzzy measure μ^r on $(X, \mathcal{F})$ is given as

$$\mu^r(A) = \frac{\#A}{\#X}$$

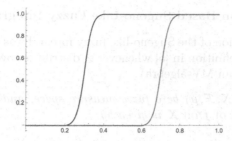

Fig. 2. The maps $\varphi^p_{l,u}$ (red) and $\varphi^{p,c}_{l,u}$ (green) determining a fuzzy measure and its conjugate fuzzy measure from Example 3. (Color figure online)

for all $A \in \mathcal{F}$, where $\#A$ and $\#X$ denote the number of elements in A and X, respectively. Let $\varphi : [0,1] \to [0,1]$ be a monotonically non-decreasing map with $\varphi(0) = 0$ and $\varphi(1) = 1$. The relative measure μ^r can be generalized as a fuzzy measure μ^r_φ on $(X, \mathcal{F})$ given by $\mu^r_\varphi(A) = \varphi(\mu^r(A))$ for any $A \in \mathcal{F}$.

Example 3. Let $(X, \mathcal{F})$ be the fuzzy measurable space from Example 2, and let $0 \le l \le u \le 1$ and $0 < p$ be a natural number. Define $\psi^p_{l,u}, \varphi^p_{l,u} : [0,1] \to [0,1]$ as follows

$$\psi^p_{l,u}(x) = \begin{cases} 0, & x \le l, \\ \frac{e^{p(2(x-l)/(u-l)-1)}}{e^{p(2(x-l)/(u-l)-1)}+1}, & l < x \le u, \\ 1, & \text{otherwise,} \end{cases} \tag{2}$$

and

$$\varphi^p_{l,u}(x) = \frac{\psi^p_{l,u}(x)(e^p+1)-1}{e^p-1} \tag{3}$$

for any $x \in (l, u]$, and $\varphi^p_{l,u}(x) = \psi^p_{l,u}(x)$, otherwise, where $\varphi^p_{l,u}$ modifies $\psi^p_{l,u}$ to get a continuous function on $[0,1]$. Since $\varphi^p_{l,u}$ is a monotonically non-decreasing map, then the map $\mu^p_{l,u} : \mathcal{F} \to [0,1]$ given by $\mu^p_{l,u} = \mu^r_{\varphi^p_{l,u}}$ is a fuzzy measure. Define $\varphi^{p,c}_{l,u}(x) = 1 - \varphi^p_{l,u}(1-x)$ for $x \in [0,1]$. One can see that the conjugate fuzzy measure to $\mu^p_{l,u}$ is then given by $\mu^{p,c}_{l,u} = \mu^r_{\varphi^{p,c}_{l,u}}$. An example of maps $\varphi^p_{l,u}$ and $\varphi^{p,c}_{l,u}$ for $l = 0.2$, $u = 0.4$ and $p = 5$ is displayed in Fig. 2. For example, if $\#X = 20$ and $A \in \mathcal{F}$ with $\#A = 6$, we get $\mu^p_{l,u}(A) = \varphi^p_{l,u}(0.3) = 0.5$ and $\mu^{p,c}_{l,u}(A) = \varphi^{p,c}_{l,u}(0.3) = 0$.

Remark 1. One can see that all fuzzy measures in the above examples are invariant with respect to the cardinality of sets, i.e. $\mu(A) = \mu(B)$, whenever A and B have the same cardinality, i.e. $\#A = \#B$. Such fuzzy measures are also referred to as *symmetric fuzzy measures*.

2.4 Multiplication Based Sugeno-Like Fuzzy Integral

The following definition of the Sugeno-like fuzzy integral was proposed in [3] and coincides with the definition in [5] whenever $\otimes$ distributes over $\bigwedge$ in the algebra of truth values (e.g. an MV-algebra).

Definition 3. *Let $(X, \mathcal{F}, \mu)$ be a fuzzy measure space, and let $f : X \to [0, 1]$. The $\otimes$-fuzzy integral of f on X is given by*

$$\int_X^\otimes f \, d\mu = \bigvee_{A \in \mathcal{F}} \mu(A) \otimes \left(\bigwedge_{x \in A} f(x) \right). \tag{4}$$

For a fuzzy measure space $(X, \mathcal{F}, \mu)$ defined over a finite set $X = \{x_1, \ldots, x_n\}$ with a symmetric fuzzy measure μ, the $\otimes$-fuzzy integral can be simply computed as follows:

$$\int_X^\otimes f \, d\mu = \bigvee_{i=1} f_i \otimes \mu_i, \tag{5}$$

where f_i is the i-th largest function value from the set $\{f(x_i) \mid i = 1, \ldots, n\}$ and $\mu_i = \mu(\{x_1, \ldots, x_i\})$.

3   Integral Transforms

A fuzzy relation $K : X \times Y \to [0, 1]$ is said to be *normal* in the second argument if $\mathrm{Core}(K_y) \neq \emptyset$ for any $y \in Y$, where $K_y(\cdot) = K(\cdot, y)$. A fuzzy relation $K^T : Y \times X \to [0, 1]$ given by $K^T(x, y) = K(y, x)$ for any $(x, y) \in X \times Y$ is called the *transpose of the fuzzy relation* K.

Definition 4. *A fuzzy relation $K : X \times Y \to L$ which is normal in the second argument is said to be an* integral kernel.

The next definition generalizes the upper and lower F-transforms and unifies the definitions of integral transforms mentioned in Introduction.

Definition 5. *Let $(X, \mathcal{F}, \mu)$ be a fuzzy measure space, let $K : X \times Y \to L$ be an integral kernel, and let $\odot \in \{\otimes, \to\}$. A map $F^\odot_{(K,\mu)} : \mathcal{F}(X) \to \mathcal{F}(Y)$ defined by*

$$F^\odot_{(K,\mu)}(f)(y) = \int_X^\otimes K(x, y) \odot f(x) \, d\mu, \tag{6}$$

is called a $(K, \mu, \odot)$-integral transform.

The elementary properties of integral transforms for lattice-valued functions can be found in [7]. The following theorem shows conditions under which a constant function (fuzzy set) a_X is transformed to a constant function a_Y, i.e., $F^\odot_{(K,\mu)}(a_X) = a_Y$.

Theorem 1. *Let $(X, \mathcal{F}, \mu)$ be a fuzzy measure space, let K be an integral kernel, and let $a \in L$.*

(i) If for any $y \in Y$ there exists $A_y \in \mathcal{F}$ such that $A_y \subseteq \mathrm{Core}(K_y)$ and $\mu(A_y) = 1$, then $F_{(K,\mu)}^{\otimes}(a_X) = a_Y$.

(ii) If for any $y \in Y$ and for any $A \in \mathcal{F}$ with $A \subseteq X \backslash \mathrm{Core}(K_y)$ it holds that $\mu(A) \leq a$, then $F_{(K,\mu)}^{\rightarrow}(a_X) = a_Y$.

It is worth noting that the standard real-valued F-transforms as well as lower and upper lattice-valued F-transforms preserve constant functions; therefore, it seems to be reasonable to assume that integral kernels and fuzzy measures as the parameters of the integral transforms satisfy the conditions under which the constant functions are preserved.

Example 4. Let $\mu = \mu_{l,u}^p$ and $\mu^c = \mu_{l,u}^{p,c}$ be fuzzy measures on $(X, \mathcal{F})$ introduced in Example 3, and let $K : X \times Y \to [0, 1]$ be an integral kernel, where $Y = \{y_1, \ldots, y_m\}$. If μ satisfies (i) of Theorem 1, then μ^c satisfies (ii) of this theorem for any $a \in [0, 1]$. Indeed, for any $y \in Y$, select a measurable set $A_y \in \mathcal{F}$ such that

(a) $A_y \subseteq \mathrm{Core}(K_y)$ and $\mu(A_y) = 1$, and
(b) if $B \in \mathcal{F}$ with $B \subseteq \mathrm{Core}(K_y)$ and $\mu(B) = 1$, $\#A_y \leq \#B$.

Obviously, for $y \in Y$, there can be more than one measurable set, for which (a) and (b) are satisfied, and only one is chosen. Put $r = \min\{\#A_y \mid y \in Y\}$ and recall that $n = \#X$. Since $\mu(A_y) = 1$ for any $y \in Y$, we find that $u \leq r/n$. Let $y \in Y$ and $B \in \mathcal{F}$ be arbitrary such that $B \subseteq X \backslash \mathrm{Core}(K_y)$, and put $s = \#B$. Since $\#\mathrm{Core}(K_y) \geq r$ for any $y \in Y$, we find that $s = \#B \leq \#X \backslash \mathrm{Core}(K_y) \leq n - r$; therefore, $s/n \leq 1 - r/n \leq 1 - u$. Since $\varphi_{l,u}^{p,c}(x) = 1 - \varphi_{l,u}^p(1-x)$ is a non-decreasing map, we obtain

$$\mu^c(B) = 1 - \varphi_{l,u}^p(1 - s/n) \leq 1 - \varphi_{l,u}^p(1 - (1-u)) = 1 - \varphi_{l,u}^p(u) = 1 - 1 = 0,$$

which concludes the verification of the first implication.

4   Application of Integral Transforms to Image Processing

In this part, we apply integral transforms to image processing, namely, filtering and compression/decompression of images. For the purpose of this paper, we restrict ourselves to grayscale images. We assume that an image h of the size $N \times M$ (the number of pixels in rows and columns) is a map $I : D \to [0, 1]$, where $D = \{(i, j) \mid 1 \leq i \leq N, 1 \leq j \leq M\}$ and the value $I(i, j)$ expresses the intensity of shades of gray from black to white for the pixel at the position $(i, j) \in D$.[3] Since an image is a two-dimensional function, we consider integral transforms from $\mathcal{F}(D)$ to $\mathcal{F}(D')$, where D and D' are the domains of images. In the following, we first describe the process of how the integral transform is applied to the above tasks and then demonstrate it in Lena image.

---

[3] For simplicity, we assume that the shade of gray can be determined for any number from $[0, 1]$.

4.1   Method Description

Let N_1, N_2, ϱ be natural numbers such that ϱ divides N_i for $i = 1, 2$, and denote $n_i = N/\varrho$ for $i = 1, 2$. The number ϱ is called the *shift* and refers to the compression ratio, which is equal to $\varrho^2 : 1$. Denote $D = \{(i,j) \mid 1 \leq i \leq N_1, 1 \leq j \leq N_2\}$ and $D_\varrho = \{(i,j) \mid 1 \leq i \leq n_1, 1 \leq j \leq n_2\}$, which expresses the domain for the compressed image ($\varrho > 1$) or filtered image ($\varrho = 1$). Let r be a natural number such that $\varrho \leq r \ll \min(N_1, N_2)$, and let $W = (w_{i,j})_{i,j=-r}^r$ be an $n \times n$ matrix of values from $[0,1]$ (which will be referred to as the *window* of size $n \times n$), where $n = 2r + 1$. In our application, we assume that $w_{00} = 1$.

Image Filtering and Compression. Both techniques present a transformation of an image from $\mathcal{F}(D)$ to an image in $\mathcal{F}(D_\varrho)$. Image filtering is obtained for $\varrho = 1$ and can be used to modify or enhance an image. Image compression is obtained for $\varrho > 1$ and one can reduce the size of an image. Our approach is based on the integral transform for lattice-valued functions, where the integral kernel $K : D \times D_\varrho \to [0,1]$ is derived from the window W as follows:

$$K_W((i,j),(i',j')) = \begin{cases} W(\pi_1(i,i'), \pi_2(j,j')), & \max(\#\pi_1(i,i'), \#\pi_2(j,j')) \leq r, \\ 0, & \text{otherwise,} \end{cases}$$

where $\pi_1(i,i') = \varrho(i'-1) + 1 - i$ and $\pi_2(j,j') = \varrho(j'-1) + 1 - j$. One can see that the integral kernel K represents a "sliding window" across the image, where the windows are centered and applied in points $(\varrho(i'-1)+1, \varrho(j'-1)+1)$ for $(i',j') \in D_\varrho$. Image filter and compression are defined together as an $(K_W, \mu, \odot)$-integral transform of $\mathcal{F}(D)$ to $\mathcal{F}(D_\varrho)$, where K_W is the integral kernel determined by a window W and μ is a fuzzy measure on $(D, \mathcal{F}(D))$ such that $F_{(K_W,\mu)}^{\odot}$ preserves constant functions. In case of image compression, we assume that K_W^T is again an integral kernel, which means that the family of sets $\{\text{Core}(K_{W,(i',j')}) \mid (i',j') \in D_\varrho\}$ covers D.

Image Decompression. This technique presents a transformation of compressed images from $\mathcal{F}(D_\varrho)$ to $\mathcal{F}(D)$. In our approach, we use $(K_W^T, \nu, \bar{\odot})$-integral transform, where K_W^T is the transpose of the integral kernel K_W, ν is a fuzzy measure on $(D_\varrho, \mathcal{F}(D_\varrho))$ such that $F_{(K_W^T, \nu)}^{\bar{\odot}}$ preserves constant functions, and $\bar{\odot}$ is the adjoined operation to $\odot$, i.e. if $\odot = \otimes$, then $\bar{\odot} = \to$ and vice versa.

By setting of the window (kernel), operation $\odot \in \{\otimes, \to\}$, and fuzzy measures μ and ν, one can determine a type of filtering and compression/decompression. For $\varrho = 1$, if $W = \{1\}_{i,j=-1}^r$, and we set $\mu = \mu_{0.5,0.5}^1$, we obtain the standard median filter. If we set $\mu = \mu_{0,0}^1$ or $\mu = \mu_{1-,1-}^1$, where $\mu_{1-,1-}^1 = \lim_{u\to 1^-} \mu_{u,u}^1$, we get minimum and maximum filter. If we consider $W = \{w_{ij}\}_{i,j=-r}^r$ and $\mu = \mu_{0.5,0.5}^1$, we obtain an weighted median filter. Therefore, our approach to filtering images can be viewed as a generalization of the mentioned techniques.

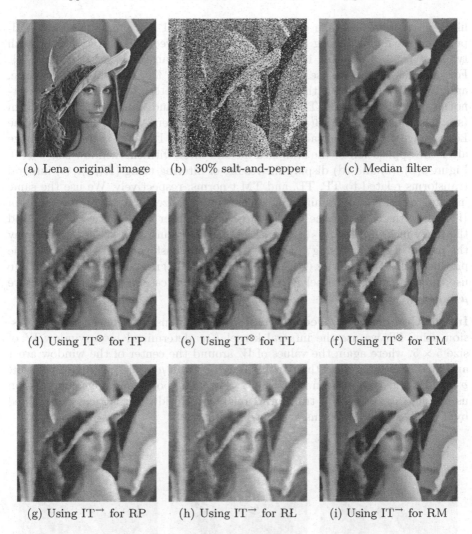

(a) Lena original image   (b) 30% salt-and-pepper   (c) Median filter

(d) Using $IT^{\otimes}$ for TP   (e) Using $IT^{\otimes}$ for TL   (f) Using $IT^{\otimes}$ for TM

(g) Using $IT^{\rightarrow}$ for RP   (h) Using $IT^{\rightarrow}$ for RŁ   (i) Using $IT^{\rightarrow}$ for RM

Fig. 3. Filtering Lena image with 30% salt-and-pepper noise using $IT^{\otimes}$ related to t-norms: TP, TŁ, TM, and $IT^{\rightarrow}$ related to residua: RP, RŁ, RM.

4.2   Illustration of Filtering and Compression/Decompression

The aim of this part is to illustrate our method based on the integral transforms for lattice-valued functions. We do not have the ambition to present results that go beyond current approaches, but we want to bring a more general method with a wide space for setting parameters that could help to improve some of the popular methods like the median, minimum, or median filter. For illustration, we use the Lena image (256×256).

Image Filtering. Our approach can be used as a non-linear filter to remove a salt-and-pepper noise, which is a consequence of the fact that the median filter is a special example of integral transform (IT for short). The salt-and-pepper noise removal using IT based filters is displayed in Fig. 3, where the both types of ITs are applied, i.e., $(K, \mu, \odot)$-integral transforms for $\odot = \{\otimes, \rightarrow\}$. For our illustration, we use the Lena image with 30% of salt-and-pepper noise, and the $IT^\otimes$ defined on the residuated lattices determined by continuous t-norms, namely, product (TP), Łukasiewicz (TŁ), and minimum (TM) t-norm (see, Example 1). Figure 3(a) shows the original Lena image, Fig. 3(b) is the Lena image with 30% of salt-and-pepper noise, and Fig. 3(c) is the Lena image after the application of the standard median filter with the window size 9×9. Figure 3(b), (c) and (d) display the results of filtering using $(K_W, \mu, \otimes)$-integral transforms related to TP, TŁ, and TM t-norms, respectively. We use the same integral kernel K_W determined by a window W of size 9×9, where the values of W around the center of the window are 1 and farther away are less than 1, and the fuzzy measure $\mu = \mu_{0.2,0.3}^5$ (see, Example 2). Figure 3(e), (f) and (g) display the results of filtering using $(K_W, \mu, \rightarrow)$-integral transforms ($IT^\rightarrow$) related to the product (RP), Łukasiewicz (RŁ), and minimum (RM) residuum, respectively. We use the same integral kernel K_W as in the previous case and the fuzzy measure $\mu = \mu_{0.48,0.49}^5$.

Image Compression/Decompression. To demonstrate the image compression using IT, we use the integral kernel K_W determined by a window W of size 5×5, where again the values of W around the center of the window are 1 and farther away are less than 1, the fuzzy measure $\mu = \mu_{0.16,0.24}^5$, and the shift $\varrho = 2$, i.e., the compression ratio is $4 : 1$. The results of Lena image compression using $(K_W, \mu, \otimes)$-integral transforms related to residuated lattices determined by TP, TŁ and TM t-norms are shown in Fig. 4.

(a) TP   (b) TŁ   (c) TM

Fig. 4. Lena image compression in a ratio of $4 : 1$ using $IT^\otimes$ related to TP, TŁ, TM t-norms.

Figure 5 shows the results of Lena image decompression using IT. We apply the $(K_W^T, \nu, \rightarrow)$-integral transforms with the conjugate fuzzy measure $\nu = \mu_{0,0.04}^{5,c}$ (see, Example 3) to the compressed Lena image obtained by the $(K_W, \mu, \otimes)$-integral transforms with the fuzzy measure $\mu_{0.16,0.24}^5$. It should be emphasized that $\otimes$ and $\rightarrow$ form the adjoined pair, i.e., if TP is used for compression, RP is then used for decompression, and similarly for other operations. Figure 5(a) presents the Lena original image. Figure 5(b), (c) and (d) display the results of the Lena image decompression using $\mathrm{IT}^{\rightarrow}$ related to RP, RŁ and RM residuum, respectively.

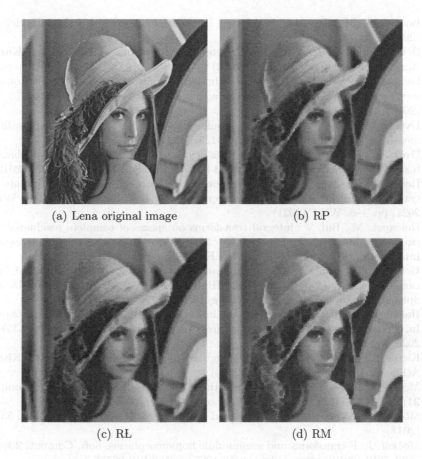

(a) Lena original image   (b) RP

(c) RŁ   (d) RM

Fig. 5. Lena image decompression using $\mathrm{IT}^{\rightarrow}$ related to RP, RŁ, RM residua.

5   Conclusion

The paper aimed to demonstrate an application of integral transforms for lattice-valued functions to image processing. We introduced the integral kernel determined by a window and fuzzy measures based on the relative cardinality, which, together with residuated lattice operations, are parameters of integral transform methods for image filtering and compression/decompression. The proposed methods are illustrated in Lena image processing. In future research, we plan to analyze the relationship between the setting of integral transform parameters and the results for image filtering and compression/decompression, and other tasks in image processing.

References

1. Baczyński, M., Jayaram, B.: Fuzzy Implications. Springer-Verlag, Heidelberg (2010)
2. Bělohlávek, R.: Fuzzy Relational Systems: Foundations and Principles. Kluwer Academic Publishers, New York (2002)
3. Dubois, D., Prade, H., Rico, A.: Residuated variants of sugeno integrals: towards new weighting schemes for qualitative aggregation methods. Inf. Sci. **329**, 765–781 (2016)
4. Dvořák, A., Holčapek, M.: L-fuzzy quantifiers of type ⟨1⟩ determined by fuzzy measures. Fuzzy Sets Syst. **160**(23), 3425–3452 (2009)
5. Dvořák, A., Holčapek, M.: Fuzzy measures and integrals defined on algebras of fuzzy subsets over complete residuated lattices. Inf. Sci. **185**(1), 205–229 (2012)
6. Holčapek, M., Quoc Bui, V.: Reconstruction of lattice-valued functions by integral transforms. In: International Workshop on Fuzzy Logic and Applications, WILF 2021, pp. 1–8. WILF (2021)
7. Holčapek, M., Bui, V.: Integral transforms on spaces of complete residuated lattice valued functions. In: Proceedings of IEEE World Congress on Computational Intelligence, WCCI 2020, pp. 1–8. IEEE (2020)
8. Holčapek, M., Bui, V.: On integral transforms for residuated lattice-valued functions. In: Lesot, M.-J., et al. (eds.) IPMU 2020. CCIS, vol. 1239, pp. 318–331. Springer, Cham (2020). https://doi.org/10.1007/978-3-030-50153-2_24
9. Holčapek, M., Rico, A.: A note on the links between different qualitative integrals. In: Proceedings of IEEE World Congress on Computational Intelligence, WCCI 2020, pp. 1–8. IEEE (2020)
10. Klement, E., Mesiar, R., Pap, E.: Triangular Norms, Trends in Logic, vol. 8. Kluwer Academic Publishers, Dordrecht (2000)
11. Močkoř, J.: Spaces with fuzzy partitions and fuzzy transform. Soft. Comput. **21**(13), 3479–3492 (2017). https://doi.org/10.1007/s00500-017-2541-7
12. Močkoř, J.: Axiomatic of lattice-valued F-transform. Fuzzy Sets Syst. **342**, 53–66 (2018)
13. Močkoř, J.: F-transforms and semimodule homomorphisms. Soft. Comput. **23**(17), 7603–7619 (2019). https://doi.org/10.1007/s00500-019-03766-1
14. Močkoř, J., Holčapek, M.: Fuzzy objects in spaces with fuzzy partitions. Soft. Comput. **21**(24), 7269–7284 (2016). https://doi.org/10.1007/s00500-016-2431-4
15. Močkoř, J., Hurtík, P.: Lattice-valued f-transforms and similarity relations. Fuzzy Sets Syst. **342**, 67–89 (2018)
16. Perfilieva, I.: Fuzzy transforms: theory and applications. Fuzzy Sets Syst. **157**(8), 993–1023 (2006)
17. Soille, P.: Morphological Image Analysis. Principle and Applications. Springer, New York (1999). https://doi.org/10.1007/978-3-662-05088-0
18. Tiwari, S., Perfilieva, I., Singh, A.: Generalized residuate lattice based F-transform. Iran. J. Fuzzy Syst. **18**(2), 165–182 (2015)

Interval Uncertainty

Why People Tend to Overestimate Joint Probabilities

Olga Kosheleva and Vladik Kreinovich(✉)

University of Texas at El Paso, El Paso, TX 79968, USA
{olgak,vladik}@utep.edu
https://www.cs.utep.edu/vladik/olgavita.html,
https://www.cs.utep.edu/vladik/longvita.html

Abstract. It is known that, in general, people overestimate the probabilities of joint events. In this paper, we provide an explanation for this phenomenon – an explanation based on Laplace Indeterminacy Principle and Maximum Entropy approach.

Keywords: Subjective probability · Interval uncertainty · Maximum Entropy approach · Laplace Indeterminacy Principle · Fuzzy logic

1 Formulation of the Problem

1.1 Description of the Situation

In many practical situations, we need to estimate the probability that two events A and B both happen – i.e., in other words, we need to estimate the joint probability $P(A \& B)$. Often, the only information that we have about two events A and B are their probabilities $a = P(A)$ and $b = P(B)$, and we have no information about the relation between these two events.

In this case, what should be a reasonable estimate for $P(A \& B)$?

1.2 A Natural Solution to Such Situations

This is an example of a situation when we need to make a decision under uncertainty, i.e., in this case, when we do not have full information about the probabilities. Such situations are ubiquitous, and in probability theory, there is a natural

---

This work was supported in part by the National Science Foundation grants 1623190 (A Model of Change for Preparing a New Generation for Professional Practice in Computer Science), and HRD-1834620 and HRD-2034030 (CAHSI Includes), and by the AT&T Fellowship in Information Technology.

It was also supported by the program of the development of the Scientific-Educational Mathematical Center of Volga Federal District No. 075-02-2020-1478, and by a grant from the Hungarian National Research, Development and Innovation Office (NRDI). The authors are thankful to the anonymous referees for valuable suggestions.

D. Ciucci et al. (Eds.): IPMU 2022, CCIS 1601, pp. 485–493, 2022.
https://doi.org/10.1007/978-3-031-08971-8_40

general approach to solving these problems. Its main idea is that different possible probability distributions correspond, in general, to different amounts of uncertainty. A natural measure of uncertainty is the average number of binary ("yes"-"no") questions that we need to ask to uniquely determine the situation. It is known that in situations when we have n alternatives with probabilities $p_1, \ldots, p_n$, this average number of questions is equal to Shannon's entropy $S = -\sum_{i=1}^{n} p_i \cdot \log_2(p_i)$; see, e.g., [15].

It is reasonable not to pretend that we have less uncertainty than we do. For example, suppose that we know only that we have n alternatives, and we do not have any information about the probabilities of these alternatives. It may be that the probability of the first alternative is 1 and the probabilities of all other alternatives are 0s. In this case, we have no uncertainty at all – so the entropy is 0. But if we select this distribution, we will be inserting certainty where there is a lot of uncertainty – e.g., we can have a probability distribution in which $p_1 = \ldots = p_n = 1/n$, in which case $S = \log_2(n)$.

To avoid artificially inserting certainty, it is reasonable to select, among all possible distributions, the one with the largest possible value of entropy. This approach is known as the *Maximum Entropy approach*; see, e.g., [7].

In particular, for the case when we have n alternatives, and we have no information about their probabilities, Maximum Entropy approach implies that we select the distribution in which all these alternatives have the same probability $1/n$. This makes perfect sense: since we have no reason to prefer one of the alternatives, it makes sense to assign the same probability to all of them. This idea was first explicitly formulated by Laplace and is known as *Laplace Indeterminacy Principle*.

1.3   What if We Apply This Approach to Our Situation

In our situation, we have four possible alternatives: $A \& B$, $A \& \neg B$, $\neg A \& B$, and $\neg A \& \neg B$. Once we select the probability $p = P(A \& B)$, we can find all other probabilities:

$$P(A \& \neg B) = P(A) - P(A \& B) = a - p,$$

$$P(\neg A \& B) = P(B) - P(A \& B) = b - p, \text{ and}$$

$$P(\neg A \& \neg B) = 1 - P(A \& B) - P(A \& \neg B) - P(\neg A \& B)$$

$$= 1 - p - (a - p) - (b - p) = 1 + p - a - b.$$

In this case, the entropy has the form

$$-p \cdot \log_2(p) - (a - p) \cdot \log_2(a - p) - (b - p) \cdot \log_2(b - p)$$
$$-(1 + p - a - b) \cdot \log_2(1 + p - a - b). \tag{1}$$

Here, for every x, we have

$$\log_2(x) = \frac{\ln(x)}{\ln(2)}.$$

Maximizing the expression (1) is equivalent to maximizing the same expression multiplied by $\ln(2)$, i.e., the expression

$$-p \cdot \ln(p) - (a - p) \cdot \ln(a - p) - (b - p) \cdot \ln(b - p) - (1 + p - a - b) \cdot \ln(1 + p - a - b). \quad (2)$$

Differentiating this expression with respect to p and equating the derivative to 0, we conclude that

$$-1 - \ln(p) + 1 + \ln(a - p) + 1 + \ln(b - p) - 1 - \ln(1 + p - a - b) = 0,$$

i.e.,

$$-\ln(p) + \ln(a - p) + \ln(b - p) - \ln(1 + p - a - b) = 0.$$

Applying the exponential function to both sides and taking into account that $\exp(0) = 1$, $\exp(\ln(x)) = x$, $\exp(a + b) = a + b$, and $\exp(a - b) = a/b$, we conclude that

$$\frac{p \cdot (1 + p - a - b)}{(a - p) \cdot (b - p)} = 1,$$

i.e., equivalently, that

$$p \cdot (1 + p - a - b) = (a - p) \cdot (b - p).$$

Opening parentheses, we get

$$p + p^2 - a \cdot p - b \cdot p = a \cdot b - a \cdot p - b \cdot p + p^2.$$

Canceling equal terms in both sides, we conclude that

$$p = a \cdot b.$$

So, in our situation, a reasonable estimate for the joint probability $P(A \& B)$ is the product $P(A) \cdot P(B)$, corresponding to the case when the events A and B are independent.

1.4 How Do People Actually Estimate the Joint Probability

Empirical data shows that in situations when people know the probabilities $P(A)$ and $P(B)$ of individual events A and B – and they have no additional information – they often overestimate the probability $P(A \& B)$ of the joint event $A \& B$; see, e.g., [1,17,22,23]. This happens both when we explicitly ask them to estimate the corresponding probabilities, and when we extract their estimated probabilities from their preferences.

In other words, they usually provide an estimate which is larger than the product $P(A) \cdot P(B)$.

1.5 Formulation of the Problem

How can we explain this phenomenon?

1.6 Important Comment

In most of the above-cited experiments, people were given:

- either situations in which both A and B are somewhat rare events with non-zero probabilities, i.e., when $0 < a < 0.5$ and $0 < b < 0.5$,
- or situations in which both A and B are rather frequent events with some uncertainty, i.e., when $0.5 < a < 1$ and $0.5 < b < 1$.

2 Our Explanation

2.1 Main Idea Behind This Explanation

In situations when the only information that we have about two events A and B are the probabilities $a = P(A)$ and $b = P(B)$ of these two events, what are the possible values of the joint probability $p = P(A \& B)$? It is known that the set of such possible values is determined by the so-called Frechet inequality (see, e.g., [20]):

$$\max(a + b - 1, 0) \leq p \leq \min(a, b).$$

In other words, possible values of the joint probability p form an interval

$$[\max(a + b - 1, 0), \min(a, b)].$$

This is an example of an *interval uncertainty*; see, e.g., [6,11,13].

All values from this interval are possible, and we have no reason to conclude that some values are more probable than others. It is therefore reasonable to assume that all these values are equally probable, i.e., that we have a uniform distribution on this interval. As we have mentioned earlier, such a conclusion – corresponding to Laplace Indeterminacy Principle – also follows from the Maximum Entropy approach.

According to decision theory (see, e.g., [4,5,9,10,14,15,19]), a rational person should make decisions based on the expected value of the utility. In case of a binary decision, this simply means using the expected (mean) value of the unknown probability p. For the uniform distribution on an interval, the mean value is the midpoint of this interval, i.e., the value

$$p = \frac{\max(a + b - 1, 0) + \min(a, b)}{2}. \tag{3}$$

2.2 This Idea Explains the Observed Overestimation: Case When $0 < a < 0.5$ and $0 < b < 0.5$

Let us show that in both above cases, our main idea explains the observed overestimation of joint probabilities.

Let us start with the case when $0 < a < 0.5$ and $0 < b < 0.5$. In this case, $a + b < 1$, so $\max(a + b - 1, 0) = 0$, and the formula (3) takes the form

$$p = \frac{\min(a, b)}{2}. \tag{4}$$

There are two possible cases here: $a \leq b$ and $b \leq a$. If $b \leq a$, then we can simply rename A and B as, correspondingly, B and A. Thus, without losing generality, we can assume that $a \leq b$. In this case, the formula (4) implies that $p = a/2$. We need to show that $a \cdot b < p = a/2$. Indeed, in this case, $b < 0.5$. Multiplying both sides of this inequality by $a > 0$, we get the desired inequality $a \cdot b < p/2$.

2.3 This Idea Explains the Observed Overestimation: Case When $0.5 < a < 1$ and $0.5 < b < 1$

Let us now consider the case when $0.5 < a < 1$ and $0.5 < b < 1$. In this case, $a + b > 1$, so $\max(a + b - 1, 0) = a + b - 1$. Similarly to the previous case, without losing generality, we can assume that $a \leq b$ and thus, $\min(a, b) = a$. Then, the formula (3) takes the form

$$p = \frac{a + b - 1 + a}{2} = \frac{2a + b - 1}{2}. \tag{5}$$

The desired inequality

$$a \cdot b < \frac{2a + b - 1}{2} \tag{6}$$

is equivalent to

$$2 \cdot a \cdot b < 2a + b - 1,$$

i.e., by moving terms between sides, to

$$1 - b < 2a - 2a \cdot b = 2a \cdot (1 - b). \tag{7}$$

Since $0.5 < a$, we have $1 < 2a$. Multiplying both sides of this inequality by $1 - b > 0$, we get the inequality (7) – and thus, the desired inequality (6) – which is equivalent to (7).

So, in both cases, the reasonable estimate (3) is larger than the product $a \cdot b$ – which explains the observed overestimation of joint probabilities.

2.4 What About the General Case?

Without losing generality, we can assume that $a \leq b$. We have considered cases when both a and b are smaller than 0.5 and when both a and b are larger than 0.5. So, the only remaining case is when $a \leq 0.5 \leq b$. We can have two subcases:

– the subcase when $a + b \leq 1$, and
– the subcase when $a + b > 1$.

In the first subcase, we have $\max(a + b - 1, 0) = 0$ and thus, $p = a/2$. In this case, since $0.5 \leq b$, we have $a/2 \leq a \cdot b$. So, we have either the exact estimate, or – when $a > 0$ and $b > 0.5$ – an *underestimation*. For example, when $a = 0.4$ and $b = 0.6$, the formula (3) leads to $p = 0.2 < 0.4 \cdot 0.6 = 0.24$.

In the second subcase, we have $\max(a + b - 1, 0) = a + b - 1$, and thus, similarly to the case when both a and b are larger than 0.5, we conclude that the value (3) is either the exact estimate – when $a = 0$ or when $b = 0.5$ – or an overestimation.

Let us describe, in the areas where $a \leq b$, subareas of overestimation $(+)$ and underestimation $(-)$:

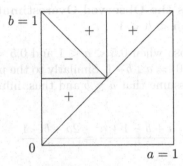

We have four equal-size triangles. In three out of four of them we have overestimation. This explains why in most cases, people overestimate joint probabilities.

3   Discussion

3.1   Is There an Inconsistency Here?

Before we discuss possible consequences of our explanation, we need to first clarify the situation, since what we described may sound fishy.

- In the first section of this paper, we used Maximum Entropy approach to conclude that, when we only know the probabilities $a = P(A)$ and $b = P(B)$, then the best estimate for $P(A \& B)$ must be the product $a \cdot b$.
- However, in the previous section, we used the same Maximum Entropy approach to come up with a completely different formula.

At first glance, this may sound like an inconsistency, but it is not.

It is well known that the same Maximum Entropy approach can lead to different answers – depending on how we formulate the problem. Let us give a simple example.

- Suppose that all we know is that a quantity x – e.g., the standard deviation – is somewhere on the interval $[0, 1]$. In this case, as we have mentioned earlier, the Maximum Entropy approach recommends that we assume that all the values from this interval are equally probable – i.e., that we have a uniform distribution on this interval.

- On the other hand, if all we know about x is that it is somewhere on the interval $[0, 1]$, then all we know about $y = x^2$ – e.g., about variance – is that it is somewhere in the interval $[0, 1]$. If we apply the same Maximum Entropy approach to the distribution of y, then we can conclude that y is also uniformly distributed on the interval $[0, 1]$.

However, if x is uniformly distributed, then the distribution of $y = x^2$ is *not* uniform, so these conclusions are indeed different.

3.2   What if We Have Three of More Events?

Suppose now that we know the probabilities $a_i = P(A_i)$ of n different events $A_1, \ldots, A_n$, and we want to estimate the joint probability $p = P(A_1 \& \ldots \& A_n)$. In this case, the only thing we know about p is that it belongs to the interval

$$[\max(a_1 + \ldots + a_n - (n - 1), 0), \min(a_1, \ldots, a_n)],$$

so the same logic as for the above case of two events leads us to the conclusion that a reasonable estimate would be the midpoint of this interval, i.e., the value

$$\frac{\max(a_1 + \ldots + a_n - (n - 1), 0) + \min(a_1, \ldots, a_n)}{2}. \tag{8}$$

It is important to mention that, e.g., for $n = 3$, this estimate is different from what we would have obtained if we:

- first use the two-event formula to estimate the probability of $A_1 \& A_2$, and
- then apply the same two-event formula to the events $A_1 \& A_2$ and A_3.

For example, if $a_1 = a_2 = a_3 = 0.6$, then:

- On the one hand, the formula (8) leads to

$$\frac{\max(1.8 - 2, 0) + 0.6}{2} = 0.3.$$

- On the other hand, our estimate for $P(A_1 \& A_2)$ is

$$\frac{\max(1.2 - 1, 0) + 0.6}{2} = \frac{0.2 + 0.6}{2} = 0.4;$$

using the formula (3) to combine 0.4 and 0.6, we get

$$\frac{\max(0.4 + 0.6 - 1, 0 + \min(0.4, 0.6)}{2} = \frac{0.4}{2} = 0.2,$$

which is indeed different from 0.3.

3.3 Computational Conclusion

As we have mentioned, there are two reasonable way to apply Maximum Entropy approach to our situation, that lead to two different formulas: the product formula $a \cdot b$, and a different formula (3). As we have also mentioned, people, in general, overestimate the joint probabilities – i.e., produce estimates which are larger than $a \cdot b$.

So, if we want to adequately describe human reasoning, we need to use general "and"-combination rules which leads to values larger than $a \cdot b$. Such rules – under the name of t-norms – are typical is fuzzy logic; see, e.g., [2,8,12,16,18,24]. So, we arrive at one more argument that fuzzy techniques are necessary if we want to adequately describe human reasoning – and an adequate description of such reasoning is one of the objectives of AI.

3.4 Physical Conclusions

In physical terns, the fact that the joint probability is, in general, larger than the probability $a \cdot b$ corresponding to independent events means that there is, in general, a correlation between many events. In plain English, this means that everything in the world is interconnected – when formulated in these terms, this becomes a truism: everything in the world *is* interconnected; see, e.g., [3,21].

References

1. Bar-Hillel, M.: On the subjective probability of compound events. Organ. Behav. Hum. Perform. **9**(4), 396–406 (1973)
2. Belohlavek, R., Dauben, J.W., Klir, G.J.: Fuzzy Logic and Mathematics: A Historical Perspective. Oxford University Press, New York (2017)
3. Feynman, R., Leighton, R., Sands, M.: The Feynman Lectures on Physics. Addison Wesley, Boston, Massachusetts (2005)
4. Fishburn, P.C.: Utility Theory for Decision Making. Wiley, New York (1969)
5. Fishburn, P.C.: Nonlinear Preference and Utility Theory. The John Hopkins Press, Baltimore, Maryland (1988)
6. Jaulin, L., Kiefer, M., Didrit, O., Walter, E.: Applied Interval Analysis. With Examples in Parameter and State Estimation, Robust Control, and Robotics. Springer, London (2001). https://doi.org/10.1007/978-1-4471-0249-6
7. Jaynes, E.T., Bretthorst, G.L.: Probability Theory: The Logic of Science. Cambridge University Press, Cambridge, UK (2003)
8. Klir, G., Yuan, B.: Fuzzy Sets and Fuzzy Logic. Prentice Hall, Upper Saddle River, New Jersey (1995)
9. Kreinovich, V.: Decision making under interval uncertainty (and beyond). In: Guo, P., Pedrycz, W. (eds.) Human-Centric Decision-Making Models for Social Sciences. SCI, vol. 502, pp. 163–193. Springer, Heidelberg (2014). https://doi.org/10.1007/978-3-642-39307-5_8
10. Luce, R.D., Raiffa, R.: Games and Decisions: Introduction and Critical Survey. Dover, New York (1989)
11. Mayer, G.: Interval Analysis and Automatic Result Verification. de Gruyter, Berlin (2017)

12. Mendel, J.M.: Uncertain Rule-Based Fuzzy Systems: Introduction and New Directions. Springer, Cham (2017). https://doi.org/10.1007/978-3-319-51370-6
13. Moore, R.E., Kearfott, R.B., Cloud, M.J.: Introduction to Interval Analysis. SIAM, Philadelphia (2009)
14. Nguyen, H.T., Kosheleva, O., Kreinovich, V.: Decision making beyond Arrow's 'impossibility theorem', with the analysis of effects of collusion and mutual attraction. Int. J. Intell. Syst. **24**(1), 27–47 (2009)
15. Nguyen, H.T., Kreinovich, V., Wu, B., Xiang, G.: Computing mean under interval uncertainty. In: Nguyen, H.T., Kreinovich, V., Wu, B., Xiang, G. (eds.) Computing Statistics under Interval and Fuzzy Uncertainty, p. 63. Springer, Heidelberg (2012). https://doi.org/10.1007/978-3-642-24905-1_12
16. Nguyen, H.T., Walker, C.L., Walker, E.A.: A First Course in Fuzzy Logic. Chapman and Hall/CRC, Boca Raton, Florida (2019)
17. Nilsson, H., Rieskamp, J., Jenny, M.A.: Exploring the overestimation of conjunctive probabilities. Front. Psychol. **4**, 101 (2013)
18. Novak, V., Perfilieva, I., Mockor, I.: Mathematical Principles of Fuzzy Logic. Kluwer, Boston, Dordrecht (1999)
19. Raiffa, H.: Decision Analysis. McGraw-Hill, Columbus, Ohio (1997)
20. Sheskin, D.J.: Handbook of Parametric and Non-Parametric Statistical Procedures. Chapman & Hall/CRC, London, UK (2011)
21. Thorne, K.S., Blandford, R.D.: Modern Classical Physics: Optics, Fluids, Plasmas, Elasticity, Relativity, and Statistical Physics. Princeton University Press, Princeton, New Jersey (2017)
22. Tversky, A., Kahneman, D.: Judgment under uncertainty: heuristics and biases. Sci. New Ser. **185**(4157), 1124–1131 (1974)
23. Wedell, D.H., Moro, R.: Testing boundary conditions for the conjunction fallacy: effects of response mode, conceptual focus and problem type. Cognition **107**, 105–136 (2008)
24. Zadeh, L.A.: Fuzzy sets. Inf. Control **8**, 338–353 (1965)

Necessary and Possibly Optimal Items in Selecting Problems

Sébastien Destercke[1] and Romain Guillaume[2(✉)]

[1] UMR CNRS 7253 Heudiasyc, Sorbonne Université, Université de Technologie de Compiègne CS 60319, 60203 Compiègne cedex, France
Sebastien.Destercke@hds.utc.fr
[2] University of Toulouse 2, IRIT, Toulouse, France
Romain.Guillaume@hds.utc.fr

Abstract. In this paper, we consider the classical and basic optimisation problem consisting in selecting a set of p items among n with minimal costs, but where the costs are ill-known or uncertain. As the optimal solution in such a case is no longer uniquely nor well-defined, we consider the issue of characterizing the set of optimal solutions, as well as those items that are necessarily or possibly in the final selection.

Keywords: Combinatorial optimisation · Interval uncertainty · Credal sets · Possibly optimal solutions

1 Introduction

As one of the most basic problem in combinatorial optimisation, item selection constitute a special case of many other well-known combinatorial optimisation problems. For instance, it corresponds to a knapsack problem with items of equal weights, or to specific one-job scheduling or assignment problems. As such, its study as a basic building block remains of interest.

This problem goes as follows: given a set $\Omega = \{x_1, \ldots, x_n\}$ of n objects, each associated with a cost c_i, find amongst those n objects the p objects that minimize the cost. In other words, if we denote by $F(X) = \sum_{x_i \in X} c_i$ the accumulated cost for the subset $X \subseteq \Omega$ of objects, then the selecting items problem consists in finding

$$X^* = \arg \min_{X \subseteq \Omega, |X|=p} F(X). \tag{1}$$

One can see that the optimal solution is obtained by taking the p objects with the smallest costs, which can be achieved in $O(n)$ time. We will denote by $\Phi = \{X \subseteq \Omega : |X| = p\}$ the set of feasible solutions of the problem.

However, previous studies have shown that this simplicity of the problem may not last when adding some uncertainty to the problem. For instance, it has been shown that computing min-max regret solutions when costs can take values in a discrete space makes the problem NP-hard [6].

It can also be argued that using min-max, regret min-max or other criterion that makes the optimal solution well-defined but unique again amounts to making a

© Springer Nature Switzerland AG 2022
D. Ciucci et al. (Eds.): IPMU 2022, CCIS 1601, pp. 494–503, 2022.
https://doi.org/10.1007/978-3-031-08971-8_41

subjective choice. An alternative, notably explored in decision making (both in multi-criteria [5] and uncertain situations [8]) and computational social choice [9], is to consider and characterize the set of possibly optimal solutions rather than searching for a unique one. While some work exists in this line for combinatorial optimisation problems [1,4], it is much less investigated.

In this paper, we discuss what happens when costs become uncertain, and when we want to characterise sets of possibly optimal solutions given this uncertainty. Such a characterization may be helpful to know on which items one should focus its investigation, or to provide a decision maker with robust and guaranteed information about the solution.

We first look at the problem when costs are known to belong to intervals, and then proceed to a more general framework where the uncertainty about costs is described by convex sets of probabilities, a model that includes as specific case most uncertainty theories, such as belief functions, probabilities or possibilities.

Section 2 discusses the problem we consider in the interval case, and notably what we mean by set of possibly optimal solutions, as well as by necessary and possibly optimal items. Section 3 then proposes a compact representation of all the possibly optimal solution by using the previously established notion, showing that this set can be obtained in polynomial time. Section 4 discusses the case where the uncertainty is described by a set of probability.

2 The Interval Case

This section introduces the simple idea of sets of possibly optimal solution (which in practice reduces to define a Pareto front), as well as the idea of necessarily and possibly optimal item, in the case where uncertainty is described by an interval.

2.1 Setting

We now consider that costs are defined by intervals, that is for object x_i we only know that its cost belong to $\mathscr{C}_i := [\underline{c}_i, \overline{c}_i]$. In practice, this means that $F(X) \in \mathscr{F}(X) := [\underline{F}(X), \overline{F}(X)]$, and that the optimal solution is not unique any more.

A regular way to solve this issue is by considering a min-max or a regret min-max criterion, where one tries to find the best solution in the worst case scenario. Let us denote by $\Gamma = \times_{i=1}^n [\underline{c}_i, \overline{c}_i]$ the hyper-cube representing the set of possible scenarios, and by $\gamma \in \Gamma$ one possible scenario. We will denote by X_γ^* the optimal solution for a scenario γ. The min-max solution is

$$X_{mM}^* = \arg \min_{X \subseteq \Omega, |X|=p} \max_{\gamma \in \Gamma} F(X)$$

In the interval valued case, such a solution is actually very easy to find, as we just have to solve Eq. (1) for $c_i = \overline{c}_i$.

However, as said in the introduction, we will be interested in this paper in characterising the whole set $\mathscr{O}$ of possibly optimal solutions. This set is defined as follows

$$\mathscr{O} = \{X \in \Phi : \exists \gamma \in \Gamma \text{ s.t. } X \in \arg \min_{X \in \Phi} F(X)\} \tag{2}$$

and includes all the solutions that, for what we know, could be optimal. In general, such a set is not obtainable through simple enumeration, nor is very practical to handle: any end-user confronted to a long list of solutions would simply not find it useful. It should however be noted that checking whether a given set $X \in \Phi$ is within $\mathcal{O}$ is very easy: simply set $c_i = \underline{c}_i$ for all $x_i \in X$ and $c_i = \overline{c}_i$ for all $x_i \notin X$, and check that X is the solution to Eq. (1). However, the number of subsets to check would still remain exponential.

For this reason, it is useful to easy to compute representations of $\mathcal{O}$, possibly approximate. This is what we do next, starting with the notion of necessary and optimal items.

2.2 Possibly and Necessarily Optimal Items

An item x_i is said possibly optimal if it is in at least one solution of $\mathcal{O}$, and necessarily optimal if it is in all the solutions of $\mathcal{O}$. For the selecting item problem, we have the following propositions:

Proposition 1. x_i *is necessarily optimal if and only if* $\overline{c}_i > \underline{c}_j$ *for at least* $n - p$ *items* x_j, *i.e.*

$$|\{x_j : \overline{c}_i < \underline{c}_j, i \neq j\}| \geq n - p$$

Proof. If part: assume $|\{x_j : \overline{c}_i < \underline{c}_j, i \neq j\}| \geq n - p$, meaning that $|\{x_j : \overline{c}_i \geq \underline{c}_j, i \neq j\}| < p$ and take a solution X of p items where x_i is not present. Among the items of this solution is at least one item x_j such that $\overline{c}_i \leq \underline{c}_j$, hence replacing this item with x_j can only improve the solution.

Only if part: let us show, by contradiction, that when $|\{x_j : \overline{c}_i \geq \underline{c}_j, i \neq j\}| \geq p$, x_i cannot be necessarily optimal. If x_i was necessarily optimal, then every solution $X \in \mathcal{O}$ would contain it and include p items. This means that at least one item within $\{x_j : \overline{c}_i \geq \underline{c}_j, i \neq j\}$ is not included in X, say x_j. Clearly, since $\overline{c}_i \geq \underline{c}_j$, by picking $c_i = \overline{c}_i$ (since x_i is necessarily optimal, any replacement would lead to include x_i in an optimal solution) and $c_j = \underline{c}_j$, we could improve the solution while excluding x_i, thus x_i cannot be necessarily optimal.

Note that Proposition 1 tells us that checking whether x_i is necessarily optimal is computationally straightforward, as one can just compare $\underline{c}_i$ to all $\overline{c}_j$. We will denote by $\nu \subseteq \Omega$ the set of necessarily optimal items.

Proposition 2. x_i *is possibly optimal if and only if* $\underline{c}_i \leq \overline{c}_j$ *for at least* $n - p$ *items* x_j, *i.e.*

$$|\{x_j : \underline{c}_i \leq \overline{c}_j, i \neq j\}| \geq n - p$$

Proof. If part: assume $|\{x_j : \underline{c}_i \leq \overline{c}_j, i \neq j\}| \geq n - p$, meaning that $|\{x_j : \underline{c}_i > \overline{c}_j, i \neq j\}| < p$. Now, consider the scenario γ where $c_i = \underline{c}_i$ and $c_j = \overline{c}_j$ for all other items x_j. Then $x_i \in X_\gamma^*$, as strictly less than p items will have a higher score than x_i in scenario γ

Only if part: again, assume by contradiction that $|\{x_j : \underline{c}_i > \overline{c}_j, i \neq j\}| \geq p$, then clearly any solution including x_i does not include at least one item within $\{x_j : \underline{c}_i > \overline{c}_j, i \neq j\}$, and replacing x_i with such an item would improve the solution, whatever the scenario γ. Therefore, x_i is not in any possible optimal solution, and is not a possibly optimal item.

As for the necessary optimal items, the procedure to detect possibly optimal items is pretty straightforward computationally speaking. We will denote by $\pi \subseteq \Omega$ the set of possibly optimal items. It should be noted that by construction, we have $v \subseteq \pi$, with the two being equal if and only if the set $\mathcal{O}$ is reduced to a singleton. It is also easy to see that $\mathcal{O} \subseteq \{X \in \Phi : v \subseteq X \subseteq \pi\}$, as all necessary items must be in all possibly optimal solutions, and any non-possibly optimal items never appears in such solutions. A natural next question is then to wonder whether we have $\mathcal{O} = \{X \in \Phi : v \subseteq X \subseteq \pi\}$? The next simple example indicates that this is not the case in general.

Example 1. Consider the following example, with 5 objects $x_1, \ldots, x_5$ and their associated interval costs:

$$c_1 \in [1,10], \quad c_2 \in [2,5], \quad c_3 \in [3,6]$$

$$c_4 \in [4,8], \quad c_5 \in [7,9].$$

We now consider the problem of selecting 3 items among those, so that $n = 5$ and $p = 3$. One can easily check that none of those item is necessarily optimal, and that all are possibly optimal. However, the subset $\{x_1, x_4, x_5\}$ is not within $\mathcal{O}$. To see this, simply consider the scenario $c_1 = 1, c_2 = 5, c_3 = 6, c_4 = 4, c_5 = 7$, whose solution is the subset $\{x_1, x_2, x_4\}$ and not $\{x_1, x_4, x_5\}$.

3 Compact Representation of Possible Optimal Solution

In this section we present a polynomial representation of all possible optimal solutions $\mathcal{O}$, together with an algorithm to build it. Before focusing on the possible optimal solutions we present how to represent all feasible solutions by a directed layered graph $G = (V, E)$ of which one example is given by Fig. 1.

The vertices of the graph are such that $V = \cup_{i=0,\ldots,n} V_i$ with $V_0 = \{0_0\}$, $V_i = \{a_i, (a+1)_i, \ldots, (b-1)_i, b_i\}$ $\forall i = 1, \ldots n-1$ with a_i and b_i respectively the smaller (the bigger) number of selected items at layer i indexed by the layer i i.e. $a_i = \max(0, p-(n-i)), b_i = \min(i,p)$ and $V_n = \{p_n\}$. a_i correspond to the minimal number of selected item after considering whether to select the ith item, and b_i the maximal number of selected items. Each value i defines a vertical layer corresponding to object x_i, while each horizontal layer (corresponding to the values going from 0 to p) correspond to the number of objects added in the selection.

The edges $E = \cup_{i=1,\ldots,n} E_i$ with $(u,v) \in E_i$ if $u \in V_{i-1}, v \in V_i$ and $u = v$ or $u = v+1$ which means respectively *The object i is not selected* or *The object i is selected*. Each path from 0_0 to p_n is a feasible solution of the problem. We can see that the number of nodes as well as the number of edge is in $O(np)$. Figure 1 provides an illustration for the case of $n = 5$ objects among which $p = 3$ must be retained.

However, what we are aiming for is not to list all feasible solutions, but to get the set $\mathcal{O}$ of possible optimal solutions, or to trim the graph from its unecessary edges and vertices. To do this, we shall denote by $v^p(I)$ the set of necessary optimal objects for a given value p with given subset $I \subseteq \Omega$ of objects and $\pi^p(I)$ the set of possibly optimal objects for a given value p with given set of object I.

When a node u_i is reached in the graph, we know that we have considered the $i-1$ first objects, and selected u of them. We therefore know that we still need to select $p - u$

objects in the remaining set $I = \{i,...n\}$. From this situation, we will see which edges must be added (if we start from the empty graph), or which edge should be removed from the complete graph, depending on the situation of object i in I when $p - u$ objects must be selected. More precisely:

- if $x_i \in v^{p-u}(I)$, only the edge *object is selected* is added to the graph, as it is necessarily selected;
- if $x_i \in \pi^{p-u}(I) \setminus v^{p-u}(I)$, both edges are added to the graph, as it is a possibly but not necessarily optimal selection;
- and if $x_i \notin \pi^{p-u}(I)$, only the edge *object is not selected* is added to the graph.

The procedure to compute the graph of all possible optimal solutions is described in Algorithm 1.

Example 2. The graph of all feasible solutions of Example 1 is represented on Fig. 1. But each path of the current graph is not possibly optimal for instance the path $(0_0, 1_1, 1_2, 1_3, 2_4, 3_5)$ which represent the solution $x_1 = 1, x_4 = 1, x_5 = 1$. Let us illustrate the algorithm on this path. At node 0_0 the object 1 is possibly optimal, hence the arc $(0_0, 1_1)$ is in the graph of possible optimal solution (we can add object x_1 to the solution). Since it is not necessarily optimal, we also add $(0_0, 0_1)$. At node 1_1 we check if object 2 is possibly optimal for the updated constraint $\sum_{i=2}^{5} x_i \geq 2$ (we still have to select 2 objects). We can see that it is possibly optimal but not necessary. Hence the path $(1_1, 1_2)$ is possible and added. At node 1_2 the constraint becomes $\sum_{i=3}^{5} x_i \geq 2$ so object 3 is necessarily optimal since $\overline{c}_3 < \underline{c}_5$, and we still have 2 objects to select. So the edge $(1_2, 1_3)$ is not in the graph of possible optimal solution. The set of all possible optimal solutions is represented on Fig. 2

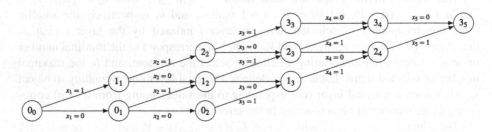

Fig. 1. Set of feasible solutions

Proposition 3. *All paths of graph returned by Algorithm 1 represent all possible optimal solution in space $O(np)$.*

Proof. We give a proof by induction on $i = 1,...,n$.

Base case with $i = 1$: by definition if x_i is possibly optimal but not necessary then $\exists X^* \in \mathscr{O}$ with $x_1 = 1$ and $\exists X^* \in \mathscr{O}$ with $x_1 = 0$, if it is necessary optimal then $\exists X^* \in \mathscr{O}$ with $x_1 = 1$ and $\nexists X^* \in \mathscr{O}$ with $x_1 = 0$ else $\exists X^* \in \mathscr{O}$ with $x_1 = 0$ and $\nexists X^* \in \mathscr{O}$ with

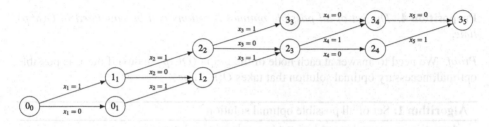

Fig. 2. Set of feasible solutions

$x_1 = 1$. So all paths form node 0_0 to node of the layer 1 are all the partial possibly optimal solutions of x_1.

Inductive step: We denote P_{i-1} the set of paths form node 0_0 to each the nodes of layer $i - 1$. Now we show that if all paths in P_{i-1} are all the partial possibly optimal solution then all paths in P_i are all the partial possibly optimal solution. We assume that is true for $i - 1$, more formally $\forall path \in P_{i-1}, \exists X^* \in \mathcal{O}$ such that $X^* = (x_1^{path}, ..., x_{i-1}^{path}, x_i^*, ...x_n^*)$ and $\nexists X \in \mathcal{O}$ such that $(x_1, ..., x_{i-1}) \in \cup_{path \in P_{i-1}} (x_1^{path}, ..., x_{i-1}^{path})$. Hence $\exists \gamma^* \in \Gamma$ such that X^* is optimal. Since Γ is hyper-cube the set of scenarios form all nodes of the layer i is $\times_{j=1}^{i-1} \gamma_j^* \times_{j=i}^{n} [\underline{c}_j, \overline{c}_j]$. Using the Bellman's principle of optimally a $X_i^* = (x_i^*, ...x_n^*) = \arg\min_{X_i \subseteq I, |X_i| = p - |X^{path}|} F(X_i)$. Since for each nodes of layer i, all paths to it have the same value of $|X^{path}| = K$ and that the scenario set on the remaining sub-set is a hyper-cube $\times_{j=i}^n [\underline{c}_j, \overline{c}_j]$ so what ever the path the possibly optimally of selected item depend only on the restricted problem to I and $|X_i| = p - K$. We can apply at each node of the layer i the Propositions 2 and 1. So if x_i is possibly optimal and not necessary optimal for a given node then they exist for each path to it a $X^* \in \mathcal{O}$ such that $X^* = (x_1^{path}, ..., x_{i-1}^{path}, 1, x_{i+1}^*, ...x_n^*)$ and if x_i is necessary optimal for a given node then they not exist for each path to it $X^* \in \mathcal{O}$ such that $X^* = (x_1^{path}, ..., x_{i-1}^{path}, 0, x_{i+1}^*, ...x_n^*)$. So all paths form node 0 to node of the layer 1 are all the partial possibly optimal solution of $(x_1, ..., x_i)$. Since both the base case and the inductive step have been proved as true, by mathematical induction All the paths of graph returned by Algorithm 1 represent all possible optimal solution. The graph returned by the algorithm has $n + 1$ layers with maximum p nodes and for each node maximal two edges.

Proposition 3 confirms that our algorithm return the expected set $\mathcal{O}$, and that this representation remains compact while listing all the elements of $\mathcal{O}$, and only those elements. Of course the number of possible paths remain exponential, but this becomes a minor issue, as we can represent them compactly. Note that the necessity or possibility of an object being in a solution can also be directly read from the graph: an object x_i is necessary if all edges from layer $i - 1$ to i go upward, and impossible if all edges from layer $i - 1$ to i are horizontal. In Fig. 2, for instance, one can check that it is not the case for any of the object/layers.

The next proposition is a simple expression of the complexity of our algorithm, which remains polynomial.

Proposition 4. *The set of all possible optimal solutions can be computed in $O(n^2 p)$ time.*

Proof. We need to answer at each node of the graph ($O(np)$ nodes) if the x_i is possible optimal, necessary optimal solution that takes $O(n)$ times.

Algorithm 1: Set of all possible optimal solution

Input: cost intervals $[\underline{c_i}, \overline{c_i}], \forall i \in \{1, ..., n\}$, minimal number p
Output: A graph $G = (V, E)$
$V_0 = \{0_0\}$
$a = max(0, p - (n - i))$
$b = min(i, p)$
$V_i = \{a_i, ..., b_i\} \forall i = 1, ... n - 1$
$V_n = \{p_i\}$
$E_i = \emptyset, \forall i = 1, ...n$
for $i \in \{1, ..., n\}$ **do**
  $\quad I = \{i, ..., n\}$
  $\quad$**for** $j_{i-1} \in V_{i-1}$ **do**
    $\quad\quad$ k=p-j
    $\quad\quad$**if** $x_i \in \pi^k(I) \setminus v^k(I)$ **then**
      $\quad\quad\quad E_i = E_i \cup \{(j_{i-1}, j+1_i)\}$
      $\quad\quad\quad E_i = E_i \cup \{(j_{i-1}, j_i)\}$
    $\quad\quad$**if** $x_i \in v^k(I)$ **then**
      $\quad\quad\quad E_i = E_i \cup \{(j_{i-1}, j+1_i)\}$
    $\quad\quad$**if** $x_i \notin \pi^k(I)$ **then**
      $\quad\quad\quad E_i = E_i \cup \{(j_{i-1}, j_i)\}$
$V = \cup_{i=0,...,n} V_i$
$E = \cup_{i=1,...,n} E_i$

---

4 Extension to the Credal Set Case

In this section, we no longer assume that c_i uncertainty is described by an interval, but by a convex set $\mathscr{P}_i$ of probabilities having for support a sub-interval of $\mathbb{R}$, often referred to as *credal sets*. Although more general models of uncertainty do exist, convex probability sets or credal sets are quite generic, as they include most uncertainty representations commonly used in practice, such as intervals, possibility distributions, belief functions, etc.

4.1 Precise Probabilities

When the sets $\mathscr{P}_i$ reduce to singletons P_i, i.e., are equivalent to specify probabilities for the costs c_i, a common way justified axiomatically to estimate the quality of a solution is by considering its expected cost. For a single item x_i, this expected cost is $\mathbb{E}_{P_i}(c_i) = \int_{\mathbb{R}} c_i p_i(c_i) dc_i$, where $p(c_i)$ is the probability density.

For the item selection issue and given a set $X \in \Phi$, this means that the solution would be evaluated as

$$\mathbb{E}[F(X)] = \mathbb{E}\left[\sum_{x_i \in X} c_i\right] = \sum_{x_i \in X} \mathbb{E}_{P_i}(c_i),$$

as the expectation is a linear operator, not depending on any possible dependencies between the distributions P_i. The problem is therefore not more complicated than in the case where costs are precisely known, and one can use all previous results on expectations, obtaining the optimal result as

$$X_P^* = \arg\min_{X \in \phi} \mathbb{E}[F(X)] \tag{3}$$

4.2 Generic Credal Sets

We now consider the case where each price is defined by a convex set of probability distributions $\mathscr{P}_i$. While precise probabilities are retrieved when those are singletons, the interval case is recovered when $\mathscr{P}_i$ contains all probabilities whose support is included in $[\underline{c}_i, \overline{c}_i]$. From a set $\mathscr{P}_i$, one can define lower and upper expectations of the cost c_i as

$$\underline{\mathbb{E}}_{\mathscr{P}_i}(c_i) = \inf_{P_i \in \mathscr{P}_i} \mathbb{E}_{P_i}(c_i), \quad \overline{\mathbb{E}}_{\mathscr{P}_i}(c_i) = \sup_{P_i \in \mathscr{P}_i} \mathbb{E}_{P_i}(c_i).$$

The question is then to know what becomes of $\mathbb{E}[F(X)]$, as in general lower and upper expectations are not additive any more[1]. However, we can easily show that, in the case where we have marginal credal sets for each costs, then they remain additive, on the proviso that the associated join model include every combinations of distributions within $\mathscr{P}_i$.

Proposition 5. *Given two credal sets $\mathscr{P}_X$ and $\mathscr{P}_Y$ defined for real-valued quantities X and Y, we have*

$$\underline{\mathbb{E}}(X + Y) = \underline{\mathbb{E}}(X) + \underline{\mathbb{E}}(Y)$$

for any joint credal set $\mathscr{P}_{X,Y}$ whose joints are built from all marginals within $\mathscr{P}_X$ and $\mathscr{P}_Y$, i.e., $\forall P_X \in \mathscr{P}_X, P_Y \in \mathscr{P}_Y, \exists P_{X,Y} \in \mathscr{P}_{X,Y}$ with those marginals.

Proof. Given a joint credal set $\mathscr{P}_{X,Y}$, we want to find

$$
\begin{aligned}
\underline{\mathbb{E}}(X + Y) &= \inf_{P_{X,Y} \in \mathscr{P}_{X,Y}} \int_x \int_y x + y p(x,y) dx dy \\
&= \inf_{P_{X,Y} \in \mathscr{P}_{X,Y}} \int_x \int_y x p(x,y) dx dy + \int_x \int_y y p(x,y) dx dy \\
&= \inf_{\Gamma_{X,Y} \in \mathscr{P}_{X,Y}} \int_x x p(x) dx + \int_y y p(y) dy \\
&= \inf_{P_X \in \mathscr{P}_X} \int_x x p(x) dx + \inf_{P_Y \in \mathscr{P}_Y} \int_y y p(y) dy
\end{aligned}
$$

---

[1] They are usually super- and sub-additive, i.e., $\underline{\mathbb{E}}(X + Y) \geq \underline{\mathbb{E}}(X) + \underline{\mathbb{E}}(Y)$.

with the last inequality being true because $\mathscr{P}_{X,Y}$ is convex and has $\mathscr{P}_X$ and $\mathscr{P}_Y$ for marginals, hence there is a joint within $\mathscr{P}_{X,Y}$ reaching simultaneously $\underline{\mathbb{E}}(X)$ and $\underline{\mathbb{E}}(Y)$

This includes most of the ways used to build to joint credal sets, i.e., from independence statements [2,3] or by using sets of copulas to model dependencies [7]. As the same holds true for upper expectations, we have that for a given solution $X \in \Phi$, we have

$$\underline{\mathbb{E}}(F(X)) = \sum_{x_i \in X} \underline{\mathbb{E}}_{\mathscr{P}_i}(c_i), \quad \overline{\mathbb{E}}(F(X)) = \sum_{x_i \in X} \overline{\mathbb{E}}_{\mathscr{P}_i}(c_i).$$

Given Eq. (3), the set of possibly optimal solution readily becomes

$$\mathscr{O} = \{X \in \Phi : \exists P_i \in \mathscr{P}_i \text{ s.t. } X_P^* \in \arg\min_{X \in \phi} \mathbb{E}[F(X)]\}$$

The transposition of all results obtained for the interval case is then direct, simply replacing the interval bounds by their lower/upper expectation counterparts.

5 Conclusion

In this paper, we investigated the problem of characterising possibly optimal solutions, and reducing them, for the simple problem of selecting optimal items when costs were interval-valued. We have also extended this analysis to much more generic uncertainty models, showing that in this case those more generic uncertainty models did not induce an increased complexity.

One obvious extension of the current work is to look for problems directly extending the selecting item problem, such as the knapsack or the assignment problem. We could also look at other simple problems issued from combinatorial optimisation where the objective function has an additive form, such as the minimum spanning tree problem. In this latter case, some existing results [10] in the vein of those of Sect. 2 could help us to obtain an efficient compact representation of possibly optimal solutions.

References

1. Benabbou, N., Perny, P.: Interactive resolution of multiobjective combinatorial optimization problems by incremental elicitation of criteria weights. EURO J. Decis. Processes **6**(3–4), 283–319 (2018). https://doi.org/10.1007/s40070-018-0085-4
2. Couso, I., Moral, S., Walley, P.: A survey of concepts of independence for imprecise probabilities. Risk Decis. Policy **5**(2), 165–181 (2000)
3. Destercke, S.: Independence and 2-monotonicity: nice to have, hard to keep. Int. J. Approx. Reason. **54**(4), 478–490 (2013)
4. Fortin, J., Zieliński, P., Dubois, D., Fargier, H.: Interval analysis in scheduling. In: van Beek, P. (ed.) CP 2005. LNCS, vol. 3709, pp. 226–240. Springer, Heidelberg (2005). https://doi.org/10.1007/11564751_19
5. Kadziński, M., Tervonen, T., Figueira, J.R.: Robust multi-criteria sorting with the outranking preference model and characteristic profiles. Omega **55**, 126–140 (2015)

6. Kasperski, A., Kurpisz, A., Zieliński, P.: Approximating the min-max (regret) selecting items problem. Inf. Process. Lett. **113**(1–2), 23–29 (2013)
7. Montes, I., Miranda, E., Pelessoni, R., Vicig, P.: Sklar's theorem in an imprecise setting. Fuzzy Sets Syst. **278**, 48–66 (2015)
8. Troffaes, M.C.: Decision making under uncertainty using imprecise probabilities. Int. J. Approx. Reason. **45**(1), 17–29 (2007)
9. Xia, L., Conitzer, V.: Determining possible and necessary winners given partial orders. J. Artif. Intell. Res. **41**, 25–67 (2011)
10. Yaman, H., Karaşan, O.E., Pınar, M.Ç.: The robust spanning tree problem with interval data. Oper. Res. Lett. **29**(1), 31–40 (2001)

Anomaly Detection in Crowdsourced Work with Interval-Valued Labels

Makenzie Spurling[1]([⊠]), Chenyi Hu[1]([⊠]), Huixin Zhan[2], and Victor S. Sheng[2]

[1] University of Central Arkansas, Conway, AR, USA
mspurling1@cub.uca.edu, chu@uca.edu
[2] Texas Tech University, Lubbock, TX, USA

Abstract. Crowdsourcing is an emerging paradigm in AI and machine learning. It involves gathering input from human crowds, usually through the Internet, to solve a given task. Due to its open nature, the selected crowd-workers usually come from a variety of social-economic backgrounds and bring with them differing levels of reliability. There is also a threat of people with adversarial intentions launching attacks to derail crowdsourced projects. In this paper, we apply interval-valued labels (IVLs) and worker reliability to detect anomalous behavior in crowd-workers. Three of the four worker reliability measures-confidence, stability, and predictability-do not rely on the correctness of a worker's label [28]. Therefore, by comparing a worker's IVLs on gold questions with regular ones, we may detect anomalies within our workers. Doing so in our computational experiments, we have successfully been able to identify adversarial attackers for quality assurance of crowdsourcing.

Keywords: crowdsourcing · reliability · interval-valued label · worker's reliability · anomaly detection

1 Introduction

In this section, we briefly introduce the research problem and motivation behind this work, along with a short literature review of related topics.

1.1 The Problem We Study

In machine learning and AI, we frequently require meaningful human knowledge as input. Crowdsourcing is the process of gathering these inputs from a large group of people (crowd-workers) using the Internet. Using online crowdsourcing marketplaces like Amazon Mechanical Turk[1] and CrowdFlower,[2] large amounts

---

[1] https://www.mturk.com/.
[2] http://crowdflowersites.com/.

This work is partially supported by the US National Science Foundation through the grant award NSF/OIA-1946391.

© Springer Nature Switzerland AG 2022
D. Ciucci et al. (Eds.): IPMU 2022, CCIS 1601, pp. 504–516, 2022.
https://doi.org/10.1007/978-3-031-08971-8_42

of manually labeled data have already been acquired. Through processing this collected data with learning algorithms, inferences are made for human users.

In this work, we assume the typical binary classification model of determining if an observation $x_i \in X$ is an instance of a given class $y \in Y$. To simplify the discussion, we assume $|Y| = 1$ without loss of generality. This is because when $|Y| = m > 1$, one may check if x_i is an instance of each of the m classes repeatedly. With the assumption of $|Y| = 1$, the problem becomes a decision problem: is $x_i \in X$ an instance of a given class y? The correct answer, either yes (1) or no (0), is called the ground truth. The basic idea of crowdsourcing is to acquire a list of answers (labels), denoted as L_i, from a crowd on the same x_i. By applying a learning strategy such as majority voting (MV) or preferred matching probability (PMP) to aggregate L_i, one can derive an inference with the objective of matching the ground truth.

The advantage of crowdsourcing is its openness and the participation of a wide range of people from different socio-economic backgrounds. On the other hand, this openness also makes it easier for people with malicious intent to launch an attack. Crowdsourcing often uses a set of gold questions with known ground truth to establish a worker's reliability. Workers with a high level of knowledge in the field tend to produce higher quality labels, although opinions may differ for each expert. Still, an expert with an antagonistic purpose can do far more damage than any other worker. For example, a naive attacker could intentionally misannotate an instance and fail a crowdsourcing task. In addition, sophisticated attackers may identify and answer gold questions correctly to establish a favorable reliability score, and then launch an attack on regular questions. Researchers have investigated ways to identify adversarial attackers in crowd-worker selection. For instances, Checco et al. discussed quality control on adversarial attacks in [1]. Li and Liu studied ways to select good workers for crowdsourcing in [21]. Qiu et al. proposed methods to select workers through behavior prediction [29]. Wang et al. reported practical strategies for adversarial detection in [30]. In terms of recent anomaly detection efforts in crowdsourcing, identifying such sophisticated attackers remains a challenge in the binary-valued labeling scheme. Kong et al. makes use of temporal and spatial segments to detect anomalies in crowdsourced traffic data through an anomaly index in [19]. In [20], Li et al. proposed a tree-modeling based approach to detect and classify anomalies based on severity within crowdsourced network data. Yan et al. deals with anomalous attackers in crowdsourced data using a generative adversarial network through an autoencoder and time series in [33]. In this work, we propose a practical strategy to detect anomalies and identify possible sophisticated attackers with interval-valued labels (IVLs) [16] rather than the commonly used binary-valued ones.

1.2   IVLs and Notations

So far, most previous studies have assumed binary-valued labels due to the binary classification model. But, a binary-valued label may lose information, especially when a worker is uncertain of the answer. Noticing the successes of interval computing in managing uncertainty such as [2–5, 7–18, 22, 25, 26], and others, Hu *et al.* introduced interval-valued labels (IVLs) in [16] recently. An IVL is a sub-interval of $[0, 1]$, which allows a worker j to include his ambiguity in selecting either 0 or 1. Following the literature on interval computing, we denote an interval object with a boldface letter to distinguish it from a real-valued one (not boldface). The greatest lower and least upper bounds of an interval object are specified with an underline and an over-line of the same letter without boldface, respectively. Hence, the IVL for an instance $x_i \in X$ made by a worker j is denoted as $\boldsymbol{l}_{ij} = [\underline{l}_{ij}, \overline{l}_{ij}] \subseteq [0, 1]$. The minimum and maximum beliefs of j on i being an instance of the given class are $\underline{l}_{ij}$ and $\overline{l}_{ij}$, respectively.

The midpoint (or centroid) of $\boldsymbol{l}_{ij}$ is point-valued. It is written as

$$\text{mid}(\boldsymbol{l}_{ij}) = \frac{\underline{l}_{ij} + \overline{l}_{ij}}{2} \quad (1)$$

without boldface l_{ij} because $\text{mid}(\boldsymbol{l}_{ij})$ is a real. Since $\boldsymbol{l}_{ij} \subseteq [0, 1]$, we have $0 \leq \text{mid}(\boldsymbol{l}_{ij}) \leq 1$. When $\text{mid}(\boldsymbol{l}_{ij}) > 0.5$, j leans toward to accepting x_i in the class. We call it a positive IVL. If $\text{mid}(\boldsymbol{l}_{ij}) < 0.5$, then j leans toward rejecting x_i from the class. We call it a negative IVL. Otherwise, it is neither positive nor negative, and implies a tie. The radius of $\boldsymbol{l}_{ij}$,

$$\text{rad}(\boldsymbol{l}_{ij}) = \frac{\overline{l}_{ij} - \underline{l}_{ij}}{2} \quad (2)$$

is point-valued too. So, the l_{ij} is not in boldface. The radius of $\boldsymbol{l}_{ij}$ specifies the range of variations from the centroid.

We denote a list of IVLs as $\boldsymbol{L} = [\boldsymbol{l}_1, \boldsymbol{l}_2, \ldots, \boldsymbol{l}_n]$, which is an interval-valued dataset. Both of its lower and upper bounds, $\underline{L}$ and $\overline{L}$ are real vectors without boldface. The element-wise midpoint and radius vectors are denoted as $\text{mid}(L)$ and $\text{rad}(L)$, respectively, without boldface. The mean of $\boldsymbol{L}$ is

$$\mu(\boldsymbol{L}) = \frac{\sum_{i=1}^{n} \boldsymbol{l}_i}{n} = \left[\frac{1}{n} \sum_{i=1}^{n} \underline{l}_i, \frac{1}{n} \sum_{i=1}^{n} \overline{l}_i \right] = [\mu(\underline{L}), \mu(\overline{L})]. \quad (3)$$

1.3   The Motivation of This Study

Very recently, researchers have established quantitative measurements of worker's reliability from IVLs [28] in terms of a worker's correctness, confidence, stability, and predictability. Reliability weighted interval majority voting (WIMV) and preferred matching probability (WPMP) algorithms have significantly improved the overall quality of crowdsourced work as illustrated in Fig. 1, which compares the F_1-score vs. worker's confidence threshold using different algorithms on a sample dataset from [32].

However, the above work assumes that every worker will perform consistently according to his/her reliability without considering anomalies. Quality assurance in real world applications requires detecting anomalies and identifying adversarial attackers. Noticing that a worker's confidence, stability, and entropy derived

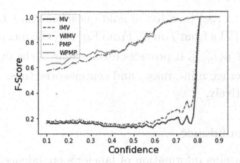

Fig. 1. F_1-score values vs. confidence threshold

from the IVLs are independent to the correctness [28], we may compare these reliability indicators on a set of gold questions (with known answer) G, and the set of regular questions X. If G well samples X, then the reliability indicators should be statistically consistent. Otherwise, a possible anomaly is detected.

The rest of this paper is organized as follows. Section 2 briefly reviews indicators of worker's reliability. Section 3 presents computational strategies for detecting anomalies and identifying possible attackers from IVLs. The results of the computational experiments are reported in Sect. 4 with Sect. 5 summarizing the work.

2 Indicators of Worker's Reliability

Unlike point-valued labels, IVLs have their own statistical and probabilistic properties. In this section, we give a short overview of the four indicators of worker's reliability: correctness, confidence, stability, and predictability. By applying them, we may be able to identify anomalous behavior in a worker.

2.1 Worker's Correctness

A common approach to estimate a worker's correctness is to employ a set of *gold questions* denoted as G. For each $g \in G$, its ground truth $o(g)$ is known (either 1 or 0) but opaque to workers. The IVL from a worker j on a $g \in G$ is denoted as $l_{gj} = [\underline{l}_{gj}, \overline{l}_{gj}]$. With the known ground truth $o(g)$, we have the *center-correctness* of l_{gj} as:

$$\text{center\_correctness}(l_{gj}) = \begin{cases} 1 - \text{mid}(l_{gj}) & \text{if } o(g) = 0, \\ \text{mid}(l_{gj}) & \text{if } o(g) = 1. \end{cases} \quad (4)$$

The center-correctness of l_{gj} relies on both $\text{mid}(l_{gj})$ and $o(g)$. To simplify our discussion, we assume $o(g) = 1$ for all $g \in G$ without loss of generality. This is because of the value of $o(g)$ is known. In the case $o(g) = 0$, we can replace l_{gj} with its difference from 1, i.e. $1 - l_{gj} = [1 - \overline{l}_{gj}, 1 - \underline{l}_{gj}]$ without changing its center-correctness.

Let $G = [g_1, g_2, \ldots, g_k]$ be a list of gold questions, and $L_G^j = [l_{g_1 j}, l_{g_2 j}, \ldots,$ $l_{g_k j}]$ be the list of k IVLs from j on G. From Eq. (3), the mean of L_G^j is the interval $\mu(L_G^j) = [\mu(\underline{L}_G^j), \mu(\overline{L}_G^j)]$. It provides estimations of the overall correctness of j in terms of his average min-, max-, and center-correctness $\mu(\underline{L}_G^j), \mu(\overline{L}_G^j)$, and $\mathrm{mid}(\mu(L_G^j))$, respectively.

2.2 Worker's Confidence

An IVL $l = [\underline{l}, \overline{l}]$ contains information of labeler's confidence. The centroid of l, $\mathrm{mid}(l)$, represents the degree of the worker's belief toward 0 or 1. When $\mathrm{mid}(l) = 0.5$, the worker has absolutely no confidence to pick either 0 or 1. The distance between $\mathrm{mid}(l)$ and 0.5, i.e. $|\mathrm{mid}(l) - 0.5|$, reflects the labeler's confidence on his belief. The radius of l, $\mathrm{rad}(l) = \frac{\overline{l} - \underline{l}}{2}$, specifies the maximum possible variation from the centroid. When $\mathrm{rad}(l) = 0$, l is point-valued; and the worker is confident of the value of l. Otherwise, the label l contains uncertainty over a range. Because the maximum possible value of $\mathrm{rad}(l)$ is 0.5, the difference between 0.5 and $\mathrm{rad}(l)$, i.e. $0.5 - \mathrm{rad}(l)$, measures labeler's confidence on the centroid. Therefore, the confidence of l is the sum of $|\mathrm{mid}(l) - 0.5|$ and $0.5 - \mathrm{rad}(l)$:

$$\mathrm{conf}(l) = |\mathrm{mid}(l) - 0.5| + 0.5 - \mathrm{rad}(l). \tag{5}$$

Obviously, the confidence of a binary-valued label (0 or 1) is always 100%. In contrast, the confidence of an IVL is between 0 and 1. Note that the confidence of an IVL is independent of the ground truth. As mentioned earlier, the mean of L_G^j, $\mu(L_G^j)$, is a sub-interval of $[0, 1]$. From $\mu(L_G^j)$, we have j's overall confidence as $|\mathrm{mid}(\mu(L_G^j)) - 0.5| + 0.5 - \mathrm{rad}(\mu(L_G^j))$. Again, unlike predicting worker's correctness, estimating worker's confidence with Eq. (5) does not require the ground truth at all. With this in mind, we can calculate j's overall level of confidence on X. Comparing j's confidences $\mathrm{conf}(L_G^j)$ and $\mathrm{conf}(L_X^j)$, we may statistically check if j performs consistently or not (see Eq. (10) for details.) If G well samples X, then $\mathrm{conf}(L_G^j)$ and $\mathrm{conf}(L_X^j)$ should be statistically consistent.

The relationship between worker's correctness and confidence is reported in [28] and illustrated as Fig. 2.

2.3 Worker's Stability and Predictability

The standard deviation of a data set is a measure of the overall stability of the data. Let L^j be a list of k IVLs made by j. We can calculate the standard deviations of $\underline{L}^j, \overline{L}^j$, $\mathrm{mid}(L^j)$, and $\mathrm{rad}(L^j)$ as usual because they are point-valued. From [14], the variance of L^j is point-valued as

$$Var(L^j) = Var(\mathrm{mid}(L^j)) + Var(\mathrm{rad}(L^j)) + \frac{2}{k} \sum_{i=1}^{k} |\Delta m_i^j \Delta r_i^j| \tag{6}$$

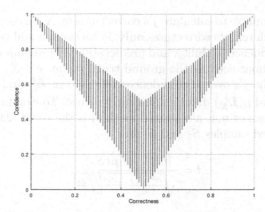

Fig. 2. Range of confidence vs. correctness

where $\Delta m_i^j = \mathrm{mid}(l_i^j) - \mu(\mathrm{mid}(L^j))$ and $\Delta r_i^j = \mathrm{rad}(l_i^j) - \mu(\mathrm{rad}(L^j))$. Hence, the standard deviation of L^j is

$$\sigma(L^j) = \sqrt{Var(L^j)}. \tag{7}$$

It measures j's overall stability. Similar to j's confidence, the standard deviation of L^j does not rely on the ground truth. So, we are able to calculate both $\sigma(L_G^j)$ and $\sigma(L_X^j)$ if L_G^j and L_X^j are provided.

To measure j's predictability, we apply the entropy of L^j according to information theory. Let s be a discrete random variable with possible outcomes $s_1, s_2, \ldots, s_n$, which occur with probability $\mathrm{p}(s_1), \mathrm{p}(s_2), \ldots, \mathrm{p}(s_n)$. Then, Shannon's entropy [27] of s is:

$$H(s) = -\sum_{i=1}^{n} p(s_i) \log p(s_i). \tag{8}$$

Algorithm 1 in [14] provides us an approach to evaluate $H(L^j)$, the entropy of L^j with Eq. (8). The $H(L^j)$ quantitatively measures j's predictability. According to the minimum entropy principle, a worker j is more predictable if the $H(L^j)$ is less than others'. The calculation of entropy does not depend on the ground truth of instances to be classified. For a specific $j \in J$, the set of crowd-workers, we can calculate and compare the values of $H(L_G^j)$ and $H(L_X^j)$ statistically as well to detect anomaly.

3   Detecting Anomaly and Adversarial Attackers

3.1   Anomaly Detection

Assuming G well samples X, the reliability indicators of j calculated from G and X should be statistically consistent. Since the ground truth of an $x \in X$ is unknown, we are unable to calculate j's correctness on X. In contrast to a binary-valued label, which reflects correctness only, IVLs contain additional information on a worker's confidence, stability, and predictability. More importantly, they can be calculated without needing the ground truth of any $x \in X$.

To compare the j's overall confidences reflected in L_G^j and L_X^j, we need to check if $\mu(L_G^j)$ and $\mu(L_X^j)$ differ significantly or not. To examine if two samples have the same mean or not, a standard method is the t-test [23]. The t-statistic of two point-valued samples S_1 and S_2 is:

$$t = \frac{|\mu(S_1) - \mu(S_2)|}{\sqrt{\frac{\sigma^2(S_1)}{|S_1|} + \frac{\sigma^2(S_2)}{|S_2|}}}. \tag{9}$$

With a specified statistical significance, we can determine if the means of S_1 and S_2 are consistent statistically. For interval-valued L_G^j and L_X^j, Eqs. (3), (6), and (7) allow us to calculate their means, variances, and standard deviations. But, both $\mu(L_G^j)$ and $\mu(L_X^j)$ are intervals. The distance between two intervals a and b is $\mathrm{dist}(a, b) = |\mathrm{mid}(a) - \mathrm{mid}(b)| + |\mathrm{rad}(a) - \mathrm{rad}(b)|$ but not $|a - b|$ [14]. Hence, the t-statistic for L_G^j and L_X^j is

$$t = \frac{\mathrm{dist}\left(\mu(L_G^j), \mu(L_X^j)\right)}{\sqrt{\frac{\sigma^2(L_G^j)}{|L_G^j|} + \frac{\sigma^2(L_X^j)}{|L_X^j|}}}. \tag{10}$$

Note: in calculating the $\mu(L_G^j)$ in Eq. (10), one should not replace l_{gj} with $1 - l_{gj}$ when $o(g) = 0$. Otherwise, it skews $\mu(L_G^j)$ to the right of 0.5.

To compare the j's overall stability reflected in L_G^j and L_X^j, we need to check if $\sigma(L_G^j)$ and $\sigma(L_X^j)$) differ significantly or not. Equation (6) enables us to calculate the variances of L_G^j and L_X^j. We can then apply the F-test [24] to compare their standard deviations. If the two variances are not significantly different, their ratio will be close to 1. When performing the t- and F-test on L_G^j and L_X^j, should a single test fail a worker is not automatically marked as an anomaly, but as likely to be one pending the results of the second test. A worker j is marked with a high possibility of being anomalous if both tests fail.

3.2   Identifying Possible Adversarial Attackers

Identifying knowledgeable attackers in crowdsourcing has been a challenging task. Such attackers can be of two types, naive or sophisticated. A well-informed naive attacker simply classifies all instances as opposite the ground truth. The attacker's answers to the gold questions result in a very low level of correctness. To use these types of labels, a replacement with its difference from 1 works in the binary classification model. In contrast, a sophisticated attacker may be able to identify gold questions and answer them with a high level of accuracy but delib-erately mislabel regular questions. Therefore, to identify potential attackers, we should focus on workers associated with a high or low correctness. The correctness of a worker j can be obtained from L_G^j. To utilize IVLs from a possible naive attacker j, we need to verify that L_G^j and L_X^j are consistent statistically. Conversely, to identify a possible sophisticated attacker, we should check if L_G^j and L_X^j are significantly different statistically. It has been reported in previous works such as [29] and others, that a very sophisticated attacker may purposely make an imperfect correctness score when answering gold questions to avoid being scrutinized. Therefore, we need to perform the t- and F-test for every $j \in J$ to identify possible attackers. Any worker j with a high level of confidence and a high correctness that fails both tests on L_G^j and L_X^j should be treated as a sophisticated attacker and removed from any inference making processes. High confidence workers with low correctness that pass both tests should be treated as naive attackers with their labels being replaced with its difference from 1.

3.3   Monitor Worker's Behavior Dynamically

Besides adversarial attacks, variations in a worker's experience, stress level, working environment, random mistakes, and others may lead to a worker's anomalous behavior. In other words, the behavior of a crowd-worker j can be time varying [31]. So, we need to monitor j's behavior dynamically. By presenting new gold questions to j periodically, the list L_G^j becomes a time series. Assuming activities prior to a fixed length of time do not influence current action and after, we use a time window T to contain the IVLs in our consideration. We denote j's IVLs on gold and regular questions within the window T as $L_{G_T}^j$ and $L_{X_T}^j$, respectively. We can perform the t- and F-tests on $L_{G_T}^j$ and $L_{X_T}^j$ to detect possible anomalies within the time-window T. For convenience, we still assume $|L_{G_T}^j| = k$. When a $l_{g_{k+1}j}$ becomes available, we move the window one step forward. By doing so, the list of IVLs on gold questions within the time-window $T+1$ is $L_{G_{T+1}}^j = \{l_{g_2j}, l_{g_3j}, \ldots, l_{g_{k+1}j}\}$. The IVLs of regular questions within the time-window $T+1$ is denoted as $L_{X_{T+1}}^j$. Performing the t- and F-tests on $L_{G_{T+1}}^j$ and $L_{X_{T+1}}^j$, we can detect possible anomalies dynamically as the T increases.

4   Computational Experiments

In this section, we report our computational experiments to investigate the effectiveness of the proposed methods for anomaly detection and identification of adversarial attackers.

4.1   The Design of Our Experiments

To carry out the experiments, we randomly generated J, a set of one hundred crowd-workers. Their levels of reliability vary. We then select three benchmark datasets in CEKA [32] named *Income94, Sick,* and *Vote* to be testing datasets because of their simplicity and the availability of ground truth. For each selected dataset, we pick a part (say one third) of it randomly to form the set of gold questions G, and the rest form the set of regular questions X. Every worker $j \in J$ provides his/her IVLs on both G and X. Thus, both L_G^j and L_X^j are available for each $j \in J$. All IVLs in L_G^j follow j's reliability indexes with some minor randomization. The labels in L_X^j also follow j's reliability, but with exceptions for some $j \in J$ that will act as attackers.

Through our experiments, we examine the effectiveness of anomaly detection and attacker identification using the t- and F-tests; and the impacts of attackers on the quality of crowdsourced work. The results are reported in the following.

4.2   The Effectiveness of Anomaly Detection and Attackers Identification

To test if our approach can effectively detect anomalies, we randomly chose a fifth of our worker pool to behave abnormally, regardless of their reliability. For each of the anomalous workers, their IVLs on X are set far away from their actual reliability indexes through large, random variation on the lower and upper bounds. For all $j \in J$, the proposed statistical tests are performed to examine if L_G^j and L_X^j have the same means and variances statistically. For our experiments, both statistical tests must fail for a worker j to be marked as anomalous. At a confidence level of at least 95%, our experiments successfully detected the anomalous workers for each of the three test datasets in CEKA. Figure 3, as an example, visually highlights the detected anomalous workers out of the hundred workers through a correctness-confidence graph. Anomalous workers are shown as dots with x's in the figure. Out of the twenty workers selected from the pool to act as attackers, sixteen were successfully identified using our proposed method. Additionally, the experiment was then run forty times and the best, worst, and average for the percentage of identified attackers versus actual attackers was collected. Over the runs, the average, best, and worst percentages were 84.1%, 100%, and 65%. This shows that in our experiments the proposed approach can detect anomalous workers effectively the majority of the time.

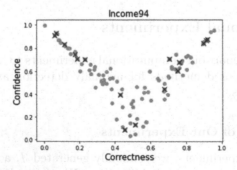

Fig. 3. Anomalous workers in Income94 dataset

To identify knowledgeable attackers, we should focus on workers with a high level of confidence (i.e., with a low or high correctness). This is because a low level of confidence reflects the worker's insufficient level of knowledge. Labels from such workers are usually ignored in practice. To identify possible attackers, we only need to check if a worker with a high level of confidence acts consistently or not. Regardless of if such a worker j is a naive or sophisticated attacker, the workers IVLs in L_G^j and L_X^j are not consistent statistically. In our experiments, we set the threshold level of confidence as 60% and pick twenty workers randomly as simulated attackers. Performing the t- and F-tests for each $j \in J$, we can determine if we should accept or reject the null hypothesis: L_G^j and L_X^j are the same statistically at a given level of significance. Figure 4 highlights these workers who fail the tests. This demonstrates the effectiveness of our approach for identifying potential attackers.

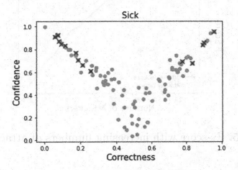

Fig. 4. Statistically inconsistent workers in Sick dataset

Scrutinizing the graph, it is shown that like with Fig. 3 only a portion (fourteen) of the twenty attackers were found. This is a normal and expected outcome. The consistency of the means and standard deviations of L_G^j and L_X^j does not mathematically ensure that j behaves normally, although the inconsistency suggests that j is likely an attacker.

4.3   Impacts of Attackers on the Quality of a Crowdsourced Work

The purpose of identifying attackers is to exclude them and improve the quality of crowdsourced work. To examine the impact of removing identified attackers, we apply the weighted interval majority voting (WIMV) algorithm defined in [28] to make inferences on the test datasets with and without removing identified attackers. We chose to use only WIMV and not the weighted preferred matching probability (WPMP) algorithm because both methods have similar performances. In one of our experiments, we collect IVLs from fifteen randomly selected j's on each $x \in X$, and then make an inference on those IVLs using WIMV. Since our test datasets come with ground truth, we are able to calculate confusion matrices for attacker-included and -excluded tests. Because the workers are randomly selected, these tests run twenty times and the average is used to form the confusion matrices. We then quantitatively measure the quality of work in terms of recall, precision, accuracy, and F_1-score. Figure 5 compares F_1-scores of attacker-included and -excluded runs on the *Vote* test dataset. The horizontal axis is the number of attackers among all workers. The figure shows that at a lower number of attackers, the non-anomalous workers in the attacker-included are able to overpower the attackers bad labels. However, as the number of attackers increases, the F_1-score for the attacker-included falls dramatically. By excluding the identified attackers, the F_1-score remains perfect or close to it even when facing a large number of adversarial attackers.

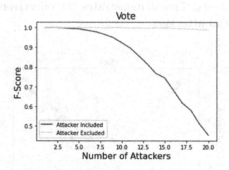

Fig. 5. F_1-score with increasing numbers of attackers

5   Summary

In this work, we have developed strategies for using IVLs to detect anomalous behavior in crowd-workers. Since the confidence, stability, and entropy of a worker j is independent to the ground truth, we are able to examine if a worker's IVLs on a set of gold questions G and regular questions X are consistent statistically. Assuming that G samples X well, any discrepancy of the means and/or standard deviations of L_G^j and L_X^j suggests j acts anomalously.

In applying the anomaly detection strategies, we have successfully been able to identify malicious attackers from regular crowd-workers as shown in Fig. 4. Figure 5 further shows an important comparison of including and excluding identified attackers. As the number of attackers increases, the quality of the crowdsourced work as measured by the F_1-score is dramatically reduced in the attacker-included runs. In contrast, the WIMV algorithm returns near perfect results after the removal of identified attackers. These experiments have shown that identifying attackers has critical importance for the quality crowdsourced work. Finally, we would like to point out that our approach does not mathematically guarantee the detection of all anomalous workers. The consistency of the means and standard deviations of L_G^j and L_X^j does not assure that j is not an attacker. Therefore, further investigations into anomaly detection are still needed, such as exploration into utilizing approximated spectrum or applying a confidence interval approach towards anomaly detection, along with detecting anomalies dynamically.

References

1. Checco, A., Bates, J., Demartini, G.: Adversarial attacks on crowdsourcing quality control. J. Artif. Intell. Res. **67**, 375–408 (2020)
2. Corliss, G.F., Hu, C., Kearfott, R.B., Walster, G.W.: Rigorous Global Search - Executive Summary. Technical report (1997)
3. Dai, J., Wang, W., Mi, J.: Uncertainty measurement for interval-valued information systems. Inf. Sci. **251**, 63–78 (2013)
4. Duan, Q., Hu, C., Wei, H.: Enhancing network intrusion detection systems with interval methods. In: SAC 2005: Proceedings of the 2005 ACM Symposium on Applied Computing, pp. 1444–1448 (2005)
5. Gan, Q., Yang, Q., Hu, C.: Parallel all-row preconditioned interval linear solver for nonlinear equations on multiprocessors. Parallel Comput. **20**(9), 1249–1268 (1994)
6. Goldstein, M., Uchida, S.: A comparative evaluation of unsupervised anomaly detection algorithms for multivariate data. PLoS ONE **11**(4), e0152173 (2016)
7. He, L., Hu, C.: Impacts of interval computing on stock market forecasting. J. Comput. Econ. **33**(3), 263–276 (2009). https://doi.org/10.1007/s10614-008-9159-x
8. Hu, C., Frolov, A., Kearfott, R., Yang, Q.: A general iterative sparse linear solver and its parallelization for interval Newton methods. Reliable Comput. **1**, 251–263 (1995)
9. Hu, C., Cardenas, A., Hoogendoorn, S., et al.: An interval polynomial interpolation problem and its Lagrange solution. Reliable Comput. **4**, 27–38 (1998)
10. Hu, C.: Using interval function approximation to estimate uncertainty. In: Huynh, V.N., Nakamori, Y., Ono, H., Lawry, J., Kreinovich, V., Nguyen, H.T. (eds.) Interval/Probabilistic Uncertainty and Non-Classical Logics. Advances in Soft Computing, vol. 46. Springer, Heidelberg (2008). https://doi.org/10.1007/978-3-540-77664-2_26
11. Hu, C., et al.: Knowledge Processing with Interval and Soft Computing. Springer, London (2008). https://doi.org/10.1007/978-1-84800-326-2
12. Hu, C., He, L.: An application of interval methods to stock market forecasting. J. Reliab. Comput. **13**, 423–434 (2007). https://doi.org/10.1007/s11155-007-9039-4
13. Hu, C.: Interval function and its linear least-squares approximation. In: ACM SNC 2011: Proceedings of the 2011 International Workshop on Symbolic-Numeric Computation, pp. 16–23. ACM (2012)
14. Hu, C., Hu, Z.H.: On statistics, probability, and entropy of interval-valued datasets. In: Lesot, M.J., et al. (eds.) IPMU 2020. CCIS, vol. 1239, pp. 407–421. Springer, Cham (2020). https://doi.org/10.1007/978-3-030-50153-2_31
15. Hu, C., Hu, Z.H.: A computational study on the entropy of interval valued datasets from the stock market. In: Lesot, M.J., et al. (eds.) IPMU 2020. CCIS, vol. 1239, pp. 422–435. Springer, Cham (2020). https://doi.org/10.1007/978-3-030-50153-2_32
16. Hu, C., Sheng, V.S., Wu, N., Wu, X.: Managing uncertainty in crowdsourcing with interval-valued labels. In: Rayz, J., Raskin, V., Dick, S., Kreinovich, V. (eds.) NAFIPS 2021. LNNS, vol. 258, pp. 166–178. Springer, Cham (2022). https://doi.org/10.1007/978-3-030-82099-2_15

17. Hu, P., Dellar, M., Hu, C.: Task scheduling on flow networks with temporal uncertainty. In: 2007 IEEE Symposium on Foundations of Computational Intelligence, pp. 128–135 (2007)

18. de Korvin, A., Hu, C., Chen, P.: Generating and applying rules for interval valued fuzzy observations. In: Yang, Z.R., Yin, H., Everson, R.M. (eds.) IDEAL 2004. LNCS, vol. 3177, pp. 279–284. Springer, Heidelberg (2004). https://doi.org/10.1007/978-3-540-28651-6_41

19. Kong, X., Song, X., Xia, F., Guo, H., Wang, J., Tolba, A.: LoTAD: long-term traffic anomaly detection based on crowdsourced bus trajectory data. World Wide Web **21**(3), 825–847 (2017). https://doi.org/10.1007/s11280-017-0487-4

20. Li, Y., Sun, J., Huang, W., Tian X.: Detecting anomaly in large-scale network using mobile crowdsourcing. In: IEEE INFOCOM 2019 - IEEE Conference on Computer Communications, pp. 2179–2187 (2019)

21. Li, H., Liu, Q.: Cheaper and Better: Selecting Good Workers for Crowdsourcing. arXiv:1502.00725 (2015)

22. Marupally, P., Paruchuri, V.S., Hu, C.: Bandwidth variability prediction with rolling interval least squares (RILS). In: Proceedings of the 50th ACM SE Conference, Tuscaloosa, AL, USA, 29–31 March 2012, pp. 209–213. ACM (2012)

23. NIST: Do two processes have the same mean? https://www.itl.nist.gov/div898/handbook/prc/section3/prc31.htm

24. NIST: F-test. www.itl.nist.gov/div898/handbook/eda/section3/eda359.htm

25. Nordin, B., Hu, C., Chen, B., Sheng, V.S.: Interval-valued centroids in K-means algorithms. In: Proceedings of the 11th IEEE International Conference on Machine Learning and Applications (ICMLA), Boca Raton, FL, USA, pp. 478–481. IEEE (2012)

26. Rhodes, C., Lemon, J., Hu, C.: An interval-radial algorithm for hierarchical clustering analysis. In: 14th IEEE International Conference on Machine Learning and Applications (ICMLA), Miami, FL, USA, pp. 849–856. IEEE (2015)

27. Shannon, C.-E.: A mathematical theory of communication. Bell Syst. Tech. J. **27**, 379–423 (1948)

28. Spurling, M., Hu, C., Sheng, V.S., Zhang, H.: Estimating crowd-worker's reliability with interval-valued labels to improve the quality of crowdsourced work (2021, to appear)

29. Qiu, L., et al.: CrowdSelect: increasing accuracy of crowdsourcing tasks through behavior prediction and user selection. In: Proceedings of the 25th ACM International Conference on Information and Knowledge Management, pp. 539–548 (2016)

30. Wang, G., Wang, T., Zheng, H., Zhao, B.: Man vs. machine: practical adversarial detection of malicious crowdsourcing workers. In: Proceedings of the 23rd USENIX Security Symposium, San Diego, CA, USA, 20–22 August 2014, pp. 239–254. USENIX Association (2014)

31. Yu, H., Liu, Y., et al.: Fair and explainable dynamic engagement of crowd workers. In: Proceedings of the Twenty-Eighth International Joint Conference on Artificial Intelligence, pp. 6575–6577 (2019)

32. Zhang, J., Sheng, V.S., Nicholson, B., Wu, X.: CEKA: a tool for mining the wisdom of crowds. J. Mach. Learn. Res. **16**, 2853–2858 (2015)

33. Zhao, Y., et al.: Outlier detection for streaming task assignment in crowdsourcing. In: WWW (2022)

Atanassov's Intuitionistic Fuzzy Sets Demystified

Eulalia Szmidt[1,2]($\boxtimes$) and Janusz Kacprzyk[1,2]

[1] Systems Research Institute Polish Academy of Sciences,
ul. Newelska 6, 01-447 Warsaw, Poland
{szmidt,kacprzyk}@ibspan.waw.pl

[2] Warsaw School of Information Technology, ul. Newelska 6, 01-447 Warsaw, Poland

Abstract. Atanassov's Intuitionistic Fuzzy Sets (IFSs for short) are a very convenient tool while making decisions, analyzing data, etc. Their structure renders a way of thinking by a human being considering pros, cons, and a lack of knowledge when faced with real problems. The IFSs are one of important and widely used extensions of fuzzy sets. They attracted a lot of attention which is confirmed by many citations. However, some problems are not clearly explained by some researchers, and some misunderstanding is caused by citing some conclusions forgetting about assumptions that were done at the beginning of some mathematical considerations. In effect, some researchers treat the IFSs as equivalent ("equipollent" should be used in that context instead) to the interval-valued fuzzy sets. It is correct, and it is not correct. The crux of a problem lies in the assumptions made at the beginning of the considerations leading to the conclusion. Our goal is to show to the reader that mechanical making use of the conclusions without paying attention to assumptions leading to the conclusions is not (and never was) justified. In other words, we stress that different models may lead to different conclusions so using specific conclusions (taking out from a context/assumptions) as the only valid conclusions is not justified. Unfortunately, such a situation occurs in the case of IFSs. The goal of this paper is to clarify it.

Keywords: Atanassov's intuitionistic fuzzy sets · Interval-valued fuzzy sets · Assumptions and conclusions

1 Introduction

Atanassov's intuitionistic fuzzy sets (IFSs, for short) (Atanassov [1–3]) are an important extension of the fuzzy sets (Zadeh [52]). The IFSs are a very convenient tool for modeling different data analysis, decision making, etc. problems in which the main difficulty is caused by a lack of knowledge. The IFSs represent the lack of knowledge by the so-called hesitation margin or intuitionistic fuzzy index. However, there are models in which the hesitation margin is not taken into account and only the membership values and the non-membership values are used. The first approach (with the hesitation margin, the membership values and the non-membership values) is called here the *three-term representation* of IFSs. The second approach (without the hesitation margin,

© Springer Nature Switzerland AG 2022
D. Ciucci et al. (Eds.): IPMU 2022, CCIS 1601, pp. 517–527, 2022.
https://doi.org/10.1007/978-3-031-08971-8_43

taking into account the membership values and the non-membership values only) we call here the *two-term representation* of IFSs. Both types of representations are mathematically correct (e.g., in the sense of fulfilling properties of some measures). Taking into account the above, we have two distinct models of the IFSs with different inputs (two terms or three terms) and different outputs (results obtained).

The motivation to write this paper are some other papers. In one of them it is stated that instead of the name "IFSs" it is better to use the "interval-valued fuzzy sets" (Klement and Mesiar [12]) which means that the two types of (fuzzy) sets are "the same". In another paper (Bustince et al. [9]) we can read about "mathematical identity" between the IFSs and the interval-valued fuzzy sets. This statement is expressed firmly also in Fig. 1. in [9]. In another paper (Deschrijver and Kerre [10]) we have again the conclusion that from the mathematical point of view, the IFSs are equivalent to the interval-valued fuzzy sets.

An interesting question arises. If we eliminate the name "IFSs", then we should forget the existence of the IFSs at all. Clearly, we do not discuss here in this context if the name is correct or not but just have in mind a separate name for IFSs, which distinguishes them from other sets. Therefore, using only the name the "interval-valued fuzzy sets", we should use then the mathematical apparatus developed for the interval-valued fuzzy sets. The operators, measures, and other characteristic tools and techniques developed for the IFSs, would not be used anymore in such a case.

It is worth stressing that in 1989 Atanassov and Gargov [5] have shown that the IFSs and interval-valued fuzzy sets are equipollent generalizations of fuzzy sets. The difference between "identical" and "eqipollent" as WolframMathWorld explains (https://mathworld.wolfram.com/Equipollent.html): *"Two statements in logic are said to be equipollent if they are deducible from each other"*.

"Two sets A and B are said to be equipollent iff there is a one-to-one correspondence (i.e., a bijection) from A onto B (Moore [13] *p. 10; Rubin* [15], *p. 67; Suppes* [16] *p. 91)*.

The above statements about equipollence are valid for the two-term model of IFSs and interval-valued fuzzy sets. However, for the three-term model of IFSs, the situation is different and we can not say at all that IFSs are equipollent to, or "the same" as interval-valued fuzzy sets. We show in this paper both the differences between the IFSs and interval-valued fuzzy sets, and more possibilities of the IFSs while making decisions.

We would like to stress firmly that mathematical conclusions are an effect of assumptions made at the beginning of mathematical considerations. Any conclusion is not generally valid, i.e., without taking into account assumptions leading to the conclusion. A change of the assumptions may result in a change the corresponding conclusions.

Moreover, there can be different models of the same phenomenon. The Feynman in his PhD dissertation [11] recalls *"a curious historical fact that modern quantum mechanics began with two quite different mathematical formulations: the differential equation of Schrödinger, and the matrix algebra of Heisenberg. The two, apparently dissimilar approaches, were proved to be mathematically equivalent.*

Even though the two theories (by Schroedinger, and by Heisenberg) are mathematically equivalent, nobody has heard about a proposal of using only one name for both of them. So why try to suggest something like this for other theories like the two-term model of the IFSs and interval-valued fuzzy sets?

Feynman continues in [11] about another model (introduced by Dirac): "... *there are no fundamentally new results. However, there is a pleasure in recognizing old things from a new point of view. Also, there are problems for which a new point of view offers a distinct advantage."* And further: *"In addition, there is always the hope that the new point of view will inspire an idea for the modification of present theories, a modification necessary to encompass present experiments."*

Indeed, the analogous situation occurs in the case of the IFSs. The IFSs can be seen not only in the equipollent way to the interval-valued fuzzy sets. We can construct the three-term model for IFSs. The three-term model is neither equipollent nor equal (in any sense) to the interval-valued fuzzy sets. It is not possible to modify the interval-value fuzzy set approach in a way that would offer the same possibilities the three-term model of the IFSs possesses. It is therefore not justified in any sense to use the name "interval-valued fuzzy sets" when we have in mind the IFSs, and this will be advocated here.

2 A Brief Introduction to the IFSs

One of the possible generalizations of a fuzzy set in X (Zadeh [52]) given by

$$A' = \{\langle x, \mu_{A'}(x)\rangle | x \in X\} \tag{1}$$

where $\mu_{A'}(x) \in [0,1]$ is the membership function of the fuzzy set A', is an IFS (Atanassov [1–3]) A is given by

$$A = \{\langle x, \mu_A(x), \nu_A(x)\rangle | x \in X\} \tag{2}$$

where: $\mu_A : X \to [0,1]$ and $\nu_A : X \to [0,1]$ such that

$$0 \le \mu_A(x) + \nu_A(x) \le 1 \tag{3}$$

and $\mu_A(x)$, $\nu_A(x) \in [0,1]$ denote a degree of membership and a degree of non-membership of $x \in A$, respectively. (See Szmidt and Baldwin [18] for assigning memberships and non-memberships for IFSs from data.)

An additional concept for each IFS in X, that is not only an obvious result of (2) and (3) but which is also relevant for applications, we will call (Atanassov [2])

$$\pi_A(x) = 1 - \mu_A(x) - \nu_A(x) \tag{4}$$

a *hesitation margin* of $x \in A$ which expresses a lack of knowledge of whether x belongs to A or not (cf. Atanassov [2]). It is obvious that $0 \le \pi_A(x) \le 1$, for each $x \in X$.

The hesitation margin turns out to be important while considering the distances (Szmidt and Kacprzyk [19,20,23,24]), entropy (Szmidt and Kacprzyk [21,25]), similarity (Szmidt and Kacprzyk [22,26]) for the IFSs, etc. i.e., the measures that play a crucial role in virtually all information processing tasks (Szmidt [17]).

The hesitation margin turns out to be relevant for applications – in image processing (cf. Bustince et al. [8]), the classification of imbalanced and overlapping classes (cf. Szmidt and Kukier [49–51]), the classification via the intuitionistic fuzzy trees (cf. Bujnowski [7]), group decision making (e.g., [4]), genetic algorithms [14], negotiations, consensus reaching, voting, etc. (cf. Szmidt and Kacprzyk papers).

The three terms describing the IFSs, i.e., the membership values, non-membership values and the hesitation margins, will be shown to get the concept of the IFS as being different from the concept of the interval-fuzzy set.

3   Expressing the IFSs by Intervals

Below we explain the representation of the IFSs by intervals showing that there are two approaches to do it.

When we use the two-term representation of the IFSs, we make use of any two terms from the triplet μ, ν, π (membership value, non-membership value, hesitation margin). In other words, we can consider a model in terms of: μ and ν or(!) μ and π or(!) ν and π.

To be more specific

– as $1 - \nu = \mu + \pi$ we can construct an interval

$$[\mu, \mu + \pi] \tag{5}$$

or(!)
– as $1 - \mu = \nu + \pi$ we can construct an interval

$$[\nu, \nu + \pi] \tag{6}$$

In such circumstances, while making use of one interval only, i.e., (5) or(!) (6), as Atanassov and Gargov noticed [5], the IFSs are equipollent to the interval-valued fuzzy sets; equipollent but not the same. The fact that both for he IFS model and for the interval-valued fuzzy sets model we use one interval does not mean that the two types of sets are "the same".

Example 1. Consider a degenerated IFS A consisting of one element x only. Assume its two-term representation, i.e., $A = \{< x, \mu, \nu >\}$. Let x be a medicine. Its advantages (positive effects) are expressed by the membership value $\mu(x)$. Its disadvantages (negative or side effects) are expressed by the non-membership value $\nu(x)$. The use of the two-term representation (μ, and ν) of the respective IFS implies therefore that the advantages of the medicine lie in the interval

$$[\mu(x), 1 - \nu(x)] = [\mu(x), \mu(x) + \pi(x)] \tag{7}$$

Instead, we could concentrate on the disadvantages of the medicine and express the disadvantages lying in the interval:

$$[\nu(x), 1 - \mu(x)] = [\nu(x), \nu(x) + \pi(x)] \tag{8}$$

For example, if $< x, 0.6, 0.3 >$, from (7) we can come to the conclusion that $\mu(x) \in [0.6, 0.7]$.

Instead(!), from (8) we have: $\nu(x) \in [0.3, 0.4]$.

However, the two term model does not make it possible to consider both intervals (7) and (8) the same time. We must decide on one interval only as we make use of $(\mu, \text{ and } \nu)$.

The situation is different when we jointly take into account all the three terms explicitly, i.e., the membership value μ, the non-membership value ν, and the value of the hesitation margin π. To be more precise, we can consider the IFSs in terms of the two intervals at the same time:

$$[\mu(x), \mu(x) + \alpha\pi(x)] \tag{9}$$

$$[\nu(x), \nu(x) + (1 - \alpha)\pi(x)] \tag{10}$$

where $\alpha \in [0, 1]$.

The differences of the two approaches (the two-term model of IFSs, and the three-term model of the IFSs) is visible in particular in decision making contexts.

Example 2. Consider again the medicine x described in Example 1 in which the two-term representation of the A-IFSs was applied. Now, we will employ the three term representation $< x, \mu, \nu, \pi >$ with the advantages given by $\mu(x)$, disadvantages expressed by $\nu(x)$, and a lack of knowledge considering both the advantages, and the disadvantages given by $\pi(x)$.

Assume $< x, 0.6, 0.3, 0.1 >$ which means that:

– in the best situation ($\alpha = 1$) from (9)–(10) we obtain $\{< x, 0.7, 0.3, 0 >\}$ as $\mu(x) = 0.6 + 0.1 = 0.7$, and $\nu(x) = 0.3$;
– in the worst situation ($\alpha = 0$) from (9)–(10) we obtain $\{< x, 0.6, 0.4, 0 >\}$ as $\mu(x) = 0.6$ and $\nu(x) = 0.3 + 0.1 = 0.4$.

Similar analyses are done in real life when extreme values of different scenarios are interesting (e.g., maximal gain or maximal risk, maximal threats or maximal opportunities).

From (9)–(10), other scenarios analyzing the same time $\mu(x)$ and $\nu(x)$ for different values of α are also possible.

For example:

– for $\alpha = 0.2$, we have $\{< x, 0.62, 0.38, 0 >\}$ as $\mu(x) = 0.6 + 0.02 = 0.62$, and $\nu(x) = 0.3 + 0.08 = 0.38$;
– for $\alpha = 0.6$, the medicine assessment is $\{< x, 0.66, 0.34, 0 >\}$ as as $\mu(x) = 0.6 + 0.06 = 0.66$, and $\nu(x) = 0.3 + 0.04 = 0.34$;
   for $\alpha = 0.5$, i.e., in an average situation, the medicine assessment is: $\{< x, 0.65, 0.35, 0 >\}$ as $\mu(x) = 0.6 + 0.05 = 0.65$, and $\nu(x) = 0.3 + 0.05 = 0.35$.

Taking into account the two-term representation of the IFSs does not make the above analysis (consideration of different scenarios) possible (only one interval, i.e., (7) or(!) (8) can be considered then).

4   Other Differences Between the IFSs and Interval-Valued Fuzzy Sets

The three-term representation of the IFSs is quite different than the representation of the IFSs by the interval-valued fuzzy sets. One of the differences makes it possible to consider scenarios concerning the future of the different real phenomena that can be described to some extent only. There are many important real processes that can not be described precisely. However, decision making is necessary for these processes. Examples are around us – voting processes, looking for a new job, introduction of a new product to the market, buying a house, using a new medicine, to name a few. A successful decision is strongly dependent on the values of the hesitation margin.

4.1   Different Measures for the IFSs and Interval-Valued Fuzzy Sets

The advantages of the three-term description of IFSs are not limited to the possibility to consider different scenarios by using two intervals. The obvious differences between the two approaches occur when considering different measures.

Szmidt and Kacprzyk [20, 24] discuss the results obtained for the most often used distances when the two and the three-term representations of the A-IFS are used.

Examples of the distances between any two A-IFSs A and B in $X = \{x_1, x_2, \ldots, x_n\}$ while using the three-term representation may be as follows (Szmidt and Kacprzyk [20]):

– the normalized Hamming distance:

$$l_{IFS}(A, B) = \frac{1}{2n} \sum_{i=1}^{n} (|\mu_A(x_i) - \mu_B(x_i)| + |\nu_A(x_i) - \nu_B(x_i)| +$$

$$|\pi_A(x_i) - \pi_B(x_i)|) \quad (11)$$

– the normalized Euclidean distance:

$$e_{IFS}(A, B) = (\frac{1}{2n} \sum_{i=1}^{n} (\mu_A(x_i) - \mu_B(x_i))^2 + (\nu_A(x_i) - \nu_B(x_i))^2$$

$$+ (\pi_A(x_i) - \pi_B(x_i))^2)^{\frac{1}{2}} \quad (12)$$

The values of both distances are from the interval $[0, 1]$.

The corresponding distances to the above ones while using the two term representation of the A-IFSs are:

– the normalized Hamming distance:

$$l'(A, B) = \frac{1}{2n} \sum_{i=1}^{n} (|\mu_A(x_i) - \mu_B(x_i)| + |\nu_A(x_i) - \nu_B(x_i)|) \quad (13)$$

– the normalized Euclidean distance:

$$q'(A, B) = (\frac{1}{2n} \sum_{i=1}^{n} (\mu_A(x_i) - \mu_B(x_i))^2 + (\nu_A(x_i) - \nu_B(x_i))^2)^{\frac{1}{2}} \quad (14)$$

Both the two-term distances and the three-term distances [17,20] are correct from the mathematical point of view, i.e., all the needed properties are fulfilled. However, the above distances are not only a theoretical "game". The three-term distances give differnt quality results e.g., when decision making (cf. e.g., Szmidt and Kacprzyk [30,42,43]). Some distances like Hausdorff distance does not work (when using the Hamming distance expressed by (13) (cf. Szmidt and Kacprzyk [35])).

The tree-term approach turned out successful when applied to:

– constructing a classifier for imbalanced and overlapping classes (cf. Szmidt and Kukier [49–51]),
– constructing intuitionistic fuzzy trees (Bujnowski [6]),
– Pearson correlation coefficient (Szmidt and Kacprzyk [32,41]), (Szmidt et al. [38, 39,44]),
– Spearman correlation coefficient (Szmidt and Kacprzyk [34]),
– Kendall correlation coefficient (Szmidt and Kacprzyk [36,37]),
– Principal Component Analysis (Szmidt and Kacprzyk [40], Szmidt et al. [45]),
– ranking procedures (Szmidt and Kacprzyk [27–31,33]).
– looking for the best attributes in classification task (Szmidt et al. [46,47]).

It is worth mentioning that the approaches presented above were successfully applied for benchmark data from
UCI Machine Learning Repository (www.ics.uci.edu/~mlearn/).

4.2 Different Operators for IFSs and Interval-Valued Fuzzy Sets. Problem of Interpretability

There are many operators introduced for IFSs (Atanassov [2]) We could insist to rewrite the operators (see below) using the two-term model of IFSs, i.e., approach which is equipollent to interval-valued fuzzy sets. However, the transparency of the formulas would decrease. The sense of the formulas, and understanding of them, would be difficult.

Even in a case of the simplest operators ([2], p. 76):

$$D_\alpha(A) = \{\langle x, \mu_A(x) + \alpha \times \pi_A(x), \nu_A(x) + (1 - \alpha) \times \pi_A(x)\rangle | x \in X\}, \quad (15)$$
$$F_{\alpha,\beta}(A) = \{\langle x, \mu_A(x) + \alpha \times \pi_A(x), \nu_A(x) + \beta \times \pi_A(x)\rangle | x \in X\} \quad (16)$$

where $\alpha, \beta \in [0, 1]$ and $\alpha + \beta \leq 1$; it is easier to understand the sense of the formulas when π is used in explicit way although the numerical results would be the same in the above two formulas if π is expressed by (4).

For other extensions of the modal operators we refer an interested reader to Atanassov's [2,3] works. What is worth stressing, the presented operators are not considered for the interval-valued fuzzy sets.

For other formulas, for example (17) making it possible to rank an alternative $Y_i(\mu_{Y_i}, \nu_{Y_i}, \pi_{Y_i})$ and compare it with other alternatives (cf. Szmidt and Kacprzyk [31, 48]) the situation is similar. Function R is expressed as

$$R(Y_i) = 0.5(1 + \pi_{Y_i})l_{IFS}(M, Y_i) \tag{17}$$

where $l_{IFS}(M, Y_i)$ is the Hamming distance of alternative Y_i from ideal positive alternative $M(1, 0, 0)$.

From (11)

$$l_{IFS}(M, Y_i) = \frac{1}{2}(|1 - \mu_{Y_i}| + |0 - \nu_{Y_i}| + |0 - \pi_{Y_i}|) = 1 - \mu_{Y_i}$$

hence

$$R(Y_i) = 0.5(1 + \pi_{Y_i})(1 - \mu_{Y_i}) \tag{18}$$

Equation (18) tells us about the "quality" of an alternative Y_i that is, the lower the value of $R(Y_i)$, (18), the better the alternative in the sense of the amount of positive information included, and of the reliability of information.

If we insist on expressing π in terms of μ and ν, we would obtain

$$R(Y_i) = 0.5(2 - \mu_{Y_i} - \nu_{Y_i})(1 - \mu_{Y_i}) \tag{19}$$

which has not clear interpretation. A similar situation occurs in many other cases.

5   Conclusions

Many problems may be solved by using not only one set of assumptions, so conclusions which are the obvious result of the made assumptions are not the only ones in all possible contexts.

There are different models of the same phenomena, concepts, and even when they lead to the same conclusions, the models may be very useful in throwing new light on the problems and/or be a starting point to new theories (approaches).

The above statements concern the IFSs too:

- it is possible to consider the IFSs under different assumptions leading to different conclusions regarding not only a general nature of the IFSs (equipollent to the interval-valued fuzzy sets or quite different from them) but also giving quite different results while solving practical problems (as the conclusions when using one interval are not the same as the conclusions obtained when using two intervals);
- we have distinct approaches to constructing models of the IFSs that is, the two-term approach leading to the construction of one interval, and the three-term approach leading to the construction of two intervals;
- it is not possible to construct for the two-term representation, which is equipollent to the interval-valued fuzzy set model, an analogical approach to the three-term approach.

References

1. Atanassov, K.: Intuitionistic Fuzzy Sets. VII ITKR Session, Sofia (Centr. Sci.-Techn. Libr. of Bulg. Acad. of Sci. 1697/1984) (in Bulgarian) (1983)
2. Atanassov, K.T.: Intuitionistic Fuzzy Sets: Theory and Applications. Springer, Heidelberg (1999). https://doi.org/10.1007/978-3-7908-1870-3
3. Atanassov, K.T.: On Intuitionistic Fuzzy Sets Theory. Springer, Heidelberg (2012). https://doi.org/10.1007/978-3-642-29127-2
4. Atanassova, V.: Strategies for decision making in the conditions of intuitionistic fuzziness. In: International Conference on 8th Fuzzy Days, Dortmund, pp. 263–269 (2004)
5. Atanassov, K., Gargov, G.: Interval-valued intuitionistic fuzzy sets. Fuzzy sets Syst. **31**(3), 343–349 (1989)
6. Bujnowski, P.: Application of intuitionistic fuzzy sets for constructing decision trees for classification tasks. Ph.D. dissertation (in Polish). SRI PAS, Warsaw (2013)
7. Bujnowski, P, Szmidt, E., Kacprzyk, J.: Intuitionistic fuzzy decision trees - a new approach. In: Rutkowski, L., et al. (eds.) ICAISC 2014. LNCS (LNAI), vol. 8467, pp. 181–192. Springer, Cham (2014). https://doi.org/10.1007/978-3-319-07173-2_17
8. Bustince, H., Mohedano, V., Barrenechea, E., Pagola, M.: An algorithm for calculating the threshold of an image representing uncertainty through A-IFSs. In: IPMU'2006, pp. 2383–2390 (2006)
9. Bustince, H., et al.: A historical account of types of fuzzy sets and their relationships. IEEE Trans. Fuzzy Syst. **24**(1), 179–194 (2016)
10. Deschrijver, G., Etienne, E., Kerre, E.: On the relationship between some extensions of fuzzy set theory. Fuzzy Sets Syst. **133**(2), 227–235 (2003)
11. Feynman, R.: Space-time approach to non-relativistic quantum mechanics. Rev. Mod. Phys. **20**, 367–387 (1948). Reprinted. In: Feynman's Thesis. A new approach to quantum theory. Ed. by Laurie M. Brown. World Scientific (2005)
12. Klement, E.P., Mesiar, R.: L-Fuzzy sets and isomorphic lattices: are all the "new" results really new? Mathematics **6**(9), 146 (2018). https://doi.org/10.3390/math6090146
13. Moore, G.H.: Zermelo's Axiom of Choice: Its Origin, Development, and Influence. Springer, New York (1982). https://doi.org/10.1007/978-1-4613-9478-5
14. Roeva, O., Michalikova, A.: Generalized net model of intuitionistic fuzzy logic control of genetic algorithm parameters. Notes IFSs **19**(2), 71–76 (2013)
15. Rubin, J.E.: Set Theory for the Mathematician. Holden-Day, New York (1967)
16. Suppes, P.: Axiomatic Set Theory. Dover, New York (1972)
17. Szmidt, E.: Distances and Similarities in Intuitionistic Fuzzy Sets. Springer, Cham (2014). https://doi.org/10.1007/978-3-319-01640-5
18. Szmidt, E., Baldwin, J.: Intuitionistic fuzzy set functions, mass assignment theory, possibility theory and histograms. IEEE World Congr. Comput. Intell. **2006**, 237–243 (2006)
19. Szmidt, E., Kacprzyk, J.: On measuring distances between intuitionistic fuzzy sets. Notes IFS **3**(4), 1–13 (1997)
20. Szmidt, E., Kacprzyk, J.: Distances between intuitionistic fuzzy sets. Fuzzy Sets Syst. **114**(3), 505–518 (2000)
21. Szmidt, E., Kacprzyk, J.: Entropy for intuitionistic fuzzy sets. Fuzzy Sets Syst. **118**(3), 467–477 (2001)
22. Szmidt, E., Kacprzyk, J.: A concept of similarity for intuitionistic fuzzy sets and its use in Group Decision Making. In: 2004 IEEE Conference on Fuzzy Systems, Budapest, pp. 1129–1134 (2004)

23. Szmidt, E., Kacprzyk, J.: Distances between intuitionistic fuzzy sets and their applications in reasoning. In: Halgamuge, S.K., Wang, L. (eds.) Computational Intelligence for Modelling and Prediction, pp. 101–116. Springer, Heidelberg (2005). https://doi.org/10.1007/10966518_8

24. Szmidt, E., Kacprzyk, J.: Distances Between Intuitionistic Fuzzy Sets: Straightforward Approaches May Not Work (IEEE IS 2006), pp. 716–721. IEEE IS (2006)

25. Szmidt, E., Kacprzyk, J.: Some problems with entropy measures for the Atanassov intuitionistic fuzzy sets. In: Masulli, F., Mitra, S., Pasi, G. (eds.) WILF 2007. LNCS (LNAI), vol. 4578, pp. 291–297. Springer, Heidelberg (2007). https://doi.org/10.1007/978-3-540-73400-0_36

26. Szmidt, E., Kacprzyk, J.: A new similarity measure for intuitionistic fuzzy sets: straightforward approaches may not work. In: 2007 IEEE Conf. on Fuzzy Systems, pp. 481–486 (2007)

27. Szmidt, E., Kacprzyk, J.: Ranking alternatives expressed via intuitionistic fuzzy sets. In: 12th International Conference IPMU 2008, pp. 1604–1611 (2008)

28. Szmidt, E., Kacprzyk, J.: A method for ranking alternatives expressed via Atanassov's intuitionistic fuzzy sets. In: Atanassov, K., et al. (Eds.) Advances in Fuzzy Sets, Intuitionistics Fuzzy Sets, Generalized Nets and Related Topics. Academic Publishing House EXIT, Warsaw 2009. Challenging Problems of Science - Computer Science, pp. 161–173 (2009)

29. Szmidt, E., Kacprzyk, J.: A new approach to ranking alternatives expressed via intuitionistic fuzzy sets. In: Ruan, D., et al. (eds.) Computational Intelligence in Decision and Control, pp. 265–270. World Scientific (2008)

30. Szmidt, E., Kacprzyk, J.: Ranking of Intuitionistic Fuzzy Alternatives in a Multi-criteria Decision Making Problem (NAFIPS 2009), Cincinnati. IEEE (2009). ISBN: 978-1-4244-4577-6

31. Szmidt, E., Kacprzyk, J.: Amount of information and its reliability in the ranking of Atanassov's intuitionistic fuzzy alternatives. In: Rakus-Andersson, E., Yager, R., Ichalkaranje, N., Jain, L.C. (eds.)Recent Advances in decision Making (SCI 222), pp. 7–19. Springer, Heidelberg (2009). https://doi.org/10.1007/978-3-642-02187-9_2

32. Szmidt, E., Kacprzyk, J.: Correlation between intuitionistic fuzzy sets. In: Hullermeier, E., Kruse, R., Hoffmann, F. (eds.) Computational Intelligence for Knowledge-Based Systems Design, LNAI, vol. 6178, pp. 169–177 (2010)

33. Szmidt, E., Kacprzyk, J.: On an enhanced method for a more meaningful ranking of intuitionistic fuzzy alternatives. Lect. Notes Artif. Intell. **6113**, 232–239 (2010)

34. Szmidt, E., Kacprzyk, J.: The Spearman rank correlation coefficient between intuitionistic fuzzy sets. In: Proceedings of the 2010 IEEE International Conference on Intelligent Systems (IEEE'IS 2010), London, pp. 276–280 (2010)

35. Szmidt, E., Kacprzyk, J.: Intuitionistic fuzzy sets - two and three term representations in the context of a Hausdorff distance. Acta Univ. Matth. Belii Ser. Math. **19**(19), 53–62 (2011). https://actamath.savbb.sk/pdf/acta1908.pdf

36. Szmidt, E., Kacprzyk, J.: The Kendall Rank correlation between intuitionistic fuzzy sets. In: Proceedings of the World Conference on Soft Computing, San Francisco, 23 May 2011 to 26 May 2011 (2011)

37. Szmidt, E., Kacprzyk, J.: The Spearman and Kendall rank correlation coefficients between intuitionistic fuzzy sets. In: Proceedings of the 7th Conference of European Society for Fuzzy Logic and Technology, Aix-Les-Bains, pp. 521–528. Antantic Press (2011)

38. Szmidt, E., Kacprzyk, J., Bujnowski, P.: Pearson's coefficient between intuitionistic fuzzy sets. Notes Intuitionist. Fuzzy Sets **17**(2), 25–34 (2011)

39. Szmidt, E., Kacprzyk, J., Bujnowski, P.: Pearson's correlation coefficient between intuitionistic fuzzy sets: an extended theoretical and numerical analysis. In: Atanassov, K.T., et al. (eds.) Recent Advances in Fuzzy Sets, Intuitionistic Fuzzy Sets, Generalized Nets and Related Topics, pp. 223–236. SRI PAS, Warsaw (2011)
40. Szmidt, E., Kacprzyk, J.: A New Approach to Principal Component Analysis for Intuitionistic Fuzzy Data Sets. In: Greco, S., Bouchon-Meunier, B., Coletti, G., Fedrizzi, M., Matarazzo, B., Yager, R.R. (eds.) IPMU 2012. CCIS, vol. 298, pp. 529–538. Springer, Heidelberg (2012). https://doi.org/10.1007/978-3-642-31715-6_56
41. Szmidt, E., Kacprzyk, J.: On an enhanced method for a more meaningful Pearson's correlation coefficient between intuitionistic fuzzy sets. ICAISC **1**, 334–341 (2012)
42. Szmidt, E., Kacprzyk, J.: Two and three term representations of intuitionistic fuzzy sets: some conceptual and analytic aspects. IEEE Int. Conf. Fuzzy Systems FUZZ-IEEE **2015**, 1–8 (2015)
43. Szmidt, E., Kacprzyk, J.: A perspective on differences between Atanassov's intuitionistic fuzzy sets and interval-valued fuzzy sets. In: Torra, V., Dahlbom, A., Narukawa, Y. (eds.) Fuzzy Sets, Rough Sets, Multisets and Clustering. SCI, vol. 671, pp. 221–237. Springer, Cham (2017). https://doi.org/10.1007/978-3-319-47557-8_13
44. Szmidt, E., Kacprzyk, J., Bujnowski, P.: Correlation between intuitionistic fuzzy sets: some conceptual and numerical extensions. In: WCCI 2012 IEEE World Congress on Computational Intelligence, Brisbane, pp. 480–486 (2012)
45. Szmidt, E., Kacprzyk, J., Bujnowski, P.: Advances in principal component analysis for intuitionistic fuzzy data sets. In: 2012 IEEE 6th International Conference "Intelligent Systems", pp. 194–199 (2012)
46. Szmidt, E., Kacprzyk, J., Bujnowski, P.: Attribute selection for sets of data expressed by intuitionistic fuzzy sets. In: 2020 IEEE International Conference on Fuzzy Systems (FUZZ-IEEE), 2020, pp. 1–7 (2020)
47. Szmidt, E., Kacprzyk, J., Bujnowski, P.: Three term attribute description of Atanassov's Intuitionistic Fuzzy Sets as a basis of attribute selection. In: 2021 IEEE International Conference on Fuzzy Systems (FUZZ-IEEE), 2021, pp. 1–6 (2021)
48. Szmidt, E., Kacprzyk, J., Bujnowski, P.: Ranking of Alternatives Described by Atanassov's Intuitionistic Fuzzy Sets - A Critical Review. Submitted (2022)
49. Szmidt, E., Kukier, M.: Classification of Imbalanced and Overlapping Classes Using Intuitionistic Fuzzy Sets (IEEE IS'06), London, pp. 722–727 (2006)
50. Szmidt, E., Kukier, M.: A new approach to classification of imbalanced classes via Atanassov's intuitionistic fuzzy sets. In: Wang, H.-F. (ed.) Intelligent Data Analysis: Developing New Methodologies Through Pattern Discovery and Recovery, pp. 85–101. Idea Group (2008)
51. Szmidt, E., Kukier, M.: Atanassov's intuitionistic fuzzy sets in classification of imbalanced and overlapping classes. In: Chountas, P., Petrounias, I., Kacprzyk, J. (eds.) Intelligent Techniques and Tools for Novel System Architectures, pp. 455–471. Springer, Heidelberg (2008). https://doi.org/10.1007/978-3-540-77623-9_26
52. Zadeh, L.A.: Fuzzy sets. Inf. Control **8**, 338–353 (1965)

Towards Explainable Summary of Crowdsourced Reviews Through Text Mining

Aaron Moody[1], Chenyi Hu[1(✉)], Huixin Zhan[2], Makenzie Spurling[1],
and Victor S. Sheng[2]

[1] University of Central Arkansas, Conway, AR, USA
chu@uca.edu
[2] Texas Tech University, Lubbock, TX, USA

Abstract. With the ever broad availability of technology, organizations
and merchants are now able to collect large amounts of reviews online.
Each review usually consists of an interval datum, such as a one to five
ranking, along with a text comment. While an aggregated numeric scale
commonly serves as an overall rating; a human user usually needs to read
text manually to comprehend it. The aim of this work is to generate an
explainable summary computationally through mining all text comments
with natural language processing (NLP). In this initial work, we are
able to derive an overall numeric scale of the reviews through sentiment
analysis. We further combine methods of text summarization together
with document clustering to obtain an explainable text summary that is
easy for human users to comprehend. As an experiment, our approach
has produced an explainable summary from a review dataset publicly
available from Amazon.

Keywords: crowdsourced reviews · explainable AI · sentiment
analysis · document clustering · text summarization

1 Introduction

In this section, we briefly introduce the problem we are studying and a sample
dataset for the purpose of illustrating our approaches.

1.1 About This Study

Nowadays, machine learning and AI have been broadly employed in real world
applications. To help a human user comprehend and trust the solutions, explainable artificial intelligence (XAI) is very much needed. The specific problem we
investigate in this work is obtaining an explainable summary from crowdsourced
reviews. A review usually consists of a numeric ranking, such as a five-star scaled
rating, along with text comments. So, we denote a review from a reviewer i as

© Springer Nature Switzerland AG 2022
D. Ciucci et al. (Eds.): IPMU 2022, CCIS 1601, pp. 528–541, 2022.
https://doi.org/10.1007/978-3-031-08971-8_44

a tuple $r_i = (s_i, d_i)$. In which, s_i and d_i represent the numeric ranking and the document containing text comments, respectively. Through machine learning, AI can then generate a summary from collected reviews for human users to make an informed decision. For instance, *"Amazon calculates a product's star rating using machine-learned models instead of a simple average."*–Amazon. While the AI generated overall numeric ranking is helpful, a human user still needs to read all the text comments to comprehend and trust the ranking. Added to this is that it is a tedious task for a human user to read such a large number of reviews manually.

Recent advances in AI and NLP have provided great tools for processing text automatically. Among them are NLTK [11], BERT (Bidirectional Encoder Representations from Transformers) [8], GPT-3 [10], Hugging Face transformers, and others. With such available tools, the aim of this work is to mine text documents in reviews computationally for an explainable summary. The methods used in this initial work include sentiment analysis, document clustering, and document summarization. Specifically, we apply sentiment analysis to derive an overall scale of the reviews, and then combine text summarization methods with document clustering to obtain an explainable and comprehensive summary for human users.

1.2   The Sample Dataset

Our approach presented in this work can be applied to all types of crowdsourced reviews. Though, to make this paper easy to read, we use a crowdsourced dataset as a sample to illustrate our ideas with experiments. The sample dataset is publicly available from Amazon; and we downloaded it on 01/25/2022. It consists of 967 reviews on a specific refurbished cellphone. Table 1 lists the count of reviews in each of the five-star rankings. From that, we have the average star ranking 3.9, which is different from Amazon's overall ranking 4.4. A human user is expected to read these 967 text comments manually to comprehend the overall ranking. Instead, we process the 967 reviews with NLP to generate an explainable summary as a case study.

Table 1. Counting of each star ranking

Ranking	1	2	3	4	5
Count	179	48	57	119	564

Beyond the main reason of readability, we use this dataset also because of that Amazon has filtered out unrelated reviews. Amazon states on its website, *"We do not consider customer ratings without an Amazon Verified Purchase status in a product's overall star rating until a customer adds more details in the form of text, image, or video."* This simplifies our study without the need to filter out unrelated reviews, which is another research topic beyond the scope of this work.

The rest of this paper is organized as the following. In Sect. 2, we apply sentiment analysis to categorize the reviews and generate an overall sentiment ranking. In Sect. 3, we use text summarization together with document clustering to discover explainable information for the overall ranking. In Sect. 4, we present an algorithm and apply it to generate an explainable summary from the sample dataset. We conclude this work in Sect. 5.

2   Overall Sentiment Ranking of the Reviews

In this section, we derive an overall sentiment ranking from all text comments. As mentioned earlier, the tuple $r_i = (s_i, d_i)$ is a review from i. The sample dataset has a five-star ranking system. So, we have $s_i \in \{1, 2, 3, 4, 5\}$. The document d_i contains the text comments from i to explain s_i. The set of all documents form a corpus D, i.e. $D = \{d_i\}$. To process a document $d \in D$ computationally, we need to break d into sentences and words as tokens. After tokenizing a document into sentences and words, one may encode (or vectorize) them with TF-IDF (Term Frequency-Inverse Document Frequency) [12], BERT, or others. The corpus D can then be processed automatically.

It is also possible that two reviewers, i and j, may not necessarily assign the same numeric ranking exactly even with similar reasons. Therefore, we need to analyze the sentiment of every $d \in D$ for consistency. The methods for accomplishing this can be supervised or unsupervised. Unsupervised learning involves using pre-defined rules when determining sentiment. An example of this would be using a list of words associated with negativity and counting how many of those words are featured in a specific sentence. Another way is supervised learning, which is far more useful. This is because context matters more than what is explicitly written down. This is accomplished by training an AI to predict sentiment based on what text is contained. Among available tools for sentiment analysis, the VADER (Valence Aware Dictionary and sEntiment Reasoner) library is broadly used and freely available [1]. It is a lexicon and rule-based sentiment analysis tool, and returns 4 values for a given document as:

- *pos*: the probability of the sentiment to be positive;
- *neu*: the probability of the sentiment to be neutral;
- *neg*: the probability of the sentiment to be negative; and
- *compound*: the normalized compound score which calculates the sum of all lexicon ratings and takes values from -1 to 1.

In this study, we opted to use the compound score as having a normalized value allows for a better comparison of overall sentiment. With this in mind, a document is deemed positive (or negative) if its compound value is greater than 0.05 (or less than -0.05). Otherwise, it is neutral. The 967 documents in the sample dataset are classified into three categories as positive (759), neutral (44), and negative (164) according to compound scores.

To match the 5-star ranking system, we classify the sentiment of each $d \in D$ into the following five categories: very negative (VN), negative (NG), neutral

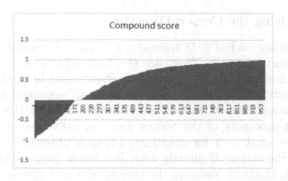

Fig. 1. Documents sorted according to their compound sentiment scores.

(NU), positive (PS), and very positive (VP). Figure 1 illustrates the documents sorted according to their compound scores. From which, we classify d_i as the following for simplicity[1]:

$$\begin{cases} \text{VN, if } \text{comp}_i \leq -0.5 \\ \text{NG, if } -0.5 < \text{comp}_i \leq -0.1 \\ \text{NU, if } -0.1 < \text{comp}_i \leq 0.1 \\ \text{PO, if } 0.1 < \text{comp}_i \leq 0.5 \\ \text{VP, if } 0.5 < \text{comp}_i \end{cases} \quad (1)$$

Table 2 lists the counts of each sentiment category. Using 1 to 5 to represent the sentiments VN to VP, respectively, we have the average sentiment ranking of 4.2, which is between the average star ranking 3.9 and Amazon's 4.4 ranking. This may suggest that sentiment analysis from the corpus can be more reliable than the average star rankings from reviewers. This is because the overall sentiment scale comes from the reasons documented specifically within each review.

Table 2. Counting of sentiments

Ranking	VN	NG	NU	PO	VP
Count	96	61	60	133	617

3 Corpus Summarization

Through sentiment analysis, we are able to generate an overall ranking successfully. However, a human user still needs explainable information to comprehend the overall ranking. In this section we summarize the corpus to obtain such information for the human user.

---

[1] Instead of Eq. (1), one may apply fuzzy memberships to categorize the sentiment of each $d \in D$.

3.1   Summarizing the Corpus Directly

Rather than reading each $d \in D$ manually, we apply document summarization to produce a short summary. There are two basic approaches to summarize a document. One is extractive; and the other is abstractive. In this study, we apply both. Using TextRank [4], we are able to rank all sentences in D according to their importance derived with latent semantic analysis (LSA). The top k most important sentences of the corpus form an extractive summary. In our experiments, we use $k = 3$ for simplicity. Figure 2 illustrates a few sentences extracted from the corpus D directly with TextRank. Researchers use ROUGE scores [3] to quantitatively measure the quality of a text summary. Table 3 lists the rouge results of Fig. 2. The recall values are 1 or very close to it because the sentences are extracted from the corpus. However, the values for precision and F-1 are very low. This implies that the extracted sentences in Fig. 2 do not well explain the overall ranking at all.

> *No carrier was able to activate the phone because there are "unpaid or overdue" charges on the AT&T account. Granted these were CARRIER UNLOCKED phones (vs FAC-TORY unlocked), which means one of them has a T-Mobile splash screen and bloatware, but that doesn't mean that the phone cannot be activated on a Verizon network since it is technically carrier unlocked, it just means I will forever see the t-mobile logo when booting, which I can get over. When they ran the part numbers, it showed that the phone was supposed to be black, but a blue case was used So, buyer beware...I can never bring myself to pay too much for a cellphone, and I don't think I ever will.*

Fig. 2. A summary of the corpus.

Table 3. Rouge results of the extractive summary in Fig. 2

	Rouge-1	Rouge-2	Rouge-l
Recall	1	0.9813	1
Precision	0.0108	0.0028	0.0108
F-1	0.0214	0.0057	0.0214

3.2   Summarizing the Corpus After Clustering Its Documents

Other than aggregating all $d \in D$ as a whole, we use the cosine similarity of two documents [2,5] to measure their distance and then group similar documents together with K-Means [7]. As illustrated in Fig. 3 on the left, the 967 documents are grouped into seven clusters. The elbow-shaped graph on the right justifies the number of clusters. Figure 4 provides the extractive summaries for the documents in each of the seven clusters. The rouge results show improvement as illustrated in Table 4.

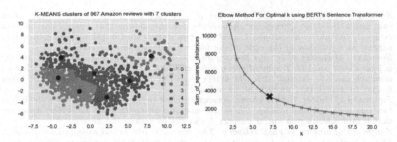

Fig. 3. K-Means clusters of the sample dataset.

Table 4. Rouge results of extractive summaries of the clusters

Summary	Clus.-1	Clus.-2	Clus.-3	Clus.-4	Clus.-5	Clus.-6	Clus.-7
Rouge-1 recall	1	1	1	1	1	1	1
Rouge-1 precision	0.0684	0.0230	0.1455	0.0897	0.0410	0.0255	0.0211
Rouge-1 F-1	0.0671	0.0995	0.1377	0.0387	0.0387	0.0352	0.0352
Rouge-2 recall	0.9780	0.9892	0.9583	0.9843	0.9795	0.9682	0.9800
Rouge-2 precision	0.0324	0.0070	0.0794	0.0502	0.0169	0.0086	0.0067
Rouge-2 F-1	0.0627	0.0156	0.1467	0.0957	0.0334	0.0086	0.0133
Rouge-1 recall	1	1	1	1	1	1	1
Rouge-1 precision	0.0684	0.0230	0.1455	0.0897	0.0410	0.0255	0.0211
Rouge-1 F-1	0.0671	0.0995	0.1377	0.0387	0.0387	0.0352	0.0352

Summaries in Fig. 4 provide explainable information but are not directly associated with a star ranking. To associate the explainable information with each star ranking, we assign two reviews (s_i, d_i) and (s_j, d_j) to the same cluster if $s_i = s_j$. Figure 5 shows the 967 documents in five clusters according to the star ranking. the rouge results have improved as shown in Table 5. Note: We have also clustered the corpus into five clusters according to sentiment categories. A careful comparison finds that the extracted information and rouge scores from the star rankings (1–5) and the sentiment categories (VN-VP), are very similar, but not identical. This is very reasonable. On one hand, the star-rankings represent the overall sentiments of the reviewers well. On the other hand, Tables 1 and 2 imply that they are not exactly the same. Due to the page limit, we do not present the details here.

– *Summary of cluster 1: I waited to review, I've had the phone now 3 months. You can watch the tons of reviews on youtube for the details, but overall the camera is great, the phone works great, you can run games and anything else you would expect, at a fraction of the cost of the latest flagship phones I received*
– *Summary of cluster 2: It says factory unlocked, but when you switch on the phone, it opens with an AT&T symbol every time and has AT&T specific apps installed on it which can't be deleted. It works better than the fingerprint reader but still takes longer to unlock that an iPhone or a Pixel 4.*
– *Summary of cluster 3: This phone arrived cracked in the corner, and the unlock button was very soft and mushy. Currently working on contacting the seller/Amazon, and if that doesn't pan out, I suspect I will get to return the device.*
– *Summary of cluster 4: Fast delivery. The phone is like brand new and works well. Minor scratches on the back glass, other than that front screen is scratch free, battery life is excellent. Phone worked as advertised no issues, phone was in above average condition*
– *Summary of cluster 5: No carrier was able to activate the phone because there are "unpaid or overdue" charges on the AT&T account. NEVER EVER BUY AMAZON RENEWED!Product arrived with a sticky substance all over it, has scratches on it, and is locked to AT&T. Not what I expected.*
– *Summary of cluster 6: Though it says as certified refurbished but got a phone which has dead pixels and also flickering screen at the bottom. Great way to save money on phone upgrade!This was a gift so I never got to test the face recognition or the fingerprint reader but the phone was in very good condition and the battery life was better than described.*
– *Summary of cluster 7: Renewed unlocked S10 looks and feels completely brand new for hundreds less. To soon to say if it the battery life is as good as I am expecting...First time buying a renewed product and so far I'm very pleased. Samsung Galaxy10S that i ordered, unlocked, arrived on time, easy swap of my sim card, no problems at all.*

Fig. 4. Summaries of D in document similarity clusters.

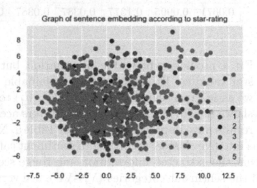

Fig. 5. Five clusters according to star ranking.

- *Summary of star 1: No carrier was able to activate the phone because there are "unpaid or overdue" charges on the AT&T account. Currently working on contacting the seller/Amazon, and if that doesn't pan out, I suspect I will get to return the device. I would of given it 5 as the phone did come looking brand new has zero scratches or paint defects, battery life is phenomenal, and the camera is a great upgrade to what I had before, but until I get a response it's staying at 1.I arrive with the back cover open and broken in a corner. The phone has had issues with apps closing since I purchased the phone.*
- *Summary of star 2: So as the title of the product listing suggests, I opted to purchase a "renewed" phone. Battery life has been pretty good–obviously it drains faster when I use it for things like Netflix, but I can go to bed with it at 15% and still have it at 13-14% when I wake up so a big improvement over my last phone (which to be fair was quite old.) Once my old SIM card (went to TMobile to try a new sim as well) was transferred to this refurbished phone, the S10 began heating up.*
- *Summary of star 3: It says factory unlocked, but when you switch on the phone, it opens with an AT&T symbol every time and has AT&T specific apps installed on it which can't be deleted. I haven't used a Samsung in decades but since I was doing the set-up and transfers, I'll make comment only on those items she's commented on.*
- *Summary of star 4: I got the phone and everything works so far. I'm just not the type who will spend $1200 for latest/bleeding edge gadget, but my old phone was so slow that I feel like I had to upgrade. Other than that the phone works great and my mom is super happy!Per description, phone did not come with factory charger.*
- *Summary of star 5: i was scared that something was going to go wrong but the phone looks like new it doesnt have 1 scratch 100% recommend it. Renewed unlocked S10 looks and feels completely brand new for hundreds less. I was skeptical on buying a refurbished phone because I'm super picky, but I figured I'd give it a shot because of the cost savings and I was in dire need of a new phone...my S7 screen was flickering and would go black when cold.*

Fig. 6. Extractive summaries according to star ranking clusters.

Table 5. Rouge results of extractive summaries of star ranking

Ext. summary	1-Star	2-Star	3-Star	4-Star	5-Star
Rouge-1 recall	1.0	1.0	1.0	1.0	1.0
Rouge-1 precision	0.0347	0.0523	0.0739	0.0197	0.0179
Rouge-1 F-1	0.0670	0.0995	0.1377	0.0387	0.0352
Rouge-2 recall	0.9813	0.9782	0.9863	0.9642	0.9913
Rouge-2 precision	0.0131	0.0237	0.0389	0.0071	0.0058
Rouge-2 F-1	0.0259	0.0463	0.0750	0.0142	0.0116
Rouge-l recall	1.0	1.0	1.0	1.0	1.0
Rouge-l precision	0.0347	0.0523	0.0739	0.0197	0.0179
Rouge-l F-1	0.0670	0.0995	0.1377	0.0387	0.0352

3.3   Investigating Information in Each Cluster Further

When noticing documents with the same star ranking in Fig. 5 are scattered, we apply k-means to further cluster the documents within the same star ranking as illustrated in Fig. 7. We then get the refined summaries for each of the five star rankings. Table 6 presents the rouge results along with the number of clusters with each star ranking in brackets. These refined summaries allow us to give human users a more explainable summarization. Looking below, a human user can find the reasons for the best and worst reviews:

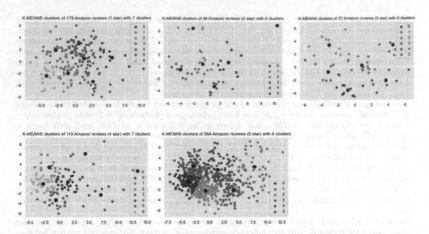

Fig. 7. Clusters within each star ranking.

- *Summary of cluster 1 (Star = 5): The phone arrived and if you told me it was a brand new one I'd have believed you. I was skeptical on buying a refurbished phone because I'm super picky, but I figured I'd give it a shot because of the cost savings and I was in dire need of a new phone...my S7 screen was flickering and would go black when cold. I was worried because when i turned it on without my SIM it said Verizon, which I thought was a different type of phone, but it fully works with my cricket SIM, having been using it for over a week.*
- *Summary of cluster 2 (Star = 5): Fast delivery. The phone is like brand new and works well. good battery, no scratches, no issues with straight talk.*
- *Summary of cluster 3 (Star = 5): Renewed unlocked S10 looks and feels completely brand new for hundreds less. the phone looks new, no scratches, no original charger, but over all im very satisfait with my purchase. I bought a Renewed Galaxy S10 from CPRTX and I was definitely skeptical when buying this phone.*
- *Summary of cluster 4 (Star = 5): I received my phone in perfect condition, it looks brand new and is fully unlocked. Camera takes quality photos, fingerprint sensor works well, battery lasts for a reasonable duration of time and I had no problems connecting this phone to Verizon. Phone had no physical defects, came with all the packaging for a new phone, and I've had no issues since I started using it.*

Table 6. Rouge results of extractive summaries of clustered star ranking

Ext. summary	1-Star [7]	2-Star [6]	3-Star [6]	4-Star [7]	5-Star [6]
Rouge-1 recall	1.0	0.8333	1.0	0.8571	1.0
Rouge-1 precision	0.1114	0.1562	0.2120	0.1389	0.0580
Rouge-1 F-1	0.1985	0.2250	0.3415	0.2233	0.1086
Rouge-2 recall	0.9790	0.8130	0.9754	0.8310	0.9776
Rouge-2 precision	0.0663	0.1001	0.1476	0.0985	0.0271
Rouge-2 F-1	0.1227	0.1731	0.2487	0.1619	0.0524
Rouge-l recall	1.0	0.8333	1.0	0.8571	1.0
Rouge-l precision	0.1114	0.1562	0.2120	0.1389	0.0580
Rouge-l F-1	0.1985	0.2250	0.3415	0.2233	0.1086

- *Summary of cluster 5 (Star = 5): I waited to review, I've had the phone now 3 months. I received a mint condition Galaxy S10, grade A+, almost like new or whatever you would call a device in flawless condition, very happy with this purchase, it has zero imperfections in simple sight, screen looking perfect and showing awesome colors as Samsung AMOLED display usually does, frame and glass in the back without any scratch or crack, I repeat: it looks just like a new S10, everything works great, camera, speakers, bluetooth, etc. Overall, the phone appears and functions brand new, and I would definitely buy renewed products from this company in the future.*
- *Summary of cluster 6 (Star = 5): i was scared that something was going to go wrong but the phone looks like new it doesnt have 1 scratch 100% recommend it. I personally hate the idea of facial recognition, but as for fingerprint and speed of the phone itself I'd say is all in all great, I was a little spooked though when I bought it and read the model number as an S10E but when I recieved it, it was just the original, so in simplistic, everything is good, though I wish there wasn't so much bloatware. Easy transition to S10 phone for an S9 user (had broken screen on previous phone, too expensive to replace). I was honestly doubting about buying this because of all the bad reviews but the phone came in great condition and with the original accessories, i couldn't ask for more:).*

Here are the top reasons for single-star reviews extracted from the corpus:

- *Summary of cluster 1 (Star = 1): ON OFF VOLUME ALWAYS CHANGED MY ASSIGNED CALLER ID. There were 2 scratches 1- 1inch and 1- 1/2 inch on the front screen. I had to buy a wireless charger and my phone won't keep a charge.*
- *Summary of cluster 2 (Star = 1): It says factory unlocked, but when you switch on the phone, it opens with an AT&T symbol every time and has AT&T specific apps installed on it which can't be deleted. It works better than the fingerprint reader but still takes longer to unlock that an iPhone or a Pixel 4.*
- *Summary of cluster 3 (Star = 1): This is a private seller selling a locked phone. A refurbished one comes with a brand new battery and all accessories described whereas a Re-newed one does not (it is just inspected for imperfections). I am not happy with this whole process and customer support was great about giving me a discount for the missing earbuds and charger, but I found out later I needed the special transfer gadget and had to cough up another $10(what a rip). I've spent a few days trying to get a Sim card to work on the phone, it was also advertised for ATT service only to find the phone was on a Sprint service.*
- *Summary of cluster 4 (Star = 1): No carrier was able to activate the phone because there are "unpaid or overdue" charges on the AT&T account. Phone was not unlocked but actually locked to T-Mobile network so it's absolutely useless to me and have received zero feedback from the seller. Could not reach the customer service department on numerous attemps.*
- *Summary of cluster 5 (Star = 1): But, I AM lucky my boyfriend works for bestbuy. I'll be more than happy to update this review if the seller can get this fixed, or walks me through what needs to be done, but I'm not expecting much as the Amazon warranty has ended. I would of given it 5 as the phone did come looking brand new has zero scratches or paint defects, battery life is phenomenal, and the camera is a great upgrade to what I had before, but until I get a response it's staying at 1.The phone has had issues with apps closing since I purchased the phone.*
- *Summary of cluster 6 (Star = 1): Though it says as certified refurbished but got a phone which has dead pixels and also flickering screen at the bottom. So I went into the AT&T store with the phone o be told they can't help me because my phone Is blacklisted and told me my phone was stolen. Beware anybody buying a refurbished phone that was checked many months before they ship it to you so the battery can easily go bad.*
- *Summary of cluster 7 (Star = 1): I am giving it only one star and I will update once I get issues cleared, if that ever happens. Currently working on contacting the seller/Amazon, and if that doesn't pan out, I suspect I will get to return the device. I bought it because I needed a Verizon locked phone not TMobile.*

3.4 Beyond Extractive Summarization

With the approaches above, we can obtain multiple views of the corpus with extractive text summarization. Recent advances in deep learning, such as convolutional and recurrent neuron networks (CNN and RNN), have provided tools for us to summarize a corpus abstractively. For instance, Zhan et al. suggest a hierarchical graph attention (HGAT) network for multiple comments integration in [13]. They have also applied a probabilistic k-hop knowledge graph neuron network (GNN) in [14] to integrate multiple users' comments very recently. Instead of optimizing rouge scores, which is NP-hard [6] and out of the scope of this work, we summarize the corpus abstractively with the HGAT for each of the five star-ranking clusters. Table 7 provides the rouge results.

Table 7. Rouge results of HGATs abstractive summaries

Abs. summary	1-Star	2-Star	3-Star	4-Star	5-Star	Total
Rouge-1 recall	0.3586	0.4539	0.4593	0.1973	0.2012	0.3077
Rouge-1 precision	1	0.9984	1	0.9978	1	0.9990
Rouge-1 F-1	0.5279	0.6241	0.6295	0.3294	0.3350	0.4467
Rouge-2 Recall	0.2517	0.3630	0.3859	0.1155	0.1183	0.1823
Rouge-2 precision	0.9946	0.9993	0.9992	0.9977	0.9991	0.9976
Rouge-2 F-1	0.4018	0.5325	0.5568	0.2071	0.2116	0.3083
Rouge-1 recall	0.3591	0.4392	0.4504	0.1793	0.2004	0.2878
Rouge-1 precision	1	0.9983	1	0.9906	1	1
Rouge-1 F-1	0.5251	0.6085	0.6041	0.3041	0.3245	0.2947

In contrast to extractive summaries, an abstractive summary does not use the original sentences directly. The recall scores are also much lower than those of the extractive summaries in the previous sections. On the other hand, an abstractive summary aims to learn knowledge from the corpus D. The obtained abstractive summary for each of the star ranking clusters contains more sentences than that of extractive summaries. This leads to a much improved precision and F-1. The abstractive summaries are not included in this paper because of their lengths.

4   Generating an Explainable Summary from the Reviews

In the section above, we have presented multiple ways to mine the corpus for explainable information. Although it is not yet perfect, we do have an algorithmic approach to obtain explainable information from crowdsourced reviews as Algorithm 1.

Algorithm 1. Finding an explainable summary from a corpus D

Inputs: $R = \{(s_i, d_i)\}$, a set of eligible reviews
Output: An explainable summery of R

for $(s_i, d_i) \in R$ **do**
   $d_i \leftarrow$ tokenize and vectorize d_i
   $stmt_i \leftarrow$ compound sentiment score d_i
end for
$D \leftarrow \{d_i\}$
$stmt_D \leftarrow$ an aggregated score from $\{stmt_i\}$
$\{D_j\} \leftarrow$ clustering D
for each cluster $D_j \subset D$ **do**
   $S_j \leftarrow$ text summary of D_j
end for
return $|D|$, $stmt_D$, and $\{S_j\}$

When applying the algorithm to the sample dataset, we may obtain a summary as the following, which is explainable to a human user though not yet perfect.

- There are 967 ($|D|$) meaningful reviews from previous buyers. An estimation of the overall sentiment is 4.2 ($stmt_D$), which is between the average star ranking 3.9 and Amazon's overall ranking 4.4 stars.
- The top three comments extracted from 5-star reviews are:
  i was scared that something was going to go wrong but the phone looks like new it doesnt have 1 scratch 100% recommend it.
  Renewed unlocked S10 looks and feels completely brand new for hundreds less.
  I was skeptical on buying a refurbished phone because I'm super picky, but I figured I'd give it a shot because of the cost savings and I was in dire need of a new phone...my S7 screen was flickering and would go black when cold.
- The top three reasons extracted from single star reviews are:
  No carrier was able to activate the phone because there are "unpaid or overdue" charges on the AT&T account. Currently working on contacting the seller/Amazon, and if that doesn't pan out, I suspect I will get to return the device.
  I would of given it 5 as the phone did come looking brand new has zero scratches or paint defects, battery life is phenomenal, and the camera is a great upgrade to what I had before, but until I get a response it's staying at 1.I arrive with the back cover open and broken in a corner.
  The phone has had issues with apps closing since I purchased the phone.

Algorithm 1 is, in fact, very flexible. One may change the parameters and obtain more or less information as is desired in practical application. Beyond adjusting the parameters in text mining, one may apply different ways to cluster the corpus, and use abstractive and/or extractive summarizations to create other views of the corpus.

5 Summary

Crowdsourced reviews can be obtained online or offline. They form a large collection of data. Aiming at XAI, this work demonstrates that one may apply currently available NLP tools to mine a corpus and produce an explainable summary automatically. Applying sentiment analysis to the corpus of the sample dataset, we are able to generate an overall ranking, which is likely more accurate than the average of star rankings. Moreover, with document clustering and summarization strategies, we are able to provide explainable information for human users without manually reading the entire corpus.

We would very much like to emphasize that this is only an initial work towards an explainable summary of crowdsourced reviews. There are certainly many other ways to improve the overall quality of the explainable summary above. For instance, recent advances in NLP and text mining continuously provide us with even more powerful tools for document summarization. One may also use time stamps to weight the reviews to discover possible dynamic trends in the reviews. Again, crowdsourced reviews form a large collection of data. Further studies into generating explainable summaries for such reviews show both scientific and practical value.

Acknowledgment. This work is partially supported by the US National Science Foundation through the grant award NSF/OIA-1946391. The authors would also very much like to express their sincere appreciations to the contributors of high quality Python software tools. Applying such publicly available tools, we are able to significantly improve the efficiency and effectiveness of this work.

References

1. Hutto C.J., Gilbert, E.E.: VADER: a parsimonious rule-based model for sentiment analysis of social media text. In: Eighth International Conference on Weblogs and Social Media, ICWSM 2914, Ann Arbor, MI, June 2014
2. Lahitani, A.R., Permanasari, A.E. Setiawan, N.A.: Cosine similarity to determine similarity measure: study case in online essay assessment. In: 4th International Conference on Cyber and IT Service Management, pp. 1–6 (2016)
3. Lin, C.-Y.: ROUGE: a package for automatic evaluation of summaries. In: Proceedings of the Workshop on Text Summarization, WAS 2004, Barcelona, Spain, July 25–26 (2004)
4. Mihalcea, R., Tarau, P.: Textrank: bringing order into text. In: Proceedings of the 2004 Conference On Empirical Methods In Natural Language Processing (2004)
5. Qurashi, A.W., Holmes, V., Johnson, A.P.: Document processing: methods for semantic text similarity analysis. In: International Conference on INnovations in Intelligent SysTems and Applications, INISTA, pp. 1–6 (2020)
6. Schluter, N.: The limits of automatic summarisation according to ROUGE. In: Proceedings of the 15th Conference of the European Chapter of the Association for Computational Linguistics, Valencia, Spain, vol. 2(Short Papers), pp. 41–45, 3–7 April (2017)

7. Singh, V.K., Tiwari, N., Garg, S.: Document clustering using k-means, heuristic k-means and fuzzy c-means. In: 2011 International Conference on Computational Intelligence and Communication Networks, pp. 297–301. IEEE (2011)
8. Tenney, I, Das, D., Pavlick, E: BERT Rediscovers the Classical NLP Pipeline (2019). https://arxiv.org/abs/1905.05950
9. Vaswani, A., et al.: Attention is all you need. In: Proceedings of the 31st International Conference on Neural Information Processing Systems, NIPS 2017, pp. 6000–6010. Curran Associates Inc., Red Hook (2017)
10. Wikipedia, GTP-3. https://en.wikipedia.org/wiki/GPT-3
11. Wikipedia, NLTK. https://en.wikipedia.org/wiki/Natural_Language_Toolkit
12. Wikipedia, tf-idf. https://en.wikipedia.org/wiki/Tf-idf
13. Zhan, H., Zhang K., Hu, C., Sheng, V.S.: HGATs: hierarchical graph attention networks for multiple comments integration. In: ASONAM 2021: Proceedings of the 2021 IEEE/ACM International Conference on Advances in Social Networks Analysis and Mining (2021)
14. Zhan, H., Zhang K., Hu, C., Sheng, V.S.: K2-GNN: multiple users' comments integration with probabilistic K-Hop knowledge graph neural networks. In: Proceedings of the 13th Asian Conference on Machine Learning (2021)

A New Similarity Measure for Real Intervals to Solve the Aliasing Problem

Pedro Huidobro[1]([✉])[iD], Noelia Rico[2][iD], Agustina Bouchet[1][iD],
Susana Montes[1][iD], and Irene Díaz[2][iD]

[1] Department of Statistics, University of Oviedo, 33003 Oviedo, Spain
{huidobropedro,bouchetagustina,montes}@uniovi.es
[2] Department of Computer Science, University of Oviedo, 33003 Oviedo, Spain
{noeliarico,sirene}@uniovi.es

Abstract. These days it is common to work with interval-valued data
in areas like fuzzy analysis, clustering, medicine or decision-making. In
this paper, we present a new similarity measure between intervals and
compare it with other measures found in the literature. We also study
some properties such as aliasing, that is obtaining the same similarity
value from very different inputs, or the behavior of the similarity when
the overlapping degree is varied, among others. The theoretical background could be found in this work as well as some artificial examples
in order to a better understanding. Finally, an experiment considering
real-life data is displayed.

Keywords: Similarity measure · Aliasing · Subsethood ·
Interval-valued data

1   Introduction

Similarity measures are very used nowadays in several areas such as fuzzy analysis [17], clustering [8], medicine [14] or decision-making [16]. In the literature,
several proposals for similarity measures can be found, with their strengths and
drawbacks. However, the most usual way to define a similarity measure is as a
real-valued function that determines the similarity between two objects, where
0 means that both objects are completely different and 1 means that they are
identical.

Under certain real-world situations, it may be difficult to determine the
appropriate value to express a variable, or the value may not be known properly.
However, we can avoid this difficulty by taking into account intervals. Multiple

This research has been partially supported by Spanish MINECO projects TIN2017-
87600-P (Noelia Rico, Agustina Bouchet and Irene Díaz) and PGC2018-098623-B-I00
(Pedro Huidobro and Susana Montes). Pedro Huidobro and Noelia Rico are also supported by the Severo Ochoa predoctoral grant program by the Principality of Asturias
(PA-20-PF-BP19-169 and PA-20-PF-BP19-167).

© Springer Nature Switzerland AG 2022
D. Ciucci et al. (Eds.): IPMU 2022, CCIS 1601, pp. 542–554, 2022.
https://doi.org/10.1007/978-3-031-08971-8_45

academics have quickly been interested in interval-valued data as a result of their strong potential for a variety of applications [3,7,11,15].

Jaccard similarity [4] and Dice similarity [2] are some of the most common similarities between intervals, that are particular cases of the Tversky's parametrized ratio model of similarity [13]. Nevertheless, we are proposing a similarity function which is based on the subsethood notion [9] and compare it to them.

Aliasing is one of the most important problems that appear when the similarity between closed intervals is calculated and it appears when the same similarity value is generated for very different intervals [6]. The reason why some similarities exhibit aliasing is a consequence of the size of intersection and union, i.e., because their sensitivity with respect to changes in the relative size of intervals is limited.

In this paper, a new similarity that takes into account the aliasing problem is presented. In Sect. 2 the definition of similarity measures and Jaccard, Dice and the bidirectional subsethood based on similarity measure are presented. In Sect. 3 the proposed similarity measure is introduced. An analysis of different properties is made in Sect. 4. In Sect. 5 an application in a real dataset is shown. Finally, some conclusions are presented in Sect. 6.

2   Similarity Measures

Let $\mathcal{L}$ be the family of closed intervals included in $\mathbb{R}$. An interval $a \in \mathcal{L}$ is denoted by $a = [\underline{a}, \overline{a}]$ with $\underline{a} \leq \overline{a}$ and $\underline{a}, \overline{a} \in \mathbb{R}$. In this work we are going to consider just those closed intervals where $\underline{a} < \overline{a}$.

First of all, we recall some basic operations we will need:

- the content relation, $a \subseteq b \Leftrightarrow \underline{b} \leq \underline{a} \leq \overline{a} < \overline{b}$
- the intersection, $a \cap b = \{x \in \mathbb{R} : x \in a \wedge x \in b\}$
- the subtraction, $a \backslash b = \{x \in \mathbb{R} : x \in a \wedge x \notin b\}$

There are several definitions of similarity in this context. Therefore, we will use the following definition [10].

Definition 1. *The function* $S : \mathcal{L} \times \mathcal{L} \rightarrow [0,1]$ *is a similarity measure for intervals if the following properties hold for any* $a, b, c \in \mathcal{L}$ *[5, 10]:*

S1: $0 \leq S(a,b) \leq 1$
S2: $S(a,b) = S(b,a)$
S3: $S(a,b) = 1$ if and only if $a = b$
S4: If $a \subseteq b \subseteq c$ then $S(a,c) \leq S(a,b)$

The width of the intervals is an important characteristic that should be taken into account in order to define similarity measures for intervals.

Definition 2. *Let* a *be an interval in* $\mathcal{L}$ *with* $a = [\underline{a}, \overline{a}]$. *The width* w *of the interval* a *is given by [1]:*

$$w(a) = \overline{a} - \underline{a}$$

In the literature, it is possible to find several definitions of similarity functions for intervals. For example, Tversky [13] proposed the following:

Definition 3. *The Ratio Model (RM) of similarity is defined as:*

$$S_{RM}(a,b) = \frac{f(a \cap b)}{f(a \cap b) + \alpha\, f(a \backslash b) + \beta\, f(b \backslash a)}$$

where $a, b \in \mathcal{L}$, $\alpha, \beta \in [0,1]$ *and* f *is a cardinality function.*

In fact, Jaccard similarity measure is obtained when $\alpha = \beta = 1$ and f is the width of the intervals:

Definition 4. *The Jaccard similarity measure (JS) between two intervals* $a, b \in \mathcal{L}$ *is given by:*

$$S_J(a,b) = \frac{w(a \cap b)}{w(a \cap b) + w(a \backslash b) + w(b \backslash a)}$$

In a similar way, Dice similarity can be obtaining through Definition 3 when $\alpha = \beta = 0.5$ and f is the width of the intervals:

Definition 5. *The Dice similarity (DS) between two intervals* $a, b \in \mathcal{L}$ *is given by:*

$$S_D(a,b) = \frac{w(a \cap b)}{w(a \cap b) + 0.5\, w(a \backslash b) + 0.5\, w(b \backslash a)}$$

In [6], the authors introduce a similarity measure using the degree to which an interval is a subset of another interval:

Definition 6. *[9] The subsethood degree between two intervals* $a, b \in \mathcal{L}$ *is a relation that indicates the degree to which* a *is a subset of* b:

$$S_h(a,b) = \frac{w(a \cap b)}{w(a)}$$

As we said previously, the intervals we consider have different endpoints. We would like to remark that it is possible to extend it to degenerate intervals, that is, a such that $\underline{a} = \overline{a}$. Considering the case when a is such that $w(a) = 0$, we could fin the following situations:

– $a \subseteq b$, then $S_h(a,b) = 1$
– $a \nsubseteq b$, thus $S_h(a,b) = 0$

However, we prefer to avoid them because in real-life problems they are really uncommon.

It is clear that there is a relation between the ratio model and the subsethood degree as the following corollary states:

Corollary 1. *The subsethood degree can be obtained from the ratio model when* $\alpha = 1$, $\beta = 0$ *and* $f = w$.

Kabir et al. introduced in [6] the bidirectional subsethood based similarity measure as follows:

Definition 7. *The bidirectional subsethood based similarity measure* S_{S_h} *for a pair of intervals* $a, b \in \mathcal{L}$ *is the t-norm of their reciprocal subsethoods* $S_h(a, b)$ *and* $S_h(b, a)$:

$$S_{S_h} = T(S_h(a, b), S_h(b, a))$$

where T *is a t-norm.*

Finally, a similarity measure is obtained if two specific t-norms are used:

Theorem 1. *[6] Let* T *be the minimum or product t-norms and* S_h *the subsethood for intervals introduced in Definition 6, then* S_{S_h} *is a similarity measure for intervals.*

From now on, S_{min} and S_{prod} represent the similarity measure defined above using the minimum t-norm and the product t-norm, respectively. Kabir et al. [6] expanded the axiomatic definition of similarities for robust similarity measures on closed and not degenerated intervals.

Definition 8. *[6] A real-valued function* $S : \mathcal{L} \times \mathcal{L} \to [0, 1]$ *is defined as a robust similarity measure for closed intervals if it fulfills the following axioms:*

A1: $0 \leq S(a, b) \leq 1$
A2: $S(a, b) = S(b, a)$
A3: $S(a, b) = 1$ *if and only if* $a = b$
A4: *If* $a \subseteq b \subseteq c$ *then* $S(a, c) \leq S(a, b)$ *and* $S(b, a) \leq S(c, b)$
A5: $S(a, b) = 0$ *if and only if* $w(a \cap b) = 0$
A6: *Consider two interval pairs* $\{a_1, b_1\}$ *and* $\{a_2, b_2\}$ *with* $w(a_1 \cap b_1) > 0$, $w(a_2 \cap b_2) > 0$, $w(a_1 \cup b_1) = w(a_2 \cup b_2)$, *and* $w(a_1 \cap b_1) = w(a_2 \cap b_2)$, $S(a_1, b_1) \neq S(a_2, b_2)$ *if* $w(a_1) \neq w(a_2)$, $w(a_1) \neq w(b_2)$, $w(b_1) \neq w(a_2)$ *and* $w(b_1) \neq w(b_2)$
A7: $S(a, b) < 1$ *if* $a \subset b$
A8: *Consider two interval pairs* $\{a_1, b_1\}$ *and* $\{a_2, b_2\}$ *with* $w(a_1 \cap b_1) > 0$, $w(a_2 \cap b_2) > 0$, $S(a_1, b_1) = S(a_2, b_2)$ *if* $a_2 = n \times a_1 = [n \times \underline{a_1}, n \times \overline{a_1}]$ *and* $b_2 = n \times b_1 = [n \times \underline{b_1}, n \times \overline{b_1}]$ *where* $n > 0$ *is a scaling factor*
A9: *Consider two interval pairs* $\{a_1, b_1\}$ *and* $\{a_2, b_2\}$ *where* $w(a_1) = w(b_1) = w(a_2) = w(b_2)$, $S(a_1, b_1) < S(a_2, b_2)$ *if* $w(a_1 \cap b_1) < w(a_2 \cap b_2)$

The axioms [A1-A4] are those established in Definition 1. Let us analyse more in depth the others (see [6] for further details). Axiom 5 forces the similarity to be 0 when there is no intersection between the intervals compared. Axiom 6 is required to avoid the problem of aliasing. Axiom 7 establishes that the degree of similarity must be less than 1 when one interval is strictly embedded in the other. Axiom 8 considers intervals where the endpoints are increased by a constant. Finally, axiom 9 establishes a greater degree of similarity when the width of the intersection is greater for intervals with the same width.

3   A New Similarity Measure

In this section it is introduced a new proposal to measure the degree of similarity between intervals. This new measure avoids the aliasing problem.

Definition 9. *The subsethood mean for two intervals $a, b \in \mathcal{L}$ is defined by:*

$$S_{mean}(a,b) = \frac{S_h(a,b) + S_h(b,a)}{2}$$

where $S_h(a,b)$ is the subsethood degree between a and b, and $S_h(b,a)$ is the subsethood degree between b and a.

The subsethood average can be rewritten as:

$$S_{mean}(a,b) = \frac{(w(a) + w(b))\, w(a \cap b)}{2\, w(a)\, w(b)}$$

The following result proves that the operator S_{mean} is a robust similarity measure.

Proposition 1. *The subsethood mean for two intervals $a, b \in \mathcal{L}$ is a robust similarity measure in the sense of Definition 8.*

Definition 8 is a particular case of Definition 1. Therefore, the following corollary is obtained:

Corollary 2. *The subsethood mean for two intervals $a, b \in \mathcal{L}$ introduced in Definition 9 is a similarity measure in the sense of Definition 1.*

Note that if $a, b \in \mathcal{L}$, then $S_{prod}(a,b) \leq S_{min}(a,b) \leq S_{mean}(a,b)$. In addition, if $a, b \in \mathcal{L}$, then $S_J(a,b) \leq S_D(a,b) \leq S_{mean}(a,b)$

4   Analysis of the Properties of the Similarity Measures

The performance of a similarity measure is often studied in terms of the properties they should fulfill. Five of these properties were presented in [6] and are the following:

- Property 1: the tendency to exhibit aliasing when interval size is varied.
- Property 2: behavior with respect to intervals where one is a complete subset of the other.
- Property 3: behavior with respect to intervals of equal size and overlapping proportion.
- Property 4: response to variations in the size of the interval maintaining the same subset level.
- Property 5: response to a linear increase of interval overlap.

In addition to these properties, we introduce a new one, Property 6, to analyse the behaviour of the overlapping degree.

4.1 Property 1

In order to analyze the tendency to exhibit aliasing when interval size is varied, Fig. 1 shows the performance of the different similarity measures for seven pairs of intervals. In all the cases, the intersection width has the same size. Jaccard and Dice similarity measures obtain the same value of similarity in all the cases, 0.4 and 0.25 respectively. These values are generated due to the aliasing because these measures are not able to distinguish the differences between the intervals. Also, the size of the union of the intervals and the intersection is constant in all the examples. Conversely, S_{mean}, S_{min} and S_{prod} provide different values for all the examples, showing a more robust behavior and avoiding aliasing.

Note that S_{mean} obtain greater values when one of the intervals is more included in the other one, which is desirable behavior. This fact is shown in Fig. 1. Note how in the first and last examples one of the intervals is totally included in the other and the value of the similarity is 0.625. In contrast, in the fourth example, in which the inclusion degree is the least the similarity value is 0.4. Moreover, the behaviour of S_{prod} is similar to S_{mean} but the values of the first one are lower as $S_{prod}(a,b) \leq S_{mean}(a,b) \ \forall a,b$. On the other hand, S_{min} shows an opposite behaviour giving the lowest values in the first and last examples while it achieves the greatest value in the fourth example. In this case, it is to the value obtained using S_{mean} (0.4).

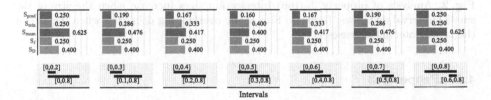

Fig. 1. Analysis of property 1: aliasing.

4.2 Property 2

In order to study this property, two situations are considered. In the first one, the size of the intersection is increased, increasing the size of the smaller interval. The idea behind this property is that the larger the value of the similarity, the larger the size of the intersection. In the second one, the size of the overlapping decreases when the larger interval increases. This means that the smaller the overlapping degree, the smaller the similarity measure. Note that in both cases one interval is totally included in the other (See Fig. 2).

In Fig. 2(top) we can see the intersection between the intervals. If we consider the similarities S_J, S_{min} or S_{prod}, then the overlap degree, in percentage, represents the 11.1%, 22.2%, 33.3%, 44.4%, 55.6%, 66.7%, 77.8% and 88.9%, respectively. The percentages are calculated using the subsethood degree. This behaviour is not identical in all similarities. On the other hand, when using

S_{mean} we obtain larger values as we want to emphasize when one interval is totally included in the other. It is possible to see that every value obtained is greater than 0.5. It is happening because one of the interval a is totally contained in the other b so $S_h(a,b) = 1$. Then, the mean between $S_h(a,b)$ and $S_h(b,a)$ is obviously greater than 0.5. In addition, Fig. 2(bottom) shows examples where the percentage decreases. Analogous behaviour is obtained with all the measures.

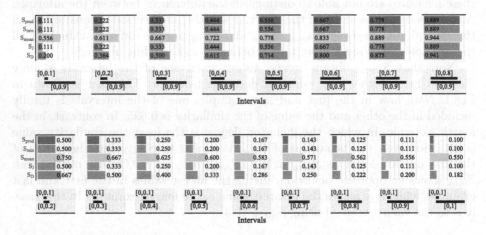

Fig. 2. Analysis of property 2. (top) Intersection sizes increase when the size of the smaller interval decreases. (bottom) Size of the overlapping decreases when the size of the larger interval increases.

4.3   Property 3

In Fig. 3(top) each example shows intervals with the same size and the same overlapping ratio. The intersection percentage decreases in the following way: 75%, 62.5%, 50%, 37.5%, 25%, 12.5% and 0%. These percentages are chosen in order to use easy-reading intervals. Here we have that $S_h(a,b) = S_h(b,a)$ as the size of the intervals in each example is equal. Thus, the similarity should be the same as the subsethood degree coincides with the overlapping degree. S_D, S_{min} and S_{mean} satisfy this property while S_J and S_{prod} do not.

4.4   Property 4

Figure 3(bottom) shows different pairs of intervals where their extremes $\underline{a}$, $\overline{a}$, $\underline{b}$ and $\overline{b}$ are multiplied by a factor to generate new intervals. Both the size of the intersection and the width of the intervals remain proportional. A similarity measure is invariant if its similarity output remains constant regardless of scaling the interval endpoints by a factor. The results show that all the similarity measures hold this property, which is what we expected according to axiom 8 in Definition 8.

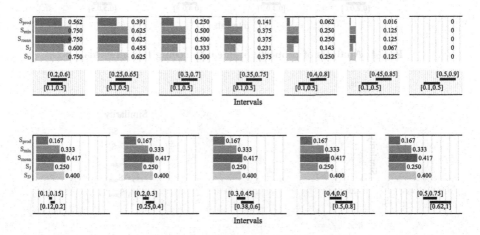

Fig. 3. Analysis of property 3: overlapping degree (top). Analysis of property 4: scaling invariant (bottom).

4.5   Property 5

The last important property considered over similarities is linearity. A similarity measure is linear if its similarity output varies linearly as to a linear change in the size of the intersection of the intervals [12]. Figures 4 and 5 display examples in which the intersection between the intervals represent, in percentage, the 25%, 50%, 75% and 100%, respectively. Again, we have chosen percentages in order to use just one decimal in the intervals for better comprehension. Then, the similarity measures S_D, S_{min} and S_{mean} show linearity.

4.6   Property 6

An interesting property that we consider important to analyse is the behaviour of the overlapping degree. If we have two pairs of intervals that have the same size of intersection, the value of the similarity should be greater in the case of the overlapping degree is greater, i.e.: Let $a, b, c, d \in \mathcal{L}$ where $w(a \cap b) = w(c \cap d)$. If $\frac{w(a \cap b)}{w(a \cup b)} \leq \frac{w(c \cap d)}{w(c \cup d)}$ then $S(a, b) < S(c, d)$ with S a similarity measure.

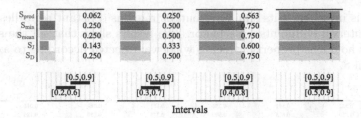

Fig. 4. Analysis of property 5: linearity seeing the intervals.

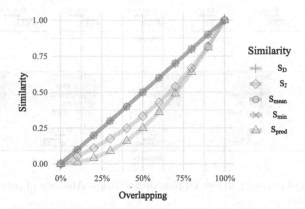

Fig. 5. Analysis of property 5: Linearity seeing the overlapping.

As Fig. 1 shows, S_{mean} and S_{prod} satisfy this property. It is obvious that S_J and S_D do not fulfill this property because they give the same value in all the cases. Also, S_{min} neither satisfies this property due to the fact that it increases when the overlapping degree decreases.

It should be highlighted that the difference between this property and property 2 lies in that in this case it is not necessary for an interval to be totally included in the other one.

Table 1 resumes the fulfillment of these properties by each similarity measure. Note the good behavior of S_{mean}.

Table 1. Summary of fulfillment of the properties by S_J, S_D, S_{prod}, S_{min} and S_{mean}.

	P1	P2	P3	P4	P5	P6
S_J	✗	✓	✗	✓	✗	✗
S_D	✗	✗	✓	✓	✓	✗
S_{prod}	✓	✓	✗	✓	✗	✓
S_{min}	✓	✓	✓	✓	✓	✗
S_{mean}	✓	✓	✓	✓	✓	✓

5   Application

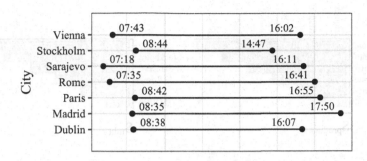

Fig. 6. Sunrise and sunset time of the cities chosen for the example.

In order to check the behaviour of the proposed measures in real data, we have applied the similarity measures to the interval given by the sunrise and sunset time of some European capital cities[1]. Figure 6 shows the intervals obtained.

The similarity measures presented in the previous sections are applied to the intervals detailed in Fig. 6. To this aim, the hour of the sunset and sunrise have been translated to the relative minute of the day. For example, the hour 07:15 am corresponds to the minute 435 of the day. Then, these minutes have been normalized in the interval $[0, 1]$ taking into account the minimum and maximum minutes of the days $[0, 1439]$.

The results obtained comparing the cities pairwisely are shown in Fig. 7. We would like to point out some of these results. For example, the pair Madrid - Vienna obtains 0.848 for S_D, 0.736 for S_J, 0.721 for S_{prod}, 0.805 for S_{min} and 0.851 for S_{mean}. Stockholm - Paris obtains 0.848 for S_D, 0.736 for S_J, 0.736 for S_{prod}, 0.736 for S_{min} and 0.868 for S_{mean}. Here it is possible to see that S_D and S_J suffer from aliasing while the others do not. Another remarkable example is the pair Sarajevo - Madrid. In this case $S_D = 0.838$, $S_J = 0.722$, $S_{prod} = 0.703$, $S_{min} = 0.822$ and $S_{mean} = 0.839$ and for Dublin - Rome $S_D = 0.945$, $S_J = 0.895$, $S_{prod} = 0.822$, $S_{min} = 0.822$ and $S_{mean} = 0.911$. In this case, the same value is obtained for S_{min} while a different value for the other similarity measures. This happens due to the fact that the overlapping degree of Dublin - Rome is greater than the overlapping degree of Sarajevo - Madrid.

---

[1] Raw data have been obtained in https://www.sunrise-and-sunset.com/.

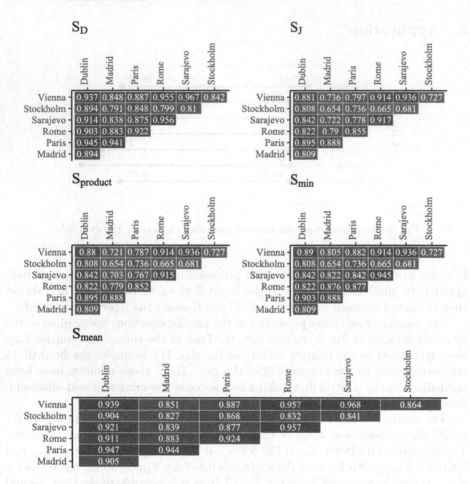

Fig. 7. Comparison of the different European cities using the different similarity measures.

6 Conclusion

Aliasing is an effect that causes equal similarity values for different pairs of intervals making them indistinguishable. In this paper a similarity measure that solves the aliasing problem is proposed. This similarity measure is based on the mean of the subsethood degree between two intervals. It is checked that this measure is robust.

Moreover, we compare our measure to four important similarity measures such as Jaccard, Dice and the bidirectional subsethood based similarity measure using the minimum and the product t-norms. Six properties have been studied in order to check the behaviour of each one, obtaining that the unique measure fulfilling all the properties is the subsethood mean. In addition, we test the behaviour of the similarity measures in a real dataset, showing again the advantages of the subsethood mean.

In the future we would like to do a more theoretical comparison with different measures based on their other mathematical properties.

References

1. Bedregal, B., Bustince, H., Fernandez, J., Deschrijver, G., Mesiar, R.: Interval-valued contractive fuzzy negations. In: International Conference on Fuzzy Systems, pp. 1–6 (2010)
2. Dice, L.R.: Measures of the amount of ecologic association between species. Ecology **26**(3), 297–302 (1945)
3. Guru, D., Kiranagi, B.B., Nagabhushan, P.: Multivalued type proximity measure and concept of mutual similarity value useful for clustering symbolic patterns. Pattern Recogn. Lett. **25**(10), 1203–1213 (2004)
4. Jaccard, P.: Nouvelles recherches sur la distribution florale. Bull. Soc. Vaud. Sci. Nat. **44**, 223–270 (1908)
5. Kabir, S., Wagner, C., Havens, T., Anderson, D., Aickelin, U.: Novel similarity measure for interval-valued data based on overlapping ratio. In: 2017 IEEE International Conference on Fuzzy Systems (FUZZ-IEEE) (2017)
6. Kabir, S., Wagner, C., Havens, T.C., Anderson, D.T.: A similarity measure based on bidirectional subsethood for intervals. IEEE Trans. Fuzzy Syst. **28**(11), 2890–2904 (2020)
7. Lai, K.K., Wang, S., Xu, J., Zhu, S., Fang, Y.: A class of linear interval programming problems and its application to portfolio selection. IEEE Trans. Fuzzy Syst. **10**(6), 698–704 (2002)
8. Lin, Y.S., Jiang, J.Y., Lee, S.J.: A similarity measure for text classification and clustering. IEEE Trans. Knowl. Data Eng. **26**(7), 1575–1590 (2013)
9. Nguyen, H., Vladik, K.: Computing degrees of subsethood and similarity for interval-valued fuzzy sets: Fast algorithms. In: Proceedings of the 9th International Conference on Information and Knowledge Technology, pp. 47–55 (2008)
10. Ontañón, S.: An overview of distance and similarity functions for structured data. Artif. Intell. Rev. **53**(7), 5309–5351 (2020). https://doi.org/10.1007/s10462-020-09821-w
11. Ren, Y., Liu, Y.H., Rong, J., Dew, R.: Clustering interval-valued data using an overlapped interval divergence. In: Proceedings of the Eighth Australasian Data Mining Conference, vol. 101, pp. 35–42 (2009)
12. Tulloss, R.E.: Assessment of similarity indices for undesirable properties and a new tripartite similarity index based on cost functions. In: Mycology in Sustainable Development: Expanding Concepts, Vanishing Borders, pp. 122–143 (1997)
13. Tversky, A.: Features of similarity. Psychol. Rev. **84**, 327–352 (1977)
14. Vilar, S., Harpaz, R., Chase, H.S., Costanzi, S., Rabadan, R., Friedman, C.: Facilitating adverse drug event detection in pharmacovigilance databases using molecular structure similarity: application to rhabdomyolysis. J. Am. Med. Inf. Assoc. **18**(Suppl. 1), i73–i80 (2011)
15. Wagner, C., Miller, S., Garibaldi, J.M., Anderson, D.T., Havens, T.C.: From interval-valued data to general type-2 fuzzy sets. IEEE Trans. Fuzzy Syst. **23**(2), 248–269 (2014)

16. Xu, Z.: Some similarity measures of intuitionistic fuzzy sets and their applications to multiple attribute decision making. Fuzzy Optim. Decis. Making **6**(2), 109–121 (2007)
17. Xuecheng, L.: Entropy, distance measure and similarity measure of fuzzy sets and their relations. Fuzzy Sets Syst. **52**(3), 305–318 (1992)

Knowledge Acquisition, Representation and Reasoning

Similarity Fuzzy Semantic Network for Social Media Analysis

Juan Luis Castro$^{(\boxtimes)}$ and Manuel Francisco

Department of Computer Science and Artificial Intelligence, University of Granada, Granada, Spain
{castro,francisco}@decsai.ugr.es

Abstract. In this paper we propose the use of the Similarity Fuzzy Semantic Networks representation model for Social Media Analysis. Similarity Fuzzy Semantic Networks are an extension of Fuzzy Semantic Networks, that incorporates reasoning by similarity through a Similarity Inference Rule. We introduce fuzzy semantic relations and similarity fuzzy semantic relations which can be used in social media analysis. To check the effectiveness we apply a similarity fuzzy semantic network in a social media complex problem, the analysis of radical discourse in Twitter, obtaining a better result than recent approaches for this problem.

Keywords: Similarity Fuzzy Semantic Networks · Similarity Fuzzy Reasoning · Social Network Analysis

1 Introduction and Motivation

Semantic Networks are a classical Knowledge Representation model that have been effectively applied over the years [6,11]. The concept of Fuzzy Semantic Network was introduced by considering fuzzy concepts and fuzzy relations between concepts, and they have been used in interesting and relevant applications [1,4]. On the other hand, reasoning by similarity is an effective approach used in fuzzy systems [10]. In this way, it would be interesting to extend the Fuzzy Semantic Network model to include similarity reasoning.

In this paper we introduce Fuzzy Similarity Semantic Networks, a model of knowledge representation which is an extension of Fuzzy Semantic Networks by adding fuzzy similarity relations between concepts. We also introduce reasoning by similarity in this model through the *inference by similarity* rule. We focus in the application of this model to social media analysis. In this way, we introduce and analyze several Similarity Fuzzy Relations for social media data (from

This work was financially supported by Junta de Andalucia, projects P18-FR-5020 and A-HUM-250-UGR18, and cofinanced by the European Social Fund (ESF). Manuel Francisco Aparicio was supported by the FPI 2017 predoctoral programme, from the Spanish Ministry of Economy and Competitiveness (MINECO), grant reference BES-2017-081202.

© Springer Nature Switzerland AG 2022
D. Ciucci et al. (Eds.): IPMU 2022, CCIS 1601, pp. 557–567, 2022.
https://doi.org/10.1007/978-3-031-08971-8_46

discourse, sentiment, emotion and appraisal analysis) and we apply Similarity Inference in order to extend an initial classification procedure, based on the classification of similar elements.

The rest of this paper is organised as follows. Sections 2 presents a brief introduction to Semantic Networks and Fuzzy Semantic Networks models. Section 3 presents Similarity Fuzzy Semantic Network model, jointly with the similarity inference rule. Section 4 introduce and analyze Similarity Fuzzy Relations for social media data. Lastly, Sect. 6 applies it to a trending and complex problem: the classification of social media data.

2   Fuzzy Semantic Networks

2.1   Semantic Networks

Semantic Networks represent knowledge with directed labelled graphs, where vertices represent concepts, which can be individuals or classes (sets of individuals), and labelled edges represent semantic relations between concepts, such that:

$$A \xrightarrow{relationS} B \tag{1}$$

represents the assertion " A $relationS$ B ". Consequently, we can represent knowledge as "Bird has-part Wings", "Animal has-part legs" or "Bird is-a Animal".

We can distinguish between two types of semantic relations:

- Hierarchical semantic relations:
  - *instance-of* (an individual is an instance of a class)
  - *is-a* (a class is a subclass of another class)
- Domain-specific semantic relations, such as *is-an-opponent-of*, *owns*...

Hierarchical semantic relations are universal, in the sense that they are present in any semantic network, meanwhile each semantic network introduces its own domain-specific relations.

The main inference rule in a Semantic Network is *inference by inheritance*. It consists of deducing new assertions in accordance with the following scheme:

$$\frac{A \quad is\text{-}a \quad B \lor A \quad instance\text{-}of \quad B}{A \quad \text{relation-S} \quad C} \tag{2}$$

2.2   Fuzzy Semantic Networks

It has been proposed to use graduations to obtain Fuzzy Semantic Networks [1, 4]. These models represent knowledge as graded labelled directed graphs. Classes are now defined as fuzzy sets of individuals, and the degree of the relation *instance-of* is the membership function of the correspondent fuzzy set. Analogously, edges represent graded semantic relations:

- *instance-of* : α stands for an instance with grade α
- *is-a* : α stands for a class that inherits from other in grade α
- Domain-specific fuzzy semantic relations, such that each relation has a an associated degree in which the assertion meets.

In this way,

$$A \xrightarrow{relation\text{-}S:\alpha} B \tag{3}$$

represents the fuzzy assertion

$$A \; relation\text{-}S \; B \; \text{in} \; \text{degree} \; \alpha \tag{4}$$

that can be abbreviated as

$$A \; relation\text{-}S{:}\alpha \; B \tag{5}$$

We can now define the *fuzzy inference by inheritance rule*. It consists of deducing new fuzzy assertions by the following scheme:

$$\frac{A \; \textit{is-a}{:}\alpha \; B \lor A \; \textit{instance-of}{:}\alpha \; B \quad B \; \textit{relation-S}{:}\beta \; C}{A \; \textit{relation-S}{:}t(\alpha, \beta) \; C} \tag{6}$$

being t a t-norm chosen to model the connective "and".

Obviously, the fuzzy inference by inheritance is a generalisation of the (non fuzzy) inference by inheritance: if we have crisp semantic relations in the premises ($\alpha = \beta = 1$), then we obtain the same crisp consequence ($t(1,1) = 1$).

2.3   Combining Inferences

After applying fuzzy inference by inheritance (or any other reasoning method), it is possible to obtain the same semantic relation between two given concepts but with different degrees. We can use an aggregation function [3] to combine both assertions in the following *combining inference rule*:

$$\frac{A \; relation\text{-}S{:}\alpha \; B \quad A \; relation\text{-}S{:}\beta \; B}{A \; relation\text{-}S{:}g(\alpha, \beta) \; B} \tag{7}$$

were g is a previously chosen aggregation function.

3   Similarity Fuzzy Semantic Networks

In the same way that classes extend its semantic relations to its sub-classes and instances by inheritance, individual or classes may transmit properties, by similarity semantic relations, to similar individual or classes [7,8]. For example, if two persons have similar opinions about political topics, then it will be reasonable to think that if we have knowledge about a property with political sense for one, it could be transmitted on some degree to the another.

In order to enrich the model of fuzzy semantic relation with this idea, we have proposed in [2] a new model for knowledge representation that we call *Similarity Fuzzy Semantic Networks*. It consist of fuzzy semantic networks with a specific family of semantic relations between classes or individuals, which we call *Similarity semantic relations*.

3.1 Similarity Semantic Relations

Similarity semantic relations are fuzzy semantic relations that represent that two individuals or two classes are similar in some sense or aspect:

$$\mathbf{A} \; is\text{-}similar\text{-}in\text{-}sense\text{-}D : \alpha \; \mathbf{B} \; , \tag{8}$$

where D may be any aspect, and it represents the assertion that concepts A and B are similar in the sense D in degree α.

We can have similarity relations between classes and also between individuals. Additionally, for every sense D, each concept will have a fuzzy neighbourhood of similar concepts in sense D.

The similarity between concepts is a knowledge that can be obtained by a knowledge acquisition technique, learned or calculated.

On the other hand, we only might transmit by *is-similar-in-sense-D* those semantic relations that are related to $sense - D$. For example we might not transmit the favourite team football property between two persons that have similar opinions about political topics. Thus, we will introduce relations between *senses* and *semantic relations of the network*.

3.2 Meta-relations

Semantic relations of the network can be considered *second order concepts*, therefore it is possible to think in *second order relations* where relations between *semantic relations of the network* are established. We call them *meta-relations*.

Particularly, we introduce in our Similarity Fuzzy Semantic Networks model a meta-relation that will be used for the Similarity inference. It is a relation that goes from domain-specific semantic relations to senses:

$$\mathbf{relation\text{-}S} \; is\text{-}related\text{-}to{:}\gamma \; \mathbf{sense\text{-}D}, \tag{9}$$

representing the assertion that *relation-S* is related to *sense-D* and thus, it can be transmitted by *is-similar-in-sense-D*.

The similarity semantic relation specifies a correspondence between concepts in a specific aspect D, meanwhile *is-related-to* delimits the domain in which similarity relations apply. In fact, when using meta-relations, we are defining a new semantic network of a higher level in which concepts are similarity relations of the principal semantic network.

3.3 Similarity Inference

These new relations enable a new kind of reasoning based on similarity. New knowledge may be extracted upon propagation of semantic relations through the *is-similar-in-sense-D* by means of the *Similarity Inference Rule*:

$$
\frac{
\begin{array}{l}
\mathbf{A}\ \textit{is-similar-in-sense-D} : \alpha\ \mathbf{B} \\
\mathbf{B}\ \textit{relation-S:}\beta\ \mathbf{C} \\
\textbf{relation-S}\ \textit{is-related-to:}\gamma\ \textbf{sense-D}
\end{array}
}{
\mathbf{A}\ \textit{relation-S:}(\gamma * t(\alpha, \beta))\ \mathbf{C}
}
\tag{10}
$$

where t is a triangular norm (t-norm).

3.4 Inference Strategy

In the proposed similarity fuzzy semantic network, the properties of the concepts may be deduced by fuzzy inheritance and/or by similarity inference. Moreover, each reasoning process results in new knowledge that may lead to new inferences. Hence, we might to establish an inference strategy.

First of all, we may choose the prevalence between inheritance and similarity inference rules. Inheritance is a *depth reasoning*, while similarity can be considered a *breadth inference*, since it is based on the neighbourhood of similar concepts. Therefore, we can use the classical Z and N models of reasoning strategy:

- Z model: first similarity, then inheritance.
- N model: first inheritance, then similarity.

Lastly, we establish iterations or cycles, as it is usual when dealing with these kinds of systems. In each step, we update the degree of every semantic relation by applying inheritance and similarity reasoning rules in the chosen order, and then applying the combining inference rule.

4 Similarity Fuzzy Semantic Network for Social Media

In this paper we propose the application of the Similarity Fuzzy Semantic Network for Social Media Analysis. We are going to enhance the Similarity Fuzzy Semantic Networks proposed in [2] by introducing some concepts, fuzzy relations and several similarity fuzzy relations specific for social media data.

4.1 Basic Concepts and Semantic Relations in Social Media

In social media we have several basic concepts which are present in any social media network: *Member*, *Post* and *Hashtag*. For some applications we can also consider the concept of *Topic*, with a finite set of domain specific instances, which must be defined for the concrete application.

With respect to semantic relations, we have several basic (crisp) domain relations: *follows* (between members), *is-author-of* (from members to posts), *is-a-repost-of* (from posts to posts), *cites-to-the-member* (from posts to members), *use-the-hashtag* (from posts to hashtag), *cites-to-the-post* (from post to post). These basic relations can be easily obtained from the tools for collecting data.

Optionally, we can consider the semantic relation *talks-about*, from posts to topics, which must be calculated by means of a named entity recognition algorithm.

Many other crisp relations can be obviously calculated from these basic relations: *is-followed-by* (between members), *has-been-posted-by* (from posts to members), *is-a-topic-of* (from topics to posts), *has-been-re-posted-by* (from posts to members), *has-re-posted* (from members to posts).

4.2 Fuzzy Semantic Relations for Social Media

We can define and calculate several fuzzy semantic relations from the basic relations, based on the number of cases of logical expressions with a semantic meaning. For example, we can consider:

- *often-talks-about*, from a member X to a topic t, based on the number of cases where "X is-author-of p and p talks-about t")
- *often-reposts-to*, from a member X to another member Y, based on the number of cases where "X is-author-of p, p is-a-re-post-of p1 and p1 has-been-posted-by Y".
- *often-use-the-hashtag*, from a member X to a hashtag h, based on the number of cases where "X is-author-of p and p use-the-hashtag h".
- *often-cites-to*, from a member X to another member Y, based on the number of cases where "X is-author-of p and p cites-to-the-member Y".
- *often-reposts-the-same-posts-that*, from a member X to another member Y, based on the number of cases where "X is-author-of p, p is-a-re-post-of p1, p2 is-a-re-post-of p and Y is-author of p2".

These fuzzy semantic relations are calculated as the fuzzy proposition "the number N of cases in which it is based is High", being *High* a fuzzy set. For example it can be defined by the membership function of the Fig. 1:

There is another kind of fuzzy relation that can be considered based on the properties of the posts. For example, if we apply an algorithm for associating a sentiment (positive, negative or neutral) for every post, then we can consider another fuzzy relations as *has-positive-opinion-about* or *has-negative-opinion-about*, from a member X to a topic t, based on the number of cases where "X is-author-of p, p talks-about t, and sentiment of p is positive (or negative)".

4.3 Similarity Fuzzy Relations in Social Media

Now we can define several similarity fuzzy semantic relations based on the fuzzy semantic relations previously defined. We will illustrate it by the following examples:

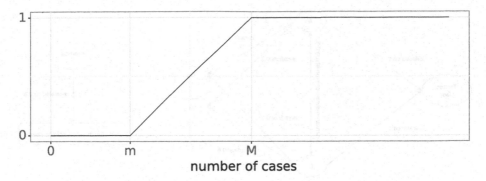

Fig. 1. Membership function of High

- **X** *is-similar-in-sense-often-repost-the-same-posts* **Y**, defined by often-re-post-the-same-posts-that, which is a symmetric relation.
- **X** *is-similar-in-sense-they-share-sentiment-about-topic-t* **Y**, defined by "X has-positive-opinion-about t and Y has-positive-opinion-about t" or "X has-negative-opinion-about t and Y has-negative-opinion-about t".
- **X** *is-similar-in-sense-they-talk-about-same-topics* **Y**, defined by the fuzzy cardinal of the fuzzy subset of topics where for every topic t, the membership function is defined by "X talks-about t and Y talks-about t".
- **X** *is-similar-in-sense-they-follow-same-members* **Y**, defined as "the number of cases where X follows m and Y follows m" is High.

These are only some examples, we can use a huge similarity semantic relations by defining symmetric logical expressions with fuzzy semantic relations and logical connectives (for example X is-similar-to Y in-the-sense they share sentiment about topic t1 and t2, and they do not talk about topic t3).

From a practical point of view, we must define the similarity fuzzy semantic relations more suitable for the problem addressed, in the sense that they might be highly related to the question we are interested in. Then we only have to calculate these similarity fuzzy semantic networks and apply the inference mechanism. In the next section we will illustrate this procedure in an real-world problem.

5   Application to Radical Discourse in Twitter

We have applied a similarity fuzzy semantic network to represent and infer new knowledge about radical discourse in Twitter.

Radical propaganda is disseminated through Social Networking Sites (SNS) such as Twitter, blogs and other platforms [9, 13]. Recruitment and radicalisation of SNS users is due to diverse factors which radicals take advantage of [12]. Identifying these radical accounts and others that are susceptible of being radicalised are important tasks in order to deal with extremism.

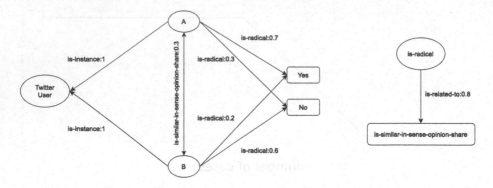

Fig. 2. Graphical representation of a similarity fuzzy semantic network for the radical discourse in Twitter.

We have used Twitter API to obtain tweets about some specific topics that are frequently found in the radical discourse. The challenge that we are facing is to detect radical users in the social network, and its main handicap is that most of the users and tweets are not radical in any form.

Given a *twitter user* U, we consider a domain-specific fuzzy semantic relation *is-radical* to represent whether a user is radical or not:

$$U \xrightarrow{is\text{-}radical:\alpha} Yes \tag{11}$$

$$U \xrightarrow{is\text{-}radical:\beta} No \tag{12}$$

being α and β the degrees in which U is radical or not, respectively. The property is-radical is considered as the aggregation of this property from different issues, and an user can be very radical in some issues and not radical in some other ones. In this way, it can be possible to have $\alpha \neq 1 - \beta$.

When two users, A and B, share opinions regarding the selected topics, we represent it by the similarity semantic relation *is-similar-in-sense-opinion-share*:

$$A \; is\text{-}similar\text{-}in\text{-}sense\text{-}opinion\text{-}share : w \; B \tag{13}$$

where w stands for the degree in which they share opinions. This enables us to propagate knowledge from user A to B and vice versa. As proposed in [5], *is-similar-to-in-sense-opinion-share* has been approximated by the relation "X is-similar-in-sense often-repost-the-same-posts Y", defined in the previous section, which is a less complex relation.

In order to determine the degree in which properties defined by the semantic fuzzy relation *is-radical* can be propagated using the similarity relation we have used the meta-relation

$$\textbf{is-radical} \; is\text{-}related\text{-}to : 0,2 \; \textbf{sense-opinion-share} \tag{14}$$

Figure 2 shows the graphic representation of the fuzzy semantic network.

Finally, we have used the product t-norm for the similarity inference rule, and the sum aggregation for the combination rule.

First, we apply the similarity inference rule for every pair of similar users (users that share opinions about the selected topics):

$$\frac{\begin{array}{l} \mathbf{A} \text{ is-similar-in-sense-opinion-share:w} \mathbf{B} \\ \mathbf{B} \text{ is-radical:p } \mathbf{Yes} \\ \mathbf{is\text{-}radical} \text{ is-related-to:0, 2 } \mathbf{sense\text{-}opinion\text{-}share} \end{array}}{\mathbf{A} \text{ is-radical:0, 2} * w * p \text{ } \mathbf{Yes}} \tag{15}$$

Then, using the combination inference rule, we obtain the degree in which every twitter user *is radical*:

$$\frac{\begin{array}{l} \mathbf{A} \text{ is-radical:} p_1 \text{ } \mathbf{Yes} \\ \mathbf{A} \text{ is-radical:} p_2 \text{ } \mathbf{Yes} \end{array}}{\mathbf{A} \text{ is-radical:} p_1 + p_2 \text{ } \mathbf{Yes}} \tag{16}$$

We have applied a cycled inference process. In each cycle the similarity inference is fired for every similar user to A, and since summation is an associative operator, the order in the combination inference rule is not relevant. Thus, we may conclude that, when the cycle i ends, it is possible to deduct that:

$$\mathbf{A} \text{ is-radical: } \left(radical^{(i)}(A) \right) \text{ } \mathbf{Yes} \tag{17}$$

being

$$radical^{(i)}(A) = radical^{(i-1)}(A) + 0, 2 * \sum_{U | w_u \in neighbours(A)} w_u * radical^{(i-1)}(u) \tag{18}$$

where $neighbours(A)$ is the fuzzy set of twitter users similar to A in the sense that they share opinions about the selected topics:

$$neighbours(A) = \{U | w_u : \mathbf{A} \text{ is-similar-in-sense-opinion-share} : w_u \text{ } \mathbf{U}\} \tag{19}$$

and being

$$radical^{(0)}(A) = \alpha \tag{20}$$

where α is the initial degree (if any) for $\mathbf{A}$ is-radical : α **Yes**.

5.1   Determining Degrees for the Fuzzy Relations

We used a human expert as an oracle for only a small number of tweets (2 of every 1000 tweets). The initial degree p for a user, would be the result of the aggregation of the degree of the tweets of the user. We have used the *mean*, that result in the ratio between user's radical tweets an the total number of them. In this way very few user had initially a non zero degree of radicalism.

Table 1. Results of the expert evaluation of the deductions made by the model. 3537 of the 4114 deductions were accepted, that yields 85.97% of accuracy.

Accepted deductions	3537
Rejected deductions	549
Undetermined deductions	28
Total deductions	4114

5.2 Real-World Experiments

We have applied this deductive system for helping to detect radicalism in twitter to a group of human experts. They classify the tweets on the basis of the keywords that appear in it, ranking users by number of positive tweets, and analyze the top ranked users. They want to improve the system to propose possible radical users to be analyzed by the experts. The main difficulty of the problem is that less than 1% of the cases are positive, and therefore it is a clearly unbalanced problem.

During the experiments they provided the system with 430000 tweets authored by more than 30000 users. The tweets were not classified in any way, and therefore the users were not ranked. Only, the initial degrees for 778 of these tweets were assigned by the experts, the rest of the tweets were unlabelled.

From these initial degrees for these 778 tweets assigned by the experts, the deductive system deduced the radical degree for 4114 users. The rest of the users have not any similarity with these users and the system can not deduce anything about them. The deductions of the system have been checked by the experts, and we obtained the results as shown in Table 1. We obtained 85.97% of accuracy, which is a clearly better result than non-deductive model such as Support Vector Machines (SVM) which is used by recent approaches [9,13] to this problem. Particularly, we trained a SVM model with the dataset of the tweets of all the 4114 users checked during the evaluation of our model, obtaining only a 68.97% accuracy in a 10 cross-validation scheme.

6 Conclusions

We extended Fuzzy Semantic Networks to Similarity Fuzzy Semantic Networks, providing them with similarity reasoning by introduced a new family of semantic relations and a higher order meta-relation that allows to apply an *inference by similarity* rule. Now, we have defined several semantic fuzzy relations and several fuzzy similarity relation for the domain of social media, in such a way that we can use a Similarity Fuzzy Semantic Network for social media analysis. We have applied this methodology to the analysis of radical discourse in Twitter. We obtain effective and sound results that shows that deductions are precise in 85.97% of the cases, that is better than non-deductive machine learning model used in recent approaches to this problem. We intend to pursue further research in the future, both at a theoretically and at application level.

References

1. Alhiyafi, J., Atta-ur-Rahman, Alhaidari, F.A., Khan, M.A.: Automatic text categorization using fuzzy semantic network. In: Benavente-Peces, C., Slama, S.B., Zafar, B. (eds.) Proceedings of the 1st International Conference on Smart Innovation, Ergonomics and Applied Human Factors (SEAHF)Smart Innovation, Systems and Technologies, pp. 24–34. Springer, Cham (2019). https://doi.org/10.1007/978-3-030-22964-1_3

2. Castro, J.L., Francisco, M.: Similarity fuzzy semantic networks and inference. An application to analysis of radical discourse in twitter. In: Artificial Intelligence and Soft Computing. Proceedings of ICAISC 2022. Lecture Notes in Computer Science. Springer, Cham (2022)

3. Dujmović, J., Torra, V.: Aggregation functions in decision engineering: ten necessary properties and parameter-directedness. In: Kahraman, C., Cebi, S., Cevik Onar, S., Oztaysi, B., Tolga, A.C., Sari, I.U. (eds.) INFUS 2021. LNNS, vol. 307, pp. 173–181. Springer, Cham (2022). https://doi.org/10.1007/978-3-030-85626-7_21

4. Flores, D.L., Rodríguez-Díaz, A., Castro, J.R., Gaxiola, C.: TA-fuzzy semantic networks for interaction representation in social simulation. In: Castillo, O., Pedrycz, W., Kacprzyk, J. (eds.) Evolutionary Design of Intelligent Systems in Modeling, Simulation and Control. Studies in Computational Intelligence, pp. 213–225. Springer, Heidelberg (2009). https://doi.org/10.1007/978-3-642-04514-1_12

5. Francisco, M., Castro, J.L.: A fuzzy model to enhance user profiles in microblogging sites using deep relations. Fuzzy Sets Syst. **401**, 133–149 (2020). https://doi.org/10.1016/j.fss.2020.05.006

6. Guo, L., Yan, F., Li, T., Yang, T., Lu, Y.: An automatic method for constructing machining process knowledge base from knowledge graph. Robot. Comput. Integrat. Manuf. **73**, 102222 (2022). https://doi.org/10.1016/j.rcim.2021.102222

7. Klawonn, F., Castro, J.L.: Similarity in fuzzy reasoning. Mathware Soft Comput. (1995)

8. Luo, M., Zhao, R.: Fuzzy reasoning algorithms based on similarity. J. Intell. Fuzzy Syst. **34**, 213–219 (2018). https://doi.org/10.3233/JIFS-171140

9. Nouh, M., Jason Nurse, R., Goldsmith, M.: Understanding the radical mind: identifying signals to detect extremist content on Twitter. 98–103 (2019). https://doi.org/10.1109/ISI.2019.8823548

10. Omri, M.N., Chouigui, N.: Measure of similarity between fuzzy concepts for identification of fuzzy user's requests in fuzzy semantic networks. Int. J. Uncertain. Fuzzin. Knowl. Based Syst. **9**, 743–748 (2001). https://doi.org/10.1016/S0218-4885(01)00119-8

11. Rahman, A.: Knowledge Representation: A Semantic Network Approach (2016). https://doi.org/10.4018/978-1-5225-0427-6

12. Spiller, P.Y.: Psicología y terrorismo: el terrorismo suicida. Estudio de variables que inciden en su aparición y desarrollo. Thesis, Universidad de Belgrano. Facultad de Humanidades. (2005). http://repositorio.ub.edu.ar/handle/123456789/225. Accessed 23 July 2011

13. Ul Rehman, Z., et al.: Understanding the language of ISIS: an empirical approach to detect radical content on twitter using machine learning. Comput. Mater. Continua **66**(2), 1075–1090 (2020). https://doi.org/10.32604/cmc.2020.012770

Management of Uncertain Data in Event Graphs

Valerio Bellandi$^{(\boxtimes)}$ ⓘ, Fulvio Frati, Stefano Siccardi, and Filippo Zuccotti

Computer Science Department, Università Degli Studi di Milano,
Via Celoria 18, Milano, MI, Italy
{valerio.bellandi,fulvio.frati,stefano.siccardi,
filippo.zuccotti}@unimi.it

Abstract. We consider graphs to model uncertain facts as edges, linking involved entities, with weights reflecting uncertainty degree. Rules are used to create new edges from the existing ones, and methods to propagate uncertainty measures are defined using a suitable theoretical framework. We also consider new rules, mined from graphs containing uncertain information and answer sets obtained using such rules. We then use Argument Graphs and Possibility Networks to evaluate the conclusions that can be drawn from the facts, taking into account their uncertainty. Finally, information revision is discussed for cases when a new piece of information is added to the graph.

Keywords: Graph · Uncertainty Data · Graph Event

1 Introduction

Graphs, both Knowledge Graphs and general graphs have been used to model facts in terms of relationships between entities and to deduce new facts from the known ones, in a similar way as using standard logic. In the real world, however, facts are often not certain, either because they still did not happen, or because our knowledge is incomplete. If uncertainty is not taken into account, the information quality, that is of primary concern when gathering large amount of data (see e.g. [2]), may be low. For this reason, methods have been devised to deal with uncertain facts, including measures for the degree of uncertainty and formulas to compute the uncertainty of deductions and so on. In the present work we discuss the impact of using such types of logic, instead of the usual Boolean one, when reasoning on graphs, looking for hidden links and mining rules. Our goal is to give to the users of a Knowledge Graph tools to evaluate, keep under control and, if necessary, filter uncertainty levels of facts and consequences that can be deduced, at each step of the graph construction and manipulation. To illustrate the situation, we make a simple example.

Example 1. Suppose that a phone P_1 makes a call C_1 to another phone P_2. Links between P_1 and C_1 and between C_1 and P_2 are certain, because we have the phone company records. If we know that P_1 is used by two siblings S_1,

ⓒ Springer Nature Switzerland AG 2022
D. Ciucci et al. (Eds.): IPMU 2022, CCIS 1601, pp. 568–580, 2022.
https://doi.org/10.1007/978-3-031-08971-8_47

S_2 fifty percent of time each, we can assign a 0.5 **probability** to links with label *calls* between both S_1 and S_2 and phone P_2. Moreover, if we observe other calls between the same phones, we can consider their temporal distribution and confirm or adjust the value. On the other hand, suppose that we *suspect* that phone P_2, owned by some person X, is actually permanently used by another person Y. We can assign a **possibility** to links between phone P_1 and persons X and Y. In this case, observation of more calls between P_1 and P_2 does not change the possibility values. However, if we observe calls between P_2 and *other* phones and we know that they are all used by friends of X, this would increase the possibility of the link between P_1 and Y.

The example shows several important points in our research: different types of uncertainty may be mixed even in a simple link chain; we need ways to evaluate uncertainty of missing links created by composition; we want to use surrounding or replicated links to refine uncertainty measures.

2   Uncertainty Management in Event Graphs

We consider graphs as Knowledge Bases (KB) or Knowledge Graphs (KG) and take into account relational facts in the form of subject-predicate-object or *triples*. These in turn can be considered propositions or logic atoms. Several types of "truth" can be applied to propositions (see e.g. [10]): *i)* Boolean truth, e.g.: is the bottle full? True or false; *ii)* Graded truth, e.g.: is the bottle full? It is three quarters full; *iii)* Uncertain Boolean truth, e.g.: is the bottle full? I believe that it is (but it might be empty instead); *iv)* Uncertain Graded truth, e.g.: is the bottle full? I believe that it is three quarters full (but it might be otherwise). The first case is managed with usual logic. The second one can be managed with three valued or multi valued logic. Case 3 is considered in possibility theory, [6,10]. A possibility level is attached to propositions, as will be detailed below. The last case should be treated with techniques derived from the cases before, but not all the details have been fully exploited. In the cases we are studying, both graded truth and uncertainty can be found, and that they may be interleaved in several ways. For instance in Example 1 the fact that P_1 is fifty percent shared by two persons is a graded truth, but (supposing that a phone call is made by just a person) a specific phone call from this phone being made by S_1 is an uncertain Boolean truth. To deal with uncertain truth we use the possibility logic framework (see [12]), that considers pairs (p, α) of a proposition p and a Necessity level α (the "weight"), that is $N(p) \geq \alpha$, where $N()$ is a necessity measure. Both numerical values and labels from an ordered scale can be used for these weights. As

$$N(p \wedge q) = min(N(p), N(q)) \tag{1}$$

we have a way to compute the level of consequences of Horn rules (see below Sect. 2.1).

Possibility theory can be equivalently defined in terms of possibility distributions and of Possibility Networks. The latter are analogous to Bayesan networks:

directed acyclic graphs, where each node represents a variable and every edge an influence between two variables. Uncertainty is expressed by means of conditional possibility distributions for each node in the context of its parents. Hybrid models, consisting of a graph to represent independence relations and possibility logic for uncertainty associated with each node and its parents, have been proposed in [6]. It is also possible to deal with inconsistency. One way consists in cutting the Knowledge Basis at some level, that is considering only propositions with weight $\geq \alpha$ for some α, such that the resulting basis is consistent. Another way requires to attach a second weight to every proposition, in order to take into account the possibility of its negation. An important point covered by possibility theories is information fusion and information revision, that is methods to adapt the KB and the weight of the propositions when a new piece of information arrives (see [5,11,13]). In particular, revision with a totally reliable input and an uncertain input have been considered, both when numerical values and ordered labels are used as proposition weights, leading to *product-based conditioning* and *minimum-based conditioning* respectively.

2.1   Rules and Rule Mining

Rules can be used to expand the data or acquire new perspectives on it. Rules are applied to KGs interpreted as conjunctions of triples of the form `subject -- predicate -- object` (see e.g. [22] for details).

Rules having only positive atoms are the simplest to deal with and are called Horn rules. Logic programs consist of sets of rules and specific techniques to find answers sets and to decide whether a given atom is entailed from the program (see e.g. [14]). We used Potassco (see [15,16]) to derive answer sets from uncertain facts and rules. Usually, the facts are assumed to be true, but, limiting ourselves to Horn rules, we can use Eq. 1 to propagate weights to the deduced propositions. An important task over KGs is rule learning or mining, that can be done in several ways, both for Horn and more general rules.

Some statistical measures are used to assess the quality of mined rules. The *support* of a rule is the number of true predictions it makes, the *head coverage* is the predicted ratio of instantiations of the head atom and the *confidence* is the proportion of true predictions out of the true predictions and false predictions. Rule mining and the above measures are defined for a KB containing certain facts only. We need some additional quality measures due to the uncertainty of the facts used for rule mining. Several programs have been published to learn Horn rules, like AMIE [19] and RDF2Rules [24]; additional steps can revise rules to incorporate exceptions in the form of negated atoms [21]. Another type of rule learning is based on embedding models. A method of this type, along with a software tool, RuLES, is described in [23]. We will limit ourselves to the Horn case; more specifically, to the possibility to use rules mined by AMIE [19] in the uncertain case. The same approach can be used with rules mined by any other programs.

2.2 Logic on Graphs

Graphs have been used in conjunction with logic by several authors with different perspectives and aims. Representing First Order Predicate Logic on graphs has been considered for instance in [20]. Logical binary relations between entities are represented by edges linking the corresponding nodes. Logical formulae are expressed as graph predicates, that are trees of connected graph morphisms, a perspective that make the approach well suited for to deal with graph rewriting, that here we are not considering at all. Proof systems on graphs have been considered for Boolean [9] and linear logic [1]. Presently we will not consider these approaches, that will be the subject of future work. Graphs have also been used to represent argumentation, including the degree of belief in arguments (see e.g. [8] for an introduction). An argument graph (AG) has arguments as nodes and arcs linking an argument attacking another. Arguments have premises from which a claim is derived by deductive reasoning using a base logic. For instance one can use the simple logic consisting of atoms and Horn rules or classical logic or some other. There are techniques to generate arguments and counterarguments from a KB. In [18] epistemic graphs with links both for supporting and attacking arguments have been defined. Moreover the degree of belief in premises, claims and deduction methods have been considered; we will consider this more complex framework in a future work. In [17] it is described a tool to reason with temporal uncertainty, that is uncertainty about which event of a pair happened before, in a temporal network. Even if in our settings events and their times can be found, we are not dealing specifically with the uncertainty in their temporal order.

3 Methodology Proposal and Real Case Study Application

The aim of the proposed methodology is to extend the graph with new relations that can be deduced by the existing ones and to deal with their logical implications, bearing in evidence their uncertain degree. It consists of the following steps, that can be iterated:

1. Define and assign weights for uncertainty of graph edges (i.e. propositions);
2. Evaluate weights of propositions derived using Horn rules (i.e. new graph edges);
3. Apply rule mining methods to weighted edges and evaluate to iterate again the step before

After the iterations phase we propose to *i)* compute answers sets with uncertainty; *ii)* build Argument Graphs with uncertainty from the KB obtained and finally *iii)* compute information fusion and revision when new input arrives. Moreover, we will consider applications of Possibility Networks, and this methodology will be illustrated using examples in the following subsections.

In many cases the graph may contain paths leading to contradictory conclusions. Argument Graphs and Possibility Networks are used to help users to evaluate their uncertainty, depending on the premises. The proposed tools can clarify each other, leaving the final decision to the users: they may choose some hypotheses highlighted by the method and decide to further investigate.

3.1   The Data Set

We adopted a subset of data from a real investigation about a case of drug trade, consisting of a list of approximately 120,000 phone calls, spanning a period of about 16 months and involving more that 14,000 phones; information about the owners of the phones was available for 4,000. Moreover, it was known that a few phones were used by people other than the formal owners or shared between two users[1].

We filtered phones whose owners or users were known, obtaining 131 nodes for persons, 129 for phones, 15796 calls and 31682 edges. The node with most edges, a phone, has 2753 edges. A sketch of the graph can be found in Fig. 1. Persons are linked by green edges (the "phones" edges, created as explained in the next section), and phones by pink edges corresponding to calls.

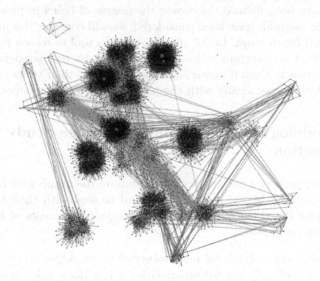

Fig. 1. The total graph of persons and calls.

The reports by the investigators described some relationships between users; using such information we manually added some links to the graph, namely

---

[1] We received the data from the investigators to produce research and proof of concepts, with permission of publishing general research results, but not to share the data. All the files we received were carefully anonymized, discarding all unnecessary information (e.g. addresses) and changing names to numerical ids, phone numbers to random digits and so on. In this way no real persons, events or places could be recognized.

being: "friends", "relatives", "indirectly linked" (when it was known or suspected that two persons communicate even if no phone call records exist, see e.g. [4] for a discussion of correlations of cascaded calls), "deals" (when it is known or suspected that one person buys drug from the other) and its negation "not deals" (when, after inquiring, the investigators think that two persons are not buying drug from each other). To prepare simple but meaningful examples, we filtered the data choosing a subset of 75 persons and approximately 13,000 phone calls and text messages involving their phones.

3.2 Assigning Weights and Creating Edges

Uncertainty weights are assigned accordingly to the user's belief, that may results in a more or less subjective procedure. In some cases, users may define some explicit rules or adopt more or less formal procedures to assign weights; however we do not deal with the specific method used and we only require that weights are assigned to the relationships as a first step. In our example, we assigned weights for uncertainty to all the edges created from the source data, that is: weight level 1 for edges linking caller and called phones to phone calls and linking phones to their owners when no other potential users were known; weight level less than 1, with values deduced by the investigation reports, for edges linking phones to persons when multiple owners and users were supposed; weight levels deduced by the investigation reports for the added relationships. The second step consists in creating new edges, with computed uncertainty weights, using rules that are known a priori, i.e. given by a field expert user. Note that we do not consider how the first set of rules is found, and assume that they are known to a field expert user. We then computed relations "phones" between persons, using the Horn rule

$$p_1 \, phones \, p_2 \quad \leftarrow \quad p_1 \, owns \, t_1, \, t_1 \, starts \, c_1, \, c_1 \, received \, t_2, \, t_2 \, owned \, p_2 \quad (2)$$

with p_1, p_2 persons, t_1, t_2 phones, c_1 phone call. The weight of the new relation was computed using the minimum formula Eq. 1. We defined similar rules for phone users (instead of owners). In order to simplify the computation, we created a single "phones" edge between persons, even if they were involved in several phone calls. We considered both the opportunity to add the number of calls as an attribute to the edge, and to define different edge types (e.g. "seldom phones", "phones", "often phones" etc.) using thresholds for the number of calls. Figure 2 (drawn using Gephi see [3]) illustrates the resulting network. The left panel shows only edges with weight level 1, considered certain, the central with weight level 0.8 or higher and the right panel all the edges. The small edges in grey or brown are communications, green edges are for friends and blue for relatives. Red edges represent the possibility that a deal for drug trade exists between two persons: there are two "almost certain" such edges (see central panel) and some more with lower confidence (right panel); purple edges, on the contrary, represent the opinion of the investigator that no drug trades involve two persons. Yellow edges represent indirectly linked persons, that is supposed but not proven communications.

3.3 Rule Mining

The next step consists in trying to complete the KB finding new rules, based on the existing edges. We applied Horn rule mining techniques to the network described above, in order to find new rules that can lead to the conclusion that two persons have a deal to trade drug. We considered Horn rules only, that is rules with only positive clauses and used AMIE to find them. Rule mining algorithms do not consider uncertainty of triples, and compute the reliability of the mined rules taking into account basically the number of examples found. On the other hand, as any uncertain fact may later prove to be false, rules based on them must be in turn somehow tagged with an uncertainty weight: one must be aware when an uncertain rule is applied to uncertain facts. To obtain such weights, at least in a coarse way, we extracted three separate sets of triples, filtering with thresholds for the weight levels and mined rules separately, looking for a "deals" relationship in the head. The certain facts network gave no results, as it contains no "deals" relationship. The almost certain facts network gave 5 rules, none with standard confidence greater than 0.07, all based on a single positive example. The network of all facts gave 42 rules. The most confident, having 0.6 standard confidence and 1 PCA confidence, simply states that being indirectly linked implies being dealing drug. Another rule found states that if a person p_1 communicates with (or more exactly phones) p_2 and is indirectly linked to p_3, then p_2 and p_3 deal drug; still other rules relate indirect links, friendship and not dealing drug. Of course, these do not describe general behaviours, but habits of the group of people under investigation. We can use the new rules either to add new edges to the network, as in Sect. 3.2, or to compute answer sets. We will concentrate on the latter choice in the following section.

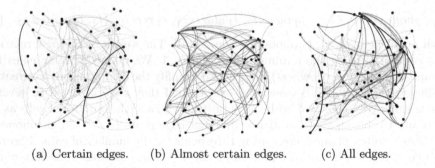

(a) Certain edges.   (b) Almost certain edges.   (c) All edges.

Fig. 2. Communications and relationships between persons with different levels of uncertainty. (Color figure online)

3.4 Answer Sets

The rules found in the previous step, with the facts contained in the KB, can be used to compute answer sets. For instance, we used the following mined rules (and some obtained exchanging X, Y and Z, as relations are symmetric):

$$ND(X,Y,U,V) : -FR(X,Z,U), \quad IL(Y,Z,V).$$
$$DL(X,Y,U,V) : -IL(X,Z,U), \quad PH(Z,Y,V). \quad (3)$$

using the syntax for clingo (see [16]); U and V are the uncertainty weights of the edges and ND, FR, IL, DL and PH stand for not deals, friend, indirectly linked, deals and phones. The uncertainty of the answers can be computed as

$$Weight(deals(X,Y,U,V)) = Min(U,V) \quad (4)$$

As the rules were mined using uncertain data, the result could be further refined using rule weights, for instance the resulting weight could be multiplied by the threshold used to mine the rules, in our case 0.7. In our experiment the answer set included 72 new "deals" and 3 "not deals" relations, including a contradictory case of a pair of persons found both dealing and not dealing drug. As the weight of the "not deals" relation was higher, the user could choose to keep it; in other cases weights could be equal so that the user should look elsewhere for hints about the preferred relation. Techniques based on Argument Graphs and Possibility Networks will be discussed in the following sections.

The above computation could find more than one answer set, that could be compared considering the weight levels of answers. In more complex cases, preference capabilites of answer set programs (see e.g. [7]) could be used to find the answer set that optimizes weight levels.

3.5   Argument Graphs

Following [8], we can generate an AG $G = (\mathcal{A}, \mathcal{R})$ from the KB K and edges added using user supplied and mined rules. It is then possible to introduce possibility measures to evaluate arguments. Here $\mathcal{A}$ is the set of simple arguments of K, that are pairs $\langle \Phi, \alpha \rangle$ with $\Phi \subseteq K$, α is the head of a rule whose body is Φ and Φ is minimal. $\mathcal{R}$ are the *attacks* of K, that is pairs $(A, B) \in \mathcal{A}$ where the head of the rule of A is the negation of one of the elements in the body of B (simple undercuts in the terminology of AGs).

As an example, we used this technique to highlight arguments related to the contradictory case regarding persons 2740 and 114 found in Sect. 3.4. The situation is shown in Fig. 3. Nodes with continuous border contain arguments supporting the hypothesis that 2740 and 114 are involved in a drug trade. Arguments are represented using simple logic in a semi formal way: the first two rows in each box are facts, the third row, marked with an asterisk, is added to have in the premises a term directly negated by the attacking arguments, the fourth row is the second of 3; the row below the horizontal line is the claim.

Numbers in square brackets near each sentence are the estimated or computed weight measures. All relationships should be considered not directional, that is, for instance "X phones Y" in this context means that there was a phone call (or more) between X and Y, disregarding who was the caller. Boxes with dashed borders are analogous, but the rule used is the first of 3 (implying "not deals") and, accordingly, facts about friendship are used instead of phone calls. These are counterargument (or attacks) for the continuous border nodes and vice versa. The box with dotted border attacks the premise "114 phones 116". In case of person 116, it was known that the phone (phone 1767) could be used by person 696 instead, with a 50% probability. Therefore there is the possibility that the phone calls considered involve user 696. As no other phone call that could involve 114 is known, we consider the above fact as a negation of "114 phones 116" even if, formally, it's implication is weaker. However partly informal, the AG can be considered a useful tool to help an agent to reason about the collected evidence and its implication. The example is quite simple, in complex cases more sophisticated tools can be used, as explained e.g. in [18].

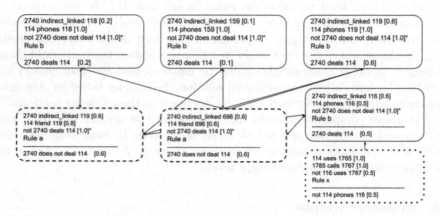

Fig. 3. AG with uncertainty for drug dealing between persons 2740 and 114.

3.6   Possibility Networks

Possibility Networks, analogous to Bayesan networks, are another tool that can be used to reason about the facts in a KG, taking into account their weights, that we denote "possibilities" in the present paragraph to conform to the usual notation for Possibility Networks.

Figure 4 shows such a network for the case of drug dealing, involving persons 2740 and 114 already considered above. Nodes are facts, here interpreted as Boolean variables; relationship names have been abbreviated as follows: IL stands for indirectly linked, FR for friends, DL for deals, PH for phones and US for uses. Edges represent dependence. Comparing to Fig. 3, we note that conditions "114 phones 118", "114 phones 159" and "114 phones 119" were not reported, because, as they are certain, they have no influence on conditioning. The situation of 116 is more complex: as it is not certain that the phone was actually used by this user, we reported the composite condition "2740 indirectly linked to 116" and "116 phones 114", together with its uncertain individual parent conditions. To compute possibility distributions for nodes we can use the formula (see [6]):

$$\pi(\omega) = \{1 \, if \, \forall (\phi, \alpha) \in \Sigma, \omega \vDash \phi \, else \, 1 - max(\alpha : \omega \nvDash \phi : (\phi, \alpha) \in \Sigma)\} \quad (5)$$

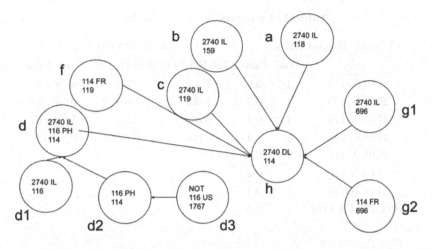

Fig. 4. Possibility Network for drug dealing between persons 2740 and 114.

where Σ is an available possibilistic KB, and (ϕ, α) its formulas; each ω is a set of values for the variables meaningful at each node and $\models$ denotes logical satisfaction. For nodes without parents, using the KB contained in the boxes of Fig. 3, we obtain the first three columns of Table 1; the last four are just the definition of logical *and* for statements "2740 indirectly linked 116" and "116 phones 114". Statements "user 116 does not use phone 1767" and "user 116 is not in touch by phone with user 114" can be considered logically equivalent. The case of node "2740 deals with 114" is more complex. To express how its possibility depends on the parent conditions we define the following formulas, using abbreviations defined in Fig. 4, e.g. "a" stands for "2740 indirectly linked 118". Moreover we define $g = g1 \wedge g2$ considering "2740 indirectly linked 696 and 114 friend 696" as a single condition for the sake of simplicity.

$$\{(a \wedge b \wedge c \wedge d \wedge \neg f \wedge \neg g \wedge h) \vee (\neg a \wedge \neg b \wedge \neg c \wedge \neg d \wedge f \wedge g \wedge \neg h), 0.5\}$$
$$\{((a \vee b \vee c \vee d) \wedge \neg f \wedge \neg g \wedge h) \vee (\neg a \wedge \neg b \wedge \neg c \wedge \neg d \wedge f \wedge g \wedge \neg h), 0.6\}$$
$$\{((a \vee b \vee c \vee d) \wedge (\neg f \vee \neg g) \wedge h) \vee (\neg a \wedge \neg b \wedge \neg c \wedge \neg d \wedge f \wedge g \wedge \neg h), 0.7\} \quad (6)$$

Formulas (6) assign maximal possibility to cases when all conditions are fulfilled and there is a deal, or no conditions are fulfilled and there is no deal; lower possibility when at least an indirect link but no friend relationships are found and there is a deal; still lower when at least an indirect link and a friend relationships are found and there is a deal; default possibility in other cases. These values are to be intended as the users' belief in the importance of conditions, and have a qualitative nature (an ordering scale between likelihood of the claims).

Using the above formulas, a global possibility distribution can be computed, so that a possibility can be assigned to every combinations of truth values of the variables. Possibility Networks can be used also to compute possibilities of a

Table 1. Local possibility distributions.

Nodes without parents			2740 IL 116 PH 114			
Node	True	False	116 PH 114	2740 IL 116	True	False
2740 IL 118	1	0.8	False	True	0	1
2740 IL 159	1	0.9	False	False	0	1
2740 IL 119	1	0.4	True	True	1	0
2740 IL 696	1	0.4	True	False	0	1
2740 IL 116	1	0.4				
114 FR 119	1	0.2				
114 FR 696	1	0.4				
NOT 116 US 1767	1	0.5				

subset of variables given evidence for some other. We will however not deal with this task here, as our example data is not well suited for this type of computation.

3.7 Revisions

In most practical cases, the KG is not given as a whole at a specific time, but it grows gradually as new data is acquired. It is also possible that the users' belief in some facts changes over time. Formal techniques are available to revise weights ("possibilities") when a new piece of information arrives, both when the weights are actually numeric, so that multiplication make sense, and when they express a belief ordering only.

We limit ourselves to consider non multiplicative weights and to an example using a totally reliable input, namely the fact "not 116 uses 1767" and consequently "not 114 phones 116" are now known to be true. Following [5], we add this formula with weight 1 to the KB; then we compute the level of inconsistency of the new KB, that is the maximum weight x such that the basis contains contradictory formulas. We have $x = 0.5$; finally we drop all formulas with weight less or equal to 0.5. The Argument Graph and the Possibility Network, accordingly, are greatly simplified.

4 Conclusion

We have shown that graphs can be a useful way to represent uncertain information. In this way a number of techniques to deal with uncertainty can be managed in a unified setting. First of all, it is possible to create new edges, with weights reflecting the user's belief in the likelihood of the represented relationship. It is then possible to mine rules, as from any KG containing certain information, filtering the edges with weights above some thresholds. The maximum threshold needed to mine a specific rule can be considered as a measure of its possibility. Mined rules can be used both to add new edges to the graph and to compute answer sets. For the latter task, standard tools can be used, appending a vector of weights to the answers. The minimum rule can then be applied to assign weights. Having completed as much as possible the KG with the above techniques, other methods can be used to evaluate the information taking the uncertainty into consideration. Argument Graphs and Possibility Networks highlight different perspectives of this task. Finally, one has at disposal formal methods to reshape the whole landscape when new information arrives. The present work touched many points which deserve to be explored in depth. In a future work we plan, in particular, to carry on computations with double weights in order to take into account inconsistencies, and to study the interplay between graded truth and uncertainty. Moreover we will mine non monotonic rules and define formulas to assign weights to rules mined from uncertain knowledge. We will also exploit the capabilities of epistemic graphs, with supporting and attacking arguments and degree of beliefs; we will experiment with evidence in Possibility Networks and revision with several types of input.

References

1. Acclavio, M., Horne, R., Strassburger, L.: Logic beyond formulas: a proof system on graphs. In: LICS 2020–35th ACM/IEEE Symposium on Logic in Computer Science, Saarbrucken, July 2020 (2020). ff10.1145/3373718.3394763ff. ffhal-02560105
2. Azzini, A., et al.: Advances in data management in the big data era. In: Goedicke, M., Neuhold, E., Rannenberg, K. (eds.) Advancing Research in Information and Communication Technology. IAICT, vol. 600, pp. 99–126. Springer, Cham (2021). https://doi.org/10.1007/978-3-030-81701-5_4
3. Bastian, M., Heymann, S., Jacomy, M.: In International AAAI Conference on Web and Social Media (2009). https://www.aaai.org/ocs/index.php/ICWSM/09/paper/view/154
4. Bellandi, V., Ceravolo, P., Maghool, S., Pindaro, M., Siccadi, S.: Correlation and pattern detection in event networks. In: 2021 BigGraphs Workshop at IEEE Big-Data 2021 (2021)
5. Benferhat, S., Didier, D., Prade, H., Williams, M.-A.: A practical approach to revising prioritized knowledge bases. Studia Logica **70** (2002)
6. Benferhat, S., Smaoui, S.: Hybrid possibilistic networks. Int. J. Approx. Reason. **44**, 224–243 (2007)
7. Brewka, G., Delgrande, J.P., Romero, J., Schaub, T.: In AAAI, pp. 1467–1474. AAAI Press (2015)
8. Besnard, P., Hunter, A.: Constructing argument graphs with deductive arguments: a tutorial. Argument Comput. **5**(1), 5–30 (2014)
9. Calk, C., Das, A., Waring, T.: Beyond formulas-as-cographs: an extension of Boolean logic to arbitrary graphs (2020). arXiv:2004.12941
10. Dubois, D., Prade, H.: Possibility theory, probability theory and multiple-valued logics: a clarification. Ann. Math. Artif. Intell. **32**, 35–66 (2001). https://doi.org/10.1023/A.1010740830286
11. Dubois, D., Prade, H.: Belief revision with uncertain inputs in the possibilistic setting (2013). arXiv:1302.3575
12. Dubois, D., Prade, H.: Possibilistic logic - an overview. In: Gabbay, D.M., Siekmann, J.H., Woods, J. (eds.) Computational Logic, Volume 9 of the Handbook of The History of Logic (2014)

13. Dubois, D., Liub, W., Mac, J., Prade, H.: The basic principles of uncertain information fusion. An organised review of merging rules in different representation frameworks. Inf. Fusion **32**, 12–39 (2016)
14. Eiter, T., Ianni, G., Krennwallner, T.: Answer set programming: a primer. In: Reasoning Web, vol. 5689, pp. 40–110 (2009)
15. Gebser, M., Kaufmann, B., Kaminski, R., Ostrowski, M., Schaub, T., Schneider, M.: Potassco: the potsdam answer set solving collection. AI Commun. **24**(2), 107–124 (2011)
16. Gebser, M., Kaminski, R., Kaufmann, B., Schaub, T.: Multi-shot ASP solving with clingo. TPLP **19**(1), 27–82 (2019)
17. Guil, F., Gomez, I., Juarez, J.M., Marin, R.: *Propos*: a dynamic web tool for managing possibilistic and probabilistic temporal constraint networks. In: Mira, J., Álvarez, J.R. (eds.) IWINAC 2007, Part II. LNCS, vol. 4528, pp. 551–560. Springer, Heidelberg (2007). https://doi.org/10.1007/978-3-540-73055-2_57
18. Hunter, A., Polberg, S., Thimm, M.: Epistemic graphs for representing and reasoning with positive and negative influences of arguments. Artif. Intell. **281** (2020). https://doi.org/10.1016/j.artint.2020.103236
19. Lajus, J., Galárraga, L., Suchanek, F.: Fast and exact rule mining with AMIE 3. In: Harth, A., et al. (eds.) ESWC 2020. LNCS, vol. 12123, pp. 36–52. Springer, Cham (2020). https://doi.org/10.1007/978-3-030-49461-2_3
20. Rensink, A.: Representing first-order logic using graphs. In: Ehrig, H., Engels, G., Parisi-Presicce, F., Rozenberg, G. (eds.) ICGT 2004. LNCS, vol. 3256, pp. 319–335. Springer, Heidelberg (2004). https://doi.org/10.1007/978-3-540-30203-2_23
21. Tran, H.D., Stepanova, D., Gad-Elrab, M.H., Lisi, F.A., Weikum, G.: Towards nonmonotonic relational learning from knowledge graphs. In: Cussens, J., Russo, A. (eds.) ILP 2016. LNCS (LNAI), vol. 10326, pp. 94–107. Springer, Cham (2017). https://doi.org/10.1007/978-3-319-63342-8_8
22. Stepanova, D., Gad-Elrab, M.H., Ho, V.T.: Rule induction and reasoning over knowledge graphs. In: d'Amato, C., Theobald, M. (eds.) Reasoning Web 2018. LNCS, vol. 11078, pp. 142–172. Springer, Cham (2018). https://doi.org/10.1007/978-3-030-00338-8_6
23. Ho, V.T., Stepanova, D., Gad-Elrab, M.H., Kharlamov, E., Weikum, G.: Rule learning from knowledge graphs guided by embedding models. In: Vrandečić, D., et al. (eds.) ISWC 2018. LNCS, vol. 11136, pp. 72–90. Springer, Cham (2018). https://doi.org/10.1007/978-3-030-00671-6_5
24. Wang, Z., Li, J.: DF2Rules: learning rules from RDF knowledge bases by mining frequent predicate cycles. preprint arXiv:1512.07734 (2015)

Possibilistic Preference Networks and Lexicographic Preference Trees – A Comparison

Nahla Ben Amor[1], Didier Dubois[2], Henri Prade[2], and Syrine Saidi[1,2(✉)]

[1] Laboratoire LARODEC, ISG de Tunis, 41 rue de la Liberté, 2000 Le Bardo, Tunisia
nahla.benamor@gmx.fr
[2] IRIT, CNRS & Univ. Paul Sabatier, 118 route de Narbonne, 31062 Toulouse Cedex 9, France
{dubois,prade,syrine.saidi}@irit.fr

Abstract. The paper compares two graphical approaches proposed for the qualitative modeling of preferences: π-pref nets and LP-trees. The former uses the graphical setting of possibilistic networks for completing partial specifications of user preferences, while the latter, which is based on lexicographic ordering, appears to offer a convenient framework for learning preferences. The π-pref network representation appears to be more flexible, even if the addition of very specific constraints allows us to recover the total order of the LP-trees.

Keywords: possibility theory · lexicographic ordering · preference representation

1 Introduction

Graphical models for the representation of qualitative preferences [3,7,17] have been motivated by the need for a compact specification of user preferences. That is to say that from a limited number of preferences, conditional or not (of the form "in the context c – which can be empty – one prefers a to not-a", where a is a Boolean variable), one must in particular be able to compare two configurations corresponding to two possible instantiations of the set of variables in question. Each preference is associated to a Boolean variable and to a node of a graph, the structure of the graph reflecting the conditionings: the parent node(s) of a node correspond(s) to the variable(s) defining the context of the preference associated to this node.

The framework of "CP-nets" [7] emerged quickly as a convenient tool for specifying conditional preferences and for completing this expression by means of a so-called "criteris paribus" principle. as a convenient tool for specifying conditional preferences and for complementing this expression of preferences by means of a so-called "ceteris paribus" principle. This principle states that conditional preferences expressed between two instantiations of a subset of Boolean variables continue to hold "all things being equal", i.e., instantiating the remaining Boolean variables in the same way in the two configurations to be compared.

Each preference thus makes it possible to compare two configurations differing by only one "worsening flip" of the Boolean variable associated with this preference. We

© Springer Nature Switzerland AG 2022
D. Ciucci et al. (Eds.): IPMU 2022, CCIS 1601, pp. 581–592, 2022.
https://doi.org/10.1007/978-3-031-08971-8_48

can then compare two configurations if we can go from one to the other by a sequence of worsening flips. In this way, an order is obtained that is generally only partial, as some pairs of configurations remain incomparable.

The CP-net framework, despite its apparent simplicity, suffers from a bias induced by a perverse effect of the "ceteris paribus" principle: It is more serious to violate a preference associated with a father node than a preference associated with an offspring node [10]. An extension of this framework, called TCP-nets [8], makes it possible to express, conditionally or unconditionally, that one node/one preference is more important than another. But this possibility unfortunately does not allow to correct the bias in favour of the father nodes.

It is only recently that it has been established that CP-nets satisfy a property that can be considered as indispensable in preference representation: the respect of the Pareto order [21]. This order means that if the preferences violated by a ω configuration all belong to the subset of those violated by another ω' configuration, the ω configuration must be preferred to ω'.

The π-pref networks (π-pref nets) [4] interpret the graph induced by conditional preferences in a different way from the CP-nets. To each node is associated a table of conditional possibilities reflecting the satisfaction of having a, or not a, in the context c. These satisfaction levels are treated as symbolic weights (the maximum satisfaction level, 1, being considered superior to any other level). The computation of preferences is then based on the chaining rule of possibilistic networks with product-based conditioning. It was established [2] that the order thus generated corresponds exactly to the Pareto (partial) order. This order can be completed by adding constraints between symbolic weights, thus expressing the relative importance between constraints. It has been shown that π-pref networks can provide a good approximation of CP-nets if explicit constraints between products of symbolic weights are added to encode preferences ceteris paribus, in the case of Boolean features. This also has a computational advantage since the comparison of configurations in the extended π-pref networks is polynomial [21].

The CP-theories [20] offer a generalization of CP-nets and TCP-nets. It allows to express that ω is preferred to ω' whatever are (i.e., "irrespective of") the values of a certain subset of variables. This framework thus makes it possible to express lexicographic preferences (the preference associated with a variable is independent of the values of the variables which follow this variable in the order of importance). The interest of lexicographic orders has also been put forward for the approximation of dominance relations between configurations in a CP-net [16].

But it is first of all in a learning perspective that the use of lexicographic preference trees (LP-trees) has been proposed [6]. They are defined both from an order relation between variables expressing their relative importance, and from local preference relations on the domains of the variables. Both the importance relationship between variables and the local preferences can be conditioned on the values of more important variables. The interest of "LP-trees" in learning user preferences has been studied in [13]. Their use in multi-agent preference aggregation procedures has also been considered in [19].

The rest of the article is organised in three main sections. Sections 2 and 3 provide the necessary reminders on possibilistic preference networks and lexicographic preference trees respectively, while Sect. 4 focuses on their comparison, before concluding in Sect. 5.

2   Possibilistic Preferences

CP-nets borrow their graphical structure from Bayesian networks, which is that of a DAG ("Directed Acyclic Graph"), but differ from them in the tables that are associated with the nodes and the way in which they are operated. Possibility networks [1,5] are a counterpart of Bayesian networks in possibility theory (the tables of conditional probabilities are replaced by tables of conditional possibilities).

Possibilistic preference networks [4] or π-pref nets are networks where the degrees of possibility are manipulated symbolically (as unspecified numerical values between 0 and 1). CP-nets and π-pref networks thus use the same specification of conditional preferences as input. But each decision variable in a π-pref graph is associated with a conditional symbolic possibility distribution.

Definition 1. *A π-pref network is a DAG composed of a set of decision variables $\mathcal{X} = \{X_1, \ldots, X_n\}$, each associated with a symbolic conditional possibilistic distribution with degrees of preference taking values in $(0, 1]$. For each instantiation of the parent(s) U_i of a node corresponding to a variable X_i, there must exist a preferred instantiation of X_i that takes a degree of possibility equal to 1. Conditional tables define an order between the instantiations of variables such that, if $x_i \succ x_i'$ (x_i preferred to x_i') then $\pi(x_i' \mid u) = \alpha$ and $\pi(x_i \mid u) = \beta$ with $\alpha < \beta \leq 1$ (X_i may not be Boolean).*

In the following one considers only choice variables X_i having x_i and $\bar{x}_i$ as possible values and a set of parents U_i. Then the preference assignment $\pi(\bar{x}_i \mid u_i) = \alpha$ (and thus $\pi(x_i \mid u_i) = 1$) expresses that *"in the context where $U_i = u_i$, x_i is preferred to $\bar{x}_i$ with a priority level $1 - \alpha$"*. That is, if $X_i = x_i$, the associated preference is completely satisfied in the context where $U_i = u_i$, and if $X_i = \bar{x}_i$ it is satisfied only to a degree α, smaller than 1 (but not specified).

In order to rank all possible complete configurations, the degree of satisfaction of each alternative must be calculated. It is calculated via the chaining rule associated with possibilistic conditioning by product, formally expressed by

$$\pi(X_i, ..., X_n) = \prod_{i=1,...,n} \pi(X_i|U_i) \tag{1}$$

The π-pref networks are based on a Markovian independence property which stipulates that each variable X_i is independent of its non-descendants in the context of its parents U_i.

Example 1. Let us consider the π-pref net of Fig. 1 expressing conditional preferences on 4 variables $\mathcal{X} = \{A, B, C, D\}$. Let us then consider the preference specification, e.g., $b\bar{c} : d \succ \bar{d}$. It is expressed by the constraint $\pi(d \mid b\bar{c}) > \pi(\bar{d} \mid b\bar{c})$. Symbolic degrees of preference are assigned: $\pi(d \mid b\bar{c}) = 1$ and $\pi(\bar{d} \mid b\bar{c}) = \delta_2$. The same procedure is followed for all the preference specifications listed in the left-hand table of Fig. 1. The degree of each configuration is calculated using the product-based chaining rule. Let us take as an illustration the configuration $\omega = a\bar{b}cd$. By applying the Eq. (1), we obtain the following result: $\pi(a\bar{b}cd) = \pi(d \mid \bar{b}c) \cdot \pi(c \mid \bar{b}) \cdot \pi(\bar{b} \mid a) \cdot \pi(a) = \delta_3 \cdot \gamma_2 \cdot \beta_1 \cdot 1 = \beta_1\gamma_2\delta_3$.

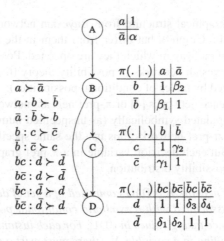

Fig. 1. Example of a π-pref net

It can be observed from the above example that if a node is associated with a conditional preference, the symbolic weights appearing in different contexts have no reason to be equal: the violation of a preference may be a source of more dissatisfaction in one context than in another.

Recall that it has been established that the partial order between configurations provided by the application of the chaining rule with symbolic weights corresponds exactly to the (partial) Pareto order on the preference violation vectors. The components of these vectors are the degrees of satisfaction of the preferences associated with each node for the considered configurations; see Fig. 2. Thus in the Example of Fig. 1, $a\bar{b}cd \succ ab\bar{c}d \succ ab\bar{c}\bar{d} \succ \bar{a}b\bar{c}\bar{d}$, but $abcd$ et $ab\bar{c}d$ are incomparable.

If we agree to associate a single symbolic weight per node (i.e., in the Example in Fig. 1, $\beta_1 = \beta_2 = \beta$, $\gamma_1 = \gamma_2 = \gamma$, $\delta_1 = \delta_2 = \delta_3 = \delta_4 = \delta$), then more comparisons become possible (thus $ab\bar{c}d \succ ab\bar{c}\bar{d}$). The partial order obtained corresponds exactly to the *order of inclusion* of the subsets of violated preferences (we consider that only one preference is associated to each node, without introducing any distinction between the contexts) [4].

The π-pref network framework allows us to add importance relations between the preferences associated with the nodes in the form of inequalities between symbolic weights, which allows us to refine the order of the inclusion [2]. For example we can add $\alpha > \beta > \gamma > \delta$. This expresses that it is less serious to violate the preference(s) on the variable A than those on the variable B, which are themselves of lesser priority than

Ω	$\vec{\omega}$
$abcd$	$(1\,1\,1\,1)$
$abc\bar{d}$	$(1\,1\,1\delta_1)$
$ab\bar{c}d$	$(1\,1\gamma_1\,1)$
$ab\bar{c}\bar{d}$	$(1\,1\gamma_1\delta_2)$
$a\bar{b}cd$	$(1\beta_1\gamma_2\delta_3)$
$a\bar{b}c\bar{d}$	$(1\beta_1\gamma_2\,1)$
$a\bar{b}\bar{c}d$	$(1\beta_1\,1\delta_4)$
$a\bar{b}\bar{c}\bar{d}$	$(1\beta_1\,1\,1)$
$\bar{a}bcd$	$(\alpha\beta_2\,1\,1))$
$\bar{a}bc\bar{d}$	$(\alpha\beta_2\,1\delta_1))$
$\bar{a}b\bar{c}d$	$(\alpha\beta_2\gamma_1\,1)$
$\bar{a}b\bar{c}\bar{d}$	$(\alpha\beta_2\gamma_1\delta_2)$
$\bar{a}\bar{b}cd$	$(\alpha\,1\gamma_2\delta_3)$
$\bar{a}\bar{b}c\bar{d}$	$(\alpha\,1\gamma_2\,1)$
$\bar{a}\bar{b}\bar{c}d$	$(\alpha\,1\,1\delta_4)$
$\bar{a}\bar{b}\bar{c}\bar{d}$	$(\alpha\,1\,1\,1)$

Fig. 2. Example 1: Vectors associated to the configurations

those on the variable C, and that the preferences on D are of greater priority than those on C. If we add this total order information between the nodes in the Example in Fig. 1, we obtain an order which now makes it possible to make the comparison $ab\bar{c}d \succ abc\bar{d}$, but which remains partial: one cannot compare $ab\bar{c}\bar{d}$ either with $\bar{a}\bar{b}\bar{c}\bar{d}$, or with $\bar{a}bcd$. This would require comparing $\gamma\delta$ with α, and with $\alpha\beta$, respectively.

Remark: One way to obtain a complete preorder in the form of an ordered partition E of configurations, is to rely on the number of nodes where the associated preference is violated. For the Example in Fig. 1, we obtain $\mathcal{E} = \{E_1, E_2, E_3, E_4, E_5\}$ consisting of 5 ordered sets of configurations from most preferred to worst:

$E_1 = \{abcd\}$ (0 violation),
$E_2 = \{abc\bar{d}, ab\bar{c}d, a\bar{b}\bar{c}\bar{d}, \bar{a}b\bar{c}\bar{d}\}$ (1 violation),
$E_3 = \{ab\bar{c}\bar{d}, a\bar{b}c\bar{d}, a\bar{b}\bar{c}d, \bar{a}bcd, \bar{a}\bar{b}c\bar{d}, \bar{a}\bar{b}\bar{c}\bar{d}\}$ (2 violations),
$E_4 = \{a\bar{b}cd, \bar{a}bc\bar{d}, \bar{a}b\bar{c}d, \bar{a}\bar{b}cd\}$ (3 violations), and
$E_5 = \{\bar{a}\bar{b}\bar{c}d\}$ (4 violations).

This pre-order refines the partial order based on inclusion. It would be possible to refine this pre-order based on importance inequalities between variables as mentioned above.

3 Lexicographic Preferences

Lexicographic preference trees (LP-trees in the following), which are said to be *complete*, require that a total order is given between *all* the variables, which reflects a relationship of relative importance between the preferences associated with them. There are several types of LP-trees [13] depending on i) whether or not the preferences are conditional, ii) whether or not the order of importance of the variables depends on the value of the variables. We give an example of the 4 possible types of complete LP-trees induced by this double dichotomy.

If the order of importance of the variables is not conditioned, i.e., it does not depend on their values, the LP-tree is *linear*, like those in Fig. 3. In all the figures an arrow in *dotted* line that goes from a node X to a node Y indicates that the node X is more important than the node Y.

Let us first examine the LP-tree of Fig. 3a. For each node/variable the preference between its two possible values is shown. None of these preferences are conditional in Fig. 3a. Comparing two configurations on the basis of a linear LP-tree with unconditional preferences is very simple: it is enough to compare them on the basis of *the most important variable for which their values differ*. Thus $abc\bar{d} \succ ab\bar{c}d$, because $c \succ \bar{c}$. This easily gives the following total order:

$$abcd \succ abc\bar{d} \succ ab\bar{c}d \succ ab\bar{c}\bar{d} \succ a\bar{b}cd \succ a\bar{b}c\bar{d} \succ a\bar{b}\bar{c}d \succ a\bar{b}\bar{c}\bar{d} \succ$$
$$\bar{a}bcd \succ \bar{a}bc\bar{d} \succ \bar{a}b\bar{c}d \succ \bar{a}b\bar{c}\bar{d} \succ \bar{a}\bar{b}cd \succ \bar{a}\bar{b}c\bar{d} \succ \bar{a}\bar{b}\bar{c}d \succ \bar{a}\bar{b}\bar{c}\bar{d}$$

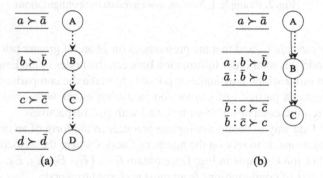

Fig. 3. Two linear LP trees. Note conditional preferences in (b).

In Fig. 3b, the preferences of nodes B and C are conditional. The comparison between 2 configurations is still made on the most important variable for which their values differ, by applying the relevant conditional preference. Thus $\bar{a}b\bar{c} \succ \bar{a}bc$ since $\bar{a} : \bar{b} \succ b$. We obtain the following total order:

$$abc \succ ab\bar{c} \succ a\bar{b}\bar{c} \succ a\bar{b}c \succ \bar{a}\bar{b}\bar{c} \succ \bar{a}\bar{b}c \succ \bar{a}bc \succ \bar{a}b\bar{c}$$

The order of importance of variables can depend on *the value of more important variables*, an idea introduced in [9]. This is the case in Fig. 4 where the preferences remain unconditional. Each new dependency induces a new sub-branch. Each path from the root to a leaf defines an order of importance of the variables, for the context of the

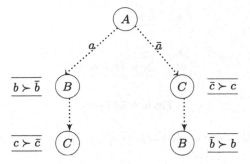

Fig. 4. Multi-branches LP-tree

value(s) that determined the branch(es) defining this path. To compare two configurations, it is necessary to know which variable(s) they differ on. If this includes one or more variables involved in defining the branches, then the preference associated with the most important of these variables determines the order. If the difference in configurations involves only variables not included in the definition of the branches, then the path corresponding to their common "context" must be identified, and the linear LP-trees procedure applied: In the example in Fig. 4 we obtain:

$$abc \succ ab\bar{c} \succ a\bar{b}c \succ a\bar{b}\bar{c} \succ \bar{a}\bar{b}\bar{c} \succ \bar{a}b\bar{c} \succ \bar{a}\bar{b}c \succ \bar{a}bc$$

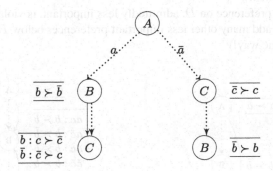

Fig. 5. A "general LP-tree"

Figure 5 is a more general example than Fig. 4, with a conditional preference. The mechanism for comparing configurations is very similar to that described for Fig. 4. It gives here (the order of $a\bar{b}\bar{c}$ and $a\bar{b}c$ is reversed compared to that of Fig. 4):

$$abc \succ ab\bar{c} \succ a\bar{b}\bar{c} \succ a\bar{b}c \succ \bar{a}\bar{b}\bar{c} \succ \bar{a}b\bar{c} \succ \bar{a}\bar{b}c \succ \bar{a}bc$$

Moreover, as in Fig. 6, there may be only one *complete preorder* between the variables, which leads to putting variables of equal importance in the same node (and to having to specify more preferences for this node!). In the case of Fig. 6 we obtain of course:

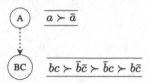

Fig. 6. A 2-LP-tree

$$abc \succ a\bar{b}\bar{c} \succ a\bar{b}c \succ ab\bar{c} \succ \bar{a}bc \succ \bar{a}\bar{b}\bar{c} \succ \bar{a}\bar{b}c \succ \bar{a}b\bar{c}$$

Note that the fact of declaring two variables of equal importance *does not authorise the separate expression of preferences concerning them*: in Fig. 6, if we had, e.g., $b \succ \bar{b}$ and $c \succ \bar{c}$, we would no longer be able to compare $ab\bar{c}$ and $a\bar{b}c$.

Moreover, there is nothing to prevent having an LP-tree like the one in Fig. 7a where the preferences of a node depend on several important variables (we have in fact $abc \succ ab\bar{c} \succ a\bar{b}c \succ a\bar{b}\bar{c} \succ \bar{a}b\bar{c} \succ \bar{a}bc \succ \bar{a}\bar{b}\bar{c} \succ \bar{a}\bar{b}c$). Even if it seems that no example can be found in the literature, conditioning could a priori also depend on less important variables. But this can lead to troubling situations as in Fig. 7b, where B is conditioned by both A more important and C less important. If we then seek to compare $ab\bar{c}\bar{d}$ and $a\bar{b}cd$, it seems that we are led to prefer the second configuration since $c \succ \bar{c}$ and no constraint concerning the more important variable B applies (yet the value of B in $ab\bar{c}\bar{d}$ is the preferred value in the context $a\bar{c}$ and the value of B in $a\bar{b}cd$ is not its preferred value in the ac context).

Moreover, the preference on D, admittedly less important, is violated by $a\bar{b}cd$ (and one could besides add many other less important preferences below D which would be violated in the same way!)

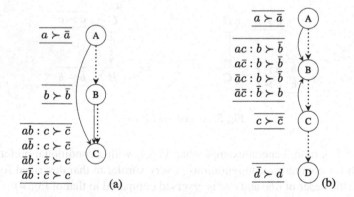

Fig. 7. Multiple conditionings

Lastly, let us also mention partial lexicographic preference trees (PLP-trees) [18] that allow tree with paths on which some variables may be missing. Hence, PLP-trees describe total preorders (instead of total orders). This relaxation is of interest in a learning perspective [18].

4 Comparison π-pref-net/LP-tree

Let's start by indicating several differences, more or less obvious, between π-pref-nets and LP-trees, after their respective presentations in the previous sections:

- complete LP-trees (where all variables are ordered) lead to a total order of configurations. The π-pref networks generally lead to only a partial order, even when adding constraints on inequalities between the symbolic weights associated with the variables, as shown in Example in Fig. 1;
- The π-pref networks allow the expression of the indifference between configurations, notably if we have conditional constraints such as $a : b \sim \bar{b}$ or if we have equalities between symbolic weights. With an LP-tree there are no tie configurations;
- For π-pref networks the structure of conditional preferences is only constrained by the structure of the DAG (more general than that of a tree);
- Even if lexicographical orders, because of their simplicity, are very present in human cognition [15], the fact of always leading to a total order of the configurations presents a forced character which can be all the less acceptable cognitively as there are many variables. In particular, the LP-tree idea is not compatible with the order provided by weighted averages of not very different weights. Indeed let us suppose that we have 4 Boolean variables A, B, C, D of respective weights α, β, γ, δ such that $\alpha + \beta + \gamma + \delta = 1$ with $\alpha \geq \beta \geq \gamma \geq \delta$; the lexicographic constraint $a \succ \bar{a}$ implies $\alpha \geq \beta + \gamma + \delta$, the lexicographic constraint $b \succ \bar{b}$ implies $\beta \geq \gamma + \delta$ the constraint $c \succ \bar{c}$ implies $\gamma \geq \delta$. We can therefore see that the weights must decrease rapidly. The networks are in comparison much more flexible.

However, let us examine whether it is possible to impose symbolic constraints in a π-pref network so that it is equivalent to an LP-tree. Let us first consider the simple case of a linear LP-tree as in Fig. 3a before dealing with the general case illustrated by Fig. 5.

For the LP-tree of Fig. 3a, each of the constraints $a \succ \bar{a}$, $b \succ \bar{b}$, $c \succ \bar{c}$, $d \succ \bar{d}$ is translated respectively by the possibility distributions $(1, \alpha)$, $(1, \beta)$, $(1, \gamma)$, $(1, \delta)$ on $\{a, \bar{a}\}$, $\{b, \bar{b}\}$, $\{c, \bar{c}\}$, $\{d, \bar{d}\}$ respectively. The order of importance of the variables induces the constraint $\alpha \leq \beta \leq \gamma \leq \delta$. But as can be seen by examining the table in Fig. 8, this constraint is not sufficient to recover the lexicographical order. We must add the constraints $\alpha \leq \beta \times \gamma \times \delta$ and $\beta \leq \gamma \times \delta$ to recover it (the first constraint, for example, ensures that $a\bar{b}\bar{c}\bar{d} \succ \bar{a}bcd$). The syntax of these products shows that it is easy to generalise the constraints to be added for a linear LP-tree with any number of variables.

The LP-tree of Fig. 5 which has for root A with preference $a \succ \bar{a}$ encoded by the distribution $(1, \alpha)$ on $\{a, \bar{a}\}$, has two branches. The one on the right (context $\bar{a}$) is coded with the two distributions $(\beta_2, 1)$, $(\gamma_3, 1)$ on $\{b, \bar{b}\}$ and on $\{c, \bar{c}\}$ respectively for the preferences $\bar{c} \succ c$ and $\bar{b} \succ b$. The constraint $\gamma_3 \leq \beta_2$ ensures the lexicographic order on this branch. As for the left branch (context a), we have on the one hand the distribution $(1, \beta_1)$ on $\{b, \bar{b}\}$ for $b \succ \bar{b}$, and on the other hand the distributions $(1, \gamma_1)$ on $\{c, \bar{c}\}$ if $B = b$ is true and $(\gamma_2, 1)$ on $\{c, \bar{c}\}$ if $B = \bar{b}$, with the importance constraints $\beta_1 \leq \min(\gamma_1, \gamma_2)$. This ensures the desired lexicographical order on this branch. The

Ω	$\vec{\omega}$
$abcd$	$(1\ 1\ 1\ 1)$
$abc\bar{d}$	$(1\ 1\ 1\ \delta)$
$ab\bar{c}d$	$(1\ 1\ \gamma\ 1)$
$ab\bar{c}\bar{d}$	$(1\ 1\ \gamma\ \delta)$
$a\bar{b}cd$	$(1\ \beta\ 1\ 1)$
$a\bar{b}c\bar{d}$	$(1\ \beta\ 1\ \delta)$
$a\bar{b}\bar{c}d$	$(1\ \beta\ \gamma\ 1)$
$a\bar{b}\bar{c}\bar{d}$	$(1\beta\ \gamma\ \delta)$
$\bar{a}bcd$	$(\alpha\ 1\ 1\ 1)$
$\bar{a}bc\bar{d}$	$(\alpha\ 1\ 1\ \delta)$
$\bar{a}b\bar{c}d$	$(\alpha\ 1\ \gamma\ 1)$
$\bar{a}b\bar{c}\bar{d}$	$(\alpha\ 1\gamma\ \delta)$
$\bar{a}\bar{b}cd$	$(\alpha\ \beta\ 1\ 1)$
$\bar{a}\bar{b}c\bar{d}$	$(\alpha\ \beta\ 1\ \delta)$
$\bar{a}\bar{b}\bar{c}d$	$(\alpha\ \beta\ \gamma\ 1)$
$\bar{a}\bar{b}\bar{c}\bar{d}$	$(\alpha\ \beta\ \gamma\ \delta)$

Fig. 8. Ex. 3a: Vectors associated to configurations

two branches correspond to the table in Fig. 9. To have $a\bar{b}c \succ \bar{a}b\bar{c}$, we must add the constraint $\beta_1 \times \gamma_2 > \alpha$. As can be seen, the process of adding constraints, which is used to represent a linear LP tree, must be repeated on each branch in the case of a general LP tree.

The study of these two examples shows that it is necessary to add in a π-pref network not only constraints between symbolic weights to reflect the order of importance of nodes in a (sub)-branch, but also constraints involving products (with a number of terms that increases with the number of variables) to obtain a fully lexicographic order. This echoes the price to be paid for obtaining such an order under all circumstances.

Ω	$\vec{\omega}$
abc	$(1\ 1\ 1)$
$ab\bar{c}$	$(1\ 1\ \gamma_1)$
$a\bar{b}\bar{c}$	$(1\ \beta_1\ 1)$
$a\bar{b}c$	$(1\ \beta_1\ \gamma_2)$
$\bar{a}b\bar{c}$	$(\alpha\ 1\ 1)$
$\bar{a}b\bar{c}$	$(\alpha\ \beta_2\ 1)$
$\bar{a}bc$	$(\alpha\ 1\ \gamma_3)$
$\bar{a}bc$	$(\alpha\ \beta_2\gamma_3)$

Fig. 9. Ex. 5: Vectors associated to configurations

Let us note finally that the 2-LP-tree of Fig. 6 does not pose any particular difficulty and is easily expressed in the form of π-pref network with the possibility distributions $(1, \alpha)$ on $\{a, \bar{a}\}$, $(1, \beta, \gamma, \delta)$ on $bc, \bar{b}\bar{c}$, $(1, \beta, \gamma, \delta)$ on $bc, \bar{b}\bar{c}, \bar{b}c, b\bar{c}$ with the constraints inequality $\alpha < \min(\beta, \gamma, \delta)$ and $\beta > \gamma > \delta$.

5 Concluding Remarks

The introduction of LP-trees has been largely motivated by their use in preference learning [13,14]. If we consider that we can extrapolate a user's preferences from the observation of her/his preferences between a rather small number of configurations, making the assumption that we are trying to learn an LP-tree can constitute a rather important representation bias: there are many ways to complete a partial order in total order in general! In fact, the natural cognitive attitude of humans to express preferences is to allow also the expression of indifference as well as to find non-comparable configurations. From this point of view, the representation offered by π-pref networks is not biased, because it obeys at least the Pareto order (which seems to be not very debatable), and can be modulated by adding constraints between the symbolic weights. Moreover one could consider learning the symbolic weights *numerically*. Indeed there is a numerical counterpart [12] to π-pref networks in terms of networks of "ordinal conditional functions" (i.e., Spohn's "kappa functions", very close to possibility theory [11]).

References

1. Ben Amor, N., Benferhat, S.: Graphoid properties of qualitative possibilistic independence relations. Int. J. Uncert. Fuzz. Know.-Based Syst. **13**, 59–96 (2005)
2. Ben Amor, N., Dubois, D., Gouider, H., Prade, H.: Preference modeling with possibilistic networks and symbolic weights: a theoretical study. In: Proceedings of the 22nd European Conference on Artificial Intelligence (ECAI 2016), The Hague, 29 August–2 September, pp. 1203–1211 (2016)
3. Ben Amor, N., Dubois, D., Gouider, H., Prade, H.: Graphical models for preference representation: an overview. In: Schockaert, S., Senellart, P. (eds.) SUM 2016. LNCS (LNAI), vol. 9858, pp. 96–111. Springer, Cham (2016). https://doi.org/10.1007/978-3-319-45856-4_7
4. Ben Amor, N., Dubois, D., Gouider, H., Prade, H.: Possibilistic preference networks. Inf. Sci. **460–461**, 401–415 (2018)
5. Benferhat, S., Dubois, D., Garcia, L., Prade, H.: On the transformation between possibilistic logic bases and possibilistic causal networks. Int. J. Approx. Reas. **29**, 135–173 (2002)
6. Booth, R., Chevaleyre, Y., Lang, J., Mengin, J., Sombattheera, C.: Learning conditionally lexicographic preference relations. In: Proceedings of the 19th European Conference on Artificial Intelligence (ECAI), pp. 269–274 (2010)
7. Boutilier, C., Brafman, R., Domshlak, C., Hoos, H., Poole, D.: CP-nets: a tool for representing and reasoning with conditional ceteris paribus preference statements. J. Artif. Intell. Res **21**, 135–191 (2004)
8. Brafman, R.I., Domshlak, C., Shimony, S.E.: On graphical modeling of preference and importance. J. Artif. Intell. Res. **25**, 389–424 (2006)
9. Bräuning, M., Hüllermeier, E.: Learning conditional lexicographic preference trees. In: Fürnkranz, J., Hüllermier (eds.) Proceedings of ECAI 2012 Workshop on Preference Learning of the European Conference on Artiticial Intelligence, Montpellier (2012)

10. Dubois, D., Hadjali, A., Prade, H., Touazi, F.: Erratum to: database preference queries - a possibilistic logic approach with symbolic priorities. Ann. Math. Artif. Intell. **73**(3–4), 359–363 (2015)
11. Dubois, D., Prade, H.: Qualitative and semi-quanlitative modeling of uncertain knowledge - a discussion. In: Computational Models of Rationality. Essays Dedicated to Gabriele Kern-Isberner on the Occasion of Her 60th Birthday, pp. 280–292. College Publications (2016)
12. Eichhorn, Ch., Fey, M., Kern-Isberner, G.: CP- and OCF-networks - a comparison. Fuzzy Sets Syst. **298**, 109–127 (2016)
13. Fargier, H., Gimenez, P.-F., Mengin, J.: Learning lexicographic preference trees from positive examples. In: Proceedings of the 32nd Conference on Artificial Intelligence (AAAI 2018), pp. 2959–2966 (2018)
14. Fürnkranz, J., Hüllermeier, E. (eds.): Preference Learning. Springer, Heidelberg (2011). https://doi.org/10.1007/978-3-642-14125-6
15. Gigerenzer, G., Goldstein, D.G.: Reasoning the fast and frugal way: models of bounded rationality. Psychol. Rev. **103**(4), 650–669 (1996)
16. Huelsman, M., Truszczynski, M.: A lexicographic strategy for approximating dominance in CP-nets. In: Proceedings of the 33rd International Florida Artificial Intelligence Research Society Conference (FLAIRS), pp. 59–74 (2020)
17. Kaci, S., Lang, J., Perny, P.: Compact representation of preferences. In: Marquis, P., Papini, O., Prade, H. (eds.) A Guided Tour of Artificial Intelligence Research, pp. 217–252. Springer, Cham (2020). https://doi.org/10.1007/978-3-030-06164-7_7
18. Liu, X., Truszczynski, M.: Learning partial lexicographic preference trees over combinatorial domains. In: Bonet, B., Koenig, S. (eds.) Proceedings of the 29th AAAI Conference on Artificial Intelligence (AAAI 2015), Austin, Texas, 25–30 January, pp. 1539–1545. AAAI Press (2015)
19. Lang, J., Mengin, J., Xia, L.: Aggregating conditionally lexicographic preferences on multi-issue domains. In: Proceedings of the 18th International Conference on Principles and Practice of Constraint Program (CP 2012), pp. 973–987 (2012)
20. Wilson, N.: Computational techniques for a simple theory of conditional preferences. Artif. Intell. **175**, 1053–1091 (2011)
21. Wilson, N., Dubois, D., Prade, H.: CP-nets, π-pref nets, and pareto dominance. In: Ben Amor, N., Quost, B., Theobald, M. (eds.) SUM 2019. LNCS (LNAI), vol. 11940, pp. 169–183. Springer, Cham (2019). https://doi.org/10.1007/978-3-030-35514-2_13

Generating Contextual Weighted Commonsense Knowledge Graphs

Navid Rezaei[1]([⊠])(iD), Marek Z. Reformat[1,2](iD), and Ronald R. Yager[3,4](iD)

[1] University of Alberta, Edmonton T6G 1H9, Canada
{nrezaeis,marek.reformat}@ualberta.ca
[2] University of Social Sciences, 90-113, Łódź, Poland
[3] Iona College, New York 10801, USA
yager@panix.com
[4] King Abdulaziz University, Jeddah, Saudi Arabia

Abstract. There has been a renewed interest in commonsense knowledge and reasoning. To achieve artificial general intelligence, systems must exhibit not only the recognition abilities of humans but also other important aspects of being human, such as commonsense and causality. Recent literature has shown that external commonsense knowledge graphs are beneficial to a variety of systems in multiple ways, including improvements in the commonsense abilities of deep learning models. This paper investigates an auto-generation of weighted commonsense knowledge graphs representing general information, as well as graphs containing contextual information. The method leads to the construction of graphs equipped with frequency based weights associated with nodes and relations. The proposed construction methodology has the advantage of a never-ending learning paradigm. We evaluate the constructed contextual knowledge graphs qualitatively and quantitatively. The commonsense knowledge graphs are inherently explainable and can support commonsense reasoning. We analyze commonsense reasoning approaches using contextual graphs and discuss the results.

Keywords: Commonsense Knowledge Graph · Context Awareness · Possibility Theory · Deep Learning

1 Introduction

There has been a renewed interest in commonsense as part of achieving human-like intelligence. Recent literature, [8,21], has shown the importance of commonsense knowledge graphs in training artificial intelligence (AI) models with commonsense. Knowledge graphs (KGs) are a semantically rich representation of data where each piece of information is represented as a triple made of a subject (s), predicate (p), and object (o) as in $s \rightarrow p \rightarrow o$. Subjects and objects are graph nodes, while predicates are edges.

This paper introduces a methodology for generating contextual weighted commonsense KGs using vision-based deep learning models. Among different

© Springer Nature Switzerland AG 2022
D. Ciucci et al. (Eds.): IPMU 2022, CCIS 1601, pp. 593–606, 2022.
https://doi.org/10.1007/978-3-031-08971-8_49

types of commonsense, such as social interactions and events, we focus on generating the physical commonsense graphs.

The choice of visual data to generate commonsense knowledge is an attempt to mimic the human way of learning. Even before developing linguistic skills, a human toddler acquires a good grasp of physical commonsense, for example, position of items in relevance to each other. This commonsense knowledge is further solidified by interacting with the real world and developing language to gain extra knowledge.

1.1 Defining Commonsense

First, it is imperative to have a clear definition of what commonsense is. A good definition paves the way to discuss the details better.

Commonsense, as John McCarthy puts it, can be distinguished in two different aspects: knowledge and ability [12]. The knowledge refers to the common knowledge gained, and the ability means to act based on the knowledge gained.

Yann LeCun, one of the inventors of convolutional neural networks, defines commonsense as a collection of models of the world, which can lead us to know what is likely, what is plausible, what is impossible [9].

The human perception gained through different senses, such as vision or touch, is the base for constructing commonsense KGs. This knowledge is context-dependent and can differ between individuals. For instance, the people who live in the northern hemisphere of the earth know the month of July to be a hot summer month, while the people in the southern hemisphere observe it as a cold winter month. Context is not limited to physical or geographical locations, but it can also include temporal aspects. For example, it is more common to see more formally dressed people in the 1960s than in the 2020s.s.

Additionally, unlike factual knowledge, commonsense knowledge is inherently uncertain. More probable phenomena are more likely part of common knowledge; while, less probable occurrences make less sense for most people.

We can also classify commonsense into different categories, including physical concepts, events, and social interactions. An example of physical commonsense is seeing desks in a classroom, and of an event one is lighting a match to start a fire. In social constructs, saying thanks after receiving a gift is commonsense.

The goal of this work is to automatically extract contextual commonsense knowledge from visual data and represent it in the format of a knowledge graph. The graph has weighted edges that illustrate levels of certainty in the extracted information. Commonsense graphs are used for many purposes, including reasoning, which is shown here.

1.2 Related Work

There have been several works in the literature regarding gathering and constructing commonsense KGs.

ConceptNet [18] originated from the crowdsourced project of Open Mind Common Sense has grown into an extensive KG that includes some degree of commonsense. It comprises 36 relations focusing on taxonomies, lexical knowledge, and physical commonsense knowledge. ConceptNet v5.7 includes around 3.4 million triples. It combines crowdsourcing with other databases, such as DBPedia, WordNet, Wikitionary, and Open Cyc. As highlighted in [8], almost 90% of the triples are related to taxonomies and lexical data.

NEIL method [3] focuses on extracting object relationships from images. It has resulted in a graph with 10,000 triples built around ten types of relations. Another process, LEVAN [4], uses a semi-automatic text processing and results in a KG with less than 100 predicate types and around 34 million triples. WebChild KB 2.0 [19] uses text and image/video captions to automatically mine commonsense knowledge. The result is a graph with over 1,000 predicate types and 18 million triples. Quasimodo [16] uses texts in logs and forums to mine commonsense. The result is 2.3 million triples, while the number of predicate types is dynamic. TransOMCS [25] mines linguistic graphs to generate a graph similar to ConceptNet with about 18.48 million triples. Such processes can be supported by other image-specific tasks [2].

World-perceiving KG (WpKG) [15] introduces a methodology to auto-generate commonsense KGs purely based on visual data. The commonsense KG includes 50 predicate types, 150 entity types, and over 7,000 triples. It can be expanded based on the vocabulary and the underlying scene graph generation models.

A recent body of work, [8,21], focuses on annotating commonsense KGs to use them for training language models to predict commonsense results given a subject and a predicate. The human-annotated KGs are typically in the size of millions and cover social interactions, events, and entity commonsense.

1.3 Contributions

As described in the introduction, commonsense knowledge is context-dependent, whether the context is temporal or spatial. To the best of our knowledge, no recent paper has focused on generating commonsense knowledge adapted to specific contexts. Current commonsense KGs, such as ConceptNet [18], lack contextual awareness.

This paper introduces a methodology to auto-generate contextual weighted commonsense knowledge using images from different contexts. We focus on the feasibility and correctness of the results obtained instead of the size of the graph.

Commonsense is inherently uncertain and subject to the amount of processed data. In order to capture this, we propose three ways to assign weights to graph edges (triples) based on the information extracted from the images. We evaluate these weighting methods to see how they resonate with human commonsense.

Using the proposed method, we generate a context-free weighted commonsense KG, as well as contextual weighted commonsense KGs for 93 physical contexts. Given the contextual commonsense KGs, we show different reasoning examples using possibilistic theory.

The code and the data are available under https://github.com/navidre/contextual_commonsense_kg.

2   Methodology

We have introduced a method for generating commonsense KGs from images using scene graph generation models in [15]. In this paper, we build on the foundations of the previously published work.

The introduced process starts with detecting objects in a set of images and predicting relationships between them. Then, based on the obtained results, it creates scene graphs (Sect. 2.1) – one per image. Finally, the method aggregates the scene graphs into a final weighted commonsense KG (Sect. 2.2). The overall process is depicted in Fig. 1.

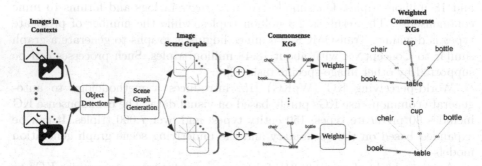

Fig. 1. The process of generating contextual commonsense KGs from images using deep learning models. Each path focuses on a single context, and the widths of edges (the right-most graphs) represent triple weights.

The previously published method [15] is improved by utilizing state-of-the-art object detection and scene graph generation models in a context-free manner. Furthermore, after minor modifications, we use the same context-free commonsense knowledge generation process to construct contextual commonsense knowledge graphs using only images as input.

2.1   Processing of Images

The first stage of the process focuses on the generation of scene graphs. A scene graph is created from a single image – detected objects are represented as nodes, and the relationships between nodes are represented as directed edges. For example, to represent a person sitting on a bench, we could have *Man-2* as the subject, where 2 is the second instance of the object *Man*, *sitting on* as the predicate, and *Bench-1* as the object.

Object and Relation Detection. To detect objects a pre-trained Faster-RCNN [14] model is used. To determine the image features, ResNeXt-101-FPN convolutional neural network (CNN) is applied instead of simpler VGG-16, which results in over 7% mAP (mean average precision) score improvement on the

COCO validation dataset [10,11,17,22]. In the Faster-RCNN algorithm, a model called Region Proposal Network (RPN) uses the CNN-generated image features to predict regions containing objects. After pooling the features with regions of interest, a classifier predicts object class scores.

Generation of Scene Graphs. In this paper, we focus on the generation of scene graphs from images with no annotations. We apply MOTIFS model [24], which has been relatively unbiased using Causal-TDE method [20]. Compared to several other models in the literature, this combination is promising. Given the predicted bounding boxes, object labels, and the regions-of-interest generated by the Fast-RCNN object detection model, the MOTIFS model uses bidirectional LSTMs (Bi-LSTMs) to predict the object features. Using these features, the MOTIFS model finetunes the object classes. Using pairwise object features, the MOTIFS model uses another set of Bi-LSTMs to predict the predicate (relation) labels. The Causal-Total Direct Effect (Causal-TDE) unbiasing method tries to mitigate the long-tail distribution among predicated types, where most predicate predictions comprise a few common types.

2.2 Formalizing Commonsense Knowledge Graph Generation

The task of aggregating scene graphs into an overall knowledge base has a few challenges of its own [15]. Some of the main challenges are: 1) quantifying and calculating the importance of scene graph triples; 2) identifying and removing incorrect data; 3) updating the graph with new knowledge; and 4) considering the different meanings of entities in different contexts.

The first task is to detect all viable objects and their relations based on the generated scene graphs. A list of the detected objects is called D_O, and a list of the detected triples is called D_T. Next, we aggregate unique triples, such as *fork-besides-plate*, to construct a KG.

Next, we calculate the weights of triples. To calculate the weights, we investigate three different methods. 1) *Detection Probability-based Method (DPbM)*. We assign to each triple a probability of its detection provided by the applied method (Sect. 2.1). Then, we aggregate all the probabilities assigned to the same triple in the form of a weighted sum. This sum is the final weight of the triple. 2) *Relative Occurrence Method (ROM)*. We calculate the number of detected occurrences of each triple in all scene graphs. Then, we divide it by the number of detected occurrences of the triple's object in the same context. 3) *Weighted Occurrence Method (WOM)*. This method is similar to the second one. The difference is that we count the 'effect' number of triples and objects by weighting each occurrence by its probability of detection. See Eq. 1 for clarification.

Detection Probability-based Method (DPbM):

$$w_{t_i} = \sum_{j=1}^{|D_T|} \delta\left(t_i, t_j\right) \cdot P(t_j) \tag{1a}$$

Relative Occurrence Method (ROM):

$$w_{t_i} = \frac{\sum_{j=1}^{|D_T|} \delta\left(t_i, t_j\right)}{\sum_{j=1}^{|D_O|} \delta\left(o_i, o_j\right)} \tag{1b}$$

Weighted Occurrence Method (WOM):

$$w_{t_i} = \frac{\sum_{j=1}^{|D_T|} \delta\left(t_i, t_j\right) \cdot P(t_j)}{\sum_{j=1}^{|D_O|} \delta\left(o_i, o_j\right) \cdot P(o_j)} \tag{1c}$$

where w_{t_i} is a weight of the t_i triple, $\delta(\cdot)$ is the Kronecker delta function, $P(t_j)$ represents the probability of detecting triple t_j by the scene graph generation model, which is made of a subject (s), predicate (p), and object (o). The weights are normalized by $\max\{w_{t_i} : t_i \in D_T\}$. Please note that all the calculations are done for each context independently as there is one generated knowledge graph per context.

To identify and remove incorrect data, a progressive method is applied. We use the triple weights to determine which triples are more commonsensical and sort the results based on the weights.

For the case of new images, new scene graphs are generated. As a result, the weights of the existing triples are updated, or new weighted triples are added. It means that our approach represents a never-ending learning paradigm, where the knowledge graph is easily updated in the presence of new data.

The generic nature of the method gives the ability to generate commonsense knowledge graphs based on context. The paper focuses on physical contexts, such as restaurants or parks. We show that the same proposed method can generate contextual commonsense knowledge when applied to different contexts. We further evaluate this claim quantitatively in the results section.

3   Generation of Commonsense Knowledge Graphs

Firstly, we construct a commonsense KG with no contexts, which is superior to the one described in [15] in size and quality. Then, we focus on generating commonsense KGs based on different contexts and their human-based evaluation.

3.1   Context-Free Commonsense Knowledge Graph

To demonstrate the generation of context-free commonsense KGs, we use the testing section of the Visual Genome (VG) dataset, which has a size of 31,876 images (around 30% of the dataset). To generate scene graphs, we use MOTIFS model unbiased with Causal-TDE method that is able to recognize 150 types of entities, such as *door*, *airplane*, or *horse*, and 50 types of predicates (relations), for example, *holding*, *sitting*, or *above*. The m R@50 (mean recall at 50) is 8.2. The weights of triples are calculated using Eq. 1.

The resulting context-free commonsense KG generation benefits from upgraded object detection and state-of-the-art scene graph generation compared to the results shown in [15]. The final context-free scene graph generated has 277,634 commonsense triples compared to around 7,000 triples in [15], which is equivalent to around 39 times improvement in size.

3.2 Contextual Commonsense Knowledge Graph

To generate a contextual commonsense knowledge graph, we start with 'raw' images from the Visual Commonsense Reasoning (VCR) dataset [23]. This dataset has around 110,000 images. The images are human-annotated regarding the places they represent. After a cleaning process and removing places with less than 100 images, we end up with 93 different locations. We consider these places as physical contexts, such as a restaurant or classroom.

As explained above (Sect. 2), we process images from each context to detect objects and then to predict relationships between the objects detected. The threshold of keeping the predicted relations is chosen as 0.1 and 0.6 for DPbM and ROM/WOM, respectively. It has ensured obtaining higher confidence in the identified relations. Given the object and relationship detected, we generate a single scene graph for each image. The scene graphs constructed from images belonging to a single context are aggregated to a single KG. The triple weights are assigned using the three different methods explained in Eq. 1. The sizes of the generated knowledge graphs varies depending on the context, but all are less than 1,000 triples, as we have tried to retain only high-quality results.

An example of a contextual commonsense knowledge graph representing a fragment of a graph that combines multiple graphs built for single contexts is illustrated in Fig. 2. It shows the object *plate* connected to tables at different locations. The thickness represents the strength/weight of the relation.

To evaluate how weight assignment mechanisms correlate with human commonsense judgment, we chose the top 100 triples based on each weighting mechanism and gave them to three humans to evaluate. The three annotators have rated each commonsense triple as: "quite commonsensical", "commonsensical", "making sense, but not in this context", and "invalid/unfamiliar in any context". The first two options are considered as accepted. To illustrate the third option, let us take a triple *car having tire* – it makes general sense, but is it not commonsensical, for example, in the restaurant context. A triple *person wearing laptop* makes little sense in any context and results in the fourth option.

Our three volunteer reviewers have evaluated the triples from two contexts: *restaurant* and *classroom*. To measure the agreement among reviewers, we use Krippendorff's Alpha [7], which is a value between 0 and 1. Zero means no agreement and one means complete agreement. As seen in Table 1, the *Detection Probability-based Method (DPbM)* gives the highest correlation with human commonsense, while other methods still show good results.

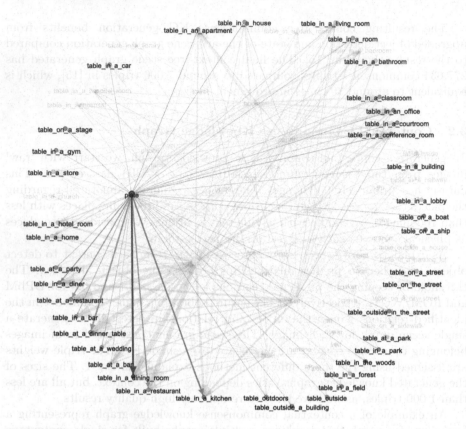

Fig. 2. Snippet of a contextual KG illustrating the item *plate* and its relation to tables at different locations; thickness of lines indicate a strength of the connection.

Table 1. Human evaluation of the three weighting strategies defined in Eq. 1. Three reviewers were given top 100 triples from each restaurant and classroom contextual commonsense knowledge graphs (total of 600 evaluations per method).

Weighing Schema	Accept	Reject	N/A	Accuracy (%)	Alpha
DPbM	560	22	18	**93.0**	**0.78**
ROM	526	60	14	87.6	0.63
WOM	538	51	11	89.7	0.72

4   Reasoning with Contextual Commonsense Knowledge Graph

The contextual commonsense KG allows for performing reasoning tasks. To illustrate a methodology that can utilize a contextual commonsense graph for possibility theory-based reasoning, we incorporate an example with *tables* positioned at different locations and *items* placed on them.

Table 2. *on table*: Number of occurrences of items on table; *total*: Total number of items; Last row: Number of tables. The contexts in this case are bar, classroom, and restaurant. The observations are made in these contexts.

location:	bar		classroom		restaurant	
item:	on table	total	on table	total	on table	total
paper	28	79	124	299	69	222
bottle	125	1562	4	52	108	634
book	20	37	164	362	47	72
laptop	4	17	47	67	37	56
cup	50	287	5	36	98	696
table	1170		837		2603	

The reasoning is based on the commonsense knowledge embedded in the auto-generated contextual knowledge graphs introduced above. The weights linked with triples are converted into occurrences of items in contexts that are considered. These are used to calculate required possibilities.

4.1 Extraction of Relevant Nodes and Occurrences

In the beginning, we extract – from the constructed contextual graph –the information about *tables* at three different places and items that are *on* the tables, i.e., are in the relation *on* with the tables. A snippet of the graph illustrating the information is shown in Figure 3. As we can see, there are several items – *paper*, *bottle*, *book*, *laptop* and *cup* – to be considered, all of which appear on *tables* at the three locations. Although the items *glass* and *plate* are 'seen' at all locations, we do not use them: a) due to ambiguity of *glass* – it can be treated as a 'cup' or as 'lenses'; and b) due to a very small number of occurrences of *plate* at tables in classrooms.

The snippet, Fig. 3, emphasizes one item – *cup* – that has been found at all three locations to a different degree. We see that it 'showed' up 696 times on the restaurant images, but only 98 times on a table in the restaurant. Similarly, there are occurrences of a cup in classroom and bar images.

The specific number of occurrences of individual items on *tables* at three locations are included in Table 2. It contains the numbers of occurrences of a given item on a *table* and the total number of occurrences of the items 'seen' at all considered images of specific locations. Additionally, the table shows the number of times a *table* appeared in pictures at each location. The numbers of pictures we have processed are 1513 of a bar, 692 of a classroom, and 2235 of a restaurant.

4.2 Reasoning: Inference with Uncertain Premises

In the presented reasoning process, we adopt a frequentist setting where possibility measures can be induced from the frequency of observations [6], and the extracted

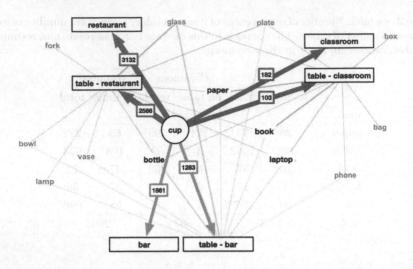

Fig. 3. Subgraph of items *on* tables in restaurant, classroom, and bar. The occurrences of *cup* are emphasized: the number of times on table versus the total number of times.

subgraph is a possibilistic graph [1]. We use a deductive inference with uncertain premises. Following analysis of *Modus Ponens* and *Modus Tollens* [5,13], we apply the following reasoning schema:

$$\Pi(q \mid p) \geq a \tag{2}$$

$$\Pi(p \mid q) \geq a' \tag{3}$$

$$\Pi(p) \in [\, b, \, b' \,] \tag{4}$$

with the consequence:

$$\Pi(q) \in \left[a * b, a' * \rightarrow b' \right] \tag{5}$$

where $*$ is a triangular norm (t-norm), and

$$a' * \rightarrow b' \text{ means } sup\{t \in [0,1], a' * t \leq b'\}.$$

Different selection of $*$ leads to different deduction schemas. For *min*, Eq. 5 becomes:

$$\Pi(q) \in \left[min(a,b), \begin{cases} 1 & if a' \leq b' \\ b' & if a' > b' \end{cases} \right] \tag{6}$$

and for *product*:

$$\Pi(q) \in \left[a \cdot b, \begin{cases} 1 & if a' = 0 \\ min(1, \frac{b'}{a'}) & if a' \neq 0 \end{cases} \right] \tag{7}$$

For calculating a possibility measure of an individual premise, we use:

$$\Pi(p) = \frac{number\ of\ observations\ of\ p}{number\ of\ observations}$$

and for complex premises:

$$\Pi(p_i \wedge p_j) = min(\Pi(p_i), \Pi(p_j))$$

In the presented example, the goal is to deduce a location of tables based on several different items seen on tables. Additionally, we consider two levels of the possibility of seeing these items – we are very confident that the items are on tables, and we are very uncertain about it.

Three different sets of items on *tables* are considered. We define the following premises:

$$p_A = (paper \wedge bottle \wedge book \wedge laptop \wedge cup)$$
$$p_B = (paper \wedge book \wedge laptop)$$
$$p_C = (bottle \wedge cup)$$

For the premises p_A and $q = table\_in\_X$, we have:

$$\Pi(table\_in\_X|p_A) = \frac{|table \wedge paper \wedge bottle \wedge book \wedge laptop \wedge cup|}{|paper \wedge bottle \wedge book \wedge laptop \wedge cup|} \tag{8}$$

The numerator is a number of observations where all items of p_A and *table* occur at the same time. The denominator, on the other hand, is a number of observations where all items of p_A occur. We also have:

$$\Pi(p_A|table\_in\_X) = \frac{|table \wedge paper \wedge bottle \wedge book \wedge laptop \wedge cup|}{|table\_occurrences\_in\_X|} \tag{9}$$

As mentioned above, two possibility measures are used when taking into account items on tables, i.e., different values of b, b' for $\Pi(p)$, Eq. 4. With that, we determine $\Pi(table\_in\_X)$ for three different locations $X = bar$, $X = classroom$, and $X = restaurant$, and we use two t-norms, Eqs. 6 and 7.

The values obtained for $b = b' = 1$, i.e., $\Pi(p_{A|B|C}) = 1$, for both types of t-norm are shown in Table 3. As we can see, different sets of items on a table lead to different values of the lower bounds of possibility intervals. The values confirm commonsense reasoning regarding occurrence of given items on tables at specific locations. It means that the items of the premise p_A lead to the conclusion that the table is in a restaurant, while for the premise p_C points to a bar.

If we change values of b and b' to 0.1, it can be observed that low possibilities of $p_{A|B|C}$ fully 'control' possibilities of locations, Table 4. It becomes evident that conditional parts of the deduction schema are suppressed, seen especially when a t-norm is *min*. On the other hand, more interesting values can be observed when a t-norm is *product*. In that case, the values of the lower bounds of possibility intervals provide more meaningful – commonsense – findings.

Table 3. $\Pi(table\_in\_X)$ for different locations and premises; possibility of premises is 1, i.e. $\Pi(p_A) = \Pi(p_B) = \Pi(p_C) = 1$.

location X:		bar	classroom	restaurant
premise:				
p_A	min	[0.2353, 1]	[0.1111, 1]	**[0.6607, 1]**
	product	[0.2353, 1]	[0.1111, 1]	**[0.6607, 1]**
p_B	min	[0.2353, 1]	**[0.7015, 1]**	[0.6607, 1]
	product	[0.2353, 1]	**[0.7015, 1]**	[0.6607, 1]
p_C	min	**[0.1742, 1]**	[0.1111, 1]	[0.1546, 1]
	product	**[0.1742, 1]**	[0.1111, 1]	[0.1546, 1]

Table 4. $\Pi(table\_in\_X)$ for different locations and premises; possibility of premises is 0.1, i.e. $\Pi(p_A) = \Pi(p_B) = \Pi(p_C) = 0.1$.

location X:		bar	classroom	restaurant
premise:				
p_A	min	[0.1000, 1]	[0.1000, 1]	[0.1000, 1]
	product	[0.0235, 1]	[0.0111, 1]	**[0.0661, 1]**
p_B	min	[0.1000, 1]	[0.1000, 1]	[0.1000, 1]
	product	[0.0235, 1]	**[0.0701, 1]**	[0.0661, 1]
p_C	min	[0.1000, 1]	[0.1000, 1]	[0.1000, 1]
	product	**[0.0174, 1]**	[0.0111, 1]	[0.0155, 1]

5   Conclusion

Commonsense knowledge graphs are shown to benefit many AI technologies, such as transformer-based language models. Hence, their construction is gaining much attention.

This paper presents a methodology for automatically building contextual weighted commonsense knowledge graphs based on the processing of images using deep learning models. Three methods are introduced to assign commonsense weights to the knowledge graph triples. The human evaluation confirms a high correlation between the generated contextual commonsense knowledge and human commonsense in the same context. Moreover, we show how the generated commonsense knowledge can be used to perform possibilistic reasoning.

References

1. Benferhat, S., Dubois, D., Garcia, L., Prade, H.: Possibilistic logic bases and possibilistic graphs. In: Proceedings of the Fifteenth Conference on Uncertainty in Artificial Intelligence, pp. 57–64. UAI 1999. Morgan Kaufmann Publishers Inc., San Francisco (1999)
2. Chamorro-Martínez, J., et al.: Referring expression generation from images via deep learning object extraction and fuzzy graphs. In: 2021 IEEE International Conference on Fuzzy Systems, FUZZ-IEEE, pp. 1–6 (2021)
3. Chen, X., Shrivastava, A., Gupta, A.: NEIL: extracting visual knowledge from web data. In: 2013 IEEE International Conference on Computer Vision, pp. 1409–1416 (2013)
4. Divvala, S.K., Farhadi, A., Guestrin, C.: Learning everything about anything: webly-supervised visual concept learning. In: 2014 IEEE Conference on Computer Vision and Pattern Recognition, pp. 3270–3277 (2014)
5. Dubois, D., Prade, H.: Possibility Theory: An Approach to Computerized Processing of Uncertainty. Springer, US (1988)
6. Dubois, D., Prade, H., Smets, P.: new semantics for quantitative possibility theory. In: Benferhat, S., Besnard, P. (eds.) ECSQARU 2001. LNCS (LNAI), vol. 2143, pp. 410–421. Springer, Heidelberg (2001). https://doi.org/10.1007/3-540-44652-4_36
7. Hayes, A.F., Krippendorff, K.: Answering the call for a standard reliability measure for coding data. Commun. Methods Meas. **1**, 77–89 (2007)
8. Hwang, J.D., et al.: COMET-ATOMIC 2020: on symbolic and neural commonsense knowledge graphs. In: The Thirty-Fifth AAAI Conference on Artificial Intelligence, pp. 6384–6392 (2021)
9. LeCun, Y.: Yann LeCun on a vision to make AI systems learn and reason like animals and humans. https://ai.facebook.com/blog/yann-lecun-advances-in-ai-research/
10. LeCun, Y., Bengio, Y.: Convolutional networks for images, speech, and time series. In: The Handbook of Brain Theory and Neural Networks, pp. 255–258. MIT Press, Cambridge (1998)
11. Lin, T.-Y., et al.: Microsoft COCO: common objects in context. In: Fleet, D., Pajdla, T., Schiele, B., Tuytelaars, T. (eds.) ECCV 2014. LNCS, vol. 8693, pp. 740–755. Springer, Cham (2014). https://doi.org/10.1007/978-3-319-10602-1_48
12. McCarthy, J., Lifschitz, V.: Formalizing Common Sense. Ablex series in artificial intelligence. Ablex Publishing Corporation (1990)
13. Prade, H.: Data bases with fuzzy information and approximate reasoning in expert systems. In: IFAC Proceedings, vol. 16, pp. 113–119 (1983)
14. Ren, S., He, K., Girshick, R.B., Sun, J.: Faster R-CNN: towards real-time object detection with region proposal networks. IEEE Trans. Pattern Anal. Mach. Intell. **39**, 1137–1149 (2015)
15. Rezaei, N., Reformat, M.Z., Yager, R.R.: Image-based world-perceiving knowledge graph (WpKG) with imprecision. In: Lesot, M.-J., et al. (eds.) IPMU 2020. CCIS, vol. 1237, pp. 415–428. Springer, Cham (2020). https://doi.org/10.1007/978-3-030-50146-4_31
16. Romero, J., Razniewski, S., Pal, K., Z. Pan, J., Sakhadeo, A., Weikum, G.: Commonsense properties from query logs and question answering forums. In: Proceedings of the 28th ACM International Conference on Information and Knowledge Management, pp. 1411–1420. Association for Computing Machinery (2019)
17. Simonyan, K., Zisserman, A.: Very deep convolutional networks for large-scale image recognition. In: International Conference on Learning Representations (2015)

18. Speer, R., Chin, J., Havasi, C.: Conceptnet 5.5: an open multilingual graph of general knowledge. In: Thirty-first AAAI Conference on Artificial Intelligence, pp. 4444–4451 (2017)
19. Tandon, N., de Melo, G., Weikum, G.: WebChild 2.0: fine-grained commonsense knowledge distillation. In: Proceedings of ACL 2017, System Demonstrations, pp. 115–120. Association for Computational Linguistics, Vancouver, July 2017
20. Tang, K., Niu, Y., Huang, J., Shi, J., Zhang, H.: Unbiased scene graph generation from biased training. In: 2020 IEEE/CVF Conference on Computer Vision and Pattern Recognition, CVPR, pp. 3713–3722 (2020)
21. West, P., et al.: Symbolic knowledge distillation: from general language models to commonsense models (2021). arXiv preprint arXiv:2110.07178
22. Xie, S., Girshick, R., Dollár, P., Tu, Z., He, K.: Aggregated residual transformations for deep neural networks. In: 2017 IEEE Conference on Computer Vision and Pattern Recognition, CVPR, pp. 5987–5995 (2017)
23. Zellers, R., Bisk, Y., Farhadi, A., Choi, Y.: From recognition to cognition: visual commonsense reasoning. In: 2019 IEEE/CVF Conference on Computer Vision and Pattern Recognition, CVPR, pp. 6713–6724 (2019)
24. Zellers, R., Yatskar, M., Thomson, S., Choi, Y.: Neural motifs: scene graph parsing with global context. In: 2018 IEEE/CVF Conference on Computer Vision and Pattern Recognition, pp. 5831–5840 (2018)
25. Zhang, H., Khashabi, D., Song, Y., Roth, D.: TransOMCS: from linguistic graphs to commonsense knowledge. In: Proceedings of the Twenty-Ninth International Joint Conference on Artificial Intelligence, IJCAI 2020, pp. 4004–4010 (2020)

Logical Structures of Opposition and Logical Syllogisms

Modelling of Fuzzy Peterson's Syllogisms Related to Graded Peterson's Cube of Opposition

Karel Fiala[1]($\boxtimes$) and Petra Murinová[2]

[1] Department of Mathematics, University of Ostrava, Ostrava, Czech Republic
karel.fiala@osu.cz

[2] Institute for Research and Application of Fuzzy Modeling, University of Ostrava, Ostrava, Czech Republic
petra.murinova@osu.cz

Abstract. In this article, we continue to study fuzzy Peterson's logical syllogisms. We will focus on new forms of fuzzy intermediate quantifiers that form a graded Peterson's cube of opposition. The main goal will be to syntactically prove new forms of valid logical syllogisms.

Keywords: Fuzzy intermediate quantifier · Graded Peterson's Cube of opposition · Fuzzy syllogism

1 Introduction

This publication builds very closely on our previous publications, in which we addressed the formal proof of fuzzy Peterson syllogisms with two or more premises (see [8,9]). Peterson syllogisms are special logical statements that work with classical/fuzzy intermediate quantifiers. Recall that fuzzy intermediate quantifiers belong to the group of fuzzy generalized quantifiers. Intermediate quantifiers are natural language expressions such as *Almost all, Most, Several, A few, etc.*. From a philosophical point of view, Peterson dealt with these quantifiers in particular in collaboration with Thompson, who showed and explained the position of these quantifiers in Peterson's square of opposition (see [15,16]). There are several authors, who devoted further generalization of the mainly classical square of opposition, who designed both the graded square and the graded cube of opposition [4,5].

When working with Peterson's syllogisms, we commonly encounter natural language expressions, for example

Almost all birds can fly.

The work was supported from ERDF/ESF by the project "Centre for the development of Artificial Inteligence Methods for the Automotive Industry of the region" No. CZ.02.1.01/0.0/0.0/17-049/0008414.

© Springer Nature Switzerland AG 2022
D. Ciucci et al. (Eds.): IPMU 2022, CCIS 1601, pp. 609–621, 2022.
https://doi.org/10.1007/978-3-031-08971-8_50

where *Almost all* is the quantifier, *birds* is the support and *can fly* is the property. The main idea for this article is to work with natural language expressions with negation in both the antecedent and the consequent, for example

Most children who don't like math can't study physics.

The main goal of this article is to first propose mathematical definitions of such quantifiers and then to verify new forms of valid syllogisms. Motivation is not only a theoretical result but also the possibility of applying these new forms of quantifiers in order to interpret natural data using natural language. Therefore continue the study proposed in [6].

2   Preliminaries

2.1   Fuzzy Type Theory

Since the article is limited by a number of pages, we will list here only the basic symbols and definitions that are necessary for our further work. For further details on these theories, we refer readers to our previous publication [11].

The model of fuzzy intermediate quantifiers which we will use in our paper was introduced by Novák [12] within Łukasiewicz fuzzy type theory (Ł-FTT). The basic syntactic objects of Ł-FTT are classical, namely the concepts of *type* and *formula*. The atomic types are ϵ (elements) and o (truth values). We denote types by Greek letters and the set of all types by *Types*. The set of all formulas of a type α is denoted by $Types_\alpha$. General types are defined as follows: if α, β are types then $(\beta\alpha)$ is a type.

The truth values considered in this paper form a linearly ordered MV_Δ-algebra[1] $\mathcal{L}_\Delta$ (see [3,13])

$$\mathcal{L}_\Delta = \langle L, \vee, \wedge, \otimes, \rightarrow, 0, 1, \Delta \rangle. \tag{1}$$

The *language* J of Ł-FTT consists of variables $x_\alpha, \ldots$, special constants $c_\alpha, \ldots$ ($\alpha \in Types$), the symbol λ, and brackets. We will consider the following concrete special constants: $\mathbf{E}_{(o\alpha)\alpha}$ (fuzzy equality) for every $\alpha \in Types$, $\mathbf{C}_{(oo)o}$ (conjunction), $\mathbf{D}_{(oo)}$ (delta operation on truth values) and the description operator $\iota_{\epsilon(o\epsilon)}$.

A (general) model of FTT is a system of sets and fuzzy equalities on them:

$$\mathcal{M} = \langle (M_\alpha, \overset{\circ}{=}_\alpha)_{\alpha \in Types}, \mathcal{L}_\Delta \rangle. \tag{2}$$

The fuzzy type theory is *complete*, i.e., a theory T is consistent iff it has a (Henkin) model ($\mathcal{M} \models T$). We can also apply its equivalent version: $T \vdash A_o$ iff $T \models A_o$.

---

[1] We write MV-algebra as a residuated lattice. Originally, it is the algebra with two binary and one unary operations, and two constants: $\langle L, \otimes, \oplus, \neg, \mathbf{0}, \mathbf{1} \rangle$.

2.2 Theory of Evaluative Linguistic Expressions

Evaluative linguistic expressions are expressions of natural language such as small, big, extremely big, etc. In our model we use basic evaluative trichotomy - *small, medium, big* as these expressions. These expressions can be modified by a linguistic hedge - with narrowing effect (*extremely, significantly, very*) or widening effect (*more or less, roughly, quite roughly, very roughly*).

Its language J^{Ev} has the following special symbols:

- The constants $\top, \bot \in Form_o$ for truth and falsity and $\dagger \in Form_o$ for the middle truth value.
- A special constant $\sim \in Form_{(oo)o}$ for additional fuzzy equality on the set of truth values L.
- A set of special constants $\nu, \ldots \in Form_{oo}$ for linguistic hedges. The J^{Ev} supposes the following special constants: $\{Ex, Si, Ve, ML, Ro, QR, VR\}$ that represent the linguistic hedges (*extremely, significantly, very, more or less, roughly, quite roughly, very roughly*, respectively).
- A set of triples of additional constants $(\mathbf{a}_\nu, \mathbf{b}_\nu, \mathbf{c}_\nu), \ldots \in Form_o$ where each hedge ν is uniquely associated with one triple of these constants.

The evaluative expressions are interpreted by special formulas $Sm \in Form_{oo(oo)}$ (*small*), $Me \in Form_{oo(oo)}$ (*medium*), $Bi \in Form_{oo(oo)}$ (*big*), and $Ze \in Form_{oo(oo)}$ (*zero*) that can be expanded by several linguistic hedges. The following formula is provable: $T^{\mathrm{Ev}} \vdash Hedge\,\nu$ for all $\nu \in \{Ex, Si, Ve, ML, Ro, QR, VR\}$. Furthermore, evaluative linguistic expressions are represented by formulas

$$Sm\,\nu, Me\,\nu, Bi\,\nu, Ze\,\nu \in Form_{oo} \tag{3}$$

where ν is a hedge. We will also assume an *empty hedge* $\bar{\nu}$ that is introduced in front of *small, medium* and *big* if no other hedge is assumed. A special hedge is Δ_{oo} that represents the expression "utmost" and occurs below in the evaluative expression $Bi\,\Delta$.

3 Fuzzy Intermediate Quantifiers

The first mathematical definition of fuzzy intermediate quantifiers can be found in [12]. This definition was later modified. Motivation and explanation can be found in (see [8,12]). The main change is the introduction of the so-called cut of a fuzzy set. We define the special operation "cut of a fuzzy set" for given fuzzy sets $y, z \in Form_{o\alpha}$: $y|z \equiv \lambda x_\alpha \cdot zx \& \Delta(\Upsilon(zx) \Rightarrow (yx \equiv zx)).^2$

Lemma 1. *[10] Let $\mathcal{M}$ be a model and p an assignment such that $B = \mathcal{M}_p(y) \subseteq_\sim M_\alpha, Z = \mathcal{M}_p(z) \subseteq_\sim M_\alpha$. Then for any $m \in M_\alpha$*

$$\mathcal{M}_p(y|z)(m) = (B|Z)(m) = \begin{cases} B(m), & \text{if } B(m) = Z(m), \\ 0 & \text{otherwise.} \end{cases}$$

---

[2] The formal definition is $\Upsilon_{oo} \equiv \lambda z_o \cdot \neg \Delta(\neg z_o)$.

As we can see in the Lemma 1 by this operation we pick elements from B exactly in their degree of membership or we do not pick them at all.

A very important role plays a fuzzy measure that fulfils the axioms of normality, monotonicity and be closed with respect to the negation. For precise definition see [12].

In the previous text, we briefly presented the necessary tools that we need to construct the mathematical definition of fuzzy intermediate quantifiers.

Definition 1. (Fuzzy intermediate quantifiers). Let Ev be a formula representing an evaluative expression, x be variables and A, B, z be formulas. Let μ be a fuzzy measure. Then either of the following formulas construes the sentence "$\langle$Quantifier$\rangle$ B's are A".

$$(Q_{Ev}^{\forall} x)(B, A) \equiv (\exists z)[(\forall x)((B|z)\, x \Rightarrow Ax) \wedge Ev((\mu B)(B|z))], \tag{4}$$

$$(Q_{Ev}^{\exists} x)(B, A) \equiv (\exists z)[(\exists x)((B|z)x \wedge Ax) \wedge Ev((\mu B)(B|z))]. \tag{5}$$

If we put instead of Ev concrete evaluative linguistic expressions we obtain the following fuzzy intermediate quantifiers:

A: All B's are $A := (Q_{Bi\Delta}^{\forall} x)(B, A) \equiv (\forall x)(Bx \Rightarrow Ax)$,

E: No B's are $A := (Q_{Bi\Delta}^{\forall} x)(B, \neg A) \equiv (\forall x)(Bx \Rightarrow \neg Ax)$,

P: Almost all B's are $A := (Q_{Bi\,Ex}^{\forall} x)(B, A)$

B: Almost all B's are not $A := (Q_{Bi\,Ex}^{\forall} x)(B, \neg A)$

T: Most B's are $A := (Q_{Bi\,Ve}^{\forall} x)(B, A)$

D: Most B's are not $A := (Q_{Bi\,Ve}^{\forall} x)(B, \neg A)$

K: Many B's are $A := (Q_{\neg\,Sm}^{\forall} x)(B, A)$

G: Many B's are not $A := (Q_{\neg\,Sm}^{\forall} x)(B, \neg A)$

F: A few (A little) B's are $A := (Q_{Sm\,Si}^{\forall} x)(B, A)$

V: A few (A little) B's are not $A := (Q_{Sm\,Si}^{\forall} x)(B, \neg A)$

S: Several B's are $A := (Q_{Sm\,Ve}^{\forall} x)(B, A)$

Z: Several B's are not $A := (Q_{Sm\,Ve}^{\forall} x)(B, \neg A)$

I: Some B's are $A := (Q_{Bi\Delta}^{\exists} x)(B, A) \equiv (\exists x)(Bx \wedge Ax)$,

O: Some B's are not $A := (Q_{Bi\Delta}^{\exists} x)(B, \neg A) \equiv (\exists x)(Bx \wedge \neg Ax)$.

In the following Theorem we will describe monotonic behavior of fuzzy intermediate quantifiers.

Theorem 1. *[12] Let $A, \ldots, O$ are intermediate quantifiers. Then the following set of implications is provable in T^{IQ}:*

1. $T^{IQ} \vdash A \Rightarrow P, T^{IQ} \vdash P \Rightarrow T, T^{IQ} \vdash T \Rightarrow K,$
   $T^{IQ} \vdash K \Rightarrow F, T^{IQ} \vdash F \Rightarrow S, T^{IQ} \vdash S \Rightarrow I.$
2. $T^{IQ} \vdash E \Rightarrow B, T^{IQ} \vdash B \Rightarrow D, T^{IQ} \vdash D \Rightarrow G,$
   $T^{IQ} \vdash G \Rightarrow V, T^{IQ} \vdash V \Rightarrow Z, T^{IQ} \vdash Z \Rightarrow O.$

By fuzzy intermediate quantifiers which we defined in the Definition 1 we are not able to mathematically describe quantifiers with negation in their support. For example, we are not able to describe:

"Most people who are not stressed do not have high blood pressure".

For the mathematical definition of these situations we modify formulas (4) (5) from Definition 1. We replace the formulas in the definition with their negations and we obtain new forms of fuzzy intermediate quantifiers.

Definition 2. (New forms of fuzzy intermediate quantifiers). Let Ev be a formula representing an evaluative expression, x be variables and A, B, z be formulas. Then either of the following formulas construes the sentence "⟨Quantifier⟩ not B's are not A".

$$(Q_{Ev}^{\forall} x)(\neg B, \neg A) \equiv (\exists z)[(\forall x)((\neg B|z) \, x \Rightarrow \neg Ax) \wedge Ev((\mu(\neg B))(\neg B|z))], \quad (6)$$

$$(Q_{Ev}^{\exists} x)(\neg B, \neg A) \equiv (\exists z)[(\exists x)((\neg B|z)x \wedge \neg Ax) \wedge Ev((\mu(\neg B))(\neg B|z))]. \quad (7)$$

If we put a concrete evaluative linguistic expression instead of Ev we obtain new forms of fuzzy intermediate quantifiers which form graded Peterson's cube of opposition. The new forms will be denoted by small letters as we can see in Fig. 1. We will not present the full overview of quantifiers here.

3.1   Cube of Opposition

Below we introduce graded Peterson's cube of opposition with new forms of quantifiers. Properties *contradictory, contrary, sub-contrary and sub-alters* between quantifiers which were syntactically proved could be found in [7]. Recall that other graded versions of the cube of opposition were proposed in [1,2,5].

Theorem 2. *The following set of implications is provable in L-FTT:*

1. $T^{IQ} \vdash a \Rightarrow p, T^{IQ} \vdash p \Rightarrow t, T^{IQ} \vdash t \Rightarrow k,$
   $T^{IQ} \vdash k \Rightarrow f, T^{IQ} \vdash f \Rightarrow s, T^{IQ} \vdash s \Rightarrow i.$
2. $T^{IQ} \vdash e \Rightarrow b, T^{IQ} \vdash b \Rightarrow d, T^{IQ} \vdash d \rightarrow g,$
   $T^{IQ} \vdash g \Rightarrow v, T^{IQ} \vdash v \Rightarrow z, T^{IQ} \vdash z \Rightarrow o.$

Proof. Analogously as in Theorem 1 by replacing each formula in the proof by its negation.

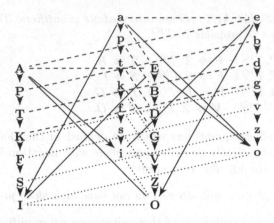

Fig. 1. Graded Peterson's cube of opposition

4   New Forms of Syllogisms

In the Sect. 3.1, we can see that between fuzzy intermediate quantifiers and their new forms exist some properties. It motivates us to find new forms of valid syllogisms which are consisted of both. In this section, we will present new forms of fuzzy syllogisms of Figure-IV. This section will be divided into three parts - depending on how monotonicity is used in the proofs of strong validity of syllogisms. First of all, we start with the definition of syllogism.

Definition 3. Let Q_1, Q_2, Q_3 be fuzzy quantifiers and $M, P, S \in \mathrm{Form}_{o\alpha}$ be formulas. Let M be a middle formula, S be a subject and P be a predicate. Then we distinguish four corresponding figures:

Figure-I	Figure-II	Figure-III	Figure-IV
$P_1 : Q_1\ M$ are P	$Q_1\ P$ are M	$Q_1\ M$ are P	$Q_1\ P$ are M
$P_2 : Q_2\ S$ are M	$Q_2\ S$ are M	$Q_2\ M$ are S	$Q_2\ M$ are S
$C : Q_3\ S$ are P	$Q_3\ S$ are P	$Q_3\ S$ are P	$Q_3\ S$ are P

By fuzzy syllogism we infer the conclusion C from two premises P_1, P_2. In Definition 3 we can see that for fuzzy syllogisms we distinguish four corresponding figures - these figures differ in the position of the middle formula in the premises.

We use letters of the alphabet to denote fuzzy intermediate quantifiers (see above for the corresponding letter for each fuzzy intermediate quantifier). These letters of the alphabet are used to write fuzzy syllogisms. To write fuzzy syllogisms of Figure-IV, we use the abbreviation $P_1 P_2 C$-IV where the abbreviation of the fuzzy intermediate quantifier (letter of the alphabet) from the first premise is located at position P_1. The abbreviation of the fuzzy intermediate quantifier from the second premise is located at position P_2. At position C is the abbreviation of the fuzzy intermediate quantifier from the conclusion.

Definition 4. Syllogism $\langle P_1, P_2, C \rangle$ is strongly valid in T^{IQ} if $T^{IQ} \vdash (P_1 \& P_2) \Rightarrow C$ or equivalently if $T^{IQ} \vdash P_1 \Rightarrow (P_2 \Rightarrow C)$.

4.1 Syllogisms by Weakening of the Conclusion

Let start with the concrete syntactic proof of strongly valid syllogism on this figure.

Theorem 3. *Syllogisms* **AAa**-*IV,* **eAe**-*IV,* **eEA**-*IV are strongly valid in* T^{IQ}.

Proof. Let us assume the syllogism as follows:

$$\textbf{AAa-IV:} \quad \frac{\begin{array}{c}(\forall x)(Px \Rightarrow Mx) \\ (\forall x)(Mx \Rightarrow Sx)\end{array}}{(\forall x)(\neg Sx \Rightarrow \neg Px)}$$

We know that

$$T^{IQ} \vdash (Px \Rightarrow Sx) \Rightarrow (\neg Sx \Rightarrow \neg Px). \tag{8}$$

We also know that

$$T^{IQ} \vdash ((Px \Rightarrow Mx)\&(Mx \Rightarrow Sx)) \Rightarrow (Px \Rightarrow Sx). \tag{9}$$

By application of transitivity on (9) and (8) we obtain

$$T^{IQ} \vdash ((Px \Rightarrow Mx)\&(Mx \Rightarrow Sx)) \Rightarrow (\neg Sx \Rightarrow \neg Px).$$

By adjunction, by generalization $(\forall x)$ and by properties of quantifiers we obtain

$$T^{IQ} \vdash (\forall x)(Px \Rightarrow Mx) \Rightarrow ((\forall x)(Mx \Rightarrow Sx) \Rightarrow (\forall x)(\neg Sx \Rightarrow \neg Px)).$$

The strong validity of the other two syllogisms can be verified similarly.

Theorem 4. *Syllogisms* **aaA**-*IV,* **EaE**-*IV,* **Eea**-*IV are strongly valid in* T^{IQ}.

Proof. We get syntactical proofs analogously to the proofs of syllogisms in Theorem 3 by replacing each formula by its negation.

In the following theorem, we will use monotonicity to prove the strong validity of other syllogisms.

Theorem 5. *Let syllogisms* **AAa**-*IV,* **eAe**-*IV,* **eEA**-*IV,* **aaA**-*IV,* **EaE**-*IV and* **Eea**-*IV be strongly valid in* T^{IQ}. *Then the following syllogisms are strongly valid in* T^{IQ}:

$$
\begin{array}{cccccc}
AAa & eAe & eEA & aaA & EaE & Eea \\
AAp & eAh & eEP & aaP & EaD & Eep \\
AAt & eAd & eET & aaT & EaD & Eet \\
AAk & eAg & eEK & aaK & EaG & Eek \\
AAf & eAv & eEF & aaF & EaV & Eef \\
AAs & eAz & eES & aaS & EaZ & Ees \\
A(*A)i & e(*A)o & e(*E)I & a(*a)I & E(*a)O & E(*e)i
\end{array}
$$

Proof. From strongly valid syllogism **AAa**-IV and from monotonicity (Theorem 2) we prove by transitivity strongly valid syllogism in the first column. Analogously we can prove the strong validity of syllogisms in the other columns by monotonicity (Theorem 1, 2).

In Theorem 5 we ordered by monotonicity strongly valid syllogisms into columns. We can see that the borders of these columns are formed by syllogisms that contain classical quantifiers or new forms of classical quantifiers. In Theorem 5 we used monotonicity to weaken the conclusion and thus we obtained other strongly valid syllogisms.

4.2   Syllogisms by Strengthening of the First Premise

Firstly we will show the syntactical proof of strongly valid syllogism.

Theorem 6. *Syllogisms* **oAO**-*IV,* **IEo**-*IV,* **oEi**-*IV,* **Oao**-*IV,* **ieO**-*IV and* **OeI**-*IV are strongly valid in* T^{IQ}.

Proof. Let us assume the syllogism as follows:

$$\textbf{oAO-IV:}\quad \frac{\begin{array}{c}(\exists x)(\neg Px \wedge Mx)\\(\forall x)(Mx \Rightarrow Sx)\end{array}}{(\exists x)(Sx \wedge \neg Px)}$$

We know that

$$T^{IQ} \vdash (Mx \Rightarrow Sx) \Rightarrow ((\neg Px \wedge Mx) \Rightarrow (Sx \wedge \neg Px)).$$

By generalization $(\forall x)$ and properties of quantifiers we obtain

$$T^{IQ} \vdash (\forall x)(Mx \Rightarrow Sx) \Rightarrow ((\exists x)(\neg Px \wedge Mx) \Rightarrow (\exists x)(Sx \wedge \neg Px)).$$

By adjunction we obtain

$$T^{IQ} \vdash ((\exists x)(\neg Px \wedge Mx)\&(\forall x)(Mx \Rightarrow Sx)) \Rightarrow (\exists x)(Sx \wedge \neg Px).$$

The strong validity of syllogisms **IEo**-IV, **oEi**-IV can be proven similarly. If we obtain syntactical proofs of syllogisms **oAO**-IV, **IEo**-IV, **oEi**-IV then we can obtain strong validity of syllogisms **Oao**-IV, **ieO**-IV, **OeI**-IV by replacing each formula in the proof by its negation.

Theorem 7. *Let syllogisms* **oAO**-*IV,* **IEo**-*IV,* **oEi**-*IV,* **Oao**-*IV,* **ieO**-*IV and* **OeI**-*IV be strongly valid in* T^{IQ}. *Then the following syllogisms are strongly valid in* T^{IQ}:

$$(*e)AO \ (*A)Eo \ (*e)Ei \ (*E)ao \ (*a)eO \ (*E)eI$$
$$(*b)AO \ (*P)Eo \ (*b)Ei \ (*B)ao \ (*p)eO \ (*B)eI$$
$$(*d)AO \ (*T)Eo \ (*d)Ei \ (*D)ao \ (*t)eO \ (*D)eI$$
$$(*g)AO \ (*K)Eo \ (*g)Ei \ (*G)ao \ (*k)eO \ (*G)eI$$
$$(*v)AO \ (*F)Eo \ (*v)Ei \ (*V)ao \ (*f)eO \ (*V)eI$$
$$(*z)AO \ (*S)Eo \ (*z)Ei \ (*Z)ao \ (*s)eO \ (*Z)eI$$
$$oAO \quad IEo \quad oEi \quad Oao \quad ieO \quad OeI$$

Proof. From strongly valid syllogism **oAO**-IV and from monotonicity (Theorem 2) we prove by transitivity strongly valid syllogism in the first column. Analogously we can prove the strong validity of syllogisms in the other columns by monotonicity (Theorem 1, 2).

In Theorem 7 we ordered by monotonicity strongly valid syllogisms into columns. Again the borders of these columns consist of syllogisms that contain classical quantifiers or new forms of classical quantifiers. In Theorem 7 we used monotonicity to strengthen the first premise.

4.3 Syllogisms by Strengthening of the Second Premise

We start this subsection with the concrete syntactical proof.

Theorem 8. *Syllogisms* **aOo**-*IV,* **EOi**-*IV,* **aII**-*IV,* **AoO**-*IV,* **eoI**-*IV and* **Aii**-*IV be strongly valid in* T^{IQ}.

Proof. Let us assume the syllogism as follows:

$$\text{aOo-IV: } \frac{\begin{array}{c}(\forall x)(\neg Px \Rightarrow \neg Mx)\\(\exists x)(Mx \wedge \neg Sx)\end{array}}{(\exists x)(\neg Sx \wedge Px)}$$

We know that

$$T^{IQ} \vdash (\neg Px \Rightarrow \neg Mx) \Rightarrow (Mx \Rightarrow Px). \tag{10}$$

We also know that

$$T^{IQ} \vdash (Mx \Rightarrow Px) \Rightarrow ((Mx \wedge \neg Sx) \Rightarrow (\neg Sx \wedge Px)). \tag{11}$$

By application transitivity on (10) and (11) we obtain

$$T^{IQ} \vdash (\neg Px \Rightarrow \neg Mx) \Rightarrow ((Mx \wedge \neg Sx) \Rightarrow (\neg Sx \wedge Px)).$$

By generalization $(\forall x)$ and properties of quantifiers we obtain

$$T^{IQ} \vdash (\forall x)(\neg Px \to \neg Mx) \Rightarrow ((\exists x)(Mx \wedge \neg Sx) \Rightarrow (\exists x)(\neg Sx \wedge Px)). \tag{12}$$

The strong validity of syllogisms **EOi**-IV, **aII**-IV can be obtain similarly. If we obtain strong validity of the syllogisms **aOo**-IV, **EOi**-IV and **aII**-IV we can prove strong validity of syllogisms **AoO**-IV, **eoI**-IV, **Aii**-IV by replacing each formula in the proof by its negation.

Theorem 9. *Let syllogisms* **aOo**-*IV,* **EOi**-*IV,* **aII**-*IV,* **AoO**-*IV,* **eoI**-*IV and* **Aii**-*IV be strongly valid in* T^{IQ}. *Then the following syllogisms are strongly valid in* T^{IQ}:

$$a(*E)o \quad E(*E)i \quad a(*A)I \quad A(*e)O \quad e(*e)I \quad A(*a)i$$
$$a(*B)o \quad E(*B)i \quad a(*P)I \quad A(*b)O \quad e(*b)I \quad A(*p)i$$
$$a(*D)o \quad E(*D)i \quad a(*T)I \quad A(*d)O \quad e(*d)I \quad A(*t)i$$
$$a(*G)o \quad E(*G)i \quad a(*K)I \quad A(*g)O \quad e(*g)I \quad A(*k)i$$
$$a(*V)o \quad E(*V)i \quad a(*F)I \quad A(*v)O \quad e(*v)I \quad A(*f)i$$
$$a(*Z)o \quad E(*Z)i \quad a(*S)I \quad A(*z)O \quad e(*z)I \quad A(*s)i$$
$$aOo \quad\quad EOi \quad\quad aII \quad\quad AoO \quad\quad eoI \quad\quad Aii$$

Proof. From strongly valid syllogism **aOo**-IV and from monotonicity (Theorem 1) we prove by transitivity strongly valid syllogism in the first column. Analogously we can prove the strong validity of syllogisms in the other columns by monotonicity (Theorem 1, Theorem 2).

We can see that we ordered strongly valid syllogisms into columns by monotonicity. Again the endpoints of these columns are syllogisms that contain classical quantifiers or new forms of classical quantifiers. In proof of Theorem 9 we use monotonicity to strengthen the second premise.

5   Example of Logical Syllogism in Finite Model

Below we will show an example of valid syllogism in a simple model with a finite set M_ϵ of elements. Details of the constructed model can be found in [8]. In Example 1 we can find a fuzzy measure that is used in Example 2.

Example 1. A measure of fuzzy sets on a finite universe can be obtained as follows. Let M be a finite set and $A, B \subseteq_{\sim} M$ be fuzzy sets. Put

$$|A| = \sum_{m \in \text{Supp}(A)} A(m). \tag{13}$$

Furthermore, let us define a function $F^R \in (L^{\mathcal{F}(M)})^{\mathcal{F}(M)}$ by[3]

$$F^R(B)(A) = \begin{cases} 1, & \text{if } B = A = \emptyset, \\ \min\left\{1, \frac{|A|}{|B|}\right\}, & \text{if } \text{Supp}(A) \subseteq \text{Supp}(B), \\ 0, & \text{otherwise} \end{cases} \tag{14}$$

for all $A, B \subseteq_{\sim} M$.

For model $\mathcal{M}$ holds true that $\mathcal{M} \models T^{IQ}$. Syllogism is valid in a model $\mathcal{M}$ if

$$\mathcal{M}(P_1) \otimes \mathcal{M}(P_2) \leq \mathcal{M}(C).$$

---

[3] By Supp(A), we denote the support of the fuzzy set A.

P_1: All people who do sports are healthy.

Example 2. **A(*g)O-IV:** P_2: Many people who are not healthy are old people.

P_3 Some old people do not do sport.

We suppose the same frame and the measure as above. Let M_ϵ be a set of people. We consider six people: $U = \{u_1, u_2, u_3, u_4, u_5, u_6\}$. We interpret the formulas in considered model as follows:

Let $Old_{o\epsilon}$ be the formula "old people" with interpretation $\mathcal{M}(Old_{o\epsilon}) = O \subseteq M_\epsilon$ defined by

$$O = \{0.2/u_1, 0.4/u_2, 0.5/u_3, 0.3/u_4, 0.8/u_5, 0.2/u_6\}.$$

Let $Health_{o\epsilon}$ be the formula "people who are healthy" with interpretation as follows: $\mathcal{M}(Health_{o\epsilon}) = H \subseteq M_\epsilon$ defined by

$$H = \{0.7/u_1, 0.4/u_2, 0.7/u_3, 0.9/u_4, 0.4/u_5, 0.9/u_6\}.$$

Let $NHealth_{o\epsilon}$ be the formula "people who are not healthy" with interpretation $\mathcal{M}(NHealth_{o\epsilon}) = \neg H \subseteq M_\epsilon$ defined by

$$\neg H = \{0.3/u_1, 0.6/u_2, 0.3/u_3, 0.1/u_4, 0.6/u_5, 0.1/u_6\}.$$

Let $Sport_{o\epsilon}$ be the formula "people who do sport" with interpretation $\mathcal{M}(Sport_{o\epsilon}) = S \subseteq M_\epsilon$ defined by

$$S = \{0.3/u_1, 0.4/u_2, 0.7/u_3, 0.9/u_4, 0.2/u_5, 0.8/u_6\}.$$

Let $NSport_{o\epsilon}$ be the formula "people who do not do sport" with interpretation $\mathcal{M}(NSport_{o\epsilon}) = \neg S \subseteq M_\epsilon$ defined by

$$\neg S = \{0.7/u_1, 0.6/u_2, 0.3/u_3, 0.1/u_4, 0.8/u_5, 0.2/u_6\}.$$

Major Premise: "All people who do sports are healthy" is the formula

$$Q_{Bi\Delta}^{\vee}(Sport_{o\epsilon}, Health_{o\epsilon}) := (\forall x_\epsilon)(Sport_{o\epsilon}(x_\epsilon) \Rightarrow Health_{o\epsilon}(x_\epsilon)),$$

which is interpreted by

$$\mathcal{M}(Q_{Bi\Delta}^{\vee}(Sport_{o\epsilon}, Health_{o\epsilon})) =$$
$$\bigwedge_{m \in M_\epsilon} (\mathcal{M}(Sport_{o\epsilon}(m)) \to \mathcal{M}(Health_{o\epsilon}(m))) = 1. \quad (15)$$

Minor Premise: "Many people who are not healthy are old people" can be represented in our model as

$$\mathcal{M}((\exists z_{o\epsilon})[(\forall x_\epsilon)((NHealth_{o\epsilon}|z_{o\epsilon})(x_\epsilon) \Rightarrow Old_{o\epsilon}(x_\epsilon)) \& (\exists x_\epsilon)(NHealth_{o\epsilon}|z_{o\epsilon})(x_\epsilon) \wedge \quad (16)$$
$$\wedge (\neg Sm)((\mu \, NHealth_{o\epsilon})(NHealth_{o\epsilon}|z_{o\epsilon}))]).$$

This leads us to find the fuzzy set $\mathcal{M}(\text{NHealth}_{o\epsilon}|z_{o\epsilon}) = C \subseteq M_\epsilon$ which gives us the greatest degree in (16). It can be verified that the fuzzy set

$$C = \{0.3/u_3, 0.1/u_4, 0.6/u_5, 0.1/u_6\} \subseteq \neg H$$

gives us the greatest degree in (16).

$$\mathcal{M}(Q^\forall_{\neg\,Sm}(\text{NHealth}_{o\epsilon}, \text{Old}_{o\epsilon})) = 1 \otimes 0.6 \wedge 1 = 0.6. \tag{17}$$

Conclusion: "Some old people do not do sport" is the formula

$$Q^\exists_{Bi\Delta}(\text{Old}_{o\epsilon}, \text{NSport}_{o\epsilon}) := (\exists x_\epsilon)(\text{Old}_{o\epsilon}(x_\epsilon) \wedge \text{NSport}_{o\epsilon}(x_\epsilon)),$$

which is interpreted by

$$\mathcal{M}(Q^\exists_{Bi\Delta}(\text{Old}_{o\epsilon}, \text{Nsport}_{o\epsilon})) = \\ \bigvee_{m \in M_\epsilon} (\mathcal{M}(\text{Old}_{o\epsilon}(m)) \wedge \mathcal{M}(\text{Nsport}_{o\epsilon}(m))) = 0.8. \tag{18}$$

From (15) (17) and (18) we can see that in our model the condition of the validity is fulfilled because $\mathcal{M}(P_1) \otimes \mathcal{M}(P_2) = 1 \otimes 0.6 = 0.6 \leq \mathcal{M}(C) = 0.8$ therefore this example of syllogism is valid in our model.

6   Conclusion and Future Directions

In this paper, we first focus on the formal definitions of new forms of intermediate quantifiers that form a graded Peterson's cube of opposition. First, we formally proved selected types of fuzzy intermediate logical syllogisms and semantically also verified their validity in the finite model. Furthermore, scientific research will focus on verifying the validity of syllogisms of all four forms. We will further extend this approach by assuming more premises, which means assuming more middle formulas and therefore more related figures (follow the work of [14]).

References

1. Boffa, S., Murinová, P., Novák, V.: Graded polygons of opposition in fuzzy formal concept analysis. Int. J. Approximate Reasoning **132**, 128–153 (2021)
2. Boffa, S., Murinová, P., Novák, V., Ferbas, P.: Graded cubes of opposition in fuzzy formal concept analysis. Int. J. Approximate Reasoning **145**, 187–209 (2022)
3. Cignoli, R.L.O., D'Ottaviano, I.M.L., Mundici, D.: Algebraic Foundations of Many-valued Reasoning. Kluwer, Dordrecht (2000)
4. Dubois, D., Prade, H., Rico, A.: Graded cubes of opposition and possibility theory with fuzzy events. Int. J. Approximate Reasoning **84**, 168–185 (2017)
5. Dubois, D., Prade, H., Rico, A.: Structures of opposition and comparisons: boolean and gradual cases. Log. Univers. **14**, 115–149 (2020)

6. Kacprzyk, J., Zadrożny, S.: Linguistic database summaries and their protoforms: towards natural language based knowledge discovery tools. Inf. Sci. **173**, 281–304 (2005)
7. Murinová, P.: Graded structures of opposition in fuzzy natural logic. Log. Univers. **265**, 495–522 (2020)
8. Murinová, P., Novák, V.: A formal theory of generalized intermediate syllogisms. Fuzzy Sets Syst. **186**, 47–80 (2013)
9. Murinová, P., Novák, V.: The structure of generalized intermediate syllogisms. Fuzzy Sets Syst. **247**, 18–37 (2014)
10. Murinová, P., Novák, V.: The theory of intermediate quantifiers in fuzzy natural logic revisited and the model of "many." Fuzzy Sets Syst. **388**, 56–89 (2020)
11. Novák, V.: On fuzzy type theory. Fuzzy Sets Syst. **149**, 235–273 (2005)
12. Novák, V.: A formal theory of intermediate quantifiers. Fuzzy Sets Syst. **159**(10), 1229–1246 (2008)
13. Novák, V., Perfilieva, I., Močkoř, J.: Mathematical Principles of Fuzzy Logic. Kluwer, Boston (1999)
14. Pereira-Fariña, M., Vidal, J.C., Díaz-Hermida, F., Bugarín, A.: A fuzzy syllogistic reasoning schema for generalized quantifiers. Fuzzy Sets Syst. **234**, 79–96 (2014)
15. Peterson, P.: Intermediate Quantifiers. Logic, linguistics, and Aristotelian semantics, Ashgate, Aldershot (2000)
16. Thompson, B.E.: Syllogisms using "few","many" and "most." Notre Dame J. Formal Logic **23**, 75–84 (1982)

Comparing Hexagons of Opposition in Probabilistic Rough Set Theory

Stefania Boffa[1]([🖂]) [ID], Davide Ciucci[1] [ID], and Petra Murinová[2]

[1] DISCo, Università degli Studi di Milano-Bicocca,
Viale Sarca 336, 20126 Milano, Italy
{stefania.boffa,davide.ciucci}@unimib.it
[2] NSC IT4Innovations, Institute for Research and Applications of Fuzzy Modeling,
University of Ostrava, 30. dubna 22, 701 03 Ostrava 1, Czech Republic
petra.murinova@osu.cz

Abstract. A hexagon of opposition built from a probabilistic rough set depends on two thresholds. This work explores the relations of opposition among vertices of hexagons obtained from pairs of thresholds. By an exhaustive analysis of the different cases that can arise, twelve patterns are defined and studied.

Keywords: Hexagon of opposition · Probabilistic rough sets · Three-way decision

1 Introduction

The *hexagon of opposition* is an extension of *Aristotle's square* (or *square of opposition*), which is a famous mathematical diagram connecting particular logical propositions [13]. The vertices of Aristotle's square represented in Fig. 1 are occupied by propositions **A**, **E**, **I**, and **O**, such that **A** and **E** are *contraries*, i.e. they cannot be true together, but they both can be false; **I** is *subaltern* of **A** and *O* is *subaltern* of **E**, i.e. **A** implies **I**, and **E** implies **O**; **I** and **O** are *sub-contraries*, i.e. they cannot be false together, but they both can be true; **A** and **O** are *contradictories* as well as **E** and **I**, i.e. **A** is the negation of **O** and **E** is the negation of **I**. In this article, we will use the lines ———, - - -, ⟶, ══ to graphically denote contrary, contradictory, subalternation, and sub-contrary relations. As shown by Fig. 2, the hexagon of opposition was originally constructed by Blanché, adding two new vertices occupied by $\mathbf{U} := \mathbf{A} \wedge \mathbf{E}$ and $\mathbf{Y} := \mathbf{I} \wedge \mathbf{O}$ to Aristotle's square. Successively, several scholars have studied the hexagon in [3,7,11] and elsewhere.

Squares and hexagons of opposition have lately been proposed in different fields, for instance, interpreting propositions with rough sets or imprecise probabilities [5,14]. An alternative hexagon has been realized in fuzzy formal concept analysis by considering instead of **U** and **Y**, an intermediate vertex between **A** and **I** and another between **E** and **O**, namely $\mathbf{U}'$ and $\mathbf{Y}'$ such that $\mathbf{I} \leq \mathbf{U}' \leq \mathbf{A}$

© Springer Nature Switzerland AG 2022
D. Ciucci et al. (Eds.): IPMU 2022, CCIS 1601, pp. 622–633, 2022.
https://doi.org/10.1007/978-3-031-08971-8_51

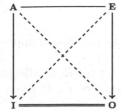

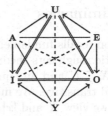

Fig. 1. Aristotle square.   **Fig. 2.** Hexagon of opposition.

and $\mathbf{O} \leq \mathbf{Y'} \leq \mathbf{E}$, where $\leq$ is the subalternation relation [4]. We here focus on the hexagon of opposition recently introduced in [1] by using Three-Way Decisions (TWD) and probabilistic rough sets. Essentially, according to TWD, a given universe is partitioned into three blocks: the *positive* (POS), *negative* (NEG), and *boundary* (BND) regions. These are respectively viewed as the regions of *acceptance*, *rejection*, and *non-commitment* in a ternary classification. Such tri-partition is mainly generated employing probabilistic rough sets, which are approximations of concepts defined from a pair of thresholds (α, β) such that $0 \leq \beta < \alpha \leq 1$ [15]. Subsequently, and similarly to the standard case [5], the sets POS, NEG, BND, $POS \cup BND$, $NEG \cup BND$, and $POS \cup NEG$ obtained from a specific pair of thresholds, are organized to form a hexagon of opposition as will be explained in Sect. 2.

It is crucial to underline that different pairs of thresholds generate different hexagons of opposition in probabilistic rough set theory. Several methods have been proposed for computing or estimating the numerical values of thresholds based on: cost or risk minimization of correct and incorrect classifications according to the Bayesian decision theory [16]; Shannon's entropy [6]; chi-square statistic [8]; and game theory [9]. Of course, using different methods, the corresponding hexagon of opposition could change. However, in dynamic and complex decision procedures, even the repeated application of the same method could produce different hexagons of opposition. Important examples include the model proposed in [16], where the loss function is defined by experts of a domain; a group of experts each one evaluating the same loss function independently from others, as considered in [2]; the model generating a collection of hexagons of opposition is the so-called *sequential three-way decision-making* analyzed in [10] and based on the concept of multilevel granular structures. Moreover, we can imagine a dynamic evolution in time, with the hexagons of opposition deriving from the evaluation of the loss function at different time steps.

Motivated by the previous considerations, we intend to explore the relations of opposition, which occur among the vertices of hexagons $\mathcal{H}_{(\alpha,\beta)}$ and $\mathcal{H}_{(\alpha',\beta')}$ generated from distinct pairs of thresholds (α, β) and (α', β'), respectively. Let us underline that the thresholds considered in this article are general, namely they do not derive from specific methods or situations. Finally, we suppose that our initial universe U is finite.

2   Preliminaries

This section recalls fundamental notions related to the hexagon of opposition in probabilistic rough sets theory.

Consider $X \subseteq U$ and an equivalence relation $\mathcal{R}$ on U, i.e. $\mathcal{R}$ is reflexive, symmetric, and transitive. We indicate the equivalence class of $x \in U$ w.r.t. $\mathcal{R}$ with $[x]_{\mathcal{R}}$, and we view X and $[x]_{\mathcal{R}}$ as events of U.

Then, $\mathcal{P}(X|[x]_{\mathcal{R}})$ denotes the *conditional probability* of X given $[x]_{\mathcal{R}}$, i.e.

$$\mathcal{P}(X|[x]_{\mathcal{R}}) = \frac{|[x]_{\mathcal{R}} \cap X|}{|[x]_{\mathcal{R}}|}. \tag{1}$$

In probabilistic rough set theory, a tri-partition of U is determined by using Eq. 1 and a pair of thresholds.

Definition 1. *Let $\alpha, \beta \in [0,1]$ such that $0 \leq \beta < \alpha \leq 1$ and let $X \subseteq U$, then the (α, β)-probabilistic positive, negative and boundary regions are respectively $POS_{(\alpha,\beta)}(X) = \{x \in U \mid \mathcal{P}(X|[x]_{\mathcal{R}}) \geq \alpha\}$, $NEG_{(\alpha,\beta)}(X) = \{x \in U \mid \mathcal{P}(X|[x]_{\mathcal{R}}) \leq \beta\}$, and $BND_{(\alpha,\beta)}(X) = \{x \in U \mid \beta < \mathcal{P}(X|[x]_{\mathcal{R}}) < \alpha\}$.*

Lemma 1. *Let $\alpha, \beta \in [0,1]$ such that $0 \leq \beta < \alpha \leq 1$ and let $X \subseteq U$. Then, $\{POS_{(\alpha,\beta)}(X), NEG_{(\alpha,\beta)}(X), BND_{(\alpha,\beta)}(X)\}$ is a partition of U.*

Based on this definition, a hexagon of opposition is built as follows.

Definition 2. *Let $A \subseteq U$, P_A denotes a property such that*

$$x \in U \text{ satisfies } P_A \text{ if and only if } x \in A.$$

Equivalently, we can say that "P_A is the property of belonging to A".

Definition 3. *Let $A, B \subseteq U$. Then,*

1. *P_A and P_B are* contrary *if and only if $A \cap B = \emptyset$;*
2. *P_A and P_B are* sub-contrary *if and only if $A \cup B = U$;*
3. *P_B is* sub-altern *of P_A if and only if $A \subseteq B$;*
4. *P_A and P_B are* contradictories *if and only if $A = U \setminus B$.*

Definition 4. *Let $A, B, C, D, E, F \subseteq U$. Then, A, B, C, D, E, and F form an hexagon of opposition if and only if*

1. *P_A and P_B are contraries, as well as P_A and P_C, and P_B and P_C;*
2. *P_A and P_E are contradictories, as well as P_B and P_D, and P_C and P_F;*
3. *P_D and P_E are sub-contraries, as well as P_D and P_F, and P_E and P_F;*
4. *P_D is sub-altern of P_A and P_C, P_E is sub-altern of P_B and P_C, and P_F is sub-altern of P_A and P_B.*

The hexagon of opposition having A, B, C, D, E, and F as vertices is represented by Fig. 3.

Furthermore, a hexagon of opposition arises whenever a tri-partition of a universe is given [5].

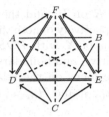
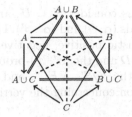

Fig. 3. Hexagon of opposition with $A, B, C, D, E, F \subseteq U$.

Fig. 4. Hexagon of opposition related to the partition $\{A, B, C\}$ of U.

Theorem 1. *Let $\{A, B, C\}$ be a partition of U. Then, $A, B, C, A \cup C, B \cup C$, and $A \cup B$ form an hexagon of opposition as in Fig. 4.*

By Lemma 1, the positive, negative, and boundary regions form a tri-partition of the initial universe. Consequently, special semantics for hexagons of opposition has been provided in the framework of probabilistic rough sets [1].

Theorem 2. *Let $X \subseteq U$ and let $0 \leq \beta < \alpha \leq 1$, then the sets $POS_{(\alpha,\beta)}(X)$, $NEG_{(\alpha,\beta)}(X)$, $BND_{(\alpha,\beta)}(X)$, $POS_{(\alpha,\beta)}(X) \cup BND_{(\alpha,\beta)}(X)$, $NEG_{(\alpha,\beta)}(X) \cup BND_{(\alpha,\beta)}(X)$, and $POS_{(\alpha,\beta)}(X) \cup NEG_{(\alpha,\beta)}(X)$ form an hexagon of opposition as in Fig. 5.*

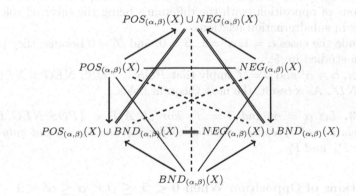

Fig. 5. Hexagon of opposition related to $\{POS_{(\alpha,\beta)}(X), NEG_{(\alpha,\beta)}(X), BND_{(\alpha,\beta)}(X)\}$.

3 Comparing Hexagons of Opposition

This section compares hexagons of opposition deriving from diverse pairs of thresholds.

Let us consider $X \subseteq U$, an equivalence relation $\mathcal{R}$ on U, and the pairs of thresholds (α, β) and (α', β'). For convenience, we respectively denote the (α, β)-probabilistic positive, negative, and boundary regions of X with POS, NEG, and BND and the (α', β')-probabilistic positive, negative, and boundary regions of X with POS', NEG', and BND'. Therefore, we focus on the relations of opposition concerning the vertices of the hexagons $\mathcal{H}_{(\alpha, \beta)}$ and $\mathcal{H}_{(\alpha', \beta')}$ depicted in Fig. 6.

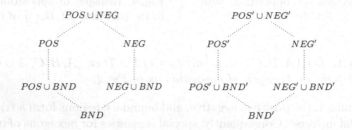

Fig. 6. Hexagons $\mathcal{H}_{(\alpha, \beta)}$ and $\mathcal{H}_{(\alpha', \beta')}$ based on (α, β) and (α', β), respectively.

Such relations change according to the mutual position of the thresholds. Hence, we analyze all possible cases that can occur: $0 < \beta' \leq \beta < \alpha \leq \alpha' < 1$, $0 < \beta' < \alpha' \leq \beta < \alpha < 1$, and $0 < \beta' \leq \beta \leq \alpha' \leq \alpha < 1$. Let us notice that by inverting (α, β) and (α', β') in the previous inequalities, we obtain the same relations of opposition, with the difference being the inverted role of the propositions in subalternation relations.

We exclude the cases $\alpha = 1$, $\alpha' = 1$, $\beta = 0$, and $\beta' = 0$ because they produce the hexagon studied in [5].

Moreover, $\alpha = \alpha'$ and $\beta = \beta'$ imply that $POS = POS'$, $NEG = NEG'$, and $BND = BND'$. As a result, the next theorem holds.

Theorem 3. *Let $\alpha = \alpha'$ and $\beta = \beta'$. For all $A, B \in \{POS, NEG, BND\}$, a certain relation of opposition is satisfied for P_A and $P_{B'}$ if and only if it is satisfied for P_A and P_B.*

3.1   Relations of Opposition When $0 < \beta' \leq \beta < \alpha \leq \alpha' < 1$

Firstly, we focus on the relations of opposition occurring when $\beta' < \beta$ and $\alpha < \alpha'$.

The proof of the next theorems are based on Definition 1, Lemma 1, and the following remark.

Remark 1. Let $0 < \beta' < \beta < \alpha < \alpha' < 1$. Then, $NEG' \subseteq NEG$, $POS' \subseteq POS$, $BND \subseteq BND'$, $NEG' \cup BND = NEG' \cup POS = BND \cup POS' = POS' \cup BND = POS' \cup NEG = \emptyset$.

Theorem 4. *The following are pairs of contraries properties:* $(P_{POS}, P_{NEG'})$, $(P_{POS'}, P_{NEG})$, $(P_{BND}, P_{POS'})$, $(P_{BND}, P_{NEG'})$, $(P_{BND}, P_{POS' \cup NEG'})$, $(P_{POS \cup BND}, P_{NEG'})$, *and* $(P_{NEG \cup BND}, P_{POS'})$.

Figure 7 shows the relations of opposition listed by Theorem 4.

Theorem 5. *The following are pairs of sub-contraries properties:* $(P_{POS}, P_{NEG' \cup BND'})$, $(P_{POS' \cup BND'}, P_{NEG \cup BND})$, $(P_{POS \cup BND}, P_{NEG' \cup BND'})$, $(P_{POS' \cup BND'}, P_{NEG})$, $(P_{POS' \cup BND'}, P_{POS \cup NEG})$, $(P_{BND'}, P_{POS \cup NEG})$, *and* $(P_{NEG' \cup BND'}, P_{POS \cup NEG})$.

Figure 8 shows the relations of opposition listed by Theorem 5.

Theorem 6. *The following are pairs of properties such that the second component is sub-altern of the first one:* $(P_{POS'}, P_{POS})$, $(P_{POS'}, P_{POS \cup NEG})$, $(P_{POS'}, P_{POS \cup BND})$, $(P_{NEG'}, P_{NEG})$, $(P_{NEG'}, P_{POS \cup NEG})$, $(P_{NEG'}, P_{NEG \cup BND})$, *and* $(P_{POS' \cup NEG'}, P_{POS \cup NEG})$.

Theorem 7. *The following are pairs of properties such that the second component is sub-altern of the first one:* $(P_{POS}, P_{POS' \cup BND'})$, $(P_{BND}, P_{POS' \cup BND'})$, $(P_{BND}, P_{NEG' \cup BND'})$, $(P_{NEG \cup BND}, P_{NEG' \cup BND'})$, $(P_{POS \cup BND}, P_{POS' \cup BND'})$, $(P_{BND}, P_{BND'})$, *and* $(P_{NEG}, P_{NEG' \cup BND'})$.

Figures 9 and 10 show the relations of opposition listed by Theorem 6 and Theorem 7, respectively.

Now, let us consider the relations of opposition occurring when $\alpha = \alpha'$ and $\beta = \beta'$. In this case, it is easy to verify that if $\alpha = \alpha'$, then $POS = POS'$ and $BND \cup NEG = BND' \cup NEG'$. Analogously, if $\beta = \beta'$, then $NEG = NEG'$ and $POS \cup BND = POS' \cup BND'$. Thus, we can prove that all relations of opposition listed by the previous theorems are preserved, except those regarding the pairs $(P_{NEG \cup BND}, P_{POS'})$, $(P_{NEG' \cup BND'}, P_{POS})$, $(P_{POS \cup BND}, P_{NEG'})$, and $(P_{POS' \cup BND'}, P_{NEG})$.

Theorem 8. (a) *If* $\alpha = \alpha'$, *then* $P_{NEG \cup BND}$ *and* $P_{POS'}$, *and* $P_{NEG' \cup BND'}$ *and* P_{POS} *are contradictories*[1].
(b) *If* $\beta = \beta'$, *then* $P_{POS \cup BND}$ *and* $P_{NEG'}$, *and* $P_{POS' \cup BND'}$ *and* P_{NEG} *are contradictories*[2].

Additionally, the following new relations of opposition are true.

Theorem 9. *Let* $\alpha = \alpha'$. *Then,* P_{POS} *and* $P_{BND'}$ *are contraries,* $P_{NEG \cup BND}$ *and* $P_{POS' \cup NEG'}$ *are sub-contraries,* $P_{POS' \cup NEG'}$ *is sub-altern of* P_{POS}, *and* $P_{NEG \cup BND}$ *is sub-altern of* $P_{BND'}$.

Theorem 10. *Let* $\beta = \beta'$. *Then,* P_{NEG} *and* $P_{BND'}$ *are contraries,* $P_{POS \cup BND}$ *and* $P_{POS' \cup NEG'}$ *are sub-contraries,* $P_{POS \cup BND}$ *is sub-altern of* $P_{BND'}$, *and* $P_{POS' \cup NEG'}$ *is sub-altern of* P_{NEG}.

---

[1] If $\alpha < \alpha'$, then $P_{NEG \cup BND}$ and $P_{POS'}$ are contraries by Theorem 4, and $P_{NEG' \cup BND'}$ and P_{POS} are sub-contraries by Theorem 5.
[2] If $\beta < \beta'$, then $P_{POS \cup BND}$ and $P_{NEG'}$ are contraries by Theorem 4, and $P_{POS' \cup BND'}$ and P_{NEG} are sub-contraries by Theorem 5.

3.2   Relations of Opposition When $0 < \beta' < \alpha' \le \beta < \alpha < 1$

The proofs of the next theorems are based on Definition 1, Lemma 1, and the following remark.

Remark 2. Let $0 < \beta' < \beta < \alpha < \alpha' < 1$. Then, $NEG' \subseteq NEG$, $BND' \subseteq NEG$, $POS \subseteq POS'$, $BND \subseteq POS'$, $NEG' \cap BND = NEG' \cap POS = BND' \cap BND = BND' \cup POS = \emptyset$.

Theorem 11. *The following are pairs of contraries properties:* $(P_{POS}, P_{BND'})$, $(P_{POS}, P_{NEG' \cup BND'})$, $(P_{POS}, P_{NEG'})$, $(P_{POS \cup BND}, P_{BND'})$, $(P_{BND}, P_{NEG'})$, $(P_{BND}, P_{NEG' \cup BND'})$, $(P_{BND}, P_{BND'})$, $(P_{POS \cup BND}, P_{NEG' \cup BND'})$, *and* $(P_{POS \cup BND}, P_{NEG'})$.

Figure 11 shows the relations of opposition listed by Theorem 11.

Theorem 12. *The following are pairs of sub-contraries properties:*
$(P_{POS' \cup BND'}, P_{POS \cup NEG})$, $(P_{POS'}, P_{NEG \cup BND})$, $(P_{POS'}, P_{POS \cup NEG})$,
$(P_{POS' \cup BND'}, P_{NEG})$, $(P_{POS' \cup BND'}, P_{NEG \cup BND})$, $(P_{POS' \cup NEG'}, P_{NEG \cup BND})$,
$(P_{POS' \cup NEG'}, P_{NEG})$, $(P_{POS'}, P_{NEG})$, *and* $(P_{POS' \cup NEG'}, P_{POS \cup NEG})$.

Figure 12 shows the relations of opposition listed by Theorem 12.

Theorem 13. *The following are pairs of properties such that the second component is sub-altern of the first one:*
$(P_{NEG'}, P_{NEG})$, $(P_{NEG'}, P_{NEG \cup BND})$, $(P_{NEG' \cup BND'}, P_{NEG})$, $(P_{NEG' \cup BND'}, P_{NEG \cup BND})$, $(P_{BND'}, P_{NEG \cup BND})$, $(P_{BND'}, P_{NEG})$, $(P_{NEG' \cup BND'}, P_{POS \cup NEG})$, $(P_{NEG'}, P_{POS \cup NEG})$, *and* $(P_{BND'}, P_{POS \cup NEG})$.

Theorem 14. *The following are pairs of properties such that the second component is sub-altern of the first one:*
$(P_{POS}, P_{POS'})$, $(P_{POS}, P_{POS' \cup BND'})$, $(P_{POS}, P_{POS' \cup NEG'})$, $(P_{BND}, P_{POS'})$,
$(P_{POS \cup BND}, P_{POS'})$, $(P_{POS \cup BND}, P_{POS' \cup NEG'})$, $(P_{BND}, P_{POS' \cup BND'})$,
$(P_{BND}, P_{POS' \cup NEG'})$, *and* $(P_{POS \cup BND}, P_{POS' \cup BND'})$.

Figures 13 and shows 14 respectively show the relations of oppositions listed by Theorem 13 and Theorem 14, respectively.

3.3   Relations of Opposition When $0 < \beta' \le \beta \le \alpha' \le \alpha < 1$

Let us first investigate the relations of opposition occurring when $0 < \beta' < \beta < \alpha' < \alpha < 1$.

The proofs of the next theorems are based on Definition 1, Lemma 1, and the following remark.

Remark 3. Let $0 < \beta' < \beta < \alpha' < \alpha < 1$. Then, $NEG' \subseteq NEG$, $POS \subseteq POS'$, $NEG' \cap BND = NEG' \cap POS = BND' \cap POS = POS' \cup NEG = \emptyset$.

Theorem 15. *The following are pairs of contraries properties:* $(P_{POS}, P_{NEG'})$, $(P_{POS}, P_{BND'})$, $(P_{POS}, P_{NEG' \cup BND'})$, $(P_{POS'}, P_{NEG})$, $(P_{POS \cup BND}, P_{NEG'})$, *and* $(P_{BND}, P_{NEG'})$.

Figure 15 shows the relations of opposition listed by Theorem 15.

Theorem 16. *The following are pairs of sub-contraries properties:*
$(P_{POS'}, P_{NEG \cup BND})$, $(P_{POS \cup BND}, P_{NEG' \cup BND'})$, $(P_{POS' \cup BND'}, P_{NEG \cup BND})$, $(P_{POS' \cup BND'}, P_{NEG})$, $(P_{POS' \cup BND'}, P_{POS \cup NEG})$, and $(P_{NEG \cup BND}, P_{POS' \cup NEG'})$.

Figure 16 shows the relations of opposition listed by Theorem 16.

Theorem 17. *The following are pairs of properties such that the second component is sub-altern of the first one:*
$(P_{POS}, P_{POS' \cup NEG'})$, $(P_{POS \cup BND}, P_{POS' \cup BND'})$, $(P_{NEG' \cup BND'}, P_{NEG \cup BND})$, $(P_{BND}, P_{POS' \cup BND'})$, $(P_{NEG'}, P_{NEG})$, $(P_{POS}, P_{POS'})$, $(P_{NEG'}, P_{NEG \cup BND})$, $(P_{NEG}, P_{NEG' \cup BND'})$, $(P_{NEG'}, P_{POS \cup NEG})$, $(P_{POS}, P_{POS' \cup BND'})$, $(P_{BND'}, P_{NEG \cup BND})$, and $(P_{POS'}, P_{POS \cup BND})$.

Figures 17 and 18 show the relations of opposition listed by Theorem 17.

When $\beta = \alpha'$, all relations of opposition shown by Theorems 15–17 are kept, except those shown in the next theorem.

Theorem 18. *Let $\beta = \alpha'$.*

(a) *If $P(X|[x]_{\mathcal{R}}) \neq \beta$ for each $x \in X$, then $P_{POS'}$ and P_{NEG} are contradictories. Otherwise, they are sub-contraries*[3].
(b) *$P_{POS \cup BND}$ and $P_{NEG' \cup BND'}$ are contraries*[4].

Also, the the following relations are added to those listed by Theorems 15–17.

Theorem 19. (a) *$P_{POS \cup BND}$ and $P_{BND'}$, P_{BND} and $P_{BND'}$, and P_{BND} and $P_{NEG' \cup BND'}$ are contraries.*
(b) *$P_{POS \cup NEG}$ and $P_{POS' \cup NEG'}$, $P_{POS'}$ and $P_{POS \cup NEG}$, and P_{NEG} and $P_{POS' \cup NEG'}$, are sub-contraries.*
(c) *$P_{POS'}$ is sub-altern of P_{BND}, $P_{POS' \cup NEG'}$ is sub-altern of $P_{POS \cup BND}$, $P_{BND'}$ is sub-altern of P_{NEG}, $P_{POS' \cup NEG'}$ is sub-altern of P_{BND}, $P_{POS \cup NEG}$ is sub-altern of $P_{NEG' \cup BND'}$.*

We can notice that $\beta = \alpha'$ if and only if $\beta < \beta'$ and $\alpha' < \alpha$ (because $\beta < \alpha$ and $\beta' < \alpha'$, by hypothesis). Consequently, it is not possible that $\beta = \alpha'$ together with $\alpha = \alpha'$ and $\beta = \beta'$.

Finally, let us analyze the cases $\alpha = \alpha'$ and $\beta = \beta'$.

Theorem 20. *Let $\beta = \beta'$. Then,*

(a) *$P_{BND'}$ and P_{NEG}, and $P_{BND'}$ and $P_{POS \cup NEG}$ are contraries;*
(b) *$P_{POS \cup BND}$ and $P_{NEG'}$, and $P_{POS' \cup BND'}$ and P_{NEG} are contradictories;*
(c) *$P_{POS \cup BND}$ and $P_{POS' \cup NEG'}$, and P_{BND} and $P_{POS' \cup NEG'}$ are sub-contraries;*

---

[3] If $\beta < \alpha'$, then $P_{POS'}$ and P_{NEG} are contraries by Theorem 15.
[4] If $\beta < \alpha'$, then $P_{POS \cup BND}$ and $P_{NEG' \cup BND'}$ are sub-contraries by Theorem 16.

(d) $P_{POSUBND}$ *is sub-altern of* $P_{BND'}$, $P_{POS'UNEG'}$ *is sub-altern of* P_{NEG}, P_{BND} *is sub-altern of* $P_{BND'}$, *and* $P_{POS'UNEG'}$ *is sub-altern of* $P_{POSUNEG}$.

Therefore, $\beta = \beta'$ implies that all relations of opposition exhibited by Theorems 15–17 hold, except those involving the pairs $(P_{POSUBND}, P_{NEG'})$ and $(P_{POS'UBND'}, P_{NEG})$: these propositions are contradictories for $\beta = \beta'$ (by Theorem 20(b)), while they are respectively contraries and sub-contraries for $\beta' < \beta$ (by Theorems 15 and 16). Moreover, items (a), (c) and (d) of Theorem 20 provide new relations of opposition being satisfied only for $\beta = \beta'$.

Theorem 21. *Let* $\alpha = \alpha'$. *Then,*

(a) $P_{POS'}$ *and* P_{BND}, *and* P_{BND} *and* $P_{POS'UBND'}$ *are contraries;*

(b) P_{POS} *and* $P_{NEG'UBND'}$ *and* $P_{POS'}$ *and* $P_{NEGUBND}$ *are contradictories;*

(c) $P_{NEG'UBND'}$ *and* $P_{POSUNEG}$, *and* $P_{BND'}$ *and* $P_{POSUNEG}$ *are sub-contraries;*

(d) $P_{POSUNEG}$ *is sub-altern of* $P_{POS'}$, $P_{POSUNEG}$ *is sub-altern of* $P_{POS'UNEG'}$, $P_{NEG'UBND'}$ *is sub-altern of* P_{BND}, *and* $P_{BND'}$ *is sub-altern of* P_{BND}.

Thus, $\alpha = \alpha'$ implies that all relations of opposition exhibited by Theorems 15–17 hold, except those involving the pairs $(P_{POS}, P_{NEG'UBND'})$ and $(P_{NEGUBND}, P_{POS'})$: these propositions are contradictories for $\alpha = \alpha'$ (by Theorem 21(b)), while they are respectively contraries and sub-contraries for $\alpha' < \alpha$ (by Theorems 15 and 16). Moreover, items (a), (c), and (d) of Theorem 21 provide new relations of opposition being satisfied only for $\alpha = \alpha'$.

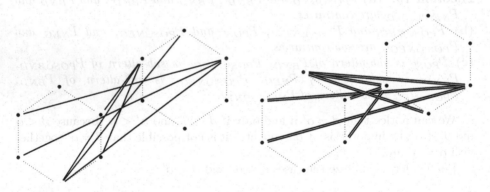

Fig. 7. $0 < \beta' < \beta < \alpha < \alpha' < 1$.   **Fig. 8.** $0 < \beta' < \beta < \alpha < \alpha' < 1$.

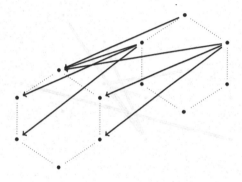

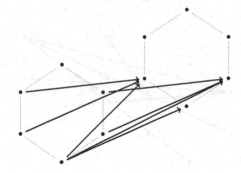

Fig. 9. $0 < \beta' < \beta < \alpha < \alpha' < 1.$ **Fig. 10.** $0 < \beta' < \beta < \alpha < \alpha' < 1.$

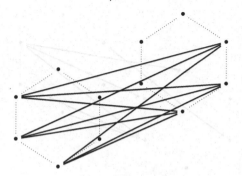

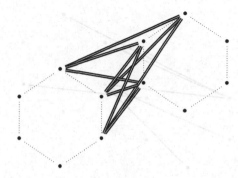

Fig. 11. $0 < \beta' < \alpha' \leq \beta < \alpha < 1.$ **Fig. 12.** $0 < \beta' < \alpha' \leq \beta < \alpha < 1.$

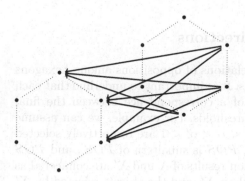

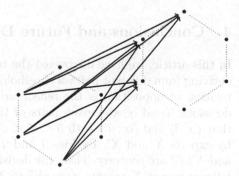

Fig. 13. $0 < \beta' < \alpha' \leq \beta < \alpha < 1.$ **Fig. 14.** $0 < \beta' < \alpha' \leq \beta < \alpha < 1.$

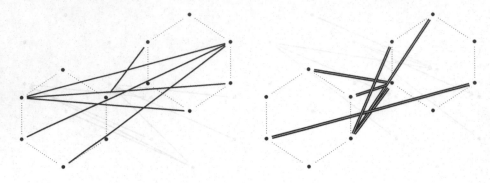

Fig. 15. $0 < \beta' < \beta < \alpha' < \alpha < 1.$ **Fig. 16.** $0 < \beta' < \beta < \alpha' < \alpha < 1.$

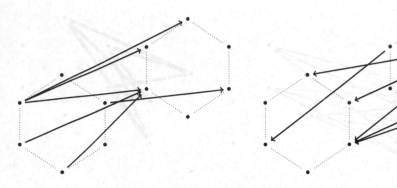

Fig. 17. $0 < \beta' < \beta < \alpha' < \alpha < 1.$ **Fig. 18.** $0 < \beta' < \beta < \alpha' < \alpha < 1.$

4   Conclusions and Future Directions

In this article, we have discovered the relations of oppositions among hexagons deriving from different pairs of thresholds. It is important to underline that each relation of opposition is the reflection of a correspondence between the final decisions based on the given pairs of thresholds. For example, we can assume that (α, β) and (α', β') with $0 < \beta' < \beta < \alpha < \alpha' < 1$ are respectively selected by experts X and X'. By Figs. 7 and 9, POS is subaltern of POS', and POS and NEG' are contrary. Then, the decision results of X and X' are connected as follows: expert X accepts more objects than X', and the objects rejected by X' cannot be accepted by X. In the future, using the relations proposed here, we intend to measure how much decisions related to diverse thresholds differ from each other. Moreover, we could generalize the hexagon in probabilistic rough sets by defining graded probabilistic rough sets based on the concept of evaluative linguistic expressions [12].

References

1. Abbruzzese, R., Gaeta, A., Loia, V., Lomasto, L., Orciuoli, F.: Detecting influential news in online communities: an approach based on hexagons of opposition generated by three-way decisions and probabilistic rough sets. Inf. Sci. **578**, 364–377 (2021)
2. Agbodah, K.: The determination of three-way decisions with decision-theoretic rough sets considering the loss function evaluated by multiple experts. Granular Comput. **4**(2), 285–297 (2018). https://doi.org/10.1007/s41066-018-0099-0
3. Béziau, J.Y.: The power of the hexagon. Log. Univers. **6**(1–2), 1–43 (2012)
4. Boffa, S., Murinová, P., Novák, V.: Graded polygons of opposition in fuzzy formal concept analysis. Int. J. Approx. Reason. **132**, 128–153 (2021)
5. Ciucci, D., Dubois, D., Prade, H.: Oppositions in rough set theory. In: Li, T., et al. (eds.) RSKT 2012. LNCS (LNAI), vol. 7414, pp. 504–513. Springer, Heidelberg (2012). https://doi.org/10.1007/978-3-642-31900-6_62
6. Deng, X., Yao, Y.: An information-theoretic interpretation of thresholds in probabilistic rough sets. In: Li, T., et al. (eds.) RSKT 2012. LNCS (LNAI), vol. 7414, pp. 369–378. Springer, Heidelberg (2012). https://doi.org/10.1007/978-3-642-31900-6_46
7. Dufatanye, A.A.: From the logical square to blanché's hexagon: formalization, applicability and the idea of the normative structure of thought. Log. Univers. **6**(1–2), 45–67 (2012)
8. Gao, C., Yao, Y.: Determining thresholds in three-way decisions with chi-square statistic. In: Flores, V., et al. (eds.) IJCRS 2016. LNCS (LNAI), vol. 9920, pp. 272–281. Springer, Cham (2016). https://doi.org/10.1007/978-3-319-47160-0_25
9. Herbert, J.P., Yao, J.: Game-theoretic rough sets. Fund. Inform. **108**(3–4), 267–286 (2011)
10. Liu, D., Li, T., Liang, D.: Three-way decisions in dynamic decision-theoretic rough sets. In: Lingras, P., Wolski, M., Cornelis, C., Mitra, S., Wasilewski, P. (eds.) RSKT 2013. LNCS (LNAI), vol. 8171, pp. 291–301. Springer, Heidelberg (2013). https://doi.org/10.1007/978-3-642-41299-8_28
11. Moretti, A.: Why the logical hexagon? Log. Univers. **6**(1), 69–107 (2012)
12. Novák, V.: A comprehensive theory of trichotomous evaluative linguistic expressions. Fuzzy Sets Syst. **159**(22), 2939–2969 (2008)
13. Parsons, T.: The traditional square of opposition (1997)
14. Pfeifer, N., Sanfilippo, G.: Probabilistic squares and hexagons of opposition under coherence. Int. J. Approx. Reason. **88**, 282–294 (2017)
15. Yao, Y.: Three-way decisions with probabilistic rough sets. Inf. Sci. **180**(3), 341–353 (2010)
16. Yao, Y., Wong, S.K.M.: A decision theoretic framework for approximating concepts. Int. J. Man Mach. Stud. **37**(6), 793–809 (1992)

Analysis of Peterson's Rules
for Syllogisms with Intermediate
Quantifiers

Vilém Novák[✉] and Petra Murinová[✉]

Institute for Research and Applications of Fuzzy Modeling,
University of Ostrava, 30. dubna 22, 701 03 Ostrava 1, Czech Republic
{vilem.novak,petra.murinova}@osu.cz
http://irafm.osu.cz/

Abstract. In our previous papers, we syntactically proved validity of
105 logical syllogisms with intermediate quantifiers. Peterson in his book
suggested 6 rules using which it is possible to verify validity of such
syllogisms in a simple way. The rules, however, are formulated in free
language and so, it is not possible to check whether they are correct. In
this paper, we focus on formalization of Peterson's rules. The main idea
is based on the graded Peterson square of opposition, which has been
formally analyzed in our previous publications.

Keywords: Peterson's rules of distributivity · quality and quantity ·
Fuzzy intermediate syllogisms · Graded Peterson square of opposition

1 Introduction

In our previous papers (see, e.g., [7,12] and others), we developed the formal
theory of intermediate quantifiers and considered five specific ones, namely *all,
almost all, most, many* and *some* (see [7,10]). Our theory formalizes the deep
analysis provided by Peterson in his book [18]. He also gave informal demonstration of validity of 105 syllogisms with intermediate quantifiers. In [8] we verified
his results using formal means of mathematical fuzzy logic.

Intermediate quantifiers belong among a wider class of fuzzy and generalized
quantifiers [17,22]. Their theory, which is mostly semantical, includes also analysis of syllogistic reasoning (see [3,16,19,23]).Our work is also related to the area
of linguistic summarization of data (cf. [5,21]).

Peterson suggested 6 extended rules using which it is possible to verify validity of syllogisms that contain also non-trivial intermediate quantifiers in a simple
way. The rules are based on the graded square of opposition that gives us information about kind of the given quantifier (*positive or negative*) and its position

The work was supported from ERDF/ESF by the project "Centre for the development of Artificial Intelligence Methods for the Automotive Industry of the region" No.
CZ.02.1.01/0.0/0.0/17-049/0008414 and partially also by the MŠMT project NPU II
project LQ1602 "IT4Innovations excellence in science".

(*majority or greater*). However, Peterson formulated the rules in free natural language and so, it is not possible to check, whether the rules do the job correctly. The goal of this paper is to suggest formalization of them.

When applying the rules to checking validity of syllogisms, important role is played by the concept of distribution that has been analyzed by many researchers (see, e.g., Gainor [4]). In the extended rules, this concept is replaced by a special number called *distribution index* (cf. also Thompson [20]). In this paper, we will modify this concept to fit our formalization. We will show that our formalized rules provide the same information as the original Peterson's ones.

2 Preliminaries

2.1 Fuzzy Type Theory

The theory of intermediate quantifiers has been developed as a special theory of fuzzy type theory Ł-FTT(higher-order fuzzy logic) with truth values forming a linearly ordered Łukasiewicz MV_Δ-algebra $\mathscr{L}_\Delta = \langle L, \vee, \wedge, \otimes, \rightarrow, 0, 1, \Delta \rangle$ (see [2, 15]). A special formula considered in the theory of intermediate quantifiers is $\dagger_o$ whose main characteristics is $\vdash \neg\dagger_o \equiv \dagger_o$. It is interpreted in the standard Łukasiewicz MV_Δ by the truth value 0.5.

The basic syntactical objects of Ł-FTT are classical: *type* and *formula* (see [1]). The atomic types are ϵ (elements) and o (truth values). General types are defined recursively from simpler type, i.e., if α, β are types then $(\beta\alpha)$ is a type. The set of all types by *Types*. .

The *language* J of Ł-FTT consists of variables $x_\alpha, \ldots$, special constants $c_\alpha, \ldots$ ($\alpha \in$ *Types*), the symbol λ, and brackets. We will consider the following concrete special constants: $\mathbf{E}_{(o\alpha)\alpha}$ (fuzzy equality) for every $\alpha \in$ *Types*, $\mathbf{C}_{(oo)o}$ (conjunction), $\mathbf{D}_{(oo)}$ (delta operation on truth values) and the description operator $\iota_{\epsilon(o\epsilon)}$.

Formulas are formed of variables, constants (each of specific type), and the symbol λ. Thus, each formula A is assigned a type and we write it as A_α. A set of formulas of type α is denoted by *Form*$_\alpha$. The set of all formulas is $Form = \bigcup_{\alpha \in Types} Form_\alpha$[1].

A (general) model of FTT is a system of sets and fuzzy equalities on them:

$$\mathscr{N} = \langle (N_\alpha, \overset{\circ}{=}_\alpha)_{\alpha \in Types}, \mathscr{L}_\Delta \rangle. \tag{1}$$

Interpretation of formulas is the following. If $\mathscr{N}$ is a model then $\mathscr{N}(A_o) \in M_o$ is a truth value, $\mathscr{N}(A_\epsilon) \in N_\epsilon$ is some element and $\mathscr{N}(A_{\beta\alpha}) : N_\alpha \rightarrow N_\beta$ is a function. For example, $\mathscr{N}(A_{o\alpha}) : N_\alpha \rightarrow N_o$ is a fuzzy set and $\mathscr{M}(A_{(o\alpha)\alpha}) : M_\alpha \times N_\alpha \rightarrow N_o$ a fuzzy relation. Note that if the truth values form the standard Łukasiewicz MV-algebra then $N_o = [0, 1]$.

Let N be a universe. A fuzzy set A in N is a function $A : N \rightarrow L$. The following well known concepts will be used below:

---

[1] To improve readability of formulas, we quite often write the type only once in the beginning of the formula and then omit it. Alternatively, we write $A \in Form_\alpha$ to emphasize that A is a formula of type α and do not repeat its type again.

(i) *Kernel* of A is a set $\mathrm{Ker}(A) = \{u \in N \mid A(u) = 1\}$.
(ii) *Support* of A is a set $\mathrm{Supp}(A) = \{u \in N \mid A(u) > 0\}$.
(iii) The set of all fuzzy sets on N is denoted by $\mathscr{F}(N)$.

For simplicity, we will denote the fuzzy set $N \setminus A$ by $\neg A$.

In the sequel we will use special (derived) formulas Υ_{oo} and $\hat{\Upsilon}_{oo}$, using which we can express that the given formula A_o has in every model a non-zero or general truth value, respectively.

$$\Upsilon_{oo} \equiv \lambda z_o \cdot \neg \Delta(\neg z_o), \qquad\qquad \text{(non-zerotruth value)}$$

$$\hat{\Upsilon}_{oo} \equiv \lambda z_o \cdot \neg \Delta(z_o \vee \neg z_o). \qquad\qquad \text{(general truth value)}$$

Both formulas Υ_{oo} as well as $\hat{\Upsilon}_{oo}$ are crisp.

Thus, if A_o is a formula representing a truth value and $p \in \mathrm{Asg}(\mathscr{M})$ then $\mathscr{M}_p(\hat{\Upsilon}A_o) = 1$ iff $\mathscr{M}_p(A_o) \in (0,1)$ and $\mathscr{M}_p(\Upsilon A_o) = 1$ iff $\mathscr{M}_p(A_o) > 0$ hold in any model $\mathscr{M}$. The formulas $\Upsilon A_o, \hat{\Upsilon}A_o$ are crisp, i.e., in any model they attain a truth value from $\{0,1\}$.

2.2 Evaluative Linguistic Expressions

The theory of intermediate quantifiers is based on the theory of evaluative linguistic expressions that are expressions of natural language such as *extremely small, roughly medium, big, very short, extremely high*, etc. The semantics of evaluative linguistic expressions is formulated in a special formal theory T^{Ev} of L-FTT.

The evaluative expressions are construed by special formulas $Sm \in Form_{oo(oo)}$ (*small*), $Me \in Form_{oo(oo)}$ (*medium*), $Bi \in Form_{oo(oo)}$ (*big*), and $Ze \in Form_{oo(oo)}$ (*zero*) that can be extended by several selected linguistic hedges. Recall that a *hedge*, which is often an adverb such as "very, significantly, about, roughly", etc. is in general construed by a formula $\nu \in Form_{oo}$ with specific properties. To classify that a given formula is a hedge, we introduced a formula $Hedge \in Form_{o(oo)}$. Then $T^{Ev} \vdash Hedge\,\nu$ means that ν is a hedge. We refer the reader to [11] for the technical details. We assume that the following is provable: $T^{Ev} \vdash Hedge\,\nu$ for all $\nu \in \{Ex, Si, Ve, ML, Ro, QR, VR\}$. Consequently, evaluative linguistic expressions are represented by formulas

$$Sm\,\nu, Me\,\nu, Bi\,\nu, Ze\,\nu \in Form_{oo} \tag{2}$$

where ν is a hedge. For example, $Bi\,Ex$ is a formula construing the evaluative expression "extremely big". We will also consider an *empty hedge* $\bar{\nu}$ that is always present in front of *small, medium* and *big* if no other hedge is given. A special hedge is Δ_{oo} that construes the expression "utmost" and occurs below in the evaluative expression $Bi\,\Delta$. Let $\nu_{1,oo}, \nu_{2,oo}$ be two hedges, i.e., $T^{Ev} \vdash Hedge\,\nu_{1,oo}$ and $T^{Ev} \vdash Hedge\,\nu_{2,oo}$. We propose a relation of partial ordering of hedges by

$$\ll := \lambda p_{oo} \lambda q_{oo} \cdot (\forall z_o)(p_{oo}z \Rightarrow q_{oo}z).$$

Lemma 1 *[11]. The following ordering the specific hedges can be proved.*

$$T^{Ev} \vdash \mathit{\Delta} \ll Ex \ll Si \ll Ve \ll \bar{\nu} \ll ML \ll Ro \ll QR \ll VR. \qquad (3)$$

Evaluative expressions characterize certain imprecisely determined positions on a bounded linearly ordered scale. As this publication is limited by the number of pages, we will refer the reader to [11, 14].

The following inequality can be proved in the theory of evaluative expressions.

Lemma 2

$$\inf \text{Supp}(\neg\, Sm) < 0.5 < \inf \text{Supp}(Bi\ Ve) \leq$$
$$\inf \text{Supp}(Bi\ Ex) \leq \inf \text{Supp}(Bi\ \mathit{\Delta}) = 1.$$

Proof. It follows from Lemma 1 and by ordering of evaluative linguistic expressions. ∎

For our analysis in this paper we also assume the following:

$$\inf \text{Supp}(\neg\, Sm) \oplus \inf \text{Supp}(Bi\ Ex) = 1, \qquad (4)$$
$$\inf \text{Supp}(\neg\, Sm) \oplus \inf \text{Supp}(Bi\ Ve) < 1. \qquad (5)$$

In this paper we will combine syntax and semantics. To simplify the notation, we will use the same symbol for a formula as well as its interpretation in a model (the reader will always know, which case is dealt with). As a special case, if Ev is an evaluative expression (a formula) then its interpretation in a model w.r.t. a standard context is a fuzzy set $Ev \in \mathscr{F}(L)$.

3 The Theory of Intermediate Quantifiers

Recall that the meaning of intermediate quantifiers lays between the meaning of the classical quantifiers $\forall$ and $\exists$. They are modeled by selected formulas of a special formal theory T^{Ev} of Ł-FTT. These formulas express quantification over the universe represented by a fuzzy set whose size is characterized by a measure due to the following definition. Formal definitions of operations on fuzzy sets can be found in [12].

3.1 Syntactic Definition of Intermediate Quantifiers

Definition 1. *Let $R \in Form_{o(o\alpha)(o\alpha)}$ be a formula where $\alpha \in Types$ is an arbitrary type.*

(i) A formula $\mu \in Form_{o(o\alpha)(o\alpha)}$ defined by

$$\mu_{o(o\alpha)(o\alpha)} \equiv \lambda z_{o\alpha}\, \lambda x_{o\alpha}\, (Rz_{o\alpha})x_{o\alpha} \qquad (6)$$

represents a measure on fuzzy sets in the universe of type $\alpha \in Types$ if it has the following properties:

(M1) $\Delta(x_{o\alpha} \subseteq z_{o\alpha}) \,\&\, \Delta(y_{o\alpha} \subseteq z_{o\alpha}) \,\&\, \Delta(x_{o\alpha} \subseteq$
      $y_{o\alpha}) \Rightarrow ((\mu z_{o\alpha})x_{o\alpha} \Rightarrow (\mu z_{o\alpha})y_{o\alpha}),$

(M2) $\Delta(x_{o\alpha} \subseteq z_{o\alpha}) \Rightarrow$
      $((\mu z_{o\alpha})(z_{o\alpha} \setminus x_{o\alpha}) \equiv \neg(\mu z_{o\alpha})x_{o\alpha}),$

(M3) $\Delta(x_{o\alpha} \subseteq y_{o\alpha}) \,\&\, \Delta(x_{o\alpha} \subseteq z_{o\alpha}) \,\&\, \Delta(y_{o\alpha} \subseteq$
      $z_{o\alpha}) \Rightarrow ((\mu z_{o\alpha})x_{o\alpha} \Rightarrow (\mu y_{o\alpha})x_{o\alpha})$

where $x_{o\alpha}, y_{o\alpha}, z_{o\alpha}$ are variables representing fuzzy sets.

(ii) *The following formula characterizes* measurable fuzzy sets *of a given type* α:

$$\mathbf{M}_{o(o\alpha)} \equiv \lambda z_{o\alpha} \cdot \neg\Delta(z_{o\alpha} \equiv \emptyset_{o\alpha}) \,\&\, \Delta(\mu z_{o\alpha})z_{o\alpha} \,\&\,$$
$$(\forall x_{o\alpha})(\forall y_{o\alpha})\Delta((M1)\,\&\,(M3)) \,\&\, (\forall x_{o\alpha})\Delta(M2) \quad (7)$$

where (M1)–(M3) are the axioms from (i).

For the definition of the intermediate quantifier, we need a special operation "cut of a fuzzy set $y \in Form_{o\alpha}$", given a fuzzy set $z \in Form_{o\alpha}$:

$$y|z \equiv \lambda x_\alpha \cdot zx \,\&\, \Delta(\Upsilon(zx) \Rightarrow (yx \equiv zx)). \quad (8)$$

Interpretation of this formula in a model is the following: if fuzzy sets $B, Z \subseteq M$ are given, then the operation $B|Z$ "cuts" B by taking only those $m \in M$ whose membership $B(m)$ is equal to $Z(m)$, otherwise $(B|Z)(m) = 0$. If there is no such element then $B|Z = \emptyset$. We can thus take various fuzzy sets Z to "pick up proper elements" from B.

Definition 2. *Let* $\mathscr{S} \subseteq Types$ *be a selected set of types and* $P = \{R \in Form_{o(o\alpha)(o\alpha)} \mid \alpha \in \mathscr{S}\}$ *be a set of new constants. Let* T *be a consistent extension of the theory* T^{Ev} *in the language* $J(T) \supseteq J^{Ev} \cup P$. *We say that the theory* T *contains* intermediate quantifiers *w.r.t. the set of types* $\mathscr{S}$ *if for all* $\alpha \in \mathscr{S}$ *the following is provable:*

(i)
$$T \vdash (\exists z_{o\alpha})\mathbf{M}_{o(o\alpha)}z_{o\alpha}. \quad (9)$$

(ii)

$$T \vdash (\forall z_{o\alpha})(\exists x_{o\alpha})(\mathbf{M}_{o(o\alpha)}z_{o\alpha} \Rightarrow (\Delta(x_{o\alpha} \subseteq z_{o\alpha}) \,\&\, \hat{\Upsilon}((\mu z_{o\alpha})x_{o\alpha})). \quad (10)$$

In the sequel, we will denote the theory due to Definition 2 by T^{IQ} and fix a selected set of types $\mathscr{S}$.

Definition 3. *Let* $Ev \in Form_{oo}$ *be a formula representing some evaluative linguistic expression,* $z \in Form_{o\alpha}$, $x \in Form_\alpha$ *be variables and* $A, B \in Form_{o\alpha}$ *be formulas such that* $T^{IQ} \vdash \mathbf{M}_{o(o\alpha)}B$, $\alpha \in \mathscr{S}$. *An intermediate quantifier of type* $\langle 1, 1 \rangle$ *is one of the following formulas:*

$$(Q_{Ev}^\forall x_\alpha)(B_{o\alpha}, A_{o\alpha}) \equiv (\exists z)[(\forall x)((B|z)\, x \Rightarrow Ax) \land Ev((\mu B)(B|z))], \quad (11)$$

$$(Q_{Ev}^{\exists} x_\alpha)(B_{o\alpha}, A_{o\alpha}) \equiv (\exists z)[(\exists x)((B|z)x \wedge Ax) \wedge Ev((\mu B)(B|z))]. \qquad (12)$$

Either of the quantifiers (11) or (12) construes the sentence

$$\langle Quantifier \rangle \ B's \ are \ A \qquad (13)$$

where $\langle Quantifier \rangle$ is a quantifier in a linguistic form.

Remark 1. As a special case, $T^{IQ} \vdash (Bi\,\Delta)(\mu B)(B|B) \equiv \top$ and $T^{IQ} \vdash (\forall z)(\neg\Delta(z \equiv B) \Rightarrow \neg(Bi\,\Delta)(\mu B)(B|z))$. Hence, the corresponding intermediate quantifiers reduce to the classical ones (cf. [10]).

Formula $B_{o\alpha}$ in (11) and (12) represents a *universe of quantification*. If we replace the metavariable Ev in (11) or (12) by a formula representing a specific evaluative linguistic expression then we obtain definition of the concrete intermediate quantifier.

Definition 4. *The following are selected intermediate quantifiers:*[2]

(A) *"All B's are A":* $(Q_{Bi\,\Delta}^{\forall}x)(B, A)$
(E) *"No B's is A":* $(Q_{Bi\,\Delta}^{\forall}x)(B, \neg A)$
(P) *"Almost all B's are A":* $(Q_{Bi\,Ex}^{\forall}x)(B, A)$
(B) *"Almost all B's are not A":* $(Q_{Bi\,Ex}^{\forall}x)(B, \neg A)$
(T) *"Most B's are A":* $(Q_{Bi\,Ve}^{\forall}x)(B, A)$
(D) *"Most B's are not A":* $(Q_{Bi\,Ve}^{\forall}x)(B, \neg A)$
(K) *"Many B's are A":* $(Q_{\neg\,Sm}^{\forall}x)(B, A)$
(G) *"Many B's are not A":* $(Q_{\neg\,Sm}^{\forall}x)(B, \neg A)$
(I) *"Some B's are A":* $(Q_{Bi\,\Delta}^{\exists}x)(B, A)$
(O) *"Some B's are not A":* $(Q_{Bi\,\Delta}^{\exists}x)(B, \neg A)$

Quantifiers **A, P, T, K, I** are called *affirmative* and **E, B, D, G, O** are called *negative*. The ordering from left to right of the symbols in the respective lists is obtained on the basis of the used evaluative expression in their definition. It will often be used below.

4   Generalized Syllogisms with Intermediate Quantifiers

4.1   Formalization of Syllogisms

The *syllogism* is a triple of formulas $\mathscr{P}_1, \mathscr{P}_2, \mathscr{C} \in Form_o$ of the theory T^{IQ} where $\mathscr{P}_1$ is a *major premise*, $\mathscr{P}_2$ a *minor premise* and $\mathscr{C}$ is a *conclusion*. We say that a syllogism is *valid* if

$$T^{IQ} \vdash \mathscr{P}_1 \,\&\, \mathscr{P}_2 \Rightarrow \mathscr{C}. \qquad (14)$$

By the completeness theorem, syllogism (14) is valid iff

$$\mathscr{M}(\mathscr{P}_1) \otimes \mathscr{M}(\mathscr{P}_2) \leq \mathscr{M}(\mathscr{C}) \qquad (15)$$

----
[2] To simplify the notation, we omit types as well as variables if unnecessary.

holds for any model $\mathscr{M} \models T^{\mathrm{IQ}}$.

Validity of (14) for all syllogisms presented in [18] was proven syntactically in [8,9]. Since Peterson's general validity rules are semantic and our goal in this paper is to explain them, we will apply semantical principles of FTT in the sequel.

Analogously as in the classical theory of syllogisms we consider four figures of syllogisms. Let Q_1, Q_2, Q_3 be quantifier symbols from (11) or (12) and $S, P, M \in Form_{o\alpha}$ be formulas representing properties of elements of type α. The following figures represent basic kinds of syllogisms with intermediate quantifiers of type $\langle 1, 1 \rangle$:

Figure I	**Figure II**	**Figure III**	**Figure IV**
Q_1 M are P	Q_1 P are M	Q_1 M are P	Q_1 P are M
Q_2 S are M	Q_2 S are M	Q_2 M are S	Q_2 M are S
Q_3 S are P	Q_3 S are P	Q_3 S are P	Q_3 S are P

where the first line in each figure is the major premise $\mathscr{P}_{1,o}$, the second line is the minor premise $\mathscr{P}_{2,o}$ and the third line is the conclusion $\mathscr{C}_o$. The formula[3] S is *subject*, P *predicate* and M is a *middle formula* (middle term). If all $Q_1, Q_2, Q_3 \in \{\forall, \exists\}$ then the corresponding syllogism is classical.

4.2 Peterson's Rules for Intermediate Syllogisms

Peterson's extended rules are based on a *distribution index* (denoted by DI). For example, formulas with $\mathrm{DI} = 5$ are more distributed than formulas with $\mathrm{DI} = 4$. The index $\mathrm{DI} = 5$ is assigned to the formulas that are in the position of subjects in the universal quantifiers (**A** and **E**) and position of predicates in the negative quantifiers **E, O, B, D** and **G**. The distribution index $\mathrm{DI} = 1$ is assigned to the subjects of particular and the predicates of affirmative quantifiers. Global overview of the assignment of distribution index is in Table 1.

1. *Rules of Distribution*
   (R1) In a valid syllogism, the sum of the distribution indices for the middle formula must exceed 5.
   (R2) No formula may be more nearly distributed in the conclusion than it is in the premises.
   The rules of quality remain unchanged.
2. *Rules of Quality*
   (R3) At least one premise must be affirmative.
   (R4) The conclusion is negative if and only if one of the premises is negative.
3. *Rules of Quantity*
   (R5) At least one premise must have a quantity of majority (**T** or **D**) or higher.
   (R6) If any premise is non-universal, the conclusion must have a quantity that is less than or equal to that premise.

---

[3] Many authors speak about *terms* instead of formulas. We call S, P, M *formulas* as is common in logic.

The validity of syllogisms using Peterson's rules is based mainly on the position of quantifiers in the Peterson's square of opposition. The main role is also played by the position of the middle formula in the individual figures. The main advantage of the proposed mathematical description of Peterson's rules will be the extension of the group of fuzzy intermediate quantifiers by other new forms. A detailed analysis of selected types of syllogisms using Peterson's rules and their verification of validity is demonstrated in [6].

Table 1. Overview of all the properties related to the Peterson's rules (B is antecedent, A is consequent)

	Quantifier	Quantity	Quality	Distribution index
All B are A	**A**	universal	affirmative	DI = 5 : antecedent, DI = 1 : consequent
No B are A	**E**	universal	negative	DI = 5 : antecedent, DI = 5 : consequent
Almost all B are A	**P**	predominant	affirmative	DI = 4 : antecedent, DI = 1 : consequent
Almost all B are not A	**B**	predominant	negative	DI = 4 : antecedent, DI = 5 : consequent
Most B are A	**T**	majority	affirmative	DI = 3 : antecedent, DI = 1 : consequent
Most B are not A	**D**	majority	negative	DI = 3 : antecedent, DI = 5 : consequent
Many B are A	**K**	common	negative	DI = 2 : antecedent, DI = 1 : consequent
Many B are not A	**G**	common	negative	DI = 2 : antecedent, DI = 5 : consequent
Some B are A	**I**	particular	affirmative	DI = 1 : antecedent, DI = 1 : consequent
Some B are not A	**O**	particular	negative	DI = 1 : antecedent, DI = 5 : consequent

4.3   Formalization of Extended Peterson's Rules

In Peterson's approach, the distribution index is based on the number of intermediate quantifiers. It means that the maximal value is 5 and the other values depend on the position in the Peterson's square of opposition. Our approach is based on the characteristics of the evaluative linguistic expressions used in the given intermediate quantifier.

Definition 5 (Distribution index). *Let* $A, B \in \mathscr{F}(N)$ *be fuzzy sets interpreting formulas* $A_{o\alpha}, B_{o\alpha}$ *in some model of* T^{IQ} *and* $Q_{Ev}(B, A)$ *be an intermediate quantifier determined by the evaluative expression Ev. The distribution index* $\mathrm{DI}(X, Q_{Ev}(B, A))$ *(or shortly,* $\mathrm{DI}(X, Q)$*) of the fuzzy set* $X \in \mathscr{F}(N)$ *interpreting a formula* $X \in Form_{o\alpha}$ *is*

$$\mathrm{DI}(X, Q_{Ev}(B, A)) = \begin{cases} \inf \mathrm{Supp}(Ev) & \text{if } X = B, \\ 0 & \text{if } X = A. \end{cases}$$

We put $\mathrm{DI}(\neg X, Q) = \neg\, \mathrm{DI}(X, Q)$ *and* $\mathrm{DI}(B, Q_{Bi\,\Delta}(B, A)) = 1$.

It is clear that the value $\inf \mathrm{Supp}(Ev) \in [0, 1]$ replaces values 1–5 in the Peterson's approach.

Let $Q_{\mathscr{P}_1}, Q_{\mathscr{P}_2}, Q_{\mathscr{C}}$ denote quantifiers occurring in the major premise, minor premise, and conclusion, respectively.

The following are Peterson's rules reformulated using our notation and concepts. To distinguish our formulation of the extended rules below from the original one, we write the rules as (ERx).

1. *Rules of Distribution*
  (ER1) $\mathrm{DI}(M, Q_{\mathscr{P}_1}) \oplus \mathrm{DI}(M, Q_{\mathscr{P}_2}) = 1$;
  (ER2a) $\mathrm{DI}(S, Q_{\mathscr{C}}) \leq \mathrm{DI}(S, Q_{\mathscr{P}_2})$;
  (ER2b) $\mathrm{DI}(P, Q_{\mathscr{C}}) \leq \mathrm{DI}(P, Q_{\mathscr{P}_1})$;

2. *Rules of Quality*
(ER3) Let $A, B \in \{S, P, M\}$, $A \neq B$. Then

$$\mathscr{P} := \begin{cases} Q^{\forall}_{Ev}(B, A), \\ Q^{\exists}_{Ev}(B, A) \end{cases}$$

  where $\mathscr{P} = \mathscr{P}_1$ or $\mathscr{P} = \mathscr{P}_2$.
(ER4) Let $A, B \in \{S, P, M\}$, $A \neq B$. Then

$$\mathscr{C} := Q^{\forall,\exists}_{Ev}(S, \neg P) \quad \text{iff} \quad \mathscr{P} := Q^{\forall,\exists}_{Ev}(B, \neg A)$$

  where $\mathscr{P} = \mathscr{P}_1$ or $\mathscr{P} = \mathscr{P}_2$.

3. *Rules of Quantity*
(ER5)
$$\inf \mathrm{Supp}_{\mathscr{P}_1}(Ev) \vee \inf \mathrm{Supp}_{\mathscr{P}_2}(Ev) > 0.5.$$

(ER6)
$$\inf \mathrm{Supp}_{\mathscr{P}_1}(Ev) \wedge \inf \mathrm{Supp}_{\mathscr{P}_2}(Ev) \geq \inf \mathrm{Supp}_{\mathscr{C}}(Ev).$$

Peterson's Rule (R1) guarantees that all syllogisms with at least one universal quantifier, or syllogisms with at least one majority quantifier lead to valid syllogism. In our approach, Rule (ER1) guarantees the same, because the rule requires the sum of the distribution indexes equal to 1.

By Rule (R2), "No formula may have a higher DI in the conclusion than it bears in the premises". This formulation is just mathematically expressed both for the subject as well as for the predicate in our Rules (ER2a) and (ER2b).

Rule (ER3) elegantly captures Peterson's rule that at least one premise is positive. In Rule (ER4), we guarantee that the conclusion is negative just when at least one premise is negative.

Rule (R5) guarantees that at least one premise contains a quantifier that has at least a majority position in the Peterson's square of opposition. In our approach, this assumption is guaranteed by the fact that at least one premise has DI > 0.5. Rule (ER6) roughly says that DI of the quantifier in the conclusion must not be greater than DI of the quantifiers in the premises.

Just as Peterson has informally demonstrated that rules (R5) and (R6) follow from (R1)–(R4), we will mathematically prove the same result below.

Lemma 3. *Let rules (ER1)–(ER4) be satisfied. Then rule (ER5) holds.*

Proof. The proof is constructed by analyzing of Figure-I as follows:

Figure-I:

$$
\begin{array}{ccc}
Q_1\,M\,P & Q_1\,M\neg P & Q_1\,M\ \ P \\
Q_2\,S\,M & Q_2\,S\ M & Q_2\,S\neg M \\
\hline
Q_C\,S\,P & Q_C\,S\neg P & Q_C\,S\ \neg P
\end{array}
$$

Let $\mathscr{P}_1 = Q_1(M,P)$ or $\mathscr{P}_1 = Q_1(M,\neg P)$ and $\mathscr{P}_2 = Q_2(S,M)$. Then $\mathrm{DI}(M,Q_{\mathscr{P}_1}) = \inf \mathrm{Supp}_{\mathscr{P}_1}(Ev)$ and $\mathrm{DI}(M,Q_{\mathscr{P}_2}) = 0$. From the assumed validity of (ER1) we know that

$$\inf \mathrm{Supp}_{\mathscr{P}_1}(Ev) = 1$$

which yields (ER5). Let $\langle M\,P, S\neg M \mid S\neg P\rangle$.[4] This situation cannot occur because rule (ER2b) is violated.

The proof for other figures is analogous.

Lemma 4. *Let rules (ER1)–(ER4) be satisfied. Then rule (ER6) holds.*

Proof. Let us consider the following cases:

Figure-I:

$$
\begin{array}{ccc}
Q_1\,M\,P & Q_1\,M\neg P & Q_1\,M\ \ P \\
Q_2\,S\,M & Q_2\,S\ M & Q_2\,S\neg M \\
\hline
Q_C\,S\ P & Q_C\,S\neg P & Q_C\,S\ \neg P
\end{array}
$$

Let us assume $\mathscr{P}_1 = Q_1(M,P)$ or $\mathscr{P}_1 = Q_1(M,\neg P)$, $\mathscr{P}_2 = Q_2(S,M)$ and $\mathscr{C} = Q_3(S,P)$ or $\mathscr{C} = Q_3(S,\neg P)$. We have $DI(S,Q_{\mathscr{C}}) = \inf \mathrm{Supp}_{\mathscr{C}}(Ev)$ and $DI(S,Q_{\mathscr{P}_2}) = \inf \mathrm{Supp}_{\mathscr{P}_2}(Ev)$. Using rule (ER2a) we have

$$\inf \mathrm{Supp}_{\mathscr{C}}(Ev) \le \inf \mathrm{Supp}_{\mathscr{P}_2}(Ev). \tag{16}$$

Similarly, we know

$$DI(M,Q_{\mathscr{P}_1}) = \inf \mathrm{Supp}_{\mathscr{P}_1}(Ev)$$

---

[4] This is shortened way how syllogisms can be written. The vertical line separates conclusion.

and $\mathrm{DI}(M, Q_{\mathscr{P}_2}) = 0$. From (ER1) we obtain $\inf \mathrm{Supp}_{\mathscr{P}_1}(Ev) = 1$ which implies

$$\inf \mathrm{Supp}_{\mathscr{C}}(Ev) \leq \inf \mathrm{Supp}_{\mathscr{P}_1}(Ev) = 1. \tag{17}$$

Finally, from (16) and (17) we obtain

$$\inf \mathrm{Supp}_{\mathscr{C}}(Ev) \leq \inf \mathrm{Supp}_{\mathscr{P}_1}(Ev) \wedge \inf \mathrm{Supp}_{\mathscr{P}_2}(Ev).$$

The last form violates the rule (ER6). Other figures are constructed analogously.

Theorem 1. *All 105 valid syllogisms satisfy Rules (ER1)–(ER4).*

Proof. The proof is technical and requires analysis of all four figures. We prove selected forms of syllogisms of Figure-I. Let us consider syllogism **AAA** of Figure I. Put

$$\mathscr{P}_1 = Q^{\forall}_{Bi\,\Delta}(M, P) = \bigwedge_{u \in N} (M(u) \rightarrow P(u)),$$

$$\mathscr{P}_2 = Q^{\forall}_{Bi\,\Delta}(S, M) = \bigwedge_{u \in N} (S(u) \rightarrow M(u)),$$

$$\mathscr{C} = Q^{\forall}_{Bi\,\Delta}(S, P) = \bigwedge_{u \in N} (S(u) \rightarrow P(u)).$$

Then $\mathrm{DI}(M, Q_{Bi\,\Delta}(M, P)) = 1$ and $\mathrm{DI}(M, Q_{Bi\,\Delta}(S, M)) = 0$. Therefore, Rule (ER1) is satisfied. Furthermore, the rule (ER1) is also satisfied for syllogisms
AAP, AAT, AAK, A(*A)I − I.

We continue with $\mathrm{DI}(S, Q_{Bi\,\Delta}(S, M)) = 1$ and $\mathrm{DI}(S, Q_{Bi\,\Delta}(S, P)) = 1$ which satisfies the Rule (ER2a). The Rule (ER2a) will be also satisfied for the syllogisms
AAP, AAT, AAK, A(*A)I − I because

$$\mathrm{DI}(S, Q_{Bi\,\Delta}(S, M)) = 1 \geq \mathrm{DI}(S, Q_{Bi\,Ex}(S, P)) \geq \mathrm{DI}(S, Q_{Bi\,Ve}(S, P)) \geq$$
$$\mathrm{DI}(S, Q_{\neg\,Sm}(S, P)).$$

Rule (ER2b) is satisfied as well because $0 = \mathrm{DI}(P, Q_{Bi\,\Delta}(S, P)) \leq \mathrm{DI}(P, Q_{Bi\,\Delta}(M, P)) = 0$. The same inequality is fulfilled for other syllogisms
AAP, AAT, AAK, A(*A)I − I.

Rule (ER3) is obviously satisfied and (ER4) does not apply.

5   Conclusion and Future Directions

In this paper, we suggested mathematical formulation of Peterson's rules. We also formally proved that the *Quantity rules* are formally provable from the *Distribution* and *Quality* rules. The first step for the next publication will be to prove that we can verify the validity of all Peterson's syllogisms using four generalized Peterson's rules.

The future research will be focused on a more detailed explanation of Peterson's rules, and also mathematical formulation of the rules for classical syllogisms. Our approach also opens the door to extension of this approach to other types of intermediate quantifiers that were introduced in [13]. Furthermore, we also plan to introduce rules for verification of valid syllogisms in the cube of opposition.

On the basis of this research we plan to develop algorithms using which it will be possible to verify validity of syllogisms automatically.

References

1. Andrews, P.: An Introduction to Mathematical Logic and Type Theory: To Truth Through Proof. Springer, Dordrecht (2002). https://doi.org/10.1007/978-94-015-9934-4
2. Cignoli, R.L.O., D'Ottaviano, I.M.L., Mundici, D.: Algebraic Foundations of Many-Valued Reasoning. Springer, Dordrecht (2000). https://doi.org/10.1007/978-94-015-9480-6
3. Dubois, D., Prade, H.: On fuzzy syllogisms. Comput. Intell. **4**, 171–179 (1988)
4. Gainor, J.: What is distribution in categorical syllogisms (2011). https://www.youtube.com/watch?v=7_Y-Bxr4apQ
5. Kacprzyk, J., Zadrożny, S.: Linguistic database summaries and their protoforms: towards natural language based knowledge discovery tools. Inf. Sci. **173**, 281–304 (2005)
6. Murinová, P.: On modeling of generalized syllogisms with intermediate quantifiers. In: Proceedings of the IFSA-NAFIPS 2019. Lafayette, USA (2019)
7. Murinová, P.: Graded structures of opposition in fuzzy natural logic. Log. Univers. **265**, 495–522 (2020)
8. Murinová, P., Novák, V.: A formal theory of generalized intermediate syllogisms. Fuzzy Sets Syst. **186**, 47–80 (2013)
9. Murinová, P., Novák, V.: The structure of generalized intermediate syllogisms. Fuzzy Sets Syst. **247**, 18–37 (2014)
10. Murinová, P., Novák, V.: The theory of intermediate quantifiers in fuzzy natural logic revisited and the model of "Many". Fuzzy Sets Syst. **388**, 56–89 (2020)
11. Novák, V.: A comprehensive theory of trichotomous evaluative linguistic expressions. Fuzzy Sets Syst. **159**(22), 2939–2969 (2008)
12. Novák, V.: A formal theory of intermediate quantifiers. Fuzzy Sets Syst. **159**(10), 1229–1246 (2008)
13. Novák, V., Murinová, P.: A formal model of the intermediate quantifiers "a few", "several" and "a little". In: Kearfott, R.B., Batyrshin, I., Reformat, M., Ceberio, M., Kreinovich, V. (eds.) IFSA/NAFIPS 2019 2019. AISC, vol. 1000, pp. 429–441. Springer, Cham (2019). https://doi.org/10.1007/978-3-030-21920-8_39
14. Novák, V., Perfilieva, I., Dvořák, A.: Insight into Fuzzy Modeling. Wiley, Hoboken (2016)
15. Novák, V., Perfilieva, I., Močkoř, J.: Mathematical Principles of Fuzzy Logic. Springer, Boston (1999). https://doi.org/10.1007/978-1-4615-5217-8
16. Pereira-Fariña, M., Vidal, J.C., Díaz-Hermida, F., Bugarín, A.: A fuzzy syllogistic reasoning schema for generalized quantifiers. Fuzzy Sets Syst. **234**, 79–96 (2014)

17. Peters, S., Westerståhl, D.: Quantifiers in Language and Logic. Claredon Press, Oxford (2006)
18. Peterson, P.: Intermediate Quantifiers. Logic, linguistics, and Aristotelian semantics. Ashgate, Aldershot (2000)
19. Schwartz, D.G.: Dynamic reasoning with qualified syllogisms. Artif. Intell. **93**, 103–167 (1997)
20. Thompson, B.: Syllogisms with statistical quantifiers. Notre Dame J. Formal Log. **27**, 93–103 (1986)
21. Yager, R.: Linguistic summaries as a tool for database discovery. In: Proceedings of FUZZIEEE 1995 Workshop on Fuzzy Database Systems and Information Retrieval, Yokohama, pp. 79–82 (1995)
22. Zadeh, L.A.: A computational approach to fuzzy quantifiers in natural languages. Comput. Math. **9**, 149–184 (1983)
23. Zadeh, L.A.: Syllogistic reasoning in fuzzy logic and its applications to usuality and reasoning with dispositions. IEEE Trans. Syst. Man Cybern. **15**, 754–765 (1985)

On Modeling of Fuzzy Peterson's Syllogisms Using Peterson's Rules

Petra Murinová[✉] and Vilém Novák

Institute for Research and Applications of Fuzzy Modeling, University of Ostrava,
30. dubna 22, 701 03 Ostrava, Czech Republic
{petra.murinova,vilem.novak}@osu.cz
http://irafm.osu.cz/

Abstract. In real world, interpretation, understanding and deriving information from natural data using natural language is very common. One of the theories that deals with this modern topic is the theory of syllogistic reasoning. There are several methods to verify the validity and invalidity of classical Aristotle's syllogisms as well as fuzzy syllogisms. In previous publications, we have focused on the mathematical construction of syntactic proofs of fuzzy Peterson's syllogisms.

The main goal of this publication is to explain Peterson's rules of *distributivy, quality* and *quantity* for verifying the validity of syllogisms and to demonstrate them on selected examples of syllogisms.

Keywords: Fuzzy intermediate quantifiers · Peterson's rules · Graded peterson's square of opposition

1 Introduction

Logical syllogisms have been studied both in terms of their formal proof and semantic verification of validity and invalidity by several authors (see [1–4]). Furthermore, a number of authors have found the application of the theory of syllogistic reasoning in various areas of applied research [5–7].

The theory of generalized syllogisms was studied by several authors as a generalization of classical Aristotle's syllogisms [8]. In this publication we will focus on a special group of syllogisms with intermediate quantifiers, which form a selected group of generalized quantifiers. Intermediate quantifiers are special linguistic expressions, for example, *Most, Several, A few, Many, A small part of, More than half*, etc. which were introduced and deeply studied by Thompson in [9] and later by Peterson in his book in [10].

Peterson in his book (see [10]) proposed intermediate syllogisms as a generalization of classical syllogisms. There are several methods how to verify the

The work was supported from ERDF/ESF by the project "Centre for the development of Artificial Inteligence Methods for the Automotive Industry of the region" No. CZ.02.1.01/0.0/0.0/17-049/0008414 and partially also by the MŠMT project NPU II project LQ1602 "IT4Innovations excellence in science".

© Springer Nature Switzerland AG 2022
D. Ciucci et al. (Eds.): IPMU 2022, CCIS 1601, pp. 647–659, 2022.
https://doi.org/10.1007/978-3-031-08971-8_53

validity of classical as well as fuzzy logical syllogisms with intermediate quantifiers. One of the best known method is the application of Venn diagram and the subsequent construction of an algebraic proof. Another idea is to use Peterson's square of opposition if we are talking about classical syllogisms. Peterson's square of opposition was proposed by Peterson as a generalization of the Aristotle's one [11–13]. Recall that graded Aristotles's square was already studied by Dubois in [14,15]. Ciucci, Dubois, and Prade [16,17] then introduced an application of the graded Aristotle's square within the possibility theory.

Another option is to find a formal mathematical proof using a formal mathematical system. This approach is based on formal definitions of fuzzy intermediate quantifiers, logical axioms of a given theory, and the help of deduction rules. The basic group of 105 fuzzy Peterson's syllogisms with *five basic fuzzy intermediate quantifiers* ("All", "Almost all", "Most", "Many" and "Some") was syntactically proved in [1].

1.1 Main Goals

The last above mentioned method is based on the mathematical definition of classical/fuzzy intermediate quantifiers. In this article, we will focus on verifying the validity of Peterson's syllogisms using *Peterson's rules of distributivity, quality and quantity*. A very detailed explanation of the true distribution was given in the presentation by Gainor in [18]. The rules for classical syllogisms were also given in another form in [19]. The main goal will be to explain the distribution rule and the distribution index for *intermediate quantifiers*. The distribution index was also discussed and explained for the percentage quantifiers in [20]. An explanation of the position of negation in individual quantifiers in relation to distribution was given in [21].

In our previous work [22], we have proposed generalized definition of Peterson's rules of distributivy, quality and quantity which are based on the position of fuzzy intermediate quantifiers inside the graded Peterson's square. In the last article devoted to Peterson's generalized rules [22], there was no place to explain the behavior of individual rules on specific examples of valid and invalid syllogisms. Furthermore, the distribution rule, which plays a very important role in verifying the validity of syllogisms, has not been thoroughly explained. The aim of this paper will therefore be to explain Peterson's rules using a graded Peterson's square of opposition apply them to selected types of syllogisms.

2 Preliminaries

The main goal of this section is to introduce the **graded** Peterson square of opposition and to recall the generalized mathematical definitions of properties *contrary, sub-contrary, contradictory and sub-alterns*. Generalized mathematical definitions of these properties have been proposed as generalizations of classical definition (see [23]).

In this section we will not explain in detail the formal mathematical system, which is based on higher-order fuzzy logic and with which mathematical definitions of fuzzy intermediate quantifiers were designed. The reader can find details in several papers [24–26].

Recall that the generalized definitions of properties that form a graded Peterson's square of opposition are proposed using the logical operations of linearly ordered MV-algebra (see [27,28]).

Definition 1. *An* MV-algebra *is a residuated lattice*

$$\langle L, \vee, \wedge, \otimes, \rightarrow, 0, 1 \rangle$$

where $a \vee b = (a \rightarrow b) \rightarrow b$, *for each* $a, b \in L$. *Furthermore, the following operations are defined on* L. *Let* $a, b \in L$,

(i) $\neg a = a \rightarrow 0$ *(negation),*
(ii) $a \oplus b = \neg(\neg a \otimes \neg b)$ *(strong summation),*
(iii) $a \leftrightarrow b = (a \rightarrow b) \wedge (b \rightarrow a)$ *(biresiduation).*

The results of this paper are based on the standard Łukasiewicz MV-algebra defined as follows.

Definition 2. *The* standard Łukasiewicz MV$_\Delta$-algebra *is a special MV-algebra extended by delta operation as follows:*

$$\langle [0,1], \vee, \wedge, \otimes, \rightarrow, 0, 1, \Delta \rangle$$

where

(i) $a \wedge b = \min(a, b)$,
(ii) $a \vee b = \max(a, b)$,
(iii) $a \otimes b = \max(0, a + b - 1)$,
(iv) $a \rightarrow b = \min(1, 1 - a + b)$, *for each* $a, b \in [0,1]$
(v) $\Delta(a) = 1$ *if* $a = 1$ *otherwise it is equal to zero.*

Therefore, $\neg a = 1 - a$ *and* $a \oplus b = \min\{1, a + b\}$, *for each* $a, b \in [0,1]$.

In the following lemma, we list some properties of the standard Łukasiewicz MV-algebra that will be used below.

Lemma 1. *Let* $\langle [0,1], \vee, \wedge, \otimes, \rightarrow, 0, 1 \rangle$ *be the standard Łukasiewicz MV-algebra and let* $I = \{1, \ldots, n\}$. *Then, the following hold for all* $a_1, \ldots, a_n$, $b_1, \ldots, b_n, a, b, c, d, e \in [0,1]$:

(a) $\neg \neg a = a$ *(double negation law).*
(b) *for each* $k \in I$, $\bigwedge_{i \in I} a_i \leq a_k$ *and* $a_k \leq \bigvee_{i \in I} a_i$.
(c) *if* $a_i \leq b_i$ *for each* $i \in I$, *then* $\bigwedge_{i \in I} a_i \leq \bigwedge_{i \in I} b_i$ *and* $\bigvee_{i \in I} a_i \leq \bigvee_{i \in I} b_i$.
(d) $\bigvee_{i \in I}(a \otimes b_i) = a \otimes \bigvee_{i \in I} b_i$.
(e) $a \oplus \neg a = 1$ *and* $a \otimes \neg a = 0$.
(f) *if* $a \otimes b \leq e$, *then* $(a \wedge c) \otimes (b \wedge d) \leq e$.
(g) *if* $a \leq b$ *and* $c \leq d$, *then* $a \otimes c \leq b \otimes d$ *and* $a \oplus c \leq b \oplus d$.
(h) $a \otimes b = \neg(a \rightarrow \neg b)$ *and* $a \rightarrow b = \neg(a \otimes \neg b)$.
(i) $a \rightarrow b \leq \neg b \rightarrow \neg a$.
(j) $\neg(a \otimes b) = \neg a \oplus \neg b$ *and* $\neg(a \oplus b) = \neg a \otimes \neg b$.

2.1   Peterson's Square

Definition 3 (Proposition). Proposition *is an expression in the form either*

$$Q(B, A) \quad or \quad Q(B, \neg A)$$

where Q is a $\langle 1, 1 \rangle$ *quantifier according to the classification introduced in [29] and A, B are terms.* $Q(B, A)$ *is an* affirmative *and* $Q(B, \neg A)$ *is a* negative *proposition.*

Quantifier Q specifies the quantity of elements satisfying B that also satisfy A.

Graded Peterson's square of opposition is formed by four main properties as follows:

Definition 4. *[23] Let T be a consistent theory of Ł-FTT,* $\mathcal{M} \models T$ *be a model, and* P_1, P_2 *be closed formulas.*

- P_1 *and* P_2 *are contraries if* $\mathcal{M}(P_1) \otimes \mathcal{M}(P_2) = 0$.
- P_1 *and* P_2 *are subcontraries if* $\mathcal{M}(P_1) \oplus \mathcal{M}(P_2) = 1$.
- P_1 *and* P_2 *are contradictories if both* $\mathcal{M}(\Delta P_1) \otimes \mathcal{M}(\Delta P_2) = 0$ *and* $\mathcal{M}(\Delta P_1) \oplus \mathcal{M}(\Delta P_2) = 1$.
- P_2 *is a subaltern of* P_1 *if* $\mathcal{M}(P_1) \leq \mathcal{M}(P_2)$.

All the properties below in the graded Peterson's square were formally proved in [24]. Recall that the straight lines mark contradictories, the dashed lines contraries, and the dotted lines subcontraries. The arrows indicate the relation subaltern.

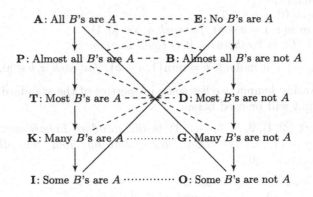

A: All B's are A --------- **E**: No B's are A

P: Almost all B's are A --- **B**: Almost all B's are not A

T: Most B's are A --- **D**: Most B's are not A

K: Many B's are A ·········· **G**: Many B's are not A

I: Some B's are A ·········· **O**: Some B's are not A

Fig. 1. graded Peterson's square of opposition

As we traditionally know, the letters **AEIO** denote the classical Aristotle's square of opposition. The quantifier labeled **A** has a *universal* position and the dual negative quantifier is labeled **E**. *Particular* quantifiers carry the letters **I** for positive and **O** for negative quantifier. The **P**redominant position is represented by the quantifier "Almost all" denoted by **P** and to it the dual negative is denoted by **B**. Quantifier "Most" is denoted as **T** (majori**T**y), and dually **D** for a negative form. The Common position is represented by the quantifier "Many" denoted by **K** and dually for the negative quantifier **G**.

Based on the position of fuzzy intermediate quantifiers, we obtain information related to Peterson's rules. Whether the quantifier is positive or negative and where it stands in the square plays an important role. So whether it has a majority and a larger position or vice versa. So we don't need to know the exact mathematical definition to work with Peter's rules if we have this knowledge with the position of quantifiers in the graded Peterson's square.

2.2 Categorical Syllogism

Definition 5 (Syllogism). *A syllogism is a triple* $\langle P_1, P_2, C \rangle$ *of three propositions.* P_1, P_2 *are called* premises *(*P_1 *is* major, P_2 *is* minor*) and* C *is called a* conclusion. *In these propositions, there appear a total of exactly three terms* S, P, M, *each of which is used exactly twice: term* S *(subject) appears somewhere in* P_2 *and as the first term of* C, *term* P *(predicate) appears somewhere in* P_1 *and as the second term of* C; *a term not present in the conclusion* C *is called a* middle term M. *A syllogism is* valid *if the conclusion* C *logically follows from premises* P_1 *and* P_2.

Syllogisms with a single middle term yield the following *four* figures:

Figure I	Figure II	Figure III	Figure IV
$Q_1\ M$ is P	$Q_1\ P$ is M	$Q_1\ M$ is P	$Q_1\ P$ is M
$Q_2\ S$ is M	$Q_2\ S$ is M	$Q_2\ M$ is S	$Q_2\ M$ is S
$Q_3\ S$ is P	$Q_3\ S$ is P	$Q_3\ S$ is P	$Q_3\ S$ is P

3 Peterson Rules for Aristotle's Syllogisms

At first, we start with two distributive rules as follow:

1. *Rules of Distribution*
   (R1)   The middle formula must be distributed at least once.
   (R2)   No formula is distributed in the conclusion unless it is distributed in one premise.

To use these rules, we have to know what distribution is. In Aristotle's syllogisms, the traditional notion of distribution is binary. If the quantifier **O** occurred in a categorical which said something about every member of the formula's extension, then the formula was said to be *distributed*. Otherwise, the formula said to be *undistributed*. So, there are only *two choices*-distributed or undistributed. Below we introduce precise definitions as follows:

Definition 6 (Distribution). *A formula in the position of subject or predicate is a claim is* distributed *when it says something definite about all members of that category.*

Definition 7 (Undistribution). *A formula in the position of subject or predicate is a claim is* undistributed *when it does not say something definite about all members of that category.*

Example 1 (Some frogs are not timid).

- This does not say anything about all frogs.
- It says that all things that are timid, at least one, is definitely not a frog.
- **There is distributivity of the predicate.**

We continue with a detailed explanation of the distribution behavior of individual quantifiers as follows:

A : *All S are P*

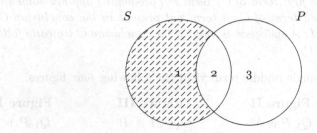

We are talking about **all** members of the category. There is a distribution of the subject.

E : *All S are not P*

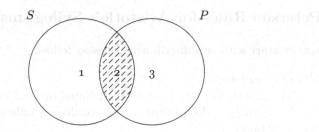

We can see that no S are included in P and no P are included in S. We have information about all S and all P. It means that **E distributes subject and predicate.**

I. Some S are P

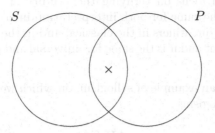

We are **not talking about all** members of the category. There is no distribution in the quantifier **I**.

O. Some S are not P

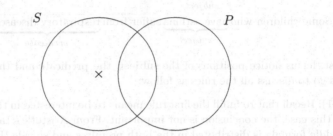

The member of S is excluded of P. We have information **about all** P that among the elements of P there is not the element contained in S. The quantifier **O** distributes predicate.

A very detailed explanation of the rule of distribution was given in the presentation by Gainor in [18]. The rules for classical syllogisms were also presented in another form in [19].

2. *Rules of quality*
  (R3)   At least one premise is positive.
  (R4)   The conclusion is negative iff at least one premise is negative.
3. *Rules of quantity*
  (R5)   At least one premise is universal.
  (R6)   If one premise is particular, the conclusion must be particular as well.

Below we summarize all properties about quantifiers, subject and predicate.

	Quantifier	Quantity	Quality	Distributed
All S are P	**A**	universal	affirmative	S
No S are P	**E**	universal	negative	S and P
Some S are P	**I**	particular	affirmative	none
Some S are not P	**O**	particular	negative	P

3.1   Example of Fuzzy Syllogisms with Classical Quantifiers

At this point we will focus on verifying the validity of syllogism of Figure-I. The construction is the same for both interpretation in classical logic and fuzzy logic. The position of quantifiers in the classical and in the generalized square of opposition is important and it is the same for universal and particular quantifiers.

Example 2. Below is an example of syllogism, on which we will demonstrate the rules for classical syllogisms.

AII-I:

P_1 : All children living in $\underbrace{\text{heavy industry}}_{middle\ formula}$ suffer from $\underbrace{\text{respiratory diseases}}_{predicate}$.

P_2 : Some children $\underbrace{\text{who have asthma}}_{subject}$ live in an environment with $\underbrace{\text{heavy industry}}_{middle\ formula}$.

C : Some children who $\underbrace{\text{have asthma}}_{subject}$ suffer from $\underbrace{\text{respiratory diseases}}_{predicate}$.

At first, let us notice positions of the subject, the predicate and the middle formula. Let us go to discuss all the rules as follow:

- (R1): Recall that to fulfill the first rule means to be interested in the middle formula. In this case, the conclusion is not important. From Aristotle's table it follows that middle formula is distributed in the both premises and so rule (R1) is fulfilled.
- (R2): Now we will be interested in (DIs) index of the subject and the predicate in both premises as well as in the conclusion. We can see that:
  - subject: the subject is not distributed in the minor premise as well in the conclusion. It means that the rule (R2) is not violated.
  - predicate: the predicate is not distributed in the major premise as well in the conclusion. It means that the rule (R2) is not violated.
- (R3), (R4), (R5) and (R6) are trivially fulfilled.

Observation: From the analysis of the validity of the example using Peterson's rules, it can be seen very quickly that if we consider the universal quantifier in the conclusion, then rule (R2) is immediately violated. In this case we can observe that the subject in the conclusion would be distributed while the subject in the minor premise would not.

4   Peterson Rules for Syllogism with Intermediate Quantifiers

In this subsection we will continue by explaining Peterson's rules for syllogisms with intermediate quantifiers. What is interesting that the rules (R2), (R3) and (R4) remain unchanged. The middle formula position and the related (R1) rule therefore play an important role. So, the first distribution rule is reformulated with respect to the number of intermediate quantifiers. Furthermore, an important role is played by the quantifier, which determines *majority*, which is used in the rule (R5).

First of all, we will explain in detail and introduce the ideological distribution for the case when we work with intermediate quantifiers. Similar to Peterson's rules for Aristotle's syllogisms positions of all quantifiers play an important role for using quality as well as distribution's rules which characterize a relationship between subjects (S) and predicates (P). These two mentioned formulas are contained in the conclusion of every syllogism, while they never occur together in the premises, and it means, their relationship must be determined by the middle formula which is guaranteed by distribution's rules.

An assumption of five basic intermediate quantifiers forming graded Peterson's square of opposition leads to the maximum DI of 5. Note that the numerical indexes (DI1 through DI5) explain the relationships between quantifiers. It means, for example, that formulas with DI5 are more distributed than those formulas with DI4. Since 5 is the maximum DI than this value of distribution index will be assigned to the traditional formulas. It will be the case that the subjects of all universal quantifiers (**A** and **E**) and predicates of all negative intermediate quantifiers **E, O, B, D** and **G** have a DI5. Let us assign DI1 to the subjects of particular and the predicates of affirmative which were in the classical approach called undistributed. From the monotonicity of positive quantifiers (it is inside of the generalized square fulfilled by subalterns property) the predicates of **P, T** and **K** are all assigned DI of 1. Finally, one more by monotonicity, the predicates of the predominant, majority, common affirmative quantifiers (**P, T, K**) have DI of 4, 3, 2, respectively. For further details on Peterson's rules, see the book [10]. The distribution index was also discussed and explained for the percentage quantifiers in [20].

1. *Rules of Distribution*
   (R1) In a valid syllogism, the sum of distribution indices for the middle formula must exceed 5.
   (R2) No formula may be more nearly distributed in the conclusion than it is in the premises.

The rules of quality remain unchanged.

2. *Rules of Quality*
   (R3) At least one premise must be affirmative.
   (R4) The conclusion is negative if and only if one of the premises is negative.
3. *Rules of Quantity*
   (R5) At least one premise must have a quantity of majority (**T** or **D**) or higher.
   (R6) If any premise is non-universal, then the conclusion must have a quantity that is less than or equal to that premise.

Table 1. Overview of all the properties related to the Peterson's rules (B is antecedent, A is consequent)

	Quantifier	Quantity	Quality	Distribution index
All B are A	**A**	universal	affirmative	DI = 5 : antecedent, DI = 1 : consequent
No B are A	**E**	universal	negative	DI = 5 : antecedent, DI = 5 : consequent
Almost all B are A	**P**	predominant	affirmative	DI = 4 : antecedent, DI = 1 : consequent
Almost all B are not A	**B**	predominant	negative	DI = 4 : antecedent, DI = 5 : consequent
Most B are A	**T**	majority	affirmative	DI = 3 : antecedent, DI = 1 : consequent
Most B are not A	**D**	majority	negative	DI = 3 : antecedent, DI = 5 : consequent
Many B are A	**K**	common	negative	DI = 2 : antecedent, DI = 1 : consequent
Many B are not A	**G**	common	negative	DI = 2 : antecedent, DI = 5 : consequent
Some B are A	**I**	particular	affirmative	DI = 1 : antecedent, DI = 1 : consequent
Some B are not A	**O**	particular	negative	DI = 1 : antecedent, DI = 5 : consequent

5 An Example of Fuzzy Non-trivial Syllogism

We continue with the example of non-trivial syllogism (both premises consist of intermediate quantifiers) of Figure-III. We will see that the presented syllogism will be valid with the particular conclusion only.

P_1 : Many $\underbrace{\text{species of whales}}_{middle\,formula}$ are about to $\underbrace{\text{become extinct}}_{predicate}$.

KAI-III: P_2 : All $\underbrace{\text{species of whales}}_{middle\,formula}$ are $\underbrace{\text{mammals}}_{subject}$.

C : Some $\underbrace{\text{mammals}}_{subject}$ are $\underbrace{\text{before extinction}}_{predicate}$.

- (R1): This rule is trivially fulfilled, because (DIs) of the middle formula is equal to 7.

- (R2):
  - subject: (DIs) of the subject in minor premise is 1.
  - predicate: (DIs) of the predicate in major premise is 1.

  (DIs) for the subject as well as for the predicate in the conclusion is equal to 1. It means that the rule (R2) is fulfilled.
- (R3) and (R4) are trivially fulfilled.

Observation: From the analysis of the validity of syllogism using Peterson's rules, we can observe that the syllogisms of the third figure are valid only with a particular conclusion. "Nothing better" can be deduced from the assumption of "large quantifiers". The reason is that the distribution index of the subject and the predicate in the premises is equal to one. In conclusion, therefore, with respect to rule (R2), only a particulate quantifier can occur.

6 Future Work and Ideas

Further directions for the continuation of this publication can be implemented in several ways. First we will continue the idea of mathematically describing Peterson's rules in order to analyze the validity of syllogisms with other kinds of fuzzy/classical intermediate quantifiers ("A few", "Several") which were proposed in [30]. Of course, the idea is to reformulate the distribution index for a larger number of quantifiers so that the majority is maintained. Another area of the research is the study of Peterson's rules for logical syllogisms with more premises.

In other publications we will also focus on verifying the validity of logical syllogisms related to the (graded/classical) Peterson's cube of opposition. Here is the idea of how to work with logical syllogisms that contain intermediate quantifiers with negation in both the antecedent and the consequent.

7 Conclusion

In this article, we focused on explaining Peterson's rules of distribution, quality and quantity. We explained the concept of distribution from the point of view of classical quantifiers. We also recalled Peterson's rules for syllogisms with intermediate quantifiers. We dealt with the concept of distribution index, which plays a very important role in verifying the veracity of syllogisms. At the end of the article we demonstrated the application of both classical and Peterson's rules on selected species of syllogisms.

References

1. Murinová, P., Novák, V.: A formal theory of generalized intermediate syllogisms. Fuzzy Sets Syst. **186**, 47–80 (2013)
2. Pereira-Fariña, M., Vidal, J.C., Díaz-Hermida, F., Bugarín, A.: A fuzzy syllogistic reasoning schema for generalized quantifiers. Fuzzy Sets Syst. **234**, 79–96 (2014)

3. Westerståhl, D.: Aristotelian syllogisms and generalized quantifiers. Stud. Logica Int. J. Symbol. Logic **48**, 577–585 (1989)
4. Zadeh, L.A.: Syllogistic reasoning in fuzzy logic and its applications to usuality and reasoning with dispositions. IEEE Trans. Syst. Man Cybern. **15**, 754–765 (1985)
5. Kacprzyk, J., Yager, R.R., Zadrożny, S.: A fuzzy logic based approach to linguistic summaries of databases. Int. J. Appl. Math. Comput. Sci. **10**(4), 813–834 (2000)
6. Wilbik, A., Kaymak, U.: Linguistic summarization of processes - a research agenda. In: Proceedings of the 2015 Conference of the International Fuzzy Systems Association and the European Society for Fuzzy Logic and Technology, pp. 136–143 (2015)
7. Wilbik, A., Dijkman, R.M.: On the generation of useful linguistic summaries of sequences. 2016 IEEE International Conference on Fuzzy Systems, pp. 555–562 (2016)
8. Wikipedia (2004). http://en.wikipedia.org/wiki/aristotle
9. Thompson, B.E.: Syllogisms using "few","many" and "most". Notre Dame J. Formal Logic **23**, 75–84 (1982)
10. Peterson, P.L.: Intermediate Quantifiers. Logic, linguistics, and Aristotelian Semantics. Ashgate, Aldershot (2000)
11. Pellissier, R.: "Setting" n-opposition. Logica Universalis **2**, 235–263 (2008)
12. Peters, S., Westerståhl, D.: Quantifiers in Language and Logic. Claredon Press, Oxford (2006)
13. Westerståhl, D.: The traditional square of opposition and generalized quantifiers. Stud. Logic **2**, 1–18 (2008)
14. Dubois, D., Prade, H.: From blanche's hexagonal organization of concepts to formal concepts analysis and possibility theory. Logica Universalis 149–169 (2012)
15. Dubois, D., Prade, H.: Gradual structures of oppositions. In: Esteva, F., Magdalena, L., Verdegay, J.L. (eds.) Enric Trillas: Passion for Fuzzy Sets, Studies in Fuzziness and Soft Computing, vol. 322, pp. 79–91 (2015)
16. Ciucci, D., Dubois, D., Prade, H.: Oppositions in rough set theory. In: Li, T., et al. (eds.) RSKT 2012. LNCS (LNAI), vol. 7414, pp. 504–513. Springer, Heidelberg (2012). https://doi.org/10.1007/978-3-642-31900-6_62
17. Ciucci, D., Dubois, D., Prade, H.: The structure of oppositions in rough set theory and formal concept analysis - toward a new bridge between the two settings. In: Beierle, C., Meghini, C. (eds.) FoIKS 2014. LNCS, vol. 8367, pp. 154–173. Springer, Cham (2014). https://doi.org/10.1007/978-3-319-04939-7_7
18. Gainor, J.: What is distribution in categorical syllogisms (2011). https://www.youtube.com/watch?v=7_Y-Bxr4apQ
19. Martin, J.N.: Distributive terms, truth, and the port royal logic. Hist. Philos. Logic (2012). https://doi.org/10.1080/01445340.2012.748331
20. Finch, H.A.: Validity rules for proportionally quantified syllogisms. Philos. Sci. **24** (1957)
21. Alvarez-Fontecilla, E., Lungenstrass, T.: Negative terms in traditional logic: distribution, immediate inference, and syllogism. The Monist **42**, 96–111 (1932)
22. Murinová, P., Pavliska, V., Burda, M.: Generalized Peterson's rules in fuzzy natural logic. In: Atlantis Studies in Uncertainty Modelling, 19 September 2021, Bratislava, pp. 383–390 (2021)
23. Murinová, P., Novák, V.: The theory of intermediate quantifiers in fuzzy natural logic revisited and the model of "many". Fuzzy Sets Syst. **388**, 56–89 (2020)
24. Murinová, P., Novák, V.: Analysis of generalized square of opposition with intermediate quantifiers. Fuzzy Sets Syst. **242**, 89–113 (2014)

25. Novák, V.: On fuzzy type theory. Fuzzy Sets Syst. **149**, 235–273 (2005)
26. Novák, V.: A comprehensive theory of trichotomous evaluative linguistic expressions. Fuzzy Sets Syst. **159**(22), 2939–2969 (2008)
27. Cignoli, R.L.O., D'Ottaviano, I.M.L., Mundici, D.: Algebraic Foundations of Many-Valued Reasoning. Kluwer, Dordrecht (2000)
28. Novák, V., Perfilieva, I., Močkoř, J.: Mathematical Principles of Fuzzy Logic. Kluwer, Boston (1999)
29. Lindström, P.: First order predicate logic with generalized quantifiers. Theoria **32**, 186–195 (1966)
30. Novák, V., Murinová, P.: A formal model of the intermediate quantifiers "a few", "several" and "a little". In: Proceedings of the IFSA-NAFIPS 2019, Lafayette (2019)

Mathematical Fuzzy Logics

Cutting of Partial Fuzzy Relations and Their Compositions – The Case of the Dragonfly Operations

Nhung Cao[ID] and Martin Štěpnička[✉][ID]

CE IT4Innovations – Institute for Research and Applications of Fuzzy Modeling, University of Ostrava, 30. dubna 22, 701 03 Ostrava, Czech Republic
{nhung.cao,martin.stepnicka}@osu.cz

Abstract. Partial fuzzy sets and relations have been recently developed in partial fuzzy set theory to handle undefined values. In this paper, we introduce the definitions of α-cut and fuzzy α-cut of partial fuzzy relations. Then some basic properties of these cuts of partial fuzzy relations are addressed. Furthermore, we study numerous properties of the compositions of α-cut or fuzzy α-cut of partial fuzzy relations. Additionally, we focus on the relationship between the compositions of the cuts of partial fuzzy relations on the one hand side, and the cuts of the compositions of the partial fuzzy relations on the other side.

Keywords: α-cut · Fuzzy α-cut · Cutability · Partial fuzzy relation · Composition · Dragonfly algebra

1 Introduction and Motivation

Alpha-cut representation of fuzzy sets was introduced in the early times of the fuzzy set theory development and since then, it has been widely applied in various studies. The motivation, theoretical and practical importance of alpha-cuts were mentioned deeply in [18]. Here, let us highlight the use of alpha-cuts in some applications. In [3], alpha-cut method was applied to build the computational procedures for simulating fuzzy cognitive maps in which the system variables and the degree of interrelationships are presented via fuzzy numbers. In [26], the authors introduced the method of alpha-cut induced fuzzy Deep Neural Network for change detection of images. The alpha-cut approach has been taken into account in constructing a Sugeno measure [5], and elaborating the new defuzzification method of generalized fuzzy sets in rule-based systems [32]. Other directions includes the comparison of fuzzy partitions based on their alpha-cuts, the cutting of intuitionistic fuzzy sets depending on connectives, and the establishment of some relationships between fuzzy sets with similarity relations and some nested systems of alpha-cuts [29,30,32].

The authors announce the support of Czech Science Foundation through the grant 20-07851S, and the partial support from ERDF/ESF project CZ.02.1.01/0.0/0.0/17-049/0008414.

© Springer Nature Switzerland AG 2022
D. Ciucci et al. (Eds.): IPMU 2022, CCIS 1601, pp. 663–675, 2022.
https://doi.org/10.1007/978-3-031-08971-8_54

Apart from dealing with alpha-cuts of fuzzy sets, several papers have been focused on studying alpha-cuts of fuzzy relations and their relevant topics of fuzzy relational compositions and fuzzy relational equations as well. For instance, for the land evaluation problem described in [25], the cutting of the output fuzzy relation at a threshold value α helps to make a clear decision regarding the suitability between the land units. The cutting of fuzzy relations involves the study of closure and interior of a relation with respect to a given property [2]. The solvability indices of fuzzy relational equations with respect to a threshold value, which provides an opportunity to look at an appropriate solution of the equations, were extensively studied in [24]. The combination of rough sets and fuzzy sets based on the cutting of fuzzy sets or fuzzy relations was addressed in [28,36]. In [18], the authors provided various valid properties concerning the preservation of the equality between the alpha-cut of compositions of fuzzy relations and the compositions of alpha-cut of the same arguments. The implementation of the Bandler-Kohout products of alpha-cuts of fuzzy relations was addressed in [10]. The efficiency and robustness of such products were examined on the real Dragonfly classification problem.

In recent years, partial fuzzy logics and related algebras for partial fuzzy set theory have been initiated and developed [4,16,21,31]. They generalized the well-known three-valued logics that allow the employment of undefined values (i.e., unknown, indeterminable, missing values, etc.). Generalized partial algebras such as the Bochvar, Sobociński, Kleene, Nelson, etc. in partial fuzzy set theory have been investigated in various aspects. In details, the compositions of partial fuzzy relations was approached [34,35], the solvability of fuzzy relational equations dealing undefined values was opened [11], and the investigation of properties of partial algebras was studied [12]. Let us note that these directions consider also the so-called Dragonfly algebra [35] which has been recently designed to model the missing values as a sort of type of undefinedness.

If we take into account both directions recalled above, in particular, the development of partial fuzzy set theory which provides the platform to deal with practical applications where the missing or unknown information may appear on the one hand side, and the usefulness of alpha-cuts in the variety of applications on the other side, their combinations seems to be a natural next step. Thus, in this article, we reasonably approach the alpha-cut systems of partial fuzzy relations and study the relevant questions. We theoretically investigate numerous properties related to the cutting of partial fuzzy relations and their compositions. For the initial investigation, let us opt for the Dragonfly operations that have been designed to deal with missing values and applied in the real application of the Dragonfly classification. Furthermore, the so-called cutability of the compositions of partial fuzzy relations is addressed as well.

We admit that one may potentially doubt about advantages of the algebraic approach to modeling the missing values. Indeed, there are other well-established theories of uncertainty theories such as possibility theory [20] or modal logics [6]. Moreover, the possibility could be also modeled by some interval-valued or bilattice fuzzy logics [14,22] and so, the connection to existing interval-valued lattices [23] might be of an interest. The algebraic approach [15] is nothing else but an approximation [19] but it is important to say that an efficient one. It can be easily implemented, e.g., in an R-package [7] and enables fast calculations, which is not always true in some other approaches correctly dealing with the uncertainty phenomenon. Also in [13] the authors recall that partial logic turned out to be useful in various areas.

2 Preliminaries

2.1 Dragonfly Algebra Dealing with Missing Values

Let us consider a complete residuated lattice $\mathcal{L} = \langle [0,1], \wedge, \vee, \otimes, \rightarrow 0, 1 \rangle$ as the underlying algebraic structure. Let $\star$ be a dummy value that represents the undefined values in the calculus. Then, we recall the Dragonfly operations [35] defined on the extension $[0,1]^\star = [0,1] \cup \{\star\}$ as follows.

Definition 1 [35]. The *Dragonfly* operations $c_D \in \{\otimes_D, \wedge_D\}$, $d_D \in \{\vee_D, \oplus_D\}$, $\rightarrow_D \colon [0,1]^\star \times [0,1]^\star \rightarrow [0,1]^\star$ are defined by $a \, c_D \, b = a \, c \, b$, $a \, d_D \, b = a \, d \, b$, $a \rightarrow_D b = a \rightarrow b$ for $a, b \in [0,1]$; and they are represented by Table 1 for $a = \star$ or $b = \star$.

Table 1. Truth table of Dragonfly operations with the occurrence of $\star$.

$a, b \in \,]0,1]$		c_D	d_D	$\rightarrow_D$
a	$\star$	$\star$	a	$\star$
$\star$	b	$\star$	b	b
$\star$	$\star$	$\star$	$\star$	1
0	$\star$	0	$\star$	1
$\star$	0	0	$\star$	$\star$

The Dragonfly algebra was designed for modeling the calculus with missing (unknown) values based on the lower estimation strategy. Consider the combination of the dummy value $\star$ and a truth value a different from $0, 1$. Their disjunction (join) $\vee_D, \oplus_D$ can be always estimated from below by a, independently on the choice of the value from $[0,1]$ that could potential replace the temporarily missing value represented by $\star$. Thus, the result of the disjunction is a. On the other hand, their conjunction (meet) $\wedge_D, \otimes_D$ result in the unknown value $\star$ as we cannot estimate the result from below by a higher value. So, the least guaranteed lower estimation is an unknown value represented by $\star$. The implication of $\star$ and a results a when $\star$ occurs in the first argument, and it results $\star$ when $\star$ is in the second argument.

The positions of $\star$ and $0, 1$ correspond to the ordering $0 \leq \star \leq 1$ which is preserved from the Kleene strategy [9]. By this ordering, $\star \wedge_D 0 = 0$, $\star \vee_D 0 = \star$,

$\star \vee_D 1 = 1, \star \wedge_D 1 = \star, 0 \rightarrow_D \star = 1$, and $\star \rightarrow_D 0 = \star$. Note, $\star \rightarrow_D \star = 1$ which preserves the well-known property in $\mathcal{L}$ that $a \rightarrow b = 1$ if and only if $a \leq b$.

We recall also the Dragonfly negation $\neg_D$ and bi-implication $\leftrightarrow_D$:

$$\neg_D a = a \rightarrow_D 0 , \quad a \leftrightarrow_D b = (a \rightarrow_D b) \wedge_D (b \rightarrow_D a) .$$

The ordering $\leq$ in the Dragonfly algebra [35] adopted in this paper reflects the chain $[0, 1]$ and fulfills that $0 \leq \star \leq 1$, so, $\star$ is incomparable with any $a \neq 0, 1$.

Let us recall the external operation $\downarrow$ which is a generalization of the well-known *Bochvar's assertion operation* (cf. [27]). This is one of several useful external auxiliary operations that have been generalized into partial fuzzy set theory, see [9]. The meaning of $\downarrow a$ can be interpreted as *"a is for sure not False"*.

Definition 2 [9]. The *external operation* $\downarrow : [0, 1]^\star \rightarrow [0, 1]^\star$ is given by: $\downarrow a = 0$ if $a = \star$ and $\downarrow a = a$ otherwise.

Several properties of the Dragonfly operations were investigated in [35]. This subsection recalls some of them and provides the additional ones that will be used in the subsequent sections.

Lemma 1 [35]. *For any $a, b, c \in [0, 1]^\star$ it holds:*

$$a \leq b \Rightarrow \downarrow (a \otimes_D c) \leq \downarrow (b \otimes_D c) ; \tag{1}$$

$$a \leq b \Rightarrow b \rightarrow_D c \leq a \rightarrow_D c . \tag{2}$$

Lemma 2. *For any $a, b \in [0, 1]^\star$ and for any $c \in \{0, \star, 1\}$ it holds:*

$$a \leq b \Rightarrow a \otimes_D c \leq b \otimes_D c .$$

Proof-sketch: We check the three cases with the occurrence of $\star$. If $a = \star$ then necessarily $b \in \{\star, 1\}$ and the right-hand side inequality clearly holds. If $b = \star$ then necessarily $a \in \{0, \star\}$ and again, the right-hand side can be checked easily. Finally, let $c = \star$. Then again, the right-hand side inequality is preserved for arbitrary $a, b \in [0, 1]$ s.t. $a \leq b$. $\qquad\square$

Lemma 3. *Consider $a, b \in [0, 1]^\star$ s.t. $(a, b) \neq (\star, 1)$. Then, for any $c \in [0, 1]^\star$:*

$$a \leq b \Rightarrow a \otimes_D c \leq b \otimes_D c .$$

Proof-sketch: Analogously to the previous case, we check all possible combinations of a, b, c with the occurrence of $\star$. $\qquad\square$

Lemma 4. *For any $a, b, c \in [0, 1]^\star$ it holds:*

$$(a \wedge_D b) \otimes_D c \geq (a \otimes_D c) \wedge_D (b \otimes_D c) .$$

Proof-sketch: Equality $(a \wedge_D b) \otimes_D c = (a \otimes_D c) \wedge_D (b \otimes_D c)$ holds on $[0, 1]$ so, we check the property with the appearance of $\star$. Take, e.g., $a = \star$ and $b, c \notin \{0, \star\}$. Then $(a \wedge_D b) \otimes_D c = \star$ while $(a \otimes_D c) \wedge_D (b \otimes_D c) = \star \wedge_D (b \otimes c)$ which is either

$\star$ or 0 (for particular choice of b, c and $\otimes$ with zero divisors) so, the inequality is preserved. The other combinations are proved analogously. $\square$

Now, we present another property that holds only in algebras with the underlying residuated lattice where $\otimes$ is without zero divisors. Firstly, let us recall that the requirement on $\otimes$ without zero divisors is equivalent to the strictness of the residuated negation.

Lemma 5 [12]. *A* $\mathcal{L} = \langle [0,1], \wedge, \vee, \otimes, \rightarrow 0, 1 \rangle$ *be a residuated lattice. Operation* $\otimes$ *is without zero divisors (i.e.,* $a \otimes b \neq 0$ *for* $a, b \neq 0$*) if and only if negation* $\neg a = a \rightarrow 0$ *satisfies that* $\neg a = 1$ *if* $a = 0$*, and* $\neg a = 0$ *otherwise.*

Lemma 6. *Let* $\otimes$ *be without zero divisors. Then, for any* $c \in [0,1]^\star$ *and for any* $a, b \in \{0, \star, 1\}$ *the following holds:*

$$a \leq b \;\Rightarrow\; c \rightarrow_D a \leq c \rightarrow_D b \,.$$

Proof-sketch: The case of $c = \star$ is trivial and also if $a = \star$, the only possibility for b is to be equal to 1 which leads to an easy proof. Let us focus on $a = 0$, $b = \star$ and $c \notin \{0, \star\}$. Then $\neg c = 0 \leq \star = c \rightarrow_D \star$ holds. $\square$

2.2 Compositions of Partial Fuzzy Relations

The Dragonfly operations has been applied to elaborate the compositions of partial fuzzy relations. Let $\mathcal{F}^\star(U) = \{A \mid U \rightarrow [0,1]^\star\}$ denote the set of all partial fuzzy sets on a universe U. Let X, Y, Z be finite non-empty universes and $R \in \mathcal{F}^\star(X \times Y)$ and $S \in \mathcal{F}^\star(Y \times Z)$. We recall the following definition.

Definition 3 [35]. Compositions $R \circ_D S$, $R \triangleleft_D S$, $R \triangleright_D S$, and $R \square_D S$ are partial fuzzy relations on $X \times Z$ given by

$$(R \circ_D S)(x,z) = \bigvee_{y \in Y} {}_D \, (R(x,y) \otimes_D S(y,z)) \,,$$

$$(R \triangleleft_D S)(x,z) = \bigwedge_{y \in Y} {}_D \, (R(x,y) \rightarrow_D S(y,z)) \,,$$

$$(R \triangleright_D S)(x,z) = \bigwedge_{y \in Y} {}_D \, (R(x,y) \leftarrow_D S(y,z)) \,,$$

$$(R \square_D S)(x,z) = \bigwedge_{y \in Y} {}_D \, (R(x,y) \leftrightarrow_D S(y,z)) \,.$$

The meaning of these compositions can be expressed similarly to that of compositions of fully defined fuzzy relations so, we only refer to the relevant literature [1, 8, 17].

3 Cutting of Partial Fuzzy Relations

Let us first recall the definitions of α-cut and fuzzy α-cut of fuzzy relations. In most of the cases, α-cut is defined as a subset of a universe s.t. the given fuzzy set (relation) attains higher or equal values than α for any element of this subset. But as pointed out in [18,33], there is a loss of information about the particular degree and for some thresholding techniques, e.g., in information retrieval, it may be beneficial to preserve the particular membership degrees for the values in the "level set". Therefore, so-called fuzzy α-cut was defined. In order to deal with both types of cuts in the same way as with the same kind of objects, we define the α-cut as the characteristic function of the "traditional" α-cut.

Definition 4. Let us consider $R \in \mathcal{F}(X \times Y)$ and let $\alpha \in \,]0,1]$. Then the α-cut $R_\alpha : X \times Y \to \{0,1\}$ and the fuzzy α-cut $\tilde{R}_\alpha \in \mathcal{F}(X \times Y)$ of R are given as

$$R_\alpha(x,y) = \begin{cases} 1 \text{ if } R(x,y) \geq \alpha \\ 0 \text{ otherwise}; \end{cases} \qquad \tilde{R}_\alpha(x,y) = \begin{cases} R(x,y) \text{ if } R(x,y) \geq \alpha \\ 0 \qquad\quad \text{otherwise}. \end{cases}$$

Remark 1. *Note that Definition 4 considers only α-cuts for non-zero values of α. This is not fully consistent with majority of the literature, however, perfectly reasonable form the practical point of view. We may recall, e.g., the claim published in [2] where the authors stated that "there is no advantage in including the case $\alpha = 0$ in the definition of the α-cut of fuzzy relations". Indeed, the 0-cut is nothing else but the whole universe, which is bringing no information but can harm proving distinct properties. So, for the sake of simplicity, instead of assuming that the properties are proved "only" for $]0,1]$, we simply assume this parametric domain for the α-cuts already in their definition and prove the properties generally.*

Now, let $R \in \mathcal{F}^\star(X \times Y)$, i.e., we consider a partial fuzzy relation. We may approach the following direction to define the α-cut and fuzzy α-cut of R.

Definition 5. Let us consider $R \in \mathcal{F}^\star(X \times Y)$ and $\alpha \in \,]0,1]$. Then the α-cut $R_\alpha \in \mathcal{F}^\star(X \times Y)$ and the fuzzy α-cut $\tilde{R}_\alpha \in \mathcal{F}^\star(X \times Y)$ of R are given as

$$R_\alpha(x,y) = \begin{cases} 1 \text{ if } R(x,y) \geq \alpha \\ 0 \text{ if } R(x,y) < \alpha \\ \star \text{ if } R(x,y) = \star; \end{cases} \qquad \tilde{R}_\alpha(x,y) = \begin{cases} R(x,y) \text{ if } R(x,y) \geq \alpha \\ 0 \qquad\quad \text{if } R(x,y) < \alpha \\ \star \qquad\quad \text{if } R(x,y) = \star. \end{cases}$$

The extensions of the α-cut as well as of the fuzzy α-cut to the cuts of partial fuzzy relations, naturally, has to return the same values for the case of defined membership degrees. Thus, we may focus only on the case of $R(x,y) = \star$ and the related (fuzzy) α-cut values. As $\star$ is not comparable with any membership degree other than 0 or 1 so, we are not able to decide whether $\star$ is smaller or greater than α. Even semantically, it makes sense to say that if the membership degree of a given pair to a given fuzzy relation is undefined (unknown), also the membership degree to the given (fuzzy) α-cut is undefined (unknown).

Now, we study the preservation of some basic properties that are well-known for the α-cut and fuzzy α-cut of fuzzy relations. It is shown that some of properties are preserved and some of them are valid only in a weaker form, e.g., the original equality is replaced by the inclusion.

Proposition 1. *Let $R, R_1, R_2 \in \mathcal{F}^\star(X \times Y)$ and $\alpha, \beta \in]0, 1]$. Then*

$$R_1 \subseteq R_2 \Rightarrow (R_1)_\alpha \subseteq (R_2)_\alpha ; \tag{3}$$

$$R_1 \subseteq R_2 \Rightarrow (\tilde{R}_1)_\alpha \subseteq (\tilde{R}_2)_\alpha ; \tag{4}$$

$$(R_1 \cup_D R_2)_\alpha \subseteq (R_1)_\alpha \cup_D (R_2)_\alpha ; \tag{5}$$

$$(\widetilde{R_1 \cup_D R_2})_\alpha \subseteq (\tilde{R}_1)_\alpha \cup_D (\tilde{R}_2)_\alpha ; \tag{6}$$

$$(R_1 \cap_D R_2)_\alpha \supseteq (R_1)_\alpha \cap_D (R_2)_\alpha ; \tag{7}$$

$$(\widetilde{R_1 \cap_D R_2})_\alpha \supseteq (\tilde{R}_1)_\alpha \cap_D (\tilde{R}_2)_\alpha ; \tag{8}$$

$$\alpha \leq \beta \Rightarrow R_\alpha \supseteq R_\beta ; \tag{9}$$

$$\alpha \leq \beta \Rightarrow \tilde{R}_\alpha \supseteq \tilde{R}_\beta . \tag{10}$$

Proof-sketch: We demonstrate the proof technique on Properties (4) and (5), (8) and (9).

Let $R_1(x, y) = a$, $R_2(x, y) = b$ for $a, b \in [0, 1]^\star$. There are three cases of pairs (a, b) that meet the assumption $R_1 \subseteq R_2$: $(0, \star)$, $(\star, 1)$, and $(a, b) \in [0, 1]^2$ s.t. $a \leq b$. In the first case, $(\tilde{R}_1)_\alpha(x, y) = 0$ which is lower or equal to anything, in the second case $(\tilde{R}_1)_\alpha(x, y) = \star$ while $(\tilde{R}_2)_\alpha(x, y) = 1$, and in the last case, the property $(\tilde{R}_1)_\alpha(x, y) \leq (\tilde{R}_2)_\alpha(x, y)$ for any α holds trivially, which proves (4).

Consider, e.g., $R_1(x, y) = \star$ and $R_2(x, y) \in]0, \alpha]$. Then $(R_1 \cup_D R_2)_\alpha(x, y) = 0 \leq (R_1)_\alpha(x, y) \vee_D (R_2)_\alpha(x, y)$. The remaining cases are checked analogously to prove that (5) holds.

Consider,e.g., $R_1(x, y) = \star$ and $R_2(x, y) \in]0, \alpha]$. Then $(\widetilde{R_1 \cap_D R_2})_\alpha(x, y) = \star$ while $(\tilde{R}_2)_\alpha(x, y) = 0$ causes that $(\tilde{R}_1)_\alpha(x, y) \wedge_D (\tilde{R}_2)_\alpha(x, y) = 0$. The remaining cases are checked analogously to prove that (8) holds.

If $R(x, y) \neq \star$ then it trivially holds that $R_\alpha(x, y) \geq R_\beta(x, y)$ for $\alpha \leq \beta$. If $R(x, y) = \star$ we get $R_\alpha(x, y) = R_\beta(x, y) = \star$ which proves (9). □

4   Compositions of Cutting Partial Fuzzy Relations

4.1   Properties

This section studies distinct properties related to the compositions of α-cuts and fuzzy α-cuts of partial fuzzy relations. It will be shown that various properties valid for the cuts of fuzzy relations are preserved for the cuts of partial fuzzy relations as well. Let symbols $\bigcap$ and $\bigcup$ stand for Gödel intersection and union, respectively, and let $R, R_1, R_2 \in \mathcal{F}^\star(X \times Y)$, $S, S_1, S_2 \in \mathcal{F}^\star(Y \times Z)$.

Proposition 2. *For any $\alpha, \beta \in]0, 1]$:*

$$R_1 \subseteq R_2 \Rightarrow (R_1)_\alpha \circ_D S_\beta \subseteq (R_2)_\alpha \circ_D S_\beta .$$

Proof-sketch: Note that $R_\alpha(x,y) \in \{0,\star,1\}$ for any partial fuzzy relation R. Then, the proof is derived using Property (3) and Lemma 2.   □

Proposition 3 ($\downarrow$-Monotonicity of $\circ_D$). *For any* $\alpha \in]0,1]$:

$$R_1 \subseteq R_2 \Rightarrow \downarrow((R_1)_\alpha \circ_D S) \subseteq \downarrow((R_2)_\alpha \circ_D S) \; ;$$
$$R_1 \subseteq R_2 \Rightarrow \downarrow\left((\tilde{R}_1)_\alpha \circ_D S\right) \subseteq \downarrow\left((\tilde{R}_2)_\alpha \circ_D S\right) \; .$$

Proof-sketch: The proof can be done using (3), (4) and Property (1).   □

Proposition 4 (Antitonicity of $\lhd_D$). *For any* $\alpha \in]0,1]$:

$$R_1 \subseteq R_2 \Rightarrow (R_1)_\alpha \lhd_D S \supseteq (R_2)_\alpha \lhd_D S \; ;$$
$$R_1 \subseteq R_2 \Rightarrow (\tilde{R}_1)_\alpha \lhd_D S \supseteq (\tilde{R}_2)_\alpha \lhd_D S \; .$$

Proof-sketch: Applying (3), (4) and the antitonicity of $\to_D$ given in (2).   □

Proposition 5 (Isotonicity of $\rhd_D$). *Assume that* $\otimes$ *has no zero divisors. Then, for any* $\alpha \in]0,1]$:

$$R_1 \subseteq R_2 \Rightarrow (R_1)_\alpha \rhd_D S \subseteq (R_2)_\alpha \rhd_D S \; .$$

Proof-sketch: Since $(R_1)_\alpha(x,y), (R_2)_\alpha(x,y) \in \{0,\star,1\}$ for any $(x,y) \in X \times Y$, we apply (3) and Lemma 6 to conclude the proof.   □

Proposition 6 (Cut embedding). *Let* $\alpha,\beta \in]0,1]$. *If* $\alpha \leq \beta$ *then,*

$$\downarrow(R_\alpha \circ_D S) \supseteq \downarrow(R_\beta \circ_D S) \; ; \qquad \downarrow\left(\tilde{R}_\alpha \circ_D S\right) \supseteq \downarrow\left(\tilde{R}_\beta \circ_D S\right) \; ;$$
$$R_\alpha \lhd_D S \subseteq R_\beta \lhd_D S \; ; \qquad\qquad \tilde{R}_\alpha \lhd_D S \subseteq \tilde{R}_\beta \lhd_D S \; .$$

Proof-sketch: It is sufficient to use Properties (9), (10), the monotonicity of $\otimes_D$ (1), and the antitonicity of $\to_D$ (2).   □

Proposition 7 (Union-$\circ$). *If* $\otimes$ *has no zero divisors then for any* $\alpha \in]0,1]$:

$$(R_1 \cup_D R_2)_\alpha \circ_D S \subseteq ((R_1)_\alpha \circ_D S) \cup_D ((R_2)_\alpha \circ_D S) \; ;$$
$$(\widetilde{R_1 \cup_D R_2})_\alpha \circ_D S \subseteq ((\tilde{R}_1)_\alpha \circ_D S) \cup_D ((\tilde{R}_2)_\alpha \circ_D S) \; .$$

Proof-sketch: Denote $(R_1 \cup_D R_2)_\alpha(x,y) = a$ and $(R_1)_\alpha(x,y) \vee_D (R_2)_\alpha(x,y) = b$. Then for any $(x,y) \in X \times Y$ and for $\alpha \in]0,1]$, the pair (a,b) differs from the pair $(\star,1)$. Because of Property (5) and because of Lemma 3, we obtain $(R_1 \cup_D R_2)_\alpha \circ_D S \subseteq ((R_1)_\alpha \cup_D (R_2)_\alpha) \circ_D S$. Then by the distributivity

$$(R_1 \cup_D R_2) \circ_D S = (R_1 \circ_D S) \cup_D (R_2 \circ_D S)$$

which holds for $\otimes$ without zero divisors (cf. [35]), we obtain the first inclusion of Proposition 7. The second inclusion is derived similarly.   □

Proposition 8 ($\downarrow$-Union-$\circ$). *For any* $\alpha \in {]}0,1]$:

$$\downarrow ((R_1 \cup_D R_2)_\alpha \circ_D S) \subseteq \downarrow (((R_1)_\alpha \circ_D S) \cup_D ((R_2)_\alpha \circ_D S)) \; ;$$

$$\downarrow \left((\widetilde{R_1 \cup_D R_2})_\alpha \circ_D S\right) \subseteq \downarrow \left(((\tilde{R}_1)_\alpha \circ_D S) \cup_D ((\tilde{R}_2)_\alpha \circ_D S)\right) \; .$$

Proof-sketch: Using (5), (6), Proposition 3, and property $\downarrow ((R_1 \cup_D R_2) \circ_D S) = \downarrow ((R_1 \circ_D S) \cup_D (R_2 \circ_D S))$, which is given in [35]. $\qquad\square$

Proposition 9 (Intersection-$\circ$). *For any* $\alpha \in {]}0,1]$:

$$(R_1 \cap_D R_2)_\alpha \circ_D S \supseteq ((R_1)_\alpha \circ_D S) \cap_D ((R_2)_\alpha \circ_D S) \; ;$$

$$(\widetilde{R_1 \cap_D R_2})_\alpha \circ_D S \supseteq ((\tilde{R}_1)_\alpha \circ_D S) \cap_D ((\tilde{R}_2)_\alpha \circ_D S) \; .$$

Proof-sketch: Denote $((R_1)_\alpha \cap_D (R_2)_\alpha)(x,y) = a$ and $(R_1 \cap_D R_2)_\alpha(x,y) = b$. Then for any $(x,y) \in X \times Y$ and $\alpha \in {]}0,1]$, the pair (a,b) differs from the pair $(\star, 1)$. Because of Property (7), and because of Lemmas 3 and 4, we get the first inclusion. The second inclusion can be inferred analogously. $\qquad\square$

4.2 Cutability of Compositions of Partial Fuzzy Relations

This section focuses on the so-called *cutability* [18] of the compositions of partial fuzzy relations using the Dragonfly algebra. In particular, we investigate the properties showing the relationship between the cut of compositions of partial fuzzy relations and the compositions of the cutting partial fuzzy relations of the same arguments. Definition 6 below, that was introduced in [18], plays an important role in investigating the cutability of the compositions.

Definition 6. Let $\mathcal{L} = \langle [0,1], \vee, \wedge, \otimes, \to 0, 1 \rangle$ and let $\alpha \in {]}0,1]$. We say, that $\otimes$ has the $G_\alpha^{\nearrow}$ property and $\to$ has the $G_\alpha^{\searrow}$ property if

$$(G_\alpha^{\nearrow}) \quad \forall a \in [\alpha, 1], b \in [\alpha, 1] : a \otimes b \geq \alpha \tag{11}$$

$$(G_\alpha^{\searrow}) \quad \forall a \in [\alpha, 1], b \in [0, \alpha[: a \to b \leq \alpha, \tag{12}$$

respectively.

Notice that $G_\alpha^{\nearrow}$ and $G_\alpha^{\searrow}$ hold for arbitrary $\alpha \in {]}0,1]$ only in the Gödel algebra. However, if it holds for a particular fixed value of α, not for arbitrary one, we may easily consider other residuated latticed based on t-norms $\otimes$ constructed as ordinal sums of other t-norms with the "Gödel part" in the rectangle $[\alpha, 1]$. This also explains the denotation pointing out to the Gödel part of the operation and the upper/lower corner of the domain where it appears.

For the sake of clarity and brevity, it will be useful to introduce a denotation of the α-cut in the classical sense, i.e., as a subset of the universe to which "our" α-cut is constructed as its characteristic set. So, let $R \subset \mathcal{F}^*(X \times Y)$ then

$$\overline{R}_\alpha = \{(x,y) \in X \times Y \mid R(x,y) \geq \alpha\} \; .$$

Now, we can introduce a proposition that extends the result published in [18]. We only recall an important fact that all the considered universes X, Y, Z are finite.

Proposition 10. *Let us consider an $\alpha \in]0,1]$, let $R \in \mathcal{F}^\star(X \times Y)$, and let $S \in \mathcal{F}^\star(Y \times Z)$. Then for any $(x,z) \in \overline{R \circ S}_\alpha$ the following holds*

$$(R \circ_D S)_\alpha(x,z) = (R_\alpha \circ_D S_\alpha)(x,z) \tag{13}$$

$$(\widetilde{R \circ_D S})_\alpha(x,z) = (\tilde{R}_\alpha \circ_D \tilde{S}_\alpha)(x,z) . \tag{14}$$

If $\otimes$ has the property $G^{\nearrow}_\alpha$ for the given α then for $(x,z) \notin \overline{R \circ S}_\alpha$:
$(R \circ_D S)_\alpha(x,z), (R_\alpha \circ_D S_\alpha)(x,z), (\widetilde{R \circ_D S})_\alpha(x,z), (\tilde{R}_\alpha \circ_D \tilde{S}_\alpha)(x,z) \in \{0, \star\}.$

Proof-sketch: Consider an $\alpha \in]0,1]$ such that $\otimes$ has the $G^{\nearrow}_\alpha$ property.

If $(x,z) \in \overline{R \circ S}_\alpha$ then there exists y such that $R(x,y) \otimes_D S(y,z) \geq \alpha$. This implies that $R(x,y), S(y,z) \geq \alpha$ and thus, $R_\alpha(x,y) = S_\alpha(y,z) = 1$. Therefore, $(R_\alpha \circ_D S_\alpha)(x,z) = 1 = (R \circ_D S)_\alpha(x,z)$ for the given pair (x,z).

Let $(x,z) \notin \overline{R \circ S}_\alpha$. Then due to property $G^{\nearrow}_\alpha$ carried by $\otimes$, there does not exist any $y \in Y$ such that it both $R(x,y)$ and $S(y,z)$ would be greater or equal to α at the same time. So, $(R_\alpha \circ_D S_\alpha)(x,z) \neq 1$. Now, if $(R \circ_D S)(x,z) = 0$, one may derive that $(R_\alpha \circ_D S_\alpha)(x,z) = (R \circ_D S)_\alpha(x,z) = 0$. If $(R \circ_D S)(x,z) \in]0, \alpha[$ then $(R \circ_D S)_\alpha(x,z) = 0$, while $(R_\alpha \circ_D S_\alpha)(x,z) \in \{0, \star\}$. The equality to $\star$ may occur if there exists $y^\star \in Y$ such that $R(x,y^\star) = S(y^\star, z) = \star$ and $\bigvee_{y \neq y^\star} R(x,y) \otimes_D S(y,z) \in]0, \alpha[$. If $(R \circ_D S)(x,z) = \star$ then $(R \circ_D S)_\alpha(x,z) = \star$ while $(R_\alpha \circ_D S_\alpha)(x,z) \in \{0, \star\}$. The case of $(R_\alpha \circ_D S_\alpha)(x,z) = 0$ can occur when for all $y \in Y : R(x,y) = \star$ and $S(y,z) \in]0, \alpha[$; or vise-versa $S(y,z) = \star$ and $R(x,y) \in]0, \alpha[$.

Proof of (14) proceeds similarly. Let us assume that $(\widetilde{R \circ_D S})_\alpha(x,z) \in [\alpha, 1]$. As $(\widetilde{R \circ_D S})_\alpha(x,z) = R(x,y') \otimes_D S(y',z)$ for some y', we get $R(x,y'), S(y',z) \in [\alpha, 1]$. Thus, $\tilde{R}_\alpha(x,y') \otimes_D \tilde{S}_\alpha(y',z) = R(x,y') \otimes_D S(y',z)$. For $y \in Y \smallsetminus \{y'\}$, we can see that if $R(x,y) \otimes_D S(y,z) \neq \star$ then due to $R(x,y) \otimes_D S(y,z) \leq R(x,y') \otimes_D S(y',z)$, it holds that $\tilde{R}_\alpha(x,y) \otimes_D \tilde{S}_\alpha(y,z) \leq \tilde{R}_\alpha(x,y') \otimes_D \tilde{S}_\alpha(y',z)$. Hence, $(\tilde{R}_\alpha \circ_D \tilde{S}_\alpha)(x,z) = \tilde{R}_\alpha(x,y') \otimes_D \tilde{S}_\alpha(y',z) = (\widetilde{R \circ_D S})_\alpha(x,z)$. The remaining part can be proved similarly to the proof of (13). □

With help of the external operation $\downarrow$, the cutability of the basic composition of partial fuzzy relations can be obtained.

Corollary 1. *Let $\alpha \in]0,1]$ and let $\otimes$ have the property $G^{\nearrow}_\alpha$ for the given α. Then*

$$\downarrow(R \circ_D S)_\alpha = \downarrow(R_\alpha \circ_D S_\alpha), \quad \downarrow(\widetilde{R \circ_D S})_\alpha = \downarrow(\tilde{R}_\alpha \circ_D \tilde{S}_\alpha).$$

The results including the sketch of the proof were presented above however, analogous approaches can be performed also when proving relevant cutability properties for the other fuzzy relational compositions. Due to the space limitations, we provide readers only with the final result aggregating them all.

Proposition 11. *Let us consider an* $\alpha \in \,]0,1]$, *let* $R \in \mathcal{F}^\star(X \times Y)$, *and let* $S \in \mathcal{F}^\star(Y \times Z)$. *Then for any* $(x,z) \in \overline{R \circ S}_\alpha$ *the following holds*

$$(R \lhd_D S)_\alpha(x,z) = (R_\alpha \lhd_D S_\alpha)(x,z) \,, \quad (\widetilde{R \lhd_D S})_\alpha(x,z) \le (\tilde{R}_\alpha \lhd_D \tilde{S}_\alpha)(x,z) \,,$$

$$(R \rhd_D S)_\alpha(x,z) = (R_\alpha \rhd_D S_\alpha)(x,z) \,, \quad (\widetilde{R \rhd_D S})_\alpha(x,z) \le (\tilde{R}_\alpha \rhd_D \tilde{S}_\alpha)(x,z) \,,$$

$$(R \square_D S)_\alpha(x,z) = (R_\alpha \square_D S_\alpha)(x,z) \,, \quad (\widetilde{R \square_D S})_\alpha(x,z) \le (\tilde{R}_\alpha \square_D \tilde{S}_\alpha)(x,z) \,.$$

If the operation $\rightarrow$ *has the property* $G_\alpha^\searrow$ *for the given* α *then*

$$\downarrow(R \lhd_D S)_\alpha \subseteq \downarrow(R_\alpha \lhd_D S_\alpha), \quad \downarrow(\widetilde{R \lhd_D S})_\alpha \subseteq \downarrow(\tilde{R}_\alpha \lhd_D \tilde{S}_\alpha) \,,$$

$$\downarrow(R \rhd_D S)_\alpha \subseteq \downarrow(R_\alpha \rhd_D S_\alpha), \quad \downarrow(\widetilde{R \rhd_D S})_\alpha \subseteq \downarrow(\tilde{R}_\alpha \rhd_D \tilde{S}_\alpha) \,,$$

$$\downarrow(R \square_D S)_\alpha \subseteq \downarrow(R_\alpha \square_D S_\alpha), \quad \downarrow(\widetilde{R \square_D S})_\alpha \subseteq \downarrow(\tilde{R}_\alpha \square_D \tilde{S}_\alpha) \,.$$

5 Conclusions

We have extended the α-cut and fuzzy α-cut of partial fuzzy relations. Then some basic properties of the cutting partial fuzzy relations were investigated. It shows that some of the properties that are valid for the cuts of fully defined fuzzy relations are preserved by the cuts of partial fuzzy relations, some of them only in a weaker form involving an inclusion instead of equality. We emphasize that the results hold for the particular algebra for partial fuzzy set theory called Dragonfly algebra. In the last section, we have investigated the cutability, i.e., the relationship between the cuts of a given composition of two partial fuzzy relations and the composition of the cuts of partial fuzzy relations. Some of the results confirm and only extend the results from [18], some of them significantly extend the knowledge provided in [18] as they focus on all the four basic compositions.

References

1. Bandler, W., Kohout, L.J.: Semantics of implication operators and fuzzy relational products. Int. J. Man Mach. Stud. **12**(1), 89–116 (1980)
2. Bandler, W., Kohout, L.J.: Special properties, closures and interiors of crisp and fuzzy relations. Fuzzy Sets Syst. **26**(3), 317–331 (1988)
3. Baykasoğlu, A., Gölcük, İ: Alpha-cut based fuzzy cognitive maps with applications in decision-making. Comput. Ind. Eng. **152**, 107007 (2021)
4. Běhounek, L., Dvořák, A.: Fuzzy relational modalities admitting truth-valueless propositions. Fuzzy Sets Syst. **388**, 38–55 (2020)
5. Bertoluzza, C., Solci, M., Capodieci, M.L.: Measure of a fuzzy set. The α-cut approach in the finite case. Fuzzy Sets Syst. **123**(1), 93–102 (2001)
6. Bou, F., Esteva, F., Godo, L.: On possibilistic modal logics defined over MTL-chains. In: Montagna, F. (ed.) Petr Hájek on Mathematical Fuzzy Logic. OCL, vol. 6, pp. 225–244. Springer, Cham (2015). https://doi.org/10.1007/978-3-319-06233-4_11

7. Burda, M., Štěpnička, M.: lfl: an R package for linguistic fuzzy logic. Fuzzy Sets Syst. **431**, 1–38 (2022)
8. Bělohlávek, R.: Fuzzy Relational Systems: Foundations and Principles. Springer New York (2002). https://doi.org/10.1007/978-1-4615-0633-1
9. Běhounek, L., Dvořák, A.: Fuzzy relational modalities admitting truth-valueless propositions. Fuzzy Sets Syst. **388**, 38–55 (2020)
10. Cao, N., Burda, M.: Triangular fuzzy relational products of level fuzzy relations. In: 19th World Congress of the International Fuzzy Systems Association (IFSA), 12th Conference of the European Society for Fuzzy Logic and Technology (EUSFLAT), and 11th International Summer School on Aggregation Operators (AGOP), pp. 32–39. Atlantis Press (2021)
11. Cao, N., Štěpnička, M.: Sufficient solvability conditions for systems of partial fuzzy relational equations. In: Lesot, M.-J., et al. (eds.) IPMU 2020. CCIS, vol. 1237, pp. 93–106. Springer, Cham (2020). https://doi.org/10.1007/978-3-030-50146-4_8
12. Cao, N., Štěpnička, M.: On preservation of residuated lattice properties for partial algebras. In: 19th World Congress of the International Fuzzy Systems Association (IFSA), 12th Conference of the European Society for Fuzzy Logic and Technology (EUSFLAT), and 11th International Summer School on Aggregation Operators (AGOP), pp. 405–412. Atlantis Press (2021)
13. Ciucci, D., Dubois, D.: A map of dependencies among three-valued logics. Inf. Sci. **250**, 162–177 (2013)
14. Cornelis, C., Arieli, O., Deschrijver, G., Kerre, E.E.: Uncertainty modeling by bilattice-based squares and triangles. IEEE Trans. Fuzzy Syst. **15**, 161–175 (2007)
15. d'Allonnes, A.R., Lesot, M.J.: If I don't know, should I infer? Reasoning around ignorance in a many-valued framework. In: Joint 17th World Congress of International Fuzzy Systems Association and 9th International Conference on Soft Computing and Intelligent Systems, IFSA-SCIS 2017, Otsu, Japan, 27–30 June 2017, pp. 1–6. IEEE (2017). https://doi.org/10.1109/IFSA-SCIS.2017.8023315
16. Daňková, M.: Functional partial fuzzy relations. Mathematics **9**(18), 2191 (2021)
17. De Baets, B., Kerre, E.: Fuzzy relational compositions. Fuzzy Sets Syst. **60**, 109–120 (1993)
18. De Baets, B., Kerre, E.: The cutting of compositions. Fuzzy Sets Syst. **62**(3), 295–309 (1994)
19. Dubois, D.: On ignorance and contradiction considered as truth-values. Log. J. IGPL **16**, 195–216 (2008)
20. Dubois, D., Prade, H.: Possibility theory and its applications: where do we stand? In: Kacprzyk, J., Pedrycz, W. (eds.) Springer Handbook of Computational Intelligence, pp. 31–60. Springer, Heidelberg (2015). https://doi.org/10.1007/978-3-662-43505-2_3
21. Dvořák, A., Holčapek, M., Rico, A.: Qualitative integrals on dragonfly algebras. In: 2021 IEEE International Conference on Fuzzy Systems (FUZZ-IEEE), pp. 1–6. IEEE (2021)
22. Esteva, F., Garcia-Calvés, P., Godo, L.: Enriched interval bilattices and partial many-valued logics: an approach to deal with graded truth and imprecision. Int. J. Uncertain. Fuzziness Knowl. Based Syst. **2**, 37–54 (1994)
23. Gasse, B.V., Cornelis, C., Deschrijver, G., Kerre, E.E.: International journal of approximate reasoning. IEEE Trans. Fuzzy Syst. **49**, 478–487 (2008)
24. Gottwald, S., Pedrycz, W.: Solvability of fuzzy relational equations and manipulation of fuzzy data. Fuzzy Sets Syst. **18**(1), 45–65 (1986)
25. Groenemans, R., Van Ranst, E., Kerre, E.: Fuzzy relational calculus in land evaluation. Geoderma **77**(2–4), 283–298 (1997)

26. Kalaiselvi, S., Gomathi, V.: α-cut induced fuzzy deep neural network for change detection of sar images. Appl. Soft Comput. **95**, 106510 (2020)
27. Karpenko, A., Tomova, N.: Bochvar's three-valued logic and literal paralogics: their lattice and functional equivalence. Log. Log. Philos. **26**(2), 207–235 (2016)
28. Liu, W.-N., Yao, J.T., Yao, Y.: Rough approximations under level fuzzy sets. In: Tsumoto, S., Słowiński, R., Komorowski, J., Grzymała-Busse, J.W. (eds.) RSCTC 2004. LNCS (LNAI), vol. 3066, pp. 78–83. Springer, Heidelberg (2004). https://doi.org/10.1007/978-3-540-25929-9_8
29. Martinetti, D., Janiš, V., Montes, S.: Cuts of intuitionistic fuzzy sets respecting fuzzy connectives. Inf. Sci. **232**, 267–275 (2013)
30. Močkoř, J.: α-cuts and models of fuzzy logic. Int. J. Gen Syst **42**(1), 67–78 (2013)
31. Novák, V.: Fuzzy type theory with partial functions. Iran. J. Fuzzy Syst. **16**(2), 1–16 (2019)
32. Pourabdollah, A., Mendel, J.M., John, R.I.: Alpha-cut representation used for defuzzification in rule-based systems. Fuzzy Sets Syst. **399**, 110–132 (2020)
33. Radecki, T.: Level fuzzy sets. J. Cybern. **7**(3–4), 189–198 (1977)
34. Štěpnička, M., Cao, N., Burda, M., Dolný, A., Ožana, S.: The concept of unavoidable features in fuzzy relational compositions. Knowl. Based Syst. **196**, 105785 (2020)
35. Štěpnička, M., Cao, N., Běhounek, L., Burda, M., Dolný, A.: Missing values and dragonfly operations in fuzzy relational compositions. Int. J. Approx. Reason. **113**, 149–170 (2019)
36. Yao, Y.: Combination of rough and fuzzy sets based on α-level sets. In: Rough Sets and Data Mining, pp. 301–321. Springer, Boston (1997). https://doi.org/10.1007/978-1-4613-1461-5_15

Rotations of Gödel Algebras with Modal Operators

Tommaso Flaminio[1]([✉]) [iD], Lluis Godo[1] [iD], Paula Menchón[2,3] [iD],
and Ricardo O. Rodriguez[4] [iD]

[1] Artificial Intelligence Research Institute (IIIA - CSIC), Barcelona, Spain
{tommaso,godo}@iiia.csic.es
[2] Nicolaus Copernicus University, Toruń, Poland
[3] CONICET, Univ. Nacional del Centro de la Provincia de Buenos Aires,
Tandil, Argentina
[4] UBA-FCEyN, Departamento de Computación, CONICET-UBA, Inst. de Invest.
en Cs. de la Computación, Buenos Aires, Argentina
ricardo@dc.uba.ar

Abstract. The present paper is devoted to study the effect of connected
and disconnected rotations of Gödel algebras with operators grounded
on directly indecomposable structures. The structures resulting from this
construction we will present are nilpotent minimum (with or without
negation fixpoint, depending on whether the rotation is connected or disconnected) with special modal operators defined on a directly indecomposable algebra. In this paper we will present a (quasi-)equational definition of these latter structures. Our main results show that directly indecomposable nilpotent minimum algebras (with or without negation fixpoint) with modal operators are fully characterized as connected and disconnected rotations of directly indecomposable Gödel algebras endowed
with modal operators.

1 Introduction

Fuzzy modal logic is an active and rapidly growing area of research that aims at
generalizing classical modal logic to a many-valued or fuzzy framework. Although
the birth of Mathematical Fuzzy logic as a discipline is usually taken with the
publication of Hájek's book [13] in 1998, the first attempts to generalize modal
logic to the setting of many-valued logic can be traced back to the 90's of the
last century. Indeed, in 1991 and 1992 Fitting published two fundamental papers
[9,10] in which, he investigates two families of many-valued modal logics: on the
side of their relational semantics, the first one is characterized by Kripke models
in which, at each possible world, formulas are evaluated by a finite Heyting
algebra; the second one allows also the accessibility relation to be many-valued.

Fitting's work on many-valued modal logics paved the way to the birth of
fuzzy modal logic as a field and inspired several other researchers who, following
his ideas, further generalized classical modal logic to the ground of infinite-valued

© Springer Nature Switzerland AG 2022
D. Ciucci et al. (Eds.): IPMU 2022, CCIS 1601, pp. 676–688, 2022.
https://doi.org/10.1007/978-3-031-08971-8_55

fuzzy logics. In this respect it is worth to remember the general approaches collected in the papers by Priest [23], by Hájek [14], by Bou, Esteva, Godo and Rodriguez [3] and by Diaconescu, Metcalfe and Schnüriger [7]. Further works which follow Fitting's ideas of generalizing Kripke models to the fuzzy environment, but focus on modal expansions of specific propositional logics, are also worth to recall. In particular the ones by Caicedo and Rodriguez [5,6] who investigate modal expansions of Gödel logic, the paper [15] by Hansoul and Teheux who instead consider modal expansions of propositional Łukasiewicz logic, and the one by Vidal, Esteva and Godo [24] where the propositional base is product fuzzy logic.

In the recent paper [11], taking inspiration on intuitionistic modal logics, we made the first steps towards an algebraic approach to modal expansions of Gödel propositional logic by introducing *finite Gödel algebras with operators* (GAOs for short) and a class of relational models which, in contrast to the original Fitting's approach, are not Kripke-like structures. Indeed, the relational duals of GAOs turn out to be frames based on *forests* rather than sets, that is, posets in which the downset of each element is totally ordered.

In the present paper, we are interested in studying *nilpotent minimum algebras with modal operators*. Nilpotent minimum algebras (NM-algebras for short) are the algebraic semantics of the so-called nilpotent minimum fuzzy logic, denoted by NM, which turns out to be sound and complete w.r.t. the algebra on $[0,1]$ defined by the so-called nilpotent minimum t-norm and its residuum [8], that is a left-continuous, but not continuous, t-norm. The results on NM-algebras with modal operators are obtained by extending the well-known construction of connected and disconnected rotations of Gödel algebras [4,18] to the modal framework.

This paper is organized as follows. Section 2 is devoted to recall basic algebraic notions and, in particular, to introduce Gödel and NM-algebras. Also we recall how NM-algebras with or without negation fixpoint can be constructed as connected or disconnected rotations of directly indecomposable Gödel algebras. In Sect. 3, after briefly recalling Gödel algebras with modal operators, we study modal expansions of NM^+ and NM^--algebras obtained by extending connected and disconnected rotations to the modal setting. In particular, Sect. 3.1 is on modal NM^+-algebras, while NM^--algebras are the subject of Sect. 3.2. Our main results, namely Theorems 3 and 4, show that for every Gödel algebra with operators whose Gödel reduct is directly indecomposable and satisfying certain properties, one can build both an NM^+ and an NM^--algebra with operators whose NM-reduct still is directly indecomposable. Indeed, each such modal NM-algebra arises in those ways. We conclude with Sect. 4 where we present some conclusions and some prospects for our future work.

2 Gödel and Nilpotent Minimum Algebras

Most of the algebraic structures we consider in this paper lay in the variety of MTL-algebras [8], namely, integral, commutative, bounded and prelinear residuated lattices which are structures of the form $\mathbf{A} = (A, *, \rightarrow, \wedge, \vee, \bot, \top)$ of type $(2, 2, 2, 2, 0, 0)$ where: $(A, *, \top)$ is a commutative monoid; $(A, \wedge, \vee, \bot, \top)$ is a bounded lattice; and the following conditions hold for all $x, y, z \in A$:

(Res) $x * y \leq z$ iff $x \leq y \to z$, where $\leq$ denotes the lattice order of $\mathbf{A}$;
(Pre) $(x \to y) \vee (y \to x) = \top$.

In every MTL-algebra, a negation operator $\neg$ can be defined as: $\neg x = x \to \bot$.

Let $\mathbf{A}$ be an MTL-algebra. A subset f of $\mathbf{A}$ is said to be a *filter* provided that: (1) $\top \in f$, (2) if $x, y \in f$, then $x * y \in f$, (3) if $x \in f$ and $y \geq x$ then $y \in f$. A filter $f \neq A$ (that is, a *proper* filter) is said to be *prime* if $x \vee y \in f$ implies that either $x \in f$ or $y \in f$. A filter f is *principal* (or *principally generated*) if there exists an element $x \in A$ such that $f = \uparrow x = \{y \in A \mid y \geq x\}$.

An MTL-algebra $\mathbf{A}$ is said to be *directly indecomposable* (d.i., henceforth) if it cannot be factorized as a non-trivial direct product $\prod_{i \in I} \mathbf{A}_i$ of MTL-algebras $\mathbf{A}_i$.

Definition 1. *A Gödel algebra is a MTL-algebra which further satisfies the following equation which expresses the idempotency property:*

(Idem) $x * x = x$.

The idempotency of Gödel algebras allows us to present them in the simplified signature in which $* = \wedge$, which coincides with the signature of Heyting algebras [16,17]. Indeed, an equivalent definition of Gödel algebras is to present them as those Heyting algebras, i.e., integral, commutative, bounded and idempotent residuated lattices, that further satisfy the prelinearity equation **(Pre)** above.

A Gödel algebra is d.i. iff $\bot$ is meet irreducible. Equivalently a Gödel algebra is d.i. iff it has a join-irreducible co-atom and hence a unique maximal filter that is in fact principally generated by its unique co-atom. In what follows we will need the following easy result.

Lemma 1. *In every d.i. Gödel algebra, if $x > \bot$, $\neg x = \bot$.*

Definition 2. *A nilpotent minimum algebra $\mathbf{A}$ is a MTL-algebra which further satisfies the following equations:*

(Inv) $\neg\neg x = x$,
(NM) $\neg(x * y) \vee (x \wedge y \to x * y) = \bot$.

In linearly ordered nilpotent minimum algebras, condition (NM) implies that either $x * y = \bot$ or $x * y = \min(x, y)$. Since the negation operator of NM-algebras is involutive, if it has a fixpoint, it is unique. The property of having a negation fixpoint or not, can be captured equationally. An NM-algebra $\mathbf{A}$ is said to be *without negation fix-point* (and we write that $\mathbf{A}$ is an NM^--algebra) if it satisfies the further equation:

(NM^-) $\neg(\neg(x * x)) * \neg(x * x) = (\neg(\neg x * \neg x)) * (\neg(\neg x * \neg x))$.

As for those NM-algebras with a negation fixpoint, we need to expand their language by a new constant $\mathbf{f}$ and an algebra $\mathbf{A} = (A, *, \rightarrow, \wedge, \vee, \mathbf{f}, \perp, \top)$ is said to be *with negation fix-point* (and we write that $\mathbf{A}$ is an NM^+-algebra) if its $\{\mathbf{f}\}$-free reduct is a NM-algebra and it further satisfies:

$(\mathbf{NM^+})$ $\neg \mathbf{f} = \mathbf{f}$.

Similarly to Gödel algebras, a NM^+ or NM^--algebra is directly indecomposable iff it has a unique maximal filter. In this case, however, the unique maximal filter is not principally generated by a unique co-atom of $\mathbf{A}$. Indeed, as we will see below, there exist d.i. NM^+ and NM^--algebras without a unique co-atom.

Now we recall a general construction which allows to define NM^- and NM^+-algebras as disconnected and connected rotations of a directly indecomposable Gödel algebra. The original ideas are from [4,18] while the proofs of next results, namely Propositions 1 and 2 and Theorems 1 and 2, can be found in [4, §4].

Let $\mathbf{A}$ be a Gödel algebra and define

$$NM^+(\mathbf{A}) = \{(a^-, a^+) \in A \times A \mid a^- \wedge a^+ = \perp\}$$
$$NM^-(\mathbf{A}) = \{(a^-, a^+) \in A \times A \mid (a^- \wedge a^+) \vee \neg(a^- \vee a^+) = \perp\}.$$

Further, for every $(a^-, a^+), (b^-, b^+) \in NM^+(A) \cup NM^-(A)$, define

$$(a^-, a^+) * (b^-, b^+) = ((a^+ \vee b^+) \rightarrow (a^- \vee b^-), a^+ \wedge b^+);$$
$$(a^-, a^+) \wedge (b^-, b^+) = (a^- \vee b^-, a^+ \wedge b^+);$$
$$\neg(a^-, a^+) = (a^+, a^-).$$

Now, denote by $\mathbf{NM^+}(\mathbf{A})$ and $\mathbf{NM^-}(\mathbf{A})$ the structures:

$$\mathbf{NM^+}(\mathbf{A}) = (NM^+(\mathbf{A}), *, \wedge, \neg, (\perp, \perp), (\top, \perp), (\perp, \top)),$$
$$\mathbf{NM^-}(\mathbf{A}) = (NM^-(\mathbf{A}), *, \wedge, \neg, (\top, \perp), (\perp, \top)).$$

It is worth pointing out that, in case $\mathbf{A}$ is a d.i. Gödel algebra, the above constructions that build the algebras $\mathbf{NM^+}(\mathbf{A})$ and $\mathbf{NM^-}(\mathbf{A})$ coincide, respectively, with the well-known *connected* and *disconnected* rotations of $\mathbf{A}$ (see [18] and [4]).

Proposition 1. *For every Gödel algebra $\mathbf{A}$, $\mathbf{NM^+}(\mathbf{A})$ is a NM^+-algebra with negation fixpoint $(\perp, \perp)$ and $\mathbf{NM^-}(\mathbf{A})$ is a NM^--algebra without negation fixpoint. Moreover, $\mathbf{A}$ is d.i. iff so are $\mathbf{NM^+}(\mathbf{A})$ and $\mathbf{NM^-}(\mathbf{A})$.*

According to the above construction, if $(a^-, a^+), (b^-, b^+)$ are elements of either $NM^+(\mathbf{A})$ or $NM^-(\mathbf{A})$, then $(a^-, a^+) \leq (b^-, b^+)$ iff $(a^-, a^+) = (a^-, a^+) \wedge (b^-, b^+) = (a^- \vee b^-, a^+ \wedge b^+)$ iff $a^- \geq b^-$ and $a^+ \leq b^+$.

Let us now start from any NM^+ or NM^--algebra $\mathbf{B}$ and define

$$G(\mathbf{B}) = \{b * b \mid b \in B\}.$$

Proposition 2. *For every NM^+ or NM^--algebra $\mathbf{B}$, the structure $\mathbf{G}(\mathbf{B}) = (G(\mathbf{B}), \wedge, \rightarrow^2, \perp, \top)$, where for every $x, y \in G(\mathbf{B})$, $x \rightarrow^2 y = (x \rightarrow y) * (x \rightarrow y)$, is a Gödel algebra. Further, $\mathbf{B}$ is d.i. iff so is $\mathbf{G}(\mathbf{B})$.*

Let **A** be a d.i. Gödel algebra and let **B** be a d.i. NM-algebra. Consider the maps $\gamma : \mathbf{A} \to \mathbf{G}(\mathbf{NM}^{\pm}(\mathbf{A}))$ and $\eta : \mathbf{B} \to \mathbf{NM}^{\pm}(\mathbf{G}(\mathbf{B}))$ defined by the following stipulations: for all $a \in A$ and $b \in B$,

$$\gamma(a) = (\bot, a) * (\bot, a), \tag{1}$$

and

$$\eta(b) = \begin{cases} (\bot, b * b) & \text{if } b > \neg b; \\ (\neg b * \neg b, \bot) & \text{if } b \le \neg b. \end{cases} \tag{2}$$

Theorem 1. *For every d.i. Gödel algebra* **A** *and for every d.i. NM-algebra* **B**:

1. *The map γ is an isomorphism between* **A** *and* $\mathbf{G}(\mathbf{NM}^{\pm}(\mathbf{A}))$;
2. *The map η is an isomorphism between* **B** *and* $\mathbf{NM}^{\pm}(\mathbf{G}(\mathbf{B}))$.

Theorem 2. *A NM-algebra* **B** *is d.i. iff there exists a d.i. Gödel algebra* **A** *such that either* $\mathbf{B} \cong \mathbf{NM}^{+}(\mathbf{A})$ *or* $\mathbf{B} \cong \mathbf{NM}^{-}(\mathbf{A})$.

3   Towards NM-Algebras with Modal Operators

We first recall the notion of Gödel algebra with two operators from [12].

Definition 3. *A Gödel algebra with operators (GAO for short) is a triple* $(\mathbf{A}, \Box, \Diamond)$ *where* **A** *is a Gödel algebra,* $\Box$ *and* $\Diamond$ *are unary operators on A satisfying the following equations:*

$$(\Box 1) \ \Box\top = \top \qquad\qquad (\Diamond 1) \ \Diamond\bot = \bot$$
$$(\Box 2) \ \Box(x \wedge y) = \Box x \wedge \Box y \quad (\Diamond 2) \ \Diamond(x \vee y) = \Diamond x \vee \Diamond y.$$

The class of Gödel algebras with operators is a variety that we denote by $\mathbb{GAO}$. It is easy to check that every $\mathbf{A} \in \mathbb{GAO}$ satisfies the following equation (algebraic counterpart of the well-known axiom K in modal logic) and inequations (monotonicity conditions for $\Box$ and $\Diamond$):

(K) $\Box(x \to y) \to (\Box x \to \Box y) = \top$.
(Mon) If $x \le y$ then $\Box x \le \Box y$ and $\Diamond x \le \Diamond y$.

In what follows we will present first steps towards expanding nilpotent minimum algebras with modal operators. In particular we will show that the construction we recalled in Sect. 2 involving d.i. Gödel and NM-algebras extends to the case of their modal expansions.

3.1   The Case of NM$^+$-Algebras with Operators

Let us start by considering a GAO $(\mathbf{A}, \Box, \Diamond)$ such that **A** is d.i. and $\Box$ satisfies the following equation:

(N1) $\Box\bot = \bot$.

Let us now define the operators $\boxminus$ and $\diamondminus$ on $NM^+(\mathbf{A})$ as follows: for all $(a^-, a^+) \in NM^+(\mathbf{A})$,

(-) $\boxminus(a^-, a^+) = (\Diamond a^-, \Box a^+)$;
(-) $\diamondminus(a^-, a^+) = (\Box a^-, \Diamond a^+)$.

Lemma 2. *For every* $(\mathbf{A}, \Box, \Diamond)$ *as above, and for all* $(a^-, a^+) \in NM^+(\mathbf{A})$, $\boxminus(a^-, a^+), \diamondminus(a^-, a^+) \in NM^+(\mathbf{A})$.

Proof. Let us prove that $\boxminus(a^-, a^+) \in NM^+(\mathbf{A})$, that is to say, $\Diamond a^- \wedge \Box a^+ = \bot$ in $\mathbf{A}$. Since $\mathbf{A}$ is d.i. , $(a^-, a^+) \in NM^+(\mathbf{A})$ iff either $a^- = \bot$ or $a^+ = \bot$. If $a^- = \bot$, then $\Diamond a^- \wedge \Box a^+ = \Diamond \bot \wedge \Box a^+ = \bot \wedge \Box a^+ = \bot$. Conversely, if $a^+ = \bot$, by $(N1)$, $\Box a^+ = \bot$, whence again $\Diamond a^- \wedge \Box a^+ = \bot$. This settles the claim. $\square$

Therefore, the operators $\boxminus$ and $\diamondminus$ are well-defined.

Definition 4. *A* NM^+-*algebra with operators* ($NMAO^+$) *is a system* $(\mathbf{B}, \boxminus, \diamondminus)$ *where* $\mathbf{B}$ *is a* NM^+-*algebra and* $\boxminus, \diamondminus : B \to B$ *satisfy the following conditions:*

$(\boxminus 1)\ \boxminus \top = \top$; $(\diamondminus 1)\ \diamondminus \bot = \bot$
$(\boxminus 2)\ \boxminus (x \wedge y) = \boxminus x \wedge \boxminus y$; $(\diamondminus 2)\ \diamondminus (x \vee y) = \diamondminus x \vee \diamondminus y$;
$(F)\ \boxminus f = f$; $(\boxminus\text{-}\diamondminus)\ \diamondminus x = \neg\, \boxminus \neg x$.

The following proposition collects some properties of $NMAO^+$s.

Proposition 3. *In every* $NMAO^+$ $(\mathbf{B}, \boxminus, \diamondminus)$ *the following properties hold:*

1. $\diamondminus f = f$;
2. *If* $a \geq f$, $\boxminus a \geq f$; *if* $a \leq f$, $\boxminus a \leq f$. *The positive and the negative elements of* $\mathbf{B}$ *are closed under* $\boxminus$;
3. *If* $a \leq f$, $\diamondminus a \leq f$; *if* $a \geq f$, $\diamondminus a \geq f$. *The positive and the negative elements of* $\mathbf{B}$ *are closed under* $\diamondminus$.

Proof. (1) By (F), $(\boxminus\text{-}\diamondminus)$ and the fact that f is the negation fixpoint, $\diamondminus f = \neg\, \boxminus \neg f = \neg\, \boxminus f = \neg f = f$.

(2) If $a \geq f$ immediately follows form (F) and the monotonicity property of $\boxminus$. If $a \leq f$, then $a \wedge f = a$, whence $\boxminus a = \boxminus(a \wedge f) = \boxminus a \wedge \boxminus f$. Thus, $\boxminus a \leq \boxminus f = f$.

(3) If $a \leq f$ the claim follows from (1) and the monotonicity property of $\diamondminus$. Conversely, if $a \geq f$, then $a \vee f = a$, whence $\diamondminus a = \diamondminus(a \vee f) = \diamondminus a \vee \diamondminus f$ which shows that $\diamondminus a \geq \diamondminus f = f$. $\square$

Now we can show that, if we start with a GAO $(\mathbf{A}, \Box, \Diamond)$ with $\mathbf{A}$ being d.i. and such that $\Box\bot = \bot$, then the operators $\boxminus$ and $\diamondminus$ endow $NM^+(\mathbf{A})$ with the structure of a NMAO.

Proposition 4. *For every GAO* $(\mathbf{A}, \Box, \Diamond)$ *which satisfies (N1) and such that* $\mathbf{A}$ *is d.i. ,* $(NM^+(\mathbf{A}), \boxminus, \diamondminus)$ *is a* $NMAO^+$. *Further,* $NM^+(\mathbf{A})$ *is d.i. as NM-algebra.*

Proof. It suffices to prove that $\boxminus$ and $\diamondsuit$ satisfy the properties of Definition 5. First of all, recall that the top element of $\mathbf{NM^+(A)}$ is the pair $(\bot, \top)$. Thus, $\boxminus(\bot, \top) = (\diamondsuit\bot, \square\top) = (\bot, \top)$ and $(\boxminus 1)$ holds. Analogously, it is easy to see that $(\diamondsuit 1)$ holds as well.

As for $(\boxminus 2)$, let $(a^-, a^+), (b^-, b^+) \in NM^+(\mathbf{A})$. Then, recalling the definition of $\wedge$ in $\mathbf{NM^+(A)}$, $\boxminus((a^-, a^+) \wedge (b^-, b^+)) = \boxminus(a^- \vee b^-, a^+ \wedge a^+) = (\diamondsuit(a^- \vee b^-), \square(a^+ \wedge a^+)) = (\diamondsuit a^- \vee \diamondsuit b^-, \square a^+ \wedge \square b^+) = \boxminus(a^-, a^+) \wedge \boxminus(b^-, b^+)$. In a similar way one can prove that $(\diamondsuit 2)$ also holds.

Now, let $(a^-, a^+) \in NM^+(\mathbf{A})$. Then, $\neg \boxminus \neg(a^-, a^+) = \neg \boxminus (a^+, a^-) = \neg(\diamondsuit a^+, \square a^-) = (\square a^-, \diamondsuit a^+) = \diamondsuit(a^-, a^+)$ and $(\boxminus\text{-}\diamondsuit)$ holds.

Let us finally prove (F). The negation fixpoint of $\mathbf{NM^+(A)}$ is $(\bot, \bot)$ and hence $\boxminus(\bot, \bot) = (\diamondsuit\bot, \square\bot)$. Since $\diamondsuit\bot = \bot$ and, by (N1), $\square\bot = \bot$, by the order relation of $\mathbf{NM^+(A)}$, $\boxminus(\bot, \bot) = (\bot, \bot)$.

That $\mathbf{NM^+(A)}$ is a d.i. NM$^+$-algebra follows directly from Theorem 2 together with the hypothesis that $\mathbf{A}$ is d.i.

Conversely, let us start with a NMAO$^+$ of the form $(\mathbf{B}, \boxminus, \diamondsuit)$ where $\mathbf{B}$ is d.i. Then, let us define $\mathbf{G(B)}$ as in Proposition 2 and unary operators $\square, \diamondsuit : G(\mathbf{B}) \to G(\mathbf{B})$ as: $\square x = \boxminus x * \boxminus x$ and $\diamondsuit x = \diamondsuit x * \diamondsuit x$. Then the following holds.

Proposition 5. *For every NMAO$^+$ $(\mathbf{B}, \boxminus, \diamondsuit)$ where $\mathbf{B}$ is d.i., $(\mathbf{G(B)}, \square, \diamondsuit)$ is a GAO in which $\mathbf{G(B)}$ is d.i. and $\square$ satisfies (N1).*

Proof. First of all $\mathbf{G(B)}$ is d.i. because of Proposition 2. Moreover (N1) easily holds because, in $\mathbf{B}$, $b * b = \bot$ iff $b \leq f$ and for all such b's, $\boxminus b \leq f$ because of Proposition 3 (2). Therefore, $\square\bot = \boxminus\bot * \boxminus\bot = \bot$. Let hence prove that $\mathbf{G(B)}$ is a GAO. The equations $(\square 1)$ and $(\diamondsuit 1)$ are easily satisfied. As for the other equations, let $x, y \in G(\mathbf{B})$, that is, there are $b_x, b_y \in B$ such that $x = b_x * b_x$ and $y = b_y * b_y$. Let us prove $(\square 2)$ distinguishing the following cases:

(-) If $b_x, b_y > f$, $x = b_x * b_x = b_x \wedge b_x = b_x$ and $y = b_y * b_y = b_y \wedge b_y = b_y$. Thus the claim follows from $(\boxminus 2)$.

(-) If $b_x, b_y \leq f$, $x = b_x * b_x = \bot = b_y * b_y = y$ and the claim trivially holds.

(-) If $b_x > f$ and $b_y \leq f$ or $b_x \leq f$ and $b_y > f$, then the claims follows from the previous cases and the observation that, since $\mathbf{B}$ is d.i. , for all $b_1 > f$ and $b_2 \leq f$, $b_1 \wedge b_2 = b_2$.

Finally, $(\diamondsuit 2)$ also holds arguing as above. For instance, if $b_x > f$ and $b_y \leq f$, then $x = b_x$ and $y = \bot$, $\diamondsuit(x \vee y) = \diamondsuit x = \diamondsuit x \vee \diamondsuit y$ because, by $(\diamondsuit 1)$, $\diamondsuit\bot = \bot$.

Theorem 3. *For every GAO $(\mathbf{A}, \square, \diamondsuit)$ which satisfies (N1) and such that $\mathbf{A}$ is d.i. and for every NMAO$^+$ $(\mathbf{B}, \boxminus, \diamondsuit)$ where $\mathbf{B}$ is d.i., the following claims hold:*

1. $(\mathbf{A}, \square, \diamondsuit) \cong (\mathbf{G(NM^+(A))}, \square, \diamondsuit)$;
2. $(\mathbf{B}, \boxminus, \diamondsuit) \cong (\mathbf{NM^+(G(B))}, \boxminus, \diamondsuit)$.

Proof. In the light of Propositions 4, 5 and Theorem 1, it suffices to prove that the maps γ and η defined in (1) and (2) respectively, preserve the modal operators.

(1) Let $a \in A$. If $a = \bot$ the claim trivially follows from (N1). Thus, let $a > \bot$ and assume $\Box a > \bot$. Then, $\gamma(\Box a) = (\bot, \Box a) * (\bot, \Box a) = (\Diamond \bot, \Box a) * (\Diamond \bot, \Box a) = ((\Box a \vee \Box a) \rightarrow (\Diamond \bot \vee \Diamond \bot), \Box a \wedge \Box a) = (\neg \Box a, \Box a) = (\bot, \Box a) = (\Diamond \bot, \Box a) = (\Diamond \neg a, \Box a) = \boxminus(\neg a, a) = \boxminus(a \rightarrow \bot, a) = \boxminus((a \vee a) \rightarrow (\bot \vee \bot), a \wedge a) = \boxminus((\bot, a) * (\bot, a)) = \Box(\gamma(a))$, where in the 5th and the 7th equalities we used Lemma 1 together with the fact that $\Box a > \bot$. If $\Box a = \bot$, $\Box(\gamma(a)) = \Box((\bot, a) * (\bot, a)) = \boxminus((a \vee a) \rightarrow (\bot \vee \bot), a \wedge a) = \boxminus(\neg a, a) = \boxminus(\bot, a) = (\Diamond \bot, \Box a) = (\bot, \bot) = \gamma(\bot) = \gamma(\Box a)$.

As for the $\Diamond$ let again $a \in A$, $a > \bot$, $\Diamond a > \bot$. Then $\gamma(\Diamond(a)) = (\bot, \Diamond a) * (\bot, \Diamond a) = (\Diamond a \rightarrow \bot, \Diamond a) = (\neg \Diamond a, \Diamond a) = (\bot, \Diamond a) = (\Box \bot, \Diamond a) = (\Box \neg a, \Diamond a) = \Diamond((a \vee a) \rightarrow (\bot \vee \bot), a \wedge a) = \Diamond((\bot, a) * (\bot, a)) = \Diamond(\gamma(a))$. Again we used Lemma 1 together with the fact that $\Diamond a > \bot$, and (N1). The case $\Diamond a = \bot$ is analogous to the above and omitted.

(2) Consider a $b \in B$. If $b = f$, $\eta(\boxminus f) = \eta(f) = f = \boxminus(f)$. Then, let us take into account the following cases:

(-) $b > f$ and hence $b > \neg b$. Thus, $\eta(\boxminus b) = (\bot, \boxminus b * \boxminus b)$. The positive elements of **B** are closed under $\boxminus$ (Proposition 3 (2)), hence $(\bot, \boxminus b * \boxminus b) = (\bot, \boxminus b) = (\Diamond \bot, \boxminus b) = \boxminus(\eta(b))$.

(-) $b < f$ and hence $b < \neg b$. In this case $\eta(\boxminus b) = (\neg \boxminus b, \bot) = (\Diamond \neg b, \bot)$. By Proposition 3 (3), $\Diamond \neg b > f$ and hence $\Diamond \neg b = \Diamond \neg b \wedge \Diamond \neg b = \Diamond \neg b * \Diamond \neg b = \Diamond \neg b$. Thus, $\eta(\boxminus b) = (\Diamond \neg b, \bot) = (\Diamond \neg b, \Box \bot) = \boxminus \eta(b)$.

As for the $\Diamond$, the proof is similar. Let us sketch, for example, the case $b < f$. Again, $\neg b > f$ and $\Diamond b \leq f$, whence $\eta(\Diamond b) = (\neg \Diamond b, \bot) = (\boxminus \neg b, \bot) = (\Box \neg b, \Diamond \bot) = \Diamond(\neg b, \bot) = \Diamond \eta(b)$.

The claim is hence settled.

Example 1. Let **A** be the Gödel algebra whose Hasse diagram is depicted in both (a) and (b) in Fig. 1 by solid lines, and let $\Box, \Diamond : A \rightarrow A$ be as defined by the dashed arrows in (a) and (b) respectively. Notice that $(\mathbf{A}, \Box, \Diamond)$ satisfies (N1).

The Hasse diagram of the algebra $\mathbf{NM}^+(\mathbf{A})$ is the one depicted in (c) and (d) in Fig. 1 with solid lines, where: $\bot = (\top, \bot)$, $x = (c, \bot)$, $y = (b, \bot)$, $z = (a, \bot)$, $f = (\bot, \bot)$, $k = (\bot, a)$, $t = (\bot, b)$, $s = (\bot, c)$, $\top = (\bot, \top)$. The operators $\boxminus$ and $\Diamond$ on $NM^+(\mathbf{A})$ defined as above correspond to the dashed arrows depicted in (c) and (d) of Fig. 1 respectively. For instance, $\boxminus z = \boxminus(a, \bot) = (\Diamond a, \Box \bot) = (\bot, \bot) = f$ and $\Diamond t = \Diamond(\bot, b) = (\Box \bot, \Diamond b) = (\bot, a) = k$.

3.2   The Case of NM⁻-Algebras with Operators

Let $(\mathbf{A}, \Box, \Diamond)$ be a GAO in which **A** is d.i. and satisfying the condition (N1) and the following additional ones:

$(SM\Box)$ If $a > \bot$, then $\Box a > \bot$; $(SM\Diamond)$ If $a > \bot$, then $\Diamond a > \bot$.

Let us define $\boxminus$ and $\Diamond$ on $NM^-(\mathbf{A})$ as above: for all $(a^-, a^+) \in NM^-(\mathbf{A})$, $\boxminus(a^-, a^+) = (\Diamond a^-, \Box a^+)$ and $\Diamond(a^-, a^+) = (\Box a^-, \Diamond a^+)$.

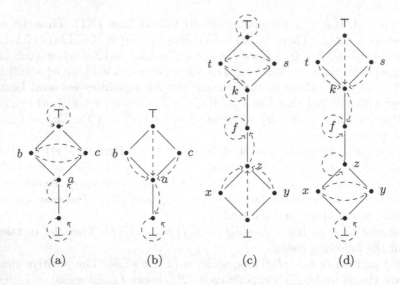

Fig. 1. A d.i. Gödel algebra with a □ operator satisfying (N1) (a) and a ◊ operator (b), and the corresponding d.i. NM$^+$-algebra with the operators ⊟ (c) and ⊟ (d).

Lemma 3. *For every* $(\mathbf{A}, \Box, \Diamond)$ *as above, and for all* $(a^-, a^+) \in NM^-(\mathbf{A})$, $\boxminus(a^-, a^+), \diamondminus(a^-, a^+) \in NM^-(\mathbf{A})$.

Proof. Let us prove the claim for the case of ⊟ and in particular that for all (a^-, a^+), if it satisfies $(a^- \wedge a^+) \vee \neg(a^- \vee a^+) = \bot$, then $(\Diamond a^- \wedge \Box a^+) \vee \neg(\Diamond a^- \vee \Box a^+) = \bot$. Since $\mathbf{A}$ is directly indecomposable, as Gödel algebra, then so is $NM^-(\mathbf{A})$ as NM-algebra. Therefore, $(a^- \wedge a^+) \vee \neg(a^- \vee a^+) = \bot$ iff either $a^- = \bot$ and $a^+ > \bot$, or $a^- > \bot$ and $a^+ = \bot$. If the former is the case, then $\Diamond a^- = \bot$ by (◊1) and $\Box a^+ > \bot$ by (SM□). If the latter is the case, similarly, $\Diamond a^- > \bot$ by (SM◊) and $\Box a^+ = \bot$ because of (N1). Thus in both cases $(\Diamond a^- \wedge \Box a^+) \vee \neg(\Diamond a^- \vee \Box a^+) = \bot$, which settles the claim.

For the following, recall the equations of Definition 5.

Definition 5. *An NM$^-$-algebra with operators (NMAO$^-$) is a system* $(\mathbf{B}, \boxminus, \diamondminus)$ *where* $\mathbf{B} = (B, *, \wedge, \neg, \bot)$ *be a NM$^-$-algebra, and* $\boxminus, \diamondminus : B \to B$ *satisfy the following conditions:* (⊟1); (⊟2); (⊟-◈); (◈1); (◈2); *and*
$(P): \boxminus(x \vee \neg x) = \boxminus x \vee \neg \boxminus x;$ $(N):$ *if* $x \leq \neg x$, *then* $\diamondminus x \leq \neg \diamondminus x$.

Proposition 6. *The following properties hold in every NMAO$^-$:*

1. *The positive and the negative elements of* $\mathbf{B}$ *are closed under* ⊟;
2. *The positive and the negative elements of* $\mathbf{B}$ *are closed under* ◈.

Proof. (1) Suppose $x \geq \neg x$. Then $x \vee \neg x = x$ and hence, by (P), $\boxminus x = \boxminus(x \vee \neg x) = \boxminus x \vee \neg \boxminus x$. Thus, $\boxminus x \geq \neg \boxminus x$. Conversely, if $x \leq \neg x$, by (P), $\boxminus \neg x = \boxminus(x \vee \neg x) = \boxminus x \vee \neg \boxminus x$, whence $\boxminus x \leq \boxminus \neg x$.

(2) The first part of the claim follows from (N), the second by the order-reversing property of $\neg$.

Now we prove that, if $\mathbf{A}$ is a d.i. Gödel algebra and $(\mathbf{A}, \Box, \Diamond)$ is a GAO satisfying (N1), (SM$\Box$) and (SM$\Diamond$), then $\mathbf{NM}^-(\mathbf{A})$ is a NM$^-$-algebra with operators.

Proposition 7. *For any GAO $(\mathbf{A}, \Box, \Diamond)$ satisfying (N1), (SM$\Box$) and (SM$\Diamond$) such that $\mathbf{A}$ is d.i., $(\mathbf{NM}^-(\mathbf{A}), \boxminus, \Diamond)$ is a NMAO$^-$ and $\mathbf{NM}^-(\mathbf{A})$ is d.i. as NM-algebra.*

Proof. The equations ($\boxminus$1), ($\boxminus$2), ($\Diamond$1), ($\Diamond$2) and ($\boxminus$-$\Diamond$) hold with the same proof of Proposition 4. Let us hence prove (P) and (N).

If $(a^-, a^+) \in NM^-(\mathbf{A})$, then either $a^- = \bot$ or $a^+ = \bot$. We assume that $a^- = \bot$ without loss of generality (the case $a^+ = \bot$ is symmetric and omitted). Then, $\boxminus((a^-, a^+) \vee \neg(a^-, a^+)) = \boxminus(a^- \wedge a^+, a^+ \vee a^-) = \boxminus(\bot, a^+) = (\Diamond\bot, \Box a^+) = (\bot, \Box a^+)$. On the other hand, $\boxminus(a^-, a^+) \vee \neg\boxminus(a^-, a^+) = (\Diamond\bot, \Box a^+) \vee \neg(\Diamond\bot, \Box a^+) = (\bot, \Box a^+) \vee (\Box a^+, \bot) = (\bot \wedge \Box a^+, \bot \vee \Box a^+) = (\bot, \Box a^+)$. Thus (P) holds.

As for (N), if $(a^-, a^+) \leq \neg(a^-, a^+)$, then $a^- \geq \bot$ and $a^+ = \bot$. Therefore, $\Diamond(a^-, a^+) = (\Box a^-, \Diamond a^+) = (\Box a^-, \bot)$. On the other hand $\neg\boxminus(a^-, a^+) = \Diamond(a^+, a^-) = (\Box a^+, \Diamond a^-) = (\bot, \Diamond a^-)$ and $(\Box a^-, \bot) \leq (\bot, \Diamond a^-)$.

And this is the converse direction, from NMAO$^-$s to GAOs.

Proposition 8. *For every NMAO$^-$ $(\mathbf{B}, \boxminus, \Diamond)$ where $\mathbf{B}$ is d.i. , $(\mathbf{G}(\mathbf{B}), \Box, \Diamond)$ is a GAO where $\mathbf{G}(\mathbf{B})$ is d.i. and $\Box$ satisfies (N1), (SM$\Box$) and (SM$\Diamond$).*

Proof. For every d.i. NM$^-$-algebra $\mathbf{B}$, Proposition 2 tells us that $\mathbf{G}(\mathbf{B})$ is a d.i. Gödel algebra. The proofs of ($\Box$1), ($\Box$2), ($\Diamond$1), ($\Diamond$2) and (N1) are as in Proposition 5, hence let us prove (SM$\Box$) and (SM$\Diamond$).

Take $a > \bot$ in $\mathbf{G}(\mathbf{B})$ and let $b \in B$ such that $a = b * b > \bot$. Thus $b > \neg b$ and $a = b \wedge b = b$. It follows that $\Box a = \boxminus a * \boxminus a = \boxminus b * \boxminus b$. By Prop. 7, $\boxminus b > \neg \boxminus b$, whence $\Box a = \boxminus b * \boxminus b = \boxminus b > \neg \boxminus b$ and hence, in $\mathbf{G}(\mathbf{B})$, $\Box a > \bot$. Similarly, $\Diamond a = \Diamond b * \Diamond b = \Diamond b$ (again by Prop. 7) whence, in $\mathbf{G}(\mathbf{B})$, $\Diamond a > \bot$.

Essentially the same proof of Theorem 3, together with the above Propositions 7 and 8, proves the following representation theorem.

Theorem 4. *For all GAO $(\mathbf{A}, \Box, \Diamond)$ which satisfies (N1), (SM$\Box$) and (SM$\Diamond$) and $\mathbf{A}$ is d.i. and for all NMAO$^-$ $(\mathbf{B}, \boxminus, \Diamond)$ where $\mathbf{B}$ is d.i., we have that $(\mathbf{A}, \Box, \Diamond) \cong (\mathbf{G}(\mathbf{NM}^-(\mathbf{A})), \Box, \Diamond)$ and $(\mathbf{B}, \boxminus, \Diamond) \cong (\mathbf{NM}^-(\mathbf{G}(\mathbf{B})), \boxminus, \Diamond)$.*

Fig. 2 shows the effect of the construction NM$^-$ to the same GAO we already discussed in Example 1 and whose Gödel algebra reduct is directly indecomposable.

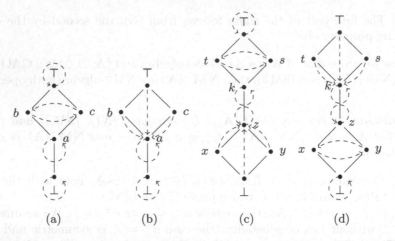

Fig. 2. A d.i. Gödel algebra endowed with a □ operator (a) and a ◊ operator (b) satisfying (N1), (SM□) and (SM◊), and the corresponding d.i. NM⁻-algebra with the operators ⊟ (c) and ⊖ (d).

4   Conclusion and Future Work

In this paper we have studied the effect of taking connected and disconnected rotations of Gödel algebras with operators whose Gödel reduct is directly indecomposable. By doing so, we have introduced the varieties of NM⁺ and NM⁻-algebras with modal operators and we have characterized the members of these varieties whose NM-reduct is directly indecomposable.

Although the aim of the present paper is to put forward an algebraic analysis of the modal structures we took into account, in [11,12] we also gave a description of the dual relational frames that arise from finite Gödel algebras with operators (*forest frames*). Those are the prelinear version of the models, based on posets, that are a semantics for intuitionistic modal logic (see e.g., [21,22]). In our future work, we plan to extend the present approach essentially in thee directions:

1. From the point of view of forest frames, taking into account that for every finite d.i. Gödel algebra **A**, **NM⁺(A)** and **NM⁻(A)** have the same prime filters, we plan to investigate how NMAO⁺ and NMAO⁻-algebras relate to forest frames and to extend to the NM-case the isomorphic representation theorem from [11].
2. From an algebraic perspective, besides connected and disconnected rotations, NM-algebras can be also seen as twist-structures obtained from Gödel algebras. It is hence interesting to deepen this latter construction for modal Gödel algebras and compare the modal NM-algebras obtained in such a way with the modal NM⁺- and NM⁻-algebras defined in the present paper, also in light of the general results proved in [19].
3. From a more general point of view, NM-algebras can be also seen as a subvariety of Nelson lattices. In [20], the authors introduce a definition of algebra

with operators more general than the one considered in the current paper in the sense that they are not required to satisfy **Mon** (monotony rules for modal operators). It will be interesting to compare this approach to ours.

Acknowledgments. The authors thank the anonymous referees for their comments. Authors acknowledge partial support by the MOSAIC project (EU H2020-MSCA-RISE-2020 Project 101007627). Flaminio and Godo also acknowledge partial support by the Spanish project PID2019-111544GB-C21 funded by MCIN/AEI/10.13039/501100011033. Menchon acknowledge partial support by argentinean projects PIP 112-20200101301CO (CONICET) and PICT-2019-2019-00882 (ANPCyT). The fourth author wants to acknowledge partial support by the following argentinean projects: PIP 112-20150100412CO (CONICET) and UBA-CyT-20020190100021BA.

References

1. Aguzzoli, S., Bova, S., Gerla, B.: Free algebras and functional representation for fuzzy logics. In: Cintula, P., et al. (eds.) Handbook of Mathematical Fuzzy Logic, Chapter IX, vol. 2. Studies in Logic, vol. 38, pp. 713–791. College Publications (2011)
2. Blackburn, P., de Rijke, M., Venema, Y.: Modal Logic. Cambridge University Press (2001)
3. Bou, F., Esteva, F., Godo, L., Rodriguez, R.: On the minimum many-values modal logic over a finite residuated lattice. JL&C **21**(5), 739–790 (2011)
4. Busaniche, M.: Free nilpotent minimum algebras. Math. Logic Quart. **52**(3), 219–236 (2006)
5. Caicedo, X., Rodriguez, R.O.: Standard Gödel modal logics. Stud. Logica **94**(2), 189–214 (2010)
6. Caicedo, X., Rodriguez, R.O.: Bi-modal Gödel logic over $[0, 1]$-valued Kripke frames. J. Logic Comput. **25**(1), 37–55 (2015)
7. Diaconescu, D., Metcalfe, G., Schnüriger, L.: A real-valued modal logic. Logical Methods Comput. Sci. **14**(1), 1–27 (2018)
8. Esteva, F., Godo, L.: Monoidal t-norm based logic: towards a logic for left-continuous t-norms. Fuzzy Sets Syst. **124**, 271–288 (2001)
9. Fitting, M.C.: Many-valued modal logics. Fundam. Informat. **15**, 235–254 (1991)
10. Fitting, M.C.: Many-valued modal logics II. Fundam. Informat. **17**, 55–73 (1992)
11. Flaminio, T., Godo, L., Rodríguez, R.O.: A representation theorem for finite Gödel algebras with operators. In: Iemhoff, R., Moortgat, M., de Queiroz, R. (eds.) WoLLIC 2019. LNCS, vol. 11541, pp. 223–235. Springer, Heidelberg (2019). https://doi.org/10.1007/978-3-662-59533-6_14
12. Flaminio, T., Godo, L., Menchón, P., Rodriguez, R.O.: Algebras and relational frames for Gödel modal logic and some of its extensions. arXiv:2110.02528. Submitted
13. Hájek, P.: Metamathematics of Fuzzy Logic. Kluwer Academic Publishers (1998)
14. Hájek, P.: On fuzzy modal logics $S5(\mathscr{C})$. Fuzzy Sets Syst. **161**(18), 2389–2396 (2010)
15. Hansoul, G., Teheux, B.: Extending łukasiewicz logics with a modality: algebraic approach to relational semantics. Stud. Logica **101**(3), 505–545 (2013)

16. Hasimoto, Y.: Heyting algebras with operators. Math. Logic. Quart. **47**(2), 187–196 (2001)
17. Horn, A.: Logic with truth values in a linearly ordered Heyting algebra. J. Symbol. Logic **34**, 395–405 (1969)
18. Jenei, S.: On the structure of rotation invariant semigroups. Archiv. Math. Logic **42**, 489–514 (2003)
19. Ono, H., Rivieccio, U.: Modal twist-structures over residuated lattices. Log. J. IGPL **22**(3), 440–457 (2014)
20. Menchón, P., Rodriguez, R.O.: Twist-structures isomorphic to modal nilpotent minimum algebras. Book of Abstracts of First Meeting Brazil-Colombia in Logic, Bogotá, Colombia, 14–17 December 2021 (2021)
21. Orłowska, E., Rewitzky, I.: Discrete dualities for Heyting algebras with operators. Fundam. Informat. **81**, 275–295 (2007)
22. Palmigiano, A.: Dualities for intuitionistic modal logics. In: Liber Amicorum for Dick de Jongh, Institute for Logic, Language and Computation, pp. 151–167. University of Amsterdam (2004). http://festschriften.illc.uva.nl/D65/palmigiano.pdf
23. Priest, G.: Many-valued modal logics: a simple approach. Rev. Symbol. Logic **1**(2), 190–2013 (2008)
24. Vidal, A., Esteva, F., Godo, L.: On modal extensions of product fuzzy logic. J. Logic Comput. **27**(1), 299–336 (2017)

On Operations of Restriction and Freezing on Monadic Fuzzy Quantifiers Over Fuzzy Domains

Antonín Dvořák[ID] and Michal Holčapek[✉][ID]

CE IT4I - IRAFM, University of Ostrava, 30. dubna 22,
701 03 Ostrava, Czech Republic
{antonin.dvorak,michal.holcapek}@osu.cz
http://ifm.osu.eu

Abstract. This article introduces important operations on the class of monadic fuzzy quantifiers, namely, restriction and freezing. These operations are introduced and investigated in the novel frame of monadic fuzzy quantifiers over fuzzy domains.

Keywords: Generalized quantifiers · Fuzzy quantifiers · Semantic properties · Restriction · Freezing

1 Introduction

The most important quantifiers of natural language are often identified with generalized monadic[1] quantifiers of type $\langle 1, 1 \rangle$ that possess two important semantic properties called *conservativity* and *extension* [9]. Both properties emphasize the special rôle of the first argument called the *restriction* in the definition of generalized quantifiers of type $\langle 1, 1 \rangle$. More specifically, the truth values of these quantifiers are not affected by these elements belonging to the second argument called *scope* that do not belong to the restriction argument.

For example, consider the quantifier "many" and a quantified sentence "Many cats are cuddly." whose truth conditions can be modeled using a type $\langle 1, 1 \rangle$ generalized quantifier over the domain of all animals denoted as M, that is, $Q_M : \mathcal{P}(M) \times \mathcal{P}(M) \to \{0, 1\}$, where $\mathcal{P}(M)$ is the power set of M, and 0 and 1 represent false and true, respectively. One can see that the truth value of this sentence should not depend on the set of cuddly animals that are not cats; in other words, only cats that are cuddly, represented by the set $A \cap B$, should count:

---

[1] Note that a generalized quantifier is said to be *monadic* if its arguments are (fuzzy) sets, such as in "Most tigers cannot swim" (type $\langle 1, 1 \rangle$). Here, the arguments of "most" are a set of tigers and a set of beings that can swim. More complicated are *polyadic* quantifiers, for which at least one of its arguments is a relation.

The second author announces a support of the ERDF/ESF project AI-Met4AI No. CZ.02.1.01/0.0/0.0/17_049/0008414.

D. Ciucci et al. (Eds.): IPMU 2022, CCIS 1601, pp. 689–702, 2022.
https://doi.org/10.1007/978-3-031-08971-8_56

$Q_M(A, B) = Q_M(A, A \cap B)$, where A denotes the set of all cats. This is exactly the definition of conservativity. Note that the set $A \cap B$ can be understood as a *restriction* of the set of all cuddly animals B to the set of all cats A. Furthermore, if the domain of all animals M is extended to a larger domain M', the truth value of our sentence should remain the same, i.e., $Q_M(A, B) = Q_{M'}(A, B)$, which defines the property of extension. Therefore, the quantifier "many" can be considered as an example of a natural language quantifier.

Moreover, the investigation of the restriction argument concerning the modeling of natural language quantifiers is also focused on two special operations, namely *restriction* and *freezing*. The first is an operation on quantifiers of type $\langle 1 \rangle$, where the resulting quantifier is restricted to a set of objects, while the second provides a mechanism reducing type $\langle 1, 1 \rangle$ generalized quantifiers to type $\langle 1 \rangle$ generalized quantifiers. Freezing can be seen as an opposite operation to *relativization*, where type $\langle 1, 1 \rangle$ quantifiers are determined from type $\langle 1 \rangle$ quantifiers.

In [4], we investigated primarily the operation of relativization and showed, among other things, that it is not possible to successfully represent this operation in the frame of fuzzy quantifiers over crisp domains. Therefore, we introduced a novel concept of *fuzzy quantifiers on fuzzy domains* and demonstrated that relativization can be in this framework defined in such a way that its essential properties are preserved. In this contribution, we continue this line of research by defining and investigating the operations of restriction and freezing.

The paper is structured as follows. In Sect. 2, we review the necessary notions from fuzzy set theory, and we also briefly introduce the definition of fuzzy domains, operations and relations on them. Section 3 discusses generalized (bivalent) quantifiers with emphasis on the operations of restriction and freezing (Sect. 3.2). The main part of the paper is in Sect. 4, which at first brings definitions of local and global fuzzy quantifiers over fuzzy domains. Then, in Sect. 4.2, novel definitions of restriction and freezing for these fuzzy quantifiers are provided, and their properties and interrelations with other notions (property of extension, operation of relativization) are discussed. Finally, Sect. 5 contains conclusions. Due to lack of space, several proofs of theorems in Sect. 4 have to be omitted.

2   Preliminaries

2.1   Algebraic Structures of Truth Values

In this paper, we assume that the algebraic structure of truth values is a *complete residuated lattice*, i.e., a six-tuple $L = \langle L, \wedge, \vee, \otimes, \rightarrow, 0, 1 \rangle$ such that $\langle L, \wedge, \vee, 0, 1 \rangle$ is a complete lattice, where 0 (1) is the least element (the greatest element) of L, and $\langle L, \otimes, 1 \rangle$ is a commutative monoid (i.e., $\otimes$ is associative and commutative, and the identity $a \otimes 1 = a$ holds for any $a \in L$). Moreover, the adjointness property is satisfied in L, that is,

$$a \leq b \rightarrow c \quad \text{iff} \quad a \otimes b \leq c \tag{1}$$

holds for each $a, b, c \in L$, where $\leq$ denotes the corresponding lattice ordering, i.e., $a \leq b$ if $a \wedge b = a$ for $a, b \in L$. As an example, it is easy to see that the two-element residuated lattice, i.e., $L = \{0, 1\}$, with obvious operations, is a Boolean algebra. We denote $\mathbf{2} = L = \{0, 1\}$. Further examples of complete residuated lattices can be determined from left-continuous t-norms on the unit interval, since the algebraic structure

$$L_T = \langle [0, 1], \min, \max, T, \rightarrow_T, 0, 1 \rangle,$$

where T is a left-continuous t-norm on $[0, 1]$ and $a \rightarrow_T b = \bigvee \{c \in [0, 1] \mid T(a, c) \leq b\}$ defines the residuum, is a complete residuated lattice (see, e.g., [1,5,8]).

2.2   Fuzzy Sets

Let L be a complete residuated lattice, and let $M \neq \emptyset$ be a universe of discourse. A function $A : M \rightarrow L$ is called a *fuzzy set on* M. A value $A(m)$ is called a *membership degree of* x *in the fuzzy set* A. The set of all fuzzy sets on M is denoted by $\mathcal{F}(M)$. A fuzzy set A on M is called *crisp* if $A(m) \in \{0, 1\}$ for any $m \in M$. The symbol $\emptyset$ denotes the empty fuzzy set on M, i.e., $\emptyset(m) = 0$ for any $m \in M$. The set of all crisp fuzzy sets on M (i.e., the power set of M) is denoted by $\mathcal{P}(M)$. The set $\mathrm{Supp}(A) = \{m \in M \mid A(m) > 0\}$ is called the *support* of a fuzzy set A.

Let $A, B \in \mathcal{F}(M)$. We say that A *is less than or equal to* B and denote it as $A \subseteq B$ if $A(m) \leq B(m)$ for any $m \in M$. Moreover, A *is equal to* B if $A \subseteq B$ and $B \subseteq A$.

2.3   Fuzzy Domains

In [3], we introduced the concept of the fuzzy universe to develop a more general framework of fuzzy quantifiers that provides a comprehensive analysis of semantic properties well known in the generalized quantifier theory. This concept was further investigated and reformulated under the name *fuzzy domain* in [4], which better corresponds to its intended meaning. For a comprehensive discussion on the motivation of fuzzy domains, see [4, Sect. 3.1]. This part presents the basic notions used in the following.

Let A be a fuzzy set on M, and let N be a set. Define $A_N : N \rightarrow L$ as

$$A_N(m) = \begin{cases} A(m), & \text{if } m \in N \cap M, \\ 0, & \text{otherwise.} \end{cases} \tag{2}$$

The fuzzy set A_N represents A (or its part) defined on M in the new domain N. It is easy to see that $A_M = A$ for any $A \in \mathcal{F}(M)$. Furthermore, $(A \odot B)_N = A_N \odot B_N$ for $A, B \in \mathcal{F}(M)$ and $\odot \in \{\cap, \cup\}$.

Definition 1. *A pair* (M, A), *where* M *is a set and* A *is a fuzzy set on* M, *is called a* fuzzy domain.

A fuzzy domain (M, A) is called *crisp* if A is crisp and $A = M$. A crisp fuzzy domain (M, M) will be denoted by (M). Let (M, A) and (N, B) be fuzzy domains. The elementary (fuzzy) set operations for fuzzy domains are given as follows:

$$(M, A) \cap (N, B) = (M \cap N, A_{M \cap N} \cap B_{M \cap N})$$
$$(M, A) \cup (N, B) = (M \cup N, A_{M \cup N} \cup B_{M \cup N})$$
$$(M, A) \backslash (N, B) = (M, A_M \backslash B_M)$$

For the sake of simplicity, we omit the expression of sets in the indexes of fuzzy sets; for example, we write simply $(M, A) \cap (N, B) = (M \cap N, A \cap B)$ assuming that $A \cap B$ is well introduced on the domain $M \cap N$ according to (2). The next definition introduces a class of fuzzy domains (see [4]).

Definition 2. *A nonempty class $\mathcal{U}$ of fuzzy domains is said to be* well defined *provided that*

C1) $(M, A) \in \mathcal{U}$ implies $(M, B) \in \mathcal{U}$ for any $B \in \mathcal{F}(M)$;
C2) $\mathcal{U}$ is closed under the intersection, union and difference.

We say that $\mathcal{U}$ is finite (countable) *if it holds for any $(M, A) \in \mathcal{U}$ that M is finite (countable).*

Let $\mathcal{U}$ be a class of fuzzy domains, and $(M, A), (N, B) \in \mathcal{U}$. We say that (M, A) *is equal to* (N, B), and denote it by $(M, A) = (N, B)$, if $M = N$ and $A = B$. Moreover, we say that (M, A) *is equal to* (N, B) *up to negligible elements*, and denote it by $(M, A) \sim (N, B)$, if $\text{Supp}(A) = \text{Supp}(B)$ and $A_{\text{Supp}(A)} = B_{\text{Supp}(A)}$. One can easily see that for any (M, A) and a set N such that $M \subseteq N$, there exists exactly one fuzzy set B on N such that $(M, A) \sim (N, B)$. This fuzzy set B is called the *extension of A from M to N*. We say that (M, A) *is a subset of* (N, B), and denote it by $(M, A) \subseteq (N, B)$, if $(M, A) \cap (N, B) \sim (M, A)$ (or, equivalently, $(M, A) \cup (N, B) \sim (N, B)$).

Theorem 1 [4]. *The binary relation $\sim$ on $\mathcal{U}$ is a congruence with respect to the intersection, union, and difference of fuzzy domains.*

3   NL-quantifiers and Generalized Quantifiers

As we mentioned in the introduction, the most important quantifiers of natural language are the type $\langle 1, 1 \rangle$ generalized quantifiers that satisfy two semantic properties: *conservativity* and *extension*. In the following, we will refer to these quantifiers as *NL-quantifiers*. They include expressions such as "all", "many", "several", etc.

3.1   Generalized Quantifiers

For generalized quantifiers, the model of an NL-quantifier, e.g. "some", takes the form of a functional (*global* quantifier) some that assigns a *local* quantifier $some_M$ to any domain (universe of discourse) M. This local quantifier assigns to any two subsets A and B of M a truth value $some_M(A, B)$. The precise definitions of local and global generalized (monadic) quantifiers are as follows. In the following, let n be a natural number, possibly equal to 0.

Definition 3 (Local generalized quantifier). *Let M be a domain. A local generalized quantifier Q_M of type $\langle 1^n, 1 \rangle$ over M is a function $\mathcal{P}(M)^n \times \mathcal{P}(M) \to \mathbf{2}$ that to any sets $A_1, \ldots, A_n$ and B from $\mathcal{P}(M)$ assigns a truth value $Q_M(A_1, \ldots, A_n, B)$ from $\mathbf{2}$.*

If $n = 0$, then we denote the type of a local generalized quantifier from the previous definition by $\langle 1 \rangle$. We will keep this notation for the remainder of the paper.

Definition 4 (Global generalized quantifier). *A global generalized quantifier Q of type $\langle 1^n, 1 \rangle$ is a functional that to any domain M assigns a local generalized quantifier $Q_M : \mathcal{P}(M)^n \times \mathcal{P}(M) \to \mathbf{2}$ of type $\langle 1^n, 1 \rangle$.*

Important examples of global bivalent generalized quantifiers of type $\langle 1 \rangle$ are $\forall$ and $\exists$, defined as $\forall_M(B) = 1$ if and only if $B = M$ and $\exists_M(B) = 1$ if and only if $B \neq \emptyset$ for any $B \in \mathcal{P}(M)$. Important examples of type $\langle 1, 1 \rangle$ generalized quantifiers are all and some, defined as $all_M(A, B) = 1$ if and only if $A \subseteq B$ and $some_M(A, B) = 1$ if and only if $A \cap B \neq \emptyset$ for any $A, B \in \mathcal{P}(M)$. One can see that the domain M has no direct effect on the definitions of all and some; therefore, the truth values of these quantifiers are not substantially influenced by their domains. Quantifiers, which possess this essential (semantic) property in the generalized quantifier theory, are said to satisfy the *property of extension*.

Definition 5. *A global generalized quantifier Q of type $\langle 1^n, 1 \rangle$ satisfies the property of extension (EXT for short) if for any M and M' such that $M \subseteq M'$ it holds that*

$$Q_M(A_1, \ldots, A_n, B) = Q_{M'}(A_1, \ldots, A_n, B)$$

for any $A_1, \ldots, A_n, B \in \mathcal{P}(M)$.

Among the further essential properties of generalized quantifiers belong *permutation* and *isomorphism invariances* and *conservativity*. More about these properties can be found in [7,9]. Finally, let us recall the definition of relativization of type $\langle 1 \rangle$ generalized quantifiers. For a more general definition, we refer to [9].

Definition 6. *Let Q be a global generalized quantifier of type $\langle 1 \rangle$. The relativization of Q is the global generalized quantifier Q^{rel} of type $\langle 1, 1 \rangle$ defined as*

$$Q_M^{\mathrm{rel}}(A, B) = Q_A(A \cap B)$$

for any M and $A, B \in \mathcal{P}(M)$.

3.2   Restriction and Freezing

In the theory of generalized quantifiers, we can distinguish two interesting notions, namely, global generalized quantifiers restricted to a set and global generalized quantifiers that freeze the restriction argument. The first notion is considered for quantifiers of type $\langle 1 \rangle$ and the second provides a mechanism reducing type $\langle 1, 1 \rangle$ generalized quantifiers to type $\langle 1 \rangle$ generalized quantifiers. First, we recall the definition of the notion of restriction.

Definition 7. *Let Q be a type $\langle 1 \rangle$ global generalized quantifier, and let A be a set. The global type $\langle 1 \rangle$ generalized quantifier $Q^{[A]}$ restricted to A is defined as follows: for any M and $B \subseteq M$ we have*

$$Q_M^{[A]}(B) = Q_A(A \cap B). \tag{3}$$

It can be seen that the quantifiers restricted to a fixed set A are obtained from local generalized quantifiers defined on A by the construction method described in (3). In other words, the restriction can be seen as an operator assigning a global quantifier restricted to a set A to each generalized quantifier through its local quantifier defined on A. Note that there is a close relation between notions of relativization and restriction. Indeed, let Q be a type $\langle 1 \rangle$ generalized quantifier. Let us define a type $\langle 1, 1 \rangle$ generalized quantifier Q' by

$$Q'_M(A, B) = (Q^{[A]})_M(B).$$

Then, it is easy to see that $Q' = Q^{\text{rel}}$.

Example 1. Let us consider a global generalized type $\langle 1 \rangle$ quantifier "more than five things" defined, for any set M and all $B \subseteq M$, as

$$(Q_{>5})_M(B) = \begin{cases} 1, & \text{if } |B| > 5, \\ 0, & \text{otherwise.} \end{cases}$$

Let T denote the set of all tanks. Then, the restriction of the quantifier "more than five things" $Q_{>5}$ to the set of all tanks T is defined as

$$(Q_{>5}^{[\text{T}]})_M(B) = (Q_{>5})_{\text{T}}(\text{T} \cap B) = \begin{cases} 1, & \text{if } |\text{T} \cap B| > 5, \\ 0, & \text{otherwise.} \end{cases}$$

If D denotes the set of all destroyed things, then the truth value of the sentence "More than five tanks were destroyed." can be evaluated by $(Q_{>5}^{[\text{T}]})_M(\text{D})$, which is equal to 1 if $|\text{T} \cap \text{D}|$ is greater than 5, and 0 otherwise.

For each set A, we can introduce two alternative definitions of restrictions of type $\langle 1 \rangle$ global generalized quantifiers. In particular, for any M and $B \subseteq M$, we can define the notion of restriction as follows (see [9]):

$$(Q^{[\underline{A}]})_M(B) = Q_{A \cap M}(A \cap B),$$

$$(Q^{[\underline{A}]})_M(B) = \begin{cases} Q_A(A \cap B), & A \subseteq M, \\ 0, & \text{otherwise.} \end{cases}$$

It is easy to see that for $A \subseteq M$, all three notions of restriction coincide.

The second concept we discuss in this subsection is called *freezing of the restriction argument* of a generalized quantifier of type $\langle 1, 1 \rangle$. Recall that the first argument of a type $\langle 1, 1 \rangle$ binary quantifier is called the *restriction* (i.e., A in $Q_M(A, B)$) and the second the *scope* (i.e., B in $Q_M(A, B)$).

Definition 8. *Let Q be a generalized quantifier of type $\langle 1, 1 \rangle$ and let A be a set. The global generalized quantifier Q^A of type $\langle 1 \rangle$, which provides freezing to A, is defined as follows: for any M and $B \subseteq M$, we have*

$$Q_M^A(B) = Q_{M \cup A}(A, B). \tag{4}$$

Example 2. The global generalized type $\langle 1, 1 \rangle$ quantifier "more than five" is defined as

$$(P_{>5})_M(A, B) = \begin{cases} 1, & \text{if } |A \cap B| > 5, \\ 0, & \text{otherwise.} \end{cases}$$

If we freeze the restriction argument of $P_{>5}$ to the set T of tanks, we obtain, using the definition above, the global type $\langle 1 \rangle$ generalized quantifier $P_{>5}^T$:

$$(P_{>5}^T)_M(B) = (P_{>5})_{M \cup T}(T, B) = \begin{cases} 1, & \text{if } |T \cap B| > 5, \\ 0, & \text{otherwise.} \end{cases}$$

Note that $P_{>5}^T = Q_{>5}^{[T]}$, where $Q_{>5}^{[T]}$ has been defined in Example 1.[2]

Similarly to the case of restriction, for each A, we can introduce two alternative definitions of freezing of type $\langle 1, 1 \rangle$ global generalized quantifiers. In particular, for any M and $B \subseteq M$, we can define (see [9]):

$$(Q^{\underline{A}})_M(B) = Q_M(A \cap M, B),$$

$$(Q^{\underline{\underline{A}}})_M(B) = \begin{cases} Q_{M \cup A}(A, B), & A \subseteq M, \\ 0, & \text{otherwise.} \end{cases}$$

Similarly to the case of restriction, for $A \subseteq M$, all three notions of freezing coincide.

The following statement provides the interrelations among the notions of relativization, restriction, and freezing (see [9, Sect. 4.5.5.2]).

Theorem 2. *For any A, $(Q^{\text{rel}})^A = Q^{[A]}$, $(Q^{\text{rel}})^{\underline{A}} = Q^{[\underline{A}]}$, and $(Q^{\text{rel}})^{\underline{\underline{A}}} = Q^{[\underline{\underline{A}}]}$.*

The next statement shows a relationship between the property of extension and various notions of restriction and freezing.

---

[2] Note that $P_{>5}$ is, in accordance with Definition 6, the *relativization* of $Q_{>5}$, cf. Theorem 2.

Theorem 3. *Let Q be a type $\langle 1 \rangle$ generalized quantifier and A be a set. Then*

(i) $Q^{[A]}$ is EXT.
(ii) $Q^{[\underline{A}]}$ is EXT whenever Q is EXT.
(iii) $Q^{[\underline{A}]}$ is not EXT in general.

Let Q be a type $\langle 1, 1 \rangle$ generalized quantifier and A be a set. Then

(i) Q^A is EXT whenever Q is EXT.
(ii) $Q^{\underline{A}}$ and $Q^{\underline{A}}$ are not EXT in general.

4   Fuzzy Quantifiers

In this section, we present the concept of fuzzy quantifiers defined over fuzzy domains, which enables us to overcome the limitations following from the definition of fuzzy quantifiers defined over crisp domains.

4.1   Fuzzy Quantifiers Over Fuzzy Domains

Similarly as in the case of generalized quantifiers (Sect. 3.1) and fuzzy quantifiers over crisp domains (see, e.g., [6] and [4, Sect. 5]), we distinguish between local and global fuzzy quantifiers over fuzzy domains. In the following, we assume that the well-defined class $\mathcal{U}$ of fuzzy domains (cf. Definition 2) is fixed.

Definition 9 (Local fuzzy quantifier). *Let (M, C) be a fuzzy domain. A local fuzzy quantifier $Q_{(M,C)}$ of type $\langle 1^n, 1 \rangle$ over (M, C) is a function $Q_{(M,C)} : \mathcal{F}(M)^n \times \mathcal{F}(M) \to L$ that to any fuzzy sets $A_1, \ldots, A_n$ and B from $\mathcal{F}(M)$ assigns a truth value $Q_{(M,C)}(A_1, \ldots, A_n, B)$ from L and*

$$Q_{(M,C)}(A_1, \ldots, A_n, B) = Q_{(M,C)}(A'_1, \ldots, A'_n, B') \tag{5}$$

holds for any $A_1, \ldots, A_n, B, A'_1, \ldots, A'_n, B' \in \mathcal{F}(M)$ such that $A_i \cap C = A'_i \cap C$ for any $i = 1, \ldots, n$ and $B \cap C = B' \cap C$.

It can be seen that the local fuzzy quantifier $Q_{(M,C)}$, which is defined over a fuzzy domain (M, C), is, in fact, a fuzzy quantifier defined over M that lives on a fuzzy set C (cf. [3, Definition 6] for details on the living-on property). The following lemma specifies this statement.

Lemma 1. *A function $Q_{(M,C)} : \mathcal{F}(M)^n \times \mathcal{F}(M) \to L$ is a local fuzzy quantifier on (M, C) if and only if the following holds:*

$$Q_{(M,C)}(A_1, \ldots, A_n, B) = Q_{(M,C)}(A_1 \cap C, \ldots, A_n \cap C, B \cap C) \tag{6}$$

for any $A_1, \ldots, A_n, B \in \mathcal{F}(M)$.

Proof. ($\Rightarrow$) This holds trivially. ($\Leftarrow$) If $A_i \cap C = A'_i \cap C$ for any $i = 1, \ldots, n$ and $B \cap C = B' \cap C$ hold, by (6) we get the desired equality.   □

As a result of this lemma, we find that the analysis of the properties of fuzzy quantifiers can be practically limited to fuzzy subsets of the fuzzy set C, as proposed in [2]. A global fuzzy quantifier is then defined in such a way that it respects the equivalence $\sim$ (i.e., to be equal up to negligible elements) defined on fuzzy domains.

Definition 10 (Global fuzzy quantifier). *A global fuzzy quantifier Q of type $\langle 1^n, 1 \rangle$ over fuzzy domains is a functional assigning to any fuzzy domain (M, C) a local fuzzy quantifier $Q_{(M,C)}$ of type $\langle 1^n, 1 \rangle$ such that for any fuzzy domains (M, C) and (M', C') with $(M, C) \sim (M', C')$, it holds that*

$$Q_{(M,C)}(A_1, \ldots, A_n, B) = Q_{(M',C')}(A_1', \ldots, A_n', B') \tag{7}$$

for any $A_1, \ldots, A_n, B \in \mathcal{F}(M)$ and $A_1', \ldots, A_n', B' \in \mathcal{F}(M')$ such that $(M, A_i) \sim (M', A_i')$ for any $i = 1, \ldots, n$ and $(M, B) \sim (M', B')$.

We should note that the condition (7) ensures that if two fuzzy domains are equal up to negligible elements, then the fuzzy quantifiers defined on them are practically identical. More precisely, their evaluations coincide for fuzzy sets that together with their domains are equal up to negligible elements. A consequence is the following useful statement. Recall that A_N denotes a fuzzy set A originally introduced on a domain M and newly defined on a domain N, see (2) for the definition. If $N \subset M$, then A_N is nothing else but a restriction of A to N.

Theorem 4. *A functional Q assigning a type $\langle 1^n, 1 \rangle$ local fuzzy quantifier $Q_{(M,C)}$ to any fuzzy domain (M, C) is a type $\langle 1^n, 1 \rangle$ global fuzzy quantifier if and only if*

$$Q_{(M,C)}(A_1, \ldots, A_n, B) = Q_{(N,C_N)}((A_1)_N, \ldots, (A_n)_N, B_N), \tag{8}$$

where $N = \mathrm{Supp}(C)$, holds for any (M, C) and $A_1, \ldots, A_n, B \in \mathcal{F}(M)$.

The following definition introduces the equality of global fuzzy quantifiers.

Definition 11. *Let Q and Q' be global fuzzy quantifiers of type $\langle 1^n, 1 \rangle$ over fuzzy domains. We say that Q is less than or equal to Q' and denote it by $Q \leq Q'$ if*

$$Q_{(M,C)}(A_1, \ldots, A_n, B) \leq Q'_{(M,C)}(A_1, \ldots, A_n, B)$$

holds for any fuzzy domain (M, C) and any $A_1, \ldots, A_n, B \in \mathcal{F}(M)$. We say that Q is equal to Q' (denoted by $Q = Q'$) if $Q \leq Q'$ and $Q' \leq Q$.

The extension property for fuzzy quantifiers over fuzzy domains follows the standard definition (Definition 5) in the following way (see [4, Definition 7.3]).

Definition 12. *A global fuzzy quantifier Q of type $\langle 1^n, 1 \rangle$ over fuzzy domains satisfies the property of extension (F-EXT for short) if for any fuzzy domains (M, C) and (N, D) such that $(M, C) \subseteq (N, D)$ it holds that*

$$Q_{(M,C)}(A_1, \ldots, A_n, B) = Q_{(N,D)}((A_1 \cap C)_N, \ldots, (A_n \cap C)_N, (B \cap C)_N) \tag{9}$$

for any $A_1, \ldots, A_n, B \in \mathcal{F}(M)$.

By definition, the inclusion of fuzzy domains $(M, C) \subseteq (N, D)$ does not guarantee that $M \subseteq N$ and thus $C(m) \leq D(m)$ for any $m \in M$, which in practice makes the verification of F-EXT more complicated. The following theorem simplifies the definition of extension for fuzzy quantifiers.

Theorem 5. *A type $\langle 1^n, 1 \rangle$ fuzzy quantifier Q satisfies F-EXT if and only if for any fuzzy domains (M, C) and (N, D) such that $M \subseteq N$ and $C \subseteq D_M$, equality (9) holds for any $A_1, \ldots, A_n, B \in \mathcal{F}(M)$.*

Finally, we define *relativization* for fuzzy quantifiers defined over fuzzy domains as follows (see Definition 8.1 in [4]).

Definition 13. *Let Q be a global fuzzy quantifier of type $\langle 1 \rangle$ over fuzzy domains. The* relativization *of Q is a global fuzzy quantifier Q^{rel} of type $\langle 1, 1 \rangle$ over fuzzy domains defined as*

$$(Q^{\mathrm{rel}})_{(M,C)}(A, B) = Q_{(M, C \cap A)}(A \cap B) \tag{10}$$

for any fuzzy domain (M, C) and $A, B \in \mathcal{F}(M)$.

4.2   Restriction and Freezing for Fuzzy Quantifiers over Fuzzy Domains

The definitions of restriction/freezing for generalized quantifiers in Sect. 3.2 suppose that the arguments of the original generalized quantifiers can be used as domains for their restriction/freezing, see equations (3) and (4). It is easy to see that, similarly as in the case of relativization, we are unable to extend the concepts of restriction and freezing for fuzzy quantifiers defined over crisp domains. Below we show that by employing fuzzy domains we can introduce these concepts in an elegant way following the definitions for bivalent generalized quantifiers (Sect. 3.2).

Fuzzy quantifiers restricted to a fixed fuzzy set are introduced as follows. This definition slightly modifies the definition in [3].

Definition 14. *Let Q be a type $\langle 1 \rangle$ global fuzzy quantifier, and let A be a fuzzy set on N. The type $\langle 1 \rangle$ fuzzy quantifier $Q^{[A]}$ restricted to A is defined as follows: for any fuzzy domain (M, C) and $B \in \mathcal{F}(M)$ we have*

$$Q^{[A]}_{(M,C)}(B) = Q_{(N,A)}((C \cap B)_N). \tag{11}$$

Note that $(C \cap B)_N$ is used in (11) to ensure that $Q^{[A]}$ is well defined. One might be surprised that $(C \cap B)_N$ is used instead of $A \cap (C \cap B)_N$, which can be expected from the corresponding definition for generalized quantifiers (cf. Definition 7). The latter expression is also correct in (11), but we applied Lemma 1 and removed A. To demonstrate that $Q^{[A]}$ is a global fuzzy quantifier, first note that $Q^{[A]}_{(M,C)}$ is a local fuzzy quantifier, since $B \cap C = B' \cap C$ implies $(B \cap C)_N = (B' \cap C)_N$. Furthermore, assume that $(M, C) \sim (M', C')$, and let

$B \in \mathcal{F}(M)$ and $B' \in \mathcal{F}(M')$ be such that $(M, B) \sim (M', B')$. Since C and C' restricted to $\mathrm{Supp}(C) = \mathrm{Supp}(C')$ coincide and the same holds for B and B' on $\mathrm{Supp}(B) = \mathrm{Supp}(B')$, we find that

$$(C \cap B)_N(m) = (C' \cap B')_N(m), \quad m \in \mathrm{Supp}(C \cap B) = \mathrm{Supp}(C' \cap B'),$$

and $(C \cap B)_N(m) = (C' \cap B')_N(m) = 0$, otherwise. Therefore, we simply obtain that $(C \cap B)_N = (C' \cap B')_N$ and, by (11), we get that $Q^{[A]}_{(M,C)}(B) = Q^{[A]}_{(M',C')}(B')$.

Example 3. Based on [4, Example 6.4], we can define a simple model of a type $\langle 1 \rangle$ fuzzy quantifier many as follows. Let $\mathcal{U}$ be a class of finite fuzzy domains, and let L be a residuated lattice with $L = [0, 1]$. A global finite fuzzy quantifier many^I of type $\langle 1 \rangle$ assigns a local fuzzy quantifier $\mathrm{many}^\mathrm{I}_{(M,C)} \colon \mathcal{F}(M) \to [0, 1]$ defined as

$$\mathrm{many}^\mathrm{I}_{(M,C)}(B) := \begin{cases} 1, & \text{if } M = \emptyset \text{ or } C = \emptyset, \\ \dfrac{\sum_{m \in M}(B \cap C)(m)}{\sum_{m \in M} C(m)}, & \text{otherwise,} \end{cases} \tag{12}$$

for any $(M, C) \in \mathcal{U}$ and any $B \in \mathcal{F}(M)$.

Let W be a set of armaments and let $O \in \mathcal{F}(W)$ denote a set of modern tanks, which is naturally imprecisely specified. Then, the global finite fuzzy quantifier $(\mathrm{many}^\mathrm{I})^{[O]}$ of type $\langle 1 \rangle$ restricted to the fuzzy set of modern tanks assigns a local fuzzy quantifier $((\mathrm{many}^\mathrm{I})^{[O]})_{(M,C)} \colon \mathcal{F}(M) \to [0, 1]$:

$$((\mathrm{many}^\mathrm{I})^{[O]})_{(M,C)}(B) = \mathrm{many}^\mathrm{I}_{(W,O)}((C \cap B)_W)$$

$$= \begin{cases} 1, & \text{if } W = \emptyset \text{ or } O = \emptyset, \\ \dfrac{\sum_{m \in W}((C \cap B)_W \cap O)(m)}{\sum_{m \in W} O(m)}, & \text{otherwise,} \end{cases} \tag{13}$$

for any $(M, C) \in \mathcal{U}$ and any $B \in \mathcal{F}(M)$.

If a crisp fuzzy domain (V) represents a set of vehicles, and $D \in \mathcal{F}(V)$ is a fuzzy set of destroyed vehicles, then the truth value of the sentence "Many modern tanks were destroyed" can be evaluated by $((\mathrm{many}^\mathrm{I})^{[O]})_{(V)}(D)$.

Similarly to the notion of restriction for generalized quantifiers, a global fuzzy quantifier restricted to a fuzzy set A on a domain N is determined from the local fuzzy quantifier defined over the fuzzy domain (N, A). Alternative definitions of the notion of restriction to a fuzzy set A on N for fuzzy quantifiers over fuzzy domains can be introduced as follows. For any fuzzy domain (M, C) and $B \in \mathcal{F}(M)$, we have:

$$(Q^{[A]})_{(M,C)}(B) = Q_{(N \cap M, A \cap C)}(B_{N \cap M}), \tag{14}$$

$$(Q^{[A]})_M(B) = \begin{cases} Q_{(N,A)}((C \cap B)_N), & (N, A) \subseteq (M, C), \\ 0, & \text{otherwise.} \end{cases} \tag{15}$$

Using Lemma 1 and $(N, A) \cap (M, C) = (N \cap M, A \cap C)$, one can simply show that

$$Q_{(N \cap M, A \cap C)}(B_{N \cap M}) = Q_{(N,A) \cap (M,C)}(A_{N \cap M} \cap (B \cap C)_{N \cap M}).$$

If $(N, A) \subseteq (M, C)$, then the three notions of restriction coincide. Trivially, we have $Q^{[A]} = Q^{\underline{[A]}}$. Furthermore, by the definition of inclusion for fuzzy domains, we have $(N, A) \sim (N \cap M, A \cap C)$. To prove that $Q^{[A]} = Q^{\underline{[A]}}$, it is sufficient to show (using (14)) that $(N \cap M, A_{N \cap M} \cap (B \cap C)_{N \cap M}) \sim (N, A \cap (B \cap C)_N)$ for any $B \in \mathcal{F}(M)$. The rest follows immediately from the fact that Q is a type $\langle 1 \rangle$ global fuzzy quantifier. Note that the equivalence holds trivially if $N \subseteq M$, but, in general, we have $N \not\subseteq M$. Since $\mathrm{Supp}(A) = \mathrm{Supp}(A_{N \cap M}) = \mathrm{Supp}(A_{N \cap M} \cap C_{N \cap M}) \subseteq N \cap M \subseteq N$, we get

$$\mathrm{Supp}(A \cap (B \cap C)_N) = \mathrm{Supp}(A) \cap \mathrm{Supp}(B_N) \cap \mathrm{Supp}(C_N)$$
$$= \mathrm{Supp}(A) \cap \mathrm{Supp}(B_N) \cap \mathrm{Supp}(C_N) \cap (N \cap M)$$
$$= \mathrm{Supp}(A_{N \cap M}) \cap \mathrm{Supp}(B_{N \cap M}) \cap \mathrm{Supp}(C_{N \cap M})$$
$$= \mathrm{Supp}(A_{N \cap M}) \cap \mathrm{Supp}((B \cap C)_{N \cap M}) = \mathrm{Supp}(A_{N \cap M} \cap (B \cap C)_{N \cap M}).$$

Furthermore, we have

$$(A \cap (B \cap C)_N)(m) = A(m) \wedge B(m) \wedge C(m) = (A_{N \cap M} \cap (B \cap C)_{N \cap M})(m)$$

for any $m \in \mathrm{Supp}(A \cap (B \cap C)_N)$, which proves the desired equivalence.

The next definition introduces the notion of freezing to a fuzzy set for fuzzy quantifiers over fuzzy domains.

Definition 15. *Let Q be a type $\langle 1, 1 \rangle$ global fuzzy quantifier and let A be a fuzzy set on N. The global fuzzy quantifier Q^A of type $\langle 1 \rangle$, which provides freezing to A, is defined as follows: for any fuzzy domain (M, C) and $B \in \mathcal{F}(M)$, we have*

$$Q^A_{(M,C)}(B) = Q_{(M \cup N, C \cup A)}(A_{M \cup N}, (B \cap C)_{M \cup N}). \tag{16}$$

Note that we use $(B \cap C)_{M \cup N}$ instead of $B_{M \cup N}$ to ensure that Q^A is a global fuzzy quantifier. In case of the use of $B_{M \cup N}$, even $Q^A_{(M,C)}$ is not a local fuzzy quantifier, particularly, $Q^A_{(M,C)}(B) \neq Q^A_{(M,C)}(B \cap C)$, in general.[3]

Similarly to the case of restriction, we can introduce two more notions of freezing of type $\langle 1, 1 \rangle$ global fuzzy quantifiers, particularly, for any (M, C) and $B \in \mathcal{F}(M)$, we define (cf. Sect. 3.2):

$$(Q^{\underline{A}})_{(M,C)}(B) = Q_{(M,C)}(A_M \cap C, B),$$

$$(Q^{\underline{A}})_{(M,C)}(B) = \begin{cases} Q_{(M \cup N, C \cup A)}(A_{M \cup N}, (B \cap C)_{M \cup N}), & (N, A) \subseteq (M, C), \\ 0, & \text{otherwise.} \end{cases}$$

Similarly to the case of restriction, all three notions of freezing coincide for $(N, A) \subseteq (M, C)$.

The following statement extends Theorem 2 for fuzzy quantifiers over fuzzy domains.

---

[3] More specifically, $(C_{M \cup N} \cup A_{M \cup N}) \cap B_{M \cup N} = (C_{M \cup N} \cup A_{M \cup N}) \cap (B_{M \cup N} \cap C_{M \cup N})$ does not hold in general; therefore, the fuzzy quantifier Q can assign different values for fuzzy sets $B_{M \cup N}$ and $(B \cap C)_{M \cup N}$.

Theorem 6. *For any fuzzy set A on N, $(Q^{\mathrm{rel}})^A = Q^{[A]}$, $(Q^{\mathrm{rel}})\underline{A} = Q^{[\underline{A}]}$, and $(Q^{\mathrm{rel}})\underline{\underline{A}} = Q^{[\underline{\underline{A}}]}$.*

Example 4. A simple model of a type $\langle 1, 1 \rangle$ fuzzy quantifier many can be defined as follows (cf. [4, Example 6.12] and Example 3). Let $\mathcal{U}$ and L have the same meaning as in Example 3. A global finite fuzzy quantifier many^{II} of type $\langle 1, 1 \rangle$ assigns a local fuzzy quantifier many$^{\mathrm{II}}_{(M,C)} : \mathcal{F}(M) \times \mathcal{F}(M) \to [0,1]$ defined as

$$\mathrm{many}^{\mathrm{II}}_{(M,C)}(A, B) := \begin{cases} 1, & \text{if } M = \emptyset \text{ or } C \cap A = \emptyset, \\ \dfrac{\sum_{m \in M}(A \cap B \cap C)(m)}{\sum_{m \in M}(A \cap C)(m)}, & \text{otherwise,} \end{cases} \tag{17}$$

for any $(M, C) \in \mathcal{U}$ and any $A, B \in \mathcal{F}(M)$.

Let W again be a set of armaments and $O \in \mathcal{F}(W)$ denote a set of modern tanks. Then, the global finite fuzzy quantifier $(\mathrm{many}^{\mathrm{II}})^O$ of type $\langle 1 \rangle$, which freezes the restriction argument of the fuzzy quantifier many^{II} to the fuzzy set of modern tanks, assigns a local fuzzy quantifier $((\mathrm{many}^{\mathrm{II}})^O)_{(M,C)} : \mathcal{F}(M) \to [0,1]$:

$$\begin{aligned} ((\mathrm{many}^{\mathrm{II}})^O)_{(M,C)}(B) &= \mathrm{many}^{\mathrm{II}}_{(M \cup W, C \cup O)}((O_{M \cup W}, (B \cap C)_{(M \cup W)}) \\ &= \begin{cases} 1, & \text{if } M \cup W = \emptyset \text{ or } O_{M \cup W} = \emptyset, \\ \dfrac{\sum\limits_{m \in (M \cup W)}(O_{(M \cup W)} \cap (B \cap C)_{(M \cup W)} \cap (C \cup O))(m)}{\sum\limits_{m \in (M \cup W)}(O_{(M \cup W)} \cap (C \cup O))(m)}, & \text{otherwise,} \end{cases} \end{aligned}$$

$$\tag{18}$$

for any $(M, C) \in \mathcal{U}$ and any $B \in \mathcal{F}(M)$.

If a crisp fuzzy domain (V) again represents a set of vehicles, and $D \in \mathcal{F}(V)$ is a fuzzy set of destroyed vehicles, then the truth value of the sentence "Many modern tanks were destroyed" can be now evaluated by $((\mathrm{many}^{\mathrm{II}})^O)_{(V)}(D)$. It is not difficult to see that $(\mathrm{many}^{\mathrm{I}})^{[O]} = (\mathrm{many}^{\mathrm{II}})^O$, where $(\mathrm{many}^{\mathrm{I}})^{[O]}$ has been defined in Example 3. More specifically, the equality is a simple consequence of Theorem 6 and the fact that many^{II} is the relativization of many^{I}, cf. [4, Example 8.4].

The last statement in this contribution extends Theorem 3 for fuzzy quantifiers over fuzzy domains.

Theorem 7. *Let Q be a type $\langle 1 \rangle$ fuzzy quantifier and A be a fuzzy set on N. Then,*

(i) $Q^{[A]}$ is F-EXT.
(ii) $Q^{[\underline{A}]}$ is F-EXT whenever Q is F-EXT.
(iii) $Q^{[\underline{\underline{A}}]}$ is not F-EXT in general.

Let Q be a type $\langle 1, 1 \rangle$ fuzzy quantifier and A be a fuzzy set on N. Then

(i) Q^A is F-EXT whenever Q is F-EXT.
(ii) $Q^{\underline{A}}$ and $Q^{\underline{\underline{A}}}$ are not F-EXT in general.

5   Conclusion

In this contribution, we investigated two important operations on fuzzy quantifiers defined over fuzzy domains. We recalled the definitions of local and global generalized quantifiers and two operations transforming one generalized quantifier into another: restriction to a set and freezing. We introduced a class of fuzzy domains and defined the basic operations and binary relations on it. Then we generalized the definitions of local and global fuzzy quantifiers over crisp domains to fuzzy quantifiers over fuzzy domains. This novel notion of fuzzy quantifiers allows us to introduce the notions of a fuzzy quantifier restricted to a fuzzy set and of freezing of fuzzy quantifiers, which could not be successfully defined for the case of fuzzy quantifiers over crisp domains.

References

1. Bělohlávek, R.: Fuzzy Relational Systems: Foundations and Principles. Kluwer Academic Publishers, New York (2002)
2. Dvořák, A., Holčapek, M.: Relativization of fuzzy quantifiers: initial investigations. In: Kacprzyk, J., Szmidt, E., Zadrożny, S., Atanassov, K.T., Krawczak, M. (eds.) IWIFSGN/EUSFLAT -2017. AISC, vol. 641, pp. 670–683. Springer, Cham (2018). https://doi.org/10.1007/978-3-319-66830-7_59
3. Dvořák, A., Holčapek, M.: On Semantic Properties of Fuzzy Quantifiers over Fuzzy Universes: Restriction and Living on. In: Lesot, M.-J., et al. (eds.) IPMU 2020. CCIS, vol. 1239, pp. 173–186. Springer, Cham (2020). https://doi.org/10.1007/978-3-030-50153-2_13
4. Dvořák, A., Holčapek, M.: Fuzzy quantifiers defined over fuzzy domains. Fuzzy Sets Syst. **431**, 39–69 (2022)
5. Hájek, P.: Metamathematics of Fuzzy Logic. Kluwer Academic Publishers, Dordrecht (1998)
6. Holčapek, M.: Monadic **L**-fuzzy quantifiers of the type $\langle 1^n, 1 \rangle$. Fuzzy Sets Syst. **159**(14), 1811–1835 (2008)
7. Keenan, E.L., Westerståhl, D.: Generalized quantifiers in linguistics and logic. In: van Benthem, J., ter Meulen, A. (eds.) Handbook of Logic and Language, 2nd edn., pp. 859–923. Elsevier, Amsterdam (2011)
8. Klement, E., Mesiar, R., Pap, E.: Triangular Norms, Trends in Logic, vol. 8. Kluwer Academic Publishers, Dordrecht (2000)
9. Peters, S., Westerståhl, D.: Quantifiers in Language and Logic. Oxford University Press, New York (2006)

Involutions on Different Goguen L-fuzzy Sets

S. Cubillo[1]([⊠]) [ID], C. Torres-Blanc[1] [ID], L. Magdalena[1],
and P. Hernández-Varela[2] [ID]

[1] Universidad Politécnica de Madrid, Campus de Montegancedo,
28660 Boadilla del Monte, Spain
{scubillo,ctorres,lmagdalena}@fi.upm.es
[2] Universidad Autónoma de Chile, Providencia 425, Santiago, Chile
p.hernandez@autonoma.cl

Abstract. J.A. Goguen introduced the L-fuzzy sets (that are extension
of Zadeh's fuzzy sets), in which the image set of the membership function
is an ordered set $(L, \leq_L)$ (base set of the L-fuzzy set). Since then, a lot of
papers studying different classes of those sets have been published. One
of the main topics in this field has been the involutions in each set L,
but these involutions are not totally independent. So the present paper is
devoted to relate the involutions on the base sets L of some L-fuzzy sets,
being L a certain bounded lattice. In particular, we consider L being the
bounded lattices defined by $[0, 1]$ and $[0, 1]^2$, as well as by the base sets
of the Atanassov's and interval-valued fuzzy sets.

Keywords: L-fuzzy sets · Bounded lattices · Order isomorphisms ·
Involutions

1 Introduction

The Goguen L-fuzzy sets on a universe X were introduced in [9], being those
determined by a membership function $f : X \to L$, where $(L, \leq)$ is a partially
ordered set (a poset). The set L is called set of membership degrees of an L-fuzzy
set. Goguen L-fuzzy sets generalize Zadeh's ordinary fuzzy sets [11], in which
$(L, \leq)$ is the set $[0, 1]$ with the usual order relation $\leq$ on the real numbers.

Since that initial definition, different L-fuzzy sets have been considered. Some
examples are Atanassov's Intuitionistic fuzzy sets [1], interval-valued fuzzy sets
[2], etc. In the first case the set L is defined as $L = \{(a, b) \in [0, 1]^2 ; a + b \leq 1\}$
which from now on we will denote as A^*. In the second case $L = \{[a, b] \subseteq
[0, 1] ; a \leq b\}$ which from now on we will refer to as I^*.

This research has been partially supported by the Government of Spain (grant
PCG2018-096509-B-100), Comunidad de Madrid (Convenio Plurianual con la Universidad Politécnica de Madrid en la línea de actuación Programa de Excelencia para el
Profesorado Universitario), Universidad Politécnica de Madrid (Spain) and Universidad Autónoma de Chile.

D. Ciucci et al. (Eds.): IPMU 2022, CCIS 1601, pp. 703–713, 2022.
https://doi.org/10.1007/978-3-031-08971-8_57

Many papers have studied in depth different Goguen L-fuzzy sets, analyzing the different connectives (t-norms, t-conorms,...) and other elements of their algebraic structures. In this sense, an essential topic is that of obtaining the complement of a given set. Involutions have usually been used for this task. Note that the definitions that we are going to introduce are applied to posets or bounded posets, although in our case we are going to use them for bounded lattices (that is, posets that have a minimum 0_L, a maximum 1_L, and every pair of elements has a supremum and an infimum). In fact, in this paper, we will focus on the posets $([0,1], \leq)$, $(A^*, \leq_{A^*})$, $(I^*, \leq_{I^*})$, and $([0,1]^2, \leq_{[0,1]^2})$, which also have a bounded lattice structure.

Definition 1. *Given a bounded poset $(L, \leq, 0_L, 1_L)$, a function $\alpha : L \to L$ is an involution if:*

1. *$\alpha(0_L) = 1_L$, $\alpha(1_L) = 0_L$.*
2. *It is strictly decreasing respect to the relation $\leq$.*
3. *It is involutive, that is, for all $x \in L$, $\alpha(\alpha(x)) = x$.*

Thus, if μ is an L-fuzzy set on X, its complement μ' can be obtained through an involution α on L, as follows:

$$\mu'(x) = \alpha(\mu(x)), \text{ for all } x \in X.$$

Hence the importance of analyzing the involutions in each bounded poset $(L, \leq, 0_L, 1_L)$. Many papers have been devoted to this study, some of them obtaining a characterization of involutions. However, a pending issue is the possible relationship between these involutions (in the corresponding bounded poset) and their characterizations. The present paper opens this study, obtaining some initial results. To do so, each Section will be devoted to compare and relate the involutions on the set of membership degrees of two Goguen L-fuzzy sets, all of them having a bounded lattice structure. Section 2 will consider Zadeh's and Attanasov's sets. In Sect. 3 the considered sets will be Attanasov's and Interval valued sets. Then, Sect. 4 will compare involutions in Interval valued sets with those defined in $[0,1]^2$. And finally, Sect. 5 will connect Zadeh's sets with those defined in $[0,1]^2$. To close the paper some conclusions are presented.

The analysis requires some background definitions that are presented here.

Definition 2. *A function $n : ([0,1], \leq) \to ([0,1], \leq)$ is a negation if*

1. *n is decreasing, and*
2. *$n(0) = 1$ and $n(1) = 0$.*

More, if $n(n(x)) = x$ for all $x \in [0,1]$, n is an involution.

Definition 3. *Given two partially ordered sets $(X, \leq_X)$ and $(Y, \leq_Y)$, a function $\varphi : X \to Y$ is an order homomorphism if φ is an order-preserving map.*

Definition 4. *Given two partially ordered sets $(X, \leq_X)$ and $(Y, \leq_Y)$, a bijective function $\varphi : X \to Y$ is an order isomorphism if φ and φ^{-1} are order-preserving maps.*

Remark 1. If $\varphi : X \rightarrow Y$ is an order isomorphism, from the above definition it directly follows:

- If X and Y are bounded partially ordered sets with X minimum element 0_X and maximum element 1_X, and with Y minimum element 0_Y and maximum element 1_Y, it is $\varphi(0_X) = 0_Y$ and $\varphi(1_X) = 1_Y$.
- If $(X, \leq_X)$ and $(Y, \leq_Y)$ are totally ordered sets, in order φ to be an order isomorphism, it suffices to be a bijective and increasing function.

Definition 5. *Let two partially ordered sets $(X, \leq_X)$ and $(Y, \leq_Y)$, and two functions $\varphi_X : X \rightarrow X$, $\varphi_Y : Y \rightarrow Y$. If $i : X \rightarrow Y$ is an inclusion (injective order homomorphism) of X in Y, we will say that φ_Y is an extension of φ_X, if for all $x \in X$, $\varphi_Y(i(x)) = i(\varphi_X(x))$.*

2   Involutions on $([0, 1], \leq)$ and on $(A^*, \leq_{A^*})$

As previously mentioned, a particular case of Goguen L-fuzzy sets are the Zadeh's fuzzy sets, in which $(L, \leq)$ is the set $[0, 1]$ with the usual relation $\leq$ in the real numbers. The involutions on this ordered set, also called strong negations, were characterized in [10] as follows: $n : [0, 1] \rightarrow [0, 1]$ is an involution if and only if there exists an order isomorphism $\varphi : ([0, 1], \leq) \rightarrow ([0, 1], \leq)$, such that for all $x \in [0, 1]$ it is $n(x) = \varphi^{-1}(1 - \varphi(x))$. It should be noted that in the characterizations of involutions that will appear in this paper, involutions in $([0, 1], \leq)$ will have an essential role.

Besides, Atanassov introduced in [1], the so called Intuitionistic fuzzy sets, which are L-fuzzy sets being $L = A^* = \{(a, b) \in [0, 1]^2 \; ; \; a + b \leq 1\}$, and the order is defined as:

$$(a, b) \leq_{A^*} (c, d) \Leftrightarrow a \leq c \text{ and } b \geq d.$$

$(A^*, \leq_{A^*})$ is a bounded lattice, where the minimum and maximum elements are, respectively, $0_{A^*} = (0, 1)$ and $1_{A^*} = (1, 0)$.

Figure 1 represents A^*, showing two elements with $(a, b) \leq_{A^*} (c, d)$.

Could we find any relationship between the involutions in $([0, 1], \leq)$ and the involutions in $(A^*, \leq_{A^*})$?

To address this problem, we will first consider the set $[0, 1]$ as a subset of A^*, for which we will define an inclusion of $[0, 1]$ in A^*, which will naturally be:

$$i : [0, 1] \rightarrow A^*, \text{ where } i(x) = (x, 0).$$

Let us note that i is an order isomorphism between $([0, 1], \leq)$ and $(S, <_{A^*})$, where $S = \{(x, 0) \; ; \; x \in [0, 1]\} \subset A^*$.

If n is an involution in $([0, 1], \leq)$, is there an extension $\mathcal{N}$ of n to A^*? That is, is there an involution $\mathcal{N}$ on A^*, such that $\mathcal{N} \circ i = i \circ n$? The answer is negative, since it must be $\mathcal{N}(1, 0) = \mathcal{N}(i(1)) = i(n(1)) = i(0) = (0, 0)$, while the image of $(1, 0)$ by any involution in $(A^*, \leq_{A^*})$, should be $(0, 1)$.

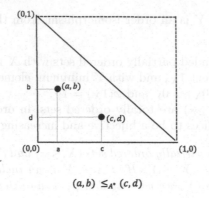

$$(a, b) \leq_{A^*} (c, d)$$

Fig. 1. The set A^* (Atanassov's Intuitionistic fuzzy sets) and two ordered elements.

However, the involutions in both sets are not totally independent, as it is demonstrated in [7], where a characterization of the involutions in $(A^*, \leq_{A^*})$ through the involutions in $([0, 1], \leq)$ was obtained.

$\mathcal{N} : A^* \to A^*$ is an involution in $(A^*, \leq_{A^*})$, if and only if there exists an involution $n : [0, 1] \to [0, 1]$ satisfying $\mathcal{N}(a, b) = (n(1 - b), 1 - n(a))$ for all $(a, b) \in A^*$. More, in this case, it is $n(a) = pr_1\mathcal{N}(a, 1 - a)$, where pr_1 is the projection on the first variable, that is, $pr_1(x, y) = x$.

This result suggests us to try to find another different inclusion, that provides us with the extension sought.

Let us consider $i^* : [0, 1] \to A^*$, where $i^*(x) = (x, 1 - x)$. i^* is an order isomorphism between $([0, 1], \leq)$ and $(M, \leq_{A^*})$, where $M = \{(x, 1 - x) \; ; \; x \in [0, 1]\} \subset A^*$. And let n be an involution on $([0, 1], \leq)$. Let us define $\mathcal{N}(a, b) = (n(1 - b), 1 - n(a))$.

In fact, according to the previous result, $\mathcal{N}$ is an involution on $(A^*, \leq_{A^*})$, and $\mathcal{N}(i^*(x)) = \mathcal{N}(x, 1 - x) = (n(x), 1 - n(x)) = i^*(n(x))$.

Figure 2 shows the inclusions i and i^* of $[0, 1]$ in A^*. In the first one the image of x is $(x, 0)$ and the image of 0 is $(0, 0)$, while in the second one the image of x is $(x, 1 - x)$, and the image of 0 is $(0, 1)$.

3   Involutions on $(A^*, \leq_{A^*})$ and on $(I^*, \leq_{I^*})$

The interval-valued Goguen L-fuzzy sets, are those in which a closed subinterval of $[0, 1]$ is assigned to each element of the universe. So, in this case $L = I^* = \{[a, b] \subseteq [0, 1]\}$, or equivalently, $I^* = \{(a, b) \in [0, 1]^2 \; ; \; a \leq b\}$. Now, the order relation in this set is defined as

$$(a, b) \leq_{I^*} (c, d) \Leftrightarrow a \leq c \text{ and } b \leq d.$$

Then $(I^*, \leq_{I^*})$ is a bounded lattice, whose minimum and maximum elements are, respectively, $0_{I^*} = (0, 0)$ and $1_{I^*} = (1, 1)$.

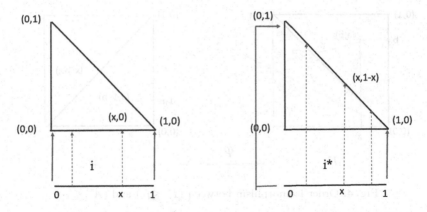

Fig. 2. Inclusions i and i^* of $([0,1], \leq)$ in $(A^*, \leq_{A^*})$

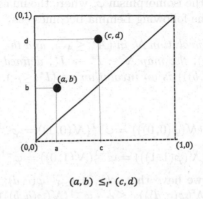

$$(a,b) \leq_{I^*} (c,d)$$

Fig. 3. Bounded partially ordered set $(I^*, \leq_{I^*})$ showing two ordered elements.

Figure 3 represents the set $(I^*, \leq_{I^*})$, and two ordered elements $(a,b) \leq_{I^*} (c,d)$.

Newly, we have that involutions in this ordered set are characterized [2,4]. Nevertheless, could we get a characterization of the involutions in $(I^*, \leq_{I^*})$, from the characterization of the involutions in $(A^*, \leq_{A^*})$?

For this, it is useful to note the existence of an order isomorphism between these two sets. In fact, the map $\varphi : (I^*, \leq_{I^*}) \rightarrow (A^*, \leq_{A^*})$, where $\varphi(a,b) = (a, 1-b)$, is an order isomorphism [8]. Note that $\varphi^{-1} = \varphi$.

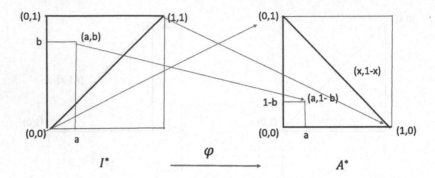

Fig. 4. Order Isomorphism between $(I^*, \leq_{I^*})$ and $(A^*, \leq_{A^*})$

Figure 4 represents the isomorphism φ, where the image of (a, b) is $(a, 1 - b)$. Now, the proof of the following Lemma becomes easy.

Lemma 1. *Given an involution $\mathcal{N}$ in $(A^*, \leq_{A^*})$, and the function $\varphi : I^* \to A^*$, with $\varphi(a, b) = (a, 1 - b)$, the map $\mathcal{N}^* : I^* \to I^*$, defined for all $(a, b) \in I^*$, by $\mathcal{N}^*(a, b) = \varphi^{-1}(\mathcal{N}(\varphi(a, b)))$ is an involution on $(I^*, \leq_{I^*})$.*

Proof.

$$\mathcal{N}^*(0, 0) = \varphi^{-1}(\mathcal{N}(\varphi(0, 0))) = \varphi^{-1}(\mathcal{N}(0, 1)) = \varphi^{-1}(1, 0) = (1, 1)$$

$$\mathcal{N}^*(1, 1) = \varphi^{-1}(\mathcal{N}(\varphi(1, 1))) = \varphi^{-1}(\mathcal{N}(1, 0)) = \varphi^{-1}(0, 1) = (0, 0)$$

If $(a, b) \leq_{I^*} (c, d)$, we have that $\varphi(a, b) \leq_{A^*} \varphi(c, d)$; then $\mathcal{N}(\varphi(c, d)) \leq_{A^*} \mathcal{N}(\varphi(a, b))$, and $\varphi^{-1}(\mathcal{N}(\varphi(c, d))) \leq_{I^*} \varphi^{-1}(\mathcal{N}(\varphi(a, b)))$; so, we have that $\mathcal{N}^*(c, d) \leq_{I^*} \mathcal{N}^*(a, b)$.

Finally, for all $(a, b) \in I^*$, $\mathcal{N}^*(\mathcal{N}^*(a, b)) = \mathcal{N}^*(\varphi^{-1}(\mathcal{N}(\varphi(a, b)))) = \varphi^{-1}(\mathcal{N}(\varphi(\varphi^{-1}(\mathcal{N}(\varphi(a, b)))))) = \varphi^{-1}(\mathcal{N}(\mathcal{N}(\varphi(a, b)))) = \varphi^{-1}(\varphi(a, b)) = (a, b)$.

That is, for each involution on $(A^*, \leq_{A^*})$ there is an involution on $(I^*, \leq_{I^*})$. Conversely, for each involution $\mathcal{N}^*$ on $(I^*, \leq_{I^*})$, it is easy to prove that there is an involution $\mathcal{N}$ on $(A^*, \leq_{A^*})$, defined as $\mathcal{N}(a, b) = \varphi(\mathcal{N}^*(\varphi^{-1}(a, b)))$.

As a consequence, it is possible to obtain the characterization of the involutions on $(I^*, \leq_{I^*})$.

In fact, $\mathcal{N}^*$ is an involution on $(I^*, \leq_{I^*})$ if and only if there exists an involution $\mathcal{N}$ on $(A^*, \leq_{A^*})$ such that for all $(a, b) \in I^*$, $\mathcal{N}^*(x, y) = \varphi^{-1}(\mathcal{N}(\varphi(x, y))) = \varphi^{-1}(\mathcal{N}(x, 1 - y))$, and by the characterization of involutions on this set, if and only if there exists an involution n in $([0, 1], \leq)$ such that $\mathcal{N}^*(x, y) = \varphi^{-1}(n(y), 1 - n(x)) = (n(y), n(x))$.

4   Involutions on $(I^*, \leq_{I^*})$ and on $(I^2, \leq_{I^2})$

In this section, we introduce a new class of Goguen L-fuzzy sets. Let $(I^2, \leq_{I^2})$ be the bounded lattice $I^2 = [0, 1]^2$, where $(a, b) \leq_{I^2} (c, d)$ if and only if $a \leq c$

and $b \leq d$. The minimum and maximum elements are, respectively, $0_{I^2} = (0,0)$ and $1_{I^2} = (1,1)$. This bounded lattice is used, for example, in measures with two fuzzy sets as arguments (see [5]).

In the previous section, we have obtained a characterization of the involutions on $(I^*, \leq_{I^*})$ from the characterization of involutions on $(A^*, \leq_{A^*})$. That has been possible, thanks to the order isomorphism between these two sets. That reasoning suggests us that, if we can find an order isomorphism between the sets $(A^*, \leq_{A^*})$ and $(I^2, \leq_{I^2})$, it would be easy to obtain a characterization of the involutions on the last one, independently of the characterization given in [5]. Nevertheless, the following theorem, shows that there is no a such isomorphism.

Theorem 1. *There is no order isomorphism between* $(I^*, \leq_{I^*})$ *and* $(I^2, \leq_{I^2})$.

Proof. If such an isomorphism $\varphi : I^* \rightarrow I^2$ exists, it would have to be $\varphi(0,0) = (0,0)$ and $\varphi(1,1) = (1,1)$.

What would be the image of $(0,1)$?

1. $\varphi(0,1) \neq (0,0)$ and $\varphi(0,1) \neq (1,1)$.
2. If $\varphi(0,1) = (a,b) \neq (1,0)$ and $(a,b) \neq (0,1)$ (see Fig. 5), there would be two non-comparable elements $(x,y), (x',y')$, satisfying at least one of the two following cases:

   (a) $(0,0) < (x,y), (x',y') < (a,b)$. In this case,

   $$\varphi^{-1}(0,0) = (0,0) < \varphi^{-1}(x,y) \,, \; \varphi^{-1}(x',y') < (0,1).$$

   But then $\varphi^{-1}(x,y)$ and $\varphi^{-1}(x',y')$ are comparable, contradicting the fact that φ is an order isomorphism.

   (b) $(a,b) < (x,y), (x',y') < (1,1)$. Then

   $$\varphi^{-1}(a,b) = (0,1) < \varphi^{-1}(x,y) \,, \; \varphi^{-1}(x',y') < \varphi^{-1}(1,1) = (1,1).$$

   Hence, $\varphi^{-1}(x,y)$ and $\varphi^{-1}(x',y')$ have to be comparable, again obtaining a contradiction.

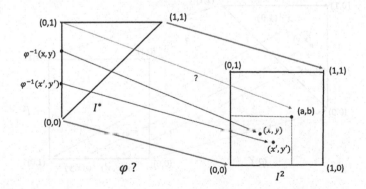

Fig. 5. It is not possible that $\varphi(0,1) \neq (1,0)$ and $\varphi(0,1) \neq (0,1)$.

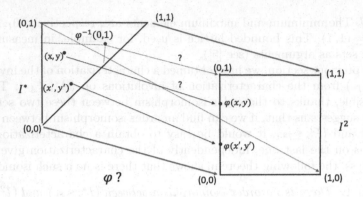

Fig. 6. It is not possible that $\varphi(0,1) = (1,0)$.

3. If $\varphi(0,1) = (1,0)$, what could be $\varphi^{-1}(0,1)$? (see Fig. 6)

$$\varphi^{-1}(0,1) \neq (1,0) \ (\text{as } (1,0) \notin I^*), \quad \varphi^{-1}(0,1) \neq (0,0),$$
$$\varphi^{-1}(0,1) \neq (1,1) \quad \text{and} \quad \varphi^{-1}(0,1) \neq (0,1).$$

Then, there exist two non-comparable elements $(x,y), (x',y')$, satisfying at least one of the two following conditions:
(a) $(0,0) < (x,y), (x',y') < \varphi^{-1}(0,1)$,
(b) $\varphi^{-1}(0,1) < (x,y), (x',y') < (1,1)$.
In a similar way to the reasoning of the previous point, we again obtain a contradiction.
4. Finally, if $\varphi(0,1) = (0,1)$, what could be the $\varphi^{-1}(1,0)$? (see Fig. 7). As before, in this case we will attain a contradiction.

Then, there is no order isomorphism between $(I^*, \leq_{I^*})$ and $(I^2, \leq_{I^2})$.

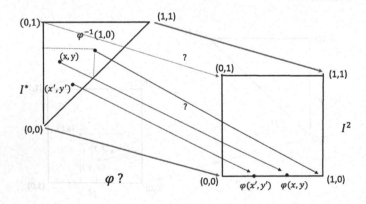

Fig. 7. It is not possible $\varphi(0,1) = (0,1)$

Nevertheless, is it possible to find a relationship between the involutions on $(I^*, \leq_{I^*})$ and the involutions on $(I^2, \leq_{I^2})$?

Lemma 2. *Every involution on* $(I^*, \leq_{I^*})$ *can be extended to an involution on* $(I^2, \leq_{I^2})$.

Proof. If $\mathcal{N}^* : I^* \to I^*$ is an involution, according to the previous Section, it can be expressed as $\mathcal{N}^*(a, b) = (n(b), n(a))$ for some involution n on $[0, 1]$.

If we define $\mathfrak{N} : I^2 \to I^2$, as $\mathfrak{N}(a, b) = (n(b), n(a))$, it is easy to prove that $\mathfrak{N}$ is an involution on $(I^2, \leq_{I^2})$ (see [5]), and it trivially is an extension of $\mathcal{N}^*$, being the trivial inclusion $i : I^* \to I^2$ such that $i(a, b) = (a, b)$.

Now we can address the reverse problem: What involutions on I^2, are such that their restriction to I^* is also an involution?

Lemma 3. *The only involutions on* $(I^2, \leq_{I^2})$ *whose restrictions to* $(I^* \leq_{I^*})$ *are also involutions, are those of the form* $\mathfrak{N}(a, b) = (n(b), n(a))$, *with* n *involution on* $[0, 1]$.

Proof. Let us remember that if $\mathfrak{N}$ is an involution on $(I^2, \leq_{I^2})$ it should be [5] either:

1. $\mathfrak{N}(a, b) = (n_1(a), n_2(b))$, with n_1 and n_2 involutions on $[0, 1]$, or
2. $\mathfrak{N}(a, b) = (n_1(b), n_1^{-1}(a))$, with n_1 bijective negation on $[0, 1]$.

Let's now consider both cases.

1. If $\mathfrak{N}(a, b) = (n_1(a), n_2(b))$, in order that its restriction to I^*, $\mathcal{N}^*$, be an involution, for all $(a, b) \in I^2$, with $a \leq b$ (that is, $(a, b) \in I^*$), it should be $\mathfrak{N}(a, b) = (n(b), n(a))$, for some involution n. But, in this case, for all $x \in [0, 1]$, it must be

$$\mathcal{N}^*(x, x) = (n_1(x), n_2(x)) = (n(x), n(x))$$

Hence, for all $x \in [0, 1]$, it is $n_1(x) = n(x) = n_2(x)$, inferring that $n_1 = n = n_2$, and $\mathfrak{N}(a, b) = (n(a), n(b))$. But if $a < b$, $(a, b) \in I^*$, $n(b) < n(a)$ and $\mathfrak{N}(a, b) = (n(a), n(b)) \notin I^*$. Then we attain a contradiction.
2. If $\mathfrak{N}(a, b) = (n_1(b), n_1^{-1}(a))$, for all $a \leq b$, $\mathcal{N}^*(a, b) = (n(b), n(a))$ for some involution n.
   Then for all $x \in [0, 1]$, $\mathcal{N}^*(x, x) = (n_1(x), n_1^{-1}(x)) = (n(x), n(x))$, and so $n_1(x) = n(x) = n_1^{-1}(x)$, n is an involution and $\mathfrak{N}(a, b) = (n(b), n(a))$.

Then if $\mathfrak{N}$ is an involution on I^2, whose restriction to I^* is also an involution, it should be $\mathfrak{N}(a, b) = (n(b), n(a))$, for some n involution on $[0, 1]$.

5   Involutions on $([0,1], \leq)$ and on $(I^2, \leq_{I^2})$

Newly, we address the task of obtaining a relationship between the involutions on $([0,1], \leq)$ and on $(I^2, \leq_{I^2})$. To do this, we define an inclusion $i : [0,1] \to I^2$, where $i(x) = (x,x)$.

If n is an involution on $[0,1]$, an extension $\mathfrak{N}$ to $(I^2, \leq_{I^2})$ should satisfy $\mathfrak{N}(i(x)) = i(n(x)) = (n(x), n(x))$.

What involutions $\mathfrak{N}$ on $(I^2, \leq_{I^2})$ are extensions of involutions on $([0,1], \leq)$?

Lemma 4. *The only involutions on $(I^2, \leq_{I^2})$ whose restrictions to $([0,1], \leq)$ are also involutions, are those of the form $\mathfrak{N}(a,b) = (n(b), n(a))$, or the form $\mathfrak{N}(a,b) = (n(a), n(b))$, with n involution on $[0,1]$.*

Proof. 1. If $\mathfrak{N}(a,b) = (n_1(a), n_2(b))$, with n_1 and n_2 involutions on $[0,1]$, we have $\mathfrak{N}(i(x)) = \mathfrak{N}(x,x) = (n_1(x), n_2(x)) = (n(x), n(x)) = i(n(x))$, and then $n_1(x) = n(x) = n_2(x)$, for all $x \in [0,1]$. Hence, the involutions n_1 and n_2 must be the same.

2. If $\mathfrak{N}(a,b) = (n_1(b), n_1^{-1}(a))$, with n_1 bijective negation on $[0,1]$, we have $\mathfrak{N}(i(x)) = \mathfrak{N}(x,x) = (n_1(x), n_1^{-1}(x)) = (n(x), n(x)) = i(n(x))$, and so $n_1(x) = n(x) = n_1^{-1}(x)$, for all $x \in [0,1]$. Hence, the negation n_1 must be an involution.

Then if an involution on $(I^2, \leq_{I^2})$ is such that its restriction to $([0,1], \leq)$ is also an involution, it should be $\mathfrak{N}(a,b) = (n(b), n(a))$ or $\mathfrak{N}(a,b) = (n(a), n(b))$, for some n involution on $[0,1]$.

6   Conclusions

This paper has been devoted to relate the involutions in some different bounded lattices. In particular, the lattices $([0,1], \leq)$, $(A^*, \leq_{A^*})$, $(I^*, \leq_{I^*})$, and $(I^2, \leq_{I^2})$, have been considered.

In a preliminary step we have reminded the definitions of involution, order homomorphism, order isomorphism and extension of a function, as tools to be used in the different discussions.

From that point we have shown that:

1. It is possible to extend any involution in $([0,1], \leq)$ to an involution in $(A^*, \leq_{A^*})$.
2. It is possible to characterize involutions in $(I^*, \leq_{I^*})$ from the characterization of the involutions in $(A^*, \leq_{A^*})$. To do so we have previously remembered an order isomorphism between the two sets.
3. There is no order isomorphism between $(I^*, \leq_{I^*})$ and $(I^2, \leq_{I^2})$.
   (a) Nevertheless, we have extended every involution on $(I^*, \leq_{I^*})$ to an involution on $(I^2, \leq_{I^2})$.
   (b) Moreover, we have determined the only involutions on $(I^2, \leq_{I^2})$ whose restriction to $(I^*, \leq_{I^*})$ is also an involution.

4. Finally, we have found the involutions on $(I^2, \leq_{I^2})$ whose restrictions to $([0,1], \leq)$ are also involutions.

In future research, new bounded lattices, sets of membership degrees of other L-fuzzy sets, will be considered, establishing relationships between the corresponding involutions.

References

1. Atanassov, K.T.: Intuitionistic Fuzzy Sets. Physica-Verlag, Heidelberg, New York (1999)
2. Barrenechea, E.: Image Processing with Interval-Valued Fuzzy Sets. Edge Detection. Contrast, Ph.D. Thesis. Universidad Púublica de Navarra (2005)
3. Bedregal, B., Mezzomo, I., Reiser, R.H.S.: n-Dimensional fuzzy negations. IEEE Trans. Fuzzy Syst. **26**(6), 3660–3672 (2018)
4. Bustince, H., Montero, J., Pagola, M., Barrenechea, E., Gómez, D.: A survey of interval-valued fuzzy sets. In: Handbook of Granular Computing, Chapter 22, pp. 491–515 . Wiley, West Sussex (2008)
5. Cubillo, S., Castiñeira, E., Montilla, W.: Supplementarity measures on fuzzy sets. In: Proceedings of the Conference EUSFLAT-LFA 2011, Aix-les-Bains, pp. 897–903 (2011)
6. Cubillo, S., Torres-Blanc, C., Hernández-Varela, P.: A characterization for some type-2 fuzzy strong negations. Knowl. Based Syst. **191**, 105281 (2020). https://doi.org/10.1016/j.knosys.2019.105281
7. Deschrijver, G., Cornelis, C., Kerre, E.: Intuitionistic fuzzy connectives revisited. In: Proceedings of Conference (IPMU 2002), Annecy, pp. 1839–1844 (2002)
8. Deschrijver, G., Kerre, E.: On the relationship between some extensions of fuzzy set theory. Fuzzy Sets Syst. **133**(2), 227–235 (2003)
9. Goguen, J.A.: L-fuzzy Sets. J. Math. Anal. Appl. **18**, 145–174 (1967)
10. Trillas, E.: On negation functions in fuzzy set theory. In: Barro et altri, S. (ed.), Advances of Fuzzy Logic, pp. 31–43 (1998). Original version in Spanish (Stochastica, 1979)
11. Zadeh, L.: Fuzzy sets. Inf. Control **8**, 338–353 (1965)

On the Order-Compatibility of Fuzzy Logic Connectives on the Generated Clifford Poset

Kavit Nanavati[iD] and Balasubramaniam Jayaram[(✉)][iD]

Department of Mathematics, Indian Institute of Techology Hyderabad,
Telangana 502284, India
ma20resch01004@iith.ac.in, jbala@math.iith.ac.in

Abstract. Fuzzy logic connectives have been order-theoretically explored in many recent works. Among them, Clifford's relations, both the additive and multiplicative versions, are prominently employed for their generality as well as utility. While the algebraic properties of the original operation are preserved, its order-theoretic properties, viz., monotonicity, boundedness, etc., are not always preserved on the obtained Clifford poset. In this work, we characterize the necessary and sufficient conditions for these and examine the behaviour of certain fuzzy logic connectives on the induced Clifford posets.

Keywords: Posets · Copulas · Fuzzy implications

1 Introduction

Order-theoretic explorations of algebraic structures lead to hitherto hidden insights. Classically, such studies have been undertaken intensively on semi-groups, see [12–14]. Chief among the proposed relations, is Clifford's relation, that stands out for its generality and utility, see [5]. The utility of the relation is evident from Clifford's seminal result which shows that if a semigroup yields a total order through Clifford's relation, it can be written as an ordinal sum of particular subsemigroups, a result that was instrumental in providing a representation for continuous t-norms, see [11].

Among the various relations that have been proposed based on fuzzy logic connectives, viz., [1,3,7], Clifford's relation is also the most general without being either domain- or operation-specific, as can be seen below.

Definition 1. *Let $\mathbb{P} \neq \emptyset$ and $F : \mathbb{P} \times \mathbb{P} \to \mathbb{P}$. The multiplicative and additive Clifford's relation, denoted by $\preceq_F$ and $\sqsubseteq_F$ respectively, are defined as follows:*

$$x \preceq_F y \iff \text{ there exists } \ell \text{ s.t. } F(\ell, y) = x \ , \qquad \text{(MCR)}$$

$$x \sqsubseteq_F y \iff \text{ there exists } \ell \text{ s.t. } F(\ell, x) = y \ . \qquad \text{(ACR)}$$

Investigation of when an operation F, associative or otherwise, yields a partial order on $\mathbb{P}$ through Clifford's relation has been done in [8] and [15] respectively.

Supported by SERB under the project MTR/2020/000506.

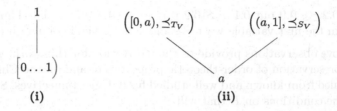

Fig. 1. (i) The Clifford poset obtained from $I_{\mathbf{GD}}$ on $\mathbb{P} = [0,1]$ in Example 1. (ii) The general structure of the Clifford poset $([0,1], \preceq_V)$ obtained from a nullnorm $V = \langle S_V, a, T_V \rangle$ on $\mathbb{P} = [0,1]$.

1.1 Motivation for This Work

While the algebraic properties of the original operation are preserved, its order-theoretic properties, viz. monotonicity, boundedness, etc., are not always preserved on the obtained Clifford poset.

For instance, consider the fuzzy implication in Example 1.

Example 1. Consider the Godel implication

$$I_{\mathbf{GD}}(x,y) = \begin{cases} 1, & \text{if } x \le y, \\ y, & \text{if } x > y. \end{cases}$$

defined on $[0,1]^2$. Clearly, $[0,1]$ w.r.t. the usual order is bounded. However, the poset obtained by (ACR)[1], given in Fig. 1(i) is not bounded below.

One might suspect it is the lack of associativity of $I_{\mathbf{GD}}$ above that leads to the lack of boundedness of the obtained Clifford poset. However, this is not the case, as can be seen if we consider a nullnorm V on $\mathbb{P} = [0,1]$, which is clearly associative. For instance, it has been shown in [8] that while all nullnorms do give rise to Clifford posets, such posets are only bounded below, thus not leading to any further interesting or richer order-theoretic structures. For instance, any nullnorm V with annihilator $a \in]0,1[$ leads to a poset whose Hasse diagram is given in Fig. 1(ii).

Similarly, even if an operation F leads to a Clifford poset, it need not be monotonic on the obtained Clifford poset. Example 2 shows such a semi-copula.

Example 2. Consider the semi-copula $S : [0,1]^2 \to [0,1]$ given as follows:

$$S(x,y) = \begin{cases} \min(x,y) & \text{if } \max(x,y) = 1, \\ 0.1, & \text{if } x = 0.2, y \in [0.7,1), \\ 0.2, & \text{if } (x,y) \in (0.2, 0.9) \times [0.7,1), \\ 0.6, & \text{if } (x,y) \in [0.9,1) \times [0.7,1), \\ 0, & \text{otherwise.} \end{cases}$$

---

[1] Note that (ACR) is employed on fuzzy implications, which are mixed monotonic functions, to obtain the order. See Sect. 4.4 for more details.

Note that $0.2 \preceq_S 0.9$ but $0.1 = S(0.2, 0.7) \npreceq_S S(0.9, 0.7) = 0.6$. Thus, S is not increasing in the first variable w.r.t $\preceq_S$ and is not a semi-copula on $([0,1], \preceq_S)$.

The above observations provide us the motivation for this work, wherein we study the preservation of order-theoretic properties of and on the Clifford poset when obtained from known and well-studied fuzzy logic connectives. Specifically, we study the conditions on F that will

(i) lead to bounded additive $(\mathbb{P}, \preceq_F)$ and multiplicative $(\mathbb{P}, \sqsubseteq_F)$ Clifford posets,
(ii) retain the original type of monotonicity in different variables even on the obtained Clifford poset.

2   Clifford Poset and Some Functional Equations

In this section, we begin by presenting the main result that characterises the operations F that lead to a partial order on the underlying set $\mathbb{P}$.

Remark 1. We employ the standard definitions of the different fuzzy logic connectives (FLCs) discussed in this work and hence refer the readers to well-known sources in the literature for these definitions[2,11]. Further, we make the following observations on the notations used in the sequel.

(i) In the sequel, $\mathbb{P}$ will always denote a non-empty set with no further structure assumed on it.
(ii) $\mathbb{L}$ will denote a bounded poset $(\mathbb{L}, \leq, 0, 1)$.
(iii) By $[a, b] \subseteq \mathbb{L}$ we denote an interval w.r.t. the order $\leq$ defined on $\mathbb{L}$, i.e., $[a, b] = \{x \in \mathbb{L} \mid a \leq x \leq b\}$.
(iv) F will denote a binary operation on $\mathbb{P}$ without any further assumption except closure, i.e., $F : \mathbb{P} \times \mathbb{P} \to \mathbb{P}$.
(v) By F^x we mean the first partial function of F, viz., $F^x(m) = F(m, x)$.
(vi) Given a function F, we shall denote its range by $\mathcal{R}an(F)$.

Definition 2. *An $F : \mathbb{P} \times \mathbb{P} \to \mathbb{P}$ is said to satisfy the*

*(i) **Local left identity** property, if for every $x \in \mathbb{P}$, there exists an $\ell \in \mathbb{P}$ such that*

$$F(\ell, x) = x. \tag{LLI}$$

*(ii) **Quasi-Projection** property, if for any $x, y, z \in \mathbb{P}$,*

$$F(x, F(y, z)) = z \implies F(y, z) = z. \tag{QP}$$

*(iii) **Generalised Quasi-Projection** property, if for any $x, y, z, w \in \mathbb{P}$,*

$$F(x, F(y, z)) = w \implies \exists \, \ell \in \mathbb{P} \text{ s.t. } F(\ell, z) = w. \tag{GQP}$$

Theorem 1 (cf. [15]). *Let $\mathbb{P} \neq \emptyset$ and $F : \mathbb{P} \times \mathbb{P} \to \mathbb{P}$ be a binary function. Let $\preceq_F$ and $\sqsubseteq_F$ be binary relations defined on $\mathbb{P}$ as in (MCR) and (ACR) respectively. Then the following are equivalent:*

(i) $(\mathbb{P}, \preceq_F)$ is a poset.
(ii) $(\mathbb{P}, \sqsubseteq_F)$ is a poset.
(iii) F satisfies (LLI), (QP), and (GQP).

2.1 FLCs that Give Rise to Clifford Posets

As can be seen above, a set of functional equations characterise the function F to lead to a Clifford poset.

The following is known about FLCs and their ability to lead to a Clifford poset when $\mathbb{L} = [0,1]$, or when $\mathbb{L}$ is only a bounded lattice, often discrete, see [4,7–9,15].

Clearly, associativity of F is a special case of (GQP), where $\ell = F(x,y)$.

  (i) A t-norm T or a t-conorm S always leads to a Clifford Poset when defined on any bounded lattice $\mathbb{L}$.
 (ii) A uninorm U defined on $\mathbb{L} = [0,1]$ does not always lead to a Clifford poset. For instance, representable uninorms do not satisfy (QP), and hence do not lead to a Clifford poset, see [8].
(iii) Any nullnorm V defined on $\mathbb{L} = [0,1]$ always leads to a Clifford poset. For some latest results on when a nullnorm V defined on a discrete lattice $\mathbb{L}$ would lead to a Clifford poset, please see [6].
(iv) Quasi-copulas and copulas on $\mathbb{L} = [0,1]$ always lead to a Clifford poset, while not all semi-copulas or fuzzy implications defined on $\mathbb{L} = [0,1]$ lead to a Clifford poset.
 (v) Overlap and grouping functions on $\mathbb{L} = [0,1]$ only lead to Clifford posets when 1 and 0 are their neutral elements respectively.
(vi) In the case of fuzzy implications I, the usual law of importation ($\mathbf{LI}(C)$), given below,

$$I(x, I(y, z)) = I(C(x, y), z), \qquad x, y, z \in \mathbb{P}, \qquad \text{(}\mathbf{LI}(C)\text{)}$$

where C is any binary operation, is a special case of (GQP), where $\ell = C(x, y)$. Thus fuzzy implications that satisfy ($\mathbf{LI}(C)$), along with (LLI), and (QP), do give rise to Clifford posets. Further, if the function C in ($\mathbf{LI}(C)$) is commutative, it implies the exchange principle given below:

$$I(x, I(y, z)) = I(y, I(x, z)). \qquad \text{(EP)}$$

Thus, in the sequel, when we discuss about the type of Clifford poset obtained from an FLC F, or the type of monotonicity on it, it is to be understood that the considered F does satisfy the requirements of Theorem 1.

2.2 Conditional Functional Equations

Similar to the important role played by the functional equations in Definition 2, the following conditional functional equations will prove immensely useful in the sequel in our quest to study the conditions on F to ensure the appropriate type of monotonicity on the Clifford poset.

Definition 3. *A function $F : \mathbb{P} \times \mathbb{P} \to \mathbb{P}$ is said to satisfy*

– **Localized[2] associativity** property, if for any $x, y, z \in \mathbb{P}$, there exists an $\ell \in \mathbb{P}$ such that

$$F(F(x, y), z) = F(\ell, F(y, z)).\tag{LA}$$

– **Localized exchange principle**, if for any $x, y, z \in \mathbb{P}$, there exists an $\ell \in \mathbb{P}$ such that

$$F(x, F(y, z)) = F(\ell, F(x, z)).\tag{LEP}$$

– **TN property**, if for any $x, y, z \in \mathbb{P}$, there exists an $\ell \in \mathbb{P}$ such that

$$F(\ell, F(F(x, y), z)) = F(y, z).\tag{TN}$$

3   FLCs and Multiplicative Clifford's Relation

In this section, we discuss the behaviour of binary operations on posets induced through the relation given in (MCR). We also discuss the behaviour of FLCs studied through (MCR) on the Clifford poset so obtained.

3.1   On the Boundedness of Multiplicative Clifford Poset

The following, easy to obtain results, show the necessary and sufficient conditions required to ensure that the multiplicative Clifford poset is both bounded below and above.

Lemma 1. $(\mathbb{P}, \preceq_F)$ is bounded below if and only if there exists an $l \in \mathbb{P}$ such that $l \in \mathcal{R}an(F^x)$ for all $x \in \mathbb{P}$.

Corollary 1. Suppose l is an annihilator of $(\mathbb{P}, F)$, then $(\mathbb{P}, \preceq_F)$ is bounded below by l.

Lemma 2. $(\mathbb{P}, \preceq_F)$ is bounded above iff there exists a $t \in \mathbb{P}$ such that $F^t : \mathbb{P} \to \mathbb{P}$ is onto.

Corollary 2. Suppose t is the identity element of $(\mathbb{P}, F)$, then $(\mathbb{P}, \preceq_F)$ is bounded above by t.

3.2   On the Monotonicity of F on the Induced Clifford Poset

We present the two important results that show the importance of the functional equations (LA) and (LEP) introduced in Definition 3.

Theorem 2. A function $F : \mathbb{P}^2 \to \mathbb{P}$ is monotonic in the first variable w.r.t $\preceq_F$ iff F satisfies (LA).

Theorem 3. A function $F : \mathbb{P}^2 \to \mathbb{P}$ is monotonic in the second variable w.r.t $\preceq_F$ iff F satisfies (LEP).

---

[2] It is worthy to highlight here that the conditional functional equations (CFEs) in Definition 3 are quite different from the usual CFEs in that we allow an argument to be substituted with another, albeit depending on the considered fixed triple and hence the nomenclature of being 'localised'.

3.3   Multiplicative Clifford Posets from FLCs

We recall that in the literature, typically, (MCR) is employed to obtain the order from FLCs that are monotonic in both the variables and whose function values do not exceed the meet of their arguments, i.e., $F \leq \wedge$, see [8,10]. Thus in this section we only consider such FLCs.

FLCs and Bounded Multiplicative Clifford Posets:

- From the properties of a t-norm T and Lemmas 1 and 2 we see that the Clifford posets obtained from T are bounded.
- Since a nullnorm V has an annihilator, we see that the Clifford poset is always bounded below. However, on general lattices, it may also be bounded above, see [6].
- Let us consider a uninorm U that leads to a Clifford poset. Since U has e as its identity and $U(0,1) = a$ as its annihilator [4], the obtained Clifford poset is bounded below by a and above by e. Note that, in a general bounded lattice $(\mathbb{L}, \leq, 0, 1)$, a need not be either 0 or 1, unlike in the case of $\mathbb{L} = [0, 1]$.
- In the case of a semi-copula, once again it is clear that if it does lead to a Clifford poset, it is always bounded.
- Overlap functions, defined on $[0, 1]$, yield a poset if and only if 1 is a neutral element. Since 0 is the annihilator, the poset is bounded below and above by 0 and 1 respectively.

Monotonicity of FLCs on Multiplicative Clifford Posets: It is clear that any associative operation F satisfies (LA), and if it is also commutative, it satisfies (LEP) as well. Thus t-norms, uninorms, and nullnorms satisfy (LA) and (LEP). However, as made clear in the following observations, the results are a tad surprising.

(i) Clearly, every t-norm T on its original poset $\mathbb{L} = (L, \leq, 0, 1)$ is also a t-norm on the Clifford poset $(\mathbb{L}, \preceq_T)$.

(ii) While a nullnorm V is monotonic on $(\mathbb{L}, \preceq_V)$, it may not become a nullnorm since the Clifford poset may not be bounded above. For some latest results in the setting of bounded lattices, please see [6].

(iii) A uninorm U is not only monotonic on the Clifford poset it gives rise to, but also becomes a t-norm on it, see [9].

(iv) Note that overlap functions, copulas, and quasi-copulas, defined on $[0, 1]$, when they yield a Clifford poset, they coincide with the usual order (see [15]), and retain their properties on the induced poset.

(v) A semi-copula, as is well known, is not associative and thus its satisfaction of (LA) does not follow directly. However, some known classes of semi-copulas are t-norms, overlap functions, copulas, and quasi-copulas, which are already accounted for above.

   In general, a semi-copula S may or may not be monotonic on the induced poset, and hence may or may not be a semi-copula. Table 1 presents some examples of semi-copulas that satisfy both (LA) and (LEP), and are thus semi-copulas on the obtained Clifford posets.

Table 1. Some examples of Multiplicative Clifford posets from Semi-copulas

Semi-copula	$([0,1], \preceq_S)$
$S_1(x,y) = \begin{cases} \min(x,y), & \text{if } \max(x,y) = 1, \\ 0, & \text{if } \min(x,y) \leq 0.4 \text{ and } \max(x,y) < 1, \\ 0.4, & \text{otherwise.} \end{cases}$	Fig. 2(i)
$S_2(x,y) = \begin{cases} \min(x,y), & \text{if } \max(x,y) = 1 \text{ or} \\ & \quad \min(x,y) \leq 0.4, \\ 0.4, & \text{otherwise.} \end{cases}$	Fig. 2(ii)
$S_3(x,y) = \begin{cases} 0, & \text{if } (x,y) \in [0,0.5] \times [0,1), \\ \min(x,y), & \text{otherwise.} \end{cases}$	Fig. 2(iii)

While the semi-copula S in Example 2 does not satisfy (LA), the semi-copula given below does not satisfy (LEP).

Example 3. Consider the semi-copula $S : [0,1]^2 \to [0,1]$ given as follows:

$$S(x,y) = \begin{cases} \min(x,y) & \text{if } \max(x,y) = 1, \\ 0.4, & \text{if } (x,y) \in [0.8,1) \times [0.5,0.6) \cup [0.5,0.6) \times [0.8,1), \\ 0.5, & \text{if } (x,y) \in [0.6,0.8) \times [0.8,1), \\ 0.6, & \text{if } (x,y) \in [0.8,1) \times [0.6,1), \\ 0, & \text{otherwise.} \end{cases}$$

Note that $S(0.8, S(0.7, 0.9)) = S(0.8, 0.5)$
$$= 0.4 \neq S(\ell, 0.6) = S(\ell, S(0.8, 0.9)) \text{ for any } \ell \in [0,1].$$

Thus (LEP) is not satisfied, and S is not increasing in the second variable w.r.t $\preceq_S$, as

$$0.5 \preceq_S 0.9 \text{ but } 0.4 = S(0.8, 0.5) \not\preceq_S S(0.8, 0.9) = 0.6.$$

4   FLCs and Additive Clifford's Relation

In this section, we discuss the behaviour of binary operations on posets induced through the relation given in (ACR). We also discuss the behaviour of FLCs studied through (ACR).

4.1   On the Boundedness of Additive Clifford Poset

Since (ACR) is the dual of the (MCR), the dual of the corresponding results given in Sect. 3.1 hold, i.e. $(\mathbb{P}, \preceq_F)$ is bounded below(above) iff $(\mathbb{P}, \sqsubseteq_F)$ is bounded above(below). It also follows from here that given the existence of an annihilator or identity element, $(\mathbb{P}, \sqsubseteq_F)$ is bounded above by the annihilator, and bounded below by the identity element.

4.2   On the Monotonicity of F on the Induced Clifford Poset

Once again, by the duality, we have the following result:

Theorem 4. *F is increasing in the first(second) variable w.r.t $\preceq_F$ iff F is increasing in the first(second) variable w.r.t $\sqsubseteq_F$.*

Note that (ACR) is employed on fuzzy implications, which are mixed monotonic functions, to obtain the order[3]. Thus, in the following theorem, we characterize the functions that are decreasing in the first variable on the induced poset, showcasing the importance of (TN).

Theorem 5. *F is decreasing in the first variable w.r.t $\sqsubseteq_F$ iff F satisfies (TN).*

4.3   Additive Clifford Posets from FLCs

Once again, in the literature, it is typical to consider (ACR) to obtain the order from FLCs whose function values always exceed the join of their arguments, i.e., $F \geq \vee$, see [7].

- By the associativity, and commutativity of t-conorms, they satisfy (LA), and (LEP). In fact, a t-conorm remains one on the obtained additive Clifford poset $(L, \sqsubseteq_S)$ too.
- Grouping functions, defined on $[0, 1]$, yield a poset if and only if 0 is a neutral element. Since they also yield a total order, their defining properties are retained on the induced poset.
- In the case of fuzzy implications, the situation is not so straight-forward and needs a deeper investigation, which is taken up in the following section.

4.4   Additive Clifford Posets from Fuzzy Implications

In case of fuzzy implications defined on $\mathbb{L}$, we consider (ACR). The reason for taking this liberty is that in case we consider (MCR), 1 would be the least element on the Clifford poset as $I(0, x) = 1$ for all $x \in L$, and $I(1, 1) = 1$, which is not the top element. Thus I won't be an implication on the induced poset. We thus investigate if and when a fuzzy implication is a fuzzy implication on the poset induced by the additive Clifford's relation.

In the following we discuss both the boundedness of additive Clifford posets obtained from an I, and also if the mixed monotonicity of an I is preserved on the obtained poset.

---

[3] See Sect. 4.4 for more details.

Bounded Additive Clifford Posets from Fuzzy Implications: We begin with the following definition.

Definition 4. *Let* $I : \mathbb{L} \times \mathbb{L} \to \mathbb{L}$ *be a fuzzy implication.*

(i) I has the neutrality property if 1 is the left-neutral element of I.
(ii) The function $N_I(x) = I^0(x) = I(x, 0)$ *is a fuzzy negation, called the natural negation of I.*

From the results and discussion in Sects. 3.1 and 4.1, we have the following result:

Lemma 3. $(L, \sqsubseteq_I)$ *is bounded below by 0 iff* I^0 *is onto.*

Corollary 3. *A fuzzy implication I on* $\mathbb{L} = [0, 1]$ *is bounded below on* $([0, 1], \sqsubseteq_I)$ *by 0 iff* N_I *is continuous.*

Corollary 4. *If* $I : \mathbb{L} \times \mathbb{L} \to \mathbb{L}$ *satisfies the neutrality property and* $\sqsubseteq_I$ *yields a bounded partial order, then 0 is its bottom element.*

Interestingly, as the following result shows, from the bottom element of the obtained poset, one may be able to determine if we have an implication on the induced poset.

Lemma 4. *Let I be an implication on the bounded poset* $(\mathbb{L}, \leq, 0, 1)$. *If* $(\mathbb{L}, \sqsubseteq_I)$ *is a poset bounded below by an* $l \neq 0$, *then I is not an implication on* $(\mathbb{L}, \sqsubseteq_I)$.

Fuzzy Implications on Additive Clifford Posets: We now turn to discuss the monotonicity of I on the obtained Clifford poset, which in essence leads to the study of (TN) for I.

Lemma 5. *Every I defined on* $\mathbb{L}$ *satisfying the neutrality property such that* $Range(I^l) = [l, 1]$, *satisfies* (TN).

Corollary 5. *Every continuous fuzzy implication* $I : [0, 1]^2 \to [0, 1]$ *with 1 as the left neutral element satisfies* (TN).

Example 4. Below presented are a couple of fuzzy implications satisfying (TN). For more examples, refer to Table 2.

(i) Yager: $I_{\mathbf{YG}}(x, y) = \begin{cases} 1, & \text{if } x = y = 0 \,, \\ y^x, & \text{otherwise} \,. \end{cases}$

(ii) Reichenbach: $I_{\mathbf{RC}}(x, y) = 1 - x + xy$.

We present now the main result of this section, that completely characterises functions that give rise to fuzzy implications on the obtained Clifford poset.

Theorem 6. *Let* $I : \mathbb{L} \times \mathbb{L} \to \mathbb{L}$. *The following statements are equivalent:*

(i) I is a fuzzy implication on $(\mathbb{L}, \sqsubseteq_I)$.
(ii) I satisfies (TN), (EP), I^0 *is onto,* $I(0, 0) = I(1, 1) = 1$, *and* $I(1, 0) = 0$.

Note that in Theorem 6, the function I need not be an implication on $([0,1], \leq)$ to begin with. Following is an example of a function that is not a fuzzy implication on $[0,1]$ but is one on the induced poset. The induced poset is shown in Fig. 2(iv). For a fixed but arbitrary $t \in (0,1)$, the function is given by:

$$I_t(x,y) = \begin{cases} 1-t, & \text{if } (x,y) \in (0,1)^2, \\ \max(1-x,y), & \text{otherwise.} \end{cases}$$

Now the following results specifying when a fuzzy implication on the original poset will again be one on the Clifford poset follow easily.

Corollary 6. *Let $I : \mathbb{L} \times \mathbb{L} \to \mathbb{L}$ be a fuzzy implication. The following statements are equivalent:*

(i) I is a fuzzy implication on $(\mathbb{L}, \sqsubseteq_I)$.
(ii) I satisfies (TN), (EP), *and I^0 is onto.*

Corollary 7. *Let $I : [0,1]^2 \to [0,1]$ be a fuzzy implication. The following statements are equivalent:*

(i) I is a fuzzy implication on $([0,1], \sqsubseteq_I)$.
(ii) I satisfies (TN), (EP), *and N_I is continuous.*

While we intend to present the study of fuzzy implications satisfying (TN) in a future work, in Table 2, we present some examples of fuzzy implications, that satisfy the conditions of Corollary 7, and hence are fuzzy implications on the additive Clifford posets as well.

Table 2. Some examples of Clifford posets from Fuzzy Implications

Implication			$([0,1], \sqsubseteq_I)$
$I_{T_{\mathbf{M}}^{\#}, N_{\mathbf{C}}}(x,y) = \begin{cases} 1, & \text{if } x \in [0,0.5] \\ & \quad \& \ y \in (0,1], \\ \max(1-x,y), & \text{otherwise.} \end{cases}$			Fig. 2(vi)
$I_{\mathbf{LK}}(x,y) = \min(1, 1-x+y)$			Usual order on $[0,1]$
$I_{\mathbf{DP}}(x,y) = \begin{cases} y, & \text{if } x = 1, \\ 1-x, & \text{if } y = 0, \\ 1, & \text{if } x < 1 \text{ and } y > 0. \end{cases}$			Fig. 2(v)

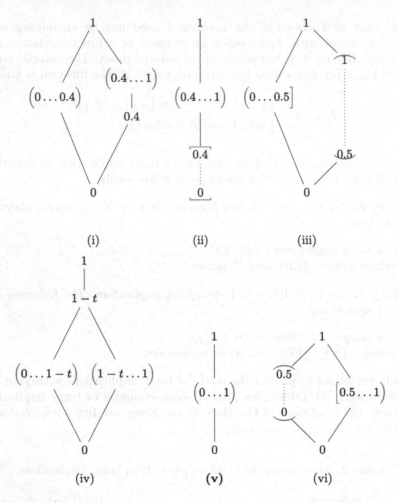

Fig. 2. Hasse diagrams of the posets obtained from semi-copulas and fuzzy implications in Tables 1 and 2, respectively.

5   Some Concluding Remarks

Clifford's relations have been extensively used to obtain order from fuzzy logic connectives. The operations that yield a partially ordered set have been completely characterized and classes of fuzzy logic connectives yielding an order have also been obtained. While the algebraic properties of an operation are preserved on the induced poset, the order dependent properties, viz., monotonicity and boundedness may not be. In this work, we have shown the importance of a few conditional functional equations, viz., (LA), (LEP), and (TN), that help us characterize the operations that preserve them. Using these, we have studied the behaviour of fuzzy logic connectives on the corresponding induced posets.

References

1. Aşıcı, E.: An order induced by nullnorms and its properties. Fuzzy Sets Syst. **325**, 35–46 (2017)
2. Baczyński, M., Jayaram, B.: Fuzzy Implications, Studies in Fuzziness and Soft Computing, vol. 231. Springer, Heidelberg (2008). https://doi.org/10.1007/978-3-540-69082-5
3. Ertuğrul, Ü., Kesicioğlu, M.N., Karacal, F.: Ordering based on uninorms. Inf. Sci. **330**, 315–327 (2016)
4. Gupta, V.K., Jayaram, B.: Clifford's order from uninorms on bounded lattices. Submitted
5. Gupta, V.K., Jayaram, B.: On a pecking order between that of Mitsch and Clifford. Submitted
6. Gupta, V.K., Jayaram, B.: On the utilitarian aspects of Clifford posets from fuzzy logic conncetives. Manuscript under preparation
7. Gupta, V.K., Jayaram, B.: Importation lattices. Fuzzy Sets Syst. **405**, 1–17 (2021)
8. Gupta, V.K., Jayaram, B.: Order based on associative operations. Inf. Sci. **566**, 326–346 (2021)
9. Gupta, V.K., Jayaram, B.: Orders from uninorms on bounded lattices: some perspectives. In: Joint Proceedings of the 19th World Congress of the International Fuzzy Systems Association (IFSA), the 12th Conference of the European Society for Fuzzy Logic and Technology (EUSFLAT), and the 11th International Summer School on Aggregation Operators (AGOP), pp. 631–638. Atlantis Press (2021)
10. Karaçal, F., Kesicioğlu, M.N.: A T-partial order obtained from t-norms. Kybernetika **47**(2), 300–314 (2011)
11. Klement, E.P., Mesiar, R., Pap, E.: Triangular Norms, Trends in Logic, vol. 8. Kluwer Academic Publishers, Dordrecht (2000)
12. Mitsch, H.: A natural partial order for semigroups. Proc. Am. Math. Soc. **97**(3), 384–388 (1986)
13. Mitsch, H.: Semigroups and their natural order. Math. Slovaca **44**(4), 445–462 (1994)
14. Nambooripad, K.S.: The natural partial order on a regular semigroup. Proc. Edinburgh Math. Soc. **23**(3), 249–260 (1980)
15. Nanavati, K., Jayaram, B.: Order based on non-associative operations. In: Joint Proceedings of the 19th World Congress of the International Fuzzy Systems Association (IFSA), the 12th Conference of the European Society for Fuzzy Logic and Technology (EUSFLAT), and the 11th International Summer School on Aggregation Operators (AGOP), pp. 675–681. Atlantis Press (2021)

Theoretical and Applied Aspects
of Imprecise Probabilities

Decision Making with State-Dependent Preference Systems

Christoph Jansen[✉] and Thomas Augustin

Department of Statistics, Ludwig-Maximilians-Universität Munich, Munich, Germany
{christoph.jansen,thomas.augustin}@stat.uni-muenchen.de

Abstract. In this paper we present some first ideas for decision making with agents whose preference system may depend on an uncertain state of nature. Our main formal framework here are commonly scalable state-dependent decision systems. After giving a formal definition of those systems, we introduce and discuss two criteria for defining optimality of acts, both of which are direct generalizations of classical decision criteria under risk. Further, we show how our criteria can be naturally extended to imprecise probability models. More precisely, we consider convex and finitely generated credal sets. Afterwards, we propose linear pogramming-based algorithms for evaluating our criteria and show how the complexity of these algorithms can be reduced by approximations based on clustering the preference systems under similar states. Finally, we demonstrate our methods in a toy example.

Keywords: State-dependent preferences · Preference system ·
Imprecise probabilities · Decision making under uncertainty · Linear
programming

1 Introduction

In many applications, the agent's preferences in a decision making problem under uncertainty can not be modeled independently of the true *state of nature*. Prominent examples for such applications can, e.g., be found in the field of insurance science. Here, often a policyholder's preferences are modelled to be dependent on her health status as, e.g., being reliant on the help of other people may lead to different preferences as being completely autonomous (see [5] for a very recent work in this direction). Further examples can, e.g., be found in problems of portfolio selection, where commonly the agent's attitude towards risky choices (and therefore indirectly the underlying preferences) are seen as depending on some exogenous environment (see, e.g., [28] for a recent work).

In such situations, the decision maker's preferences are called *state-dependent*: The knowledge of the true state of nature might force the decision maker to completely (or partially) rearrange the ranking of the consequences different decisions may lead to. Given their practical relevance, it is not surprising that many fundamental works have dealt with state-dependent preferences.

© Springer Nature Switzerland AG 2022
D. Ciucci et al. (Eds.): IPMU 2022, CCIS 1601, pp. 729–742, 2022.
https://doi.org/10.1007/978-3-031-08971-8_59

For instance, one can consult the classic sources [11] or [21,22], but many more exist. See also [2] for a modern reappraisal. Most of these works are in the classical Anscombe and Aumann framework of 'preferences over horse lotteries' (see [1]): Starting from a preference relation on the domain of all horse lotteries, they derive 'conditional' preference relations for every state fixed and then say the original relation is state-dependent whenever there exist distinct (non-null) states for which these conditional relations differ (see, e.g., [12]).

In the present work, we choose a more direct and applied view on the notion of state dependence. Instead of over horse lotteries, we model preferences directly on a finite consequence set and assume that the uncertainty about the states is externally given by an imprecise probability model. Moreover, under each state we allow the agent to express also partial preferences with respect to both the ordering itself and the strength of preferences. The practical evaluation of consequences often relies on reference points external to the consequence itself (see, e.g., [10] for impactful psychological research), and indeed these reference points may also be related to other consequences. A quite prominent example for such a setting is obtained by rigorously formalizing the notion of regret familiar from classical decision theory: measuring the "inappropriateness" of an action in a particular state, as [20, p.59] originally had put it, is impossible "unless [...] state-contingent consequences can be specified" ([16, p. 810]), see also, for instance, [23] on axiomatizations of the minimax regret principle and, e.g., [17] for a recent application in the context of climate model uncertainty.

The paper is organized as follows: Sect. 2 discusses the required mathematical definitions and concepts. After that, Sect. 3 introduces the notion of state-dependent decision systems and proposes two classes of decision criteria for both the case of precise and imprecise probabilistic information about the states. In Sect. 4, we first demonstrate how the proposed criteria can be evaluated by using linear optimization theory and then discuss different possibilities for reducing the complexity of the obtained linear programs by grouping the variables under 'similar' states. Section 5 illustrates the discussed concepts in a toy example. Section 6 concludes the paper.

2   Preliminaries

We start by recalling our central concept for modelling a decision maker's preferences, namely the concept of a *preference system* as introduced in [9]. The basic idea here is very natural: the ordinal and the cardinal part of the preferences are modeled by two separate pre-orders (i.e. transitive and reflexive binary relations). The ordinal order is a pre-order on the set of consequences, while the cardinal order formally corresponds to a pre-order on the ordinal order - conceived as a set. Note that the following Definitions 1, 2 and 3 are (essentially) taken from [9].

Definition 1. *Let A be a non-empty set and let $R_1 \subseteq A \times A$ denote a pre-order on A. Moreover, let $R_2 \subseteq R_1 \times R_1$ denote a pre-order on R_1. Then the triplet $\mathcal{A} = [A, R_1, R_2]$ is called a **preference system** on A. The preference system $\mathcal{A}' = [A, R_1', R_2']$ is called **sub-system** of $\mathcal{A}$ if $R_1' \subseteq R_1$ and $R_2' \subseteq R_2$.*

The relations R_1 and R_2 are usually interpreted in terms of behavior: If a pair $(a, b) \in R_1$, this means that a *is at least as desirable as* b, whereas if a pair of pairs $((a, b), (c, d)) \in R_2$, this means that *exchanging* b *by* a *is at least as desirable as exchanging* d by c. To ensure that the orders of a preference system do not contradict, a consistency criterion is introduced. Roughly speaking, a preference system is consistent if there exists a utility function on the set of consequences which represents both involved pre-orders simultaneously. As usual, we will use the following notation: For a pre-order $R \subseteq M \times M$ on a set M, we denote by $P_R \subseteq M \times M$ its *strict part*[1] and by $I_R \subseteq M \times M$ its *indifference part*[2].

Definition 2. *Let* $\mathcal{A} = [A, R_1, R_2]$ *be a preference system. Then* $\mathcal{A}$ *is said to be* **consistent** *if there exists a function* $u : A \rightarrow [0, 1]$ *such that for all* $a, b, c, d \in A$ *the following properties hold:*

i) If $(a, b) \in R_1$, *then* $u(a) \geq u(b)$ *with equality iff* $(a, b) \in I_{R_1}$.
ii) If $((a, b), (c, d)) \in R_2$, *then*

$$u(a) - u(b) \geq u(c) - u(d)$$

with equality iff $((a, b), (c, d)) \in I_{R_2}$.

Every such function u *is then said to* **(weakly) represent** *the preference system* $\mathcal{A}$. *The set of all (weak) representations* u *of* $\mathcal{A}$ *is denoted by* $\mathcal{U}_{\mathcal{A}}$.

For consistent preference systems whose ordinal order has minimal and maximal elements, it may be useful to consider only utility functions that measure the utility of consequences on the same scale. This is, for example, central for defining an expected value generalized to preference systems.

Definition 3. *Let* $\mathcal{A} = [A, R_1, R_2]$ *be a consistent preference system. Assume there exist elements* $a_*, a^* \in A$ *such that* $(a^*, a) \in R_1$ *and* $(a, a_*) \in R_1$ *for all* $a \in A$. *Then the set*

$$\mathcal{N}_{\mathcal{A}} := \left\{ u \in \mathcal{U}_{\mathcal{A}} : u(a_*) = 0 \ \wedge \ u(a^*) = 1 \right\}$$

is called the **normalized representation set** *of* $\mathcal{A}$. *Further, for a number* $\delta \in [0, 1)$, *we denote by* $\mathcal{N}_{\mathcal{A}}^{\delta}$ *the set of all* $u \in \mathcal{N}_{\mathcal{A}}$ *satisfying*

$$u(a) - u(b) \geq \delta \quad \wedge \quad u(c) - u(d) - u(e) + u(f) \geq \delta$$

for all $(a, b) \in P_{R_1}$ *and for all* $((c, d), (e, f)) \in P_{R_2}$. *Then,* $\mathcal{N}_{\mathcal{A}}^{\delta}$ *is called the* **normalized representation set of granularity** δ *of* $\mathcal{A}$.

3 State-Dependent Decision Systems

We now come to the central concept of this paper, namely that of state-dependent decision systems. The idea is very natural: Instead of a fixed preference system, we now want to allow the decision maker's preferences to be dynamic in the states of nature of a decision problem under uncertainty.

---

[1] Defined by: $(m_1, m_2) \in P_R \Leftrightarrow (m_1, m_2) \in R \wedge (m_2, m_1) \notin R$.
[2] Defined by: $(m_1, m_2) \in I_R \Leftrightarrow (m_1, m_2) \in R \wedge (m_2, m_1) \in R$.

3.1   The Basic Model

We start by giving the fundamental definition. Note that for simplicity and to avoid measure-theoretic problems, the sets $A = \{a_1, \ldots, a_n\}$ and $S = \{s_1, \ldots, s_m\}$ are assumed to be finite throughout the rest of the paper.

Definition 4. *Let S denote some non-empty set of states of nature and A denote some non-empty set of consequences. For every $s \in S$, let $\mathcal{A}_s = [A, R_1^s, R_2^s]$ be a preference system on A. For a non-empty subset $\mathcal{G} \subseteq A^S := \{f : S \to A\}$, representing the acts available to the decision maker, we call the pair*

$$\mathcal{D} = \left[\mathcal{G}, (\mathcal{A}_s)_{s \in S}\right]$$

*a **decision system**. A decision system $\mathcal{D}$ is called **state-independent** if it holds that $\mathcal{A}_s = \mathcal{A}_{s'}$ for all $s, s' \in S$. Otherwise, $\mathcal{D}$ will be called **state-dependent**.*

Especially in the case of a state-dependent decision system, it is useful to consider only utility functions that measure the utility on the same scale. In contrast to non-dynamic preference systems, however, this requires a stronger assumption: The maximal and minimal elements of the ordinal orders of all preference systems involved must be independent of the state of the nature.

Definition 5. *Let $\mathcal{D} = \left[\mathcal{G}, (\mathcal{A}_s)_{s \in S}\right]$ be a decision system. Then $\mathcal{D}$ is called **commonly scalable** if there exist elements $a_*, a^* \in A$ such that $(a^*, a) \in R_1^s$ and $(a, a_*) \in R_1^s$ for all $a \in A$ and $s \in S$, i.e. if there exist common maximal and minimal elements which are independent of the state of nature. Further, for $\delta \in [0, 1)$, $\mathcal{D}$ is called δ-**consistent** if $\mathcal{N}_{\mathcal{A}_s}^\delta \neq \emptyset$ for all $s \in S$. Finally, $\mathcal{D}$ is called **consistent** if it is 0-consistent.*

Note that the definition of a state-dependent commonly scalable decision system $\mathcal{D} = \left[\mathcal{G}, (\mathcal{A}_s)_{s \in S}\right]$ does not rule out the possibility that there are states under which the decision maker has coinciding preference systems. From now on we assume, *without restricting generality of what follows*, that for some $\ell \in \{1, \ldots m\}$ there is a partition $\mathbb{S} := \{S_1, \ldots, S_\ell\}$ of S that satisfies the following properties:

i) For all $d \in \{1, \ldots, \ell\}$ and all $s_{i_1}, s_{i_2} \in S_d$ it holds $\mathcal{A}_{s_{i_1}} = \mathcal{A}_{s_{i_2}}$.
ii) For all $c \neq d \in \{1, \ldots, \ell\}$ and all $s_{i_1} \in S_c$ and $s_{i_2} \in S_d$ it holds $\mathcal{A}_{s_{i_1}} \neq \mathcal{A}_{s_{i_2}}$.
iii) For $c < d \in \{1, \ldots, \ell\}$, if $s_{i_1} \in S_c$ and $s_{i_2} \in S_d$, then $i_1 < i_2$.

We then denote by $\mathcal{A}_{S_d}$ the preference system $\mathcal{A}_s$ for arbitrary $s \in S_d$. Note that this assumption simply ensures that the states of nature are already grouped in classes containing coinciding preference systems.

3.2   Criteria for Decision Making

We will now consider two different types of decision criteria in state-dependent decision systems: Criteria based on numerical representations of a generalized expected value and those that select undominated elements of a generalized stochastic dominance relation. For the first type of criterion, we first need to define what is meant by expected value in our context.

Definition 6. *Let* $\mathcal{D} = [\mathcal{G}, (\mathcal{A}_s)_{s \in S}]$ *be a commonly scalable and* δ*-consistent decision system and let* π *denote a probability measure on* $(S, 2^S)$*. For* $X \in \mathcal{G}$*, we define the expressions*

$$
L_\pi^\delta(X) = \min\left\{ \sum_{d=1}^{\ell} \left(\sum_{s \in S_d} u_{S_d}(X(s)) \cdot \pi(\{s\}) \right) : (u_{S_1}, \dots, u_{S_\ell}) \in \bigtimes_{d=1}^{\ell} \mathcal{N}_{\mathcal{A}_{S_d}}^\delta \right\}
$$

$$
U_\pi^\delta(X) = \max\left\{ \sum_{d=1}^{\ell} \left(\sum_{s \in S_d} u_{S_d}(X(s)) \cdot \pi(\{s\}) \right) : (u_{S_1}, \dots, u_{S_\ell}) \in \bigtimes_{d=1}^{\ell} \mathcal{N}_{\mathcal{A}_{S_d}}^\delta \right\}
$$

Then, the (possibly degenerated) interval

$$
E_\pi^\delta(X) = [L_\pi^\delta(X), U_\pi^\delta(X)]
$$

*is called the **state-dependent expectation** of* X *with respect to the prior distribution* π *and granularity* δ*.*

In principle, there are many different criteria thinkable that are based on the state-dependent expectations $E_\pi^\delta(X)$ of the different acts in $X \in \mathcal{G}$. Here, we want to stick with the most conservative one among them, namely the one taking into account only the lower bound $L_\pi^\delta(X)$ of each of these intervals.

Definition 7. *Let* $\mathcal{D} = [\mathcal{G}, (\mathcal{A}_s)_{s \in S}]$ *be a commonly scalable and* δ*-consistent decision system and let* π *denote a probability measure on* $(S, 2^S)$*. An act* $X^* \in \mathcal{G}$ *is called* $(\mathcal{D}, \pi, \delta)$*-**maximin** if* $L_\pi^\delta(X^*) \geq L_\pi^\delta(X)$ *for all* $X \in \mathcal{G}$*.*

Some remarks on Definition 7: in the case of a state-independent decision system, the criterion essentially reduces to the $\mathcal{D}_\delta$-maximin criterion as introduced in [9, Definition 6 i)]. If further the then constant relations R_1 and R_2 satisfy the axioms in [14, p. 147, Definition 1] and thus admit a cardinal utility representation that is unique up to positive linear transformations, the criterion reduces to the principle of maximizing expected utility (note that of course in this case it is implied that both relations R_1 and R_2 have to be complete).

The second type of criterion is based on a generalization of the concept of first order stochastic dominance. The idea is first to define a partial order on the set of available acts and then to call optimal those among them that are undominated with respect to this relation. We start with defining the dominance relation.

Definition 8. *Let* $\mathcal{D} = [\mathcal{G}, (\mathcal{A}_s)_{s \in S}]$ *be a commonly scalable and consistent decision system and let* π *denote a probability measure on* $(S, 2^S)$*. For an act* $X \in \mathcal{G}$ *and a collection of functions* $u := (u_d)_{d=1,\dots,\ell}$ *such that it holds that* $u_d \in \mathcal{N}_{\mathcal{A}_{S_d}}$ *for each* $d = 1, \dots, \ell$*, the expression*

$$
E_{(\pi, u)}(X) = \sum_{d=1}^{\ell} \left(\sum_{s \in S_d} u_{S_d}(X(s)) \cdot \pi(\{s\}) \right)
$$

*is called the (π, u)-__expectation__ of X. Further, for two acts $X, Y \in \mathcal{G}$, we say
that X $(\mathcal{D}, \pi)$-__dominates__ Y, abbreviated with $X \geq_{(\mathcal{D},\pi)} Y$, if it holds that*

$$E_{(\pi,u)}(X) \geq E_{(\pi,u)}(X)$$

*for every $u := (u_d)_{d=1,\dots,\ell}$ with $u_d \in \mathcal{N}_{A_{S_d}}$ for each $d = 1, \dots, \ell$. Finally, an
act $X^* \in \mathcal{G}$ is called $(\mathcal{D}, \pi)$-__undominated__ if there is no act $Y \in \mathcal{G}$ such that
$Y \geq_{(\mathcal{D},\pi)} X^*$ but not $X^* \geq_{(\mathcal{D},\pi)} Y$, that is if X^* is an undominated element of
the dominance relation $\geq_{(\mathcal{D},\pi)}$.*

Some remarks on the dominance relation: First, it is immediate that for a state-
independent decision system in which, in addition, the cardinal relation R_2
involved is empty, classical stochastic dominance for partial orders is equivalent
to it. Further, it can be easily shown that for the case of a state-independent
decision system with constant, but not necessarily empty, R_2, it reduces to the
order $R_{\forall\forall}$ as defined in [9, p. 123] and also considered in [7, Definition 4 ii)].
Finally, one sees immediately that the dominance relation is a pre-order on $\mathcal{G}$,
i.e., a reflexive and transitive, but not necessarily complete, binary relation.

3.3 Generalizing the Criteria to Imprecise Probabilities

So far, we have limited our considerations to decision systems under precise
probabilities. In this section we want to show how the decision criteria discussed
so far can also be generalized most naturally to decision systems under imprecise
probabilities. Although different generalizations are often conceivable (analogous
as in the case with cardinal utility, see, e.g., [24,27]), we restrict ourselves to one
particular generalization each for reasons of simplicity and space. As a generalized uncertainty model, we consider convex and finitely generated credal sets
$\mathcal{M}$, i.e., convex sets of probability measures on $(S, 2^S)$ with a finite number of
extreme points collected in

$$\mathcal{E}(\mathcal{M}) = \{\pi^{(1)}, \dots \pi^{(K)}\}.$$

We start by generalizing $(\mathcal{D}, \pi, \delta)$-maximin. As already mentioned, many different generalizations are plausible, depending on the decision maker's attitude
towards ambiguity. Consistent with our previous restriction to the lower bound,
we will again examine only the absolute ambiguity-averse variant.

__Definition 9.__ *Let $\mathcal{D} = [\mathcal{G}, (\mathcal{A}_s)_{s\in S}]$ be a commonly scalable and δ-consistent
decision system and let $\mathcal{M}$ be a convex and finitely generated credal set on $(S, 2^S)$.
An act $X^* \in \mathcal{G}$ is called $(\mathcal{D}, \mathcal{M}, \delta)$-__maximin__ if*

$$L^\delta_{(\mathcal{D},\mathcal{M})}(X^*) := \min_{\pi \in \mathcal{M}} L^\delta_\pi(X^*) \geq \min_{\pi \in \mathcal{M}} L^\delta_\pi(X) =: L^\delta_{(\mathcal{D},\mathcal{M})}(X)$$

for all $X \in \mathcal{G}$.

This decision criterion also has a well-known special case: If the underlying decision system is state-independent and the then constant relations of the preference

system guarantee a unique utility representation up to for positive linear transformations (see above), then the criterion reduces to the Γ-maximin criterion known from decision making under imprecise probabilities (see, e.g., [24]).

Also the dominance relation $\geq_{(\mathcal{D},\pi)}$ from Definition 8 can naturally be adapted to the case of imprecise probabilities by demanding the involved acts to be in relation for all probability measures from the underlying credal set.

Definition 10. *Let $\mathcal{D} = [\mathcal{G}, (\mathcal{A}_s)_{s \in S}]$ be a commonly scalable and consistent decision system and let $\mathcal{M}$ be a convex and finitely generated credal set on $(S, 2^S)$. For acts $X, Y \in \mathcal{G}$, we say X $(\mathcal{D}, \mathcal{M})$-**dominates** Y, abbreviated with $X \geq_{(\mathcal{D},\mathcal{M})} Y$, if it holds that $X \geq_{(\mathcal{D},\pi)} Y$ for every $\pi \in \mathcal{M}$. Further, an act $X^* \in \mathcal{G}$ is called $(\mathcal{D}, \mathcal{M})$-**undominated** if X^* is $(\mathcal{D}, \pi)$-undominated for every $\pi \in \mathcal{M}$.*

Before turning to the computation of the different criteria just discussed, we end the paragraph by briefly commenting on how two other well-known criteria from decision theory with imprecise probabilities, namely E-admissibility and maximality, could be most naturally generalized to the state-dependent framework presented in this paper.

The criterion of *E-admissibility* (see [15]) - in its original state-*in*dependent version - demands an act to maximize expected utility for at least one compatible pair (u, π) of utility function and probability measure. This can be easily adapted to our setting by demanding the same for at least one probability measure from $\mathcal{M}$ and at least one *family* of utility functions $(u_d)_{d=1,\dots,\ell}$ with $u_d \in \mathcal{N}_{\mathcal{A}_{S_d}}$ for each $d = 1, \dots, \ell$. To calculate this generalized criterion, an adaptation of the algorithm from [26, Sect. 5.2] would presumably be applicable.

The criterion of *maximality* (see [27]) - in its original state-*in*dependent version[3] - demands an act to dominate every other available act Y in expectation for at least one compatible pair (u_Y, π_Y) of utility function and probability measure. In contrast to E-admissibility, this pair is allowed to depend on the respective competing act Y under consideration. Also this criterion can be easily adapted to the state-dependent setting by demanding the same for at least one probability measure from $\pi_Y \in \mathcal{M}$ and at least one *family* of utility functions $(u_d^Y)_{d=1,\dots,\ell}$ with $u_d^Y \in \mathcal{N}_{\mathcal{A}_{S_d}}$ for each $d = 1, \dots, \ell$. For the computation of this state-dependent maximality, an adaptation of the algorithm from [8, Proposition 2] would presumably be applicable.

4 Algorithms for Determining Optimal Acts

In this section we show how optimal acts can be determined with respect to the discussed decision criteria using linear optimization as has been extensively done before in the context of decision making with imprecise probabilities (see,

---

[3] Note that maximality originally is defined for a fixed cardinal utility function u (and thus in particular for complete preferences), such that actually also the state-independent version given above is an adaptation of maximality to decision making with preference system-valued acts. So, actually, the adaptation given above is an adaptation of this adaptation.

e.g., [6,13,25,26]). For this purpose, we first discuss two basic algorithms for the optimization of the two criteria discussed and then demonstrate how the complexity of these algorithms can be reduced by suitable approximations. The idea of the approximation is to group the preference systems under certain, in a certain sense similar, states and then to consider only decision variables for each cluster of states in the optimization. All discussed optimization problems are given directly for the criteria under imprecise probabilities, since these contain the criteria under precise probabilities in each case as a special case.

4.1   Two Basic Linear Programs

We start with the basic linear program for computing the criterion value of any fixed act with respect to the $(\mathcal{D}, \mathcal{M}, \delta)$-maximin criterion. For this let $\mathcal{A} = [A, R_1, R_2]$, with $A = \{a_1, \ldots, a_n\}$, be a consistent preference system for which there exist elements $a_{k_1}, a_{k_2} \in A$ such that $(a_{k_1}, a) \in R_1$ and $(a, a_{k_2}) \in R_1$ for all $a \in A$. The property of a vector $(v_1, \ldots, v_n)$ to contain exactly the images of a utility function $u : A \to [0,1]$ from the set $\mathcal{N}_{\mathcal{A}}^{\delta}$ is then describable by the system of linear (in-)equalities given through

- $v_{k_1} = 1$ and $v_{k_2} = 0$,
- $v_i = v_j$ for every pair $(a_i, a_j) \in I_{R_1}$,
- $v_i - v_j \geq \delta$ for every pair $(a_i, a_j) \in P_{R_1}$,
- $v_k - v_l = v_p - v_q$ for every pair of pairs $((a_k, a_l), (a_p, a_q)) \in I_{R_2}$ and
- $v_k - v_l - v_p + v_q \geq \delta$ for every pair of pairs $((a_k, a_l), (a_p, a_q)) \in P_{R_2}$.

Denote by $\Delta_{\mathcal{A}}^{\delta}$ the set of all vectors $(v_1, \ldots, v_n) \in [0,1]^n$ satisfying all these (in)equalities. Equipped with this, we receive the following proposition which can be proven by slightly adapting the proof of [9, Prop. 3].

Proposition 1. *Let $\mathcal{D} = [\mathcal{G}, (\mathcal{A}_s)_{s \in S}]$ be a commonly scalable and δ-consistent decision system with common maximal and minimal elements $a_{k_1}, a_{k_2} \in A$, respectively, and let $A = \{a_1, \ldots, a_n\}$ and $S = \{s_1, \ldots s_m\}$. Let $\mathcal{M}$ be a convex and finitely generated credal set on $(S, 2^S)$. For $X \in \mathcal{G}$, denote by w_j the unique $i \in \{1, \ldots, n\}$ with $X(s_j) = a_i$. For every fixed $t \in \{1, \ldots, K\}$, consider the linear program*

$$\sum_{d=0}^{\ell-1} \left(\sum_{j=c_d+1}^{c_{d+1}} v_{w_j}^d \cdot \pi^{(t)}(\{s_j\}) \right) \longrightarrow \min_{(v_1^1, \ldots, v_n^1, \ldots, v_1^\ell, \ldots v_n^\ell)}$$

with constraints $(v_1^d, \ldots, v_n^d) \in \Delta_{\mathcal{A}_{S_d}}^{\delta}$ for every $d \in \{1, \ldots, \ell\}$ and the conventions $S_0 = \emptyset$ and $c_d = |\cup_{j=0}^d S_j|$. Denote by $opt(t)$ the optimal value of the linear program with t fixed. It then holds:

$$L_{(\mathcal{D}, \mathcal{M})}^{\delta}(X) = \min \left\{ opt(t) : t \in \{1, \ldots, K\} \right\}$$

We now turn to the basic linear program for checking $(\mathcal{D}, \mathcal{M})$-dominance. The proposition can be proven by slightly modifying the proof of [9, Prop. 5 i)].

Proposition 2. *Consider the same situation as in Proposition 1. For $X, Y \in \mathcal{G}$, denote by x_j and y_j the unique $i_X, i_Y \in \{1, \ldots, n\}$ such that $X(s_j) = a_{i_X}$ and $Y(s_j) = a_{i_Y}$ hold, respectively. For every fixed $t \in \{1, \ldots, K\}$, consider the linear optimization problem*

$$\sum_{d=0}^{\ell-1} \left(\sum_{j=c_d+1}^{c_{d+1}} (v_{x_j}^d - v_{y_j}^d) \cdot \pi^{(t)}(\{s_j\}) \right) \longrightarrow \min_{(v_1^1, \ldots, v_n^1, \ldots, v_1^\ell, \ldots v_n^\ell)}$$

with constraints $(v_1^d, \ldots, v_n^d) \in \Delta_{\mathcal{A}_{S_d}}^0$ for every $d \in \{1, \ldots, \ell\}$ and the conventions $S_0 = \emptyset$ and $c_d = | \cup_{j=0}^d S_j |$. Denote by $opt(t)$ the optimal value of the linear program with t fixed. It then holds:

$$X \geq_{(\mathcal{D}, \mathcal{M})} Y \quad \Leftrightarrow \quad \min\left\{ opt(t) : t \in \{1, \ldots, K\} \right\} \geq 0$$

We end the paragraph with two brief comments: First, to check whether an act X is undominated, Proposition 2 can simply be applied several times: If $Y \geq_{(\mathcal{D}, \mathcal{M})} X$ does *not* hold for all acts $Y \in \mathcal{G} \setminus \{X\}$, then one can directly infer the undominatedness of X. Second, both propositions can also be applied to precise probability measures. In this case, one simply chooses the credal set $\mathcal{M} = \{\pi\}$ as a singleton consisting only of the precise probability in question. The propositions then simplify considerably, since in each case only one instead of a set of linear programs has to be solved.

4.2 Approximating the Linear Programs by Grouping the States

The linear programs from Propositions 1 and 2 possess a separate set of variables and constraints for each preference system $\mathcal{A}_{S_d}$ under each partition class $S_d \in \mathbb{S}$. This may produce very complex optimization tasks if the considered decision problem is large. In this section, we will look at how to significantly reduce both the number of variables and the number of constraints without sacrificing too much accuracy. The main idea is to approximate the discussed basic algorithms by grouping the preference systems under in a certain sense similar states of nature. However, before turning to the approximations just mentioned, let us first note a fundamental property of preference and, as a consequence, also decision systems. It follows by observing that the intersection of pre-orders is again a pre-order that preserves minimal and maximal elements

Proposition 3. *Let $\mathcal{D} = [\mathcal{G}, (\mathcal{A}_s)_{s \in S}]$ be a commonly scalable decision system with state space S and let $\mathbb{V}$ be some partition of S. Then it holds that*

$$\mathcal{D}_{\mathbb{V}} := [\mathcal{G}, (\mathcal{A}_s^{\mathbb{V}})_{s \in S}]$$

is a commonly scalable decision system, where for every $V \in \mathbb{V}$ and $s \in V$:

$$\mathcal{A}_s^{\mathbb{V}} := \left[A, \bigcap_{d \in V} R_1^d, \bigcap_{d \in V} R_2^d \right].$$

Note that this implies $\mathcal{A}_{s_1}^{\mathbb{V}} = \mathcal{A}_{s_2}^{\mathbb{V}}$ for $s_1, s_2 \in V \in \mathbb{V}$, i.e. the preference systems are constant within the partition classes.

In what follows we are interested in partitions $\mathbb{V}$ of the state space S of which the partition $\mathbb{S}$ already discussed is a *refinement*: For every element $S_d \in \mathbb{S}$ there exists an element $V \in \mathbb{V}$ such that $S_d \subseteq V$. We denote this by $\mathbb{S} \# \mathbb{V}$ and also call $\mathbb{V}$ a *coarsening* of $\mathbb{S}$ in this case.

Let us assume that we already found a suitable partition $\mathbb{V} = \{V_1, \ldots, V_r\}$ of the state space, where $r \leq \ell$ and $\mathbb{S} \# \mathbb{V}$. Similar as already done for $\mathbb{S}$, we assume without loss of generality that for $c < d \in \{1, \ldots, r\}$, if $s_{i_1} \in V_c$ and $s_{i_2} \in V_d$, then $i_1 < i_2$. The idea to approximate our basic algorithms by less complex, but preferably information-preserving surrogate algorithms is then very simple: Instead of considering separate variables and constraints for each preference system under each state, we only consider separate variables and constraints for each element of the partition provided with the common preference system.

Technically, this is achieved by replacing the series of linear programming problems from Proposition 1 by the series of problems (for every $t \in \{1, \ldots, K\}$)

$$\sum_{d=0}^{r-1} \left(\sum_{j=p_d+1}^{p_{d+1}} v_{w_j}^d \cdot \pi^{(t)}(\{s_j\}) \right) \longrightarrow \min_{(v_1^1, \ldots, v_n^1, \ldots, v_1^r, \ldots v_n^r)}$$

with constraints $(v_1^d, \ldots, v_n^d) \in \Delta_{\mathcal{A}_{V_d}^{\mathbb{V}}}^{\delta}$ for every $d \in \{1, \ldots, r\}$ and the conventions $V_0 = \emptyset$ and $p_d = |\cup_{j=0}^d V_j|$ and by, respectively, replacing the series of linear programming problems from Proposition 2 by the series of linear programming problems (for every $t \in \{1, \ldots, K\}$)

$$\sum_{d=0}^{\ell-1} \left(\sum_{j=p_d+1}^{p_{d+1}} (v_{x_j}^d - v_{y_j}^d) \cdot \pi^{(t)}(\{s_j\}) \right) \longrightarrow \min_{(v_1^1, \ldots, v_n^1, \ldots, v_1^r, \ldots v_n^r)}$$

with constraints $(v_1^d, \ldots, v_n^d) \in \Delta_{\mathcal{A}_{V_d}^{\mathbb{V}}}^{0}$ for every $d \in \{1, \ldots, r\}$ and, again, $V_0 = \emptyset$ and $p_d = |\cup_{j=0}^d V_j|$. As the approximation quality heavily depends on it, the partition should be chosen in an information-preserving manner.

4.3   Different Choices for the Partition

So far, we have restricted the partition $\mathbb{V}$ of the state space only in that it had to be a coarsening of the partition $\mathbb{S}$. In this section, we will now briefly discuss two concrete choices for $\mathbb{V}$ that have other desirable properties besides this minimal requirement.[4] For that, assume that $(\mathcal{A}_s)_{s \in S}$ denotes the family of preference systems corresponding to a (potentially state-dependent) decision system.

Pattern Clustering: The first possibility for a partition of the state space is to group preference systems that contain a certain predefined preference pattern. Let $\mathcal{P}_1, \ldots, \mathcal{P}_z$, where $z < \ell$, denote pairwisely conflicting[5] preference systems on A. Then, a partition $\mathbb{V}_{pa}$ in at most $z + 1$ partition classes is obtained by

$$\mathbb{V}_{pa} = \Big\{ \{ s \in S : \mathcal{P}_t \preceq \mathcal{A}_s \} : t = 1, \ldots, z \Big\} \cup \Big\{ \{ s \in S : \mathcal{P}_t \not\preceq \mathcal{A}_s \text{ for all } t \} \Big\},$$

where for preference systems $\mathcal{B} = [A, R_1^B, R_2^B]$ and $\mathcal{C} = [A, R_1^C, R_2^C]$ we denote by $\mathcal{B} \preceq \mathcal{C}$ that $P_{R_1^B} \subseteq P_{R_1^C}$, $I_{R_1^B} \subseteq I_{R_1^C}$, $P_{R_2^B} \subseteq P_{R_2^C}$ and $I_{R_2^B} \subseteq I_{R_2^C}$ hold.

Distance-Based Clustering: Another possibility for finding a partition of the state space is to group states $s \in S$ whose associated ordinal relations R_1^s are not 'too far' away from each other: As described in [29, Algorithm 1], for some distance d between pre-orders (like, e.g., the normalized cardinality of their symmetric difference), one first picks a threshold $\xi \in (0, 1)$ and computes the distances $d(R_1^s, R_1^{s^*})$ for all $s \neq s^* \in S$. Afterwards, we put such states in the same cluster between which there exists a 'path of ordinal relations' with distances lower or equal than ξ. This gives a partition of S into some number of clusters $C_1, \ldots, C_b$. If one now extends the distance function to clusters by setting $D(C_{l_1}, C_{l_2}) := \min\{d(R_1^s, R_1^{s^*}) : s \in C_{l_1}, s^* \in C_{l_2}\}$, one can repeat this step until the partition does no longer change.

5   An Illustrative Toy Example

As an illustrative example, we consider the simple commonly scalable decision system given in Table 1 with only two acts taking values in the consequence set $A = \{a_*, b, c, d, a^*\}$, where a_* and a^* denote the common minimal and maximal elements of A, respectively. Under each state $s \in \{s_1, s_2, s_3\}$, we assume that R_1^s is given by the transitive hull of of the chain $a^* P_{R_1^s} d P_{R_1^s} c P_{R_1^s} b P_{R_1^s} a_*$. Thus, the ordinal part of the preferences is state independent. In contrast, the cardinal part of the preferences does depend on the state of nature: For $a_1, a_2 \in A$, denote by $e_{a_1 a_2}$ the pair (a_1, a_2). Then, under s_1 the cardinal part $R_2^{s_1}$ is given as

Table 1. A compact representation of the decision system.

	s_1	s_2	s_3
X_1	d	c	b
X_2	a^*	d	a_*

---

[4] One easily verifies that both of the partitions discussed in this section are indeed coarsenings of $\mathbb{S}$.

[5] For $d_1 \neq d_2 \in \{1, \ldots, z\}$ we have $\mathcal{U}_{\mathcal{P}_{d_1}} \cap \mathcal{U}_{\mathcal{P}_{d_2}} = \emptyset$. This makes $\mathbb{V}_{pa}$ a partition.

the transitive hull of $e_{ba_*}I_{R_2^{s_1}}e_{cb}I_{R_2^{s_1}}e_{dc}I_{R_2^{s_1}}e_{a^*d}$, under s_2 the cardinal part $R_2^{s_2}$ is given as the transitive hull of $e_{ba_*}P_{R_2^{s_2}}e_{cb}P_{R_2^{s_2}}e_{a^*d}P_{R_2^{s_2}}e_{dc}$ and under s_3 the cardinal part $R_2^{s_3}$ is given as the transitive hull of $e_{ba_*}P_{R_2^{s_3}}e_{a^*d}P_{R_2^{s_3}}e_{cb}P_{R_2^{s_3}}e_{dc}$.

We make the following three observations: (1) The preference system $\mathcal{A}_{s_1}$ *uniquely* specifies a utility function $u_{s_1} \in \mathcal{N}_{\mathcal{A}_{s_1}}$, which is given by

$$(u_{s_1}(a_*), u_{s_1}(b), u_{s_1}(c), u_{s_1}(d), u_{s_1}(a^*)) = (0, 0.25, 0.5, 0.75, 1).$$

(2) The preference system $\mathcal{A}_{s_2}$ restricts all utility functions $u_{s_2} \in \mathcal{N}_{\mathcal{A}_{s_2}}$ to satisfy the inequality $u_{s_2}(d) - u_{s_2}(c) \leq 0.25$. (3) The preference system $\mathcal{A}_{s_3}$ restricts all utility functions $u_{s_3} \in \mathcal{N}_{\mathcal{A}_{s_3}}$ to satisfy the inequality $u_{s_3}(b) - u_{s_3}(a_*) \geq 0.25$.

Now, assume the uncertainty about the states of nature is characterized by the credal set $\mathcal{M} = \{\pi : \pi(\{s_1\}) \leq 0.2 \ \wedge \ \pi(\{s_2\}) \leq 0.2\}$. Then, for arbitrary $\pi \in \mathcal{M}$, $u_{s_1} \in \mathcal{N}_{\mathcal{A}_{s_1}}$, $u_{s_2} \in \mathcal{N}_{\mathcal{A}_{s_2}}$ and $u_{s_3} \in \mathcal{N}_{\mathcal{A}_{s_3}}$ the expression $E_{(\pi,u)}(X_1) - E_{(\pi,u)}(X_2)$ can be computed by

$$-\underbrace{\pi_1(u_{s_1}(a^*) - u_{s_1}(d))}_{\leq 0.2 \cdot 0.25} - \underbrace{\pi_2(u_{s_2}(d) - u_{s_2}(c))}_{\leq 0.2 \cdot 0.25} + \underbrace{\pi_3(u_{s_3}(b) - u_{s_3}(a_*))}_{\geq 0.6 \cdot 0.25} > 0.$$

Thus, as the probability and the utility are arbitrary, this inequality demonstrates that $X_1 \geq_{(\mathcal{D},\mathcal{M})} X_2$. An approximation under distance-based clustering yields the same: Since the ordinal relations are state-independent, any distance produces only one cluster $\{S\}$. Thus, we obtain a state-independent decision system and the intersection of $R_2^{s_1}$, $R_2^{s_2}$ and $R_2^{s_3}$ contains (e_{ba_*}, e_{dc}) and (e_{ba_*}, e_{a^*d}). Thus, the above inequality still holds since $\pi_1 + \pi_2 < \pi_3$ for all $\pi \in \mathcal{M}$.

6   Outlook

In this paper, we have presented some initial ideas on decision theory with state-dependent preference systems. Besides the conceptual foundation and the differentiation from existing notions of state-dependence, we have focused on the computation of the presented decision criteria. We proposed different linear programs and showed how they can be approximated by less complex ones if the states are clustered appropriately. While we think that our paper gives a solid formal basis for decision making with state-dependent preference systems, we are also aware there is still a lot left open for future research, including:

- **Comparison of Cluster Techniques:** To be able to assess the quality of the different cluster techniques from Sect. 4.3, a systematic comparative analysis of the exact and approximate algorithms – both in terms of similarity of solutions and of computational complexity – would be necessary. In this way, it would be possible to systematically investigate which technique to use in what type of concrete application example.
- **Other Approximation Approaches:** If the credal set in the criteria from Sect. 3.3 arises from a two-monotone lower probability, the computation of

the associated criterion values simplifies considerably (compare the discussion in [9, p. 120]). If the credal set does not arise from a two-monotone lower probability, then an alternative approximation approach would be to approximate it by one, using the techniques described in [3,18]. Such approximation has recently been carried out, e.g., in [4,19]. Here, of course, it would be of particular interest to combine both approximation approaches.

- **Adapt Other Decision Criteria:** As already briefly discussed at the end of Sect. 3.3, there exist many optimality criteria for decision making with imprecise probabilities apart from the ones discussed here. An adaptation of these criteria to the state-dependent setting discussed in this paper would certainly deserve further research.

- **Real World Application:** Finally, the framework presented in this paper needs to be applied and tested in real world decision making problems in order to practically analyze what are the benefits and shortcomings compared to classical – state-independent – decision models.

Acknowledgments. We thank the three anonymous reviewers for their constructive and insightful comments that helped to improve the paper.

References

1. Anscombe, F., Aumann, R.: A definition of subjective probability. Ann. Math. Statist. **43**(1), 199–205 (1963)
2. Baccelli, J.: The problem of state-dependent utility: a reappraisal. Br. J. Philos. Sci. **72**(2), 617–634 (2020)
3. Bronevich, A., Augustin, T.: Approximation of coherent lower probabilities by 2-monotone measures. In: Augustin, T., Coolen, F., Moral, S., Troffaes, M. (eds), Proceedings of Sixth Symposium on Imprecise Probability: Theories and Applications, pp. 61–69. SIPTA (2009)
4. Cinfrignini, A., Petturiti, D., Vantaggi, B.: Envelopes of equivalent martingale measures and a generalized no-arbitrage principle in a finite setting. arXiv preprint arXiv:2107.01240 (2021)
5. De Donder, P., Leroux, M.-L.: Long term care insurance with state-dependent preferences. Health Econ. **30**(12), 3074–3086 (2021)
6. Jansen, C., Augustin, T., Schollmeyer, G.: Quantifying degrees of E-admissibility in decision making with imprecise probabilities. In: Augustin, T., Cozman, F., Wheeler, G. (eds.), Reflections on the Foundations of Probability and Statistics: Essays in Honor of Teddy Seidenfeld, Theory and Decision Library A. Springer (in press)
7. Jansen, C., Blocher, H., Augustin, T., Schollmeyer, G.: Information efficient learning of complexly structured preferences: elicitation procedures and their application to decision making under uncertainty. Int. J. Approx. Reason. **144**, 69–91 (2022)
8. Jansen, C., Augustin, T., Schollmeyer, G.: Decision theory meets linear optimization beyond computation. In: Antonucci, A., Cholvy, L., Papini, O. (eds.) ECSQARU 2017. LNCS (LNAI), vol. 10369, pp. 329–339. Springer, Cham (2017). https://doi.org/10.1007/978-3-319-61581-3_30
9. Jansen, C., Schollmeyer, G., Augustin, T.: Concepts for decision making under severe uncertainty with partial ordinal and partial cardinal preferences. Int. J. Approx. Reason. **98**, 112–131 (2018)

10. Kahneman, D., Tversky, A.: Prospect theory: an analysis of decision under risk. Econometrica **47**, 263–291 (1979)
11. Karni, E.: Decision Making Under Uncertainty: The Case of State-Dependent Preferences. Harvard University Press (1985)
12. Karni, E.: State-Dependent Preferences. In: Vernengo, M., Perez Caldentey, E., Rosser Jr, B. (eds.) The New Palgrave Dictionary of Economics. Palgrave Macmillan (2018)
13. Kikuti, D., Cozman, F., Shirota Filho, R.: Sequential decision making with partially ordered preferences. Artif. Intell. **175**, 1346–1365 (2011)
14. Krantz, D., Luce, D., Suppes, P., Tversky, A.: Foundations of Measurement. Vol. I: Additive and Polynomial Representations. Academic Press (1971)
15. Levi, I.: On indeterminate probabilities. J. Philos. **71**, 391–418 (1974)
16. Loomes, G., Sugden, R.: Regret theory: an alternative theory of rational choice under uncertainty. Econ. J. **92**(386), 805–824 (1982)
17. Manski, C., Sanstad, A., De Canio, S.: Addressing partial identification in climate modeling and policy analysis. Proc. Natl. Acad. Sci. **118**(15), 1–10 (2021)
18. Montes, I., Miranda, E., Vicig, P.: 2-Monotone outer approximations of coherent lower probabilities. Int. J. Approx. Reason. **113**, 14–38 (2019)
19. Petturiti, D., Vantaggi, B.: Conditional submodular Choquet expected values and conditional coherent risk measures. Int. J. Approx. Reason. **101**, 181–205 (2018)
20. Savage, L.: The theory of statistical decision. J. Am. Statist. Assoc. **46**(253), 55–67 (1951)
21. Schervish, M., Seidenfeld, T., Kadane, J.: State-dependent utilities. J. Am. Statist. Assoc. **85**(411), 840–847 (1990)
22. Schervish, M., Seidenfeld, T., Kadane, J.: Shared preferences and state-dependent utilities. Manag. Sci. **37**(12), 1575–1589 (1991)
23. Stoye, J.: Axioms for minimax regret choice correspondences. J. Econ. Theory **146**(6), 2226–2251 (2011)
24. Troffaes, M.: Decision making under uncertainty using imprecise probabilities. Int. J. Approx. Reason. **45**, 17–29 (2007)
25. Troffaes, M., Hable, R.: Computation. In: Augustin, T., Coolen, F., de Cooman, G., Troffaes, M. (eds.) Introduction to Imprecise Probabilities. Wiley (2014)
26. Utkin, L., Augustin, A.: Powerful algorithms for decision making under partial prior information and general ambiguity attitudes. In: Cozman, F., Nau, R., Seidenfeld, T. (eds.) Proceedings of Fourth Symposium on Imprecise Probability: Theories and Applications, pp. 349–358. SIPTA (2005)
27. Walley, P.: Statistical Reasoning with Imprecise Probabilities. Chapman and Hall (1991)
28. Wei, J., Shen, Y., Zhao, Q.: Portfolio selection with regime-switching and state-dependent preferences. J. Comput. Appl. Math. **365**, 1–27 (2020)
29. Zhu, C., Wen, F., Sun, J.: A rank-order distance based clustering algorithm for face tagging. In: Conference on Computer Vision and Pattern Recognition, pp. 481–488 (2011)

Inner Approximations of Credal Sets
by Non-additive Measures

Enrique Miranda(✉) [ID], Ignacio Montes[ID], and Andrés Presa

Department of Statistics and Operations Research, University of Oviedo,
Oviedo, Spain
{mirandaenrique,imontes,UO264980}@uniovi.es

Abstract. We consider the problem of transforming a coherent lower probability into another one that (i) belongs to some subclass with better mathematical properties, such as 2- or complete monotonicity; (ii) is at least as informative as the original model, while being as close as possible to it. We show that the problem can be approached in terms of linear programming and that it can be connected with the one of determining the incenter of a credal set. Finally, we compare the performance of the original and the transformed model in a decision problem.

Keywords: Coherent lower probabilities · 2-Monotone capacities · Belief functions · Distortion models · Optimality criteria

1 Introduction

This paper deals with *coherent lower probabilities*, that are non-additive measures that can be obtained as lower envelopes of a closed and convex set of probability measures. They constitute an *imprecise probability* model [1], and include as particular cases the majority of models for uncertainty and imprecision that have been proposed in the literature. However, this generality comes with a price: given a coherent lower probability, there is not an easy procedure for determining the extreme points of the associated set of probabilities, and neither there is a unique extension to expectation operators; this hampers the use of coherent lower probabilities in practice. This motivates the quest for transformations of a coherent lower probability into another one with better mathematical properties. In past works [9,12,13] we considered *outer approximations* of a coherent lower probability, that were less informative than the original model. Here we move in the opposite direction, and look for transformations that shrink the credal set and where the associated lower probability belongs to a subfamily of interest.

In Sect. 2, we consider the inner approximations of a coherent lower probability by 2-monotone capacities or belief functions, and compare the results with those in [9,12,13]; in Sect. 3, we consider the particular case of distortion models, and establish a connection with the notion of incenter of a credal set from [7,8];

Supported by grant PGC2018-098623-B-I00.

Sect. 4 studies the relationship between the optimal alternatives with respect to the initial and the transformed model according to a number of criteria; and Sect. 5 gives some final comments and remarks. Due to the space limitations, proofs have been omitted.

2 Inner Approximations of Coherent Lower Probabilities

Let $\mathcal{X}$ be a finite possibility space. We call *lower probability* a function $\underline{P} : \mathcal{P}(\mathcal{X}) \to [0,1]$ that is monotone ($A \subseteq B \Rightarrow \underline{P}(A) \leq \underline{P}(B)$) and normalised ($\underline{P}(\emptyset) = 0, \underline{P}(\mathcal{X}) = 1$). Its associated set of dominating probabilities, or *credal set*, is given by:

$$\mathcal{M}(\underline{P}) = \{P \text{ probability measure } | P(A) \geq \underline{P}(A) \ \forall A \subseteq \mathcal{X}\}.$$

Following [17], $\underline{P}$ *avoids sure loss* when $\mathcal{M}(\underline{P}) \neq \emptyset$, and it is *coherent* when it is the lower envelope of $\mathcal{M}(\underline{P})$: $\underline{P}(A) = \min_{P \in \mathcal{M}(\underline{P})} P(A)$ for every $A \subseteq \mathcal{X}$. Its conjugate *upper* probability is given by $\overline{P}(A) = 1 - \underline{P}(A^c)$ for every $A \subseteq \mathcal{X}$.

As particular instances of coherent lower probabilities, we have those that are 2-monotone, meaning that

$$\underline{P}(A \cup B) + \underline{P}(A \cap B) \geq \underline{P}(A) + \underline{P}(B) \quad \forall A, B \subseteq \mathcal{X};$$

they are called *completely monotone*, or a *belief function*, when

$$\underline{P}\left(\cup_{i=1}^k A_i\right) \geq \sum_{\emptyset \neq I \subseteq \{1,\ldots,k\}} (-1)^{|I|+1} \underline{P}\left(\cap_{i \in I} A_i\right)$$

for every $A_1, \ldots, A_k$ in $\mathcal{P}(\mathcal{X})$ and every $k \in \mathbb{N}$. We denote by $\mathcal{C}_2$ and $\mathcal{C}_\infty$ the families of 2-monotone lower probabilities and belief functions, respectively.

Any coherent lower probability $\underline{P}$ can be alternatively expressed using the *Möbius* transformation

$$m_{\underline{P}}(A) = \sum_{B \subseteq A} (-1)^{|A \setminus B|} \underline{P}(B) \quad \forall A \subseteq \mathcal{X},$$

and conversely $m_{\underline{P}}$ allows to retrieve the initial coherent lower probability by:

$$\underline{P}(A) = \sum_{B \subseteq A} m_{\underline{P}}(B) \quad \forall A \subseteq \mathcal{X}.$$

Definition 1. *Let $\underline{P}$ be a coherent lower probability and let $\mathcal{C}$ be a class of coherent lower probabilities. $\underline{Q} \in \mathcal{C}$ is an* inner approximation *of $\underline{P}$ in $\mathcal{C}$ if $\underline{Q}(E) \geq \underline{P}(E)$ for every $E \subseteq \mathcal{X}$. It is called* non-dominating *inner approximation in $\mathcal{C}$ if there is no other $\underline{Q}' \in \mathcal{C}$ such that $\underline{P} \leq \underline{Q}' \nleq \underline{Q}$.*

In terms of credal sets, $\underline{Q}$ is an inner approximation of $\underline{P}$ if $\mathcal{M}(\underline{P}) \supseteq \mathcal{M}(\underline{Q})$ and it is non-dominating if there is no other $\underline{Q}' \in \mathcal{C}$ such that $\mathcal{M}(\underline{P}) \supseteq \mathcal{M}(\underline{Q}') \supsetneq \mathcal{M}(\underline{Q})$.

Following our previous work in [9,12,13], one way of obtaining inner approximations of a coherent lower probability $\underline{P}$ in a subclass $\mathcal{C}$ is to consider those that minimise the distance with $\underline{P}$, in the sense of Baroni and Vicig [2]:

$$d_{BV}(\underline{P}, \underline{Q}) = \sum_{E \subseteq \mathcal{X}} |\underline{P}(E) - \underline{Q}(E)| = \sum_{E \subseteq \mathcal{X}} \left| \underline{P}(E) - \sum_{B \subseteq E} m_{\underline{Q}}(B) \right|. \qquad (1)$$

Given a family $\mathcal{C}$ of non-additive measures, we shall denote by $\mathcal{C}_{BV}(\underline{P})$ the class of optimal inner approximations, in the sense that they minimise the BV distance:

$$\mathcal{C}^{BV}(\underline{P}) = \left\{ \underline{Q} \in \mathcal{C} \mid \underline{Q} \geq \underline{P}, d_{BV}(\underline{P}, \underline{Q}) = \min_{\underline{Q}' \in \mathcal{C}} d_{BV}(\underline{P}, \underline{Q}') \right\}.$$

Note that when $\underline{Q}$ is an inner approximation of $\underline{P}$ we can get rid of the absolute values in Eq. (1), since in that case $d_{BV}(\underline{P}, \underline{Q}) = \sum_{E \subseteq \mathcal{X}} (\underline{Q}(E) - \underline{P}(E))$. Moreover, the connections between the different properties of non-additive measures allow us to establish inclusion relationships (for instance $\mathcal{C}_\infty \subseteq \mathcal{C}_2$). In this respect, the following simple result shall come in handy:

Proposition 1. *Let $\underline{P}$ be a coherent lower probability. Consider two classes of coherent lower probabilities $\mathcal{C}$ and $\mathcal{C}'$ such that $\mathcal{C}' \subseteq \mathcal{C}$.*

1. *If $\underline{Q}$ is a non-dominating inner approximation of $\underline{P}$ in $\mathcal{C}'$, then it is also a non-dominating inner approximation of $\underline{P}'$ in $\mathcal{C}'$ for some non-dominating inner approximation $\underline{P}'$ of $\underline{P}$ in $\mathcal{C}$.*
2. *If moreover $\underline{Q} \in \mathcal{C}'^{BV}(\underline{P})$, then also $\underline{Q} \in \mathcal{C}'^{BV}(\underline{P}')$ for some $\underline{P}' \in \mathcal{C}^{BV}(\underline{P})$.*

Let us consider the problem of inner approximating a coherent lower probability $\underline{P}$ by another one $\underline{Q}$ that is 2- or completely monotone. One important assumption throughout this paper is that there are no zero lower probabilities involved, in the sense that $\underline{P}(A) > 0$ for every $A \neq \emptyset$. This helps simplifying some of the results we shall establish later on.

It is straightforward to establish the following result, using similar arguments to those in [9,12,13]:

Proposition 2. *Let $\underline{P}$ be a coherent lower probability. Consider the following conditions:*

$$\sum_{A \subseteq \mathcal{X}} m_{\underline{Q}}(A) = 1, \quad m_{\underline{Q}}(\emptyset) = 0. \qquad (2\text{monot.}1)$$

$$\sum_{\{x_i, x_j\} \subseteq B \subseteq A} m_{\underline{Q}}(B) \geq 0, \quad \forall A \subseteq \mathcal{X}, \forall x_i, x_j \in A, x_i \neq x_j. \qquad (2\text{monot.}2)$$

$$m_{\underline{Q}}(\{x_i\}) \geq 0, \quad \forall x_i \in \mathcal{X}. \qquad (2\text{monot.}3)$$

$$\sum_{B \subseteq E} m_{\underline{Q}}(B) \geq \underline{P}(E) \quad \forall E \neq \mathcal{X}, \emptyset. \qquad (2\text{monot.}4)$$

$$m_{\underline{Q}}(A) \geq 0 \quad \forall A \subseteq \mathcal{X}. \qquad (\text{C-monot.})$$

1. *The optimal solutions of the linear programming problem of minimising Eq.* (1) *subject to* (2monot.1) $\div$ (2monot.4) *are non-dominating inner approximations of $\underline{P}$ in C_2.*
2. *The optimal solutions of the linear programming problem of minimising Eq.* (1) *subject to* (2monot.1), (2monot.4) *and* (C-monot.) *are non-dominating inner approximations of $\underline{P}$ in C_∞.*

Example 1. Let $\mathcal{X} = \{x_1, x_2, x_3, x_4\}$ and let $\underline{P}$ be the coherent lower probability on $\mathcal{P}(\mathcal{X})$ that is the lower envelope of the mass functions $(0.25, 0.25, 0.25, 0.25)$ and $(0.5, 0.5, 0, 0)$. This coherent lower probability is not 2-monotone, because

$$\underline{P}(\{x_1, x_2, x_3\}) + \underline{P}(\{x_3\}) = 0.75 < 1 = \underline{P}(\{x_1, x_3\}) + \underline{P}(\{x_2, x_3\}).$$

If we solve the linear programming problem in Proposition 2 we obtain that the 2-monotone inner approximations that minimise the BV-distance with $\underline{P}$ correspond to the probability measures in $\mathcal{M}(\underline{P})$; as a consequence, they also coincide with the non-dominating inner approximations in C_∞. ◆

Although in this example the non-dominating inner approximations in C_2 and C_∞ coincide, this will not be the case in general: simply take a coherent lower probability $\underline{P}$ that is 2-monotone but not completely monotone. The example also shows that, in contradistinction with what we proved in [12] for the outer approximations, the non-dominating inner approximations in C_2 need not agree with $\underline{P}$ on singletons.

We see from the example that there may be more than one non-dominating inner approximation of a coherent lower probability $\underline{P}$ in C_2 or in C_∞. Considering the lessons learned from [9], we believe that the best procedure to choose one non-dominating inner approximation is to select the one that minimises the quadratic distance, given by:

$$d_q(\underline{P}, \underline{Q}) = \sum_{E \subseteq \mathcal{X}} \left(\underline{P}(E) - \underline{Q}(E)\right)^2 = \sum_{E \subseteq \mathcal{X}} \left(\underline{P}(E) - \sum_{B \subseteq E} m_{\underline{Q}}(B)\right)^2, \qquad (2)$$

among those in $C_2^{BV}(\underline{P})$ or $C_\infty^{BV}(\underline{P})$ (that is, among the optimal solutions of the linear programming problem). We obtain the following result:

Proposition 3. *Let $\underline{P}$ be a coherent lower probability on $\mathcal{P}(\mathcal{X})$.*

1. *The quadratic programming problem of minimising Eq.* (2) *subject to* (2monot.1) $\div$ (2monot.4) *and*

$$d_{BV}(\underline{P}, \underline{Q}) = \min_{\underline{Q}' \in C_2} d_{BV}(\underline{P}, \underline{Q}') \qquad \text{(2.monot-BV)}$$

has a unique solution which is a non-dominating inner approximation in C_2.
2. *The quadratic programming problem of minimising Eq.* (2) *subject to* (2monot.1), (2monot.4), (C-monot.) *and*

$$d_{BV}(\underline{P}, \underline{Q}) = \min_{\underline{Q}' \in C_\infty} d_{BV}(\underline{P}, \underline{Q}') \qquad \text{(C.monot-BV)}$$

has a unique solution which is a non-dominating inner approximation in C_∞.

Note that the restrictions 2.monot-BV and C.monot-BV are necessary, in that if we do not impose them the solutions of the quadratic problem may not minimise the distance of Baroni and Vicig; we are thus imposing a lexicographic order between this and the quadratic distance.

3 Incenters of Credal Sets

We shift our attention to the problem of inner approximating a coherent lower probability by some *distortion model* [10,11]. Distortion models are determined by a probability measure P_0, a distorting function d and a distortion parameter δ. These elements determine the set of probability measures given by:

$$B_d^\delta(P_0) = \{P \mid d(P, P_0) \leq \delta\}.$$

Our focus in this paper shall be on the linear vacuous [17], pari mutuel [14,17] and total variation [15] models. These classes will be denoted by $\mathcal{C}_{\mathrm{LV}}$, $\mathcal{C}_{\mathrm{PMM}}$ and $\mathcal{C}_{\mathrm{TV}}$, respectively. Other distortion models of interest are the constant odds ratio [3], the ones associated with the L_1 or Kolmogorov distances [6,11], or those obtained as monotone transformations of a probability measure [4]. We refer to [5,10,11] for a comparative analysis.

3.1 Inner Approximations in $\mathcal{C}_{\mathrm{LV}}$

Definition 2. *Given a probability measure P_0 and a distortion parameter $\delta \in (0,1)$, the associated* linear vacuous *model is the coherent lower probability*

$$\underline{P}_{\mathrm{LV}}(\mathcal{X}) = 1 \quad and \quad \underline{P}_{\mathrm{LV}}(A) = (1-\delta)P_0(A) \ \forall A \subset \mathcal{X}. \tag{3}$$

Its associated credal set can be represented as:

$$\mathcal{M}(\underline{P}_{LV}) = \{\delta P + (1-\delta)P_0 \mid P \in \mathbb{P}(\mathcal{X})\}.$$

The existence of an inner approximation of a coherent lower probability in $\mathcal{C}_{\mathrm{LV}}$ can be easily characterised using convex combinations of extreme points of $\mathcal{M}(\underline{P}_{LV})$:

Proposition 4. *Let $\underline{P}$ be a coherent lower probability with conjugate upper probability $\overline{P}$. There exists a linear vacuous model $\underline{P}_{\mathrm{LV}}$ such that $\underline{P} \leq \underline{P}_{\mathrm{LV}}$ if and only if $\underline{P}(A) < \overline{P}(A)$ for any $A \neq \emptyset, \mathcal{X}$.*

The inner approximation in $\mathcal{C}_{\mathrm{LV}}$ may not be unique.

Example 2. Consider a three-element possibility space $\mathcal{X} = \{x_1, x_2, x_3\}$ and the coherent lower probability $\underline{P}$ given by:

A	$\{x_1\}$	$\{x_2\}$	$\{x_3\}$	$\{x_1, x_2\}$	$\{x_1, x_3\}$	$\{x_2, x_3\}$
$\underline{P}(A)$	0.2	0.05	0.1	0.4	0.4	0.5
$\underline{P}_{\mathrm{LV}}^1(A)$	0.2	0.2	0.3	0.4	0.5	0.5
$\underline{P}_{\mathrm{LV}}^2(A)$	0.2	0.3	0.2	0.5	0.4	0.5

Then the lower probabilities $\underline{P}_{\mathrm{LV}}^1$ and $\underline{P}_{\mathrm{LV}}^2$ in the table above are two different elements of $\mathcal{C}_{\mathrm{LV}}$. ♦

On the other hand, it is possible to characterise the set of non-dominating inner approximations of a coherent lower probability $\underline{P}$ in $\mathcal{C}_{\mathrm{LV}}$. For this aim, for any $\delta \in (0,1)$ we define the lower probability $\underline{Q}_\delta$ by:

$$\underline{Q}_\delta(\mathcal{X}) = 1, \quad \text{and} \quad \underline{Q}_\delta(A) = \frac{\underline{P}(A)}{1-\delta} \ \forall A \subset \mathcal{X}.$$

Proposition 5. *1. There exists a linear vacuous model with a distortion factor δ that inner approximates $\underline{P}$ if and only if $\underline{Q}_\delta$ avoids sure loss.*
2. In that case, for any $P_0 \in \mathcal{M}(\underline{Q}_\delta)$ the linear vacuous model determined by (P_0, δ) by Eq. (3) determines an inner approximation of $\underline{P}$ in $\mathcal{C}_{\mathrm{LV}}$.
3. The set $\Lambda_{\mathrm{LV}} := \{\delta \in (0,1) \mid \mathcal{M}(\underline{Q}_\delta) \neq \emptyset\}$ has a maximum value δ_{LV}.

It is not difficult to see that, given an inner approximation $\underline{Q}$ of $\underline{P}$ in $\mathcal{C}_{\mathrm{LV}}$ determined by (P_0, δ), the distance $d_{\mathrm{LV}}(\underline{P}, \underline{Q})$ depends on δ only, and it is minimised when δ is maximised. Therefore, the non-dominating inner approximations are the ones associated with linear vacuous models with distortion factor δ_{LV}, where δ_{LV} is the maximum of Λ_{LV}, that exists by Proposition 5, and P_0 is any element of $\mathcal{M}(\underline{Q}_{\delta_{\mathrm{LV}}})$.

Next we give a manageable expression of the value δ_{LV}. Let

$$\mathbb{A}(\mathcal{X}) = \left\{ \mathcal{A} = (A_i)_{i=1,\ldots,k} \mid \exists \beta_\mathcal{A} \in \mathbb{N} \text{ such that } \sum_{i=1}^{k} I_{A_i} = \beta_\mathcal{A} \right\}$$

be the class of all finite families of subsets of $\mathcal{X}$ such that every $x \in \mathcal{X}$ belongs to the same number of elements in the family.

Theorem 1. *Let $\underline{P}$ be a coherent lower probability satisfying $\underline{P}(A) < \overline{P}(A)$ for every $A \neq \emptyset, \mathcal{X}$. Then:*

$$\delta_{\mathrm{LV}} = \min_{\mathcal{A} \in \mathbb{A}(\mathcal{X})} \left(1 - \frac{1}{\beta_\mathcal{A}} \sum_{A \in \mathcal{A}} \underline{P}(A)\right). \tag{4}$$

If in addition $\underline{P}$ is 2-monotone, then

$$\delta_{\mathrm{LV}} = \min_{\mathcal{A} \in \mathbb{A}^*(\mathcal{X})} \left(1 - \sum_{A \in \mathcal{A}} \underline{P}(A), \frac{\sum_{A \in \mathcal{A}} \overline{P}(A) - 1}{|\mathcal{A}| - 1}\right), \tag{5}$$

where $\mathbb{A}^*(\mathcal{X})$ denotes the set of partitions of $\mathcal{X}$.

The proof of Eq. (4) is based on suitable manipulations of the definition of avoiding sure loss from [17], while that of Eq. (5) is related to some results from the framework of incenters of credal sets [7,8] (see Theorem 3 later on).

Theorem 1 and Proposition 1 give us a simple procedure to obtain a non-dominating linear vacuous model inner approximating $\underline{P}$: we first obtain a 2-monotone non-dominating inner approximation $\underline{Q}$ of $\underline{P}$ (for instance one minimising the BV-distance, following the linear programming approach described in Sect. 2), and then apply Theorem 1 to $\underline{Q}$. This procedure is graphically represented in Fig. 1.

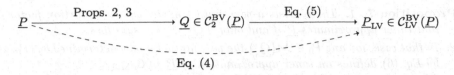

Fig. 1. Graphical description of the procedure for obtaining an element of $\mathcal{C}_{\mathrm{LV}}^{\mathrm{BV}}(\underline{P})$.

3.2 Inner Approximations in $\mathcal{C}_{\mathrm{PMM}}$

The second family of distortion models we study is the pari mutuel:

Definition 3. *Given a probability measure P_0 and a distortion parameter $\delta > 0$, the associated* pari mutuel *model is defined as the coherent conjugate lower and upper probabilities:*

$$\underline{P}_{\mathrm{PMM}}(A) = \max\{(1+\delta)P_0(A) - \delta, 0\} \tag{6}$$
$$\overline{P}_{\mathrm{PMM}}(A) = \min\{(1+\delta)P_0(A), 1\} \quad \forall A \subseteq \mathcal{X}.$$

Next, we follow the same steps as in previous subsection in the analysis of the inner approximations in $\mathcal{C}_{\mathrm{PMM}}$.

Proposition 6. *Let $\underline{P}$ be a coherent lower probability with conjugate upper probability $\overline{P}$. There exists an inner approximation of $\underline{P}$ in $\mathcal{C}_{\mathrm{PMM}}$ if and only if $\underline{P}(A) < \overline{P}(A)$ for any $A \neq \emptyset, \mathcal{X}$.*

There may be more than one non-dominating inner approximation:

Example 3. Consider the same coherent lower probability as in Example 2. The coherent lower probabilities $\underline{Q}_{\mathrm{PMM}}^1$ and $\underline{Q}_{\mathrm{PMM}}^2$ with conjugates given by:

A	$\{x_1\}$	$\{x_2\}$	$\{x_3\}$	$\{x_1, x_2\}$	$\{x_1, x_3\}$	$\{x_2, x_3\}$
$\overline{Q}_{\mathrm{PMM}}^1(A)$	0.5	0.4	0.4	0.9	0.9	0.8
$\overline{Q}_{\mathrm{PMM}}^2(A)$	0.5	0.35	0.45	0.85	0.95	0.8

are two different non-dominating inner approximations in $\mathcal{C}_{\mathrm{PMM}}$. ◆

Next we are going to characterise the inner approximations in $\mathcal{C}_{\mathrm{PMM}}$ of a coherent lower probability $\underline{P}$. For any $\delta > 0$, let us define the upper probability:

$$\overline{Q}_\delta = \begin{cases} \frac{\overline{P}(A)}{1+\delta} & \text{if } \overline{P}(A) < 1. \\ 1 & \text{if } \overline{P}(A) = 1. \end{cases} \quad \underline{Q}_\delta(A) = 1 - \overline{Q}_\delta(A^c) \ \forall A \subseteq \mathcal{X}.$$

With the same steps as for the LV model, we obtain the following result.

Proposition 7. *1. There exists a pari mutuel model with a distortion factor δ that inner approximates $\underline{P}$ if and only if $\underline{Q}_\delta$ avoids sure loss.*

2. In that case, for any $P_0 \in \mathcal{M}(\underline{Q}_\delta)$ the pari mutuel model determined by (P_0, δ) by Eq. (6) defines an inner approximation of $\underline{P}$ in $\mathcal{C}_{\mathrm{PMM}}$.

3. The set $\Lambda_{\mathrm{PMM}} := \{\delta \in (0,1) \mid \mathcal{M}(\underline{Q}_\delta) \neq \emptyset\}$ has a maximum value δ_{PMM}.

As was the case in Sect. 3.1, the BV distance between the initial and the transformed models only depends on the distortion parameter δ, and it is minimised when δ is maximised. Our aim now is to give a more manageable expression of the maximum δ_{PMM} of the set Λ_{PMM}, which exists from the previous result.

Theorem 2. *Let $\underline{P}$ be a coherent lower probability with conjugate $\overline{P}$ satisfying $\underline{P}(A) < \overline{P}(A)$ for every $A \neq \emptyset, \mathcal{X}$. Then:*

$$\delta_{\mathrm{PMM}} = \min_{\mathcal{A} \in \mathbb{A}(\mathcal{X})} \left(\frac{1}{\beta_{\mathcal{A}}} \sum_{A \in \mathcal{A}} \overline{P}(A) - 1 \right). \tag{7}$$

If in addition $\underline{P}$ is 2-monotone, then

$$\delta_{\mathrm{PMM}} = \min_{\mathcal{A} \in \mathbb{A}^*(\mathcal{X})} \left(\sum_{A \in \mathcal{A}} \overline{P}(A) - 1, \frac{1 - \sum_{A \in \mathcal{A}} \underline{P}(A)}{|\mathcal{A}| - 1} \right). \tag{8}$$

As with the LV model, Theorem 2 together with Proposition 1 give a procedure for computing the value δ_{PMM}. It is illustrated in Fig. 2.

$$\underline{P}, \overline{P} \xrightarrow{\text{Props. 2, 3}} \underline{Q} \in \mathcal{C}_2^{\mathrm{BV}}(\underline{P}) \xrightarrow{\text{Eq. (8)}} \underline{P}_{\mathrm{PMM}} \in \mathcal{C}_{\mathrm{PMM}}^{\mathrm{BV}}(\underline{P})$$

Eq. (7)

Fig. 2. Graphical description of the procedure for obtaining an element of $\mathcal{C}_{\mathrm{PMM}}^{\mathrm{BV}}(\underline{P})$.

3.3 Inner Approximations in $\mathcal{C}_{\mathrm{TV}}$

The third and last distortion model we investigate in this paper is the total variation model.

Definition 4. *Given a probability measure P_0 and a distortion parameter $\delta \in (0,1)$, the associated total variation model is defined as the coherent lower probability:*

$$\underline{P}_{\mathrm{TV}}(\mathcal{X}) = 1 \quad and \quad \underline{P}_{\mathrm{TV}}(A) = \max\{0, P_0(A) - \delta\} \quad \forall A \subset \mathcal{X}. \tag{9}$$

This corresponds to the lower envelope of the set of those probability measures whose total variation distance with P_0 is at most δ. Our first result characterises the existence of a TV inner approximation in the same conditions as in the other two cases previously analysed. Note that, when $\underline{P}(A) > 0$ for any non-trivial event A, as we are assuming in the paper, any inner approximation Q of $\underline{P}$ in $\mathcal{C}_{TV}$ will also satisfy $\underline{Q}(A) > 0$ for any $A \neq \emptyset$, which means that its expression can be simplified to $\underline{Q}(A) = P_0(A) - \delta$ for any $A \neq \emptyset, \mathcal{X}$ and $\underline{Q}(\emptyset) = 0, \underline{Q}(\mathcal{X}) = 1$.

Proposition 8. *Let $\underline{P}$ be a coherent lower probability with conjugate upper probability $\overline{P}$. There exists a total variation model $\underline{P}_{TV}$ such that $\underline{P} \leq \underline{P}_{TV}$ if and only if $\underline{P}(A) < \overline{P}(A)$ for any $A \neq \emptyset, \mathcal{X}$.*

Again, there may be more than one inner approximation minimising the BV distance with respect to the original model:

Example 4. Consider the same coherent lower probability as in Example 2. The following coherent lower probabilities:

A	$\{x_1\}$	$\{x_2\}$	$\{x_3\}$	$\{x_1, x_2\}$	$\{x_1, x_3\}$	$\{x_2, x_3\}$
$\underline{Q}^1_{TV}(A)$	0.2	0.05	0.3	0.4	0.65	0.5
$\underline{Q}^2_{TV}(A)$	0.2	0.25	0.1	0.6	0.45	0.5

are two different non-dominating inner approximations in $\mathcal{C}^{BV}_{TV}(\underline{P})$. ◆

The inner approximations of $\underline{P}$ in $\mathcal{C}_{TV}$ can be characterised in a similar manner as in the previous two subsections. Given the coherent lower probability $\underline{P}$ and $\delta > 0$, let us define the lower probability $\underline{Q}_\delta$ by

$$\underline{Q}_\delta(\mathcal{X}) = 1 \text{ and } \underline{Q}_\delta(A) = \underline{P}(A) + \delta \ \forall A \subset \mathcal{X}. \tag{10}$$

Then we have the following:

Proposition 9. *1. There exists a total variation model with a distortion factor δ that inner approximates $\underline{P}$ if and only if $\underline{Q}_\delta$ avoids sure loss.*
2. In that case, for any $P_0 \in \mathcal{M}(\underline{Q}_\delta)$ the total variation model determined by (P_0, δ) by Eq. (9) determines an inner approximation of $\underline{P}$ in $\mathcal{C}_{TV}$.
3. The set $\Lambda_{TV} := \{\delta \in (0, 1) \mid \mathcal{M}(\underline{Q}_\delta) \neq \emptyset\}$ has a maximum value δ_{TV}.

As before, the distance between the total variation model determined by (P_0, δ) is only a function of δ, and it is minimised for the maximum value δ_{TV}, existing by Proposition 9.

3.4 Incenters of Credal Sets

The above results lead us naturally to look for more manageable expressions of the value δ_{TV}, in the lines of Theorems 1 and 2. Indeed, this was already done in [7,8], and δ_{TV} corresponds to what we called *incenter radius* of the credal set $\mathcal{M}(\underline{P})$. The results from that paper give us a simple formula for computing δ_{TV} when the initial coherent lower probability is 2-monotone.

Theorem 3. *[7, 8] Let $\underline{P}$ be a 2-monotone lower probability with conjugate $\overline{P}$ satisfying that $\underline{P}(A) < \overline{P}(A)$ for every $A \neq \emptyset, \mathcal{X}$. Then:*

$$\delta_{\mathrm{TV}} = \min_{A \in \mathcal{A}^*(\mathcal{X})} \left\{ \frac{1 - \sum_{A \in \mathcal{A}} \underline{P}(A)}{|\mathcal{A}|}, \frac{\sum_{A \in \mathcal{A}} \overline{P}(A) - 1}{|\mathcal{A}|} \right\}. \tag{11}$$

With this result, we obtain a simple procedure for computing a TV inner approximation. It is illustrated in Fig. 3.

$$\underline{P} \xrightarrow{\text{Props. 2, 3}} Q \in \mathcal{C}_2^{\mathrm{BV}}(\underline{P}) \xrightarrow{\text{Eq. (11)}} \underline{P}_{\mathrm{TV}} \in \mathcal{C}_{\mathrm{TV}}^{\mathrm{BV}}(\underline{P})$$

Fig. 3. Graphical description of the procedure for obtaining an element of $\mathcal{C}_{\mathrm{TV}}^{\mathrm{BV}}(\underline{P})$.

Using the above ideas, we next investigate whether it is also possible to obtain incenters in terms of LV or PMM models instead of the TV distance. Indeed,

$$\delta_{\mathrm{LV}} = \max \left\{ \delta \in (0,1) \mid \exists P_0 \in \mathbb{P}(\mathcal{X}) \text{ such that } B_{\mathrm{LV}}^\delta(P_0) \subseteq \mathcal{M}(\underline{P}) \right\},$$

$$\delta_{\mathrm{PMM}} = \max \left\{ \delta \in (0,1) \mid \exists P_0 \in \mathbb{P}(\mathcal{X}) \text{ such that } B_{\mathrm{PMM}}^\delta(P_0) \subseteq \mathcal{M}(\underline{P}) \right\},$$

where $B_{\mathrm{LV}}^\delta(P_0)$ and $B_{\mathrm{PMM}}^\delta(P_0)$ denote the credal sets of the linear vacuous and pari mutuel models determined by (P_0, δ), respectively. We may then refer to δ_{LV} and δ_{PMM} as the *incenter radius* with respect to the LV or PMM model, respectively. Moreover, any P_0 such that $B_{\mathrm{LV}}^{\delta_{\mathrm{LV}}}(P_0) \subseteq \mathcal{M}(\underline{P})$ (respectively, $B_{\mathrm{LV}}^{\delta_{\mathrm{PMM}}}(P_0) \subseteq \mathcal{M}(\underline{P})$) is called *incenter* with respect to the LV (resp., PMM) model. It is quite straightforward to prove that $\delta_{\mathrm{TV}} \leq \min\{\delta_{\mathrm{LV}}, \delta_{\mathrm{PMM}}\}$ and that the three values $\delta_{\mathrm{TV}}, \delta_{\mathrm{LV}}$ and δ_{PMM} may be different.

Example 5. Let us consider Example 1 from [7]. Take $\mathcal{X} = \{x_1, x_2, x_3\}$ and the coherent lower and upper probabilities $\underline{P}$ and $\overline{P}$ given by:

A	$\{x_1\}$	$\{x_2\}$	$\{x_3\}$	$\{x_1, x_2\}$	$\{x_1, x_3\}$	$\{x_2, x_3\}$
$\underline{P}(A)$	0.5	0.1	0.1	0.65	0.75	0.2
$\overline{P}(A)$	0.8	0.25	0.35	0.9	0.9	0.5

In [7], it was shown that $\delta_{TV} = 0.075$, and that, following the notation in Eq. (10):

$$\mathcal{M}(Q_{\alpha_I}) = \{\beta(0.575, 0.175, 0.35) + (1 - \beta)(0.65, 0.175, 0175) \mid \beta \in [0,1]\}.$$

For computing the values α_{LV} and α_{PMM}, we notice that any coherent lower probability in a 3-element possibility space is 2-monotone too, hence we can use Eqs. (5) and (8), respectively.

For the LV, we obtain $\delta_{LV} = 0.15$. Moreover, the set of incenters, that coincides with $\mathcal{M}(Q_{LV})$, is given by:

$$\mathcal{M}(Q_{LV}) = \{\beta(11/17, 2/17, 4/17) + (1 - \beta)(13/17, 2/17, 2/17) \mid \beta \in [0,1]\}.$$

With respect to the PMM, $\delta_{PMM} = 0.3$. In this case, there is a unique incenter, given by the probability mass distribution $(13/23, 5/23, 5/23)$. Hence, the set of incenters, that coincides with $\mathcal{M}(\overline{Q}_{\alpha_{PMM}})$, is the singleton:

$$\mathcal{M}(\overline{Q}_{\alpha_{PMM}}) = \{(13/23, 5/23, 5/23)\}.$$

We see that the (sets of) incenters are different for the three models: TV, LV and PMM. ♦

4   Comparison of Decision Rules

We conclude our work by comparing the decisions stemming from the original lower probability $\underline{P}$ and its inner approximation $\underline{Q}$ by a number of rules; for a deeper discussion of these rules and some relevant references, we refer to [16].

Consider a decision problem where we must choose from a set of alternatives D, whose reward depends on the outcome of an experiment. The set of possible outcomes is a finite possibility space $\mathcal{X}$, and our information about the probabilities of these outcomes is modelled in terms of a coherent lower probability $\underline{P}$ on $\mathcal{P}(\mathcal{X})$. In such a context, there are a number of decision criteria that generalise the expected utility paradigm to an imprecise context. If we denote J_d the gamble associated with the alternative d, so that $J_d(x)$ gives the reward associated with the alternative d if the outcome of the experiment turns out to be x, then we have the following:

Definition 5. *Consider the following subset of alternatives:*

$$opt_{\geq} = \{d \in D \mid \nexists e \in D \setminus \{d\} \text{ such that } J_e(x) \geq J_d(x) \; \forall x \in \mathcal{X}\}.$$

The optimal alternatives according to the:

- *Γ-maximin criterion are $opt_{\underline{P}}(D) = \{d \in opt_{\geq} \mid \underline{P}(J_d) = \max_{e \in D} \underline{P}(J_e)\}$;*
- *Γ-maximax criterion are $opt_{\overline{P}}(D) = \{d \in opt_{\geq} \mid \overline{P}(J_d) = \max_{e \in D} \overline{P}(J_e)\}$;*
- *Maximality are $opt_{>_{\underline{P}}} = \{d \in opt_{\geq} \mid \underline{P}(J_e - J_d) \leq 0 \; \forall e \in D\}$;*
- *Interval dominance are $opt_{\sqsupseteq_{\underline{P}}} = \{d \in opt_{\geq} \mid \overline{P}(J_d) \geq \underline{P}(J_e) \; \forall e \in opt_{\geq}\}$;*
- *E-admissibility are $opt_{\mathcal{M}(\underline{P})} = \{d \in opt_{\geq} \mid \exists P \in \mathcal{M}(\underline{P}) \text{ such that } E_P(J_e) \leq E_P(J_d) \; \forall e \in opt_{\geq}\}$.*

The computation of these decisions is at times difficult, and may require determining the set of extreme points of $\mathcal{M}(\underline{P})$ or its natural extension to the space of gambles on $\mathcal{X}$. For this reason, it may be of interest to consider a simpler model such as 2-monotone lower probabilities, where the computation of the natural extension can be done efficiently in terms of the Choquet integral and where the extreme points are easy to obtain. Nevertheless, it is important to clarify the relationship between the sets of optimal solutions obtained with the initial model and its transformation.

In this sense, it is easy to see that, if $\underline{Q}$ is an inner approximation of $\underline{P}$, and as a consequence $\mathcal{M}(\underline{P}) \supseteq \mathcal{M}(\underline{Q})$, the set of optimal decisions with respect to

Q in terms of maximality (resp., interval dominance, E-admissibility) shall be included in those that are optimal with respect to $\underline{P}$ in terms of maximality (resp., interval dominance, E-admissibility):

$$\mathrm{opt}_{>_{\underline{P}}} \supseteq \mathrm{opt}_{>_{\underline{Q}}}, \qquad \mathrm{opt}_{\sqsupset_{\underline{P}}} \supseteq \mathrm{opt}_{\sqsupset_{\underline{Q}}} \qquad \mathrm{opt}_{\mathcal{M}(\underline{P})} \supseteq \mathrm{opt}_{\mathcal{M}(\underline{Q})}.$$

Let us show that these inclusions may be strict, and that there is no inclusion relationship between the sets of optimal alternatives in the case of Γ-maximin and Γ-maximax:

Example 6. Consider the possibility space $\mathcal{X} = \{x_1, x_2, x_3, x_4\}$, the coherent lower probability $\underline{P}$ and a non-dominating inner approximation $\underline{Q} \in \mathcal{C}_2^{\mathrm{BV}}(\underline{P})$ given by:

A	$\{x_1\}$	$\{x_2\}$	$\{x_3\}$	$\{x_4\}$	$\{x_1, x_2\}$	$\{x_1, x_3\}$	$\{x_1, x_4\}$
$\underline{P}(A)$	0.1	0	0	0.3	0.1	0.3	0.6
$\underline{Q}(A)$	0.1	0.1	0.1	0.3	0.2	0.3	0.6

A	$\{x_2, x_3\}$	$\{x_2, x_4\}$	$\{x_3, x_4\}$	$\{x_1, x_2, x_3\}$	$\{x_1, x_2, x_4\}$	$\{x_1, x_3, x_4\}$	$\{x_2, x_3, x_4\}$
$\underline{P}(A)$	0.3	0.4	0.4	0.5	0.6	0.7	0.6
$\underline{Q}(A)$	0.3	0.4	0.4	0.5	0.7	0.8	0.6

Consider the alternatives $D = \{d_1, d_2, d_3, d_4, d_5\}$ whose utilities are given by:

$$J_1 = (3, 2, {-9}/{10}, 3), \quad J_2 = (2, 3, {2}/{3}, 2), \quad J_3 = (3, -2, -2, 4),$$
$$J_4 = (-1, -1, 2.7, 2.7), \quad J_5 = (3, 3.5, -1, -1).$$

For them, it holds that:

	J_1	J_2	J_3	J_4	J_5	$J_1 - J_2$	$J_2 - J_1$
$\underline{P}$	1.44	1.4$\overline{6}$	1.5	0.48	-0.6	$-0.02\overline{6}$	-0.4
$\overline{P}$	2.7	2.3	1.9	2.33	1.55	0.4	0.02$\overline{6}$
$\underline{Q}$	1.73	1.7	1.3	0.46	-0.15	0.03	$-0.34\overline{3}$
$\overline{Q}$	2.41	2.0$\overline{6}$	2	1.96	1.5	0.34$\overline{3}$	-0.03

With this information, we obtain the following optimal decisions:

- For $D_1 = \{d_1, d_2, d_3\}$, $\mathrm{opt}_{\underline{P}}(D) = \{d_3\}$ and $\mathrm{opt}_{\underline{Q}}(D) = \{d_1\}$.
- For $D_2 = \{d_2, d_3, d_4\}$, $\mathrm{opt}_{\overline{P}}(D) = \{d_4\}$ and $\mathrm{opt}_{\overline{Q}}(D) = \{d_2\}$.
- For $D_3 = \{d_1, d_2\}$, $\mathrm{opt}_{>_{\underline{Q}}} = \{d_1\}$ and $\mathrm{opt}_{>_{\underline{P}}} = \{d_1, d_2\}$.
- For $D_4 = \{d_1, d_5\}$, $\mathrm{opt}_{\sqsupset_{\underline{Q}}} = \{d_1\}$ and $\mathrm{opt}_{\sqsupset_{\underline{P}}} = \{d_1, d_5\}$.
- Finally, considering again D_1, $\mathrm{opt}_{\mathcal{M}(\underline{Q})} = \{d_1\}$ and $\mathrm{opt}_{\mathcal{M}(\underline{P})} = \{d_1, d_3\}$. ◆

5   Concluding Remarks

The results in this paper show that it is possible to transform a coherent lower probability into a more manageable model with a minimal loss of information; nevertheless, and in contrast to what we showed in the case of the outer approximations [9,12,13], the non-dominating inner approximation will not be unique in the majority of classes. In addition to the results reported in this paper, we have also analysed the set of inner approximations in the family of probability intervals and p-boxes; space limitations have prevented us from reporting those results here.

With this, we should obtain a broader picture of the problem, and it should also help us in choosing the subfamily of coherent lower probabilities where we want our inner approximation to belong; we should find a balance between the closeness to the original model that we can get with the more general class of 2-monotone lower probabilities and the simplicity and better mathematical properties that we can get in some particular cases, such as the distortion models.

As future lines of research, we would like to deepen in the comparison between the initial and the transformed models; to consider other distances or divergences between the two; and to provide a geometric perspective on the transformations, along the lines of our comments on the incenters.

References

1. Augustin, T., Coolen, F., de Cooman, G., Troffaes, M. (eds.) Introduction to Imprecise Probabilities. In: Wiley Series in Probability and Statistics. Wiley (2014)
2. Baroni, P., Vicig, P.: An uncertainty interchange format with imprecise probabilities. Int. J. Approx. Reason. **40**, 147–180 (2005)
3. Berger, J.: Robust Bayesian analysis: sensitivity to the prior. J. Statist. Plan. Inference **25**, 303–328 (1990)
4. Bronevich, A.: Necessary and sufficient consensus conditions for the eventwise aggregation of lower probabilities. Fuzzy Sets Syst. **158**, 881–894 (2007)
5. Destercke, S., Montes, I., Miranda, E.: Processing distortion models: a comparative study. Int. J. Approx. Reason. **145**(C), 91–120 (2022)
6. Huber, P.: Robust Statistics. Wiley, New York (1981)
7. Miranda, E., Montes, I.: Centroids of Credal sets: a comparative study. In: Vejnarová, J., Wilson, N. (eds.) ECSQARU 2021. LNCS (LNAI), vol. 12897, pp. 427–441. Springer, Cham (2021). https://doi.org/10.1007/978-3-030-86772-0_31
8. Miranda, E., Montes, I.: Centroids of credal sets: a comparative study. Submitted for publication (2021)
9. Miranda, E., Montes, I., Vicig, P.: On the selection of an optimal outer approximation of a coherent lower probability. Fuzzy Sets Syst. **424C**, 1–36 (2021)
10. Montes, I., Miranda, E., Destercke, S.: Unifying neighbourhood and distortion models. Part I- New results on old models. Int. J. Gen. Syst. **49**(6), 605–635 (2020)
11. Montes, I., Miranda, E., Destercke, S.: Unifying neighbourhood and distortion models: Part II- New models and synthesis. Int. J. Gen. Syst. **49**(6), 636–674 (2020)
12. Montes, I., Miranda, E., Vicig, P.: 2-Monotone outer approximations of coherent lower probabilities. Int. J. Approx. Reason. **101**, 181–205 (2018)

13. Montes, I., Miranda, E., Vicig, P.: Outer approximating coherent lower probabilities with belief functions. Int. J. Approx. Reason. **110**, 1–30 (2019)
14. Pelessoni, R., Vicig, P., Zaffalon, M.: Inference and risk measurement with the pari-mutuel model. Int. J. Approx. Reason. **51**, 1145–1158 (2010)
15. Seidenfeld, T., Wasserman, L.: Dilation for sets of probabilities. Ann. Statist. **21**, 1139–54 (1993)
16. Troffaes, M.C.M.: Decision making under uncertainty using imprecise probabilities. Int. J. Approx. Reason. **45**(1), 17–29 (2007)
17. Walley, P.: Statistical Reasoning with Imprecise Probabilities. Chapman and Hall, London (1991)

A Robust Bayesian Estimation Approach for the Imprecise Plackett–Luce Model

Tathagata Basu$^{(\boxtimes)}$, Sébastien Destercke , and Benjamin Quost

UMR CNRS 7253 Heudiasyc, Sorbonne Université, Université de Technologie de
Compiègne, 60319 - 60203 Compiègne cedex, France
{tathagata.basu,sebastien.destercke,benjamin.quost}@hds.utc.fr

Abstract. Learning to rank has become an important part in the fields
of machine learning and statistical learning. Rankings are indeed present
in many applications, including cognitive psychology, recommender systems, sports tournament or automated algorithm choices. Rankings are
however prone to subjectivity (when provided by users) and to incom-
pleteness (when a contestant is missing, or users only report partial
preferences). Robust or cautious approaches may overcome such issues.
In this paper, we develop a Bayesian robust approach for a commonly
used parametric model, the Plackett-Luce (PL) model. This allows us to
obtain interval-valued parameter estimates for the strength parameter of
the Plackett-Luce model. We illustrate our method with both synthetic
and real data to show the usefulness of skeptic inference.

Keywords: preference learning · Plackett-Luce model · Bayesian
analysis · imprecise probability

1 Introduction

Dealing with preferences and rankings is an old topic in both statistics, AI and
machine learning. They are present in cognitive psychology [12], recommender
systems [7] or automated algorithm choices [11]. However, it always had an
important role in sports or related events, where rankings or pairwise comparisons of participants are commonly used. One of the earliest works (dating back
to the 30's) on pairwise comparisons [13] laid the foundations of the Bradley-
Terry model [2]. When multiple comparisons are involved, this model naturally
extends to the Plackett-Luce model, which is based on (and named after) the
works of Plackett [10] and Luce [9].

Several estimation strategies were proposed for both models. In particular,
Hunter [8] provided a class of minorisation-maximisation (or simply MM) algorithms, which are iterative optimisation methods to estimate the strength parameters of generalised Bradley-Terry models. Later on, several Bayesian methods
were introduced, such as the expectation propagation method for the Plackett-
Luce model [6], a latent variable approach for the generalised Bradley-Terry

This research was funded by the project PreServe (ANR Grant ANR-18-CE23-0008).

© Springer Nature Switzerland AG 2022
D. Ciucci et al. (Eds.): IPMU 2022, CCIS 1601, pp. 757–769, 2022.
https://doi.org/10.1007/978-3-031-08971-8_61

models [3], etc. However, such strategies rely on a number of assumptions, and provide precise estimates whatever the amount and quality of available data.

In presence of limited information, however, it seems preferable to estimate a cautious ranking model, which would provide sets of possible rankings as outputs, or even abstain from making a prediction. Such a lack of information can occur in many different scenarios. For instance, we might have very little information before initialising a recommender system, or we may only observe partial rankings (e.g., pairwise comparisons or top-k rankings). Moreover, rank data, especially those obtained by user feedback, can be subjective and uncertain, and should be treated accordingly. Therefore, it seems beneficial to carry on within a cautious framework such as described above.

Note that there exist a couple of existing such frameworks for the PL model. For instance, Cheng *et al.* [4] propose to threshold pairwise ranking probabilities to obtain partial rankings, but are still based on a precise estimate and all the biases that can come with it. In Adam *et al.* [1], an imprecise Plackett-Luce model was proposed for rank data; the α-cut of the contour likelihood was used to obtain robust estimates. This latter approach has the advantage that cautiousness directly depends on the lack of information; however, it has the drawbacks of likelihood-based approaches, notably a high sensitivity to the data at hand (especially for small sample sizes). In this paper, we consider using imprecise probabilities to develop a robust Bayesian PL model, where the imprecise posterior inference is the consequences of considering a set of possible priors.

The rest of the paper is organised as follows. In Sect. 2, we discuss our robust Bayesian approach for imprecise label ranking. Section 3 presents the proposed maximum a posteriori estimation strategy of the model. In Sect. 4, we illustrate our method on synthetic and real data, and we compare our strategy with other methods. Finally, we conclude this paper in Sect. 5.

2   Our Robust PL Model

This section introduces the model, and shows how we can perform robust Bayesian inference over such a model.

2.1   The Plackett-Luce Model

Assume we want to learn a probabilistic model over rankings of p objects. A naive computation of the empirical frequencies of the rankings at hand is doomed to fail, since although the initial space is discrete, its size is factorial in p. The recourse to a parametric model seems therefore desirable. We consider the Plackett-Luce (PL for short) model, which relies on the Luce choice axiom for choosing an item from a subset of a set of items. The axiom states that the probability of selecting one object over another from an urn containing many objects is not affected by the presence or absence of other objects in the urn [9]. Therefore, this axiom allows us to define a probabilistic model over the total order of the labels.

Let there be a total of p horses participating to n different races. Then, the PL model [10] can be defined in the following way:

$$P(X \mid \lambda) = \prod_{i=1}^{n} \prod_{j=1}^{p_i-1} \frac{\lambda_{x_{ij}}}{\sum_{m=j}^{p_i} \lambda_{x_{im}}}. \tag{1}$$

where $p_i \leq p$ is the number of horses in the i-th race, $\lambda := (\lambda_1, \cdots, \lambda_p)$ is the vector of strength parameters and $X := [x_{ij}]$ is the $n \times p$ matrix containing the rankings (i.e., x_{ij} is the rank of the jth object/participant in the ith observed ranking, $i = 1, \ldots, n, j = 1, \ldots, p$). Sometimes, Eq. (1) is also called the Plackett-Luce distribution because of its probabilistic formulation.

Example 1. Consider the following ranking data from $n = 2$ races involving $p = 4$ different horses 'A', 'B', 'C' and 'D'. For instance, we have $x_{12} = 1$ and $x_{11} = 4$ (B and A have rank 1 and 4 in the first observation) (Table 1).

Table 1. A toy example

	1	2	3	4
1	B	D	C	A
2	B	A	C	–

Then, the PL model is given by

$$P(X \mid \lambda) = \left[\frac{\lambda_B}{\lambda_B + \lambda_D + \lambda_C + \lambda_A} \cdot \frac{\lambda_D}{\lambda_D + \lambda_C + \lambda_A} \cdot \frac{\lambda_C}{\lambda_C + \lambda_A} \right] \tag{2}$$
$$\cdot \left[\frac{\lambda_B}{\lambda_B + \lambda_A + \lambda_C} \cdot \frac{\lambda_A}{\lambda_A + \lambda_C} \right].$$

We then use this expression to estimate the strength parameters. For instance, we can empoly the MM algorithm by Hunter [8] to compute the maximum likelihood estimates.

We also have a Thurstonian interpretation for the PL model. A Thurstonian model considers a random score variable for each label. Drawing from the score distributions, and sorting based on these sampled scores, gives a sample ranking: that is, a distribution over the scores leads to a distribution over the rankings. Yellott [12] showed that a score distribution boils down to the PL model if and only if the scores follow a Gumbel distribution with fixed shape parameter.

2.2 Hierarchical Model

For the robust Bayesian analysis, we adopt the latent variable model suggested by Caron and Doucet [3]. The latent variable Z_{ij} in the data augmentation process stands for the arrival time of the j-th item in the i-th race; it is assumed to be exponential:

$$Z_{ij} \overset{\text{ind}}{\sim} \text{Exp}\left(\sum_{m=j}^{p_i} \lambda_{x_{im}} \right).$$

Then, a natural choice for prior distribution over the strength parameters is the (conjugate) Gamma distribution, which ensures that $\lambda_k > 0$ for all $k = 1, \cdots, p$. This gives the following hierarchical model (assuming X are i.i.d. observations):

$$X \mid \lambda \sim \prod_{i=1}^{n} \prod_{j=1}^{p_i-1} \frac{\lambda_{x_{ij}}}{\sum_{m=j}^{p_i} \lambda_{x_{im}}}, \tag{3}$$

$$Z \mid X, \lambda \sim \prod_{i=1}^{n} \prod_{j=1}^{p_i-1} \left(\sum_{m=j}^{p_i} \lambda_{x_{im}} \right) \exp\left(-Z_{ij} \sum_{m=j}^{p_i} \lambda_{x_{im}} \right), \tag{4}$$

$$\lambda \sim \prod_{k=1}^{p} \frac{b_k^{a_k} \lambda_k^{a_k-1} e^{-b_k \lambda_k}}{\Gamma(a_k)}, \tag{5}$$

where $a_k > 0$ and $b_k > 0$.

In this paper, we will partially specify the prior parameters a_k by intervals $[\underline{a_k}, \overline{a_k}]$, in order to perform robust Bayesian analysis. This can also be seen as a scaled bound of the prior expectation of the k-th strength parameter. Therefore, for very limited information, we can simply consider a wider interval for a_k to perform a near-vacuous analysis.

3   Parameter Estimation

For parameter estimation, we need to investigate the posterior distributions of the strength parameters. The use of conjugate priors allows us to obtain analytic expressions of the full conditional as well as of the posteriors. However, the sensitivity analysis over a_k increases the computation cost. Therefore, we only compute the maximum a posteriori (MAP) estimates of the strength parameters instead of the full posterior analysis. We will see that this allows us to have efficient estimation procedures.

3.1   Maximum a Posteriori Estimation

We typically obtain MAP estimates by maximizing the posterior distribution $P(\lambda \mid X)$ with respect to λ, using an EM procedure. We first compute the complete log-likelihood which includes the latent variables in the likelihood function. From Eqs. (1) and (4), we get

$$\ell(\lambda) := \log P(X, Z \mid \lambda) = \sum_{i=1}^{n} \sum_{j=1}^{p_i-1} \left[\log(\lambda_{x_{ij}}) - Z_{ij} \sum_{m=j}^{p_i} \lambda_{x_{im}} \right]. \tag{6}$$

Computing the log-posterior from the log-prior defined above and this complete log-likelihood gives

$$\log(P(\lambda \mid X, Z)) = \ell(\lambda) + \log(P(\lambda)) + T \tag{7}$$

where T is an additive constant independent of λ—and therefore irrelevant for computing the MAP estimate. Therefore, for this latter purpose, following [3], we apply the EM algorithm [5] to $\ell(\lambda) + \log(P(\lambda))$.

E-step: In the E-step, we compute the expectation of $\ell(\lambda) + \log(P(\lambda))$ with respect to the latent variables Z, conditional on observing the data X and a current estimate λ^* for λ. This gives us a function of λ and λ^*:

$$Q(\lambda, \lambda^*) = \mathbb{E}_{Z|X,\lambda^*}\left[\ell(\lambda)\right] + \log(P(\lambda)),$$

$$= \mathbb{E}_{Z|X,\lambda^*}\left[\sum_{i=1}^{n}\sum_{j=1}^{p_i-1}\left[\log(\lambda_{x_{ij}}) - Z_{ij}\sum_{m=j}^{p_i}\lambda_{x_{im}}\right]\right] + \log(P(\lambda)),$$

$$= \sum_{i=1}^{n}\sum_{j=1}^{p_i-1}\left[\log(\lambda_{x_{ij}}) - \mathbb{E}_{Z|X,\lambda^*}(Z_{ij})\sum_{m=j}^{p_i}\lambda_{x_{im}}\right] + \log(P(\lambda));$$

since Z_{ij} follows an exponential distribution, we have

$$= \sum_{i=1}^{n}\sum_{j=1}^{p_i-1}\left[\log(\lambda_{x_{ij}}) - \frac{\sum_{m=j}^{p_i}\lambda_{x_{im}}}{\sum_{m=j}^{p_i}\lambda_{x_{im}}^*}\right] + \log(P(\lambda));$$

now, from Eq. (5), we have

$$= \sum_{i=1}^{n}\sum_{j=1}^{p_i-1}\left[\log(\lambda_{x_{ij}}) - \frac{\sum_{m=j}^{p_i}\lambda_{x_{im}}}{\sum_{m=j}^{p_i}\lambda_{x_{im}}^*}\right] + \sum_{k=1}^{p}\left[(a_k - 1)\log(\lambda_k) - b_k\lambda_k\right] + C,$$

where C is additive constant independent of λ. Therefore,

$$Q(\lambda, \lambda^*) \equiv \sum_{i=1}^{n}\sum_{j=1}^{p_i-1}\left[\log(\lambda_{x_{ij}}) - \frac{\sum_{m=j}^{p_i}\lambda_{x_{im}}}{\sum_{m=j}^{p_i}\lambda_{x_{im}}^*}\right] + \sum_{k=1}^{p}\left[(a_k - 1)\log(\lambda_k) - b_k\lambda_k\right] \tag{8}$$

M-step: In the M-step, we need to differentiate the function $Q(\lambda, \lambda^*)$ with respect to each λ_k to obtain the iterative formulation.

$$\frac{\partial Q}{\partial \lambda_k} = \frac{\partial}{\partial \lambda_k}\left[\sum_{i=1}^{n}\sum_{j=1}^{p_i-1}\left[\log(\lambda_{x_{ij}}) - \frac{\sum_{m=j}^{p_i}\lambda_{x_{im}}}{\sum_{m=j}^{p_i}\lambda_{x_{im}}^*}\right] + \sum_{k=1}^{p}\left[(a_k - 1)\log(\lambda_k) - b_k\lambda_k\right]\right],$$

$$= \left[\sum_{i=1}^{n}\mathbb{I}_{k\in\{x_{i1},\cdots,x_{i(p_i-1)}\}} + a_k - 1\right]\frac{\partial \log(\lambda_k)}{\partial \lambda_k} - \left[\sum_{i=1}^{n}\sum_{j=1}^{p_i-1}\frac{\mathbb{I}_{k\in\{x_{ij},\cdots,x_{ip_i}\}}}{\sum_{m=j}^{p_i}\lambda_{x_{im}}^*} + b_k\right]\frac{\partial \lambda_k}{\partial \lambda_k},$$

$$= \frac{1}{\lambda_k}\left[\sum_{i=1}^{n}\mathbb{I}_{k\in\{x_{i1},\cdots,x_{i(p_i-1)}\}} + a_k - 1\right] - \left[\sum_{i=1}^{n}\sum_{j=1}^{p_i-1}\frac{\mathbb{I}_{k\in\{x_{ij},\cdots,x_{ip_i}\}}}{\sum_{m=j}^{p_i}\lambda_{x_{im}}^*} + b_k\right].$$

Computing the MAP estimate requires to set this derivative to zero, which gives

$$\lambda_k = \frac{a_k + w_k - 1}{b_k + \sum_{i=1}^n \sum_{j=1}^{p_i-1} \frac{\delta_{ijk}}{\sum_{m=j}^{p_i} \lambda_{x_{im}}^*}}, \tag{9}$$

where $w_k = \sum_{i=1}^n \mathbb{I}_{k \in \{x_{i1}, \cdots, x_{i(p_i-1)}\}}$ and $\delta_{ijk} = \mathbb{I}_{k \in \{x_{ij}, \cdots, x_{ip_i}\}}$. Now, to show that Eq. (9) gives a maximum for $Q(\lambda, \lambda^*)$, we investigate the Hessian matrix

$$H_Q = \begin{bmatrix} -\frac{a_1+w_1-1}{\lambda_1^2} & 0 & \cdots & 0 \\ 0 & -\frac{a_2+w_2-1}{\lambda_2^2} & \cdots & 0 \\ \vdots & \vdots & \vdots & \vdots \\ 0 & \cdots & 0 & -\frac{a_p+w_p-1}{\lambda_p^2} \end{bmatrix}. \tag{10}$$

Assuming that a horse does not come last in every race ($w_k \geq 1$, for all k), H_Q is negative definite for all values of λ. Therefore, the Q function attains its maximum when Eq. (9) is satisfied. This gives us the following iterative formula to obtain an approximate solution for λ:

$$\lambda_k^{(t)} = \frac{a_k + w_k - 1}{b_k + \sum_{i=1}^n \sum_{j=1}^{p_i-1} \frac{\delta_{ijk}}{\sum_{m=j}^{p_i} \lambda_{x_{im}}^{(t-1)}}}. \tag{11}$$

3.2   Imprecise MAP Estimation

Remark that after Eq. (11), we have

$$\lambda_k^{(t)} \propto a_k \quad \text{and} \quad \lambda_k^{(t)} \propto \sum_{m=j}^{p_i} \lambda_{x_{im}}^{(t-1)};$$

Therefore, bounds on the parameter value $\lambda_k^{(t)}$ estimated in the t-th iteration can be computed as

$$\underline{\lambda}_k^{(t)} = \frac{a_k + w_k - 1}{b_k + \sum_{i=1}^n \sum_{j=1}^{p_i-1} \frac{\delta_{ijk}}{\sum_{m=j}^{p_i} \underline{\lambda}_{x_{im}}^{(t-1)}}}, \quad \overline{\lambda}_k^{(t)} = \frac{\overline{a}_k + w_k - 1}{b_k + \sum_{i=1}^n \sum_{j=1}^{p_i-1} \frac{\delta_{ijk}}{\sum_{m=j}^{p_i} \overline{\lambda}_{x_{im}}^{(t-1)}}}. \tag{12}$$

To show that these bounds reflect epistemic uncertainty (i.e., the larger the dataset, the closer the bounds are to each other), we make the following simple but necessary assumption.

Assumption 1. (Boundedness of λ_k) *There exists a global bound $M < \infty$ such that $0 < \underline{\lambda}_k^{(t)} \leq \overline{\lambda}_k^{(t)} \leq M$ for each parameter k and all iteration t.*

Note that this assumption is not very limiting, as in practice we will start from bounded initial estimates, and (12) will not diverge. Given this assumption is satisfied, we can show that our estimates become more and more precise as data are gathered.

Theorem 1 (Convergence of imprecision). *Let* $\Delta_k^{(t)}(n) := \overline{\lambda}_k^{(t)} - \underline{\lambda}_k^{(t)}$ *denote the imprecision in the k-th strength parameter estimated at the t-th iteration. Let* $p = \max_i\{p_i\}$, *and let* $\lambda^{(0)} = (1/p, \cdots, 1/p)$ *be the initial guess of the strength parameter vector. Then, as* $n \to \infty$, *we have* $\Delta_k^{(t)}(n) \to 0$ *for each parameter k and all iteration t.*

Proof. Since we obtain the lower and upper estimates by an iterative algorithm, we will prove the theorem by induction.

For $t = 1$ From Eq. (12), we have

$$\Delta_k^{(1)}(n) = \frac{\overline{a}_k + w_k - 1}{b_k + \sum_{i=1}^n \sum_{j=1}^{p_i-1} \frac{\delta_{ijk}}{\sum_{m=j}^{p_i} 1/p}} - \frac{\underline{a}_k + w_k - 1}{b_k + \sum_{i=1}^n \sum_{j=1}^{p_i-1} \frac{\delta_{ijk}}{\sum_{m=j}^{p_i} 1/p}}$$

$$= \frac{\overline{a}_k - \underline{a}_k}{b_k + p\sum_{i=1}^n \sum_{j=1}^{p_i-1} \frac{\delta_{ijk}}{p_i+1-j}}$$

Note that by construction, we have $w_k = \sum_{i=1}^n \mathbb{I}_{k \in \{x_{i1}, \cdots, x_{i(p_i-1)}\}}$ and $\delta_{ijk} = \mathbb{I}_{k \in \{x_{ij}, \cdots, x_{ip_i}\}}$. Then there exists a sequence of numbers $\{k_s\}^\infty$, and a sequence $\{j_{k_s} | j_{k_s} < p_{k_s}, \forall k_s \in \{k_s\}^\infty\}^\infty$, such that

$$\Delta_k^{(1)}(n) = \frac{\overline{a}_k - \underline{a}_k}{b_k + \sum_{i \in \{k_s\}^\infty} \sum_{j=1}^{j_i} \frac{p}{p_i+1-j}}.$$

As $n \to \infty$, we have $\sum_{i \in \{k_s\}^\infty} \sum_{j=1}^{j_i} \frac{p}{p_i+1-j} \to \infty$, and therefore $\Delta_k^{(1)}(n) \to 0$.

For $t = 2$

As previously, we have

$$\Delta_k^{(2)}(n) = \frac{\overline{a}_k + w_k - 1}{b_k + \sum_{i=1}^n \sum_{j=1}^{p_i-1} \frac{\delta_{ijk}}{\sum_{m=j}^{p_i} \overline{\lambda}_{x_{im}}^{(1)}}} - \frac{\underline{a}_k + w_k - 1}{b_k + \sum_{i=1}^n \sum_{j=1}^{p_i-1} \frac{\delta_{ijk}}{\sum_{m=j}^{p_i} \underline{\lambda}_{x_{im}}^{(1)}}}$$

$$= \frac{\overline{a}_k + w_k - 1}{b_k + \sum_{i=1}^n \sum_{j=1}^{p_i-1} \frac{\delta_{ijk}}{\sum_{m=j}^{p_i} \overline{\lambda}_{x_{im}}^{(1)}}} - \frac{\underline{a}_k + w_k - 1}{b_k + \sum_{i=1}^n \sum_{j=1}^{p_i-1} \frac{\delta_{ijk}}{\sum_{m=j}^{p_i} \left(\overline{\lambda}_{x_{im}}^{(1)} - \Delta_{x_{im}}^{(1)}(n)\right)}}$$

$$= \delta_k^{(2)}(n) + S_k^{(2)}(n),$$

where

$$\delta_k^{(2)}(n) = \left[\frac{\overline{a}_k}{b_k + \sum_{i=1}^n \sum_{j=1}^{p_i-1} \frac{\delta_{ijk}}{\sum_{m=j}^{p_i} \overline{\lambda}_{x_{im}}^{(1)}}} - \frac{\underline{a}_k}{b_k + \sum_{i=1}^n \sum_{j=1}^{p_i-1} \frac{\delta_{ijk}}{\sum_{m=j}^{p_i} \left(\overline{\lambda}_{x_{im}}^{(1)} - \Delta_{x_{im}}^{(1)}(n)\right)}}\right] \tag{13}$$

$$S_k^{(2)}(n) = \left[\frac{w_k - 1}{b_k + \sum_{i=1}^n \sum_{j=1}^{p_i-1} \frac{\delta_{ijk}}{\sum_{m=j}^{p_i} \overline{\lambda}_{x_{im}}^{(1)}}} - \frac{w_k - 1}{b_k + \sum_{i=1}^n \sum_{j=1}^{p_i-1} \frac{\delta_{ijk}}{\sum_{m=j}^{p_i} \left(\overline{\lambda}_{x_{im}}^{(1)} - \Delta_{x_{im}}^{(1)}(n)\right)}}\right]. \tag{14}$$

To show $\lim_{n\to\infty} \Delta_k^{(2)}(n) \to \infty$, we need that both $\delta_k^{(2)}(n) \to 0$ and $S_k^{(2)}(n) \to 0$ as $n \to \infty$. Due to space limitations, we will only provide details for the former. Now, from Eq. (13), we have

$$\lim_{n\to\infty} \delta_k^{(2)}(n) = \lim_{n\to\infty} \left[\frac{\overline{a_k}}{b_k + \sum_{i=1}^n \sum_{j=1}^{p_i-1} \frac{\delta_{ijk}}{\sum_{m=j}^{p_i} \overline{\lambda}_{x_{im}}^{(1)}}} - \frac{a_k}{b_k + \sum_{i=1}^n \sum_{j=1}^{p_i-1} \frac{\delta_{ijk}}{\sum_{m=j}^{p_i} \left(\overline{\lambda}_{x_{im}}^{(1)} - \lim_{n\to\infty} \Delta_{x_{im}}^{(1)}(n) \right)}} \right].$$

Since $\Delta_k^{(1)}(n) \to 0$ as $n \to \infty$, we have

$$\lim_{n\to\infty} \delta_k^{(2)}(n) = \lim_{n\to\infty} \left[\frac{\overline{a_k}}{b_k + \sum_{i=1}^n \sum_{j=1}^{p_i-1} \frac{\delta_{ijk}}{\sum_{m=j}^{p_i} \overline{\lambda}_{x_{im}}^{(1)}}} - \frac{a_k}{b_k + \sum_{i=1}^n \sum_{j=1}^{p_i-1} \frac{\delta_{ijk}}{\sum_{m=j}^{p_i} \overline{\lambda}_{x_{im}}^{(1)}}} \right]$$

$$= \lim_{n\to\infty} \left[\frac{\overline{a_k} - a_k}{b_k + \sum_{i=1}^n \sum_{j=1}^{p_i-1} \frac{\delta_{ijk}}{\sum_{m=j}^{p_i} \overline{\lambda}_{x_{im}}^{(1)}}} \right].$$

From the boundedness assumption on λ_k, we have

$$\lim_{n\to\infty} \delta_k^{(2)}(n) \leq \lim_{n\to\infty} \left[\frac{\overline{a_k} - a_k}{b_k + \sum_{i=1}^n \sum_{j=1}^{p_i-1} \frac{\delta_{ijk}}{\sum_{m=j}^{p_i} M}} \right]$$

which becomes, after applying previous arguments,

$$\leq \lim_{n\to\infty} \left[\frac{\overline{a_k} - a_k}{b_k + \frac{1}{Mp} \sum_{i\in\{k_s\}}^\infty \sum_{j=1}^{j_i} \frac{p}{p_i+1-j}} \right].$$

Since Mp is finite and the term $\sum_{i\in\{k_s\}}^\infty \sum_{j=1}^{j_i} \frac{p}{p_i+1-j}$ diverges to ∞ as $n \to \infty$, we therefore have

$$\lim_{n\to\infty} \delta_k^{(2)}(n) = 0. \tag{15}$$

Coupled with the same result for $S_k^{(2)}(n)$, we get $\Delta_k^{(2)}(n) \to 0$ as $n \to \infty$.

Now, by mathematical induction, we can assume that $\lim_{n\to\infty} \Delta_k^{(t)}(n) \to 0$ for $t = 1, 2, \cdots, r$. Using the same reasoning as above (which is not detailed here, due to the lack of place), we can show that this holds for $t = r + 1$ as well, which proves our theorem.

4   Illustration

For the illustration of our method, we use both synthetic and real-life datasets. We show that as we accumulate more data or ignore sparse information, our method gives us a more precise answer. To do so, we first define completeness as

$$\text{Completeness} = \frac{\text{nb observed comparisons}}{\text{nb possible comparisons}}. \tag{16}$$

Here, for two strength parameters λ_i and λ_j, we consider that $\lambda_i > \lambda_j$ if

$$\inf_{a_1, \cdots, a_P} \{\lambda_i(a_1, \cdots, a_P) - \lambda_j(a_1, \cdots, a_P)\} > 0; \tag{17}$$

note that if $\lambda_i \not> \lambda_j$ and $\lambda_j \not> \lambda_i$, we call the objects (drivers) incomparable.

4.1 Synthetic Dataset

For the synthetic dataset, we set $\lambda_k = (81 - k)$ for $1 \leq k \leq 80$. We then use these fixed values of λ to generate 10000 observations of rankings. We also add some noise in the data by adding 100 observations obtained by using a different set of λ_k such that $\lambda_k = (21 - k)$ for $1 \leq k \leq 20$ and $\lambda_k \sim U(0, 1)$ for $21 \leq k \leq 80$.

To perform our analyses, we consider two different settings. In one case, we consider the completeness of our estimate for different top k-rankings and in the other case, we consider the completeness against the total number of observations.

In the Fig. 1, we show these analyses of completeness averaged over 10 replications. We start our analyses with 20 observations and keep adding 5 observations in each step. We notice that the estimates become more complete as we increase the number of observations. It tends to be monotone except for few cases. This happens as in the new observations, a parameter may perform unexpectedly better/worse and force the estimates to be more imprecise. We also check this for 4 different values of top k-ranks. In one case, we consider all the rankings and the completeness is equal to 1 even after repeating for 10 times. But, this value changes for other cases. It is usually lower for smaller values of k. However, we notice that for $k = 20$, this completeness increases faster than the others and at a certain point the completeness is better than the completeness for $k = 40$.

4.2 NASCAR Dataset

We use the NASCAR 2002 dataset to illustrate our method with a real dataset. This dataset contains the results of 2002 season where a total of 36 races took place. In each race, 43 drivers participate and across the season 87 different drivers participate. This dataset was studied by Hunter [8] for illustration. Note that the data are pre-processed so as to eliminate 4 drivers, who always come last.

We aim at using these data in order to infer a ranking model of the drivers. More precisely, we aim at showing that as we infer from more complete data (see below for a definition of completeness), or as we ignore sparse information, our method results in a more precise ranking model.

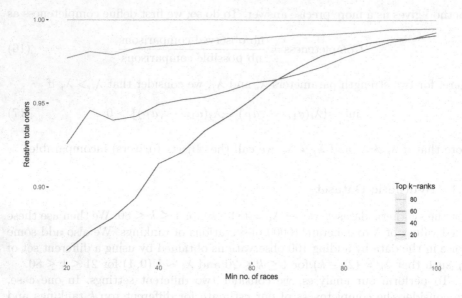

Fig. 1. Completeness of the estimated rankings with respect to different size of observations and different top k-rankings.

Cautious Ranking Inference. First, we simply estimate the rankings of the drivers. For this purpose, we consider the whole dataset with 83 drivers. We set $a_1 = a_2 = \cdots = a_P = a$ for near vacuous analysis and consider $a \in (1/83, 82/83)$. We set $b_1 = b_2 = \cdots = b_P = 1$ and perform our robust Bayesian analysis over a to obtain the bounds for the strength parameters. We display these strength parameters (in the increasing order) of their lower bounds in Fig. 2.

Note that $\lambda_i > \lambda_j$ (or ith driver is better than the jth) in the sense of Eq. (17) whenever $\underline{\lambda}_i > \underline{\lambda}_j$ and $\overline{\lambda}_i > \overline{\lambda}_j$, due to their dependencies to a_i values. We can see that a majority of drivers can be ordered; some of them are however incomparable, such as for instance driver 58, whose 4th place in one race led our robust approach to be cautious about its potential strength.

Sensitivity to Completeness of Training Data. In a second step, we analyse what becomes of our predictions if we consider more complete rankings in order to infer our model. Since all races contain different drivers, we do this in two ways.

First, we consider those drivers that have participated in at least r races. Obviously, for $r = 1$, we consider all drivers; by letting r increase, we eliminate some of them: then, we get more complete information about the remaining ones. In addition, we consider only the top-k information corresponding to race outcomes, thereby truncating the observed rankings.

Figure 3 summarises this analysis, showing that globally, the completeness of the inferred rankings increases as we get more information. We can see that as we increase r (required number of races for a driver to be included in the data),

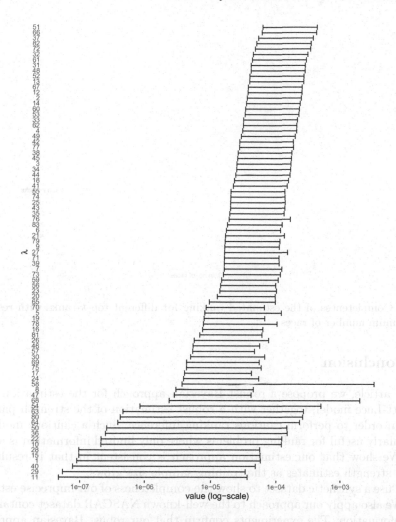

Fig. 2. MAP estimate of λ with 83 drivers

the comparisons become more complete. This is also the case when we use the complete racing outcomes instead of the top k-ranks. In this latter case, since some drivers may perform well in some races and arrive below the kth position in others, this selection is likely to change the bounds of the estimated strength parameters, thus resulting in incomplete comparisons. We also notice that for smaller values of r, completeness is better for top 15-rankings than for top 20-rankings. This may seem contradictory, but this behaviour is actually plausible, since for those particular cases, the refined race results are more consistent for the first 15 ranks, and therefore the strength parameter bounds are tighter.

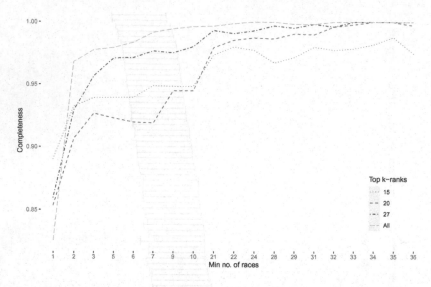

Fig. 3. Completeness of the estimated ranking for different top k-ranks with respect to minimum number of races

5   Conclusion

In this article, we propose a robust Bayesian approach for the estimation of a Plackett-Luce model, together with a robust estimation of the strength parameters, in order to perform cautious ranking inference. Such a cautious model is particularly useful for ranking problems where only limited information is available. We show that our estimation approach is consistent in that it results in tighter strength estimates as the training sample size grows.

We use a synthetic dataset to show the completeness of our imprecise estimation. We also apply our approach to the well-known NASCAR dataset containing race information. The experiments confirm that our robust Bayesian approach tends to be more complete when we have more information, satisfying our theoretical result on the imprecision of the posterior estimates.

We plan to extend our approach in several ways: studying the effect of adding prior information; using expected estimates rather than MAP ones; extending our model to mixture of PL, for instance to perform preference clustering.

References

1. Adam, L., Van Camp, A., Destercke, S., Quost, B.: Inferring from an imprecise Plackett–Luce model: application to label ranking. In: Davis, J., Tabia, K. (eds.) SUM 2020. LNCS (LNAI), vol. 12322, pp. 98–112. Springer, Cham (2020). https://doi.org/10.1007/978-3-030-58449-8_7
2. Bradley, R.A., Terry, M.E.: Rank analysis of incomplete block designs: I. the method of paired comparisons. Biometrika **39**(3/4), 324–345 (1952)

3. Caron, F., Doucet, A.: Efficient Bayesian inference for generalized Bradley-Terry models. J. Comput. Graph. Stat. **21**(1), 174–196 (2012)
4. Cheng, W., Hüllermeier, E., Waegeman, W., Welker, V.: Label ranking with partial abstention based on thresholded probabilistic models. In: Advances in Neural Information Processing Systems, vol. 25 (2012)
5. Dempster, A.P., Laird, N.M., Rubin, D.B.: Maximum likelihood from incomplete data via the EM algorithm. J. R. Stat. Soc. Ser. B (Methodol.) **39**(1), 1–38 (1977)
6. Guiver, J., Snelson, E.: Bayesian inference for Plackett-Luce ranking models. In: Proceedings of the 26th Annual International Conference on Machine Learning, ICML 2009, pp. 377–384. Association for Computing Machinery, New York, NY, USA (2009). https://doi.org/10.1145/1553374.1553423
7. He, J., Li, X., Liao, L.: Category-aware next point-of-interest recommendation via listwise Bayesian personalized ranking. IJCAI **17**, 1837–1843 (2017)
8. Hunter, D.R.: MM algorithms for generalized Bradley-Terry models. Ann. Stat. **32**(1), 384–406 (2004). https://doi.org/10.1214/aos/1079120141
9. Luce, R.D.: Individual Choice Behavior: A Theoretical analysis. Wiley, New York (1959)
10. Plackett, R.L.: The analysis of permutations. J. Roy. Stat. Soc.: Ser. C (Appl. Stat.) **24**(2), 193–202 (1975). https://doi.org/10.2307/2346567
11. Tornede, A., Wever, M., Hüllermeier, E.: Algorithm selection as recommendation: From collaborative filtering to dyad ranking. In: CI Workshop, Dortmund (2019)
12. Yellott, J.I.: The relationship between Luce's choice axiom, Thurstone's theory of comparative judgment, and the double exponential distribution. J. Math. Psychol. **15**(2), 109–144 (1977). https://doi.org/10.1016/0022-2496(77)90026-8
13. Zermelo, E.: Die Berechnung der Turnier-Ergebnisse als ein Maximumproblem der Wahrscheinlichkeitsrechnung. Math. Z. **29**(1), 436–460 (1929). https://doi.org/10.1007/BF01180541

A Discussion About Independence and Correlation in the Framework of Coherent Lower Conditional Probability

Giulianella Coletti[1] , Sara Latini[2] , and Davide Petturiti[3]($\boxtimes$)

[1] Department of Mathematics and Computer Science, University of Perugia, Perugia, Italy
giulianella.coletti@unipg.it
[2] Department of Information Engineering, Computer Science and Mathematics, University of L'Aquila, L'Aquila, Italy
sara.latini@graduate.univaq.it
[3] Department of Economics, University of Perugia, Perugia, Italy
davide.petturiti@unipg.it

Abstract. Aim of the paper is to put under the right perspective the concepts of independence and correlation in the framework of coherent lower conditional probability, taking suitably into account also events whose lower probability is zero or one.

Keywords: Coherent lower probability · Zero-layers · Independence · Positive and negative correlation

1 Introduction

Coherent lower conditional probability plays an important role in decision making models in presence of ambiguity, such as in the (pessimistic) synthesis of probabilistic information coming from multiple sources or of judgments of a pool of experts. On the one hand, if one cannot ignore the consideration of null or almost certain events in the framework of coherent conditional probabilities, this is even more compelling when dealing with coherent lower conditional probabilities.

As far as stochastic independence and positive and negative correlation are concerned, the shortcomings of classical definitions have been pointed out in a series of papers (see, for instance, [1–3,10,11]). For this reason, suitable definitions have been proposed in a way to avoid those counterintuitive situations, in particular when the given events have probability equal to 0 or 1. These definitions of independence and of correlation between two events agree with the classical ones and their variations when the probabilities of the relevant events are not both equal to 0 and 1. In particular, they are able to avoid the situations, where logical dependence does not (contrary to intuition) imply stochastic dependence, or logical constraints do not imply (positive or negative) correlation.

© Springer Nature Switzerland AG 2022
D. Ciucci et al. (Eds.): IPMU 2022, CCIS 1601, pp. 770–783, 2022.
https://doi.org/10.1007/978-3-031-08971-8_62

The aim of this paper is to set forth a concise picture of our previous results on stochastic independence and positive and negative correlation, mainly, to discuss their extension to coherent lower conditional probabilities.

In the literature, the issue of providing a suitable notion of independence or irrelevance in the context of imprecise probabilities has been already investigated (see, e.g., [2,5,12]). In particular, in [2] a definition of independence of events E and H, with respect to a coherent lower conditional probability is proposed. Such definition requires independence for every element of the dominating class, which attains the minimum in one of the elements of $\{E, H, E^*|H^*, H^*|E^*\}$. However this definition is too stringent, as it is verified only when the restriction of $\underline{P}$ to the above family is a coherent conditional probability.

In this paper, we propose a definition of independence for events that permits to capture non-degenerate coherent lower conditional probabilities. Our definition of independence differs from the definition of epistemic irrelevance due to Walley [5,12]. The latter is given for random variables and can be expressed in terms of convex hulls of marginal and conditional credal sets. Our definition works with sets of coherent conditional probabilities under different conditioning events, and, as is well-known, the convex combination of coherent conditional probabilities is not necessarily a coherent conditional probability.

Besides independence, the concepts of correlation and dependence are gathering increasing attention in the context of imprecise probabilities and, in case of random variables, they can be connected to imprecise copula theory [8,9]. For this, with the same rationale behind our definition of independence, we provide an analogous definition of positive/negative correlation for events with respect to a coherent lower conditional probability that is sound also for extreme lower probability values.

The paper is organized as follows. In Sect. 2 we recall the necessary notions on coherent (lower) conditional probability. In Sect. 3 we collect (without proofs, but correcting some typos present in the representation theorem given in [4]) previous results on stochastic independence and correlation for coherent conditional probabilities. Finally, in Sect. 4 we introduce the new definition of independence and positive and negative correlation in the framework of coherent lower conditional probabilities. In particular, due to a lack of space, we only provide a characterization of independence when $\underline{P}(E|H) = \underline{P}(E|H^c) = \alpha \in]0,1]$ and of correlation when $\underline{P}(E|H) = \underline{P}(E|H^c) = 1$, showing non-triviality of the given definitions.

2   The Reference Framework

We refer to the framework where conditional probability is the basic concept introduced as a function of two variables (precisely an ordered pair of events) ruled by a set of axioms.

2.1   Coherent Conditional Probability

We consider an *event* to be any fact described by a Boolean sentence, indicating by Ω the *sure event* and using $\varnothing$ for the *impossible event*. Given an event E, we will use the symbol E^* to denote either E or its contrary E^c. We recall that an *additive class* of events is a set of events closed under taking disjunction $\vee$. A *Boolean algebra* of events is an additive class which is further closed under taking the contrary $(\cdot)^c$, and hence under conjunction $\wedge$. We further take a *conditional event* $E|H$ to be an ordered pair of events E, H with $H \neq \varnothing$.

In the sequel, for any Boolean algebra $\mathcal{A}$, we write $\mathcal{A}^0$ to indicate $\mathcal{A} \setminus \{\varnothing\}$. For an arbitrary family of events $\mathcal{E} = \{E_1, \ldots, E_n\}$, we use $\mathbf{alg}(\mathcal{E})$ to denote the minimal Boolean algebra of events containing $\mathcal{E}$ and $\mathbf{add}(\mathcal{E})$ to denote the minimal additive class of events containing $\mathcal{E}$. By $\mathbf{at}(\mathcal{E})$ we indicate the finest partition of Ω contained in $\mathbf{alg}(\mathcal{E})$, in particular, the events in $\mathcal{E}$ are said to be *logically independent* if the cardinality of $\mathbf{at}(\mathcal{E})$ is 2^n.

Definition 1. *Let $\mathcal{A}$ be a Boolean algebra of events and let $\mathcal{H}$ be an additive class with $\mathcal{H} \subseteq \mathcal{A}^0$. A **conditional probability** on $\mathcal{A} \times \mathcal{H}$ is a function $P : \mathcal{A} \times \mathcal{H} \rightarrow [0, 1]$ that satisfies the following conditions:*

(i) $P(E|H) = P(E \wedge H|H)$, for every $E \in \mathcal{A}$ and $H \in \mathcal{H}$;
(ii) $P(\cdot|H)$ is a finitely additive probability on $\mathcal{A}$, for every $H \in \mathcal{H}$;
(iii) $P(E \wedge F|H) = P(E|H) \cdot P(F|E \wedge H)$, for every $H, E \wedge H \in \mathcal{H}$ and $E, F \in \mathcal{A}$.

As usual, whenever $\Omega \in \mathcal{H}$, we will write $P(E) = P(E|\Omega)$ for all $E \in \mathcal{A}$. Following [6], we say that a conditional probability $P(\cdot|\cdot)$ is *full* on the algebra $\mathcal{A}$ if it is defined on $\mathcal{A} \times \mathcal{A}^0$.

For every finite Boolean algebra of events $\mathcal{A}$ and additive class $\mathcal{H} \subseteq \mathcal{A}^0$, every conditional probability $P(\cdot|\cdot)$ on $\mathcal{A} \times \mathcal{H}$ determines a linearly ordered class $\{H_0^0, \ldots, H_0^k\}$ of decreasing elements of $\mathcal{H}$, such that

- $H_0^0 = \bigvee_{H \in \mathcal{H}} H$;
- for $\alpha = 1, \ldots, k$, $H_0^\alpha = \bigvee \{H \in \mathcal{H} : H \subseteq H_0^{\alpha-1}, P(H|H_0^{\alpha-1}) = 0\}$.

The last event H_0^k is such that $P(H|H_0^k) > 0$ for all $H \in \mathcal{H}$ with $H \subseteq H_0^k$. The events $\{H_0, \ldots, H_k\}$ give rise to a class $\{\mathcal{I}_0, \ldots, \mathcal{I}_k\}$ of decreasing Boolean ideals of $\mathcal{A}$, where $\mathcal{I}_\alpha = \{A \in \mathcal{A} : A \subseteq H_0^\alpha\}$. In turn, the class of ideals $\{\mathcal{I}_0, \ldots, \mathcal{I}_k\}$ is associated to a class of unconditional probabilities $\{P_0, \ldots, P_k\}$ where each P_α is the restriction of $P(\cdot|H_0^\alpha)$ to $\mathcal{I}_\alpha$. In particular, each P_α is completely determined by its values on $\mathcal{I}_\alpha \cap \mathbf{at}(\mathcal{A})$ through additivity. For every event $H \in \mathcal{H}$, there is a unique index $\alpha_H \in \{0, \ldots, k\}$ such that $H \in \mathcal{I}_{\alpha_H}$ and $P_{\alpha_H}(H) > 0$. Moreover, for every conditional event $E|H \in \mathcal{A} \times \mathcal{H}$ we have that

$$P(E|H) = \frac{P_{\alpha_H}(E \wedge H)}{P_{\alpha_H}(H)}. \tag{1}$$

The class $\{P_0, \ldots, P_k\}$ is said $\mathcal{H}$-*minimal agreeing class* and allows to represent the conditional probability $P(\cdot|\cdot)$ on $\mathcal{A} \times \mathcal{H}$ through (1). In particular, a $\mathcal{A}^0$-minimal agreeing class allows to represent a full conditional probability $P(\cdot|\cdot)$ on $\mathcal{A}$ and is referred to as *complete agreeing class*.

In the sequel, we call *assessment* a function $P : \mathcal{G} \rightarrow [0, 1]$ with $\mathcal{G}$ an arbitrary set of conditional events and, given $\mathcal{D} \subseteq \mathcal{G}$, $P_{|\mathcal{D}}$ stands for the *restriction* of P to $\mathcal{D}$. The following definition and characterization theorem can be found in [1].

Definition 2. *Let $\mathcal{G} = \{E_i|H_i\}_{i \in I}$ be an arbitrary family of conditional events. An assessment $P : \mathcal{G} \to [0,1]$ is a* **coherent conditional probability** *if there exists a conditional probability $P' : \mathcal{A} \times \mathcal{H} \to [0,1]$, with $\mathcal{A} = \textbf{alg}(\{E_i, H_i\}_{i \in I})$ and $\mathcal{H} = \textbf{add}(\{H_i\}_{i \in I})$, such that $P'_{|\mathcal{G}} = P$.*

Theorem 1. *Let $\mathcal{G}$ be an arbitrary family of conditional events. Then, for any function $P : \mathcal{G} \to [0,1]$, the following statements are equivalent:*

(i) P is a coherent conditional probability on $\mathcal{G}$;
(ii) for every finite subfamily $\mathcal{F} = \{E_1|H_1, \ldots, E_n|H_n\} \subseteq \mathcal{G}$, denoting by $\mathcal{A} = \textbf{alg}(\{E_i, H_i\}_{i=1}^n)$ and $\mathcal{H} = \textbf{add}(\{H_i\}_{i=1}^n)$, there exists a $\mathcal{H}$-minimal agreeing class $\{P_0, \ldots, P_k\}$ corresponding to a conditional probability $P'(\cdot|\cdot)$ on $\mathcal{A} \times \mathcal{H}$ extending $P_{|\mathcal{F}}$, i.e., such that, for $i = 1, \ldots, n$, it holds that

$$P(E_i|H_i) = \frac{P_{\alpha_{H_i}}(E_i \wedge H_i)}{P_{\alpha_{H_i}}(H_i)}.$$

We recall, see e.g. [7] and [1], that coherence is a necessary and sufficient condition for the extendibility of an assessment P on any larger set $\mathcal{G}' \supset \mathcal{G}$ of conditional events. In particular, a coherent conditional probability P can be always extended (generally not in a unique way) to a full conditional probability on $\mathcal{A} = \textbf{alg}(\{E_i, H_i\}_{i \in I})$.

2.2 Zero-Layers

To conclude our review of the setting of coherent conditional probability, we recall the concept of *zero-layer* from [1], which naturally arises from the structure of conditional probability described in Theorem 1.

Definition 3. *Let $\mathcal{A}$ be a finite Boolean algebra of events and let $\{P_0, \ldots, P_k\}$ be a complete agreeing class on $\mathcal{A}$. For every event $H \in \mathcal{A}^0$, the* **zero-layer** *of H with respect to $\{P_0, \ldots, P_k\}$ is the non-negative number*

$$o(H) = \alpha_H,$$

where $\alpha_H \in \{0, \ldots, k\}$ is the unique index such that $H \in \mathcal{I}_{\alpha_H}$ and $P_{\alpha_H}(H) > 0$; the zero layer of the impossible event is set to $o(\varnothing) = +\infty$. For every conditional event $E|H \in \mathcal{A} \times \mathcal{A}^0$, the **zero-layer** *of $E|H$ with respect to $\{P_0, \ldots, P_k\}$ is the non-negative number*

$$o(E|H) = o(E \wedge H) - o(H).$$

The zero-layer of $E|H$ is easily seen to have a behavior that is independent of the chosen complete agreeing class in case $E \wedge H = \varnothing$ or $P(E|H) > 0$ since it reduces, respectively, to $+\infty$ and to 0. The following Theorem 2, summarizing results given in Theorem 2 in [2] and Theorem 4.8 in [4], shows the robustness of the zero-layer of a conditional event with respect to the choice of the agreeing class, when E, H are logically independent events and extreme and equal probabilities are given to $E|H$ and $E|H^c$. This paves the way to using zero-layers for distinguishing between independence and correlation when extreme probability events are involved.

Theorem 2. *Let E, H be logically independent events and let P be a coherent conditional probability on a family of conditional events $\mathcal{G}$ containing the set $\mathcal{D} = \{E^*|H^*, H^*|E^*\}$. Let $P(E|H) = P(E|H^c) = 0$ or 1. If there exists a complete agreeing class $\{P_\alpha\}$ on $\mathbf{alg}(\{E, H\})$ that agrees with $P_{|\mathcal{D}}$, such that one of the following conditions holds:*

(a) $o(E|H) = o(E|H^c)$ and $o(E^c|H) = o(E^c|H^c)$;
(b) $o(E|H) < [>]o(E|H^c)$;
(c) $o(E^c|H) > [<]o(E^c|H^c)$;

then the same condition holds true for any other complete agreeing class on $\mathbf{alg}(\{E, H\})$ that agrees with $P_{|\mathcal{D}}$.

Notice that, if $P(E|H) = P(E|H^c) = \delta \in]0, 1[$, then it trivially holds that $o(E|H) = o(E|H^c) = o(E^c|H) = o(E^c|H^c) = 0$.

2.3   Coherent Lower Conditional Probability

Given an arbitrary set $\mathcal{G}$ of conditional events, a *coherent lower conditional probability* on $\mathcal{G}$ is a non-negative function $\underline{P}$ such that there exists a non-empty family $\mathcal{P}$ of coherent conditional probabilities on $\mathcal{G}$, said *dominating family*, whose lower envelope agrees with $\underline{P}$, that is, for every $E|H \in \mathcal{G}$,

$$\underline{P}(E|H) = \inf_{P \in \mathcal{P}} P(E|H).$$

In particular, $\mathcal{P}$ can be taken equal to the set $\mathcal{Q}$ of all dominating coherent conditional probabilities on $\mathcal{G}$

$$\mathcal{Q} = \{P : P \text{ is a coherent conditional probability on } \mathcal{G}, P \geq \underline{P}\},$$

and in this case the pointwise infima are attained (see [13]). The family $\mathcal{Q}$ will be referred to as *maximal dominating family*.

When $\mathcal{G}$ is finite, if $\underline{P}$ is a coherent lower conditional probability, then there exists a finite dominating family $\mathcal{P}$ such that

$$\underline{P}(E|H) = \min_{P \in \mathcal{P}} P(E|H),$$

whose elements are called *i-minimal* according to the following definition.

Definition 4. *Let $\underline{P}$ be a coherent lower conditional probability on a finite set of conditional events $\mathcal{G} = \{E_1|H_1, \ldots, E_n|H_n\}$. For any conditional event $E_i|H_i \in \mathcal{G}$, an element P^i of the maximal dominating family $\mathcal{Q}$ such that $P^i(E_i|H_i) = \underline{P}(E_i|H_i)$ will be called i-**minimal** coherent conditional probability.*

3   Independence and Correlation in the Framework of Coherent Conditional Probabilities

Inspired by what is proposed in [2–4, 10, 11] and trying to solve some weaknesses, we recall here the following definitions of independence and correlation in the framework of coherent conditional probability.

We first recall the definition of stochastic independence given in [1, 2] that goes under the name of *cs-independence*, where "cs" reads as "coherent setting".

Definition 5. *Let P be a coherent conditional probability defined on an arbitrary family of conditional event $\mathcal{G}$ containing $\mathcal{D} = \{E^*|H^*, H^*|E^*\}$. We say that E is **cs-independent** of H with respect to P, denoted as $E \perp\!\!\!\perp_{cs} H$, if the following two conditions hold:*

- $P(E|H) = P(E|H^c)$;
- *there exists a complete agreeing class $\{P_\alpha\}$ on $\mathbf{alg}(\{E, H\})$ that agrees with $P_{|\mathcal{D}}$ such that*

$$o(E|H) = o(E|H^c) \quad and \quad o(E^c|H) = o(E^c|H^c).$$

Notice that if $P(E|H) = P(E|H^c) = \delta \in]0, 1[$, then the second condition is automatically verified and so $E \perp\!\!\!\perp_{cs} H$. Next, we recall the definition of positive and negative cs-correlation given in [4], that is obtained as a natural counterpart of cs-independence.

Definition 6. *Let P be a coherent conditional probability defined on an arbitrary family of conditional events $\mathcal{G}$ containing $\mathcal{D} = \{E^*|H^*, H^*|E^*\}$. We say that:*

- *E is **positively cs-correlated** with H with respect to P, denoted as $E \perp^+_{cs} H$, if one of the following conditions holds:*
  - $P(E|H) > P(E|H^c)$;
  - *$P(E|H) = P(E|H^c) = 0$, and there exists a complete agreeing class $\{P_\alpha\}$ on $\mathbf{alg}(\{E, H\})$ that agrees with $P_{|\mathcal{D}}$ such that*

$$o(E|H) < o(E|H^c);$$

  - *$P(E|H) = P(E|H^c) = 1$, and there exists a complete agreeing class $\{P_\alpha\}$ on $\mathbf{alg}(\{E, H\})$ that agrees with $P_{|\mathcal{D}}$ such that*

$$o(E^c|H) > o(E^c|H^c);$$

- *E is **negatively cs-correlated** with H with respect to P, denoted as $E \perp^-_{cs} H$, if one of the following conditions holds:*
  - $P(E|H) < P(E|H^c)$;
  - *$P(E|H) = P(E|H^c) = 0$, and there exists a complete agreeing class $\{P_\alpha\}$ on $\mathbf{alg}(\{E, H\})$ that agrees with $P_{|\mathcal{D}}$ such that*

$$o(E|H) > o(E|H^c),$$

- $P(E|H) = P(E|H^c) = 1$, *and there exists a complete agreeing class* $\{P_\alpha\}$ *on* $\mathbf{alg}(\{E, H\})$ *that agrees with* $P_{|\mathcal{D}}$ *such that*

$$o(E^c|H) < o(E^c|H^c);$$

– E *is* **not cs-correlated** *with* H *with respect to* P, *denoted as* $E \not\perp_{cs} H$, *if it is not positively nor negatively cs-correlated with* H.

The next Proposition 1 shows that two events not cs-independent are necessarily either positively or negatively cs-correlated.

Proposition 1. *For every* E, H *it holds that*

$$E \not\perp_{cs} H \iff E \perp\!\!\!\perp_{cs} H.$$

As proved in [2] and [4], the above definitions of stochastic independence and positive/negative correlation in a coherent setting avoid the counterintuitive situations arising from the adoption of the classical definitions. In fact, as shown in the following theorem, in the presence of extreme probability events, these definitions allow the identification of a correlation between events which are logically related, and that, therefore, cannot be stochastically independent.

Theorem 3. *Let* P *be a coherent conditional probability defined on an arbitrary family of conditional events* $\mathcal{G}$ *containing the set* $\mathcal{D} = \{E^*|H^*, H^*|E^*\}$. *Then, the following properties hold:*

(i) if either $E \wedge H = \varnothing$ *or* $E^c \wedge H^c = \varnothing$, *then* $E \perp_{cs}^- H$;
(ii) if either $E^c \wedge H = \varnothing$ *or* $E \wedge H^c = \varnothing$ *then* $E \perp_{cs}^+ H$;
(iii) if $E \perp\!\!\!\perp_{cs} H$ *then* E *and* H *are logically independent.*

Detecting correlation and independence in the presence of extreme probability events by means of the definitions recalled above involves the construction of a complete agreeing class for $P_{|\mathcal{D}}$ that, in turn, can be found solving a sequence of linear systems (see [2,4]). Such class is then used to determine the zero-layers of the involved conditional events.

Definition 6 allows to clearly establish a positive/negative correlation between E and H when $P(E|H) \neq P(E|H^c)$. On the other hand, the distinction between correlation and independence according to Definition 5 becomes much more involved in case $P(E|H) = P(E|H^c) = 0$ or 1. The following Theorem 4 provides a complete characterization of correlation and independence between the logically independent events E and H without the need to explicitly identify the zero-layers for the conditional events involved. Such theorem corrects some typos present in the statement of Theorem 6.1 in [4]. We point out that, once the value of P on $\mathcal{D} = \{E^*|H^*, H^*|E^*\}$, where E, H are logically independent, has been fixed and $P(E|H) = P(E|H^c) = 0$ or 1, then its extension to $H|\Omega$ is uniquely determined. In detail, Theorem 4 relies just on probabilities $P(H), P(E^*|H^*)$ and $P(H^*|E^*)$.

Theorem 4. *Let* E, H *be logically independent events and let* P *be a coherent conditional probability on a family of conditional events* $\mathcal{G}$ *containing the set* $\mathcal{D} = \{E^*|H^*, H^*|E^*\}$, *with* $P(E|H) = P(E|H^c)$. *Then, the following properties hold:*

(i) $E \perp_{cs}^+ H$ *if and only if one of the following conditions holds:*
   (a) $P(E|H) = 0$ *and the extension of* P *to* H *and* $H|E$ *meets either of the following conditions:*
      1. $P(H) = 0$ *and* $P(H|E) > 0$;
      2. $0 < P(H) < 1$ *and* $P(H|E) = 1$;
   (b) $P(E|H) = 1$ *and the extension of* P *to* H *and* $H|E^c$ *meets either of the following conditions:*
      1. $0 < P(H) < 1$ *and* $P(H|E^c) = 0$;
      2. $P(H) = 1$ *and* $P(H|E^c) < 1$;

(ii) $E \perp_{cs}^- H$ *if and only if one of the following conditions holds:*
   (c) $P(E|H) = 0$ *and the extension of* P *to* H *and* $H|E$ *meets either of the following conditions:*
      1. $0 < P(H) < 1$ *and* $P(H|E) = 0$;
      2. $P(H) = 1$ *and* $P(H|E) < 1$;
   (d) $P(E|H) = 1$ *and the extension of* P *to* H *and* $H|E^c$ *meets either of the following conditions:*
      1. $P(H) = 0$ *and* $P(H|E^c) > 0$;
      2. $0 < P(H) < 1$ *and* $P(H|E^c) = 1$.

(iii) $E \perp\!\!\!\perp_{cs} H$ *if and only if one of the following conditions holds:*
   (e) $0 < P(E|H) < 1$;
   (f) $P(E|H) = 0$ *and the extension of* P *to* H *and* $H|E$ *meets either of the following conditions:*
      1. $P(H) = 0$ *and* $P(H|E) = 0$;
      2. $P(H) = 1$ *and* $P(H|E) = 1$;
      3. $0 < P(H) < 1$ *and* $0 < P(H|E) < 1$;
   (g) $P(E|H) = 1$ *and the extension of* P *to* H *and* $H|E^c$ *meets either of the following conditions:*
      1. $P(H) = 0$ *and* $P(H|E^c) = 0$;
      2. $P(H) = 1$ *and* $P(H|E^c) = 1$;
      3. $0 < P(H) < 1$ *and* $0 < P(H|E^c) < 1$.

4   Independence and Correlation in the Framework of Coherent Lower Conditional Probabilities

In [2] a definition of cs-independence for a coherent conditional lower probability $\underline{P}$ has been introduced. Two events E and H are defined to be independent with respect to $\underline{P}$ if there exists a dominating class $\mathcal{P}$ of coherent conditional probabilities on $\mathcal{G}$ such that, for every $P \in \mathcal{P}$, E is cs-independent of H. However, this definition is too demanding, since it involves too many conditional events. The strength of this definition is testified by the fact that it is satisfied only if $\underline{P}$, restricted to $\{E, H, E^*|H^*, H^*|E^*\}$, is a coherent conditional probability [2].

In this paper a different definition is proposed: it involves only two probabilities P^1 and P^2 dominating $\underline{P}$ on $\mathcal{D}$ and i-minimal on $E|H$ and $E|H^c$, respectively, such that E is cs-independent of H with respect to both. Nevertheless this *local* condition does not prevent that together with a pair of such i-minimal probabilities there exists also a pair $P^{1'}$ and $P^{2'}$ of i-minimal probabilities such that E is positively (or negatively) cs-correlated with H with respect to both. Therefore, here we provide a sound definition, where we explicitly require the non-existence of such a pair.

Definition 7. *Let $\underline{P}$ be a coherent lower conditional probability defined on an arbitrary family of conditional events $\mathcal{G}$ containing $\mathcal{D} = \{E^*|H^*, H^*|E^*\}$. We say that E is* **cs-independent** *of H with respect to $\underline{P}$, denoted as $E\underline{\perp\!\!\!\perp}_{cs}H$, if $\underline{P}_{|\mathcal{D}}$ admits P^1 and P^2, i-minimal for $E|H$ and $E|H^c$, respectively, such that E is cs-independent of H with respect to both P^1 and P^2, and do not exist $P^{1'}$ and $P^{2'}$, i-minimal for $E|H$ and $E|H^c$, respectively, such that E is either positively cs-correlated or negatively cs-correlated with H with respect to both $P^{1'}$ and $P^{2'}$.*

Condition *(iii)* of Theorem 3 immediately implies the following corollary.

Corollary 1. *Let $\underline{P}$ be a coherent lower conditional probability defined on an arbitrary family of conditional events $\mathcal{G}$ containing the set $\mathcal{D} = \{E^*|H^*, H^*|E^*\}$. It holds that if $E\underline{\perp\!\!\!\perp}_{cs}H$ then E and H are logically independent.*

It is natural to extend the above definition to positive/negative correlation.

Definition 8. *Let $\underline{P}$ be a coherent lower conditional probability defined on an arbitrary family of conditional events $\mathcal{G}$ containing $\mathcal{D} = \{E^*|H^*, H^*|E^*\}$. We say that:*

- *E is* **positively cs-correlated** *with H with respect to $\underline{P}$, denoted as $E\underline{\perp}^+_{cs}H$, if $\underline{P}_{|\mathcal{D}}$ admits P^1 and P^2, i-minimal for $E|H$ and a $E|H^c$, respectively, such that E is positively cs-correlated with H with respect to both P^1 and P^2, and do not exist $P^{1'}$ and $P^{2'}$, i-minimal for $E|H$ and $E|H^c$, respectively, such that E is either negatively cs-correlated with H or cs-independent of H with respect to both $P^{1'}$ and $P^{2'}$;*
- *E is* **negatively cs-correlated** *with H with respect to $\underline{P}$, denoted as $E\underline{\perp}^-_{cs}H$, if $\underline{P}_{|\mathcal{D}}$ admits P^1 and P^2, i-minimal for $E|H$ and $E|H^c$, respectively, such that E is negatively cs-correlated with H with respect to both P^1 and P^2, and do not exist $P^{1'}$ and $P^{2'}$, i-minimal for $E|H$ and $E|H^c$, respectively, such that E is either positively cs-correlated with H or cs-independent of H with respect to both $P^{1'}$ and $P^{2'}$.*

We point out that the coherent conditional probabilities P^1, P^2 and $P^{1'}, P^{2'}$ appearing in Definitions 7 and 8 are defined only on $\mathcal{D}$ since they refer to $\underline{P}_{|\mathcal{D}}$. Moreover, the two elements of pairs P^1, P^2 and $P^{1'}, P^{2'}$ are not necessarily distinct, in the sense that the same coherent conditional probability on $\mathcal{D}$ can be i-minimal for both $E|H$ and $E|H^c$, thus it can happen $P^1 = P^2$ and $P^{1'} = P^{2'}$.

Let us stress that, for having $\neg(E \underline{\perp\!\!\!\perp}_{cs} H)$, either there is no pair P^1, P^2 of coherent conditional probabilities on $\mathcal{D}$ which are i-minimal for $E|H$ and $E|H^c$, respectively, and unanimously establish cs-independence of E and H, or there exists a pair $P^{1'}, P^{2'}$ of coherent conditional probabilities on $\mathcal{D}$ which are i-minimal for $E|H$ and $E|H^c$, respectively, and unanimously establish positive [negative] cs-independence of E and H. Therefore, under the existence of P^1, P^2, if all pairs $P^{1'}, P^{2'}$ express mixed correlation and independence statements, then $E \underline{\perp\!\!\!\perp}_{cs} H$. Analogous considerations apply to $\neg(E \underline{\perp}_{cs}^+ H)$ and $\neg(E \underline{\perp}_{cs}^+ H)$.

From Definition 8 and Theorem 3 the following Corollary 2 immediately follows.

Corollary 2. *Let $\underline{P}$ be a coherent lower conditional probability defined on an arbitrary family of conditional events $\mathcal{G}$ containing the set $\mathcal{D} = \{E^*|H^*, H^*|E^*\}$. Then, the following properties hold:*

(i) *if either $E \wedge H = \varnothing$ or $E^c \wedge H^c = \varnothing$, then $E \underline{\perp}_{cs}^- H$;*
(ii) *if either $E^c \wedge H = \varnothing$ or $E \wedge H^c = \varnothing$ then $E \underline{\perp}_{cs}^+ H$.*

The following Example 1 shows that there are $\underline{P}$ such that there is a pair P^1, P^2 for which E, H are cs-independent, a pair $P^{1'}, P^{2'}$ for which E, H are positively cs-correlated, and a pair $P^{1''}, P^{2''}$ for which E, H are negatively cs-correlated. In Example 1 we have $P^1 = P^2$, $P^{1'} = P^{2'}$ and $P^{1''} = P^{2''}$.

Example 1. Let E, H be logically independent events and let $\mathrm{at}(\{E, H\}) = \{C_1, C_2, C_3, C_4\}$ with $C_1 = E \wedge H, C_2 = E \wedge H^c, C_3 = E^c \wedge H, C_4 = E^c \wedge H^c$. Take $\mathcal{D} = \{E^*|H^*, H^*|E^*\}$ and consider the class $\mathcal{P} = \{P^1, P^2, P^3\}$ of coherent conditional probabilities on $\mathcal{D}$ such that

$\mathcal{D}$	$E|H$	$E|H^c$	$E^c|H$	$E^c|H^c$	$H|E$	$H|E^c$	$H^c|E$	$H^c|E^c$
P^1	1	1	0	0	1	1	0	0
P^2	1	1	0	0	1	0	0	1
P^3	1	1	0	0	0	1	1	0
$\underline{P}$	1	1	0	0	0	0	0	0

Since $\underline{P}(E|H) = \underline{P}(E|H^c) = 1$, all coherent conditional probabilities dominating $\underline{P}$ on $\mathcal{D}$ are automatically i-minimal for both the conditional events $E|H$ and $E|H^c$ and it always holds $o(E|H) = o(E|H^c) = 0$. Each coherent conditional probability P^i, for $i = 1, 2, 3$, can be associated to a complete agreeing class $\{P_\alpha^i\}$ on $\mathrm{alg}(\{E, H\})$ as follows

	C_1	C_2	C_3	C_4
P_0^1	1	0	0	0
P_1^1	•	1	0	0
P_2^1	•	•	1	0
P_3^1	•	•	•	1

	C_1	C_2	C_3	C_4
P_0^2	1	0	0	0
P_1^2	•	1	0	0
P_2^2	•	•	0	1
P_3^2	•	•	1	•

	C_1	C_2	C_3	C_4
P_0^3	0	1	0	0
P_1^3	1	•	0	0
P_2^3	•	•	1	0
P_3^3	•	•	•	1

$o(E^c|H) = 2 = o(E^c|H^c)$ $o(E^c|H) = 3 > 1 = o(E^c|H^c)$ $o(E^c|H) = 1 < 3 = o(E^c|H^c)$

We have that P^1 is i-minimal for both $E|H$ and $E|H^c$ and such that E is cs-independent of H. Moreover, P^2 is i-minimal for both $E|H$ and $E|H^c$ and such that E is positively cs-correlated with H. Finally, P^3 is i-minimal for both $E|H$ and $E|H^c$ and such that E is negatively cs-correlated with H. Hence, we have that $\neg(E \perp\!\!\!\perp_{cs} H)$ and $\neg(E \perp^+_{cs} H)$ and $\neg(E \perp^-_{cs} H)$. ♦

We first consider the case of cs-independence when $\underline{P}(E|H)$ and $\underline{P}(E|H^c)$ are both different from extreme values 0 and 1.

Theorem 5. *Let E, H be logically independent events and let $\underline{P}$ be a coherent lower conditional probability defined on an arbitrary set of conditional events $\mathcal{G}$ containing the set $\mathcal{D} = \{E^*|H^*, H^*|E^*\}$ such that $\underline{P}(E|H) = \alpha$ and $\underline{P}(E|H^c) = \beta$, with $\alpha, \beta \in]0,1[$. Then, $E \perp\!\!\!\perp_{cs} H$ if and only if $\alpha = \beta$, and there is $\delta \in [0,1]$ such that*

$$\max\{\underline{P}(H|E), \underline{P}(H|E^c)\} \le \delta \quad and \quad \max\{\underline{P}(H^c|E), \underline{P}(H^c|E^c)\} \le 1 - \delta.$$

Proof. Let P^1, P^2 be coherent conditional probabilities on $\mathcal{D}$ which are i-minimal for $E|H$ and $E|H^c$, respectively. Then we have $P^1(E|H) = \alpha$, $P^1(E|H^c) \ge \beta$, $P^2(E|H) \ge \alpha$, $P^2(E|H^c) = \beta$, and, so, every complete agreeing class on $\mathbf{alg}(\{E, H\})$ representing P^i, for $i = 1, 2$, is such that $o(E|H) = o(E|H^c) = 0$. Let $\mathbf{at}(\{E, H\}) = \{C_1, C_2, C_3, C_4\}$ with $C_1 = E \wedge H, C_2 = E \wedge H^c, C_3 = E^c \wedge H, C_4 = E^c \wedge H^c$.

If $\alpha > \beta$ or $\alpha < \beta$, then we cannot find a pair P^1, P^2 such that $E \perp\!\!\!\perp_{cs} H$ with respect to both, so, $\alpha = \beta$ is necessary to have $E \perp\!\!\!\perp_{cs} H$. If $\alpha = \beta$, then we always have $0 < P^1(E|H) \le P^1(E|H^c) \le 1$ and $1 \ge P^2(E|H) \ge P^2(E|H^c) > 0$, therefore, we cannot have a pair P^1, P^2 such that $E \perp^+_{cs} H$ with respect to both, nor a pair P^1, P^2 such that $E \perp^-_{cs} H$ with respect to both. Thus, it remains to prove the existence of a pair P^1, P^2 such that $E \perp\!\!\!\perp_{cs} H$ with respect to both. Since it must be $P^i(E|H) = P^i(E|H^c) = \alpha$ for $i = 1, 2$, every such P^i will be i-minimal both for $E|H$ and $E^c|H$ and $o(E^c|H) = o(E^c|H^c) = 0$. Let δ be an arbitrary number in $]0,1[$. Below we report all the possible complete agreeing classes $\{P^i_\alpha\}$ on $\mathbf{alg}(\{E, H\})$ that agree with $P^i(E|H) = P^i(E|H^c) = \alpha$:

(A)			
	C_1	C_2	C_3	C_4
P^i_0	α	0	$1-\alpha$	0
P^i_1	$\bullet$	α	$\bullet$	$1-\alpha$

$P^i(H|E) = P^i(H|E^c) = 1$

(B)			
	C_1	C_2	C_3	C_4
P^i_0	0	α	0	$1-\alpha$
P^i_1	α	$\bullet$	$1-\alpha$	$\bullet$

$P^i(H|E) = P^i(H|E^c) = 0$

(C)			
	C_1	C_2	C_3	C_4
P^i_0	$\alpha\delta$	$\alpha(1-\delta)$	$(1-\alpha)\delta$	$(1-\alpha)(1-\delta)$

$P^i(H|E) = P^i(H|E^c) = \delta$

Therefore, $E \perp\!\!\!\perp_{cs} H$ if and only if $\alpha = \beta$, and there is $\delta \in [0,1]$ such that $\max\{\underline{P}(H|E), \underline{P}(H|E^c)\} \le \delta$ and $\max\{\underline{P}(H^c|E), \underline{P}(H^c|E^c)\} \le 1 - \delta$. □

We notice that, in case $\underline{P}$ is a coherent conditional probability, then the inequalities in Theorem 5 are satisfied as equalities and the theorem collapses in condition *(iii.e)* of Theorem 4.

It is possible to prove that when $\underline{P}(E|H) = \alpha$ and $\underline{P}(E|H^c) = \beta$, with $\alpha, \beta \in]0,1[$, the condition $\alpha > \beta$ [$\alpha < \beta$] is necessary for $E \perp^+_{cs} H$ [$E \perp^-_{cs} H$].

In this case, to get a characterization of $E\perp^+_{cs}H$ $[E\perp^-_{cs}H]$ some domination conditions on $\underline{P}(H^*|E^*)$ need to be added in order to guarantee the existence of a pair P^1, P^2 of coherent conditional probabilities on $\mathcal{D}$ which are i-minimal for $E|H$ and $E|H^c$, respectively, and such that $E\perp^+_{cs}H$ $[E\perp^-_{cs}H]$ with respect to both. Since the quoted conditions and the proof do not fit the space limitations of the paper, they are reserved for an extended version.

It remains to consider the case in which $\underline{P}(E|H), \underline{P}(E|H^c)$ take extreme values 0 or 1. Still due to a lack of space, below we analyze cs-independence and cs-correlation with respect to $\underline{P}$ in the case $\underline{P}(E|H) = \underline{P}(E|H^c) = 1$ showing that, yet in this particular case, non-trivial situations arise. The complete characterization is reserved for an extended version of the paper.

Theorem 6. *Let E, H be logically independent events and let $\underline{P}$ be a coherent lower conditional probability defined on an arbitrary set of conditional events $\mathcal{G}$ containing the set $\mathcal{D} = \{E^*|H^*, H^*|E^*\}$ such that $\underline{P}(E|H) = \underline{P}(E|H^c) = 1$. Then the following statements hold:*

(i) $E\perp\!\!\!\perp_{cs}H$ *if and only if one of the following conditions holds:*
   (a) $0 < \underline{P}(H|E) < 1, 0 < \underline{P}(H^c|E) < 1, 0 < \underline{P}(H|E^c) < 1$ *and* $0 < \underline{P}(H^c|E^c) < 1$;
   (b) $\underline{P}(H|E) = \underline{P}(H|E^c) = 1$;
   (c) $\underline{P}(H^c|E) = \underline{P}(H^c|E^c) = 1$;
(ii) $E\perp^+_{cs}H$ *if and only if* $0 < \underline{P}(H|E) \leq 1$ *and* $0 < \underline{P}(H^c|E^c) \leq 1$ *and*
$$\max\{\underline{P}(H|E), \underline{P}(H^c|E^c)\} = 1;$$

(iii) $E\perp^-_{cs}H$ *if and only if* $0 < \underline{P}(H^c|E) \leq 1$ *and* $0 < \underline{P}(H|E^c) \leq 1$ *and*
$$\max\{\underline{P}(H^c|E), \underline{P}(H|E^c)\} = 1.$$

Proof. Since $\underline{P}(E|H) = \underline{P}(E|H^c) = 1$, every coherent conditional probability P^1 which is i-minimal for $E|H$ is also i-minimal for $E|H^c$, and an analogous situation happens for a probability P^2 which is i-minimal for $E|H^c$. Thus we can limit to consider a single i-minimal coherent conditional probability that we denote as P^i on $\mathcal{D}$ which satisfies $P^i(E|H) = P^i(E|H^c) = 1$, for which it always holds $o(E|H) = o(E|H^c) = 0$. We further have that every coherent conditional probability on $\mathcal{D}$ that dominates $\underline{P}_{|\mathcal{D}}$ is i-minimal for both $E|H$ and $E|H^c$.

Let $\mathbf{at}(\{E, H\}) = \{C_1, C_2, C_3, C_4\}$ with $C_1 = E \wedge H, C_2 = E \wedge H^c, C_3 = E^c \wedge H, C_4 = E^c \wedge H^c$. Take δ, ε be arbitrary real numbers in $]0, 1[$. Below we report all the possible complete agreeing classes $\{P^i_\alpha\}$ on $\mathbf{alg}(\{E, H\})$ that agree with $P^i(E|H) = P^i(E|H^c) = 1$:

(A)

	C_1	C_2	C_3	C_4
P^i_0	δ	$1-\delta$	0	0
P^i_1	•	•	1	0
P^i_2	•	•	•	1

(B)

	C_1	C_2	C_3	C_4
P^i_0	δ	$1-\delta$	0	0
P^i_1	•	•	0	1
P^i_2	•	•	1	•

(C)

	C_1	C_2	C_3	C_4
P^i_0	δ	$1-\delta$	0	0
P^i_1	•	•	ε	$1-\varepsilon$

$o(E^c|H) = 1 < 2 = o(E^c|H^c)$
$P^i(H|E) = \delta$
$P^i(H|E^c) = 1$

$o(E^c|H) = 2 > 1 = o(E^c|H^c)$
$P^i(H|E) = \delta$
$P^i(H|E^c) = 0$

$o(E^c|H) = 1 = o(E^c|H^c)$
$P^i(H|E) = \delta$
$P^i(H|E^c) = \varepsilon$

(D)

	C_1	C_2	C_3	C_4
P_0^i	1	0	0	0
P_1^i	•	1	0	0
P_2^i	•	•	1	0
P_3^i	•	•	•	1

$o(E^c|H) = 2 = o(E^c|H^c)$
$P^i(H|E) = 1$
$P^i(H|E^c) = 1$

(E)

	C_1	C_2	C_3	C_4
P_0^i	1	0	0	0
P_1^i	•	1	0	0
P_2^i	•	•	0	1
P_3^i	•	•	1	•

$o(E^c|H) = 3 > 1 = o(E^c|H^c)$
$P^i(H|E) = 1$
$P^i(H|E^c) = 0$

(F)

	C_1	C_2	C_3	C_4
P_0^i	1	0	0	0
P_1^i	•	1	0	0
P_2^i	•	•	ε	$1-\varepsilon$

$o(E^c|H) = 2 > 1 = o(E^c|H^c)$
$P^i(H|E) = 1$
$P^i(H|E^c) = \varepsilon$

(G)

	C_1	C_2	C_3	C_4
P_0^i	1	0	0	0
P_1^i	•	0	1	0
P_2^i	•	1	•	0
P_3^i	•	•	•	1

$o(E^c|H) = 1 = o(E^c|H^c)$
$P^i(H|E) = 1$
$P^i(H|E^c) = 1$

(H)

	C_1	C_2	C_3	C_4
P_0^i	1	0	0	0
P_1^i	•	ε	$1-\varepsilon$	0
P_2^i	•	•	•	1

$o(E^c|H) = 1 = o(E^c|H^c)$
$P^i(H|E) = 1$
$P^i(H|E^c) = 1$

(I)

	C_1	C_2	C_3	C_4
P_0^i	0	1	0	0
P_1^i	1	•	0	0
P_2^i	•	•	1	0
P_3^i	•	•	•	1

$o(E^c|H) = 1 < 3 = o(E^c|H^c)$
$P^i(H|E) = 0$
$P^i(H|E^c) = 1$

(L)

	C_1	C_2	C_3	C_4
P_0^i	0	1	0	0
P_1^i	1	•	0	0
P_2^i	•	•	0	1
P_3^i	•	•	1	•

$o(E^c|H) = 2 = o(E^c|H^c)$
$P^i(H|E) = 0$
$P^i(H|E^c) = 0$

(M)

	C_1	C_2	C_3	C_4
P_0^i	0	1	0	0
P_1^i	1	•	0	0
P_2^i	•	•	ε	$1-\varepsilon$

$o(E^c|H) = 1 < 2 = o(E^c|H^c)$
$P^i(H|E) = 0$
$P^i(H|E^c) = \varepsilon$

(N)

	C_1	C_2	C_3	C_4
P_0^i	0	1	0	0
P_1^i	0	•	0	1
P_2^i	1	•	0	•
P_3^i	•	•	1	•

$o(E^c|H) = 1 = o(E^c|H^c)$
$P^i(H|E) = 0$
$P^i(H|E^c) = 0$

(O)

	C_1	C_2	C_3	C_4
P_0^i	0	1	0	0
P_1^i	ε	•	0	$1-\varepsilon$
P_2^i	•	•	1	•

$o(E^c|H) = 1 = o(E^c|H^c)$
$P^i(H|E) = 0$
$P^i(H|E^c) = 0$

By the previous discussion we have that $\underline{P}_{|\mathcal{D}}$ is always the lower envelope of a finite class $\mathcal{P}$ whose elements can be represented by some of the complete agreeing classes (A)–(O).

For the statement (i) it follows that the class $\mathcal{P}$ can be formed only by elements of type (C) or only of types (D)-(G)-(H) or only of types (L)-(N)-(O). In particular, it cannot be that $\mathcal{P}$ contains elements of two different groups of those above since this would imply that $\underline{P}_{|\mathcal{D}}$ is dominated by elements that result in a positive/negative cs-correlation.

For the statement *(ii)* *[(iii)]* it follows that the class $\mathcal{P}$ can be formed only by elements of types *(B)-(E)* *[(A)-(I)]* or only of types *(E)-(F)* *[(I)-(M)]*. In particular, it cannot be that $\mathcal{P}$ contains elements of two different groups of those above since this would imply that $\underline{P}_{|\mathcal{D}}$ is dominated by elements of type *(C)* that result in a cs-independence.   □

We notice that, in case $\underline{P}$ is a coherent conditional probability, then, since $P(H) = P(H|E)$ when $P(E|H) = P(E|H^c) = 1$, the theorem collapses in conditions *(i.b)*, *(ii.d)* and *(iii.g)* of Theorem 4.

5   Conclusion

We proposed a definition of independence and positive/negative correlation for events, in the context of coherent lower conditional probability. Due to space limitations, we provided a characterization of cs-independence when $\underline{P}(E|H) = \underline{P}(E|H^c) = \alpha$ for $\alpha \in]0,1]$ and of cs-correlation for $\alpha = 1$. To complete the characterization of cs-independence, the case $\alpha = 0$ needs to be analyzed, while cs-correlation requires to consider both the cases $\alpha = 0$ and $\underline{P}(E|H) \neq \underline{P}(E|H^c)$.

References

1. Coletti, G., Scozzafava, R.: Probabilistic Logic in a Coherent Setting, Trends in Logic, vol. 15. Kluwer Academic Publisher, Dordrecht/Boston/London (2002)
2. Coletti, G., Scozzafava, R.: Stochastic independence in a coherent setting. Ann. Math. Artif. Intell. **35**(1), 151–176 (2002)
3. Coletti, G., Scozzafava, R.: Stochastic independence for upper and lower probabilities in a coherent setting. In: Technologies for Constructing Intelligent Systems 2. Studies in Fuzziness and Soft Computing, vol. 90, pp. 17–30. Physica, Heidelberg (2002)
4. Coletti, G., van der Gaag, L., Petturiti, D., Vantaggi, B.: Detecting correlation between extreme probability events. Int. J. Gen. Syst. **49**(1), 64–87 (2020)
5. Cozman, F., Walley, P.: Graphoid properties of epistemic irrelevance and independence. Ann. Math. Art. Intell. **45**(1), 173–195 (2005)
6. Dubins, L.: Finitely additive conditional probabilities, conglomerability and disintegrations. Ann. Probab. **3**(1), 89–99 (1975)
7. Holzer, S.: On coherence and conditional prevision. Boll. UMI **6**(4), 441–460 (1985)
8. Montes, I., Miranda, E., Pelessoni, R., Vicig, P.: Sklar's theorem in an imprecise setting. Fuzzy Sets Syst. **278**, 48–66 (2015)
9. Omladič, M., Stopar, N.: Multivariate imprecise Sklar type theorems. Fuzzy Sets Syst. **428**, 80–101 (2022)
10. Vantaggi, B.: Conditional independence in a coherent finite setting. Ann. Math. Art. Intell. **32**(1), 287–313 (2001)
11. Vantaggi, B.: Conditional independence structures and graphical models. Int. J. Uncert. Fuzz. Knowl. Based Syst. **11**(05), 545–571 (2003)
12. Walley, P.: Statistical Reasoning with Imprecise Probabilities. Chapman and Hall, London (1991)
13. Williams, P.: Notes on conditional previsions. Int. J. Approx. Reas. **44**(3), 366–383 (2007)

Markov and Time-Homogeneity Properties in Dempster-Shafer Random Walks

Andrea Cinfrignini[1] , Davide Petturiti[2]([✉]) , and Barbara Vantaggi[1]

[1] Department of MEMOTEF, "La Sapienza" University of Rome, Rome, Italy
{andrea.cinfrignini,barbara.vantaggi}@uniroma1.it
[2] Department of Economics, University of Perugia, Perugia, Italy
davide.petturiti@unipg.it

Abstract. We generalize discrete-time finite-horizon random walks in order to deal with ambiguity or mis-specification inside the framework of belief functions. Referring to the product rule of conditioning for belief functions, we propose suitable definitions of Markov and time-homogeneity properties. Moreover, we investigate to what extent such properties can be constrained by means of one-step time-homogeneity.

Keywords: Belief functions · Random walk · Markov property · Time-homogeneity

1 Introduction

Uncertainty is usually modelled through a probability measure, however deviations from the classical theory are justified by empirically documented phenomena in different fields such as decision theory and artificial intelligence.

Decision models involving sets of probability measures or non-additive uncertainty measures have been extensively studied in a way to capture situations of *ambiguity* (see, e.g., [8,10] and also [3]). More recently, stochastic processes under imprecise probabilities or non-linear expectations have been deeply investigated (see, e.g., [5,6,12,14,16,19]). In this context, many of the quoted papers try to enforce a version of the classical Markov property, often together with a companion version of time-homogeneity.

The cited papers can be broadly divided into those focusing on local belief models and those relying on a global belief model. Approaches based on local models deal with the process by considering one-step transitions and then extending it to more steps by working in analogy with the probabilistic case. Though the Markov property in the probabilistic framework leads to a unique probability measure due to additivity, in the imprecise case things become much more involved. On the other hand, approaches based on a global model look for a form of conditional uncertainty measures, that extends the information contained in the local models by requiring a set of mathematical properties. For instance, in [19] a global model based on a conditional upper expectation is proposed.

© Springer Nature Switzerland AG 2022
D. Ciucci et al. (Eds.): IPMU 2022, CCIS 1601, pp. 784–797, 2022.
https://doi.org/10.1007/978-3-031-08971-8_63

In this paper we focus on particular imprecise (discrete-time finite-horizon) random walks, where uncertainty is modelled inside Dempster-Shafer theory [7,15], that we call *Dempster-Shafer random walks*. We look for a global belief function for the process that enforces a suitable version of the Markov and time-homogeneity properties. Our approach differs from other proposals present in the literature (such as [19]) since we work with belief functions and the local transition models are obtained from the global one through the product (or geometric) conditioning rule [18]. Our choice of the product conditioning rule is motivated by a nice parametrization of the model: indeed, the model specification is known to be a hard problem in the imprecise setting [16]. The price we pay is that the conditional belief functions we get are generally not coherent in the sense of Williams [21] and Walley [20]. As a consequence, a Dempster-Shafer random walk will not be in general equal to the lower envelope of a family of precise random walks. For other approaches generalizing Markov chains in the framework of Walley see [13,17,19]. Another peculiarity of our proposal, distinguishing it from the quoted approaches, is that we consider t-step transitions for all the possible t's and rely on the global belief function through the product conditioning rule, in order to ensure their consistency.

We propose a construction that generalizes the probabilistic one and reduces to it when additivity of the global belief function is required. Such construction constrains the global model by imposing one-step time-homogeneity. We show that, among the global models, there are those where both the Markov property and time-homogeneity fail and those where just one property fails. It is actually possible to prove that a global belief function ensuring both properties always exists: we do not report this part here for lack of space. However, we show that uniqueness of such a belief function generally fails. It turns out that the global model is characterized by a family of transition belief functions. Thus, the problem is to select a particular "canonical" belief function Bel that makes the process a Dempster-Shafer random walk and ensures a particular structure for the family of transition belief functions. This last point is particularly relevant in facing the problem of convergence of belief functions when passing from discrete to continuous time [9].

It turns out that the global model we get gives rise to a conditional Choquet expectation that can be locally interpreted as a completely monotone lower expectation. Thus, a deeper comparison with the existing literature [5,6,14,16], that mainly copes with lower/upper expectations, can be considered. Though such conditional Choquet expectation is generally not the lower envelope of conditional expectations related to precise random walks, it can be locally associated to a closed and convex set of probability measures given by a conditional core.

2   Preliminaries

Let Ω be a finite non-empty set of states of the world and take $\mathcal{F} = \mathcal{P}(\Omega)$, where the latter denotes the power set of Ω. We denote by $\mathbb{R}^{\Omega}$ the set of all random variables on Ω and by $\mathbf{1}_E$ the *indicator* of event E, for every $E \in \mathcal{F}$.

As is well-known, the Dempster-Shafer theory of evidence (see [7,15]) is based on a pair of non-additive set functions said, respectively, *belief* and *plausibility functions*. In particular, a *belief function* is a mapping $Bel : \mathcal{F} \to [0,1]$ satisfying:

(i) $Bel(\emptyset) = 0$ and $Bel(\Omega) = 1$;

(ii) $Bel \left(\bigcup_{i=1}^{k} E_i \right) \geq \sum_{\emptyset \neq I \subseteq \{1,\ldots,k\}} (-1)^{|I|+1} Bel \left(\bigcap_{i \in I} E_i \right)$, for every $k \geq 2$ and $E_1, \ldots, E_k \in \mathcal{F}$.

Condition *(ii)* is called *complete monotonicity* and together with *(i)* it implies *monotonicity*: $Bel(A) \leq Bel(B)$ when $A \subseteq B$, with $A, B \in \mathcal{F}$. The function Bel is associated to a *dual* set function Pl on $\mathcal{F}$ called *plausibility function* and defined, for every $A \in \mathcal{F}$, as $Pl(A) = 1 - Bel(A^c)$. Moreover, both Bel and Pl are completely characterized by the *Möbius inverse* of Bel (see, e.g., [11,15]) that goes also under the name of *basic probability assignment*. Such function $m : \mathcal{F} \to [0,1]$ is non-negative and satisfies $m(\emptyset) = 0$ and $\sum_{B \in \mathcal{F}} m(B) = 1$, and also

$$Bel(A) = \sum_{B \subseteq A} m(B) \quad \text{and} \quad Pl(A) = \sum_{B \cap A \neq \emptyset} m(B), \tag{1}$$

where the last two equations hold for all $A \in \mathcal{F}$.

We also recall that every belief function induces a non-empty, closed and convex set of probability measures on $\mathcal{F}$ called *core* (see, e.g., [11]) and denoted

$$\mathbf{core}(Bel) = \{P : P \text{ is a probability measure on } F, P \geq Bel\}, \tag{2}$$

such that $Bel = \min \mathbf{core}(Bel)$ and $Pl = \max \mathbf{core}(Bel)$, where minima and maxima are pointwise on $\mathcal{F}$. Therefore, belief and plausibility functions are particular coherent lower and upper probabilities [20,21]. We also recall that probability measures are particular belief functions that turn out to be *additive*, i.e., satisfy *(ii)* with an equality sign.

The problem of conditioning for belief functions has been deeply investigated in the literature and several proposals have been considered (see, e.g., [7,18] and [2] for a deeper discussion). In this work we refer to the *product (or geometric) conditioning rule* for belief functions introduced in [18]: for every $E, H \in \mathcal{F}$ with $Bel(H) > 0$

$$Bel(E|H) = \frac{Bel(E \cap H)}{Bel(H)}. \tag{3}$$

Notice that the above rule of conditioning can be reformulated as a *chain rule* for belief functions: for every $E, H \in \mathcal{F}$ with $Bel(H) > 0$ it holds that

$$Bel(E \cap H) = Bel(E|H)Bel(H). \tag{4}$$

We notice that, whenever $Bel(H) > 0$, $Bel(\cdot|H)$ is a belief function on $\mathcal{F}$ inducing $\mathbf{core}(Bel(\cdot|H))$. Thus, locally on every H with positive belief, $Bel(\cdot|H)$ can be interpreted as a coherent lower probability on $\mathcal{F}$. Nevertheless, setting

$\mathcal{H} = \{H \in \mathcal{F} : Bel(H) > 0\}$, the function $Bel(\cdot|\cdot)$ on $\mathcal{G} = \mathcal{F} \times \mathcal{H}$ may fail to be a coherent lower conditional probability in the sense of Williams [21] (see [2]).

Though a conditional belief function under the product rule (3) is defined whenever the conditioning event has positive belief, this conditioning rule can be generalized axiomatically as done in [2], in order to deal with conditioning events with null belief.

3   Dempster-Shafer Random Walks

Consider a discrete-time finite-horizon process $\{X_0, \ldots, X_T\}$ with $T \in \mathbb{N}$, $X_0 = x_0 \in \mathbb{R}$ and, for $n = 1, \ldots, T$,

$$X_n = \begin{cases} X_{n-1} + u \text{ if "up"}, \\ X_{n-1} + d \text{ if "down"}, \end{cases} \tag{5}$$

where $u > d$ are the "up" and "down" coefficients. Typical choices are $x_0 = 0$, $u = 1$ and $d = -1$. The process above is defined on a filtered measurable space $(\Omega, \mathcal{F}, \{\mathcal{F}_n\}_{n=0}^T)$, where $\Omega = \{1, \ldots, 2^T\}$ and $\mathcal{F}_n$ is the algebra generated by random variables $\{X_0, \ldots, X_n\}$, for $n = 0, \ldots, T$, with $\mathcal{F}_0 = \{\emptyset, \Omega\}$ and $\mathcal{F}_T = \mathcal{F} = \mathcal{P}(\Omega)$.

The trajectories of $\{X_0, \ldots, X_T\}$ can be represented graphically on a binomial tree. In particular, every state $\omega \in \Omega$ is identified with the path corresponding to the T-digit binary expansion of number $\omega - 1$, in which zeroes are interpreted as "up" movements and ones as "down" movements. Figure 1 shows a binomial tree for $T = 3$.

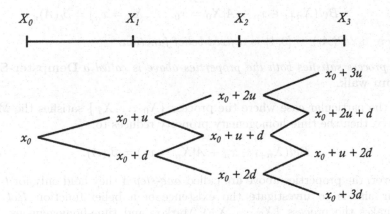

Fig. 1. Binomial tree for $T = 3$.

The process $\{X_1, \ldots, X_T\}$ is usually introduced to model a *random walk* (see [1]) that can be obtained as an additive transformation of a sequence of binary random variables forming a *Bernoulli process*. The assumptions of a classical

Bernoulli process can be relaxed due to imprecision on the knowledge of probability distributions and an imprecise Bernoulli process can be formulated as the lower envelope of a set of Bernoulli processes (see [4]).

In this work we assume that uncertainty on the evolution of the process is not necessarily additive but is handled in the Dempster-Shafer theory of evidence through a belief function. Thus, in what follows we will endow the filtered measurable space $(\Omega, \mathcal{F}, \{\mathcal{F}_n\}_{n=0}^T)$ with a belief function $Bel : \mathcal{F} \to [0, 1]$.

For $n = 1, \ldots, T$, denote

$$\mathcal{A}_n = \{a_k = ku + (n - k)d : k = 0, \ldots, n\}, \tag{6}$$

for which we have $a_0 < a_1 < \ldots < a_n$. Moreover, for every $x \in \mathbb{R}$ and $A \in \mathcal{P}(\mathcal{A}_n)$, denote

$$x + A = \{x + a_k : a_k \in A\}, \tag{7}$$

where $x + A = \emptyset$ if $A = \emptyset$. In particular, each random variable X_n takes values in the set $\mathcal{X}_n = x_0 + \mathcal{A}_n$ and a generic element of $\mathcal{X}_n$ will be denoted as x_n.

Definition 1. *Given a filtered belief space* $(\Omega, \mathcal{F}, \{\mathcal{F}_n\}_{n=0}^T, Bel)$, *the process* $\{X_0, \ldots, X_T\}$ *is said to satisfy the:*

Markov Property: *if for every* $0 \leq n \leq T - 1$ *and* $1 \leq t \leq T - n$, $A \in \mathcal{P}(\mathcal{A}_t)$, *and* $x_0 \in \mathcal{X}_0, \ldots, x_n \in \mathcal{X}_n$ *on a trajectory it holds that*

$$Bel(X_{n+t} \in x_n + A | X_0 = x_0, \ldots, X_n = x_n) = Bel(X_{n+t} \in x_n + A | X_n = x_n);$$

time-homogeneity property: *if for every* $0 \leq n \leq T - 1$ *and* $1 \leq t \leq T - n$, $A \in \mathcal{P}(\mathcal{A}_t)$, *and* $x_0 \in \mathcal{X}_0, \ldots, x_n \in \mathcal{X}_n$ *on a trajectory it holds that*

$$Bel(X_{n+t} \in x_n + A | X_0 = x_0, \ldots, X_n = x_n) = \beta_t(A),$$

where $\beta_t : \mathcal{P}(\mathcal{A}_t) \to [0, 1]$ *is a fixed belief function.*

If the process satisfies both the properties above is called a **Dempster-Shafer random walk**.

In the particular case where the process $\{X_0, \ldots, X_T\}$ satisfies the Markov property, then the time-homogeneity property reduces to

$$Bel(X_{n+t} \in x_n + A | X_n = x_n) = \beta_t(A). \tag{8}$$

Moreover, the properties above are called *one-step* if they hold only for $t = 1$.

Our aim is to investigate the existence of a belief function Bel on $\mathcal{F}$ that makes the process $\{X_0, \ldots, X_T\}$ Markov and time-homogeneous, i.e., a Dempster-Shafer random walk. We stress that a Dempster-Shafer random walk singles out a family of belief functions $\{\beta_t : t = 1, \ldots, T\}$ defined on the family of power sets $\{\mathcal{P}(\mathcal{A}_t) : t = 1, \ldots, T\}$ that, in turn, are determined by the particular Bel that is chosen. Let us point out that, if Bel is not additive, then we need the entire family of β_t's since the usual *Chapman-Kolmogorov equation* (see, e.g., [1]) does not apply. Such β_t's are actually *t-step transition* belief functions.

The Markov and time-homogeneity properties can be expressed also in terms of the *conditional Choquet expectation* functional associated to Bel. For a fixed Bel on $\mathcal{F}$, for every $0 \leq n \leq T - 1$ and $1 \leq t \leq T - n$, and $\varphi(x)$ a real-valued function of one real variable defined on $\mathcal{X}_{n+t}$, one can define the random variables $\mathbb{C}[\varphi(X_{n+t})|X_0, \ldots, X_n]$ and $\mathbb{C}[\varphi(X_{n+t})|X_n]$ through the Choquet integral (see, e.g., [11]). We let $x_0 \in \mathcal{X}_0, \ldots, x_n \in \mathcal{X}_n$ vary on the trajectories of the tree. For all $\omega \in \{X_0 = x_0, \ldots, X_n = x_n\}$ we set

$$\mathbb{C}[\varphi(X_{n+t})|X_0, \ldots, X_n](\omega) = \oint \varphi(X_{n+t}) \, \mathrm{d}Bel(\cdot|X_0 = x_0, \ldots, X_n = x_n), \quad (9)$$

while for all $\omega \in \{X_n = x_n\}$ we set

$$\mathbb{C}[\varphi(X_{n+t})|X_n](\omega) = \oint \varphi(X_{n+t}) \, \mathrm{d}Bel(\cdot|X_n = x_n). \quad (10)$$

It is easily seen that if Bel satisfies the Markov property then

$$\mathbb{C}[\varphi(X_{n+t})|X_0, \ldots, X_n] = \mathbb{C}[\varphi(X_{n+t})|X_n]. \quad (11)$$

Furthermore, if Bel satisfies also the time-homogeneity property, then both $\mathbb{C}[\varphi(X_{n+t})|X_0, \ldots, X_n]$ and $\mathbb{C}[\varphi(X_{n+t})|X_n]$ can be expressed in terms of the belief function β_t defined on $\mathcal{P}(\mathcal{A}_t)$.

More generally, we can define $\mathbb{C}[\cdot|\mathcal{F}_n] := \mathbb{C}[\cdot|X_0, \ldots, X_n]$ on the entire $\mathbb{R}^{\Omega}$, by generalizing (9), provided all conditional belief functions are well-defined. The mentioned properties of the conditional Choquet expectation functional allow us to appreciate the implication of Markov and time-homogeneity properties.

4 Construction of Dempster-Shafer Random Walks

As is well-known, in the classical theory of random walks (see, e.g., [1]), Bel is assumed to be a probability measure P which is completely characterized by a single parameter $p \in (0, 1)$ that expresses the conditional probability of a one-step "up" movement. In particular, in the classical case, the process $\{X_0, \ldots, X_T\}$ can be defined through a finite sequence of stochastically independent events $\{E_1, \ldots, E_T\}$ with $P(E_n) = p$, for $n = 1, \ldots, T$. In turn, the process $\{X_0, \ldots, X_T\}$ is defined setting

$$X_0 = x_0 \quad \text{and} \quad X_n = x_0 + \sum_{i=1}^{n} [(u - d)\mathbf{1}_{E_i} + d], \quad \text{for } n = 1, \ldots, T. \quad (12)$$

Indeed, in the probabilistic setting, the independence assumption on P singles out the joint distribution of the process: for every trajectory on the binomial tree with $x_0 \in \mathcal{X}_0, \ldots, x_T \in \mathcal{X}_T$ and $x_T = x_0 + ku + (T - k)d$ we have

$$P(X_0 = x_0, \ldots, X_T = x_T) = p^k (1 - p)^{T-k}. \quad (13)$$

Moreover, since $p \in (0, 1)$, such joint probability distribution alone gives rise through additivity to all conditional probability distributions that automatically satisfy Markov and time-homogeneity properties.

If we give up on the additivity of Bel, then the above construction necessarily breaks down. Our goal then, is to propose a construction that generalizes the classical one and reduces to it in case of additivity.

At this aim, we consider two parameters $b_u, b_d > 0$ with $b_u + b_d \leq 1$ to be intuitively interpreted as one-step "up" and "down" conditional beliefs.

A first idea to try to recover the probabilistic construction is to impose that the belief function Bel satisfies an analogue of (13): for every trajectory on the binomial tree with $x_0 \in \mathcal{X}_0, \ldots, x_T \in \mathcal{X}_T$ and $x_T = x_0 + ku + (T - k)d$ we have

$$Bel(X_0 = x_0, \ldots, X_T = x_T) = b_u^k b_d^{T-k}. \tag{14}$$

The above equation gives rise to a "partially specified" belief model on the trajectories: we will show in the following that there can be infinitely many global belief models agreeing with the above assessment and we will restrict to those satisfying specific properties.

In particular, since the event $\{X_0 = x_0, \ldots, X_T = x_T\}$ corresponding to a trajectory reduces to a singleton $\{\omega\}$ for a $\omega \in \Omega$, equation (14) implies

$$m(X_0 = x_0, \ldots, X_T = x_T) = b_u^k b_d^{T-k}, \tag{15}$$

where m is the Möbius inverse of Bel. An immediate consequence of this fact is that a Bel satisfying (14) is positive on $\mathcal{F} \setminus \{\emptyset\}$, therefore conditioning through the product rule is always well-defined.

Summing over all the possible trajectories of the binomial tree we get that

$$\sum_{x_0, \ldots, x_T} m(X_0 = x_0, \ldots, X_T = x_T) = (b_u + b_d)^T. \tag{16}$$

Therefore, if $b_u + b_d < 1$, equation (14) provides very few constraints for the belief function Bel as we need to allocate a remaining mass of $1 - (b_u + b_d)^T$ and this provides many degrees of freedom.

It actually turns out that between the infinite number of belief functions satisfying equation (14) there are some failing both the Markov and time-homogeneity properties and some failing just one of them, while our target are those satisfying both.

The following proposition introduces a belief function on $\mathcal{F}$ satisfying (14) under which the process $\{X_0, \ldots, X_T\}$ is Markov.

Proposition 1. *Let Bel be the belief function on $\mathcal{F}$ whose Möbius inverse satisfies (15) and $m(\Omega) = 1 - (b_u + b_d)^T$. Then the process $\{X_0, \ldots, X_T\}$ satisfies the Markov property.*

Proof. We first notice that Bel is additive on $\mathcal{F} \setminus \{\Omega\}$, i.e., $Bel(A \cup B) = Bel(A) + Bel(B)$ for every disjoint $A, B \in \mathcal{F}$ with $A \cup B \neq \Omega$. Furthermore, $Bel(X_0 = x_0) = Bel(\Omega) = 1$, while $Bel(X_0 = x_0, \ldots, X_T = x_T)$ is determined by (14) for all the trajectories on the binomial tree.

For $0 < n \leq T-1$, let $\{X_0 = x_0, \dots, X_n = x_n\}$ be a partial trajectory on the binomial tree with $x_n = x_0 + ku + (n-k)d$. Then, summing over the trajectories on the binomial tree completing the fixed partial trajectory we have that

$$Bel(X_0 = x_0, \dots, X_n = x_n) = \sum_{x_{n+1}, \dots, x_T} Bel(X_0 = x_0, \dots, X_T = x_T)$$

$$= b_u^k b_d^{n-k} (b_u + b_d)^{T-n}.$$

Now, for every $1 \leq t \leq T - n$ and $A \in \mathcal{P}(\mathcal{A}_t)$, let $a_h \in A$. Then, summing over the partial trajectories up to time $n + t$ completing $\{X_0 = x_0, \dots, X_n = x_n\}$ and ending with $X_{n+t} = x_n + a_h$ we obtain

$$Bel(X_0 = x_0, \dots, X_n = x_n, X_{n+t} = x_n + a_h)$$

$$= \sum_{x_{n+1}, \dots, x_{n+t-1}} Bel(X_0 = x_0, \dots, X_{n+t} = x_n + a_h)$$

$$= \binom{t}{h} b_u^{h+k} b_d^{n+t-h-k} (b_u + b_d)^{T-n-t}.$$

Hence, we get that

$$Bel(X_{n+t} = x_n + a_h | X_0 = x_0, \dots, X_n = x_n) = \frac{\binom{t}{h} b_u^h b_d^{t-h}}{(b_u + b_d)^t},$$

$$Bel(X_{n+t} \in x_n + A | X_0 = x_0, \dots, X_n = x_n) = \sum_{a_h \in A} \frac{\binom{t}{h} b_u^h b_d^{t-h}}{(b_u + b_d)^t}.$$

For $0 < n \leq T - 1$, let $x_n = x_0 + ku + (n-k)d \in \mathcal{X}_n$. Summing over all the partial trajectories from time 0 to time n ending with $X_n = x_n$ we get that

$$Bel(X_n = x_n) = \sum_{x_0, \dots, x_{n-1}} Bel(X_0 = x_0, \dots, X_n = x_n) = \binom{n}{k} b_u^k b_d^{n-k} (b_u + b_d)^{T-n}.$$

Now, for every $1 \leq t \leq T-n$ and $A \in \mathcal{P}(\mathcal{A}_t)$, let $a_h \in A$. Then, summing over the partial trajectories from time 0 to time $n+t$ with $X_n = x_n$ and $X_{n+t} = x_n + a_h$ we obtain

$$Bel(X_n = x_n, X_{n+t} = x_n + a_h)$$

$$= \sum_{\substack{x_0, \dots, x_{n-1} \\ x_{n+1}, \dots, x_{n+t-1}}} Bel(X_0 = x_0, \dots, X_{n+t} = x_n + a_h)$$

$$= \binom{n}{k} \binom{t}{h} b_u^{h+k} b_d^{n+t-h-k} (b_u + b_d)^{T-n-t}.$$

Hence, we get that

$$Bel(X_{n+t} = x_n + a_h | X_n = x_n) = \frac{\binom{t}{h} b_u^h b_d^{t-h}}{(b_u + b_d)^t},$$

$$Bel(X_{n+t} \in x_n + A | X_n = x_n) = \sum_{a_h \in A} \frac{\binom{t}{h} b_u^h b_d^{t-h}}{(b_u + b_d)^t}.$$

Finally, since $Bel(X_{n+t} \in x_n + A | X_0 = x_0, \ldots, X_n = x_n) = Bel(X_{n+t} \in x_n + A | X_n = x_n)$ the claim follows. $\qquad\square$

The belief function defined in Proposition 1 could be seen as the most imprecise model satisfying (15), while other belief functions satisfying (15) have Möbius inverse distributing the mass $1 - (b_u + b_d)^T$ on all the events different from the atoms of $\mathcal{F}$. In other terms, every other belief function on $\mathcal{F}$ satisfying (15) will dominate the belief function defined in Proposition 1, pointwise on $\mathcal{F}$.

The following example shows that, even though the above belief function satisfies the Markov property, it fails time-homogeneity.

Example 1. Let $T = 3$ and consider the belief function Bel defined in Proposition 1. Simple computations show that

$$Bel(X_3 = x_0 + u + 2d | X_0 = x_0, X_1 = x_0 + u, X_2 = x_0 + u + d) = \frac{b_d}{b_u + b_d},$$
$$Bel(X_1 = x_0 + d | X_0 = x_0) = b_d(b_u + b_d)^2,$$

therefore the time-homogeneity property does not hold and even one-step time-homogeneity fails. $\qquad\blacklozenge$

Besides violating time-homogeneity, the belief function introduced in Proposition 1 does not respect the intuitive meaning of parameters b_u, b_d since, for every $0 < n \leq T - 1$, we have that

$$Bel(X_{n+1} = x_n + u | X_0 = x_0, \ldots, X_n = x_n) = \frac{b_u}{b_u + b_d},$$
$$Bel(X_{n+1} = x_n + d | X_0 = x_0, \ldots, X_n = x_n) = \frac{b_d}{b_u + b_d}.$$

Hence, a different approach is to impose one-step time-homogeneity requiring Bel to satisfy, for every $0 \leq n \leq T - 1$, and $x_0 \in \mathcal{X}_0, \ldots, x_n \in \mathcal{X}_n$ on a trajectory

$$Bel(X_{n+1} = x_n + u | X_0 = x_0, \ldots, X_n = x_n) = b_u, \tag{17}$$
$$Bel(X_{n+1} = x_n + d | X_0 = x_0, \ldots, X_n = x_n) = b_d. \tag{18}$$

Indeed, a straightforward application of the chain rule (4) allows to show that (17)–(18) imply (14). It turns out that imposing (17)–(18) produces much more constraints for the belief function Bel.

Proposition 2. *A belief function Bel on $\mathcal{F}$ satisfies (17)–(18) if and only if the corresponding Möbius inverse m satisfies the following conditions:*

(i) $m(\{X_0 = x_0, \ldots, X_T = x_T\}) = b_u^k b_d^{T-k}$, *for* $x_T = x_0 + ku + (T - k) \in \mathcal{X}_T$;

(ii) $m(\{X_0 = x_0, \ldots, X_{T-1} = x_{T-1}\}) = b_u^k b_d^{T-1-k}(1 - b_u - b_d)$, *for* $x_{T-1} = x_0 + ku + (T - 1 - k)d \in \mathcal{X}_{T-1}$;

(iii) for every $0 < n < T - 1$, for $x_n = x_0 + ku + (n - k)d \in \mathcal{X}_n$

$$\sum_{\substack{B \subseteq \{X_0 = x_0, \ldots, X_n = x_n\} \\ B \not\subseteq \{X_0 = x_0, \ldots, X_{n+1} = x_n + u\} \\ B \not\subseteq \{X_0 = x_0, \ldots, X_{n+1} = x_n + d\}}} m(B) = b_u^k b_d^{n-k} (1 - b_u - b_d);$$

(iv)

$$\sum_{\substack{B \subseteq \{X_0 = x_0\} \\ B \not\subseteq \{X_0 = x_0, X_1 = x_0 + u\} \\ B \not\subseteq \{X_0 = x_0, X_1 = x_0 + d\}}} m(B) = 1 - b_u - b_d;$$

where all events $\{X_0 = x_0, \ldots, X_n = x_n\}$ correspond to partial trajectories on the binomial tree.

Proof. We prove necessity of *(i)–(iv)*. Since $Bel(X_0 = x_0) = 1$ and, for every $0 \le n \le T - 1$, we have that

$$Bel(X_{n+1} = x_{n+1}|X_0 = x_0, \ldots, X_n = x_n) = \frac{Bel(X_0 = x_0, \ldots, X_{n+1} = x_{n+1})}{Bel(X_0 = x_0, \ldots, X_n = x_n)},$$

by applying progressively the chain rule (4) to (17)–(18) we get that

$$Bel(X_0 = x_0, \ldots, X_{n+1} = x_{n+1}) = \prod_{j=1}^{n} Bel(X_{j+1} = x_{j+1}|X_0 = x_0, \ldots, X_j = x_j).$$

Condition *(i)* is readily verified to hold. Moreover, for $0 \le n \le T - 1$, conditions *(ii)–(iv)* immediately follow by expressing $Bel(X_0 = x_0, \ldots, X_n = x_n)$ in terms of the corresponding Möbius inverse m and deleting the expressions of $Bel(X_0 = x_0, \ldots, X_{n+1} = x_n + u)$ and $Bel(X_0 = x_0, \ldots, X_{n+1} = x_n + d)$ in terms of m. Sufficiency of *(i)–(iv)* can be proved reverting the construction. $\square$

The following example shows that one-step time-homogeneity does not imply either time-homogeneity or the Markov property.

Example 2. Let $T = 3$ and take $\Omega = \{1, \ldots, 8\}$ with

Ω	X_0	X_1	X_2	X_3
1	x_0	$x_0 + u$	$x_0 + 2u$	$x_0 + 3u$
2	x_0	$x_0 + u$	$x_0 + 2u$	$x_0 + 2u + d$
3	x_0	$x_0 + u$	$x_0 + u + d$	$x_0 + 2u + d$
4	x_0	$x_0 + u$	$x_0 + u + d$	$x_0 + u + 2d$
5	x_0	$x_0 + d$	$x_0 + u + d$	$x_0 + 2u + d$
6	x_0	$x_0 + d$	$x_0 + u + d$	$x_0 + u + 2d$
7	x_0	$x_0 + d$	$x_0 + 2d$	$x_0 + u + 2d$
8	x_0	$x_0 + d$	$x_0 + 2d$	$x_0 + 3d$

Consider the Möbius inverse m on $\mathcal{F}$ satisfying conditions *(i)* and *(ii)* of Proposition 2 and

$$m(\{2,3\}) = b_u(1 - b_u - b_d) \quad m(\{5,6,7,8\}) = b_d(1 - b_u - b_d),$$
$$m(\{3,5\}) = m(\Omega) = \tfrac{1}{2}(1 - b_u - b_d),$$

while it is zero elsewhere. Such m is easily verified to satisfy also conditions *(iii)* and *(iv)* of Proposition 2, thus the corresponding Bel satisfies one-step time-homogeneity. Nevertheless, such Bel does not satisfy the Markov property as

$$Bel(X_3 = x_0 + 2u + d | X_0 = x_0, X_1 = x_0 + u, X_2 = x_0 + u + d) = b_u,$$
$$Bel(X_3 = x_0 + 2u + d | X_2 = x_0 + u + d) = \tfrac{2b_u^2 b_d + \frac{1}{2}(1 - b_u - b_d)}{2b_u b_d + \frac{1}{2}(1 - b_u - b_d)}.$$

The corresponding Bel does not satisfy time-homogeneity as well since for $a_1 = u + d \in \mathcal{A}_2$ we have

$$Bel(X_3 = x_0 + u + a_1 | X_0 = x_0, X_1 = x_0 + u) = 2b_u b_d + 1 - b_u - b_d,$$
$$Bel(X_2 = x_0 + a_1 | X_0 = x_0) = 2b_u b_d + \tfrac{1}{2}(1 - b_u - b_d).$$

◆

The following example shows that one-step time-homogeneity and the Markov property do not imply time-homogeneity.

Example 3. Let $T = 3$ and take $\Omega = \{1, \ldots, 8\}$ with the same identification of states as Example 2. Let $b_u = b_d = \delta \in (0, \tfrac{1}{2})$ and consider the Möbius inverse m on $\mathcal{F}$ satisfying conditions *(i)* and *(ii)* of Proposition 2 and such that

$$m(\{1,2,3,4\}) = m(\{5,6,7,8\}) = m(\{3,5\}) = m(\{4,6\}) = \delta(1 - 2\delta),$$
$$m(\{3,4,5,6\}) = (1 - 2\delta)^2,$$

while it is zero elsewhere. Such m is easily verified to satisfy also conditions *(iii)* and *(iv)* of Proposition 2, thus the corresponding Bel satisfies one-step time-homogeneity. We notice that, working over trajectories of the tree, since $Bel(X_3 \in x_1 + A | X_0 = x_0, X_1 = x_1) = Bel(X_3 \in x_1 + A | X_1 = x_1)$ for every $A \in \mathcal{P}(\mathcal{A}_2)$, then the one-step Markov property implies the Markov property in this case, and the former holds by one-step time-homogeneity and since

$$Bel(X_3 = x_3 | X_0 = x_0, X_1 = x_1, X_2 = x_2) = Bel(X_3 = x_3 | X_2 = x_2) = \delta.$$

Nevertheless, since for $a_1 = u + d \in \mathcal{A}_2$ we have

$$Bel(X_3 = x_0 + u + a_1 | X_0 = x_0, X_1 = x_0 + u) = 2\delta^2,$$
$$Bel(X_2 = x_0 + a_1 | X_0 = x_0) = 2\delta^2 + 1 - 2\delta.$$

Hence the time-homogeneity property does not hold.   ◆

Finally, the following example shows that there can be infinitely many belief functions satisfying the Markov and time-homogeneity properties.

Example 4. Let $T = 3$ and take $\Omega = \{1, \ldots, 8\}$ with the same identification of states as Example 2. Let $\alpha \in [0,1]$ and consider the Möbius inverse m_α on $\mathcal{F}$ satisfying conditions *(i)* and *(ii)* of Proposition 2 and such that

$$m_\alpha(\{1,2,3,4\}) = b_u(1 - b_u - b_d), \quad m_\alpha(\{5,6,7,8\}) = b_d(1 - b_u - b_d),$$
$$m_\alpha(\{1,2,3,4,5,6,7\}) = \alpha(1 - b_u - b_d),$$
$$m_\alpha(\{2,3,4,5,6,7,8\}) = (1 - \alpha)(1 - b_u - b_d),$$

while it is zero elsewhere. Also in this case, conditions *(iii)* and *(iv)* of Proposition 2 are shown to hold. It is easily verified that the corresponding belief function Bel_α satisfies the Markov and time-homogeneity properties. In particular, for $n = 1, 2, 3$, denoting $\mathcal{A}_n = \{a_k^n = ku + (n-k)d : k = 0, \ldots, n\}$, we write $A_{i_1, \ldots, i_t}^n := \{a_{i_1}^n, \ldots, a_{i_t}^n\}$, $k_\alpha := \alpha(1 - b_u - b_d)$ and $h_\alpha := (1 - \alpha)(1 - b_u - b_d)$. Then, time-homogeneity holds with respect to the family of belief functions $\{\beta_1^\alpha, \beta_2^\alpha, \beta_3^\alpha\}$ reported below:

$\mathcal{P}(\mathcal{A}_1)$	$\emptyset$	A_0^1	A_1^1	$\mathcal{A}_1$
β_1^α	0	b_d	b_u	1

$\mathcal{P}(\mathcal{A}_2)$	$\emptyset$	A_0^2	A_1^2	A_2^2	$A_{0,1}^2$	$A_{0,2}^2$	$A_{1,2}^2$	$\mathcal{A}_2$
β_2^α	0	b_d^2	$2b_u b_d$	b_u^2	$b_u b_d + b_d$	$b_u^2 + b_d^2$	$b_u b_d + b_u$	1

$\mathcal{P}(\mathcal{A}_3)$	$\emptyset$	A_0^3	A_1^3	A_2^3
β_3^α	0	b_d^3	$3b_u b_d^2$	$3b_u^2 b_d$
$\mathcal{P}(\mathcal{A}_3)$	A_3^3	$A_{0,1}^3$	$A_{0,2}^3$	$A_{0,3}^3$
β_3^α	b_u^3	$2b_u b_d^2 + b_d^3$	$b_d^3 + 3b_u^2 b_d$	$b_d^3 + b_u^3$
$\mathcal{P}(\mathcal{A}_3)$	$A_{1,2}^3$	$A_{1,3}^3$	$A_{2,3}^3$	$A_{0,1,2}^3$
β_3^α	$b_u b_d^2 + b_u^2 b_d + 2b_u b_d$	$3b_u b_d^2 + b_u^3$	$2b_u^2 b_d + b_u^2$	$b_d(b_u^2 + b_u + 1) + h_\alpha$
$\mathcal{P}(\mathcal{A}_3)$	$A_{0,1,3}^3$	$A_{0,2,3}^3$	$A_{1,2,3}^3$	$\mathcal{A}_3$
β_3^α	$2b_u b_d^2 + b_d^2 + b_u^3$	$2b_u^2 b_d + b_u^2 + b_d^3$	$b_u(b_d^2 + b_d + 1) + k_\alpha$	1

Therefore, we have an infinite class of belief functions $\{Bel_\alpha : \alpha \in [0,1]\}$ satisfying the Markov and time-homogeneity properties.   ◆

It is possible to show that, for every $T \in \mathbb{N}$, there exists a belief function (generally not unique) that guarantees both the Markov and time-homogeneity properties. The proof is omitted for lack of space. In particular, the goal is to single out a particular Bel of this type that results in a family of transition belief functions $\{\beta_t : t = 1, \ldots, T\}$ with a particular structure. The characterization of such a "canonical" belief function will be the aim of future research.

5 Conclusion

In this paper we have defined a Dempster-Shafer random walk as a (discrete-time finite-horizon) process defined on a filtered belief space, that satisfies a suitable definition of Markov and time-homogeneity properties. We showed how one-step time-homogeneity can be used to constrain a belief function in order to match both properties. In general, though existence of such a belief function can be proved, we showed here that there can be infinitely many choices, thus the selection of a "canonical" belief function requires to add some extra requirement. Here, we provided a characterization of the one-step time-homogeneity property, but a characterization of t-step time-homogeneity is necessary to single out particular families of transition belief functions. This last point will be the aim of future research.

Acknowledgements. The second author was partially supported by Fondazione Cassa di Risparmio di Perugia (grant n. 2018.0427).

References

1. Çinlar, E.: Introduction to Stochastic Processes. Prentice-Hall (1975)
2. Coletti, G., Petturiti, D., Vantaggi, B.: Conditional belief functions as lower envelopes of conditional probabilities in a finite setting. Inf. Sci. **339**, 64–84 (2016)
3. Coletti, G., Petturiti, D., Vantaggi, B.: A Dutch book coherence condition for conditional completely alternating Choquet expectations. Bollet. dell'Unione Mate. Italiana **13**(4), 585–593 (2020). https://doi.org/10.1007/s40574-020-00251-8
4. De Bock, J., de Cooman, G.: Imprecise Bernoulli processes. In: Greco, S., Bouchon-Meunier, B., Coletti, G., Fedrizzi, M., Matarazzo, B., Yager, R.R. (eds.) IPMU 2012. CCIS, vol. 299, pp. 400–409. Springer, Heidelberg (2012). https://doi.org/10.1007/978-3-642-31718-7_42
5. de Cooman, G., De Bock, J., Lopatatzidis, S.: Imprecise stochastic processes in discrete time: global models, imprecise Markov chains, and ergodic theorems. Int. J. Approx. Reason. **76**, 18–46 (2016)
6. de Cooman, G., Hermans, F., Quaeghebeur, E.: Imprecise Markov chains and their limit behaviour. Probab. Eng. Inf. Sci. **23**(4), 597–635 (2009)
7. Dempster, A.: Upper and lower probabilities induced by a multivalued mapping. Ann. Math. Stat. **38**(2), 325–339 (1967)
8. Etner, J., Jeleva, M., Tallon, J.M.: Decision theory under ambiguity. J. Econ. Surv. **26**(2), 234–270 (2012)
9. Feng, D., Nguyen, H.: Choquet weak convergence of capacity functionals of random sets. Inf. Sci. **177**(16), 3239–3250 (2007)
10. Gilboa, I., Marinacci, M.: Ambiguity and the Bayesian paradigm. In: Arló-Costa, H., Hendricks, V.F., van Benthem, J. (eds.) Readings in Formal Epistemology. SGTP, vol. 1, pp. 385–439. Springer, Cham (2016). https://doi.org/10.1007/978-3-319-20451-2_21
11. Set Functions, Games and Capacities in Decision Making. TDLC, vol. 46. Springer, Cham (2016). https://doi.org/10.1007/978-3-319-30690-2_7
12. Hartfiel, D., Seneta, E.: On the theory of Markov set-chains. Adv. Appl. Probab. **26**(4), 947–964 (1994)
13. Krak, T., T'Joens, N., de Bock, J.: Hitting times and probabilities for imprecise Markov chains. Proc. Mach. Learn. Res. **103**, 265–275 (2019)
14. Nendel, M.: On nonlinear expectations and Markov chains under model uncertainty. Int. J. Approx. Reason. **130**, 226–245 (2021)
15. Shafer, G.: A Mathematical Theory of Evidence. Princeton University Press, Princeton (1976)
16. Škulj, D.: Discrete time Markov chains with interval probabilities. Int. J. Approx. Reason. **50**(8), 1314–1329 (2009)

17. Škulj, D.: Random walks on graphs with interval weights and precise marginals. Int. J. Approx. Reason. **73**, 76–86 (2016)
18. Suppes, P., Zanotti, M.: On using random relations to generate upper and lower probabilities. Synthese **36**(4), 427–440 (1977)
19. T'Joens, N., De Bock, J., de Cooman, G.: A particular upper expectation as global belief model for discrete-time finite-state uncertain processes. Int. J. Approx. Reason. **131**, 30–55 (2021)
20. Walley, P.: Statistical Reasoning with Imprecise Probabilities. Chapman and Hall, London (1991)
21. Williams, P.: Notes on conditional previsions. Int. J. Approx. Reason. **44**(3), 366–383 (2007)

Correlated Boolean Operators
for Uncertainty Logic

Enrique Miralles-Dolz[1,2]([envelope])[iD], Ander Gray[1,2]([envelope])[iD], Edoardo Patelli[3][iD],
and Scott Ferson[1][iD]

[1] Institute for Risk and Uncertainty, University of Liverpool, Liverpool, UK
{enmidol,akgray,ferson}@liverpool.ac.uk
[2] United Kingdom Atomic Energy Authority, Abingdon, UK
[3] Centre for Intelligent Infrastructure, University of Strathclyde, Glasgow, UK
edoardo.patelli@strath.ac.uk

Abstract. We present a correlated *and* gate which may be used to propagate uncertainty and dependence through Boolean functions, since any Boolean function may be expressed as a combination of *and* and *not* operations. We argue that the *and* gate is a bivariate copula family, which has the interpretation of constructing bivariate Bernoulli random variables following a given Pearson correlation coefficient and marginal probabilities. We show how this copula family may be used to propagate uncertainty in the form of probabilities of events, probability intervals, and probability boxes, with only partial or no knowledge of the dependency between events, expressed as an interval for the correlation coefficient. These results generalise previous results by Fréchet on the conjunction of two events with unknown dependencies. We show an application propagating uncertainty through a fault tree for a pressure tank. This paper comes with an open-source Julia library for performing uncertainty logic.

Keywords: Imprecise probability · Uncertainty logic · Boolean functions · Uncertainty propagation · Copula

1 Introduction

The logical conjunction ($\wedge$) is a function $f : \{0,1\}^2 \to \{0,1\}$ that returns a value of 1 if and only if both of the inputs are 1. The logical values assigned to the inputs represent the truth value of certain propositions or events, and in Boolean algebra it is required absolute certainty about these truth values (i.e. they are either *true* (1) or *false* (0)). That is, variables take the form $p \in \{0,1\}$. However, this requirement is often too restrictive to be used in practical applications where truth values have some degree of uncertainty, and therefore an extension of classical Booleans to uncertain Booleans would be desirable. We define uncertain Booleans as probabilities $p \in [0,1]$ defining a precise Bernoulli distribution (an event), interval probabilities $p \subseteq [0,1]$ defining a set of Bernoulli distributions (a credal set), and probability boxes with range$(p) \subseteq [0,1]$. This paper presents a method to perform uncertainty logic with these structures.

© Springer Nature Switzerland AG 2022
D. Ciucci et al. (Eds.): IPMU 2022, CCIS 1601, pp. 798–811, 2022.
https://doi.org/10.1007/978-3-031-08971-8_64

Note that it is possible to build any binary Boolean operation from two primitive operations, for example from *and* and *not*. Table 1 shows the 16 (2^4) possible binary and unary Boolean operations, written in terms of two primitives operations $\wedge$ and $\neg$. Note that some of these operations (e.g. Identity and Zero) are trivial, and with the other operations being written in terms of previously derived operations for brevity. Since all of these operations may be written in terms of an $\wedge$ and a $\neg$ operation, and since the *not* operation is $not(A) = \neg A = 1 - A$, it follows that we therefore only need to describe a correlated *and* operator, and all other binary operators, and further more complicated Boolean functions, may be calculated in terms of these two operators.

Table 1. Summary of the 16 possible binary and unary Boolean operations written in terms of two primitive operations $\wedge$ and $\neg$.

A	1100	Adopted name	Adopted symbol	Expansion
B	1010			
w_1	1100	Identity	A	Trivial
w_2	1010	Identity	B	Trivial
w_3	0000	Zero	0	Trivial
w_4	1111	One	1	Trivial
w_5	1000	And	$A \wedge B$	Primitive
w_6	0011	Not	$\neg A$	$1 - A$
w_7	0101	Not	$\neg B$	$1 - B$
w_8	1110	Or	$A \vee B$	$\neg((\neg A) \wedge (\neg B))$
w_9	0111	Nand	A nand B	$\neg(A \wedge B)$
w_{10}	0001	Nor	A nor B	$\neg(A \vee B)$
w_{11}	0110	Exclusive Or	A xor B	$(A \vee B) \wedge (A$ nand $B)$
w_{12}	1001	Equivalence	$A \equiv B$	$\neg(A$ xor $B)$
w_{13}	1011	Implication	$A \implies B$	$\neg A \vee B$
w_{14}	1101	Implication	$B \implies A$	$A \vee \neg B$
w_{15}	0100	Inhibition	$A \not\Longrightarrow B$	$\neg(A \implies B)$
w_{16}	0010	Inhibition	$B \not\Longrightarrow A$	$\neg(B \implies A)$

When events A and B are independent, their logical conjunction is calculated as $\mathbb{P}(A \wedge B) = \mathbb{P}(A)\mathbb{P}(B)$. However, the assumption of independence has a significant consequence quantitatively, as shown in [3]. Therefore, after extending the mathematical structures to describe events A and B from classical Booleans to uncertain Booleans, the next desirable extension would be on this assumption of independence between their probabilities. For example, consider the two following random bit-vectors each with the same marginal probabilities $P(A) = P(B) = 0.5$ (a sequence of two fair coin tosses)

$$A = \{0, 1, 1, 1, 1, 0, 0, 1, 1, 1, 0, 0, 1\},$$
$$B = \{0, 0, 0, 1, 1, 1, 1, 1, 1, 1, 0, 0, 1\}. \tag{1}$$

Although the individual coin tosses is fair (the sample mean for these 12 tosses is ~ 0.6 for each vector), the vectors are corrected, that is, the outcome of one throw can influence the other, with $\rho_{AB} = 0.3$ (sample correlation is ~ 0.35).

In [9], it is derived a model for the conjunction employing the Pearson correlation coefficient to capture dependence (referred to as the Lucas model). Unlike for continuous distributions, two marginals and a correlation coefficient is sufficient to completely define a bivariate Bernoulli random variable [7]. The Lucas model is defined as

$$\mathbb{P}(A \wedge B) = \mathbb{P}(A)\mathbb{P}(B) + \rho_{AB}\sqrt{\mathbb{P}(A)\mathbb{P}(\neg A)\mathbb{P}(B)\mathbb{P}(\neg B)}\,, \tag{2}$$

where ρ_{AB} is the Pearson correlation coefficient of A and B.

However, this model can return misleading results when certain combinations of probabilities of events and correlations are employed. For example, considering $\mathbb{P}(A) = 0.3$ and $\mathbb{P}(B) = 0.2$ with $\rho_{AB} = -1$ (opposite dependence), the Lucas model returns $\mathbb{P}(A \wedge B) = -0.123$, which is obviously erroneous. The fact that Eq. 2 is returning a negative probability is simply because the probability assigned for events A and B cannot have a correlation of -1. This means that, for some probabilities of events, the Pearson correlation coefficient cannot take any value in $[-1, 1]$, but in some subset $S \subseteq [-1, 1]$.

This subset S can be found through the Fréchet inequalities, which define the lower and upper bounds of the logical conjunction given the probability of its events [5], and are written as

$$\mathbb{P}(A \wedge B) \in [\max(\mathbb{P}(A) + \mathbb{P}(B) - 1, 0), \min(\mathbb{P}(A), \mathbb{P}(B))]\,. \tag{3}$$

Substituting the bounds in Eq. 2, and rearranging for ρ_{AB}, the subset $S = [\underline{\rho}_{AB}, \overline{\rho}_{AB}] \subseteq [-1, 1]$ can be found as

$$\begin{cases} \underline{\rho}_{AB} = \dfrac{\max(\mathbb{P}(A) + \mathbb{P}(B) - 1, 0) - \mathbb{P}(A)\mathbb{P}(B)}{\sqrt{\mathbb{P}(A)\mathbb{P}(\neg A)\mathbb{P}(B)\mathbb{P}(\neg B)}} \\[4mm] \overline{\rho}_{AB} = \dfrac{\min(\mathbb{P}(A), \mathbb{P}(B)) - \mathbb{P}(A)\mathbb{P}(B)}{\sqrt{\mathbb{P}(A)\mathbb{P}(\neg A)\mathbb{P}(B)\mathbb{P}(\neg B)}}\,. \end{cases} \tag{4}$$

With these definitions for the lower and upper bound of the Pearson correlation coefficient, the subset S for the previous example with $\mathbb{P}(A) = 0.3$ and $\mathbb{P}(B) = 0.2$ is $[-0.327, 0.763]$, and not $[-1,1]$ as previously guessed.

The proposed correlated *and* operation combines the Lucas model and the Fréchet inequalities to restrict the former to return probabilities in [0,1] for any specified Pearson correlation. If the introduced correlation is greater than $\overline{\rho}$, then the upper Fréchet bound is returned. On the other hand, if it is lower than $\underline{\rho}$, then the model gives the lower Fréchet bound. Lastly, when the introduced correlation is in S, then the probability is calculated following the Lucas model. Therefore, the correlated *and* operator is written as

$$P(A \wedge B) = \begin{cases} \max(P(A) + P(B) - 1, 0) & \text{if } \rho_{AB} \leq \underline{\rho}_{AB} \\ \min(P(A), P(B)) & \text{if } \rho_{AB} \geq \overline{\rho}_{AB} \\ P(A)P(B) + \rho(A, B)\sqrt{P(A)P(\neg A)P(B)P(\neg B)} & \text{otherwise .} \end{cases} \quad (5)$$

We present an extension for the Boolean operators allowing for uncertainty not only in the inputs, but also in the dependence, which now can be specified for any interval correlation $\rho \subseteq [-1, 1]$, having the Fréchet bounds as a special case when $\rho = [-1, 1]$. Functions of Bernoulli random variables with uncertainty in dependence generally yield interval probabilities, we thus show how intervals may also be propagated through the derived operations.

2   Correlated *and* as a Copula

In this section we argue that the above derived correlated *and* is a bivariate copula (2-copula) family, parameterised by a correlation coefficient ρ. Rewritten in a more standard copula notation:

$$C_\rho(u, v) = \begin{cases} W(u, v) & \text{if } \rho \leq \underline{\rho}_{uv} \\ M(u, v) & \text{if } \rho \geq \overline{\rho}_{uv} \\ uv + \rho\sqrt{u(1-u)v(1-v)} & \text{otherwise ,} \end{cases}$$

where $W(u, v) = \max(u + v - 1, 0)$ and $M(u, v) = \min(u, v)$ are the Fréchet-Hoeffding copula bounds. A 2-copula C is any function $C : [0, 1]^2 \rightarrow [0, 1]$ with the following properties:

1. Grounded: $C(0, v) = C(u, 0) = 0$,
2. Uniform margins: $C(u, 1) = u$; $C(1, v) = v$,
3. 2-increasing:
   $C(u_2, v_2) - C(u_2, v_1) - C(u_1, v_2) + C(u_1, v_1) \geq 0$
   for all $0 \leq u_1 \leq u_2 \leq 1$ and $0 \leq v_1 \leq v_2 \leq 1$.

It is easy to see that the first two properties hold. The third property is harder to demonstrate, and in this work we provide no proof, despite the Lucas model $uv + \rho\sqrt{u(1-u)v(1-v)}$ is non-decreasing in u and v. However, non-decreasing is a necessary but not sufficient criteria for 2-increasing [12]. Yet Durante and Jaworski [2] prove that C is a copula iff it satisfies criteria 1. and 2. and if the partial derivatives are increasing (Corollary 2.4). That is, for every $u \in [0, 1]$,

$$v \mapsto \frac{\delta C(u, v)}{\delta u}$$

is increasing on $[0, 1]$. The partial derivatives of the above *and* gate is

$$\frac{\delta C_\rho(u, v)}{\delta u} = \begin{cases} 0 & \text{if } \rho_{uv} \leq \underline{\rho}_{uv} \\ 1 & \text{if } \rho_{uv} \geq \overline{\rho}_{uv} \\ v + \rho\frac{v(1-u)(1-v)-uv(1-v)}{2\sqrt{uv(1-u)(1-v)}} & \text{otherwise} \end{cases}$$

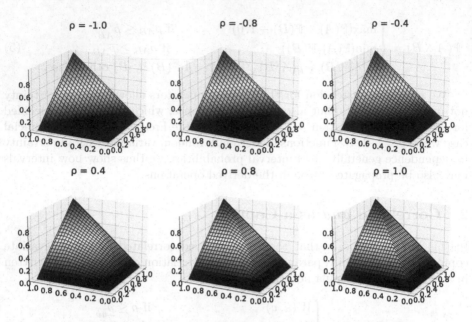

Fig. 1. $C_\rho(u,v)$ for $\rho = \{-1, -0.8, -0.4, 0.4, 0.8, 1\}$

which from observation C_ρ follows. Figure 1 shows $C_\rho(u,v)$ for various values of ρ. If $C_\rho(u,v)$ is a copula family, then it is a *complete* copula family, as it includes the two Fréchet-Hoeffding bounds W and M, corresponding to minimal (when $\rho = -1$) and maximal (when $\rho = 1$) correlation respectively, and the independence copula $\Pi(u,v) = uv$ when $\rho = 0$.

For the main results of this paper it is not required that the presented operator is a copula, only that it is non-decreasing. However it is interesting since t-norms, which are similar functions to copulas, are widely used in fuzzy logic to model *and* operations [8]. The interpretation of t-norms in fuzzy logic is often unclear, whilst the presented C_ρ has a clear probabilistic interpretation. Given two marginal Bernoulli random variables with $\mathbb{P}(A)$ and $\mathbb{P}(B)$, and Pearson correlation coefficient ρ, $C_\rho(\mathbb{P}(A), \mathbb{P}(B))$ returns the joint probability of events A and B occurring, i.e. $\mathbb{P}(A = 1, B = 1)$, which is one element of the joint probability of the bivariate Bernoulli distribution, with the other elements being $\mathbb{P}(A = 1, B = 0)$, $\mathbb{P}(A = 0, B = 1)$, and $\mathbb{P}(A = 0, B = 0)$.

3   Interval Probabilities

Since $C_\rho(u,v)$ is non-decreasing in u and v, interval values for u and v can be simply evaluated with endpoints. Moreover, in $C_\rho(u,v)$ the correlation ρ only has a single occurrence, and so it can be evaluated exactly with interval arithmetic. However, a useful observation is that $C_\rho(u,v)$ is also non-decreasing in ρ, and an interval value for ρ induces an imprecise copula. The concept of imprecise

Table 2. Interval bounds on the joint probability of a bivariate Bernoulli with marginals $\mathbb{P}(u = 1) = [0.2, 0.3]$, $\mathbb{P}(v = 1) = [0.45, 0.5]$ and interval correlation $\rho = [-0.2, 0.4]$.

$\mathbb{P}(u,v)$	0	1	$\mathbb{P}(u)$
0	$[0.304, 0.52]$	$[0.223, 0.44]$	$[0.7, 0.8]$
1	$[0.02, 0.2106]$	$[0.0502, 0.2417]$	$[0.2, 0.3]$
$\mathbb{P}(v)$	$[0.5, 0.55]$	$[0.45, 0.5]$	

copulas, which are a bounded set of copulas, has been discussed in [10]. From Fig. 1 it can be seen that increasing ρ yields larger or equal values of joint probabilities, i.e. $C_{\rho_1} \leq C_{\rho_2}$ for $\rho_1 \leq \rho_2$, and therefore interval uncertainty in ρ may also be evaluated with endpoints. Therefore, given two events with interval probabilities $u = [\underline{u}, \overline{u}]$ and $v = [\underline{v}, \overline{v}]$, and partially known correlation $\rho = [\underline{\rho}, \overline{\rho}]$, the interval probability of their conjunction can be evaluated as

$$\underline{\mathbb{P}}(u = 1, v = 1) = C_{\underline{\rho}}(\underline{u}, \underline{v}),$$

$$\overline{\mathbb{P}}(u = 1, v = 1) = C_{\overline{\rho}}(\overline{u}, \overline{v}).$$

As an example, for $u = [0.2, 0.3]$, $v = [0.45, 0.6]$ and $\rho = [-0.2, 0.4]$, rigorous bounds on their conjunction can be calculated as $\mathbb{P}(u = 1, v = 1) = [0.0502, 0.2417]$.

The full joint probability distribution of the bivariate Bernoulli can also be found by noticing that, for example, $\mathbb{P}(u = 1, v = 0) = \mathbb{P}(u \wedge \neg v)$, with the *not* operator defined as $\neg v = 1 - v$, which may be evaluated with C_ρ. However, some careful consideration is required regarding the correlation coefficient. If probabilities u and v have correlation ρ_{uv}, then u and $1 - v$ will have $\rho_{u \neg v} = -1 * \rho_{uv}$ [11], i.e. when complementing an event, the correlation must be reversed. The other elements of the joint distribution of the bivariate Bernoulli can be calculated as

$$\mathbb{P}(u = 1, v = 0) = C_{-1 * \rho}(u, 1 - v),$$

$$\mathbb{P}(u = 0, v = 1) = C_{-1 * \rho}(1 - u, v),$$

$$\mathbb{P}(u = 0, v = 0) = C_\rho(1 - u, 1 - v).$$

Notice that when the probabilities are complemented twice, the correlation stays the same, since it has been negated twice: $\rho_{\neg u, \neg v} = -(-\rho_{uv}) = \rho_{uv}$. Table 2 shows the computed joint distribution using the previous example of $u = [0.2, 0.3]$, $v = [0.45, 0.6]$ and $\rho = [-0.2, 0.4]$.

3.1   Other Boolean Operations

Once a correlated *and* operation has been constructed, other correlated Boolean operations can be defined in terms of this operation and a *not*, shown in Table 1. For example, *or* can be defined as

$$A \text{ or } B = \mathbb{P}(A \vee B) = 1 - \mathbb{P}((1 - A) \wedge (1 - B)),$$

which may be written in terms of C_ρ is

$$A \vee B = 1 - C_\rho(1 - A, 1 - B). \tag{6}$$

The other operations can be similarly expanded, taking care to negate ρ appropriately.

4 Probability Boxes

The previous section describes a method to perform logical operations on uncertain Booleans characterised by interval probabilities $p \subseteq [0,1]$, which define a bounded set of Bernoulli distributions. A possible generalisation of this is to have a distributional or imprecise distributional (p-box) characterisation, e.g., any p-box p whose range is a subset of the unit interval range$(p) \subseteq [0,1]$. The binary events involved with Boolean operations can be expressed in the form of Bernoullis (precise), set of Bernoullis (interval), or distributional Bernoullis (p-box). Note that here we are not describing the arithmetic of real functions $(f : R^m \to R^n)$, but are describing an extension of Boolean functions with p-box inputs, i.e., events or uncertain Booleans with uncertainty characterised by p-boxes. This is particularly relevant for c-boxes [4], which are p-box shaped confidence distributions for binomial inference with limited data. That is, they are a confidence characterisation of an uncertain Boolean given some sample set, e.g., the data for A in Eq. 1.

Since C_ρ is a non-decreasing binary operator, it can also be readily evaluated with the convolutions used in p-box arithmetic. Given two random variables with distribution functions F_X and F_Y, correlated by copula C_{XY}, a binary operation $Z = f(X, Y)$ can be evaluated with the following Lebesgue-Stieltjes integral

$$F_Z(z) = \int_{f\{z\}} dC_{XY}(F_X(x), F_Y(y)),$$

where the integration domain is the set $f\{z\} = \{(x, y)|x, y \in \mathbb{R}, f(x, y) < z\}$ (the set of all x and y for which $f(x, y) < z$). Note that the copula C_{XY} is not the same copula used to define the correlated *and* operation C_ρ, where C_{XY} defines the dependence between the random variables X and Y (which defines the uncertainty we have about the events), and C_ρ defines the correlation between the events themselves. We elaborate on this difference in Sect. 4.1.

Inserting $f = C_\rho$ into the above equation, and since the operation is non-decreasing we have

$$\underline{F_Z}(z) = \int_{C_\rho} dC_{XY}\left(\underline{F_X}(x), \underline{F_Y}(y)\right), \tag{7}$$

$$\overline{F_Z}(z) = \int_{C_{\overline{\rho}}} dC_{XY}\left(\overline{F_X}(x), \overline{F_Y}(y)\right). \tag{8}$$

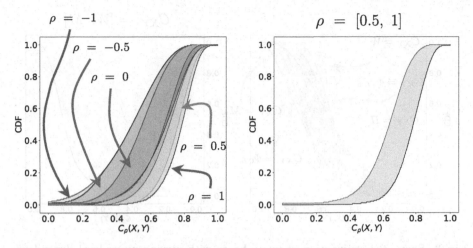

Fig. 2. (Left) Show logical *and* between the two K-out-of-N c-boxes $X \sim \mathrm{KN}(5,6)$, $Y \sim \mathrm{KN}(16,20)$ for different values of precise correlation. **(Right)** shows logical *and* with the interval correlation $\rho = [0.5, 1]$, and is the envelope of the orange and purple c-boxes. Independence is used in the upper level throughout $C_{XY} = \Pi$.

for two p-boxes $X = [\underline{F}_X, \overline{F}_X]$, $Y = [\underline{F}_Y, \overline{F}_Y]$, and interval correlation $\rho = [\underline{\rho}, \overline{\rho}]$. Software for performing rigorous correlated p-box arithmetic is readily available for bounding the above integrals efficiently [6]. The above integrals are those usually used in p-box arithmetic, except that the binary operation C_ρ is parameterised by ρ, which could be an interval. In the interval case, the envelope of the two end points yields the bounds on the output p-box. Figure 2 shows Eqs. 7 and 8 evaluated for two K-out-of-N c-boxes [4] $X \sim \mathrm{KN}(5,6)$, $Y \sim \mathrm{KN}(16,20)$ for different values of event correlations, shown in different colours. The right figure shows logical *and* with an interval correlation $\rho = [0.5, 1]$, which is the envelope of the purple and orange c-boxes. Note in Fig. 2 independence was used for the upper level C_{XY}, but independence is not necessarily the only choice for C_{XY}. In fact, any copula C_{XY} can be used in Equations (7) and (8), which can greatly influence results, as much as the choice of correlation ρ does. We explore this difference in the next section.

4.1 Two Levels of Dependence

The copula C_{XY} in the *and* operation (7) and (8) plays a different role to the correlation ρ. The correlation ρ is the dependence between the events $\mathbb{P}(A) = a$ and $\mathbb{P}(B) = b$, i.e., the correlation between the two random bit-vectors (1), and is the only dependence that plays a role when two uncertain Booleans are characterised by precise probabilities as real values. When considering two interval probabilities, two distributions, or two p-boxes, ρ still correlates the events as before, however one could worry that the uncertainty characterising the marginal probabilities might share some bivariate information. That is, the p-boxes have

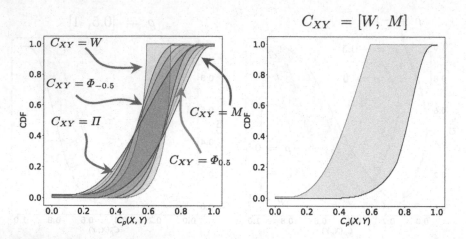

Fig. 3. Shows the conjunction of two p-boxes with varying upper-level dependence. (**Left**) Show logical *and* between the two K-out-of-N c-boxes $X \sim \mathrm{KN}(5,6)$, $Y \sim \mathrm{KN}(16,20)$ for constant independent event correlation ρ, but different values of upper-level dependence. Φ_r is the Gaussian copula with parameter value r. (**Right**) shows logical *and* with independence for the lower-level ρ, but unknown dependence in the upper-level.

a dependence which the copula C_{XY} characterises, distinctly from the event correlation ρ. We call the event correlation ρ as "lower-level dependence" and the copula C_{XY} as the "upper-level dependence". This upper-level dependence can have a profound impact on the conjunction of two uncertain Booleans. The left of Fig. 3 shows the variation in the same two c-boxes as Fig. 2, but with a constant lower-level independence and a varying upper-level C_{XY}. The copula Φ_r is a Gaussian copula with parameter r. Note that the green p-box, showing independence on both levels, is the same in both Figs. 2 and 3.

As for the lower-level, the dependence on the upper-level could be imprecisely known, that is, it may not be possible to know C_{XY}. Using p-box arithmetic, unknown dependence can be propagated through a non-decreasing binary operation using the following convolutions [3] which has been adapted using the imprecise probabilistic conjunction C_ρ

$$\underline{F_Z}(z) = \inf_{C_\rho(x,y)=z} \left[W\left(\underline{F}_X(x), \underline{F}_Y(y)\right) \right], \tag{9}$$

$$\overline{F_Z}(z) = \sup_{C_{\overline{\rho}}(x,y)=z} \left[W^d\left(\overline{F}_X(x), \overline{F}_Y(y)\right) \right], \tag{10}$$

where C^d is the dual copula of C: $C^d(u,v) = u + v - C(u,v)$. The right of Fig. 3 shows the result of the p-box conjunction with unknown upper-level dependence and with lower-level independence.

The p-box bounds from unknown upper-level dependence are not only rigorous but are also best-possible in the sense that they cannot be made tighter without introducing additional dependence assumptions. One may find the breath (grey shaded area) of this p-box surprising, and how strong the independence assumption is. One may also wonder why the p-box on the right is not a simple envelope of the p-boxes on the left. This is because the left p-boxes only consider Gaussian dependencies, whilst the right p-box considers all possible copulas C_{XY}, of which there are an infinite number.

Risk analysts tell us that for a fault tree analysis to be probabilistic the event probabilities should be characterised by distributions [1]. If so, then the issue of the two levels of dependence immediately arises. As far as we are aware, this issue has not been widely addressed. Generally, the upper-level independence is assumed. This section has shown that this assumption has a strong effect on the results of logical operations involving uncertainty.

5 Application

In fault tree analysis, Boolean operators are employed to calculate a system's probability of failure. These are useful to, for example, understand what are the most likely routes of failure, show compliance with the reliability requirements, or designing monitoring strategies. To carry out these analyses it is required to define an event tree, where the connections between events are made with Boolean operators, with their respective event probabilities and dependencies. Then, the Boolean operators are calculated backwards from the top event to find its probability of failure.

Figure 4 represents a fault tree for a pressure tank system, derived in [3,13]. It displays the Boolean operators $\wedge$ (AND) and $\vee$ (OR) connecting the failure events E_i (with E_1 being the top event), and the system components tank (T), relay (K2), pressure switch (S), on-switch (S1), timer relay (R), and relay (K1). For the sake of brevity, the function of these components will not be explained in this paper.

To measure the probability of failure of the system (event E_1), it is necessary to estimate the failure rates for its components T, K2, S, S1, R and K1, and the dependence of the events in the Boolean operations. The most common method of calculation, as in [13], is to calculate the probability of failure assuming independence and known rates of failure for the components. In [3], the assumption of lower-level independence was relaxed including some known/unknown dependence, and extending the point probabilities to intervals, showing that the assumptions in [13] underestimate the probability of failure. To demonstrate the capabilities of the method derived in this paper, two scenarios on the components probability of failure will be calculated, with three lower-level dependence cases for each (independence, mixed dependence, and unknown dependence):

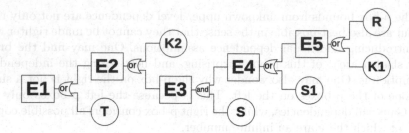

Fig. 4. Fault tree diagram for the pressure tank system.

1. An interval scenario, where the probability of failure of the components is modeled as intervals.
2. A p-box scenario, which generalises [3] combining p-boxes and intervals. The probabilities of failure of the relays (K1, K2, and R) have been extended to follow a K-out-of-N c-box [4].

The specific values for each scenario and dependence are indicated in Tables 3 and 4 respectively.

Table 3. Probability of failure for the tank pressure system components. In the interval scenario, all probabilities are modeled in the form of intervals. In the p-box scenario, tank and switches have an interval probability, whilst the relays follow a K-out-of-N c-box.

Component	Interval scenario	P-box scenario
T	$[4.5 \times 10^{-6}, 5.5 \times 10^{-6}]$	$[4.5 \times 10^{-6}, 5.5 \times 10^{-6}]$
K2	$[2.5 \times 10^{-5}, 3.5 \times 10^{-5}]$	$KN(3, 10^5)$
S	$[0.5 \times 10^{-4}, 1.5 \times 10^{-4}]$	$[0.5 \times 10^{-4}, 1.5 \times 10^{-4}]$
K1	$[2.5 \times 10^{-5}, 3.5 \times 10^{-5}]$	$KN(3, 10^5)$
R	$[0.5 \times 10^{-4}, 1.5 \times 10^{-4}]$	$KN(1, 10^4)$
S1	$[2.5 \times 10^{-5}, 3.5 \times 10^{-5}]$	$[2.5 \times 10^{-5}, 3.5 \times 10^{-5}]$

Table 4. Dependence in the system's events for the three different cases: independence, mixed dependence, and unknown dependence.

Event	Independence	Mixed dependence	Unknown dependence
E_1	$\rho = 0$	$\rho = 0$	$\rho = [-1, 1]$
E_2	$\rho = 0$	$\rho = [-1, 1]$	$\rho = [-1, 1]$
E_3	$\rho = 0$	$\rho = 0.15$	$\rho = [-1, 1]$
E_4	$\rho = 0$	$\rho = [-0.2, 0.2]$	$\rho = [-1, 1]$
E_5	$\rho = 0$	$\rho = 1$	$\rho = [-1, 1]$

5.1   Interval Scenario

On the left of Fig. 5 it is shown the probability of failure E_1 for the interval scenario, where the red area belongs to the independence case, blue to the mixed dependence case, and green to the unknown dependence. It is possible to see how the uncertainty increases as the dependence assumptions are removed from the Boolean operations. Intervals for the probability of E_1 are indicated in Table 5.

Table 5. Probability of E_1 in the interval scenario.

Case	$\mathbb{P}(E_1)$
Independence	$[2.950 \times 10^{-5}, 4.053 \times 10^{-5}]$
Mixed dependence	$[2.949 \times 10^{-5}, 6.551 \times 10^{-5}]$
Unknown dependence	$[2.499 \times 10^{-5}, 1.905 \times 10^{-4}]$

5.2   P-Box Scenario

The results in the P-box scenario are more complicated to interpret since the calculations are probabilities of the probability of the event E_1. However, meaningful analyses can be drawn from them. For example, assuming the required failure probability of the tank system is no more than 10^{-4}, a possible question could be what is the probability of it being lower or equal than 10^{-4}, or how likely is the system to comply with that requirement. Table 6 includes the results of such inquiry. In the case of all the events being independent, the probability of fulfilling the requirements goes from 0.969 to 1, so one can infer the tank pressure system is likely to fulfil the requirements. When the independence assumption is removed, and the mixed dependence scenario is adopted, it is possible to see how the uncertainty on the assessment increases. Finally, if all the dependence assumptions are relaxed, the probability goes from 0 to 1, meaning that no guarantees can be given on the reliability of the tank pressure system. These results are illustrated in Fig. 5 (right), which depicts how dramatic the consequences can be when assuming certain dependencies for the events.

Table 6. Probability of $\mathbb{P}(E_1) <= 10^{-4}$ in the P-box scenario.

Case	$\mathbb{P}(E_1) <= 10^{-4}$
Independence	$[0.969, 1]$
Mixed dependence	$[0.88, 1]$
Unknown dependence	$[0, 1]$

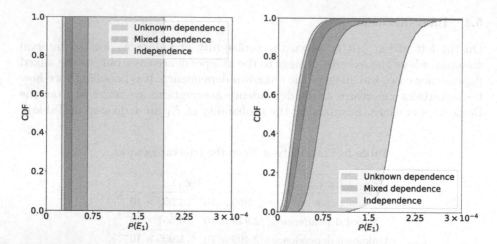

Fig. 5. (Left) Interval of $\mathbb{P}(E_1)$ for different dependence assumptions. **(Right)** Probability box of $\mathbb{P}(E_1)$ for different dependence assumptions.

6   Conclusion

In this paper, classical Boolean functions have been generalised to be able to operate with precise probabilities, intervals, p-boxes, and with any input correlation. We show an application of the generalisation of Boolean operations calculating the probability of failure of a pressure tank system. The uncertainty is propagated through the fault tree with different combinations of probabilities of the events, intervals, and p-boxes, under different dependence assumptions. The results suggest that assumptions on the probability or dependence of the events have a strong impact on the outcome of the analysis, and these should be carefully addressed in any serious assessment.

Also, the issue of the two levels of dependence has been introduced, and shown that it can have a dramatic effect on the results of a probabilistic risk assessment.

The computational resources to perform correlated Boolean operations are available in the following open-source Julia package: https://github.com/Institute-for-Risk-and-Uncertainty/UncLogic.jl

Acknowledgements. We thank William (Bill) Huber (from Analysis & Inference) for his advice in the early stages of this research. This research was funded by the EPSRC and ESRC CDT in Risk and Uncertainty (EP/L015927/1), established within the Institute for Risk and Uncertainty at the University of Liverpool. This work has been carried out within the framework of the EUROfusion Consortium, funded by the European Union via the Euratom Research and Training Programme (Grant Agreement No 101052200 - EUROfusion). Views and opinions expressed are however those of the author(s) only and do not necessarily reflect those of the European Union or the European Commission. Neither the European Union nor the European Commission can be held responsible for them.

References

1. Atwood, C., et al.: Handbook of Parameter Estimation for Probabilistic Risk Assessment. US Nuclear Regulatory Commission (2003)
2. Durante, F., Jaworski, P.: A new characterization of bivariate copulas. Commun. Statist. Theory Methods **39**(16), 2901–2912 (2010)
3. Ferson, S., et al.: Dependence in probabilistic modeling Dempster-Shafer theory and probability bounds analysis. Tech. rep., Sandia National Lab. (SNL-NM), Albuquerque, NM (United States) (2015)
4. Ferson, S., O'Rawe, J., Balch, M.: Computing with confidence: imprecise posteriors and predictive distributions. In: Vulnerability, Uncertainty, and Risk: Quantification, Mitigation, and Management, pp. 895–904 (2014)
5. Fréchet, M.: Généralisation du théoreme des probabilités totales. Fundam. Math. **1**(25), 379–387 (1935)
6. Gray, A., Ferson, S., Patelli, E.: ProbabilityBoundsAnalysis.jl: arithmetic with sets of distributions. Submitted to the Proceedings of JuliaCon (2021)
7. Joe, H.: Multivariate Models and Multivariate Dependence Concepts. CRC Press (1997)
8. Klir, G.J., Folger, T.A.: Fuzzy Sets, Uncertainty, and Information. Prentice-Hall, Inc. (1987)
9. Lucas, D.J.: Default correlation and credit analysis. J. Fixed Income **4**(4), 76–87 (1995)
10. Montes, I., Miranda, E., Pelessoni, R., Vicig, P.: Sklar's theorem in an imprecise setting. Fuzzy Sets Syst. **278**, 48–66 (2015)
11. Nelsen, R.B.: An Introduction to Copulas. Springer, New York (2007). https://doi.org/10.1007/0-387-28678-0
12. Schweizer, B., Sklar, A.: Probabilistic Metric Spaces. Courier Corporation (2011)
13. Vesely, W.E., Goldberg, F.F., Roberts, N.H., Haasl, D.F.: Fault Tree Handbook. Tech. rep. Nuclear Regulatory Commission, Washington, DC (1981)

Author Index

Adamczyk, David II-418, II-431
Aguiló, Isabel I-410
Alfonso-Robaina, Daniel I-155
Almeida, Rui Jorge II-223
Amini, Mehran II-288
Anseán, David II-748
Antunes-Santos, Felipe II-259, II-443
Anzilli, Luca I-34
Aragón, Roberto G. I-107
Araújo, Juscelino I-460
Arendsen, Jasper II-248
Asmus, Tiago I-359
Augustin, Thomas I-729, II-532

Baczyński, Michał I-182, I-194
Baelde, Aurélien II-735
Balicki, Krzysztof I-421
Ballarino, Andrea II-547
Baştürk, Nalan II-223
Basu, Tathagata I-757
Baz, Juan I-11, II-483
Bedregal, Benjamín I-206, I-460
Bedychaj, Andrzej II-3
Belabbes, Sihem II-652
Bellandi, Valerio I-568
Ben Amor, Nahla I-581
Ben Yaghlane, Boutheina II-624
Benferhat, Salem II-379, II-652
Benítez-Caballero, María José I-142
Bēts, Raivis I-270
Blanche-Alcócer, Juan Carlos I-294
Blocher, Hannah II-17
Boffa, Stefania I-622
Borges, Eduardo I-359
Bouchet, Agustina I-542
Bouraoui, Zied II-379
Bouyssou, Denis II-197
Brusaferri, Alessandro II-547
Burda, Michal I-25
Bustince, Humberto I-359, II-355

Cabrera, Inma P. I-77, I-100, I-118
Cabrera-Cuevas, Marcelino II-163

Çakır, Esra II-141
Calcagnì, Antonio II-457
Calvo Sánchez, Tomasa I-47
Campagner, Andrea II-761
Cao, Nhung I-233, I-663
Cardin, Marta I-34
Carvalho, Joao Paulo II-69
Castro, Javier II-151, II-367
Castro, Juan Luis I-557
Chacón-Gómez, Fernando I-63
Chalco-Cano, Yurilev I-245, I-294
Chebbah, Mouna II-624
Christen, Ramón II-469
Cinelli, Matteo II-681
Cinfrignini, Andrea I-784
Ciucci, Davide I-622, II-761
Coletti, Giulianella I-770
Coquin, Didier II-54
Cordero, Pablo I-77, I-87, I-100, I-118
Córdoba-Hidalgo, Patricia II-329
Cordon, Oscar II-355
Costa, Nahuel II-748
Costa, Tiago Mendoça da I-245
Couso, Inés II-748
Crespo, Luis G. II-99
Cubillo, S. I-703

Damiani, Ernesto II-560
Daňková, Martina I-25
de Andrés Calle, Rocio II-173
De Baets, Bernard I-3, I-100, II-443
de Blas, Clara Simón I-398
De Tré, Guy II-572
Demircioğlu, Emre II-141
Denzler, Alexander II-469
Destercke, Sébastien I-494, I-757
Detyniecki, Marcin II-707
Díaz, Irene I-11, I-542
Díaz-García, J. Angel II-275, II-317
Díaz-Moreno, Juan Carlos I-155
Dimuro, Graçaliz P. I-359
Djouadi, Yassine II-638
Doria, Serena II-667

Drygaś, Paweł   I-421
Dubois, Didier   I-581, II-508
Dujmović, Jozo   II-572
Dvořáček, Petr   II-696
Dvořák, Antonín   I-689
Dyczkowski, Krzysztof   I-307

Elouedi, Zied   II-612
Enciso, Manuel   I-87
Eugenia Cornejo, Maria   I-63

Fernandez, F. Javier   II-259
Fernandez-Basso, Carlos   II-275, II-317
Fernández-Martínez, Manuel   II-163
Fernandez-Peralta, Raquel   I-182
Ferreira de Carvalho, Danilo   II-235
Ferson, Scott   I-798
Fiala, Karel   I-609
Flaminio, Tommaso   I-676, II-584
Flores-Vidal, Pablo A.   II-367
Francisco, Manuel   I-557
Franco, Camilo   II-85
Frati, Fulvio   I-568
Fumanal-Idocin, Javier   II-355
Fuster-Parra, Pilar   I-47

García-Zamora, Diego   I-11
Gianini, Gabriele   II-560
Gilio, Angelo   II-584
Godo, Lluis   I-676, II-584
Gómez González, Daniel   I-398
Gómez, Daniel   II-151, II-367
Gómez-Romero, Juan   II-306
Gómez-Sánchez, Jesica   II-317
Gray, Ander   I-798
Grigorenko, Olga   I-448
Grina, Fares   II-612
Grzegorowski, Marek   II-44
Grzegorzewski, Przemyslaw   II-494, II-520
Guevara, Juan Antonio   I-398, II-151
Guillaume, Romain   I-494
Gupta, Megha   I-169
Gutiérrez, Inmaculada   II-151
Gutiérrez-Batista, Karel   II-275, II-317

Habtewold, Tesfa Dejenie   II-223
Hanoch, Ofir   II-223
Harispe, Sébastien   II-185
Hatwagner, Miklos F.   II-288

Hernández-Jiménez, Beatriz   I-245
Hernández-Varela, P.   I-703
Hidouri, Amel   II-624
Holčapek, Michal   I-471, I-689
Horanská, Ľubomíra   II-355
Hu, Chenyi   I-504, I-528
Hudec, Miroslav   I-372
Huidobro, Pedro   I-542
Hula, Jan   II-431
Hurtik, Petr   II-343, II-696

Imoussaten, Abdelhak   II-185, II-774

Jabbour, Said   II-624
Janeček, Jiří   II-405
Janicki, Ryszard   I-332
Jankowska, Monika   II-44
Jansen, Christoph   I-729, II-17
Janusz, Andrzej   II-44
Jayaram, Balasubramaniam   I-169, I-714
Jean, Pierre-Antoine   II-185
Jendoubi, Siwar   II-735
Jeyasothy, Adulam   II-707

Kacprzyk, Janusz   I-517
Kaldjob Kaldjob, Paul Alain   II-197
Kaymak, Uzay   II-235, II-248
Kebir, Sara   II-598
Kenny, Sean P.   II-99
Koczy, Laszlo T.   II-288
Kosheleva, Olga   I-485
Kosior, Dawid   I-307
Kralj Novak, Petra   II-681
Kreinovich, Vladik   I-485
Kulkarni, Chinmay   II-31
Kupka, Jiří   I-258

Latini, Sara   I-770
Laugel, Thibault   II-707
Łażewski, Stanisław   II-44
Lefevre, Eric   II-612
Lesot, Marie-Jeanne   II-707, II-720
Lin, Jianyi   II-560
Lobo, David   I-130
Lombardi, Luigi   II-457
López-Marchante, Víctor   I-130
Lopez-Molina, Carlos   II-259, II-443
López-Rodríguez, Domingo   I-87
Lucca, Giancarlo   I-359

Ma, Truong-Thanh   II-379
Magdalena, L.   I-703
Malleuve-Martínez, Annette   I-155
Marín, Nicolás   II-329
Marsala, Christophe   I-345, II-707
Martín-Bautista, Maria J.   II-275, II-306,
    II-317
Martínez, Luis   I-11
Massanet, Sebastia   I-182, I-410
Matteucci, Matteo   II-547
Mauris, Gilles   II-54
Mayag, Brice   II-197, II-210
Mazzola, Luca   II-469
Medina, Jesús   I-63, I-107, I-130, I-142,
    I-155
Mencar, Corrado   II-508
Menchón, Paula   I-676
Mendioroz, Maite   II-443
Mesiar, Radko   I-359, I-372
Mihailovs, Valerijs   I-448
Miķelsons, Emīls Miķelis   I-270
Mináriková, Erika   I-372
Mio, Corrado   II-560
Mir, Arnau   I-182, II-259
Miralles-Dolz, Enrique   I-798
Miranda, Enrique   I-743
Mir-Fuentes, Arnau   II-259, II-443
Miś, Katarzyna   I-219
Močkoř, Jiří   I-320
Mojzisek, David   II-431
Molek, Vojtech   II-343
Monks, Eduardo   I-434
Montero, Javier   II-85, II-367
Montes, Ignacio   I-743
Montes, Susana   I-11, I-542
Montmain, Jacky   II-185
Moody, Aaron   I-528
Mora, Ángel   I-87
Morales-Garzón, Andrea   II-306
Morillo, Jaime   I-398
Moś, Grzegorz   I-384
Moura, Bruno   I-434
Mozetič, Igor   II-681
Muñoz-Velasco, Emilio   I-77, I-100
Murinová, Petra   I-609, I-622, I-634, I-647

Nanavati, Kavit   I-169, I-714
Neres, Fernando   I-206

Novák, Vilém   I-634, I-647
Nowak, Aleksandra   II-3

Ojeda-Aciego, Manuel   I-100, I-118
Ojeda-Hernández, Manuel   I-77
Omar, Aziz   II-532
Osuna-Gómez, Rafaela   I-245

Pagnier, Fanny   II-54
Patelli, Edoardo   I-798
Pavliska, Viktor   I-25
Peelman, Milan   II-572
Pękala, Barbara   I-307
Peláez-Moreno, Carmen   I-118
Pelicon, Andraž   II-681
Pelta, David A.   II-163
Pérez-Fernández, Raúl   I-3, II-483
Pérez-Gámez, Francisco   I-87
Perfilieva, Irina   I-282, II-394, II-405, II-418
Petturiti, Davide   I-770, I-784
Pham, Tam   I-282
Pieszczek, Mateusz   I-194
Pinheiro, Jocivania   I-359
Pivert, Olivier   II-720
Poignant, Floriane A.   II-99
Portmann, Edy   II-469
Portolani, Pietro   II-547
Pourraz, Frédéric   II-54
Prade, Henri   I-581
Presa, Andrés   I-743
Prieto-Herráez, Silvia   II-173

Quoc, Viec Bui   I-471
Quost, Benjamin   I-757

Raddaoui, Badran   II-624
Radja, Hakim   II-638
Rajesh, Mohith   II-31
Ramírez-Poussa, Eloísa   I-63, I-107
Reformat, Marek Z.   I-593
Reiser, Renata   I-434
Rezaei, Navid   I-593
Rico, Noelia   I-542
Riera, Juan Vicente   I-182, I-410
Rietjens, Kim   II-248
Rijcken, Emil   II-248
Robles, José Manuel   II-151

Rodríguez, J. Tinguaro   II-85
Rodriguez, Ricardo O.   I-676
Rodriguez-Martinez, Iosu   I-359
Romaniuk, Maciej   II-494
Rubio-Manzano, Clemente   I-155
Ruiz, M. Dolores   II-275, II-317

Sachan, Swati   II-128
Saidi, Syrine   I-581
Sánchez, Daniel   II-329
Sánchez, Luciano   II-748
Sánchez-Lozano, Juan Miguel   II-163
Sanfilippo, Giuseppe   II-584
Santiago, Regivan   I-206, I-460
Santos, Helida   I-359, I-434
Scantamburlo, Teresa   II-681
Schneider, Guilherme   I-434
Schollmeyer, Georg   II-17
Sheng, Victor S.   I-504, I-528
Shylaja, S. S.   II-31
Siccardi, Stefano   I-568
Simões, Artur   II-69
Slaba, Tony C.   II-99
Smits, Grégory   II-720
Šostak, Alexander   I-270
Spurek, Przemysław   II-3
Spurling, Makenzie   I-504, I-528
Štěpnička, Martin   I-233, I-663
Świechowski, Maciej   II-44
Szkoła, Jarosław   I-307
Szmidt, Eulalia   I-517

Tabia, Karim   II-379, II-598, II-638
Tabor, Jacek   II-3
Takáč, Zdenko   II-355
Taş, Mehmet Ali   II-141
Tchantcho, Bertrand   II-210
Torres-Blanc, C.   I-703

Valášek, Radek   I-233
Valverde-Albacete, Francisco José   I-118
Van Gorp, Pieter   II-235
van Riel, Natal   II-235
Vantaggi, Barbara   I-784
Verjus, Hervé   II-54
Vlems, Femke   II-248
von Oertzen, Timo   II-532

Xie, Shengkun   II-115

Yager, Ronald R.   I-593
Yamin, Adenauer   I-434
Yepmo Tchaghe, Véronne   II-720

Zámečníková, Hana   II-343, II-394
Zervanou, Kalliopi   II-248
Zhan, Huixin   I-504, I-528
Zhang, Jin   II-115
Zollo, Fabiana   II-681
Zuccotti, Filippo   I-568

Printed in the United States
by Baker & Taylor Publisher Services

Printed in the United States
by Baker & Taylor Publisher Services